Rick Steves'

GREAT BRITAIN

2011

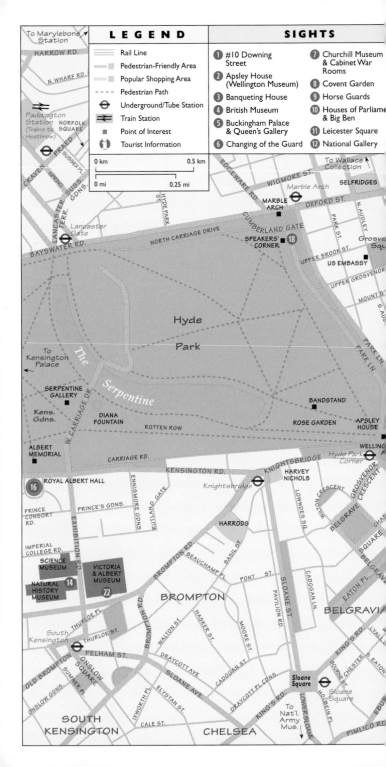

LEGEND

	Rail Line
	Pedestrian-Friendly Area
	Popular Shopping Area
- - -	Pedestrian Path
Ⓤ	Underground/Tube Station
🚉	Train Station
■	Point of Interest
🛈	Tourist Information

0 km   0.5 km

0 mi   0.25 mi

SIGHTS

① #10 Downing Street
② Apsley House (Wellington Museum)
③ Banqueting House
④ British Museum
⑤ Buckingham Palace & Queen's Gallery
⑥ Changing of the Guard
⑦ Churchill Museum & Cabinet War Rooms
⑧ Covent Garden
⑨ Horse Guards
⑩ Houses of Parliament & Big Ben
⑪ Leicester Square
⑫ National Gallery

To Marylebone Station

HARROW RD.

N. WHARF RD.

Paddington Station (Trains to Heathrow)

NORFOLK SQUARE

PRAED ST.

CRAVEN

SPRING

SUSSEX PL.

SUSS. GDNS.

LANCASTER TERR.

Lancaster Gate

BAYSWATER RD.

To Kensington Palace

The Serpentine

SERPENTINE GALLERY

Kens. Gdns.

DIANA FOUNTAIN

W. CARRIAGE DR.

ALBERT MEMORIAL

CARRIAGE RD.

① ROYAL ALBERT HALL

PRINCE CONSORT RD.

PRINCE'S GDNS.

EXHIBITION RD.

IMPERIAL COLLEGE RD.

SCIENCE MUSEUM

NATURAL HISTORY MUSEUM ⑭

VICTORIA & ALBERT MUSEUM ㉒

South Kensington

THURLOE PL.

THURLOE ST.

PELHAM ST.

ONSLOW SQUARE

OLD BROMPTON RD.

SUMNER PL.

ONSLOW GDNS.

AXWORTH PL.

ELYSTAN ST.

SOUTH KENSINGTON

CALE ST.

EDGWARE RD.

WIGMORE ST.

To Wallace Collection

Marble Arch

SELFRIDGES

MARBLE ARCH

OXFORD ST.

CUMBERLAND GATE

SPEAKERS' CORNER ⑱

NORTH CARRIAGE DRIVE

N. AUDLEY ST.

PARK ST.

UPPER BROOK ST.

US EMBASSY

UPPER GROSVENOR

Grosve Squ

MOUNT S

S. AUD

Hyde

Park

PARK LN.

PARK LN.

BANDSTAND

ROSE GARDEN

ROTTEN ROW

APSLEY HOUSE

WELLING

WELLING
Hyde Park Corner Ⓤ

KENSINGTON RD.

KNIGHTSBRIDGE

HARVEY NICHOLS

GROSVENOR CRESCENT

CRESCENT

Knightsbridge Ⓤ

RUTLAND GATE

ENNISMORE GDNS.

LOWNDES ST.

WILTON

BELGRAVE SQ.

BELGRAVE

EATON PL.

HARRODS

BROMPTON RD.

BEAUCHAMP PL.

BASIL ST.

PONT ST.

SLOANE ST.

CADOGAN LN.

SQUARE

BELGRAVIA

BROMPTON

WALTON ST.

HASKER ST.

MOORE ST.

PAVILION RD.

CADOGAN ST.

DRAYCOTT PL. GDNS.

KING'S RD.

DRAYCOTT AVE.

SLOANE AVE.

Sloane Square

Sloane Square Ⓤ

BOURNE ST.

CHESTER ST.

S. EATON

LYALL

HOLBEIN PL.

LOWER SLOANE

To Nat'l. Army Mus.

CHELSEA

PIMLICO RD.

EBUR

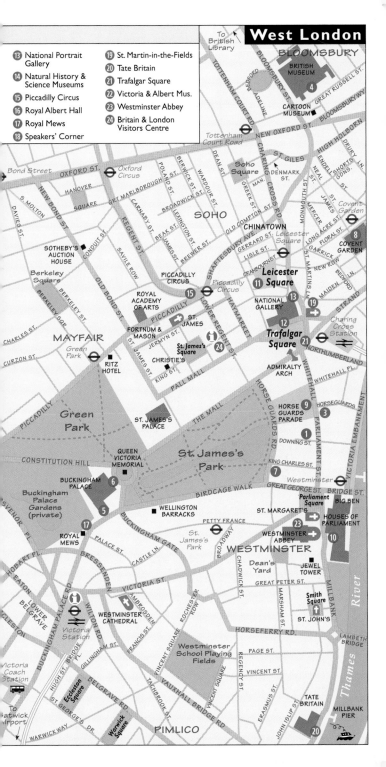

West London

13 National Portrait Gallery
14 Natural History & Science Museums
15 Piccadilly Circus
16 Royal Albert Hall
17 Royal Mews
18 Speakers' Corner
19 St. Martin-in-the-Fields
20 Tate Britain
21 Trafalgar Square
22 Victoria & Albert Mus.
23 Westminster Abbey
24 Britain & London Visitors Centre

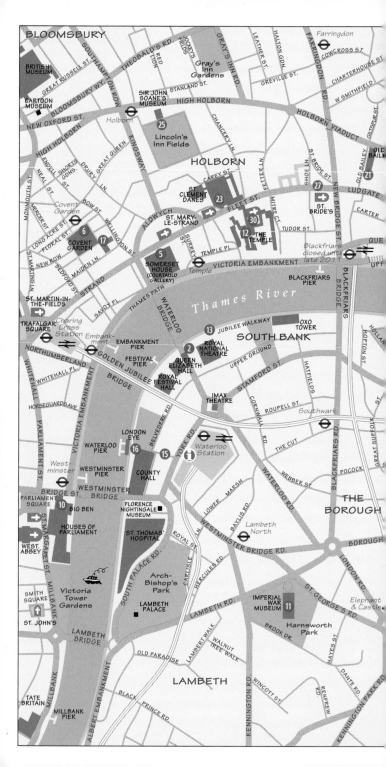

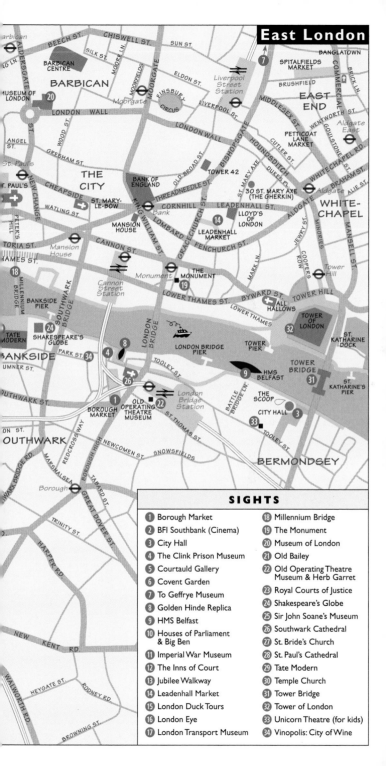

East London

SIGHTS

1. Borough Market
2. BFI Southbank (Cinema)
3. City Hall
4. The Clink Prison Museum
5. Courtauld Gallery
6. Covent Garden
7. To Geffrye Museum
8. Golden Hinde Replica
9. HMS Belfast
10. Houses of Parliament & Big Ben
11. Imperial War Museum
12. The Inns of Court
13. Jubilee Walkway
14. Leadenhall Market
15. London Duck Tours
16. London Eye
17. London Transport Museum
18. Millennium Bridge
19. The Monument
20. Museum of London
21. Old Bailey
22. Old Operating Theatre Museum & Herb Garret
23. Royal Courts of Justice
24. Shakespeare's Globe
25. Sir John Soane's Museum
26. Southwark Cathedral
27. St. Bride's Church
28. St. Paul's Cathedral
29. Tate Modern
30. Temple Church
31. Tower Bridge
32. Tower of London
33. Unicorn Theatre (for kids)
34. Vinopolis: City of Wine

Edinburgh

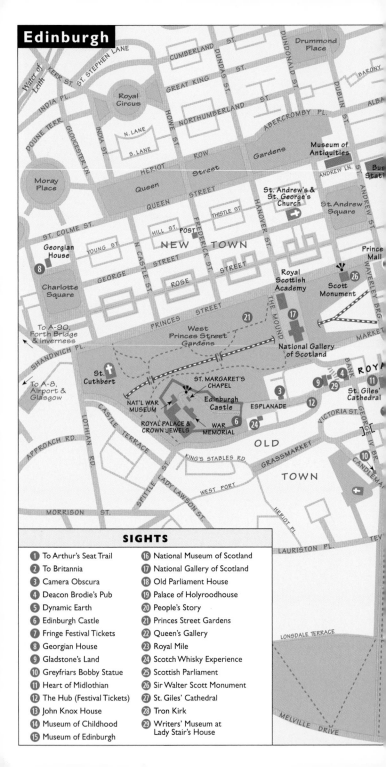

SIGHTS

1. To Arthur's Seat Trail
2. To Britannia
3. Camera Obscura
4. Deacon Brodie's Pub
5. Dynamic Earth
6. Edinburgh Castle
7. Fringe Festival Tickets
8. Georgian House
9. Gladstone's Land
10. Greyfriars Bobby Statue
11. Heart of Midlothian
12. The Hub (Festival Tickets)
13. John Knox House
14. Museum of Childhood
15. Museum of Edinburgh
16. National Museum of Scotland
17. National Gallery of Scotland
18. Old Parliament House
19. Palace of Holyroodhouse
20. People's Story
21. Princes Street Gardens
22. Queen's Gallery
23. Royal Mile
24. Scotch Whisky Experience
25. Scottish Parliament
26. Sir Walter Scott Monument
27. St. Giles' Cathedral
28. Tron Kirk
29. Writers' Museum at Lady Stair's House

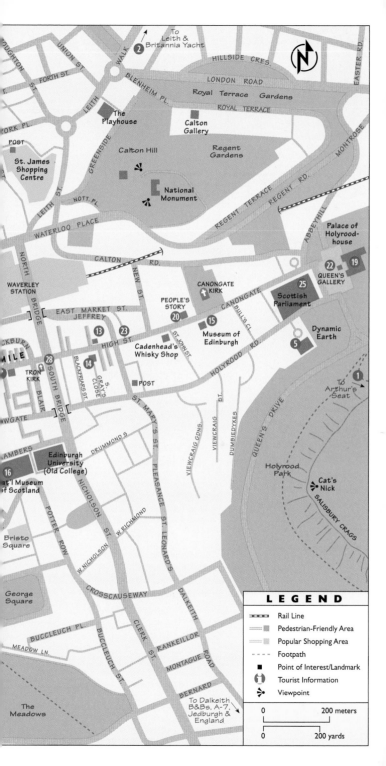

CONTENTS

Great Britain

What's so great about Britain? Plenty. You can watch a world-class Shakespeare play, do the Beatles blitz in Liverpool, and walk along a windswept hill in the footsteps of Wordsworth. Climb cobblestone streets as you wander Edinburgh's Royal Mile, or take a ferry to a windswept isle. Ponder a moody glen, wild-ponied moor, lonesome stone circle, or ruined abbey. Try getting your tongue around a few Welsh words, taste "candy floss" by the beach, and enjoy evensong at Westminster Cathedral. Stroll through a cute-as-can-be Cotswold town, try to spot an underwater monster in a loch, and sail along the Thames past Big Ben. Great Britain has it all.

Regardless of the revolution we had 230-some years ago, many American travelers feel that they "go home" to Britain. This most popular tourist destination has a strange influence and power over us. The more you know of Britain's roots, the better you'll get in touch with your own.

The Isle of Britain is small (about the size of Idaho)—600 miles long and 300 miles at its widest point. Britain's highest mountain (Scotland's Ben Nevis) is 4,409 feet, a foothill by our standards. The population is a fifth that of the United States. At its peak in the mid-1800s, Britain owned one-fifth of the world and accounted for more than half the planet's industrial output. Today, the empire is down to the Isle of Britain itself and a few token scraps, such as Northern Ireland, Gibraltar, and the Falklands.

And yet, culturally, Britain remains a world leader. Her heritage, culture, and people cannot be measured in traditional units of power. London is a major exporter of actors, movies, and theater; of rock and classical music; and of writers, painters, and sculptors.

On the other hand, when it comes to cuisine, Britain has given the world...fish-and-chips and haggis. Bad, bland British food is almost a universal joke, headed by dishes with funny names like "bubble and squeak" and "toad in the hole." Traditionally, Britain was known for heavy, no-nonsense meals. The day started with a hearty breakfast of eggs and bacon, followed by meat pies and beer for lunch, and finished with a filling dinner of red meat and thick sauces.

But the cuisine has improved in recent years. The British have added fresh fruits and vegetables to their diet, and many regions pride themselves on using locally grown foods to make lighter, more creative variations of old favorites. Foreign influ-

ences—especially Indian and Chinese imports—are especially popular, having been adapted to local tastes.

Thankfully, one distinctive British tradition remains popular: afternoon tea served with biscuits, cookies, or little sandwiches. This four o'clock break is part pick-me-up and part social ritual.

Ethnically, the British Isles are a mix of the descendants of the early Celtic natives (in Scotland, Ireland, Wales, and Cornwall), descendants of the invading Anglo-Saxons who took southeast England in the Dark Ages, and descendants

of the conquering Normans of the 11th century...not to mention more recent immigrants from around the world. Cynics call the United Kingdom an English Empire ruled by London, whose dominant Anglo-Saxon English (50 million) far outnumber their Celtic brothers and sisters (10 million).

It's easy to think that "Britain" and "England" are one and the same. But actually, three very different countries make up Great Britain: England, Wales, and Scotland. (Add Northern Ireland and you've got the United Kingdom—but you'll need a different guidebook.) Let's take a quick cultural tour through Great Britain's three nations.

England

Even today, England remains a cultural and linguistic touchstone for the almost one billion humans who speak English. It's the center of the United Kingdom in every way: home to four out of five UK citizens, the seat of government, the economic powerhouse, the center of higher

Britain Almanac

Official Name: The United Kingdom of Great Britain and Northern Ireland (locals say "the UK" or "Britain").

Population: Britain's 61 million people are a mix of Celtic DNA, plus a sizable and growing minority of recent immigrants, largely from India, Pakistan, and Eastern Europe. Seven in ten British call themselves Christian (half of those are Anglican), but in any given week, more Brits visit a mosque than an Anglican church.

Latitude and Longitude: 54°N and 2°W. The latitude is similar to Alberta, Canada.

Area: From "Britannia's" 19th-century peak of power, when it dominated much of the globe, the British Empire shrunk to a quarter of its former size. Today, this nation is 95,000 square miles (about the size of Michigan). It's comprised of one large island and a chunk of another large island.

Geography: Most of the British Isles consist of low hills and rolling plains, with a generally moderate climate. The country's highest point is 4,409-foot Ben Nevis in western Scotland. Britain's longest river, the Severn, loops 220 miles from the mountains of Wales east into England, then south to the Bristol Channel. The Thames River runs 215 miles east–west through the heart of southern England (including London).

Biggest Cities: London is the capital, with 8 million people. Industrial Birmingham has 2.6 million, Glasgow has 1.5 million, and the port of Liverpool has 1.1 million.

Economy: The Gross Domestic Product is $2.2 trillion and the GDP per capita is $36,500. Moneymakers include banking, insurance

and business services, energy production, agriculture, shipping, and trade with the US and Germany. Heavy industry—which once drove the Industrial Revolution—is now in decline. The economy and pound sterling have weakened a bit against the euro and the dollar in recent years.

Government: Queen Elizabeth II officially heads the country, but in practice it's the prime minister, who leads the majority party in Parliament. The British House of Commons has 659 seats. (The House of Lords is now a mere advisory body.) Britain's traditional two-party system—Labour and Conservatives ("Tories")—now has a smaller third player, the Liberal Democrats ("Lib Dems"). The current prime minister, Conservative leader David Cameron, came to power in May 2010, unseating Labour Party rival Gordon Brown. Britain is a member of the European Union (but not the euro system) and is one of the five permanent members (with veto power) of the UN Security Council. In 1999, Scotland, Wales, and Northern Ireland were each granted its own Parliament—and, with that, more autonomy in their domestic affairs.

Flag: The "Union Jack" has two red crosses on a field of blue: the English cross of St. George and the Scottish cross of St. Andrew.

The Average Brit: Eats 35 pounds of pizza and 35 pounds of chocolate a year, and weighs 12 stone (170 pounds). He or she is 40 years old, has 1.66 children, and will live to age 79. He/she drinks 2.5 cups of tea a day and 2.5 glasses of wine a week (Americans drink less than half that). He/she has free health care, and gets 23 vacation days a year (versus 12 in the US and 39 in France). He/she sleeps 7.5 hours a night, speaks one language, and loves soccer.

learning, and the cultural heart. And, although it lacks some of the Celtic color of other parts of Britain, you'll find plenty of variety even in "plain vanilla" England.

North England tends to be hilly with poor soil, so the traditional economy was based on livestock (grazing cows and sheep).

Today it has some of England's most beautiful landscapes, but in the 19th century it was dotted with belching smokestacks as its major cities and heartland became centers of coal and iron mining and manufacturing. Now its working-class cities and ports (such as Liverpool) are experiencing a comeback, buoyed by higher employment, tourism, and vibrant arts scenes.

South England, including London, has always had more people and more money than the north. Blessed with rolling hills, wide plains, and the Thames River, in the past this area was rich with farms, its rivers flowed with trade, and high culture flourished around the epicenter in London. And today, even though London is a thriving metropolis of eight million people, much the same could still be said.

The English people have a worldwide reputation (or stereotype) for being cheerful, courteous, and well-mannered. Cutting in line is very gauche. On the other hand, English soccer

fans can be notorious "hooligans." The English are not known for being touchy-feely or physically demonstrative (hugging and kissing), but they sure do love to talk. When times get tough, they persevere with a stiff upper lip. The understated English wit is legendary—if someone dies, it's "a bit of a drag" (but if the tea is cold, it's "ghastly"!).

For the tourist, England offers a little of everything we associate with Britain: castles, cathedrals, and ruined abbeys; chatty locals nursing beers in village pubs; mysterious prehistoric stone circles and Roman ruins; tea, scones, and clotted cream; hikes across unspoiled, sheep-speckled hillsides; and drivers who cheerfully wave from the "wrong" side of the road. And then there's London, a world in itself, with monuments (Big Ben), museums (the British Museum), royalty (Buckingham Palace), theater, and nightlife, throbbing with the pulse of the global community.

You can trace England's illustrious history by roaming the countryside. Prehistoric peoples built the mysterious stone circles of Stonehenge and Avebury. Then came the Romans, who built Hadrian's Wall and baths at Bath. Viking invaders left their mark in York, and the Normans built the Tower of London. As England Christianized and unified, the grand cathedrals of Salisbury, Wells, and Durham arose. Next came

the castles and palaces of the English monarchs (Windsor and Warwick) and the Shakespeare sights from the era of Elizabeth I (Stratford-upon-Avon). In following centuries, tiny England became a maritime empire (the *Cutty Sark* at Greenwich) and the world's first industrial power (Ironbridge Gorge).

England's Romantic poets were inspired by the unspoiled nature and time-passed villages of the Lake District and the Cotswolds. In the 20th century, the gritty urban world of 1960s Liverpool gave the world the Beatles (and the tacky tourist world of Blackpool). Finally, end your

journey through English history in London—on the cutting edge of 21st-century trends.

For a thousand years, England has been a major cultural center. Parliamentary democracy, science (Isaac Newton), technology (Michael Faraday), and education (Oxford and Cambridge) were nurtured here. In literature, England has few peers in any language, producing some of the greatest legends (King Arthur, *Beowulf,* and *The Lord of the Rings*), poems (by Chaucer, Wordsworth, and Byron), novels (by Dickens, Austen, and J. K. Rowling), and plays (by William Shakespeare, England's greatest writer). London rivals

Broadway as the best scene for live theater. England is a major exporter of movies and movie actors—Laurence Olivier, Alec Guinness, Ian McKellen, Helen Mirren, Judi Dench, Kate Winslet, Keira Knightley, Ralph Fiennes, Hugh Grant, Ricky Gervais, and on and on.

In popular music, England remains almost America's equal. It started in the 1960s with the "British invasion" of bands that reinfused rock and blues into America—the Beatles, the Rolling Stones, and the Who. Then came successive waves in the 1970s (Elton John, Led Zeppelin, David Bowie, Pink Floyd, Queen, and the Sex Pistols), the '80s (Dire Straits, The Clash, The Cure, Elvis Costello, the Smiths, the Police, and Duran Duran), the '90s (Oasis, Spice Girls, and the rave scene), and into the 21st century (Coldplay, Amy Winehouse, Lily Allen, and Radiohead).

Wales

Humble, charming little Wales is traditional and beautiful—it sometimes feels trapped in a time warp. When you first enter Wales, it may seem like you're still in England. But soon you'll awaken to the uniqueness and crusty yet poetic vitality of this small country, and realize...you're not in Oxford anymore. And don't ask for an "English breakfast"

at your Welsh B&B—they'll smile politely and remind you that it's a "Welsh breakfast," made with Welsh ingredients.

For the tourist, Wales is a land of stout castles (the best are at Conwy and Caernarfon), salty harbors, chummy community choirs, slate-roofed villages, and a landscape of mountains, moors, and lush green fields dotted with sheep. Snowdonia National Park is a hiker's paradise, with steep but manageable mountain trails, cute-as-a-Hobbit villages (Beddgelert and Betws-y-Coed), and scenery more striking than most

anything in England. Fascinating slate-mine museums (such as at Blaenau Ffestiniog), handy home-base towns (Conwy and Ruthin), and enticing, offbeat attractions round out Wales' appeal.

Perhaps Wales' best attraction is hearing the locals speak Welsh (or Cymraeg, pronounced kum-RAH-ig). The Welsh people often use this tongue-twisting and fun-to-listen-to Celtic language when speaking with one another, smoothly switching to English when a visitor asks a question. With its sometimes harsh, sometimes melodic tones, Welsh transports listeners to another time and place.

Culturally, Wales is "a land of poets and singers"—or so says the national anthem. From the myths of Merlin and King Arthur to the poetry of Dylan Thomas (1914–1953), Wales has a long literary tradition. In music, the country nourishes its traditional Celtic folk music

(especially the harp), and exports popular singers such as Tom Jones, Charlotte Church, and Jem. Popular actors born in Wales include Richard Burton and Catherine Zeta-Jones.

Scotland

Rugged, feisty, colorful Scotland is the yin to England's yang. Whether it's the looser, less-organized nature of the people, the stone and sandstone architecture, the unmanicured landscape, or simply the haggis, go-its-own-way Scotland still stands apart. The home of kilts, bagpipes, whisky, golf, lochs, and shortbread lives up to its clichéd image—and then some.

While the Scots are known for their telltale burr—and more than a few unique words (aye, just listen for a wee blether)—they're also trying to keep alive their own Celtic tongue: Gaelic (pronounced "gallic"). While few Scots speak Gaelic in everyday life, legislation protects it, and it's beginning to be used on road signs.

That's just one small sign of the famously independent Scottish spirit. Since the days of William "Braveheart" Wallace, the Scots have chafed under English rule. Thanks to the recent trend of "devolution," Scotland is increasingly autonomous (even opening their own Parliament in 1999).

Visitors divide their time between the two Scotlands: the Lowlands (the flatter, southern area around Edinburgh and Glasgow, populated by mobile phone–toting yuppies) and the Highlands (the remote, rugged northern area, where proudly traditional Scots eke out a living).

In the Lowlands, don't miss the impressive Scottish capital of Edinburgh, with its attractions-lined Royal Mile and stirring hilltop castle. Nearby, the rival city of Glasgow offers a grittier (but quickly gentrifying) urban ambience. And golfers can't miss the seaside town of St. Andrews, with its world-famous links, vast sandy beaches, colorful university life, and an evocative ruined cathedral.

To commune with the traditional Scottish soul, head for the Highlands. Here you'll find hills, lochs (lakes), "sea lochs" (inlets), castles, and a feeling of remoteness. The "Weeping Glen" of Glencoe offers grand views and a sad tale of Scottish history. The provincial city of Inverness is a handy home base for venturing to uniquely Scottish sights (including the historic site of "Bonnie" Prince Charlie's disastrous Battle of Culloden). Ever-present whisky distilleries offer the chance to sample another uniquely

Scottish "spirit," and viewing the engineering feat of the Caledonian Canal—not to mention famous Loch Ness—inspires awe (say hi to Nessie). Hardy souls can set sail for some of Scotland's islands: Iona and Mull (from Oban), or the super-scenic Isle of Skye.

Whether going to England, Wales, Scotland, or (my choice) all three, you'll have a grand adventure—and a great experience—in Britain. Cheerio!

INTRODUCTION

This book breaks Great Britain into its top big-city, small-town, and rural destinations. It gives you all the information and opinions necessary to wring the maximum value out of your limited time and money in each of these locations. If you plan a month or less for Britain and have a normal appetite for information, this book is all you need. If you're a travel-info fiend, this book sorts through all the superlatives and provides a handy rack upon which to hang your supplemental information.

Experiencing British culture, people, and natural wonders economically and hassle-free has been my goal for more than three decades of traveling, tour guiding, and travel writing. With this new edition, I pass on to you the lessons I've learned, updated for your trip in 2011. (Note that Northern Ireland—which is part of the UK, but technically not Great Britain—is covered in my book *Rick Steves' Ireland*.)

While including the predictable biggies (such as Big Ben, Edinburgh, Stratford-upon-Avon, and Stonehenge), the book also mixes in a healthy dose of Back Door intimacy (windswept Roman lookouts, angelic boys' choirs, and nearly edible Cotswold villages). This book is selective. For example, there are plenty of great countryside palaces; I recommend just the best—Blenheim.

The best is, of course, only my opinion. But after spending half my adult life researching Europe, I've developed a sixth sense for what travelers enjoy. The places featured in this book will knock your spots off.

About This Book

Rick Steves' Great Britain 2011 is a personal tour guide in your pocket. The book is organized by destination. Each destination is a mini-vacation on its own, filled with exciting sights, strollable

Key to This Book

Updates

This book is updated every year, but things change. For the latest, visit www.ricksteves.com/update, and for a valuable list of reports and experiences—good and bad—from fellow travelers, check www.ricksteves.com/feedback.

Abbreviations and Times

I use the following symbols and abbreviations in this book:

Sights are rated:

▲▲▲	**Don't miss**
▲▲	**Try hard to see**
▲	**Worthwhile if you can make it**
No rating	**Worth knowing about**

Tourist information offices are abbreviated as **TI,** and bathrooms are **WC**s. To categorize accommodations, I use a **Sleep Code** (described on page 24).

Like Britain, this book uses the **24-hour clock** for schedules. It's the same through 12:00 noon, then keep going: 13:00, 14:00, and so on. For anything over 12, subtract 12 and add p.m. (14:00 is 2:00 p.m.).

When giving **opening times,** I include both peak season and off-season hours if they differ. So, if a museum is listed as "May–Oct daily 9:00–16:00," it should be open from 9 a.m. until 4 p.m. from the first day of May until the last day of October (but expect exceptions).

For **transit** or **tour departures,** I first list the frequency, then the duration. So, a train connection listed as "2/hour, 1.5 hours" departs twice each hour, and the journey lasts an hour and a half.

neighborhoods, homey and affordable places to stay, and memorable places to eat. In the following chapters, you'll find these sections:

Planning Your Time suggests a schedule with thoughts on how best to use your limited time.

Orientation includes specifics on public transportation, helpful hints, local tour options, easy-to-read maps, and tourist information.

Sights describes the top attractions and includes their cost and hours.

Self-Guided Walks take you through interesting neighborhoods, with a personal tour guide in hand.

Sleeping describes my favorite hotels, from good-value deals to cushy splurges.

Eating serves up a range of options, from inexpensive pubs to fancy restaurants.

Connections outlines your options for traveling to destinations by train, bus, and plane, plus route tips for drivers.

British History and Culture is a quick overview of Britain, past and present.

The **appendix** is a traveler's tool kit, with telephone tips, useful phone numbers, transportation basics (on trains, buses, car rentals, driving, and flights), recommended books and films, a festival list, a climate chart, a handy packing checklist, a hotel reservation form, and a fun British–Yankee dictionary.

Browse through this book and select your favorite sights. Then have a brilliant trip! Traveling like a temporary local, you'll get the absolute most out of every mile, minute, and dollar. I'm happy that you'll be visiting places I know and love, and meeting my favorite British people.

Planning

This section will help you get started on planning your trip—with advice on trip costs, when to go, and what you should know before you take off.

Travel Smart

Your trip to Britain is like a complex play—easier to follow and to really appreciate on a second viewing. While no one does the same trip twice to gain that advantage, reading this book in its entirety before your trip accomplishes much the same thing.

Design an itinerary that enables you to visit sights at the best possible times. Note holidays, specifics on sights, and days when sights are closed. If you're using public transportation, read up on the tips for trains and buses (see pages 812 and 819 of the appendix). If you're renting a car, study my driving tips and the examples of road signs (see page 822).

Mix intense and relaxed periods in your itinerary. To maximize rootedness, minimize one-night stands. It's worth a long drive after dinner to be settled into a town for two nights. B&Bs are also more likely to give a better price to someone staying more than one night. Every trip (and every traveler) needs at least a few slack days (for picnics, laundry, people-watching, and so on). Pace yourself. Assume you will return.

Reread this book as you travel, and visit local TIs. Upon arrival in a new town, lay the groundwork for a smooth departure; write down (or print out from an online source) the schedule for the train or bus that you'll take when you depart. Drivers can study the best route to their next destination.

Get online at Internet cafés or at your hotel, and buy a phone card or carry a mobile phone: You can get tourist information,

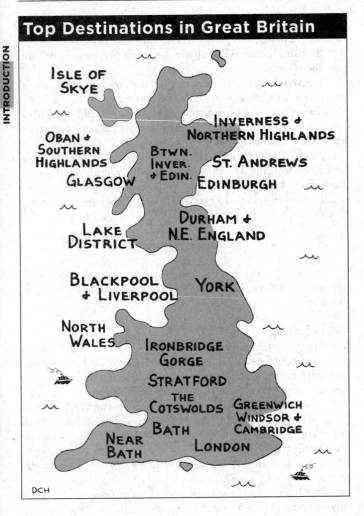

Top Destinations in Great Britain

ISLE OF SKYE

OBAN & SOUTHERN HIGHLANDS

GLASGOW

BTWN. INVER. & EDIN.

INVERNESS & NORTHERN HIGHLANDS

ST. ANDREWS

EDINBURGH

LAKE DISTRICT

DURHAM & N.E. ENGLAND

BLACKPOOL & LIVERPOOL

YORK

NORTH WALES

IRONBRIDGE GORGE

STRATFORD

THE COTSWOLDS

GREENWICH WINDSOR & CAMBRIDGE

NEAR BATH

BATH

LONDON

DCH

learn the latest on sights (special events, tour schedules, etc.), book tickets and tours, make reservations, reconfirm hotels, research transportation connections, check weather, and keep in touch with your loved ones.

Connect with the culture. Set up your own quest for the best pub, cathedral, or chocolate bar. Be open to unexpected experiences. Slow down and enjoy the friendliness of your British hosts. You speak the language—use it! Ask questions; most locals are eager to point you in their idea of the right direction. Keep a notepad in your pocket for organizing your thoughts. Wear your money belt, and figure out how to estimate prices in dollars. Those who expect to travel smart, do.

Trip Costs

Five components make up your trip costs: airfare, surface transportation, room and board, sightseeing and entertainment, and shopping and miscellany. Note that the global economic crisis—and the UK's own budget woes—have prompted the government to increase the VAT (Value-Added Tax, like a national sales tax) from 17.5 percent to 20 percent, effective January 1, 2011. Because prices already include VAT, don't be surprised if things cost more than what I've listed in this book.

Airfare: A basic round-trip US-to-London flight costs $700–1,200, depending on where you fly from and when (cheaper in winter). If your trip extends beyond Great Britain, consider saving time and money by flying "open jaw" (into one city and out of another; for instance, into London and out of Amsterdam).

Surface Transportation: For a three-week whirlwind trip of all my recommended British destinations, allow $550 per person for public transportation (train pass, key buses, and Tube fare in London) or $900 per person (based on two people sharing) for a three-week car rental, parking, gas, and insurance. Leasing is worth considering for trips of two and a half weeks or more. Car rental and leases are cheapest when arranged from the US. Train passes are normally available only outside of Europe (although you can buy a bus pass in Britain). You may save money by simply buying tickets as you go. For more on public transportation and car rental, see "Transportation" in the appendix.

Room and Board: You can thrive in Britain on $115 per day per person for room and board (less in villages). A $115-per-day budget allows an average of $15 for lunch, $30 for dinner, $5 for snacks, and $65 for lodging (based on two people splitting a $130 double room that includes breakfast). Students and tightwads can do it on $60 ($35 for hostel bed, $25 for groceries).

Sightseeing and Entertainment: Figure on paying roughly $10–30 apiece for the major sights that charge admission (Stonehenge-$11, Shakespeare's Birthplace in Stratford-$20, Westminster Abbey-$24, Tower of London-$27), $7 for minor ones (climbing church towers), $12 for guided walks, and $20–40 for bus tours and splurge experiences (such as Scottish folk evenings). For information on various sightseeing passes, see page 21.

Fortunately, many of the best sights in London are free, including the British Museum, National Gallery, National Portrait Gallery, Tate Britain, Tate Modern, Victoria & Albert Museum, and the British Library (though most request donations). An overall average of $30 a day works in most cities (allow $50 for London). Don't skimp here. After all, this category is the driving force behind your trip—you came to sightsee, enjoy, and experience Britain.

Great Britain at a Glance

England

▲▲▲London Thriving metropolis packed with world-class museums, monuments, churches, parks, palaces, theaters, pubs, Beefeaters, telephone boxes, double-decker buses, and all things British.

▲▲Greenwich, Windsor, and Cambridge Easy side-trips from London: famous observatory at the maritime center of Greenwich, the Queen's palace at Windsor, and England's best university town, Cambridge.

▲▲▲Bath Genteel Georgian showcase city, built around the remains of an ancient Roman bath.

▲▲Near Bath England's mysterious heart, including the prehistoric-meets–New Age hill at Glastonbury, spine-tingling stone circles at Stonehenge and Avebury, enjoyable cathedral towns of Wells and Salisbury, delightful Dorset countryside, and rugged sights of South Wales.

▲▲The Cotswolds Remarkably quaint villages—including the cozy market town Chipping Campden, popular hamlet Stow-on-the-Wold, and handy transit hub Moreton-in-Marsh—scattered over a hilly countryside, and near one of England's top palaces at Blenheim.

▲Stratford-upon-Avon Shakespeare's hometown and top venue for seeing his plays performed, plus the medieval Warwick Castle and Coventry's inspiring cathedral nearby.

▲Ironbridge Gorge Birthplace of the Industrial Revolution, with sights and museums that tell the earth-changing story.

▲Blackpool and Liverpool England's tackiest, most fun-loving beach resort at Blackpool, and the increasingly rejuvenated port city (and Beatles hometown) of Liverpool.

▲▲The Lake District Idyllic lakes-and-hills landscape, with enjoyable hikes and joyrides, time-passed valleys, William Wordsworth and Beatrix Potter sights, and the charming home-base town of Keswick.

▲▲▲York Walled medieval town with grand Gothic cathedral, excellent museums (Viking, Victorian, Railway), and atmospheric old center, with the windswept North York Moors at its doorstep.

▲**Durham and Northeast England** Youthful working-class town with magnificent cathedral, plus (nearby) an open-air museum, the Roman remains of Hadrian's Wall, Holy Island, and Bamburgh Castle.

Wales
▲▲▲**North Wales** Scenically rugged land with the castle towns of Conwy, Caernarfon, and Beaumaris; natural beauty of Snowdonia National Park; tourable slate mines at Blaenau Ffestiniog; colorful Welsh villages like Beddgelert and Ruthin; and charming locals who speak a tongue-twisting old language.

Scotland
▲▲▲**Edinburgh** Proud and endlessly entertaining Scottish capital, with an imposing castle, attractions-studded Royal Mile, excellent museums, and atmospheric neighborhoods.

▲**St. Andrews** Sandy beach town that gave birth to golf and hosts Scotland's top university.

▲**Glasgow** Scotland's gritty but gentrifying "second city," a hotbed of modern architecture.

▲**Oban and the Southern Highlands** Handy home-base town of Oban—with boat trips to the isles of Mull and Iona—and the stirring "Weeping Glen" of Glencoe.

▲**Isle of Skye** Remote, dramatically scenic island with craggy mountainscapes, jagged Trotternish Peninsula, castles, distilleries, and the handy home-base towns of Portree and Kyleakin.

▲**Inverness and the Northern Highlands** Regional capital with easy access to more Highlands sights, including Culloden Battlefield (Scotland's Alamo) and monster-spotting at the famous Loch Ness.

▲**Between Inverness and Edinburgh** Whisky mecca of Pitlochry and stately castle and battlefield at Stirling.

Shopping and Miscellany: Figure roughly $2 per postcard, $3 for tea or an ice-cream cone, and $5 per pint of beer. Shopping can vary in cost from nearly nothing to a small fortune. Good budget travelers find that this category has little to do with assembling a trip full of lifelong and wonderful memories.

Sightseeing Priorities

Depending on the length of your trip, and taking geographic proximity into account, here are my recommended priorities.

3 days:	London
5 days, add:	Bath and the Cotswolds
7 days, add:	York
9 days, add:	Edinburgh
11 days, add:	Stratford, Warwick, Blenheim
14 days, add:	North Wales, Wells/Glastonbury/Avebury
17 days, add:	Lake District, Hadrian's Wall, Durham
21 days, add:	Ironbridge Gorge, Blackpool, Scottish Highlands
24 days, add:	Choose two of the following—St. Andrews, Glasgow, Cambridge, South Wales

This list includes virtually everything on "Britain's Best Three-Week Trip by Car" itinerary and map on pages 10 and 11.

Your itinerary will depend on your interests. Nature-lovers will likely put the lovely Lake District, the Scottish Highlands, and North Wales nearer the top of their list, while engineers are drawn like a magnet to Ironbridge Gorge. Coastal Blackpool offers lowbrow, amusement-park fun, refreshing for families and those who've had enough of museums.

When to Go

In Britain, July and August are peak season—my favorite time—with very long days, the best weather, and the busiest schedule of tourist fun. For Scotland, the weather is best in May and June.

Prices and crowds don't go up during peak times as dramatically in Britain as they do in much of Europe, except for holidays and festivals (see "Holidays and Weekends" sidebar, later). Still, travel during "shoulder season" (May, early June, Sept, and early Oct) is easier and can be a bit less expensive. Shoulder-season travelers usually enjoy smaller crowds, decent weather, the full range of sights and tourist fun spots, and the ability to grab a room almost whenever and wherever they like—often at a flexible price. Winter travelers find absolutely no crowds and soft room prices, but shorter sightseeing hours and reliably bad weather. Some attractions are open only on weekends or are closed entirely in the winter (Nov–Feb). The weather can be cold and dreary, and nightfall draws the shades on sightseeing well before dinnertime. While rural charm falls with the leaves, city sightseeing is fine in the winter.

Holidays and Weekends

Popular places are even busier on weekends—especially sunny weekends, which are sufficient cause for an impromptu holiday in this soggy corner of Europe. Three-day weekends can make towns, trains, buses, roads, and hotels even more crowded. Book your accommodations well in advance if you'll be traveling during busy times.

A few national holidays jam things up, especially Bank Holiday Mondays. Mark these dates in red on your travel calendar: New Year's Day, Good Friday through Easter Monday (April 22–25 in 2011), the Bank Holidays that occur on the first and last Mondays in May (May 2 and 30 in 2011), the first Monday in August (Aug 1 in 2011—Scotland only), the last Monday in August (Aug 29 in 2011—England and Wales only), Christmas, and December 26 (Boxing Day). For more information, check the list of holidays and festivals on page 834.

Many businesses, as well as many museums, close on Good Friday, Easter, and New Year's Day. On Christmas, virtually everything closes down, even the Tube in London (taxi rates are high). Museums are also generally closed December 24 and 26; smaller shops are usually closed December 26.

Plan for rain no matter when you go. Just keep traveling and take full advantage of bright spells. The weather can change several times in a day, but rarely is it extreme. As the locals say, "There is no bad weather, only inappropriate clothing." Bring a jacket and dress in layers. Temperatures below 32°F cause headlines, and days that break 80°F—while increasingly frequent in recent years—are still rare in Britain. July and August are not much better than shoulder months. May and June can be lovely anywhere in Britain. (For more information, see the climate chart in the appendix.) While sunshine may be rare, summer days are very long. The midsummer sun is up from 6:30 until 22:30. It's not uncommon to have a gray day, eat dinner, and enjoy hours of sunshine afterward.

Know Before You Go

Your trip is more likely to go smoothly if you plan ahead. Check this list of things to arrange while you're still at home.

You need a **passport**—but no visa or shots—to travel in Great Britain. You may be denied entry into certain European countries if your passport is due to expire within three to six months of your ticketed date of return. Get it renewed if you'll be cutting it close. It can take up to six weeks to get or renew a passport (for more on passports, see www.travel.state.gov). Pack a photocopy of your passport in your luggage in case the original is lost or stolen.

Book rooms well in advance if you'll be traveling during peak

INTRODUCTION

Britain's Best Three-Week Trip by Car

Day	Plan	Sleep in
1	Arrive in London, bus to Bath	Bath
2	Bath	Bath
3	Pick up car, Avebury, Wells, Glastonbury	Bath
4	South Wales, St. Fagans, Tintern	Chipping Campden
5	Explore the Cotswolds, Blenheim	Chipping Campden
6	Stratford, Warwick, Coventry	Ironbridge Gorge
7	Ironbridge Gorge, to North Wales	Conwy
8	Highlights of North Wales	Conwy
9	Liverpool, Blackpool	Blackpool
10	South Lake District	Keswick area
11	North Lake District	Keswick area
12	Drive up west coast of Scotland	Oban
13	Highlands, Loch Ness, Scenic Highlands Drive	Edinburgh
14	Edinburgh	Edinburgh
15	Edinburgh	Edinburgh
16	Hadrian's Wall, Beamish, Durham's Cathedral and evensong	Durham
17	North York Moors, York, turn in car	York
18	York	York
19	Early train to London	London
20	London	London
21	London	London
22	Whew!	

While this three-week itinerary is designed to be done by car, it can be done by train and bus or, better yet, with a BritRail & Drive Pass (best car days: the Cotswolds, North Wales, Lake District, Scottish Highlands, Hadrian's Wall); for more on the pass, see page 816. For three weeks without a car, I'd cut back on the recommended sights with the most frustrating public transportation (South and North Wales, Ironbridge Gorge, and the Scottish Highlands). (Drivers can save a couple of days and a lot of miles by going directly from the Lake District to Edinburgh and skipping the long ride through the Highlands.) Lacing together the cities by train is very slick, and buses get you where the trains don't go. With more time, everything is workable without a car.

season and any major **holidays.**

Most people fly into London and remain there for a few days. Instead, consider a gentler **small-town start** in Bath (the ideal jet-lag pillow), and let London be the finale at the end of your trip. You'll be more rested and ready to tackle England's greatest city. Heathrow Airport has direct bus connections to Bath and other cities. (Bristol Airport is also near Bath.)

If you'll be in London or Stratford and want to **see a play,** check theater schedules ahead of time. For simplicity, I book plays while in Britain, but if there's something you just have to see, consider buying tickets before you go. For the current schedule of London plays and musicals, visit www.officiallondontheatre.co.uk. Because Stratford's main theater recently reopened after a long renovation, tickets to Shakespeare performances there are likely to sell out even earlier than usual (see www.rsc.org.uk for details). Note that if it's just Shakespeare you're after—with or without Stratford—you can see his plays in London, too.

To attend the **Edinburgh Festival** (Aug 12–Sept 4 in 2011), you can book tickets in advance (for details, see page 634).

If you want to **golf at St. Andrews' famous Old Course,** reserve a year ahead, or for other courses, reserve two weeks ahead. You can also try for a tee time when you arrive, but to play the Old Course, you'll need a golf handicap certificate (see page 669).

At **Stonehenge,** anyone can see the stones from behind the rope line, but if you want to go inside the stone circle, you'll need advance reservations (see page 294).

Call your **debit- and credit-card companies** to let them know the countries you'll be visiting, to ask about fees, and more (see page 16).

Do your homework if you want to buy **travel insurance.** Compare the cost of the insurance to the likelihood of your using it and your potential loss if something goes wrong. For more information, see www.ricksteves.com/insurance.

If you're bringing an MP3 player, you can download free information from **Rick Steves Audio Europe,** featuring hours of travel interviews on Great Britain, audio tours of major sights in London, and more (at www.ricksteves.com/audioeurope and in iTunes; for details, see page 828).

If you're planning on **renting a car** in Great Britain, you'll need your driver's license. An International Driving Permit is recommended (see page 820).

If traveling to continental Europe on the **Eurostar** train, consider ordering a ticket in advance (or buy it in Britain); for details, see page 194.

Because **airline carry-on restrictions** are always changing, visit the Transportation Security Administration's website (www.tsa.gov/travelers) for an up-to-date list of what you can bring on the plane with you...and what you have to check. Some airlines may restrict you to only one carry-on (no extras like a purse or daypack); check with your airline or at the British transportation website (www.dft.gov.uk).

Practicalities

Emergency and Medical Help: Dial 999 for police or medical emergencies. If you get sick, do as the Brits do and go to a pharmacist for advice. Or ask at your B&B or hotel for help—they'll know the nearest medical and emergency services.

Lost or Stolen Passport: To replace a passport, you'll need to go in person to a US embassy or consulate (see page 809). While not required, having a backup form of ID—ideally a photocopy of your passport and driver's license—speeds up a replacement. For more info, see www.ricksteves.com/help.

Time Zones: Britain is one hour earlier than most of continental Europe and five/eight hours ahead of the East/West coasts of the US. The exceptions are the beginning and end of Daylight Saving Time: Britain and Europe "spring forward" the last Sunday in March (two weeks after most of North America), and "fall back" the last Sunday in October (one week before North America). For a handy online time converter, try www.timeanddate.com/world clock.

Business Hours: In Britain, most stores are open Monday through Saturday from roughly 10:00 to 17:00. In London, stores stay open later on Wednesday or Thursday (until 19:00 or 20:00), depending on the neighborhood. Sundays have the same pros and cons as they do for travelers in the US (special events, limited hours, banks and many shops closed, limited public transportation, no rush hours, street markets lively with shoppers). Saturdays are virtually weekdays with earlier closing hours and no rush hour (though transportation connections can be less frequent than on weekdays).

Watt's Up? Britain's electrical system is different from North America's in two ways: the shape of the plug (three square prongs—not the two round prongs used in continental Europe) and the voltage of the current (220 volts instead of 110 volts). For your North American plug to work in Britain, you'll need a three-prong adapter plug, sold inexpensively at travel stores in the US, and in British airports and drugstores. As for the voltage, most newer electronics or travel appliances (such as hair dryers, laptops, and battery chargers) automatically convert the voltage—if you see a range of voltages printed on the item or its plug (such as "110–220"), it'll work in Great Britain and Europe. Otherwise, you can buy a converter separately in the US (about $20), though these tend to be heavy and unreliable, and get really hot when in use. For small appliances that don't automatically convert voltage, I suggest going without or buying a cheap replacement in Britain. Low-cost hairdryers and other small appliances are sold at Superdrug, Boots, or Argos stores (ask your hotelier for the closest branch).

Discounts: Discounts (called "concessions" or "concs" in Britain) aren't listed in this book. However, many British sights offer discounts for seniors (loosely defined as those who are retired or willing to call themselves a senior), youths (ages 8–18), groups of 10 or more, families, and students or teachers with proper identification cards (www.isic.org). Always ask. Some discounts are available only for EU citizens.

News: British papers cover global events, and Americans can also keep in touch via the *International Herald Tribune* (published almost daily throughout Europe and online at www.iht.com). Other newsy sites are http://news.bbc.co.uk and www.europeantimes.com. Every Tuesday, the European editions of *Time* and *Newsweek* hit the stands with articles of particular interest to travelers in Europe. Sports addicts can get their daily fix online at www.espn.com or from *USA Today*. Many hotels have BBC News (of course) and CNN television channels.

Money

This section offers advice on how to pay for purchases on your trip (including getting cash from ATMs and paying with plastic), dealing with lost or stolen cards, VAT (sales tax) refunds, and tipping.

What to Bring

Bring both a credit card and a debit card. You'll use the debit card at cash machines (ATMs) to withdraw pounds for most purchases, and the credit card to pay for larger items. Some travelers carry a third card as a backup, in case one gets demagnetized or eaten by a temperamental machine.

As an emergency backup, bring several hundred dollars in hard cash (in easy-to-exchange $20 bills). Avoid using currency exchange booths (lousy rates and/or outrageous fees); if you have foreign currency to exchange, take it to a bank. Don't use traveler's checks—they're a waste of time (long waits at slow banks) and a waste of money in fees.

Exchange Rate

I list prices in pounds (£) throughout this book.

1 British pound (£1) = about $1.60

While the euro (€) is now the currency of most of Europe, Britain is sticking with its pound sterling. The British pound (£), also called a "quid," is broken into 100 pence (p). Pence means "cents." You'll find coins ranging from 1p to £2, and bills from £5 to £50. Counterfeit pound coins are easy to spot (real coins have an inscription on their outside rims; the fakes look like tree bark).

London is so expensive that some travelers try to kid themselves that pounds are dollars. But when they get home, that £1,000 Visa bill isn't asking for $1,000...it wants $1,600. (To get the latest rate and print a cheat sheet, see www .oanda.com.)

Scotland and Northern Ireland issue their own currency in pounds, worth the same as an English pound. English, Scottish, and Northern Ireland's Ulster pounds are technically interchangeable in each region, although Scottish and Ulster pounds are considered "undesirable" and sometimes not accepted in England. Banks in any of the three regions will convert your Scottish or Ulster pounds into English pounds for no charge. Don't worry about the coins, which are accepted throughout Britain.

Cash

Cash is just as desirable in Britain as it is at home. Small businesses (hotels, restaurants, and shops) prefer that you pay your bills with cash. Some vendors will charge you extra for using a credit card, and some won't take credit cards at all.

Throughout Britain, ATMs (which locals call "cashpoints") are the standard way for travelers to get cash. To withdraw money from an ATM, you'll need a debit card (ideally with a Visa or MasterCard logo for maximum usability), plus a PIN code. Know your PIN code in numbers because there are no letters on European keypads. You could use a credit card for ATM transactions, but it's generally more expensive (since it's considered a "cash advance" rather than a "withdrawal"). For security, it's best to shield the keypad when entering your PIN at the ATM.

When using an ATM, taking out large sums of money can reduce the number of per-transaction bank fees you'll pay. If the machine refuses your request, try again and select a smaller amount (some cash machines limit the amount you can withdraw—don't take it personally). If that doesn't work, try a different machine.

Most ATMs in Britain are located outside of a bank. Try to use the ATM when the branch is open; if your card is eaten by a machine, you can immediately go inside for help. If the ATM dispenses big bills, try to break them at a bank or larger store, since it's easier to pay for purchases at small businesses using smaller bills.

Even in Britain, you'll need to keep your cash safe. Use a money belt—a pouch with a strap that you buckle around your waist like a belt and wear under your clothes. Pickpockets target tourists. A money belt provides peace of mind, allowing you to carry lots of cash safely. Don't waste time every few days tracking down a cash machine—withdraw a week's worth of money, stuff it in your money belt, and travel!

Credit and Debit Cards

Visa and MasterCard are more commonly accepted than American Express. While you can use either a credit or a debit card for most transactions, using a credit card offers a greater degree of fraud protection (since debit cards draw funds directly from your account).

Just like at home, credit and debit cards are accepted by larger hotels, restaurants, and shops. I typically use my debit card for withdrawing cash from ATMs, and I use my credit card only in a few specific situations: to book hotel reservations by phone, to make major purchases (such as car rentals, plane tickets, and long hotel stays), and to pay for things near the end of my trip (to avoid another visit to the ATM).

Ask Your Credit- or Debit-Card Company: Before your trip, contact the company that issued your debit or credit cards.

• Confirm your card will work overseas, and alert them that you'll be using it in Europe; otherwise, they may deny transactions if they perceive unusual spending patterns.

• Ask for the specifics on transaction **fees.** When you use your credit or debit card—either for purchases or ATM withdrawals—you'll often be charged additional "international transaction" fees of up to 3 percent (1 percent is normal) plus $5 per transaction. If your fees are too high, consider getting a card just for your trip: Capital One (www.capitalone.com) and most credit unions have low-to-no international fees.

• If you plan to withdraw cash from ATMs, confirm your daily **withdrawal limit** (£300 is usually about the maximum). Some travelers prefer a high limit that allows them to take out more cash at each ATM stop, while others prefer to set a lower limit in case their card is stolen.

• Ask for your credit card's **PIN** in case you encounter Europe's chip-and-PIN system. For security reasons, most banks will only mail a PIN, so give yourself plenty of time to get the code if you don't already know it.

Chip and PIN: If your card is declined for a purchase in Europe, it may be because of chip and PIN, which requires cardholders to punch in a PIN instead of signing a receipt. Much of Europe, including Great Britain, Ireland, France, the Netherlands, and Scandinavia, is adopting this system. Chip and PIN is used by some merchants and also at automated payment machines—such as those at train stations, parking garages, luggage lockers, and self-serve pumps at gas stations. If you're prompted to enter your PIN (but don't know it), ask if the cashier can print a receipt for you to sign instead, or just pay cash. If you're dealing with an automated machine that won't take your card, look for a cashier nearby who can make your card work. The easiest solution is to carry sufficient cash.

Dynamic Currency Conversion: If merchants offer to convert your purchase price into dollars (called dynamic currency conversion, or DCC), refuse this "service." You'll pay even more in fees for the expensive convenience of seeing your charge in dollars.

Damage Control for Lost Cards

If you lose your credit, debit, or ATM card, you can stop people from using it by reporting the loss immediately to the respective global customer-assistance centers. Call these 24-hour US numbers collect: Visa (410/581-9994), MasterCard (636/722-7111), and American Express (623/492-8427). Diner's Club has offices in Britain (0870-1900-011) and the US (702/797-5532, call collect).

At a minimum, you'll need to know the name of the financial institution that issued you the card, along with the type of card (classic, platinum, or whatever). Providing the following information will allow for a quicker cancellation of your missing card: full card number, whether you are the primary or secondary cardholder, the name exactly as printed on the card, billing address, home phone number, circumstances of the loss or theft, and identification verification (your birth date, your mother's maiden name, or your Social Security number—memorize this, don't carry a copy). If you are the secondary cardholder, you'll also need to provide the primary cardholder's identification-verification details. You can generally receive a temporary card within two or three business days.

If you promptly report your card lost or stolen, you typically won't be responsible for any unauthorized transactions on your account, although many banks charge a liability fee of $50.

Tipping

Tipping in Britain isn't as automatic and generous as it is in the US, but for special service, tips are appreciated, if not expected. As in the US, the proper amount depends on your resources, tipping philosophy, and the circumstances, but some general guidelines apply.

INTRODUCTION

Restaurants: At a pub or restaurant with waitstaff, check the menu or your bill to see if the service is included; if not, tip about 10 percent. Many restaurants in London now add a 12 percent "optional" tip onto the bill—read your bill carefully, and tip only what you think the service warrants. At pubs where you order at the counter, you don't have to tip. (Regular customers ordering a round sometimes say, "Add one for yourself" as a tip for drinks ordered at the bar—but this isn't expected.)

Taxis: To tip the cabbie, round up. For a typical ride, round up to a maximum of 10 percent (to pay a £4.50 fare, give £5; for a £28 fare, give £30). If the cabbie hauls your bags and zips you to the airport to help you catch your flight, you might want to toss in a little more. But if you feel like you're being driven in circles or otherwise ripped off, skip the tip.

Special Services: Tour guides at public sights sometimes hold out their hands for tips after they give their spiel. If I've already paid for the tour, I don't tip extra unless they've really impressed me. At hotels, if you let porters carry your luggage, it's polite to give them 50p for each bag (another reason to pack light). I don't tip the maid, but if you do, you can leave 50p per overnight at the end of your stay.

In general, if someone in the service industry does a super job for you, a small tip of a pound or two is appropriate, but not required.

When in doubt, ask. If you're not sure whether (or how much) to tip for a service, ask your hotelier or the TI; they'll fill you in on how it's done on their turf.

Getting a VAT Refund

Wrapped into the purchase price of your British souvenirs is a Value-Added Tax (VAT) of 20 percent (as of January 1, 2011). If you purchase more than £20 (about $32) worth of goods at a store that participates in the VAT-refund scheme, you're entitled to get most of that tax back. Getting your refund is usually straight-forward and, if you buy a substantial amount of souvenirs, well worth the hassle. If you're lucky, the merchant will subtract the tax when you make your purchase. (This is more likely to occur if the store ships the goods to your home.) Otherwise, you'll need to:

Get the paperwork. Have the merchant completely fill out the necessary refund document, called a "Tax-Free Shopping Cheque." You'll have to present your passport at the store.

Get your stamp at the border or airport. Process your cheque(s) at your last stop in the EU (e.g., at the airport) with the customs agent who deals with VAT refunds. It's best to keep your purchases in your carry-on for viewing, but if they're too large or dangerous (such as knives) to carry on, track down the proper customs agent to inspect them before you check your bag. You're not supposed to use your purchased goods before you leave. If you show up at customs wearing your new Wellingtons, officials might look the other way—or deny you a refund.

Collect your refund. You'll need to return your stamped document to the retailer or its representative. Many merchants work with a service, such as Global Refund (www.globalrefund.com) or Premier Tax Free (www.premiertaxfree.com), which have offices at major airports, ports, or border crossings. These services, which extract a 4 percent fee, can refund your money immediately in your currency of choice or credit your card (within two billing cycles). If the retailer handles VAT refunds directly, it's up to you to contact the merchant for your refund. Or you can mail the documents from your point of departure (using a stamped, addressed envelope you've prepared or one that's been provided by the merchant). You'll then have to wait—it can take months.

Customs for American Shoppers

You are allowed to take home $800 worth of items per person duty-free, once every 30 days. The next $1,000 is taxed at a flat 3 percent. After that, you pay the individual item's duty rate. You can also bring in duty-free a liter of alcohol (slightly more than a standard-size bottle of wine; you must be at least 21), 200 cigarettes, and up to 100 non-Cuban cigars.

As for food, you can take home vacuum-packed cheeses; dried herbs, spices, or mushrooms; and canned fruits or vegetables, including jams and vegetable spreads. Baked goods, candy, chocolate, oil, vinegar, mustard, and honey are OK. Fresh fruits or vegetables (even that banana from your airplane breakfast) are not permitted. Meats are generally not allowed. Just because a duty-free shop in an airport sells a food product doesn't mean it will automatically pass US customs. Be prepared to lose your investment.

Note that you'll need to carefully pack any bottles of wine, jam, honey, oil, and other liquid-containing items in your checked luggage, due to the three-ounce limit on liquids in carry-on baggage. To check customs rules and duty rates before you go, visit www.cbp.gov, and click on "Travel," then "Know Before You Go."

Sightseeing

Sightseeing can be hard work. Use these tips to make your visits to Britain's finest sights meaningful, fun, efficient, and painless.

Plan Ahead

Set up an itinerary that allows you to fit in all your must-see sights. For a one-stop look at opening hours in the bigger cities, see the

"At a Glance" sidebars throughout this book. Most sights keep stable hours, but you can easily confirm the latest by checking their website or asking at the local TI.

Don't put off visiting a must-see sight—you never know when a place will close unexpectedly for a holiday, strike, or restoration. On holidays (see list on page 834), expect shorter hours or closures.

When possible, visit major sights in the morning (when your energy is best) and save other activities for the afternoon. Hit the museum highlights first, then see the rest if you have the stamina and time.

Going at the right time helps avoid crowds. This book offers tips on specific sights. Try visiting very early, at lunch, or very late. Evening visits are usually peaceful, with fewer crowds. For specifics on London at night, see the sidebar on page 94.

Study up. To get the most out of the self-guided walks and sight descriptions in this book, read them before you visit.

At Sights

Here's what you can typically expect:

Some important sights may have metal detectors or conduct bag searches that will slow your entry, while others may require you to check daypacks and coats. They'll be kept safely. If you have something you can't bear to part with, stash it in a pocket or purse. To avoid checking a small backpack, carry it under your arm like a purse as you enter. From a guard's point of view, a backpack is generally a problem while a purse is not.

At churches—which often offer interesting art (usually free) and a cool, welcome seat—a modest dress code (no bare shoulders or shorts) is encouraged.

Flash photography is sometimes banned, but taking photos without a flash is usually OK. Look for signs or ask. Flashes damage oil paintings and distract others in the room. Even without a flash, a handheld camera will take a decent picture (or buy postcards or posters at the museum bookstore). If photos are permitted, video cameras are generally OK, too.

Museums have special exhibits in addition to their permanent collection. Some exhibits are included in the entry price; others come at an extra cost (which you may have to pay even if you don't want to see the exhibit).

Many sights rent audioguides, which generally offer excellent recorded descriptions (about £3.50; sometimes included with admission). If you bring along your own pair of headphones and a Y-jack, you can sometimes share one audioguide with your travel partner and save money. Or download my free London audio tours—covering the British Museum, British Library, St. Paul's Cathedral, and the City of London and Westminster walks—onto your MP3 player and bring them along (see page 828). Guided tours, which usually cost around £3–8 and vary widely in quality, are most likely to occur during peak season.

Some sights run short films featuring their highlights and history. These are generally well worth your time. I make it standard operating procedure to ask when I arrive at a sight if there is a film.

Expect changes—artwork can be on tour, on loan, out sick, or shifted at the whim of the curator. To adapt, pick up any available free floor plans as you enter. Ask the museum staff if you can't find a particular piece.

Important sights often have an on-site café or cafeteria (usually a good place to rest and have a snack or light meal). The WCs are usually free and nearly always clean (it's smart to carry tissues in case a WC runs out of TP).

Many places sell postcards that highlight their attractions. Before you leave, scan the postcards and thumb through the biggest guidebook (or skim its index) to be sure you haven't overlooked something you'd like to see.

Most sights stop admitting people 30–60 minutes before closing time, and some rooms close early (often 45 minutes before the actual closing time). Guards usher people out, so don't save the best for last.

Every sight or museum offers more than what is covered in this book. Use the information in this book as an introduction—not the final word.

Sightseeing Passes and Memberships

Many sights in Britain are covered by the Great British Heritage Pass or these memberships: English Heritage or National Trust. If you're a whirlwind sightseer, seriously consider the Great British Heritage Pass, which covers the most sights.

Great British Heritage Pass: The best deal for busy travelers, this pass covers all of the major English Heritage and National Trust sights, plus many others (including several major attractions in Scotland, Wales, and Northern Ireland). Covering about 600 historic sights, this pass is good for a certain number of consecutive days (£45/4 days, £65/7 days, £85/15 days, £115/30 days; £99/£143/£187/£253 family pass also available for up to 2 adults and 3 kids ages 5–15—though note that kids already get discounts at sights; tel. 0870-242-9988, www.britishheritagepass.com). You can buy this pass online (£6.50 extra for shipping) or at various tourist information centers in Britain; for example, in London, this pass is sold by the Britain and London Visitors Centre on Lower Regent Street.

Memberships: Many sights in Britain are managed by either

Get It Right

Americans tend to use "England," "Britain," and "UK" interchangeably, but they're not the same:

- **England** is in the southeast part of Britain.
- **Britain** is the name of the island.
- **Great Britain** is the political union of England, Scotland, and Wales.
- The **United Kingdom** adds Northern Ireland.
- The **British Isles** (not a political entity) also includes the independent Republic of Ireland.
- The **British Commonwealth** is a loose association of possessions and former colonies (including Canada, Australia, and India) that profess at least symbolic loyalty to the Crown.

the English Heritage or the National Trust (the sights don't overlap). Both organizations sell annual memberships that allow free or discounted entry to the sights they supervise; the English Heritage also sells passes. You can join the National Trust or English Heritage online or at just about any of their sights.

Membership in **English Heritage** includes free entry to more than 400 sights in England and half-price admission to about 100 more sights in Scotland and Wales. For most travelers, the **Overseas Visitor Pass** is a better choice than the pricier one-year membership (Visitor Pass: £20/7 days, £24.50/14 days, discounts for couples and families; Membership: £44 for one person, £77 for two, discounts for seniors and students, children under 19 free; toll tel. 0870-333-1182, www.english-heritage.org.uk).

Membership in the **National Trust** is best suited for garden-and-estate enthusiasts, ideally those traveling by car. It covers more than 300 historic houses, manors, and gardens throughout Great Britain (£48.50 for one year, student and family discounts, children under 5 free, www.nationaltrust.org.uk).

CADW, the Welsh version of the National Trust, sells an **Explorer Pass** that covers many sights in Wales. If you're planning to visit at least three castles or other historic places on their list, the pass will probably save you money (3-day pass: £11/1 person, £18/2 people, £26.50/family; 7-day pass: £17.50/1 person, £29/2 people, £36/family; available at www.cadw.wales.gov.uk or individual sights).

Things to Consider: If you have children and you're all avid sightseers, consider the Great British Heritage family pass; otherwise don't get a pass or membership for them, because they get in free or cheap at most sights. Similarly, people over 60 get "concessions" (discounted prices) at many British sights (and can get a senior discount on an English Heritage membership). If you're traveling by car and can get to the more remote sights, you're more likely to get your money's worth out of a pass or membership, especially during peak season (Easter–Oct). If you're traveling off-season (Nov–Easter) when many of the sights are closed, the deals are a lesser value.

The Bottom Line: These various deals can save a busy sight-seer money...but only if you choose carefully. Make a list of the sights you plan to see, check which sights are covered (visit the websites listed above), and then add up the total if you were to pay individual admissions to the covered sights. Compare the total to the cost of the pass or membership. Keep in mind that an advantage to any of these deals is that you'll feel free to dip into lesser sights that normally aren't worth the cost of their admission.

Sleeping

I favor accommodations (and restaurants) handy to your sight-seeing activities. In Britain, small bed-and-breakfast places (B&Bs) generally provide the best value, though I also include some bigger hotels. Rather than list lodgings scattered throughout a city, I choose two or three favorite neighborhoods and recommend the best accommodations values in each, from $30 bunk beds to fancy-for-my-book $300 doubles. Outside of pricey London, you can expect to find good doubles for $80–160, including cooked breakfasts and tax. (For specifics on London, see page 145.)

I look for places that are friendly; clean; a good value; located in a central, safe, quiet neighborhood; and not mentioned in other guidebooks. I'm more impressed by a handy location and a fun-loving philosophy than flat-screen TVs and shoeshine machines. For tips on making reservations, see page 31.

Rates and Deals

I've described my recommended accommodations using a Sleep Code (see sidebar on next page). Prices listed are for one-night stays in peak season, usually include a hearty breakfast, and assume you're booking directly (not through a TI or online hotel-booking engine).

You should find prices listed in this book to be good through 2011 (except during major holidays and festivals—see page

INTRODUCTION

Sleep Code

(£1 = about $1.60, country code: 44)
To help you easily sort through these listings, I've divided the rooms into three categories, based on the price for a double room with bath:

$$$	**Higher Priced**
$$	**Moderately Priced**
$	**Lower Priced**

To give maximum information in a minimum of space, I use the following code to describe accommodations. Prices in this book are listed per room, not per person. When a price range is given for a type of room (such as "Db-£80–120"), it means the price fluctuates with the season, size of room, or length of stay.

S = Single room, or price for one person in a double.

D = Double or twin room. (I specify double- and twin-bed rooms only if they are priced differently, or if a place has only one or the other. When reserving, you should specify.)

T = Three-person room (often a double bed with a single).

Q = Four-person room (adding an extra child's bed to a T is usually cheaper).

b = Private bathroom with toilet and shower or tub.

s = Private shower or tub only. (The toilet is down the hall.)

According to this code, a couple staying at a "Db-£80" hotel would pay a total of £80 (about $130) per night for a room with a private toilet and shower (or tub). Unless otherwise noted, credit cards are accepted and breakfast is included.

If I mention "Internet access" in a listing, there's a public terminal in the lobby for guests to use. If I include "Wi-Fi," you can generally access it in your room (usually for free), but only if you have your own laptop.

834)—though some might increase slightly due to the January 2011 VAT tax hike. B&B rates tend to be pretty straightforward, but can be soft in slow times. However, at hotels, the official "rack rates" (the highest rates a hotel charges) can be misleading, since they omit lower promotional rates, cheaper oddball rooms, and special clearance deals. (Some fancy £120 rooms can rent for a third off if you arrive late on a slow day and ask for a deal.)

Given the economic downturn, hoteliers are willing and eager to make a deal. I'd suggest emailing several hotels to ask for their best price. Comparison-shop and make your choice.

As you look over the listings, you'll notice that some accommodations promise special prices to my readers who book direct (without using a room-finding service or hotel-booking website, which take a commission). To get these rates, mention this book when you reserve, then show the book upon arrival. Many B&Bs now take credit cards, but many add the card service fee to your bill (about 3 percent of the price).

In general, prices can soften up if you do any of the following: offer to pay cash, stay at least three nights, or mention this book. You can also try asking for a cheaper room or a discount, or offer to skip breakfast. To save money off-season, consider arriving without a reservation and dropping in at the last minute.

When establishing prices, confirm if the charge is per person or per room (if a price is too good to be true, it's probably per person). Because many places in Britain charge per person, small groups often pay the same for a single and a double as they would for a triple. In this book, however, room prices are listed per room, not per person.

Helpful Hints

Many places listed have three floors of rooms and steep stairs; expect good exercise and be happy you packed light. You'll generally find an elevator (called a "lift" here) only at larger hotels. If you're concerned about stairs, call and ask about ground-floor rooms or pay for a hotel with a lift. Air-conditioning is rare (I've noted which of my listings have it), but most places have fans. On hot summer nights, you'll want your window open—though in big cities, you may have to put up with street noise.

Learn the terminology: An "en suite" room has a bathroom (toilet and shower/tub) actually inside the room; a room with a "private bathroom" can mean that the bathroom is all yours, but it's across the hall; and a "standard" room has access to a bathroom down the hall that's shared with other rooms. (Confusingly, pricey hotels might call an en suite room "standard" to differentiate it from a fancier "superior" or "deluxe" room—if you're not sure, ask for clarification.)

Figuring there's little difference between "en suite" and "private" rooms, some places charge the same for both. If you want your own bathroom inside the room, request "en suite."

If money's tight, ask for a standard room. You'll almost always have a sink in your room. And, as more rooms go "en suite," the hallway bathroom is shared with fewer standard rooms.

"Twin" means two single beds, and "double" means one double bed (in my listings, I list all two-person rooms as "doubles"). If you will take either one, let them know, or you might be needlessly turned away. Most hotels offer family deals, which means that parents with young children can easily get a room with an extra child's bed or a discount for larger rooms. Call to negotiate the price. Teenage kids are generally charged as adults. Kids under five almost always sleep free.

Note that to be called a "hotel," a place technically must have certain amenities, including a 24-hour reception (though this rule is loosely applied). A place called "townhouse" or "house" (such as "London House") is like a big B&B or a small family-run hotel—with fewer amenities but more character than a "hotel."

Britain has a rating system for hotels and B&Bs. These diamonds and stars are supposed to imply quality, but I find that they mean only that the place sporting these symbols is paying dues to the tourist board. Rating systems often have little to do with value.

Hoteliers and B&B hosts can be a great help and source of advice. Most know their city well and can assist you with everything from public transit and airport connections to finding a good restaurant, the nearest Internet café, or launderette.

Even at the best places, mechanical breakdowns occur: Air-conditioning malfunctions, sinks leak, hot water turns cold, and toilets gurgle and smell. Report your concerns clearly and calmly at the front desk. For more complicated problems, don't expect instant results.

If you suspect night noise will be a problem, ask for a quiet room in the back or on an upper floor. To guard against theft in your room, keep valuables out of sight. Some rooms come with a safe, and others have safes at the front desk. Use them if you're concerned.

Checkout can pose problems if surprise charges pop up on your bill. If you settle up your bill the day before you leave, you'll have time to discuss and address any points of contention (before 19:00, when the night shift usually arrives).

If you're traveling beyond my recommended destinations, you'll find accommodations where you need them. Any town with tourists has a TI that books rooms or can give you a list and point you in the right direction. In the absence of a TI, ask people on the street or in pubs or restaurants for help. Online, visit www.smoothhound.co.uk, which offers a range of accommodations for towns throughout the UK (searchable by town, airport, hotel name, or price range).

Types of Accommodations
B&Bs

Compared to hotels, bed-and-breakfast places give you double the cultural intimacy for half the price. While you may lose some of the conveniences of a hotel—such as lounges, in-room phones,

Smoke-Free Great Britain

Great Britain's public places are now smoke-free. Hotels, B&Bs, and restaurants are required to be non-smoking (though hoteliers are permitted to designate specific rooms for smokers). In the "Sleeping" sections of each chapter, I've listed the rare instance where a hotel has smoking rooms—but for the most part, the smoke truly has cleared in Britain.

frequent bed-sheet changes, and being able to pay with a credit card—I happily make the trade-off for the lower rates and personal touches. Some B&Bs now take credit cards, but may add the card service fee to your bill (about 3 percent of the price). If you have a reasonable but limited budget, skip hotels and go the B&B way.

You'll generally pay £25–50 (about $40–80) per person for a double room in a B&B in Britain. Lately the big, impersonal chain hotels are offering rooms cheaper than the mom-and-pop places (but without breakfast); see "Big, Cheap, Modern Hotels," later. When considering the price of a B&B or small hotel, remember you're getting two breakfasts (up to a £25 value) for each double room.

B&Bs range from large guest houses with 15–20 rooms to small homes renting out a spare bedroom, but they typically have six rooms or fewer. The philosophy of the management determines the character of a place more than its size and facilities offered. I avoid places run as a business by absentee owners. My top listings are run by people who enjoy welcoming the world to their breakfast table.

B&B proprietors are selective as to whom they invite in for the night. At some B&Bs, children are not welcome. Risky-looking people (two or more single men are often assumed to be potential troublemakers) find many places suddenly full. If you'll be staying for more than one night, you are a "desirable." In popular weekend-getaway spots, you're unlikely to find a place to take you for Saturday night only. If my listings are full, ask for guidance. Mentioning this book can help. Owners usually work together and can call up an ally to land you a bed.

B&Bs come with their own etiquette and quirks. Owners are at the whim of their guests—if you're getting up early, so are they; and if you check in late, they'll wait up for you. Be considerate. It's polite to call ahead to confirm your reservation the day before and give them a rough estimate of your arrival time. This allows them to plan their day and run errands before or after you arrive...and it also allows them to give you specific directions for driving or walking to their place.

B&Bs serve a hearty fried breakfast of eggs and much more (for details on breakfast, see page 36). Because your B&B owner is also the cook, there's usually a limited time span when breakfast is served (typically about an hour—make sure you know when it is). Sometimes they'll even designate a specific time when all guests are expected to gather to eat. It's an unwritten rule that guests shouldn't show up at the very end of the breakfast period and expect a full cooked breakfast. If you do arrive late (or need to leave before breakfast is served), most B&B hosts are happy to let you help yourself to cereal, fruit, and coffee; ask politely if it's possible.

B&Bs are not hotels. Think of your host as a friendly acquaintance who's invited you to stay in her home, rather than someone you're paying to wait on you.

Americans sometimes assume they'll get new towels each day. The British don't, and neither should you. Hang towels up to dry and reuse.

Be aware of luggage etiquette. A large bag in a compact older building can easily turn even the most graceful of us into a bull in a British china shop. If you've got a backpack, don't wear it indoors. If your host offers to carry your bag upstairs, accept—they're adept at maneuvering luggage up tiny staircases without damaging their walls and banisters. Finally, use your room's luggage racks—putting bags on empty beds can dirty and scuff nice comforters. Treat these lovingly maintained homes as you would a friend's house.

In almost every B&B, you'll encounter unusual bathroom fixtures. The "pump toilet" has a flushing handle that doesn't kick in unless you push it just right: too hard or too soft, and it won't go. Be decisive but not ruthless. There's also the "dial-a-shower," an electronic box under the shower head where you'll turn a dial to select the heat of the water and (sometimes with a separate dial or button) turn on or shut off the flow of water. If you can't find the switch to turn on the shower, it may be just outside the bathroom.

Most rooms in most B&Bs come with a hot-water pot, cups, tea bags, and coffee packets (if you prefer decaf, buy a jar at a grocery before leaving home, and dump into a baggie for easy packing). Electrical outlets have switches that turn the current on or off; if your electrical appliance isn't working, flip the switch at the outlet.

Most B&Bs come with thin walls and doors. This can make for a noisy night, especially with people walking down the hall to use the bathroom. If you're a light sleeper, bring earplugs. And please be quiet in the halls and in your rooms (talk softly, and keep the TV volume low). Those of us getting up early will thank you for it.

Your B&B bedroom probably won't include a phone. In this mobile-phone age, street phone booths can be few and far between. Some B&B owners will allow you to use their phone (with an international phone card), but many are disinclined to let you ring up charges. That's because most British people pay for each local call (whether from a fixed line or a mobile phone), and rates are expensive. Therefore, to be polite, ask to use their phone only in an emergency—and offer to use an international calling card or to pay for the call. If you plan to be staying in B&Bs and making frequent calls, consider buying a British mobile phone (see page 808). And if you're bringing your laptop, look for places with Wi-Fi (noted in my hotel listings).

Many B&B owners are also pet owners. And, while pets are rarely allowed into guest rooms, and B&B proprietors are typically very tidy, those with pet allergies might be bothered. I've tried to list which B&Bs have pets, but if you're allergic, ask about pets when you reserve.

Remember that you'll likely need to pay cash for your room. Plan ahead so you have enough cash to pay up when you check out.

Big, Cheap, Modern Hotels

American-style hotel chains—popular with budget tour groups—offer all the predictable comforts in a no-frills, practical package. While most travelers prefer the classic British B&B experience, chain hotels—which are popping up in bigger cities all over Britain—can be a great value. They offer simple, clean, and modern rooms for up to four people (two adults/two children) for £60–100, depending on the location. Some are located near the train station, on major highways, or outside the city center. What you lose in charm, you gain in savings.

These hotels are especially worth considering for families, as kids generally stay for free (but check details on the websites). Most rooms have a double bed, single bed, five-foot trundle bed, private shower, WC, and TV. There's usually an attached restaurant, good security, an elevator, and a 24-hour staffed reception desk. Breakfast is always extra. Of course, they're as cozy as a Motel 6, but many travelers love them...or, at least, the value they provide.

Here are some tips for getting the best deal:

Book through their websites, as they are often the easiest way to make reservations, and will generally net you a discount. Midweek prices are generally higher than weekend rates, and Sunday nights can be shockingly cheap. The price ranges I list tend to be wide, as the specific rates vary dramatically with demand. In fact, the rates for a particular room for a specific date can change from day to day or week to week (like airline tickets), making it difficult to know when to book. On the hotel's online reservation form, punch in the dates you're considering to see what the going rate is. Also on the websites, look for special offers. For the best deals, book at least three weeks in advance, prepay in full...and hope you don't have to change your plans (since these promotional rates are nonrefundable).

The biggest chains are **Premier Travel Inn** (www.premier inn.com, reservations tel. 0870-242-8000) and **Travelodge** (www .travelodge.co.uk, reservations tel. 0870-085-0950). Premier Inn has a "Premier Offer" non-flexible booking option on certain dates, but you have to book at least three weeks in advance and prepay for your room in its entirety (not changeable or refundable). Travelodge has a similar, nonrefundable "Saver" rate, where you prepay for your stay at least three weeks in advance (changes possible for a small fee until up to a week ahead).

Other chains with locations in Britain include the Irish chain **Jurys Inn** (www.jurysinns.com) and the French-owned **Ibis** (www .ibishotel.com). Couples could also consider **Holiday Inn Express,** which are spreading throughout Britain. These are like a Holiday Inn Lite, with cheaper prices and no restaurant. Many of their hotels allow only two per room, but some take up to four (doubles cost about £60–100, make sure Express is part of the name or you'll pay more for a regular Holiday Inn, www.hiexpress.co.uk, reservations tel. 0871-423-4896).

Meanwhile, **easyHotel** is a different animal—an extremely basic, pay-as-you-go bargain chain with several branches in London (see page 162 for details).

For recommendations for online hotel deals in London, as well as using auction-type sites, see page 146.

Hostels

Britain has hundreds of hostels of all shapes and sizes. Choose your hostel selectively. Hostels can be historic castles or depressing tenements, serene and comfy or overrun by noisy school groups.

You'll pay about £20–25 for a bed. People of any age are welcome, if you don't mind dorm-style accommodations (usually in rooms of four to eight beds) and meeting other travelers. Cheap meals are sometimes offered, and kitchen facilities may be available.

There are two basic types of hostels: official and independent. Unfortunately, many of the official hostels (overseen by Hostelling International) have become overpriced and, in general, I no longer recommend them. Many of the independent hostels are more fun, easygoing, and cheaper. Hostels of Europe (www.hostelseurope .com) and Hostels.com have good listings. You can also book online for many hostels (for London: www.hostellondon.com; for Britain and Wales: www.yha.org.uk; and for Scotland: www .hostel-scotland.co.uk).

Phoning

To call Britain from the US or Canada, you'll need to know Britain's country code: 44. To call from the US or Canada, dial 011-44-local number (drop the initial 0 from the local number). If calling Britain from another European country, dial 00-44-local number (without its initial zero). For more tips on calling, see page 804.

Making Reservations

Given the quality of the places I've found for this book, I'd recommend that you reserve your rooms in advance, particularly if you'll be traveling during peak season. Book several weeks ahead or as soon as you've pinned down your travel dates. Note that some national holidays jam things up and merit your making reservations far in advance (see "Holidays and Weekends" sidebar on page 9). Just like at home, holidays that fall on a Monday, Thursday, or Friday can turn the weekend into a long holiday, so book the entire weekend well in advance.

Requesting a Reservation: To make a reservation, contact hotels directly by email, phone, or fax. Email is the clearest and most economical way to make a reservation. Or you can go straight to the hotel website; many have secure online reservation forms and can instantly inform you of availability and any special deals. But be sure you use the hotel's official site and not a booking agency's site—otherwise you may pay higher rates than you should. If phoning from the US, be mindful of time zones (see page 13).

The hotelier wants to know these key pieces of information (also included in the sample request form in the appendix):
- number and type of rooms
- number of nights
- date of arrival
- date of departure
- any special needs (e.g., bathroom in the room or down the hall, twin beds vs. double bed, air-conditioning, quiet, view, ground floor, etc.)

When you request a room, use the European style for writing dates: day/month/year. For example, a two-night stay in July would be "2 nights, 16/07/11 to 18/07/11." Consider in advance how long you'll stay; don't just assume you can tack on extra days once you arrive. Mention any discounts offered—for Rick Steves readers or otherwise—when you make the reservation.

If you don't get a reply to your email or fax, it usually means the hotel is already fully booked (but you can try sending the message again, or call to follow up).

Confirming a Reservation: If the hotel's response includes its room availability and rates, it's not a confirmation. You must tell them that you want that room at the given rate. Most hoteliers will request your credit-card number for a one-night deposit to hold the room. While you can email your credit-card information (I do), it's safer to share that confidential info via phone call, fax, two successive emails, or secure online reservation form (if the hotel has one on its website).

Canceling a Reservation: If you must cancel your reservation, it's courteous to do so with as much advance notice as possible—at least three days. Simply make a quick phone call or send an email. Family-run hotels and B&Bs lose money if they turn away customers while holding a room for someone who doesn't show up. Understandably, many places bill no-shows for one night.

Hotels in larger cities such as London sometimes have strict cancellation policies. For example, you might lose a deposit if you cancel within two weeks of your reserved stay, or you might be billed for the entire visit if you leave early. Internet deals may require prepayment, with no refunds for cancellations. If concerned, ask about cancellation policies before you book.

If canceling via email, request confirmation that your cancellation was received to avoid being billed accidentally.

Reconfirming Your Reservation: Always call to reconfirm your room reservation a day or two in advance from the road. Smaller hotels and B&Bs appreciate knowing your time of arrival. If you'll be arriving after 17:00, be sure to let your hotelier know. On the small chance that a hotel loses track of your reservation, bring along a hard copy of their emailed or faxed confirmation. Don't have the TI reconfirm rooms for you; they'll take a commission.

Reserving Rooms as You Travel: You can make reservations as you travel, calling hotels or B&Bs a few days to a week before your arrival. If everything's full, don't despair. Call a day or two in advance and fill in a cancellation. If you'd rather travel without any reservations at all, you'll have greater success snaring rooms if you arrive at your destination early in the day. When you anticipate crowds (weekends are worst), call hotels at about 9:00 or 10:00 on the day you plan to arrive, when the hotel clerk knows who'll be checking out and just which rooms will be available.

Most TIs in Britain can book you a room in their town, and also often in nearby towns. They generally charge a £4 fee, and you'll pay a 10 percent "deposit" at the TI and the rest at the B&B (meaning that you pay extra and the B&B loses money, as the TI keeps the "deposit"). While this can be useful in a pinch, it's a better deal for everyone (except the TIs) to book direct, using the listings in this book.

Eating

Britain's reputation for miserable food, while once well-deserved, is now dated. The British cuisine scene is lively, trendy, and pleasantly surprising. (Unfortunately, it's also expensive.) Even the basic, traditional pub grub has gone "upmarket," with gastropubs that serve fresh vegetables rather than soggy fries and mushy peas.

All British eateries are now smoke-free. Restaurants and pubs that sell food are non-smoking indoors; establishments keep their smokers contented by allowing them to light up in doorways and on outdoor patios.

Budget Eating Tips

You have plenty of inexpensive choices: pub grub, daily lunch and early-bird specials, ethnic restaurants, cafeterias, fast food, picnics, fish-and-chips, greasy-spoon cafés, pizza, and more.

I've found that portions are huge and, with locals feeling the pinch of their recession, **sharing plates** is generally just fine. Ordering two drinks, a soup or side salad, and splitting a £10 meat pie can make a good, filling meal. If you are on a limited budget, share a main course in a more expensive place for a nicer eating experience.

Pub grub is the most atmospheric budget option. You'll usually get fresh, tasty buffets under ancient timbers, with hearty lunches and dinners priced reasonably at £6–10 (see "Pubs," later).

Classier restaurants have some affordable deals. Lunch is usually cheaper than dinner; a top-end, £25-for-dinner-type restaurant often serves the same quality two-course lunch deals for £10. Look for early-bird dinner specials, allowing you to eat well and affordably (generally two courses-£17, three courses-£20), but early (about 17:30–19:00, last order by 19:00).

Ethnic restaurants from all over the world add spice to Britain's cuisine scene. Eating Indian, Bangladeshi, Chinese, or Thai is cheap (even cheaper if you do take-out). Middle Eastern stands sell gyro sandwiches, falafel, and *shwarmas* (lamb in pita bread). An Indian samosa (greasy, flaky meat-and-vegetable pie) costs £2, can be microwaved, and makes a very cheap, if small, meal. (For more, see "Indian Food," later.) You'll find all-you-can-eat Chinese and Thai places serving £6 meals and offering £3.50 take-away boxes. While you can't "split" a buffet, you can split a take-away box. Stuff the box full, and you and your partner can eat in a park for less than £2 each—making this Britain's cheapest hot meal.

Most large **museums** (and some historic **churches**) have handy, moderately priced cafeterias.

Fast food places, both American and British, are everywhere.

Cheap chain restaurants, such as steak houses and pizza places, serve no-nonsense food in a family-friendly setting (steak-house meals about £10; all-you-can-stomach pizza about £5). For specific chains to keep an eye out for, see "Good Chain Restaurants," below.

Bakeries sell yogurt, cartons of "semi-skimmed" milk, pastries, and pasties (PASS-teez). Pasties are heavy, savory meat pies that originated in the Cornish mining country; they had big crust handles so miners with filthy hands could eat them and toss the crust. The most traditional filling is beef stew, but you'll also find them with chicken, vegetable, lamb and mint, and even Indian flavors inside.

Picnicking saves time and money. You can easily get prepared food to go. Munch a relaxed "meal on wheels" picnic during your open-top bus tour or river cruise to save 30 precious minutes for sightseeing.

Good **sandwich shops** and corner **grocery stores** are a hit with local workers eating on the run. Try boxes of orange juice (pure, by the liter), fresh bread, tasty British cheese, meat, a tube of Colman's English mustard, local eatin' apples, bananas, small tomatoes, a small tub of yogurt (drinkable), trail mix, nuts, plain or chocolate-covered digestive biscuits, and any local specialties. At **open-air markets** and **supermarkets,** you can get produce in small quantities (3 tomatoes and 2 bananas cost about £1). Supermarkets often have good deli sections, even offering Indian dishes, and sometimes salad bars. Decent packaged sandwiches (£3–4) are sold everywhere (for a few options, see "Carry-Out Chains," later).

Good Chain Restaurants

I know—you're going to Britain to enjoy characteristic little hole-in-the-wall pubs, so mass-produced food is the furthest thing from your mind. But several excellent chains with branches across the UK can be a nice break from pub grub. I've recommended these restaurants throughout this book, but if you see a location that I haven't listed...go for it.

Sit-Down Chains

Wagamama Noodle Bar, serving up fresh and reliably delicious pan-Asian cuisine, is stylish, youthful, and mod. There's one in almost every midsize city in the UK, and after you've sampled

Sounds Bad, Tastes Good

The British have a knack for making food sound funny. Here are a few examples:

Toad in the Hole: Sausage dipped in batter and fried

Bubble and Squeak: Leftovers, usually potatoes, veggies, and meat, all fried up together

Bap: Small roll

Treacle: Golden syrup, similar to light molasses

their udon noodles, fried rice, or curry dishes, you'll know why. They're usually in a sprawling, loud, and modern hall filled with long shared tables and busy servers who scrawl your order on the placemat. Portions are huge enough for light eaters on a tight budget to share (typically £7–10 entrées, good vegetarian options).

At **Yo! Sushi,** freshly prepared sushi dishes trundle past on a conveyor belt. Color-coded plates tell you how much each dish costs (£1.75–5), and a picture-filled menu explains what you're eating. Just help yourself.

Gourmet Burger Company (GBK) offers burgers that are, if not quite gourmet, very good. Choices range from a simple cheeseburger to more elaborate options, such as Jamaican (£7-8 burgers). Choose a table and order at the counter—they'll bring the food to you.

Loch Fyne Fish Restaurant, a Scottish chain, serves up fish, oysters, and mussels in a lively, upscale-but-unpretentious setting (£10–15 entrées, early-bird deals).

Ask and **Pizza Express** serve quality pasta and pizza in a pleasant, sit-down atmosphere that's family-friendly. **Jamie's Italian** (from celebrity chef Jamie Oliver) is hipper and pricier, and feels more upmarket.

Carry-Out Chains

While the following places might have some seating, they're an easy place to grab some prepackaged food on the go.

Major supermarket chains have smaller, offshoot branches that specialize in sandwiches, salads, and other prepared foods "to go." These can be a picnicker's dream come true. Some shops are stand-alone, while others are located inside a larger store. The most prevalent—and best—is **M&S Simply Food** (an offshoot of the Marks & Spencer department-store chain; no seating but plasticware is provided). **Sainsbury's Local** grocery stores also offer some decent prepared food; **Tesco Express** and **Tesco Metro** are a distant third.

Other "cheap and cheery" chains, such as **Pret à Manger** and **Eat,** provide office workers with good, healthful sandwiches, salads, and pastries to go.

West Cornwall Pasty Company sells a variety of these traditional savory pies for around £3—as do many smaller, independent bakeries.

The Great British Breakfast

The traditional "fry," or "full English/Scottish/Welsh breakfast"—generally included in the cost of your room—is famous as a hearty way to start the day. Also known as a "heart attack on a plate," the breakfast is especially feast-like if you've just come from the land of the skimpy continental breakfast across the Channel.

The standard fry gets off to a healthy start with juice and cereal or porridge. (Try Weetabix, a soggy British cousin of shredded wheat and perhaps the most absorbent material known to humankind.) Next, with tea or coffee, you get a heated plate with a fried egg, Canadian-style bacon or sausage, a grilled tomato, sautéed mushrooms, and baked beans. Toast comes in a rack (to cool quickly and crisply) with butter and marmalade. This protein-stuffed meal is great for stamina and tides many travelers over until dinner.

You'll figure out quickly which parts of the "fry" you like and don't like. Your host appreciates knowing this up front, rather than serving you the whole shebang and having to throw out uneaten food. There's nothing wrong with skipping some or all of the fry—few Brits actually start their day with this heavy breakfast. Many progressive B&B owners offer vegetarian, organic, or other creative variations on the traditional breakfast.

These days, the best coffee is served in a *cafetière* (also called a "French press"). When your coffee has steeped as long as you like, plunge down the filter and pour.

Afternoon Tea

People of leisure punctuate their day with an "afternoon tea" at a tearoom. You'll get a pot of tea, small finger foods (like cucumber sandwiches), homemade scones, jam, and thick clotted cream. A lighter "cream tea" gets you tea and a scone or two. Tearooms, which often serve appealing light meals, are usually open for lunch and close at about 17:00, just before dinner. For more on this most British of traditions, see page 180.

Pubs

Pubs are a basic part of the British social scene, and, whether you're a teetotaler or a beer-guzzler, they should be a part of your travel here. "Pub" is short for "public house." It's an extended living room where, if you don't mind the stickiness, you can feel the pulse of Britain.

Smart travelers use the pubs to eat, drink, get out of the rain, watch sporting events, and make new friends. Unfortunately, many city pubs have been afflicted with an excess of brass, ferns, and video games. Most traditional atmospheric pubs are in the countryside and in smaller towns.

Pub Grub

Pub grub gets better each year. In London, it offers the best indoor eating value. For £6–10, you'll get a basic budget hot lunch or dinner in friendly surroundings. (For something more refined, try a gastropub, which serves higher-quality meals for £12–18.) The *Good Pub Guide* is excellent (www.thegoodpubguide.co.uk). Pubs that are attached to restaurants, advertise their food, and are crowded with locals are more likely to have fresh food and a chef—and less likely to be the kind of pub that sells only lousy microwaved snacks.

Pubs generally serve traditional dishes, such as fish-and-chips, vegetables, "bangers and mash" (sausages and mashed potatoes),

roast beef with Yorkshire pudding (batter-baked in the oven), and assorted meat pies, such as steak-and-kidney pie or shepherd's pie (stewed lamb topped with mashed potatoes). Side dishes include salads (sometimes even a nice self-serve salad bar), vegetables, and—invariably—"chips" (French fries). "Crisps" are potato chips. A "jacket potato" (baked potato stuffed with fillings of your choice) can almost be a meal in itself. A "ploughman's lunch" is a "traditional British meal" of bread, cheese, and sweet pickles that nearly every tourist tries...once. These days, you'll likely find more Italian pasta, curried dishes, and quiche on the menu than traditional fare.

Meals are usually served 12:00–14:00 and 18:00–20:00—generally not throughout the day. Since they make more money selling beer, many pubs stop serving meals early in the evening. There's often no table service. Order at the bar, then take a seat and they'll bring the food when it's ready (or sometimes you pick it up at the bar). Pay at the bar (sometimes when you order, sometimes after you eat). Don't tip unless it's a place with full table service. Servings are hearty, service is quick, and you'll rarely spend more than £10. (If you're on a tight budget, consider sharing a meal—note the size of portions around you before ordering.) A beer or cider adds another couple of pounds. (Free tap water is always available.)

Beer

The British take great pride in their beer. Many Brits think that drinking beer cold and carbonated, as Americans do, ruins the taste. Most pubs will have **lagers** (cold, refreshing, American-style beer), **ales** (amber-colored, cellar-temperature beer), **bitters** (hop-flavored ale, perhaps the most typical British beer), and **stouts** (dark and somewhat bitter, like Guinness). At pubs, long-handled pulls are used to pull the traditional, rich-flavored "real ales" up from the cellar. These are the connoisseur's favorites: fermented naturally, varying from sweet to bitter, often with a hoppy or nutty flavor. Notice the fun names. Short-hand pulls at the bar mean colder, fizzier, mass-produced, and less interesting keg beers. Mild beers are sweeter, with a creamy malt flavoring. Irish cream ale is a smooth, sweet experience. Try the draft cider (sweet or dry)... carefully.

Order your beer at the bar and pay as you go, with no need to tip. An average beer costs £3. Part of the experience is standing before a line of "hand pulls," or taps, and wondering which beer to choose.

Drinks are served by the pint (20-ounce imperial size) or the half-pint. (It's almost feminine for a man to order just a half; I order mine with quiche.) Proper British ladies like a half beer and half 7-Up **shandy**.

Besides beer, many pubs actually have a good selection of wines by the glass, a fully stocked bar for the gentleman's "G and T" (gin and tonic), and the increasingly popular bottles of alcohol-plus-sugar (such as Bacardi Breezers) for the younger, working-class set. **Pimm's** is a refreshing and fruity summer cocktail, traditionally popular during Wimbledon. It's an upper-class drink—a rough bloke might insult a pub by claiming it sells more Pimm's than beer. Teetotalers can order from a wide variety of soft drinks. Children are served food and soft drinks in pubs, but you must be 18 to order a beer.

Pub hours vary. Pubs generally serve beer Monday–Saturday 11:00–23:00 and Sunday 12:00–22:30, though many are open later, particularly on Friday and Saturday. As it nears closing time, you'll hear shouts of "Last orders." Then comes the 10-minute warning bell. Finally, they'll call "Time!" to pick up your glass, finished or not, when the pub closes.

A cup of darts is free for the asking. People go to a public house to be social. They want to talk. Get vocal with a local. This is easiest at the bar, where people assume you're in the mood to talk (rather than at a table, where you're allowed a bit of privacy). The pub is the next best thing to having relatives in town. Cheers!

Indian Food

Eating Indian food is "going local" in cosmopolitan, multiethnic Britain. You'll find recommended Indian restaurants in most British cities, and even in small towns. Take the opportunity to sample food from Britain's former colony. Indian cuisine is as varied as the country itself. In general, they use more exotic spices than British or American cuisine—some hot, some sweet. Indian food is very vegetarian-friendly, offering many meatless dishes to choose from on any given menu.

For a simple meal that costs about £10–12, order one dish with rice and *naan* (Indian flatbread that can be served plain, with garlic, or other ways). You'll generally pay separately for the rice (it's not included in the entrée price, as it often is at Indian restaurants in the US). Many restaurants have a fixed-price combination meal that offers more variety, and is simpler and cheaper than ordering à la carte. For about £20, you can make a mix-and-match platter out of several sharable dishes, including *dal* (lentil soup) as a starter; one or two meat or vegetable dishes with sauce (for example, chicken curry, chicken *tikka masala* in a creamy tomato sauce, grilled fish tandoori, chickpea *chana masala*, or the spicy *vindaloo* dish); *raita* (a cooling yogurt that's added to spicy dishes); rice; *naan;* and an Indian beer (wine and Indian food don't really mix) or chai (a cardamom- and cinnamon-spiced tea, usually served with milk). An easy way to taste a variety of dishes (especially for a single diner) is to order a *thali*—a sort of sampler plate, generally served on a metal tray, with small servings of various specialties.

Desserts (Sweets)

To the British, the traditional word for dessert is "pudding," although it's also referred to as "sweets" these days. Sponge cake, cream, fruitcake, and meringue are key players.

Trifle is the best-known British concoction, consisting of sponge cake soaked in brandy or sherry (or orange juice for children), then covered with jam and/or fruit and custard cream. Whipped cream can sometimes put the final touch on this "light" treat.

Castle puddings are sponge puddings cooked in small molds and topped with Golden Syrup (a popular brand and a cross between honey and maple syrup). Bread-and-butter pudding

British Chocolate

My chocoholic readers are enthusiastic about British chocolates. As with other dairy products, chocolate seems richer and creamier here than it does in the US, so even the basics like Kit Kat and Twix have a different taste. Some favorites include Cadbury Gold bars (filled with liquid caramel), Cadbury Crunchie bars, Nestlé's Lion bars (layered wafers covered in caramel and chocolate), Cadbury's Boost bars (a shortcake biscuit with caramel in milk chocolate), Cadbury Flake (crumbly folds of melt-in-your-mouth chocolate), Galaxy chocolate bars (especially the ones with hazelnuts), and Aero (a light-as-air chocolate bar filled with little bubbles). Thornton shops (in larger train stations) sell a box of sweets called the Continental Assortment, which comes with a tasting guide. The highlight is the mocha white-chocolate truffle. British M&Ms, called Smarties, are better than American ones. At ice-cream vans, look for the beloved traditional "99p"—a vanilla soft-serve cone with a small Flake bar stuck right into the middle. For a break from chocolate, buy a roll of wine gums—similar to Jujubes, but tangier and less sweet (Maynards is the biggest brand).

consists of slices of French bread baked with milk, cream, eggs, and raisins (similar to the American preparation), served warm with cold cream. Hasty pudding, supposedly the invention of people in a hurry to avoid the bailiff, is made from stale bread with dried fruit and milk. Queen of puddings is a breadcrumb pudding topped with warm jam, meringue, and cream. Treacle pudding is a popular steamed pudding whose "sponge" mixture combines flour, suet (animal fat), butter, sugar, and milk. Christmas pudding (also called plum pudding) is a dense mixture with dried and candied fruit served with brandy butter or hard sauce. Sticky toffee pudding is a moist cake made with dates, heated and drizzled with toffee sauce, and served with ice cream or cream. Banoffee pie is the delicious British answer to banana cream pie.

The British version of custard is a smooth, yellow liquid. Cream tops most everything custard does not. There's single cream for coffee. Double cream is really thick. Whipped cream is familiar, and clotted cream is the consistency of whipped butter.

Fool is a dessert with sweetened pureed fruit (such as rhubarb, gooseberries, or black currants) mixed with cream or custard and chilled. Elderflower is a popular flavoring for sorbet.

Scones are tops, and many inns and restaurants have their secret recipes. Whether made with fruit or topped with clotted cream, scones take the cake.

How Was Your Trip?

Were your travels fun, smooth, and meaningful? If you'd like to share your tips, concerns, and discoveries, please fill out the survey at www.ricksteves.com/feedback. I value your feedback. Thanks in advance—it helps a lot.

Traveling as a Temporary Local

We travel all the way to Europe to enjoy differences—to become temporary locals. You'll experience frustrations. Certain truths that we find "God-given" or "self-evident," such as cold beer, ice in drinks, bottomless cups of coffee, hot showers, and bigger being better, are suddenly not so true. One of the benefits of travel is the eye-opening realization that there are logical, civil, and even better alternatives.

Europeans generally like Americans. But if there is a negative aspect to their image of us, it's that we are loud, aggressive, impolite, rich, superficially friendly, and a bit naive.

The British (and Europeans in general) place a high value on speaking quietly in restaurants and on trains. Listen while on the bus or in a restaurant—the place can be packed, but the decibel level is low. Try to adjust your volume accordingly to show respect for their culture.

While the British look bemusedly at some of our Yankee excesses—and worriedly at others—they nearly always afford us individual travelers all the warmth we deserve. Judging from all the happy feedback I receive from travelers who have used this book, it's safe to assume you'll enjoy a great, affordable vacation—with the finesse of an independent, experienced traveler.

Thanks, and have a brilliant holiday!

Back Door Travel Philosophy
From *Rick Steves' Europe Through the Back Door*

Travel is intensified living—maximum thrills per minute and one of the last great sources of legal adventure. Travel is freedom. It's recess, and we need it.

Experiencing the real Europe requires catching it by surprise, going casual..."Through the Back Door."

Affording travel is a matter of priorities. (Make do with the old car.) You can travel—simply, safely, and comfortably—anywhere in Europe for $120 a day plus transportation costs (allow more for bigger cities). In many ways, spending more money only builds a thicker wall between you and what you came to see. Europe is a cultural carnival, and, time after time, you'll find that its best acts are free and the best seats are the cheap ones.

A tight budget forces you to travel close to the ground, meeting and communicating with the people, not relying on service with a purchased smile. Never sacrifice sleep, nutrition, safety, or cleanliness in the name of budget. Simply enjoy the local-style alternatives to expensive hotels and restaurants.

Connecting with people carbonates your experience. Extroverts have more fun. If your trip is low on magic moments, kick yourself and make things happen. If you don't enjoy a place, maybe you don't know enough about it. Seek the truth. Recognize tourist traps. Give a culture the benefit of your open mind. See things as different but not better or worse. Any culture has much to share.

Of course, travel, like the world, is a series of hills and valleys. Be fanatically positive and militantly optimistic. If something's not to your liking, change your liking.

Travel can make you a happier American as well as a citizen of the world. Our Earth is home to six and a half billion equally important people. It's humbling to travel and find that people don't have the "American Dream"—they have their own dreams. Europeans like us, but, with all due respect, they wouldn't trade passports.

Thoughtful travel engages us with the world. In tough economic times, it reminds us what is truly important. By broadening perspectives, travel teaches new ways to measure quality of life.

Globetrotting destroys ethnocentricity, helping you understand and appreciate different cultures. Rather than fear the diversity on this planet, celebrate it. Among your prized souvenirs will be the strands of different cultures you choose to knit into your own character. The world is a cultural yarn shop, and Back Door travelers are weaving the ultimate tapestry. Join in!

ENGLAND

ENGLAND

England (pop. 50 million) is a hilly country the size of Louisiana (50,346 square miles) and located in the lower two-thirds of the isle of Britain. Scotland is to the north and the English Channel to the south, with the North Sea to the east and Wales (and the Irish Sea) to the west. Fed by ocean air from the southwest, the climate is mild, with a chance of cloudy, rainy weather almost any day of the year.

England has an economy that can stand alongside many much larger nations. It boasts high-tech industries (software, chemicals, aviation), international banking, and textile manufacturing, and is a major exporter of beef. While farms and villages remain, England is now an urban, industrial, and post-industrial colossus.

England traditionally has been very class-conscious, with the wealthy landed aristocracy, the middle-class tradesmen, and the lower-class farmers and factory workers. While social stratification is fading with the new global economy, regional differences remain strong. Locals can often identify where someone is from by their dialect or local accent—Geordie, Cockney, or Queen's English.

One thing that sets England apart from its fellow UK countries (Scotland, Wales, and Northern Ireland) is its ethnic makeup. Traditionally, those countries had Celtic roots, while the English mixed in Saxon and Norman blood. In the 20th century, England welcomed many Scots, Welsh, and Irish as low-wage workers. More recently, it's become home to immigrants from former colonies of its worldwide empire—

England

particularly from India/Pakistan/Bangladesh, the Caribbean, and Africa—and to many workers from poorer Eastern European countries. These days it's not a given that every "English" person speaks English. Nearly one in three citizens does not profess the Christian faith. As the world becomes interconnected by communications technology, it's possible for many immigrants to physically inhabit the country while remaining closely linked to their home culture—rather than truly assimilating into England.

This is the current English paradox. England—the birthplace and center of the extended worldwide family of English-speakers—is losing its traditional Englishness. Where Scotland, Wales, and Northern Ireland have cultural movements to preserve their local languages and customs, England does not. Politically, there is no "English" party in the UK Parliament. While Scotland, Wales, and Northern Ireland have their own parliaments to decide local issues, England must depend on the decisions of the UK government at large. Except for the occasional display of an English flag at a soccer match (the red St. George's cross on a white background), many English people don't really think of themselves as "English"—more as "Brits," a part of the wider UK.

Today, England tries to preserve its rich past as it races forward as a leading global player. There  are still hints of its legacy of farms, villages, Victorian lamplighters, and upper-crust dandies. But it's also a jostling world of unemployed factory workers, investment bankers, soccer matches, rowdy "stag" parties, and faux-Tudor suburbs. Modern England is a culturally diverse land in transition. Catch it while you can.

LONDON

London is more than 600 square miles of urban jungle. With eight million people, it's a world in itself and a barrage on all the senses. On my first visit, I felt extremely small.

London is more than its museums and landmarks. It's a living, breathing, thriving organism...a coral reef of humanity. The city has changed dramatically in recent years, and many visitors are surprised to find how "un-English" it is. ESL (English as a second language) seems like the city's first language, as white people are now a minority in major parts of the city that once symbolized white imperialism. Arabs have nearly bought out the area north of Hyde Park. Chinese takeouts outnumber fish-and-chips shops. Eastern Europeans pull pints in British pubs. Many hotels are run by people with foreign accents (who hire English chambermaids), while outlying suburbs are home to huge communities of Indians and Pakistanis. London is a city of eight million separate dreams, inhabiting a place that tolerates and encourages them. With the English Channel Tunnel and discount airlines making travel between Britain and the Continent easier than ever, London is learning—sometimes fitfully—to live as a microcosm of its formerly vast empire.

London, which has long attracted tourists, seems perpetually at your service, with an impressive slate of sights, entertainment, and eateries, linked by a great transit system. In anticipation of the 2012 Olympic Games and a greater onslaught of tourists than usual, London is busy spiffing up the place, especially its rapidly developing Olympic Park in East London.

With just a few days here, you'll get no more than a quick splash in this teeming human tidal pool. But with a good orientation, you'll find London manageable and fun. You'll get a sampling of the city's top sights, history, and cultural entertainment, and a good look at its ever-changing human face.

Blow through the city on the open deck of a double-decker orientation tour bus, and take a pinch-me-I'm-in-London walk through the West End. Ogle the crown jewels at the Tower of London, hear the chimes of Big Ben, and see the Houses of Parliament in action. Cruise the Thames River, and take a spin on the London Eye. Hobnob with the tombstones in Westminster Abbey, and visit with Leonardo, Botticelli, and Rembrandt in the National Gallery. Enjoy Shakespeare in a replica of the Globe Theatre and marvel at a glitzy, fun musical at a modern-day theater. Whisper across the dome of St. Paul's Cathedral, then rummage through our civilization's attic at the British Museum. And sip your tea with pinky raised and clotted cream dribbling down your scone.

Planning Your Time

The sights of London alone could easily fill a trip to Britain. It's a great one-week getaway. But on a three-week tour of Britain, I'd give London three busy days. You won't be able to see everything, so don't try. You'll keep coming back to London. After dozens of visits myself, I still enjoy a healthy list of excuses to return. If you're flying in, consider starting your trip in Bath and making London your British finale. Especially if you hope to enjoy a play or concert, a night or two of jet lag is bad news.

Here's a suggested three-day schedule:

Day 1

9:00   Tower of London (crown jewels first, then Beefeater tour, then White Tower).

13:00   Grab a picnic, catch a boat at Tower Pier, and relax with lunch on the Thames while cruising to Westminster Pier.

14:30   Tour Westminster Abbey, and consider their evensong service (at 15:00 Sat–Sun, at 17:00 Mon–Fri).

Evening   Follow my self-guided Westminster Walk. When you're finished, if it's a Monday or Tuesday, you could return to the Houses of Parliament and pop in to see the House of Commons in action (until 22:30).

Day 2

8:30   Take a double-decker hop-on, hop-off London sightseeing bus tour (from Green Park or Victoria) and hop off for the Changing of the Guard.

11:00   Buckingham Palace (guards change most days May–July at 11:30, alternate days Aug–April—confirm).

12:00   Walk through St. James' Park to enjoy London's delightful park scene.

13:00   Covent Garden for lunch, shopping, and people-watching.

14:30   Tour the British Museum.

Evening   Have a pub dinner before a play, concert, or evening walking tour.

Day 3 (or More)

If traveling around Britain, spend 30 minutes on the phone this morning getting all essential elements of your trip nailed down. If you know where you'll be and when, call those B&Bs now.

Then, choose among these remaining London highlights: National Gallery, British Library, Cabinet War Rooms and Churchill Museum, Imperial War Museum, the two Tates (Tate Modern on the south bank for modern art, Tate Britain on the north bank for British art), St. Paul's Cathedral, or the Museum of London; take a spin on the London Eye or a cruise to Kew or Greenwich; enjoy a Shakespearean play at Shakespeare's Globe; do some serious shopping at one of London's elegant department stores or open-air markets; or take another historic walking tour.

No matter how long your visit, take advantage of the free, self-guided **Rick Steves audio tours** of major London sights and neighborhoods (download them from www.ricksteves.com/audio europe or search for "Rick Steves' Audio Tours" in iTunes); these are available for the British Museum, the British Library, St. Paul's Cathedral, the Westminster neighborhood, and The City.

Orientation to London

(area code: 020)

To grasp London more comfortably, see it as the old town in the city center without the modern, congested sprawl. (Even at that, it's still huge.)

The Thames River (pronounced "tems") runs roughly west to east through the city, with most of the visitor's sights on the north bank. Mentally, maybe even physically, with scissors, trim down your map to include only the area between the Tower of London (to the east), Hyde Park (west), Regent's Park (north), and the South Bank (south). This is roughly the area bordered by the

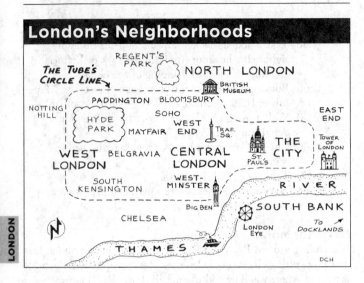

LONDON

Tube's Circle Line. This four-mile stretch between the Tower and Hyde Park (about a 1.5-hour walk) looks like a milk bottle on its side (see map above), and holds 80 percent of the sights mentioned in this chapter.

Sprawling London becomes much more manageable if you think of it as a collection of neighborhoods:

Central London: This area contains Westminster and what Londoners call the West End. The **Westminster** district includes Big Ben, Parliament, Westminster Abbey, and Buckingham Palace—the grand government buildings from which Britain is ruled. Trafalgar Square, London's gathering place, has many major museums. The **West End** is the center of London's cultural life, with bustling squares: Piccadilly Circus and Leicester Square (pronounced "LESS-ter") host cinemas, tourist traps, and nighttime glitz. Soho and Covent Garden are thriving people-zones with theaters, restaurants, pubs, and boutiques. And Regent and Oxford streets are the city's main shopping zones.

North London: Neighborhoods in this part of town—including Bloomsbury, Fitzrovia, and Marylebone—contain such major sights as the British Museum and the overhyped Madame Tussauds Waxworks. Nearby, along busy Euston Road, is the British Library plus a trio of train stations (one of them, St. Pancras International Station, is linked to Paris and Brussels by the Eurostar "Chunnel" train).

The City: Today's modern financial district, called simply "The City," was a walled town in Roman times. Gleaming skyscrapers are interspersed with historical landmarks such as St. Paul's Cathedral, legal sights (Old Bailey), and the Museum of

London. The Tower of London and Tower Bridge lie at The City's eastern border.

The South Bank: The South Bank of the Thames River offers major sights (Tate Modern, Shakespeare's Globe, London Eye) linked by a riverside walkway. Within this area, **Southwark** (SUTH-uck) stretches from the Tate Modern to London Bridge. Pedestrian bridges connect the South Bank with The City and Trafalgar Square.

West London: This huge area contains neighborhoods such as Mayfair, Belgravia, Chelsea, South Kensington, and Notting Hill. It's home to London's wealthy, and has many trendy shops and enticing restaurants. Here you'll find a range of museums (Victoria and Albert Museum, Tate Britain, and more), my top hotel recommendations, lively Victoria Station, and the vast green expanses of Hyde Park and Kensington Gardens.

East London: Just east of The City is the **East End**—the increasingly gentrified former stomping ground of Cockney ragamuffins and Jack the Ripper. Even farther to the east, London's version of Manhattan—the **Docklands**—has sprung up around Canary Wharf. Energized by big businesses, the Docklands show you London at its most modern. Historic **Greenwich** lies just south of the Docklands/Canary Wharf area, across the Thames. And the **2012 Olympic Park** is being built in the once-dreary Stratford district, a short train ride to the north.

Tourist Information

The **Britain and London Visitors Centre,** just a block off Piccadilly Circus, is the best tourist information service in town (June–Sept Mon–Fri 9:30–18:30, Sat 9:00–17:00, Sun 10:00–16:00; Oct–May Mon–Fri 9:30–18:00, Sat–Sun 10:00–16:00; 1 Lower Regent Street, tel. 020/8846-9000, toll tel. 0870-156-6366, www.visitbritain .com, www.visitlondon.com). If you visit only one TI, make it this one. Unfortunately, London's many "Tourist Information Centres" (which represent themselves as TIs at major train and bus stations and airports) are now simply businesses, selling advertising space to companies with fliers to distribute.

The Britain and London Visitors Centre has many different departments. It's a great one-stop shopping place to get tourist information, buy advance tickets to big sights, buy sightseeing passes, arrange coach tours, buy theater tickets, plan travel beyond London, and even book trains to the Continent. Bring your itinerary and a checklist of questions.

Entering the lobby, check out the various departments and get in the right line for what you need. At the Tourist Information desk handling both London and Britain inquiries, pick up various free publications: the *London Planner* (a free monthly that lists all

Affording London's Sights

London is one of Europe's most expensive cities, with the dubious distinction of having some of the world's most expensive admission prices. Fortunately, many of its best sights are free.

Free Museums: Many of the city's biggest and best museums won't cost you a dime. Free sights include the British Museum, British Library, National Gallery, National Portrait Gallery, Tate Britain, Tate Modern, Wallace Collection, Imperial War Museum, Victoria and Albert Museum, Natural History Museum, Science Museum, National Army Museum, Sir John Soane's Museum, the Museum of London, the Geffrye, and on the outskirts of town, the Royal Air Force Museum London.

About half of these museums request a donation of a few pounds, but whether you contribute or not is up to you. If I spend money for an audioguide, I feel fine about not otherwise donating. If that makes you uncomfortable, donate.

Free Churches: Smaller churches let worshippers (and tourists) in free, although they may ask for a donation. The big sightseeing churches—Westminster Abbey and St. Paul's—charge steep admission fees, but offer free evensong services daily. Westminster Abbey also offers free organ recitals most Sundays at 17:45.

Other Freebies: There are plenty of free performances, such as lunch concerts at St. Martin-in-the-Fields (see page 90) and summertime movies at The Scoop amphitheater near City Hall (Tube: London Bridge, schedule at www.morelondon.com—click on "The Scoop"). For other freebies, check out www.freelondonlistings.co.uk. There's no charge to enjoy the pageantry of the Changing of the Guard, rants at Speaker's Corner in Hyde Park, displays at Harrods, the people-watching scene at Covent Garden, and the colorful streets of the East End. It's free to view the legal action at the Old Bailey and the legislature at work in the Houses of Parliament.

And you can get into a bit of the Tower of London by attending Sunday services in the Tower's chapel (chapel access only).

Greenwich makes for a very cheap day out (see next chapter). Its many good museums are all free, and the journey there is covered by a cheap Zones 1-2 Tube ticket.

Sightseeing Deals: If you buy a paper One-Day Travelcard or rail ticket at a National Rail station (such as Paddington or Victoria), you may be eligible for two-for-one discounts at many popular sights, such as the London Eye, Tower of London, Tate Modern, and Madame Tussauds Waxworks. Get details and print vouchers at www.daysoutguide.co.uk, or look for brochures with coupons at major train stations.

Good-Value Tours: The £5-8 city walking tours with professional guides are one of the best deals going. (Note that the guides for the "free" walking tours are unpaid and expect tips—I'd pay for a professionally guided tour instead.) Hop-on, hop-off big-bus tours (£22–26), while expensive, provide a great overview, and include free boat tours as well as city walks. A one-hour Thames ride to Greenwich costs £9.50 one-way, but most boats come with an entertaining commentary. A three-hour bicycle tour is about £16–19.

Pricey...But Worth It? Big-ticket sights worth their hefty admission fees are Kew Gardens (£13.50), Shakespeare's Globe (£10.50), and the Cabinet War Rooms, with its fine Churchill Museum (£14.95).

The London Eye has become a London must-see—though if you're on a tight budget, it's difficult to justify its very high cost (£18). While Hampton Court Palace (£14) is expensive, it is well-presented and a reasonable value if you have an interest in royal history. The Queen charges big time to open her palace to the public: Buckingham Palace (£16.50, Aug–Sept only) and her art gallery and carriage museum (adjacent to the palace, £8.75 and £7.75, £15 for both) are expensive but interesting. Madame Tussauds Waxworks is pricey but still fun and popular (£28, £22.50 if purchased at TI, drops to £14 after 17:00 if booked online). The Vinopolis wine museum provides a way to get a buzz and call it museum-going (from £20, entry includes tastes of wine).

Many smaller museums cost only around £5. My favorites include the Courtauld Gallery (free on Mon until 14:00) and the Wellington Museum at Apsley House (£6, www.english-heritage .org.uk).

Not Worth It: The London Dungeon, at £22.50, is gimmicky, overpriced, and a terrible value...despite the long line at the door.

Theater: Compared with Broadway's prices, London theater is a bargain. Seek out the freestanding "tkts" booth at Leicester

Square to get discounts from 25 to 50 percent on good seats (though not necessarily for the hottest shows; see page 140). If you're willing to settle for the cheapest seats (possibly with obstructed views), ask the theater's box office for their best deal (even the hottest shows generally have some £10–20 tickets). A £5 "groundling" ticket for a play at Shakespeare's Globe is the best theater deal in town (see page 142). Tickets to the Open Air Theatre at north London's Regent's Park start at £12 (see page 143).

London doesn't come cheap. But with its many free museums and affordable plays, this cosmopolitan, cultured city offers days of sightseeing thrills without requiring you to pinch your pennies (or your pounds).

the sights, events, and hours), walking tours info, a theater guide, a London bus map, and the *Guide to River Thames Boat Services*. The staff sells a good £1 map and all the various sightseeing passes (both the nationwide passes described on page 21, and the London Pass described below).

The Entertainment and Tickets desk sells tickets to plays (steep 20 percent booking fee). The Hotels and Travel desk sells long-distance bus tickets and passes, train tickets (convenient for reservations), and Fast Track tickets to some of London's attractions. These tickets, which allow you to skip the queue at the sights at no extra cost, are worthwhile for places that can have long ticket lines, such as the Tower of London, the London Eye, and Madame Tussauds Waxworks. (If you're going to the Waxworks, buy tickets here, since—at £22.50—they're cheaper than at the sight itself.)

The Visitors Centre reserves hotel rooms, but you can avoid their £5 booking fee by contacting hotels on your own. A Rail Europe section books the Eurostar and train travel or train passes on the Continent.

Upstairs, you'll find more brochures, Internet access (£1/20 minutes), and comfy chairs where you can read or get organized.

The **London Pass** is pricey, and only worth considering for the most rabid sightseer (£40/1 day, £55/2 days, £63/3 days, £90/6 days; days are calendar days rather than 24-hour periods; includes 160-page guidebook, toll tel. 0870-242-9988, www.londonpass.com). It lets you skip the lines and covers plenty of sights that cost £11–17, including the Tower of London, St. Paul's Cathedral, Shakespeare's Globe, Cabinet War Rooms, Windsor Castle, and Kew Gardens. If you saw just these sights without the pass, you'd pay about £90, the cost of a six-day London Pass. Busy sightseers can make a short pass work for a longer trip by seeing only covered sights during the validity of the pass, and touring London's many free sights (listed on page 52) before or after the pass' validity period. Note that the pass doesn't include Westminster Abbey, the London Eye, or Madame Tussauds Waxworks. Think through your sightseeing plans carefully, and do the math before you buy.

Arrival in London

By Train: London has nine major train stations, all connected by the Tube (subway). All have ATMs, and many of the larger stations also have shops, fast food, exchange offices, and luggage storage. From any station, you can ride the Tube or taxi to your hotel. For more info on train travel, see www.nationalrail.co.uk.

By Bus: The main intercity bus station is Victoria Coach Station, one block southwest of Victoria train station (and the Victoria Tube station). For more on bus travel, see www.nationalexpress.com.

By Plane: London has five airports. Most tourists arrive at Heathrow or Gatwick airports, although flights from elsewhere in Europe may land at Stansted, Luton, or London City airports. For specifics on getting from London's airports to downtown London, see "London Connections" on page 182; for hotels near Heathrow and Gatwick, see page 163.

Helpful Hints

Theft Alert: Wear your money belt. The Artful Dodger is alive and well in London. Be on guard, particularly on public transportation and in places crowded with tourists, who, considered naive and rich, are targeted. The Changing of the Guard scene is a favorite for thieves. And more than 7,500 purses are stolen annually at Covent Garden.

Pedestrian Safety: Cars drive on the left side of the road—which can be as confusing for foreign pedestrians as for foreign drivers. Before crossing a street, I always look right, look left, then look right again just to be sure. Most crosswalks are even painted with instructions, reminding foreign guests to "Look right" or "Look left."

Medical Problems: Local hospitals have good-quality 24-hour-a-day emergency care centers where any tourist who needs help can drop in and, after a wait, be seen by a doctor. Your hotel has details. St. Thomas' Hospital, immediately across the river from Big Ben, has a fine reputation.

Getting Your Bearings: London is well-signed for visitors. A new initiative called Legible London is erecting thoughtfully designed, pedestrian-focused maps around town. In this sprawling city—where predictable grid-planned streets are relatively rare—it's also smart to buy and use a good map. The *Benson's London Street Map* (£2.75), sold at many newsstands and bookstores, is my favorite for efficient sightseeing.

Festivals: For one week in February and another in September, fashionistas descend on the city for **London Fashion Week** (www.londonfashionweek.co.uk). The famous **Chelsea Flower Show** blossoms in late May (book ahead for this popular event at www.rhs.org.uk/chelsea). During the annual **Trooping the Colour** in June, there are military bands and pageantry, and the Queen's birthday parade (www.trooping-the-colour.co.uk). Tennis fans pack the stands at the **Wimbledon Tennis Championship** on June 20–July 3 in 2011 (www.wimbledon.org), and partygoers head for the **Notting Hill Carnival** in late August.

Winter: London dazzles year-round, so consider visiting in winter, when airfares and hotel rates are generally cheaper and there are fewer tourists. For ideas on what to do, see the "Winter

Activities in London" article at www.ricksteves.com/winter acts.

Internet Access: As nearly all hotels offer Internet access and cafés all over town have free Wi-Fi, there are fewer actual Internet cafés. If you need to get online, you'll find Internet cafés near Trafalgar Square (456 Strand), on Oxford Street (at #358, opposite Bond Street Tube station), and near Victoria Station (at 164 Victoria Street).

Travel Bookstores: Located between Covent Garden and Leicester Square, the very good **Stanfords Travel Bookstore** stocks current editions of many of my books (Mon–Fri 9:00–19:30, Thu 9:00–20:00, Sat 10:00–20:00, Sun 12:00–18:00, 12–14 Long Acre, Tube: Leicester Square, tel. 020/7836-1321, www.stanfords.co.uk).

Two impressive **Waterstone's** bookstores have the biggest collection of travel guides in town: on Piccadilly (Mon–Sat 9:00–22:00, Sun 12:00–18:00, Costa Café, 203 Piccadilly, tel. 020/7851-2400) and on Trafalgar Square (Mon–Sat 9:30–21:00, Sun 12:00–18:00, Costa Café on second floor, tel. 020/7839-4411).

Baggage Storage: Train stations have replaced their lockers with more secure baggage storage counters, known locally as "left luggage." Each bag must go through a scanner (just like at the airport), so lines can be slow. Expect long waits in the morning to check in (up to 45 minutes) and in the afternoon to pick up (each item-£8/24 hours, most stations daily 7:00–23:00). You can also store bags at the airports (similar rates and hours, www.excess-baggage.com). If leaving London and returning later, you may be able to leave a box or bag at your hotel for free—assuming you'll be staying there again.

Bike Rental: Barclays Cycle Hire rents bikes from self-service docking stations (most likely won't work with US credit or debit cards, www.tfl.gov.uk).

Getting Around London

To travel smart in a city this size, you must get comfortable with public transportation. London's excellent taxis, buses, and subway (Tube) system make a private car unnecessary.

If you do have a car, stow it—you don't want to drive in London. If you need convincing, here's one more reason: An £8 **congestion charge** is levied on any private car entering the city center during peak hours (Mon–Fri 7:00–18:00, no charge Sat–Sun and holidays, fee payable at gas stations, convenience stores, and self-service machines at public parking lots, or online at www.cclondon.com). Traffic cameras photograph and identify every vehicle that enters the fee zone; if you get spotted and don't pay up by midnight that day (or pay £10 until midnight of the following day), you'll get socked with at least a £60 penalty. The system has been effective in cutting down traffic jam delays and bolstering London's public transit. The revenue that's raised subsidizes the buses, which are now cheaper, more frequent, and even more user-friendly than before. Today, the vast majority of vehicles in the city center are buses, taxis, and service trucks. (Drivers—or American city planners—can find out more information on the congestion charge at www.cclondon.com.)

Public-Transit Passes

London has the most expensive public transit in the world—save money on your Tube and bus rides using a multi-ride pass. You have three options: pay double by buying individual tickets as you go; buy a £3 Oyster card and top it up as needed to travel like a local for about £1–2 per ride; or get a Travelcard for unlimited travel on one or seven days.

The transit system has six zones. Since almost all of my recommended accommodations, restaurants, and sights are within Zones 1 and 2, those are the prices I've listed here—but you'll pay more to go farther afield. Specific fares and other details change constantly; for a complete and updated list of prices, check www.tfl.gov.uk.

Individual Transit Tickets

These days in London, individual paper tickets are dinosaurs; there's no point buying one unless you're literally taking just one ride your entire time in the city. Because individual fares (£4 per Tube ride, £2 per bus ride) are about double the cost of using a pay-as-you-go Oyster card (explained below), in just two or three rides you'll recoup the £3 added deposit for the Oyster. If you do buy a single ticket, avoid ticket-window lines in Tube stations by using the coin-op machines; practice on the punchboard to see how the system works (hit "Adult Single" and your destination). These tickets are valid only on the day of purchase.

Oyster Cards

A pay-as-you-go Oyster card (a plastic card embedded with a computer chip) is the standard, smart way to economically ride the Tube, buses, Docklands Light Railway (DLR), and Overground. On each type of transport, you simply lay the card flat against the yellow card reader at the turnstile or entrance, it flashes green, and the fare is automatically

deducted. (You'll also touch your card again to exit the Tube and DLR turnstiles, but not to exit buses.)

With an Oyster card, rides cost about half the price of individual paper tickets (£1.80 or £2.30 per Tube ride—depending on time of day, £1.20 per bus ride). You buy the card itself at any Tube station ticket window for a £3 deposit, then load it up with as much credit as you want. (For extra peace of mind, ask about registering your card against theft or loss.) When your balance gets low, you simply add credit—or "top up"—at a ticket window or machine. A price cap on the pay-as-you-go Oyster card guarantees you'll never pay more than the One-Day Travelcard price within a 24-hour period.

You can see how much credit remains on your card or review the trips you've taken so far by swiping it at any automatic ticket machine. Oyster card balances never expire (though they need reactivating at a ticket window every two years), so you can use the card whenever you're in London, or lend it to someone else. If you're done with the card (and don't mind a short wait), you can turn it in to reclaim your £3 deposit at any ticket window.

Travelcards

Like the Oyster card, Travelcards are valid on the Tube, buses, Docklands Light Railway (DLR), and Overground. The difference is that Travelcards let you ride as many times as you want within a one- or seven-day period for one fixed price.

Before you buy a card, estimate where you'll be going; there's a card for Zones 1 and 2, and another for Zones 1–6 (which includes Heathrow Airport). If Heathrow is the only ride you're taking outside Zones 1–2 (which is likely), you can pay a small supplement to make the Zones 1–2 Travelcard stretch to cover that one ride.

The **One-Day Travelcard** gives you unlimited travel for a day (Zones 1–2: £7.20, off-peak version £5.60; Zones 1–6: £15, off-peak version £7.50; cheaper off-peak versions are good for travel after 9:30 on weekdays and anytime on weekends). This Travelcard works like a traditional paper ticket: You buy it at any Tube station ticket window or machine, then feed it into a turnstile (and retrieve it) to enter and exit the Tube. On a bus, just show it to the driver when you get on.

The **Seven-Day Travelcard** is a great option if you're staying four or more days and plan to use the buses and Tube a lot. It's actually issued on a plastic Oyster card, but gives you unlimited travel anytime, anywhere in Zones 1 and 2 for a week (£25.80 plus the refundable £3 deposit for the Oyster card). As with an Oyster card, you'll touch it to the yellow pad when entering or exiting a Tube turnstile, or when boarding a bus.

Discounts

Groups: A gang of 10 or more adults can travel all day on the Tube for £3.70 each (but not on buses). Kids ages 11–17 pay £1 when part of a group of 10.

Families: A paying adult can take up to four kids (aged 10 and under) for free on the Tube, Docklands Light Railway (DLR), and Overground all day, every day (kids 10 and under are always free on buses). At the Tube station, use the manual gate, rather than the turnstiles, to be waved in. Other child and student discounts are explained at www.tfl.gov.uk/tickets.

River Cruises: A Travelcard gives you a 33 percent discount on most Thames cruises (see "Cruises" on page 72). If you pay for Thames Clippers (including the Tate-to-Tate museum boat) with your pay-as-you go Oyster card, you'll get a 10 percent discount.

Sightseeing Deal: Buy a paper One-Day Travelcard or rail ticket at a National Rail station, and you may qualify for two-for-one discounts at many popular sights (look for brochures with coupons at major train stations, or print vouchers at www.daysout guide.co.uk).

Transit Passes: The Bottom Line

Struggling to choose which pass works best for your trip? First of all, skip the individual tickets. On a short visit (three days or fewer), if you think you'll be zipping around a lot, consider a One-Day Travelcard for each day you're here (or at least for your busiest days); if you'll be taking fewer, more focused rides, get an Oyster card and pay as you go. If you're in London four days or longer, the Seven-Day Travelcard will likely pay for itself.

By Tube

London's subway system (called the Tube or Underground—but never "subway," which refers to a pedestrian underpass) is one of this planet's great people-movers and often the fastest long-distance transport in town (runs Mon–Sat about 5:00–24:00, Sun about 7:00–23:00). While technically not part of the Tube, two other commuter rail lines are tied into the network: The Docklands Light Railway (called DLR, runs to the Docklands, 2012 Olympics site, and Greenwich) and the Overground.

Get your bearings by studying a map of the system (free at any station). Each line has a name (such as Circle, Northern, or Bakerloo) and two directions (indicated by the end-of-the-line stops). Find the line that will take you to your destination, and figure out roughly what direction (north, south, east, or west) you'll need to go to get there.

You can use an Oyster card, a Travelcard, or individual tickets (all explained earlier) to pay for your journey. At the Tube station, touch your Oyster card flat against the turnstile's yellow card reader, both when you enter and exit the station. If you have a regular paper ticket or a One-Day Travelcard, feed it into the turnstile, reclaim it, and hang on to it—you'll need it later.

Find your train by following signs to your line and the (general) direction it's headed (such as Central Line: east). Since some tracks are shared by several lines, double-check before boarding a train: First, make sure your destination is one of the stops listed on the sign at the platform. Also, check the electronic signboards that announce which train is next, and make sure the destination (the end-of-the-line stop) is the direction you want. Some trains,  particularly on the Circle and District lines, split off for other directions, but each train has its final destination marked above its windshield.

Trains run roughly every 3–10 minutes. If one train is absolutely packed and you notice another to the same destination is coming in three minutes, wait to avoid the sardine routine. Rush hours (8:00–10:00 and 16:00–19:00) can be packed and sweaty. Bring something to do to make your waiting time productive. If you get confused, ask for advice from a local, a blue-vested staff person, or at the information window located before the turnstile entry.

You can't leave the system without touching your Oyster card to an electronic reader, or feeding your ticket or One-Day Travelcard into the turnstile. (If you have a single-trip paper ticket,  the turnstile will eat your now-expired ticket; if it's a One-Day Travelcard, it will spit out your still-valid card.) Save walking time by choosing the best street exit—check the maps on the walls or ask any station personnel.

The system can be fraught with construction delays and breakdowns (the Circle Line is notorious for problems). This will be especially noticeable in 2011, as London gears up for the 2012 Olympics. Most construction is scheduled for weekends. Closures are known and publicized in advance (online at www.tfl.gov.uk and with posters in the Tube). Pay attention to signs and announcements explaining necessary detours. Closed Tube lines are often replaced by temporary bus service, but it can be faster to figure out alternate routes on the Tube; since the lines cross each other constantly, there are several ways to make any journey. For help, check out the "Journey Planner" at www.tfl.gov.uk.

Tube Etiquette

- When your train arrives, stand off to the side and let riders exit the train before you try to board.
- Avoid using the hinged seats near the doors of some trains when the car is jammed; they take up valuable standing space.
- If you're blocking the door when the train stops, step out of the car and off to the side, let others off, then get back on.
- Talk softly in the cars. Listen to how quietly Londoners communicate and follow their lead.
- On escalators, stand on the right and pass on the left. But note that in some passageways or stairways, you might be directed to walk on the left (the direction Brits go behind the wheel).
- When leaving a station, it's polite to hold the door for the person behind you.
- Discreet eating and drinking are fine (nothing smelly); drinking alcohol and smoking are not.

By Bus

If you figure out the bus system, you'll swing like Tarzan through the urban jungle of London. Pick up a free bus map at a TI, transport office, or some major museums; it will list the bus routes best for sightseeing. Also see the "Handy Bus Routes" sidebar (next page).

Buses are covered by Travelcards and Oyster cards. Or you can buy individual tickets from a machine at bus stops (no change

Oakwood ⊖	N91	⊕ ⊗
Old Coulsdon	N68	Aldwych
Old Ford	N8	Oxford Circus
Old Kent Road Canal Bridge	53, N381	⊙
	453	⊙ ⊙
	N21	⊙
Old Street ⊖ ≹	243	Aldwych
Orpington ≹	N47	⊙
Oxford Circus ⊖	Any bus	⊙
	N18	⊙
Paddington ⊖ ≹	23, N15	⊙ ⊙ ⊙
Palmers Green ≹	N29	⊙
Park Langley	N3	⊙ ⊙
Peckham	12	⊙ ⊙
	N89, N343	⊙
	N136	⊙ ⊙
	N381	⊙
Penge Pawleyne Arms	176	⊙
	N3	⊙ ⊙
Petts Wood ≹	N47	⊙
Pimlico Grosvenor Road	24	⊙ ⊙
Plaistow Greengate	N15	⊙ ⊙
Plumstead ≹	53	⊙
Plumstead Common	53	⊙

given). Any bus ride in downtown London costs £2 for those paying cash, or £1.20 if using an Oyster card (with a cap of £3.90 maximum per day). If you're staying longer, consider the £16.60 Seven-Day bus pass.

The first step in mastering London's bus system is learning how to decipher the bus stop signs (see photo). In the first column, find your destination on the list—e.g., Paddington. In the next column, find a bus that goes there—the #23. The final column has a letter within a circle (e.g., "M") that tells you exactly

LONDON

Handy Bus Routes

Since London instituted a congestion charge for cars, the bus system has gotten faster, easier, and cheaper than ever. Tube-oriented travelers need to get over their tunnel vision, learn the bus system, and get around fast and easy. The best views are upstairs on a double-decker.

Here are some of the most useful routes:

Route #9: Knightsbridge (Harrods) to Hyde Park Corner to Piccadilly Circus to Trafalgar Square. This is one of two "Heritage Routes" using old-style double-decker buses.

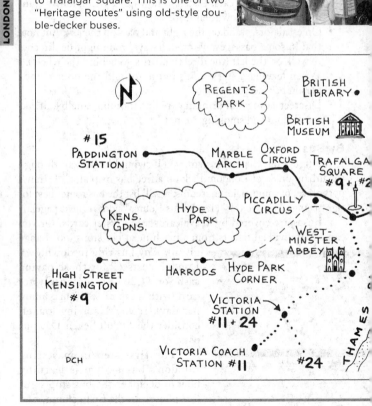

Routes #11 and #24: Victoria Station to Westminster Abbey to Trafalgar Square (#11 continues to St. Paul's and Liverpool Street Station).

Route #RV1 (a scenic South Bank joyride): Tower of London to Tower Bridge to Southwark Street (five-minute walk behind Tate Modern/Shakespeare's Globe) to London Eye/Waterloo Station/County Hall, then over Waterloo Bridge to Aldwych and Covent Garden.

Route #15: Paddington Station to Oxford Circus to Regent Street/TI to Piccadilly Circus to Trafalgar Square to Fleet Street to St. Paul's to Tower of London. This is the other "Heritage Route" using old-style double-decker buses.

In addition, several buses (including #6, #13, #15, #23, #139, and #159) make the corridor run from Trafalgar, Piccadilly Circus, and Oxford Circus to Marble Arch. Check the bus stop closest to your hotel—it might be convenient to your sightseeing plans.

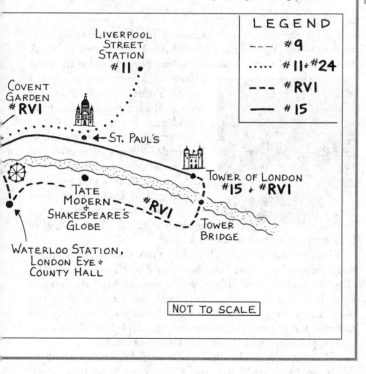

which bus stop you need to stand at to catch your bus. (You'll find the same letter marked on a neighborhood map nearby.) Make your way to that stop—you'll know it's yours because it will have the same letter on its pole—and wait for the bus with your number on it to arrive. Hop on, and you're good to go.

As you board, touch your Oyster card to the electronic card reader, or, if you have a paper ticket or a One-Day Travelcard, show it to the driver. On "Heritage Routes" #9 and #15 (which use older double-decker buses), you may still pay a conductor; take a seat, and he or she will come around to collect your fare or verify your pass. There's no need to tap your card or show your ticket when you hop off.

If you have an Oyster card or Travelcard, save your feet and get in the habit of hopping buses for quick little straight shots, even just to get to a Tube stop. During bump-and-grind rush hours (8:00–10:00 and 16:00–19:00), you'll usually go faster by Tube.

By Taxi

London is the best taxi town in Europe. Big, black, carefully regulated cabs are everywhere. (While historically known as "black cabs," some of London's official taxis are now covered with wildly

colored ads.) Some cabs are switching to biofuels—a good use for frying oil used for all those fish-and-chips.

I've never met a crabby cabbie in London. They love to talk, and they know every nook and cranny in town. I ride in a taxi each day just to get my London questions answered (drivers must pass a rigorous test on "The Knowledge" of London geography to earn their license).

If a cab's top light is on, just wave it down. Drivers flash lights when they see you wave. They have a tight turning radius (on new cabs, the back tires actually pivot), so you can hail cabs going in either direction. If waving doesn't work, ask someone where you can find a taxi stand. Telephoning a cab will get you one in a few minutes, but costs a little more (toll tel. 0871-871-8710; £2 surcharge, plus extra fee to book ahead by credit card).

Rides start at £2.20. The regular tariff #1 covers most of the day (Mon–Fri 6:00–20:00), tariff #2 is during "unsociable hours" (Mon–Fri 20:00–22:00 and Sat–Sun 6:00–22:00), and tariff #3 is at night (nightly 22:00–6:00) and on holidays. Rates go up about 15–20 percent with each higher tariff. All extra charges are explained in writing on the cab wall. Tip a cabbie by rounding up (maximum 10 percent).

Connecting downtown sights is quick and easy, and will cost you about £6–8 (for example, St. Paul's to the Tower of London). For a short ride, three adults in a cab generally travel at close to Tube prices—and groups of four or five adults should taxi everywhere. All cabs can carry five passengers, and some take six, for the same cost as a single traveler.

Don't worry about meter cheating. Licensed British cab meters come with a sealed computer chip and clock that ensures you'll get the correct tariff. The only way a cabbie can cheat you is by taking a needlessly long route. Another pitfall is taking a cab when traffic is bad to a destination efficiently served by the Tube. On one trip to London, I hopped in a taxi at South Kensington for Waterloo Station and hit bad traffic. Rather than spending 20 minutes and £2 on the Tube, I spent 40 minutes and £16 in a taxi.

If you overdrink and ride in a taxi, be warned: Taxis charge £40 for "soiling" (a.k.a., pub puke). If you forget this book in a taxi, call the Lost Property office and hope for the best (toll tel. 0845-330-9882).

Tours in London

▲▲▲Hop-on, Hop-off Double-Decker Bus Tours

Two competitive companies (Original and Big Bus) offer essentially the same two tours of the city's sightseeing highlights, with nearly 30 stops on each route. Big Bus tours are a little more expensive (£26), while Original tours are cheaper (£22 with this book) and nearly as good.

These once-over-lightly bus tours drive by all the famous sights, providing a stress-free way to get your bearings and see the biggies. They stop at a core group of sights regardless of which overview tour you're on: Piccadilly Circus, Trafalgar Square, Big Ben, St. Paul's, the Tower of London, Marble Arch, Victoria Station, and elsewhere. With a good guide and nice weather, I'd sit back and enjoy the entire tour. (If you don't like your guide, you can hop off and try your luck with the next departure in 10–20 minutes.)

Each company offers at least one route with live (English-only) guides, and a second (sometimes slightly different route) comes with recorded, dial-a-language narration. In addition to the overview tours, both Original and Big Bus include the Thames River boat trip by City Cruises (similar to the £13 "River Red Rover" ticket explained on page 74) and three 1.5-hour walking tours.

Pick up a map from any flier rack or from one of the countless

LONDON

salespeople, and study the complex system. Sunday morning—when the traffic is light and many museums are closed—is a fine time for a tour. Unless you're using the bus tour mainly for hop-on, hop-off transportation, consider saving time and money by taking a night tour (described later).

Buses run about every 10–15 minutes in summer, every 20 minutes in winter, and operate daily. They start at about 8:30 and run until early evening in summer, or until late afternoon in winter. The last full loop usually leaves Victoria Station about 17:00 (confirm by checking the schedule or asking the driver).

You can buy tickets from drivers or from staff at street kiosks (credit cards accepted at kiosks at major stops such as Victoria, ticket good for 24 hours).

Original London Sightseeing Bus Tour—There are two versions of their basic highlights loop: **The Original Tour** (live guide, marked with a yellow triangle on the front of the bus) and the **City Sightseeing Tour** (essentially the same route but with recorded narration, a kids' soundtrack option, and a stop at Madame Tussauds; bus marked with a red triangle). Other routes include the blue-triangle **Museum Tour** (connecting far-flung museums and major shopping

stops), and green, black, and purple triangle routes (linking major train stations to the central route). All routes are covered by the same ticket. Keep it simple and just take one of the city highlights tours (£25, £22 after £3 discount with this book, limit two discounts per book, they'll rip off the corner of this page—raise bloody hell if the staff or driver won't honor this discount; also online deals, info center at 17 Cockspur Street, tel. 020/8877-1722, www.theoriginaltour.com).

Big Bus London Tours—For £26 (up to 30 percent discount if you book low-use times online—requires printer), you get the same basic overview tours: Red buses come with a live guide, while the blue route has a recorded narration and a longer path (one hour longer) around Hyde Park. These pricier Big Bus tours tend to have better, more dynamic guides than the Original tours, and more departures as well—meaning shorter waits for those hopping on and off (daily 8:30–18:00, winter until 16:30, info center at 48 Buckingham Palace Road, tel. 020/7233-9533, www.bigbustours.com).

London by Night Sightseeing Tour—This tour offers a two-hour circuit, but after hours, with no extras (e.g., walks, river cruises), and at a lower price. While the narration can be pretty

> ## Combining a London Bus Tour and the Changing of the Guard
>
> For a grand and efficient intro to London, consider catching either of the bus companies' overview tours at 8:30, riding 90 percent of the loop (which takes just over two hours, depending on traffic), and hopping off at Buckingham Palace in time to catch the Changing of the Guard ceremony. Both tours depart at 8:30 every morning—choose between the Big Bus Tour (live guide, catch it at the Green Park Tube station) or the Original Bus Tour (recorded narration, catch it at Grosvenor Gardens a block from Victoria Station). If you miss the 8:30 bus, there's generally another departure in 20 minutes that might get you to the ceremony a bit late (confirm with the driver).

lame, the views at twilight are grand—though note that it stays light until late on summer nights, and London just doesn't do floodlighting as well as Paris (£16, £11 online, drivers take cash only). From May through late September, there are nightly departures at 19:30 (open top), 20:00 (open top), 20:30 (closed top), and 21:30 (open top) from Victoria Station (Jan–April and late Sept–late Dec departs at 19:30 only with closed-top bus, no tours between Christmas and New Year). Buses leave from the curb immediately in front of Victoria Station (closest to building at muster point C; or you can board at any stop, such as Paddington Station, Marble Arch, Trafalgar Square, London Eye, or Tower of London; tel. 020/8545-6109, www.london-by-night.net). For a memorable and economical evening, munch a scenic picnic dinner on the top deck. (There are plenty of take-away options within the train stations and near the various stops.)

▲▲Walking Tours

Several times a day, top-notch local guides lead (sometimes big) groups through specific slices of London's past. Look for brochures at TIs or ask at hotels, although the latter usually push higher-priced bus tours. *Time Out*, the weekly entertainment guide (£3 at newsstands), lists some, but not all, scheduled walks. Check with the various tour companies by phone or online to get their full picture.

To take a walking tour, you simply show up at the announced location and pay the guide. Then enjoy two chatty hours of Dickens, Harry Potter, the Plague, Shakespeare, Legal London, the Beatles, Jack the Ripper, or whatever is on the agenda.

The Essential London Walk—Blue Badge Tourist Guides offer a basic two-hour walk for £5, 365 days a year at 10:00 (from the

Eros statue on Piccadilly Circus—look for the guide with the Blue Badge umbrella, www.touristguides.org.uk). Tours go rain or shine, and there's no need to pre-book—just show up. This is the best deal going, as you know you'll get a well-trained guide leading you through the historic core of London (from Piccadilly, you walk to Trafalgar Square, Whitehall, Westminster Abbey, the Houses of Parliament, and the Thames, and end at Buckingham Palace—just in time for the last part of the Changing of the Guard).

London Walks—This leading company lists its extensive and creative daily schedule in a beefy, plain *London Walks* brochure. Pick it up at TIs, hotels, or St. Martin-in-the-Fields' Café in the Crypt on Trafalgar Square, or access it on their website. Just perusing their fascinating lineup of tours inspires me to stay longer in London. Their two-hour walks, led by professional guides and actors, cost £8 (cash only, walks offered year-round, private tours for groups-£120, tel. 020/7624-3978 for a live person, tel. 020/7624-9255 for a recording of today's or tomorrow's walks and the Tube station they depart from, www.walks.com).

London Walks also offers "Explorer Days" tours into the countryside, a good option for those with limited time and transportation (£14 plus £10–46 for transportation and any admission costs, cash only: Stonehenge/Salisbury, Oxford/Cotswolds, Cambridge, Bath, and so on). These are economical in part because everyone gets group discounts for transportation and admissions.

Sandemans New London "Free Royal London Tour"—This company employs English-speaking students (rather than licensed guides) who recite three-hour spiels covering the basic London sights. While the fast-moving, youthful tours are light and irreverent, and can be both entertaining and fun, it's misleading to call the tours "free," as tips are expected (the guides are unpaid). With the Essential London Walk (listed earlier) offered daily at a reasonable price by professional Blue Badge guides, taking this "free" tour makes no sense to me (daily at 11:00 and 13:00, meet at Wellington Arch, Tube: Hyde Park Corner, Exit 2). Sandemans also has other guided tours for a charge, including a Pub Crawl (£12, Tue–Sat at 19:30, meet at Belushi's at 9 Russell Street, Tube: Covent Garden, www.newlondon -tours.com).

Beatles Walks—Fans of the still–Fab Four can take one of three Beatles walks (London Walks, listed earlier, has two that run 5 days/week; Big Bus, above, includes a daily walk with their bus tour). For more on the Beatles, see page 105.

Jack the Ripper Walks—Each walking tour company seems to make most of its money with "haunted" and Jack the Ripper tours. Many guides are historians and would rather not lead these lightweight tours—but, in tourism as in journalism, "if it bleeds, it leads" (which is why the juvenile London Dungeon is one of London's busiest sights).

Two reliably good two-hour tours start every night at the Tower Hill Tube station exit. **Ripping Yarns** is guided by off-duty Yeoman Warders—the Tower of London "Beefeaters" (£7, pay at end, nightly at 18:45, no tours between Christmas and New Years, mobile 07813-559-301, www.jack-the-ripper-tours.com). **London Walks'** guides leave from the same spot later each night (£7, pay at the start, nightly at 19:30, tel. 020/7624-3978, recorded info tel. 020/7624-9255, www.jacktheripperwalk.com). After taking both, I found the London Walks more entertaining, informative, and with a better route (along quieter, once-hooker-friendly lanes, with less traffic), starting at Tower Hill and ending at Liverpool Street Station rather than returning to Tower Hill. Groups can be huge for both, but there's always room—just show up.

Private Walks with Local Guides—Standard rates for London's registered Blue Badge guides are about £125 for four hours, and £200 or more for nine hours (tel. 020/7780-4060, www.tourist guides.org.uk or www.blue-badge.org.uk). I know and like four fine local guides: **Sean Kelleher** (tel. 020/8673-1624, mobile 07764-612-770, seankelleher@btinternet.com), **Britt Lonsdale** (£150/half-day, £250/day, great with families, tel. 020/7386-9907, mobile 07813-278-077, brittl@btinternet.com), and two others who work in London when they're not on the road leading my Britain tours, **Tom Hooper** (mobile 07986-048-047, tomh@ricksteves.net) and **Gillian Chadwick** (mobile 07889-976-598, gillianc@ricksteves .net).

Driver-Guides—These two guides have cars or a minibus (particularly helpful for travelers with limited mobility) and charge around £290/half-day and £420/day for London tours (see websites and contact them for details): **Robina Brown** (tel. 020/7228-2238, www.driverguidetours.com, robina@driverguidetours.com) and **Janine Barton** (tel. 020/7402-4600, http://seeitinstyle.synthasite .com, jbsiis@aol.com).

London Duck Tours

A bright-yellow amphibious WWII-vintage vehicle (the model that landed troops on Normandy's beaches on D-Day) takes a gang of 30 tourists past some famous sights on land—Big Ben, Trafalgar Square, Piccadilly Circus—then splashes into the Thames for a cruise. All in all, it's good fun at a rather steep price. The live guide works hard, and it's kid-friendly to the point of goofiness (£20,

Daily Reminder

Sunday: The Tower of London and British Museum are both especially crowded today. The Speakers' Corner in Hyde Park rants from early afternoon until early evening. These places are closed: Banqueting House, Sir John Soane's Museum, and legal sights (Houses of Parliament, City Hall, and Old Bailey; the neighborhood called The City is dead). Westminster Abbey and St. Paul's are open during the day for worship but closed to sightseers. With all these closures, this morning is a good time to take a bus tour. Most big stores are open 12:00–18:00. Street markets are flourishing at Camden Lock, Spitalfields, Petticoat Lane, Brick Lane, and Greenwich, but Portobello Road and Brixton markets are closed (though the Brixton farmer's market is open 10:00–14:00). Theaters are quiet, as most actors take today off. (There are a few exceptions, such as *The Lion King* and Shakespeare's Globe, which offer Sunday performances in summer.)

Monday: Virtually all sights are open except for Apsley House, Sir John Soane's Museum, Vinopolis, and a few others. The Courtauld Gallery is free until 14:00. The Houses of Parliament are usually open until 22:30.

Tuesday: Virtually all sights are open, except for Vinopolis and Apsley House. The British Library is open until 20:00. On the first Tuesday of the month, Sir John Soane's Museum is also open 18:00–21:00. The Houses of Parliament are usually open until 22:30.

Wednesday: Virtually all sights are open, except for Vinopolis.

April–Sept daily 10:30–18:00, shorter hours Oct–March, 1–4/hr, 1.25 hours—45 minutes on land and 30 minutes in the river, £3 booking fee online, these book up in advance, departs from Chicheley Street—you'll see the big, ugly vehicle parked 100 yards behind the London Eye, Tube: Waterloo or Westminster, tel. 020/7928-3132, www.londonducktours.co.uk).

Bike Tours

London, like Paris, is committed to creating more bike paths, and many of its best sights can be laced together with a pleasant pedal through its parks. A bike tour is a fun way to see the sights and enjoy the city on two wheels.

London Bicycle Tour Company—Three tours covering London are offered daily from their base at Gabriel's Wharf on the south bank of the Thames. Sunday is the best, as there is less car traffic (**Central Tour**—£15.95, April–Oct daily at 10:30, Nov–March only on Mon–Fri, 6 miles, 2.5 hours, includes Westminster, Covent Garden, and St. Paul's; **Royal West Tour**—£18.95, April–Oct Sat–Sun at 12:00, Nov–March only on Sun, 9 miles, 3.5

Thursday: All sights are open, plus evening hours at the British Museum (selected galleries until 20:30), National Portrait Gallery (until 21:00), and Vinopolis (until 22:00).

Friday: All sights are open, except the Houses of Parliament. Sights open late include the British Museum (selected galleries until 20:30), National Gallery (until 21:00), National Portrait Gallery (until 21:00), Vinopolis (until 22:00), Victoria and Albert Museum (until 22:00), and Tate Modern (until 22:00). Best street market today: Spitalfields.

Saturday: Most sights are open except legal ones (Old Bailey, City Hall, Houses of Parliament; skip The City). Vinopolis is open until 22:00, the Tate Modern is open until 22:00. Today's the day to hit the Portobello Road street market; the Camden Lock and Greenwich markets are also good.

Notes: The St. Martin-in-the-Fields church offers concerts at lunchtime (Mon, Tue, and Fri at 13:00) and in the evening (jazz Wed at 20:00; classical at 19:30 Thu-Sat, sometimes Tue). Evensong occurs daily at St. Paul's (Mon-Sat at 17:00 and Sun at 15:15), Westminster Abbey (Mon-Fri at 17:00—may be spoken on Wed, Sat-Sun at 15:00), and Southwark Cathedral (weekdays at 17:30, Sat at 16:00, Sun at 15:00, no service on Wed or alternate Mon). London by Night Sightseeing Tour buses leave from Victoria Station every evening (19:30-21:30, only at 19:30 in winter). The London Eye spins nightly (last departure between 20:00 and 21:30, depending on the season).

hours, includes Westminster, Hyde Park, Buckingham Palace, and Covent Garden; **East Tour**—£18.95, April–Oct Sat–Sun at 14:00, Nov–March only on Sat at 12:00, 9 miles, 3.5 hours, includes south side of the river to Tower Bridge, then The City to the East End; book ahead for off-season tours). They also rent bikes (£3.50/hour, £20/day; office open daily 10:00–18:00, west of Blackfriars Bridge on the South Bank, 1a Gabriel's Wharf, tel. 020/7928-6838, www .londonbicycle.com).

Fat Tire Bike Tours—Daily bike tours cover the highlights of downtown London on two different itineraries (£2 discount with this book): Royal London (£20, daily March–Nov at 11:00, June–Aug also at 15:30, 7 miles, 4 hours, meet at Queensway Tube station; includes Parliament, Buckingham Palace, Hyde Park, and Trafalgar Square) and the Thames River (£30, mid-March–Nov Thu–Sat at 10:30, 5 hours, meet at Waterloo Tube station—exit 2; includes London Eye, St. Paul's, Tower of London, Trafalgar Square, Covent Garden, and boat trip on the Thames). The spiel is light and irreverent rather than scholarly, but the price is right. Reservations are easy online and required for Thames River tours

London

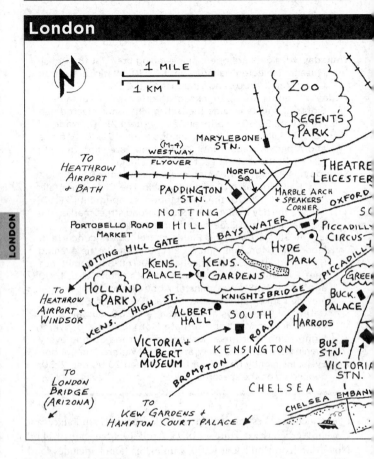

and kids' bikes (off-season tours by arrangement, mobile 078-8233-8779, www.fattirebiketourslondon.com). The schedule changes often—confirm online or by phone.

▲▲Cruises

Boat tours with entertaining commentaries sail regularly from many points along the Thames. The options are confusing, since several companies offer essentially the same trip. Your basic options are to use the boats either for a scenic joyride cruise within central London, or for transportation to an outlying sight (such as Greenwich or Kew Gardens).

Boats come and go from several docks in central London (see sidebar page 74). The most popular places to embark are Westminster Pier (at the base of Westminster Bridge across the street from Big Ben) and Waterloo Pier (at the London Eye, across the river).

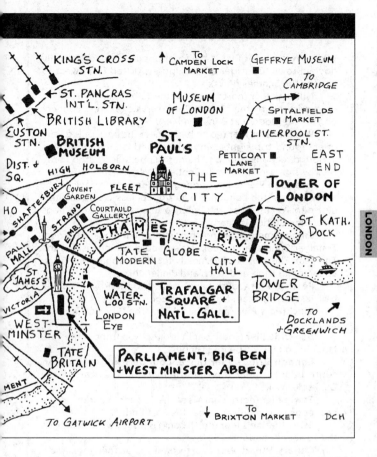

KING'S CROSS STN.

To CAMDEN LOCK MARKET

GEFFRYE MUSEUM

To CAMBRIDGE

ST. PANCRAS INT'L. STN.

MUSEUM OF LONDON

SPITALFIELDS MARKET

BRITISH LIBRARY

EUSTON STN.

BRITISH MUSEUM

ST. PAUL'S

LIVERPOOL ST. STN.

PETTICOAT LANE MARKET

EAST END

DIST. & SQ.

HIGH HOLBORN

THE CITY

TOWER OF LONDON

HO

SHAFTESBURY

COVENT GARDEN

FLEET

STRAND

COURTAULD GALLERY

ST. KATH. DOCK

PALL MALL

EMB.

THAMES

RIVER

ST. JAMES'S

TATE MODERN

GLOBE

CITY HALL

TOWER BRIDGE

VICTORIA

WATER-LOO STN.

London Eye

TO DOCKLANDS & GREENWICH

WEST-MINSTER

TATE BRITAIN

TRAFALGAR SQUARE & NAT'L. GALL.

MENT

PARLIAMENT, BIG BEN & WESTMINSTER ABBEY

To BRIXTON MARKET

DCH

TO GATWICK AIRPORT

LONDON

Buy boat tickets at the kiosks on the docks. While individual Tube and bus tickets don't work on the boats, a Travelcard can snare you a 33 percent discount on most cruises (just show the card when you pay for the cruise; no discount with the pay-as-you-go Oyster card except on Thames Clippers). Because different companies vary in the discounts they offer, always ask. Children and seniors generally get discounts. You can purchase drinks and scant, pricey snacks on board. Clever budget travelers pack a picnic and munch while they cruise.

Round-trip fares are only a bit more than one-way. Still, for pleasure and efficiency, consider combining a one-way cruise (to Kew, Greenwich, or wherever) with a Tube or train ride back.

Tourist-Oriented Cruises in Central London

London offers many made-for-tourist cruises on slow-moving, open-top boats accompanied by commentary about passing sights.

Thames Boat Piers

While Westminster Pier is the most popular, it's not the only dock in town. Consider all the options (listed from west to east, as the Thames flows):

Millbank Pier (north bank), at the Tate Britain Museum, is used primarily by the "Tate to Tate" service (express connection to Tate Modern at Bankside Pier).

Westminster Pier (north bank), near the base of Big Ben, offers round-trip sightseeing cruises and lots of departures in both directions (though Thames Clippers don't stop here). Nearby sights include Parliament and Westminster Abbey.

Waterloo Pier (a.k.a. **London Eye Pier**, south bank), right at the base of the London Eye, is a good, less-crowded alternative to Westminster, with many of the same cruise options (Waterloo Station is nearby).

Embankment Pier (north bank) is near Covent Garden, Trafalgar Square, and Cleopatra's Needle (the obelisk on the Thames). This pier is used mostly for special boat trips (such as some RIB trips, and lunch and dinner cruises).

Festival Pier (south bank) is next to the Royal Festival Hall, just downstream from the London Eye.

Blackfriars Pier (north bank) is in The City, not far from St. Paul's.

Bankside Pier (south bank) is directly in front of the Tate Modern and Shakespeare's Globe.

London Bridge Pier (a.k.a. **London Bridge City Pier,** south bank) is near the HMS *Belfast* and the start of my Bankside Walk.

Tower Pier (north bank) is at the Tower of London, at the east edge of The City and near the East End.

St. Katharine's Pier (north bank) is just downstream from the Tower of London.

Canary Wharf Pier (north bank) is at the Docklands, London's new "downtown."

In outer London, you might also use the piers at **Greenwich, Kew Gardens,** and **Hampton Court.**

City Cruises runs boats from Westminster Pier across the river to Waterloo Pier, then downriver to Tower Pier and on to Greenwich (tel. 020/7740-0400, www.citycruises.com). If you want just a sample, hop on their 30-minute cruise only as far as Tower Pier (£8 one-way, £10.50 round-trip, daily April–Oct roughly 10:00–19:00, until 18:00 in winter, 2/hr). City Cruises also

offers a £13 "River Red Rover" ticket good for all-day hop-on, hop-off travel (also included with the bus tours described on page 65)—though the line's limited stops in central London make this a lesser deal than it might seem.

Thames River Services runs a similar service with even fewer stops: Westminster to St. Katharine's Pier to Greenwich (tel. 020/7930-4097, www.thamesriverservices.co.uk). They have classic boats and feel a little friendlier and more old-fashioned. For more details, see "Cruising Downstream, to Greenwich and the Docklands," later.

The **Circular Cruise** offered by Crown River Services is a handy hop-on, hop-off route with stops at the Westminster, Festival, Embankment, Bankside, London Bridge, and St. Katharine's piers (£3 to go one stop, £8 one-way for a longer trip, £10.50 for an all-day ticket, daily 11:00-18:30, every 30 minutes late May–early Sept, fewer stops and less frequent off-season, tel. 020/7936-2033, www.crownriver.com).

The **London Eye** operates its own river cruise, offering a 40-minute live-guided circular tour from Waterloo Pier. As it's much pricier than the alternatives for just a short loop, it's a poor value (£12, reservations recommended, 10 percent discount if you pre-book online, no Travelcard discounts, departures daily generally at :45 past the hour, April–Oct 10:45–18:45, Nov–March 11:45–16:45, closed mid-Jan–mid-Feb, toll tel. 0870-500-0600, www.londoneye.com).

Careening at Top Speed Along the Thames: Two competing companies invite you aboard a small, 12-person, high-speed rigid inflatable boat (RIB—similar to a Zodiac) for an adrenaline-fueled tour of the city (London RIB Voyages: stand-up comedian guides, £32.50/50 minutes, £45/1.25 hours, tel. 020/7928-8933, www.londonribvoyages.com; Thames RIB Experience: £29/50 minutes, £45/1.5 hours, toll tel. 0870-224-4200, www.thamesrib experience.com).

Away from the Thames, on Regent's Canal: Consider exploring London's canals by taking a cruise on historic Regent's Canal in north London. The good ship *Jenny Wren* offers 1.5-hour guided canal boat cruises from Walker's Quay in Camden Town through scenic Regent's Park to Little Venice (£9; Aug daily at 10:30, 12:30, 14:30, and 16:30; April–July and Sept–Oct daily at 12:30 and 14:30, Sat–Sun also at 16:30; Walker's Quay, 250 Camden High Street, 3-minute walk from Tube: Camden Town; tel. 020/7485-4433, www.walkersquay.com). While in Camden Town, stop by the popular, punky Camden Lock Market to browse through trendy arts and crafts (daily 10:00–18:00, busiest on weekends, a block from Walker's Quay, www.camdenlockmarket .com).

Commuting by Clipper

Thames Clippers, with their fast, sleek, 220-seat catamarans, are designed for commuters rather than sightseers. Think of the clippers as express buses in the river—they zip no-nonsense through London every 20 minutes, stopping at most of the major docks en route: Embankment, Waterloo, Blackfriars or Bankside, London Bridge, Tower, Canary Wharf (Docklands), and Greenwich (roughly 20 minutes from Embankment to Tower, 10 more minutes to Docklands, 10 more minutes to Greenwich). However, the clippers are less pleasant for joyriding than the cruises described earlier. There's no commentary, and no open deck up top (the only outside access is on a crowded deck at the exhaust-choked back of the boat, where you're jostling for photos). Any one-way ride costs £5.30, and a River Roamer all-day ticket costs £12 (33 percent discount with Travelcard, 10 percent off with a pay-as-you-go Oyster card, tel. 020/7001-2222, www.thamesclippers.com).

The company also offers two express trips. The **"Tate to Tate"** boat service, which directly connects Tate Britain (Millbank Pier) and the Tate Modern (Bankside Pier), is made for art-lovers (£5 one-way, covered by £12 River Roamer day ticket; buy ticket at gallery desk, at kiosk by the dock, or onboard; daily 10:00–17:00, runs every 40 minutes, 18-minute trip, www.tate.org.uk/tatetotate). The **O$_2$ Express** runs only on nights when there are events going on at the O$_2$ Arena (formerly the Millennium Dome; from Waterloo Pier, £6 one-way, £12 round-trip, 30 minutes).

Cruising Downstream, to Greenwich and the Docklands

Greenwich: Both of the big tour companies (City Cruises and Thames River Services, described earlier) head to Greenwich from Westminster Pier. The cruises are usually narrated by the captain, with most commentary given on the way to Greenwich. The companies' prices are the same (£9.50 one-way, £12.50 round-trip), though their itineraries are slightly different: **City Cruises** stops at Waterloo/London Eye Pier and Tower Pier on the way to Greenwich (if you buy their £13 River Red Rover ticket, you can hop on and off all day long; daily April–Oct generally 10:00–17:00, less off-season, 2/hour, 1.25 hours from Westminster to Greenwich; cheaper to go from Tower Pier to Greenwich—£8 one-way, £10.50 round-trip, only 30 minutes to Greenwich—but you miss all the scenery in central London). **Thames River Services** stops only at St. Katharine's Pier on the way to Greenwich, making the trip a little faster (April–Oct 10:00–16:00, July–Aug until 17:00, daily 2/hour; Nov–March shorter hours and runs every 40 minutes; 1 hour from Westminster to Greenwich).

The **Thames Clippers,** described earlier, are cheaper, faster, and make more stops downtown, but have no commentary and no seating up top (£5.30 one-way, £12 for an all-day pass, 3/hour, about 45 minutes from Westminster to Greenwich).

To maximize both efficiency and sightseeing, I'd take a boat to Greenwich one way, and go the other way on the DLR (Docklands Light Railway), with a stop in the Docklands (Canary Wharf station).

The Docklands: Thames Clippers connect the Docklands' Canary Wharf Pier to both central London and Greenwich (£5.30 one-way, £12 for an all-day pass, no commentary, 3/hour, roughly 10 minutes to Tower, 30 minutes to Waterloo, 15 minutes to Greenwich).

Cruising Upstream, to Kew Gardens and Hampton Court Palace

Boats operated by the Westminster Passenger Services Association leave for Kew Gardens from Westminster Pier (£12 one-way, £18 round-trip, cash only; 4/day, April–Oct daily at 10:30, 11:15, 12:00, and 14:00; 1.5 hours, about half the trip is narrated, tel. 020/7930-2062, www.wpsa.co.uk). Most boats continue on to Hampton Court Palace for an additional £3 (and another 1.5 hours). Because of the river current, you'll sometimes save 30 minutes cruising from Hampton Court back into town (depends on the tide—ask before you commit to the boat). Romantic as these rides sound, it can be a long trip...especially upstream.

Self-Guided Walk

Westminster Walk

Just about every visitor to London strolls along historic Whitehall from Big Ben to Trafalgar Square. This quick, nine-stop walk gives meaning to that touristy ramble. Under London's modern traffic and big-city bustle lie 2,000 fascinating years of history. You'll get a whirlwind tour as well as a practical orientation to London. (Those traveling with an iPod or other MP3 player can download a free **Rick Steves audio tour** of this walk at www.ricksteves.com, or search for "Rick Steves Audio Tours" in iTunes.)

Start halfway across **Westminster Bridge (❶)** for that "Wow, I'm really in London!" feeling. Get a close-up view of the **Houses of Parliament** and **Big Ben** (floodlit at night). Downstream you'll see the **London Eye.** Down the stairs to Westminster Pier are boats to the Tower of London and Greenwich (downstream) or Kew Gardens (upstream).

En route to Parliament Square, you'll pass a **statue of Boadicea (❷)**, the Celtic queen defeated by Roman invaders in A.D. 60.

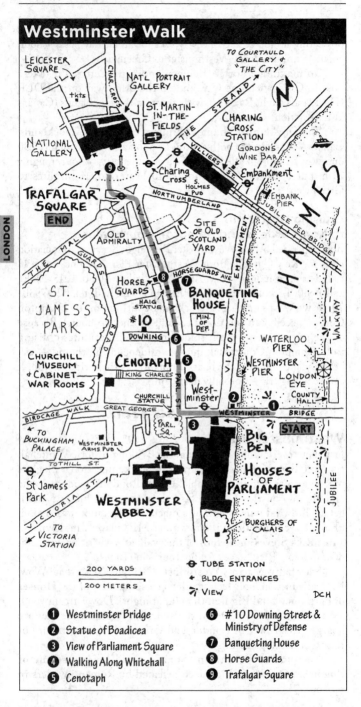

Westminster Walk

TO COURTAULD GALLERY & "THE CITY"

LEICESTER SQUARE

NAT'L PORTRAIT GALLERY

St. Martin-in-the-Fields

NATIONAL GALLERY

CHARING CROSS STATION

Gordon's Wine Bar

Charing Cross

S. HOLMES PUB

Embankment

EMBANK. PIER

JUBILEE PED. BRIDGE

TRAFALGAR SQUARE
END

NORTHUMBERLAND

Site of Old Scotland Yard

THE MALL

OLD ADMIRALTY

ST. JAMES'S PARK

Horse Guards

HAIG STATUE

Horse Guards Ave.

Banqueting House

CHURCHILL MUSEUM & CABINET WAR ROOMS

#10 DOWNING

MIN. OF DEF.

Cenotaph

KING CHARLES

WATERLOO PIER

WESTMINSTER PIER

LONDON EYE

COUNTY HALL

BIRDCAGE WALK

GREAT GEORGE

CHURCHILL STATUE

West-minster

WESTMINSTER BRIDGE

START

TO BUCKINGHAM PALACE

WESTMINSTER ARMS PUB

PARL. SQ.

BIG BEN

TOTHILL ST.

St James's Park

HOUSES OF PARLIAMENT

VICTORIA ST.

TO VICTORIA STATION

WESTMINSTER ABBEY

BURGHERS OF CALAIS

JUBILEE

THAMES

WALKWAY

VICTORIA EMBANKMENT

200 YARDS
200 METERS

⊖ TUBE STATION
← BLDG. ENTRANCES
↗ VIEW

DCH

1. Westminster Bridge
2. Statue of Boadicea
3. View of Parliament Square
4. Walking Along Whitehall
5. Cenotaph
6. #10 Downing Street & Ministry of Defense
7. Banqueting House
8. Horse Guards
9. Trafalgar Square

LONDON

For fun, call home from a pay phone near Big Ben at about three minutes before the hour, to let your loved one hear the bell ring. You'll find four red phone booths lining the north side of **Parliament Square** (❸) along Great George Street.

Wave hello to Churchill in Parliament Square. To his right is **Westminster Abbey** with its two stubby, elegant towers.

Head north up Parliament Street, which turns into **Whitehall** (❹), and walk toward Trafalgar Square. You'll see the thought-provoking **Cenotaph** (❺) in the middle of the street, reminding passersby of Britain's many war dead. To visit the Churchill Museum and Cabinet War Rooms (see page 84), take a left before the Cenotaph, on King Charles Street.

Continuing on Whitehall, stop at the barricaded and guarded #10 Downing Street (❻) to see the British "White House," home of the prime minister. Break the bobby's boredom and ask him a question. The huge building across Whitehall from Downing Street is the **Ministry of Defense** (MOD), the "British Pentagon."

Nearing Trafalgar Square, look for the 17th-century **Banqueting House** across the street (❼) and the **Horse Guards** (❽) behind the gated fence (Changing of the Horse Guards Mon–Sat at 11:00, Sun at 10:00, dismounting ceremony daily at 16:00).

The column topped by Lord Nelson marks **Trafalgar Square** (❾). The stately domed building on the far side of the square is the **National Gallery** (free), which has a classy café upstairs in the Sainsbury wing. To the right of the National Gallery is **St. Martin-in-the-Fields Church** and its Café in the Crypt.

To get to Piccadilly from Trafalgar Square, walk up Cockspur Street to Haymarket, then take a short left on Coventry Street to colorful **Piccadilly Circus.**

Near Piccadilly, you'll find the **Britain and London Visitors Centre** (on Lower Regent Street) and piles of theaters. **Leicester Square** (with its half-price "tkts" booth for plays—see page 137) thrives just a few blocks away. Walk through seedy **Soho** (north of Shaftesbury Avenue) for its fun pubs (consider my recommended Soho "Food Is Fun" Three-Course Dinner Crawl on page 173). From Piccadilly or Oxford Circus, you can take a taxi, a bus, or the Tube home.

Sights in London

Central London

Westminster

▲▲▲**Westminster Abbey**—The greatest church in the English-speaking world, Westminster Abbey is the place where England's kings and queens have been crowned and buried since 1066. Like

a stony refugee camp huddled outside St. Peter's Pearly Gates, Westminster Abbey has many stories to tell. The steep admission includes an excellent audioguide, worthwhile if you have the time and interest. To experience the church more vividly, take a live tour, or attend evensong or an organ concert (see next page).

Two tiny **museums** ring the cloisters. The Chapter House, where the monks had daily meetings, features fine architecture and stained glass with faded but well-described medieval art. The Abbey Museum has exhibits on royal coronations, funerals, Abbey history, a close-up look at medieval stained glass, and replicas of the crown jewels used for coronation practice. Look into the impressively realistic eyes of Elizabeth I, Charles II, Admiral Nelson, and a dozen others, part of a compelling series of wax-and-wood statues that, for three centuries, graced coffins during funeral processions.

Cost: £15, £30 family ticket (covers 2 adults and 1 child), cash only, includes cloisters, audioguide, and Abbey Museum.

Hours: Abbey open Mon–Fri 9:30–16:30, Wed until 19:00 (main church only), Sat 9:30–14:30, last entry one hour before closing, closed Sun to sightseers but open for services; Abbey Museum open daily 10:30–16:00; cloisters open daily 8:00–18:00; 1.5-hour guided tour-£3, up to 5/day in summer; Tube: Westminster or St. James's Park. Info desk tel. 020/7222-5152 or 020/7654-4834, www.westminster-abbey.org.

Crowd-Beating Tips: The main entrance, on the Parliament Square side, often has a sizable line; visit early, during lunch, or late to avoid tourist hordes. Sat and Mon are worst. Midmornings are also crowded, while weekdays after 14:30 are less congested; come then and stay for the 17:00 evensong.

Music: The church hosts evensong performances daily, sung every night but Wednesday, when it may be spoken (Mon–Fri at 17:00; Sat–Sun at 15:00). A free 30-minute organ recital is often held on Sunday at 17:45.

▲▲Houses of Parliament (Palace of Westminster)—This Neo-Gothic icon of London, the royal residence from 1042 to 1547, is now the meeting place of the legislative branch of government. The Houses of Parliament are located in what was once the Palace of Westminster—long the palace of England's medieval kings—until it was largely destroyed by fire in 1834. The palace was rebuilt in the Victorian Gothic style (a move away from Neoclassicism

▲▲London Eye Enormous observation wheel, dominating—and offering commanding views over—London's skyline. **Hours:** Daily July–Aug 10:00–21:30, June and Sept 10:00–21:00, Oct–May 10:00–20:00. See page 112.

▲▲Imperial War Museum Examines the military history of the bloody 20th century. **Hours:** Daily 10:00–18:00. See page 114.

▲▲Tate Modern Works by Monet, Matisse, Dalí, Picasso, and Warhol displayed in a converted powerhouse. **Hours:** Daily 10:00–18:00, Fri–Sat until 22:00. See page 116.

▲▲Shakespeare's Globe Timbered, thatched-roofed reconstruction of the Bard's original wooden "O." **Hours:** Theater complex, museum, and actor-led tours generally daily 9:00–17:00; in summer, morning theater tours only. Plays are also held here. See page 116.

▲▲Tate Britain Collection of British paintings from the 16th century through modern times, including works by William Blake, the Pre-Raphaelites, and J. M. W. Turner. **Hours:** Daily 10:00–18:00, first Fri of the month until 22:00. See page 120.

▲▲Natural History Museum Packed with stuffed creatures, engaging exhibits, and enthralled kids. **Hours:** Daily 10:00–17:50. See page 124.

▲▲The Docklands London's emerging new "Manhattan," with a forest of skyscrapers. **Hours:** Always open, but most interesting at the end of the workday. See page 129.

▲Courtauld Gallery Fine collection of paintings filling one wing of the Somerset House, a grand 18th-century palace. **Hours:** Daily 10:00–18:00. See page 95.

▲Buckingham Palace Britain's royal residence with the famous Changing of the Guard. **Hours:** Palace—Aug–Sept only, daily 9:45–18:00; Guard—generally May–July daily at 11:30, Aug–April every other day. See page 96.

▲Old Operating Theatre Museum 19th-century hall where surgeons performed amputations for an audience of aspiring med students. **Hours:** Daily 10:30–16:45. See page 120.

Vinopolis Offering a breezy history of wine with plenty of tasting opportunities. **Hours:** Thu–Sat 12:00–22:00, Sun 12:00–18:00, closed Mon–Wed. See page 118.

during much of August and September, you can get a behind-the-scenes peek at the royal chambers of both houses during these months with a tour (£14, 1.25 hours, generally Mon–Fri, times vary, so confirm in advance; book ahead through www.ticketmaster.co.uk). The same tours are offered Saturdays year-round.

Jewel Tower: Across the street from the Parliament building's St. Stephen's Gate, the Jewel Tower is a rare remnant of the old Palace of Westminster used by kings until Henry VIII. The crude stone tower (1365–1366) was a guard tower in the palace wall, overlooking a moat. It contains a fine little exhibit on Parliament and the tower (£3, daily March–Oct 10:00–17:00, Nov–Feb 10:00–16:00, tel. 020/7222-2219). Next to the tower (and free) is a quiet courtyard with picnic-friendly benches.

Big Ben: The clock tower (315 feet high) is named for its 13-ton bell, Ben. The light above the clock is lit when the House of Commons is sitting. The face of the clock is huge—you can actually see the minute hand moving. For a good view of it, walk halfway over Westminster Bridge.

▲▲▲**Churchill Museum and Cabinet War Rooms**—This is a fascinating walk through the underground headquarters of the British government's fight against the Nazis in the darkest days of the Battle for Britain. The attraction includes two parts: the war rooms themselves, and a top-notch museum dedicated to the man who steered the war from here, Winston Churchill. For details on all the blood, sweat, toil, and tears, pick up the excellent, essential, and included audioguide at the entry, and dive in.

Cabinet War Rooms: The 27-room, heavily fortified nerve center of the British war effort was used from 1939 to 1945. Churchill's room, the map room, and other rooms are just as they were in 1945. As you follow the one-way route, be sure to take advantage of the audioguide, which explains each room and offers first-person accounts of wartime happenings here (it takes about 45 minutes,  not counting the Churchill Museum). Be patient—it's well worth it. While the rooms are spartan, you'll see how British gentility survived even as the city was bombarded—posted signs informed those working underground what the weather was like outside, and a cheery notice reminds you to turn off the light switch to conserve electricity.

Churchill Museum: Don't bypass this museum, which occupies a large hall about a half-dozen rooms into the war rooms. It dissects every aspect of the man behind the famous cigar, bowler hat, and V-for-victory sign. It's extremely well-presented and engaging, using artifacts, quotes, political cartoons, clear explanations, and high-tech interactive exhibits to bring the colorful statesman to life; this museum alone deserves an hour. You'll get a taste of Winston's wit, irascibility, work ethic, passion for painting, American ties, writing talents, and drinking habits. The exhibit shows Winston's warts as well: It questions whether his party-switching was just political opportunism, examines the basis for his opposition to Indian self-rule, and reveals him to be an intense taskmaster who worked 18-hour days and was brutal to his staffers (who deeply respected him nevertheless).

A long touch-the-screen timeline lets you zero in on events in his life from birth (November 30, 1874) to his first appointment as prime minister in 1940. Many of the items on display—such as a European map divvied up in permanent marker, which Churchill brought home from the postwar Potsdam Conference—drive home the remarkable span of history this man lived through. Imagine: Churchill began his military career riding horses in the cavalry, and ended it speaking out against the proliferation of nuclear armaments. It's all the more amazing considering that, in the 1930s, the man who would become my vote for greatest statesman of the 20th century was once considered a washed-up loony ranting about the growing threat of fascism.

Cost and Hours: £14.95, daily 9:30–18:00, last entry one hour before closing; on King Charles Street, 200 yards off Whitehall, follow the signs, Tube: Westminster. Tel. 020/7930-6961, www.iwm.org.uk. The museum's gift shop is great for anyone nostalgic for the 1940s. Note that this wonderful museum is far superior to the Winston Churchill's Britain at War Experience (next to the London Dungeon on the South Bank); give that one—and the London Dungeon—a miss.

Eating: If you're hungry, get your rations at the Switch Room café (in the museum) or, for a nearby pub lunch, try the Westminster Arms (food served downstairs, on Storey's Gate, a couple of blocks south of Cabinet War Rooms).

Horse Guards—The Horse Guards change daily at 11:00 (10:00 on Sun), and there's a colorful dismounting ceremony daily at 16:00. The rest of the day, they just stand there—terrible for video cameras (on Whitehall, between Trafalgar Square and #10 Downing Street, Tube: Westminster, www.changing-the-guard.com).

Buckingham Palace pageantry is canceled when it rains, but the horse guards change regardless of the weather.

▲**Banqueting House**—England's first Renaissance building (1619–1622) was designed by Inigo Jones. Built by King James I and decorated by his son Charles I, the Banqueting House came to symbolize the Stuart kings' "divine right" management style—the belief that God himself had anointed them to rule. The house is one of the few London landmarks spared by the 1698 fire, and the only surviving part of the original Palace of Whitehall. Today it opens its doors to visitors, who enjoy a restful 20-minute audio-visual history, a 30-minute audio tour, and a look at the exquisite banqueting hall itself. As a tourist attraction, it's basically one big room—but what a grand room it is, with sumptuous ceiling paintings by Peter Paul Rubens. At Charles I's request, these paintings drove home the doctrine of the legitimacy of the divine right of kings. Ironically, in 1649—divine right ignored—King Charles I was famously executed right here.

Cost and Hours: £4.80, includes audioguide, Mon–Sat 10:00–17:00, closed Sun, last entry at 16:30, subject to closure for government functions, aristocratic WC, immediately across Whitehall from the Horse Guards, Tube: Westminster. Tel. 020/3166-6154 or 020/3166-6155, www.hrp.org.uk.

On Trafalgar Square

▲▲**Trafalgar Square**—London's recently renovated central square, the climax of most marches and demonstrations, is a thrilling place to simply hang out. Lord Nelson stands atop his 185-foot-tall fluted granite column, gazing out toward Trafalgar, where he lost his life but defeated the French fleet. Part of this 1842 memorial is made from his victims' melted-down cannons. He's surrounded by spraying fountains, giant  lions, hordes of people, and—until recently—even more pigeons. A former London mayor decided that London's "flying rats" were a public nuisance and evicted Trafalgar Square's venerable seed salesmen (Tube: Charing Cross).

▲▲▲**National Gallery**—Displaying Britain's top collection of European paintings from 1250 to 1900—including works by Leonardo, Botticelli, Velázquez, Rembrandt, Turner, Van Gogh, and the Impressionists—this is one of Europe's great galleries. You'll peruse 700 years of art—from gold-backed Madonnas to Cubist bathers. The newly remodeled museum is surprisingly

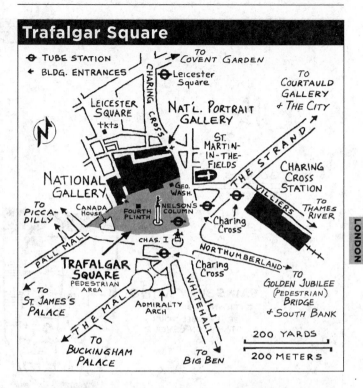

Trafalgar Square

- ⊕ TUBE STATION
- ← BLDG. ENTRANCES

TO COVENT GARDEN

⊕ Leicester Square

LEICESTER SQUARE tkts

CHARING CROSS

NAT'L. PORTRAIT GALLERY

ST. MARTIN-IN-THE-FIELDS

TO COURTAULD GALLERY & THE CITY

THE STRAND

CHARING CROSS STATION

VILLIERS

NATIONAL GALLERY

GEO. WASH.

NELSON'S COLUMN

Canada House

FOURTH PLINTH

TO PICCA-DILLY

PALL MALL

CHAS. I

TRAFALGAR SQUARE PEDESTRIAN AREA

ADMIRALTY ARCH

TO ST. JAMES'S PALACE

THE MALL

TO BUCKINGHAM PALACE

WHITEHALL

Charing Cross

Charing Cross

NORTHUMBERLAND

TO THAMES RIVER

TO GOLDEN JUBILEE (PEDESTRIAN) BRIDGE & SOUTH BANK

TO BIG BEN

200 YARDS
200 METERS

family-friendly (especially on Sunday mornings), with a variety of kids' activities. While the collection is huge, following the route suggested on my "National Gallery Highlights" map on pages 88–89 will give you my best quick visit. For a more thorough tour, the £3.50 audioguide is excellent.

Cost and Hours: Free, but suggested donation of £2–3; daily 10:00–18:00, Fri until 21:00; last entry to special exhibits 45 minutes before closing, free one-hour overview tours daily

at 11:30 and 14:30, plus Fri at 19:00; no photography, on Trafalgar Square, Tube: Charing Cross or Leicester Square. Recorded info tel. 020/7747-2885, switchboard tel. 020/7839-3321, www.national gallery.org.uk.

Eating: The excellent-but-pricey museum restaurant called the National Dining Rooms is a good spot to split afternoon tea (see page 181). Two cheaper eateries, also in the museum, are located near the Getty Entrance: the National Café (with both

National Gallery Highlights

☒ ELEVATOR / LIFT

🗐 STAIRS

30 YARDS

30 METERS

SAINSBURY WING
ENTRANCE ON LEVEL 0
SELF-GUIDED TOUR
STARTS ON LEVEL 2

**SAINSBURY
ENTRANCE**

MEDIEVAL & EARLY RENAISSANCE

1. ANONYMOUS – The Wilton Diptych
2. UCCELLO – Battle of San Romano
3. VAN EYCK – The Arnolfini Marriage

ITALIAN RENAISSANCE

4. BOTTICELLI – Venus and Mars
5. CRIVELLI – The Annunciation, with Saint Emidius

HIGH RENAISSANCE

6. MICHELANGELO – Entombment
7. RAPHAEL – Pope Julius II
8. HOLBEIN – The Ambassadors
9. DA VINCI – The Virgin of the Rocks; Virgin and Child with St. Anne and St. John the Baptist

VENETIAN RENAISSANCE

10. TINTORETTO – The Origin of the Milky Way
11. TITIAN – Bacchus and Ariadne

NORTHERN PROTESTANT ART

12. VERMEER – A Young Woman
13. "A Peepshow"
14. REMBRANDT – Belshazzar's Feast
15. REMBRANDT – Self-Portrait

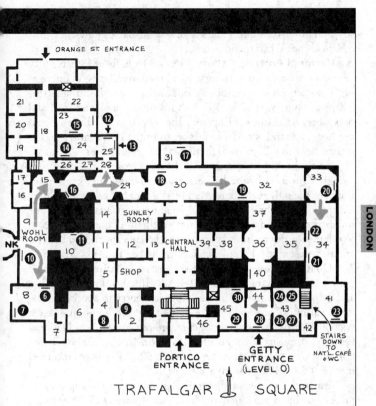

ORANGE ST. ENTRANCE

LONDON

WOHL ROOM

NK

SUNLEY ROOM

CENTRAL HALL

SHOP

PORTICO ENTRANCE

GETTY ENTRANCE (LEVEL 0)

STAIRS DOWN TO NAT'L CAFÉ & WC

TRAFALGAR SQUARE

BAROQUE & ROCOCO

16 RUBENS –
The Judgment of Paris

17 VAN DYCK –
Equestrian Portrait of Charles I

18 VELÁZQUEZ –
The Rokeby Venus

19 CARAVAGGIO –
The Supper at Emmaus

20 BOUCHER –
Pan and Syrinx

BRITISH

21 CONSTABLE – The Hay Wain

22 TURNER –
The Fighting Téméraire

23 DELAROCHE –
The Execution of Lady Jane Grey

IMPRESSIONISM & BEYOND

24 MONET –
Gare St. Lazare

25 MONET –
The Water-Lily Pond

26 MANET –
Corner of a Café-Concert
(a.k.a. The Waitress)

27 RENOIR –
Boating on the Seine

28 SEURAT –
Bathers at Asnières

29 VAN GOGH –
Sunflowers

30 CÉZANNE – Bathers

a table-service restaurant and an easier-on-the-budget sandwich/soup/salad/pastry buffet) and the Espresso Bar (sandwiches, soft couches, and ArtStart computers).

▲▲National Portrait Gallery—Put off by halls of 19th-century characters who meant nothing to me, I used to call this "as interesting as someone else's yearbook." But a selective walk through this 500-year-long *Who's Who* of British history is quick and free, and puts faces on the story of England. The collection is well-described, not huge, and in historical sequence, from the 16th century on the second floor to today's royal family on the ground floor.

Some highlights: Henry VIII and wives; portraits of the "Virgin Queen" Elizabeth I, Sir Francis Drake, and Sir Walter Raleigh; the only real-life portrait of William Shakespeare; Oliver Cromwell and Charles I with his head on; portraits by Gainsborough and Reynolds; the Romantics (William Blake, Lord Byron, William Wordsworth, and company); Queen Victoria and her era; and the present royal family, including the late Princess Diana.

Cost and Hours: Free, but suggested donation of £5, temporary exhibits extra; daily 10:00–18:00, Thu–Fri until 21:00, first and second floors open Mon at 11:00, last entry to special exhibits 45 minutes before closing, excellent themed audioguides-£3; entry 100 yards off Trafalgar Square, around corner from National Gallery, opposite Church of St. Martin-in-the-Fields; Tube: Charing Cross or Leicester Square. Tel. 020/7306-0055, recorded info tel. 020/7312-2463, www.npg.org.uk.

Eating: The elegant Portrait Restaurant on the top floor is pricey but has a fine view of Trafalgar Square (£15-20 entrées, reservations smart, tel. 020/7312-2490). The Portrait Café in the basement (take the lift down) is cheaper and offers sandwiches, salads, and pastries.

▲St. Martin-in-the-Fields—The church, built in the 1720s with a Gothic spire atop a Greek-type temple, is an oasis of peace on the wild and noisy Trafalgar Square. St. Martin cared for the poor. "In

the fields" was where the first church stood on this spot (in the 13th century), between Westminster and The City. Stepping inside, you still feel a compassion for the needs of the people in this neighborhood—the church serves the homeless and houses a Chinese community center. The modern east window—with grillwork bent into the shape of a warped cross—was installed in 2008 to replace one damaged in World War II.

A new freestanding glass pavilion

to the left of the church serves as the entrance to the church's underground areas. There you'll find the concert ticket office, a gift shop, brass-rubbing center, and the recommended support-the-church Café in the Crypt.

Cost and Hours: Church entry free, donations welcome, £3.50 audioguide at shop downstairs; hours vary but generally Mon–Fri 8:30–13:00 & 14:00–18:00, Sat 9:30–13:00 & 14:00–18:00, Sun 15:30–17:00; Tube: Charing Cross. Tel. 020/7766-1100, www2 .stmartin-in-the-fields.org.

Music: The church is famous for its concerts. Consider a free lunchtime concert (Mon, Tue, and Fri at 13:00), an evening concert (£6–25, several nights a week at 19:30), or Wednesday night jazz in the church's café (£5–10, at 20:00). See the website for the concert schedule.

The West End and Nearby

To explore this area during dinner, see my recommended Soho "Food Is Fun" Three-Course Dinner Crawl, and munch your way from Covent Garden to Soho (see sidebar on page 173).

▲**Piccadilly Circus**—Although this square is slathered with neon billboards and tacky attractions, the surrounding streets are packed with great shopping opportunities and swimming with youth on the rampage. For overstimula-
tion in a grimy mall that smells like teen spirit, drop by the extremely trashy Trocadero Center for its Funland arcade games, multiplex cinema, and 10-lane bowling alley (admission to Trocadero is free; individual attractions have separate admissions; located between
Piccadilly and Leicester squares on Coventry Street). Nearby Shaftesbury Avenue and Leicester Square teem with fun-seekers, theaters, Chinese restaurants, and street singers. To the north-east is London's Chinatown and, beyond that, the funky Soho neighborhood (described next). And curling to the northwest from Piccadilly Circus is genteel Regent Street, lined with the city's most exclusive shops.

▲**Soho**—North of Piccadilly, seedy Soho has become seriously trendy and is well worth a gawk. It's the epicenter of London's thriving and colorful youth, a fun and funky *Sesame Street* scene populated by people of every color of the racial rainbow...straight, gay, and everything in between.

Soho is also London's red light district (especially near Brewer and Berwick Streets), where "friendly models" wait in tiny rooms

West End & Nearby

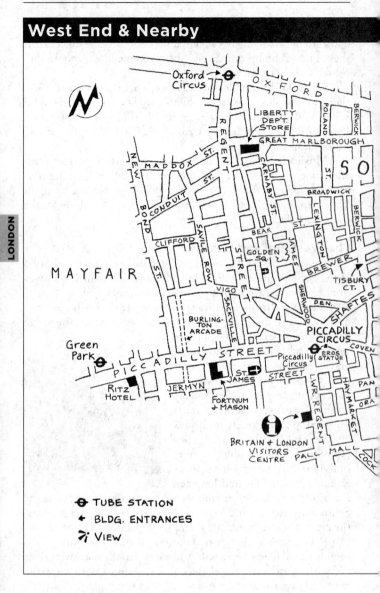

up dreary stairways, and voluptuous con artists sell strip shows. Though venturing up a stairway to check out a model is interesting, anyone who goes into any one of the shows will be ripped off. Every time. Even a £5 show in a "licensed bar" comes with a £100 cover or minimum (as it's printed on the drink menu) and a "security man." You may accidentally buy a £200 bottle of bubbly. And suddenly, the door has no handle. While this all sounds creepy, it's

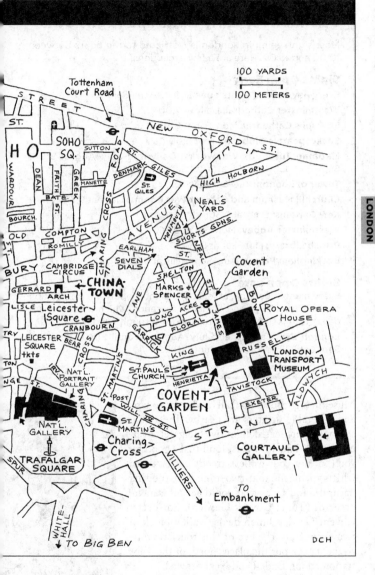

easy to avoid trouble if you're not looking for it. In fact, the sleazy joints share the block with respectable pubs and restaurants, and elderly couples out for a stroll pass neon signs that flash *Licensed Sex Shop in Basement.*

▲▲**Covent Garden**—The centerpiece of this boutique-ish shopping district is an iron-and-glass arcade. The "Actors' Church" of St. Paul, the Royal Opera House, and the London Transport

London for Early Birds and Night Owls

Most sightseeing in London is restricted to the hours between 10:00 and 18:00. Here are a few exceptions:

Sights Open Early

Every day, several sights open at 9:45 or earlier.

Westminster Cathedral: Daily at 7:00.

St. Paul's Cathedral: Mon–Sat at 8:30.

Shakespeare's Globe: Daily at 9:00.

Madame Tussauds Waxworks: Daily mid-July–Aug at 9:00, Sept–mid-July Mon–Fri at 9:30, Sat–Sun at 9:00.

Tower of London: Tue–Sat at 9:00.

Churchill Museum and Cabinet War Rooms: Daily at 9:30.

Kew Gardens: Daily at 9:30.

Westminster Abbey: Mon–Sat at 9:30.

British Library: Mon–Sat at 9:30.

Buckingham Palace: Aug–Sept daily at 9:45.

Sights Open Late

Every night in London, at least one sight is open late (in addition to the London Eye and Madame Tussauds, which are open late daily). Here's the scoop from Monday through Sunday:

London Eye: Last ascent July–Aug daily until 21:30, June and Sept until 21:00, otherwise until 20:00.

Museum (described next) all border the square, and venerable theaters are nearby. The area is a people-watcher's delight, with cigarette eaters, Punch-and-Judy acts, food that's good for you (but not your wallet), trendy crafts, sweet whiffs of marijuana, two-tone hair (neither natural), and faces that could set off a metal detector (Tube: Covent Garden). For better Covent Garden lunch deals, walk a block or two away from the eye of this touristic hurricane (check out the places north of the Tube station, along Endell and Neal Streets).

▲**London Transport Museum**—This modern, well-presented museum, located right at Covent Garden, is fun for kids and thought-provoking for adults (if a bit overpriced). Whether you're cursing or marveling at the buses and Tube, the growth of Europe's third-biggest city (after Moscow and Istanbul) has been made possible by its public transit system.

Cost and Hours: £10, includes optional £2 donation, Sat–Thu

Madame Tussauds: Mid-July–Aug daily until 21:00; Sept–mid-July Mon–Fri until 19:30, Sat–Sun until 20:00.

Clink Prison Museum:
July–Sept daily until 21:00,
Oct–June Sat–Sun until
19:30.

Houses of Parliament
(when in session, roughly
Oct–July): Mon–Tue until
22:30.

British Library: Tue until
20:00.

Sir John Soane's Museum: First Tue of month until 21:00.

British Museum (some galleries): Thu–Fri until 20:30.

National Portrait Gallery: Thu–Fri until 21:00.

Vinopolis: Thu–Sat until 22:00, Sun until 18:00.

National Gallery: Fri until 21:00.

Victoria and Albert Museum: Fri until 22:00.

London Transport Museum: Some Fri until 22:00.

Tate Modern: Fri–Sat until 22:00.

Tate Britain: First Fri of the month until 22:00.

10:00–18:00, Fri 11:00–18:00, open some Fri until 22:00 for special events, last entry 45 minutes before closing, pleasant upstairs café with Covent Garden view, in southeast corner of Covent Garden courtyard, Tube: Covent Garden. Switchboard tel. 020/7379-6344 or recorded info tel. 020/7565-7298, www.ltmuseum.co.uk.

▲**Courtauld Gallery**—While less impressive than the National Gallery, this wonderful collection of paintings is still a joy. The gallery is part of the Courtauld Institute of Art, and the thoughtful description of each piece of art reminds visitors that the gallery is still used for teaching. You'll see medieval European paintings and works by Rubens, the Impressionists (Manet, Monet, and Degas), Post-Impressionists (such as Cézanne), and more. Besides the permanent collection, a quality selection of loaners and temporary exhibits are often included in the entry fee.

Cost and Hours: £5, free Mon until 14:00; open daily 10:00–18:00, last entry at 17:30; downstairs cafeteria, lockers, and WC; bus #6, #9, #11, #13, #15, or #23 from Trafalgar Square; Tube: Temple or Covent Garden. Shop tel. 020/7848-2579, recorded info tel. 020/7848-2526, www.courtauld.ac.uk.

Somerset House: The Courtauld Gallery is located at Somerset House, a grand 18th-century civic palace that offers a marvelous public space (housing temporary exhibits) and a riverside terrace with several eateries (between the Strand and the Thames). The palace once held the national registry that recorded Britain's births, marriages, and deaths: "...where they hatch 'em, match 'em, and dispatch 'em." Step into the courtyard to enjoy the fountain. Go ahead...walk through it. The 55 jets get playful twice an hour. In the winter, this becomes a popular ice-skating rink with a toasty café for viewing (www.somerset-house.org.uk).

Buckingham Palace

There are three palace sights that require admission: the State Rooms (Aug–Sept only), Queen's Gallery, and Royal Mews. You can pay for each separately, or buy a combo-ticket. The combo-ticket for £30.50 admits you to all three sights; a cheaper version for £15 covers the Queen's Gallery and Royal Mews. Many  tourists are more interested in the Changing of the Guard, which costs nothing at all to view.

▲**State Rooms at Buckingham Palace**—This lavish home has been Britain's royal residence since 1837. When the Queen's at home, the royal standard flies (a red, yellow, and blue flag); otherwise, the Union Jack flaps in the wind. The Queen opens her palace to the public—but only in August and September, when she's out of town.

Cost and Hours: £17 for lavish State Rooms and throne room, includes audioguide; Aug–Sept only, daily 9:45–18:00, last admission 15:45; only 8,000 visitors a day by timed entry; come early to the palace's Visitor Entrance (opens 9:15) or book ahead in person or by phone or online (£1.25 extra); Tube: Victoria. Tel. 020/7766-7300, www.royalcollection.org.uk.

▲**Queen's Gallery at Buckingham Palace**—Queen Elizabeth's personal collection of art is on display in a wing adjoining the palace. Her 7,000 paintings make up the finest private art collection in the world, rivaling Europe's biggest national art galleries. It's actually a collection of collections, built on by each successive monarch since the 16th century. She rotates her paintings, enjoying some privately in her many palatial residences while sharing others with her subjects in public galleries in Edinburgh and London. Small, thoughtfully presented, and always exquisite displays fill the five rooms open to the public. As you're in "the most important building in London," security is tight.

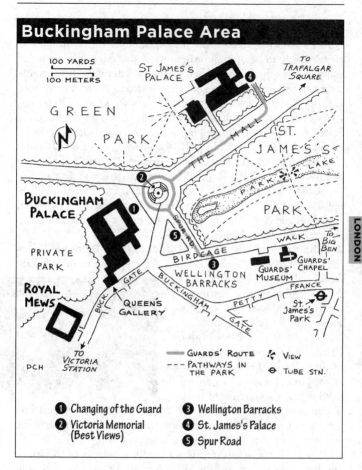

Buckingham Palace Area

100 YARDS
100 METERS

TO TRAFALGAR SQUARE

ST JAMES'S PALACE

GREEN PARK

N

THE MALL

ST. JAMES'S PARK

LAKE

BUCKINGHAM PALACE

Victoria Memorial

SPUR RD

PARK

PRIVATE PARK

WALK

To Big Ben

SPUR ROAD

BIRDCAGE

GUARDS' CHAPEL

ROYAL MEWS

BUCK. GATE

QUEEN'S GALLERY

BUCKINGHAM GATE

WELLINGTON BARRACKS

GUARDS' MUSEUM

FRANCE

PETTY

St James's Park

TO VICTORIA STATION

PCH

— GUARDS' ROUTE
--- PATHWAYS IN THE PARK

VIEW
TUBE STN.

❶ Changing of the Guard
❷ Victoria Memorial (Best Views)
❸ Wellington Barracks
❹ St. James's Palace
❺ Spur Road

LONDON

In addition to the permanent collection, you'll see temporary exhibits and a small room glittering with the Queen's personal jewelry. Compared to the crown jewels at the Tower, it may be Her Majesty's bottom drawer—but it's still a dazzling pile of diamonds. Temporary exhibits change about twice a year, and are lovingly described by the included audioguide. While admission tickets come with an entry time, this is only enforced during rare days when crowds are a problem.

The gallery is scheduled to close from early 2011 until mid-April, when it reopens with an all-new exhibit (possibly "Dutch Landscapes").

Cost and Hours: £8.75, daily 10:00–17:30, last entry one hour before closing, Tube: Victoria. Tel. 020/7766-7301, but Her Majesty rarely answers. Men shouldn't miss the mahogany-trimmed urinals.

Royal Mews—Located to the left of Buckingham Palace, the Queen's working stables, or "mews," are open to visitors. The visit is likely to be disappointing unless you follow the included audioguide or the hourly guided tour, in which case it's thoroughly entertaining—especially if you're interested in horses and/or royalty. The 40-minute tours show off a few of the Queen's 30 horses, a fancy car, and a bunch of old carriages, finishing with the Gold State Coach (c. 1760, 4 tons, 4 mph). Queen Victoria said absolutely no cars. When she died, in 1901, the mews got its first Daimler. Today, along with the hay-eating transport, the stable is home to five Bentleys and Rolls-Royce Phantoms, with one on display.

Cost and Hours: £7.75, April–July and Oct Sat–Thu 11:00–16:00, Aug–Sept 10:00–17:00, last entry 45 minutes before closing, closed Fri and Nov–March, guided tours on the hour, Buckingham Palace Road, Tube: Victoria. Tel. 020/7766-7302.

▲▲Changing of the Guard at Buckingham Palace—This is the spectacle every visitor to London has to see at least once: stone-

faced, red-coated, bearskin-hatted guards changing posts with much fanfare, in an hour-long ceremony accompanied by a brass band.

It's 11:00 at Buckingham Palace, and the on-duty guards are ready to finish their shift. Nearby at St. James's Palace (a half-mile northwest), a second set of guards is also ready for a break. At a third location, fresh replacement guards gather for a review and inspection at Wellington Barracks, 500 yards east of the palace (on Birdcage Walk).

At 11:15, the tired St. James's guards head out to the Mall, and then take a right turn for Buckingham Palace. At 11:30, the replacement troops, led by the band, also head for Buckingham Palace. Meanwhile, a fourth group—the Horse Guard—passes by along the Mall on their way back to Hyde Park Corner from their own changing-of-the-guard ceremony on Whitehall (which just took place at Horse Guards Parade at 11:00, or 10:00 on Sun).

At 11:45, the tired and fresh guards converge on Buckingham Palace in a perfect storm of Red Coat pageantry. Everyone parades around, the guard changes (passing the regimental flag, or "color") with much shouting, the band plays a happy little concert, and then they march out. At noon, two bands escort two detachments of guards away: the tired guards to Wellington Barracks and the fresh guards to St. James's Palace. As the fresh guards set up at St. James's Palace and the tired ones dress down at the barracks, the tourists disperse.

Cost and Hours: Free, daily May–July at 11:30, every other day Aug–April, no ceremony in very wet weather; exact schedule subject to change—call 020/7766-7300 for the day's plan, or check www.changing-the-guard.com or www.royalcollection.org.uk (click "Visit," then "Changing the Guard"); Buckingham Palace, Tube: Victoria, St. James's Park, or Green Park. Or hop into a big black taxi and say, "Buck House, please" (a.k.a. Buckingham Palace).

Sightseeing Strategies: Most tourists just show up and get lost in the crowds, but those who know the drill will enjoy the event more. The action takes place in stages over the course of an hour, at several different locations. The main event is in the fore-court right in front of Buckingham Palace (between Buckingham Palace and the fence) from 11:30 to 12:00. To see it close up, you'll need to get here no later than 10:30 to get a place right next to the fence.

But there's plenty of pageantry elsewhere. Get out your map and strategize. You could see the guards mobilizing at Wellington Barracks or St. James's Palace (11:00–11:15). Or watch them parade with bands down The Mall and Spur Road (11:15–11:30). After the ceremony at Buckingham Palace is over (and many tourists have gotten bored and gone home), the parades march back along those same streets (12:10).

Pick one event and find a good, unobstructed place from which to view it. The key is to either get right up front along the road or fence, or find some raised elevation to stand or sit on—a balustrade or a curb—so you can see over people's heads.

For the best overall view, stake out the high ground on the circular Victoria Memorial (come before 11:00 to get a place). From the Memorial, you have good views of the palace as well as the arriving and departing parades along The Mall and Spur Road. The actual changing of the guard in front of the palace is a nonevent. It is interesting, however, to see nearly every tourist in London gathered in one place at the same time. Afterward, stroll through nearby St. James's Park.

North London

▲▲▲**British Museum**—Simply put, this is the greatest chronicle of civilization...anywhere. A visit here is like taking a long hike through *Encyclopedia Britannica* National Park. While the vast British Museum wraps around its Great Court (the huge entrance hall), the most popular sections of the museum fill the ground floor: Egyptian, Assyrian, and ancient Greek, with the famous Elgin Marbles from the Athenian Parthenon. The museum's stately Reading Room—famous as the place where Karl Marx hung out

British Museum Overview

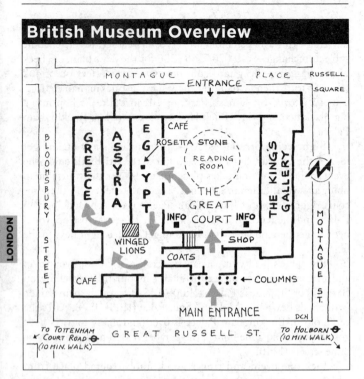

while formulating his ideas on communism and writing *Das Kapital*—sometimes hosts special exhibits.

From the Great Court, doorways lead to all wings. Huge winged lions (which guarded an Assyrian palace 800 years before Christ) guard these great galleries. For a brief tour, connect these ancient dots:

Start with the **Egyptian** section. Wander from the Rosetta Stone past the many statues. At the end of the hall, climb the stairs to mummy land.

Back at the winged lions, explore the dark, violent, and mysterious **Assyrian** rooms. The Nimrud Gallery is lined with royal propaganda reliefs and wounded lions (from the ninth century B.C.).

The most modern of the ancient art fills the **Greek** section. Find Room 11, behind the winged lions, and start your walk through Greek art history with the simple and primitive Cycladic

North London

fertility figures. Later, painted vases show a culture really into partying. The finale is the Elgin Marbles. The much-wrangled-over bits of the Athenian Parthenon (from about 450 B.C.) are even more impressive than they look. To best appreciate these ancient carvings, take the audioguide tour (described later).

Be sure to venture upstairs to see artifacts from **Roman Britain** (Room 50) that surpass anything you'll see at Hadrian's Wall or elsewhere in Britain. Nearby, the Dark Age Britain exhibits offer a worthwhile peek at that bleak era; look for the Sutton Hoo Burial Ship artifacts from a seventh-century royal burial on the east coast of England (Room 41). A rare Michelangelo cartoon (preliminary sketch) is in Room 90.

Cost and Hours: Free but a £4, $6, or €5 donation requested; temporary exhibits extra, daily 10:00–17:30, Thu–Fri until 20:30—but not all galleries open after 17:30, least crowded weekday late afternoons, Great Russell Street, Tube: Tottenham Court Road. Switchboard tel. 020/7323-8000, general info tel. 020/7323-8299, collection questions tel. 020/7323-8838, www.britishmuseum.org.

Tours: The 1.5-hour Highlights tours, led by licensed guides, are expensive but meaty, giving an introduction to the museum's masterpieces (£8, daily at 10:30, 13:00, and 15:00). The free 30- to 40-minute eyeOpener tours are led by volunteers, who focus on select rooms (daily 11:00–15:30, generally every half-hour, plus Thu at 18:15 and 19:15).

The £4.50 **audioguide** (called a "Multimedia Guide") offers dial-up audio commentary and video on 200 objects, as well as several theme tours (for example, 1.5-hour Highlights tour or Parthenon Sculptures tour). They're substantial and cerebral (must leave photo ID). There's also a fun children's audioguide (£3).

Those traveling with an iPod or other MP3 player can download a free **Rick Steves audio tour** of the British Museum at www .ricksteves.com (or search for "Rick Steves' Audio Tours" in iTunes).

▲▲▲**British Library**—Here, in just two rooms, called "The Treasures of the British Library," are the literary treasures of Western civilization, from early Bibles to the Magna Carta to Shakespeare's *Hamlet* to Lewis Carroll's *Alice's Adventures in Wonderland.* You'll see the Lindisfarne Gospels transcribed on an illuminated manuscript, as well as Beatles lyrics scrawled on the back of a greeting card. The British Empire built its greatest monuments out of paper, and it's with literature that England made her lasting contribution to civilization and the arts.

Cost and Hours: Free but £2 suggested donation, temporary exhibits extra, Mon–Fri 9:30–18:00, Tue until 20:00, Sat 9:30–17:00, Sun 11:00–17:00, helpful free computers give you extra info, ground-floor café, self-service cafeteria upstairs, Tube: King's Cross St. Pancras—walk a block west to 96 Euston Road, Euston Tube station is also nearby; bus #10, #30, #73, #91, #205, or #390. Tel. 019/3754-6060 or 020/7412-7676, www.bl.uk.

Tours: Those traveling with an iPod or other MP3 player can download a free **Rick Steves audio tour** of the British Library at www.ricksteves.com (or search for "Rick Steves' Audio Tours" in iTunes).

▲**Wallace Collection**—Sir Richard Wallace's fine collection of 17th-century Dutch Masters, 18th-century French Rococo, medi-

eval armor, and assorted aristocratic fancies fills the sumptuously furnished Hertford House on Manchester Square. From the rough and intimate Dutch lifescapes of Jan Steen to the pink-cheeked Rococo fantasies of François Boucher, a wander through this little-visited mansion makes you nostalgic for the days of the empire. While this collection would be a big deal in a mid-sized city, it's small potatoes here in London...but enjoyable nevertheless.

Cost and Hours: Free, daily 10:00–17:00, £4 audioguide, free

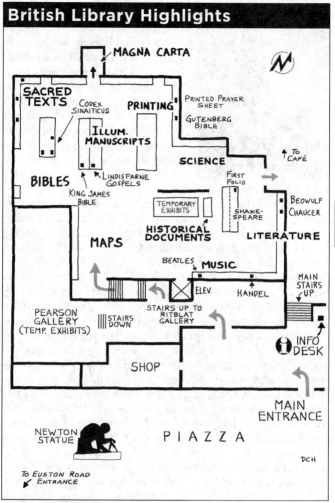

British Library Highlights

MAGNA CARTA

SACRED TEXTS

Codex Sinaiticus

ILLUM. MANUSCRIPTS

PRINTING

PRINTED PRAYER SHEET

GUTENBERG BIBLE

SCIENCE

→ TO CAFÉ

BIBLES

Lindisfarne Gospels

KING JAMES BIBLE

FIRST FOLIO

SHAKE-SPEARE

BEOWULF CHAUCER

TEMPORARY EXHIBITS

HISTORICAL DOCUMENTS

MAPS

LITERATURE

BEATLES

MUSIC

ELEV.

HANDEL

MAIN STAIRS UP

PEARSON GALLERY (TEMP. EXHIBITS)

STAIRS DOWN

STAIRS UP TO RITBLAT GALLERY

INFO DESK

SHOP

MAIN ENTRANCE

NEWTON STATUE

PIAZZA

DCH

To EUSTON ROAD ENTRANCE

guided tours or lectures almost daily—call to confirm times, just north of Oxford Street on Manchester Square, Tube: Bond Street. Tel. 020/7563-9500, www.wallacecollection.org.

▲**Madame Tussauds Waxworks**—This is gimmicky and expensive, but dang good...a hit with the kind of travelers who skip the British Museum. The original Madame Tussaud did wax casts of heads lopped off during the French Revolution (such as Marie-Antoinette's). She took her show on the road and ended up in London in 1835. Now it's all about squeezing Tom Cruise's bum, gambling with George Clooney, and partying with Beyoncé, Britney, and Brangelina. In addition to posing with all the eerily

realistic wax dummies—from Johnny Depp to Barack Obama to the Beatles—you'll have the chance to tour a hokey haunted-house exhibit; learn how they create this waxy army; hop on a people-mover and cruise through a kid-pleasing "Spirit of London" time trip; and meet your favorite Marvel super heroes before heading into an auditorium for a nine-minute "4-D" show—a 3-D movie heightened by wind, "back ticklers," and other special effects.

Cost and Hours: £28, no waiting in line if you buy ticket on their website (10 percent discount), or TI (£22.50), £41 combo-ticket with London Eye, cheaper for kids. From 17:00 to closing, it's £14 if you buy in advance online. Children under 5 are always free. Open Mon–Fri 9:30–19:30, Sat–Sun 9:00–20:00, mid-July–Aug and school holidays daily 9:00–21:00, last entry two hours before closing; Marylebone Road, Tube: Baker Street. Toll tel. 0871-894-3000, www.madametussauds.com. Check the website for discounts on this pricey waxtravaganza.

Crowd-Beating Tips: This popular attraction can be swamped by crowds. To avoid the hassle, buy your tickets and reserve an entry time in advance, either online (10 percent discount) or by phone (same price as box office). If you wait to buy tickets at the attraction, you'll discover that the ticket-buying line twists endlessly once inside the door (believe the posted signs warning you how long the wait will be—an hour or more is not unusual at busy times). If you buy your tickets at the door, try to arrive after 15:00.

▲**Sir John Soane's Museum**—Architects love this quirky place, as do fans of interior decor, eclectic knickknacks, and Back Door sights. Tour this furnished home on a bird-chirping square and see 19th-century chairs, lamps, and carpets, wood-paneled nooks and crannies, and stained-glass skylights. The townhouse is cluttered with Soane's (and his wife's) collection of ancient relics, curios, and famous paintings, including Hogarth's series on *The Rake's Progress* (read the fun plot) and several excellent Canalettos. In 1833, just before his death, Soane established his house as a museum, stipulating that it be kept as nearly as possible in the state he left

it. If he visited today, he'd be entirely satisfied. You'll leave wishing you'd known the man.

Cost and Hours: Free but donations much appreciated, Tue–Sat 10:00–17:00, first Tue of the month also 18:00–21:00, closed Sun–Mon, last entry 30 minutes before closing, long entry lines on Sat and first Tue, good £1 brochure, £5 guided tour Sat at 11:00, 13 Lincoln's Inn Fields, quarter-mile southeast of British Museum, Tube: Holborn. Tel. 020/7405-2107, www.soane.org.

Cartoon Museum—This humble but interesting museum is located in the shadow of the British Museum. While its three rooms are filled with British cartoons unknown to most Americans, the satire of famous bigwigs and politicians—from Napoleon to Margaret Thatcher, the Queen, and Tony Blair—shows the power of parody to deliver social commentary. Upstairs, you'll see pages spanning from *Tarzan* to *Tank Girl,* and *Andy Capp* to the British *Dennis the Menace*—interesting only to comic-book diehards.

LONDON

Cost and Hours: £5.50, Tue–Sat 10:30–17:30, Sun 12:00–17:30, closed Mon, 35 Little Russell Street—go one block south of the British Museum on Museum Street and turn right, Tube: Tottenham Court Road. Tel. 020/7580-8155, www.cartoon museum.org.

Pollock's Toy Museum—This rickety old house, with glass cases filled with toys and games lining its walls and halls, is a time-warp experience that brings back childhood memories to people who grew up without batteries or computer chips. Though the museum is small, you could spend a lot of time here, squinting at the fascinating toys and dolls that entertained the children of 19th- and early 20th-century England. The included information is great. The story of Theodore Roosevelt refusing to shoot a bear cub while on a hunting trip was celebrated in 1902 cartoons, resulting in a new, huggable toy: the Teddy Bear. It was popular for good reason: it could be manufactured during World War I without rationed products; it coincided with the new belief that soft toys were good for a child's development; it was an acceptable "doll for boys"; and it's *the* toy children keep long after they've grown up.

Cost and Hours: £5, kids–£2, generally Mon–Sat 10:00–17:00, closed Sun, last entry 30 minutes before closing, 1 Scala Street, Tube: Goodge Street. Tel. 020/7636-3452, www.pollockstoy museum.com.

Beatles and Beyond—Central London is surprisingly devoid of sights associated with the famous '60s rock band. To see much of anything, consider taking a guided walk (described on page 68).

For a photo op, go to **Abbey Road** and walk the famous crosswalk pictured on the *Abbey Road* album cover (Tube: St. John's Wood, get information and buy Beatles memorabilia at the small kiosk in the station). From the Tube station, it's a five-minute walk west down Grove End Road to the intersection with Abbey Road. The Abbey Road recording studio is the low-key, white building to the right of Abbey House (it's still a working studio, so you can't go inside). Ponder the graffiti on the low wall  outside, and...imagine. To re-create the famous cover photo, shoot the crosswalk from the roundabout as you face north up Abbey Road. Shoes are optional.

Nearby is **Paul McCartney's current home** (7 Cavendish Avenue): Continue down Grove End Road, turn left on Circus Road, and then right on Cavendish. Please be discreet.

The **Beatles Store** is at 231 Baker Street (Tube: Baker Street). It's small—some Beatles-logo T-shirts, mugs, pins, and old vinyls like you might have your closet—and has nothing of historic value (open eight days a week, 10:00–18:30, tel. 020/7935-4464, www.beatlesstorelondon.co.uk; another rock memorabilia store is across the street).

A few doors down is the **Sherlock Holmes Museum,** a  meticulous re-creation of the (fictional) apartment of the (fictional) detective at the (real) address of 221b Baker Street. Fans will like it. Others might enjoy the Victorian-era furniture, clothes, pipes, paintings, and chamber pots, which give a glimpse at daily life from the time (£6, daily 9:30-18:30, large gift shop for Holmes connoisseurs, Tube: Baker Street, tel. 020/7935-8866, www.sherlock-holmes.co.uk).

The City

When Londoners say "The City," they mean the one-square-mile business center in East London that 2,000 years ago was Roman Londinium. The outline of the Roman city walls can still be seen in the arc of roads from Blackfriars Bridge to Tower Bridge. Within The City are 23 churches designed by Sir Christopher Wren, mostly just ornamentation around St. Paul's Cathedral. Today, while home to only 5,000 residents, The City thrives with nearly 500,000 office workers coming and going daily. It's a fascinating district to wander on weekdays, but since almost nobody actually lives there, it's dull in the evenings and on Saturday and Sunday.

The City

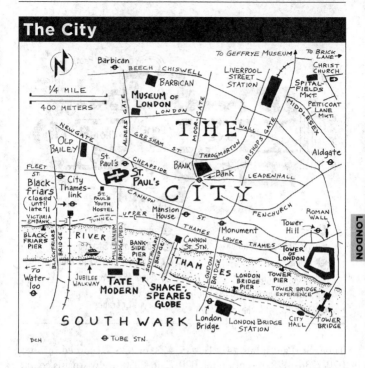

St. Paul's Cathedral and Nearby

▲▲▲**St. Paul's Cathedral**—Wren's most famous church is the great St. Paul's, its elaborate interior capped by a 365-foot dome.

Since World War II, St. Paul's has been Britain's symbol of resistance. Despite 57 nights of bombing, the Nazis failed to destroy the cathedral, thanks to the St. Paul's volunteer fire watchmen, who stayed on the dome. During your visit, you can climb the dome for a great city view. The crypt (included with admission) is a world of historic bones and memorials (including Admiral Nelson's tomb) and interesting cathedral models.

Cost and Hours: £12.50, includes church entry and dome climb; Mon–Sat 8:30–16:30, last church entry for sightseeing 16:00, last dome entry 16:15, closed Sun except for worship, £3 tours and £4 audioguides; download free Rick Steves audio tour for your iPod/MP3 player at www.ricksteves.com or iTunes; no photography allowed, cheery café and pricier restaurant in crypt,

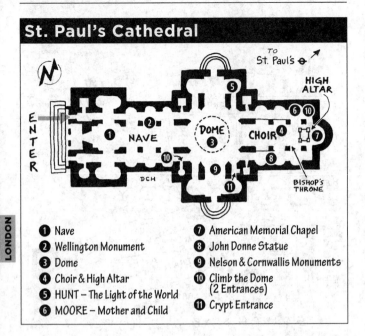

St. Paul's Cathedral

1. Nave
2. Wellington Monument
3. Dome
4. Choir & High Altar
5. HUNT – The Light of the World
6. MOORE – Mother and Child
7. American Memorial Chapel
8. John Donne Statue
9. Nelson & Cornwallis Monuments
10. Climb the Dome (2 Entrances)
11. Crypt Entrance

Tube: St. Paul's; bus #4, #11, #15, #23, or #26. Recorded info tel. 020/7236-4128, reception tel. 020/7246-8350, www.stpauls.co.uk.

Music: The evensong services are free, but nonpaying visitors are not allowed to linger afterward (Mon–Sat at 17:00, Sun at 15:15, 40 minutes).

▲**Old Bailey**—To view the British legal system in action—lawyers in little blond wigs speaking legalese with a British accent—spend a few minutes in the visitors' gallery at the Old Bailey, called the "Central Criminal Court." Don't enter under the dome; signs point you to the two visitors' entrances.

Cost and Hours: Free, generally Mon–Fri 10:00–13:00 & 14:00–16:30 depending on caseload, closed Sat–Sun, reduced hours in Aug; no kids under 14; no bags, mobile phones, cameras, iPods, or food, but small purses OK; Eddie at Bailey's Café across the street at #27 stores bags for £2; 2 blocks northwest of St. Paul's on Old Bailey Street, follow signs to public entrance, Tube: St. Paul's. Tel. 020/7248-3277.

▲**Museum of London**—This museum tells the fascinating story of London, taking you on a walk from its pre-Roman beginnings to the present. It features London's distinguished citizens through history—from Neanderthals to Romans to Elizabethans to Victorians to Mods to today. The museum's displays are chronological, spacious, and informative without being overwhelming. Scale models and costumes help you visualize everyday life in the city at different periods. There are enough whiz-bang multimedia displays (including the Plague and the Great Fire) to spice up otherwise humdrum artifacts. This regular stop for the local school kids gives the best overview of London history in town.

Cost and Hours: Free, daily 10:00–18:00, last entry 30 minutes before closing, see the day's events board for special talks and tours, Tube: Barbican or St. Paul's plus a five-minute walk. Tel. 020/7814-5530, recorded info tel. 020/7001-9844, www.museumof london.org.uk.

The Monument—Wren's 202-foot-tall tribute to London's Great Fire was recently restored. Climb the 331 steps inside the column for a view of The City that is still monumental (£3, daily 9:30–17:30, last entry at 17:00, junction of Monument Street and Fish Street Hill, Tube: Monument, tel. 020/7626-2717, www.the monument.info).

Tower of London and Nearby

▲▲▲**Tower of London**—The Tower has served as a castle in wartime, a king's residence in peacetime, and, most notoriously, as the

prison and execution site of rebels. You can see the crown jewels, take a witty Beefeater tour, and ponder the executioner's block that dispensed with troublesome heirs to the throne and a couple of Henry VIII's wives.

William I, still getting used to his new title of "the Conqueror," built the stone "White Tower" (1077–1097) to keep the Londoners in line. The Tower also served as an effective lookout for seeing invaders coming up the Thames. His successors enlarged it to its present 18-acre size. Because of the security it provided, the Tower served over the centuries as a royal residence, the Royal Mint, the Royal Jewel House, and, most famously, as the prison and execution site of those who dared oppose the Crown.

The Tower's hard stone and glittering jewels represent the ultimate power of the monarch. So does the executioner's block. You'll find more bloody history per square inch in this original tower of power than anywhere else in Britain. Today, though its military purpose is history, it's still home to the Yeoman Warders, a.k.a. the "Beefeaters," who host three million visitors a year.

Cost and Hours: £17, family-£47; audioguide-£4; March–Oct Tue–Sat 9:00–17:30, Sun–Mon 10:00–17:30; Nov–Feb Tue–Sat 9:00–16:30, Sun–Mon 10:00–16:30; last entry 30 minutes before

LONDON

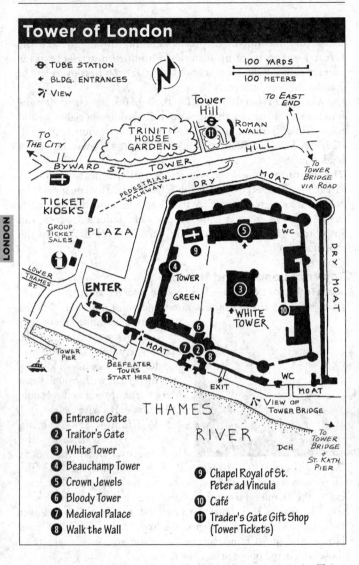

Tower of London

- ⊕ TUBE STATION
- ← BLDG. ENTRANCES
- ⌐ VIEW

100 YARDS
100 METERS

1 Entrance Gate
2 Traitor's Gate
3 White Tower
4 Beauchamp Tower
5 Crown Jewels
6 Bloody Tower
7 Medieval Palace
8 Walk the Wall
9 Chapel Royal of St. Peter ad Vincula
10 Café
11 Trader's Gate Gift Shop (Tower Tickets)

closing; no photography allowed of jewels or in chapels; Tube: Tower Hill. Switchboard toll tel. 0844-482-7777.

Getting Tickets: The long but fast-moving ticket lines are worst on Sundays. Avoid lines anytime by buying your ticket online (www.hrp.org.uk), at the Trader's Gate gift shop down the steps from the Tower Hill Tube stop, at the Tower Welcome Centre to the left of the normal ticket line (credit card only), in advance at any London TI (no extra charge), or by phone (£2 extra fee, tel. 0844-482-7799 within UK, tel. 011-44-20-3166-

6000 from the US). After your visit, consider taking the boat to Greenwich from here (see "Cruises" on page 72).

More Sights near the Tower—The best remaining bit of London's **Roman Wall** is just north of the Tower (at the Tower Hill Tube station).

The iconic **Tower Bridge** (often mistakenly called London Bridge) has been freshly painted and is undergoing restoration. The hydraulically powered drawbridge was built in 1894 to accommodate the growing East End. While fully modern, its design was a retro Neo-Gothic look.

You can tour the bridge at the **Tower Bridge Experience,** with a history exhibit and a peek at the Victorian engine room that lifts the span (£7, daily 10:00–18:00 in summer, 9:30–17:30 in winter, last entry 30 minutes before closing, good view, poor value, enter at the northwest tower, tel. 020/7403-3761, Tube: Tower Hill, www.towerbridge.org.uk). The visit is most interesting when the drawbridge lifts to let ships pass, as it does a thousand times a year; for the bridge-lifting schedule, see the website or call 020/7940-3984.

The chic **St. Katharine Dock,** just east of Tower Bridge, has private yachts, mod shops, and the classic Dickens Inn, fun for a drink or pub lunch. Across the bridge is the South Bank, with the upscale Butlers Wharf area, City Hall, museums, and the Jubilee Walkway.

Northeast of The City

▲**Geffrye Museum**—This low-key but well-organized museum—housed in an 18th-century almshouse—is located north

of Liverpool Street Station in the trendy Shoreditch area. Walk past 11 English living rooms, furnished and decorated in styles from 1600 to 2000, then descend the circular stairs to see changing exhibits on home decor. In summer, explore the fragrant herb garden.

Cost and Hours: Free, Tue–Sat 10:00–17:00, Sun 12:00–17:00, closed Mon, garden open April–Oct, 136 Kingsland Road. Tel. 020/7739-9893, www.geffrye-museum.org.uk. To get here, take the Tube to Liverpool Street, then it's a 10-minute ride north on bus #149 or #242. Or take the East London line on the Overground to the Hoxton stop, which is right next to the museum.

The South Bank

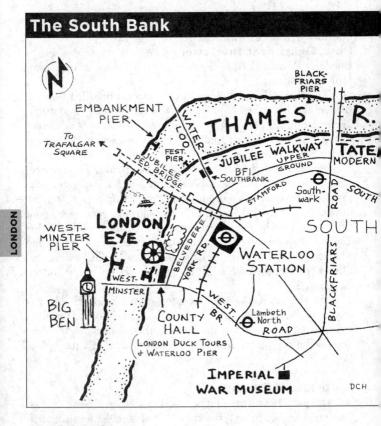

LONDON

South Bank

▲**Jubilee Walkway**—The South Bank is a thriving arts and cultural center tied together by this riverside path, a popular, pub-crawling pedestrian prom-

enade called the Jubilee Walkway. Stretching from Tower Bridge past Westminster Bridge, it offers grand views of the Houses of Parliament and St. Paul's. On a sunny day, this is the place to see London out strolling. The Walkway hugs the river except just east of London Bridge, where it cuts inland for a couple of blocks. Plans are underway to expand the path into a 60-mile "Greenway" encircling the city, scheduled to open in 2012 for the Olympic Games and Elizabeth's 60th year as queen (www.jubileewalkway.org.uk).

▲▲**London Eye**—This giant Ferris wheel, towering above London opposite Big Ben, is the world's highest observational

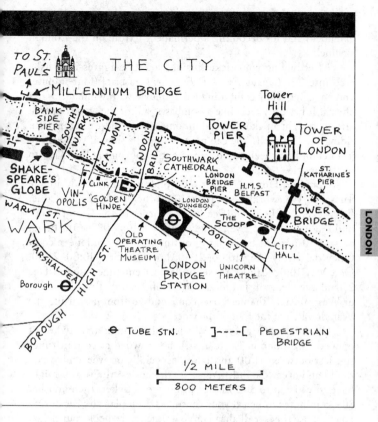

THE CITY

TO ST. PAUL'S

MILLENNIUM BRIDGE

Tower Hill

BANK-SIDE PIER

SOUTHWARK

CANNON

LONDON BRIDGE

TOWER PIER

TOWER OF LONDON

ST. KATHARINE'S PIER

SHAKE-SPEARE'S GLOBE

SOUTHWARK CATHEDRAL

LONDON BRIDGE PIER

H.M.S. BELFAST

VIN-OPOLIS

CLINK

"GOLDEN HINDE"

WARK ST.

WARK

LONDON DUNGEON

THE SCOOP

TOWER BRIDGE

MARSHALSEA

OLD OPERATING THEATRE MUSEUM

TOOLEY

CITY HALL

Borough

HIGH ST.

BOROUGH

LONDON BRIDGE STATION

UNICORN THEATRE

⊖ TUBE STN.   ]----[PEDESTRIAN BRIDGE

1/2 MILE

800 METERS

LONDON

wheel and London's answer to the Eiffel Tower. While the experience is memorable, London doesn't have much of a skyline, and the price is borderline outrageous. But whether you ride or not, the wheel is a sight to behold.

Designed like a giant bicycle wheel, it's a pan-European undertaking: British steel and Dutch engineering, with Czech, German, French, and Italian mechanical parts. It's also very "green," running extremely efficiently and virtually silently. Twenty-five

people ride in each of its 32 air-conditioned capsules for the 30-minute rotation (you go around only once). Each capsule has a bench, but most people stand. From the top of this 443-foot-high wheel—the highest public viewpoint in the city—even Big Ben looks small. Built to celebrate the new millennium, the Eye's original five-year lease has been extended, and it's becoming a permanent fixture on the London skyline.

After buying your ticket inside, you'll be aggressively ushered into *The London Eye 4-D Experience*, a brief (four-minute) and engaging show combining a 3-D movie with wind and water effects. It basically feels like a bombastic ad for the attraction you already bought a ticket for, and in some ways is more exciting than riding the Eye itself. You can politely skip the show if you want to just get on the wheel, and have the option of coming back later to see the movie.

Cost and Hours: £18, or £41 combo-ticket with Madame Tussauds Waxworks—see page 104, other packages available. Buy tickets at the box office (in the corner of the County Hall building nearest the Eye), in advance by calling 0870-500-0600, or save 10 percent by booking online at www.londoneye.com. Open daily July–Aug 10:00–21:30, June and Sept 10:00–21:00, Oct–May 10:00–20:00, these are last-ascent times, closed Dec 25 and a few days in Jan for annual maintenance, Tube: Waterloo or Westminster. Thames boats come and go from here using the Waterloo Pier at the foot of the wheel.

Crowd-Beating Tips: While not as popular as when it opened, the London Eye can still be crowded at certain times (busiest between 11:00 and 17:00, especially on weekends year-round and every day July–Aug). At the busiest times, you might have to wait up to 30 minutes to buy your ticket, then another 30–45 minutes to board your capsule. If you plan to visit during one of those times, call ahead or go online to pre-book your ticket, then punch your confirmation code into the automated machine in the ticket office (no wait to get the ticket, but you'll still wait to board the wheel). You can pay an extra £10 for a Fast Track ticket that lets you jump the queue, but the time savings are probably not worth the expense.

By the Eye: The area next to the London Eye has developed a cotton-candy ambience of kitschy, kid-friendly attractions. There's an aquarium, game arcade, and "Movieum" dedicated to movies filmed in London, from *Harry Potter* to *Star Wars*.

▲▲**Imperial War Museum**—This impressive museum covers the wars of the last century—from World War I biplanes to the rise of fascism to Montgomery's Africa campaign tank to the Cold War, the Cuban Missile Crisis, the Troubles in Northern Ireland, the wars in Iraq, and terrorism.

Allow plenty of time, as this powerful museum—with lots of artifacts and video clips—can be engrossing. The core of the permanent collection, located downstairs, takes you step by step through World Wars I and II. A special exhibit called "Monty:

Master of the Battlefield" celebrates Field Marshal Bernard Montgomery. Then you move on to conflicts since 1945. Most of the displays are low-tech—glass cases hold dummies in uniforms, weapons, newspaper clippings, ordinary objects from daily life—but have excellent explanations and video clips. The Trench Experience lets you walk through a dark, chaotic, smelly WWI trench. The Blitz Experience film assaults the senses with the noise and intensity of a WWII air raid on London. Also, the cinema shows a rotating selection of films.

In the entry hall are the large exhibits—including Monty's tank, several field guns, and, dangling overhead, vintage planes.

Imagine the awesome power of the 50-foot V-2 rocket, the kind the Nazis rained down on London, which could arrive silently and destroy a city block. Its direct descendant is the Polaris missile, capable of traveling nearly 3,000 miles in 20 minutes and obliterating an entire city.

Two other sections are not to be missed: The "Secret War" peeks into the intrigues of espionage in World Wars I and II and in conflicts since. The section on the Holocaust, one of the best on the subject anywhere, tells the story with powerful videos, artifacts, and fine explanations.

War wonks will love the place, as will general history buffs who enjoy patiently reading displays. For the rest, there are enough multimedia exhibits and submarines for the kids to climb in to keep it interesting.

Rather than glorify war, the museum does its best to shine a light on the 100 million deaths of the 20th century. It shows everyday life for people back home and never neglects the powerful human side of one of humankind's most persistent traits.

The museum (which sits in an inviting park equipped with an equally inviting café) is housed in what was the Royal Bethlam Hospital. Also known as "the Bedlam asylum," the place was so wild that it gave the world a new word for chaos. Back in Victorian times, locals—without reality shows and YouTube—paid admission to visit the asylum on weekends for entertainment.

Cost and Hours: Free, daily 10:00–18:00, temporary exhibits extra, often guided tours on weekends—ask at info desk, £4 audioguide, Tube: Lambeth North or bus #12 or bus #159. Tel. 020/7416-5000, www.iwm.org.uk.

▲▲**Tate Modern**—Dedicated in the spring of 2000, the striking museum across the river from St. Paul's opened the new century with art from the previous one. Its powerhouse collection of Monet, Matisse, Dalí, Picasso, Warhol, and much more is displayed in a converted powerhouse. Of equal interest are the many temporary exhibits featuring cutting-edge art. Each year, the main hall features a different monumental installation by a prominent artist.

Cost and Hours: Free but £3 donations appreciated, fee for special exhibitions, daily 10:00–18:00, Fri–Sat until 22:00—good times to visit, last entry to temporary exhibitions 45 minutes before closing, audioguide-£3.50; free 45-minute guided tours at 11:00, 12:00, 14:00, and 15:00—confirm at info desk; view restaurant on top floor, cross the Millennium Bridge from St. Paul's; Tube: Southwark, London Bridge or Mansion House plus a 10–15-minute walk; or connect by "Tate to Tate" boat from Tate Britain for £5 one-way or £12 for day ticket, 33 percent discount with Travelcard or Oyster card, buy ticket on board. Tel. 020/7887-8888, www.tate.org.uk.

▲**Millennium Bridge**—The pedestrian bridge links St. Paul's Cathedral and the Tate Modern across the Thames. This is London's first new bridge in a century. When it first opened, the $25 million bridge wiggled when people walked on it, so it promptly closed for an $8 million, 20-month stabilization; now it's stable and open again. Nicknamed the "blade of light" for its sleek minimalist design (370 yards long, 4 yards wide, stainless steel with teak planks), its clever aerodynamic handrails deflect wind over the heads of pedestrians.

▲▲**Shakespeare's Globe**—This replica of the original Globe

Theatre was built, half-timbered and thatched, as it was in Shakespeare's time. (This is the first thatched roof constructed in London since they were outlawed after the Great Fire of 1666.) The Globe originally accommodated 2,200 seated

Crossing the Thames on Foot

You can cross the Thames on any of the bridges that carry car traffic over the river, but London's two pedestrian bridges are more fun. The Millennium Bridge (see photo) connects the sedate St. Paul's Cathedral with the great Tate Modern. The Golden Jubilee Bridge, well-lit with a sleek, futuristic look, links bustling Trafalgar Square on the North Bank with the London Eye and Waterloo Station on the South Bank.

and another 1,000 standing. Today, slightly smaller and leaving space for reasonable aisles, the theater holds 800 seated and 600 groundlings. Its promoters brag that the theater melds "the three A's"—actors, audience, and architecture—with each contributing to the play. The working theater hosts authentic performances of Shakespeare's plays with actors in period costumes, modern interpretations of his works, and some works by other playwrights (generally all summer at 14:00 and 19:30—but confirm). For details on seeing a play, see page 141.

The complex has three parts: the theater itself, the box office, and a museum. The Globe Exhibition ticket (£10.50) includes both a tour of the theater and the museum. First, you browse on your own through the **museum's** displays of Elizabethan-era costumes, music, script-printing, and special effects. There are early folios and objects that were dug up onsite. A video and scale models help put Shakespearean theater within the context of the times. (The Globe opened one year after England mastered the seas by defeating the Spanish Armada. The debut play was Shakespeare's *Julius Caesar*.)

Next comes the tour of the **theater**—you must take the tour at the time stamped on your ticket, but you can come back to the museum afterward; tickets are good all day. The guide (usually an actor) leads you into the theater to see the stage and the different seating areas for the different classes of people. You take a seat and learn how the new Globe is similar to the old Globe (open-air performances, standing-room by the stage, no curtain) and how it's different (female actors today, lights for night performances, concrete floor). It's not a backstage tour—you don't see dressing rooms or costume shops or sit in on rehearsals, though you may see workers building sets for a new production. You mostly sit and listen. The guides are energetic, theatrical, and knowledgeable, bringing the Elizabethan period to life.

When matinee performances are going on, you can't tour the theater. But you can see the museum, then tour the nearby (and less interesting) Rose Theatre instead.

Cost and Hours: £10.50 includes museum and 40-minute tour, £7.50 when only the Rose Theatre is available for touring, tickets good all day; complex open daily 9:00–17:00; exhibition and tours: May–Sept—Globe tours offered mornings only with Rose Theatre tours in afternoon; Oct–April—Globe tours run all day, tours start every 15–30 minutes; on the South Bank directly across Thames over Southwark Bridge from St. Paul's, Tube: Mansion House or London Bridge plus a 10-minute walk. Tel. 020/7902-1400 or 020/7902-1500, www.shakespeares-globe.org.

Eating: The Swan at the Globe café offers a sit-down restaurant (for lunch and dinner, reservations recommended, tel. 020/7928-9444), a drinks-and-plates bar, and a sandwich-and-coffee cart (daily 9:00–closing, depending on performance times).

Vinopolis: City of Wine—While it seems illogical to have a huge wine museum in beer-loving London, Vinopolis makes a good case.

Built over a Roman wine store and filling the massive vaults of an old wine warehouse, the museum offers an excellent audioguide with a light yet earnest history of wine to accompany your sips of various mediocre reds and whites, ports, and champagnes. Allow some time, as the audioguide takes 1.5 hours—and the sipping can slow things down pleasantly. This place is popular. Booking ahead for Friday and Saturday nights is a must.

Cost and Hours: Self-guided tour options range from £20 to £65—each includes about five wine tastes and an audioguide. Other options are available for guided tours. Some packages also include whiskey (the new wine), other spirits, or a meal. Thu–Sat 12:00–22:00, Sun 12:00–18:00, closed Mon–Wed, last entry 2.5 hours before closing, between the Globe and Southwark Cathedral at 1 Bank End, Tube: London Bridge. Tel. 020/7940-8300, www.vinopolis.co.uk.

Southwark

These sights are in Southwark, on the South Bank. The area stretching from the Tate Modern to London Bridge, known as Southwark (SUTH-uck), was for centuries the place Londoners would go to escape the rules and decency of the city and let their hair down. Bearbaiting, brothels, rollicking pubs, and theater—you name the dream, and it could be fulfilled just across the Thames. A run-down warehouse district through the 20th century, it's been gentrified with classy restaurants, office parks, pedestrian promenades, major sights (such as the Tate Modern and Shakespeare's Globe), and this colorful collection of lesser sights. The area is easy on foot and a scenic—though circuitous—way to connect the Tower of London with St. Paul's.

The Clink Prison Museum—Proudly the "original clink," this was, until 1780, where law-abiding citizens threw Southwark troublemakers. Today, it's a low-tech torture museum filling grotty old rooms with papier-mâché gore. Unfortunately, there's little that seriously deals with the fascinating problem of law and order in Southwark, where 18th-century Londoners went for a good time.

Cost and Hours: Overpriced at £5; July–Sept daily 10:00–21:00; Oct–June Mon–Fri 10:00–18:00, Sat–Sun until 19:30; 1 Clink Street, Tube: London Bridge. Tel. 020/7403-0900, www.clink.co.uk.

***Golden Hinde* Replica**—This is a full-size replica of the 16th-century warship in which Sir Francis Drake circumnavigated the globe from 1577 to 1580. Commanding this ship, Drake earned the reputation as history's most successful pirate. The original is long gone, but this boat has logged more than 100,000 miles, including a voyage around the world. While the ship is fun to see, its interior is not worth touring.

Cost and Hours: £6, daily 10:00–17:00; may be closed if rented out for pirate birthday parties, school groups, or weddings; Tube: London Bridge. Tel. 020/7403-0123, www.goldenhinde.com.

Southwark Cathedral—While made a cathedral only in 1905, it's been the neighborhood church since the 13th century, and comes with some interesting history. The enthusiastic docents give impromptu tours if you ask.

Cost and Hours: Free but £4 suggested donation, daily 8:00–18:00, last entry 30 minutes before closing, £2.50 guidebook, no photos without permission, Tube: London Bridge. Tel. 020/7367-6700, http://cathedral.southwark.anglican.org.

Music: The cathedral hosts evensong services (weekdays at 17:30, Sat at 16:00, Sun at 15:00, no service on Wed or alternate Mon).

▲**Old Operating Theatre Museum and Herb Garret**—Climb a tight and creaky wooden spiral staircase to a church attic where you'll find a garret used to dry medicinal herbs, a fascinating exhibit on Victorian surgery, cases of well-described 19th-century medical paraphernalia, and a special look at "anesthesia, the defeat of pain." Then you stumble upon Britain's oldest operating theater, where limbs were sawed off way back in 1821.

Cost and Hours: £5.80, cash only, daily 10:30–16:45, 9a St. Thomas Street, Tube: London Bridge. Tel. 020/7188-2679, www.thegarret.org.uk.

HMS *Belfast*—"The last big-gun armored warship of World War II" clogs the Thames just upstream from the Tower Bridge. This huge vessel—now manned with wax sailors—thrills kids who always dreamed of sitting in a turret shooting off their imaginary guns. If you're into WWII warships, this is the ultimate. Otherwise, it's just lots of exercise with a nice view of the Tower Bridge.

Cost and Hours: £12.95, includes audioguide, daily March–Oct 10:00–18:00, Nov–Feb 10:00–17:00, last entry one hour before closing, Tube: London Bridge. Tel. 020/7940-6300, www.hmsbelfast.iwm.org.uk.

City Hall—The glassy, egg-shaped building near the south end of Tower Bridge is London's City Hall, designed by Sir Norman Foster, the architect who worked on London's Millennium Bridge and Berlin's Reichstag. City Hall houses the office of London's mayor—the blonde, flamboyant, conservative former journalist and author Boris Johnson. He consults here with the Assembly representatives of the city's 25 districts. An interior spiral ramp allows visitors to watch and hear the action below in the Assembly Chamber—ride the lift to the second floor (the highest visitors can go) and spiral down. On the lower ground floor is a large aerial photograph of  London, an information desk, and a handy cafeteria. Next to City Hall is the outdoor amphitheater called The Scoop.

Cost and Hours: City Hall is free and open to visitors Mon–Thu 8:00–18:00, Fri 8:00–17:30, closed Sat–Sun; Tube: London Bridge station plus 10-minute walk, or Tower Hill station plus 15-minute walk. Tel. 020/7983-4000.

West London

▲▲**Tate Britain**—One of Europe's great art houses, Tate Britain specializes in British painting from the 16th century through modern times. The museum has a good representation of William Blake's religious sketches, the Pre-Raphaelites' realistic art, and J.

West London

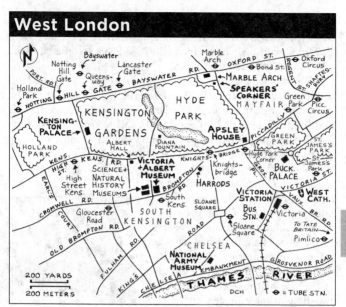

M. W. Turner's swirling works. This is people's art, with realistic paintings rooted in the people, landscape, and stories of the British Isles. You'll see Hogarth's stage sets, Gainsborough's ladies, Blake's angels, Constable's clouds, Turner's tempests, the swooning realism of the Pre-Raphaelites, and the camera-eye portraits of Hockney and Freud. What you won't see here are the fleshy goddesses, naked baby angels, and Madonna-and-child altarpieces so popular elsewhere in Europe. The largely Protestant English abhorred the "graven images" of the wealthy Catholic world.

The collection is constantly in motion but the basic layout stays the same: a roughly chronological walk through British paintings from 1500 to 1901 in the west half of the building, the 20th century in the east, and the works of J. M. W. Turner in the adjoining Clore Gallery.

Cost and Hours: Free, £2 donation requested, temporary exhibits extra; daily 10:00–18:00, last entry to special exhibitions at 17:15, first Fri of the month until 22:00, last entry to special exhibitions at 20:30; no photography allowed without advance permission, café and restaurant; Tube: Pimlico, then 7-minute walk;

take the "Tate to Tate" boat directly to the museum from Tate Modern; or take bus #87 from National Gallery or bus #88 from Oxford Circus. Switchboard tel. 020/7887-8888, recorded info tel. 020/7887-8008, www.tate.org.uk.

Tours: Free tours are offered Mon–Fri at 11:00 (art from 1500 to 1800), 12:00 (art from 1800 to 1900), 14:00 (Turner), and 15:00 (art from the 20th century). Weekend tours cover the collection's highlights (Sat–Sun 12:00 and 15:00); call to confirm schedule. The £3.50 audioguide (with photos and video clips) is useful.

▲**Apsley House (Wellington Museum)**—Having beaten Napoleon at Waterloo, Arthur Wellesley, the First Duke of Wellington, was once the most famous man in Europe. He was given a huge fortune with which he purchased London's ultimate address, #1 London. His refurbished mansion offers a nice interior, a handful of world-class paintings, and a glimpse at the life of the great soldier and two-time prime minister. Those who

LONDON

know something about Wellington ahead of time will appreciate the place much more than those who don't, as there's scarce biographical background. The place is well-described by the included audioguide, which has sound bites from the current Duke of Wellington (who still lives at Apsley).

Cost and Hours: £6, free on June 18—Waterloo Day, April–Oct Wed–Sun 11:00–17:00, Nov–March until 16:00, closed Mon–Tue, 20 yards from Hyde Park Corner Tube station. Tel. 020/7499-5676, www.english-heritage.org.uk. Hyde Park's pleasant and picnic-friendly rose garden is nearby.

Note that the **Wellington Arch,** which stands just across the street, is open to the public but not worth the £4 charge (elevator up, lousy views and boring exhibits).

▲**Hyde Park and Speakers' Corner**—London's "Central Park," originally Henry VIII's hunting grounds, has more than 600 acres of lush greenery, the huge manmade Serpentine Lake, the royal Kensington Palace and Orangery (described later), and the ornate Neo-Gothic Albert Memorial across from the Royal Albert Hall. The western half of the park is known as Kensington Gardens.

On Sundays, from just after noon until early evening, **Speakers' Corner** offers soapbox oratory at its best (northeast corner of the park, Tube: Marble Arch). Characters climb their stepladders, wave their flags, pound emphatically on their sandwich boards, and share what they are convinced is their wisdom. Regulars have resident hecklers who know their lines and are always ready with a verbal jab or barb. "The grass roots of democracy" is actually a holdover from when the gallows stood here and the criminal was allowed to say just about anything he wanted to before he swung. I dare you to raise your voice and gather a crowd—it's easy to do.

The **Princess Diana Memorial Fountain** honors the "People's Princess," who once lived in nearby Kensington Palace. The low-key circular stream, great for cooling off your feet on a hot day, is in the south central part of the park, near the Albert Memorial and Serpentine Gallery. (Don't be confused by signs to the Diana, Princess of Wales Memorial Playground, in the northwest corner of the park.)

▲▲▲**Victoria and Albert Museum**—The world's top collection of decorative arts (vases, stained glass, fine furniture, clothing, jewelry, carpets, and more) is a surprisingly interesting assortment of crafts from the West, as well as Asian and Islamic cultures. The British Galleries are grand, but there's much more to see, including Raphael's tapestry cartoons and a cast of Trajan's Column that depicts the emperor's conquests.

The V&A grew out of the Great Exhibition of 1851, that ultimate celebration of the Industrial Revolution. Now "art" could be brought to the masses through modern technology and mass production. The museum was founded on the idealistic Victorian notion that anyone can be continually improved by education and example. After much support from Queen Victoria and Prince Albert, the museum was renamed for the royal couple, and its present building was opened in 1909.

The V&A is in the midst of a 10-year update and expansion. Changes so far include a new café, sculpture gallery, Islamic room, and refurbished Medieval and Renaissance galleries. During this chaotic time, exhibits may be rearranged, so check with the information desk for current room closures, carry a copy of the museum's detailed map, and ask a nearby guard if you can't find one of the objects I mention below.

You could spend days in this place. The museum is large and gangly, with 150 rooms and more than 12 miles of corridors. Pick up the much-needed museum map (£1 suggested donation). While just wandering works well here, consider catching one of the free one-hour orientation tours or buying the fine £5 *V&A Guide Book*.

Here are a few highlights:

The **British Galleries** sweeps chronologically through 400 years of British high-class living (1500–1900)—all laid out over two floors, and beautifully described.

In Room 46A are the plaster casts of **Trajan's Column**—a copy of Rome's 140-foot spiral relief telling the story of the conquest of Dacia (modern-day Romania).

Room 46B has plaster casts of **Renaissance sculptures** by Michelangelo and others, which allowed 19th-century art students who couldn't afford a railpass to go study the classics. Compare Michelangelo's monumental *David* with Donatello's girlish *David* (at the other end of the room), and see Ghiberti's bronze Baptistery doors that inspired the Florentine Renaissance.

In Room 48A are **Raphael's "cartoons,"** seven of the full-size designs by Raphael that were used to produce tapestries for the Sistine Chapel (approximately 13 feet by 17 feet, done in tempera on paper, now mounted on canvas). The cartoons were sent to factories in Brussels, cut into strips (see the lines), and placed on the looms. The scenes are the reverse of the final product—lots of left-handed saints.

Cost and Hours: Free, £3 donation requested, possible pricey fee for special exhibits, daily 10:00–17:45, Fri until 22:00, free one-hour tours daily on the half-hour 10:30–15:30, Tube: South Kensington, from the Tube station a long tunnel leads directly to museum. Tel. 020/7942-2000, www.vam.ac.uk.

▲▲**Natural History Museum**—Across the street from Victoria and Albert, this mammoth museum is housed in a giant and wonderful Victorian, Neo-Romanesque building. In the main hall, above a big dinosaur skeleton and under a massive slice of sequoia tree, Charles Darwin sits as if upon a throne overseeing it all. Built in the 1870s specifically for the huge collection (50 million specimens), the building  has two halves: the Life Galleries (creepy-crawlies, human biology, "our place in evolution," and awe-inspiring dinosaurs) and the Earth Galleries (meteors, volcanoes, earthquakes, and so on).

Exhibits are wonderfully explained, with lots of creative, interactive displays. Pop in, if only for the wild collection of dinosaurs and to hear English children exclaim, "Oh my goodness!" Get oriented by talking with one of the many "visit planners" (helpful guides scattered throughout the museum), review the "What's on Today" board for special events and tours, and note which sections are closed (rather than "renovating," they say "we are evolving"). While the dinosaur hall often has a long line, everything else is wide open. Don't miss the vault in the mineralogy section (top floor of the green zone), with rare and precious stones (including a meteorite from Mars and the Aurora Pyramid of Hope, displaying 296 diamonds showing their full range of natural colors).

Cost and Hours: Free, fees for special exhibits, daily 10:00–17:50, last entry at 17:30, occasional tours, long tunnel leads directly from South Kensington Tube station to museum. Tel. 020/7942-5000, exhibit info and reservations tel. 020/7942-5011, www.nhm .ac.uk.

▲**Science Museum**—Next door to the Natural History Museum, this sprawling wonderland for curious minds is kid-perfect, with themes such as measuring time, exploring space, and the evolution of modern medicine. It offers hands-on fun, from moonwalks to deep-sea exploration, with trendy technology exhibits, an IMAX theater (£8, kids-£6.25), and cool rotating themed exhibits, including "Climate Science—The Science behind Climate Change," on display through 2011.

Cost and Hours: Free, daily 10:00–18:00, Exhibition Road, Tube: South Kensington. Toll tel. 0870-870-4868, www.science museum.org.uk.

Kensington Palace—In 1689, King William and Queen Mary moved from Whitehall in central London to the more pristine and peaceful village of Kensington (now engulfed by London). Sir Christopher Wren renovated an existing house into Kensington Palace, which became the center of English court life until 1760, when the royal family moved into Buckingham Palace. Since then, lesser royals have bedded down in Kensington Palace. Princess Diana lived here from her 1981 marriage to Prince Charles until her death in 1997. Today it's home to three of Charles' cousins. The palace, while still functioning as a royal residence, also welcomes visitors with an impressive string of royal apartments and a few rooms of royal dresses.

While generally a ▲▲ attraction, the palace is currently being renovated, and until June 2012 it's not worth your time or money. Rather than close it during restoration, they've created a silly "Enchanted Palace" theatrical show replacing the historic artifacts of the palace (such as the wonderful royal dress collection, splendid 17th-century furniture of the William and Mary apartments, and the bed where Queen Victoria was born—fully clothed, it is said) with cheesy modern props. The only good thing about the Enchanted Palace is that it enables unwitting tourists to help pay for the £12 million renovation.

Cost and Hours: £12.50, daily 10:00–18:00, until 17:00 in winter, last entry one hour before closing, a 10-minute hike through Kensington Gardens from either Queensway or High Street Kensington Tube station. Toll tel. 0870-751-5170 or 0844-482-7777, www.hrp.org.uk.

Eating: Garden enthusiasts enjoy popping into the secluded Sunken Garden, 50 yards from the exit. Consider afternoon tea at the nearby Orangery (see page 180), built as a greenhouse for Queen Anne in 1704.

Victoria Station—From underneath this station's iron-and-glass canopy, trains depart for the south of England and Gatwick Airport. While Victoria Station is famous and a major Tube stop, few tourists actually take trains from here—most just come to take in the exciting bustle. It's a fun place to just be a "rock in a river" teeming with commuters and services. The station is surrounded by big red buses, taxis, travel agencies, and lousy eateries. It's next to the main intercity bus station (Victoria Coach Station) and the best inexpensive lodgings in town.

Westminster Cathedral—This cathedral, the largest Catholic church in England and just a block from Victoria Station, is striking, but not very historic or important to visit. Opened in 1903,

it has a brick Neo-Byzantine flavor (surrounded by glassy office blocks). While it's definitely not Westminster Abbey, half the tourists wandering around inside seem to think it is. The highlight is the lift to the viewing gallery atop its 273-foot bell tower (£5 for the lift, tower open daily 9:30–12:30 & 13:00–17:00).

Cost and Hours: Free entry, daily 7:00–19:00; 5-minute walk from Victoria Station or take bus #11, #24, #148, #211, or #507 to museum's door; just off Victoria Street, Tube: Victoria; www.westminstercathedral .org.uk.

National Army Museum—This museum is not as awe-inspiring as the Imperial War Museum, but it's still fun, especially for kids into soldiers, armor, and guns. And while the Imperial War Museum is limited to wars of the 20th century, the National Army Museum tells the story of the British army from 1415 through the Bosnian conflict and Iraq, with lots of Redcoat lore and a good look at Waterloo. Kids enjoy trying on a Cromwellian helmet, seeing the skeleton of Napoleon's horse, and peering out from a World War I trench through a working periscope.

Cost and Hours: Free, daily 10:00–17:30, Royal Hospital Road, Chelsea, Tube: Sloane Square. Tel. 020/7730-0717 or 020/7881-2455, www.national-army-museum.ac.uk.

Greater London
West of Central London

▲▲**Kew Gardens**—For a fine riverside park and a palatial green-house jungle to swing through, take the Tube or the boat to every botanist's favorite escape, Kew Gardens.

While to most visitors the Royal Botanic Gardens of Kew are simply a delightful opportunity to wander among 33,000 different types of plants, to the hardworking organization that runs the gardens, it's a way to promote understanding and preservation of the botanical diversity of our planet. The Kew Tube station drops you in an herbal little business community, a two-block walk from Victoria Gate (the main garden entrance). Pick up a map brochure and check at the gate for a monthly listing of best blooms.

Garden-lovers could spend days exploring Kew's 300 acres. For a quick visit, spend a fragrant hour wandering through three

buildings: the **Palm House**, a humid Victorian world of iron, glass, and tropical plants built in 1844; a **Waterlily House** that Monet would swim for; and the **Princess of Wales Conservatory**, a modern greenhouse with many different climate zones growing countless cacti, bug-munching carnivorous plants, and more. The latest addition to the gardens is the **Rhizotron and Xstrata Treetop Walkway**, a 200-yard-long scenic steel walkway that puts you high in the canopy 60 feet above the ground.

Cost and Hours: £13.50, discounted to £11.50 45 minutes before closing, kids under 17 free, £5 for Kew Palace only; April–Aug Mon–Fri 9:30–18:30, Sat–Sun 9:30–19:30; closes earlier Sept–March, last entry to gardens 30 minutes before closing, galleries and conservatories close at 17:30 in high season—earlier off-season; free one-hour walking tours daily at 11:00 and 14:00; £4 narrated 40-minute hop-on, hop-off joyride on Kew Explorer tram departs on the hour from 11:00 from near Victoria Gate; Tube: Kew Gardens, boats run April–Oct between Kew Gardens and Westminster Pier—see page 77. Switchboard tel. 020/8332-5000, recorded info tel. 020/8332-5655, www.kew.org.

Eating: For a sun-dappled lunch or afternoon tea, walk 10 minutes from the Palm House to the Orangery (£8–12 lunches,

Greater London

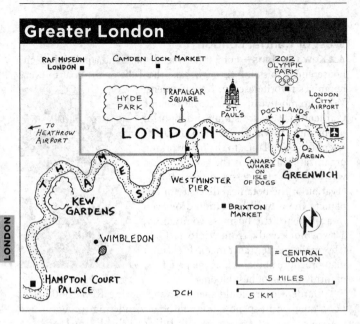

£15–18 afternoon tea, daily 10:00–18:00, until 17:00 in winter, closes early for events, tel. 0844-482-7777 www.hrp.org.uk).

▲**Hampton Court Palace**—Fifteen miles up the Thames from downtown (a £15 taxi ride from Kew Gardens), and worth ▲▲ for palace aficionados, is the 500-year-old palace of Henry VIII. Actually, it was originally the palace of his minister, Cardinal Wolsey. When Wolsey, a clever man, realized Henry VIII was experiencing a little palace envy, he gave the mansion to his king. The Tudor palace was also home to Elizabeth I and Charles

I. Sections were updated by Christopher Wren for William and Mary. The stately palace stands overlooking the Thames and includes some impressive Tudor rooms, including a Great Hall with a magnificent hammer-beam ceiling. The industrial-strength Tudor kitchen was capable of keeping 600 schmoozing courtiers thoroughly—if not well—fed. The sculpted garden features a rare Tudor tennis court and a popular maze.

The palace, fully restored after a 1986 fire, tries hard to please, but it doesn't quite sparkle. From the information center in the main courtyard, pick up audioguides for self-guided tours of various wings of the palace (free). The Tudor kitchens, Henry VIII's apartments, and the King's apartments are most interesting; the Georgian rooms are pretty dull. The maze in the nearby garden is a curiosity some find fun (maze free with palace ticket, otherwise £3.50).

Cost and Hours: The palace costs £14, or £38 for families, online discounts, daily April–Oct 10:00–18:00, Nov–March 10:00–16:30, last entry one hour before closing, café. Toll tel. 0844-482-7777, www.hrp.org.uk.

Getting There: The train (2/hour, 35 minutes) from London's Waterloo Station drops you across the river from the palace (just walk across the bridge). Consider arriving at or departing from the palace by boat (connections with London's Westminster Pier, see page 77); it's a relaxing and scenic three- to four-hour cruise past two locks and a fun new/old riverside mix.

Royal Air Force Museum London—A hit with aviation enthusiasts, this huge aerodrome and airfield contain planes from World War II's Battle of Britain up through the Gulf War. You can climb inside some of the planes, try your luck in a cockpit, and fly with the Red Arrows in a flight simulator.

Cost and Hours: Free, daily 10:00–18:00, last entry 30 minutes before closing, café, shop, parking-£2.50, Grahame Park Way, 30-minute ride from central London, Tube: Colindale—top of Northern Line Edgware branch. Tel. 020/8205-2266, www.raf museum.org.uk.

▲▲The Docklands

London is growing east. The Docklands, at a bend in the Thames dubbed the Isle of Dogs, were once the primary harbor for the Port of London—the world's largest, with direct connections to the North Sea. But in the 20th century, World War II damage and the transition to container shipping left the Docklands a derelict and deserted no-man's-land...the most miserable place in London. However, over the last couple of decades, things have changed dramatically, and the Docklands have been transformed into a vibrant business center. Shipping canals and a few old brick warehouses survive, but everything has been spiffed up and gentrified. Some of the UK's tallest skyscrapers tower overhead, and underfoot are sprawling subterranean supermalls.

While not full of the touristy sights that many are seeking in London, the Docklands offer a refreshing look at the British version of a 21st-century city. You can see the highlights in a short visit. It's best at the end of the workday, when it's lively with office workers (it's ideal on the way back from Greenwich—covered in the next chapter—since Greenwich and the Docklands line up on the same train tracks). Ride the Tube or the Docklands Light Railway (DLR) to the Canary Wharf stop, and go for a stroll. Explore the ultra-modern malls and delightfully peaceful parks with pedestrian bridges looping over the now-tranquil canals. Though you can't get up in the skyscrapers, the ground-floor levels are welcoming with fun art. Photographers can't help but capture jumbo jets gliding past gleaming towers, goofy pose-with-me statues, and trendy pubs filled with trendier young professionals. Then head over to West India Quay to visit the Museum of London Docklands (see below). If you're at the Docklands, it's a relatively straightforward detour to see the Olympics 2012 sights in Stratford (see next section).

▲Museum of London Docklands—Illuminating the gritty and fascinating history of this site, this museum traces the story of what was London's primary harbor (free, daily 10:00–18:00, West India Quay, Tube: West India Quay or Canary Wharf, tel. 020/7001-9844, www.museumindocklands.org.uk).

2012 London Olympic Park, in Stratford

From July 27 to August 12, 2012, all eyes will be on London as it hosts athletes from 205 nations in the 30th Olympiad. Though events will take place throughout the city, festivities will center around Olympic Park, filling the Lea Valley, about seven miles northeast of central London. Once voted the worst place to live in London, Lea Valley was the site of derelict factories, mountains of discarded tires, and Europe's biggest refrigerator

dump. Now it's Europe's biggest construction site, with a veritable army of workers, fleets of trucks, clusters of concrete-mixing towers, and forests of cranes working furiously to get everything ready on time. Work is scheduled to be complete in July of 2011, when a rigorous 12-month testing process will begin. (For now, you can either view the site on your own, or go on a guided tour—both explained later.)

London is the first city to host the modern games three times—first in 1908, and then in 1948 (the first post-World-War-II Olympics, known as the "Austerity Games"). The city won the 2012 bid for its grand and green vision, including a promise to permanently improve the least desirable part of the city. The site's connection to the broader world will be extraordinary: It will take just two hours to go from Paris to Olympic Park (ride the Eurostar to St. Pancras International Station in downtown London, and connect via a seven-minute bullet train to Stratford Station).

These will be the greenest games ever. There will be no public parking at the site—event tickets will include an all-day London

2012 Olympics Venues

Although most of the Olympic Games will be held in London's East End, there will be sports and activities all over London and Britain. These are the main venues:

Olympic Park, in the Stratford district of East London, is the heart of the games. Here you'll find the 80,000-seat Olympic Stadium (for opening and closing ceremonies) and the Olympic Village, where the athletes will stay. A 12,000-seat basketball arena is under construction—and will be completely dismantled when the games are over. The Aquatics Centre, with its swooping wave-like roofline, may become the architectural "face" of the games.

Central London will be the site of—really?—beach volleyball. Tons of sand will be spread across the parking lot behind #10 Downing Street and Horse Guards, creating an urban beach ringed with bleachers. Triathletes will compete in **Hyde Park,** swimming in the Serpentine lake, then biking and running around the park. **Greenwich Park** (near the *Cutty Sark,* see page 200) will hold equestrian events, while the nearby **O₂ Arena** (formerly the "Millennium Dome") will host gymnastics and more basketball.

Farther afield, you'll find tennis at **Wimbledon** (of course), volleyball at **Earl's Court,** and football/soccer at **Wembley Stadium.** The Olympic torch will wend its way through various communities. And anywhere you go, you can't avoid the universally ridiculed Olympic mascots—those alien/Gumby/Cyclops-like creatures named Wenlock and Mandeville.

Tickets go on sale spring 2011 by lottery for British and EU residents only (US residents can check www.tickets .london2012.com for up-to-date info).

Tube pass. About 90 percent of demolition material has been recycled. More than half of the deliveries will be by train or boat rather than by truck. Half a million trees are being planted, and 1.4 million tons of dirt have been cleansed of arsenic, lead, and other toxic chemicals—a reminder of this site's dirty industrial past. Locals whine about the cost—as locals have whined about big public building projects, I imagine, since the days when great cities built great Gothic churches. But the $14 billion project is a stimulus plan, with 90 percent local investment and employment.

About 75 percent of the construction will be "legacy building," giving these structures a practical life in a reinvigorated community after the games. Many of the buildings will be converted to housing (enough for 16,000 residents), with half of these units designated for low-income people. Bridges leading to the site, built double-wide for huge crowds, will be scaled back. The commercial zone, Stratford City, will become the biggest shopping center in

Europe. Between the bullet trains, Tube, regional rail services, and DLR, residents of post-Olympics Stratford will enjoy the best public transit in town, with multiple connections to central London. (Don't confuse it with Stratford-upon-Avon, the famous Warwickshire town where Shakespeare was born. That's two hours northwest of London.)

Suddenly, Stratford is a place with a future (and poor little Grandmas who've called it home are now worth something to their relatives and developers...and chocolate and flowers appear on Sundays). It seems fitting that this most multiethnic part of London will host these famously multiethnic games.

Visiting the Olympic Park Site

On Your Own: A viewpoint on the greenway (called "The View Tube") comes with information boards, a lookout tower, a café (already well-known for its coffee and brownies), and a WC. It's free and a short walk from the Pudding Mill Lane DLR station. Along the way, you'll see some of the legion of Nepali Gurkhas employed here for security.

Getting There: Ride the Tube (Jubilee Line) from central London to Stratford, where you can change to the DLR to Pudding Mill Lane. To go direct on the DLR, take a Stratford-bound train from Bank (in central London, also accessible from the Monument Tube station) or from Canary Wharf (in the Docklands), and get off at Pudding Mill Lane.

On a Tour: Blue Badge guides lead 1.5-hour guided walks of the area, weaving background about its Industrial Age heritage into the excitement of today's building project and impressive vision (£8, pay guide directly in cash, online reservations recommended but not required, daily at 11:00, www.toursof2012sites.com). Meet at Bromley-by-Bow Tube station (District or Hammersmith Line).

Note that the Stratford, Pudding Mill Lane, and Bromley-by-Bow stations are (barely) inside Zone 2, which means the trip is covered by any Tube ticket or pass covering Zones 1-2.

Shopping in London

Department Stores

Harrods—Harrods is London's most famous and touristy department store. With more than four acres of retail space covering seven floors, it's a place where some shoppers could spend all day. (To me, it's still just a department store.) Big yet classy, Harrods has everything from elephants to toothbrushes (Mon–Sat 10:00–20:00, Sun 12:00–18:00, mandatory storage for big backpacks-£3, no shorts or flip-flops, on Brompton Road, Tube: Knightsbridge, tel. 020/7730-1234, www.harrods.com).

While the store is famous partly for its Egyptian theme and its memorials to Princess Diana and her boyfriend, Dodi Fayed, those were the pet projects of Harrods' former owner, Mohamed Al Fayed (Dodi's Egyptian father). Al Fayed sold the store in May of 2010 to a Qatari investment group, so it's possible some of these features (especially the Di and Dodi stuff) could change.

Sightseers should pick up the free *Store Guide* at any info post. Here's what I enjoy: On the ground floor, find the Food Halls, with their Edwardian tiled walls, creative and exuberant displays, and staff in period costumes—not quite like your local supermarket back home.

Descend to the lower ground floor and follow signs to the Egyptian Escalator (in the center of the store), where you'll likely find a memorial to Dodi Fayed and Princess Diana. Photos and flowers honor the late Princess and her lover, who both died in a car crash in Paris in 1997. Inside a small, clear pyramid, you can see a wine glass still dirty from their last dinner and the engagement ring that Dodi purchased the day before they died. True Di-hards can go back up one level to the ground floor and follow signs to Door #3 in Menswear (near Men's Designer and Men's Tailoring, at the escalator). A huge (and more than a little creepy) bronze statue shows Di and Dodi releasing a symbolic albatross.

Back in the center of the store, ride the Egyptian Escalator—lined with pharaoh-headed sconces, papyrus-plant lamps, and hieroglyphic balconies—to the fourth floor. From the escalator, make a U-turn left and head to the far corner of the store (toys) to find child-size luxury cars that actually work. If you have £10,000 to spare, these are the perfect gift for the child who has everything.

Also on the fourth floor is **The Georgian Restaurant,** where you can enjoy a fancy afternoon tea (see page 181). For non-tea drinkers, 27 other eateries are scattered throughout the store, including a sushi bar, kosher deli, pizzeria, classic pub, and—for the truly homesick—a Krispy Kreme.

Many of my readers report that Harrods is overpriced, snooty, and teeming with American and Japanese tourists. It's the only shopping mall I've seen with its own gift store. Still, it's the palace of department stores. The nearby Beauchamp Place is lined with classy and fascinating shops.

Harvey Nichols—Once Princess Diana's favorite, "Harvey Nick's" remains the department store *du jour* (Mon–Sat 10:00–20:00, Sun 12:00–18:00, near Harrods, 109–125 Knightsbridge, Tube: Knightsbridge, tel. 020/7235-5000, www.harveynichols.com). Want to pick up a little £20 scarf for the wife? You won't do it here, where they're more like £200. The store's fifth floor is a veritable food fest, with a gourmet grocery store, a fancy restaurant, a Yo! Sushi bar, and a lively café. Consider a take-away tray of sushi to eat on a bench in the Hyde Park rose garden two blocks away.

Street Markets

Antique buffs, people-watchers, and folks who brake for garage sales love London's street markets. There's good early-morning market activity somewhere any day of the week. The best—which combine lively stalls and a colorful neighborhood with cute and characteristic shops of its own—are Portobello Road and Camden Market. Any London TI has a complete, up-to-date list. If you like to haggle, there are no holds barred in London's street markets. Warning: Markets attract two kinds of people: tourists and pickpockets.

In Notting Hill

Portobello Road Market—Arguably London's best street market, Portobello Road stretches for several blocks through the delightful, colorful, funky-yet-quaint Notting Hill neighborhood (immortalized by the Hugh Grant/Julia Roberts film of the same name). Already charming streets lined with pastel-painted houses and offbeat antiques shops are enlivened on Saturdays with 2,000 additional stalls (5:30-17:00), plus food, live music, and more. (It's also extremely crowded.) If you start at Notting Hill Gate and work your way north, you'll find these general sections: antiques, new goods, produce, more new goods, and a flea market. While Portobello Road is best on Saturdays, it's enjoyable to stroll this street on most other days as well, since the characteristic shops are fun to explore—but skip it on Sundays, when virtually everything is closed (Tube: Notting Hill Gate, near recommended accommodations, tel. 020/7229-8354, www.portobelloroad.co.uk).

In the East End

All three of these East End markets are busiest and most interesting on Sundays.

Spitalfields Market—This huge, mod-feeling market hall (pronounced "spittle-fields") combines a shopping mall with old brick buildings and sleek modern ones, all covered by a giant glass roof. While the shops and a rainbow of restaurant options are open every day, the open space between them is filled with stalls during the week. It's best on Sundays (9:00–17:00), when all stalls and shops are open; you'll find a lively organic food market, many ethnic eateries, crafts, trendy clothes, bags, and an antique-and-junk market. Thursdays are for antiques, Fridays specialize in cutting-edge fashion and art, and the first and third Wednesday of every month feature a record and book fair (all 10:00–16:00). It's quietest on Saturdays, Mondays, and Tuesdays, when only the shops are open—no stalls (shops open daily 11:00–19:00, Tube: Liverpool Street; from the Tube stop, take Bishopsgate East exit, turn left, walk 2 blocks, and turn right on Brushfield Street; tel. 020/7375-2963, www.visitspitalfields.com).

Petticoat Lane Market—Just a block from Spitalfields Market, this is a line of stalls on an otherwise dull, glass-skyscraper-lined Middlesex Street; adjoining Wentworth Street is grungier and more characteristic. Expect budget clothing, leather, shoes, watches, jewelry, and crowds (Sun 9:00–14:00, sometimes later; smaller market Mon–Fri 10:00–16:30 on Wentworth Street only; closed Sat; Middlesex Street and Wentworth Street, Tube: Liverpool Street). The Columbia Road flower market is nearby (Sun 8:00–15:00, http://columbiaroad.info).

Brick Lane Market—Housed in the former Truman Brewery, this market is in the heart of the "Banglatown" Bangladeshi community (Sun 10:00–17:00, tel. 020/7770-6028, www.bricklane market.com).

Other Markets

Camden Lock Market—This huge, trendy arts-and-crafts festival has become quite punky to many travelers. Still, it's London's fourth-most-popular tourist attraction (daily 10:00–18:00, busiest on weekends, Tube: Camden Town, tel. 020/7284-2084, www.camdenlockmarket.com).

Covent Garden Market—Originally the convent garden for Westminster Abbey, the iron-and-glass market hall hosted a produce market until the 1970s (earning it the name "Apple Market"). Yesteryear's produce stalls are now open 10:00–18:00 daily with antiques (Mon); clothes, gifts, and foods (Tue–Fri); and handmade crafts (Sun; tel. 020-7836-9136, www.coventgardenlife .com/shopping/markets). The **Jubilee Hall Market** to the south follows a similar schedule (antiques Mon 5:00–18:00, general market Tue–Fri 9:30–18:00, handcrafts Sat–Sun 9:00–18:00, tel. 020/7379-4242, www.jubileemarket.co.uk).

Brixton Market—Here the food, clothing, records, and hair-braiding throb with an Afro-Caribbean beat (stalls open Mon–Tue and Thu–Sat 8:00–18:00, Wed 8:00–15:00, closed Sun; farmer's market Sun 10:00–14:00 but otherwise dead on Sundays; Tube: Brixton, www.brixtonmarket.net).

Greenwich—With several sightseeing treats just a quick DLR ride from central London, Greenwich has its share of great markets. They're especially lively on weekends. For details, see page 207.

Famous Auctions

London's famous auctioneers welcome the curious public for viewing and bidding. You can preview estate catalogs or browse auction calendars online. To ask questions or set up an appointment, contact **Sotheby's** (Mon–Fri 9:00–16:30, closed Sat–Sun, café, 34–35 New Bond Street, Tube: Oxford Circus, tel. 020/7293-5000, www.sothebys.com) or **Christie's** (Mon–Fri 9:00–17:00, Sat–Sun usually 12:00–17:00 but weekend hours vary—call ahead, 8 King Street, Tube: Green Park, tel. 020/7839-9060, www.christies.com). See map on page V for locations of both.

Entertainment in London

Theater (a.k.a. "Theatre")

London's theater rivals Broadway's in quality and usually beats it in price. Choose from 200 offerings—Shakespeare, musicals, comedies, thrillers, sex farces, cutting-edge fringe, revivals starring movie celebs, and more. London does it all well. I prefer big, glitzy—even bombastic—musicals over serious chamber dramas, simply because London can deliver the lights, sound, dancers, and multimedia spectacle I rarely get back home. (If you're a regular visitor to Broadway or Las Vegas—where you have access to similar spectacles—you might prefer some of London's more low-key offerings.)

There are also plenty of enticing plays to choose from, ranging from revivals of classics to cutting-edge works by the hottest young playwrights. Many star huge-name celebrities (you'll see the latest offerings advertised all over the Tube and elsewhere). London is a magnet for movie stars who want to stretch their acting chops. For example, since 2003, Kevin Spacey has been the artistic director of the Old Vic theatre. He has directed and appeared in several productions, and has enlisted many big-name film directors and actors for others (www.oldvictheatre.com).

Most theaters, marked on tourist maps, are found in the West End between Piccadilly and Covent Garden. Box offices, hotels, and TIs offer a handy free *London Theatre Guide* and *Entertainment Guide*. From home, it's easy to check www.officiallondontheatre.co.uk for the latest on what's currently playing in London.

Performances are nightly except Sunday, usually with one or two matinees a week (Shakespeare's Globe is the rare theater that does offer performances on Sun, May–Sept). Tickets range from about £15 to £60. Matinees are generally cheaper and rarely sell out.

To book a seat, simply call the theater box office (which may ring through to a central ticketing office), ask about seats and available dates, and buy a ticket with your credit card. You can call from the US as easily as from England. Arrive about 30 minutes before the show starts to pick up your ticket and avoid lines.

For a booking fee, you can reserve online. Most theater websites link you to a preferred ticket vendor, usually www.ticket master.co.uk or www.seetickets.com. In the US, Keith Prowse Ticketing is also handy by phone or online (US tel. 212/398-4175, www.keithprowse.com).

Although booking through an agency is quick and easy, prices are inflated by a standard 25 percent fee. Ticket agencies (whether in the US, at London's TIs, or scattered throughout the city) are scalpers with an address. If you're buying from an agency, look at the ticket carefully (your price should be no more than 30 percent over the printed face value; the 20 percent VAT is already included in the face value), and understand where you're sitting according to the floor plan (if your view is restricted, it will state this on the ticket; for floor plans of the various theaters, see www.theatre monkey.com).

Agencies are worthwhile only if a show you've just got to see is sold out at the box office. They scarf up hot tickets, planning to make a killing after the show is sold out. US booking agencies get their tickets from another agency, adding even more to your expense by involving yet another middleman. Many tickets sold on the street are forgeries. Although some theaters use booking agencies to handle their advance sales, you'll stand a good chance of saving money by avoiding the middleman and simply calling the box office directly to purchase your tickets (international phone calls are cheap, and credit cards make booking a snap).

Theater Lingo: stalls (ground floor), dress circle (first balcony), upper circle (second balcony), balcony (sky-high third balcony), slips (cheap seats on the fringes). Many cheap seats have a restricted view (behind a pillar).

Cheap Theater Tricks: Most theaters offer cheap returned tickets, standing-room, matinee, and senior or student standby deals. These "concessions" (discounted tickets) are indicated with a "conc" or "s" in the listings. Picking up a late return can get you a great seat at a cheap-seat price. Even if a show is "sold out," there's usually a way to get a seat. Call the theater box office and ask how.

If you don't care where you sit, you can often buy the absolutely cheapest seats—those with an obstructed view or in the nosebleed section—at the box office; these tickets generally cost less than £20. Many theaters are so small that there's hardly a bad seat. After the lights go down, scooting up is less than a capital offense. Shakespeare did it.

Half-Price "tkts" Booth: This famous ticket booth at Leicester Square sells discounted tickets for top-price seats to

London's Major Theaters

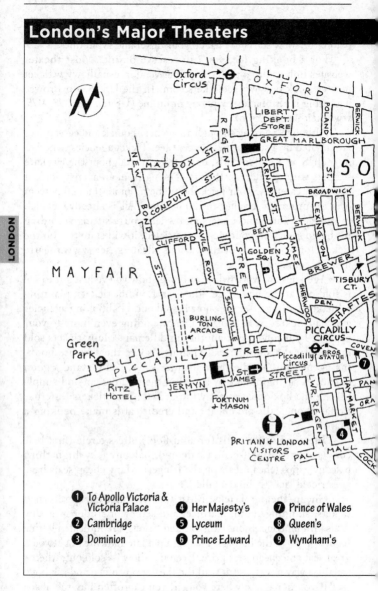

1. To Apollo Victoria & Victoria Palace
2. Cambridge
3. Dominion
4. Her Majesty's
5. Lyceum
6. Prince Edward
7. Prince of Wales
8. Queen's
9. Wyndham's

shows on the push list—but only on the day of the performance (generally £3 service charge per ticket, Mon–Sat 10:00–19:00, Sun 11:00–16:00, lines often form early, list of shows available online at www.tkts.co.uk). Most tickets are half-price; other shows are discounted 25 percent. Note that the real half-price booth (with its "tkts" name) is a freestanding kiosk at the edge of the garden in Leicester Square. Several dishonest outfits nearby advertise

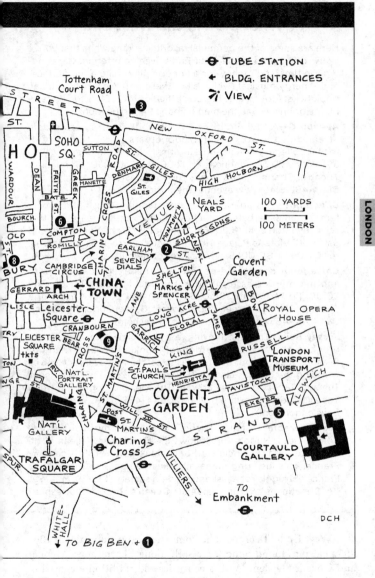

"official half-price tickets"—avoid these.

Here are sample prices: A top-notch seat to *Chicago* costs £59 if you buy directly from the theater; the same seat costs £32.50 at Leicester Square. The cheapest balcony seat is £25 through the theater. Half-price tickets can be a good deal, unless you want the cheapest seats or the hottest shows. But check the board; occasionally they sell cheap tickets to good shows.

What's On in the West End

Here are some of the perennial favorites and new hits that you're likely to find among the West End's evening offerings. If spending the time and money for a London play, I like a full-fledged, high-energy musical (which all of these are). Generally you can book tickets for free at the box office or for a £2-3 fee by telephone or online. See the map on page 94 for locations.

Avenue Q—A foul-mouthed but hilarious send-up of *Sesame Street*, this show uses actor/puppeteers to tell the story of recent college graduates making their way in the big city (£10-55, nightly 20:00, matinees Fri 17:00 and Sat 16:30, Wyndham's Theatre, Charing Cross Road, Tube: Leicester Square, toll tell. 0844-482-5141, www.avenueqthemusical.co.uk).

Billy Elliot—This adaptation of the popular British film is part family drama, part story of a boy who just has to dance, set to a score by Elton John (£20–65, Mon–Sat 19:30, matinees Thu and Sat 14:30, Victoria Palace Theatre, Victoria Street, Tube: Victoria, toll tel. 0844-811-0055, www.billyelliotthemusical.com).

Chicago—A chorus-girl-gone-bad forms a nightclub act with another murderess to bring in the bucks (£25–59, Mon–Thu 20:00, Fri 17:30 and 20:30, Sat 15:00 and 20:00, Cambridge Theatre, Earlham Street, Tube: Covent Garden, booking toll tel. 0844-412-4652, www.chicagothemusical.com).

Jersey Boys—This fast-moving, easy-to-follow show tracks the rough start and rise to stardom of Frankie Valli and The Four Seasons. It's light, but the music is so catchy that everyone leaves whistling the group's classics (£20–65, Mon–Sat 19:30, matinees Tue and Sat 14:30, Prince Edward Theatre, Old Compton Street, Tube: Leicester Square, toll tel. 0844-482-5138, www.jersey boyslondon.com).

Les Misérables—Claude-Michel Schönberg's musical adaptation of Victor Hugo's epic follows the life of Jean Valjean as he struggles with the social and political realities of 19th-century France. This inspiring mega-hit takes you back to the days of France's struggle for a just and modern society (£15–59, Mon–Sat 19:30, matinees Wed and Sat 14:30, Queen's Theatre, Shaftesbury

West End Theaters: The commercial (nonsubsidized) theaters cluster around Soho (especially along Shaftesbury Avenue) and Covent Garden. With a centuries-old tradition of pleasing the masses, these present London theater at its glitziest. See the "What's On in the West End" sidebar.

Royal Shakespeare Company: If you'll ever enjoy Shakespeare, it'll be in Britain. The RSC performs at various theaters around London and in Stratford-upon-Avon year-round. To get a schedule, contact the RSC (Royal Shakespeare Theatre, Stratford-upon-Avon, toll tel. 0844-800-1110, www.rsc.org.uk).

Avenue, Tube: Piccadilly Circus, box office toll tel. 0844-482-5138, www.lesmis.com).

The Lion King—In this Disney extravaganza, Simba the lion learns about the delicately balanced circle of life on the savanna (£20–62.50, Tue–Sat 19:30, matinees Wed and Sat 14:00, Sun 15:00, Lyceum Theatre, Wellington Street, Tube: Charing Cross or Covent Garden, booking toll tel. 0844-844-0005, theater info tel. 020/7420-8100, www.thelionking.co.uk).

Mamma Mia!—This energetic, spandex-and-platform-boots musical weaves together a slew of ABBA hits to tell the story of a bride in search of her real dad as her promiscuous mom plans her Greek Isle wedding. The production has the audience dancing by the time it reaches its happy ending (£20–85, Mon–Thu and Sat 19:30, Fri 20:30, matinees Fri 17:00 and Sat 15:00, Prince of Wales Theatre, Coventry Street, Tube: Piccadilly Circus, box office toll tel. 0844-482-5115, www.mamma-mia.com).

Phantom of the Opera—A mysterious masked man falls in love with a singer in this haunting Andrew Lloyd Webber musical about life beneath the stage of the Paris Opera (£20–59, Mon–Sat 19:30, matinees Tue and Sat 14:30, Her Majesty's Theatre, Haymarket, Tube: Piccadilly Circus or Leicester Square, US toll-free tel. 800-334-8457, London booking toll tel. 0844-412-2707, www.thephantomoftheopera.com).

We Will Rock You—Whether or not you're a Queen fan, this musical tribute (more to the band than to Freddie Mercury) is an understandably popular celebration of their work (£28–60, Mon–Sat 19:30, matinee Sat 14:30, Dominion Theatre, Tottenham Court Road, Tube: Tottenham Court Road, Ticketmaster toll tel. 0844-847-1775, www.queenonline.com/wewillrockyou).

Wicked—This lively prequel to *The Wizard of Oz* examines how the Witch of the West met Glinda the Good Witch, and later became so, you know...(£15–62.50, Mon–Sat 19:30, matinee Wed and Sat 14:30, Apollo Victoria Theatre, just east of Victoria Station, Tube: Victoria, Ticketmaster toll tel. 0844-826-8000, www.wickedthemusical.co.uk).

Shakespeare's Globe: To see Shakespeare in a replica of the theater for which he wrote his plays, attend a play at the Globe. In this round, thatch-roofed, open-air theater the plays are performed much as Shakespeare intended—under the sky with no amplification.

The play's the thing from late April through early October (usually Mon 19:30, Tue–Sat 14:00 and 19:30, Sun either 13:00 and/or 18:30, tickets can be sold out months in advance). You'll pay £5 to stand and £15–35 to sit, usually on a backless bench. Because only a few rows and the pricier Gentlemen's Rooms have seats with backs, £1 cushions and £3 add-on back rests are considered a good investment by many. Dress for the weather. The £5 "groundling" tickets—which are open to rain—are most fun. Scurry in early to stake out a spot on the stage's edge, where the most interaction with the actors occurs. You're a crude peasant. You can lean your elbows on the stage, munch a picnic dinner (yes, you can bring in food), or walk around. I've never enjoyed Shakespeare as much as here, performed as it was meant to be in the "wooden O." If you can't get a ticket, consider waiting around. Plays can be long, and many groundlings leave before the end. Hang around outside and beg or buy a ticket from someone leaving early (groundlings are allowed to come and go). A few non-Shakespeare plays are also presented each year.

To reserve tickets for plays, call or drop by the theater box office (Mon–Sat 10:00–18:00, Sun 10:00–17:00, open one hour later on performance days, New Globe Walk entrance, no extra charge to book by phone, tel. 020/7401-9919). You can also reserve online (www.shakespeares-globe.org, £2 booking fee). If the tickets are sold out, don't despair; a few often free up at the last minute. Try calling around noon the day of the performance to see if the box office expects any returned tickets. If so, they'll advise you to show up a little more than an hour before the show, when these tickets are sold (first-come, first-served).

The theater is on the South Bank, directly across the Thames over the Millennium Bridge from St. Paul's Cathedral (Tube: Mansion House or London Bridge). The Globe is inconvenient for public transport, but the courtesy phone in the lobby lets you get a minicab in minutes. (These minicabs have set fees—e.g., £8 to South Kensington—but generally cost less than a metered cab and provide fine and honest service.) During theater season, there's a regular supply of black cabs outside the main foyer on New Globe Walk.

Outdoor Theater in Summer: Enjoy Shakespearean drama and other plays under the stars at the Open Air Theatre, in leafy Regent's Park in north London. Food is allowed: You can bring your own picnic; order à la carte from the theater menu; or pre-order a £22.50 picnic supper from the theater at least 36 hours in advance (tickets £12–50; season runs late May–mid-Sept, box office open April–late May Mon–Sat 10:00–18:00, closed Sun; late May–mid-Sept Mon–Sat 10:00–20:00, Sun 10:00–until start of play on performance days only; order tickets online after mid-Jan or by phone Mon–Sun 9:00–21:00; £1 booking fee by phone, no fee if ordering online or in person; toll tel. 0844-826-4242, www.openairtheatre.org; grounds open 1.5 hours prior to evening performances, one hour prior to 14:30 matinee, and 30 minutes prior to earlier matinees; 10-minute walk north of Baker Street Tube, near Queen Mary's Gardens within Regent's Park; detailed directions and more info at www.openairtheatre.org).

Fringe Theater: London's rougher evening-entertainment scene is thriving, filling pages in *Time Out*. Choose from a wide range of fringe theater and comedy acts (generally £5).

Classical Music

Concerts at Churches—For easy, cheap, or free concerts in historic churches, ask the TI (or check *Time Out*) about **lunch concerts,** especially:

- St. Bride's Church, with free lunch concerts twice a week at 13:15 (generally Tue, Wed, or Fri—confirm by phone or online, church tel. 020/7427-0133, www.stbrides.com).
- St. James's at Piccadilly, with 50-minute concerts on Monday, Wednesday, and Friday at 13:10 (suggested £3.50 donation, info tel. 020/7381-0441, www.st-james-piccadilly.org).
- St. Martin-in-the-Fields, offering free concerts on Monday, Tuesday, and Friday at 13:00 (suggested £3.50 donation, church tel. 020/7766-1100, www.smitf.org).

St. Martin-in-the-Fields also hosts fine **evening concerts** by candlelight (£6–26, several nights a week at 19:30,) and live jazz in its underground Café in the Crypt (£5.50–9 tickets, Wed at 20:00).

Evensong and Organ Recitals at Churches—Evensong services are held at several churches, including:

- St. Paul's Cathedral (Mon–Sat at 17:00, Sun at 15:15).
- Westminster Abbey (Mon–Tue and Thu–Fri at 17:00, Sat–Sun at 15:00; there's a service on Wed, but it may be spoken, not sung).
- Southwark Cathedral (Mon–Tue and Thu–Fri at 17:30, Sat at 16:00, Sun at 15:00, no service on Wed or alternate Mon, tel. 020/7367-6700, www.southwark.anglican.org/cathedral).
- St. Bride's Church (Sun at 17:30, tel. 020/7427-0133, www .stbrides.com).

Free **organ recitals** are often held on Sunday at 17:45 in Westminster Abbey (30 minutes, tel. 020/7222-5152). Many other churches have free concerts; ask for the *London Organ Concerts Guide* at the TI.

Prom Concerts, Opera, and Dance—For a fun classical event (mid-July–mid-Sept), attend a **Prom Concert** (shortened from "Promenade Concert") during the annual festival at the Royal Albert Hall. Nightly concerts are offered at give-a-peasant-some-culture prices to "Promenaders"—those willing to stand throughout the performance (£5 standing-room spots sold at the door, £7 restricted-view seats, most £20–54 but depends on performance, Tube: South Kensington, toll tel. 0845-401-5045, www.bbc.co.uk/proms).

Some of the world's best **opera** is belted out at the prestigious Royal Opera House, near Covent Garden (box office tel. 020/7304-4000, www.roh.org.uk), and at the London Coliseum (English National Opera, St. Martin's Lane, Tube: Leicester Square, box office toll tel. 0871-911-0200, www.eno.org).

For **dance,** try Sadler's Wells Theatre (Rosebery Avenue, Islington, Tube: Angel, info tel. 020/7863-8198, box office toll tel. 0844-412-4300, www.sadlerswells.com).

Other Nightlife

Evening Museum Visits—Many museums are open an evening or two during the week, offering fewer crowds. See a list on page 94.

Tours—Guided walks are offered several times a day. **London Walks** is the most established company. Daytime walks vary by theme: ancient London, museums, legal London, Dickens, Beatles, Jewish quarter, Christopher Wren, and so on. In the evening, expect a more limited choice: ghosts, Jack the Ripper, pubs, or literary-themed. Get the latest from their brochure or website, or call for a recorded listing of that day's walks. Show up at the listed time and place, pay the guide, and enjoy the two-hour tour (£8, cash only, tel. 020/7624-3978, recorded info tel. 020/7624-9255, www.walks.com).

To see the city illuminated at night, consider a bus tour. A two-hour **London by Night Sightseeing Tour** leaves every evening from Victoria Station and other points (see page 66).

Summer Evenings Along the South Bank—If you're visiting London in summer, consider the South Bank.

Take a trip around the **London Eye** while the sun sets over the city (the wheel spins until late—last ascent at 21:30 July–Aug, 21:00 in June and Sept). Then cap your night with an evening walk along the pedestrian-only **Jubilee Walkway,** which runs east–west along the river. It's where Londoners go to escape the heat. This pleasant stretch of the walkway—lined with pubs and casual eateries—goes from the London Eye past Shakespeare's Globe to Tower Bridge (you can walk in either direction).

If you're in the mood for a movie, take in a flick at the **BFI Southbank,** located just across the river, alongside Waterloo Bridge. Run by the British Film Institute, the state-of-the-art theater shows mostly classic films, as well as art cinema (£9, £5 on Tue and weekday matinees, Tube: Waterloo or Embankment, box office tel. 020/7928-3232, check www.bfi.org.uk for schedules).

Farther east along the South Bank is **The Scoop**—an outdoor amphitheater next to City Hall. It's a good spot for outdoor movies, concerts, dance, and theater productions throughout the summer—with Tower Bridge as a scenic backdrop. These events are free, nearly nightly, and family-friendly. For the latest event schedule, see www.morelondon.com and click on "The Scoop" (next to City Hall, Riverside, The Queen's Walkway, Tube: London Bridge).

Cruises—During the summer, boats sail as late as 19:00 between Westminster Pier (near Big Ben) and the Tower of London. (For details, see page 74.)

A handful of outfits run Thames River evening cruises with four-course meals and dancing. **London Showboat** offers the best value (£75, April–Oct Wed–Sun, March and Nov–Dec Thu–Sat, Jan–Feb Fri–Sat, 3.5 hours, departs at 19:30 from Westminster Pier and returns by 23:00, reservations necessary, tel. 020/7740-0400, www.citycruises.com). Dinner cruises are also offered by **Bateaux London** (£75–125, tel. 020/7695-1800, www.bateauxlondon.com). For more on cruising, get the *River Thames Boat Services* brochure from a London TI.

Sleeping in London

London is an expensive city for rooms. Cheaper rooms are relatively dumpy. Don't expect £130 cheeriness in an £80 room. For £70, you'll get a double with breakfast in a safe, cramped, and dreary place with minimal service and the bathroom down the hall. For £90, you'll get a basic, clean, reasonably cheery double in a usually cramped, cracked-plaster building with a private bath, or a soulless but comfortable room without breakfast in a huge Motel 6–type place. My London splurges, at £160–260, are spacious, thoughtfully appointed places good for entertaining or romancing. Off-season, it's possible to save money by arriving late without a reservation and looking around. Competition softens prices, especially for multinight stays. Check hotel websites for special deals. Remember, all of Britain's accommodations are now non-smoking.

Looking for Hotel Deals Online

Given London's high hotel prices, consider using the Internet to help score a hotel deal. Various websites list rooms in high-rise, three- and four-star business hotels. You'll give up the charm and warmth of a family-run establishment, and breakfast will probably not be included, but you might find that the price is right.

Start by checking the websites of several chains to get an idea of typical rates and to check for online-only deals. Big London hotel chains include the following: Millennium/ Copthorne (www.millenniumhotels.com), Thistle (www.thistle .com), Intercontinental/Holiday Inn (www.ichotelsgroup.com), Radisson (www.radisson.com), Hilton (www.hilton.com), and

London's Hotel Neighborhoods

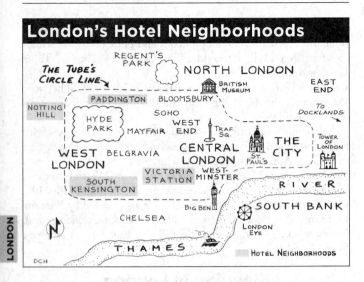

THE TUBE'S CIRCLE LINE

REGENT'S PARK

NORTH LONDON

EAST END

BRITISH MUSEUM

NOTTING HILL

PADDINGTON

BLOOMSBURY

To DOCKLANDS

HYDE PARK

SOHO

WEST END

MAYFAIR

TRAF. SQ.

WEST LONDON

BELGRAVIA

CENTRAL LONDON

ST. PAUL'S

THE CITY

TOWER OF LONDON

SOUTH KENSINGTON

VICTORIA STATION

WEST-MINSTER

R I V E R

CHELSEA

BIG BEN

SOUTH BANK

London Eye

N

T H A M E S

Hotel Neighborhoods

DCH

LONDON

Red Carnation (www.redcarnationhotels.com). For information on no-frills, Motel 6–type chains, see "Big, Good-Value, Modern Hotels," later.

Auction-type sites (such as www.priceline.com or www.hotwire.com) can be great for matching flexible travelers with empty hotel rooms, often at prices well below the hotel's normal rates.

Other favorite accommodation discount sites mentioned by my readers include www.londontown.com (an informative site with a discount booking service), http://athomeinlondon.co.uk and www.londonbb.com (both list central B&Bs), www.lastminute.com, www.visitlondon.com, http://roomsnet.com, and www.eurocheapo.com. Read candid reviews of London hotels at www.tripadvisor.com. And check the "Graffiti Wall" at www.ricksteves.com for the latest tips and discoveries.

For a good overview on finding London hotel deals, go to www.smartertravel.com and click on "Travel Guides," then "London."

Victoria Station Neighborhood (Belgravia)

The streets behind Victoria Station teem with little, moderately-priced-for-London B&Bs. It's a safe, surprisingly tidy, and decent area without a hint of the trashy, touristy glitz of the streets in front of the station. I've divided these accommodations into two broad categories: west or east of

Sleep Code

(£1 = about $1.60, country code: 44, area code: 020)
S = Single, **D** = Double/Twin, **T** = Triple, **Q** = Quad, **b** = bathroom,
s = shower only. Unless otherwise noted, credit cards are
accepted and prices include breakfast.

To help you sort through these listings easily, I've divided
the rooms into three categories, based on the price for a
double room with bath:

$$$ Higher Priced—Most rooms £115 or more.
  $$ Moderately Priced—Most rooms between £70-115.
    $ Lower Priced—Most rooms £70 or less.

Prices can change without notice; verify the hotel's
current rates online or by email. For other updates, see www
.ricksteves.com/update.

---

the station. Decent eateries abound in both areas (see page 175).
All the recommended hotels are within a five-minute walk of the
Victoria Tube, bus, and train stations. On hot summer nights,
request a quiet back room.

Near the hotels on the west side is the 400-space Semley
Place NCP **parking garage** (£32/day, possible discounts with hotel
voucher, just west of the Victoria Coach Station at Buckingham
Palace Road and Semley Place, toll tel. 0845-050-7080, www
.ncp.co.uk). The best laundry options are on the east side: The
handy **Pimlico Launderette** is about five blocks southwest of
Warwick Square (daily 8:00–19:00, self- or full service, south of
Sutherland Street at 3 Westmoreland Terrace, tel. 020/7821-8692),
and **Launderette Centre** is a block northeast of Warwick Square
(Mon–Fri 8:00–22:00, Sat 8:00–20:00, Sun 9:00–20:00, last wash
2 hours before closing, about £7 wash and dry, £9 full-service, 31
Churton Street, tel. 020/7828-6039).

West of Victoria Station
Here in Belgravia, the prices are a bit higher and your neighbors include Andrew Lloyd Webber and Margaret Thatcher (her
policeman stands outside 73 Chester Square). All of these places
line up along tranquil Ebury Street, two blocks over from Victoria
Station.

$$$ Lime Tree Hotel, enthusiastically run by Charlotte and
Matt, comes with 25 spacious, stylish, comfortable, thoughtfully
decorated rooms and a fun-loving breakfast room (Sb-£85–95,
Db-£120–140, larger superior Db-£140–160, Tb-£150–185, fam-
ily room-£170–200, free Internet access and Wi-Fi, small lounge

Victoria Station Neighborhood

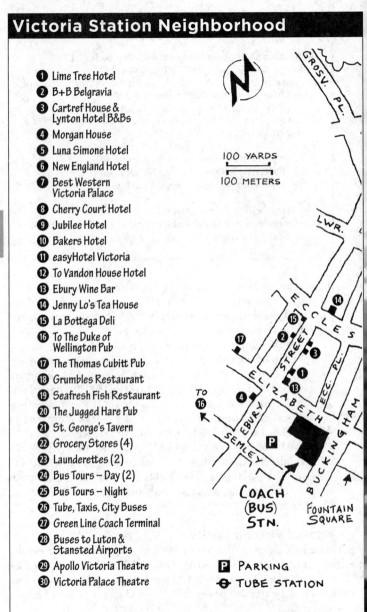

1. Lime Tree Hotel
2. B+B Belgravia
3. Cartref House & Lynton Hotel B&Bs
4. Morgan House
5. Luna Simone Hotel
6. New England Hotel
7. Best Western Victoria Palace
8. Cherry Court Hotel
9. Jubilee Hotel
10. Bakers Hotel
11. easyHotel Victoria
12. To Vandon House Hotel
13. Ebury Wine Bar
14. Jenny Lo's Tea House
15. La Bottega Deli
16. To The Duke of Wellington Pub
17. The Thomas Cubitt Pub
18. Grumbles Restaurant
19. Seafresh Fish Restaurant
20. The Jugged Hare Pub
21. St. George's Tavern
22. Grocery Stores (4)
23. Launderettes (2)
24. Bus Tours – Day (2)
25. Bus Tours – Night
26. Tube, Taxis, City Buses
27. Green Line Coach Terminal
28. Buses to Luton & Stansted Airports
29. Apollo Victoria Theatre
30. Victoria Palace Theatre

100 YARDS
100 METERS

P PARKING
⊖ TUBE STATION

GROSV. PL.

LWR.

ECCLES

STREET

ELIZABETH

ECC. PL.

EBURY

SEMLEY

BUCKINGHAM

TO 16

P

COACH (BUS) STN.

FOUNTAIN SQUARE

LONDON

LONDON

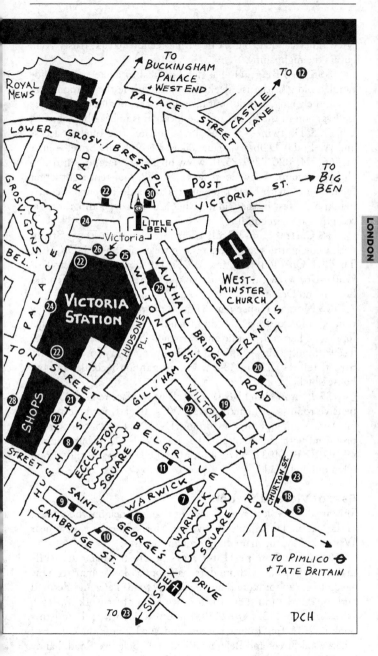

opens onto quiet garden, 135 Ebury Street, tel. 020/7730-8191, www.limetreehotel.co.uk, info@limetreehotel.co.uk, trusty Alan covers the night shift).

$$$ B+B Belgravia has done its best to make a tight-and-tangled old guesthouse sleek and mod. While the 17 rooms are small, the young, can-do staff takes good care of guests, the coffee is always on in the lobby, and the location is unbeatable (Sb-£99, Db-£125, Db twin-£135, Tb-£155, Qb-£165, free Internet access and Wi-Fi, DVD library, loaner bikes, 64–66 Ebury Street—enter at #66, tel. 020/7259-8570, www.bb-belgravia.com, info@bb-belgravia.com). A few doors down, at #82, they rent eight larger "apartments" with basic kitchenettes and a do-it-yourself continental breakfast in the fridge (Db-£120–160 depending on size, reception at main building).

$$ Cartref House B&B offers rare charm on Ebury Street, with 10 delightful rooms and a warm welcome (Sb-£73, Db-£102, Tb-£133, Qb-£164, fans, free Wi-Fi, 129 Ebury Street, tel. 020/7730-6176, www.cartrefhouse.co.uk, info@cartrefhouse.co.uk, Sharon and Derek).

$$ Morgan House rents 11 good rooms and is entertainingly run, with lots of travel tips and friendly chat from owner Rachel Joplin and her staff, Danilo and Fernanda (S-£58, D-£78, Db-£98, T-£98, family suites-£138–148 for 3–4 people, Wi-Fi, 120 Ebury Street, tel. 020/7730-2384, www.morganhouse.co.uk, morgan house@btclick.com).

$$ Lynton Hotel B&B is a well-worn place renting 13 inexpensive rooms with small prefab WCs. It's a fine value run by brothers Mark and Simon Connor (D-£80, Db-£95, these prices promised with this book in 2011, free Wi-Fi, 113 Ebury Street, tel. 020/7730-4032, www.lyntonhotel.co.uk, mark-and-simon @lyntonhotel.co.uk).

East of Victoria Station

This area is a bit less genteel-feeling than the neighborhood west of the station, but still plenty inviting. Most of these are on or near Warwick Way, the main drag through this area.

$$ Luna Simone Hotel rents 36 fresh, spacious, well-maintained rooms with modern bathrooms. It's a smartly managed place, run for more than 40 years by twins Peter and Bernard and son Mark, and they still seem to enjoy their work (Sb-£70, Db-£100, Tb-£120, Qb-£150, these prices with cash and this book in 2011, free Internet access and Wi-Fi, near the corner of Charlwood Street and Belgrave Road at 47 Belgrave Road, handy bus #24 to Victoria Station and Trafalgar Square stops out front, tel. 020/7834-5897, www.lunasimonehotel.com, stay@lunasimone hotel.com).

$$ New England Hotel, run by Jay and the Patel family, has slightly worn but well-priced rooms in a tight old corner building (small Sb-£59, Db-£89, Tb-£109, Qb-£119, pay Internet access and Wi-Fi, 20 Saint George's Drive, tel. 020/7834-1595, fax 020/7834-9000, www.newenglandhotel.com, stay@newenglandhotel.com).

$$ Best Western Victoria Palace offers modern business-class comfort compared with the other creaky old hotels listed here. Choose between the 43 rooms in the main building (Db-£120, includes breakfast, elevator, 60-64 Warwick Way), or 22 rooms in the annex a half-block away (Db-£89, breakfast-£8.50, no elevator, 17 Belgrave Road, reception at main building); both have been recently renovated (air-con, free Wi-Fi, tel. 020/7821-7113, fax 020/7630-0806, www.bestwesternvictoriapalace.co.uk, info @bestwesternvictoriapalace.co.uk).

$ Cherry Court Hotel, run by the friendly and industrious Patel family, rents 12 very small but bright and well-designed rooms in a central location (Sb-£50, Db-£55, Tb-£80, Qb-£95, Quint/b-£110, these prices are promised with this book through 2011, 5 percent fee to pay with credit card, fruit-basket breakfast in room, air-con, free Internet access and Wi-Fi, laundry, peaceful garden patio, 23 Hugh Street, tel. 020/7828-2840, fax 020/7828-0393, www.cherrycourthotel.co.uk, info@cherrycourthotel .co.uk).

$ Jubilee Hotel is a well-run slumbermill with 24 tiny rooms and many tiny beds. It's a bit musty and its windows only open a few inches, but the price is right (S-£39–45, Sb-£59–65, tiny D-£55–59, Db-£69–79, Tb-£79–95, Qb-£99–109, higher prices are for Fri–Sun, ask for the 5 percent Rick Steves discount when booking, pay Internet access and Wi-Fi, 31 Eccleston Square, tel. 020/7834-0845, www.jubileehotel.co.uk, stay@jubileehotel.co.uk, Bob Patel).

$ Bakers Hotel is a well-worn cheapie, with 11 tight rooms, but it's conveniently located and offers near-youth-hostel prices and a small breakfast (S-£40, D-£55, Db-£65, T-£65, Tb-£75, family room-£85, less for longer stays and on weeknights, pay Wi-Fi, 126 Warwick Way, tel. 020/7834-0729, www.bakershotel.co.uk, reservations@bakershotel.co.uk, Amin Jamani).

$ easyHotel Victoria, at 36 Belgrave Road, is part of the budget chain described on page 162.

"South Kensington," She Said, Loosening His Cummerbund

To stay on a quiet street so classy it doesn't allow hotel signs, surrounded by trendy shops and colorful restaurants, call "South Ken" your London home. Shoppers like being a short walk from Harrods and the designer shops of King's Road and Chelsea. When I

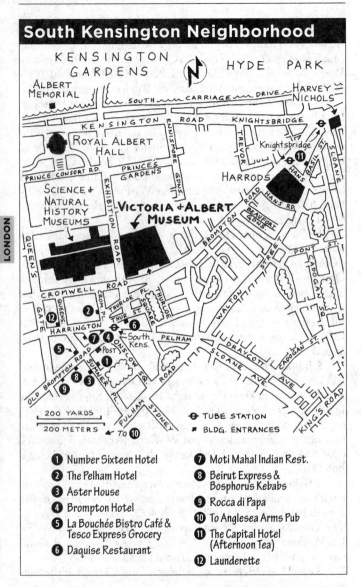

South Kensington Neighborhood

KENSINGTON GARDENS

HYDE PARK

ALBERT MEMORIAL

SOUTH CARRIAGE DRIVE

HARVEY NICHOLS

KENSINGTON ROAD

KNIGHTSBRIDGE

ROYAL ALBERT HALL

Knightsbridge ⊖ ❶❶

PRINCE CONSORT RD.

PRINCE'S GARDENS

HARRODS

SCIENCE & NATURAL HISTORY MUSEUMS

VICTORIA & ALBERT MUSEUM

ENNISMORE GDNS.

TREVOR

BASIL ST.

SLOANE ST.

HANS RD.

BEAUFORT GDNS.

BROMPTON ROAD

HANS ST.

PON ST.

CADOGAN

EXHIBITION ROAD

QUEEN'S GATE

CROMWELL ROAD

CROM. PL.

THURLOE PL.

THURLOE SQUARE

WALTON STREET

CADOGAN ST.

❶❷ HARRINGTON

❷

THUR. ST.

❻

⊖ South Kens.

PELHAM

DRAYCOTT AVE.

❺

❼ ❹

QUEEN'S

Post ⊖

ONSLOW SQ.

SLOANE AVE.

CADOGAN ST.

❽ ❸

SUMNER PL.

❶

ROAD

❾

OLD BROMPTON ROAD

FULHAM ROAD

SYDNEY

KING'S ROAD

200 YARDS

200 METERS ← TO ❿

⊖ TUBE STATION

❋ BLDG. ENTRANCES

❶ Number Sixteen Hotel
❷ The Pelham Hotel
❸ Aster House
❹ Brompton Hotel
❺ La Bouchée Bistro Café & Tesco Express Grocery
❻ Daquise Restaurant
❼ Moti Mahal Indian Rest.
❽ Beirut Express & Bosphorus Kebabs
❾ Rocca di Papa
❿ To Anglesea Arms Pub
❶❶ The Capital Hotel (Afternoon Tea)
❶❷ Launderette

splurge, I splurge here. Sumner Place is just off Old Brompton Road, 200 yards from the handy South Kensington Tube station (on Circle Line, two stops from Victoria Station; and on Piccadilly Line, direct from Heathrow). There's a handy **launderette** on the corner of Queensberry Place and Harrington Road (Mon–Fri 7:30–21:00, Sat 9:00–20:00, Sun 10:00–19:00, bring 50p and £1 coins).

$$$ Number Sixteen, for well-heeled travelers, packs over-the-top formality and class into its 42 rooms, plush lounges, and tranquil garden. It's in a labyrinthine building, with modern decor—perfect for an urban honeymoon (Db-from £200—but soft, ask for discounted "seasonal rates," especially on weekends and in Aug—subject to availability, does not include 20 percent VAT, breakfast buffet in the garden-£17, elevator, 16 Sumner Place, tel. 020/7589-5232, fax 020/7584-8615, US tel. 800-553-6674, www.firmdalehotels.com, sixteen@firmdale.com).

$$$ The Pelham Hotel, a 52-room business-class hotel with a pricey mix of pretense and style, is not quite sure which investment company owns it. It's genteel, with low lighting and a pleasant drawing room among the many perks (Db-£180–260, breakfast extra, does not include 20 percent VAT, lower prices Aug and weekends, Web specials can include free breakfast, air-con, elevator, free Internet access, pay Wi-Fi, gym, 15 Cromwell Place, tel. 020/7589-8288, fax 020/7584-8444, US tel. 1-888-757-5587, www.pelhamhotel.co.uk, reservations@pelhamhotel.co.uk).

$$$ Aster House, run by friendly and accommodating Simon and Leonie Tan, has a cheerful lobby, lounge, and breakfast room. Its rooms are comfy and quiet, with TV, phone, and air-conditioning. Enjoy breakfast or just lounging in the whisper-elegant Orangery, a Victorian greenhouse. Simon and Leonie offer free loaner mobile phones to their guests (Sb-£120, Db-£180, bigger Db-£225, rates do not include 20 percent VAT, 20 percent discount with this book through 2011 if you book three or more nights, 25 percent off for five or more nights, additional 5 percent off with cash, check website for specials, free Wi-Fi, 3 Sumner Place, tel. 020/7581-5888, fax 020/7584-4925, www.asterhouse.com, asterhouse@btinternet.com).

$$ Brompton Hotel is a humble, borderline-dreary place with 17 rooms above a jumble of cafés and clubs. There's a noisy bar and some street noise, so ask for a room in the back if you want quiet. It has old carpets and no public spaces, and they serve breakfast in your room. In spite of all this, it's cheap for London and very well-located (Sb-£85, Db-£90, Tb-£130, "deluxe" rooms are just like the others but with a tub, save a little by booking via their website, includes continental breakfast, Wi-Fi, across from the South Kensington Tube station at 30 Brompton Road, tel. 020/7584-4517, fax 020/7823-9936, www.bromhotel.com, book@bromhotel.com).

Notting Hill and Bayswater Neighborhoods

Residential Notting Hill has quick bus and Tube access to downtown, and, for London, is very "homely" (Brit-speak for cozy). It's also peppered with trendy bars and restaurants, and is home to the

Notting Hill & Bayswater Neighborhoods

⊖ TUBE STN.

1/4 MILE

400 METERS

SATURDAY MARKET

KENSINGTON GARDENS SQUARE

Post

TO PADDINGTON STATION

Bayswater

Queensway

TO MARBLE ARCH

Notting Hill Gate

KENSINGTON GARDENS

PLAY-GROUND

KENSINGTON PALACE

HOLLAND PARK

High Street Kensington

❶ Phoenix Hotel
❷ Vancouver Studios
❸ Kensington Gardens Hotel
❹ Princes Square Guest Accommodation
❺ Westland Hotel
❻ London Vicarage Hotel
❼ The Gate Hotel
❽ To Norwegian YWCA
❾ Maggie Jones Restaurant

❿ The Churchill Arms Pub & Thai Kitchens
⓫ The Prince Edward Pub
⓬ Café Diana
⓭ Royal China Restaurant
⓮ Whiteleys Mall (Food Court, Grocery, Internet)
⓯ Tesco Grocery
⓰ Spar Market
⓱ The Orangery (Afternoon Tea)
⓲ Launderette

LONDON

famous Portobello Road Market (see page 134).

Popular with young international travelers, Bayswater's Queensway street is a multicultural festival of commerce and eateries. The neighborhood does its dirty clothes at **Galaxy Launderette** (£6 self-service, £8–10 full-service, daily 8:00–20:00, staff on hand with soap and coins, 65 Moscow Road, at corner of St. Petersburgh Place and Moscow Road, tel. 020/7229-7771). For **Internet access,** you'll find several stops along busy Queensway, and a self-serve bank of computer terminals on the food circus level—third floor—of Whiteleys Shopping Centre (daily 8:30–24:00, corner of Queensway and Porchester Gardens).

Near Kensington Gardens Square

Several big, old hotels line the quiet Kensington Gardens Square (not to be confused with the much bigger Kensington Gardens adjacent to Hyde Park), a block west of bustling Queensway, north of Bayswater Tube station. These hotels are quiet for central London, but the area feels a bit sterile, and (aside from Vancouver Studios) the hotels here tend to be quite impersonal.

$$$ Vancouver Studios offers 45 modern rooms with fully equipped kitchenettes (utensils, stove, microwave, and fridge) rather than breakfast (Sb-£89, Db-£130, Tb-£170, extra bed-£20, can be more at busy times, 10 percent discount for week-long stay or more, pay Internet access, free Wi-Fi, welcoming lounge and wonderful garden, near Kensington Gardens Square at 30 Prince's Square, tel. 020/7243-1270, fax 020/7221-8678, www.vancouver studios.co.uk, info@vancouverstudios.co.uk).

$$ Phoenix Hotel, a Best Western modernization of a 125-room hotel, offers American business-class comforts; spacious, plush public spaces; and big, fresh, modern-feeling rooms. Its prices—which range from fine value to rip-off—are determined by a greedy computer program, with huge variations according to expected demand. Book online to save money (flexible prices, but usually Sb-£65, Db-£90, elevator, free Wi-Fi, 1–8 Kensington Gardens Square, tel. 020/7229-2494, fax 020/7727-1419, US tel. 800-528-1234, www.phoenixhotel.co.uk, info@phoenixhotel .co.uk).

$$ Kensington Gardens Hotel, an annex of Phoenix Hotel down the street (see above), laces 17 pleasant rooms together in a tall, skinny building with lots of stairs and no elevator (Ss-£57, Sb-£64, Db-£86, Tb-£105; book by phone or email for these special Rick Steves prices, rather than through the pricier website; continental breakfast served at Phoenix Hotel, free Wi-Fi, 9 Kensington Gardens Square, tel. 020/7243-7600, fax 020/7792-8612, www.kensingtongardenshotel.co.uk, info@kensingtongardens hotel.co.uk, Rowshanak).

$$ Princes Square Guest Accommodation is a big 50-room place that's well-located, practical, and a good value, especially with its online discounts (Sb-£50–60, Db-£60–80, Tb-£80–100, elevator, pay Wi-Fi, 23–25 Princes Square, tel. 020/7229-9876, www.princessquarehotel.co.uk, info@princessquarehotel.co.uk).

Near Kensington Gardens

$$$ Westland Hotel, conveniently located on a busy street a five-minute walk from the Notting Hill neighborhood, feels like a wood-paneled hunting lodge with a fine lounge. The 32 spacious rooms are comfortable, with old-fashioned charm. Their £130 doubles are the best value, but check their website for specials. It's been run by the Isseyegh family for three generations (Sb-£110, deluxe Sb-£124, Db-£130, deluxe Db-£152, cavernous premier Db-£172, sprawling Tb-£165–193, gargantuan Qb-£186–220, Quint/b-£234, 10 percent discount on your first-time stay in 2011 if you book direct and show the current edition of this book on arrival, discount not valid for e-books, elevator, pay Wi-Fi, garage-£12/day, between Notting Hill Gate and Queensway Tube stations at 154 Bayswater Road, tel. 020/7229-9191, fax 020/7727-1054, www.westlandhotel .co.uk, reservations@westlandhotel.co.uk, Shirley and Bertie).

$$$ London Vicarage Hotel is family-run, understandably popular, and elegantly British in a quiet, classy neighborhood. It has 17 rooms furnished with taste and quality, a TV lounge, a grand staircase, and facilities on each floor. Mandy and Monika maintain a homey atmosphere (S-£56, Sb-£95, D-£95, Db-£125, T-£120, Tb-£160, Q-£130, Qb-£176, 20 percent less in winter— check website, free Wi-Fi; 8-minute walk from Notting Hill Gate and High Street Kensington Tube stations, near Kensington Palace at 10 Vicarage Gate; tel. 020/7229-4030, fax 020/7792-5989, www .londonvicaragehotel.com, vicaragehotel@btconnect.com).

$$ The Gate Hotel has seven cramped, tired rooms on a delightful curved street near the start of the Portobello Road Market, in the heart of the characteristic Notting Hill neighborhood. While the lodgings are basic, the location is wonderful (Sb-£60, Db-£85, bigger "luxury" Db-£95, Tb-£115, each room £10 more Fri-Sat, 5 percent more if paying with credit card, continental breakfast in room, no elevator, pay Wi-Fi, 6 Portobello Road, Tube: Noting Hill Gate, tel. 020/7221-0707, fax 020/7221-9128, www.gatehotel.co.uk, bookings@gatehotel.co.uk, Jasmine).

Near Holland Park

$ Norwegian YWCA (Norsk K.F.U.K.)—where English is definitely a second language—is open to any Norwegian woman, and to non-Norwegian women under 30. (Men must be under 30 with a Norwegian passport.) Located on a quiet, stately street, it offers a study, TV room, piano lounge, and an open-face Norwegian ambience (goat cheese on Sundays!). They have mostly quads, so those willing to share with strangers are most likely to get a bed (July–Aug: Ss-£37.50, shared double-£36.50/bed, shared triple-£31.50/bed, shared quad-£28/bed, includes breakfast year-round plus sack lunch and dinner Sept–June, £20 key deposit and £2 membership fee required, pay Wi-Fi, 52 Holland Park, Tube: Holland Park, tel. 020/7727-9346 or 020/7727-9897, www.kfukhjemmet.org.uk, kontor@kfukhjemmet.org.uk). With each visit, I wonder which is easier to get—a sex change or a Norwegian passport?

Paddington Station Neighborhood

The neighborhood near Paddington Station—while a bit less charming than the other areas I've recommended—is pleasant enough, and very convenient to the Heathrow Express airport train. The area is flanked by the Paddington and Lancaster Gate Tube stops. Most of my recommendations circle Norfolk Square, just two blocks in front of Paddington Station, yet still quiet and comfortable. Its main drag, London Street, is lined with handy eateries—pubs, Indian, Italian, Greek, Lebanese, and more—plus convenience stores and an Internet café. To reach this area, exit the station toward Praed Street (with your back to the tracks, it's to the left). Once outside, continue straight across Praed Street and down London Street; Norfolk Square is a block ahead on the left.

On Norfolk Square

These places (and many more on the same street) are essentially interchangeable; all offer small rooms at a reasonable price, in tall buildings with lots of stairs and no elevator. I've chosen the ones that offer the most reasonable prices and the warmest welcome.

$$ St. David's Hotels, run by the hospitable Neokleous family, has 60 tight rooms in several adjacent buildings (S-£60, Sb-£70, D-£70, Db-£90, Tb-£100, free Wi-Fi, 14–20 Norfolk Square, tel. 020/7723-3856, fax 020/7402-9061, www.stdavids hotels.com, info@stdavidshotels.com).

$$ Tudor Court Hotel has 38 rooms run by the Gupta family (S-£39, Sb-£82, Db-£89, Tb-£108, family room-£132, 10–12 Norfolk Square, tel. 020/7723-5157, fax 020/7723-0727, www .tudorcourtpaddington.co.uk, reservations@tudorcourtpaddington .co.uk).

$$ Falcon Hotel has 19 small rooms wrapped around a tight staircase (S-£50, Sb-£55, D-£69, Db-£75, pay Wi-Fi, 11 Norfolk Square, tel. 020/7723-8603, fax 020/7402-7009, www.falcon-hotel .com, info@falcon-hotel.com).

$$ Ashley Hotel, next door, is a classic old place with 54 rooms (S-£35–40, Sb-£50–60, Db-£70–80, pay Wi-Fi, 15-17 Norfolk

Square, tel. 020/7723-3375, fax 020/7723-0173, www.ashleyhotel
london.com, info@ashleyhotellondon.com).

$ easyHotel, the budget chain described on page 162, has a
branch at 10 Norfolk Place.

Elsewhere near Paddington Station

To reach these hotels, follow the earlier Paddington Station directions, but continue past Norfolk Square to the big intersection
with Sussex Gardens; the Royal Park is to the right, and Springfield Hotel is immediately to the left.

$$$ The Royal Park is the neighborhood's classy splurge,
with 48 plush rooms, polished service, a genteel lounge (free
champagne for guests nightly 19:00–20:00), and all the little
extras (standard Db-£139–149, bigger "executive" Db-£169–179,
prices vary with demand and do not include 20 percent VAT or
breakfast, free Internet access and Wi-Fi, 3 Westbourne Terrace,
tel. 020/7479-6600, fax 020/7479-6601, www.theroyalpark.com,
info@theroyalpark.com).

$$ Springfield Hotel is efficiently run and old-school simple,
with 17 well-worn rooms. It sits on the wide, busy street called
Sussex Gardens (request a quieter back room), with several other
similar hotels nearby if you're in a pinch (Sb-£60, Db-£80–90,
Tb-£100, check online for deals, extra fee for paying with credit
card, 154 Sussex Gardens, tel. 020/7723-9898, fax 020/7723-0874,
www.springfieldhotellondon.co.uk, info@springfieldhotellondon
.co.uk).

Other Neighborhoods

North of Marble Arch: **$$$ The 22 York Street B&B** offers
a casual alternative in the city center, renting 10 traditional,
hardwood, comfortable rooms (Sb-£89, Db-£120, free Internet
access and Wi-Fi, inviting lounge; from Baker Street Tube sta-
tion, walk 2 blocks down Baker Street and take a right to 22 York
Street—since there's no sign, just look for #22; tel. 020/7224-2990,
www.22yorkstreet.co.uk, mc@22yorkstreet.co.uk, energetically
run by Liz and Michael Callis).

$$$ The Sumner Hotel, renting 19 rooms in a 19th-century
Georgian townhouse, is located a few blocks north of Hyde Park
and Oxford Street, a busy shopping destination. Decorated with
fancy modern Italian furniture, this swanky place packs in all the
extras (Db-£160–190 depending on size, 20 percent discount with
this book in 2011, extra bed-£30, air-con, elevator, free Wi-Fi, 54
Upper Berkeley Street just off Edgware Road, Tube: Marble Arch,
tel. 020/7723-2244, fax 0870-705-8767, www.thesumner.com,
hotel@thesumner.com, manager Peter).

Near Buckingham Palace: **$$ Vandon House Hotel,** run by

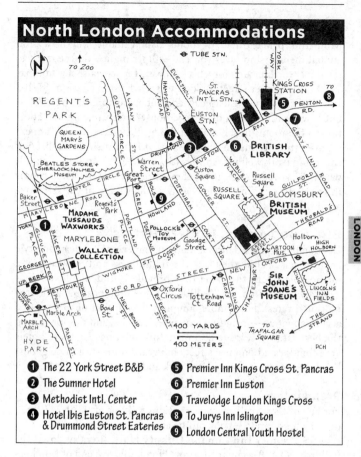

North London Accommodations

- ① The 22 York Street B&B
- ② The Sumner Hotel
- ③ Methodist Intl. Center
- ④ Hotel Ibis Euston St. Pancras & Drummond Street Eateries
- ⑤ Premier Inn Kings Cross St. Pancras
- ⑥ Premier Inn Euston
- ⑦ Travelodge London Kings Cross
- ⑧ To Jurys Inn Islington
- ⑨ London Central Youth Hostel

Central College in Iowa, is packed with students most of the year, but rents its 32 rooms to travelers from late May through August at great prices. The rooms, while institutional, are comfy, and the location is excellent (S-£46, D-£70, Db-£90, Tb-£99, Qb-£119, only twin beds, elevator, pay Internet access and Wi-Fi; 3-minute walk west of St. James's Park Tube station or 7-minute walk from Victoria Station, near west end of Petty France Street on a tiny road, 1 Vandon Street; tel. 020/7799-6780, www.vandonhouse.com, info@vandonhouse.com).

Near Euston Station and the British Library: The **$$$ Methodist International Centre (MIC),** a modern, youthful Christian hotel and conference center, fills its lower floors with international students and its top floor with travelers. The 28 rooms are modern and sleek yet comfortable, with fine bathrooms, phones, and desks. The atmosphere is friendly, safe, clean, and controlled; it also has a spacious lounge and game room (Sb-£117 on Fri–Sun, £137 on Mon–Thu; Db-£130 on Fri–Sun, £149 on Mon–Thu; pricier "deluxe" rooms also available, buying a £100 annual membership saves you £30–40 per night—do the math to see if it's worth paying for, check website for specials, elevator, pay Wi-Fi, on a quiet street a block west of Euston Station, 81–103 Euston Street—not Euston Road, Tube: Euston, tel. 020/7380-0001, www.micentre.com, reservations@micentre.com). In addition to the rooms in the main building, they have several "annex" rooms—three rooms in one house that share a single bathroom; this could work well for families (S-£85, D-£95). In June–August, when the students are gone, they also rent simpler twin rooms in the main building (S or D-£75, includes one breakfast, extra breakfast-£13).

Big, Good-Value, Modern Hotels

London has an abundance of modern, impersonal, American-style chain hotels. While they lack the friendliness and funkiness of a memorable B&B, the value they provide is undeniable; doubles generaly go for around £90–100 (or less—often possible with promotional rates). For a more complete description of this type of accommodation—including amenities, caveats, and tips for getting the best rates—see page 29 in the Introduction. As these hotels are often located on busy streets in dreary train-station neighborhoods, use common sense after dark and wear your money belt.

Premier Inn

For any of these, call their reservations toll line at 0870-242-8000 or—the best option—book online at www.premierinn.com.

$$ Premier Inn London County Hall, literally down the hall from a $400-a-night Marriott Hotel, fills one end of London's massive former County Hall building. This family-friendly place is wonderfully located near the base of the London Eye and across the Thames from Big Ben. Its 313 efficient rooms come with all the necessary comforts, though it's quite anonymous—rather than a real reception desk, you'll find self-service check-in kiosks with a couple of clerks standing by to help (Db-£109–150 for 2 adults and up to 2 kids under age 16, elevator, pay Wi-Fi, some easy-access rooms, 500 yards from Westminster Tube stop and Waterloo Station, Belvedere Road, central reservations toll tel. 0870-242-8000, reception desk toll tel. 0870-238-3300, easiest to book online at www.premierinn.com).

$$ Premier Inn London Southwark, with 59 rooms, is near Shakespeare's Globe on the South Bank (Db for up to 2 adults and 2 kids-£91–150, elevator, pay Wi-Fi, Bankside, 34 Park Street, Tube: London Bridge, toll tel. 0870-990-6402, www.premierinn.com).

$$ Premier Inn Kings Cross St. Pancras, with 276 rooms, is across the street from the east end of King's Cross Station and near the Eurostar terminus at St. Pancras Station (Db-£96–150, air-con, elevator, pay Wi-Fi, 26–30 York Way, Tube: King's Cross St. Pancras, toll tel. 0870-990-6414, www.premierinn.com).

Other **$$ Premier Inns** charging £90-150 per room include **London Euston** (big, blue Lego-type building packed with vacationing families, on handy but noisy street at corner of Euston Road and Dukes Road, Tube: Euston, toll tel. 0870-238-3301), **London Kensington Earl's Court** (11 Knaresborough Place, Tube: Earl's Court or Gloucester Road, toll tel. 0870-238-3304), **London Victoria** (82–83 Eccleston Square, Tube: Victoria, toll tel. 0870-423-6494), and **London Putney Bridge** (farther out, 3 Putney Bridge Approach, Tube: Putney Bridge, toll tel. 0870-238-3302). Avoid the **Tower Bridge** location, which is an inconvenient 15-minute walk from the nearest Tube stop.

Other Chains

Travelodge: **$$ Travelodge London Kings Cross** is another typical chain hotel with 140 cookie-cutter rooms, just 200 yards south (in front) of King's Cross Station (Db-usually £85, family rooms, can be noisy, elevator, pay Wi-Fi, Grays Inn Road, Tube: King's Cross St. Pancras, tel. 020/7278-5179). Other convenient Travelodge London locations are nearby **Kings Cross Royal Scot, Euston, Marylebone, Covent Garden, Liverpool Street,** and **Farringdon.** For details on all Travelodge hotels, see www.travelodge.co.uk.

Ibis: **$$ Hotel Ibis London Euston St. Pancras** rents 380 rooms on a quiet street a block west of Euston Station (Db-£89–149, usually £129, no family rooms, elevator, pay Internet access and Wi-Fi, 3 Cardington Street, Tube: Euston, tel. 020/7388-7777 or 020/7304-7712, fax 020/7388-0001, www.ibishotel.com, h0921@accor.com). There's also an **Ibis London City** (5 Commercial Street, Tube: Aldgate East, tel. 020/7422-8400), but the other Ibis locations are far from the center.

Jurys Inn: **$$ Jurys Inn Islington** rents 200-plus compact, comfy rooms near King's Cross Station (Db/Tb-£109–169, some discounted rooms available online, 2 adults and 2 kids under age 12 can share one room, 60 Pentonville Road, Tube: Angel, tel. 020/7282-5500, fax 020/7282-5511, www.jurysinns.com). You'll also find Jurys Inns at **Chelsea** (Imperial Road, Tube: Imperial Wharf, tel. 020/7411-2200) and near **Heathrow Airport** (see "Heathrow and Gatwick Airports," later).

easyHotel

With several hotels in good neighborhoods around London,

easyHotel is a radical concept—offering what you need to sleep well and safe, and nothing more. Most of them are fitted into old buildings, so the rooms are all odd shapes, from tiny windowless closets to others that are quite spacious. All rooms are well-ventilated and come with an efficient "bathroom pod" that looks like it was popped out of a plastic mold—just big enough to take care of business. While they do have a 24-hour reception, everything else is spartan: you get two towels, liquid soap, and a clean bed—no breakfast, no fresh towels, and no daily cleaning. The base rate ranges from £21 to £65, depending on the room size and when you book—"The earlier you book, the less you pay." Prices are the same for one person or two, but then you're nickel-and-dimed with optional charges for the TV, Wi-Fi, luggage storage, and so on.

London

If you go with the basic package, it's like hosteling with privacy—a hard-to-beat value. But you get what you pay for; in my experience, easyHotels are cheap in every sense of the word (no elevator, thin walls, noisy halls filled with loud travelers seeking bargain beds, flimsy construction that often results in broken things in the room). And they're only a good deal if you book far enough ahead to get a good price, and skip the many extras...which can add up fast. Regardless of the location, reserve through their website (www.easyhotel.com).

$ easyHotel Victoria is well-located in an old building near Victoria Station (77 rooms, 36 Belgrave Road—for location, see map on page 148, Tube: Victoria, tel. 020/7834-1379, enquiries @victoria.easyhotel.com). They also have branches at **South Kensington** (34 rooms, 14 Lexham Gardens, Tube: Earl's Court or Gloucester Road, tel. 020/7136-2870, enquiries@southken.easy hotel.com), **Earl's Court** (80 rooms, 44-48 West Cromwell Road, Tube: Earl's Court, tel. 020/7373-4546, enquiries@earlscourt.easy hotel.com), **Paddington** (47 rooms, 10 Norfolk Place, Tube: Paddington, tel. 020/7706-9911, enquiries@paddington.easy hotel.com), and **Heathrow** and **Luton** airports (Heathrow location described on page 164).

Hostels

$ London Central Youth Hostel is the flagship of London's hostels, with 300 beds and all the latest in security and comfortable efficiency. Families and travelers of any age will feel welcome in this wonderful facility. You'll pay the same price for any bed in a 4- to 8-bed single-sex dorm—with or without private bathroom—so try to grab one with a bathroom (£20–30 per bunk bed—fluctuates with demand, £3/night extra for nonmembers, breakfast-£4; includes sheets, towel and locker; families welcome to book an entire room, free Wi-Fi, members' kitchen, laundry, book long in advance, between Oxford Street and Great Portland Street Tube stations at 104 Bolsover Street, toll tel. 0870-770-6144 or 0845-371-9154, www.yha.org.uk, londoncentral@yha.org.uk).

$ St. Paul's Youth Hostel, near St. Paul's, is clean, modern, friendly, and well-run. Most of the 190 beds are in shared, single-sex 3- to 11-bunk rooms (bed-around £20 depending on demand, twin D-£60, includes locker and sheets but not breakfast, non-members pay £3 extra, cheap meals, open 24 hours, 36 Carter Lane, Tube: St. Paul's, tel. 020/7236-4965 or toll tel. 0845-371-9012, www.yha.org.uk, stpauls@yha.org.uk).

$ A cluster of three **St. Christopher's Inn** hostels, south of the Thames near London Bridge, have cheap dorm beds; one branch is for women only (£22–32, 161–165 Borough High Street, Tube: Borough or London Bridge, reservations tel. 020/8600-7500, www.st-christophers.co.uk).

Dorms

$ The **University of Westminster** opens its dorm rooms to travelers during summer break, from mid-June through late September. Located in several high-rise buildings scattered around central London, the rooms—some with private bathrooms, others with shared bathrooms nearby—come with access to well-equipped kitchens and big lounges (S-£25–35, Sb-£35–54, D-£40–60, Db-£50–95, apartment Sb-£43–71, apartment Db-£56–82, weekly rates, tel. 020/7911-5181, www.wmin.ac.uk/comserv, unilet vacations@westminster.ac.uk).

$ University College London also has rooms for travelers, from mid-June until mid-September (S-£30–32, D-£55–65, breakfast extra, pay Internet access, tel. 020/7278-3895, www.ucl.ac.uk /residences).

$ Ace Hotel, a budget hotel within four townhouses set in a residential neighborhood, has contemporary decor (£21–32 per bed in 3- to 8-bed dorms, bunk-bed D-£53–58, bunk-bed Db-£57–68, Db with patio-£105, pay Internet access, lounge and garden, 16–22 Gunterstone Road, Tube: Baron's Court or West Kensington, tel. 020/7602-6600, www.ace-hotel.co.uk, reception@ace-hotel .co.uk).

$ The **London School of Economics** has openings in its dorms from late July through September (S-£33–43, Sb-£59–65, D-£52–60, Db-£76–94, tel. 020/7955-7575, www.lsevacations .co.uk, vacations@lse.ac.uk).

Heathrow and Gatwick Airports
At or near Heathrow Airport

It's so easy to get to Heathrow from central London, I see no reason to sleep there. But if you do, here are some options. The

Yotel is actually inside the airport, while the rest are a short bus or taxi ride away. In addition to public buses, the cleverly named £4 "Hotel Hoppa" shuttle bus connects the airport to many nearby hotels (different routes serve the various hotels and terminals).

$$ Yotel, at the airport, has small sleep dens that offer a place to catch a quick nap (£37–64/4 hours), or to stay overnight (tiny "standard cabin"—£60/8 hours, "premium cabin"—£82/8 hours; cabins sleep 1–2 people; price is per cabin not person, reserve online for free or by phone for small fee). Prices vary by day, week, and time of year, so check their website. All rooms are only slightly larger than a double bed, and have private bathrooms and free Internet access and Wi-Fi. These windowless rooms have oddly purplish lighting (Heathrow Terminal 4, tel. 020/7100-1100, www.yotel.com, customer@yotel.com).

$ easyHotel, your cheapest bet, is in a low-rent residential neighborhood a £5 taxi ride from the airport. Its 53 no-frills, pod-like rooms are on two floors. Before booking at this very basic place, read the explanation on page 162 (Db-£25–45, no breakfast, no elevator, pay Internet access and Wi-Fi, Brick Field Lane; take local bus #140 from airport's Central Bus Station or the "Hotel Hoppa" #H8 from Terminals 1 or 3, or the hotel can arrange a £5 taxi to the airport; tel. 020/8897-9237, www.easyhotel.com, enquiries@heathrow.easyhotel.com).

$$ Hotel Ibis London Heathrow is a chain hotel offering predictable value (Db-£77, Db-£52 on Fri–Sun, check website for specials as low as £45, breakfast-£7, pay Internet access and Wi-Fi; 112–114 Bath Road, take local bus #105, #111, #140, #285, #423, or #555 from airport's Central Bus Station or #555 direct from Terminal 4, or the "Hotel Hoppa" #H6 from Terminals 1 or 3, or #H56 from Terminals 4 or 5; tel. 020/8759-4888, fax 020/8564-7894, www.ibishotel.com, h0794@accor.com).

$$ Jurys Inn, another hotel chain, tempts tired travelers with 300-plus cookie-cutter rooms (Db-£89–105, check website for deals, breakfast extra; on Eastern Perimeter Road, Tube: Hatton Cross plus 5-minute walk; take the Tube one stop from Terminals 1, 2, or 3; or two stops from Terminals 4 or 5; or the "Hotel Hoppa" #H9 from Terminals 1 or 3, or #H53 from Terminals 4 or 5; or buses #285, #482, #490, or #555; tel. 020/8266-4664, fax 020/8266-4665, www.jurysinns.com).

At or near Gatwick Airport

$$ Yotel, with small rooms, has a branch right at the airport (Gatwick South Terminal; see prices and contact info in Heathrow listing, earlier).

$$ Gatwick Airport Central Premier Inn rents cheap rooms 350 yards from the airport (Db-£40–75, breakfast-£8, £2 shuttle bus from airport—must reserve in advance, Longbridge Way, North Terminal, toll tel. 0871-527-8406, frustrating phone tree, www.premierinn.com). Four more Premier Inns are within a five-mile radius from the airport.

$$ Barn Cottage, a converted 16th-century barn flanked by a tennis court and swimming pool, sits in the peaceful countryside, with a good pub just two blocks away. Its two wood-beamed rooms, antique furniture, and large garden makes you forget Gatwick is 10 minutes away (S-£55, D-£75, cash only, Church Road, Leigh, Reigate, Surrey, tel. 01306/611-347, www.a1tourism.com/uk /barncott.html, warmly run by Pat and Mike Comer). Don't confuse this place with others of the same name. A taxi from Gatwick to here runs about £15; the Comers can take you back to the airport or train station for about £10.

$ Gatwick Airport Travelodge has budget rooms about two miles from the airport (Db-£39–57, breakfast extra, pay Wi-Fi, Church Road, Lowfield Heath, Crawley, £3 shuttle bus from airport, toll tel. 0871-984-6031, www.travelodge.co.uk).

Eating in London

In London, the sheer variety of foods—from every corner of its former empire and beyond—is astonishing. You'll be amazed at the number of hopping, happening new restaurants of all kinds.

If you want to dine (as opposed to eat), drop by a London newsstand to get a weekly entertainment guide or an annual restaurant guide (both have extensive restaurant listings). Visit www .london-eating.co.uk or www.squaremeal.co.uk for more options.

The thought of a £50 meal in Britain generally ruins my appetite, so my London dining is limited mostly to easygoing, fun, moderately priced alternatives. I've listed places by neighborhood—handy to your sightseeing or hotel. Considering how expensive London can be, if there's any good place to cut corners to stretch your budget, it's by eating cheaply. Pub grub (at one of London's 7,000 pubs) and ethnic restaurants (especially Indian and Chinese) are good low-cost options. Of course, picnicking is the fastest and cheapest way to go. Good grocery stores and sandwich shops, fine park benches, and polite pigeons abound in Britain's most expensive city.

Remember, London (and all of Britain) is smoke-free. Expect restaurants and pubs that sell food to be non-smoking indoors, with smokers occupying patios and doorways outside.

Central London
Near Trafalgar Square
These places are within about 100 yards of Trafalgar Square.

Central London Eateries

LONDON

1 St. Martin-in-the-Fields
  Café in the Crypt
2 The Chandos Pub's Opera Room
3 Gordon's Wine Bar
4 The Lord Moon of the Mall Pub
5 Stockpot & Woodlands South
  Indian Vegetarian Restaurant
6 West End Kitchen
7 Criterion Restaurant
8 The Wolseley

9 Joe Allen
10 Loch Fyne Fish Restaurant
11 Sofra Turkish Restaurant
12 Sitar Indian Restaurant
13 Belgo Centraal
14 Neal's Yard Eateries
15 Food for Thought Café

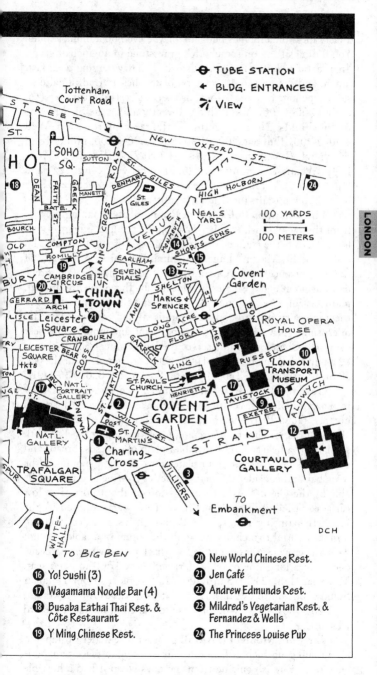

LONDON

TUBE STATION
BLDG. ENTRANCES
VIEW

Tottenham Court Road

STREET
ST.
SOHO SQ.
HO
SUTTON
DEAN
FRITH
GREEK
MANETTE
BATE.
BOURCH.
COMPTON
OLD
ROMILLY
BURY
CAMBRIDGE CIRCUS
GERRARD
ARCH
CHINA-TOWN
LISLE
Leicester Square
CRANBOURN
LEICESTER SQUARE tkts
BEAR
NAT'L. PORTRAIT GALLERY
NAT'L. GALLERY
TRAFALGAR SQUARE
SPUR
WHITE-HALL
↓ TO BIG BEN

NEW OXFORD ST.
DENMARK
GILES
ST.
ST. GILES
HIGH HOLBORN
AVENUE
CHARING CROSS
EARLHAM
SEVEN DIALS
SHELTON
LANE
GARRICK
LONG ACRE
FLORAL
KING
ST. PAUL'S CHURCH
HENRIETTA
COVENT GARDEN
Post
ST. MARTIN'S
WILL.
IV ST.
Charing Cross
VILLIERS
STRAND
TO Embankment

Neal's Yard
MONMOUTH
SHORTS GDNS.
ST. PL.
Marks & Spencer
Covent Garden
JAMES
ROYAL OPERA HOUSE
RUSSELL
LONDON TRANSPORT MUSEUM
TAVISTOCK
EXETER
ALDWYCH
COURTAULD GALLERY

100 YARDS
100 METERS

DCH

⑯ Yo! Sushi (3)
⑰ Wagamama Noodle Bar (4)
⑱ Busaba Eathai Thai Rest. & Côte Restaurant
⑲ Y Ming Chinese Rest.
⑳ New World Chinese Rest.
㉑ Jen Café
㉒ Andrew Edmunds Rest.
㉓ Mildred's Vegetarian Rest. & Fernandez & Wells
㉔ The Princess Louise Pub

St. Martin-in-the-Fields Café in the Crypt is just right for a tasty meal on a monk's budget—maybe even on a monk's tomb. You'll dine sitting on somebody's gravestone in an ancient crypt. Their enticing buffet line is kept stocked all day, serving breakfast, lunch, and dinner (£6–10 cafeteria plates, hearty traditional desserts, free jugs of water). They also serve a restful cream tea (£6, daily 14:00–17:00). You'll find it directly under the St. Martin-in-the-Fields Church, facing Trafalgar Square (Mon–Wed 8:00–20:00, Thu–Sat 8:00–21:00, Sun 11:00–18:00, profits go to the church, Tube: Charing Cross, tel. 020/7766-1158 or 020/7766-1100). Wednesday evenings at 20:00 come with a live jazz band (£6-9 tickets). While here, check out the concert schedule for the busy church upstairs (or visit www.smitf.org).

The Chandos Pub's Opera Room floats amazingly apart from the tacky crush of tourism around Trafalgar Square. Look for it opposite the National Portrait Gallery (corner of William IV Street and St. Martin's Lane) and climb the stairs (to the right of the pub entrance) to the Opera Room. This is a fine Trafalgar rendezvous point and a wonderfully local pub. They serve traditional, plain-tasting £6–7 pub meals—meat pies and fish-and-chips are their specialty. The ground-floor pub is stuffed with regulars and offers snugs (private booths), the same menu, and more serious beer drinking. Chandos proudly serves the local Samuel Smith beer at £2 a pint (kitchen open daily 11:00–19:00, order and pay at the bar, 29 St. Martin's Lane, Tube: Leicester Square, tel. 020/7836-1401).

Gordon's Wine Bar, with a simple, steep staircase leading into a candlelit 15th-century wine cellar, is filled with dusty old bottles, faded British memorabilia, and nine-to-fivers. At the "English rustic" buffet, choose a hot meal or cold meat dish with a salad, or a hearty (and splittable) plate of cheeses, bread, and pickles (£7.75)—or share four plates for £12. Then step up to the wine bar and consider the many varieties of wine and port available by the glass. This place is passionate about port. The low carbon-crusted vaulting deeper in the back seems to intensify the Hogarth-painting atmosphere. Although it's crowded, you can normally corral two chairs and grab the corner of a table. On hot days, the crowd spills out onto a leafy back patio, where a barbecue cooks for a long line of tables (arrive before 17:00 to get a seat, Mon–Sat 11:00–23:00, Sun 12:00–22:00, 2 blocks from Trafalgar Square, bottom of Villiers Street at #47, Tube: Embankment, tel. 020/7930-1408, www.gordonswinebar.com, manager Gerard Menan).

The Lord Moon of the Mall pub, with real ales on tap and cheap pub grub such as fish-and-chips, is a good place to experience retro English cuisine from the days when it had a horrible reputation. The pub fills a great, old former Barclays Bank building a block down Whitehall from Trafalgar Square (daily 9:00–22:00, kid-friendly menu but no kids after 20:00, 16–18 Whitehall, Tube: Charing Cross or Embankment, tel. 020/7839-7701).

Near Piccadilly

Hungry and broke in the theater district? Head for Panton Street (off Haymarket, two blocks southeast of Piccadilly Circus), where several hardworking little places compete, all seeming to offer a three-course meal for about £8.50. Peruse the entire block (vegetarian, Pizza Express, Moroccan, Thai, Chinese, and two famous diners) before making your choice.

Stockpot is a meat, potatoes, gravy, and mushy-peas kind of place, famous and rightly popular for its edible, cheap English meals (Mon–Sat 7:00–23:30, Sun 7:00–22:00, 38–40 Panton Street, cash only). The **West End Kitchen** (across the street at #5, same hours and menu) is a direct competitor that's also well-known and just as good. Vegetarians may prefer the **Woodlands South Indian Vegetarian Restaurant,** which serves an impressive £18 *thali* (37 Panton Street).

The palatial **Criterion** offers grand-piano ambience beneath gilded tiles and chandeliers in a dreamy Byzantine church setting from 1880. It's right on Piccadilly Circus but a world away from the punk junk. It's a deal for the visual experience during lunch and before 19:00—but after 19:00, the menu becomes really expensive...and, at any hour, the service could care less. Anyone can drop in for coffee or a drink (£17–20 fixed-price meals, daily 12:00–14:30 & 17:30–19:00 & 22:00–23:30, 224 Piccadilly, tel. 020/7930-0488).

The Wolseley is the grand 1920s showroom of a long-defunct British car. The last Wolseley drove out with the Great Depression, but today this old-time bistro bustles with formal waiters serving traditional Austrian and French dishes in an elegant black-marble-and-chandeliers setting fit for its location next to the Ritz. Although the food can be unexceptional, prices are reasonable, and the presentation and setting are grand. Reservations are a must (£16.50 plates; cheaper soup, salad, and sandwich menu available; Mon–Fri 7:00–24:00, Sat 8:00–24:00, Sun 8:00–23:00, 160 Piccadilly—for exact location see map on page 166, tel. 020/7499-6996). They're popular for their fancy cream or afternoon tea (for details, see page 180).

Near Covent Garden

Covent Garden bustles with people and touristy eateries. The area feels overrun, but if you must eat around here, there are some good options.

Joe Allen, tucked in a basement a block away, serves modern

Pub Appreciation

The pub is the heart of the people's England, where all manner of folks have, for generations, found their respite from work and a home-away-from-home. England's classic pubs are national treasures, with great cultural value and rich history, not to mention good beer and grub.

The Golden Age for pub-building was in the late Victorian era (c. 1880–1905), when pubs were independently owned and land prices were high enough to make it worthwhile to invest in fixing up pubs. The politics were pro-pub as well: Conservatives, backed by Big Beer, were in, and temperance-minded Liberals were out.

Especially in class-conscious Victorian times, traditional pubs were divided into sections by elaborate screens (now mostly gone), allowing the wealthy to drink in a more refined setting, while commoners congregated on the pub's rougher side. These were really "public houses," featuring nooks (snugs) for groups and clubs to meet, friends and lovers to rendezvous, and families to get out of the house at night. Because many pub-goers were illiterate, pubs were simply named for the picture hung outside (e.g., The Crooked Stick, The Queen's Arms—meaning her coat of arms).

Historic pubs still dot the London cityscape. The only place to see the very oldest-style tavern in the "domestic tradition" is at **Ye Olde Cheshire Cheese,** which was rebuilt in 1667 (after the Great Fire) from a 16th-century tavern (£6–7 pub grub, £9–12 meals in the restaurant, open daily, 145 Fleet Street; Tube: Temple or St. Paul's, Blackfriars station is nearest but is closed until late 2011; tel. 020/7353-6170). Imagine this place in the pre-Victorian era: With no bar, drinkers gathered around the fireplaces, while tap boys shuttled tankards up from the cellar. (This was long before barroom taps were connected to casks in the cellar. Oh, and don't say "keg"—that's a gassy modern thing.)

Late-Victorian pubs, such as the lovingly restored 1897 **Princess Louise** (Mon-Fri 11:30–23:00, Sat 12:00–23:00, Sun 12:00–22:30, 208 High Holborn, Tube: Holborn, tel. 020/7405-8816), are more common. These places are fancy, often with heavy embossed wallpaper ceilings, decorative tile work, fine-etched glass, ornate carved stillions (the big central hutch for storing bottles and glass), and even urinals equipped with a place to set your glass.

London's best Art Nouveau pub is **The Black Friar** (c. 1900–1915), with fine carved capitals, lamp holders, and quirky phrases worked into the decor (£7–10 meals, open daily, Tube: Temple or St. Paul's, across from the Blackfriars Tube station—closed until late 2011—at 174 Queen Victoria Street, tel. 020/7236-5474).

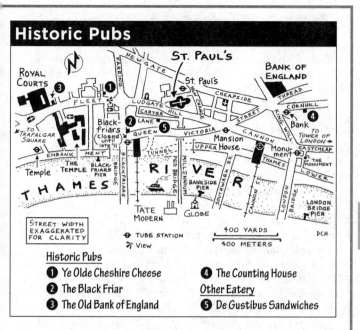

Historic Pubs

STREET WIDTH
EXAGGERATED
FOR CLARITY

⊖ TUBE STATION

🔭 VIEW

400 YARDS

400 METERS

DCH

Historic Pubs

1 Ye Olde Cheshire Cheese

2 The Black Friar

3 The Old Bank of England

4 The Counting House

Other Eatery

5 De Gustibus Sandwiches

LONDON

The "former-bank pubs" represent a more modern trend in pub building. As banks increasingly go electronic, they're moving out of lavish, high-rent old buildings. Many of these former banks are being refitted as pubs with elegant bars and free-standing stillions, providing a fine centerpiece. Three such pubs are **The Old Bank of England** (Mon–Fri 11:00–23:00, closed Sat–Sun,

194 Fleet Street, Tube: Temple, tel. 020/7430-2255), **The Jugged Hare** (open daily, 172 Vauxhall Bridge Road—see map on page 148, Tube: Victoria, tel. 020/7828-1543, also see listing on page 176), and **The Counting House** (Mon–Fri 11:00–23:00, closed Sat–Sun, 50 Cornhill, Tube: Bank, tel. 020/7283-7123, also see listing on page 179).

Go pubbing in the evening for a lively time, or drop by during the quiet late morning (from 11:00), when the pub is empty and filled with memories. For a guided tour, check out Bob Steel's London Heritage pub walks (about £50/group for a leisurely half-day private walk, www.aletrails.com, bsteel@blueyonder.co.uk).

international and American cuisine with both style and hubbub. Downstairs off a quiet street with candles and white tablecloths, it's comfortably spacious and popular with the theater crowd (meals for about £30, £16 two-course specials and £18 three-course specials 17:00–18:45, open daily 11:30–23:00, piano music after 21:00, 13 Exeter Street, tel. 020/7836-0651).

Loch Fyne Fish Restaurant is part of a Scottish chain that grows its own oysters and mussels. It offers an inviting atmosphere with a fine fishy energy and no pretense (£10–15 entrées, £12.50 two-course early dinner served until 18:30, open daily, a couple of blocks behind Covent Garden at 2 Catherine Street, tel. 020/7240-4999).

Sofra Turkish Restaurant is good for quality Turkish with a touch of class. They have several menus: *meze* (Turkish tapas), vegetarian, and set (£8 before 18:00, £10 after 18:00, open long hours daily, 36 Tavistock Street, tel. 020/7240-3773).

Sitar Indian Restaurant is a well-respected Indian/Bangladeshi place serving dishes from many regions, fine fish, and a tasty £17 vegetarian *thali*. It's small and dressy, with snappy service (£15 entrées, daily 12:00–24:00, next to Somerset House at 149 Strand—see map on page 166, tel. 020/7836-3730).

Belgo Centraal serves hearty Belgian specialties in a vast 400-seat underground lair. It's a mussels, chips, and beer emporium dressed up as a mod-monastic refectory—with noisy acoustics and waiters garbed as Trappist monks. The classy restaurant section is more comfortable and less rowdy, but usually requires reservations. It's often more fun just to grab a spot in the boisterous beer hall, with its tight, communal benches (no reservations accepted). Both sides have the same menu and specials. Belgians claim they eat as well as the French and as heartily as the Germans. Belgo, which offers a stunning array of dark, blond, and fruity Belgian beers, actually makes Belgian things trendy—a formidable feat (£10–14 meals, open daily 12:00–23:00; Mon–Fri £5–6.30 "beat the clock" meal specials 17:00–18:30—the time you order is the price you pay—including main dishes and fries; no meal-splitting after 18:30, and you must buy food with beer; daily £8 lunch special 12:00–17:00; 1 kid eats free for each parent ordering a regular entrée; 1 block north of Covent Garden Tube station at 50 Earlham Street, tel. 020/7813-2233).

Neal's Yard is *the* place for cheap, hip, and healthy eateries near Covent Garden. The neighborhood is a tabouli of fun, hippie-type cafés. One of the best is the venerable and ferociously vegetarian **Food for Thought,** packed with local health nuts (good £5 vegetarian meals, £7.50 dinner plates, Mon–Sat 12:00–20:30, Sun 12:00–17:00, 2 blocks north of Covent Garden Tube station, 31 Neal Street, near Neal's Yard, tel. 020/7836-0239).

The Soho "Food Is Fun" Three-Course Dinner Crawl

For a multicultural, movable feast, consider enjoying a drink and eating (or splitting) one course at each of these places. Start around 17:30 to avoid lines, get in on early-bird specials, and find waiters willing to let you split a meal. Prices, though reasonable by London standards, add up. Servings are large enough to share. All are open nightly. Arrive at 17:30 at **Belgo Centraal** and split the early-bird dinner special: a kilo of mussels, fries, and dark Belgian beer. At **Yo! Sushi,** have beer or sake and a few dishes, then slurp your last course at **Wagamama Noodle Bar.** For dessert, people-watch at Leicester Square.

Near Soho and Chinatown

London has a trendy scene that most Beefeater-seekers miss entirely. These restaurants are scattered throughout the hipster, gay, and strip-club district, teeming each evening with fun-seekers and theater-goers. Even if you plan to have dinner elsewhere, it's a treat just to wander around this lively area.

Beware of the extremely welcoming women standing outside the strip clubs (especially on Great Windmill Street). Enjoy the sales pitch—but only fools fall for the "£5 drink and show" lure. They don't get back out without emptying their wallet...literally.

Yo! Sushi is a futuristic-Japanese-food-extravaganza experience, complete with thumping rock, Japanese cable TV, and a 195-foot-long conveyor belt. For £1.25, you get unlimited green tea or water. Snag a bar stool and grab dishes as they rattle by (priced by color of dish; check the chart: £1.75–5 per dish, daily 12:00–23:00, 2 blocks south of Oxford Street, where Lexington Street becomes Poland Street, 52 Poland Street, tel. 020/7287-0443). If you like Yo!, there are about 40 other locations around town, including a handy branch a block from the London Eye on Belvedere Road, as well as outlets within Selfridges, Harvey Nichols department stores, Victoria train station, and Whiteleys Mall on Queensway.

Wagamama Noodle Bar is a noisy, pan-Asian, organic slurp-pathon. As you enter, check out the kitchen and listen to the roar of the basement, where benches rock with happy eaters. Everybody sucks. Portions are huge and splitting is allowed (£7–10 meals, Mon–Sat 11:30–23:00, Sun 12:00–22:00, crowded after 19:00, 10A Lexington Street, tel. 020/7292-0990 but no reservations taken). If you like this place, handy branches are all over town, including one near the British Museum (4 Streatham Street), Kensington (26 High Street), in Harvey Nichols (109 Knightsbridge), Covent

Garden (1 Tavistock Street), Leicester Square (14 Irving Street), Piccadilly Circus (8 Norris Street), Fleet Street (#109), and next to the Tower of London (Tower Place).

Busaba Eathai Thai Restaurant is a hit with locals for its snappy service, casual-yet-high-energy ambience, and good, inexpensive Thai cuisine. You'll sit communally around big, square 16-person hardwood tables or at two-person tables by the window—with everyone in the queue staring at your noodles. They don't take reservations, so arrive by 19:00 or line up (£7–10 meals, Mon–Thu 12:00–23:00, Fri–Sat 12:00–23:30, Sun 12:00–22:00, 106 Wardour Street, tel. 020/7255-8686). They have three other handy locations: on nearby Panton Street, just below Piccadilly Circus; at 22 Store Street, near the British Museum and Goodge Street Tube; and at 8–13 Bird Street, just off Oxford Street and across from the Bond Street Tube.

Côte Restaurant is a contemporary French bistro chain, serving good-value French cuisine with no pretense at the right prices (£9–13 mains, £12 three-course early dinner specials if you order by 19:00, open Mon–Wed 8:00–23:00, Thu–Fri 8:00–24:00, Sat 10:00–24:00, Sun 10:00–22:30, 124–126 Wardour Street, tel. 020/7287-9280).

Y Ming Chinese Restaurant—across Shaftesbury Avenue from the ornate gates, clatter, and dim sum of Chinatown—has dressy European decor, serious but helpful service, and authentic Northern Chinese cooking (good £10 meal deal offered 12:00–18:00, £7–10 plates, open Mon–Sat 12:00–23:45, closed Sun, 35–36 Greek Street, tel. 020/7734-2721).

New World Chinese Restaurant is a sprawling old-fashioned Chinese diner that just feels real. It's a fixture in Chinatown, serving cheap Cantonese food, including dim sum lunch and a similar dinner menu with an array of little £3 dishes (daily 11:00–24:00, 1 Gerrard Place, tel. 020/7734-0677).

Jen Café, across the street, is a humble Chinese corner eatery much loved for its homemade dumplings (£3–5 plates, long hours daily, 4 Newport Place, tel. 020/7287-9708).

On Lexington Street, in the Heart of Soho

Andrew Edmunds Restaurant is a tiny, candlelit place where you'll want to hide your camera and guidebook and not act like a tourist. This little place—with a jealous and loyal clientele—is the closest I've found to Parisian quality in a cozy restaurant in London. The modern European cooking and creative seasonal menu are worth the splurge (£6–8 starters, £11–18 entrées, Mon–Sat 12:30–15:00 & 18:00–22:45, Sun 13:00–15:30 & 18:00–22:30, come early or call ahead, request ground floor rather than basement, 46 Lexington Street, tel. 020/7437-5708).

Mildred's Vegetarian Restaurant, across from Andrew Edmunds, has cheap prices, an enjoyable menu, and a pleasant interior filled with happy eaters (£7–9 meals, Mon–Sat 12:00–23:00, closed Sun, vegan options, 45 Lexington Street, tel. 020/7494-1634).

Fernandez & Wells is a delightfully simple little wine, cheese, and ham bar. Drop in and grab a stool as you belly up to the big wooden bar. Share a plate of top-quality cheeses and/or Spanish or French hams with fine bread and oil, while sipping a nice glass of wine and talking with Dean or his staff (Mon–Sat 11:00–22:00, Sun 12:00–19:00, quality sandwiches at lunch, wine/cheese/ham bar after 16:00, 43 Lexington Street, tel. 020/7734-1546).

West London
Near Victoria Station Accommodations

These restaurants are within a few blocks of Victoria Station—and all are places I've enjoyed eating at. As with the accommodations in this area, I've grouped them by location: east or west of the station (see the map on page 148).

Cheap Eats: For groceries, a handy **M&S Simply Food** is inside Victoria Station (Mon–Sat 7:00–24:00, Sun 8:00–22:00), along with a **Sainsbury's Market** (daily 6:00–23:00, at rear entrance, on Eccleston Street). A second Sainsbury's is just north of the station on Victoria Street, and a larger Sainsbury's is on Wilton Road near Warwick Way, a couple of blocks southeast of the station (Mon–Fri 7:00–23:00, Sat 7:00–22:00, Sun 11:00–17:00). A string of good ethnic restaurants lines Wilton Road (near the recommended Seafresh Fish Restaurant). For affordable if forgettable meals, try the row of cheap little eateries on Elizabeth Street.

West of Victoria Station

Ebury Wine Bar, filled with young professionals, provides a cut-above atmosphere, delicious £13–18 entrées, and a £21 three-course and £16 two-course special anytime (it includes a glass of champagne, but you're welcome to swap it for wine). In the delightful back room, the fancy menu features modern European cuisine with a French accent; at the wine bar, find a cheaper bar menu that's better than your average pub grub. This is emphatically a "traditional wine bar," with no beers on tap (daily 11:00–23:00, reserve after 20:00, at intersection of Ebury and Elizabeth Streets, 139 Ebury Street, tel. 020/7730-5447).

Jenny Lo's Tea House is a simple budget place serving up reliably tasty £7–9 eclectic Chinese-style meals to locals in the know. While the menu is small, everything is high quality. Jenny clearly learned from her father, Ken Lo, one of the most famous Cantonese chefs in Britain, whose fancy place is just around the corner (Mon–Fri 11:30–15:00 & 18:00–22:00, closed Sat–Sun, cash only, 14 Eccleston Street, tel. 020/7259-0399).

La Bottega is an Italian delicatessen that fits its upscale Belgravia neighborhood. It offers tasty, freshly cooked pastas (£6), lasagnas, and salads (lasagna and salad meal-£8), along with great sandwiches (£3) and a good coffee bar with pastries. While not cheap, it's fast (order at the counter), and the ingredients would please an Italian chef. Grab your meal to go, or enjoy the Belgravia good life with locals, either sitting inside or on the sidewalk (Mon–Fri 8:00–19:00, Sat 9:00–18:00, Sun 10:00–17:00, on corner of Ebury and Eccleston Streets, tel. 020/7730-2730).

The Duke of Wellington Pub is a classic neighborhood place with forgettable grub, woodsy sidewalk seating, and an inviting interior (dinner served Mon–Sat 18:00–21:00, 63 Eaton Terrace, tel. 020/7730-1782).

The Thomas Cubitt Pub, packed with young professionals, is a trendy neighborhood gastropub, great for a drink or pricey meal (44 Elizabeth Street, tel. 020/7730-6060).

LONDON

East of Victoria Station

Grumbles brags it's been serving "good food and wine at nonscary prices since 1964." Offering a delicious mix of "modern eclectic French and traditional English," this unpretentious little place with cozy booths inside (on two levels, including a cellar) and four nice sidewalk tables is *the* spot to eat well in this otherwise workaday neighborhood. Their traditional dishes are their forte (£9–18 plates, £10 early-bird specials 18:00–19:00, open daily 12:00–14:30 & 18:00–23:00, reservations wise, half a block north of Belgrave Road at 35 Churton Street, tel. 020/7834-0149, Alex).

Seafresh Fish Restaurant is the neighborhood place for plaice—and classic and creative fish-and-chips cuisine. You can either take out on the cheap or eat in, enjoying a white fish ambience. Though Mario's father started this place in 1965, it feels like the chippie of the 21st century (meals-£5 to go, £10–14 to sit, Mon–Sat 12:00–15:00 & 17:00–22:30, closed Sun, 80–81 Wilton Road, tel. 020/7828-0747).

The Jugged Hare pub, a 10-minute walk from Victoria Station, sits in a lavish old bank building, with vaults replaced by tankards of beer and a fine kitchen. They have a fun, traditional menu with more fresh veggies than fries, and a plush, vivid pub scene good for a meal or just a drink (£6.25 sandwiches, £8–10 meals, food served daily 12:00–21:30, drinks served daily 11:00–23:00, 172 Vauxhall Bridge Road, tel. 020/7828-1543).

St. George's Tavern is *the* pub for a meal in this neighborhood. They serve dinner from the same fun menu in three zones: on the sidewalk to catch the sun and enjoy some people-watching, in the sloppy pub, and in a classier back dining room. They're proud of their sausages and "toad in the hole." The scene is inviting for just a beer, too (£7–10 meals, Mon–Sat 10:00–22:00, Sun until 21:00, corner of Hugh Street and Belgrave Road, tel. 020/7630-1116).

Near Notting Hill and Bayswater Accommodations

For locations, see the map on page 154.

Maggie Jones, a Charles Dickens-meets-Ella Fitzgerald splurge, is exuberantly rustic and very English, with a 1940s-jazz soundtrack. You'll get solid English cuisine, including huge plates of crunchy vegetables, served by a young and casual staff. It's pricey, but the portions are huge (especially the meat-and-fish pies, their specialty). You're welcome to save lots by splitting your main course. The candlelit upstairs is the most romantic, while the basement is kept lively with the kitchen, tight seating, and lots of action. If you eat well once in London, eat here—and do it quick, before it burns down (lunch—£5 starters, £7 entrées; dinner—£6–9 starters, £13–19 entrées; Mon–Sat 12:30–14:30 & 18:30–23:00, Sun 12:30–16:00 & 18:30–22:30, reservations recommended, 6 Old Court Place, just east of Kensington Church Street, near High Street Kensington Tube stop, tel. 020/7937-6462).

The Churchill Arms pub and **Thai Kitchens** (same location) are local hangouts, with good beer and a thriving old-English ambience in front, and hearty £6.50 Thai plates in an enclosed patio in the back. You can eat the Thai food in the tropical hideaway (table service) or in the atmospheric pub section (order at the counter and they'll bring it to you). They also serve basic English pub food (£3 sandwiches, £6 meals). The place is festooned with Churchill memorabilia and chamber pots (including one with Hitler's mug on it—hanging from the ceiling farthest from Thai Kitchen—sure to cure the constipation of any Brit during World War II). Arrive by 18:00 or after 21:00 to avoid a line. During busy times, diners are limited to an hour at the table (daily 12:00–22:00, 119 Kensington Church Street, tel. 020/7792-1246).

The Prince Edward serves good grub in a quintessential pub setting (£7–12 meals, Mon–Wed 10:00–23:00, Thu–Sat 10:00–23:30, Sun 10:00–22:30, plush-pubby indoor seating or sidewalk tables, family-friendly, pay Wi-Fi, 2 blocks north of Bayswater Road at the corner of Dawson Place and Hereford Road, 73 Prince's Square, tel. 020/7727-2221).

Café Diana is a healthy little eatery serving sandwiches, salads, and Middle Eastern food. It's decorated—almost shrine-like—with photos of Princess Diana, who used to drop by for pita sandwiches. You can dine in the simple interior, or order some food from the counter to go (£3–4 sandwiches, £6–8 meat dishes, daily 8:00–23:00, 5 Wellington Terrace, on Bayswater Road, opposite Kensington Palace Garden Gates, where Di once lived, tel. 020/7792-9606, Abdul).

On Queensway: The road called Queensway is a multiethnic food circus, lined with lively and inexpensive eateries—browse the options along here and choose your favorite. For a cut above, head for **Royal China Restaurant**—filled with London's Chinese, who consider this one of the city's best eateries. It's dressed up in black, white, and gold, with candles and brisk waiters. While it's pricier than most neighborhood Chinese restaurants, the food is noticeably better (£9–13 dishes, Mon–Thu 12:00–23:00, Fri–Sat 12:00–23:30, Sun 11:00–22:00, dim sum until 17:00, 13 Queensway, tel. 020/7221-2535). For a lowbrow alternative, **Whiteleys Mall Food Court**—at the top end of Queensway—offers a fun selection of ethnic and fast-food chain eateries among Corinthian columns, and a multiscreen theater in a delightful mall (daily 9:00–23:00; options include Yo! Sushi, good salads at Café Rouge, pizza, Starbucks, and a coin-op Internet place; third floor, corner of Porchester Gardens and Queensway).

Supermarkets: **Tesco** is a half-block from the Notting Hill Gate Tube stop (Mon–Sat 7:00–23:00, Sun 12:00–18:00, near intersection with Pembridge Road, 114–120 Notting Hill Gate). The smaller **Spar Market** is at 18 Queensway (Mon–Sat 7:00–24:00, Sun 9:00–24:00), and **Marks & Spencer** can be found in Whiteleys Mall (Mon–Sat 10:00–20:00, Sun 12:00–18:00).

Near South Kensington Accommodations

Popular eateries line Old Brompton Road and Thurloe Street (Tube: South Kensington), and a good selection of cheap eateries are clumped around the Tube station. For locations, see the map on page 152.

La Bouchée Bistro Café is a classy hole-in-the-wall touch of France. This candlelit and woody bistro, with very tight seating, serves a two-course, £11.50 special on weekdays during lunch and from 17:30–18:30, and £17 *plats du jour* all *jour*. Reservations are smart in the evening (daily 12:00–15:00 & 17:30–23:30, 56 Old Brompton Road, tel. 020/7589-1929).

Daquise, run by a well-established Warsaw restaurateur, is ideal if you're in the mood for kielbasa and kraut (£12 meals, weekday lunch special, daily 12:00–23:00, 20 Thurloe Street, tel. 020/7589-6117).

Moti Mahal Indian Restaurant, with minimalist-yet-classy mod ambience and attentive service, serves mostly Bangladeshi cuisine that's delicious. Consider chicken *jalfrezi* if you like spicy food, and buttery chicken if you don't (£10 dinners, daily 12:00–14:30 & 17:30–23:00, 3 Glendower Place, tel. 020/7584-8428).

Beirut Express has fresh, well-prepared Lebanese cuisine. In the front, you'll find take-away service as well as barstools for quick service (£4 sandwiches). In the back is a sit-down restaurant with £14 plates (daily 12:00–23:00, 65 Old Brompton Road, tel. 020/7591-0123).

Bosphorus Kebabs is the student favorite for a quick, fast, and hearty Turkish dinner. While mostly for take-away, they have a few tight tables indoors and on the sidewalk (£5 meals, Turkish kebabs, daily until 24:00, 59 Old Brompton Road, tel. 020/7584-4048).

Rocca di Papa is a bright and dressy Italian place with a heated terrace (£8 pizza, pasta, and salads; open daily, 73 Old Brompton Road, tel. 020/7225-3413).

The Anglesea Arms, with a great terrace surrounded by classy South Kensington buildings, is a destination pub that feels like the classic neighborhood favorite. It's a thriving and happy place, with a woody ambience and a mellow back dining room a world away from any tourism. Chef Julian Legge freshens up traditional English cuisine and prints up a daily menu listing his creative meals. While it'd be a shame to miss his cooking, this is also a fine place for simply a beer (£6 starters, £13 entrées, meals served daily 12:00–15:00 & 18:00–22:00, a couple of blocks off Old Brompton Road at 15 Selwood Terrace, tel. 020/7373-7960).

Supermarket: **Tesco Express** is handy for picnics (daily 7:00–24:00, 50–52 Old Brompton Road).

Elsewhere in London

Between St. Paul's and the Tower: **The Counting House,** formerly an elegant old bank, offers great £8–10 meals, nice homemade meat pies, fish, and fresh vegetables. The fun "nibbles menu" is available starting in the early evening until 22:00 (or until 21:00 on Mon–Tue; open Mon–Fri 11:00–23:00, closed Sat–Sun, gets really busy with the buttoned-down 9-to-5 crowd after 12:15, near Mansion House in The City, 50 Cornhill—see map on page 171, tel. 020/7283-7123).

Near St. Paul's: **De Gustibus Sandwiches** is where a top-notch artisan bakery meets the public, offering fresh, you-design-it sandwiches, salads, and soups. Just one block below St. Paul's, it has simple seating or take-out picnic sacks for lugging to one of the great nearby parks (Mon–Fri 7:00–17:00, closed Sat–Sun, from church steps follow signs to youth hostel a block downhill—see map on page 171, 53–55 Carter Lane, tel. 020/7236-0056; another outlet is inside the Borough Market in Southwark).

Near the British Library: Drummond Street (running just west of Euston Station) is famous in London for cheap and good Indian vegetarian food (£5–10 dishes). Consider **Chutneys**

(124 Drummond, tel. 020/7388-0604) and **Ravi Shankar** (133–135 Drummond, tel. 020/7388-6458) for a good *thali* (both open long hours daily).

Taking Tea in London

Once the sole province of genteel ladies in fancy hats, afternoon tea has become more democratic in the 21st century. While some tearooms—such as the £37-a-head tea service at the Ritz and the finicky Fortnum & Mason—still require a jacket and tie (and a bigger bank account), most happily welcome tourists in jeans and sneakers.

Tea Terms

The cheapest "tea" on the menu is generally a "cream tea"; the most expensive is the "champagne tea." **Cream tea** is simply a pot of tea and a homemade scone or two with jam and thick clotted cream. For maximum pinkie-waving taste per calorie, slice your scone thin like a miniature loaf of bread. **Afternoon tea** generally is a cream tea, plus a tier of three plates holding small finger foods (such as cucumber sandwiches) and an assortment of small pastries. **Champagne tea** includes all of the goodies, plus a glass of champagne. **High tea** generally means a more substantial late-afternoon or early-evening meal, often served with meat or eggs.

Tearooms, which often also serve appealing light meals, are usually open for lunch and close about 17:00, just before dinner. At all the places listed below, it's perfectly acceptable to order one afternoon tea and one cream tea (at about £5) and split the afternoon tea goodies.

Places to Sip Tea

The Wolseley serves a good afternoon tea in between their meal service (£10 cream teas, £20 afternoon tea, served Sun–Fri 15:30–18:30, Sat 15:30–17:30, see full listing on page 169). If you split their afternoon tea, you can actually enjoy two light meals at a great price in classic elegance.

The Orangery at Kensington Palace serves four different varieties of tea meals, from the £15 "Orangery tea" to the £35 "Tregothnan tea," in its bright white hall near Princess Di's former residence. You can also order treats à la carte. The portions aren't huge, but who can argue with eating at a princess' orangery or on its deck? (Tea served 12:00–18:00, no reservations taken; a 10-minute walk through Kensington Gardens from either Queensway or High Street Kensington Tube stations to the orange brick building, about 100 yards from Kensington Palace—see map on page 154; tel. 020/3166-6113, www.hrp.org.uk.)

The National Dining Rooms, a restaurant/café within the National Gallery on Trafalgar Square, is convenient and has a nondescript modern ambience. Although the restaurant can book up in advance, you can generally waltz in for afternoon tea at the café. To play it safe, arrive in the early afternoon to reserve a tea time, then take the self-guided National Gallery Tour (page 88) before or after your appointed time (£4 cakes and tarts, £5.50 cream tea, £16.50 afternoon tea, tea served 15:00–17:30, located in Sainsbury Wing of National Gallery, Tube: Charing Cross or Leicester Square, tel. 020/7747-2525, www.thenationaldiningrooms.co.uk).

The National Café, at the other end of the building (across the street from St. Martin–in–the–Fields), also serves tea in a more appealing, old-fashioned atmosphere—and their afternoon tea is a bit cheaper (£5.50 cream tea, £14.50 afternoon tea, tea served 15:00–17:30).

The Café at Sotheby's, located on the ground floor of the auction giant's headquarters, is manna for shoppers taking a break from fashionable New Bond Street. There are no windows—just a long leather bench, plenty of mirrors, and a dark-wood room where waiters serve sweet treats and the £6.50 mix-and-match Neal's Yard cheese plate to locals in the know (£3 cakes and creams, £6.50 "small tea," £11 afternoon tea, £18.75 champagne tea, café open Mon–Fri only 9:30–11:30 & 12:00–16:45, afternoon tea served 15:00–16:45, reservations recommended, 34–35 New Bond Street—see map on page V, Tube: Bond Street or Oxford Circus, tel. 020/7293-5077, www.sothebys.com/cafe/restaurant.html).

The Capital Hotel, a luxury hotel a half-block from Harrods, caters to weary shoppers with its intimate five-table, linen-tablecloth tearoom. It's where the ladies-who-lunch meet to decide whether to buy that Versace gown they've had their eye on. Even so, casual clothes, kids, and sharing plates are all OK (£18.50 afternoon tea, daily 14:30–17:30, call to book ahead—especially on weekends, see map on page 152, 22 Basil Street, Tube: Knightsbridge, tel. 020/7589-5171, www.capitalhotel.co.uk).

Fortnum & Mason's St. James's Restaurant, on the fourth floor, offers plush seats under the elegant tearoom's chandeliers. You'll get the standard three-tiered silver tea tray: finger sandwiches on the bottom, fresh scones with jam and clotted cream on the first floor, and decadent pastries and "tartlets" on the top floor, with unlimited tea. Consider it dinner (about £30–38, Mon–Sat 14:00–18:30, Sun 12:00–16:30, dress up a bit for this—no shorts, "children must be behaved," see map on page V, 181 Piccadilly, reserve in advance online or at toll tel. 0845-602-5694, www.fortnumandmason.com).

Harrods' Georgian Restaurant is where you (along with 200 of your closest friends) can enjoy a fancy tea under a skylight as a pianist tickles the keys of a Bösendorfer, the world's most expensive piano (£24 afternoon tea, includes finger sandwiches and pastries with free refills, tea served Mon–Fri from 15:00, Sat–Sun from 15:45, last order at 17:15, on Brompton Road, Tube: Knightsbridge, reservations tel. 020/7225-6800, www.harrods.com).

Cheaper Options: Taking tea is not just for tourists and the wealthy—it's a true English tradition. If you want the teatime experience but are put off by the price, most department stores on Oxford Street (including those between Oxford Circus and Bond Street Tube stations) offer an afternoon tea (some more affordable than others). For example, **John Lewis** has a mod third-floor brasserie that serves a nice £10 afternoon tea platter from 15:00 (on Oxford Street one block west of the Bond Street Tube station, tel. 020/3073-0626, www.johnlewis.com). Many museums and bookstores have cafés serving afternoon tea goodies à la carte, where you can put together a spread for less than £10—**Waterstone's** fifth-floor café and the **Victoria and Albert Museum** café are two of the best. **Teapod,** a modern option near the Tower Bridge, advertises the "best-value afternoon tea in London," serving cream tea for £5 and afternoon tea for £10, along with sandwiches, soups, salads, and pastries (Mon–Fri 8:30–18:00, Sat 9:00–19:00, Sun 10:00–19:00, 31 Shad Thames, 200 yards from the Tower Bridge on the South Bank, tel. 020/7407-0000).

In Bath: The **Pump Room** is reason enough to put off tea in London—assuming you're visiting the city of Bath. This historic, elegant Georgian hall with live music lets anyone enjoy the ritual of tea in grand style (see page 243).

London Connections

Airports

Phone numbers and websites for London's airports and major airlines are listed in the appendix. For accommodations at or near the major airports, see page 163.

Heathrow Airport

Heathrow Airport is one of the world's busiest airports. Think about it: 68 million passengers a year on 470,000 flights from 180 destinations riding 90 airlines, like some kind of global maypole dance. Read signs and ask questions. For Heathrow's airport, flight, and transfer information, call the switchboard at toll tel. 0844-335-1801, or visit the help-

London's Airports

ful website at www.heathrowairport.com.

Heathrow has five terminals: T-1 (mostly domestic and Irish flights, with some service to Europe and the US); T-2 (closed for renovation, should reopen in 2013); T-3 (North and South American, Asian, and some European flights); T-4 (European and US flights); and T-5 (British Airways flights only). You can walk between T-1 and T-3. To travel between the other terminals, you can take the Heathrow Express trains (free), buses (free), or the Tube (requires a ticket). Unlike most American airports, there is no train that links all the terminals together on one line, so you may have to transfer if you're going to T-4 or T-5.

If you're flying out of Heathrow, it's critical to confirm which terminal your flight will use (check the Web or call your airline in advance)—because if it's T-4 or T-5, you'll need to allow extra time. Taxi drivers generally know which terminal you'll need, but bus drivers may not.

Each terminal has an airport information desk (generally daily 6:00–22:00), car-rental agencies, exchange bureaus, ATMs, a pharmacy, a **VAT refund desk** (tel. 020/8910-3682; you must present the VAT claim form from the retailer here to get your tax rebate on items purchased in Britain—see page 18 for details), and **baggage storage** (£8/item for 24 hours, hours vary by terminal but generally daily 5:30–23:00, www.left-baggage.co.uk). Get online 24 hours a day at Heathrow's **Internet access points** (at each terminal—T-4's is up on the mezzanine level) or with your laptop (pay Wi-Fi provided by Boingo, www.boingo.com). There's a **post office** on the first floor of T-3. Each terminal has cheap **eateries.**

Heathrow's small **"TI"** (tourist info shop), even though it's a for-profit business, is worth a visit to pick up free information: a simple map, the *London Planner*, and brochures (daily 6:30–22:00, 5-minute walk from T-3 in Tube station, follow signs to Underground; bypass queue for transit info to reach window for London questions).

Getting to London from Heathrow Airport

You have five basic options for traveling the 14 miles between Heathrow Airport and downtown London: Tube (£4.50/person), bus (£5/person), direct shuttle bus (£21.50/person), express train with connecting Tube or taxi (about £20/person), or taxi (about £55 per group).

By Tube (Subway): For £4.50, the Tube takes you from any Heathrow terminal to downtown London in 50–60 minutes on the Piccadilly Line (6/hour; depending on your destination, may require a transfer, buy ticket at the Tube station ticket window). If you plan to use the Tube for transport in London, it may make sense to buy a Travelcard or pay-as-you-go Oyster card at the Tube station ticket window at the airport. (For information on these passes, see page 57.) If your Travelcard covers only Zones 1-2, it does not include Heathrow (Zone 6); however, you can pay a small supplement for the initial trip from Heathrow to downtown.

If you're taking the Tube from downtown London *to* the airport, note that the Piccadilly Line trains don't stop at every terminal. Trains either stop at T-4, then T-1/T-3 (also called Heathrow Central), in that order; or T-1/T-3 and T-5. When leaving central London on the Tube, allow extra time if going to T-4 or T-5, since you have to be sure you get on a train going to your terminal; carefully check the destination information before you board.

By Bus: Most buses depart from the outdoor common area in the heart of the Heathrow complex called the Central Bus Station. It serves T-1 and T-3, and is a 5-minute walk from these terminals. To get to T-4 or T-5 from the Central Bus Station, go inside, downstairs, and follow signs to take Heathrow Express trains to your terminal (free, but only runs every 15–20 minutes to those terminals); or catch one of the free buses that circulate between terminals.

National Express has regular service from Heathrow's Central Bus Station to Victoria Coach Station in downtown London, near several of my recommended hotels. While slow, the bus is affordable and convenient for those staying near Victoria Station (£5,

1–2/hour, less frequent from Victoria Station to Heathrow, 45–60 minutes depending on time of day, toll tel. 0871-781-8181, www .nationalexpress.com).

By Shuttle: SkyShuttle operates buses about every half hour between all Heathrow terminals and hotels in central London (£21.50/person one-way, £34.40/person round-trip; reservations toll tel. 0845-481-0960, call between 6:00-22:00; www.skyshuttle .co.uk).

By Train: Two different trains (slow for £8, fast for £18) run between Heathrow Airport and London's Paddington Station. At Paddington Station, you're in the thick of the Tube system, with easy access to any of my recommended neighborhoods—my Paddington hotels are just outside the front door, and Notting Hill Gate is just two Tube stops away. The **Heathrow Connect** train is the slightly slower, much cheaper option, serving T-1 and T-3 at one station called Heathrow Central; use free transfers if you're coming from either T-4 or T-5 (£8 one-way, 2/hour, 30 minutes, toll tel. 0845-678-6975, www.heathrowconnect.com). The **Heathrow Express** train is fast (15 minutes to downtown from T-1 and T-3; 21 minutes from T-5; transfer required from T-4) and runs more frequently (4/hour), but it's pricey (£18 "express class" one-way, £32 round-trip, ask about discount promos at ticket desk, buy ticket before you board or pay a £3 surcharge to buy it on the train, covered by BritRail pass, daily 5:10–23:25, toll tel. 0845-600-1515, www.heathrowexpress.co.uk). At the airport, you can use Heathrow Express as a free transfer between terminals.

By Taxi: Taxis from the airport cost about £45–70 to west and central London (one hour). For four people traveling together, this can be a deal. Hotels can often line up a cab back to the airport for about £30–40. For the cheapest taxi to the airport, don't order one from your hotel. Simply flag down a few and ask them for their best "off-meter" rate. Locals refer to hired cars that do the trip off-meter as "mini-cabs." These are reliable and generally cost about what you'd pay for a taxi in good traffic, but—with a fixed price—they can save you money when taxis are snarled in congestion with the meter running.

Getting to Bath from Heathrow Airport

Direct buses run daily from Heathrow to Bath (£19.10, 10/day direct, 2–3 hours, more frequent but slower with transfer in London, toll tel. 0871-781-8181, www.nationalexpress.com). BritRail passholders may prefer the 2.5-hour Heathrow–Bath bus/train connection via Reading (BritRail passholders just pay £15 for bus; otherwise £46–65 depending on time of day, about £20 cheaper when bought in advance; tel. 0118-957-9425, buy bus ticket from www.railair.com, train ticket from www.firstgreatwestern.co.uk).

First catch the RailAir Link shuttle bus (2/hour, 45 minutes) to Reading (RED-ding), then hop on the express train (2/hour, 1 hour) to Bath. Factoring in the connection in Reading—which can add at least an hour to the trip—the train is a less convenient option than the direct bus to Bath.

Gatwick Airport

More and more flights land at Gatwick Airport, halfway between London and the South Coast (toll tel. 0844-335-1802, www.gatwickairport.com). Gatwick has two terminals, North and South, which are easily connected by a free monorail (2-minute trip, runs 24 hours daily). Note that boarding passes say "Gatwick N" or "Gatwick S" to indicate your terminal. British Airways flights generally use Gatwick North. The Gatwick Express trains (described next) stop only at Gatwick South. Schedules in each terminal show only arrivals and departures from that terminal.

Getting to London: Gatwick Express trains are clearly the best way into London from this airport. They shuttle conveniently between Gatwick South and London's Victoria Station, with many of my recommended hotels (£17, £29 round-trip, 4/hour, 30 minutes, runs 5:00–24:00 daily, purchase tickets on train at no extra charge, toll tel. 0845-850-1530, www.gatwickexpress.com). If you buy your tickets at the station before boarding, ask about their deal where three adults travel for the price of two, or four for the price of three. (If you see others in the ticket line, suggest buying your tickets together—you'll save more than £5 each.)

You can save a few pounds by taking Southern Railway's slower and less frequent **shuttle train** between Gatwick South and Victoria Station (£10.90, up to 4/hour, 45 minutes, toll tel. 0845-127-2920, www.southernrailway.com).

A train also runs from Gatwick South to **St. Pancras International Station** (£8.90, 8/hour, 1 hour, www.firstcapital connect.co.uk)—useful for travelers taking the Eurostar train (to Paris or Brussels) or staying in the St. Pancras/King's Cross neighborhood.

Even slower, but cheap and handy to the Victoria Station neighborhood, you can take the **bus** from Gatwick to Victoria (£7.50, hourly, 1.5 hours, toll tel. 0871-781-8181, www.national express.com).

Getting to Bath: To get to Bath from Gatwick, you can catch a bus to Heathrow and take the bus to Bath from there (10/day, 4–5 hours total, £25 one-way, transfer at Heathrow Airport, www.nationalexpress.com—see "Getting to Bath from Heathrow Airport," earlier). By train, the best Gatwick–Bath connection involves a transfer in Reading (£45–54 one-way depending on time of day, £12 in advance, hourly, 2.5 hours, www.firstgreatwestern

.co.uk; avoid transfer in London, where you'll have to change stations).

London's Other Airports

Stansted Airport: If you're using Stansted (toll tel. 0870-0000-303, www.stanstedairport.com), you have several options for getting into or out of London. Two different **buses** connect the airport and downtown London's Victoria Station neighborhood: National Express (£10, £17 round-trip, every 20 minutes, 1.75 hours, runs 24 hours a day, picks up and stops throughout London, ends at Victoria Coach Station, toll tel. 0871-781-8181, www.national express.com) and Terravision (£9, 2–3/hour, 1.25 hours, ends at Green Line Coach Station just south of Victoria Station). Or you can take the faster, pricier Stansted Express **train** (£18-20 one-way, £25-27 round-trip, connects to London's Tube system at Tottenham Hale and Liverpool Street, 4/hour, 45 minutes, 5:00–23:00, toll tel. 0845-850-0150, www.stanstedexpress.com). Stansted is expensive by **cab;** figure £120 one-way from central London.

Luton Airport: For Luton (airport tel. 01582/405-100, www.london-luton.co.uk), there are two choices into or out of London. The fastest way to go is by **rail** to London's St. Pancras International Station (£12 one-way, 1–5/hour, 25–45 minutes—check schedule to avoid the slower trains, toll tel. 0845-712-5678, www.east midlandstrains.co.uk); catch the 10-minute shuttle bus (£1) from outside the terminal to the Luton Airport Parkway Station. The Green Line express **bus** #757 runs to Buckingham Palace Road, just south of London's Victoria Station (£13 one-way, £16 round-trip, small discount for easyJet passengers who buy online, 2–4/hour, 1.25–1.5 hours, 24 hours a day, toll tel. 0844-801-7261, www.greenline.co.uk). If you're sleeping at Luton, consider easyHotel (see listing on page 164).

London City Airport: There's a slim chance you might use London City Airport (tel. 020/7646-0088, www.londoncity airport.com). To get into London, take the Docklands Light Railway (DLR) to the Bank Tube station, which is one stop east of St. Paul's on the Central Line (£4 one-way, covered by Travelcard, £2.20–2.70 on Oyster card, 22 minutes, tel. 020/7222-1234, www.tfl.gov.uk/dlr).

Connecting London's Airports by Bus

More and more travelers are taking advantage of cheap flights out of London's smaller airports. A handy **National Express bus** runs between Heathrow, Gatwick, Stansted, and Luton airports—easier than having to cut through the center of London—although traffic can be bad and increase travel times (toll tel. 0871-781-8181, www.nationalexpress.com).

From **Heathrow Airport to: Gatwick Airport** (1–4/hour, 1.25–1.5 hours, £19.50 one-way, £36.50 round-trip, allow at least three hours between flights), **Stansted Airport** (1–2/hour, 1.5–1.75 hours, £22.50 one-way, £29.30 round-trip), **Luton Airport** (hourly, 1–1.5 hours, £20.30 one-way, £25.60 round-trip).

Discounted Flights from London

London is one of Europe's cheapest places to fly into and out of. For information, see "Cheap Flights" on page 827.

Trains and Buses

Britain is covered by a myriad of rail systems (owned by different companies), which together are called National Rail. London, the country's major transportation hub, has a different train station for each region. There are nine main stations (see the route map on next page):

Euston—Serves northwest England, North Wales, and Scotland.

King's Cross—Serves northeast England and Scotland, including York and Edinburgh.

Liverpool Street—Serves east England, including Essex and Harwich.

London Bridge—Serves south England, including Brighton.

Marylebone—Serves southwest and central England, including Stratford-upon-Avon.

Paddington—Serves south and southwest England, including Heathrow Airport, Windsor, Bath, South Wales, and the Cotswolds.

St. Pancras International—Serves north and south England, plus the Eurostar to Paris or Brussels (see "Crossing the Channel," later).

Victoria—Serves Gatwick Airport, Canterbury, Dover, and Brighton.

Waterloo—Serves southeast England, including Salisbury.

In addition, there are other, smaller train stations in London that you are not likely to use, such as **Charing Cross** or **Blackfriars.**

Any train station has schedule information, can make reservations, and can sell tickets for any destination. Most stations offer a baggage-storage service (£8/bag for 24 hours, look for *left luggage* signs); because of long security lines, it can take a while to check or pick up your bag (www.excess-baggage.com). For more details on the services available at each station, see www.nationalrail.co.uk /stations.

Buying Tickets: For general information, call 0845-748-4950 (or visit www.nationalrail.co.uk or www.eurostar.com; £5 book-

London's Train Stations

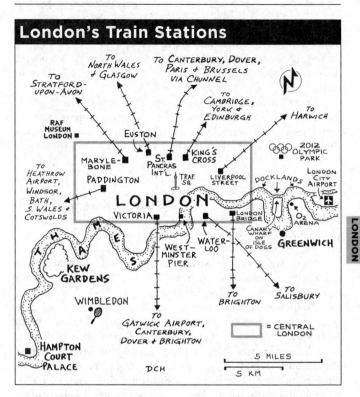

TO NORTH WALES & GLASGOW

TO CANTERBURY, DOVER, PARIS & BRUSSELS VIA CHUNNEL

TO STRATFORD-UPON-AVON

TO CAMBRIDGE, YORK & EDINBURGH

N

TO HARWICH

RAF MUSEUM LONDON ■

EUSTON

2012 OLYMPIC PARK

MARYLE-BONE

ST. PANCRAS INT'L.

KING'S CROSS

LONDON CITY AIRPORT

TO HEATHROW AIRPORT, WINDSOR, BATH, S. WALES & COTSWOLDS

PADDINGTON

TRAF. SQ.

LIVERPOOL STREET

DOCKLANDS

LONDON

VICTORIA

LONDON BRIDGE

O2 ARENA

THAMES

WEST-MINSTER PIER

WATER-LOO

CANARY WHARF ON ISLE OF DOGS

GREENWICH

KEW GARDENS

WIMBLEDON

TO BRIGHTON

TO SALISBURY

TO GATWICK AIRPORT, CANTERBURY, DOVER & BRIGHTON

☐ = CENTRAL LONDON

■ HAMPTON COURT PALACE

DCH

5 MILES

5 KM

LONDON

ing fee for telephone reservations). If you book far enough ahead, you might find discounted train tickets on certain routes at www.megatrain.com (toll tel. 0871-266-3333; as they also sell bus tickets, be careful to specify that you want to take the train).

Railpasses: For train travel outside London, consider getting a BritRail pass. Options include passes that cover England as well as Scotland and Wales, England-only passes, England/Ireland passes, "London Plus" passes (good for travel in most of southeast England but not in London itself), and BritRail & Drive passes (which offer you some rail days and some car-rental days). For specifics, contact your travel agent, or see www.ricksteves.com/rail.

By Train
To Points West
From Paddington Station to: Bath (2/hour, 1.5 hours; also consider a guided Evan Evans tour by bus—see page 191), **Oxford** (2/hour direct, 1 hour, more possible with transfer in Reading, 1 hour), **Penzance** (every 1–2 hours, 5–5.5 hours, possible change in Plymouth), and **Cardiff** (2/hour, 2.25 hours).

To Points North

From King's Cross Station: Trains run at least hourly, stopping in **York** (2 hours), **Durham** (3 hours), and **Edinburgh** (4.5 hours). Trains to **Cambridge** also leave from here (3/hour, 45–60 minutes).

From Euston Station to: **Conwy** (nearly hourly, 3.25 hours, transfer in Chester), **Liverpool** (hourly, 2 hours, more with transfer), **Blackpool** (hourly, 3 hours, transfer at Preston), **Keswick** (hourly, 4.5 hours, transfer to bus at Penrith), and **Glasgow** (1–2/hour, 4.5–5 hours).

From London's Other Stations

Trains run between London and **Canterbury,** leaving from St. Pancras International Station and arriving in Canterbury West (1–2/hour, 1 hour), as well as from London's Victoria Station and arriving in Canterbury East (2/hour, 1.5 hours).

Direct trains leave for **Stratford-upon-Avon** from Marylebone Station, located near the southwest corner of Regents Park (5/day direct, more with transfers, 2.25 hours).

To Other Destinations: Dover (hourly, 1 hour, direct from St. Pancras International Station; also hourly, 2 hours, direct from Victoria Station or Charing Cross Station), **Brighton** (4–5/hour, 1 hour, from Victoria Station and London Bridge Station), **Portsmouth** (3/hour, 1.5–2 hours, most from Waterloo Station, a few from Victoria Station), and **Salisbury** (1–2/hour, 1.5 hours, from Waterloo Station). For trains to **Windsor, Cambridge, Greenwich,** or **Bath,** see those chapters.

By Bus

Buses are slower but considerably cheaper than trains for reaching destinations around Britain, and beyond. Most depart from **Victoria Coach Station,** which is one long block south of Victoria Station (near many recommended accommodations and Tube: Victoria). Inside the station, you'll find basic eateries, kiosks, and a helpful information desk stocked with schedules and ready to point you to your bus or answer any questions.

Most domestic buses are operated by **National Express** (toll tel. 0871-781-8181, www.nationalexpress.com); their international departures are called **Eurolines** (toll tel. 0871-781-8177, www.eurolines.co.uk). A newer, smaller company called **Megabus** undersells National Express with deeply discounted promotional fares—the farther ahead you buy, the less you pay (trips tend to take longer than those on National Express, toll tel. 0900-160-0900, www.megabus.com). They also sell discounted train tickets on selected routes.

Try to avoid bus travel on Friday and Sunday evenings, when

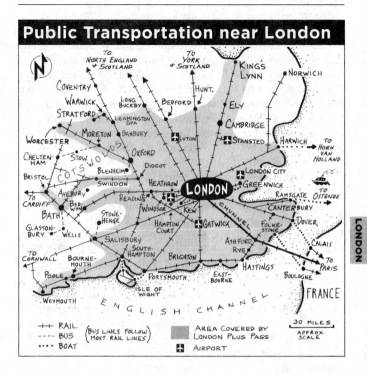

Public Transportation near London

TO NORTH ENGLAND & SCOTLAND — TO YORK & SCOTLAND — KING'S LYNN — NORWICH — COVENTRY — WARWICK — STRATFORD — LONG BUCKBY — BEDFORD — HUNT. — ELY — CAMBRIDGE — STANSTED — HARWICH — TO HOEK VAN HOLLAND — WORCESTER — MORETON — BANBURY — LUTON — LEAMINGTON SPA — CHELTENHAM — STOW — OXFORD — DIDCOT — COTSWOLDS — BLENHEIM — BRISTOL — SWINDON — HEATHROW — LONDON — LONDON CITY — GREENWICH — AVEBURY — READING — KEW — RAMSGATE — TO OSTENDE — TO CARDIFF — BED. WYN — STONE-HENGE — WINDSOR — CANTERBURY — CHANNEL — BATH — HAMPTON COURT — GATWICK — FOLKE-STONE — DOVER — GLASTON-BURY — WELLS — SALISBURY — ASHFORD, RYE — CALAIS — TO CORNWALL — BOURNE-MOUTH — SOUTH-HAMPTON — BRIGHTON — HASTINGS — TO PARIS — POOLE — PORTSMOUTH — EAST-BOURNE — BOULOGNE — FRANCE — WEYMOUTH — ISLE OF WIGHT — ENGLISH CHANNEL

+++ RAIL
- - - BUS (BUS LINES FOLLOW MOST RAIL LINES)
.... BOAT

AREA COVERED BY LONDON PLUS PASS
✈ AIRPORT

30 MILES APPROX. SCALE

LONDON

weekend travelers are more likely to make buses sell out.

To ensure getting a ticket—and to save money with special promotions—you can book your ticket in advance online (see websites above). The cheapest pre-purchased tickets can be changed (for a £5 fee), but they're nonrefundable. If you have a British mobile phone, you can buy an "M-Ticket," which sends your paperless confirmation number right to your phone.

If you're planning to buy your ticket at the station, try to arrive an hour before the bus departs—or drop by the day before. (For buses to Stansted Airport and Oxford, you can buy the ticket on board; otherwise you'll buy it at a ticket window.) Watch your bags carefully—luggage thieves thrive at the station.

To Bath: The National Express bus leaves from Victoria Coach Station (9/day, 2.75–3.75 hours, avoid those with layover in Bristol, sample fares: one-way-£22, round-trip-£29).

To get to Bath via Stonehenge, consider taking a guided bus tour from London to Stonehenge, Salisbury, and Bath, and abandoning the tour in Bath (be sure to confirm that Bath is the last stop on that particular tour). **Evan Evans'** tour is £69 and includes admissions. The tour leaves from Victoria Coach Station every morning at 8:45 (you can stow your bag under the bus), stops in Salisbury (for a look at its magnificent cathedral) and Stonehenge, and then stops in Bath for a city tour before returning to London (offered year-round; they also offer another tour to Stonehenge and Bath via Windsor Castle). You can book the tour at the Victoria Coach Station or the Evan Evans office (258 Vauxhall Bridge Road, near Victoria Coach Station, tel. 020/7950-1777, US tel. 866-382-6868, www.evanevans.co.uk). **Golden Tours** also runs a Stonehenge–Bath tour (£59, check website for seasonal tour days; departs from Fountain Square, located across from Victoria Coach Station, US tel. 800-548-7083, toll tel. 0844-880-6981, www.goldentours.co.uk).

To Other Destinations: Oxford (2–4/hour, about 1.5 hours), **Cambridge** (hourly, 2–2.5 hours), **Canterbury** (about hourly, 2–2.5 hours), **Dover** (about hourly, 2.5–3.25 hours), **Penzance** (5/day, 8.5–10 hours, overnight available), **Cardiff** (hourly, 3.25 hours), **Liverpool** (8/day direct, 5.25–6 hours, overnight available), **Blackpool** (4/day direct, 6.25–7 hours, overnight available), **York** (4/day direct, 5.25 hours), **Durham** (4/day direct, 6.5–7.5 hours), **Glasgow** (3/day direct, 8–9 hours, train is a much better option), **Edinburgh** (2/day direct, 8.75–9.75 hours, go by train instead).

To Dublin, Ireland: This bus/boat journey, operated by National Express, takes 10–12 hours (£35–45, 1/day, departs Victoria Coach Station at 18:00, check in with passport one hour before). Consider a cheap 1.25-hour Ryanair flight instead (www.ryanair.com).

To the Continent: Especially in summer, buses run to destinations all over Europe, including Paris, Amsterdam, Brussels, and Germany (sometimes crossing the Channel by ferry, other times through the Chunnel). For any international connection, you need to check in with your passport one hour before departure. For details, call toll tel. 0871-781-8177 or visit www.eurolines.co.uk. For information on crossing the Channel by bus, see the end of this chapter.

Crossing the Channel
By Eurostar Train

The fastest and most convenient way to get from Big Ben to the Eiffel Tower is by rail. Eurostar, a joint service of the Belgian, British, and French railways, is the speedy passenger train that zips you (and up to 800 others in 18 sleek cars) from downtown London to downtown Paris or Brussels (15+/day, 2.25–2.5 hours) faster and more easily than flying. The actual tunnel crossing is a 20-minute, silent, 100-mile-per-hour non-event. Your

ears won't even pop. Eurostar's monopoly expired at the beginning of 2010, and Air France has already announced plans to start a competing high-speed rail service between London and Paris (possibly in 2011). Press reports say Germany's national railroad wants to run its high-speed trains to London by the 2012 Olympics.

Eurostar Fares

Channel fares are reasonable but complicated. Prices vary depending on how far ahead you reserve, whether you can live with restrictions, and whether you're eligible for any discounts (children, youths, seniors, round-trip travelers, and railpass holders all qualify).

Fares can change without notice, but typically a **one-way, full-fare ticket** (with no restrictions on refundability) runs about $425 first-class and $300 second-class. **Cheaper seats** come with more restrictions and can sell out quickly (figure $100–160 for second-class, one-way). Those traveling with a railpass that covers France or Britain should look first at the **passholder** fare ($85–130 for second-class, one-way Eurostar trips). For more details, visit my *Guide to Eurail Passes* (www.ricksteves.com/eurostar), Rail Europe (www.raileurope.com), or go directly to Eurostar (www.eurostar.com).

A tour company called **BritainShrinkers** sells one- or two-day tours via the Eurostar to Paris, Brussels, or Bruges, enabling you to side-trip to these cities from London for less than most train tickets alone. For example, you'll pay £109 for a one-day Paris "tour" (unescorted Mon–Sat day trip with Métro pass; tel. 207-713-1311 or www.britainshrinkers.com). This can be a particularly good option if you need to get to Paris from London on short notice, when only the costliest fares are available.

Buying Eurostar Tickets

Because only the most expensive (full-fare) ticket is fully refundable, don't reserve until you're sure of your plans. But if you wait too long, the cheapest tickets will get bought up.

Once you're confident about the time and date of your crossing, you can check and book fares by phone or online. Ordering online through Eurostar or major agents offers a print-at-home e-ticket option. You can also order by phone through Rail Europe at US tel. 800-EUROSTAR for home delivery before you go, or through Eurostar (French toll tel. 08 92 35 35 39, priced in euros) and pick up your ticket at the train station. In continental Europe, you can buy your Eurostar ticket at any major train station in any country or at any travel agency that handles train tickets (expect a booking fee). In Britain, tickets can be issued only at the Eurostar office in St. Pancras International Station. You can purchase

passholder discount tickets at
Eurostar departure stations,
through US agents, or by phone
with Eurostar, but they may be
harder to get at other train stations and travel agencies, and
are a discount category that can
sell out.

Remember that Britain's
time zone is one hour earlier
than France or Belgium. Times
listed on tickets are local times
(departure from London is
British time, arrival in Paris in
French time).

LONDON

Taking the Eurostar

Eurostar trains depart from and arrive at London's St. Pancras
International Station. Check in at least 30 minutes in advance for
your Eurostar trip. It's very similar to an airport check-in: You pass
through airport-like security, show your passport to customs officials, and find a TV monitor to locate your departure gate. There
are a few airport-like shops, newsstands, horrible snack bars, and
cafés (bring food for the trip from elsewhere), pay-Internet terminals, and a currency-exchange booth with rates about the same as
you'll find on the other end.

Crossing the Channel Without Eurostar

The old-fashioned ways of crossing the Channel are cheaper than
Eurostar (taking the bus is cheapest). They're also twice as romantic, complicated, and time-consuming.

By Train and Boat

To Paris: You'll take a train from London to the port of Dover,
then catch a ferry to Calais, France, before boarding another train
for Paris. Trains go from London's St. Pancras International to
Dover's Priory Station (hourly, 1.25 hours; bus or taxi from train
station to ferry dock). P&O Ferries sail from Dover to Calais;
TGV trains run from Calais to Paris. You'll need to book your
own train tickets to Dover and from Calais to Paris. The prices
listed here are for the ferry only (from £30 one-way or £60 round-
trip online, more at dock or by phone, book early for best fares; 22/
day, 1.5 hours, toll tel. 08716-645-645, www.poferries.com).

To Amsterdam: Stena Line's Dutchflyer service combines
train and ferry tickets between London and Amsterdam via the
ports of **Harwich** and Hoek van Holland. Trains go from London's

Liverpool Street Station to Harwich (hourly, 1.75 hours). Stena Line ferries sail from Harwich to Hoek van Holland (7.5 hours), where you can transfer to a train to Amsterdam or other Dutch cities (ferry—from £35, from £57 with cabin, book at least 2 weeks in advance for best price, 13 hours total travel time, Dutchflyer toll tel. 0844-576-2762, www.stenaline.co.uk, Dutch train info at www.ns.nl).

For additional European ferry info, visit www.aferry.to. For UK train and bus info, go to www.traveline.org.uk.

By Bus

You can take the bus from London direct to **Paris** (4/day, 8.25–9.75 hours), **Brussels** (3–4/day, 12 hours), or **Amsterdam** (4/day, 12 hours) from Victoria Coach Station (via ferry or Chunnel, day or overnight). You'll pay the same to Paris, Brussels, or Amsterdam. The price depends on when you book (for example: £28 one-way, £38 round-trip if purchased at least a week ahead; £40 one-way, £55 round-trip if purchased the day before; £44 one-way, £61 round-trip if purchased same day; no discounts and £5 more for any ticket during peak times such as holiday weekends; toll tel. 0871-781-8177; visit www.eurolines.co.uk and look for "funfares").

By Plane

Check with budget airlines for inexpensive round-trip fares to Paris or Brussels (see "Cheap Flights" on page 827).

GREENWICH, WINDSOR, AND CAMBRIDGE

Three of the best day-trip possibilities near London are Greenwich, Windsor, and Cambridge (listed from nearest to farthest). Greenwich is England's maritime capital; Windsor has a very famous castle; and Cambridge is England's best university town.

Getting Around

By Train: The British rail system uses London as a hub and normally offers same-day round-trip fares that cost virtually the same as one-way fares. For day trips, these "off-peak day return" tickets, available if you depart London outside rush hour (usually after 9:30 on weekdays and anytime Sat–Sun), are best. You can also save a little money if you purchase tickets before 18:00 the day before your trip.

By Train Tour: London Walks offers a variety of "Explorer Days" tours year-round by train, including a Cambridge itinerary (£14 plus transportation and admissions costs, pick up their brochure at the TI or hotels, tel. 020/7624-3978, www.walks.com, see listing on page 68).

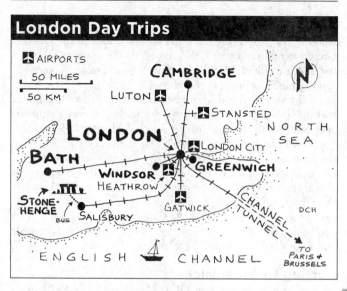

London Day Trips

Greenwich

Tudor kings favored the palace at Greenwich (GREN-ich). Henry VIII was born here. Later kings commissioned Inigo Jones and

Christopher Wren to beautify the town and palace, and built a grand hospital to care for retired seamen (which later became a college for training naval officers). Visitors also come here for all things salty. Greenwich is England's maritime capital, and though its main attraction—the *Cutty Sark* clipper—is closed for restoration until at least late 2011, the town is still worth a visit.

Greenwich is synonymous with timekeeping and astronomy, and at the Royal Observatory Greenwich, you can learn how those pursuits tie into its seafaring status. The town also has stunning Baroque architecture, appealing markets, a fleet of nautical shops, plenty of parks, kid-friendly museums, and hordes of tourists. Since all the major sights here are free to enter, and you can travel between central London and Greenwich on a cheap Tube ticket, it's a wonderfully inexpensive day out. And where else can you set your watch with such accuracy?

Planning Your Time

Upon arrival, stroll past the *Cutty Sark* dry dock to the Discover Greenwich exhibit and TI, then drop into the grand buildings of the Old Royal Naval College and walk the shoreline promenade. Enjoy a lunch or drink in the venerable Trafalgar Tavern, before heading to the National Maritime Museum and then through the park up to the Royal Observatory Greenwich. The town's sights are open daily, but its popular market is closed Monday and Tuesday.

If you like to mix and match public transit, I'd suggest taking the boat to Greenwich for the scenery and commentary, and the DLR (Docklands Light Railway) back, especially if you want to stop at the Docklands on the way home. To visit the Docklands—the glittering forest of skyscrapers rising from a once-derelict port—hop out of the train at the Canary Wharf stop for a quick stroll (see page 129). From there, you can tack on a small detour to check out the Olympics 2012 site (see page 130).

Getting to Greenwich

It's a joy by boat, or a snap by DLR (Docklands Light Railway).

By Boat: From central London, you can cruise scenically down the Thames to Greenwich. Various tour boats—with commentary and open-deck seating up top—leave from the piers at Westminster, Waterloo, and the Tower of London (2/hour, about 1 hour); note that most boats have commentary only on the way to Greenwich, not on the way back.

Thames Clippers offer faster trips, with no commentary and only a small deck at the stern (departs every 20 minutes from several piers in central London, 45 minutes). Thames Clippers also connect Greenwich to the Docklands' Canary Wharf Pier (3/hour, 10 minutes).

For cruising details, see page 74.

By DLR (Docklands Light Railway): From Bank station (also accessible from the Monument Tube station) in central London, take the DLR to Cutty Sark station in central Greenwich; it's one stop before the main—but less central—Greenwich station (departs at least every 10 minutes, 20 minutes, all in Zone 2, covered by any Tube pass). Some DLR trains terminate at Island Gardens (from which you can generally catch another train to Greenwich's Cutty Sark station within a few minutes, though it may be more memorable to walk under the river through the long Thames pedestrian tunnel). Many DLR trains terminate at Canary Wharf, so make sure you get on one that continues to Lewisham or Greenwich.

By Train: Mainline trains also go from London (Cannon Street and London Bridge stations) several times an hour to Greenwich station (10-minute walk from the sights). Although the train is fast and cheap, the DLR is preferable because it drops you right in the heart of town.

By Bus: Catch bus #188 from Russell Square near the British Museum (about 45 minutes to Greenwich).

Orientation to Greenwich

(area code: 020)

Still well within the city limits of London, Greenwich feels like a small town all its own. Covered markets and outdoor stalls

make for lively weekends. Save time to browse the town. Wander beyond the touristy Church Street and Greenwich High Road to where flower stands spill onto the side streets, and antique shops sell brass nautical knickknacks. King William Walk, College Approach, Nelson Road, and Turnpin Lane are all worth a look. If you need pub grub, Greenwich has almost 100 pubs, with some boasting that they're mere milliseconds from the prime meridian.

Markets: Thanks to its markets, Greenwich throbs with day-trippers on weekends. The **Greenwich Market** is an entertaining mini-Covent Garden, located in the middle of the block between the Cutty Sark DLR station and the Old Royal Naval College—right on your way to the sights (Wed 11:00–18:00, Thu–Sun 10:00–17:30, closed Mon–Tue; farmer's market on Wed, food court on Thu–Sun, antiques on Thu–Fri, arts and crafts on Fri–Sun; tel. 020/7515-7153, www.greenwichmarket.net). The **Clocktower Market** sells old odds and ends at high prices on Greenwich High Road, near the post office (Sat–Sun only 10:00–16:00, www.clocktowermarket.co.uk).

Tourist Information

The TI is inside the Discover Greenwich information center (described later, under "Sights in Greenwich"). From the DLR station, exit straight ahead to the monumental gateway for the Old Royal Naval College complex; Discover Greenwich is just inside the gate on the left (daily 10:00–17:00, Pepys House, 2 Cutty Sark Gardens, toll tel. 0870-608-2000, www.visitgreenwich.org.uk).

Guided walks, which depart from the TI, offer an overview of the town and go past most of the big sights (£6, daily at 12:15 and 14:15, 1.5 hours; the only sights entered are the Painted Hall and Chapel, and only on the 14:15 tour).

Sights in Greenwich

I've organized these listings as a handy sightseeing walk through town, starting right next to the Cutty Sark DLR station.

▲▲**Cutty Sark**—The Scottish-built *Cutty Sark* was the last of the great China tea clippers, and was the queen of the seas when first launched in 1869. With 32,000 square feet of sail, she could blow with the wind 300 miles in a day. The ship is closed for renovation until at least late 2011—check www.cuttysark.org.uk for updates.

Discover Greenwich—This new visitors center (which also houses the TI) is located at the corner of the Old Royal Naval College closest to the *Cutty Sark*. While it's hardly a museum, it offers a decent introduction to Greenwich. In the center, a model of the town lights up to tell its history. Surrounding the model are displays and artifacts from various people who have left their mark on the town, and exhibits about the architecture and construction of Greenwich's fine buildings (free, daily 10:00–17:00).

Adjoining Discover Greenwich are the TI and a recommended pub, The Old Brewery.

▲**Old Royal Naval College**—The college was originally a hospital founded by Queen Mary II and King William III in 1692 as a charity to care for retired or injured naval officers (called pensioners). William and Mary spared no expense, hiring the great Christopher Wren to design the complex (though other architects completed it). Its days as a hospital ended in 1869, and it served as a college for training naval officers from 1873 to 1998. Now that the Royal Navy has moved out, the public is invited to view the college's elaborate Painted Hall and Chapel, which are in symmetrical buildings that face each other overlooking a broad riverfront park.

Cost and Hours: Free, daily 10:00–17:00, sometimes closed for private events, choral service Sun at 11:00 in chapel—all are welcome. Guides give 1.5-hour tours covering the hall and chapel, along with other areas not open to the general public (£5, daily at 11:30 and 14:00, call ahead to check availability). Tel. 020/8269-4799, www.oldroyalnavalcollege.org.

❷ **Self-Guided Tour:** Good descriptions are free to borrow in each building, or you can buy the fun *Nasty Naval College* brochure, with offbeat facts about the place (50p). Guides called Yeoman Warders are often standing by to answer questions.

Here's an overview of what you'll see:

Painted Hall: Originally intended as a dining hall for pensioners, this sumptuously painted room was deemed too glorious (and, in the winter, too cold) for that purpose. So almost as soon as it was completed, it became simply a place to impress visitors.

Enter the hall, climb the stairs, and gape up at one of the largest painted ceilings in Europe—112 feet long. It's a big propaganda

Greenwich

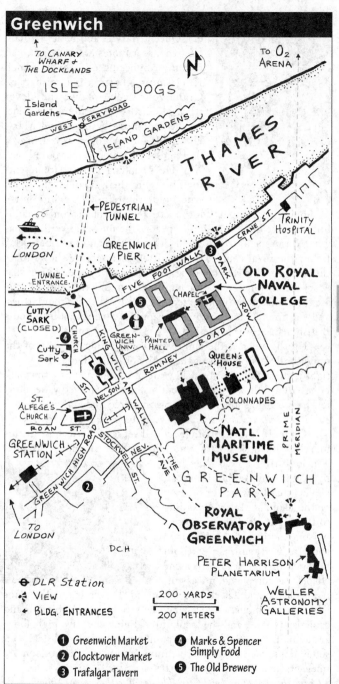

TO CANARY
WHARF &
THE DOCKLANDS

TO O₂
ARENA

ISLE OF DOGS

Island
Gardens

WEST FERRY ROAD

Island Gardens

THAMES RIVER

PEDESTRIAN TUNNEL

CRANE ST.

TRINITY HOSPITAL

GREENWICH PIER

FIVE FOOT WALK

TO LONDON

TUNNEL ENTRANCE

OLD ROYAL NAVAL COLLEGE

CHAPEL

PARK ROW

CUTTY SARK (CLOSED)

GREENWICH UNIV.

PAINTED HALL

ROMNEY ROAD

Cutty Sark

CHURCH ST.

KING WILLIAM WALK

NELSON

QUEEN'S HOUSE

COLONNADES

ST. ALFEGE'S CHURCH

ROAN ST.

STOCKWELL ST.

NEV. ST.

THE AVE.

NAT'L. MARITIME MUSEUM

PRIME MERIDIAN

GREENWICH STATION

GREENWICH HIGH ROAD

GREENWICH PARK

TO LONDON

ROYAL OBSERVATORY GREENWICH

DCH

PETER HARRISON PLANETARIUM

WELLER ASTRONOMY GALLERIES

⊕ DLR Station
⚡ VIEW
↟ BLDG. ENTRANCES

200 YARDS
200 METERS

❶ Greenwich Market
❷ Clocktower Market
❸ Trafalgar Tavern

❹ Marks & Spencer
Simply Food
❺ The Old Brewery

GREENWICH

scene, glorifying the building's founders, Queen Mary II and King William III (who, as a Protestant monarch, had recently trounced the Catholic French King Louis XIV in a pivotal battle). Crane your neck—or use the clever wheeled mirrors—to examine the scene. In the center are William and Mary. Under his foot, William is crushing a dark figure with a broken sword...Louis XIV. He is handing a red cap (representing liberty) to the woman on the right, who holds the reins of a white horse (symbolizing Europe). On the left, a white-robed woman hands him an olive branch, a sign of peace. The message: William has granted Europe liberty by saving it from the tyranny of Louis XIV. Below the royal couple, the Spirit of Architecture shows them the plans for this very building (commemorating the sad fact that Mary died before she saw it completed). Ringing the central image are the four seasons (represented by Zodiac signs), the four virtues, and—at the top and bottom—a captured Spanish galleon and a British man-of-war battleship.

Up the steps at the end of the room, along the wall of the **upper hall,** is a portrait of the family of King George I. On the right is the artist who spent 19 years of his life painting this hall, James Thornhill. He's holding out his hand—reportedly, he didn't feel he was paid enough for this Sistine-sized undertaking.

• *Exit the hall, and cross the field to enter the building with the...*

Chapel: Not surprisingly, you'll sense a nautical air in this fine chapel. Notice the rope motif in the floor tiles down the aisle.

The painting above the altar, by American Benjamin West, depicts the shipwreck of St. Paul on the island of Malta. According to the Bible, Paul came across a poisonous viper and threw it in the fire, miraculously without being injured. Soon after the chapel was completed, it was gutted by a fire, and had to be redecorated all over again. The plans were too ambitious, so they cut corners. Some of the columns and capitals are fake, and the "sculptures" lining the nave high above are actually *trompe l'oeil*—3-D paintings meant to look real. But some items, such as the marble frame around the main door, are finely crafted.

• *Leave the chapel, and walk straight down to the water—enjoying the sweeping views across to the Docklands. When you hit the river, turn right for the...*

Thames to Trafalgar Tavern Stroll—Wander east along the Thames on Five Foot Walk (named for the width of the path). Notice that the Old Royal Naval College is split into two parts; reportedly, Queen Mary didn't want the view from the Queen's House blocked. Looking up from the river, you'll see the college's twin-domed towers (one giving the time, the other the direction of the wind) framing the Queen's House, and the Royal Observatory Greenwich crowning the hill beyond.

Continuing downstream, just past the college, you'll find the **Trafalgar Tavern.** Dickens knew the pub well, and he used

it as the setting for the wedding breakfast in *Our Mutual Friend.* Built in 1837 in the Regency style to attract Londoners downriver, the tavern is popular with locals (and tourists) for its fine lunches. The upstairs Nelson Room is still used for weddings. Its formal moldings and elegant windows with balconies over the Thames

are a step back in time. In addition to the casual pub, they also have an elegant ground-floor dining room (£6–11 pub grub; £6–8 starters and £11–17 entrées in restaurant; food served Mon–Sat 12:00–22:00, Sun 12:00–17:00, Park Row, tel. 020/8858-2909).

A mile downstream from the pub, the **O₂ Arena** (formerly the "Millennium Dome") languished for nearly a decade after its con-

troversial construction and brief life as a millennial "world's fair" site. Plans for a casino and hotel project fell through, although it has come in handy as an emergency homeless shelter. It was finally bought by a developer a few years ago and rechristened "The O₂" in honor of the telecommunications company that paid for the naming rights. Currently, it hosts concerts and sporting events, and will see action during the 2012 Summer Olympics. Whatever it's called, locals will no doubt continue to grumble about its original cost.

• *From the Trafalgar Tavern, walk two long blocks up Park Row, and turn right (through the gate near the corner) into the park. The palatial buildings in the middle of the park are the Queen's House and the Maritime Museum; the Royal Observatory Greenwich is on the hilltop beyond.*

GREENWICH

Queen's House—This building, the first Palladian-style villa in Britain, was designed in 1616 by Inigo Jones for James I's wife, Anne of Denmark. All traces of the queen are long gone, and the Great Hall and Royal Apartments now serve as an art gallery for the National Maritime Museum. Predictably, most of the art is nautical-themed, with plenty of paintings of ships and sea battles, and portraits of admirals and captains. The Orangery is home to various Christ-like paintings depicting the death of Admiral Nelson—the naval hero who is so adored here in England's naval capital. Among these is the great J. M. W. Turner painting *Battle of Trafalgar*, his largest and only royal commission. The painting is often out on loan, so ask at the entry before you look for it (free, daily 10:00–17:00, last entry 30 minutes before closing, tel. 020/8858-4422, www.nmm.ac.uk).

▲**National Maritime Museum**—Great for anyone interested in the sea, this museum holds everything from a *Titanic* passenger's pocket watch to the uniform Admiral Nelson wore when he was killed at Trafalgar (look for the bullet hole, in the left shoulder). A big glass roof tops three levels of slick, modern, kid-friendly exhibits about all things seafaring.

The Explorers exhibit covers early expeditions and an ill-fated Arctic trip, complete with a soundtrack of creaking wooden ships and crashing waves. One room displays stained-glass windows honoring members of London's Baltic Exchange (an important shipping consortium) killed in World War I. Kids like the All Hands and Bridge galleries, where they can send secret messages by Morse code and operate a miniature dockside crane. Along with displays of lighthouse technology, a whaling cannon, and a Greenpeace "survival pod," you'll see model ships, nautical paintings, and various salty odds and ends. Note that some parts of the museum are closed for renovation until 2012, though there's still plenty to see.

Cost and Hours: Free, daily 10:00–17:00, last entry 30 minutes before closing; look for family-oriented events posted at entrance—singing, treasure hunts, storytelling—particularly on weekends; tel. 020/8312-6608, www.nmm.ac.uk.

• *The final sight in town—the Royal Observatory—is at the top of the hill just behind the National Maritime Museum. To reach it, you'll cross through the colonnade connecting the museum and the Queen's House, then follow the crowds as they huff up the steep hill (allow 10-15 minutes).*

▲▲**Royal Observatory Greenwich**—Located on the prime meridian (0° longitude), the observatory is famous as the point from which all time is measured. However, the observatory's early work had nothing to do with coordinating the world's clocks to Greenwich Mean Time (GMT). The observatory was founded in 1675 by Charles II for the purpose of improving navigation by more accurately charting the night sky. Today, the Greenwich time signal is linked with the BBC (which broadcasts the famous "pips" worldwide at the top of the hour). A visit here gives you a taste of the science of astronomy, timekeeping, and seafaring—and how they all meld together—along with great views over Greenwich and the distant London skyline.

Cost and Hours: Free entry to observatory, daily 10:00–17:00, later in summer—can be as late as 20:00, courtyard sometimes open later than buildings, last entry 30 minutes before closing. Tel. 020/8858-4422, www.nmm.ac.uk.

Planetarium: Shows cost £6.50, last 30 minutes, and generally run every hour (usually Mon–Fri 13:00–16:00, Sat–Sun 11:00–16:00, fewer shows in winter, schedule can change from day to day). Confirm times by calling ahead, checking online, or picking up a flier (which you'll see around the observatory). As these shows can sell out, consider calling ahead to order tickets (see phone number above).

❷ Self-Guided Tour: As you hike up the hill to the observatory, look along the roof to see the orange **Time Ball**—also visible from the Thames—which drops daily at 13:00. Nearby, under the analog clock just outside the courtyard, see how your foot measures up to the foot where the public standards of length are cast in bronze.

Entering the observatory, you're directed to choose between two routes: the meridian route, to the right; and the astronomy route, to the left. Since the meridian route is more interesting, do that first.

Meridian Route: Following signs, you'll have the chance to rent an audioguide (£3.50, 1 hour), then enter the courtyard.

Running through the middle of this space is The Line—the **prime meridian.** Visitors wait patiently in line to have their photographs taken as they straddle the line in front of the monument, with one foot in each hemisphere. While watching all this fuss over a little line, consider that—unlike the equator—the placement of the prime meridian is totally arbitrary. It could well have been at my house, in Timbuktu, or just a few feet over—as, for a time, it was (the trough along the building's roofline shows where one astronomer had placed

GREENWICH

The Longitude Problem

Around 1700, as England's ships began to venture farther from their home island, the alarming increase in the number of shipwrecks made it clear that navigational tools had to be improved. Determining latitude—the relative position between the equator and the North or South Pole—was straightforward; sailors needed only to measure the angle of the sun at noon. But figuring out longitude, or their east-west position, was not as easy without a fixed point (such as the equator) from which to measure.

In 1714, the British government offered the £20,000 Longitude Prize. Two successful solutions emerged, and both are tied to Greenwich.

The first approach was to map the stars in the night sky over Greenwich. Then, sailors at sea could compare the stars overhead to the Greenwich map and calculate their east-west position. Visitors to the Royal Observatory can still see the giant telescopes—under retractable roofs—that were used to carefully chart the movement of the stars night after night.

The second approach was to create a clock that would remain completely accurate on voyages—no easy feat back then, when turbulence and changes in weather and humidity made timepieces notoriously unreliable at sea. John Harrison spent 45 years working on this problem, finally succeeding in 1760 with his fourth effort, the H4 (which won him the Longitude Prize). You can see all four of his attempts at the Royal Observatory.

So, how can a clock determine longitude? Every 15° of longitude equals an hour when comparing the difference in sunrise or sunset times between two places. For example, the time gap between Greenwich and New York City is five hours, which translates into a longitudinal difference of 75°. Equipped with an accurate timepiece set to Greenwich Mean Time, sailors could figure out their longitude by comparing sunset time at their current position with sunset time back in Greenwich.

Notice that both approaches use Greenwich as a baseline—either on an astral map or on a clock. That's why, to this day, the prime meridian and official world time are both centered in this unassuming London suburb.

it). While waiting for your turn, set your wristwatch to the digital clock showing GMT to a tenth of a second.

Three different attractions are scattered around this courtyard. First, hiding in a corner is the **camera obscura.** This thrillingly low-tech device projects a live image from Greenwich onto a flat disc in a darkened room, simply by manipulating light, without electricity or machinery. Bizarre as this seems today, imagine how astonishing it was in the days before television.

The smaller building is the **Flamsteed House,** named for the first king-appointed Astronomer Royal (in 1675). It contains the apartments that he lived in, and the Wren-designed Octagon Room, where Flamsteed carried out some of his work. Downstairs is a fascinating exhibit on the "Longitude Problem" and how it was solved (see sidebar). Also on display are all four of John Harrison's sea clocks. Compared to his other contraptions, the fourth and final attempt looks like an oversized pocket watch. But, in terms of its impact, this little timepiece is right up there with the printing press, the cotton gin, the telegraph, and the money belt on the scale of human achievement.

Finally, the **Telescopes Exhibition,** in the larger house, has a wide assortment of historical telescopes, including a couple of room-sized ones.

• *Now head out back for the...*

Astronomy Route: Walk past the giant rusted-copper cone top of the planetarium. The building beyond houses the **Weller Astronomy Galleries,** where interactive, kid-pleasing displays allow you to guide a space mission and touch a 4.5-billion-year-old meteorite. You can also buy tickets for and enter the state-of-the-art, 120-seat **Peter Harrison Planetarium** from here (for details, see "Planetarium," earlier).

Before you leave the observatory grounds, enjoy the **view** from the overlook—the symmetrical royal buildings, the Thames, the

Docklands and its busy cranes (including the tallest building in Britain, Canary Wharf Tower, a.k.a. One Canada Square), the huge O_2 Arena, and the square-mile City of London, with its skyscrapers and the dome of St. Paul's Cathedral. At night (17:00–24:00), look for the green laser beam the observatory projects into the sky (best viewed in winter), extending along the prime meridian for 15 miles.

Eating in Greenwich

If you're in town on a weekend, be sure to drop by the **Greenwich Market,** which hosts a sprawling food court (Thu–Sun 10:00–17:30, directly in front of Cutty Sark DLR station). Another handy place to pick up ready-made food is **M&S Simply Food,** between the DLR station and the *Cutty Sark* dry dock (Mon–Sat 8:30–21:00, Sun 10:00–21:00, 55 Greenwich Church Street, tel. 020/7228-2545).

The Trafalgar Tavern, described under "Sights in Greenwich" on page 203, is good (Mon–Sat 12:00–22:00, Sun 12:00–17:00, Park Row, tel. 020/8858-2909).

The Old Brewery, in the Discover Greenwich center on the Old Royal Naval College grounds, is an upscale gastropub decorated with all things beer. A brewery formerly on this site used to provide the daily ration of four pints of beer for pensioners at the hospital. Today it's a microbrewery offering 50 different beers, while a beer sommelier suggests the right pairings with food on the menu (£6–12 pub grub; part of the pub becomes a fancier restaurant in the evenings with £5–6 starters and £11–17 entrées; daily 10:00–23:00, lunch 12:00–17:00, dinner from 18:00, tel. 020/3327-1280).

Windsor

Windsor, a compact and easy walking town of about 30,000 people, originally grew up around the royal residence. In 1070, William the Conqueror continued his habit of kicking Saxons out of their various settlements, taking over what the locals called "Windlesora" (meaning "riverbank with a hoisting crane")—which later became "Windsor." William built the first fortified castle on a chalk hill above the Thames; later, kings added on to his early designs, rebuilding and expanding the castle and surrounding gardens.

By setting up primary residence here, modern monarchs increased Windsor's popularity and prosperity—most notably, Queen Victoria, whose stern statue glares at you as you approach the castle. After her death, Victoria rejoined her beloved husband Albert in the Royal Mausoleum at Frogmore House, a mile south of the castle in a private section of the Home Park (house and mausoleum rarely open). The current Queen considers Windsor her primary residence, and the one where she feels most at home. You can tell if Her Majesty is in residence by checking to see which flag is flying above the round tower: If it's the royal standard (a red, yellow, and blue flag) instead of the Union Jack, the Queen is at home.

While 99 percent of visitors just come to see the castle and go, some enjoy spending the night. Windsor's charm is most evident when the tourists are gone. Consider overnighting here—parking and access to Heathrow Airport are easy, day-tripping into London is feasible, and an evening at the horse races (on Mondays) is hoof-pounding, heart-thumping fun.

Getting to Windsor

By Train: Windsor has two train stations—Windsor & Eton Central (5-minute walk to palace, TI inside) and Windsor & Eton Riverside (5-minute walk to palace and TI). First Great Western trains run between London's Paddington Station and Windsor & Eton Central (3/hour, 35 minutes, change at Slough; £8 one-way standard class, £8.50–11 same-day return, www.firstgreatwestern .co.uk). South West Trains run between London's Waterloo Station and Windsor & Eton Riverside (2/hour, 1 hour; £8.20 one-way standard class, £9–15 same-day return, info toll tel. 0845-748-4950, www.nationalrail.co.uk).

If you're day-tripping into London from Windsor, ask at the train station about combining a same-day return train ticket with a One-Day Travelcard as one ticket (£12–21, lower price for travel after 9:30, covers rail transportation to and from London and doubles as an all-day Tube and bus pass in town, rail ticket may also qualify you for half-price London sightseeing discounts—ask or look for brochure at station, or go to www.daysoutguide.co.uk).

By Bus: Green Line buses #701 and #702 run from London's Victoria Colonnades (between the Victoria train and coach stations) to the Parish Church stop on Windsor's High Street, before continuing on to Legoland (£1–9 one-way, £9.50–13.50 round-trip, prices vary depending on time of day, 1–2/hour, 1.25 hours to Windsor, tel. 01344/782-222, www.rainbowfares.com).

By Car: Windsor is about 20 miles from London, and just off Heathrow Airport's landing path. The town (and then the castle and Legoland) is well-signposted from the M4 motorway. It's a convenient first stop if you're arriving at and renting a car from Heathrow, and saving London until the end of your trip.

From Heathrow Airport: Buses #71 and #77 run between Terminal 5 and Windsor, dropping you in the center of town on Peascod Street (about £7, 1–2/hour, 45 minutes, toll tel. 0871-200-2233, www.firstgroup.com). London black cabs can charge whatever they like from Heathrow to Windsor (and do); avoid them by calling a local cab company, such as Windsor Radio Cars (£20, tel. 01753/677-677, www.windsorcars.com).

Orientation to Windsor

(area code: 01753)

Windsor's pleasant pedestrian shopping zone litters the approach to its famous palace with fun temptations. You'll find most shops and restaurants around the castle on High and Thames Streets, and down the pedestrian Peascod Street (PESS-cot), which runs perpendicular to High Street.

WINDSOR

Windsor

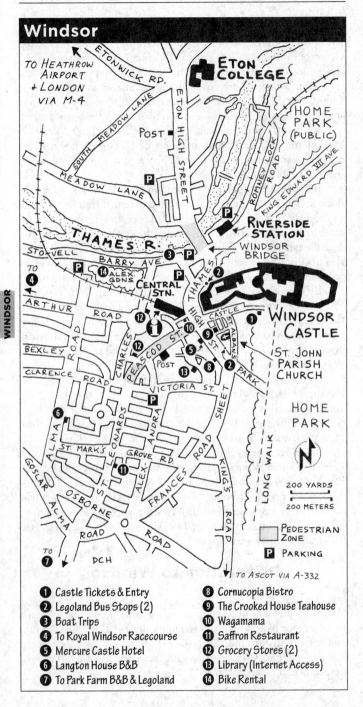

TO HEATHROW
AIRPORT
& LONDON
VIA M-4

ETONWICK RD.

ETON COLLEGE

HOME PARK (PUBLIC)

SOUTH MEADOW LANE

POST

ETON HIGH STREET

MEADOW LANE

ROMNEY LOCK ROAD

KING EDWARD VII AVE

P

P

RIVERSIDE STATION

THAMES R.

STOVELL

BARRY AVE.

❸

P

WINDSOR BRIDGE

WINDSOR

P

❷

TO
❹

P

⑭ ALEX. GDNS.

Central Stn.

Thames

High St.

WINDSOR CASTLE

❶

ARTHUR

ROAD

⑫

ℹ

PEASCOD ST.

Castle

St. Albans Park

St. John Parish Church

❷

BEXLEY

ROAD

⑫

CHARLES

POST

❺

⑩

❾

❽

⑬

HOME PARK

CLARENCE ROAD

VICTORIA ST.

SHEET

LEONARDS ROAD

ALMA

ROAD

❻

ST. MARK'S

GROVE RD.

ALEX. ANDRA

ROAD

KING'S ROAD

LONG WALK

GOSLAR

ALMA

OSBORNE

⑪

FRANCES ROAD

N

200 YARDS

200 METERS

TO
❼

DCH

TO ASCOT VIA A-332

PEDESTRIAN ZONE

P PARKING

❶ Castle Tickets & Entry
❷ Legoland Bus Stops (2)
❸ Boat Trips
❹ To Royal Windsor Racecourse
❺ Mercure Castle Hotel
❻ Langton House B&B
❼ To Park Farm B&B & Legoland
❽ Cornucopia Bistro
❾ The Crooked House Teahouse
⑩ Wagamama
⑪ Saffron Restaurant
⑫ Grocery Stores (2)
⑬ Library (Internet Access)
⑭ Bike Rental

WINDSOR

Tourist Information

The TI is adjacent to Windsor & Eton Central Station, in the Windsor Royal Shopping Centre's Old Booking Hall (May–Sept Mon–Fri 9:30–17:30, Sat 9:30–17:00, Sun 10:00–16:00; Oct–April Mon–Sat 10:00–17:00, Sun 11:00–16:00; tel. 01753/743-900, www.windsor.gov.uk). The TI sells discount tickets to Legoland (adults-£33, children-£23).

Arrival in Windsor

By Train: The train to Windsor & Eton Central Station from Paddington (via Slough) will spit you out in a shady shopping pavilion (which houses the TI), only a few minutes' walk from the castle. If you arrive instead at Windsor & Eton Riverside Station (from Waterloo Station), you'll see the castle as you exit—just follow the wall to the castle entrance.

By Car: Follow signs from the M4 motorway for pay-and-display parking in the center. River Street Car Park is closest to the castle, but pricey and often full. The cheaper, bigger Alexandra Car Park (near the riverside Alexandra Gardens) is farther west. To walk to the town center from the Alexandra Car Park, head east through the tour-bus parking lot toward the castle. At the souvenir shop, walk up the stairs (or take the elevator) and cross the overpass to the Windsor & Eton Central Station. Just beyond the station, you'll find the TI in the Windsor Royal Shopping Centre.

Helpful Hints

Internet Access: Get online for free at the **library,** located on Bachelors' Acre, between Peascod and Victoria Streets (Mon and Thu 9:30–17:00, Tue 9:30–20:00, Wed 14:00–17:00, Fri 9:30–19:00, Sat 9:30–15:00, closed Sun, tel. 01753/743-940, www.rbwm.gov.uk).

Supermarkets: Pick up picnic supplies at **Marks & Spencer** (Mon–Sat 9:00–18:00, Sun 11:00–17:00, 130 Peascod Street, tel. 01753/852-266) or at **Waitrose** (Mon–Tue and Sat 8:30–19:00, Wed–Fri 8:30–20:00, Sun 11:00–17:00, King Edward Court Shopping Centre, just south of the Windsor & Eton Central Station, tel. 01753/860-565). Just outside the castle, you'll find long benches near the statue of Queen Victoria—great for people-watching while you munch.

Bike Rental: Extreme Motion, near the river in Alexandra Gardens, rents 21-speed mountain bikes as well as helmets (£12/4 hours, £17/day, helmets-£1–1.50, £100 credit-card deposit required, bring passport as ID, summer daily 10:00–22:00, tel. 01753/830-220, www.extrememotion.com).

Sights in Windsor

▲▲Windsor Castle

Windsor Castle, the official home of England's royal family for 900 years, claims to be the largest and oldest occupied castle in the world. Thankfully, touring it is simple. You'll see immense grounds, lavish staterooms, a crowd-pleasing dollhouse, an art gallery, and the chapel.

Cost and Hours: £16, family pass-£42, daily March–Oct 9:45–17:15, Nov–Feb 9:45–16:15, last entry 1.25 hours before closing, tel. 020/7766-7304, www.royalcollection.org.uk.

Tours: As you enter, ask about the warden's free 30-minute guided walks around the grounds (2/hour). They cover the grounds but not the castle, which is well-described by the included audioguide (skip the official guidebook).

Other Activities: The **Changing of the Guard** takes place Monday through Saturday at 11:00 (April–July) and on alternating days the rest of the year (check website to confirm schedule; ceremonies begin a little earlier—get there by 10:45). There is no Changing of the Guard on Sundays or in very wet weather. There's an **evensong** in the chapel nightly at 17:15—free for worshippers.

◑ Self-Guided Tour: Immediately upon entering, you pass through a simple modern building housing a **historical overview** of the castle. This excellent intro

is worth a close look—you're basically on your own after this. Inside, you'll find the motte (artificial mound) and bailey (fortified stockade around it) of William the Conqueror's castle. Dating from 1080, this was his first castle in England.

Follow the signs to the staterooms/gallery/dollhouse. **Queen Mary's Dollhouse**—a palace in miniature (1:12 scale, from 1924) and "the most famous dollhouse in the world"—often has the longest wait. If dollhouses aren't your cup of tea, you can skip that line and go immediately into the lavish **staterooms.** Strewn with history and the art of a long line of kings and queens, they're the best I've seen in Britain—and well-restored after the devastating 1992 fire. Take advantage of the talkative docents in each room, who are happy to answer your questions.

The adjacent gallery is a changing exhibit featuring the **royal art collection** (and some big names, such as Michelangelo and Leonardo). Signs direct you (downhill) to **St. George's Chapel.** Housing numerous royal tombs, it's a fine example of Perpendicular

Gothic, with classic fan vaulting spreading out from each pillar (dating from about 1500). The simple chapel containing the tombs of the current Queen's parents, King George VI and "Queen Mother" Elizabeth, and younger sister, Princess Margaret, is along the church's north aisle. Next door is the sumptuous 13th-century **Albert Memorial Chapel,** redecorated after the death of Prince Albert in 1861 and dedicated to his memory.

More Sights in Windsor

Legoland Windsor—Paradise for Legomaniacs under 12, this huge kid-pleasing park has dozens of tame but fun rides (often with very long lines) scattered throughout its 150 acres. The

impressive Miniland has 40 million Lego pieces glued together to create 800 tiny buildings and a mini-tour of Europe; the Creation Centre boasts an 80 percent-scale Boeing 747 cockpit, made of two million bricks. Several of the more exciting rides involve getting wet, so dress accordingly or buy a cheap disposable poncho in

the gift shop. While you may be tempted to hop on the Hill Train at the entrance, it's faster and more convenient to walk down into the park. Food is available in the park, but you can save money by bringing a picnic.

Cost: Adults-£38, £34.20 in advance online, £33 from Windsor TI; children-£28, £25.20 online, £23 from TI; free for ages 3 and under; optional Q-Bot or Q-Bot Express ride-reservation gadget allows you to bypass lines (£10–40 depending on when you go and how much time you want to save); coin lockers-£1.

Hours: Convoluted schedule, but generally mid-March–July Mon–Fri 10:00–17:00, Sat–Sun 10:00–18:00, sometimes closed Tue–Wed in spring; Aug daily 9:30–20:00; Sept–Oct Thu–Mon 10:00–17:00, until 18:00 Sat–Sun, closed Tue–Wed; closed Nov–mid-March. Call or check website for exact schedule. Toll tel. 0871-222-2001, www.legoland.co.uk.

Getting There: A £4.50 round-trip shuttle bus runs from opposite Windsor's Theatre Royal on Thames Street, and from the Parish Church stop on High Street (2/hour). If day-tripping from London, ask about rail/shuttle/park admission deals from Paddington or Waterloo train stations. For drivers, the park is on B3022 Windsor/Ascot road, two miles southwest of Windsor and 25 miles west of London. Legoland is clearly signposted from the M3, M4, and M25 motorways. Parking is easy and free.

Eton College—Across the bridge from Windsor Castle you'll find many post-castle tourists filing toward the most famous "public" (the equivalent of our "private") high school in Britain. Eton was founded in 1440 by King Henry VI; today it educates about 1,300 boys (ages 13–18), who live on campus. Eton has molded the characters of 19 prime ministers, as well as members of the royal family, most recently princes William and Harry. The college is sparse on sights, but the public is allowed into the schoolyard, chapel, cloisters, and the Museum of Eton Life (£6.20, access only by one-hour guided tour at 14:00 and 15:15; tours available late-March–Sept, usually Wed and Fri–Sun but daily during spring and summer holiday; closed Oct–late March and about once a month for special events, so call ahead; no photos in chapel, no food or drink allowed; tel. 01753/671-177, www.etoncollege.com).

Boat Trips—Cruise up and down the Thames River for relaxing views of the castle, the village of Eton, Eton College, and the Royal Windsor Racecourse. Relax onboard and nibble a picnic (£5.20, family pass-from £13, 40 minutes; mid-Feb–Oct 1–2/hour daily 10:00–17:00; Nov Sat–Sun hourly 10:00–16:00, closed Mon–Fri; closed Dec–mid-Feb; tel. 01753/851-900, www.frenchbrothers .co.uk). The same company also offers a longer two-hour circular trip (£8.40, 1–2/day).

Horse Racing—The horses race near Windsor every Monday evening at the Royal Windsor Racecourse (£9–23 entry, off A308 between Windsor and Maidenhead, tel. 01753/498-400, www .windsor-racecourse.co.uk). The romantic way to get there is by a 10-minute shuttle boat (£6 round-trip, www.frenchbrothers.co.uk). The famous Ascot Racecourse (described below) is also nearby.

Near Windsor

Ascot Racecourse—Located seven miles southwest of Windsor and just north of the town of Ascot, this royally owned racecourse is one of the most famous horse-racing venues in the world. Originally opened in 1711, it is best known for June's five-day Royal Ascot race meeting, attended by the Queen and 299,999 of her loyal subjects. For many, the outlandish hats worn on Ladies Day (Thursday) are more interesting than the horses. Royal Ascot is usually the third week in June (June 14–18 in 2011), and the pricey tickets go on sale the preceding November (see website for details). In addition to Royal Ascot, the racecourse runs the ponies year-round—funny hats strictly optional (regular tickets generally £10–20, online discounts, children 17 and under free; parking-£5–7, more for special races; dress code enforced in some areas and on certain days, toll tel. 0870-727-1234, www.ascot.co.uk).

Sleeping in Windsor

(area code: 01753)

Most visitors stay in London and do Windsor as a day trip. But here are a few suggestions for those staying the night.

$$$ Mercure Castle Hotel, with 108 business-class rooms, is as central as can be, just down the street from Her Majesty's weekend retreat (Db-£120–165, nonrefundable online deals, breakfast-£16, air-con, free Wi-Fi, 18 High Street, tel. 01753/851-577, www.mercure.com, h6618@accor.com).

$$ Langton House B&B is a stately Victorian home with three well-appointed rooms lovingly maintained by Paul and Sonja Fogg (Sb-£60, Db-£95, Tb-£115, Qb-£135, 5 percent extra if paying by credit card, lower prices during slow times, family-friendly, guest kitchen, free Internet access and Wi-Fi, 46 Alma Road, tel. 01753/858-299, www.langtonhouse.co.uk, paul@langtonhouse.co.uk).

$$ Park Farm B&B, bright and cheery, is convenient for drivers visiting Legoland (Sb-£65, Db-£85, Tb-£95, Qb-£105, ask about family room with bunk beds, cash only—credit card solely for reservations, free Wi-Fi, access to shared fridge and microwave, free off-street parking, 1 mile from Legoland on St. Leonards Road near Imperial Road, 5-minute bus ride or 1-mile walk to castle, £4 taxi ride from station, tel. 01753/866-823, www.parkfarm.com, stay@parkfarm.com, Caroline and Drew Youds).

WINDSOR

Sleep Code

(£1 = about $1.60, country code: 44)

S = Single, **D** = Double/Twin, **T** = Triple, **Q** = Quad, **b** = bathroom, **s** = shower only. Unless otherwise noted, credit cards are accepted.

To help you sort through these listings easily, I've divided the rooms into three categories based on the price for a standard double room with bath:

$$$ Higher Priced—Most rooms £100 or more.
$$ Moderately Priced—Most rooms between £60-100.
$ Lower Priced—Most rooms £60 or less.

Prices can change without notice; verify the hotel's current rates online or by email. For other updates, see www.ricksteves.com/update.

Eating in Windsor

Elegant Spots with River Views: Several places flank Windsor Bridge, offering romantic dining after dark. The riverside promenade, with cheap take-away stands scattered about, is a delightful place for a picnic lunch or dinner with the swans.

Touristy Places Around the Palace: Strolling the streets and lanes around the palace entrance, you'll find countless trendy and inviting eateries. **Cornucopia Bistro** serves tasty international dishes (£11 two-course lunches, £10–14 dinner entrées, closed Mon, 6 High Street). **The Crooked House** is a touristy 17th-century timber-framed teahouse, serving fresh, hearty £8–10 lunches and cream teas in a tipsy interior or outdoors on its cobbled lane (daily 10:30–18:00, 51 High Street). **Wagamama** offers modern Asian food, mostly in the form of noodle soups, in an informal and communal setting (£7–10 dishes, daily 12:00–23:00, on the left as you face the Windsor Royal Shopping Centre).

Ethnic Food Along St. Leonards Road: Locals enjoy the vast selection of unpretentious little eateries (including a fire-station-turned-pub) just past the end of pedestrian Peascod Street. You'll also find a handful of ethnic eateries. **Saffron Restaurant** is the local choice for South Indian cuisine, with a modern interior and attentive waiters who struggle with English but are fluent at bringing out tasty dishes. Their vegetarian *thali* is a treat (open daily for lunch from noon, dinner 17:30–23:00, 99 St. Leonards Road, tel. 01753/855-467).

Cambridge

Cambridge, 60 miles north of London, is world-famous for its prestigious university. Wordsworth, Isaac Newton, Tennyson, Darwin, and Prince Charles are a few of its illustrious alumni. The university dominates—and owns—most of Cambridge, a historic town of 100,000 people. Cambridge is the epitome of a university town, with busy bikers, stately residence halls, plenty of bookshops, and proud locals who can point out where DNA was originally modeled, the atom was first split, and electrons were initially discovered.

In medieval Europe, higher education was the domain of the Church, and was limited to ecclesiastical schools. Scholars lived in "halls" on campus. This academic community of residential halls, chapels, and lecture halls connected by peaceful garden courtyards survives today in the colleges that make up the universities of Cambridge and Oxford. By 1350 (Oxford is roughly 100 years older), Cambridge had eight colleges, each with a monastic-type courtyard, chapel, library, and lodgings. Today, Cambridge has 31 colleges, each with its own facilities. In the town center, these grand old halls date back centuries, with ornately decorated facades that try to one-up each other. While students' lives revolve around their independent college, the university organizes lectures, presents degrees, and promotes research.

The university schedule has three terms: the Lent term from mid-January to mid-March, the Easter term from mid-April to mid-June, and the Michaelmas term from early October to early December. During exam time (roughly the month of May), the colleges are closed to visitors, which can impede access to all the picturesque little corners of the town. But the main sights—King's College Chapel and Trinity Library—stay open, and Cambridge is never sleepy.

If you're choosing between England's two university towns—Cambridge and Oxford—it's hard to go wrong. I prefer Cambridge as a town—it's cozier, more appealing, and very handy from London. However, Cambridge is not really on the way to anything, making it better as a side-trip than as a stopover. For convenience, you can't beat Oxford, which sits near the Cotswolds, Stratford-upon-Avon, and other major sights.

Planning Your Time

Cambridge is worth most of a day but not an overnight. Start by taking the TI's walking tour, which includes a visit to the town's only must-see sight, the King's College Chapel (first tour at 11:00, later on Sun, call ahead to confirm and reserve—see "Tours in Cambridge," later). Spend the afternoon touring the Fitzwilliam Museum (closed Mon), or simply enjoying the ambience of this stately old college town.

Getting to Cambridge

By Train: It's an easy trip from London and less than an hour away. Catch the train from London's King's Cross Station (3/hour, fast trains leave at :15 and :45 past the hour and run in each direction, 45 minutes, £20 one-way standard class, £21 same-day return after 9:30, operated by First Capital Connect, toll tel. 0845-748-4950, www.firstcapitalconnect.co.uk or www.nationalrail.co.uk). Trains also run from London's Liverpool Street Station—though more frequent, they take longer (4/hour, 1.25 hours).

By Bus: National Express coaches run from London's Victoria

Coach Station to the Parkside stop in Cambridge (hourly, 2–2.5 hours, £11.50, toll tel. 08717-818-181).

Orientation to Cambridge

(area code: 01223)

Cambridge is congested but small. Everything is within a pleasant walk. There are two main streets, separated from the Cam River by the most interesting colleges. The town center, brimming with tearooms, has a TI and a colorful open-air market square. The train station is about a mile to the southeast.

Tourist Information

Cambridge's TI is well-run and well-signposted, just off Market Square in the town center. They book rooms for £5, and sell bus tickets, a £0.50 town map, and a bigger £1 map/guide (Mon–Sat 10:00–17:00, Easter–Sept also Sun 11:00–15:00—otherwise closed Sun, phones answered from 9:00, Peas Hill, toll tel. 0871-226-8006, room-booking tel. 01223/457-581, www.visitcambridge .org).

Arrival in Cambridge

By Train: Cambridge's train station doesn't have baggage storage, but you can pay to leave your bags at the nearby bike-rental shop (see "Helpful Hints," below). The station also lacks a TI, but it does have automated machines that dispense city maps for a £1 coin.

To get from the station to downtown Cambridge, you have several options. You can **walk** for about 25 minutes (exit straight ahead on Station Road, bear right at the war memorial onto Hills Road, and follow it into town); take a public **bus** marked *Citi1*, *Citi3*, or *Citi7* (£1.30, pay driver, runs every 5–10 minutes, get off at Emmanuel Street stop—look for Grand Arcade shopping mall on the left); pay about £5 for a **taxi;** or book a City Sightseeing **bus tour** (described later).

By Car: Drivers can follow signs from the M11 motorway to any of the handy and central short-stay parking lots. Or you can leave the car at one of five park-and-ride lots outside the city, then take the shuttle into town (free parking, shuttle costs £2.30 round-trip if you buy ticket from machine, or £2.60 from driver).

Helpful Hints

Festival: The **Cambridge Folk Festival** gets things humming and strumming (July 28–31 in 2011, www.cambridgefolkfestival .co.uk).

Bike Rental: Station Cycles, located about a block to your right as you exit the station, rents bikes (£8/4 hours, £10/day,

Cambridge

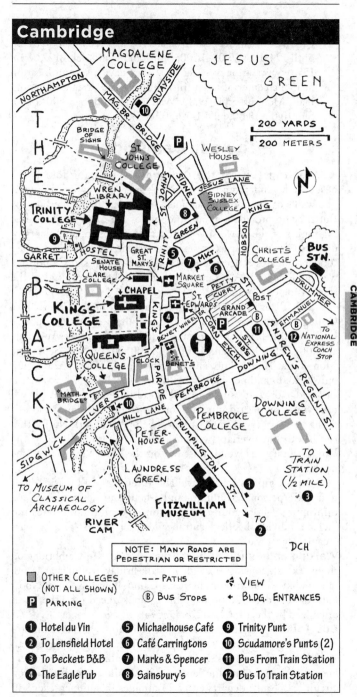

MAGDALENE COLLEGE

JESUS GREEN

NORTHAMPTON

MAG. BR.

QUAYSIDE

BRIDGE

T H E

BRIDGE OF SIGHS

ST. JOHN'S COLLEGE

WREN LIBRARY

TRINITY COLLEGE

GARRET HOSTEL

ST. JOHN'S ST.

SIDNEY ST.

WESLEY HOUSE

JESUS LANE

SIDNEY SUSSEX COLLEGE

HOBSON ST.

KING ST.

CHRIST'S COLLEGE

200 YARDS
200 METERS

N

BUS STN.

SENATE HOUSE

TRINITY ST.

GREAT ST. MARY'S

CLARE COLLEGE

CHAPEL

KING'S COLLEGE

B A C K S

QUEEN'S COLLEGE

CLOCK TOWER

"MATH. BRIDGE"

SIDGWICK

SILVER ST.

HILL LANE

PETER-HOUSE

TO MUSEUM OF CLASSICAL ARCHAEOLOGY

LAUNDRESS GREEN

RIVER CAM

MARKET SQUARE

KING'S PARADE

MKT.

ST. EDWARD'S

PETTY CURY

BENET WHEELER

CORN EXCH.

ST. BENET'S

PEMBROKE ST.

PEMBROKE COLLEGE

TRUMPINGTON ST.

FITZWILLIAM MUSEUM

ST. POST

GRAND ARCADE

ST. TIBB'S

DOWNING ST.

ST. ANDREW'S ST.

REGENT ST.

DRUMMER

EMMANUEL

CAMBRIDGE

DOWNING COLLEGE

TO NATIONAL EXPRESS COACH STOP

TO TRAIN STATION (½ MILE)

TO

DCH

NOTE: MANY ROADS ARE PEDESTRIAN OR RESTRICTED

☐ OTHER COLLEGES (NOT ALL SHOWN)

☐ PARKING

--- PATHS

Ⓑ BUS STOPS

↙ VIEW

✦ BLDG. ENTRANCES

❶ Hotel du Vin
❷ To Lensfield Hotel
❸ To Beckett B&B
❹ The Eagle Pub

❺ Michaelhouse Café
❻ Café Carringtons
❼ Marks & Spencer
❽ Sainsbury's

❾ Trinity Punt
❿ Scudamore's Punts (2)
⓫ Bus From Train Station
⓬ Bus To Train Station

helmets-50p, £75 deposit, cash or credit card) and stores luggage (£3–4/bag depending on size; Mon–Fri 8:00–18:00, Wed until 19:00, Sat 9:00–17:00, Sun 10:00–17:00, tel. 01223/307-125, www.stationcycles.co.uk). They have a second location near the center of town (inside the Grand Arcade shopping mall, Mon–Fri 8:00–19:00, Wed until 20:00, Sat 9:00–18:00, Sun 10:00–18:00, tel. 01223/307-655).

Tours in Cambridge

▲▲**Walking Tour of the Colleges**—A walking tour is the best way to understand Cambridge's mix of "town and gown." The walks can be more educational (read: dry) than entertaining. But they do provide a good rundown of the historic and scenic highlights of the university, some fun local gossip, and plenty of university trivia. For example, why are entering students called "undergraduates"? Because long ago, new students at Cambridge were assigned a B.A. to mentor them...so they were "under" the supervision of a "graduate."

The TI offers **daily walking tours** that include the King's College Chapel, as well as another college—usually Queen's College (£12.50, 2 hours, includes admission fees; July–Aug daily at 11:00, 12:00, 13:00, and 14:00, no 11:00 tour on Sun; Sept–June Mon–Sat at 11:00, 13:00, and another time—likely at 12:00, Sun only at 13:00 and possibly at 12:00; tel. 01223/457-574, www.visit cambridge.org). It's smart to call ahead to reserve a spot (they'll take your credit-card number), or you can drop by in person (if doing this, try to arrive 30 minutes before the tour). Notice that the 12:00 tour overlaps with the limited opening times of the Wren Library—so you'll miss out on the library if you take the noon tour.

Private guides are also available through the TI (basic 1-hour tour-£3.75/person, £55 minimum; 1.5-hour tour-£4.25/person, £62 minimum; 2-hour tour-£4.75/person, £70 minimum; does not include individual college entrance fees, tel. 01223/457-574, tours @cambridge.gov.uk).

Walking and Punting Ghost Tour—If you're in Cambridge on the weekend, consider a £5 ghost walk Friday evenings at 18:00, or a spooky £17.50 trip on the River Cam followed by a walk most Saturdays at dusk (20:00 in summer; book ahead for either tour, organized by the TI, tel. 01223/457-574).

Bus Tours—City Sightseeing hop-on, hop-off bus tours are informative and cover the outskirts, including the American WWII Cemetery. But keep in mind that walking tours go where buses can't—right into the center (£13, 80 minutes for full 21-stop circuit, cash only, departs every 20 minutes in summer, every 40 minutes in winter, first bus leaves train station at 10:06, last bus at 17:46, recorded commentary, tel. 01223/423-578, www.city-sight seeing.com). If arriving by train, you can buy your ticket from their kiosk directly in front of the station, then ride the bus into town.

Sights in Cambridge

Cambridge has many impressive old college buildings to explore, with fancy facades and tranquil grassy courtyards. I've featured the two most interesting (King's and Trinity), but feel free to wander beyond these. You might notice several bricked-up windows on the old buildings around town. This dates from a time when taxes were calculated per window...so filling them in saved money.

▲**King's Parade and Nearby**—The lively street in front of King's College, called King's Parade, seems to be where every-

one in Cambridge gathers. Looming across the street from the college is **Great St. Mary's Church**, with a climbable bell tower (£3, Mon–Sat 9:30–16:30, Sun 12:30–16:00, 123 stairs). The street out front is where students hawk punting tours on the Cam River (generally £12–15 for 45 minutes; described later, under "Punting on the Cam").

Behind the church is the thriving **Market Square.** The big market is on Sunday (9:30–16:30) and features produce, arts, and crafts. On other days, you'll find mostly clothes and food (Mon–Sat 9:30–16:00).

The imposing Neoclassical building at the top (north) end of the street is the **Senate House,** the meeting place of the university's governing body. In June, you might see green boxes lining the front of this house. Traditionally at the end of the term, students would come to these boxes to see whether or not they'd earned their degree; if their name was not on the list, they had flunked. Amazingly, until 2010 this was the only notification students received about their status. (Now they also get an email.)

In the opposite direction (south), at Benet Street, look for the strikingly modern **Corpus Clock.** Designed and commissioned by alum John Taylor, the clock was ceremonially unveiled by Stephen Hawking in 2008. It uses concentric golden dials with blue LED lights to tell the time, but it's precise only every five minutes; its otherwise-irregular timekeeping mimics the unpredictability of life. Perched on top is Chronophage, the "eater of time"—a grotesque giant grasshopper that keeps the clock moving and periodically winks at passersby. Creepy and disturbing? Exactly, says Taylor...so is the passage of time.

Just down Benet Street on the left is the **Eagle Pub**—Cambridge's oldest pub, and a sight in itself; it's worth poking into the courtyard to learn about its dynamic history, even if you don't eat or drink here (see page 228). Across the street from the pub stands the oldest surviving building in Cambridgeshire, **St. Benet's Church.** The Saxons who built the church included circular holes in its bell tower, to encourage owls to roost there and keep the mouse population under control.

▲▲**King's College Chapel**—Built from 1446 to 1515 by Henrys VI through VIII, England's best example of Perpendicular Gothic is the single most impressive building in town.

Cost and Hours: £5, erratic hours depending on school schedule and events; during academic term usually Mon–Fri 9:30–15:30, Sat 9:30–15:15, Sun 13:15–14:15; during breaks (see page 217) usually Mon–Sat 9:30–16:30, Sun 10:00–17:00. Tel. 01223/331-212, recorded info tel. 01223/331-155, www.kings.cam.ac.uk/chapel.

Evensong: When school's in session, you're welcome to enjoy an evensong service in this glorious space, with a famous choir made up of men and boys (free, Mon–Sat at 17:30, Sun at 15:30).

Getting There: You'll see the regal front facade of King's College along King's Parade. To enter the chapel, curl around the back: Facing the college on King's Parade, head right and take the first left possible (just after the Senate House, on Senate House passage); at the dead-end, bear left on Trinity Lane to reach the gate where you can pay to enter the chapel.

◑ Self-Guided Tour: Stand inside, look up, and marvel, as Christopher Wren did, at what was the largest single span of

vaulted roof anywhere—2,000 tons of incredible fan vaulting, held in place by the forces of gravity (a careful balancing act resting delicately on the buttresses visible outside the building).

While Henry VI—who began work on the chapel—wanted it to be austere, his descendants decided instead to use it to glorify the House of Tudor (of which his son, Henry VII, was the first king). Lining the walls are giant **Tudor coats-of-arms.** The shield includes a fleur-de-lis because an earlier ancestor, Edward III, woke up one day and—citing his convoluted lineage—somewhat arbitrarily declared himself king of France. The symbols on the left (a rose and the red dragon of Wales, holding the shield) represent the family of Henry VII's father, the Tudors. On the right, the greyhound holding the shield and the portcullis symbolize the family of Henry VII's mother, Lady Margaret Beaufort, who prodded her son for years to complete this chapel.

The 26 **stained-glass windows** date from the 16th century. It's the most Renaissance stained glass anywhere in one spot. (Most

of the stained glass in English churches dates from Victorian times, but this glass is much older.) The lower panes show scenes from the New Testament, while the upper panes feature corresponding stories from the Old Testament. Considering their turbulent history, it's miraculous that these windows have survived for nearly half a millennium in such a pristine state. After Henry VIII separated from the Catholic Church in 1534, many such windows and other Catholic features around England were destroyed. (Think of all those ruined abbeys dotting the English countryside.) However, since Henry had just paid for these windows, he couldn't bear to get rid of them. A century later, in the days of Oliver Cromwell, another wave of iconoclasm destroyed more windows around England. Though these windows were slated for removal, they stayed put. (Historians speculate that Cromwell's troops, who were garrisoned in this building, didn't want the windows removed in the chilly wintertime.) Finally, during World War II, the windows were taken out and hidden away to keep them safe and then painstakingly replaced.

The **choir screen** that bisects the church was commissioned by King Henry VIII to commemorate his marriage to Anne Boleyn. By the time it was finished, so was she (beheaded). But it was too late to remove her initials, which were carved into the screen (look for *R.A.*, for *Regina Anna*—"Queen Ann").

Behind the screen is the **choir** area, where the King's College Choir performs a daily evensong (see details earlier). On Christmas Eve, a special service is held here and broadcast around the world on the BBC—a tradition near and dear to the hearts of Brits.

Finally, walk to the altar and admire Rubens' masterful *Adoration of the Magi.* It's actually a family portrait: The admirer in the front (wearing red) is a self-portrait of Rubens, Mary looks an awful lot like his much-younger wife, and the Baby Jesus resembles their own newborn at the time.

▲▲**Trinity College and Wren Library**—More than a third of Cambridge's 83 Nobel Prize winners have come from this richest and biggest of the town's colleges, founded in 1546 by Henry VIII. There are three sights to see at the college: the entrance gate, the grounds, and the magnificent Wren Library.

Trinity Gate: You'll notice gates like these adorning facades of colleges around town. Above the door is a statue of **King Henry**

VIII, who founded Trinity because he feared that Cambridge's existing colleges were too cozy with the Church. Notice Henry's right hand holding a chair leg instead of the traditional crown jewels scepter. This is courtesy of Cambridge's Night Climbers, who first replaced the scepter a century ago, and continue to periodically switch it out for other items. According to campus legend, decades ago some of the world's most talented mountaineers enrolled at Cambridge... in one of the flattest parts of England. (Cambridge was actually a seaport until Dutch engineers drained the surrounding swamps.) Lacking opportunities to practice their skill, they began scaling the frilly facades of Cambridge's college buildings under cover of darkness (if caught, they'd be expelled). In the 1960s, climbers actually managed to haul an entire automobile onto the roof of the Senate House. The university had to bring in the army to cut it into pieces and remove it. Only 50 years later, at a class reunion, did the guilty parties finally 'fess up.

In the little park to the right, notice the lone **apple tree.** Supposedly, this tree is a descendant of the very one that once stood in the garden of Sir Isaac Newton (who spent 30 years at Trinity). According to legend, Newton was inspired to investigate gravity when an apple fell from the tree onto his head. This tree stopped bearing fruit long ago; if you do see apples, they've been tied on by mischievous students.

If you like, head through the gate into the...

Trinity Grounds: The grounds are enjoyable to explore, if not quite worth the cost of admission (£3, daily 9:30–17:00, last entry 45 minutes before closing, tel. 01223/338-400, www.trin .cam.ac.uk).

Inside the **Great Court,** the clock (on the tower on the right) double-rings at the top of each hour. It's a college tradition to take off running from the clock when the high noon bells begin (it takes 43 seconds to clang 24 times), race around the courtyard, touching each of the four corners without setting foot on the cobbles, and return to the same

spot by the time the ringing ends. Supposedly only one student (a young lord) ever managed the feat—a scene featured in *Chariots of Fire* (but filmed elsewhere).

The **chapel** (entrance under clock)—which pales in comparison to the stunning King's College Chapel—feels like a shrine to thinking, with statues honoring great Trinity minds both familiar (Isaac Newton, Alfred Lord Tennyson, Francis Bacon) and unfamiliar. Who's missing? The poet Lord Byron, who was such a hell-raiser during his time at Trinity that a statue of him was deemed unfit for Church property; his statue stands in the library instead.

Wren Library: Don't miss the 1695 Christopher Wren-designed library, with its wonderful carving and fascinating original manuscripts (free, Mon–Fri 12:00–14:00, Nov–mid-June also Sat 10:30–12:30, always closed Sun; only 19 people allowed in at a time). Just outside the library entrance, Sir Isaac Newton clapped his hands and timed the echo to measure the speed of sound as it raced down the side of the cloister and back. In the library's 12 display cases (covered with cloth that you flip back), you'll see handwritten works by Sir Isaac Newton and John Milton, alongside A. A. Milne's original *Winnie the Pooh* (the real Christopher Robin attended Trinity College). If you just want to see Wren Library (without paying for the grounds), enter from the riverside entrance, located by the Garret Hostel Bridge.

▲▲**Fitzwilliam Museum**—Britain's best museum of antiquities and art outside of London is the Fitzwilliam, housed in a grand Neoclassical building a 10-minute walk south of Market Square. The Fitzwilliam's broad collection is like a mini-British Museum/National Gallery rolled into one. The ground floor features an extensive range of antiquities and applied arts—everything from Greek vases, Mesopotamian artifacts, and Egyptian sarcophagi to Roman statues, fine porcelain, and suits of armor. Upstairs is the painting gallery, with works that span art history: Old Masters (such as Titian and Canaletto), a fine English section (featuring Gainsborough, Reynolds, Hogarth, and others), and a nice array of modern and contemporary art (including Picasso, Manet, and Renoir). Rounding out the collection are old manuscripts, including some musical compositions from Handel. Watch your step—in 2006, a visitor tripped and accidentally smashed three 17th-century Chinese vases. Amazingly, the vases were restored and are now on display in Gallery 17...in a protective case (free, suggested £3 donation, audio/videoguide-£3, Tue–Sat 10:00–17:00, Sun 12:00–17:00, closed Mon except Bank Holidays, no photos, Trumpington Street, tel. 01223/332-900, www.fitzmuseum.cam.ac.uk).

Museum of Classical Archaeology—Although this museum contains no originals, it offers a unique chance to see accurate copies (19th-century casts) of virtually every famous ancient Greek and Roman statue. More than 450 statues are on display. If you've seen the real things in Greece, Istanbul, Rome, and elsewhere, touring this collection is like a high school reunion..."Hey, I know you!" But since it takes some time to get here, this museum is best left to devotees of classical sculpture (free, Mon–Fri 10:00–17:00, Sat 10:00–13:00 during term, closed Sun, Sidgwick Avenue, tel. 01223/335-153, www.classics.cam.ac.uk/museum).

Getting There: The museum is a five-minute walk west of Silver Street Bridge; after crossing the bridge, continue straight until you reach a sign reading *Sidgwick Site*. The museum is in the long building on the corner to your right; the entrance is on the opposite side, and the museum is upstairs.

▲**Punting on the Cam**—For a little levity and probably more exercise than you really want, try hiring one of the traditional flat-

bottom punts at the river and pole yourself up and down (or around and around, more likely) the lazy Cam. Once you get the hang of it, it's a fine way to enjoy the scenic side of Cambridge. It's less crowded in late afternoon (and less embarrassing).

Several companies rent punts and offer tours. Hawkers try to snare passengers in the thriving people zone in front of King's College. Prices are soft in slow times—try talking them down a bit before committing.

Trinity Punt, just north of Garret Hostel Bridge, is run by Trinity College students (£12/hour, £40 deposit, 45-minute tours-£30/boat, can share ride and cost with up to 2 others, cash only, ask for quick and free lesson, Easter–mid-Oct Mon–Fri 11:00–17:30, Sat–Sun 10:00–17:30, return punts by 18:30, no rentals mid-Oct–Easter, tel. 01223/338-483). **Scudamore's** has two locations: Mill Lane, just south of the central Silver Street Bridge, and the less convenient Quayside at Magdalene Bridge, at the north end of town (rentals-£16–18/hour, £80 deposit required—can use credit card; 45-minute tours-£15/person; open daily June–Aug 9:00–22:00 or later, Sept–May at least 10:00–16:00, weather permitting, tel. 01223/359-750, www.scudamores.com).

Near Cambridge

Imperial War Museum Duxford—This former airfield, nine miles south of Cambridge, is nirvana for aviation fans and WWII buffs. Wander through seven exhibition halls housing 200 vintage aircraft (including Spitfires, B-17 Flying Fortresses, a Concorde, and a Blackbird), as well as military land vehicles and special displays on Normandy and the Battle of Britain. On many weekends, the museum holds special events, such as air shows (extra fee)—check the website for details (£16.50, show local bus ticket for discount, daily mid-March–late Oct 10:00–18:00, late Oct–mid-March 10:00–16:00, last entry one hour before closing; Concorde interior open Mon–Fri until 15:00, Sat–Sun until 16:00; tel. 01223/835-000, http://duxford.iwm.org.uk).

Getting There: The museum is located off A505 in Duxford. From Cambridge, you can take the bus marked *Citi7* from the train station (45 minutes) or from Emmanuel Street's Stop A (55 minutes, bus runs 2/hour Mon–Sat, www.stagecoachbus.com /cambridge). On Sundays and Bank Holidays, catch the #132 bus, run by private bus operator Myalls, from the train station or the Drummer Street bus station (40 minutes, first bus around 10:00, then every 2 hours until 18:00, tel. 01763/243-225).

Sleeping in Cambridge

(£1 = about $1.60, country code: 44)
While Cambridge is an easy side-trip from London, its subtle charms might convince you to spend the night. Cambridge has very few accommodations in the city center, and none in the tight maze of colleges and shops where you'll spend most of your time. These recommendations are about a 10- to 15-minute walk south of the town center, toward the train station.

$$$ Hotel du Vin blends France, England, and wine. This worthwhile splurge has 41 comfortable, spacious rooms above a characteristic bistro that offers good deals for guests and non-guests. This mod place manages to be classy yet unpretentious (Db-£120–150, fancier suites available, check online for special offers, optional £11 continental or £14 full English breakfast, air-con, elevator, pay Wi-Fi, just down the street from the Fitzwilliam Museum at Trumpington Street 15–17, tel. 01223/227-330, fax 01223/227-331, www.hotelduvin.com).

$$ Lensfield Hotel is a traditional, crank-'em-out hotel with 30 nicely appointed rooms (Sb-£65, Db-£99, pricier rooms also available, pay Wi-Fi, 53 Lensfield Road, tel. 01223/355-017, fax 01223/312-022, www.lensfieldhotel.co.uk, enquiries@lensfield hotel.co.uk).

$ Debbie and Michael Beckett rent one room in their modern home, next door to a big church halfway between downtown and the train station. The room, with a private bathroom in the hall, makes you feel like a houseguest (S-£45, D-£55, includes breakfast, 15 St. Paul's Road, tel. 01223/315-832, debbie.beckett2 @googlemail.com).

Eating in Cambridge

While picnicking is scenic and saves money, the weather may not always cooperate. Here are a few ideas for fortifying yourself with a lunch in central Cambridge.

The Eagle Pub, near the TI, is the oldest pub in town, and a Cambridge institution with a history so rich that a visit here practically qualifies as sight-

seeing. Find your way into the delightful courtyard, with outdoor seating and a good look at the place's past. The second-floor windows were once guest rooms, back when this was a coachmen's inn as well as a pub. Notice that the window on the right end is open; any local will love to tell you why. Follow the signs into the misnamed "RAF Bar," where US Air Force pilots signed the ceiling while stationed here during World War II. Science fans can celebrate the discovery of DNA—Francis Crick and James Watson first announced their findings here in 1953 (£6–8 lunches, £6–11 dinners, food served daily 10:00–22:00, drinks until 23:00, 8 Benet Street, tel. 01223/505-020).

The **Michaelhouse Café** is a heavenly respite from the crowds, tucked into the repurposed St. Michael's Church, just north of Great St. Mary's Church. At lunch, choose from salads, soups, and sandwiches, as well as a few hot dishes and a variety of tasty baked goods (£5–10 light meals, Mon–Sat 8:00–17:00, breakfast served 8:00–11:00, lunch served 11:30–15:30, hot drinks and baked goods always available, closed Sun, Trinity Street, tel. 01223/309-147). Near the end of the day—after 14:30—you can pay £4 to fill your plate with whatever they have left.

Café Carringtons is a cozy cafeteria that serves traditional British food at reasonable prices, including a Sunday roast lunch (£6–8 meals, £5 sandwiches, Mon–Sat 8:00–17:00, Sun 10:00–16:00, down the stairs at 23 Market Street, tel. 01223/361-792).

Supermarkets: There's an **M&S Simply Food** at the train station and a larger Marks & Spencer department store on Market Square (Mon–Thu 9:00–18:00, Wed until 20:00, Fri 9:00–19:00, Sat 9:00–18:30, Sun 11:00–17:00, tel. 01223/355-219). **Sainsbury's** supermarket has longer hours (Mon–Sat 8:00–23:30, Sun 11:00–17:00, 44 Sidney Street, at the corner of Green Street).

A good picnic spot is Laundress Green, a grassy park on the river, at the end of Mill Lane near the Silver Street Bridge punts. There are no benches, so bring something to sit on. Remember, the college lawns are private property, so walking or picnicking on the

CAMBRIDGE

grass is generally not allowed. When in doubt, ask at the college's entrance.

Cambridge Connections

From Cambridge by Train to: York (1–2/hour, 2.5 hours, transfer in Peterborough), **Oxford** (2/hour, 2.5 hours, change in London involves Tube transfer between train stations), **London** (King's Cross Station: 3/hour, 45–60 minutes; Liverpool Street Station: 4/hour, 1.25 hours). Train info: Toll tel. 0845-748-4950, www .nationalrail.co.uk.

By Bus to: London (hourly, 2–2.5 hours), **Heathrow Airport** (1–2/hour, 2–3 hours). Bus info: Toll tel. 08717-818-181, www .nationalexpress.com.

BATH

The best city to visit within easy striking distance of London is Bath—just a 1.5-hour train ride away. Two hundred years ago, this city of 85,000 was the trendsetting Hollywood of Britain. If ever a city enjoyed looking in the mirror, Bath's the one. It has more "government-listed" or protected historic buildings per capita than any other town in England. The entire city, built of the creamy warm-tone limestone called "Bath stone," beams in its cover-girl complexion. An architectural chorus line, it's a triumph of the Georgian style. Proud locals remind visitors that the town is routinely banned from the "Britain in Bloom" contest to give other towns a chance to win. Bath's narcissism is justified. Even with its mobs of tourists (2 million per year) and greedy prices, Bath is a joy to visit.

Bath's fame began with the allure of its (supposedly) healing hot springs. Long before the Romans arrived in the first century, Bath was known for its warm waters. Romans named the popular spa town Aquae Sulis, after a local Celtic goddess. The town's importance carried through Saxon times, when it had a huge church on the site of the present-day abbey and was considered the religious capital of Britain. Its influence peaked in 973 with King Edgar's sumptuous coronation in the abbey. Later, Bath prospered as a wool town.

Bath then declined until the mid-1600s, wasting away to just a huddle of huts around the abbey, with hot, smelly mud and 3,000 residents, oblivious to the Roman ruins 18 feet below their dirt floors. In fact, with its own walls built upon ancient ones, Bath was no bigger than that Roman town. Then, in 1687, Queen Mary, fighting infertility, bathed here. Within 10 months she gave birth to a son...and a new age of popularity for Bath.

The revitalized town boomed as a spa resort. Ninety percent of the buildings you'll see today are from the 18th century. A father-and-son team of local architects—both named John Wood (the Elder and the Younger)—were inspired by the Italian architect Andrea Palladio to build a "new Rome." The town bloomed in the Neoclassical style, and streets were lined not with scrawny sidewalks but with wide "parades," upon which the women in their stylishly wide dresses could spread their fashionable tails.

Beau Nash (1673–1762) was Bath's "master of ceremonies." He organized both the daily regimen of aristocratic visitors and the city, lighting the streets, improving security, banning swords, and opening the Pump Room. Under his fashionable baton, Bath became a city of balls, gaming, and concerts—the place to see and be seen in England. This most civilized place became even more so with the great Neoclassical building spree that followed.

These days, modern tourism has stoked the local economy, as has the fast morning train to London. (A growing number of Bath professionals catch the 7:13 train to Paddington Station every morning.) With renewed access to Bath's soothing hot springs at the Thermae Bath Spa, the venerable waters are in the spotlight again, attracting a new generation of visitors in need of a cure or a soak.

Planning Your Time

Bath deserves two nights even on a quick trip. On a three-week Britain getaway, spend three nights in Bath, with one day for the city and one day for side-trips (see next chapter). Ideally, use Bath as your jet-lag recovery pillow, and do London at the end of your trip.

Consider starting a three-week British vacation this way:

Day 1: Land at Heathrow. Connect to Bath by National Express bus—the better option—or the less convenient bus/train combination (for details, see page 186). While you don't need or want a car in Bath, and some rental companies have an office there, those who land early and pick up their cars at the airport can visit Windsor Castle (near Heathrow) and/or Stonehenge on their way to Bath. (You can also consider flying into Bristol.) If you have the evening free in Bath, take a walking tour.

Day 2: 9:00–Tour the Roman Baths; 10:30–Catch the free city walking tour; 12:30–Picnic on the open deck of a Bath tour bus; 14:00–Free time in the shopping center of old Bath; 15:30–Tour the Fashion Museum or Museum of Bath at Work. Take the evening walking tour (unless you did last night), enjoy the Bizarre Bath comedy walk, consider seeing a play, or go for a nighttime soak in the Thermae Bath Spa.

Bath

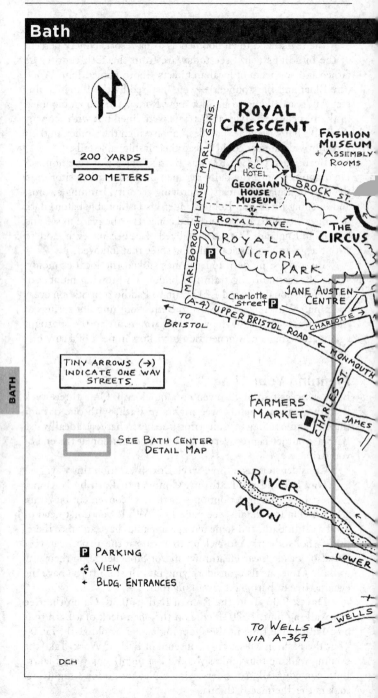

N

200 YARDS
200 METERS

ROYAL CRESCENT

FASHION MUSEUM & ASSEMBLY ROOMS

MARL. GDNS.

MARLBOROUGH LANE

R.C. HOTEL

GEORGIAN HOUSE MUSEUM

BROCK ST.

ROYAL AVE.

THE CIRCUS

P

ROYAL VICTORIA PARK

JANE AUSTEN CENTRE

Charlotte Street P

(A-4) UPPER BRISTOL ROAD

TO BRISTOL

CHARLOTTE

MONMOUTH

TINY ARROWS (→) INDICATE ONE WAY STREETS.

FARMERS' MARKET

CHARLES ST.

JAMES

SEE BATH CENTER DETAIL MAP

RIVER AVON

P PARKING
⚶ VIEW
← BLDG. ENTRANCES

LOWER

TO WELLS VIA A-367

WELLS

DCH

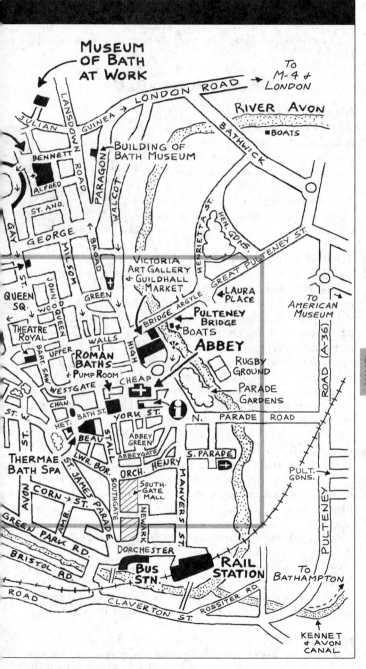

Day 3 (and possibly 4): By car, explore nearby sights. Without a car, consider a one-day Avebury/Stonehenge/cute towns minibus tour from Bath (Mad Max tours are best; see "Tours in Bath," later).

Orientation to Bath

(area code: 01225)

Bath's town square, three blocks in front of the bus and train station, is a cluster of tourist landmarks, including the abbey, Roman and Medieval Baths, and the Pump Room. Bath is hilly. In general, you'll gain elevation as you head north from the town center.

Tourist Information

The TI is in the abbey churchyard (Mon–Sat 9:30–18:00, Sun 10:00–16:00, closes one hour earlier Mon–Sat Oct–May, pricey toll tel. 0906-711-2000—50p/minute, www.visitbath.co.uk). The TI sells various visitor guides and maps—survey your options before buying one (£1-1.50). Only the most basic visitor guide—with a very rudimentary map—is free. The TI books rooms and theater tickets for no extra fee (booking tel. 0844-847-5256). If you're a Jane Austen fan, ask about the walking tours that leave from the TI on weekends. Entertainment listings from the local paper are posted on their bulletin board. You can also buy the Great British Heritage Pass here (see page 22).

Arrival in Bath

The Bath Spa **train station** has a national and international tickets desk and a privately run travel agency masquerading as a TI. Directly in front of the train station is Bath's brand-new SouthGate Bath shopping center. To get from the train station to the TI, exit straight ahead, walk two blocks up Manvers Street, and turn left at the triangular "square" overlooking the riverfront park, following the small TI arrow on a signpost.

The **bus station** is west of the train station, along Dorchester Street.

My recommended B&Bs are all within a 10- to 15-minute walk or a £4-5 taxi ride from the train and bus stations.

Helpful Hints

Festivals: The **Bath Literature Festival** is an open book February 26–March 6 in 2011 (www.bathlitfest.org.uk). The **Bath**

International Music Festival bursts into song every spring (classical, folk, jazz, contemporary; May 25–June 5 in 2011, www.bathmusicfest.org.uk), overlapped by the eclectic **Bath Fringe Festival** (theater, walks, talks, bus trips; generally similar dates to the Music Festival, www.bathfringe.co.uk). The **Jane Austen Festival** unfolds genteelly in late September (www.janeausten.co.uk/festival). And for three weeks in December, the squares around the abbey are filled with a **Christmas market.**

Bath's festival **box office** sells tickets for most events and can tell you exactly what's on tonight (a block down from the TI at 2 Church Street, tel. 01225/463-362, www.bathfestivals .org.uk). The city's weekly local paper, the *Bath Chronicle,* publishes a "What's On" event listing (www.thisisbath.com).

Internet Access: Ask your hotel or the TI for the closest Internet café. You can also get online at the Bath **library** (£1.20/20 minutes, slightly cheaper with free library membership, Mon 9:30–18:00, Tue–Thu 9:30–19:00, Fri–Sat 9:30–17:00, Sun 13:00–16:00, in the Podium Shopping Centre on Northgate Street near Pulteney Bridge, tel. 01225/394-041, www.bathnes.gov.uk).

Bookstore: Topping & Company, an inviting bookshop, has posters in the windows advertising frequent author readings, free coffee and tea for browsers, and tables filled with tidy stacks of carefully selected volumes (daily 9:00–20:00, near the bottom of the street called "The Paragon"—where it meets George Street, tel. 01225/428-111, www.toppingbooks .co.uk).

Laundry: The **Spruce Goose Launderette** is between the Circus and the Royal Crescent, on the pedestrian lane called Margaret's Buildings. Bring lots of £1 coins for washing and £0.20 coins for drying, as there are no change machines (self-service: about £4–5/load, daily 8:00–20:00, last load at 19:00; full-service: £12/load, Mon–Fri 8:00–12:00; tel. 01225/483-309). **Speedy Wash** can pick up your laundry anywhere in town on weekdays before 11:00 for same-day service (£12/small bag, Mon–Fri 7:30–17:30, Sat 8:30–13:00 but no pickup, closed Sun, no self-service, most hotels work with them, 4 Mile End, London Road, tel. 01225/427-616).

Car Rental: Enterprise provides a pickup service for customers to and from their hotels (extra fee for one-way rentals, at Lower Bristol Road outside Bath, tel. 01225/443-311, www .enterprise.com). Others include **Thrifty** (pickup service and one-way rentals available, in the Burnett Business Park in Keynsham—between Bath and Bristol, tel. 01179/867-997, www.thrifty.co.uk), **Hertz** (one-way rentals possible, at

BATH

Bath at a Glance

▲▲▲**Roman and Medieval Baths** Ancient baths that gave the city its name, tourable with good audioguide. **Hours:** Daily July–Aug 9:00–22:00, March–June and Sept–Oct 9:00–18:00, Nov–Feb 9:30–17:30. See page 239.

▲▲▲**Walking Tours** Free top-notch tours, helping you make the most of your visit, led by The Mayor's Corps of Honorary Guides. **Hours:** Sun–Fri at 10:30 and 14:00, Sat at 10:30 only; additional evening walks offered May–Sept Tue and Fri at 19:00. See below.

▲▲ **The Circus and the Royal Crescent** Stately Georgian (Neo-classical) buildings from Bath's late-18th-century glory days. **Hours:** Always viewable. See page 246.

▲▲**Fashion Museum** 400 years of clothing under one roof, plus opulent Assembly Rooms. **Hours:** Daily March–Oct 10:30–18:00, Nov–Feb 10:30–17:00. See page 248.

▲▲**Museum of Bath at Work** Gadget-ridden circa-1900 engineer's shop, foundry, factory, and office, best enjoyed with a live tour. **Hours:** April–Oct daily 10:30–17:00, Nov and Jan–March weekends only, closed in Dec. See page 249.

▲**Pump Room** Swanky Georgian hall, ideal for a spot of tea or a taste of unforgettably "healthy" spa water. **Hours:** Daily 9:30–12:00 for coffee and breakfast, 12:00–14:30 for lunch, 14:30–16:30 for afternoon tea (open for dinner during Bath International Music Festival, July–Aug, and Christmas holidays only). See page 243.

Windsor Bridge, tel. 0870-850-2691, www.hertz.co.uk), and **National/Europcar** (one-way rentals available, £7 by taxi from the train station, at Brassmill Lane—go west on Upper Bristol Road, tel. 01225/481-982 or 01761/479-205). Skip **Avis**—it's a mile from the Bristol train station; you'd need to rent a car to get there. Most offices close Saturday afternoon and all day Sunday, which complicates weekend pickups. Ideally, take the train or bus from downtown London to Bath, and rent a car as you leave Bath.

Parking: Parking in the city center is difficult. Short-term street parking is available but pricey (about £2.50/hour, 2-hour maximum, buy pay-and-display tickets from machine). You'll pay less per hour in long-stay lots (figure £9/24 hours; the Charlotte Street car park is handy). For more info on parking, visit www.bathnes.gov.uk/bathnes.

▲**Thermae Bath Spa** Relaxation center that put the bath back in Bath. **Hours:** Daily 9:00–22:00. See page 244.

▲ **Abbey** 500-year-old Perpendicular Gothic church, graced with beautiful fan vaulting and stained glass. **Hours:** April–Oct Mon–Sat 9:00–18:00, Sun 13:00–14:30 & 16:30–17:30; Nov–March Mon–Sat 9:00–16:30, Sun 13:00–14:30 & 16:30–17:30. See page 245.

▲**Pulteney Bridge and Parade Gardens** Shop-strewn bridge and relaxing riverside gardens. **Hours:** Bridge—always open; gardens—Easter–Sept daily 11:00–17:00, shorter hours off-season. See page 246.

▲**Georgian House at No. 1 Royal Crescent** Best opportunity to explore the interior of one of Bath's high-rent Georgian beauties. **Hours:** Mid-Feb–Oct Tue–Sun 10:30–17:00, Nov Tue–Sun 10:30–16:00, closed Mon and Dec–mid-Feb. See page 247.

▲**American Museum** An insightful look primarily at colonial/early-American lifestyles, with 18 furnished rooms and eager-to-talk guides. **Hours:** Mid-March–Oct Tue–Sun 12:00–17:00, closed Mon and Nov–mid-March. See page 250.

Jane Austen Centre Exhibit on 19th-century Bath-based novelist, best for her fans. **Hours:** Mid-March–mid-Nov daily 9:45–17:30, July–Aug Thu–Sat until 19:00; mid-Nov–mid-March Sun–Fri 11:00–16:30, Sat 9:45–17:30. See page 249.

BATH

Tours in Bath

▲▲▲**Walking Tours**—Free two-hour tours are offered by **The Mayor's Corps of Honorary Guides,** led by volunteers who want to share their love of Bath with its many visitors (as the city's mayor first did when he took a group on a guided walk back in the 1930s). Their chatty, historical, and gossip-filled walks are essential for your understanding of this town's amazing Georgian social scene. How else would you learn that the old "chair ho" call for your sedan chair evolved into today's "cheerio" farewell? Tours leave from outside the Pump Room in the abbey churchyard (free, no tips, year-round Sun–Fri at 10:30 and 14:00, Sat at 10:30 only; additional evening walks May–Sept Tue and Fri at 19:00; tel. 01225/477-411, www.bathguides.co.uk). Tip for theatergoers: When your guide stops to talk outside the Theatre Royal, skip out for a moment, pop into the box office, and see about snaring a great deal on a play for tonight.

For a **private tour,** call the local guides' bureau, Bath Parade Guides (£60/2 hours, tel. 01225/337-111, www.bathparadeguides .co.uk, bathparadeguides@yahoo.com). For **Ghost Walks** and **Bizarre Bath** tours, see "Nightlife in Bath," later.

▲▲**City Bus Tours**—City Sightseeing's hop-on, hop-off bus tours zip through Bath. Jump on a bus anytime at one of 17 signposted pickup points, pay the driver, climb upstairs, and hear recorded commentary about Bath. City Sightseeing has two 45-minute routes: a city tour (unintelligible audio recording on half the buses, live guides on the other half—choose the latter), and a "Skyline" route outside town (all live guides, stops near the American Museum—15-minute walk). On a sunny day, this is a multitasking tourist's dream come true: You can munch a sandwich, work on a tan, snap great photos, and learn a lot, all at the same time. Save money by doing the bus tour first—ticket stubs get you minor discounts at many sights (£11.50, ticket valid for 2 days and both tour routes, generally 4/hour daily in summer 9:30–18:30, in winter 10:00–15:00, tel. 01225/330-444, www.city-sightseeing.com).

Taxi Tours—Local taxis, driven by good talkers, go where big buses can't. A group of up to four can rent a cab for an hour (about £20) and enjoy a fine, informative, and—with the right cabbie—entertaining private joyride. It's probably cheaper to let the meter run than to pay for an hourly rate, but ask the cabbie for advice.

To Stonehenge, Avebury, and the Cotswolds

Bath is a good launch pad for visiting Wells, Avebury, Stonehenge, and more.

Mad Max Minibus Tours—Operating daily from Bath, Maddy and Paul offer thoughtfully organized, informative tours that run with entertaining guides. Book ahead—as far ahead as possible in summer—for these popular tours. Their **Stone Circles** full-day tour covers 110 miles and visits Stonehenge, the Avebury Stone Circles, and two cute villages: Lacock and Castle Combe. Photogenic Lacock (LAY-cock) is featured in parts of the BBC's *Pride and Prejudice* and the Harry Potter movies, and Castle Combe, the southernmost Cotswold village, is as sweet as they come (£32.50 plus £6.90 Stonehenge entry, tours run daily 8:45–16:30, arrive 15 minutes early, leaves early to beat the Stonehenge hordes). Their shorter tour of **Stonehenge and Lacock** leaves daily at 13:15 and returns at 17:15; occasionally, it also leaves at 8:45 and returns at 12:45 (£17.50 plus £6.90 Stonehenge entry). Most of their tours are limited to 16 people, though on busy days, the half-day tour might have up to 24.

Mad Max also offers a **Cotswold Discovery** full-day tour,

a picturesque romp through the countryside with stops and a cream-tea opportunity in the Cotswolds' quainter villages, including Stow-on-the-Wold, Bibury, Tetbury, the Coln Valley, The Slaughters (optional walk between the two villages), and others (£35; runs Sun, Tue, and Thu 8:45–17:15; arrive 15 minutes early). If you request it in advance, you can bring your luggage along and use the tour as transportation to Stow or, for £5 extra, Moreton-in-Marsh, with easy train connections to Oxford.

All tours depart from Bath at the Glass House shop on the corner of Orange Grove, a one-minute walk from the abbey. Arrive 15 minutes before your departure time and bring cash (it's possible to pay with credit card only if you book online at least 48 hours in advance—£1 discount). Online or email reservations are preferable to calling (phone answered daily 8:00–18:00, tel. 07990/505-970, www.madmax.abel.co.uk, maddy@madmax.abel.co.uk). Please honor or cancel your seat reservation.

More Bus Tours—If Mad Max is booked up, don't fret. Plenty of companies in Bath offer tours of varying lengths, prices, and destinations. Note that the cost of admission to sights is usually not included with any tour.

Scarper Tours runs a minibus tour to Stonehenge (£14, 10 percent Rick Steves discount if you book direct, doesn't include £6.90 Stonehenge entry fee, departs from behind the abbey; daily mid-June–Aug at 9:30, 13:00, and 16:30; mid-March–mid-June and Sept–mid-Oct at 10:00 and 14:00; mid-Oct–mid-March at 13:00; tel. 07739/644-155, www.scarpertours.com). The three-hour tour (two hours there and back, an hour at the site) includes driver narration en route.

Celtic Horizons, run by retired teacher Alan Price, offers tours from Bath to a variety of destinations, such as Stonehenge, Avebury, and Wells. He can provide a convenient transfer service (to or from London, Heathrow, Bristol Airport, the Cotswolds, and so on), with or without a tour itinerary en route. Allow about £25/hour for a group (his comfortable minivan seats up to 8 people) and £125 for Heathrow–Bath transfers. It's best to make arrangements and get pricing information by email at alan@celtichorizons.com (cash only, tel. 01373/461-784, http://celtichorizons.com).

Sights in Bath

In the Town Center

▲▲▲**Roman and Medieval Baths**—In ancient Roman times, high society enjoyed the mineral springs at Bath. From Londinium—and throughout the empire—Romans traveled so often to Aquae Sulis, as the city was called, to "take a bath" that finally it became known simply as Bath. Today, a fine museum

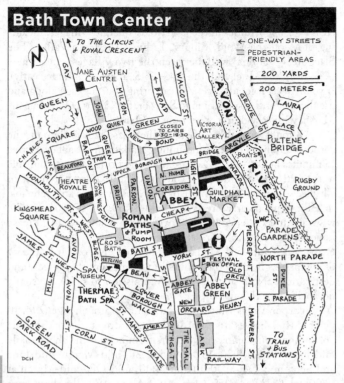

Bath Town Center

TO THE CIRCUS & ROYAL CRESCENT

← ONE-WAY STREETS
▭ PEDESTRIAN-FRIENDLY AREAS

200 YARDS
200 METERS

JANE AUSTEN CENTRE

GAY

QUEEN

JOHN

MILSOM

BROAD

WALCOT ST.

AVON

GROVE

LAURA PLACE

CHARLES STREET

QUEEN SQUARE

WOOD

QUIET

GREEN

VICTORIA ART GALLERY

ARGYLE ST.

PULTENEY BRIDGE

PRINCES ST.

BEAUFORD

BARTON

QUEEN

TRIM

NEW BOND

BRIDGE

GR. PARADE

BOATS

RIVER

MONMOUTH ST.

THEATRE ROYALE

BEAUFORD

CLOSE

BRIDE

WESTGATE

UPPER BOROUGH WALLS

PARSON.

N. HUMB.

CORRIDOR

UNION

HIGH ST.

GUILDHALL MARKET

RUGBY GROUND

KINGSMEAD SQUARE

WEST ST.

HETLING

BIGGS

ROMAN BATHS & PUMP ROOM

ABBEY

CHEAP

WC

PIERREPONT ST.

PARADE GARDENS

JAMES ST. WEST

AVON

CROSS BATH

BATH ST.

BEAU

YORK ST.

i

FESTIVAL BOX OFFICE

NORTH PARADE

MILK

SPA MUSEUM

THERMAE BATH SPA

LOWER BOROUGH WALLS

ABBEY GATE

OLD ORCH.

ABBEY GREEN

NEW ORCHARD

HENRY

DUKE ST.

S. PARADE

GREEN PARK ROAD

ST.

CORN ST.

ST. JAMES'S PARADE

SOUTHGATE

AMERY

NEWARK

THE MALL

MANVERS ST.

TO TRAIN & BUS STATIONS

RAILWAY

DCH

BATH

surrounds the ancient bath. With the help of a great audioguide,
you'll wander past well-docu-
mented displays, Roman artifacts,
a temple pediment with an evocative bearded face, a bronze head of
the goddess Sulis Minerva, excavated ancient foundations, and
the actual mouth of the spring.
At the end you'll have a chance
to walk around the big pool itself,

where Romans once lounged, splished, splashed, and thanked the
gods for the gift of naturally hot water.

Cost and Hours: £11.50, £0.75 more in July–Aug, includes
audioguide, £15 combo-ticket includes Fashion Museum—a £3.50
savings, family ticket available, daily July–Aug 9:00–22:00, March–
June and Sept–Oct 9:00–18:00, Nov–Feb 9:30–17:30, last entry one
hour before closing, tel. 01225/477-785, www.romanbaths.co.uk.

Crowd-Beating Tips: As this is the top sight in this touristy
town, it can be very busy on Saturdays and any day in the summer
(though you'll never wait longer than about 30 minutes to get in).

On any day, the least crowded time to visit is before 11:00. If you're here in the summer (July–Aug), the best time is after 19:00, when the baths are romantic, gas-lit, and all yours.

Tours: Take advantage of the included, essential **audioguide,** which will make your visit easy and informative. In addition to the basic commentary, look for posted numbers to key into your audioguide for specialty topics—including a kid-friendly tour and insightful musings from American expat writer Bill Bryson. For those with a big appetite for Roman history, in-depth **guided tours** leave from the end of the museum at the edge of the actual bath (included with ticket, on the hour, a poolside clock is set for the next departure time, 20–40 minutes depending on the guide). You can revisit the museum after the tour.

➲ **Self-Guided Tour:** Follow the one-way route through the bath and museum complex. This self-guided tour offers a basic overview; for more in-depth commentary, make ample use of the included audioguide.

You'll begin by walking around the upper **terrace,** overlooking the Great Bath. This terrace—lined with sculptures of VIRs (Very Important Romans)—evokes ancient times, but was built in the 1890s. The ruins of the bath complex sat undisturbed for centuries before finally being excavated and turned into a museum in the late 19th century.

Head inside to the museum, where exhibits explain the **dual purpose** of the buildings that stood here in Roman times: a bath complex, for relaxation and for healing; and a temple dedicated to the goddess Sulis Minerva, who was believed to be responsible for the mysterious and much-appreciated thermal springs. Cut-away diagrams and models help resurrect both parts of this complex and give you your bearings for the actual fragments and foundations you'll see.

Peer down into the **spring,** where little air bubbles remind you that 240,000 gallons of water a day emerge from the earth—magically, it must have seemed to Romans—at a constant 115°F.

Go downstairs to get to know the Romans who built and enjoyed these baths. The fragments of the **temple pediment**—carved by indigenous Celtic craftsmen, but employing Roman themes—represent a remarkable cultural synthesis. Sit and watch for a while, as a slide projection fills in historians'

best guess as to what once occupied the missing bits. The identity of the circular face in the middle puzzles researchers. (God? Santa Claus?) It could be the head of the Gorgon monster after it was slain by Perseus—are those snakes peeking through its hair and beard? And yet, the Gorgon was traditionally depicted as female. Perhaps instead it's Neptune, the god of water—appropriate for this aquatic site.

The next exhibits examine the **importance** of Aquae Sulis (the settlement here) in antiquity. Much like the pilgrimage sites of the Middle Ages, this spot exerted a powerful pull on people from all over the realm, who were eager to partake in its healing waters and to worship at the religious site. You'll see some of the small but extremely heavy carved-stone tables that pilgrims hauled here as an offering to the gods.

Walking through the temple's original foundations, keep an eye out for the sacrificial altar. The gilded-bronze head of the

goddess **Sulis Minerva** (in the display case) once overlooked a flaming cauldron inside the temple, where only priests were allowed to enter. Similar to the Greek goddess Athena, Sulis Minerva was considered to be a life-giving mother goddess. The next room displays some of the requests (inscribed on sheets of pewter or iron) that visitors made of the goddess. Take time to read some of these—many are comically spiteful and petty, offering a warts-and-all glimpse into day-to-day Roman culture.

Engineers enjoy a close-up look at the **spring overflow** and the original drain system—built two millennia ago—that still carries excess water to the River Avon. Marvel at the cleverness and durability of Roman engineering, created in (what we usually imagine to be) a "primitive" time.

Then you'll head outside to the **Great Bath** itself (where you can join one of the included guided tours—look for the clock with the next start time). Take a slow lap (by foot) around the perimeter, imagining the frolicking Romans who once immersed themselves up to the neck in this five-foot-deep pool. (On busy days, when costumed characters hang out by the bath, you may not have to imagine.) The water is greenish because of algae—don't drink it. The best views are from the west end, looking back toward the abbey. Nearby is a giant chunk of roof span, from a time when this was a cavernous covered swimming hall. At the corner, you'll step over a small canal where hot water still trickles into the main pool. Nearby, find a length of original lead pipe, remarkably well-preserved since antiquity.

Symmetrical bath complexes branch off at opposite ends of the Great Bath (perhaps dating from a conservative period when the Romans maintained separate facilities for men and women). The **East Baths** show off changing rooms and various bathing rooms, each one designed for a special therapy or recreational purpose (immersion therapy tub, sauna-like heated floor, and so on), as described in detail by the audioguide.

When you're ready to leave, head for the **West Baths,** with more facilities (including a sweat bath and a *frigidarium*, or "cold plunge" pool), another look at the spring, and more foundations. After returning your audioguide, you'll exit through the gift shop and have the opportunity to dip into the attached **Pump Room** to drink a spot of tea or to gag on the spa water (described next; for your free sample, head to the little alcove on the right and show them your bath ticket).

▲**Pump Room**—For centuries, Bath was forgotten as a spa. Then, in 1687, the previously barren Queen Mary bathed here, became

pregnant, and bore a male heir to the throne. A few years later, Queen Anne found the water eased her painful gout. Word of its wonder waters spread, and Bath earned its way back on the aristocratic map. High society soon turned the place into one big pleasure palace. The Pump Room, an elegant Georgian hall just above the Roman Baths, offers visitors their best chance to raise a pinky in this Chippendale grandeur. Above the newspaper table and sedan chairs, a statue of Beau Nash himself sniffles down at you. Drop by to sip coffee or tea or to enjoy a light meal (daily 9:30–12:00 for coffee and £6–9 breakfast, 12:00–14:30 for £6–16 lunches, 14:30–16:30 for £17.50 traditional afternoon tea, tea/coffee and pastries also available in the afternoons; open for dinner July–Aug, during Bath International Music Festival, and Christmas holidays only; live music daily—string trio or piano, times vary; tel. 01225/444-477). For just the price of a coffee (£3), you're welcome to drop in anytime—except during lunch—to enjoy the music and atmosphere.

The Spa Water: This is your chance to eat a famous (but forgettable) "Bath bun" and split a drink of the awful curative water (£0.50 or free with your Roman and Medieval Baths ticket). The water comes from the King's Spring and is brought to you by an appropriately attired server, who explains that the water is 10,000 years old, pumped up from nearly 100 yards deep, and marinated in 43 wonderful minerals. Convenient public WCs (which use plain

BATH

old tap water) are in the entry hallway that connects the Pump Room with the baths.

▲**Thermae Bath Spa**—After simmering unused for a quarter-century, Bath's natural thermal springs once again offer R&R for the masses. The state-of-the-art

spa is housed in a complex of three buildings that combine historic structures with controversial (and expensive) new glass-and-steel architecture.

Is the Thermae Bath Spa worth the time and money? The experience is pretty pricey and humble compared to similar German and Hungarian spas. Because you're in a tall, modern building in the city center, it lacks a certain old-time elegance. Jets are very limited, and the only water toys you'll see are big foam noodles. There's no cold plunge—the only way to cool off between steam rooms is to step onto a small, unglamorous balcony. The Royal Bath's two pools are essentially the same, and the water isn't particularly hot in either—in fact, the main attraction is the rooftop view from the top one (best with a partner or as a social experience).

That said, this is the only natural thermal spa in the UK, and a chance to bathe in Bath. If you visit, bring your own swimsuit and come for a couple of hours (Fri night and all day Sat-Sun are most crowded). Or consider an evening visit, when—on a chilly day—Bath's twilight glows through the steam from the rooftop pool.

Cost: The cheapest spa pass is £24 for two hours, which gains you access to the Royal Bath's large, ground-floor "Minerva Bath"; the four steam rooms and the waterfall shower; and the view-filled, open-air, rooftop thermal pool. If you want to stay longer, it's £34/4 hours and £54/day (towel, robe, and slippers-£9). The much-hyped £39 Twilight Package includes three hours and a meal (one plate, drink, robe, towel, and slippers). The appeal of this package is not the mediocre meal, but being on top of the building at a magical hour (which you can do for less money at the regular rate).

Thermae also has all the "pamper thyself" extras: massages, mud wraps, and various healing-type treatments, including "watsu"—water shiatsu (£40–70 extra). Book treatments at www .thermaebathspa.com.

Hours: Daily 9:00–22:00, last entry at 19:30. No kids under 16 are allowed. It's 100 yards from the Roman and Medieval Baths, on Beau Street. Tel. 01225/331-234. There's a salad-and-smoothies café for guests.

The Cross Bath: This renovated, circular Georgian structure across the street from the main spa provides a simpler and less-expensive bathing option. It has a hot-water fountain that taps directly into the spring, making its water temperature higher than the spa's (£14/1.5 hours, daily 10:00–20:00, last entry at 18:30, check in at the bath's main office across the street and you'll be escorted to the Cross Bath, changing rooms, no access to Royal Bath, no kids under 12).

Spa Visitor Centre: Also across the street, in the Hetling Pump Room, this free, one-room exhibit explains the story of the spa (Mon–Sat 10:00–17:00, Sun 10:00–16:00, £2 audioguide).

▲**Abbey**—The town of Bath wasn't much in the Middle Ages, but an important church has stood on this spot since Anglo-Saxon

times. King Edgar I was crowned here in 973, when the church was much bigger (before the bishop packed up and moved to Wells). Dominating the town center, today's abbey—the last great medieval church of England—is 500 years old and a fine example of Late Perpendicular Gothic, with breezy fan vaulting and enough stained glass to earn it the nickname "Lantern of the West."

The **facade** (c. 1500, but mostly restored) is interesting for some of its carvings. Look for the angels going down the ladder. The statue of Peter (to the left of the door) lost his head to mean iconoclasts; it was re-carved out of his once supersized beard. Take a moment to appreciate the abbey's architecture from the Abbey Green square.

Going **inside** is worth the £2.50 suggested donation (April–Oct Mon–Sat 9:00–18:00, Sun 13:00–14:30 & 16:30–17:30; Nov–March Mon–Sat 9:00–16:30, Sun 13:00–14:30 & 16:30–17:30; handy flier narrates a self-guided 19-stop tour, tel. 0122/422-462, www.bathabbey.org). The glass, red-iron gas-powered lamps, and heating grates on the floor are all remnants of the 19th century. The window behind the altar shows 52 scenes from the life of Christ. A window to the left of the altar shows Edgar's coronation.

Posted on the door (and on the abbey website) is the schedule for **events,** including concerts, services, and evensong.

Climbing to the top of the **tower** is only possible with an official 50-minute guided tour. You'll climb 212 steps for views across the rooftops of Bath and down into the Roman and Medieval Baths complex (£5, sporadic schedule but generally at the top of each hour Mon–Sat April–Oct 10:00–16:00, Nov–March 11:00–14:00, more often during busy times, no tours Sun, buy tickets in abbey gift shop).

A small but worthwhile exhibit, the abbey's **Heritage Vaults** tell the story of Christianity in Bath since Roman times (free, Mon–Sat 10:00–17:30, until 16:30 Nov–March, closed Sun, entrance just outside church, south side).

▲**Pulteney Bridge, Parade Gardens, and Cruises**—Bath is inclined to compare its shop-lined Pulteney Bridge to Florence's Ponte Vecchio. That's pushing it.

But to best enjoy a sunny day, pay £1 to enter the Parade Gardens below the bridge (Easter–Sept daily 11:00–17:00, shorter hours off-season, includes deck chairs, ask about concerts held some Sun at 15:00 in summer, entrance a block south of bridge, www.bathnes.gov.uk). Taking a siesta to relax peacefully at the riverside provides a wonderful break (and memory).

Across the bridge at Pulteney Weir, tour boat companies run **cruises** (£8 round-trip, £4 one-way, up to 7/day if the weather's good, one hour to Bathampton and back, WCs on board, tel. 01225/312-900). Just take whatever boat is running—all stop in Bathampton (allowing you to hop off and walk back—about 45–60 minutes). Boats come with picnic-friendly sundecks.

Guildhall Market—The little, old-school shopping mall located across from Pulteney Bridge is a frumpy time warp in this affluent town. It's fun for browsing and picnic-shopping. Its cheap Market Café is recommended in "Eating in Bath," later.

Victoria Art Gallery—This gallery, next to Pulteney Bridge, has two parts: the ground floor houses temporary exhibits, while the upstairs is filled with paintings from the late 17th century to the present, along with a small collection of decorative arts (free, Tue–Sat 10:00–17:00, Sun 13:30–17:00, closed Mon, WC, tel. 01225/477-233, www.victoriagal.org.uk).

Northwest of the Town Center

Several worthwhile public spaces and museums can be found a slightly uphill 10-minute walk away.

▲▲**The Circus and the Royal Crescent**—If Bath is an architectural cancan, these are its knickers. These first Georgian "condos"—built by the John Woods (the Circus by the Elder, the Royal Crescent by the Younger)—are well-explained by the city walking tours. "Georgian" is British for "Neoclassical," or dating from the 1770s. These two building complexes, conveniently located a block apart from each other, are quintessential Bath.

Circus: True to its name, this is a circular housing complex. Picture it as a coliseum turned inside out. Its Doric, Ionic, and

Corinthian capital decorations pay homage to its Greco-Roman origin, and are a reminder that Bath (with its seven hills) aspired to be "the Rome of England." The frieze above the first row of columns has hundreds of different panels, each representing the arts, sciences, and crafts. The first floor was high off the ground, to accommodate aristocrats on sedan chairs and women with sky-high hairdos. The tiny round windows on the top floors were the servants' quarters. While the building fronts are uniform, the backs are higgledy-piggledy, infamous for their "hanging loos." Stand in the middle of the Circus among the grand plane trees, on the capped old well. Imagine the days when there was no indoor plumbing, and the servant girls gathered here to fetch water—this was gossip central. If you stand on the well, your clap echoes three times around the circle (try it).

Royal Crescent: A long, graceful arc of buildings—impossible to see in one glance unless you step way back to the edge of the big park in front—evokes the wealth and gentility of Bath's glory days. As you cruise the Crescent, pretend you're rich. Then

pretend you're poor. Notice the "ha ha fence," a drop-off in the front yard that acted as a barrier, invisible from the windows, for keeping out sheep and peasants. The refined and stylish **Royal Crescent Hotel** sits unmarked in the center of the Crescent (with the giant rhododendron growing over the door). You're welcome to (politely) drop in to explore its fine ground-floor public spaces and back garden. A gracious and traditional tea is served in the garden out back (£12.50 cream tea, £22.50 afternoon tea, daily 15:00–17:00, sharing is OK, reserve a day in advance in summer, tel. 01225/823-333).

▲**Georgian House at No. 1 Royal Crescent**—This museum (corner of Brock Street and Royal Crescent) offers your best look into a period house. Your visit is limited to four roped-off rooms, but if you take your time and talk to the docents stationed in each room, it's worth the £6 admission to get behind one of those classy Georgian facades. The docents are determined to fill you in on all the fascinating details of Georgian life...like how high-class women shaved their eyebrows and pasted on carefully trimmed strips of furry mouse skin in their place. On the bedroom dresser sits a bowl of black beauty marks and a head-scratcher from those pre-shampoo days. Fido spent his days in the kitchen treadmill powering the rotisserie (mid-Feb–Oct Tue–Sun 10:30–17:00, Nov Tue–Sun 10:30–16:00, last entry 30 minutes before closing, closed Mon and Dec–mid-Feb, £2 guidebook available, no photos, "no stiletto heels, please," tel. 01225/428-126, www.bath-preservation -trust.org.uk). Its WC is accessible from the street (under the entry steps, across from the exit and shop).

▲▲**Fashion Museum**—Housed underneath Bath's Assembly Rooms, this museum displays four centuries of fashion on one floor.

It's small, but the fact-filled, included audioguide can stretch a visit to an informative and enjoyable hour. Like fashion itself, the collection changes all the time. A major feature is usually the museum's choices for "Dress of the Year" dating back to 1963—a fascinating opportunity to see nearly a half-century's fashion trends in one sweep of the head. (The menswear version—awarded sporadically—shows a bit less variation, but has flashes of creativity.) Many of the exhibits are organized by theme (bags, shoes, underwear, wedding dresses, and so on). You'll see how fashion evolved—just like architecture and other arts—from one historical period to the next: Georgian, Regency, Victorian, the Swinging '60s, and so on. If you're intrigued by all those historic garments, take a chance to lace up your own trainer corset (which looks more like a lifejacket) and try on a hoop underdress (£7, £15 combo-ticket covers Roman Baths—saving you £3.50, family ticket available, daily March–Oct 10:30–18:00, Nov–Feb 10:30–17:00, last entry one hour before closing, on-site self-service café, tel. 01225/477-789, www.fashionmuseum.co.uk).

Assembly Rooms: Whether or not you're touring the Fashion Museum, poke into the building that houses it, where you can wander the big, grand, empty Assembly Rooms. Card games, concerts, tea, and dances were held here in the 18th century, before the advent of fancy hotels with grand public spaces made them obsolete. Note the extreme symmetry (pleasing to the aristocratic eye) and the high windows (assuring privacy). After the Allies bombed the historic and well-preserved German city of Lübeck, the Germans picked up a Baedeker guide and chose a similarly lovely city to bomb: Bath. The Assembly Rooms—gutted in this wartime tit-for-tat by WWII bombs—have since been restored to their original splendor. (Only the chandeliers are original.)

Nearby: Below the Fashion Museum (to the left as you leave, 20 yards away, at the door marked *14* and *Alfred House*) is one of the few surviving sets of **iron house hardware**. "Link boys" carried torches through the dark streets, lighting the way for big shots in their sedan chairs as they traveled from one affair to the next. The link boys extinguished their torches in the black conical "snuffers." The lamp above was once gas-lit. The crank on the left was used to hoist bulky things to various windows (see the hooks). Few of these sets survived the dark days of the WWII Blitz, when most were collected and melted down, purportedly to make weapons to feed the British war machine. (Not long ago, these well-meaning Brits finally found out that all of their patriotic extra commitment to the national struggle had been for naught, since the metal ended up in junk heaps.)

Shoppers head down **Bartlett Street,** just below the Fashion Museum, to browse the antique shops.

▲▲**Museum of Bath at Work**—This modest but lovable place explains the industrial history of Bath. The museum is more

interesting than it sounds, serving as a vivid reminder that there's always been a grimy, workaday side to this spa town. The core of the museum is the well-preserved, circa-1900 fizzy-drink business of Mr. Bowler, which includes a Dickensian office, engineer's shop, brass foundry, and factory floor. It's just a pile of meaningless old gadgets—until the included audioguide resurrects Mr. Bowler's creative genius. You'll find that each item has its own story. Upstairs are display cases featuring other Bath creations through the years, including a 1914 Horstmann car, wheeled

sedan chairs (this *is* Bath, after all), and the versatile plasticine (colorful proto-Play-Doh—still the preferred medium of Aardman Studios, creators of the stop-motion animated *Wallace and Gromit* movies). At the snack bar, you can buy your own historic fizzy drink (a descendant of the ones once made here). On your way out, don't miss the small collection of exhibits on the ground floor, featuring cabinetmaking, the traditional methods for cutting the local "Bath Stone," a locally produced six-stroke engine, and more (£5, people over 60 pay £3.50, April–Oct daily 10:30–17:00, Nov–March weekends only except closed in Dec, last entry at 16:00, Julian Road, 2 steep blocks up Russell Street from Assembly Rooms, tel. 01225/318-348, www.bath-at-work.org.uk).

Sightseeing Tip: Notice the proximity of this museum to the very different Fashion Museum (described earlier). Museum attendants told me that—while open-minded spouses appreciate both places—it's standard for husbands to visit the Museum of Bath at Work while their wives are touring the Fashion Museum. Maybe it's time to divide and conquer?

Jane Austen Centre—This exhibition focuses on Jane Austen's tumultuous, sometimes-troubled five years in Bath (circa 1800, during which time her father died), and the influence the city had on her writing. There's little of historic substance here; you'll walk through a Georgian townhouse that she didn't live in (one of her real addresses in Bath was a few houses up the road, at 25 Gay Street), and you'll see mostly enlarged reproductions of things associated with her writing. The museum describes various places from two novels set in Bath (*Persuasion* and *Northanger Abbey*). After a live intro (15 minutes, 2/hour, starts at :15 and :45 past the hour) explaining how this romantic but down-to-earth woman dealt with the silly, shallow, and arrogant aristocrats' world, where "the doing of nothings all day prevents one from doing anything," you'll see a 15-minute video and wander through the rest of the exhibit. The well-stocked gift shop—with "I love Mr. Darcy" tote bags and Colin Firth's visage emblazoned on teacups, postcards, and more—is worthy of a shopping spree for Jane Austen fans (£7; mid-March–mid-Nov daily 9:45–17:30, July–Aug Thu–Sat until 19:00; mid-Nov–mid-March Sun–Fri 11:00–16:30, Sat 9:45–17:30; between Queen's Square and the Circus at 40 Gay Street, tel. 01225/443-000, www.janeausten.co.uk).

Upstairs, the award-winning **Regency Tea Rooms** hits the spot for Austenites, with costumed waitstaff and themed teas (£6–10), including the all-out "Tea with Mr. Darcy" for £11.50 (also £6 sandwiches, open same hours as the Centre, last orders 45 minutes before closing).

Jane Austen–themed **walking tours** of the city begin at the TI and end at the Centre (£5, 1.5 hours, Sat–Sun at 11:00, July–Aug also Fri–Sat at 16:00, no reservation necessary).

Building of Bath Collection—This offers an intriguing behind-the-scenes look at how the Georgian city was actually built (£4, mid-Feb–Nov Sat–Mon 10:30–17:00, last entry 30 minutes before closing, closed Tue–Fri and Dec–mid-Feb, a short walk north of the city center on a street called "The Paragon," tel. 01225/333-895, www.bath-preservation-trust.org.uk).

Outer Bath

▲**American Museum**—I know, you need this in Bath like you need a Big Mac. The UK's only museum dedicated to American history, this may be the only place that combines Geronimo and Groucho Marx. It has thoughtful exhibits on the history of Native Americans and the Civil War, but the museum's heart is with the decorative arts and cultural artifacts that reveal how Americans lived from colonial times to the mid-19th century. Each of the 18 completely furnished rooms (from a plain 1600s Massachusetts dining/living room to a Rococo Revival explosion in a New Orleans bedroom) is hosted by eager guides, waiting to fill you in on the everyday items that make domestic Yankee history surprisingly interesting. (In the Lee Room, look for the original mouse holes, lovingly backlit, in the floor boards.) One room is a quilter's nirvana. You could easily spend an afternoon here, enjoying the surrounding gardens, arboretum, and trails (£8, mid-March–Oct Tue–Sun 12:00–17:00, closed Mon and Nov–mid-March, last entry one hour before closing, at Claverton Manor, tel. 01225/460-503, www.americanmuseum.org). The museum is outside of town and a headache to reach if you don't have a car (10–15-minute walk from bus #18 or the hop-on, hop-off bus stop).

Activities in Bath

Walking—The Bath Skyline Walk is a six-mile wander around the hills surrounding Bath (leaflet at TI). Plenty of other scenic paths are described in the TI's literature. For additional options, get *Country Walks around Bath,* by Tim Mowl (£4.50 at TI or bookstores).

Hiking the Canal to Bathampton—An idyllic towpath leads two miles from the Bath Spa train station, along the Kennet and Avon canal, to the sleepy village of Bathampton. Immediately behind the station in Bath, cross the footbridge, turn left, and find where the canal hits the River Avon. Head northeast along the small canal, noticing the series of Industrial Age locks and giving thanks that you're not a horse pulling a barge. After the path criss-crosses the canal a few times, you'll mostly walk with the water on your right. You'll be in Bathampton in less than an hour, where The George, a classic pub, awaits with a nice meal and cellar-temp beer (reservations smart, tel. 01225/425-079).

Boating—The Bath Boating Station, in an old Victorian boat-house, rents rowboats, canoes, and punts (£7 per person/first hour, then £3/additional hour, Easter–Sept daily 10:00–18:00, closed off-season, Forester Road, one mile northeast of center, tel. 01225/312-900, www.bathboating.co.uk).

Swimming and Kids' Activities—The Bath Sports and Leisure Centre has a fine pool for laps as well as lots of water slides. Kids have entertaining options in the mini-gym "Active Club" area, which includes a rock wall and a "Zany Zone" indoor playground (swimming: £3.70 for adults, £2.30 for kids; kids and their parents pay £4 each to use "Active Club" plus pool; Mon–Fri 6:30–22:00, Sat 6:30–19:00, Sun 8:00–20:00, kids' hours limited, call for open-swim times, just across North Parade Bridge, tel. 01225/486-905, www.aquaterra.org).

Shopping—There's great browsing between the abbey and the Assembly Rooms (Fashion Museum). Shops close at about 17:30, and many are open on Sunday (11:00–16:00). Explore the antique shops lining Bartlett Street, below the Fashion Museum.

BATH

Nightlife in Bath

For an up-to-date list of events, pick up the local weekly newspaper, the *Bath Chronicle,* which includes a "What's On" schedule (www .thisisbath.com). Younger travelers may enjoy the party-ready bar, club, and nightlife recommendations at www.itchybath.co.uk.

▲▲Bizarre Bath Street Theater—For an entertaining walking-tour comedy act "with absolutely no history or culture," follow Dom, J. J., or Noel Britten on their creative and lively Bizarre Bath walk. This 1.5-hour "tour," which combines stand-up comedy with cleverly executed magic tricks, plays off unsuspecting passersby as well as tour members. It's a belly laugh a minute (£8, or £7 if you show your Rick Steves book, April–Oct nightly at 20:00, smaller groups Mon–Thu, promises to insult all nationalities and sensitivities, just racy enough but still good family fun, leaves from The Huntsman pub near the abbey, confirm at TI or call 01225/335-124, www.bizarrebath.co.uk).

▲Theatre Royal Performance—The 18th-century, 800-seat Theatre Royal, newly restored and one of England's loveliest, offers a busy schedule of London West End–type plays, including many "pre-London" dress-rehearsal runs (£15–39, shows generally start at 19:30 or 20:00, matinees at 14:30, box office open Mon–Sat 10:00–20:00, Sun 12:00–20:00, £3 extra to book online or by phone with a credit card, tel. 01225/448-844, www.theatreroyal .org.uk).

Forty nosebleed spots on a bench (misnamed "standbys") go on sale at noon Monday through Saturday for that day's evening performance (£5, 2 tickets maximum). If the show is sold out, same-day "standing places" go on sale at 18:00 (12:00 for matinees) for £3 (2 tickets maximum). For either of these cheap options, it's better to pay cash at the box office (£3 fee for online or phone purchases). Also at the box office, you can snatch up any "last minute" seats for £10–15 a half-hour before "curtain up."

A handy, cheap sightseers' tip: During the free Bath walking tour, your guide stops here. Pop into the box office, ask what's playing tonight, and see if there are many seats left. If the play sounds good and plenty of seats remain unsold, you're fairly safe to come back 30 minutes before curtain time to buy a ticket at that cheaper price. Oh...and if you smell jasmine, it's the ghost of Lady Grey, a mistress of Beau Nash.

Evening Walks—Take your choice: comedy (Bizarre Bath, described earlier), history, or ghost tour. The free **city history walks** (a daily standard described on page 237) are offered on some summer evenings (2 hours, May–Sept Tue and Fri at 19:00, leave from Pump Room). **Ghost Walks** are a popular way to pass the after-dark hours (£7, cash only, 1.5 hours, year-round Thu–Sat at

20:00, leave from The Garrick's Head pub to the left and behind Theatre Royal as you face it, tel. 01225/350-512, www.ghostwalks ofbath.co.uk). The cities of York and Edinburgh—which have houses thought to be actually haunted—are better for these walks.

Pubs—Most pubs in the center are very noisy, catering to a rowdy twentysomething crowd. But on the top end of town, you can still find some classic old places with inviting ambience and live music. These are listed in order from closest to farthest away:

The **Old Green Tree,** the most convenient of all these pubs, is a rare traditional pub right in the town center (locally brewed real ales, no children, 12 Green Street; also recommended for lunch— see "Eating in Bath," later).

The **Star Inn** is much appreciated by local beer-lovers for its fine ale and "no machines or music to distract from the chat." It's a "spit 'n' sawdust" place, and its long bench, nicknamed "death row," still comes with a complimentary pinch of snuff from tins on the ledge. Try the Bellringer Ale, made just up the road (Mon–Fri 12:00–14:30 & 17:30–24:00, Sat–Sun 12:00–24:00, no food served, 23 The Vineyards, top of The Paragon/A4 Roman Road, tel. 01225/425-072, generous and friendly welcome from Paul, who runs the place).

The **Bell** has a jazzy, pierced-and-tattooed, bohemian feel, but with a mellow older crowd. There's some kind of activity nearly every night, usually involving live music (the only food served is £2.50 sandwiches, Mon–Sat 11:30–23:00, Sun 12:00–22:30, 103 Walcot Street, tel. 01225/460-426, www.walcotstreet.com).

Summer Nights at the Baths—In July and August, you can stretch your sightseeing day at the Roman Baths, open nightly until 22:00 (last entry 21:00), when the gas lamps flame and the baths are far less crowded and more atmospheric. To take a dip yourself, consider popping in to the Thermae Bath Spa (last entry at 19:30).

Sleeping in Bath

Bath is a busy tourist town. Accommodations are expensive, and low-cost alternatives are rare. By far the best budget option is the

YMCA—it's central, safe, simple, very well-run, and has plenty of twin rooms available. To get a good B&B, make a telephone reservation in advance. Competition is stiff, and it's worth asking any of these places for a weekday, three-nights-in-a-row, or off-season deal. Friday and Saturday nights are tightest (with many rates

Sleep Code

(£1 = about $1.60, country code: 44, area code: 01225)
S = Single, **D** = Double/Twin, **T** = Triple, **Q** = Quad, **b** = bathroom,
s = shower only. Unless otherwise noted, credit cards are accepted.

To help you sort easily through these listings, I've divided the rooms into three categories based on the price for a standard double room with bath:

$$$ Higher Priced—Most rooms £100 or more.
 $$ Moderately Priced—Most rooms between £60-100.
  $ Lower Priced—Most rooms £60 or less.

Prices can change without notice; verify the hotel's current rates online or by email. For other updates, see www.ricksteves.com/update.

going up by about 25 percent)—especially if you're staying only one night, since B&Bs favor those lingering longer. If staying only Saturday night, you're very bad news to a B&B hostess. If you're driving to Bath, stowing your car near the center will cost you (though some less-central B&Bs have parking)—see "Parking" on page 236, or ask your hotelier. Almost every place provides Wi-Fi at no charge to its guests.

BATH

B&Bs near the Royal Crescent

These listings are all a 15-minute uphill walk or an easy £4–5 taxi ride from the train station. Or take any hop-on, hop-off bus tour from the station, get off at the stop nearest your B&B (likely Royal Avenue—confirm with driver), check in, then finish the tour later in the day. The Marlborough Lane places have easier parking, but are less centrally located.

$$$ The Town House, overlooking the Assembly Rooms, is genteel and deluxe, yet homey, with three fresh, mod rooms that have a hardwood stylishness. In true B&B style, you'll enjoy a gourmet breakfast, likely at a big family table with the other guests. This is a great value for the quality and location (Db-£95–100 or £120–130 Fri–Sat, 2-night minimum, free Wi-Fi, 7 Bennett Street, tel. & fax 01225/422-505, www.thetownhousebath.co.uk, stay@thetownhousebath.co.uk, Alan and Brenda Willey).

$$$ Marlborough House, exuberantly run by Peter, is the most mod-and-trendy B&B I've seen in Bath. Each of the six rooms comes with a sip of brandy (Sb-£70–95, standard Db-£70–110, superior Db-£85–125, Tb-£95–135, organic breakfasts and toiletries, free Wi-Fi, free parking, some street noise, 1 Marlborough

Lane, tel. 01225/318-175, fax 01225/466-127, www.marlborough -house.net, mars@manque.dircon.co.uk).

$$ Brocks Guest House has six rooms in a Georgian townhouse built by John Wood in 1765. Located between the prestigious Royal Crescent and the courtly Circus, it was redone in a way that would make the great architect proud (standard Db-£79–85, superior Db-£87–95, Tb-£99–125, Qb-£115–125, higher rates are for Fri–Sat, free Wi-Fi, little top-floor library, 32 Brock Street, tel. 01225/338-374, fax 01225/334-245, www.brocksguesthouse.co.uk, brocks@brocksguesthouse.co.uk, Richard).

$$ Parkside Guest House has five thoughtfully appointed Edwardian rooms. It's a bit older, but it's tidy, clean, homey, and well-priced—and has a spacious back garden (Sb-£60, Db-£80, these prices are for Rick Steves readers, free Wi-Fi, limited free parking, 11 Marlborough Lane, tel. & fax 01225/429-444, www .parksidebandb.co.uk, post@parksidebandb.co.uk, kind Inge Lynall).

$$ Cornerways B&B, located on a noisy street, is simple and well-worn, with three rooms and old-fashioned homey touches (Sb-£45–55, Db-£65–75, 15 percent discount with this book and 3-night stay in 2011, free Wi-Fi, DVD library, free parking, 47 Crescent Gardens, tel. 01225/422-382, www.cornerwaysbath .co.uk, info@cornerwaysbath.co.uk, Sue Black).

B&Bs East of the River

These listings are a 10-minute walk from the city center. While generally a better value, they are not quite as conveniently located.

$$$ Villa Magdala rents 18 stately, hotelesque rooms in a freestanding Victorian townhouse opposite a park. In a city that's so insistently Georgian, it's fun to stay in a mansion that's decorated so enthusiastically Victorian (Db-£95–130 depending on size and demand, family rooms, inviting lounge, free Wi-Fi, free parking, in quiet residential area on Henrietta Street, tel. 01225/ 466-329, fax 01225/483-207, www.villamagdala.co.uk, enquiries @villamagdala.co.uk, Roy and Lois).

$$$ The Kennard, immaculately maintained by proud owners Giovanni and Mary Baiano, rents 12 rooms a short walk through a genteel neighborhood from the Pulteney Bridge. Each of the rooms is different, but all are colorfully and elaborately decorated (prices are for Sun-Thu/Fri-Sat: S-£58/£65, Sb-£79/£120, Db-£98/£120, Tb-£138/£160, free Wi-Fi, free street parking permits, thoughtfully planned Georgian garden out back, 11 Henrietta Street, tel. 01225/310-472, fax 01225/460-054, www .kennard.co.uk, reception@kennard.co.uk).

$$$ The Ayrlington, next door to a lawn-bowling green, has 16 attractive rooms with Asian decor and hints of a more genteel

Bath Accommodations

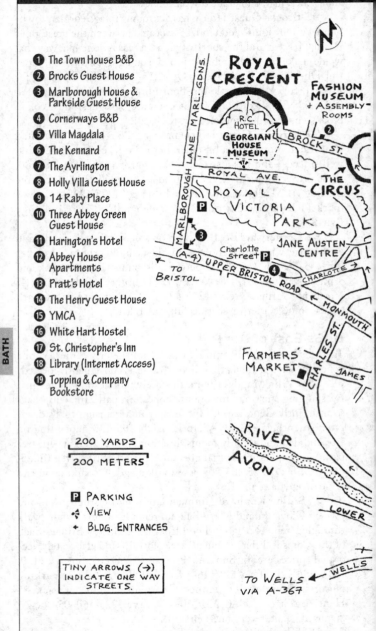

1. The Town House B&B
2. Brocks Guest House
3. Marlborough House & Parkside Guest House
4. Cornerways B&B
5. Villa Magdala
6. The Kennard
7. The Ayrlington
8. Holly Villa Guest House
9. 14 Raby Place
10. Three Abbey Green Guest House
11. Harington's Hotel
12. Abbey House Apartments
13. Pratt's Hotel
14. The Henry Guest House
15. YMCA
16. White Hart Hostel
17. St. Christopher's Inn
18. Library (Internet Access)
19. Topping & Company Bookstore

BATH

ROYAL CRESCENT

FASHION MUSEUM + ASSEMBLY ROOMS

R.C. HOTEL

GEORGIAN HOUSE MUSEUM

BROCK ST.

MARL. GDNS.

MARLBOROUGH LANE

ROYAL AVE.

ROYAL VICTORIA PARK

THE CIRCUS

JANE AUSTEN CENTRE

Charlotte Street

(A-4) UPPER BRISTOL ROAD

CHARLOTTE

TO BRISTOL

MONMOUTH

FARMERS' MARKET

CHARLES ST.

JAMES

RIVER AVON

LOWER

WELLS

TO WELLS VIA A-367

200 YARDS

200 METERS

P PARKING

VIEW

BLDG. ENTRANCES

TINY ARROWS (→) INDICATE ONE WAY STREETS.

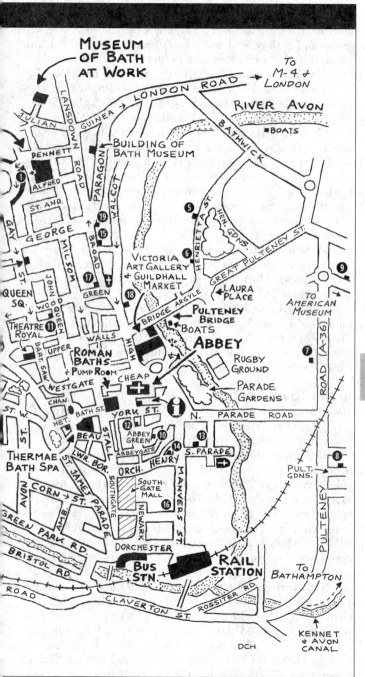

MUSEUM OF BATH AT WORK

To M-4 & LONDON

RIVER AVON

BOATS

LONDON ROAD

JULIAN

LANSDOWN ROAD

GUINEA

PARAGON

BATHWICK

Building of BATH MUSEUM

BENNETT

ALFRED

ST. AND.

GAY

ST.

GEORGE

WALCOT

5

HENRIETTA ST.

HEN. GDNS.

GREAT PULTENEY ST.

9

19

15

BROAD

MILSOM

JOHN

QUEEN

GREEN

17

18

Victoria Art Gallery & Guildhall Market

6

Laura Place

To AMERICAN MUSEUM

QUEEN SQ.

WOOD

BART. SAW.

THEATRE ROYAL

11

UPPER

WALLS

HIGH

BRIDGE ARGYLE

PULTENEY BRIDGE

BOATS

ABBEY

ROMAN BATHS + Pump Room

CHEAP

Rugby Ground

Parade Gardens

7

ROAD (A-36)

WESTGATE

CHAN.

ST. W.

HET.

BATH ST.

YORK ST.

N. PARADE ROAD

ST.

BEAU

STALL

LWR. BOR.

12

Abbey Green

10

Abbeygate

14

13

S. PARADE

8

PULT. GDNS.

Thermae BATH SPA

ST. JAMES PARADE

ORCH.

HENRY

SOUTHGATE

MANVERS ST.

SOUTH-GATE MALL

16

NEWARK

PULTENEY

AVON

CORN

ST.

GREEN PARK RD.

AMB.

DORCHESTER

BUS STN

RAIL STATION

To BATHAMPTON

BRISTOL RD.

ROAD

CLAVERTON ST.

ROSSITER RD.

KENNET & AVON CANAL

DCH

BATH

time. Though this well-maintained hotel fronts a busy street, it's quiet and tranquil. Rooms in the back have pleasant views of sports greens and Bath beyond. For the best value, request a standard top-floor double with a view of Bath (twin Db-£80–100, standard Db-£100–125, superior Db-£120–150, big deluxe Db-£130–170, higher price is for Fri–Sun, free Wi-Fi, fine garden, free and easy parking, 24–25 Pulteney Road, tel. 01225/425-495, fax 01225/469-029, www.ayrlington.com, mail@ayrlington.com, Ling Roper).

$$ Holly Villa Guest House, with a cheery garden, six bright rooms, and a cozy TV lounge, is enthusiastically and thoughtfully run by chatty, friendly Jill and Keith McGarrigle (Db-£70–80, Tb-£90–100, cash only, free Wi-Fi in some areas, free parking; 8-minute walk from station and city center—walk over North Parade Bridge, take the first right, and then take the second left to 14 Pulteney Gardens; tel. 01225/310-331, www.hollyvilla.com, jill@hollyvilla.com).

$$ 14 Raby Place is another good value, mixing Georgian glamour with homey warmth and modern, artistic taste within its five rooms. Muriel Guy—a no-high-tech Luddite—keeps things simple and endearingly friendly. She's a fun-loving live wire who serves organic food for breakfast (S with private bathroom on the hall-£35, Db-£70–75, Tb-£80, cash only; 14 Raby Place—go over bridge on North Parade Road, left on Pulteney Road, cross to church, Raby Place is first row of houses on hill; tel. 01225/465-120).

In the Town Center

You'll pay a premium to sleep right in the center. And, since Bath is so pleasant and manageable by foot, a downtown location isn't essential. Still, these are particularly well-located.

$$$ Three Abbey Green Guest House, with seven rooms, is bright, cheery, and located in a quiet, traffic-free courtyard only 50 yards from the abbey and the Roman Baths. Its spacious rooms are a fine value (Db-£95–145, four-poster Db-£145–175, family rooms-£135–195, price depends on season and size of room, 2-night minimum on weekends, free Internet access and Wi-Fi, tel. 01225/428-558, www.threeabbeygreen.com, stay@threeabbeygreen.com, Sue and Derek). They also rent self-catering apartments (Db-£135–165, Qb-£160–195, 2-night minimum).

$$$ Harington's Hotel rents 13 fresh, modern rooms on a quiet street in the town center. This stylish place feels like a boutique hotel, but with a friendlier, laid-back vibe (Sb-£79–155, standard Db-£88–135, superior Db-£98–145, large superior Db-£108–155, Tb-£138–185, prices vary substantially depending on demand, free Wi-Fi, attached bistro for guests only, 10 Queen Street, tel. 01225/461-728, fax 01225/444-804, www.haringtons

hotel.co.uk, post@haringtonshotel.co.uk). Melissa and Peter offer a 5 percent discount with this book for two-night stays except on Fridays, Saturdays, and holidays. They also rent two self-catering apartments down the street—one can sleep up to three (Db-£130, Tb-£145), and the other can sleep up to nine (prices on request; for apartments: 2-night minimum on weekdays, 3-night minimum on weekends).

$$$ Abbey House Apartments consist of three flats on Abbey Green and several others scattered around town—all tastefully restored by Laura (who, once upon a time, was a San Francisco rock musician). The apartments called Abbey View and Abbey Green (which comes with a washer and dryer) both have views of the abbey from their nicely equipped kitchens. These are especially practical and economical if you plan on cooking. Laura provides everything you need for simple breakfasts, and it's fun and cheap to stock the fridge or get take-away for a meal in your flat. When Laura meets you to give you the keys, you become a local (Sb-£90, Db-£100–175, price depends on size, 2-night minimum, rooms can sleep four with Murphy and sofa beds, apartments clearly described on website, free Wi-Fi, Abbey Green, tel. 01225/464-238, www.laurastownhouseapartments.co.uk, laura @laurastownhouseapartments.co.uk).

$$$ Pratt's Hotel is as proper and olde English as you'll find in Bath. Its creaks and frays are aristocratic, and even its public places make you want to sip a brandy. The 46 rooms show their age a bit, but are comfy and spacious. Since it's near a busy street, occasionally it can get noisy—request a quiet room, away from the street (Sb-£60–100, Db-£90–140, price depends on demand, check website for current rates and specials, dogs-£7.50 but children under 15 free with 2 adults, elevator, pay Wi-Fi, attached restaurant-bar, 4–6 South Parade, tel. 01225/460-441, fax 01225/448-807, www .forestdale.com, pratts@forestdale.com).

$$ The Henry Guest House is a simple, vertical place, renting eight clean rooms. It's friendly, well-run, and just two blocks in front of the train station (Sb-£55–65, Db-£85–105, higher prices are for bigger "premier" rooms, extra bed-£15, family room-£135, 2-night minimum on weekends, free Wi-Fi, 6 Henry Street, tel. 01225/424-052, www.thehenry.com, stay@thehenry.com). Steve and Liz also rent two self-catering apartments nearby that sleep up to eight with cots and a sleeper couch (email them for rates).

Bargain Accommodations

Bath's Best Budget Beds: **$** The **YMCA,** centrally located on a leafy square, has 210 beds in industrial-strength rooms—all with sinks and prison-style furnishings. The place is a godsend for budget travelers—safe, secure, quiet, and efficiently run. With lots of twin rooms and no double beds, this is the only easily accessible budget option in downtown Bath (rates for Sun–Thu/Fri–Sat: S-£28/£32, twin D-£44/£52, T-£60/£69, Q-£72/£84, dorm beds-£16/£19, WCs and showers down the hall, includes continental breakfast, cooked breakfast-£2.30, cheap lunches, free linens, rental towels, lockers, pay Internet access, free Wi-Fi, laundry facilities, down a tiny alley off Broad Street on Broad Street Place, tel. 01225/325-900, fax 01225/462-065, www.bathymca.co.uk, stay@bathymca.co.uk).

Sloppy Backpacker Dorms: **$ White Hart Hostel** is a simple nine-room place offering adults and families good, cheap beds in two- to six-bed dorms (£15/bed, S-£25, D-£40, Db-£50–70, kitchen, fine garden out back, 5-minute walk behind train station at Widcombe—where Widcombe Hill hits Claverton Street, tel. 01225/313-985, www.whitehartbath.co.uk). The White Hart also has a pub with a reputation for decent food. **$ St. Christopher's Inn,** in a prime, central location, is part of a chain of low-priced, high-energy hubs for backpackers looking for beds and brews. Their beds are so cheap because they know you'll spend money on their beer. It sits above the lively, youthful Belushi's pub, which is also where you'll find the reception (54 beds in 6- to 12-bed rooms-£15–21, D-£52–58, higher prices are for weekends and walk-ins—it's always cheaper to book online, check website for specials, pay Internet access, free Wi-Fi, laundry facilities, lounge, 9 Green Street, tel. 01225/481-444, www.st-christophers.co.uk).

Eating in Bath

Bath is bursting with eateries. There's something for every appetite and budget—just stroll around the center of town. A picnic dinner of deli food or take-out fish-and-chips in the Royal Crescent Park or down by the river is ideal for aristocratic hoboes. The restaurants I recommend are small and popular—reserve a table on Friday and Saturday evenings. Most pricey little bistros offer big savings with their two- and three-course lunches and "pre-theatre" specials. In general, you can get two courses for £10 at lunch or £12 in the early evening (compared with £15 for a main course after 18:30 or 19:00). Restaurants advertise their early-bird specials, and as long as you order within the time window, you're in for a cheap meal.

Romantic, Upscale French and English

Tilleys Bistro serves healthy French, English, and vegetarian meals with candlelit ambience. Owners Dawn and Dave make you feel as if you are guests at a dinner party in their elegant living room. Their fun menu lets you build your own meal, and there's an interesting array of £6–9 starters. If you cap things off with the cheese plate and a glass of the house port, you'll realize that's a passion of Dave's. While it's pricey and the portions are modest, this is a memorable splurge (£10–19 entrées; lunch specials: £12.50/2 courses, £15/3 courses; Mon–Sat 12:00–14:30 & 18:00–22:30, Sun 18:00–21:00 only, reservations smart, 3 North Parade Passage, tel. 01225/484-200).

The Garrick's Head is an elegantly simple gastropub right around the corner from the Theatre Royal, with a pricey restaurant on one side and a bar serving affordable snacks on the other. You're welcome to eat from the bar menu, even if you're in the fancy dining room or outside enjoying some great people-watching (£6–10 pub grub, £11–16 entrées on the fancier menu, Mon–Sat 11:00–22:00, Sun 12:00–22:00, drinks until later, 8 St. John's Place, tel. 01225/318-368).

The Circus Café and Restaurant is a relaxing little eatery serving well-executed English cuisine with European flair. Choose between the interior—with a clean, minimalist modern atmosphere either on the main floor or in the cellar—and the four tables on the peaceful street connecting the Circus and the Royal Crescent (£8 lunches, £7 starters and £13 entrées at dinner, open Mon–Sat 12:00–15:00 & 18:00–20:00, closed Sun, reservations smart, 34 Brock Street, tel. 01225/466-020).

Casanis French Bistro-Restaurant is a local hit. Chef Laurent, who hails from Nice, cooks "authentic Provençal cuisine" from the south of France, while his wife, Jill, serves. The decor matches the cuisine—informal, relaxed, simple, and top-quality. The intimate Georgian dining room upstairs is a bit nicer and more spacious than the ground floor (lunch specials: £13.50/2 courses, £17/3 courses; dinner special available 18:00–19:00: £17/2 courses, £21/3 courses; open Tue–Sat 12:00–14:00 & 18:00–22:00, closed Sun–Mon, immediately behind the Assembly Rooms at 4 Saville Row, tel. 01225/780-055).

Casual, Non-Traditional Alternatives

Whether ethnic food or vegetarian, there are plenty of ways to get some fun culinary variation in this town.

Demuths Vegetarian Restaurant is highly rated and ideal for the well-heeled vegetarian. Its tight, stark, understated interior comes with a vegan vibe (£6–11 lunches, £7 starters and £13–15 entrées at dinner, daily 10:00–16:00 & 17:30–21:00, later on weekends, 2 North Parade Passage, tel. 01225/446-059).

Yen Sushi is your basic little sushi bar—plain and sterile, with stools facing a conveyor belt that constantly tempts you with a variety of freshly made delights on color-coded plates. When you're done, they tally your plates and give you the bill (£1.50–4 plates, you can fill up for £12 or so, daily 12:00–15:00 & 17:30–22:30, 11 Bartlett Street, tel. 01225/333-313).

BATH

Bath Restaurants

1. Tilleys Bistro & Demuths Vegetarian Rest.
2. The Garrick's Head
3. The Circus Café & Rest.
4. Casanis French Bistro-Rest.
5. Yen Sushi
6. Martini Restaurant
7. Rajpoot Tandoori
8. Thai Balcony, Boston Tea Party & Seafoods Fish & Chips
9. Yak Yeti Yak
10. Ocean Pearl Oriental Buffet & Waitrose Supermarket
11. Wagamama
12. Ask Restaurant
13. Loch Fyne
14. Crystal Palace Pub
15. The Old Green Tree
16. Chandos Deli
17. The Cornish Bakehouse
18. Guildhall Market
19. M&S Kitchen & Café Revive
20. Royal Crescent Hotel (Afternoon Tea)
21. The Star Inn
22. The Bell

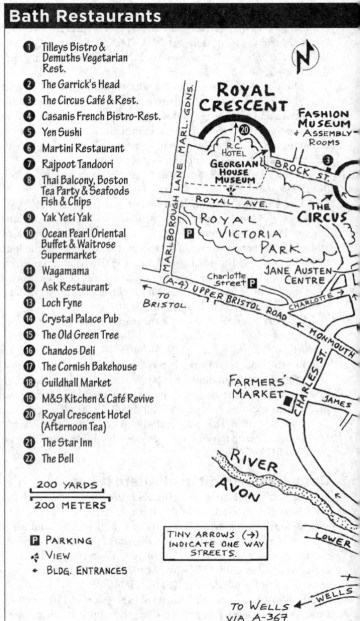

200 YARDS
200 METERS

P PARKING
↙ VIEW
← BLDG. ENTRANCES

TINY ARROWS (→) INDICATE ONE WAY STREETS.

ROYAL CRESCENT
FASHION MUSEUM & ASSEMBLY ROOMS
R.C. HOTEL
GEORGIAN HOUSE MUSEUM
BROCK ST.
THE CIRCUS
MARLBOROUGH LANE
MARL. GDNS.
ROYAL AVE.
ROYAL VICTORIA PARK
JANE AUSTEN CENTRE
Charlotte Street
(A-4) UPPER BRISTOL ROAD
TO BRISTOL
CHARLOTTE
MONMOUTH
CHARLES ST.
FARMERS' MARKET
JAMES
RIVER AVON
LOWER
WELLS
TO WELLS VIA A-367

BATH

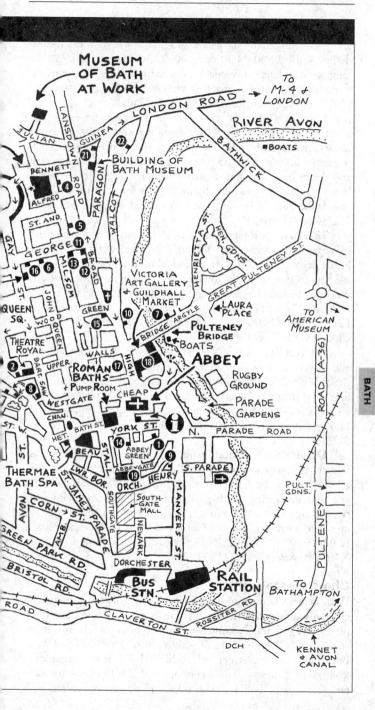

MUSEUM OF BATH AT WORK

TO M-4 & LONDON

LONDON ROAD

RIVER AVON

BOATS

BATHWICK

JULIAN

LANSDOWN ROAD

GUINEA

22

21

BENNETT

4

ALFRED

PARAGON

WALCOT

BUILDING OF BATH MUSEUM

HENRIETTA ST.

HEN. GDNS.

ST. AND.

5

GEORGE

11

GAY

MILSOM

BROAD

16 6 13 12

JOHN

QUEEN SQ.

WOOD

QUEEN

GREEN

10

15

VICTORIA ART GALLERY + GUILDHALL MARKET

GREAT PULTENEY ST.

LAURA PLACE

7

BRIDGE ARGYLE

PULTENEY BRIDGE

BOATS

ABBEY

TO AMERICAN MUSEUM

THEATRE ROYAL

2

BART. SAW

UPPER

WALLS

HIGH

ROMAN BATHS + PUMP ROOM

17

18

CHEAP

RUGBY GROUND

PARADE GARDENS

ROAD (A-36)

8

WESTGATE

CHAN.

HET.

BATH ST.

BEAU

STALL

YORK ST.

14

ABBEY GREEN

1

9

ABBEYGATE

N. PARADE ROAD

THERMAE BATH SPA

LWR. BOR.

ST. JAMES PARADE

SOUTHGATE

ORCH. HENRY

19

S. PARADE

PULT. GDNS.

AVON

CORN

ST.

SOUTH-GATE MALL

NEWARK

MANVERS ST.

GREEN PARK RD.

BRISTOL RD.

ROAD

DORCHESTER

BUS STN.

CLAVERTON ST.

RAIL STATION

ROSSITER RD.

TO BATHAMPTON

DCH

KENNET & AVON CANAL

PULTENEY

BATH

Martini Restaurant, a hopping, purely Italian place, has class and jovial waiters (£9–12 pastas and pizzas, £14–19 meat and fish dishes, daily 12:00–14:30 & 18:00–22:30—except open all day long on Sat, plenty of veggie options, daily fish specials, extensive wine list, reservations smart on weekends, 9 George Street, tel. 01225/460-818; Nunzio, Franco, and chef Luigi).

Rajpoot Tandoori serves—by all assessments—the best Indian food in Bath. You'll hike down deep into a sprawling cellar, where the plush Indian atmosphere and award-winning cooking make paying the extra pounds palatable. The seating is tight and the ceilings low, but it's air-conditioned (£8.25 three-course lunch special, £9–11 entrées; figure £20 per person with rice, naan, and drink; daily 12:00–14:30 & 18:00–23:00, 4 Argyle Street, tel. 01225/466-833, Ali).

Thai Balcony Restaurant's open, spacious interior is so plush, it'll have you wondering, "Where's the Thai wedding?" While locals debate which of Bath's handful of Thai restaurants serves the best food or offers the lowest prices, there's no doubt that Thai Balcony's fun and elegant atmosphere makes for a memorable and enjoyable dinner (£9 two-course lunch special, £8–9 plates, daily 12:00–14:00 & 18:00–22:00, reservations smart on weekends, Saw Close, tel. 01225/444-450).

Yak Yeti Yak is a fun Nepalese restaurant, with both Western and sit-on-the-floor seating. Sera and his wife, Sarah, along with their cheerful, hardworking Nepali team, cook up great traditional food (and plenty of vegetarian plates) at prices that would delight a sherpa (£7–9 lunches, £5 veggie plates, £8–9 meat plates, daily 12:00–14:30 & 17:00–22:30, downstairs at 5 Pierrepont Street, tel. 01225/442-299).

Ocean Pearl Oriental Buffet is famous for being the restaurant Asian tourists eat at repeatedly. It offers a practical, 40-dish, all-you-can-eat buffet in the modern Podium Shopping Centre and spacious seating in a high, bright dining hall overlooking the river. You'll pay £6.50 for lunch, £11.50 for dinner, or you can fill up a take-away box for just £3.50 at lunch or £4.50 at dinner (daily 12:00–15:00 & 18:00–22:30, in the Podium Shopping Centre on Northgate Street, tel. 01225/331-238).

Chain Restaurants

With so many homegrown favorites, I see little reason to frequent a chain restaurant in Bath. But if you're a fan, you'll find these three places: **Wagamama Noodle Bar** specializes in pan-Asian cuisine (£7–9 meals, Mon–Sat 12:00–23:00, Sun 12:00–22:00, 1 York Buildings, George Street, tel. 01225/337-314, www.wagamama.com); **Ask** dishes up Italian comfort food (£8–10 pizzas and pastas, good salads, daily 12:00–23:00, George Street but entrance on

Broad Street, tel. 01225/789-997); and **Loch Fyne,** which serves fresh fish at reasonable prices, fills what was once a lavish bank building with a bright, airy, youthful, high-energy atmosphere (£10–18 meals, £10 two-course special from lunch until 19:00 on weekdays, daily 12:00–22:30, 24 Milsom Street, tel. 01225/750-120). All of these chains are found all over Britain (see descriptions on page 34).

Pubs

With so many other tempting options (and since this is not a good pub-grub town), eating at a pub in Bath isn't as appealing as elsewhere. For the best pub grub, head for **The Garrick's Head** gastropub (described earlier). But if you're looking for a more traditional, lowbrow place, consider these options.

Crystal Palace Pub is an inviting place just a block away from the abbey, facing the delightful little Abbey Green. With a focus on food rather than drink, they serve "pub grub with a Continental flair" in three different spaces, including a picnic-table back patio (£9–12 meals, food served Mon–Fri 11:00–21:00, Sat 11:00–20:00, Sun 12:00–20:00, last orders for drinks at 23:00, no kids after 16:30, Abbey Green, tel. 01225/482-666).

The Old Green Tree, in the old town center, serves satisfying lunches to locals in a characteristic pub setting (real ales on tap, £6–7 sandwiches, £9 meals, food served for lunch Mon–Sat 12:00–15:00 only, open daily for drinks, no children, can be crowded on weekend nights, 12 Green Street, tel. 01225/448-259).

If you're looking for a pub to drink and hang out in, rather than eat at, check out **The Star Inn** and **The Bell** (described on page 253).

Simple Options

These are excellent options for a fast, handy, and tasty meal on the go. If you get take-away (possible at most of these), you can munch your picnic while watching street musicians from a bench on the Abbey Square.

Boston Tea Party feels like a Starbucks—if there were only one. It's fresh and healthy, serving extensive breakfasts, light lunches, and salads. The outdoor seating overlooks a busy square. They also host musical events, and their walls are decorated with works by local artists (£3–7 breakfasts, £5–7 lunches, Mon–Sat 7:30–19:00, Sun 9:00–19:00, free Wi-Fi, 19 Kingsmead Square, tel. 01225/313-901).

Chandos Deli has good coffee and tasty £3–5 sandwiches made on artisan breads. This upscale but casual five-table place serves breakfast pastries and lunch to dedicated foodies who don't want to pay too much (Mon–Sat 9:00–17:00, Sun 11:00–17:00, 12

BATH

George Street, tel. 01225/314-418).

Seafoods Fish & Chips is respected by lovers of greasy fried fish in Bath. There's diner-style and outdoor seating, or you can get your food to go for a bit cheaper (£4–5 meals, Mon–Sat 11:30–22:00, closed Sun, 38 Kingsmead Square, tel. 01225/465-190).

The Cornish Bakehouse, tucked down a shopping gallery across from the Guildhall Market, has freshly baked £3 take-away pasties (Mon–Sat 8:30–17:30, Sun 10:00–17:00, off High Street at 11A The Corridor, tel. 01225/426-635).

Produce Market and Café: **Guildhall Market,** across from Pulteney Bridge, has produce stalls with food for picnickers. At its inexpensive **Market Café,** you can slurp a curry or sip a tea while surrounded by stacks of used books, bananas on the push list, and honest-to-goodness old-time locals (£3–5 traditional English meals including fried breakfasts all day, Mon–Sat 8:00–17:00, closed Sun, tel. 01225/461-593 a block north of the abbey, on High Street).

Supermarkets: **Waitrose,** at the Podium Shopping Centre, is great for picnics, with a good salad bar (Mon–Fri 8:30–20:00, Sat 8:30–19:00, Sun 11:00–17:00, just west of Pulteney Bridge and across from post office on High Street). **Marks & Spencer,** near the train station, has a grocery at the back of its department store and two eateries: **M&S Kitchen** on the ground floor; and the pleasant, inexpensive **Café Revive** on the top floor (Mon–Fri 8:30–19:00, Sat 8:30–18:00, Sun 11:00–17:00, 16–18 Stall Street).

Bath Connections

Bath's train station is called Bath Spa (toll tel. 0845-748-4950). The National Express bus station is just west of the train station (bus info toll tel. 0871-781-8181, www.nationalexpress.com). For all public bus services in southwestern England, see www.travelinesw.com.

From London to Bath: To get from London to Bath and see Stonehenge to boot, consider an all-day organized **bus tour** from London (and skip out of the return trip; see page 191).

From Bath to London: You can catch a **train** to London's Paddington Station (2/hour, 1.5 hours, best deals for travel after 9:30 and when purchased in advance, www.firstgreatwestern.co.uk), or save money—but not time—by taking the National Express **bus** to Victoria Coach Station (direct buses nearly hourly, 3–3.75 hours, one-way-£19.10, round-trip-£27.80).

From Heathrow to Bath: See page 186. Also consider taking a minibus with Alan Price (see "Celtic Horizons" on page 239).

From Bath to London's Airports: You can reach **Heathrow** directly and easily by National Express bus (10/day, 2–3 hours, £19.10 one-way, toll tel. 0871-781-8181, www.nationalexpress.com)

or by a train-and-bus combination (take twice-hourly train to Reading, catch twice-hourly airport shuttle bus from there, allow 2.5 hours total, £46–65 depending on time of day, about £10 cheaper when bought in advance, BritRail passholders just pay £15 for bus). Or take the Celtic Horizons minibus to Heathrow.

You can get to **Gatwick** by train (about hourly, 2.5 hours, £45–54 one-way depending on time of day, cheaper in advance, transfer in Reading) or by bus (10/day, 4–5 hours, £25 one-way, transfer at Heathrow Airport).

Between Bristol Airport and Bath: Located about 20 miles west of Bath, this airport is closer than Heathrow, but they haven't worked out good connections to Bath yet. From Bristol Airport, your most convenient options are to take a taxi (£35) or call Alan Price (see "Celtic Horizons" on page 239). Otherwise, at the airport you can hop aboard the Bristol Airport Flyer (bus #A1), which takes you to the Temple Meads train station in Bristol (£7, 2–6/hour, 30 minutes, buy bus ticket at airport info counter or from driver, tell driver you want the Temple Meads train station). At the Temple Meads Station, check the departure boards for trains going to the Bath Spa train station (4/hour, 15 minutes, £6). To get from Bath to Bristol Airport, just reverse these directions: Take the train to Temple Meads, then catch the Bristol Airport Flyer bus.

From Bath by Train to: Salisbury (1–2/hour, 1 hour), **Portsmouth** (hourly, 2.25 hours), **Exeter** (1–2/hour, 1.5–2 hours, transfer in Bristol or Westbury), **Penzance** (1–2/hour, 4.5–5 hours, one direct, most 1–2 transfers), **Moreton-in-Marsh** (hourly, 2.5–3 hours, 2–3 transfers), **York** (2/hour, 4.25–4.5 hours, 1–2 transfers in Birmingham, Bristol, and/or London), **Oxford** (hourly, 1.25 hours, transfer in Didcot), **Cardiff** (hourly, 1–1.5 hours), **Birmingham** (2/hour, 2 hours, transfer in Bristol), and **points north** (from Birmingham, a major transportation hub, trains depart for Blackpool, Scotland, and North Wales; use a train/bus combination to reach Ironbridge Gorge and the Lake District).

From Bath by Bus to: Salisbury (hourly, 2.75 hours, transfer in Warminster; or 1/day direct at 10:35, 1.5 hours on National Express #300), **Portsmouth** (1/day direct, 3 hours), **Exeter** (4/day, 3.5–4 hours, transfer in Bristol), **Penzance** (2/day, 7–8 hours, transfer in Bristol), **Cheltenham** or **Gloucester** (4/day, 2.5 hours, transfer in Bristol), **Stratford-upon-Avon** (1/day, 4 hours, transfer in Bristol), and **Oxford** (1/day direct, 2 hours, more with transfer). Buses to **Wells** depart nearly hourly, but the last direct bus back leaves before the evensong service is finished (1.25 hours, last return 17:43—except Sun, when there are also buses at 18:46 and 20:16; or take 18:15 bus to Bristol, then train to Bath—see page 288). For bus connections to **Avebury** and **Glastonbury,** see the next chapter.

NEAR BATH

Glastonbury • Wells • Avebury • Stonehenge
• Salisbury • South Wales

Ooooh, mystery, history. Glastonbury is the ancient home of Avalon, King Arthur, and the Holy Grail. Nearby, medieval Wells gathers around its grand cathedral, where you can enjoy an evensong service. Then get Neolithic at every Druid's favorite stone circles, Avebury and Stonehenge. Salisbury is known for its colorful markets and soaring cathedral.

An hour west of Bath, at St. Fagans National History Museum, you'll find South Wales' story vividly told in a park full of restored houses. Relish the romantic ruins and poetic wax of Tintern Abbey, the lush Wye River Valley, and the quirky Forest of Dean.

Planning Your Time

In England: Avebury, Glastonbury, and Wells make a wonderful day out from Bath. With a car, you can do all three in a day if you're selective with your sightseeing in each town (no lingering). Splicing in Stonehenge is possible, but really stretching it. If you want to squeeze a little less into each day, choose either the sights to the west (Wells and Glastonbury), or those to the east (Avebury, Stonehenge, and Salisbury). Ideally, try to see Stonehenge on your way from London, saving your Bath side-tripping day for the other sights.

Everybody needs to see Stonehenge, but I'll tell you now, it looks just like it looks. You'll know what I mean when you pay to get in and rub up against the rope fence that keeps tourists at a distance. Avebury is the connoisseur's circle: more subtle and welcoming.

Wells is simply a cute town, much smaller and more medieval than Bath, with a uniquely beautiful cathedral that's best experienced at the 17:15 evensong service (Sun at 15:00). Glastonbury can be covered well in three to four hours: See the abbey, climb the tor, and ponder your hippie past (and where you are now). Just an hour from Bath, Salisbury makes a pleasant stop, particularly on a market day (Tue, Sat, and every other Wed), though its cathedral looks striking anytime.

In Wales: Think of the South Wales sights as a different grouping. Ideally, they fill the day you leave Bath for the Cotswolds. Anyone interested in Welsh culture can spend four hours in St. Fagans National History Museum. Castle-lovers and romantics will want to consider seeing Tintern Abbey, the Forest of Dean, and the castles of Cardiff, Caerphilly, and Chepstow.

For a great day in South Wales, consider this schedule:

9:00 Leave Bath for South Wales.

10:30 Tour St. Fagans.

15:00 Stop at Tintern Abbey and/or a castle of your choice, then drive to the Cotswolds.

18:00 Set up in your Cotswolds home base.

Getting Around the Region

By Car: Drivers can do a 133-mile loop, from Bath to Avebury (25 miles) to Stonehenge (30 miles) to Glastonbury (50 miles) to Wells (6 miles) and back to Bath (22 miles). A loop from Bath to South Wales is 100 miles, mostly on the 70-mph motorway. Each of the Welsh sights is just off the motorway.

By Bus and Train: Wells and Glastonbury are both easily accessible by bus from Bath. Bus #173 goes direct from Bath to **Wells** (hourly, less frequent on Sun, 1.25 hours), where you can catch bus #375, #376, or #377 to continue on to **Glastonbury** (4/hour, 20 minutes). Note that there are no direct buses between Bath and Glastonbury. Wells and Glastonbury are also connected to each other by a 9.5-mile foot and bike path (though, alas, neither town has bike rental).

Many different buses run between Bath and **Avebury,** all requiring one or two transfers (hourly, 2 hours). There is no bus between Avebury and Stonehenge.

A one-hour train trip connects Bath to **Salisbury** (1–2/hour). With the best public transportation of all these towns, Salisbury is a good jumping-off point for Stonehenge or Avebury by bus or car. The Stonehenge Tour runs buses between Salisbury, Old Sarum, and Stonehenge (see page 300). Buses also run regularly from Salisbury to Avebury (1–2/hour, 1.5–2.5 hours; Wilts & Dorset bus #2 leaves from bus station on Endless Street and also from St. Paul's Church on Fisherton Street, near the train station; transfer in Devizes to Stagecoach's bus #49 to Avebury; other combinations possible, some with 2 transfers).

Sights near Bath

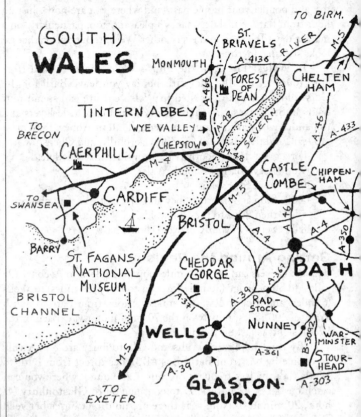

Various bus companies run these routes, including Stagecoach, Bodmans Coaches, the First Bus Company, and Wilts & Dorset. To find fare information, check with Traveline South West, which combines all the information from these companies into an easy-to-use website that covers all the southwest routes (www .travelinesw.com, toll tel. 0871-200-2233). Buses run much less frequently on Sundays.

To get to **South Wales** from Bath, take a train to Cardiff, then connect by bus (or train) to the sights.

By Tour: From Bath, if you don't have a car, the most convenient and quickest way to see Avebury and Stonehenge is to take an all-day bus tour, or a half-day tour just to Stonehenge. Of those tours leaving from Bath, Mad Max is the liveliest (see "Tours in Bath" on page 238).

Glastonbury

Marked by its hill, or "tor," and located on England's most powerful line of prehistoric sites (called a "ley line"), the town of Glastonbury gurgles with history and mystery.

In A.D. 37, Joseph of Arimathea—Jesus' wealthy uncle—brought vessels containing the blood of Jesus to Glastonbury, and, with them, Christianity came to England. (Joseph's visit is plausible—long before Christ, locals traded lead to merchants from the Levant.) While this story is "proven" by fourth-century writings and accepted by the Church, the King-Arthur-and-the-Holy-Grail legends it inspired are not.

Those medieval tales came when England needed a morale-boosting folk hero for inspiration during a war with France. They pointed to the ancient Celtic sanctuary at Glastonbury as proof enough of the greatness of the fifth-century warlord Arthur. In 1191, his supposed remains (along with those of Queen Guinevere) were dug up from the abbey garden, and Glastonbury became woven into the Arthurian legends. Reburied in the abbey choir, their gravesite is a shrine today. Many think the Grail trail ends at the bottom of the Chalice Well, a natural spring at the base of the Glastonbury Tor.

The Glastonbury Abbey was England's most powerful by the 10th century, and was part of a nationwide network of monasteries that by 1500 owned one-sixth of all English land and had four times the income of the Crown. Then Henry VIII dissolved the abbeys in 1536. He was particularly harsh on Glastonbury—he not only destroyed the abbey but also hung and quartered the abbot, sending the parts of his body on four different national tours...at the same time.

But Glastonbury rebounded. In an 18th-century tourism campaign, thousands signed affidavits stating that they'd been healed by water from the Chalice Well, and once again Glastonbury was on the tourist map. Today, Glastonbury and its Tor are a center for searchers, too creepy for the mainstream church but just right for those looking for a place to recharge their crystals.

Part of the fun of a visit to Glastonbury is just being in a town where every other shop and eatery is a New Age place. If you need spiritual guidance or just a rune reading, wander through the Glastonbury Experience, a New Age mall at the bottom of High Street. Locals who are not into this complain that on High Street you can buy any kind of magic crystal or incense, but not a roll of TP. But, as this counterculture is their town's bread and butter, they do their best to sit in their pubs and go "Ommmmm."

Orientation to Glastonbury

(area code: 01458)

Tourist Information

The TI is on High Street—as are many of the dreadlocked folks who walk it. It occupies a fine 15th-century townhouse called The

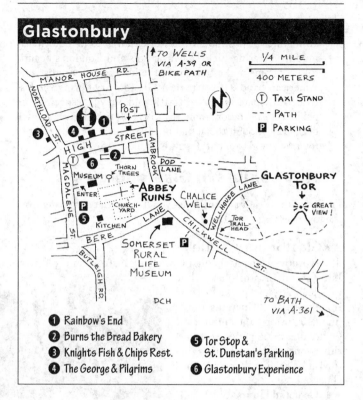

Glastonbury

↑ TO WELLS
VIA A-39 OR
BIKE PATH

¼ MILE

400 METERS

MANOR HOUSE RD.

NORTHLOAD ST.

POST

③ ④ ① ①

HIGH STREET

LAMBROOK ST.

⑦ TAXI STAND
- - - PATH
P PARKING

N

T ⑥ ②

MUSEUM Ø

POP LANE

THORN TREES

**GLASTONBURY
TOR**

MAGDALENE ST.

ENTER

ABBEY
RUINS

CHALICE
WELL

WELLHOUSE LANE

☀ GREAT
VIEW!

P

CHURCHYARD

⑤

KITCHEN

TOR
TRAIL-
HEAD

LANE

CHILKWELL

BERE

SOMERSET
RURAL
LIFE
MUSEUM

P

ST.

BUTLEIGH RD.

DCH

TO BATH
VIA A-361 →

① Rainbow's End
② Burns the Bread Bakery
③ Knights Fish & Chips Rest.
④ The George & Pilgrims

⑤ Tor Stop &
St. Dunstan's Parking
⑥ Glastonbury Experience

Tribunal (Mon–Thu 10:00–16:00, Fri–Sat 10:00–16:30, closed Sun, pay Internet access, 9 High Street, tel. 01458/832-954, www .glastonburytic.co.uk). The TI sells several booklets about cycling and walking in the area, including the *Glastonbury and Street Guide,* with local listings and a map (£1.50); and the *Glastonbury Millennium Trail* pamphlet, which sends visitors on a historical scavenger hunt, following 20 numbered marble plaques embedded in the pavement throughout the town (£0.60).

Above the TI is the marginally interesting **Lake Village Museum** with two humble rooms featuring tools made of stones, bones, and antlers. Preserved in and excavated from the local peat bogs, these tools offer a look at the lives of marshland people in pre-Roman times (£2.50, extensive descriptions, same hours as TI).

Helpful Hints

Market Day: Tuesday is market day for crafts, knickknacks, and produce on the main street. There's also a country market Tuesday mornings in the Town Hall.

Glastonbury Festival: Every summer (June 22–26 in 2011), the gigantic Glastonbury Festival—billing itself as the "largest music and performing arts festival in the world"—brings all manner of postmodern flower children to its notoriously muddy "Healing Fields." Music fans and London's beautiful people make the trek to see the hottest new English and American bands. If you're near Glastonbury during the festival, anticipate increased traffic and crowds (especially on public transportation; more than 135,000 tickets generally sell out), even though the actual music venue is six miles east of town (www.glastonburyfestivals.co.uk).

Sights in Glastonbury

I've listed these sights in the order you'll reach them, moving from the town center to the Tor.

▲▲Glastonbury Abbey

The evocative ruins of the first Christian sanctuary in the British Isles stand mysteriously alive in a lush 36-acre park. Because it comes with a fine museum, a dramatic history, and enthusiastic guides dressed in period costume, this is one of the most engaging to visit of England's many ruined abbeys.

Cost and Hours: £5.50, daily June–Aug 9:00–18:00, Sept–May 9:30 or 10:00 to dusk, closing times vary in the winter, last entry 30 minutes before closing, nearby pay parking, informative but long-winded 40-minute audioguide-£1, tel. 01458/832-267, www.glastonburyabbey.com. Enter the abbey from Magdalene Street (around the corner from High Street, near the St. Dunstan's parking lot).

Tours and Demonstrations: Costumed guides offer tours and presentations throughout the day (all included with your ticket). These include a fun medieval kitchen demo (described later) and earnest, costumed "Living History" reenactments (generally daily March–Oct at 10:30, 12:00, 14:00, and 16:00). As you enter, confirm these times, and ask about other tour and show times. Or, if you're coming on a slow day (off-season weekdays), call ahead to get the schedule.

Eating: Picnicking is encouraged—bring something from one of the shops in town (see "Eating in Glastonbury," later), or buy food at the small café on site.

Background: The space that these ruins occupy has been sacred ground for centuries. The druids used it as a pagan holy site, and during Joseph of Arimathea's supposed visit here, he built a simple place of worship. In the 12th century—because of that legendary connection with Joseph of Arimathea—Glastonbury was the leading Christian pilgrimage site in all of Britain. The popular abbey grew very wealthy and employed a thousand people to serve the needs of the pilgrims. Then, in 1171, Thomas Becket was martyred at Canterbury, and immediately canonized by the pope (who thanked God for the opportunity to rile up the Christian public in England against King Henry II). This was a classic church-state power struggle. The king was excommunicated, and had to crawl through the streets of London on his knees and submit to a whipping from each bishop in England. Religious pilgrims abandoned Glastonbury for Canterbury, leaving Glastonbury suddenly a backwater.

In 1184, there was a devastating fire in the monastery, and in 1191, the abbot here "discovered"—with the help of a divine dream—the tomb and bodies of King Arthur and Queen Guinevere. Of course, this discovery rekindled the pilgrim trade in Glastonbury.

Then, in 1539, King Henry VIII ordered the abbey's destruction. When Glastonbury Abbot Richard Whiting questioned the king's decision, he was branded a traitor, hung at the top of Glastonbury Tor (after carrying up the plank that would support his noose), and his body cut into four pieces. His head was stuck over the gateway to the former abbey precinct. After this harsh example, the other abbots accepted the king's dissolution of England's abbeys. Many returned to monastic centers in France.

Today, the abbey attracts people who find God within. Tie-dyed, starry-eyed pilgrims seem to float through the grounds, naturally high. Others lie on the grave of King Arthur, whose burial site is marked off in the center of the abbey ruins.

◐ Self-Guided Tour: After buying your ticket, tour the informative **museum** at the entrance building. A model shows the abbey in its pre–Henry VIII splendor, and exhibits tell the story of a place "grandly constructed to entice the dullest minds to prayer." You'll often see costumed guides here who are eager to share the site's story, and might even offer an impromptu tour.

Then head out to explore the green park, dotted with bits of the **ruined abbey.** You come face-to-face with the abbey's west (entrance) end. The abbey was long and skinny, but vast. At 580 feet long, it was the longest in Britain.

Before poking around the ruins, circle to the left behind the entrance building to find the two **thorn trees.** According to legend, when Joseph of Arimathea came here, he climbed nearby Warrell Hill and stuck his staff into the soil. A thorn tree sprouted that still stands there today; these are its offspring. The trees bloom twice a year, at Easter and at Christmas. If the story seems far-fetched to you, don't tell the Queen—a blossom from this tree sits proudly on her breakfast table every Christmas morning.

Now hike along the ruins to the far end of the abbey. You can stand and, from what was the altar, look down at what was the nave. In this area, you'll find the tombstone (formerly in the floor of the church's choir) where the supposed relics of Arthur and Guinevere were interred.

Continue around the far side of the abbey ruins, feeling free to poke around the park. Head back toward the front of the church,

 noticing all of the foundation rubble in the field adjoining the abbey; among these were the former churchyard, where Arthur and Guinevere's bones were originally found.

Head for the only surviving intact building on the grounds—the abbot's conical **kitchen.** Here, you'll often find Matilda the pilgrim (or another costumed docent) demonstrating life in the abbey kitchen in a kind of medieval cooking show.

Near Glastonbury Tor

These sights are about a 15-minute walk from the town center, toward the Tor (see "Getting There," on page 277).

Somerset Rural Life Museum—Exhibits in this free and extremely kid-friendly museum include peat digging, cider-making, and cheesemaking. The Abbey Farmhouse is now a collection of domestic and work mementos that illustrate the life of Victorian farm laborer John Hodges "from the cradle to the grave." The fine 14th-century tithe barn (one of 30 such structures that funneled tithes to the local abbey), with its beautifully preserved wooden ceiling, is filled with Victorian farm tools and enthusiastic schoolchildren (free, Tue–Sat 10:00–17:00, closed Sun–Mon, last entry 30 minutes before closing, free parking, at intersection of Bere Lane and Chilkwell Street, tel. 01458/831-197, www.somerset.gov.uk/museums).

Chalice Well—According to tradition, Joseph of Arimathea brought the chalice from the Last Supper to Glastonbury in A.D. 37. Supposedly it ended up in the bottom of a well, which is now the centerpiece of a peaceful and inviting garden. Even if the chalice is not in the bottom of the well and the water is red from iron ore and not Jesus' blood, the tranquil setting is one where nature's harmony is a joy to ponder. To find the well itself, follow the gurgling stream uphill, passing several places to drink from or wade in the

healing water, as well as areas designated for silent reflection. The stones of the well shaft date from the 12th century, and are believed to have come from the church in Glastonbury Abbey (which was destroyed by fire). During the 18th century, pilgrims flocked to Glastonbury for the well's healing powers. Have a drink or take some of the precious water home—they sell empty bottles to fill (entry-£3.50, daily April–Oct 10:00–18:00, Nov–March 10:00–16:30, last entry 30 minutes before closing, on Chilkwell Street/A361, drivers park at Rural Life Museum and walk 5 minutes—see instructions on page 278, tel. 01458/831-154, www.chalicewell.org.uk).

▲Glastonbury Tor

Seen by many as a Mother Goddess symbol, the Tor—a natural plug of sandstone on clay—has an undeniable geological charisma.

Climbing the Tor is the essential activity on a visit to Glastonbury. A fine Somerset view rewards those who hike to its 520-foot summit. From its top you can survey a former bogland that is still below sea level at high tide. The ribbon-like man-made drainage canals that glisten as they slice through the farmland are the work of Dutch engineers, imported centuries ago to turn the marshy wasteland into something usable.

Looking out, find Glastonbury (at the base of the hill) and Wells (marked by its cathedral) to the right. Above Wells, a TV tower marks the 996-foot high point of the Mendip Hills. It was lead from these hills that attracted the Romans (and, perhaps, Jesus' uncle Joe) so long ago. Stretching to the left, the hills define what was the coastline before those Dutch engineers arrived.

The Tor-top tower is the remnant of a chapel dedicated to St. Michael. Early Christians often employed St. Michael, the warrior angel, to combat pagan gods. When a church was built upon a pagan holy ground like this, it was frequently dedicated to Michael. But apparently those pagan gods fought back: St. Michael's Church was destroyed by an earthquake in 1275.

Getting There: The Tor is a steep hill at the southeastern edge of the town (it's visible from just about everywhere). The base of the Tor is a 20-minute **walk** from the TI and town center. From the base, a trail leads up to the top (figure another 15–20 uphill minutes, if you keep a brisk pace). While you can hike up the Tor from either end, the less-steep approach (which most people take) starts next to the Chalice Well.

NEAR BATH

If you have a **car,** drive to the Somerset Rural Life Museum, where you can park for free, then walk five minutes to the trailhead (walk up the lane between the parking lot and the museum, turn right onto Chilkwell Street, and watch on the left for the Chalice Well, then the trailhead).

If you're without a car and don't want to walk to the Tor trailhead, you have two options: The **Tor Bus** shuttles visitors from the town center to the base of the Tor. If you ask, the bus will also stop at the Somerset Rural Life Museum and the Chalice Well (£3 round-trip, 2/hour, on the half-hour, Easter–Sept daily 9:30–13:00 & 14:00–19:30, doesn't run Oct–Easter, catch bus at St. Dunstan's parking lot in the town center—to the right as you face the abbey entrance, pick up schedule at TI). A **taxi** to the Tor trailhead costs about £5 one-way—an easier and more economical choice for couples or groups. Remember, these take you only to the bottom of the Tor; to reach the top, you have to hike.

Eating in Glastonbury

Rainbow's End is one of several fine, healthy, vegetarian lunch cafés for hot meals (different every day), salads, herbal teas, yummy homemade sweets, and New Age people-watching (£7–8 meals, cheaper salads sold by the portion, vegan and gluten-free options, counter service, daily 10:00–16:00, a few doors up from the TI, 17 High Street, tel. 01458/833-896). If you're looking for a midwife or a male-bonding tribal meeting, check their notice board.

Burns the Bread makes hearty pasties (savory meat pies) as well as fresh pies, sandwiches, delicious cookies, and pastries. Ask about the Torsy Moorsy Cake (a type of fruitcake made with cheddar), or try a gingerbread man made with real ginger. Grab a pasty and picnic with the ghosts of Arthur and Guinevere in the abbey ruins (£1.50 pasties and pastries, Mon–Sat 6:00–17:00, Sun 11:00–17:00, 14 High Street, tel. 01458/831-532).

Knights Fish and Chips Restaurant, which has been in the same family since 1909, is the town's top chippy—and another fine option for a picnic at the abbey (£6 to go, about £1 more for table service, Mon 17:00–21:30, Tue–Sat 12:00–14:15 & 17:00–21:30, closed Sun, 5 Northload Street, tel. 01458/831-882).

The George & Pilgrims Hotel's wonderfully Old World pub might be exactly what the doctor ordered for visitors suffering a New Age overdose. The French owners mix a few French dishes into the traditional pub-grub menu (£5 sandwiches, £8–11 meals, Mon–Sat 11:00–23:00, Sun 12:00–22:30, food served 12:00–15:00 & 18:00–21:00, 1 High Street, tel. 01458/831-146). They also rent rooms (Db-£70).

Glastonbury Connections

The nearest train station is in Bath. Local buses are run by First Bus Company (toll tel. 0845-606-4446, www.firstgroup.com).

From Glastonbury by Bus to: Wells (4/hour, 20 minutes, bus #375/#376/#377 runs frequently, bus #29 only 6/day), **Bath** (hourly, allow 2 hours, take bus #375/#376/#377 or #29 to Wells, transfer to bus #173 to Bath, 1.25 hours between Wells and Bath). Buses are sparse on Sundays (generally one bus every other hour). If you're heading to points west, you'll likely connect through **Taunton** (which is a transfer point for westbound buses from Bristol).

Wells

Because this well-preserved little town has a cathedral, it can be called a city. While it's the biggest town in Somerset, it's England's smallest cathedral city (pop. 9,400), with one of its most interesting cathedrals and a wonderful evensong service. Wells has more medieval buildings still doing what they were originally built to do than any town you'll visit. Market day fills the town square on Wednesday (farmers market) and Saturday (general goods).

Orientation to Wells

(area code: 01749)

Tourist Information

The TI, on the main square, has information about the town's sights and nearby cheese factories (April–Oct Mon–Sat 10:00–17:00, Sun 10:00–16:00; Nov–March Mon–Sat 11:00–16:00, closed Sun; tel. 01749/672-552, www.wellstourism.com). They have pay Internet access, give out a free schematic map of town, and sell a better one for £0.10. Consider the *Wells City Trail* booklet for £0.60. On Wednesdays and Saturdays at 11:00, they offer a one-hour walking tour of town for £4.

Arrival in Wells

If you're coming by **bus,** you'll arrive at the big, well-organized but unstaffed bus parking lot, about a five-minute walk from the town center. (The big church tower you see is *not* the cathedral.)

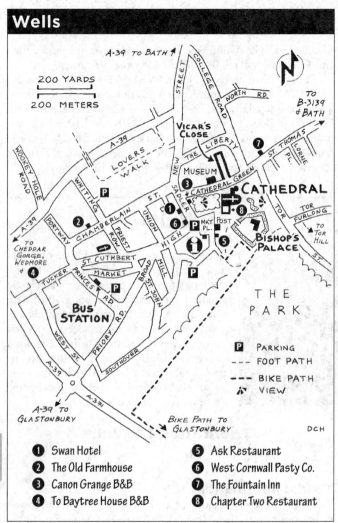

Wells

A-39 TO BATH

200 YARDS
200 METERS

COLLEGE ROAD / STREET
NORTH RD.
TO B-3139 & BATH

LOVERS WALK
A-39

WOOKEY HOLE ROAD

VICAR'S CLOSE
THE LIBERTY
MUSEUM
CATHEDRAL GREEN
CATHEDRAL
ST. THOMAS PL.
LORNE

WHITING
CHAMBERLAIN
PRIEST ROW
UNION ST.
SADLER ST.
NEW ST.

③
①
⑦
⑧
⑥ MKT PL. POST
HIGH ST.

A-39
PORTWAY
②

TO CHEDDAR GORGE, WEDMORE
④

ST. CUTHBERT
TUCKER
PRINCES RD.
MARKET
BROAD ST.
ST. JOHN
MILL ST.

①
⑤
BISHOP'S PALACE
TOR
TOR FURLONG
TO TOR HILL
TOR ST.

BUS STATION
WEST ST.
PRIORY RD.
SOUTHOVER

THE PARK

A-39 TO GLASTONBURY
A-371

BIKE PATH TO GLASTONBURY

P PARKING
--- FOOT PATH
--- BIKE PATH
👁 VIEW

DCH

① Swan Hotel
② The Old Farmhouse
③ Canon Grange B&B
④ To Baytree House B&B
⑤ Ask Restaurant
⑥ West Cornwall Pasty Co.
⑦ The Fountain Inn
⑧ Chapter Two Restaurant

NEAR BATH

Find the Wells map at the head of the stalls to get oriented; the signpost at the main exit directs you downtown. **Drivers** will find pay parking right on the main square, but because of confusing one-way streets, it's hard to reach; instead, it's simpler to park at the Princes Road lot near the bus station (enter on Priory Road) and walk five minutes to the cathedral.

Helpful Hints

Local Guide: Edie Westmoreland offers town walks in the summer by appointment (£15/group of 2–5 people, £4/person for

8 or more, 1.5-hour tours usually start at Penniless Porch on town square, book three days in advance, tel. 01934/832-350, mobile 07899-836-706, ebwestmoreland@btinternet.com).

Best Views: It's hard to beat the grand views of the cathedral from the green in front of it...but the reflecting pool tucked inside the Bishop's Palace grounds tries hard. For a fine cathedral-and-town view from your own leafy hilltop bench, hike 10 minutes up Tor Hill.

Sights in Wells

▲▲Wells Cathedral

England's first completely Gothic cathedral (dating from about 1200) is the highlight of the city. Locals claim this church has the largest collection of medieval statuary north of the Alps. It certainly has one of the widest and most elaborate facades I've seen, and unique figure-eight supports in the nave to boot.

Cost and Hours: Requested £5.50 donation—not intended to keep you out, daily Easter–Sept 7:00–19:00, Oct–Easter 7:00–18:00; to take pictures, pay £3 photography fee at info desk or at coin-op machine inside cathedral, no flash in choir; one-hour tours Mon–Sat April–Oct at 10:00, 12:00, 13:00, 14:00, and 15:00—unless other events are going on in the cathedral; good shop, handy Chapter Two restaurant, tel. 01749/674-483, www.wellscathedral.org.uk.

𝕆 Self-Guided Tour: Begin on the vast, inviting **green** in front of the cathedral. In the Middle Ages, the cathedral was enclosed within the "Liberty," an area free from civil jurisdiction until the 1800s. The Liberty included the green on the west side of the cathedral, which, from the 13th to the 17th centuries, was a burial place for common folk, including 17th-century plague victims. During the Edwardian period, a local character known as Boney Foster used to dig up the human bones and sell them to tourists. The green later became a cricket pitch, then a field for grazing animals. Today, it's the perfect setting for an impressive cathedral.

Peer up at the impressive **facade.** The newly restored west front displays almost 300 original 13th-century carvings of kings and the Last Judgment. The bottom row of niches is empty, too easily reached by Cromwell's men, who were hell-bent on destroying "graven images." Stand back and imagine it as a grand Palm Sunday welcome with a cast of hundreds—all gaily painted back then, choristers singing boldly from holes above the doors and trumpets tooting through the holes up by the 12 apostles.

Now head **inside.** Most of the time, visitors enter by going to the right, through the door under the small spire into the lobby

NEAR BATH

and welcome center. (At certain times—generally 7:00-9:00 and 17:00–19:00—you can enter through the cathedral's main door.)

At the **welcome center,** you'll be warmly greeted and reminded how expensive it is to maintain the cathedral. Pay the donation, buy a £3 photo-permission sticker (if you choose), and pick up a map of the cathedral's highlights. Then head through the cloister and into the cathedral.

At your first glance down the nave, you're immediately struck by the general lightness and the unique "scissors" or hourglass-

shaped **double arch** (added in 1338 to transfer weight from the west—where the foundations were sinking under the tower's weight—to the east, where they were firm). The warm tones of the stone interior give the place a modern feel. Until Henry VIII and the Reformation, the interior was painted a gloomy red and green. Later it was whitewashed. Then, in the 1840s, the church experienced the Victorian "great scrape," as locals peeled moldy whitewash off and revealed the bare stone we see today. The floral ceiling painting is based on the original medieval design. A single pattern was discovered under the 17th-century whitewash and repeated throughout.

Small, ornate 15th-century pavilion-like chapels flank the altar, carved in lacy Gothic for wealthy townsmen. The **pulpit** features a post-Reformation, circa-1540 English script—rather than the standard Latin. Since this was not a monastery church, the Reformation didn't destroy it as it did the Glastonbury Abbey church.

We'll do a quick clockwise spin around the cathedral's interior. First walk down the left aisle until you reach the north transept. The medieval **clock** does a silly but much-loved joust on the quar-

ter-hour. If you get to watch the show, notice how—like clockwork—every other rider gets clobbered. The clock's face, which depicts the earth at the center of the universe, dates from 1390. The outer ring shows hours, the second ring shows minutes, and the inner ring shows the dates of the month and phases of the moon. Beneath the clock, the fine **crucifix** was carved out of a yew tree by a German prisoner of war during World War II. After the war ended, many of England's German prisoners figured

there was little in Germany to go home to, so they stayed, assimilating into English culture. Also in the north transept is the door with well-worn steps leading up to the grand fan-vaulted **Chapter House**—an intimate place for the theological equivalent of a huddle among church officials.

Now continue down the left aisle. On the right is the entrance to the **choir** (or "quire," the central zone where the daily services are sung). Go in and take a close look at the embroidery work on the cushions, which celebrate the hometowns of important local church leaders. Up above the east end of the choir is "Jesse's Window," depicting Jesus' family tree. It's also called the "Golden Window," because it's bathed in sunlight each morning.

Head back out to the aisle the way you came in, and continue to the end of the church. In the apse you'll find the **Lady Chapel.** Examine the medieval stained-glass windows. Do they look jumbled? In the 17th century, Puritan troops trashed the precious original glass. Much was repaired, but many of the broken panes were like a puzzle that was never figured out. That's why today many of the windows are simply kaleidoscopes of colored glass.

Now circle around and head up the other aisle. As you walk, notice that many of the black **tombstones** set in the floor have decorative recesses that aren't filled with brass (as they once were). After the Reformation in the 1530s, the church was short on cash, so they sold the brass to raise money for roof repairs.

Once you reach the south transept, you'll find several items of interest. The **old font** survives from the previous church (A.D. 705) and has been the site of Wells baptisms for almost a thousand years. In the far end of this transept, a little of the muddy green and red that wasn't whitewashed survives.

Nearby, notice the **carvings** at the tops of the pillars, which depict medieval life. On the first pillar, notice the man with a toothache, and another man with a thorn in his foot. The second pillar tells a story of medieval justice: On the left, we see thieves

stealing grapes; on the right, the wood-cutter (with an axe) is warning the farmer (with the pitchfork) what's happening. Circle around to the back of the pillar for the rest of the story: On the left, the farmer chases one of the thieves, grabbing him by the ear. On the right, he clobbers the thief over the head with his pitchfork—so hard the farmer's hat falls off.

Also in the south transept, you'll find the entrance to the cathedral **Reading Room.** Housing a few old manuscripts, it offers a peek into a real 15th-century library (£1, Fri–Sat 14:30–16:30 only; might also be possible to step in for a quick look on weekday mornings and afternoons).

And finally, the south transept is also where you'll exit the cathedral: Head out into the cloister, then cross the courtyard back to the welcome center, shop, Chapter Two restaurant, and exit. Go in peace.

More Cathedral Sights

▲▲**Cathedral Evensong Service**—The cathedral choir takes full advantage of heavenly acoustics with a nightly 45-minute evensong service. You will sit right in the old "quire" as you listen to a great pipe organ and boys', girls', and men's voices (Mon–Sat at 17:15, Sun at 15:00, generally no service when school is out July–Aug unless a visiting choir performs, to check call 01749/674-483 or visit www.wellscathedral.org.uk). At 17:05 (Sun at 15:05) the verger ushers visitors to their seats. There's usually plenty of room.

On weekdays and Saturdays, if you need to catch the 17:43 bus to Bath, request a seat on the north side of the presbytery, so you can slip out the side door without disturbing the service (10-minute walk to station from cathedral; or go at 18:15 via Bristol—explained under "Wells Connections," later).

The cathedral also hosts several evening **concerts** each month (£10–26, most about £18, generally Thu–Sat at 19:00 or 19:30, box office in cathedral gift shop, open Mon–Sat 14:00–16:30, closed Sun, tel. 01749/832-201). Concert tickets are also available at the TI.

Vicar's Close—Lined with perfectly pickled 14th-century houses, this is the oldest continuously occupied complete street in Europe (since 1348, just a block north of the cathedral—go under the big arch and look left). It was built to house the vicar's choir, and it still houses church officials (and some of the houses can be rented for a weeklong holiday; contact the cathedral office for details).

▲**Bishop's Palace**—Next to the cathedral stands the moated Bishop's Palace, built in the 13th century and still in use today as

the residence of the Bishop of Bath and Wells. While the interior of the palace itself is dull, the grounds and gardens surrounding it are spectacular—the most tranquil and scenic spot in Wells, with wonderful views of the cathedral. It's just the place for a relaxing walk in the park (£5.50, April–Oct daily 10:30–18:00, closed Nov–March, often closed on Sat for special events—call to confirm, last entry one hour before closing, tel. 01749/988-111, www.bishopspalace .org.uk).

The palace's spring-fed moat was built in the 14th century to protect the bishop during squabbles with the borough. Now it serves primarily as a pool for mute swans, who have been trained to ring a bell to ask for food. The bridge was last drawn in 1831. Crossing that bridge, you'll buy your ticket and enter the grounds (past the old-timers playing a proper game of croquet—daily after 13:30). Pass through the evocative ruins of the Great Hall (which was deserted and left to gradually deteriorate), and stroll through the chirpy south lawn. If you're feeling energetic, hike up to the top of the ramparts that encircle the property.

Circling around the far side of the mansion, cross the little bridge and follow the path to the wells (springs) that gave the city

its name. Surrounding a reflecting pool with the cathedral towering overhead, these flower-bedecked pathways are idyllic. Nearby are an arboretum, picnic area, and sweet little pea-patch gardens.

After touring the gardens, the mansion's interior is a letdown—despite the borrowable descriptions that struggle to make the dusty old place meaningful. Have a spot of tea in the café (with outdoor garden seating), or climb the creaky wooden staircase to wander long halls lined with portraits of bishops past.

NEAR BATH

Near Wells

The following stops are best for drivers.

Cheddar Cheese—If you're in the mood for a picnic, drop by any local aromatic cheese shop for a great selection of tasty Somerset cheeses. Real farmhouse cheddar puts American cheddar to Velveeta shame. The **Cheddar Gorge Cheese Company,** eight miles west of Wells, is a dairy farm with a guide and viewing area, giving guests a chance to see the cheesemaking process and enjoy a sample (£2, daily 10:00–16:00; take A39, then A371 to Cheddar Gorge; tel. 01934/742-810, www.cheddargorgecheeseco.co.uk).

Scrumpy Farms—Scrumpy is the wonderfully dangerous hard cider brewed in this part of Britain. You don't find it served in many pubs because of the unruly crowd it attracts. Scrumpy, at 8 percent alcohol, will rot your socks. "Scrumpy Jack," carbonated mass-produced cider, is not real scrumpy. The real stuff is "rough farmhouse cider." This is potent stuff. It's said some farmers throw a side of beef into the vat, and when fermentation is done only the teeth remain.

TIs list local cider farms open to the public, such as **Mr. Wilkins' Land's End Cider Farm,** a great Back Door travel experience (free, Mon–Sat 10:00–20:00, Sun 10:00–13:00; west of Wells in Mudgley, take B3139 from Wells to Wedmore, then B3151 south for 2 miles, farm is a quarter-mile off B3151—tough to find, get close and ask locals; tel. 01934/712-385).

Apples are pressed from August through December. Hard cider, while not quite scrumpy, is also typical of the West Country, but more fashionable, "decent," and accessible. You can get a pint of hard cider at nearly any pub, drawn straight from the barrel—dry, medium, or sweet.

Castle of Nunney—The centerpiece of the charming village of Nunney (between Bath and Glastonbury, off A361) is a striking 14th-century castle surrounded by a fairy-tale moat. Its rare, French-style design brings to mind the Paris Bastille. The year 1644 was a tumultuous one for Nunney. Its noble family was royalist (and likely closet Catholics). They defied Parliament, so Parliament ordered their castle "slighted" (deliberately destroyed) to ensure that it would threaten the order of the land no more. Looking at this castle, so daunting in the age of bows and arrows, you can see how it was no match for the modern cannon. The pretty Mendip village of Nunney, with its little brook, is also worth a wander.

Sleeping in Wells

Wells is a pleasant overnight stop, with a handful of agreeable B&Bs. The first three places listed below are within a short walk of the cathedral.

Sleep Code

(£1 = about $1.60, country code: 44, area code: 01749)
S = Single, **D** = Double/Twin, **T** = Triple, **Q** = Quad, **b** = bathroom,
s = shower only. Unless otherwise indicated, you can assume
credit cards are accepted and breakfast is included.

To help you sort easily through these listings, I've divided
the rooms into two categories based on the price for a
standard double room with bath:

$$ Higher Priced—Most rooms £80 or more.
$ Lower Priced—Most rooms less than £80.

Prices can change without notice; verify the hotel's
current rates online or by email. For other updates, see www
.ricksteves.com/update.

$$ Swan Hotel, a Best Western facing the cathedral, is a big,
comfortable 50-room hotel. Prices for their Tudor-style rooms vary
based on whether you want extras like a four-poster bed or a view
of the cathedral (Sb-£104, Db-£136, superior Db-£156, deluxe
Db-£176, ask about weekend deals, free Wi-Fi, Sadler Street, tel.
01749/836-300, fax 01749/836-301, www.swanhotelwells.co.uk,
info@swanhotelwells.co.uk).

$ The Old Farmhouse, a five-minute walk from the town cen-
ter, welcomes you with a secluded front garden and two tastefully
decorated rooms (Db-£75–80, 2-night minimum, secure parking, next to the gas station at 62 Chamberlain Street, tel. 01749/
675-058, www.wellsholiday.com, theoldfarmhousewells@hotmail
.com, charming owners Felicity and Christopher Wilkes).

$ Canon Grange B&B is a 15th-century watch-your-head
beamed house directly in front of the cathedral. It has seven
homey rooms and a cozy charm (S-£45, Sb-£50, Db-£68, Db
with spectacular cathedral view-£74, family room, free Wi-Fi, on
the cathedral green, tel. 01749/671-800, www.canongrange.co.uk,
canongrange@email.com, Annette and Ken).

$ Baytree House B&B is a modern and practical home at
the edge of town (on a big road, a 10-minute walk to the center)
renting five fresh, bright, and comfy rooms. Amanda and Paulo
Bellini run the place with Italian enthusiasm (Db-£68, Tb-£80,
two rooms have private bathrooms on the hall, family rooms, free
Wi-Fi, plush lounge, free parking, near where Strawberry Way
hits the A39 road to Cheddar at 85 Portway, tel. 01749/677-933,
mobile 07745-287-194, www.baytree-house.co.uk, stay@baytree
-house.co.uk).

Eating in Wells

Downtown Wells is tiny. A fine variety of eating options is within a block or two of its market square, including classic pubs, **Ask Restaurant** (a popular Italian chain, £8–10 pizza and pastas, £9–12 entrées, open daily, right on the square in the Market Hall, outdoor tables, tel. 01749/677-681), a branch of **West Cornwall Pasty Company** selling good savory pasties to go (Mon–Sat 8:00–18:00, Sun 10:00–17:00, 1a Sadler Street, tel. 01749/671-616), and little delis and bakeries serving light meals.

The Fountain Inn, on a quiet street 50 yards behind the cathedral, serves good pub grub (£9–10 lunches, £10–13 dinners, open daily, St. Thomas Street, tel. 01749/672-317).

Chapter Two, the modern restaurant in the cathedral welcome center, offers a handy if not heavenly lunch (£6–7 lunches, Mon–Sat 10:00–17:00, Sun 11:00–17:00, may close earlier in winter, tel. 01749/676-543).

Wells Connections

The nearest train station is in Bath. The bus station in Wells is at a well-organized bus parking lot at the intersection of Priory and Princes roads. Local buses are run by First Bus Company (for Wells, toll tel. 0845-606-4446, www.firstgroup.com), while buses to and from London are run by National Express (toll tel. 0871-781-8181, www.nationalexpress.com).

From Wells by Bus to: Bath (hourly, 1.25 hours, last bus #173 leaves at 17:43—except Sun, when there are also buses at 18:46 and 20:16; if you miss the Mon–Sat 17:43 bus to Bath, catch the 18:15 bus to Bristol, then a 15-minute train ride to Bath, arriving 19:35), **Glastonbury** (4/hour, 20 minutes, bus #375/#376/#377 runs frequently, bus #29 only 6/day), **London's** Victoria Coach Station (£28–30, 1/day direct, departs Wells at 6:55, arrives London at 11:20; otherwise hourly with a change in Bristol, 4 hours).

Avebury

Avebury is a prehistoric open-air museum, with a complex of fascinating Neolithic sites all gathered around the great stone henge (circle). Because the area sports only a thin skin of top-soil over chalk, it is naturally treeless (similar to the area around Stonehenge). Perhaps this unique landscape—where the land connects with the big sky—made it the choice of pre-historic societies for their religious monuments. Whatever

the case, Avebury dates to 2800 B.C.—six centuries older than Stonehenge. This complex, the St. Peter's Basilica of Neolithic civilization, makes for a fascinating visit. Many enjoy it more than Stonehenge.

Orientation to Avebury

(area code: 01672)
Avebury, just a little village with a big stone circle, is easy to reach by car, but may not be worth the hassle by public transportation (see "Getting Around the Region" on page 269).

Tourist Information
The TI is located within the town chapel. Notice the stone work: It's a mix of bricks and broken stones from the ancient circle (April–Oct Tue–Sat 9:30–17:00, Sun 9:30–14:30, closed Mon; Nov–March likely open Thu–Sat 9:30–16:00, Sun 9:30–14:30, likely closed Mon–Wed; Green Street, tel. 01672/539-179, www .visitwiltshire.co.uk). For good information on the Avebury sights, see the websites of the English Heritage (www.english -heritage.org.uk) and the National Trust (www.nationaltrust .org.uk).

Arrival in Avebury
If driving, you must pay to park in Avebury, and your only real option is the flat-fee National Trust parking lot, which is a three-minute walk from the village (£5, £3 after 15:00, summer 9:00–18:00, off-season 9:00–16:00). No other public parking is available in the village.

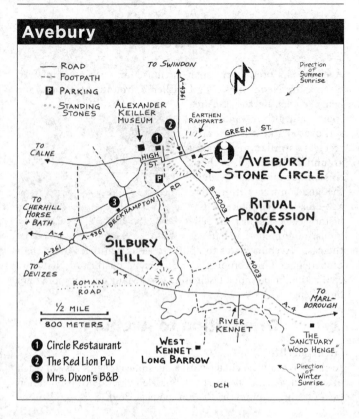

Avebury

ROAD
FOOTPATH
P PARKING
STANDING STONES

TO SWINDON

N

Direction of Summer Sunrise

A-4361

ALEXANDER KEILLER MUSEUM

❷

EARTHEN RAMPARTS

GREEN ST.

TO CALNE

❶

HIGH ST.

i AVEBURY STONE CIRCLE

P

B-4003

TO CHERHILL HORSE & BATH

❸

BECKHAMPTON RD.

RITUAL PROCESSION WAY

A-4

A-4361

SILBURY HILL

B-4003

A-361

A-4

TO DEVIZES

ROMAN ROAD

TO MARL-BOROUGH

A-4

½ MILE
800 METERS

❶ Circle Restaurant
❷ The Red Lion Pub
❸ Mrs. Dixon's B&B

WEST KENNET LONG BARROW

RIVER KENNET

THE SANCTUARY "WOOD HENGE"

Direction of Winter Sunrise

DCH

Sights in Avebury

NEAR BATH

▲▲**Avebury Stone Circle**—The stone circle at Avebury is bigger (16 times the size), less touristy, and, for many, more interesting than Stonehenge. You're free to wander among 100 stones, ditches, mounds, and curious patterns from the past, as well as the village of Avebury, which grew up in the middle of this fascinating 1,400-foot-wide Neolithic circle.

In the 14th century, in a kind of frenzy of religious paranoia, Avebury villagers buried many of these mysterious pagan stones. Their 18th-century descendants hosted social events in which they broke up the remaining pagan stones (topple, heat up, douse with cold water, and scavenge broken stones as building blocks). In modern times, the buried stones were dug up and re-erected. Concrete markers show where the missing broken-up stones once stood.

To make the roughly half-mile walk around the circle, you'll hike along an impressive earthwork henge—a 30-foot-high outer bank surrounding a ditch 30 feet deep, making a 60-foot-high rampart. This earthen rampart once had stones standing around the perimeter, placed about every 30 feet, and four grand causeway entries. Originally, two smaller circles made of about 200 stones stood within the henge (free, always open).

▲**Ritual Procession Way**—Also known as West Kennet Avenue, this double line of stones provided a ritual procession way leading from Avebury to a long-gone wooden circle dubbed "The Sanctuary." This "wood henge," thought to have been 1,000 years older than everything else in the area, is considered the genesis of Avebury and its big stone circle. Most of the stones standing along the procession way today were reconstructed in modern times.

▲**Silbury Hill**—This pyramid-shaped hill is a 130-foot-high, yet-to-be-explained mound of chalk just outside of Avebury.

More than 4,000 years old, this mound is considered the largest man-made object in prehistoric Europe (with the surface area of London's Trafalgar Square and the height of the Nelson Column). It's a reminder that we've only just scratched the surface of England's mysterious and ancient religious landscape.

Inspired by a legend that the hill hid a gold statue in its center, locals tunneled through Silbury Hill in 1830, undermining the structure. Work is currently underway to restore the hill, which remains closed to the public. Archaeologists (who date things like this by carbon-dating snails and other little critters killed in its construction) figure Silbury Hill took only 60 years to build in about 2200 B.C. This makes Silbury Hill the last element built at Avebury and contemporaneous with Stonehenge. Some think it may have been an observation point for all the other bits of the Avebury site. You can still see evidence of a spiral path leading up the hill, and a moat at its base.

The Roman road detoured around Silbury Hill. (Roman engineers often used features of the landscape as visual reference points when building roads. Their roads would commonly kink at the crest of hills or other landmarks, where they realigned with a new visual point.) Later, the hill sported a wooden Saxon fort, which likely acted as a look-out for marauding Vikings. And in World War II, the Royal Observer Corps stationed men up here to count and report Nazi bombers on raids.

West Kennet Long Barrow—A pull-out on the road just past Silbury Hill marks the West Kennet Long Barrow (a 15-minute walk from Silbury Hill). This burial chamber, the best-preserved Stone Age chamber tomb in the UK, stands intact on the ridge. It lines up with the rising sun on the summer solstice. You can walk inside the barrow.

Cherhill Horse—Heading west from Avebury on A4 (toward Bath), you'll see an obelisk (a monument to some important earl) above you on the downs, or chalk hills, near the village of Cherhill. You'll also see a white horse carved into the chalk hillside. Above it are the remains of an Iron Age hill fort known as Oldbury Castle—described on an information board at the roadside pull-out. There is one genuinely prehistoric white horse in England (the Uffington White Horse); the Cherhill Horse, like all the others, is just an 18th-century creation. Prehistoric discoveries were all the rage in the 1700s, and it was a fad to make your own fake ones. Throughout southern England, you can cut into the thin layer of topsoil and find chalk. Now, so they don't have to weed, horses like this are cemented and painted white.

Alexander Keiller Museum—This archaeology museum has an interactive exhibit in a 17th-century barn (£4.50, daily April–Oct 10:00–18:00, Nov–March 10:00–16:30, last entry 30 minutes before closing, tel. 01672/539-250).

Sleeping and Eating in Avebury

Sleeping in Avebury makes lots of sense, since the stones are lonely and wide-open all night. **$ Mrs. Dixon's B&B,** up the road from the public parking lot, rents three cramped and homey rooms. Look for the green-and-white *Bed & Breakfast* sign from the main road (S-£40, D-£60, these prices promised with this book in 2011, cash only, parking available in back, 6 Beckhampton Road, tel. 01672/539-588, run by earthy Mrs. Dixon and crew).

The pleasant **Circle Restaurant** serves healthy, hearty à la carte lunches, including vegan and gluten-free dishes, and cream teas on most days (daily April–Oct 10:00–17:30, Nov–March 10:00–15:30, next to National Trust store and the Alexander Keiller museum, tel. 01672/539-514).

The Red Lion has inexpensive, greasy pub grub; a creaky, well-worn, dart-throwing ambience; and a medieval well in its dining room (£6–12 meals, daily 12:00–22:00, tel. 01672/539-266).

NEAR BATH

Stonehenge

As old as the pyramids, and older than the Acropolis and the Colosseum, this iconic stone circle amazed medieval Europeans, who figured it was built by a race of giants. And it still impresses visitors today. As one of Europe's most famous sights, Stonehenge does a valiant job of retaining an air of mystery and majesty (partly because cordons, which keep hordes of tourists from trampling all over it, foster the illusion that it stands alone in a field). Although some people are underwhelmed by Stonehenge, most of its almost one million annual visitors find that it's worth the trip. And the ancient site continues to reveal its mysteries: In 2010, within sight of Stonehenge, archaeologists discovered another 5,000-year-old henge, or ditch, which they believe once encircled a wooden "twin" of the famous circle.

Getting to Stonehenge

By Public Transportation: Catch a train to Salisbury, then go by bus or taxi to Stonehenge (for details, see page 298). Note that there is no public transportation between Avebury and Stonehenge.

    By Car: Stonehenge is well-signed just off A303. It's about 15 minutes north of Salisbury, an hour east of Glastonbury, and an hour south of Avebury. From Salisbury, head north on A345 (Castle Road) through Amesbury, go west on A303 for 1.5 miles, veer right onto A344, and it's just ahead on the left, with the parking lot on the right.

    By Bus Tour: For tours of Stonehenge from Bath, see page 239 (Mad Max is best); for tours from Salisbury, see page 300.

Orientation to Stonehenge

Cost: £6.90, covered by English Heritage Pass and Great British Heritage Pass (see page 22).

Hours: Daily June–Aug 9:00–19:00, mid-March–May and Sept–mid-Oct 9:30–18:00, mid-Oct–mid-March 9:30–16:00, last entry 30 minutes before closing.

When to Go: Shorter hours and possible closures June 20–22 due to huge, raucous solstice crowds; £3 parking fee likely in summer—refundable with paid admission.

Information: Entry includes a worthwhile hour-long audio-guide—though they sometimes run out. Tel. 01980/623-108 or toll tel. 0870-333-1181, www.english-heritage.org.uk/stonehenge.

Reaching the Inner Stones: Special one-hour access to the stones' inner circle—before or after regular visiting hours—costs an extra £14.50 and must be reserved well in advance. Details are on the English Heritage website (go to "Explore Stonehenge," then click on the Stone Circle Access link) or by calling 01722/343-830.

Planned Changes: Future plans for Stonehenge call for the creation of a new visitors center and museum, designed to blend in with the landscape and make the stone circle feel more pristine. Visitors will park farther away and ride a shuttle bus to the site.

Self-Guided Tour

The entrance fee includes a good audioguide, but this commentary will help make your visit even more meaningful.

Walk in from the parking lot, buy your ticket, pick up your included audio-guide, and head through the ugly underpass beneath the road. On the way up the ramp, notice the artist's rendering of what Stonehenge once looked like. As you approach the massive structure, walk right up to the knee-high cordon and let your fellow 21st-century tourists melt away. It's just you and the druids....

England has hundreds of stone circles, but Stonehenge—which literally means "hanging stones"—is unique. It's the only one that has horizontal cross-pieces (called lintels) spanning the vertical monoliths, and the only one with stones that have been made smooth and uniform. What you see here is a bit more than half the original structure—the rest was quarried centuries ago for other buildings.

Now do a slow counterclockwise spin around the monument, and ponder the following points. As you walk, mentally flesh out

Stonehenge

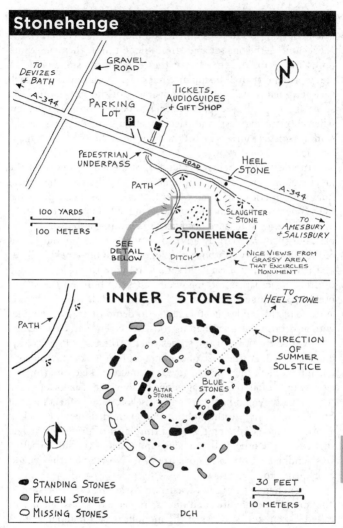

TO DEVIZES & BATH

GRAVEL ROAD

N

A-344

PARKING LOT
P

TICKETS, AUDIOGUIDES & GIFT SHOP

PEDESTRIAN UNDERPASS

ROAD

HEEL STONE

PATH

A-344

100 YARDS
100 METERS

SLAUGHTER STONE

STONEHENGE

TO AMESBURY & SALISBURY

SEE DETAIL BELOW

DITCH

NICE VIEWS FROM GRASSY AREA THAT ENCIRCLES MONUMENT

INNER STONES

TO HEEL STONE

PATH

DIRECTION OF SUMMER SOLSTICE

ALTAR STONE

BLUE-STONES

N

● STANDING STONES
◐ FALLEN STONES
○ MISSING STONES

30 FEET
10 METERS

DCH

the missing pieces and re-erect the rubble. Knowledgeable guides posted around the site are happy to answer your questions.

This was a hugely significant location to prehistoric peoples. There are some 500 burial mounds within a three-mile radius of Stonehenge—most likely belonging to kings and chieftains. Built in phases between 3000 and 1000 B.C., Stonehenge's original function may have been simply as a monumental gravestone for a ritual burial site. (So goes one recently popular theory.) But that's not the end of the story, as the monument was expanded over the millennia.

NEAR BATH

Stonehenge still functions as a remarkably accurate celestial calendar. As the sun rises on the summer solstice (June 21), the "heel stone"—the one set apart from the rest, near the road—lines up with the sun and the altar at the center of the stone circle. A study of more than 300 similar circles in Britain found that each was designed to calculate the movement of the sun, moon, and stars, and to predict eclipses in order to help early societies know when to plant, harvest, and party. Even in modern times, as the summer solstice sun sets in just the right slot at Stonehenge, pagans boogie.

In addition to being a calendar, Stonehenge is built at the precise point where six ley lines intersect. Ley lines are theoretical lines of magnetic or spiritual power that crisscross the globe. Belief in the power of these lines has gone in and out of fashion over time: They are believed to have been very important to prehistoric peoples, but then were largely ignored until the New Age movement of the 20th century. Without realizing it, you follow these ley lines all the time: Many of England's modern highways are built on top of prehistoric paths, and many churches are built on the site of prehistoric monuments where ley lines intersect. If you're a skeptic, ask one of the guides at Stonehenge to demonstrate the ley lines with a pair of L-shaped divining rods...it's creepy and convincing.

Notice that two of the stones (facing the entry passageway) are blemished. At the base of one monolith, it looks like someone has pulled back the stone to reveal a concrete skeleton. This is a clumsy repair job to fix damage done by souvenir-seekers long ago, who actually rented hammers and chisels to take home a piece of Stonehenge. Look to the right of the repaired stone: The back of another stone is missing the same thin layer of protective lichen that covers the others. The lichen—and some of the stone itself—was sandblasted off to remove graffiti. (No wonder they've got Stonehenge roped off now.)

Stonehenge's builders used two different types of stones. The tall, stout monoliths and lintels are made of sandstone blocks called sarsen stones. Most of the monoliths weigh about 25 tons (the largest is 45 tons), and the lintels are about seven tons apiece. These sarsen stones were brought from "only" 20 miles away. The shorter stones in the middle, called "bluestones," came from the south coast of Wales—240 miles away. (Close if you're taking a train, but far if you're packing a megalith.) Imagine the logistical puzzle of floating six-ton stones up the River Avon, then rolling them on logs about 20 miles to this position...an impressive feat, even in our era of skyscrapers.

Why didn't the builders of Stonehenge use what seem like perfectly adequate stones nearby? This, like many other questions about Stonehenge, remains shrouded in mystery. Think again about the ley lines. Ponder the fact that many experts accept none of the explanations of how these giant stones were transported. Then imagine congregations gathering here 5,000 years ago, raising thought levels, creating a powerful life force transmitted along the ley lines. Maybe a particular kind of stone was essential for maximum energy transmission. Maybe the stones were levitated here. Maybe psychics really do create powerful vibes. Maybe not. It's as unbelievable as electricity used to be.

Salisbury

Salisbury, set in the middle of the expansive Salisbury Plain, is a favorite stop for its striking cathedral and intriguing history.

Salisbury was originally settled during the Bronze Age, possibly as early as 600 B.C., and later became a Roman town called Sarum. The modern city of Salisbury developed when the old settlement outgrew its boundaries, prompting the townspeople to move the city from a hill to the river valley below. Most of today's visitors come to marvel at the famous Salisbury Cathedral, featuring England's tallest spire and largest cathedral green. Collectors, bargain hunters, and foodies will savor Salisbury's colorful market days. And archaeologists will dig the region around Salisbury, with England's highest concentration of ancient sites. The town itself is pleasant and walkable, and is a convenient base camp for visiting the ancient sites of Stonehenge and Avebury, or for exploring the countryside.

Orientation to Salisbury

(area code: 01722)

Salisbury (pop. 45,000) stretches along the River Avon in the shadow of its huge landmark cathedral. The heart of the city clusters around Market Square, which is also a handy parking lot on non-market days. High Street, a block to the west, leads to the medieval North Gate of the Cathedral Close. Shoppers explore the streets south of the square. The area north of Market Square is generally residential, with a few shops and pubs.

Tourist Information

The TI, just off Market Square, hands out free city maps, books rooms for no fee, and sells train tickets with a £1.10 surcharge (May Mon–Sat 9:30–17:00, Sun 10:00–16:00; June–Sept Mon–Sat 9:30–18:00, Sun 10:00–16:00; Oct–April Mon–Sat 9:30–17:00, closed Sun; Fish Row, tel. 01722/334-956, www.visitwiltshire .co.uk).

Ask the TI about 1.5-hour **walking tours** (£4, April–Oct daily at 11:00, Nov–March Sat–Sun only, depart from TI; other itineraries available, including £4 Ghost Walk May–Sept Fri at 20:00; tel. 01722/320-349, www.salisburycityguides.co.uk).

Arrival in Salisbury

By Train: From the train station, it's a 10-minute walk into the town center. Leave the station to the left, walk about 50 yards down South Western Road, and take the first right (at The Railway Tavern) onto Mill Road, following it around the bend and through the traffic roundabouts. Soon you'll see the Queen Elizabeth Gardens and the cathedral spire on your right. The road becomes Crane Bridge Road, then Crane Street, and finally New Street before intersecting with Catherine/St. John Street. Market Square and the TI are one long block north (left) on Catherine Street, and it's another two short blocks beyond that to the bus station. The Salisbury Cathedral and recommended Exeter Street B&Bs are to the south (right), down St. John Street (which becomes Exeter Street).

By Car: Drivers will find several pay parking lots in Salisbury—simply follow the blue *P* signs. The "Central" lot, behind the giant red-brick Sainsbury's store, is within a 10-minute walk of the TI or cathedral and is best for overnight stays (enter from Churchill Way West or Castle Street, lot open 24 hours). The "Old George Mall" parking garage is closer to the cathedral and has comparable daytime rates (£1/hour, 1 block north of cathedral, enter from New Street; garage open Mon–Sat 7:00–20:00, Sun 10:00–17:00).

Helpful Hints

Market Days: For centuries, Salisbury has been known for its lively markets. On Tuesdays and Saturdays, Market Square hosts the charter market, with general goods. Every other Wednesday is the farmers market. There are also special markets, such as one with French products. Ask the TI for a current schedule.

Festivals: The **Salisbury International Arts Festival** runs for just over two weeks at the end of May and beginning of June (likely May 20–June 4 in 2011, www.salisburyfestival.co.uk).

NEAR BATH

Salisbury

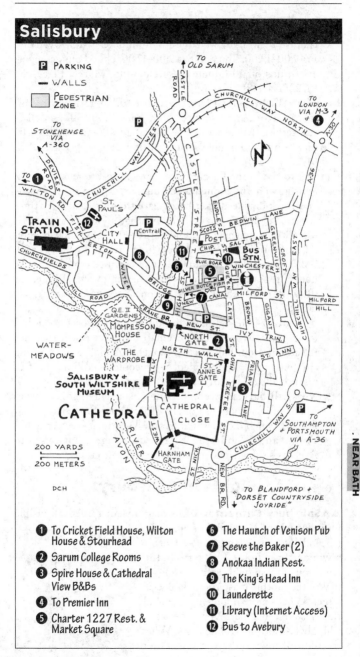

P PARKING
— WALLS
PEDESTRIAN ZONE

TO OLD SARUM
TO LONDON VIA M-3
TO STONEHENGE VIA A-360
TO DEVIZES ROAD
WILTON RD.
TRAIN STATION
CHURCHFIELDS
ST. PAUL'S
CITY HALL
CASTLE ROAD
CHURCHILL WAY NORTH
A-36
CHURCHILL WAY
WEST
CASTLE STREET
SCOTS STREET
ENDLESS ST.
BEDWIN LANE
GREENWICH
CROFT
EAST
CHURCHILL WAY EAST
POST
CHIP.
SALT LANE
BUS STN.
BLUE BOAR
QUEEN ST.
WINCHESTER
MILFORD ST.
GIGANT ST.
MILFORD HILL
SILVER BUTCH FISH
NEW CANAL
CATH.
BROWN ST.
IVY ST.
TRIN.
ST. ANN ST.
FRIARY LANE
Q.E. II GARDENS
MOMPESSON HOUSE
THE WARDROBE
WATER-MEADOWS
CRANE BR.
BRIDGE
FISHERTON ST.
WATER ST.
MILL ROAD
NORTH GATE
NORTH WALK
NEW ST.
ST. JOHN ST.
ST. EXETER ST.
ST. ANNE'S GATE
WEST WALK
SALISBURY & SOUTH WILTSHIRE MUSEUM
CATHEDRAL
CATHEDRAL CLOSE
RIVER AVON
ST. NICH
NEW BR. RD.
HARNHAM GATE
CHURCHILL WAY S.
TO SOUTHAMPTON & PORTSMOUTH VIA A-36
TO BLANDFORD & "DORSET COUNTRYSIDE JOYRIDE"

200 YARDS
200 METERS

DCH

❶ To Cricket Field House, Wilton House & Stourhead
❷ Sarum College Rooms
❸ Spire House & Cathedral View B&Bs
❹ To Premier Inn
❺ Charter 1227 Rest. & Market Square
❻ The Haunch of Venison Pub
❼ Reeve the Baker (2)
❽ Anokaa Indian Rest.
❾ The King's Head Inn
❿ Launderette
⓫ Library (Internet Access)
⓬ Bus to Avebury

Internet Access: The **library** has 12 terminals for visitors, who can use them free of charge for 30 minutes (Mon–Wed and Fri 9:00–19:00, Thu and Sat 9:00–17:00, closed Sun, computers turned off 10 minutes before closing, Market Place, tel. 01722/324-145).

Laundry: Washing Well has full-service (£7.50–13/load depending on size, 2-hour service, Mon–Sat 8:30–17:30) as well as self-service (Mon–Sat 16:00–20:30, Sun 7:00–20:30, last self-service wash 30 minutes before closing; 28 Chipper Lane, tel. 01722/421-874).

Getting to the Stone Circles: You can get to Stonehenge from Salisbury on **The Stonehenge Tour** bus. Their distinctive red-and-black double-decker buses leave from the Salisbury train station and make a circuit to Stonehenge and Old Sarum (£11, £18 with Stonehenge and Old Sarum admission, tickets good all day, buy ticket from driver, June–Aug daily 9:30–17:00, 1–2/hour, may not run June 21 due to solstice crowds, shorter hours off-season, 30 minutes from station to Stonehenge, tel. 01983/827-005, check www.thestonehengetour.info for timetable).

A **taxi** from Salisbury to Stonehenge can be a good deal for groups (£40–50, call or email for exact price, includes round-trip from Salisbury to Stonehenge plus an hour at the site, entry fee not included, 5–6 people maximum, best to reserve ahead, tel. 01722/339-781 or mobile 07971-255-690, www.salisburytaxis.com, brian@salisburytaxis.co.uk, Brian MacNeillie). Brian also offers a three-hour Stonehenge visit for £80, which includes Old Sarum, Woodhenge, Durrington Walls, and Woodford's thatched cottages. For buses to Avebury's stone circle, see "Salisbury Connections," later.

Sights in Salisbury

▲▲**Salisbury Cathedral**—This magnificent cathedral, visible for miles around because of its huge spire (the tallest in England at 404 feet), is a wonder to behold. The surrounding enormous grassy field (called a "close") makes the Gothic masterpiece look even larger. What's more impressive is that all this was built in a mere 38 years—astonishingly fast for the Middle Ages. When the old hill town of Sarum was moved down to the valley, its cathedral had to be replaced in a hurry. So, in 1220, the townspeople began building, and in 1258

NEAR BATH

their sparkling-new cathedral was ready for ribbon-cutting. Since the structure was built in just a few decades, its style is uniform, rather than the patchwork of styles common in cathedrals of the time (which often took centuries to construct).

Cost and Hours: £5.50 suggested donation; mid-June–Aug Mon–Sat 7:15–19:15, Sun 7:15–18:15; Sept–mid-June daily 7:15–18:15; Chapter House usually opens Mon–Sat at 9:30, Sun at 12:45, closes 30–45 minutes before the rest of the cathedral, and closes entirely for special events; choral evensong Mon–Sat at 17:30, Sun at 15:00; excellent cafeteria, tel. 01722/555-120, recorded info tel. 01722/555-113, www.salisburycathedral.org.uk. This working cathedral opens early for services—be respectful if you arrive when one is in session.

Tower Tours: Imagine building a cathedral on this scale before the invention of cranes, bulldozers, or modern scaffolding. An excellent tower tour (1.5–2 hours) helps visitors understand how it was done. You'll climb in between the stone arches and the roof to inspect the vaulting and trussing; see a medieval winch that was used in the construction; and finish with the 330-step climb up the narrow tower for a sweeping view of the Wiltshire country-side (£8.50; early June–Aug Mon–Sat at 11:15, 13:15, 14:15, and 15:15, Sun at 14:00 and 16:00; May–early June and Sept Mon–Sat at 11:15, 14:15, and 15:15, Sun at 14:00 and 16:00; fewer off-season but usually one at 14:15, no tours in Dec except Christmas week; maximum 12 people, can reserve by calling 01722/555-156).

❍ Self-Guided Tour: Entering the church, you'll instantly feel the architectural harmony. Volunteer guides posted at the entry are ready to answer your questions. (Free guided tours of the cathedral nave are offered—about twice hourly—when enough people assemble.)

As you look down the nave, notice how the stone columns march identically down the aisle, like a thick gray forest of tree trunks. The arches overhead soar to grand heights, helping church-goers appreciate the vast and amazing heavens.

From the entrance, head to the far wall (the back-left cor-ner). You'll find a model showing how this cathedral was built so quickly in the 13th century. Next to that is the "oldest working clock in existence," dating from the 14th century (the hourly bell has been removed, so as not to interrupt worship services). On the wall by the clock is a bell from the decommissioned ship HMS *Salisbury*. Look closely inside the bell to see the engraved names of crew members' children who were baptized on the ship.

Wander down the aisle past monuments and knights' tombs. When you get to the transept, examine the columns where the arms of the church cross. These posts were supposed to support a more modest bell tower, but when a heavy tower was added 100 years later, the columns bent under the enormous weight, causing the tower to lean sideways. Although the posts were later reinforced, the tower still tilts about two and a half feet.

Continue down the left side of the choir and dip into the Morning Chapel. At the back of this chapel, find the spectacular glass prism engraved with images of Salisbury—donated to the church in memory of a soldier who died at the D-Day landing at Normandy.

The oldest part of the church is at the apse (far end), where construction began in 1220: the Trinity Chapel. The giant, modern stained-glass window ponders the theme "prisoners of conscience."

After you leave the nave, pace the cloister and follow signs to the medieval **Chapter House.** All English cathedrals have a chapter house, so called because it's where the daily Bible verse, or chapter, is read. These spaces often served as gathering places for conducting church or town business. Here you can see a modest display of cathedral items plus one must-see display: one of the four original copies of the Magna Carta, a document as important to the English as the Constitution is to Americans. This "Great Charter," dating from 1215, settled a dispute between the slimy King John and some powerful barons. Revolutionary for limiting the monarch's power, the Magna Carta constitutionally guaranteed that the monarch was not above the law. This was one of the first major victories in the long battle between monarchs and nobles.

▲**Cathedral Close**—The enormous green surrounding the cathedral is the largest in England, and one of the loveliest. It's cradled in the elbow of the River Avon and ringed by row houses, cottages, and grand mansions. The church owns the houses on the green and rents them to lucky people with holy connections. A former prime minister, Edward Heath, lived on the green, not  because of his political influence, but because he was once the church organist.

The benches scattered around the green are an excellent place for having a romantic moonlit picnic or for gazing thoughtfully at the leaning spire. Although you may be tempted to linger until it's late, don't—this is still private church property...and the heavy medieval gates of the close shut at about 23:00.

A few houses are open to the public, such as the overpriced Mompesson House and the medieval Wardrobe. The most interesting attraction is the...

NEAR BATH

▲**Salisbury and South Wiltshire Museum**—Occupying
the building just opposite the cathedral entry, this eclectic and
sprawling collection was heralded by American expat travel writer
Bill Bryson as one of England's best. While that's a stretch, the
museum does offer a little something for everyone, including
exhibits on local archaeology and history, a costume gallery, the
true-to-its-name "Salisbury Giant" puppet once used by the tai-
lors' guilds during parades, some J. M. W. Turner paintings of the
cathedral interior, and a collection of exquisite Wedgwood china
and other ceramics. The highlight is the "Stonehenge Gallery,"
with informative and interactive exhibits explaining the ancient
structure. Since there's not yet a good visitors center at the site
itself, this makes for a good pre- or post-Stonehenge activity (£6,
Mon–Sat 10:00–17:00, July–Aug Sun 12:00–17:00, Sept–June
closed Sun, 65 The Close, tel. 01722/332-151, www.salisbury
museum.org.uk).

Sleeping in Salisbury

(£1 = about $1.60, country code: 44, area code: 01722)
Salisbury's town center has very few affordable accommodations,
and I've listed them below—plus a couple of good choices a little
farther out. The town gets particularly crowded during the arts
festival (late May through early June).

$$ Cricket Field House, outside of town on A36 toward
Wilton, overlooks a cricket pitch and golf course. It has 17 clean,
comfortable rooms, a gorgeous garden, and plenty of parking (Sb-
£60–68, Db-£85–105, price depends on season, Wilton Road, tel.
& fax 01722/322-595, www.cricketfieldhouse.co.uk, cricketfield
cottage@btinternet.com, Brian and Margaret James). While this
place works best for drivers, it's just a 15-minute walk from the
train station or a five-minute bus ride from the city center.

$$ Sarum College is a theological college that rents 48 rooms
in its building right on the peaceful Cathedral Close. Much of
the year, it houses visitors to the college, but it usually has rooms
for tourists as well—except the week after Christmas, when they
close. The slightly institutional but clean rooms share hallways with
libraries, bookstores, and offices, and the five attic rooms come
with grand cathedral views (S-£45, Sb-£60, D-£70, Db-£95–105
depending on size, meals available at additional cost, elevator, 19
The Close, tel. 01722/424-800, fax 01722/338-508, www.sarum
.ac.uk, hospitality@sarum.ac.uk).

$$ Spire House B&B, just off the Cathedral Close, is
classy and cozy. The four bright, surprisingly quiet rooms come
with busy wallpaper, and two have canopied beds (Db-£80,
Tb-£90, cash only, no kids under age 8, free Wi-Fi, 84 Exeter

Street, tel. 01722/339-213, www.salisbury-bedandbreakfast.com, spire.enquiries@btinternet.com, friendly Lois).

$ Cathedral View B&B, with four rooms next door at #83, is similar and offers a good value in an outstanding location (Db-£75, Tb-£90, cash only, 2-night minimum on weekends, no kids under age 10, free Wi-Fi, 83 Exeter Street, tel. 01722/502-254, www .cathedral-viewbandb.co.uk, enquiries@cathedral-viewbandb.co .uk, Wenda and Steve).

$ Premier Inn, two miles from the city center, offers dozens of prefab and predictable rooms ideal for drivers and families (Db-£66–87, more during special events, 2 kids ages 15 and under sleep free, breakfast-£5–8, pay Wi-Fi, possible noise from nearby trains, off roundabout at A30 and Pearce Way, toll tel. 0871-527-8956, toll fax 0871-527-8957, www.premierinn.com).

Eating in Salisbury

There are plenty of atmospheric pubs all over town. For the best variety of restaurants, head to the Market Square area. Many places offer great "early bird" specials before 20:00.

Charter 1227, an upstairs eatery overlooking Market Square, is a handy place for a nice meal (£12.50 two-course lunch, open Tue–Sat 12:00–14:30 & 18:00–21:30, closed Sun–Mon, dinner reservations smart, 6 Ox Row, tel. 01722/333-118).

The Haunch of Venison, possibly dating back to 1320, is a Salisbury institution with creaky, crooked floors and the mummified hand of a cheating card player on display (actually a replica; to the left of the fireplace in the House of Lords room). Downstairs, the "occasionally haunted" half-timbered pub serves nouvelle pub grub (£5–8 meals). The restaurant upstairs, while a little pretentious, has a good reputation for its traditional fare (£8–13 entrées; pub open Mon–Sat 11:00–23:00, Sun 12:00–22:00, food served 12:00–14:30 & 18:00–21:00, reservations smart for dinner, 1 Minster Street, tel. 01722/411-313).

Reeve the Baker, with a branch just up the street from the TI, crafts an array of high-calorie delights and handy pick-me-ups for a fast and affordable lunch. The long cases of pastries and savory treats will make you drool (Mon–Fri 8:00–17:30, Sat 8:00–17:00, Sun 10:00–16:00, cash only; one location is next to the TI at 2 Butcher Row, another is at the corner of Market and Bridge streets at 61 Silver Street, tel. 01722/320-367).

Anokaa is a splurge that's highly acclaimed for its updated Indian cuisine. You won't find the same old chicken *tikka* here, but clever newfangled variations on Indian themes, dished up in a dressy, contemporary setting (£9–15 entrées, £9 lunch buffet, daily 12:00–14:00 & 17:30–22:30, 60 Fisherton Street, tel. 01722/414-142).

The King's Head Inn is a youthful chain pub with a big, open, modern interior and fine outdoor seating overlooking the pretty little River Avon. Its extensive menu has something for everyone (£3–5 sandwiches, £4–9 entrées, Mon–Fri 7:00–24:00, Sat–Sun 8:00–24:00, food served until 22:00, kids welcome during the day but they must order meals by 20:30, free Wi-Fi, 1 Bridge Street, tel. 01722/342-050).

Salisbury Connections

From Salisbury by Train to: London's Waterloo Station (1–2/ hour, 1.5 hours), **Bath** (1–2/hour, 1 hour), **Oxford** (hourly, 2 hours, transfer in Reading and Basingstoke), **Portsmouth** (hourly, 1.25 hours), **Exeter** (1–2/hour, 2 hours, some require transfers), **Penzance** (about hourly, 5.5–6 hours, 1–2 transfers). Train info: toll tel. 0845-748-4950, www.nationalrail.co.uk.

By Bus to: Bath (hourly, 2.75 hours, transfer in Warminster, www.travelinesw.com; or one direct bus/day at 10:35, 1.5 hours on National Express #300, toll tel. 0871-781-8181, www.national express.com), **Avebury** (1–2/hour, 1.5–2.5 hours, transfer in Devizes, Pewsey, or Marlborough, www.travelinesw.com). Many of Salisbury's long-distance buses are run by Wilts & Dorset (tel. 01722/336-855 or 01983/827-005, www.wdbus.co.uk). National Express buses go once a day to **Bath** (morning only at 10:35, 1.5 hours) and **Portsmouth** (evenings only at 18:25, 1.5 hours, toll tel. 0871-781-8181, www.nationalexpress.com).

Near Salisbury

Old Sarum

Right here, on a hill overlooking the plain below, is where the original town of Salisbury was founded many centuries ago. While little remains of the old town, the view of the valley is amazing...and a little imagination can transport you back to *very* olde England.

Human settlement in this area stretches back to the Bronze Age, and the Romans, Saxons, and Normans all called this hilltop home. From about 500 B.C. through A.D. 1220, Old Sarum flourished, giving rise to a motte-and-bailey castle, a cathedral, and scores of wooden homes along the town's outer ring. The town grew so quickly that by the Middle Ages, it had outgrown its spot on the hill. In 1220, the local bishop successfully petitioned to move the entire city to the valley below, where space and water was plentiful. So, stone by stone, Old Sarum was packed up and shipped to New Sarum, where builders used nearly all the rubble

Near Salisbury

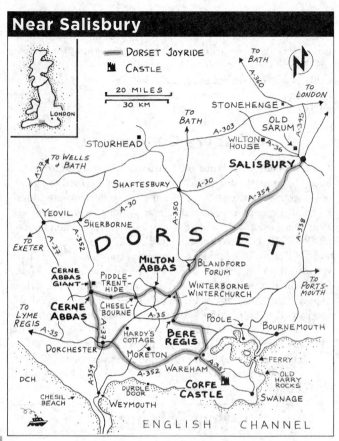

from the old city to create a brand-new town with a magnificent cathedral.

Old Sarum was eventually abandoned altogether, leaving only a few stone foundations. The grand views of Salisbury from here have "in-spired" painters for ages and provided countless picnickers with a scenic backdrop: Grab a sandwich or snacks from one of the grocery stores in Salisbury or at the excellent Waitrose supermarket at the north end of town—just west of where A36 meets A345.

Cost and Hours: £3.50, daily July–Aug 9:00–18:00, April–June and Sept 10:00–17:00, Feb–March and Oct 10:00–16:00, Nov–Jan 11:00–15:00, last entry 30 minutes before closing, tel. 01722/335-398, www.english-heritage.org.uk.

Getting There: It's two miles north of Salisbury off A345, accessible by Wilts & Dorset bus #5 or #6 or via The Stonehenge Tour bus (see page 300).

Wilton House

This sprawling estate, with a grand mansion and lush gardens, has been owned by the Earls of Pembroke since King Henry VIII's time. Inside the mansion, you'll find a collection of paintings by Rubens, Rembrandt, Van Dyck, and Brueghel, along with quirky odds-and-ends, such as a lock of Queen Elizabeth I's hair. The perfectly proportioned Double Cube Room has served as everything from a 17th-century state dining room to a secret D-Day planning room during World War II...if only the portraits could talk. The Old Riding School houses a skippable 20-minute film that dramatizes the history of the family. Outside, classic English gardens feature a river lazily winding its way through grasses and under Greek-inspired temples. Jane Austen fans particularly enjoy this stately home, where parts of 2005's Oscar-nominated *Pride and Prejudice* were filmed. But, alas, Mr. Darcy has checked out.

Cost and Hours: House and gardens-£12, gardens only-£5; house open Easter weekend and May–Aug Sun–Thu 11:30–16:30, last entry 45 minutes before closing, closed Fri–Sat except holiday weekends; gardens open 2 weeks in mid-April and May–Aug daily 11:00–17:00, Sept Sat–Sun 11:00–17:00, last entry 30 minutes before closing; house and gardens closed Oct–April, except house open Easter weekend and gardens open mid-April; recorded info tel. 01722/746-729, tel. 01722/746-714, www.wiltonhouse.com.

Getting There: It's five miles west of Salisbury via A36 to Wilton's Minster Street; or buses #2, #13, #25, #26, #27, or #R3 from Salisbury to Wilton.

Stourhead

For a serious taste of traditional English landscape, don't miss this 2,650-acre delight. Stourhead, designed by owner Henry Hoare II in the mid-18th century, is a wonderland of rolling hills, meandering paths, placid lakes, and colorful trees, punctuated by classically inspired bridges and monuments. It's what every other English estate aspires to be—like nature, but better (house and garden-£11.60, or £7 to see just one; house open mid-March–Oct Fri–Tue 11:00–17:00, closed Wed–Thu; garden open year-round daily 9:00–18:00, last entry 30 minutes before closing, 28 miles west of Salisbury off B3092 in town of Stourton, 3 miles northwest of Mere, tel. 01747/841-152, www.nationaltrust.org.uk).

Drivers or ambitious walkers can visit nearby **King Alfred's Tower** and climb its 205 steps for glorious views of the estate and surrounding countryside (£2.80 to climb tower, same opening times as house, 2.5 miles northwest of Stourhead, off Tower Road).

Dorset Countryside Joyride

The region of Dorset, just southwest of Salisbury, is full of rolling fields, winding country lanes, quaint cottages, and villages stuffed with tea shops. Anywhere you go in the area will take you some-place charming, so consider this tour only a suggestion and feel free to get pleasantly lost in the English countryside. You'll be tak-ing some less-traveled roads, so bring along a good map.

Starting in Salisbury, take A354 through Blandford Forum to Winterborne Whitechurch. From here, follow signs and small back roads to the village of Bere Regis, where you'll find some lovely 15th-century buildings, including one with angels carved on the roof. Follow A35 and B3075 to Wareham, where T. E. Lawrence (a.k.a. Lawrence of Arabia) lived; he's buried in nearby Moreton. Continue south on A351 to the dramatic and romantic **Corfe Castle.** This was a favorite residence for medieval kings until it was destroyed by a massive gunpowder blast during a 17th-century siege (£6.20, daily April–Sept 10:00–18:00, March and Oct 10:00–17:00, Nov–Feb 10:00–16:00, last entry 30 minutes before closing, tel. 01929/481-294, www.nationaltrust.org.uk). Retrace A351 to Wareham, and then take A352 to Dorchester.

Just northeast of Dorchester on A35, near the village of Stinsford, novelist Thomas Hardy was born in 1840; you'll find **Hardy's family's cottage** nearby in Higher Bockhampton (£4, May–Oct Thu–Mon 11:00–17:00, closed Tue-Wed and Nov–April, last entry 30 minutes before closing, tel. 01305/262-366, www .nationaltrust.org.uk). While Hardy's heart is buried in Stinsford with his first wife, Emma, the rest of him is in Westminster Abbey's Poets' Corner. Take A35 back to Dorchester. Just west of Dorchester, stay on A35 until it connects to A37; then follow A352 north toward Sherborne.

About eight miles north of Dorchester, on the way to Sherborne, you'll find the little town of **Cerne Abbas** (surn AB-iss), named for an abbey in the center of town. There are only two streets to wander down, so take this opportunity to recharge with a cup of tea and a scone. Abbots Tea Room has a nice cream tea (pot of tea, scone, jam, and clotted cream, 7 Long St., tel. 01300/341-349). Up the street, you can visit the abbey and its well, reputed to have healing powers.

Just outside of town, a large chalk figure, the **Cerne Abbas Giant,** is carved into the green hillside. Chalk figures such as this one can be found in many parts of the region. Because the soil is only a few inches deep, the overlying grass and dirt can easily be removed to expose the bright white chalk bedrock beneath, creat-ing the outlines. While nobody is sure exactly how old the figures are, or what their original purpose was, they are faithfully maintained by the locals, who mow and clear the fields at least once a year. This particular figure, possibly a fertility god, looks friendly... maybe a little too friendly. Locals claim that if a woman who's having trouble getting pregnant sleeps on the giant for one night, she will soon be able to conceive a child. (A few years back, controversy surrounded this giant, as a 180-foot-tall, donut-hoisting Homer Simpson was painted onto the adjacent hillside. No kidding.)

Leaving Cerne Abbas on country roads toward Piddletrenthide (on the aptly named River Piddle), continue through Cheselbourne to **Milton Abbas.** (This area, by the way, has some of the best town names in the country, such as Droop, Plush, Pleck, and Folly.) The village of Milton Abbas looks overly perfect. In the 18th century, a wealthy man bought up the town's large abbey and estate. His new place was great...except for the neighbors, a bunch of vulgar villagers with houses that cluttered his view from the garden. So, he had the town demolished and rebuilt a mile away. What you see now is probably the first planned community, with identical houses, a pub, and a church. The estate is now a "public school," which is what the English call an expensive private school. From Milton Abbas, signs lead you back to Winterborne Whitechurch, and A354 to Salisbury.

South Wales

Although the best bits of Wales lie to the north (see North Wales chapter), there are a few worthwhile sights in the southern part of the country, not far from Bath (see map on page 270). Note that many of the sights mentioned here—including Caerphilly Castle, Chepstow Castle, and Tintern Abbey—are included in Wales' Explorer Pass (described on page 22).

Cardiff and Nearby

The Welsh capital of Cardiff (pop. 320,000) has a newly renovated waterfront area, with shops and entertainment. It's also home to the 74,000-seat Millennium Stadium, which will see football (soccer) action during the 2012 London Summer Olympics.

Cardiff's helpful **TI** is located in the Old Library, a five-minute walk from Cardiff Castle and a 10-minute walk from the train station (Mon–Sat 9:30–18:00, Sun 10:00–16:00, The Hayes, tel. 02920/873-573, www.visitcardiff.com). They have Internet access (£1/30 minutes) and storage lockers (small-£3, large-£5, both require refundable £3 deposit, lockers open Mon–Sat 9:30–17:30, Sun 10:00–15:30).

Sights in and near Cardiff

In Cardiff

Cardiff Castle (Castell Caerdydd)—A visit to Cardiff's castle is interesting only if you catch one of the entertaining tours of the interior. With its ornate clock tower, the castle is the latest in a series of fortresses erected on the site by Romans, Normans, and assorted British lords. The interior is a Victorian fantasy, and there's a visitors center, with a film and exhibits (£13.50 with 45-minute tour, £10.50 without tour, tours at least every 20 minutes, either ticket includes audioguide, daily March–Oct 9:00–18:00, Nov–Feb 9:00–17:00, last tour and entry one hour before closing, tel. 02920/878-100, www.cardiffcastle.com).

Near Cardiff

▲▲St. Fagans National History Museum/ Amgueddfa Werin Cymru (Museum of Welsh Life)

This best look at traditional Welsh folk life has three sections: open-air folk museum, main museum (which you walk through as you enter), and castle/garden.

Outside, in a 100-acre park that surrounds a castle, you'll find displays of more than 40 carefully reconstructed old houses from all corners of this little country. Each house is fully furnished and comes equipped with a local expert warming up beside a toasty fire, happy to tell you anything you want to know about life in this old cottage. Ask questions!

Cost and Hours: Free entry, parking-£3, daily 10:00–17:00, tel. 02920/573-500, www.museumwales.ac.uk/en/stfagans. While everything is well-explained, the £2 museum guidebook (or £0.30 map)—available at the information desk as you enter—is a good investment. If you see construction in process, it's to build more storage for the museum's sizable collection of artifacts.

Getting There: To get from the Cardiff train station to the museum in the village of St. Fagans, catch bus #32 (hourly, 25 minutes, toll tel. 0871-200-2233, www.traveline-cymru.info). Drivers leave M4 at Junction 33 and follow the signs. Leaving the museum, jog left on the freeway, take the first exit, and circle back, following signs to M4.

➋ **Self-Guided Tour:** If the sky's dry, see the scattering of houses first. Otherwise, in the main museum building, head to Gallery One, a recently renovated multimedia gallery with artifacts from Welsh life—including elaborately carved "love spoons" as well as new memorabilia near and dear to local hearts (such as mementos from triumphant rugby teams). Don't miss the costume exhibit, hidden behind a gallery of farming equipment. Spend an hour in the large building's fascinating museum.

Head outside, where a small train trundles among the exhibits from Easter to October (five stops, £0.50/stop, whole circuit takes 45 minutes). The castle interior is royal enough and surrounded by a fine garden.

The highlight of the open-air museum is the Rhyd-y-Car 1805 row house, which displays ironworker cottages as they might have looked in 1805, 1855, 1895, 1925, 1955, and 1985, offering a fascinating zip through Welsh domestic life from hearths to microwaves.

Step into an old schoolhouse, a chapel, or a blacksmith's shop to see traditional craft makers in action. Head over to the farm and wander among the livestock and funky old outbuildings. Then beam a few centuries forward to the House for the Future, an optimistic projection of domestic life in Wales 50 years from now. The timber house blends traditional building techniques with new technologies aimed at sustainability. The roof collects water and soaks up solar energy. The earth that was removed to make way for the foundation was formed into bricks that were then used in the structure.

Eating at St. Fagans: The coffee shop near the entrance and the restaurant upstairs are both handy, but you'll eat light lunches better, cheaper, and with more atmosphere in the park at the Gwalia Tea Room. The Plymouth Arms pub just outside the museum serves the best food.

▲Caerphilly Castle

The impressive but gutted old castle, spread over 30 acres, is the second largest in Europe after Windsor. English Earl Gilbert

de Clare erected this squat behemoth to try to establish a stronghold in Wales. With two concentric walls, it was considered to be a brilliant arrangement of defensive walls and moats. Attackers had to negotiate three drawbridges and four sets of doors and portcullises just to reach the main entrance. For the record, there were no known successful enemy forays beyond the current castle's inner walls.

The castle has its own leaning tower—the split and listing tower reportedly out-leans Pisa's. Some also believe there to be a resident ghost. Legend has it that de Clare, after learning of his wife Alice's infidelity, exiled her back to France and had her lover killed. Upon discovering her paramour's fate, Alice died of a broken heart. Since then, the "Green Lady," named for her husband's jealousy, has reportedly roamed the ramparts.

Exhibits at the castle display clever catapults, castle-dwellers' tricks for harassing intruders, and a good dose of Welsh history.

Cost and Hours: £3.60; March–Oct daily 9:30–17:00, until 18:00 July–Aug; Nov–Feb Mon–Sat 10:00–16:00, Sun 11:00–16:00; last entry 30 minutes before closing, tel. 02920/883-143, www.cadw.wales.gov.uk.

Getting There: The town of Caerphilly—the castle is located right in the center—is nine miles north of Cardiff. To get there, take the train from Cardiff to Caerphilly (2–4/hour, 20 minutes) and walk five minutes. It's 20 minutes by car from St. Fagans (exit #32, following signs from M4).

Cardiff Connections

From Cardiff by Train to: Caerphilly (2–4/hour, 20 minutes), **Bath** (hourly, 1–1.5 hours), **Birmingham** (1/hour direct, more with change in Bristol, 2 hours), **London**'s Paddington Station (2/hour, 2.25 hours), **Chepstow** (every 1-2 hours, 40 minutes; then bus #69 to **Tintern**—runs every 2 hours, 20 minutes). Train info: toll tel. 0871-200-2233, www.traveline-cymru.info.

By Car: For driving directions from Bath to Cardiff, see "Route Tips for Drivers," at the end of this chapter.

Between Bath and the Cotswolds

While there are more direct driving routes from Bath to the Cotswolds, the sights listed here are handy if you're connecting those two areas via a South Wales detour. If you're seduced into spending the night in this charming area, you'll find plenty of B&Bs near the Tintern Abbey or in the castle-crowned town of Chepstow, located just down the road (a one-hour drive from Bath).

The **Chepstow TI** is helpful (April–early Oct 9:30–17:00, off-season 10:00–15:30, Bridge Street, tel. 01291/623-772, www.visit wyevalley.com). For a 21-stop, 1.5-hour **stroll** around the village, pick up the £1.50 *Chepstow Town Trail* guide from the Chepstow Museum (free, Mon–Sat July–Sept 10:30–17:30, Oct–June 11:00–13:00 & 14:00–17:00, Sun year-round 14:00–17:00, across the street from Chepstow Castle). The walk begins at the town gate, where, in medieval times, folks arriving to sell goods or livestock were hit up for tolls.

The **Tintern TI,** north of the abbey and the village of Tintern, is housed within a former railway station (March–Oct

daily 10:30–17:30, closed Nov–
Feb, café, railway exhibit, The
Old Station, tel. 01291/689-566,
www.visitwyevalley.com).

Chepstow Castle

Perched on a hill overlooking
the pleasant village of Chepstow
on one side and the Wye River
on the other, this castle is worth a short stop for drivers heading
for Tintern Abbey, or it's a 10-minute walk from the Chepstow
train station (uphill going back).

The stone-built bastion dating to 1066 was among the first
castles the Normans plunked
down to secure their turf in
Wales, and it remained in use
through 1690. While many
castles of the time were built first
in wood, Chepstow, then a key
foothold on the England–Wales
border, was built from stone from
the start for durability. As you
clamber along the battlements, you'll find architectural evidence
of military renovations through the centuries, from Norman to
Tudor right up through Cromwellian additions. You can tell which
parts date from Norman days—they're the ones built from yellow
sandstone instead of the grayish limestone that makes up the rest
of the castle.

Cost and Hours: £3.60; March–Oct daily 9:30–17:00, until
18:00 July-Aug; Nov–Feb Mon–Sat 10:00–16:00, Sun 11:00–16:00;
last entry 30 minutes before closing, guidebook-£3.50, in Chepstow
village a half-mile from train station, tel. 01291/624-065, www
.cadw.wales.gov.uk.

▲▲Tintern Abbey

Inspiring monks to prayer, William Wordsworth to poetry, J. M.
W. Turner to a famous painting, and rushed tourists to a thoughtful moment, this verse-worthy ruined-castle-of-an-abbey merits
a five-mile detour off the motorway. Founded in 1131 on a site
chosen by Norman monks for its tranquility, it functioned as an
austere Cistercian abbey until its dissolution in 1536. The monks
followed a strict schedule. They rose several hours after midnight
for the first of eight daily prayer sessions, and spent the rest of their
time studying, working the surrounding farmlands, and meditat-
ing. Dissolved under Henry VIII's Act of Suppression in 1536, the
magnificent church moldered in relative obscurity until tourists in

the Romantic era (mid-18th century) discovered the wooded Wye valley and abbey ruins. J. M. W. Turner made his first sketches in 1792, and William Wordsworth penned "Lines Composed a Few Miles Above Tintern Abbey..." in 1798.

Most of the external walls of the 250-foot-long, 150-foot-wide church still stand, along with the exquisite window tracery and outlines of the sacristy, chapter house, and dining hall. The daylight that floods through the roofless ruins highlights the Gothic decorated arches—in those days a bold departure from Cistercian simplicity.

In summer, the abbey is flooded with tourists, so visit early or late to miss the biggest crowds. The shop sells Celtic jewelry and other gifts. Take an easy 15-minute walk up to St. Mary's Church for a view of England just over the River Wye.

Cost and Hours: £3.60; March–Oct daily 9:30–17:00, until 18:00 July–Aug; Nov–Feb Mon–Sat 10:00–16:00, Sun 11:00–16:00; last entry 30 minutes before closing, occasional summertime events in the cloisters (check website for schedule), tel. 01291/689-251, www.cadw.wales.gov.uk.

Getting There: From Cardiff, catch a 40-minute train to Chepstow; from there, take a 20-minute ride on bus #69 (runs every 2 hours) or a taxi to the abbey.

▲Wye River Valley and Forest of Dean

This land is lush, mellow, and historic. Local tourist brochures explain the Forest of Dean's special dialect, its strange political autonomy, and its oaken ties to Trafalgar and Admiral Nelson.

Sleeping in the Wye River Valley: **$ The Florence,** snuggled

in the lower Wye Valley north of Tintern on the way to Monmouth, is located just off the 177-mile-long Offa's Dyke Path. On a nice day, hotel guests can eat on the garden terrace of this 17th-century hotel and share the scenery with the cows lazing along the riverbanks (Sb-£35, Db-£70, request river view, includes breakfast, no kids under 10, tel. 01594/530-830, www.florencehotel.co.uk, enquiries@florencehotel.co.uk, kind owners Dennis and Kathy).

For a medieval night, check into the **$ St. Briavels Castle B&B/Youth Hostel.** An 800-year-old Norman castle used by King John in 1215 (the year he signed the Magna Carta), the hostel is comfortable (as castles go), friendly, and in the center of the quiet village of St. Briavels just north of Tintern Abbey (70 beds, £18–22 beds in 8- to 16-bed dorms, non-members-£3 extra, includes breakfast, private 4- to 8-bed rooms available, reception open daily 6:30–10:00 & 17:00–23:00, hostel closed to guests daily 10:00–17:00, curfew at 23:30, kitchen and lounge, brown-bag lunches and evening meals available, toll tel. 0845-371-9042, www .yha.org.uk, stbriavels@yha.org.uk).

Eating: For dinner, eat at the **hostel**, which hosts medieval banquets on most Wednesday and Saturday nights in summer (£15, open to public, must book several days in advance—see hostel listing above for contact info), or walk "just down the path and up the snyket" to **The Crown Inn** (decent food and local pub atmosphere).

South Wales Connections

Route Tips for Drivers

Bath to Cardiff and St. Fagans: Leave Bath following signs for A4, then M4. It's 10 miles north (on A46 past a village called Pennsylvania) to the M4 freeway. Zip westward, crossing a huge suspension bridge into Wales (£5.50 toll westbound only). Stay on M4 (not M48) past Cardiff, take exit 33, and follow the brown signs south to *St. Fagans National History Museum/Amgueddfa Werin Cymru/Museum of Welsh Life.*

Bath to Tintern Abbey: Follow the directions above to M4. Take M4 to exit 21 and get on M48. The abbey is six miles (up A466, follow signs to *Chepstow,* then *Tintern*) off M48 at exit 2, right where the northern bridge across the Severn hits Wales.

Cardiff to the Cotswolds via Forest of Dean: On the Welsh side of the big suspension bridge, take the Chepstow exit and follow signs up A466 to *Tintern Abbey* and the *Wye River Valley.* Carry on to Monmouth, and follow A40 and M50 to the Tewkesbury exit, where small roads lead to the Cotswolds.

THE COTSWOLDS

Chipping Campden • Stow-on-the-Wold
• Moreton-in-Marsh • Blenheim Palace

The Cotswold Hills, a 25-by-90-mile chunk of Gloucestershire, are dotted with enchanting villages and graced with England's greatest countryside palace, Blenheim. As with many fairy-tale regions of Europe, the present-day beauty of the Cotswolds was the result of an economic disaster. Wool was a huge industry in medieval England, and Cotswold sheep grew the best wool. A 12th-century saying bragged, "In Europe the best wool is English. In England the best wool is Cotswold." The region prospered. Wool money built fine towns and houses. Local "wool" churches are called "cathedrals" for their scale and wealth. Stained-glass slogans say things like "I thank my God and ever shall, it is the sheep hath paid for all."

With the rise of cotton and the Industrial Revolution, the woolen industry collapsed. Ba-a-a-ad news. The wealthy Cotswold towns fell into a depressed time warp; the homes of impoverished nobility became gracefully dilapidated. Today, visitors enjoy a harmonious blend of man and nature—the most pristine of English countrysides decorated with time-passed villages, rich wool churches, tell-me-a-story stone fences, and "kissing gates" you wouldn't want to experience alone. Appreciated by throngs of 21st-century Romantics, the Cotswolds are enjoying new prosperity.

The north Cotswolds are best. Two of the region's coziest towns, Chipping Campden and Stow-on-the-Wold, are eight and four miles, respectively, from Moreton-in-Marsh, which has the best public transportation connections. Any of these three towns makes a fine home base for your exploration of the thatch-happiest of Cotswold villages and walks.

Planning Your Time

The Cotswolds are an absolute delight by car and, with patience, enjoyable even without a car. On a three-week British trip, I'd spend at least two nights and a day in the Cotswolds. The Cotswolds' charm has a softening effect on many uptight itineraries. You could enjoy days of walking from a home base here.

Home Bases: Chipping Campden and Stow-on-the-Wold are quaint without being overrun, and both have good accommodations. Stow has a bit more character for an overnight stay, and offers the widest range of choices. The plain town of Moreton-in-Marsh is the only one of the three with a train station, and only worth visiting as a transit hub. While Moreton has the most convenient connections, non-drivers can also make it work to home-base in Chipping Campden or Stow—especially if you don't mind sorting through bus schedules or springing for the occasional taxi to connect towns. (But note that this becomes even more challenging on Sundays, when bus schedules are dramatically reduced.) With a car, consider really getting away from it all by staying in one of the smaller villages.

Nearby Sights: England's top countryside palace, Blenheim, is located at the eastern edge of the Cotswolds, between Moreton and Oxford (see end of this chapter). If you want to take in some Shakespeare, note that Stow, Chipping Campden, and Moreton are only a 30-minute drive from Stratford, which offers a great evening of world-class entertainment (see Stratford-upon-Avon chapter).

One-Day Driver's 100-Mile Cotswold Blitz: Use a good map and reshuffle this plan to fit your home base:

9:00   Browse through Chipping Campden, following my self-guided walk.

10:30 Joyride through Snowshill, Stanway, and Stanton.

12:30 Have lunch in Stow-on-the-Wold, then follow my self-guided walk there.

15:00 Drive to the Slaughters, Bourton-on-the-Water, and Bibury; or, if you're up for a hike instead of a drive, walk from Stow to the Slaughters to Bourton, then catch the bus back to Stow.

18:00 Have dinner at a countryside gastropub (reserve in advance by phone), then head home; or drive 30 minutes to Stratford-upon-Avon for a Shakespeare play.

Cotswold Appreciation 101

History can be read into the names of the area. *Cotswold* could come from the Saxon phrase meaning "shelters for sheep," or more likely, from the Old English for shelter ("cot" as in cottage) or on an open upland ("wold").

In the Cotswolds, a town's main street (called High Street) needed to be wide to accommodate the sheep and cattle being marched to market (and today, to park tour buses). Some of the most picturesque cottages were once humble row houses of weavers' cottages, usually located along a stream for their waterwheels (good examples in Bibury and Lower Slaughter). The towns run on slow clocks and yellowed calendars. An entire village might not have a phone booth.

Fields of yellow (rapeseed) and pale blue (linseed) separate pastures dotted with black and white sheep. In just about any B&B, when you open your window in the morning you'll hear sheep baa-ing. The decorative "toadstool" stones dotting front yards throughout the region are medieval staddle stones, which buildings were set upon to keep the rodents out.

Cotswold walls and roofs are made of the local limestone. The limestone roof tiles hang by pegs. To make the weight more bearable, smaller and lighter tiles are higher up. An extremely strict building code keeps towns looking what many locals call "overly quaint."

Don't miss Blenheim Palace, which deserves a half-day. Thanks to its location at the Cotswolds' eastern edge, Blenheim fits well on the way into or out of the region.

Two-Day Plan by Public Transportation: This plan is best for any day except Sunday—when virtually no buses run—and assumes you're home-basing in Moreton-in-Marsh.

Day 1: Take the morning bus (likely around 9:30) to Chipping Campden to explore that town. If you want to stretch your legs, hike 30 minutes (each way) into Broad Campden. Then take the bus from Chipping Campden to Moreton and transfer to a Stow-bound bus. After poking around Stow, hike from Stow through the Slaughters to Bourton-on-the-Water (about 3 hours at a relaxed pace), then return by bus to Moreton for dinner. (For less walking and more time for an early dinner in Stow, do just part of the hike, or take the bus from Stow to Bourton and back.) Note that the last bus back to Moreton departs Stow at about 19:20 (departs Bourton at 19:10, this bus runs Mon–Sat only—sparse connections on Sun,

While you'll still see lots of sheep, the commercial wool industry is essentially dead. It costs more to shear a sheep than the 50 pence the wool will fetch. In the old days, sheep lived long lives, producing lots of wool. When they were finally slaughtered, the meat was tough and eaten as "mutton." Today, you don't find mutton much because the sheep are raised primarily for their meat, and slaughtered younger. When it comes to Cotswold sheep these days, it's lamb (not mutton) and dinner (not sweaters).

Towns are small, and everyone seems to know everyone. The area is provincial yet ever-so-polite, and people commonly rescue themselves from a gossipy tangent by saying, "It's all very...mmm...yaaa."

In contrast to the village ambience are the giant manors and mansions whose private, gated driveways you'll drive past. Many of these now belong to A-list celebrities, who have country homes here. If you live in the Cotswolds, you can call Madonna, Elizabeth Hurley, Kate Moss, and Kate Winslet your neighbors.

This is walking country. The English love their walks and vigorously defend their age-old right to free passage. Once a year the Rambling Society organizes a "Mass Trespass," when each of the country's 50,000 miles of public footpaths is walked. By assuring that each path is used at least once a year, they stop landlords from putting up fences. Any paths found blocked are unceremoniously unblocked.

Questions to ask locals: Do you think foxhunting should have been banned? Who are the Morris men? What's a kissing gate?

confirm times locally).

Day 2: Take a day trip to Blenheim Palace via Oxford (train to Oxford, bus to palace); or rent a bike and ride to Chastleton House; or take a daylong countryside walk (best to bus to Stow or Chipping Campden and walk from there).

Tourist Information

Local TIs stock a wide array of helpful resources. Ask for the *Cotswold Lion* weekly newspaper, which includes suggestions for walks and hikes (summers only); the monthly *Cotswold Events* guide; the *Explore the Cotswolds by Public Transport* bus timetable brochure, as well as individual bus schedules for the routes you'll be using; and the *Attractions and Events Guide 2011* (with updated prices and hours for Cotswolds sights). Each village also has its own assortment of brochures about the place itself, and the surrounding countryside, often for a small fee (£0.50–1). While paying for these items seems chintzy, realize that Cotswolds TIs have lost much of their funding and are struggling to make ends meet (some even have volunteer staff).

Getting Around the Cotswolds
By Bus

The Cotswolds are so well-preserved, in part, because public transportation to and within this area has long been miserable.

Fortunately, a train line and a few key buses connect the more interesting villages. Centrally located Moreton-in-the-Marsh is the region's transit hub—with the only train station and several bus lines.

To explore the towns, use the bus routes that hop through the Cotswolds about every 1.5 hours, lacing together main stops and ending at rail stations. In each case, the entire trip takes about an hour. Individual fares are around £2. (There is an all-day, unlimited Cotswold Rover Ticket for £6, but of the handy buses described below, it covers only #855. You can buy it from the driver on participating routes.)

The TI hands out easy-to-read bus schedules for the key lines described below (or check www.traveline.org.uk, or call the Traveline info line, toll tel. 0871-200-2233). Put together a one-way or return trip by public transportation, making for a fine Cotswolds day. Ask the TI for the *Explore the Cotswolds by Public Transport* timetables, which summarize all of the bus routes in the area in separate central, north, and south sections (or download them at www.cotswoldsaonb.org.uk). If you're traveling one-way between two train stations, remember that the Cotswold villages—generally pretty clueless when it comes to the needs of travelers without a car—have no official baggage-check services. You'll need to improvise; ask sweetly at the nearest TI or business. Note that bus service is essentially nonexistent on Sundays.

Here are the most helpful bus lines:

Buses **#21** and **#22** run from Moreton-in-Marsh to Batsford to Bourton-on-the-Hill to Blockley, then either to Broadway (#21) or Broad Campden (#22) on their way to Chipping Campden, before ending at Stratford-upon-Avon (operated by Johnsons Coaches, tel. 01564/797-000, www.johnsonscoaches.co.uk). Note that this route is the only one that goes all the way through to Chipping Campden.

Bus **#801** goes from Moreton-in-Marsh to Stow-on-the-Wold to "Slaughter Pike" (on the main road just south of the two Slaughters) to Bourton-on-the-Water, and then usually continues on to Cheltenham (operated by Pulham & Sons Coaches, tel.

01451/820-369, www.pulhamscoaches.com).

Bus **#855** (called the Fosse Link) goes from Moreton-in-Marsh to Stow-on-the-Wold to Bourton-on-the-Water to Northleach to Cirencester, and then (in the morning and evening) on to the Kemble train station (operated by Pulham & Sons Coaches, tel. 01451/820-369, www.pulhamscoaches.com).

Note that no single bus connects the three major towns described in this chapter (Chipping Campden, Stow, and Moreton); to get between Chipping Campden and Stow, you'll have to change buses in Moreton.

By Bike

Despite narrow roads, high hedgerows (blocking some views), and even higher hills, bikers enjoy the Cotswolds free from the constraints of bus schedules. For each area, TIs have fine route planners that indicate which peaceful, paved lanes are particularly scenic for biking. In summer, it's smart to book your rental bike a couple of days ahead.

In **Moreton-in-Marsh,** the nice folks at the **Toy Shop** rent mountain bikes. You can stop in the shop to rent a bike, or call ahead to pick up or drop off at other times—they're flexible (£15/day with route maps, bike locks, and helmets; shop open Mon and Wed–Fri 9:00–13:00 & 14:00–17:00, Sat 9:00–17:00, closed Sun and Tue, High Street, tel. 01608/650-756).

In **Chipping Campden,** you have two options: **Cycle Cotswolds,** right in town at the Volunteer Inn pub, is the most convenient (£10/day, £15/24 hours, daily 7:00–21:00, Lower High Street, tel. 01789-720-193, www.cyclecotswolds.co.uk). Otherwise, try **Cotswold Country Cycles** (£15/day, tandem-£30/day, includes helmets and route maps, delivery for a fee, daily 9:30–dusk, 2 miles north of town at Longlands Farm Cottage, tel. 01386/438-706, mobile 07746-107-728, www.cotswoldcountrycycles.com); they also offer self-led bike tours of the Cotswolds and surrounding areas (2–7 days, see website for details).

Stow-on-the-Wold does not have any bike rental shops.

By Foot

Walking guidebooks and leaflets abound, giving you a world of choices for each of my recommended stops (choose a book with clear maps). If you're doing any hiking whatsoever, get the excellent Ordnance Survey Explorer OL #45 map, which shows every road, trail, and ridgeline (£8 at local TIs). Nearly every hotel and B&B has a box or shelf of local walking guides and maps, including Ordnance Survey #45. Don't hesitate to ask for a loaner. For a quick circular hike from a particular village, peruse the books and brochures offered by that village's TI. Villages are generally no

The Cotswolds

THE COTSWOLDS

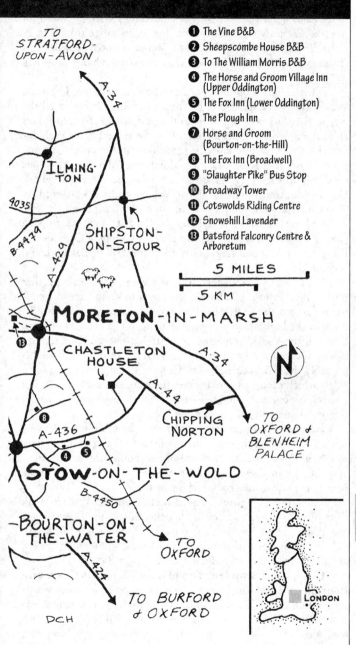

1 The Vine B&B
2 Sheepscombe House B&B
3 To The William Morris B&B
4 The Horse and Groom Village Inn (Upper Oddington)
5 The Fox Inn (Lower Oddington)
6 The Plough Inn
7 Horse and Groom (Bourton-on-the-Hill)
8 The Fox Inn (Broadwell)
9 "Slaughter Pike" Bus Stop
10 Broadway Tower
11 Cotswolds Riding Centre
12 Snowshill Lavender
13 Batsford Falconry Centre & Arboretum

TO STRATFORD-UPON-AVON

A.34

ILMINGTON

A4035

B.4479

A.429

SHIPSTON-ON-STOUR

5 MILES
5 KM

MORETON-IN-MARSH

CHASTLETON HOUSE

A.44

A.34

N

CHIPPING NORTON

TO OXFORD & BLENHEIM PALACE

A-436

8

4 5

STOW-ON-THE-WOLD

B-4450

BOURTON-ON-THE-WATER

TO OXFORD

A.424

TO BURFORD & OXFORD

DCH

LONDON

THE COTSWOLDS

more than three miles apart, and most have pubs that would love to feed and water you. For a list of guided walks, ask at any TI for the free *Cotswold Lion* newspaper. The walks range from 2 to 12 miles, and often involve a stop at a pub or tearoom (April–Sept; *Lion* newspaper also online at www.cotswoldsaonb.org.uk—click on "Publications").

There are many options for hikers, ranging from the "Cotswold Way" path that leads 100 miles from Chipping Campden all the way to Bath, to easy loop trips to the next village. Serious hikers enjoy doing a several-day loop, walking for several hours each day and sleeping in a different village each night. One popular route is the **"Cotswold Ring"**: Day 1—Moreton-in-Marsh to Stow-on-the-Wold to the Slaughters to Bourton-on-the-Water (12 miles); Day 2—Bourton-on-the-Water to Winchcombe (13 miles); Day 3—Winchcombe to Stanway to Stanton (7 miles), or all the way to Broadway (10.5 miles total); Day 4—On to Chipping Campden (just 5.5 miles, but steeply uphill); Day 5—Chipping Campden to Broad Campden, Blockley, Bourton-on-the-Hill or Batsford, and back to Moreton (7 miles).

Realistically, on a short visit, you won't have time for that much hiking. But if you have a few hours to spare, consider venturing across the pretty hills and meadows of the Cotswolds. Each of the home-base villages I recommend has several options. Stow-on-the-Wold, immersed in pretty but not-too-hilly terrain, is within easy walking distance of several interesting spots, and is probably the best starting point. Chipping Campden sits along a ridge, which means that hikes from there are extremely scenic, but also more strenuous. Moreton—true to its name—sits on a marsh, offering flatter and less picturesque hikes.

Here are a few hikes to consider, in order of difficulty (easiest first). I've selected these for their convenience to the home-base towns, and because the start and/or end points are on bus lines, allowing you to hitch a ride back to where you started (or on to the next town) rather than backtracking by foot.

Stow, the Slaughters, and Bourton-on-the-Water: Walk from Stow to Upper and Lower Slaughter, then on to Bourton-on-the-Water (which has bus service back to Stow on #801 or #855). One big advantage of this walk is that it's mostly downhill (4 miles, about 2–3 hours one-way). For details, see page 348.

Chipping Campden, Broad Campden, Blockley, and Bourton-on-the-Hill: From Chipping Campden, it's an easy mile walk into charming Broad Campden, and from there, a more strenuous hike to Blockley and Bourton-on-the-Hill (which are both connected by bus #21/#22 to Chipping Campden and Moreton). For more details, see page 328.

Winchcombe, Stanway, Stanton, and Broadway: You can

reach the charming villages of Stanway and Stanton by foot, but it's tough going—lots of up and down. The start and end points (Winchcombe and Broadway) have decent bus connections, and in a pinch some buses do serve Stanton (but carefully check schedules before you set out).

Broadway to Chipping Campden: The hardiest hike of those I list here, this takes you along the Cotswold Ridge. Attempt it only if you're a serious hiker (5.5 miles).

Bibury and the Coln Valley are pretty, but lack of bus access makes hiking there less appealing.

By Car

Joyriding here truly is a joy. Winding country roads seem designed to spring bucolic village-and-countryside scenes on the driver at every turn. Distances here are wonderfully short—but only if you invest in the Ordnance Survey map of the Cotswolds, sold locally at TIs and newsstands (the £8 Explorer OL #45 map is excellent but almost too detailed for drivers; the £5 Tour Map #8 covers a wider area in less detail). Here are driving distances from Moreton: **Stow-on-the-Wold** (4 miles), **Chipping Campden** (8 miles), **Broadway** (10 miles), **Stratford-upon-Avon** (17 miles), **Warwick** (23 miles), **Blenheim Palace** (20 miles).

Car hiking is great. In this chapter, I cover the postcard-perfect (but discovered) villages. With a car and the local Ordnance Survey map, you can easily ramble about and find your own gems. The problem with having a car is that you are less likely to walk. Consider taking a taxi or bus somewhere, so that you can walk back to your car and enjoy the scenery (see suggestions earlier).

Car Rental: Two places near Moreton-in-Marsh rent cars by the day. **Value Self Drive,** based in Shipston-on-Stour (about six miles north of Moreton) and run by accommodating Julian, has affordable rates (£23–33/day including insurance and taxes, automatic for no extra charge, Mon–Sat 8:30–19:00, might also be open Sun, call ahead to arrange, mobile 07974-805-485, valueselfdrive @btinternet.com). Conveniently, Julian will deliver a car to you in Moreton for £5 extra, provided you drive him back to Shipston (or a taxi from Moreton to Shipston costs £20). **Robinson Goss Self Drive,** also six miles north of Moreton-in-Marsh, is a bit more expensive, and won't bring the car to you in Moreton (£29–58/day including everything but gas, Mon–Fri 8:30–17:00, Sat 8:30–12:00, closed Sun, tel. 01608/663-322, www.robgos.co.uk).

By Taxi

Two or three town-to-town taxi trips can make more sense than renting a car. While taking a cab cross-country seems extravagant (about £2.50/mile), the distances are short (Stow to Moreton is 4 miles, Stow to Chipping Campden is 10), and one-way walks are lovely. If you call a cab, confirm that the meter will start only when you are actually picked up. Consider hiring a cab at the hourly "touring rate" (generally around £30), rather than the meter rate (e.g., £20–25 Stow to Chipping Campden). For a few more bucks, you can have a joyride peppered with commentary.

Note that the drivers listed are not typical city taxi services (with many drivers on call), but are mostly individuals—it's smart to book ahead if you're arriving in high season, since they can book up in advance on weekends.

To scare up a driver in Moreton, call **Moreton Taxis** (toll-free tel. 0800-955-8584), Richard at **Four Shires** (mobile 07747-802-555), or **Iain's Taxis** (mobile 07789-897-966); in Stow, call Iain (above) or **Tony Knight** (mobile 07887-714-047); and in Chipping Campden, call Iain (above) or Paul at **Cotswold Private Hire** (mobile 07980-857-833). Tim Harrison at **Tour the Cotswolds** specializes in tours of the Cotswolds and its gardens (mobile 07779-030-820, www.tourthecotswolds.co.uk; Tim co-runs a recommended B&B in Snowshill—see page 341).

By Tour

Departing from Bath, **Mad Max Minibus Tours** offers a "Cotswold Discovery" full-day tour, and can drop you off in Stow with your luggage if you arrange it in advance (see page 238 of the Bath chapter).

While none of the Cotswold towns offers regularly scheduled walks, many have voluntary warden groups who love to meet visitors and give walks for just a small donation (about £3/person; specific contact information appears below for Chipping Campden).

Chipping Campden

Just touristy enough to be convenient, the north Cotswolds town of Chipping Campden (CAM-den) is a ▲▲ sight. This market town, once the home of the richest Cotswold wool merchants, has some incredibly beautiful thatched roofs. Both the great British historian G. M. Trevelyan and I call Chipping Campden's High Street the finest in England.

THE COTSWOLDS

Orientation to Chipping Campden

(area code: 01386)

Walk the full length of High Street; its width is characteristic of market towns. Go around the block on both ends. On one end, you'll find impressively thatched homes (out Sheep Street, past the public WC, and right on Westington Street). Walking north on High Street, you'll pass the Market Hall, the wavy roof of the first great wool mansion, a fine and free memorial garden, and, finally, the town's famous 15th-century Perpendicular Gothic "wool" church. (This route is the same as my self-guided town walk.)

Tourist Information

Chipping Campden's TI is tucked away in the old police station on High Street. Get the £1 town guide, which includes a map (April–Oct daily 9:30–17:00; Nov–March Mon–Thu 10:00–13:00, Fri–Sun 10:00–16:00; tel. 01386/841-206, www.chippingcampden online.org).

Helpful Hints

Festivals: Chipping Campden's biggest festival is the **Cotswold Olimpicks,** a series of tongue-in-cheek countryside games (such as competitive shin-kicking) atop Dover's Hill, just above town (first Fri–Sat after Late May Bank Holiday, www .olimpickgames.co.uk). They also have an **open gardens festival** the third weekend in June and a **music festival** in mid-May.

Internet Access: Try the occasionally open **library** (closed Tue, Thu, and Sun; High Street, tel. 01386/840-692) or **Butty's at the Old Bakehouse,** a casual eatery and Internet café (£1.50/15 minutes, £2.50/30 minutes, £4/hour, free Wi-Fi, Mon–Sat 7:30–14:30, closed Sun, Lower High Street, tel. 01386/840-401).

Bike Rental: Call **Cycle Cotswolds** or **Cotswold Country Cycles** (see page 321).

Taxi: Try **Cotswold Private Hire** or **Tour the Cotswolds** (see page 326).

Parking: Find a spot anywhere along High Street and park for free with no time limit. There's also a pay-and-display lot (1.5-hour maximum) on High Street (across from TI).

Tours: The local members of the **Cotswold Voluntary Wardens** would be happy to show you around town for a small donation to their conservation society (£3/person, 1-hour walk, walks July–Sept Tue at 14:30, meet at Market Hall). Tour guide and coordinator Ann Colcomb can help arrange for a walk on other days as well (tel. 01386/832-131, www.cotswoldsaonb.com).

Walks and Hikes from Chipping Campden: Since this is a particularly hilly area, long-distance hikes are challenging. The easiest and most rewarding stroll is to the thatch-happy Hobbit village of **Broad Campden** (about a mile, mostly level). From there, you can walk or take the bus (#22) back to Chipping Campden.

Or, if you have more energy, continue from Broad Campden up over the ridge and into picturesque **Blockley**—and, if your stamina holds out, all the way to **Bourton-on-the-Hill** (Blockley and Bourton-on-the-Hill are also connected by bus #21/#22 to Chipping Campden and Moreton).

Alternatively, you can hike up to **Dover's Hill,** just north of the village. Ask locally about this easy circular one-hour walk that takes you on the first mile of the 100-mile-long Cotswold Way (which goes from here to Bath).

For more about hiking, see "Getting Around the Cotswolds—By Foot" on page 321.

Self-Guided Walk

Welcome to Chipping Campden

This stroll through "Campden" (as locals call their town) takes you from the Market Hall west to the old silk mill, and then back east the length of High Street to the church. It takes about an hour.

Market Hall: Begin at Campden's most famous monument—the Market Hall. It stands in front of the TI, marking the town center. The Market Hall was built in 1627 by the 17th-century Lord of the Manor, Sir Baptist Hicks. (Look for the Hicks family coat of arms in the building's facade.) Back then, it was an elegant—even over-the-top—shopping hall for the townsfolk who'd come here to buy their produce. In the

1940s, it was almost sold to an American, but the townspeople heroically raised money to buy it first, then gave it to the National Trust for its preservation.

The timbers inside are true to the original. Study the classic Cotswold stone roof, still held together with wooden pegs nailed in from underneath. (Tiles were cut and sold with peg holes, and stacked like waterproof scales.) Buildings all over the region still use these stone shingles. Today, the hall, which is rarely used, stands as a testimony to the importance of trade to medieval Campden.

Adjacent to the Market Hall is the sober WWI monument—a

THE COTSWOLDS

reminder of the huge price paid by every little town. Walk around it, noticing how 1918 brought the greatest losses.

The TI is just across the street, in the old police courthouse. If it's open, you're welcome to climb the stairs and peek into the **Magistrate's Court** (free, same hours as TI, ask at TI to go up). Under the open-beamed courtroom, you'll find a humble little exhibit on the town's history.

• *Walk west a few steps, to the Red Lion Pub. Across High Street (and a bit to the right) from the pub, look for the house with a sundial, called...*

"Green Dragons": The house's decorative black cast-iron fixtures once held hay and functioned much like salad bowls for horses. Fine-cut stones define the door, but "rubble stones" make up the rest of the wall. The pink stones are the same limestone but have been heated, and likely were scavenged from a house that burned down.

• *At the Red Lion Pub, leave High Street and walk a block down Sheep Street. Just past the public loo, on the right-hand side, is the old...*

Silk Mill: The tiny Cam River powered a mill here since about 1790. Today it houses the handicraft workers guild and some interesting history. In 1902, Charles Robert Ashbee (1863–1942) revitalized this sleepy hamlet of 2,500 by bringing a troupe of London artisans and their families (160 people in all) to town. Ashbee was a leader in the romantic Arts and Crafts movement—craftspeople repulsed by the Industrial Revolution who idealized the handmade crafts and preindustrial ways. Ashbee's idealistic craftsmen's guild lasted only until 1908, when most of his men grew bored with their small-town, back-to-nature ideals. Today, the only shop surviving from the originals is that of **silversmith David Hart.** His grandfather came to town with Ashbee, and the workshop (upstairs in the mill building) is an amazing time warp—little changed since 1902. Mr. Hart is a gracious man as well as a fine silversmith, and he welcomes browsers six days a week. (While you could continue 200 yards farther to see some fine thatched houses, this walk doesn't.)

• *Return to High Street, turn right, and walk through town.*

High Street: Chipping Campden's High Street has changed little architecturally since 1840. (The town's street plan and property lines survive from the 12th century.) Notice the harmony of the long rows of buildings. While the street comprises different styles through the centuries, everything you see was made of the same Cotswold stone—the only stone allowed today.

To remain level, High Street arcs with the contour of the hillside. Because it's so wide, you know this was a market town. In

Chipping Campden

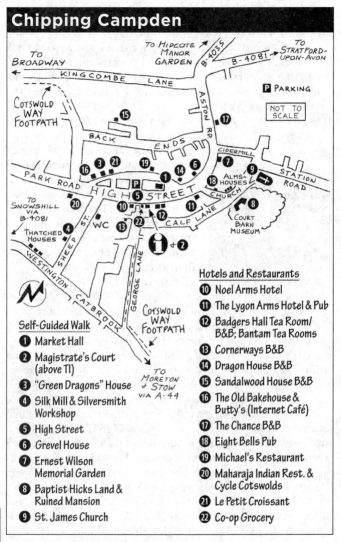

TO HIDCOTE MANOR GARDEN
TO STRATFORD-UPON-AVON
TO BROADWAY
KINGCOMBE LANE
B-4035
B-4081
ASTON RD.
P PARKING
NOT TO SCALE
COTSWOLD WAY FOOTPATH
BACK ENDS
CIDERMILL
STATION ROAD
PARK ROAD
HIGH STREET
ALMS-HOUSES
CHURCH
TO SNOWSHILL VIA B-4081
SHEEP ST.
WC
CALF LANE
COURT BARN MUSEUM
THATCHED HOUSES
WESTINGTON
CATBROOK
GEORGE LANE
COTSWOLD WAY FOOTPATH
TO MORETON & STOW VIA A-44

Self-Guided Walk
1. Market Hall
2. Magistrate's Court (above TI)
3. "Green Dragons" House
4. Silk Mill & Silversmith Workshop
5. High Street
6. Grevel House
7. Ernest Wilson Memorial Garden
8. Baptist Hicks Land & Ruined Mansion
9. St. James Church

Hotels and Restaurants
10. Noel Arms Hotel
11. The Lygon Arms Hotel & Pub
12. Badgers Hall Tea Room/ B&B; Bantam Tea Rooms
13. Cornerways B&B
14. Dragon House B&B
15. Sandalwood House B&B
16. The Old Bakehouse & Butty's (Internet Café)
17. The Chance B&B
18. Eight Bells Pub
19. Michael's Restaurant
20. Maharaja Indian Rest. & Cycle Cotswolds
21. Le Petit Croissant
22. Co-op Grocery

THE COTSWOLDS

past centuries, livestock and packhorses laden with piles of freshly shorn fleece would fill the streets. Campden was a sales and distribution center for the wool industry, and merchants from as far away as Italy would come here for the prized raw wool.

High Street has no house numbers: Locals know the houses by their names. In the distance, you'll see the town church (where this walk ends). Notice that the power lines are buried underground, making the scene delightfully uncluttered.

As you stroll High Street, you'll find the finest houses on the uphill side—which gets more sun. You'll pass several old sundials as you wander. Decorative features (like the Ionic capitals near the TI) are added for non-structural touches of class. Most High Street buildings are half-timbered, but with cosmetic stone facades. You may see some exposed half-timbered walls. Study the crudely beautiful framing, made of hand-hewn oak (you can see the adze marks) and held together by wooden pegs.

Peeking down alleys, you'll notice how the lots are narrow but very deep. Called "burgage plots," this platting goes back to 1170. In medieval times, rooms were lined up long and skinny like train cars: Each building had a small storefront, followed by a workshop, living quarters, staff quarters, stables, and a pea patch-type garden at the very back. Now the private alleys that still define many of these old lots lead to comfy gardens. While some of today's buildings are wider, virtually all the widths are exact multiples of that basic first unit (for example, a modern building may be three times wider than its medieval counterpart).

• *Hike up High Street toward the church, to just before the first intersection, to find the...*

Grevel House: In 1367, William Grevel built what's considered Campden's first stone house (on the left). Sheep tycoons had big homes. Imagine back then, when this fine building was surrounded by humble wattle-and-daub huts. It had newfangled chimneys, rather than a crude hole in the roof. (No more rain inside!) Originally a "hall house" with just one big, tall room, it got its upper floor in the 16th century. The finely carved central bay window is a good early example of the Perpendicular Gothic style. The gargoyles scared away bad spirits—and served as rain spouts. The boot scrapers outside each door were fixtures in that muddy age—especially in market towns, where the streets were filled with animal dung.

• *Continue up High Street for about 100 yards. Go past Church Street (which we'll walk up later). On the right, you'll find a small Gothic arch leading into a garden.*

Ernest Wilson Memorial Garden: Once the church's vegetable patch, this small and secluded garden is a botanist's delight today. It's filled with well-labeled plants that the Victorian botanist Ernest Wilson brought back to England from his extensive travels in Asia. There's a complete history of the garden on the board to the left of the entry (free, open daily until dusk).

• *Backtrack to Church Street. Turn left, walk past the recommended Eight Bells Inn, and hook left with the street. Along your right-hand side stretches...*

Baptist Hicks Land: Sprawling adjacent to the town church, the area known as Baptist Hicks Land held Hicks' huge estate and manor house. This influential Lord of the Manor was from "a family of substance," who were merchants of silk and fine clothing as well as moneylenders. Beyond the ornate gate (which you'll see ahead, near the church), only a few outbuildings and the charred corner of his mansion survive. The **mansion** was burned by Royalists in 1645 during the Civil War—notice how Cotswold stone turns red when burned. Hicks housed the poor, making a show of his

generosity, adding a long row of almshouses (with his family coat of arms) for neighbors to see as they walked to church. These almshouses (lining Church Street on the left) house pensioners today, as they have since the 17th century.

On the right, filling the old **Court Barn,** is a museum about crafts and designs from the Arts and Crafts movement, with works by Ashbee and his craftsmen (£3.50, Tue–Sun 10:30–17:30, closed Mon, tel. 01386/841-951, www.courtbarn.org.uk).

• *Next to the Court Barn, a scenic, tree-lined lane leads to the front door of the church. On the way, notice the 12 lime trees, one for each of the apostles, that were planted in about 1760 (sorry, no limes).*

St. James Church: One of the finest churches in the Cotswolds, St. James Church graces one of its leading towns. Both the town and the church were built by wool wealth. Go inside. The church is Perpendicular Gothic, with lots of light and strong verticality. Notice the fine vestments and altar hangings (intricate c. 1460 embroidery) behind protective blue curtains (near the back of the church). Tombstones pave the floor in the chancel (often under protective red carpeting)—memorializing great wool merchants through the ages.

At the altar is a brass relief of William Grevel, the first owner of the Grevel House (described earlier), and his wife. But it is Sir

Baptist Hicks who dominates the church. His huge, canopied tomb is the ornate final resting place for Hicks and his wife, Elizabeth. Study their faces, framed by fancy lace ruffs (trendy in the 1620s). Adjacent—as if in a closet— is a statue of their daughter, Lady Juliana, and her husband, Lutheran Yokels. Juliana commissioned the statue in 1642, when her husband died, but had it closed until *she* died in 1680. Then, the doors were opened, revealing these two people holding hands and living happily ever after—at least in marble. The hinges were likely used only once.

As you leave the church, look immediately around the corner to the left of the door. A small tombstone reads "Thank you Lord for Simon, a dearly loved cat who greeted everyone who entered this church. RIP 1980."

Sleeping in Chipping Campden

In Chipping Campden—as in any town in the Cotswolds—B&Bs offer a better value than hotels. Rooms are generally tight on Saturdays (when many charge a bit more and are reluctant to rent to one-nighters) and in September, which is considered a peak month. Parking is never a problem. Always ask for a discount if staying longer than one or two nights.

$$$ Noel Arms Hotel, the characteristic old hotel on the main square, has welcomed guests for 600 years. Its lobby was recently remodeled in a medieval-meets-modern style, and its 27 rooms are well-furnished with antiques (Sb-£110, standard Db-£130, bigger Db-£160, fancier four-poster Db-£180–200, midweek deals, some ground-floor doubles, free Wi-Fi in lobby, attached restaurant/bar and café, free parking, High Street, tel. 01386/840-317, fax 01386/841-136, www.noelarmshotel.com, reception@noelarmshotel.com).

$$$ The Lygon Arms Hotel (pronounced "lig-un"), attached to the popular pub of the same name, has small public areas and 10 cheery, open-beamed rooms (one small older Db-£75–80, huge "superior" Db-£100–120, lovely courtyard Db-£130–160, lower prices are for midweek or multi-night stays, family deals, free

---

Sleep Code

(£1 = about $1.60, country code: 44, area code: 01386)
S = Single, **D** = Double/Twin, **T** = Triple, **Q** = Quad, **b** = bathroom, **s** = shower only. Unless noted otherwise, you can assume credit cards are accepted and breakfast is included.

To help you sort easily through these listings, I've divided the rooms into three categories based on the price for a standard double room with bath:

$$$ Higher Priced—Most rooms £90 or more.
  $$ Moderately Priced—Most rooms between £65-90.
    $ Lower Priced—Most rooms £65 or less.

Prices can change without notice; verify the hotel's current rates online or by email. For other updates, see www.ricksteves.com/update.

Wi-Fi, free parking, High Street, go through archway and look for hotel reception on the left, tel. 01386/840-318, www.lygonarms.co.uk, sandra@lygonarms.co.uk, Sandra Davenport).

$$$ Badgers Hall Tea Room, also listed later under "Eating in Chipping Campden," rents three pricey rooms (Db-£98, or £110 on weekends, 2-night minimum, includes breakfast and tea, no kids under age 10, free Wi-Fi, High Street, tel. 01386/840-839, www.badgershall.com, Karen).

$$ Cornerways B&B is a fresh, bright, and comfy modern home (not "oldie worldie") a block off High Street. It's run by the delightful Carole Proctor, who can "look out the window and see the church where we were married." The two huge, light, airy loft rooms are great for families (Db-£70, Tb-£90, Qb-£110, 2-night minimum, £5 off for 3 or more nights, children's discount, cash only, free Wi-Fi, off-street parking, George Lane, just walk through the arch beside Noel Arms Hotel, tel. 01386/841-307, www.cornerways.info, carole@cornerways.info).

$$ Dragon House B&B rents two tidy rooms—with medieval beams and a shared lounge—right on the center of High Street. They have laundry machines and a sumptuous, stay-awhile garden (Db-£68, £5 off for 3 or more nights, cash only, free Wi-Fi, free off-street parking available, near Market Hall, tel. & fax 01386/840-734, www.dragonhouse-chipping-campden.com, info@dragonhouse-chipping-campden.co.uk, Valerie and Graeme the retired potter). They also have a cottage that sleeps up to six (Sat–Sat only, £250–750/week depending on month).

$$ Sandalwood House B&B is a big, comfy, heavily potpourri-scented home with a pink flowery lounge and a sprawling back garden. Just a five-minute walk from the center of town, it's in a quiet, woodsy setting. Its two cheery, pastel rooms are bright and spacious (D/Db-£73, T-£90, 2-night minimum, cheaper if you order a light breakfast instead of full, self-catering apartment sleeps four-£450/week, cash only, no kids under age 10, free Wi-Fi, free off-street parking, tel. & fax 01386/840-091, sandalwoodhouse @hotmail.com, Diana Bendall). To get to Sandalwood House, go west on High Street, and at the church and the Volunteer Inn, turn right and then right again; look for a sign in the hedge on the left, and head up the long driveway.

$$ The Old Bakehouse rents two small but pleasant twin-bedded rooms in a 600-year-old home with a plush fireplace lounge. As this place is under new management in 2011, some of these details might change (Sb-£45, Db-£70, family deals, £5 off for 2 or more nights, cash only, free Wi-Fi, Lower High Street, tel. & fax 01386/840-979, www.chippingcampden-cotswolds.co.uk, oldbakehouse@chippingcampden-cotswolds.co.uk).

$ The Chance B&B rents two rooms in a modern home with Cotswolds charm about a 10-minute walk from the town center (Db-£65, cash only, free Wi-Fi, free parking, 1 Aston Road, tel. 01386/849-079, www.the-chance.co.uk, enquiries@the-chance .co.uk, Sally and Paul).

Eating in Chipping Campden

This town—so filled with wealthy residents and tourists—comes with many choices. I've listed some local favorites below. If you have a car, consider driving to one of the excellent countryside pubs mentioned in the sidebar on page 352.

Eight Bells Pub is a charming 14th-century inn on Leysbourne with a classy and woody restaurant and a more colorful pub. For over a decade now, Neil and Julie have enjoyed keeping their seasonal menu as locally sourced as possible. They serve a daily special, are proud of their fish dishes, and always have a good vegetarian dish. As this is rightly considered deli best deal going in town for top-end pub dining, reservations are smart (£13–16 dinners, daily 12:00–14:00 & 18:30–21:00, later Fri–Sat, tel. 01386/840-371).

The Lygon Arms Pub is cozy and inviting, with a good, basic bar menu. You can order from the same menu in the colorful pub or the more elegant dining room across the passage (£7 sandwiches, £8–15 meals, daily 11:30–14:30 & 18:00–22:00).

Michael's, a fun Mediterranean restaurant on High Street, serves hearty portions and breaks plates at closing every Saturday night. Michael, who runs his place with a contagious passion and love of life, is from Cyprus: The forte here is Greek, with plenty of *mezes*—small dishes for £5–10 (also £14–17 entrées, Tue–Sun 11:00–14:30 & 19:00–22:00, closed Sun nights and Mon, tel. 01386/840-826).

Maharaja Indian Restaurant in the Volunteer Inn, while forgettable, is the only Indian place in town (£8–12 meals, daily 17:00–22:30, grassy courtyard out back, Lower High Street, tel. 01386/849-281).

Light Meals

If you want a quick, take-away sandwich, consider these options. Munch your lunch on the benches on the little green near the Market Hall.

Le Petit Croissant, a cheery little French deli with a tearoom in the back, serves pastries, quiche, cheese, and wine (£4 sandwiches, more to eat in, Mon–Fri 9:00–17:00, Sat 8:30–17:00, closed Sun, Lower High Street, tel. 01386/841-861).

THE COTSWOLDS

Butty's at the Old Bakehouse offers tasty £2–4 sandwiches and wraps made to order (Mon–Sat 7:30–14:30, closed Sun, Lower High Street, tel. 01386/840-401). They also have Internet access (see "Helpful Hints," earlier).

Picnic: The **Co-op** grocery store is the town's small "supermarket" (Mon–Sat 7:00–22:00, Sun 8:00–22:00, next to TI on High Street).

Tearooms

To visit a cute tearoom, try one of these places, located in the town center.

Badgers Hall Tea Room is great for a wide selection of savory dishes and desserts. A tempting table of homemade cakes, crumbles, and scones just inside the door lures passersby into its delightful half-timbered dining room. Along with light lunches, they serve a generous afternoon tea—a tall and ritualistic tray of dainty sandwiches, pastries, and scones with tea—for half the London price (£25 for 2 people, daily 10:00–17:00, High Street).

Bantam Tea Rooms, near the Market Hall, is also a good value (£7 teas, £6 sandwiches, Mon–Sat 10:00–17:00, Sun 10:30–17:00, High Street, tel. 01386/840-386).

Near Chipping Campden

Because the countryside around Chipping Campden is particularly hilly, it's also especially scenic. This is a very rewarding area to poke around and discover little thatched villages.

West of Chipping Campden

Due west of Chipping Campden lies the famous and touristy town of Broadway. Just south of that, you'll find my nominations for the cutest Cotswold villages. Like marshmallows in hot chocolate, Stanway, Stanton, and Snowshill nestle side by side, awaiting your arrival. (Note the Stanway House's limited hours when planning your visit.)

Broadway

This postcard-pretty town, a couple of miles west of Chipping Campden, is filled with inviting shops and fancy teahouses. With a "broad way" indeed running through its middle, it's one of the bigger towns in the area. This means you'll likely pass through at some point if you're driving—but, since all the big bus tours seem to stop here, I usually give Broadway a miss. However, with a new road that allows traffic to skirt the town, Broadway has gotten cuter than ever. Broadway has good bus connections with Chipping Campden (on bus #21).

Just outside Broadway, on the road to Chipping Campden, you might spot signs for the **Broadway Tower,** which looks like a turreted castle fortification stranded in the countryside without a castle in sight. This 55-foot-tall observation tower is a "folly"—a uniquely English term for a quirky, outlandish novelty erected as a giant lawn ornament by some aristocrat with more money than taste. If you're also weighted down with too many pounds, you can relieve yourself of £4 to climb to its top for a view over the pastures.

Stanway

More of a humble crossroads community than a true village, sleepy Stanway is worth a visit mostly for its manor house, which offers an intriguing insight into the English aristocracy today. If you're in the area when it's open, it's well worth visiting.

▲▲**Stanway House**—The Earl of Wemyss (pronounced "Weemz"), whose family tree charts relatives back to 1202, opens

his melancholy home and grounds to visitors just two days a week in the summer. Walking through his house offers a unique glimpse into the lifestyles of England's eccentric and fading nobility.

Cost and Hours: £7, June–Aug Tue and Thu only 14:00–17:00, tel. 01386/584-469, www.stanwayfountain.co.uk. His lordship himself narrated the audioguide to his home (£2).

Getting There: By car, leave B4077 at a statue of (the Christian) George slaying the dragon (of pagan superstition); you'll round the corner and see the manor's fine 17th-century Jacobean gatehouse. There's no public transportation to Stanway.

⊙ **Self-Guided Tour:** Start with the grounds, then head into the house itself.

The Earl recently restored "the tallest **fountain** in Britain" on the grounds—300 feet tall, gravity-powered, and quite impressive (fountain spurts for 30 minutes at 14:45 and 16:00 on opening days).

The bitchin' **Tithe Barn** (near where you enter the grounds) dates to the 14th century, and predates the manor. It was originally where monks—in the days before money—would accept one-tenth of whatever the peasants produced. Peek inside: This is a great hall for village hoedowns. While the Tithe Barn is no longer used to greet motley peasants and collect their feudal "rents," the lord still gets rent from his vast landholdings, and hosts community fêtes in his barn.

Stepping into the obviously very lived-in **manor,** you're free to wander around pretty much as you like, but keep in mind that a family does live here. His lordship is often roaming about as well. The place feels like a time warp. Ask a staff member to demonstrate the spinning rent-collection table. In the great hall, marvel at the one-piece oak shuffleboard table and the 1780 Chippendale exercise chair (half an hour of bouncing on this was considered good for the liver).

The manor dogs have their own cutely painted "family tree," but the Earl admits that his last dog, C. J., was "all character and no breeding." Poke into the office. You can psychoanalyze the lord by the books that fill his library, the videos stacked in front of his bed (with the mink bedspread), and whatever's next to his toilet.

The place has a story to tell. And so do the docents stationed in each room—modern-day peasants who, even without family trees, probably have relatives going back just as far in this village. Really. Talk to these people. Probe. Learn what you can about this side of England.

From Stanway to Stanton: These towns are separated by a row of oak trees and grazing land, with parallel waves echoing

the furrows plowed by medieval farmers. Centuries ago, farmers were allotted long strips of land called "furlongs." The idea was to dole out good and bad land equitably. (One square furlong equals an acre.) Over centuries of plowing these, furrows were formed. Let someone else drive, so you can hang out the window under a canopy of oaks, passing stone walls and sheep. Leaving Stanway on the road to Stanton, the first building you'll see (on the left, just outside Stanway) is a thatched cricket pavilion overlooking the village cricket green. Dating only from 1930, it's raised up (as medieval buildings were) on rodent-resistant staddle stones. Stanton is just ahead; follow the signs.

▲Stanton

Pristine Cotswold charm cheers you as you head up the main street of the village of Stanton. Go on a photo safari for flower-bedecked doorways and windows. (A scant few buses serve Stanton, but they're unpredictable—inquire locally.)

Stanton's **Church of St. Michael** (with the pointy spire) betrays a pagan past. It's safe to assume any church dedicated to St. Michael (the archangel who fought the devil) sits upon a sacred pagan site. Stanton is actually at the intersection of two ley lines (geographic lines along which many prehistoric sights are found). You'll see St. Michael's well-worn figure (and, above that, a sundial) over the door as you enter. Inside, above the capitals in the nave, find

the pagan symbols for the sun and the moon. While the church probably dates back to the ninth century, today's building is mostly from the 15th century, with 13th-century transepts. On the north transept (far side from entry), medieval frescoes show faintly through the 17th-century whitewash. (Once upon a time, these frescoes were considered too "papist.") Imagine the church interior colorfully decorated throughout. Original medieval glass is behind the altar. The list of rectors (at the very back of the church, under the organ loft) goes back to 1269. Finger the grooves in the back pews, worn away by sheepdog leashes. (A man's sheepdog accompanied him everywhere.)

Horse Riding—Anyone can enjoy the Cotswolds from the saddle. Jill Carenza's **Cotswolds Riding Centre,** set just out-

side Stanton village, is in the most scenic corner of the region. The facility has 50 horses, and takes rank beginners on a scenic "hack" through the village and into the high country (per-hour prices: £29/person for a group hack, £39/person for a semi-private hack, £49 for a private one-person hack;

lessons, longer rides, rides for experts, and pub tours available; tel. 01386/584-250, www.cotswoldsriding.co.uk). From Stanton, head toward Broadway and watch for the riding center on your right after about a third of a mile.

Sleeping in Stanton: **$$ The Vine B&B** has five rooms in a characteristic old Cotswolds house near the center of town. Owned by Jill from the riding center (described above), it takes a backseat to the horses: It's basically self-service, so there's no greeting or check-in, and guests wander around wondering which room is theirs. Still, it's the best option in Stanton, and convenient if you want to ride all day (Ds-£69, Db-£95, cottage with kitchen and 2 bedrooms-£150, most rooms with 4-poster beds, some stairs, tel. 01386/584-250, info@cotswoldsriding.co.uk).

Snowshill

Another nearly edible little bundle of cuteness, the village of Snowshill (SNOWS-hill) has a photogenic triangular square with a characteristic pub at its base.

▲Snowshill Manor—Dark and mysterious, this old palace is filled with the lifetime collection of Charles Paget Wade. It's one

big, musty celebration of craftsmanship, from finely carved spinning wheels to frightening samurai armor to tiny elaborate figurines carved by prisoners from the bones of meat served at dinner. Taking seriously his family motto, "Let Nothing Perish," Wade dedicated his life and fortune to preserving things finely crafted. The house (whose management made me promise not to promote it as an eccentric collector's pile of curiosities) really shows off Mr. Wade's ability to recognize and acquire fine examples of craftsmanship. It's all very...mmm...yaaa.

Cost and Hours: £9, manor house open mid-March–Oct Wed–Sun 12:00–17:30, gardens and ticket window open at 11:00, last entry 50 minutes before closing, closed Mon–Tue and Nov–March, restaurant, tel. 01386/852-410, www.nationaltrust.org.uk /snowshillmanor.

Getting There: The manor overlooks the town square, but there's no direct access from the square; instead, the entrance and parking lot are about a half-mile up the road toward Broadway. Park there and follow the long walkway through the garden to get to the house. A golf-cart-type shuttle to the house is available for those who need assistance.

Getting In: This popular sight strictly limits the number of entering visitors by doling out entry times. No reservations are possible; to get a slot, you must report to the ticket desk. It can be up to an hour's wait—even more on busy days, especially weekends (when they can sell out for the day as early as 14:00). Tickets go on sale and the gardens open at 11:00; the manor house opens at 12:00. Therefore, a good strategy is to arrive close to the opening time, and if there's a wait, enjoy the gardens (it's a 10-minute walk to the manor). If you have more time to kill, head into the village of Snowshill itself (a half-mile away) to wander and explore—or get a time slot for later in the day, and return in the afternoon.

Snowshill Lavender—In 2000, farmer Charlie Byrd realized that tourists love lavender. He planted his farm with 250,000

plants, and now visitors come to wander among his 53 acres, which burst with gorgeous lavender blossoms from mid-June through late August. His fragrant fantasy peaks late each July. Lavender—so famous in France's Provence—is not indigenous to this region, but it fits the climate and soil just fine. A free flier in the shop explains the variations of flowers blooming. Farmer Byrd produces lavender oil (an herbal product valued since ancient times for its healing, calming, and fragrant qualities) and sells it in a delightful shop, along with many other lavender-themed items. In the café, enjoy a pot of lavender-flavored tea with a lavender scone.

Cost and Hours: £2.50 to walk through the fields and the distillery, free to enter shop and café; late May–late Aug daily 10:00–17:00; Easter–late May and late Aug–Christmas Wed–Sun 10:00–17:00, closed Mon–Tue; closed Jan–Easter; tel. 01386/854-821, www.snowshill-lavender.co.uk, info@snowshill-lavender.co.uk.

Getting There: It's a half-mile out of Snowshill on the road toward Chipping Campden (easy parking). Entering Snowshill from the road to the manor (described above), take the left fork, then turn left again at the end of the village.

Sleeping near Snowshill: The pretty, one-pub village of Snowshill holds a gem of a B&B. **$$$ Sheepscombe House B&B** is a clean and pristine home on a working sheep farm. It's immersed in the best of Cotswold scenery, with plenty of sheep in the nearby fields. Jacki and Tim Harrison rent three modern, spacious, and thoughtfully appointed rooms (Db-£100–115, Tb-£160–165, folding cots available, free Wi-Fi, just a third of a mile south of Snowshill—look for signs, tel. 01386/853-769, www.broadway-cotswolds.co.uk/sheepscombe.html, reservations @snowshill-broadway.co.uk). Tim, who's happy to give you a local's perspective on this area, also runs Tour the Cotswolds car service (see page 326).

East of Chipping Campden

These lie roughly between Chipping Campden and Stow (or Moreton)—handy if you're connecting those towns.

▲Hidcote Manor Garden

Located northeast of Chipping Campden, this is less "on the way" to other towns than the other sights in this section—but the

THE COTSWOLDS

grounds around this manor house are still worth a look if you like gardens. Hidcote is where garden designers pioneered the notion of creating a series of outdoor "rooms," each with a unique theme (e.g., maple room, red room, and so on) and separated by a yew-tree hedge. The manor house itself is closed to the public, but you're invited to follow your nose through a clever series of small gardens that lead delightfully from one to the next. Among the best in England, Hidcote Gardens are at their fragrant peak from May through August.

Cost and Hours: £9.50; July–Aug daily 10:00–18:00; mid-March–June and Sept Sat–Wed 10:00–18:00, closed Thu–Fri; Oct Sat–Wed 10:00–17:00, closed Thu–Fri; last entry one hour before closing; closed Nov–mid-March except Nov–Christmas Sat–Sun 12:00–15:00; tearoom, restaurant, 4 miles northeast of Chipping Campden—roughly toward Ilmington, tel. 01386/438-333, www.nationaltrust.org.uk/hidcote.

▲Broad Campden, Blockley, and Bourton-on-the-Hill

This trio of pleasant villages lines up along an off-the-beaten-path road between Chipping Campden and Moreton or Stow. **Broad Campden,** just on the outskirts of Chipping Campden, has some of the cutest thatched-roof houses I've seen. **Blockley,** nestled higher in the picturesque hills, is a popular setting for films. The same road continues on to **Bourton-on-the-Hill** (pictured), with fine views looking down into a valley and an excellent gastropub (Horse and Groom, described on page 352). All three of these towns

are connected to Chipping Campden by bus #22 (#21 goes only to Bourton and Blockley), or you can walk (easy to Broad Campden, more challenging to the other two—see page 328).

THE COTSWOLDS

Stow-on-the-Wold

Located 10 miles south of Chipping Campden, Stow-on-the-Wold—with a name that means "meeting place on the uplands"—

is the highest point of the Cotswolds. Despite its crowds, it retains its charm, and it merits ▲▲. Most of the tourists are day-trippers, so nights—even in the peak of summer—are peaceful. Stow has no real sights other than the town itself, some good pubs, antiques stores, and cute shops draped seductively around a big town square. Visit the church, with its evocative old door guarded by ancient yew trees and the tombs of wool tycoons. A visit to Stow is not complete until you've locked your partner in the stocks on the village green.

Orientation to Stow-on-the-Wold

(area code: 01451)

Tourist Information

Stow's TI, an independent business called Go Stow, is on a little alley right between the main street and Market Square. Get the handy little £0.50 walking-tour brochure called *Town Trail* and the free monthly *Cotswold Events* guide (Mon–Sat 10:00–17:00, Sun 11:00–16:00—except Oct–April until 16:30, 12 Talbot Court, tel. 01451/870-150, www.go-stow.co.uk).

At the TI, you can rent an **audioguide** town tour (£8, £12/2 people). You'll borrow an iPod Shuffle with the tour, and follow it to a dozen or so points around town for 80 minutes. While well-produced and easy to follow, there's not a lot of substance beyond my self-guided walk.

Helpful Hints

Internet Access: Try the erratically open **library** in St. Edwards Hall on the main square (closed Sun–Mon and Thu, tel. 01451/830-352), or the **youth hostel** (open long hours daily).

Taxi: See "Getting Around the Cotswolds—By Taxi" (page 325).

Parking: Park anywhere on Market Square free for two hours, or overnight between 16:00 and 11:00 (free 18:00–9:00 plus any 2 hours—they note your license, so you can't just move

THE COTSWOLDS

to another spot; £50 tickets for offenders). There's a pay-and-display lot for longer stays at the bottom of town (toward the Oddingtons), and a free long-stay lot 400 yards north of the town square at the Tesco supermarket (follow the signs).

Self-Guided Walk

Welcome to Stow-on-the-Wold

This little four-stop walk covers about 500 yards and takes about 45 minutes.

Start at the **Stocks on the Market Square.** Imagine this village during the time when people were publicly ridiculed here as

a punishment. Stow was born in pre-Roman times; it's where three trade routes crossed at a high point in the region (altitude: 800 feet). This square was the site of an Iron Age fort, and then a Roman garrison town. This main square hosted an international fair starting in 1107, and people came from as far away as Italy

for the wool fleeces. This grand square was a vast, grassy expanse. Picture it in the Middle Ages (before the buildings in the center were added): a public commons and grazing ground, paths worn through the grass, and no well. Until the late 1800s, Stow had no running water; women fetched water from the "Roman Well" a quarter-mile away.

With as many as 20,000 sheep sold in a single day, this square was a thriving scene. And Stow was filled with inns and pubs to keep everyone housed, fed, and watered. A thin skin of topsoil covers the Cotswold limestone, from which these buildings were made. The **Stow Lodge** (next to the church) lies a little

lower than the church; the lodge sits on the spot where locals quarried stones for the church. That building, originally the rectory, is now a hotel. The church (where we'll end this little walk) is made of Cotswold stone, and marks the summit of the hill upon which the town was built. The stocks are a great photo op (lock dad up for a great family Christmas card).

• *Walk past the youth hostel and White Hart inn to the market, and cross to the other part of the square. Notice how locals seem to be a part of a tight-knit little community.*

For 500 years, the **Market Cross** stood

Stow-on-the-Wold

TO MORETON-IN-MARSH, STRATFORD-UPON-AVON, WARWICK

TO BROADWAY & CHIPPING CAMPDEN

A-429

A-424

B-4077

TO UPPER SWELL, FORD & STANWAY

TESCO SUPERMKT

P Free

PATH TO BROADWELL

NOT TO SCALE

Bus Stop

High St.

PARSON'S CORNER

FOSSE WAY

WC

START

Stocks

THE SQUARE

⓫

❶

❸

❾

⓯

P PARKING
SELF-GUIDED WALK

N

ELL LANE

CHURCH ✚

TO LOWER SWELL

POST

B-4068

❼

CHURCH ST.

⓭   ⓮   ❷

⓬

DIGBETH ST.

SHEEP ST.

ℹ "GO STOW"

❻

FLEECE ALLEY

BACK WALLS

A-429

DCH

TO
UPPER & LOWER ODDINGTON

PARK ST.

❹

❺

❽

WC

P

Pay & Display

TO
❿

TO BOURTON-ON-THE-WATER & THE SLAUGHTERS

❶ The Stow Lodge Hotel & Rest.
❷ The Kings Arms Hotel & Pub; Co-op Grocery
❸ The Old Stocks Hotel & Rest.
❹ Number Nine B&B; Park Street Eateries
❺ Cross Keys Cottage; Chipping House B&B
❻ The Pound B&B
❼ West Deyne B&B

❽ Tall Trees B&B
❾ Youth Hostel & Café
❿ To Little Broom B&B
⓫ The Queen's Head Pub
⓬ The Talbot Restaurant
⓭ The Coffee House
⓮ Market Cross
⓯ St. Edwards Hall & Library (Internet)

THE COTSWOLDS

in the market reminding all Christian merchants to "trade fairly under the sight of God." Notice the stubs of the iron fence in the concrete base—a reminder of how countless wrought-iron fences were cut down and given to the government to be melted down during World War II. (Recently, it's been disclosed that all that iron ended up in junk heaps—frantic patriotism just wasted.) The plaque on the cross honors the Lord of the Manor, who donated money back to his tenants, allowing the town to finally finance running water in 1878.

Scan the square for a tipsy shop that locals call the "wonky house" (next to The Kings Arms). Because it lists (tilts) so severely, it's a listed building—the facade is protected (but the interior is modern and level). The Kings Arms, with its great gables and scary chimney, was once where travelers parked their horses before spending the night. In the 1600s, this was considered the premium "posting house" between London and Birmingham. Today, the Kings Arms cooks up pub grub and rents rooms upstairs.

During the English Civil War, which pitted Parliamentarians against Royalists, Stow-on-the-Wold remained staunchly loyal to the king. (Charles I is said to have eaten at the Kings Arms before a great battle.) Because of its allegiance, the town has an abundance of pubs with royal names (King's This and Queen's That).

The stately building in the center of the square with the wooden steeple is **St. Edwards Hall.** Back in the 1870s, a bank couldn't locate the owner of an account containing a small fortune, so it donated the funds to the town to build this civic center. It serves as a city hall, library, and meeting place. When it's open for some local event, you can wander around upstairs to see the largest collection of Civil War portrait paintings in England.

• *Walk past The Kings Arms down Digbeth Street to the little triangular park located in front of the Methodist Church and across from the Royalist Hotel. This hotel—along with about 20 others—claims to be the oldest in England, dating from 947.*

Just beyond the small grassy triangle with benches was the place where locals gathered for bloody cockfights and bearbaiting (watching packs of hungry dogs tear at bears). Today this is where—twice a year, in May and October—the Stow Horse Fair attracts nomadic Roma (Gypsies) and Irish Travellers from far and wide. They congregate down the street on the Maugersbury Road. Locals paint a colorful picture of the Roma, Travellers, and horses inundating the town. The young women dress up because the fair also functions as a marriage market.

• *Hook right and hike up the wide street.*

As you head up **Sheep Street,** you'll pass a boutique-filled former brewery yard (on the left). Notice its fancy street-front office, with a striking flint facade. Sheep Street was originally not a street, but a staging place for medieval sheep markets. The sheep would be gathered here, then paraded into the Market Square down narrow alleys—just wide enough for a single file of sheep to walk down, making it easier to count them. You'll see several of these so-called "fleece alleys" as you walk up the street.

• *Just past a fine antique bookstore (Wychwood Books), turn right onto*

Church Street, which leads past the best coffee shop in town (The Coffee House), and find the church.

Before entering the **church,** circle it. On the back side, a door is flanked by two ancient yew trees. While many view it as the Christian "Behold, I stand at the door and knock" door, J. R. R. Tolkien fans see something quite different. Tolkien hiked the Cotswolds, and had a passion for sketching evocative trees such as this. *Lord of the Rings* enthusiasts are convinced this must be the inspiration for the door into Moria.

While the church (open daily—apart from services—9:00–18:00) dates from Saxon times, today's structure is from the 15th century. Its history is played up in leaflets and plaques just inside the door. The floor is paved with the tombs of big shots who made their money from wool and are still boastful in death. (Find the tombs crowned with the bales of wool.) Most of the windows are Victorian (19th-century), but the two sets high up in the clerestory are from the dreamier Pre-Raphaelite school (c. 1920).

On the right wall as you approach the altar, a monument remembers the many boys from this small town who were lost in World War I (50 out of a population of 2,000). There were far fewer in World War II. The biscuit-shaped plaque (to the left) remembers an admiral from Stow who lost four sons defending the realm. It's sliced from an ancient fluted column (which locals believe is from Ephesus, Turkey).

During the English Civil War (1615), the church was ransacked, and more than 1,000 soldiers were imprisoned here. The tombstone in front of the altar remembers the Royalist Captain Keyt. His long hair, lace, and sash indicate he was a "cavalier," and true-blue to the king (Cromwellians were called "round heads"—named for their short hair). Study the crude provincial art—childlike skulls and (in the upper corners) symbols of his service to the king (armor, weapons).

Finally, don't miss the kneelers tucked in the pews. These are made by a committed band of women known as "the Kneeler Group." They meet most Tuesday mornings (except sometimes in summer) at 10:30 in the Church Room to needlepoint, sip coffee, and enjoy a good chat. (The vicar assured me that any tourist wanting to join them would be more than welcome. The help would be appreciated and the company would be excellent.)

Hiking from Stow

Stow/Lower Slaughter/Bourton Day Hike

Stow is made-to-order for day hikes. The most popular is the downhill, four-mile stroll to Lower Slaughter, then on to Bourton-on-the-Water. It's a two-hour walk if you don't stop. Allow about three hours if you dawdle. From Bourton-on-the-Water, a bus can bring you back to Stow. Any B&B or hotel can loan you a map for this hike. Note that these three towns are described in more detail starting on page 354.

Leaving Stow, walk through the cemetery and down the big A429 road for about 200 yards, then cross the road and catch the well-marked trail. Follow it for a delightful hour across farms, over romantic gates, and past Gainsborough-painting vistas. You'll enjoy an intimate backyard look at local farm life. Although it seems like you might lose the trail, tiny signs keep you on target. Finally, passing a cricket pitch, you reach **Lower Slaughter,** with its fine church and a mill creek leading up to its mill.

Hiking from Lower Slaughter up to **Upper Slaughter** is a worthwhile one-mile, 15-minute detour each way, if you have the time and energy.

From Lower Slaughter, it's a less-scenic 15-minute walk to the bigger town of **Bourton-on-the Water.** Leave Lower Slaughter along its mill creek, then follow a bridle path back to A429 and into Bourton. Walking into Bourton, you'll pass the bus stop for the ride back to Stow (buses #801 or #855 depart roughly hourly Mon-Sat, only 3/day Sun, 10-minute ride, £1.30).

Sleeping in Stow

(£1 = about $1.60, country code: 44, area code: 01451)

$$$ The Stow Lodge Hotel fills the historic church rectory with lots of old English charm. Facing the town square, with its own sprawling and peaceful garden, this lavish old place offers 21 large, thoughtfully appointed rooms with soft beds, stately public spaces, and a cushy-chair lounge (slippery rates but generally Db-£120, £10 extra on Sat, cheaper Oct–April, closed Jan, pay Internet access and free Wi-Fi, free off-street parking, The Square, tel. 01451/830-485, fax 01451/831-671, www.stowlodge.com, enquiries@stowlodge.com, helpful Hartley family).

$$$ The Kings Arms, with nine rooms above a pub, manages to keep its historic Cotswolds character while still feeling fresh and modern in all the right ways (Sb-£60, Db-£100, steep stairs, three "cottages" out back, free Wi-Fi, free off-street parking, Market Square, tel. 01451/830-364, www.kingsarmsstow.co.uk, info@kingsarmsstow.co.uk, Lucinda and Richard).

$$$ The Old Stocks Hotel, facing the town square, is a good value, even though the building itself is classier than its 18 big, simply furnished rooms. It's friendly and family-run, yet professional as can be. With man-killer beams and all beds equipped with footboards, it's a challenge for anyone over six feet tall (Sb-£45, standard Db-£90, refurbished "superior" Db-£110, Tb-£120, each room £10 extra on Sat, family deals, ground-floor room, free Wi-Fi in some rooms, attached bar and restaurant, garden patio, free off-street parking, The Square, tel. 01451/830-666, fax 01451/870-014, www.oldstockshotel.co.uk, info@oldstockshotel .co.uk, Allen family).

$$ Number Nine has three large, bright, recently refurbished, and tastefully decorated rooms. This 200-year-old home comes with watch-your-head beamed ceilings and old wooden doors (Sb-£45-55, Db-£60-75, free Internet access and Wi-Fi, 9 Park Street, tel. 01451/870-333, mobile 07779-006-539, www.number-nine .info, enquiries@number-nine.info, James and Carol Brown).

$$ Cross Keys Cottage offers four smallish but smartly updated rooms with bright floral decor and modern bathrooms. Kindly Margaret and Roger Welton take care of their guests in this 350-year-old beamed cottage (Sb-£55-65, Db-£65-75, cash discount if you book direct, free Wi-Fi, Park Street, tel. & fax 01451/831-128, rogxmag@hotmail.com).

$ Chipping House B&B is a fine, warm old place with three rooms with modern touches and a welcoming lounge—it feels like a visit to Auntie's house (Db-£65, cash only, free Wi-Fi, Park Street, tel. 01451/831-756, chippinghouse@tesco.net, dog-lovers Merv and Carolyne Oliver).

$ The Pound is the quaint, 500-year-old, slanty, cozy, and low-beamed home of Patricia Whitehead. She offers two bright, inviting, twin-bedded rooms and a classic old fireplace lounge (D-£50-60, T-£85, cash only, downtown on Sheep Street, tel. & fax 01451/830-229, patwhitehead1@live.co.uk).

$ West Deyne B&B has two grandmotherly rooms, a garden, a fountain, and a small conservatory overlooking the countryside (D-£50-60, T-£85, cash only, a short walk across the busy road from downtown Stow on Lower Swell Road, tel. 01451/831-011, Joan Cave).

$ Tall Trees B&B, on Oddington Road at the bottom end of Stow, comes with horses and chickens on four acres of land. Run by no-nonsense Jennifer, the five contemporary rooms are in an old-style building (Sb-£40–50, Db-£60–70, price depends on size, family room-£100; she also rents out the whole place for up to 8 people—£400/3 days, £800/week; cash only, two ground-floor rooms, free Wi-Fi, free off-street parking, tel. 01451/831-296, fax 01451/870-049, www.self-cateringcotswolds.co.uk, talltreestow @aol.com).

$ *Hostel:* The **Stow-on-the-Wold Youth Hostel,** on Stow's main square, is the only hostel in the Cotswolds, with 48 beds in nine rooms. It has a friendly atmosphere and a members' kitchen (dorm bed-£18, non-members-£3 extra, includes sheets, some family rooms with private bathrooms, evening meals, pay Internet access and Wi-Fi, lockers, reserve long in advance, tel. 01451/830-497, fax 01451/870-102, www.yha.org.uk, stow@yha.org.uk, manager Rob).

Near Stow

$$ Little Broom B&B hides out in the neighboring hamlet of Maugersbury, which enjoys the peace Stow once had. It rents three cozy rooms that share a fine garden and a pool (S-£30, Sb-£45–65, D-£50, Db-£55–75, apartment Db-£75–85 for two people plus £10–15 for each extra person, cash only, pay Wi-Fi, tel. & fax 01451/830-510, www.cotswolds.info/webpage/little-broom.htm, brendarussell@hotmail.co.uk). Brenda has racehorses, and her greenhouse keeps the pool warm throughout the summer (guests welcome). It's an easy eight-minute walk from Stow: Head east on Park Street until the fork. Take the gravel road (marked *private property/no parking*) to the right of the toilet kiosk, and it'll take you to the B&B.

Eating in and near Stow

While Stow has several good dining options, consider venturing out of town for a meal. You can walk to the pub in nearby Broadwell, or—better yet—drive to one of the many enticing gastropubs in the surrounding villages (see sidebar on pages 352–353).

In Stow

These places are all within a five-minute walk of one another, either on the main square or downhill on Queen and Park streets. For dessert, consider munching a treat or fruit (there's plenty for sale at the late-hours grocery on the square) under the trees on the square's benches and watching the sky darken, the lamps come on, and visitors having their photo fun in the stocks.

Restaurants and Pubs

The Stow Lodge is the choice of the town's proper ladies. There are two parts: The formal but friendly bar serves fine pub grub (hearty £8–11 lunches and dinners, daily 12:00–14:00 & 19:00–20:30); and the restaurant serves a popular £25 three-course dinner (nightly, veggie options, good wines, just off main square, tel. 01451/830-485, Val). On a sunny day, the pub serves lunch in the well-manicured garden, where you'll feel quite aristocratic.

The Old Stocks Hotel Restaurant, which might at first glance seem like a tired and big hotel dining room, is actually a classy place to dine. With attentive service and an interesting menu, they provide tasty and well-presented food. It's good, basic pub grub at pub prices served in a fancy dining room with views of the square. In good weather, the garden out back is a hit (£8–9 lunches, £10–13 dinners, cheaper "snack" menu before 17:00, dinner served nightly 18:30–20:30, reservations recommended on weekends, tel. 01451/830-666).

The Queen's Head faces the Market Square, next to the Stow Lodge. With a classic pub vibe, it's a great place to bring your dog and watch the eccentrics while you eat pub grub and drink the local Cotswold brew, Donnington Ale (£6–7 sandwiches, £8–10 lunches, £9–13 dinners, beer garden out back, daily 12:00–14:30 & 18:30–21:00, tel. 01451/830-563, John).

The Talbot has a more stylish and contemporary feel, with creative, modern dishes (£6–8 lunches, £10–12 dinners). They serve drinks until midnight or later (meals served 12:00–14:30 & 18:30–21:00). With couches to cuddle up on and free Wi-Fi, it works hard to be a popular hangout. On Friday and Saturday evenings after 22:00, they crank up the music, making it the liveliest place in town (The Square, tel. 01451/870-934).

The Old Butchers feels like a breath of fresh air in staid old Stow. Trendy, with good food and slow, snooty service, it dishes up classic English cuisine with a French foodie flair and a passion for meat (£14–18 entrées, daily 11:00–15:30 & 18:00–21:30, open all day long Sat–Sun, 7 Park Street, reservations likely necessary, tel. 01451/831-700).

Cheaper Options and Ethnic Food

Head to the grassy triangle where Digbeth hits Sheep Street; there you'll find take-out fish-and-chips, Chinese, and Indian food. You can picnic at the triangle, or on the benches by the stocks on Market Street.

Greedy's Fish and Chips, on Park Street, is a favorite with locals for take-out. There's no seating, but they do have benches in front (£4.50 fish-and-chips, Mon–Sat 12:00–14:00 & 16:30–21:00, closed Sun, tel. 01451/870-821).

Great Country Gastropubs

These places—known for their high-quality meals and fine settings—are very popular. Arrive early or phone in a reservation. (If you show up at 20:00, it's unlikely that they'll be able to seat you for dinner if you haven't called first.) These pubs allow "well-behaved children," and are practical only for those with a car. If you have wheels, make a point to dine at one (or more) of these—no matter where you're sleeping.

Near Stow

The first two (in Oddington, about three miles from Stow) are more trendy and fresh, yet still in a traditional pub setting. The Plough (in Ford, a few miles farther away) is your jolly olde dark pub.

The Horse and Groom Village Inn in Upper Oddington is a smart place in a 16th-century inn, serving modern English and Continental food with a good wine list (32 wines by the glass) and serious beer (lunch: £7–10 sandwiches, £10–15 entrées; dinner: £14–17 main dishes; daily 12:00–14:00 & 18:30–21:00, tel. 01451/830-584).

The Fox Inn, a different Fox Inn than the one in Broadwell (see "Pub Dinner Hike from Stow"), is old but fresh and famous among locals for its quality cooking (£12–17 entrées, daily 12:00–14:00 & 18:30–22:00, garden and winter garden, in Lower Oddington, tel. 01451/870-555). They also rent three rooms (Db-£75–95, www.foxinn.net)

Jade Garden Chinese Take-Away is appreciated by locals who don't want to cook (Wed–Sun 17:00–23:00, closed Tue, Park Street, tel. 01451/870-288).

The Prince of India offers good Indian food to take out or eat in (£7–8 entrées, nightly 18:00–23:30, 5 Park Street, tel. 01451/830-099).

The Coffee House provides a nice break from the horses-and-hounds traditional cuisine found elsewhere. You can get your food to go, or eat here—there's pleasant garden seating out back (£9–10 soups, salads, and sandwiches; good coffee, Mon–Sat 9:30–17:00, Sun 10:00–16:00, Church Street, tel. 01451/870-802).

The **Youth Hostel Café** (facing the Market Square) serves drinks and meals all day and is family-friendly, with great prices and tables in the backyard garden (£5 breakfast, £6–7 dinner, tel. 01451/830-497).

The Plough Inn, in the hamlet of Ford, fills a fascinating old building, once an old coaching inn and later a courthouse. Ask the bar staff for some fun history—like what "you're barred" means. Eat from the same traditional English menu in the restaurant, bar, or garden. They are serious about both their beer and—judging by the extensive list of homemade temptations—their desserts (£11-16 meals, food served daily 12:00-14:00 & 18:00-21:00, all day long Fri–Sun and June–Aug, 4 miles from Stow on Tewkesbury Road, reservations smart, tel. 01386/584-215).

Near Moreton-in-Marsh, in Bourton-on-the-Hill

The hill-capping Bourton—about a five-minute drive (or two-mile uphill walk) above Moreton—offers sweeping views over the Cotswold countryside. Perched at the top of this steep, picturesque burg is an enticing destination pub.

Horse and Groom is a new-feeling gastropub serving delicious modern English fare in a light and spacious modern-meets-traditional interior. The service is friendly, and the place is lively (£12-19 meals, food served daily 12:00-14:00 & 19:00-21:00, until 21:30 on Fri–Sat, tel. 01386/700-413). They also rent rooms (Db-£110-160 depending on size, www.horseandgroom.info). Don't confuse this with The Horse and Groom Village Inn in Upper Oddington, near Stow (described earlier).

Even Cheaper: Small grocery stores face the main square (**Co-op,** open daily 7:00–22:00, is next to the Kings Arms), and a big **Tesco** supermarket is 400 yards north of town.

Pub Dinner Hike from Stow

From Stow, consider taking a half-hour countryside walk to the village of Broadwell, where you'll find a traditional old pub serving good basic grub in a convivial atmosphere. **The Fox Inn** serves pub dinners and draws traditional ales—including the local Donnington ales (£8-10 meals, food served Mon–Sat 11:30–14:00 & 18:30–21:00, Sun 12:00–14:00 only, outdoor tables in garden out back, on the village green, tel. 01451/870-909, Mike and Carol).

Getting There: If you walk briskly, it's just 20 minutes downhill from Stow. While the walk is not particularly scenic (it's one-third paved lane, and the rest on an arrow-straight bridle

THE COTSWOLDS

path), it is peaceful, and the exercise is a nice way to start and finish your meal. The trail is poorly marked, but it's hard to get lost: Leave Stow at Parson's Corner, continue downhill, pass the town well, follow the bridle path straight until you hit the next road, then turn right at the road and walk downhill into the village of Broadwell. You can often hitch a ride with someone from the pub back to Stow after you eat.

Near Stow-on-the-Wold

These sights are all south of Stow: Some are within walking distance (the Slaughters and Bourton-on-the-Water), and one is 20 miles away (Cirencester). The Slaughters and Bourton are tied together by the countryside walk described on page 348.

▲Lower and Upper Slaughter

"Slaughter" has nothing to do with lamb chops. It comes from the sloe tree (the one used to make sloe gin). You can reach these towns on bus #801 at the "Slaughter Pike" stop (along the main road, near the villages).

Lower Slaughter is a classic village, with ducks, a charming little church, a working water mill, and usually an artist busy at her easel somewhere. The Old Mill Museum is a folksy ensemble with a tiny museum, shop, and tea house complete with a delightful terrace overlooking the mill pond, enthusiastically run by Gerald and his daughter Laura (who just can't resist giving generous tastes of their homemade ice cream). Just behind the Old Mill, two kissing gates lead to the path that goes to nearby Upper Slaughter (a 15-minute walk or 2-minute drive away). And if you follow the mill creek downstream, a bridle path leads to Bourton-on-the-Water (described next).

In **Upper Slaughter,** walk through the yew trees (sacred in  pagan days) down a lane through the raised graveyard (a buildup of centuries of graves) to the peaceful church. In the back of the fine graveyard, the statue of a wistful woman looks over the tomb of an 18th-century rector (sculpted by his son).

If driving, the small roads from Upper Slaughter to **Ford** and **Kineton** (and the Cotswold Farm Park, described later) are some of England's most scenic. Roll your window down and joyride slowly.

▲Bourton-on-the-Water

I can't figure out whether they call this "the Venice of the Cotswolds" because of its quaint canals or its miserable crowds.

Either way, it's very pretty. This town—four miles south of Stow and a mile from Lower Slaughter—gets overrun by midday and weekend hordes. Surrounding Bourton's green are sidewalks jammed with disoriented tourists wearing nametags. If you can avoid them, it's worth a drive-through and maybe a short stop. While it can be mobbed with tour groups during the day, it's pleasantly empty in the early evening and after dark. It's conveniently connected to Stow and Moreton by buses #801 and #855.

Parking: Finding a spot here is predictably tough. Even during the busy business day, rather than park in the pay-and-display parking lot a five-minute walk from the center, drive right into town and wait for a spot on High Street just past the village green (where the road swings left, turn right to go down High Street; there's a long row of free two-hour spots in front of the Edinburgh Woolen Mills Shop, on the right).

Tourist Information: The TI is tucked across the stream a short block off the main drag, just off Victoria Street (April–Oct Mon–Fri 9:30–17:00, Sat 9:30–17:30, closed Sun, closes one hour earlier Nov–March, tel. 01451/820-211, www.bourtoninfo.com).

Sights: Bourton's attractions are tacky tourist traps, but the three listed below might be worth considering. All are on High Street in the town center. In addition to these, families also enjoy Bourton's kid-perfect **leisure centre** (big pool and sauna, 5-minute walk from town center, open daily, call for public hours, tel. 01451/824-024).

▲**Motor Museum**—Lovingly presented, this good, jumbled museum shows off a lifetime's accumulation of vintage cars, old lacquered signs, threadbare toys,

and prewar memorabilia. If you appreciate old cars, this is nirvana. Wander the car-and-driver displays, from the automobile's early days to the stylish James Bond era. Don't miss the back door (marked *village life exhibition*), which leads to old carriage houses filled with even more cars. Talk to an elderly Brit who's touring the place for some personal memories (£4.10, mid-Feb–early Dec daily 10:00–18:00, closed off-season, in the mill facing the town center, tel. 01451/821-255, www.cotswold-motor-museum.com).

Model Railway Exhibition—This exhibit of three model railway layouts is impressive only to train buffs (£2.50, June–Aug daily 11:00–17:00, Sept–May Sat–Sun only, limited Jan hours, located in the back of a hobby shop, tel. 01451/820-686, www.bourtonmodel railway.co.uk).

Model Village—This light but fun display re-creates the town on a 1:9 scale in a tiny outdoor park, and has an attached room full of tiny models showing off various bits of British domestic life (£3.50 for the park, £1 more for the model room, daily 10:00–17:45, until 15:45 in winter, tel. 01451/820-467).

Walk to the Slaughters—From Bourton-on-the-Water, it's about a 30-minute walk (or a two-minute drive) to Upper and Lower Slaughter (described previously); taken together, they make for an easy two-hour round-trip walk from Bourton. (You could also walk from Stow through the Slaughters to Bourton—hike described on page 348.)

▲Cotswold Farm Park

Here's a delight for young and old alike. This park is the private venture of the Henson family, who are passionate about preserving rare and endangered breeds of local animals. While it feels like a kids' zone (with all the family-friendly facilities you can imagine), it's actually a fascinating chance for anyone to get up close and (very) personal with piles of mostly cute animals, including the sheep that made this region famous—the big and woolly Cotswold Lion. A busy schedule of demonstrations gives you a look at local farm life—check the events board as you enter for times for the milking, "farm safari," shearing, and well-done "sheep show." Join the included, 20-minute tractor ride, with recorded narration by the founder's son, Adam Henson, filled with the family passion for the farm's mission. Buy a bag of seed (£0.50) upon arrival, or have your map eaten by munchy goats as I did. Tykes love the little tractor rides, maze, and zip line, but the "touch barn" is where it's at for little kids.

Cost and Hours: £7, kids-£5.65, family ticket for 2 adults and 2 kids-£22.75, daily mid-March–early Sept 10:30–17:00, last entry 30 minutes before closing, closed off-season, good £2 guidebook, decent cafeteria, tel. 01451/850-307, www.cotswoldfarmpark.co.uk.

Getting There: It's well-signposted about halfway between Stow and Stanway (15 minutes from either) just off Tewkesbury Road (B4077, toward Ford from Stow). A visit here makes sense if you're traveling from Stow to Chipping Campden.

Northleach

One of the "untouched and untouristed" Cotswold villages, Northleach is worth a short stop. The town's impressive main

square and church attest to its position as a major wool center in the Middle Ages. Park in the square called The Green or the adjoining Market Place. The town has no TI, but you can pick up a free town map and visitor guide at Keith Haring's World of Mechanical Music (described next) or at the post office on the Market Place (Mon–Fri 9:00–13:00 & 14:00–17:30, Sat 9:00–12:30, closed Sun) and at other nearby shops. Information: www.northleach.gov.uk.

Getting There: Northleach is nine miles south of Stow, down A429. Bus #855 connects it to Stow and Moreton (toll tel. 0871-200-2233, www.traveline.org.uk).

▲**Keith Harding's World of Mechanical Music**—In 1962, Keith Harding, tired of giving ad-lib "living room tours," opened this delightful little one-room place. It offers a unique opportunity to listen to 300 years of amazing self-playing musical instruments. It's run by people who are passionate about the restoration work they do on these musical marvels. The curators delight in demonstrating about 20 of the museum's machines with each hour-long tour. You'll hear Victorian music boxes and the earliest polyphones (record players) playing cylinders and then discs—all from an age when music was made mechanically, without the help of electricity. The admission fee includes an essential hour-long tour (£8, daily 10:00–17:00, last entry at 16:00, tours go constantly—join one in progress, High Street, Northleach, tel. 01451/860-181, www.mechanicalmusic.co.uk).

Church of Saints Peter and Paul—This fine Perpendicular Gothic church has been called the "cathedral of the Cotswolds." It's one of the Cotswolds' finest two "wool" churches (along with Chipping Campden's), paid for by 15th-century wool tycoons. Find the oldest tombstone. The

THE COTSWOLDS

brass plaques on the floor memorialize big shots, showing sheep and sacks of wool at their long-dead feet, and inscriptions mixing Latin and the old English.

▲Bibury

Six miles northeast of Cirencester, this village is a favorite with British picnickers fond of strolling and fishing. Bibury (BYE-bree) offers some relaxing sights, including a row of very old weavers' cottages, a trout farm, a stream teeming with fat fish and proud ducks, and a church surrounded by rosebushes, each tended by a volunteer of the parish. A protected wetlands area on the far side of the stream hosts

newts and water voles. Walk up the main street, then turn right along the old weavers' Arlington Row and back on the far side of the marsh, peeking into the rushes for wildlife.

For a closer look at the fish, cross the little bridge to the 15-acre **Trout Farm,** where you can feed them—or catch your own (£3.75 entrance fee to walk the grounds, fish food-£0.50, rod rental-£3.75, daily April–Sept 9:00–18:00, March and Oct 9:00–17:00, Nov–Feb daily 9:00–16:00, catch-your-own only available weekends daily July–Aug and March–June and Sept–Oct, tel. 01285/740-215, www.biburytroutfarm.co.uk).

Don't miss the scenic **Coln Valley drive** from A429 to Bibury through the enigmatic villages of Coln St. Dennis, Coln Rogers, Coln Powell, and Winson. Unfortunately, no buses reach Bibury.

Sleeping in Bibury: If you'd like to spend the night in tiny Bibury, consider **$$ The William Morris B&B,** named for the 19th-century designer and writer (small Db-£75, big Db-£85, £10 more Fri–Sun, cash only, 2 rooms, 200 yards from the bridge toward the church at 11 The Street, tel. 01285/740-555, www.thewilliammorris.com, info@thewilliammorris.com).

▲Cirencester

Almost 2,000 years ago, Cirencester (SIGH-ren-ses-ter) was the ancient Roman city of Corinium. It's 20 miles from Stow down A429, which was called Fosse Way in Roman times. Bus #855 connects Cirencester to Stow and Moreton. Drivers follow *town centre* signs and try to find parking right on the market square; if it's parked up, retreat to the Waterloo pay-and-display lot (a five-minute walk away).

In Cirencester, stop by the impressive **Corinium Museum** to find out why they say, "If you scratch Gloucestershire, you'll

find Rome." The museum chronologically displays well-explained artifacts from the town's rich history, with a focus on Roman times—when Corinium was the second-biggest city in the British Isles (after Londinium). You'll see column capitals and fine mosaics, before moving on to the Anglo-Saxon and Middle Ages exhibits (£4.50; April–Oct Mon–Sat 10:00–17:00, Sun 14:00–17:00; Nov–March Mon–Sat 10:00–16:00, Sun 14:00–16:00; Park Street, tel. 01285/655-611,www.cirencester.co.uk/corinium museum).

The **TI,** in the Corinium Museum shop, answers questions and sells a £0.50 town map and a £1 town walking-tour brochure (same hours as museum, tel. 01285/654-180).

Cirencester's church is the largest of the Cotswolds "wool" churches. The cutesy New Brewery Arts crafts center entertains visitors with traditional weaving and potting, workshops, an interesting gallery, and a good coffee shop. Monday and Friday are general-market days, Friday features an antiques market, and a crafts market is held on most Saturdays.

Moreton-in-Marsh

This workaday town—worth ▲—is like Stow or Chipping Campden without the touristy sugar. Rather than gift and antiques

shops, you'll find streets lined with real shops: ironmongers selling cottage nameplates and carpet shops strewn with the remarkable patterns that decorate B&B floors. A shin-kickin' traditional market of 100-plus stalls fills High Street each Tuesday, as it has for the last 400 years (8:00–16:00, handicrafts, farm produce, clothing, great people-watching, best if you go early). The Cotswolds has an economy aside from tourism, and you'll feel it here.

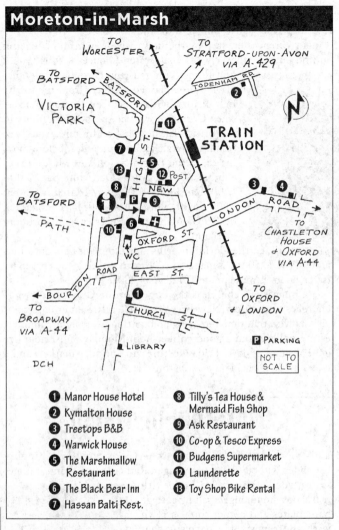

Moreton-in-Marsh

TO WORCESTER

TO STRATFORD-UPON-AVON VIA A-429

TO BATSFORD

BATSFORD

TODENHAM RD.

❷

VICTORIA PARK

N

❶

HIGH ST.

TRAIN STATION

❼

❺

❶❸

❶❷ POST

❽

NEW

❸

❹

LONDON ROAD

TO BATSFORD

PATH

P

❾

TO CHASTLETON HOUSE & OXFORD VIA A-44

❶⓪

❻

OXFORD ST.

WC

BOURTON ROAD

EAST ST.

TO OXFORD & LONDON

TO BROADWAY VIA A-44

❶

CHURCH ST.

LIBRARY

DCH

P PARKING

NOT TO SCALE

❶ Manor House Hotel
❷ Kymalton House
❸ Treetops B&B
❹ Warwick House
❺ The Marshmallow Restaurant
❻ The Black Bear Inn
❼ Hassan Balti Rest.

❽ Tilly's Tea House & Mermaid Fish Shop
❾ Ask Restaurant
❶⓪ Co-op & Tesco Express
❶❶ Budgens Supermarket
❶❷ Launderette
❶❸ Toy Shop Bike Rental

Orientation to Moreton-in-Marsh

(area code: 01608)

Moreton has a tiny, sleepy train station two blocks from High Street, lots of bus connections, and the best **TI** in the region. The TI offers a room-booking service, pay Internet access, and discounted tickets for major sights (such as Blenheim Palace). Peruse the racks of fliers, confirm rail and bus schedules, and consider the £0.50 *Town Trail* self-guided walking tour leaflet (Mon 8:45–16:00, Tue–Thu 8:45–17:15, Fri 8:45–16:45, Sat 10:00–

13:00—or until 12:30 in winter, closed Sun, good public WC, tel. 01608/650-881).

Helpful Hints

Internet Access: It's available for a price at the **TI,** and free at the erratically open **library** (down High Street where it becomes Stow Road, tel. 01608/650-780).

Baggage Storage: While there is no formal baggage storage in town, the **Black Bear Inn** (next to the TI) might let you leave bags there—especially if you buy a drink. Or you can pay £2 to leave a bag at the **launderette** (see below).

Laundry: The handy launderette is a block in front of the train station on New Road (daily 7:00–19:00, last wash at 18:00, £3.40 self-service wash, £2–3 self-service dry, or drop off Mon–Fri 8:00–11:00 for £2.50 extra and same-day service—pick up by 17:00, tel. 01608/650-888).

Bike Rental, Taxis, and Car Rental: See "Getting Around the Cotswolds" (page 320).

Parking: It's easy—anywhere on High Street is fine any time, as long as you want, for free (though there's a 2-hour limit for parking in the small lot in the middle of the street). On Tuesdays, when the market makes parking tricky, you can park at the Budgens supermarket for £3—refundable if you spend at least £5 in the store.

Hikes and Walks from Moreton-in-Marsh: As its name implies, Moreton-in-Marsh sits on a flat, boggy landscape, making it a bit less appealing for hikes; I'd bus to Chipping Campden or to Stow, both described earlier, for a better hike (this is easy, since Moreton is a transit hub). If you do have just a bit of time to kill in Moreton, consider walking a mile out to the arboretum and falconry center in **Batsford** (described later).

Sleeping in Moreton-in-Marsh

(£1 = about $1.60, country code: 44, area code: 01608)

$$$ Manor House Hotel is Moreton's big old hotel, dating from 1545 but sporting such modern amenities as toilets and electricity. Its 35 classy-for-the-Cotswolds rooms and its garden invite relaxation (Sb-£115, Db-£145, family suite-£210, £40 more for Sat night, rates are soft—often a bit less, includes breakfast, elevator, pay Wi-Fi, log fire in winter, attached restaurants, free parking, on far end of High Street away from train station, tel. 01608/650-501, fax 01608/651-481, www.cotswold-inns-hotels.co.uk, info @manorhousehotel.info).

$$ Kymalton House (KYE-mal-ton) has two bright, tastefully decorated rooms in a gracious modern house. With a pleasant garden, it's set back off of a busy street just outside the town center (Db-£70, cheaper for 3 or more nights, double beds only, cash only, closed Dec–Jan, tel. 01608/650-487, kymalton@uwclub.net, Sylvia and Doug Gould). It's a seven-minute walk from town (walk past Budgens supermarket, turn right on Todenham Road, look for house on the right). They'll happily pick up and drop off train travelers at the station.

$ **Treetops B&B** is plush, with seven spacious, attractive rooms, a sun lounge, and a three-quarter-acre backyard. Liz and Ben (the family dog) will make you feel right at home—if you meet their two-night minimum on weekends (large Db-£65, gigantic Db-£70, two wheelchair-accessible ground-floor rooms have patios, free Wi-Fi, set far back from the busy road, London Road, tel. & fax 01608/651-036, www.treetopscotswolds.co.uk, treetops1@talk21.com, Liz and Brian Dean). It's an eight-minute walk from town and the railway station (exit station, keep left, go left on bridge over train tracks, look for sign, then long driveway).

$ **Warwick House,** just down the road from Treetops, is where "half-American" Charlie Grant rents three rooms in a contemporary, casual, slightly rough-around-the-edges house. It's on a busy road, but the windows keep out most noise. Charlie will do your laundry if you stay three or more nights (Sb-£38, Db-£62, Tb-£75, 3 percent extra with credit card, no kids under age 12, healthy breakfast option, free Wi-Fi and loaner laptop, free parking, will pick up from train station, London Road, tel. 01608/650-773, www.snoozeandsizzle.com, whbandb@yahoo.com).

Eating in Moreton-in-Marsh

A stroll up and down High Street lets you survey your small-town options.

The Marshmallow is relatively upscale but affordable, with a menu that includes traditional English dishes as well as lasagna and salads (£9–11 entrées, 14 fancy teas, Sun–Mon 10:00–19:00, Tue 10:00–16:00, Wed–Sat 10:00–20:00, reservations smart, shady back garden for summer dining, tel. 01608/651-536).

The Black Bear Inn offers traditional English food. As you enter, choose between the dining room on the left or the pub on the right (£5–10 meals and daily specials, restaurant open daily 12:00–14:00 & 18:30–21:00—except no dinner on Sun, pub open daily 11:00–1:00 in the morning, tel. 01608/652-992).

Hassan Balti, with tasty Bangladeshi food, is a fine value for sit-down or take-out (£7–12 meals, daily 12:00–14:00 & 17:30–23:30, High Street, tel. 01608/650-798).

Tilly's Tea House serves fresh soups, salads, sandwiches, and pastries for lunch in a cheerful spot on High Street across from the

TI (£5–7 light meals, good cream tea-£5, Mon–Sat 9:00–16:30, closed Sun, tel. 01608/650-000).

Ask, a chain restaurant across the street, has decent pastas, pizzas, and salads, and a breezy, family-friendly atmosphere (£8–11 pizzas, daily 12:00–23:00, take-out available, tel. 01608/651-119).

Mermaid fish shop is popular for its take-out fish and tasty selection of traditional savory pies (£5 fish-and-chips, £2 pies, Mon–Sat 12:00–14:00 & 17:00–22:30, closed Sun).

Picnic: There's a small **Co-op** grocery on High Street in the town center (Mon–Sat 7:00–20:00, Sun 8:00–20:00), and a **Tesco Express** one door down (Mon–Fri 6:00–23:00, Sat–Sun 7:00–23:00). The big **Budgens** supermarket is indeed super (Mon–Sat 8:00–22:00, Sun 10:00–16:00, far end of High Street). There are picnic tables across the busy street, in pleasant Victoria Park.

Nearby: The excellent **Horse and Groom** gastropub in Bourton-on-the-Hill is a quick drive or uphill two-mile walk away (see page 352).

Moreton-in-Marsh Connections

Moreton, the only Cotswolds town with a train station, is also the best base for exploring the region by bus (see "Getting Around the Cotswolds," page 320).

From Moreton by Train to: London's Paddington Station (one-way-£27–29, round-trip after 8:15-£27, every 1–2 hours, 1.5–1.75 hours), **Bath** (hourly, 2.5–3 hours, 2–3 transfers), **Oxford** (about hourly, 40 minutes), **Ironbridge Gorge** (hourly, 2.75–3.5 hours, 2–3 transfers; arrive Telford, then catch bus or cab 7 miles to Ironbridge Gorge—see page 406). While you can reach **Stratford** by train, it's faster by bus (#21 and #22 end there, Mon–Sat about hourly, none on Sun, 1–1.25 hours). Train info: tel. 0845-748-4950, www.nationalrail.co.uk.

Near Moreton-in-Marsh

▲Chastleton House

This stately home, located about five miles southeast of Moreton-in-Marsh, was actually lived in by the same family from 1607 until 1991. It offers a rare peek into a Jacobean gentry house. (Jacobean, which comes from the Latin for "James," indicates the style

THE COTSWOLDS

from the time of King James I—the early 1600s.) Built, like most Cotswold palaces, with wool money, it gradually declined with the fortunes of its aristocratic family until, according to the last lady of the house, it was "held together by cobwebs." It came to the National Trust on the condition that they would maintain its musty Jacobean ambience. Wander on creaky floorboards, many of them original, and chat with volunteer guides stationed in each room. It's an uppity place that doesn't encourage spontaneity. The docents are proud to play on one of the best croquet teams in the region (the rules of croquet were formalized in this house in 1868). Page through the early-20th-century family photo albums in the room just off the entry.

Cost and Hours: £8.65; April–Sept Wed–Sat 13:00–17:00, closed Sun–Tue; Oct Wed–Sat 13:00–16:00, closed Sun–Tue; last entry one hour before closing; closed Nov–March; 10-minute drive southeast of Moreton, well-signposted, 5-minute hike to house from free parking lot, recorded info tel. 01494/755-560, www.nationaltrust.org.uk/chastleton.

Getting In: Only 175 visitors a day are allowed into the home (25 people every 30 minutes), and reservations are not possible—it's first-come, first served. At the busiest times, you might have to wait a bit to enter the house. Wednesday and Thursday are the quietest days, with the shortest wait times.

Batsford

This village, just a mile west of Moreton, has two side-by-side attractions that might appeal if you have a special interest or time to kill. These are also connected to Moreton by buses #21 and #22.

Cotswold Falconry Centre—Along with the Cotswolds' hunting heritage comes falconry—and this place, with dozens of specimens of eagles, falcons, owls, and other birds, gives a sample of what these deadly birds of prey can do. You can peruse the cages to see all the different birds, but there's little point in visiting unless you make it to the hour-long falconry presentation (£6.50, £11 combo-ticket with Arboretum, mid-Feb–mid-Nov daily 10:00–17:30, last entry at 17:00; flying displays at 11:30, 13:30, and 15:00, plus in summer at 16:30; Batsford Park, tel. 01386/701-043, www.cotswold-falconry.co.uk).

Batsford Arboretum—This sleepy grove, with 2,800 trees from around the world, pales in comparison to some of the Cotswolds' genteel manor gardens. But it's next door to the Falconry Centre, and handy to visit if you'd enjoy strolling through a diverse wood (£6.50, £11 combo-ticket with Falconry Centre, daily 9:00–18:00, last entry at 16:45, closed Wed in Dec–Jan, tel. 01386/701-441, www.batsarb.co.uk).

THE COTSWOLDS

Blenheim Palace

Just 30 minutes' drive from Oxford (and convenient to combine with a drive through the Cotswolds), Blenheim Palace is one of

England's best—worth ▲▲▲. Too many palaces can send you into a furniture-wax coma, but everyone should see Blenheim. The Duke of Marlborough's home—the largest in England—is still lived in, which is wonderfully obvious as you prowl through it. The 2,000-acre yard, well-designed by Lancelot "Capability" Brown, is as majestic to some as the palace itself. The view just past the outer gate as you enter is a classic. Note: Americans who pronounce the place "blen-HEIM" are the butt of jokes. It's "BLEN-em."

Cost and Hours: £18, discount tickets that save £2.50 are available at TIs in surrounding towns—including Moreton-in-Marsh and Oxford; family ticket for two adults and two kids-£48, £5 guidebook; open mid-Feb–Oct daily 10:30–17:30, last tour departs at 16:45; Nov–mid–Dec Wed–Sun 10:30–17:30; park open but palace closed Nov–mid-Dec Mon–Tue and mid-Dec–mid-Feb; tel. 01993/810-530, recorded info tel. 0800-849-6506, www.blenheimpalace.com.

Getting There: Blenheim Palace sits at the edge of the cute cobbled town of Woodstock. The train station nearest the palace (Hanborough, 1.5 miles away) has no taxi or bus service.

From **Oxford,** take bus #S3 (Mon–Sat 2/hour, less frequent on Sun, 30 minutes; bus tel. 01865/772-250, www.stagecoachbus.com). It departs from downtown Oxford at George Street (near the corner with Magdalen Street), then stops at Oxford's bus station at Gloucester Green and sometimes also at Oxford's train station (check the schedule). It stops twice near Blenheim Palace: the "Blenheim Palace Gates" stop is along the main road about a half-mile walk to the palace itself; the "Woodstock/Marlborough Arms" stop puts you right in the heart of the village of Woodstock (handy if you want to poke around town before heading to the palace; this adds just a few more minutes' walking than the other bus stop). The Woodstock gate also offers the most spectacular view of the palace and lake.

If you're coming from the **Cotswolds,** your easiest train connection is from Moreton-in-Marsh to Oxford, where you can catch the bus to Blenheim (note that bus #S3 doesn't always stop at the

THE COTSWOLDS

Oxford train station—you may have to walk five minutes to the bus station).

Drivers head for Woodstock (from the Cotswolds, follow signs for *Oxford* on A-44); the palace is well-signposted once in town, just off the main road. Buy your ticket at the gate, then drive up the long driveway to park near the palace.

Background: John Churchill, first duke of Marlborough, defeated Louis XIV's French forces at the Battle of Blenheim in 1704. This pivotal event marked a turning point in the centuries-long struggle between the English and the French, and some historians claim that if not for his victory, we'd all be speaking French today. (They're probably exaggerating, but *qui sait?*) A thankful Queen Anne rewarded Churchill by building him this nice home, perhaps the finest Baroque building in England (designed by playwright-turned-architect John Vanbrugh). Ten dukes of Marlborough later, it's as impressive as ever. (The current, 11th duke considers the would-be 12th more of an error than an heir, and what to do about him is quite an issue.) In 1874, a later John Churchill's daughter-in-law, Jennie Jerome, gave birth at Blenheim to another historic baby in that line...and named him Winston. The history continues.

● **Self-Guided Tour:** From the parking lot, stop off at the "Falstaff" info booth to pick up a free map and head through the small courtyard. You'll emerge into a grand courtyard in front of the palace's columned yellow facade. Most of the attractions are reached by going through the palace's main entry.

You'll enter into the truly great **Great Hall.** Before taking the well-organized tour, spend some time on your own in the fine **Winston Churchill Exhibition,** displaying letters, paintings, and other artifacts of the great statesman who was born here. The highlight is the bed in which Sir Winston was born in 1874 (prematurely...his mother went into labor suddenly while attending a party here).

When you've had your fill of Churchill, catch the 45-minute guided tour of the **state rooms**—the fancy halls the dukes use to impress visiting dignitaries (tours leave every 10 minutes, included with ticket, last one at 16:45). This fascinating tour lets visitors ogle some of the most sumptuous rooms in the palace, ornamented with fine porcelain, gilded ceilings, portraits of past dukes (and photos of the present duke's family), and "chaperone" sofas designed to give courting couples just enough privacy...but not too much. When the palace is really busy (most likely on Sun), they dispense with guided tours and go "free flow," allowing those with an appetite for learning to strike up conversations with docents in each room.

Enjoy the series of 10 Brussels tapestries that commemorate

military victories of the First Duke of Marlborough, including the Battle of Blenheim. After winning that pivotal conflict, he scrawled a quick note on the back of a hotel bill notifying the Queen of his victory (you'll see a replica). The tour offers insights into the quirky ways of England's fading nobility—for example, in exchange for this fine palace, the duke still pays "rent" to the Queen in the form of one ornamental flag per year (called "quit-rent standard").

The palace items come with tales of past dukes of Marlborough and their families. You'll learn about Consuelo Vanderbilt—of the New York Vanderbilts—who was forced against her will to marry into this aristocratic family. She was miserable, but dutifully produced two sons (whom she dubbed "the heir and the spare") before the marriage fell apart after 10 years.

Finish with the remarkable "long library"—with its tiers of books and stuccoed ceilings—before exiting through the chapel, near the entrance to the gardens (described below). But before taking off to explore the gardens, consider two more attractions inside the main palace.

Blenheim Palace: The Untold Story (to the left as you enter the Great Hall) is a modern, 45-minute, multimedia "visitors' experience" (runs every 10 minutes, included in your ticket). You'll travel from room to room—as doors open and close behind you—guided through 300 years of history by a maid named Grace Ridley. (If you have limited time to spend at the palace, this is skippable.)

For a more extensive visit, follow up the general tour with a 30-minute guided walk through the **private apartments** of the duke. Tours leave at the top and bottom of each hour; however, since you'll see where the duke's family actually resides today, tours are cancelled if His Grace is in his jammies (£4.50, irregular schedule but generally May–Sept daily 12:00–16:30, tickets are limited, buy from table in library or at Flagstaff info booth outside main gates, enter in corner of courtyard to left of grand palace entry).

The palace's expansive **gardens** stretch nearly as far as the eye can see in every direction. Access them from the courtyard, by going through the little door near the "Churchill Shop" (as you face the main palace entrance, it's to the right). You'll emerge into the Water Terraces; from there, you can loop around to the left, behind the palace, to see (but not enter) the Italian Garden. Or, head down to the lake to walk along the waterfront trail; going left takes you to the rose gardens and arboretum, while turning right brings you to the Grand Bridge. You can explore on your own (using the map and good signposting), or rent a £3 audioguide that outlines three different walks around the property (40–90 minutes depending on tour; rent it in the "Churchill Shop" next to the door to the gardens).

Finally, in the "stables block" (under the gateway to the right, as you face the main palace entrance) is the **"Churchill's Destiny" exhibit,** which traces the military leadership of two great men who shared that name: John, who defeated Louis XIV at the Battle of Blenheim in the 18th century, and in whose honor this palace was built; and Winston, who was born in this palace, and who won the Battle of Britain and helped defeat Hitler in the 20th century. The exhibit offers a painstaking, blow-by-blow account of each of the battles. It's remarkable that arguably two of the most important military victories in the nation's history were overseen by distant cousins—England is a small island indeed. (Winston Churchill fans can visit his tomb, just over a mile away in the Bladon town churchyard—the church is faintly visible from inside the palace.)

The final attraction is actually on the way out of the palace complex: the kid-friendly **pleasure garden,** where a lush and humid greenhouse flutters with butterflies. A kid zone includes a few second-rate games and the "world's largest symbolic hedge maze." The maze is worth a look if you haven't seen one and could use some exercise. If you have a car, you'll pass these gardens as you drive down the road toward the exit; otherwise, you can take the tiny train from the palace parking lot to the garden (2/hour).

Sleeping near Blenheim Palace, in Woodstock

(£1 = about $1.60, country code: 44, area code: 01993)

$$ Blenheim Guest House, charming and 200 years old, has six rooms in the town center. A bit musty, it's located above a tearoom literally next door to the gateway into the palace grounds (Sb-£55, Db-£65–75 depending on size, free Wi-Fi, 17 Park Street, tel. 01993/813-814, fax 01993/813-810, www.theblenheim.com, theblenheim@aol.com).

$$ The Townhouse is a refurbished 18th-century stone house where Eddie rents five plush rooms (Sb-£55, Db-£75–90 depending on size, includes breakfast, free Wi-Fi in garden, in town center at 15 High Street, tel. & fax 01993/810-843, www.woodstock-townhouse.com, info@woodstock-townhouse.com).

STRATFORD-UPON-AVON

Stratford is Shakespeare's hometown. To see or not to see? Stratford is a must for every big bus tour in England, and one of the most popular side-trips from London. English majors and actors are in seventh heaven here. Sure, it's touristy, and non-literary types might find it's much ado about nothing. But nobody back home would understand if you skipped Shakespeare's house.

Shakespeare connection aside, the town's riverside and half-timbered charm, coupled with its hardworking tourist industry, makes Stratford a fun stop. But the play's the thing to bring the Bard to life—and with the Royal Shakespeare Company (the world's best Shakespeare ensemble) finally moving back into its newly renovated home in 2011, this is sure to be a banner year for visitors. If you'll ever enjoy a Shakespeare performance, it'll be here...even if you flunked English Lit.

While you're in the area, explore Warwick, England's finest medieval castle, and stop by Coventry, a blue-collar town with a spirit that the Nazis' bombs couldn't destroy.

Planning Your Time

Stratford, Warwick, and Coventry are a made-to-order day for drivers connecting the Cotswolds with points north (such as Ironbridge Gorge or North Wales). While connections from the Cotswolds to Ironbridge Gorge are tough, Stratford, Warwick, and Coventry are well-served by public transportation.

If you're just passing through Stratford, it's worth a half-day, but to see a play, you'll need to spend the night, or drive in from the nearby Cotswolds (doable—just 30 minutes away; see previous chapter).

Warwick is England's single most spectacular castle. It's very touristy, but it's also historic and fun (worth three hours of your time). Have lunch in Warwick town. Coventry, the least important stop on a quick trip, is most interesting as a chance to see a real, struggling, Midlands industrial city (with some decent sightseeing).

If you're very speedy, you can hit all three sights on a one-day drive-through (you'll find driving tips at the end of this chapter). If you're more relaxed, see a play and stay in Stratford, then stop at Warwick and Coventry the following morning en route to your next destination.

Orientation to Stratford

(area code: 01789)

Stratford's old town is compact, with the TI and theater along the riverbank, and Shakespeare's Birthplace a few blocks inland; you can easily walk to everything except Anne Hathaway's and Mary Arden's places. The core of town is lined with half-timbered houses. The river has an idyllic yet playful feel, with a park along both banks, paddleboats, hungry swans, and a fun old crank-powered ferry.

Arrival in Stratford

By Train: It's simple: Exit straight ahead from the train station, bear right up the hill (alongside the parking lot), and you'll follow the main drag straight to the river. (For the Grove Road B&Bs, turn right at the first big intersection.) If you need to buy a picnic for your return train trip, there's a Morrison's grocery store nearby (you can see it across the tracks).

By Car: If you're sleeping in Stratford, ask your B&B for arrival and parking details (many have a few free parking spaces, but it's best to reserve ahead). If you're just here for the day, and coming from the south (i.e., the Cotswolds), cross the big bridge and pass the TI for the best parking. Veer right (following *Through Traffic, P,* and *Wark* signs), go around the block—turning right and right and right—and enter the multistory Bridgefoot garage (first hour free, £6/6 hours, £20/10–24 hours, you'll find no place easier or cheaper). The TI and City Sightseeing bus stop are a block away.

Tourist Information

The TI has moved around in recent years, but in 2011 you'll probably find it where the main street hits the river. Otherwise, ask around, or get information from your B&B (likely open daily 9:00–16:00, on Bridgefoot, tel. 01789/264-293, www.shakespeare -country.co.uk).

Helpful Hints

Name That Stratford: If you're coming by train or bus, be sure to request a ticket for "Stratford-upon-Avon," not just "Stratford." Another Stratford—also known as Stratford Langthorne, just outside London—is the location for several events in the 2012 Olympics, and is nowhere near where you're trying to go.

Festival: Every year on the weekend following Shakespeare's birthday (traditionally considered to be April 23—also the day he died), Stratford celebrates. The town hosts free events, including activities for children. In 2011, expect tours and hotels to be booked up long in advance surrounding the weekend of April 23–24.

Internet Access: Get online at **Cyber Junction** (£3.50/hour, Mon–Thu and Sat 10:30–20:00, Fri 10:30–17:00, closed Sun, 28 Greenhill Street, tel. 01789/263-400, www.thecyber junction.co.uk) or the **library,** on Henley Street just a few doors down from Shakespeare's Birthplace (£5/hour, Mon–Fri 9:00–17:30, Sat 9:30–17:00, Sun 12:00–16:00; if all computers are in use, reserve a time at the desk; tel. 01789/292-209).

Baggage Storage: Located directly behind the TI, **The Old Barn** shop stores bags—but be back to pick them up before the store closes, or you're out of luck for the night (£2/bag, Mon–Sat 10:00–17:00, Sun 10:00–16:00, tel. 01789/269-567).

Laundry: Sparklean is a 10-minute walk from the city center, or about five minutes from the Grove Road B&Bs (self-serve wash-£8.50, daily 8:00–21:00, last wash at 20:00, 74 Bull Street, tel. 01789/269-075). On weekdays, Sparklean's kindly Jane will do the wash for you for £10–12 in a few hours if you drop it off by 12:00 (if you're in a pinch, she may even be able to pick up or drop off at your B&B). **Greenhill Launderette** is more central, but also more expensive and not as friendly (self-service wash and dry-about £10–12, daily 8:00–22:00, last wash at 20:45, Greenhill Street).

Taxis: Try **007 Taxis** (tel. 01789/414-007) or the taxi stand on Woodbridge, near the intersection with High Street. To arrange for a private car and driver, contact **Platinum Cars** (£25/hour, tel. 01789/264-626, www.platinum-cars.co.uk).

Stratford-upon-Avon

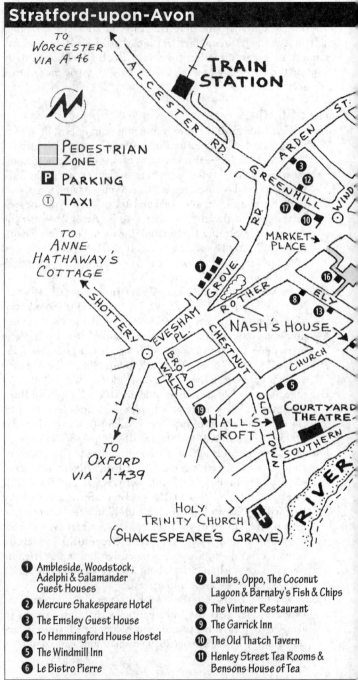

TO
WORCESTER
VIA A-46

ALCESTER RD.

TRAIN
STATION

M

PEDESTRIAN
ZONE

P PARKING

T TAXI

ARDEN

ST.

GREENHILL

❸

⓬

WIND...

TO
ANNE
HATHAWAY'S
COTTAGE

⓱

⓾

MARKET
PLACE

SHOTTERY

EVESHAM
PL.

GROVE
RD.

❶

ROTHER

⓰

❽

ELY

⓭

NASH'S HOUSE

BROAD
WALK

CHESTNUT

CHURCH

TO
OXFORD
VIA A-439

⓳

HALL'S
CROFT

OLD
TOWN

❺

COURTYARD
THEATRE

SOUTHERN

HOLY
TRINITY CHURCH
(SHAKESPEARE'S GRAVE)

RIVER

❶ Ambleside, Woodstock, Adelphi & Salamander Guest Houses
❷ Mercure Shakespeare Hotel
❸ The Emsley Guest House
❹ To Hemmingford House Hostel
❺ The Windmill Inn
❻ Le Bistro Pierre
❼ Lambs, Oppo, The Coconut Lagoon & Barnaby's Fish & Chips
❽ The Vintner Restaurant
❾ The Garrick Inn
⓾ The Old Thatch Tavern
⓫ Henley Street Tea Rooms & Bensons House of Tea

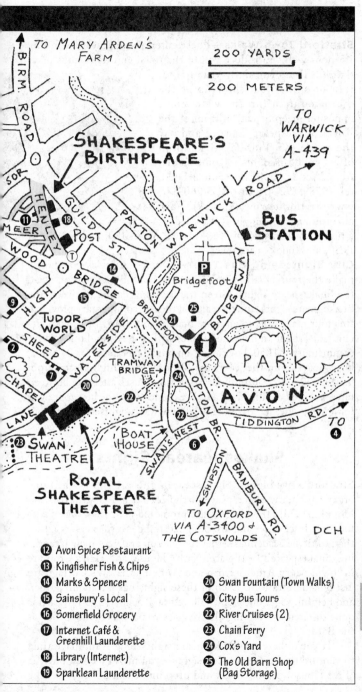

- ⑫ Avon Spice Restaurant
- ⑬ Kingfisher Fish & Chips
- ⑭ Marks & Spencer
- ⑮ Sainsbury's Local
- ⑯ Somerfield Grocery
- ⑰ Internet Café & Greenhill Launderette
- ⑱ Library (Internet)
- ⑲ Sparklean Launderette
- ⑳ Swan Fountain (Town Walks)
- ㉑ City Bus Tours
- ㉒ River Cruises (2)
- ㉓ Chain Ferry
- ㉔ Cox's Yard
- ㉕ The Old Barn Shop (Bag Storage)

Tours in Stratford

Stratford Town Walks—These entertaining, award-winning 1.5-hour walks introduce you to the town and its famous playwright. Tours run daily year-round, rain or shine. Just show up at the Swan fountain (on the waterfront, opposite Sheep Street) in front of the Royal Shakespeare Theatre and pay the guide (£5, kids-£2, ticket stub offers good discounts to some sights, Mon–Wed at 11:00, Thu–Sun at 14:00, tel. 01789/292-478 or 07855/760-377, www.stratfordtownwalk.co.uk). They also run an evening ghost walk led by

a professional magician (£6, kids-£3, Mon, Thu, and Fri–Sat at 19:30, must book in advance).

City Sightseeing Bus Tours—Open-top buses constantly make the rounds, allowing visitors to hop on and hop off at all the Shakespeare sights. Given the far-flung nature of two of the Shakespeare sights, and the value of the fun commentary provided, this tour makes the town more manageable. The full 12-stop circuit takes about an hour, and comes with a steady and informative commentary (£11.50, buy tickets on bus, ticket good for 24 hours, buses leave from the TI every 20 minutes in high season from 9:30–17:00, every 30 minutes off-season; buses alternate between tape-recorded commentary and live guides—for the best tour, wait for a live guide; tel. 01789/412-680, www.citysightseeing-stratford.com).

Shakespearean Sights

Stratford's five biggest Shakespeare sights are run by the same organization, the Shakespeare Birthplace Trust (www.shakespeare.org.uk). While these sights are promoted as if they were tacky tourist attractions—and are designed to be crowd-pleasers rather than to tickle academics—they're well-run and genuinely interesting. Shakespeare's Birthplace, Nash's House, and Hall's Croft are in town; Mary Arden's Farm and Anne Hathaway's Cottage are just outside Stratford. Each of these sights has a tranquil garden and helpful, eager docents who love to tell a story; and yet, each is quite different, so visiting all five gives you a well-rounded look at the Bard.

If you're here for Shakespeare sightseeing—and have time to venture to the countryside sights—you might as well buy the "Five House" combo-ticket and drop into them all. If your time is more limited, visit only Shakespeare's Birthplace, which is the most convenient to reach (right in the town center) and offers the best historical introduction to the playwright.

Combo-Tickets: Admission to the three Shakespeare Birthplace Trust sights in town requires one of two combo-tickets; no individual tickets are sold. Individual tickets are sold for the outlying sights, Anne Hathaway's Cottage (£7.50) and Mary Arden's Farm (£8.50), but make sense only if you visit just these two sights. To visit only Shakespeare's Birthplace, Hall's Croft, and Nash's House, get the £12.50 **Shakespeare Birthplace combo-ticket.** To add Anne Hathaway's Cottage and Mary Arden's Farm, get the £19 **Shakespeare Five House combo-ticket.** If you've taken a walking tour with Stratford Town Walks (described under "Tours in Stratford," earlier), show your ticket stub to get the Shakespeare Five House combo-ticket for just £12.50. Tickets are sold at participating sights, and are good for one year. Shakespeare's grave isn't covered by either combo-ticket.

Closing Times: What the Shakespeare sights list as their "closing time" is actually their last-entry time. If you show up at the closing time I've noted below, you'll still be able to get in, but will have limited time to enjoy the sight (since they start closing things down soon after).

In Stratford
▲▲Shakespeare's Birthplace
Touring this sight, you'll experience a modern multimedia exhibit before seeing Shakespeare's actual place of birth. While the birthplace itself is a bit underwhelming, the exhibit, helpful docents, and sense that Shakespeare's ghost still haunts these halls make it good introduction to the Bard.

Cost and Hours: Covered by either combo-ticket, daily April–Oct 9:00–17:00, July–Aug until 18:00, Nov–March 10:00–16:00, in town center on Henley Street, tel. 01789/204-016.

◒ Self-Guided Tour: The **"Shakespeare: Life, Love, and Legacy"** exhibit provides an entertaining and easily digestible introduction (or, for some, review) about what made the Bard so great. You'll walk through a series of four rooms, and in each one you'll watch a four-minute video clip about Shakespeare's life and career: movie clips of his works; his upbringing in Stratford and his family life; his career in London; and the impact he's had on many facets of our culture. You'll also see fancy displays (such as a mannequin Shakespeare hunched over his desk), as well as actual historic artifacts that are illuminated when they're described in the video presentation, including an original 1623 First Folio of Shakespeare's work. It would be nice to linger over the First Folio, but the presentation hustles you into the next

William Shakespeare
(1564–1616)

William Shakespeare is the greatest author in any language, period. He expanded and helped define modern English. In one fell swoop, he made the language of every-day people as important as Latin. In the process, he gave us phrases like "one fell swoop," which we quote without knowing it's Shakespeare.

William Shakespeare was born in Stratford-upon-Avon (at today's Shakespeare's Birthplace attraction, described on page 375), and married local girl Anne Hathaway at the age of 18. A few years later, he moved to London, where he spent most of his career and founded (along with his troupe) the Globe Theatre, a replica of which now sits along the Thames' South Bank (see page 116). It was in London that Shakespeare taught his play-going public about human nature, with plots that entertained both the highest and the lowest minds. His tool was an unrivaled mastery of the English language. He retired—rich and famous—back in Stratford, spending his last five years at a house called New Place (now long gone, but its foundations next to Nash's House are being excavated—see page 378).

Using borrowed plots, outrageous puns, and poetic language, Shakespeare wrote comedies (c. 1590—*Taming of the Shrew, As You Like It*), tragedies (c. 1600—*Hamlet, Othello, Macbeth, King Lear*), and fanciful combinations (c. 1610—*The Tempest*), exploring the full range of human emotions and reinventing the English language.

Perhaps as important was his insight into humanity. Think of his stock of great characters and great lines: Hamlet ("To be or not to be, that is the question"), Othello and his jealousy ("It is the green-eyed monster"), ambitious Mark Antony ("Friends,

room after just a short glance.

Leaving the exhibit, you'll walk through the garden and to the **birthplace,** a half-timbered Elizabethan building where young William grew up. I find the old house a bit disappointing, as if millions of visitors have rubbed it clean of anything authentic. It was restored in the 1800s, and, while the furnishings seem tacky and modern, they're supposed to be true

Romans, countrymen, lend me your ears"), rowdy Falstaff ("The better part of valor is discretion"), and the star-crossed lovers Romeo and Juliet ("But soft, what light through yonder window breaks"). Shakespeare probed the psychology of human beings 300 years before Freud. Even today, his characters strike a familiar chord.

Shakespeare wrote his plays to be performed, not read. He published a few, but as his reputation grew, unauthorized "bootleg" versions began to circulate. Some of these were written by actors who were trying (with faulty memories) to re-create plays they had appeared in years before. It wasn't until seven years after his death, in 1623, that a complete collection of Shakespeare's plays was published, commonly known as the First Folio. Of the 700 printed, about 150 survive. (Most are in the US, but three are in Stratford.) Western literature owes much to this folio, which collects 36 of the 37 known Shakespeare's plays (*Pericles* missed out). It came with an engraving of the only portrait from living memory of Shakespeare, and likely the most accurate depiction of the great playwright.

Little is known about Shakespeare the man. The scope of his brilliant work, his humble beginnings, and the fact that no original Shakespeare manuscripts survive raise a few scholarly eyebrows. Some scholars have wondered if maybe Shakespeare had help on several of his plays. After all, they reasoned, how could a journeyman actor, with little education, have written so many masterpieces? And he was surrounded by other great writers, such as his friend and fellow poet, Ben Jonson. Most modern scholars, though, agree that Shakespeare did indeed write the plays and sonnets attributed to him.

to 1575, when William was 11. To liven up the otherwise dead-feeling house, chat up the well-versed attendants posted here and there, eager to answer your questions. You'll be greeted by a costumed guide who offers an introductory talk, then set free to explore on your own. Shakespeare's father, John—who came from humble beginnings, but bettered himself by pursuing a career in glove-making (you'll see the window where he sold them to customers on the street)—provided his family with a comfortable, upper-middle-class existence. The guest bed in the parlor was a major status symbol: They must have been rich to afford such a nice bed that wasn't even used every day. This is also the house where Shakespeare and his bride, Anne Hathaway, began their married life together. Upstairs you'll see the rooms where young Will, his siblings, and his parents slept. After Shakespeare's father died and William inherited the building, the thrifty playwright converted it into a pub to make a little money.

You'll exit into the fine **garden.** The ugly modern building in the middle of the complex sometimes hosts temporary exhibits.

If you hear a commotion in the garden, it's likely Shakespearean **actors,** who perform brief scenes here. Pull up a bench and listen, imagining the playwright as a young boy stretching his imagination in this very place.

Nash's House—Nash was the first husband of Shakespeare's granddaughter...not exactly a close connection. However, this house is next to the garden that was once the site of New Place, the house where Shakespeare retired. Archaeologists have recently been excavating the remains of New Place, and an engaging, kid-friendly temporary exhibit (called "Dig for Shakespeare") has filled the otherwise dull parlor of Nash's House. Even better, you might be able to walk around the

garden, watch the archaeologists at work, and (sometimes) lend a hand with the excavation and cleaning of the artifacts. Because Shakespeare is, in many ways, still shrouded in mystery, this work is important to learn about his lifestyle. This opportunity will only last as long as the excavation does, so the house might be back to its boring old self for your visit (covered by either combo-ticket, daily April–Oct 10:00–17:00, Nov–March 11:00–16:00, Chapel Street, tel. 01789/292-325).

Hall's Croft—This former home of Shakespeare's daughter, Susanna, is in the Stratford town center. A fine old Jacobean house,

it's the fanciest of the group. Since she married a doctor, the exhibits here are focused on 17th-century medicine. If you have time to spare and one of the combo-tickets, it's worth a quick pop-in. To make the exhibits interesting, ask the docent for the 15- to 20-minute introduction, which helps bring the plague—and some of the bizarre remedies of the time—to life (covered by either combo-ticket, same hours as Nash's House, on-site tearoom, between Church Street and the

Stratford Thanks America

Residents of Stratford are thankful for the many contributions Americans have made to their city and its heritage. Along with pumping up the economy day in and day out with tourist visits, Americans paid for half the rebuilding of the Royal Shakespeare Theatre after it burned down in 1926. The Swan Theatre renovation was funded entirely by American aid. Harvard University inherited—you guessed it—the Harvard House, and it maintains the house today. London's much-loved theater, Shakespeare's Globe, was the dream (and gift) of an American. And there's even an odd but prominent "American Fountain" overlooking Stratford's market square on Rother Street, which was given in 1887 to celebrate the Golden Jubilee of the rule of Queen Victoria.

river on Old Town Street, tel. 01789/292-107).

Shakespeare's Grave—To see his final resting place, head to the riverside Holy Trinity Church. Shakespeare was a rector for this church when he died. While the church is surrounded by an evocative graveyard, the Bard is entombed in a place of honor, right in front of the altar inside (£1.50, not covered by either combo-ticket, free to view for churchgoers, April–Sept Mon–Sat 8:30–17:30, Sun 12:30–17:00, Oct–March until 17:00 or 16:00, 10-minute walk past  the theater—see its graceful spire as you gaze down the river, tel. 01789/266-316, www.stratford-upon-avon.org). The church marks the ninth-century birthplace of the town, which was once a religious settlement.

Just Outside Stratford

To reach either of these sights, it's best to drive or take the hop-on, hop-off bus tour (see "Tours in Stratford," earlier). Both sights are well-signposted (with brown signs) from the major streets and ring roads around Stratford. If driving between the sights, ask for directions at the sight you're leaving.

▲▲**Mary Arden's Farm**—Along with Shakespeare's Birthplace, this is my favorite of the Shakespearean sights. Famous as the girlhood home of William's mom, this homestead is in Wilmcote (about three miles from Stratford). Built around two historic farmhouses, it's an open-air folk museum depicting 16th-century farm life...which happens to have ties to Shakespeare. The Bard is basically an afterthought here.

The museum hosts many special **events,** including the falconry show described below. The day's events are listed on a chalkboard by the entry, or you can call ahead to find out what's on. There are always plenty of activities to engage kids: It's an active, hands-on place.

Follow the Tudor roses from building to building, through farmhouses with good displays about farm life. Throughout the complex, you'll see period interpreters in Tudor costumes. They'll likely be going through the day's chores as people back then would have done—activities such as milking the sheep and cutting wood to do repairs on the house. They're there to answer questions and provide fun, gossipy insight into what life was like at the time.

The first building, **Palmer's farm** (mistaken for Mary Arden's home for hundreds of years, and correctly identified in 2000), is furnished as it would have been in Shakespeare's day.

Mary Arden actually lived in the neighboring **farmhouse,** seemingly less impressive and covered in brick facade. Dorothy Holmes, who lived here until 1979, left it as a 1920s time warp, and that's just what you'll see today.

Of the many events here, the most enjoyable is the **falconry demonstration** with lots of mean-footed birds (only on weekends and local school holidays—including July–Aug; usually at 11:00, 13:00, and 15:00). Chat with the falconer about their methods for earning

the birds' trust. The birds' hunger sets them to flight (a round-trip earns the bird a bit of food; the birds fly when hungry—but don't have the energy if they're *too* hungry). Like Katherine, the wife described as "my falcon" in *The Taming of the Shrew*, these birds are tamed and trained with food as a reward. If things are slow, ask if you can feed one.

Cost and Hours: £8.50 or covered by £19 combo-ticket, daily April–Oct 10:00–17:00, visitors must leave by 17:30, likely closed Nov–March, tel. 01789/293-455.

Getting There: The most convenient way to get here is by car (free parking) or the hop-on, hop-off bus tour, but it's also possible to reach by train. The Wilmcote train station is directly across the street from Mary Arden's House (£2 round-trip fare, one stop from Stratford-upon-Avon on Birmingham-bound train, 5-minute trip, train runs about every hour, call London Midland to confirm departure time—tel. 0844-811-0133, www.london midland.com).

▲**Anne Hathaway's Cottage**—Located 1.5 miles out of Stratford (in Shottery), this home is a 12-room farmhouse where the Bard's

wife grew up. William courted Anne here—she was 26, he was only 18—and his tactics proved successful. (Maybe a little too much, as she was several months pregnant at their wedding.) They were married for 34 years, until his death in 1616 at age 52. The Hathaway family lived here for 400 years, until 1911, and much of the family's 92-acre farm remains part of the sight.

After buying your ticket, turn left and head down through the garden to the thatch-roofed **cottage,** which looks cute enough to eat. The house offers an intimate peek at life in Shakespeare's day. In some ways, it even feels more authentic than his birthplace, and it's fun to imagine the writer of some of the world's greatest romances wooing his favorite girl right here during his formative years. Docents are posted in the first and last rooms to provide meaning and answer questions; while most tourists just stampede through, you'll have a more informative visit if you pause to listen to their commentary. (If the place shakes, a tourist has thunked his or her head on the low beams.)

Maybe even more interesting than the cottage are the **gardens,** which have several parts (including a prizewinning "traditional cottage garden"). If you head uphill (to the right from the entry), you'll find a "Woodland Walk," along with a fun sculpture garden littered with modern interpretations of Shakespearean characters (such as Falstaff's mead gut, and a great photo-op statue of the British Isles sliced out of steel). In the middle is a yew maze (planted only in 2001, so not yet a challenge). You might also find rotating exhibits, generally on a gardening theme.

Cost and Hours: £7.50 or covered by £19 combo-ticket, daily April–Oct 9:00–17:00, Nov–March 10:00–16:00, tel. 01789/ 292-100.

Getting There: It's a 30-minute walk, a stop on the hop-on, hop-off tour bus, or a quick taxi ride from Stratford; well-signposted for drivers entering Stratford from any direction, easy £1 parking.

▲▲▲Plays Performed by the Royal Shakespeare Company

The Royal Shakespeare Company (RSC), undoubtedly the best Shakespeare company on earth, performs year-round in Stratford and in London (see page 140). Seeing a play here in the Bard's birthplace is a must for Shakespeare fans, and a memorable experience for anybody. Between its excellent acting and remarkable staging, the RSC makes Shakespeare as accessible and enjoyable as it gets.

The RSC expects to have a banner year in 2011, as their completely refurbished flagship theater is finally re-opening after a three-year renovation. In addition to the main Royal Shakespeare Theatre, the smaller, attached Swan Theatre is also coming out of mothballs. Meanwhile, the Courtyard Theatre—which filled in for the other two theaters while they were out of commission—will continue to operate at some capacity, likely staging mostly non-Shakespearean plays. All told, Stratford now has three great venues.

The Royal Shakespeare Company makes it easy to take in some theater, thanks to their very user-friendly website (www.rsc .org.uk), painless ticket-booking system, and chock-a-block schedule that fills the summer with mostly big-name Shakespeare plays (with a few more obscure titles to please the die-hard aficionados, as well).

Performances: Performances take place most days (Mon–Sat generally around 19:00 or 19:30, matinees around 13:00, sporadic Sun shows). Shows generally last three hours or more, with one intermission; for an evening show, don't count on getting home much before 23:00. There's no strict dress code—and people dress casually (nice jeans and short-sleeve shirts are fine)—but shorts are discouraged. You can buy a program for £3.50. If you're feeling bold, buy a £5 standing ticket and then slip into an open seat as the lights dim—if there's not something available during the play's first half, something might open up after intermission.

Getting Tickets: Tickets range from £5 (standing) to £45, with most around £35. Saturday evening shows—the most popular—are most expensive. You can book tickets as you like it: online (www.rsc.org.uk), by phone (toll tel. 0844-800-1110), or in person at the box office (Mon–Sat 9:30–20:00, closed Sun). You'll pay by credit card, get a confirmation number, then pick up your tickets at the theater 30 minutes before "curtain up." Because it's so easy to get tickets online or by phone, it makes absolutely no sense to pay extra to book tickets through any other source.

Tickets go on sale months in advance. Saturdays and very famous plays (such as *Romeo and Juliet* or *Hamlet*) sell out the fastest; the earlier in the week the performance is, the longer it takes to sell out (e.g., Thursdays sell out faster than Mondays). Before your trip, check the schedule on their website, and consider buying tickets if something strikes your fancy. But demand is difficult to predict, and some tickets do go unsold. On my last visit, on a sunny Friday in June, the riverbank was crawling with tourists. I stepped into the RSC on a lark to see if they had any tickets. An hour later, I was watching King Lear lose his marbles.

Even if there aren't any seats available, you can sometimes buy a returned ticket on the evening of an otherwise sold-out show. Ask for details at the box office.

Theaters

The Royal Shakespeare Theatre—The newly restored flagship theater of the RSC has an interesting past. The original theater

was built in 1879 to honor the Bard, but burned down in 1926. The big replacement building you see today (facing the riverside park) was erected in 1932. During the design phase, no actors were consulted; as a result, they built the stodgy Edwardian "picture frame"–style stage, even though the more dynamic "thrust"-style stage—which makes it easier for the audience to become engaged—is the actors' choice. (It's also closer in design to Shakespeare's Globe stage, which juts into the crowd.) The original, ill-conceived design was the reason for the recent multiyear renovation. Now, post-renovation, the theater has an updated, thrust-style stage. While the new theater is bigger, it still respects its history; for example, floorboards from the 1932 stage have been re-laid in the theater's entry foyer, so as you wait for your play, you're walking on theater history.

The Swan Theatre—Adjacent to the RSC Theatre is the smaller, Elizabethan-style Swan Theatre, a galleried playhouse that opened in 1986. Seating about 450, this venue is a much smaller space.

The Courtyard Theatre—A two-minute walk down Southern Lane from the original Royal Shakespeare Theatre, this 1,000-seat theater was expanded (and the so-called "giant rusty box" attached to its side) as a replacement venue while the Royal Shakespeare Theatre was being renovated. It was actually designed as a prototype for the main theater—a testing ground for the lights, seats, and structure of its big brother. With a dramatic thrust stage and a vertical, wrap-around seating arrangement that makes it unusually intimate for a theater of its size, the Courtyard Theatre puts you right on top of the action—literally, as the cheapest "gallery" seats literally look down onto Othello's bald spot.

Non-Shakespearean Sights

Tudor World at the Falstaff Experience—This attraction is tacky, gimmicky, and more about entertainment than educa-

tion. (And, while it's named for a Shakespeare character, the exhibit isn't about the Bard.) Filling Shrieve's House Barn with fun exhibits (mannequins and descriptions, but few real artifacts), it sweeps through Tudor history from the plague to Henry VIII's privy chamber to a replica 16th-century tavern. If you're into ghost-spotting, their nightly ghost tours may be your best shot (museum-£5, daily 10:30–17:30, last entry 30 minutes before closing; ghost tours-£7.50, daily at 18:00; Sheep Street, tel. 01789/298-070, www.falstaffexperience.co.uk).

Avon Riverfront—The River Avon is a playground of swans and canal boats. The swans have been the mascots of Stratford since 1623, when, seven years after the Bard's death, a poem in his First Folio nicknamed him "the sweet swan of Avon." Join in the bird-scene fun and buy **swan food** (£0.50) to feed swans and ducks; ask at the ice-cream stand for details. Don't feed the Canada geese, which locals disdain (they say the geese are vicious and have been messing up the eco-balance since they were imported by a king in 1665).

The **canal boats** saw their workhorse days during the short window of time between the start of the Industrial Revolution and

the establishment of the railways. Today, they're mostly pleasure boats. The boats are long and narrow, so two can pass in the slim canals. There are 2,000 miles of canals in England's Midlands, built to connect centers of industry with seaports and provide vital transportation during the early days of the Industrial Revolution. Stratford was as far inland as you could sail on natural rivers from

Bristol; it was the terminus of the man-made Birmingham Canal, built in 1816. Even today, you can motor your canal boat all the way to London from here.

For a little bit of mellow river action, rent a **rowboat** (£4/hour per person) or, for more of a challenge, pole yourself around on a Cambridge-style **punt** (canal is poleable—only 4 or 5 feet

The Look of Stratford

There's much more to Stratford than Shakespeare sights. Take time to appreciate the look of the town itself. While the main street goes back to Roman times, the key date for the city was 1196, when the king gave the town "market privileges." Stratford was shaped by its marketplace years. The market's many "departments" were located on logically named streets, whose names still remain: Sheep Street, Corn Street, and so on. Today's street plan—and even the 57' 9" width of the lots—survives from the 12th century. (Some of the modern storefronts in the town center are still that exact width.)

Starting about 1600, three great fires gutted the town, leaving very few buildings older than that era. Since those fires, tinderbox thatch roofs were prohibited—the Old Thatch Tavern on Greenhill Street is the only remaining thatch roof in town, predating the law and grandfathered in.

The town's main drag, Bridge Street, is the oldest street in town, but looks the youngest. It was built in the Regency style—a result of a rough little middle row of wattle-and-daub houses being torn down in the 1820s to double the street's width. Today's Bridge Street buildings retain that early 19th-century style: Regency.

Throughout Stratford, you'll see striking black-and-white, half-timbered buildings, as well as half-timbered structures that were partially plastered over and covered up in the 19th century. During Victorian times, the half-timbered style was considered low-class, but in the 20th century—just as tourists came, preferring the ye olde style—timbers came back into vogue, and the plaster was removed on many old buildings. But any black and white you see is likely to be modern paint. The original coloring was "biscuit yellow" and brown.

deep; same price as the rowboat and more memorable/embarrassing if you do the punting—don't pay £8/hour per person for a waterman to do the punting for you). Take a short stop on your lazy tour of the English countryside, and moor your canal boat at Stratford's Canal Basin. You can try a sleepy half-hour **river cruise** (£4.50, no commentary, Avon Boating, board boat

in Bancroft Gardens near the RSC theater or at Swan's Nest Boathouse across the Tramway Footbridge, tel. 01789/267-073, www.avon-boating.co.uk), or jump on the oldest surviving **chain ferry** (c. 1937) in Britain (£0.50), which shuttles people across the river just beyond the theater.

Cox's Yard, a riverside timber yard until the 1990s, is a rare physical remnant of the days when Stratford was an industrial port. Today, Cox's is a touristy entertainment center with pubs that have live music most nights (£5–15, schedule at tel. 01789/404-600 or www.coxsyard.co.uk).

Sleeping in Stratford

If you want to spend the night after you catch a show, options abound. Ye olde timbered hotels are scattered through the city center. Most B&Bs are a short walk away on the fringes of town, right

on the busy ring roads that route traffic away from the center. (The recommended places below generally have double-paned windows for rooms in the front, but still get some traffic noise.)

Local hoteliers expect huge demand in 2011 since the Royal Shakespeare Theatre is finally reopening: Book as far ahead as possible. In general, the weekend after Shakespeare's birthday (April 23–24 in 2011) is particularly tight, but Fridays and Saturdays are busy through the season. This town is so reliant upon the theater for its business that some B&Bs have secondary insurance covering their loss if the Royal Shakespeare Company ever stops performing in Stratford.

On Grove Road

These accommodations are at the edge of town on busy Grove Road, across from a grassy park. From here, it's about a 10-minute walk either to the town center or to the train station (opposite directions).

$$ Ambleside Guest House is run with quiet efficiency and attentiveness by owners Peter and Ruth. Each of the seven rooms has been completely renovated, including the small but tidy bathrooms. The place has a homey, airy feel, with none of the typical B&B clutter (S-£28–38, Db-£60–80, Tb-£85–115, Qb-£100–140, ground-floor rooms, free parking, free Wi-Fi, 41 Grove Road, tel. 01789/297-239, fax 01789/295-670, www.amblesideguesthouse .com, ruth@amblesideguesthouse.com—include your phone number in your request, since they like to call you back to confirm with

Sleep Code

(£1 = about $1.60, country code: 44, area code: 01789)
S = Single, **D** = Double/Twin, **T** = Triple, **Q** = Quad, **b** = bathroom,
s = shower only. Unless noted otherwise, you can assume
credit cards are accepted and breakfast is included.

To help you sort easily through these listings, I've divided
the rooms into three categories based on the price for a
standard double room with bath:

$$$ **Higher Priced**—Most rooms £90 or more.
$$ **Moderately Priced**—Most rooms between £60–90.
$ **Lower Priced**—Most rooms £60 or less.

Prices can change without notice; verify the hotel's
current rates online or by email. For other updates, see www
.ricksteves.com/update.

a personal touch).

$$ Woodstock Guest House is a friendly, frilly, family-
run, and flowery place with five comfortable rooms (Sb-£35–45,
Db-£60–80, family room-£75–120 depending on number of
people, cash only, deals for 2 or more nights, ground-floor room,
free Wi-Fi, free parking, 30 Grove Road, tel. 01789/299-881, www
.woodstock-house.co.uk, jackie@woodstock-house.co.uk, owners
Denis and bubbly Jackie).

$$ Adelphi Guest House has six rooms, two with four-poster
beds. Martin and Ellen have filled the house with antiques and
run the place with Scottish charm. For breakfast, they offer a wide
variety beyond the standard "English fry" (S-£40, Db-£75–80,
Tb-£120, 5 percent surcharge on credit cards, 10 percent discount
if you stay at least 2 nights in 2011—mention this book when you
reserve, free Wi-Fi, free parking if booked in advance, 39 Grove
Road, tel. 01789/204-469, www.adelphi-guesthouse.com, info
@adelphi-guesthouse.com).

$ Salamander Guest House, run by gregarious Frenchman
Pascal and his wife, Anna, rents seven well-priced but basic rooms
(S-£30–35, Db-£50–60, Tb-£60–75, Qb-£80–90, free Wi-Fi, free
on-site parking, 40 Grove Road, tel. & fax 01789/205-728, www
.salamanderguesthouse.co.uk, p.delin@btinternet.com).

Elsewhere in Stratford

$$$ Mercure Shakespeare Hotel, centrally located in a black-
and-white building just up the street from Nash's House, has 73
spacious and elegant rooms, each one named for a Shakespearean
play or character. Some of the rooms are old-style Elizabethan

higgledy-piggledy (with modern finishes), while others are contemporary style—note your preference when you reserve (Sb-£80, standard Db-£100, deluxe Db-£130–150, breakfast-£15/person, prices soft depending on demand, parking-£10/day, free Wi-Fi in lobby, pay Wi-Fi in rooms, Chapel Street, tel. 01789/294-997, fax 01789/415-411, www.mercure.com, h6630-re@accor.com).

$$ The Emsley Guest House holds five bright, modern rooms named after different counties in England. It's conscientiously run by Melanie and Ray Coulson, who give it a homey and inviting atmosphere (Sb-£45–50, Db-£60–80, Tb-£90–120, Q-£120–160, 5-person family room with extra bathroom-£150–200, families welcome, free Wi-Fi, free off-street parking, 5 minutes from station at 4 Arden Street, tel. 01789/299-557, www.theemsley.co.uk, mel@theemsley.co.uk).

$ *Hostel:* **Hemmingford House,** with 130 beds in 2- to 10-bed rooms, is a 10-minute bus ride from town (from £26 for non-members, includes breakfast; take bus #15, #18, or #18A two miles to Alveston; tel. 01789/297-093 or 0845-371-9661, stratford @yha.org.uk).

Eating in Stratford

Stratford's numerous eateries vie for your pre-theater business, with special hours and meal deals. (Most offer light two- and three-course menus from 17:30–19:00.) You'll find many hardworking places lined up along Sheep Street and Waterside. Unfortunately, post-theater dinners are more challenging, as most eateries close early.

The Windmill Inn serves modestly priced but elegant fare in a 17th-century inn. It combines old and new style, and—since it's a few steps beyond the heart of the tourist zone—actually attracts some locals as well. Order drinks and food at the bar, settle into a comfy chair, and wait for your meal to be served (£7–10 pub grub, daily 12:00–22:00, Church Street, tel. 01789/297-687).

Le Bistro Pierre, across the river near the boating station, is a relatively new French eatery that's been impressing Stratford residents. They have indoor or outdoor seating and slow service (£9.25 two-course lunches; £13.50 two-courses meals before 19:00, otherwise £10–13 entrées; Mon–Fri 12:00–15:00 & 17:00–22:30, Sat 12:00–16:00 & 17:00–23:00, Sun 12:30–16:00 & 18:00–22:00, Swan's Nest, Bridgefoot, tel. 01789/264-804). They also have a pub with a different menu.

The next three places, part of the same chain, line up along Sheep Street, offering trendy ambience and "modern English" cuisine, with relatively high prices and small portions (you'll pay separately for side dishes): **Lambs** is intimate, and serves meat, fish, and veggie dishes with panache. The upstairs feels dressy, under low half-timbered beams (specials before 19:00: £11.50 two-course meals, £15 three-course meals; otherwise £12–16 entrées, Mon 17:00–21:30, Tue–Sat 12:00–14:00 & 17:00–21:30, Sun 12:00–14:00 & 18:00–21:00, 12 Sheep Street, tel. 01789/292-554). **Oppo,** next door, has a less formal "bistro" ambience (£11.50 two-course meals before 19:00; otherwise £8–10 light meals, £13–15 entrées; Mon–Thu 12:00–14:00 & 17:00–21:30, Fri–Sat 12:00–14:00 & 17:00–23:00, Sun 18:00–21:00, tel. 01789/269-980). **The Vintner,** just up the street, feels even trendier than its siblings, but still with old style. They're known for their £10 burger (£7–10 light meals, £11–15 entrées, Mon–Thu 12:00–21:45, Fri–Sat 12:00–22:00, Sun 12:00–21:00, 4–5 Sheep Street, tel. 01789/297-259).

The Garrick Inn bills itself as the oldest pub in town, and comes with a cozy, dimly lit restaurant vibe. Choose between the pub or table-service section; either way, you'll dine on pricey pub grub (£8–11 dishes, daily 12:00–23:00, 25 High Street, tel. 01789/292-186).

Drinking: **The Old Thatch Tavern** is, according to natives, the best place in town for beer, including local brews from the Purity Brewery. Since the food is mediocre, come here only to drink—not to eat (daily 11:00–23:00, on Greenhill Street overlooking the market square).

Tea Room: **Henley Street Tea Rooms,** across the street from Shakespeare's Birthplace, has indoor seating plus outdoor tables right on the main pedestrian mall (£4 cream tea, £10 afternoon tea, teas available all day, daily 9:00–17:30, 40 Henley Street, tel. 01789/415-572). The same people run Bensons House of Tea & Gift Shop, just down the street (at #33).

Indian: **The Coconut Lagoon** serves tasty, spicy nouvelle South Indian cuisine and offers pre-theater specials until 19:00: a £10.50 two-course deal or £13.25 for three courses (otherwise £10–13 entrées, daily 12:00–14:30 & 17:00–23:00, 21 Sheep Street, tel. 01789/293-546). Closer to the Grove Road B&Bs, the simpler **Avon Spice** has a good reputation and lower prices (£7–11 entrées, daily 17:00–23:30, 7 Greenhill Street, tel. 01789/267-067).

Fish-and-Chips: **Barnaby's** is a greasy fast-food fish-and-chips joint near the waterfront—but it's convenient if you want to get takeout for the riverside park just across the street (£4–6 fish-and-chips, daily 11:00–20:00, at Sheep Street and Waterside). For better food, queue up with the locals at **Kingfisher** (£6–7 fish-and-chips, Mon–Sat 11:30–13:45 & 17:00–22:00, closed Sun, a long block up at 13 Ely Street, tel. 01789/292-513).

Picnics: For groceries, you'll find **Marks & Spencer** on Bridge Street (Mon–Sat 9:00–18:00, Sun 10:30–16:30, small coffee-and-sandwiches café upstairs, tel. 01789/292-430). Across the street, the **Sainsbury's Local** stays later than other supermarkets in town (daily 7:00-22:00). Nearby, **Somerfield** is in the Town Centre mall (Mon–Sat 8:00–19:00, Sun 10:00–16:00, tel. 01789/292-604). To picnic, head to the canal and riverfront park between the Royal Shakespeare Theatre and the TI. Choose a bench with views of the river or of vacation houseboats, and munch your fish-and-chips while tossing a few fries into the river to attract swans. It's a fine way to spend a midsummer night's eve.

Stratford Connections

Remember: When buying tickets or checking schedules, ask for "Stratford-upon-Avon," not just "Stratford" (which is a different town). Notice that a single train (running about every 2 hours) connects most of these destinations: Warwick, Leamington Spa (change for Coventry or Oxford), then London.

From Stratford-upon-Avon by Train to: London (every 2 hours, 2.25 hours, direct to Marylebone Station), **Warwick** (10/day, 30 minutes), **Coventry** (at least hourly, 1.75 hours, change in Leamington Spa or Birmingham), **Oxford** (every 2–3 hours, 1.25, change in Leamington Spa or Banbury). Train info: toll tel. 0845-748-4950, www.nationalrail.co.uk.

By Bus to: Cotswolds towns (bus #21 or #22, Mon–Sat about hourly, none on Sun, 35 minutes to **Chipping Campden**, 1–1.25 hours to **Moreton-in-Marsh;** also stops at Broadway, Blockley, and Bourton-on-the-Hill; Johnsons Coaches, tel. 01564/797-000, www.johnsonscoaches.co.uk), **Warwick** (hourly by bus, 20 minutes, tel. 01788/535-555, www.stagecoachbus.com), **Coventry** (hourly, 1.25 hours, tel. 01788/535-555, www.stagecoachbus.com). A direct bus runs to **Oxford** only on Sundays; otherwise, you'll change in Chipping Norton (train is better). Most intercity buses stop on Stratford's Bridge Street (a block up from the TI). For bus info that covers all the region's companies, call Traveline at toll tel. 0871-200-2233 (www.travelinemidlands.co.uk).

By Car: Driving is easy and distances are brief: **Stow-on-the-Wold** (22 miles), **Warwick** (8 miles), **Coventry** (19 miles).

Route Tips for Drivers: Stratford to Points North via Warwick and Coventry

Leaving the Bridgefoot garage in downtown Stratford (see page 370), circle to the right around the same block, but stay on "the Wark" (Warwick Road, A439). Warwick is eight miles away. The castle is just south of town on the right. (For parking advice, see page 395.) When you're trying to decide whether to stop in Coventry or not, factor in Birmingham's rush hour—try to avoid driving through that city between 14:00–20:00, if you can.

If You're Including Coventry: After touring Warwick Castle, carry on through the center of Warwick town and follow signs to Coventry (still A439, then A46). If you're stopping in Coventry, follow signs painted on the road to the *City Centre*, and then to *Cathedral Parking*. Grab a place in the high-rise parking lot. Leaving Coventry, follow signs to *Nuneaton* and *M6 North* through lots of sprawl, and you're on your way. (See below.)

If You're Skirting Coventry: Take M69 (direction: Leicester) and follow M6 as it threads through giant Birmingham.

Once You're on M6: The highway divides into a free M6 and an "M6 Toll" road (designed to help drivers cut through the Birmingham traffic chaos). Take the toll road—£5 is a small price to pay to avoid all the nasty traffic (www.m6toll.co.uk).

When battling through sprawling Birmingham, keep your sights on M6. If you're heading for any points north—Ironbridge Gorge (Telford), North Wales, Liverpool, Blackpool, or the Lakes (Kendal for the South Lake District, Keswick for the North Lake District)—just stay relentlessly on M6 (direction: North West). Each destination is clearly signed directly from M6. For specifics on getting to Ironbridge Gorge, see page 406.

Near Stratford-upon-Avon

Warwick

The pleasant town of Warwick—home to England's finest medieval castle—goes about its business almost oblivious to the busloads of tourists passing through. From the castle, a lane leads into the old town center a block away, where you'll find the **TI** (Mon–Fri 9:30–17:00, Sat–Sun 10:00–16:30, closes earlier in winter, tel. 01926/492-212, www.warwick-uk.co.uk), plenty of eateries (including the Ask restaurant chain), and several minor attractions. The TI can also sell same-day tickets to Warwick Castle; there's no discount, but it can save you time in line at the castle.

Sights in Warwick

▲▲Warwick Castle

Almost *too* groomed and organized, this theme park of a castle gives its crowds of visitors a decent value for the stiff entry fee. The cash-poor but enterprising lord hired the folks at Madame Tussauds (now part of Merlin Entertainments, which also owns the London Eye and Legoland) to wring maximum tourist dollars out

Stratford Area

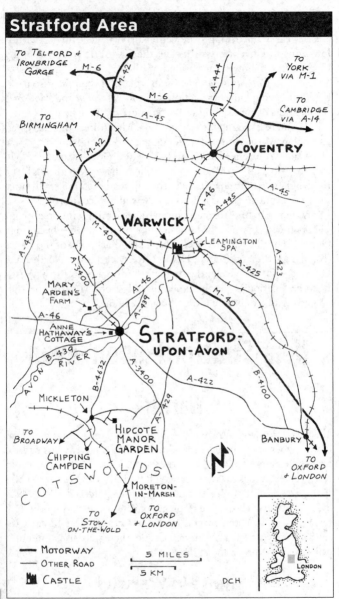

TO TELFORD &
IRONBRIDGE
GORGE

M-6

M-42

TO BIRMINGHAM

M-42

A-435

M-40

A-3400

MARY ARDEN'S FARM

A-46

ANNE HATHAWAY'S COTTAGE

B-439

AVON RIVER

B-4632

A-3400

MICKLETON

TO BROADWAY

CHIPPING CAMPDEN

C O T S W O L D S

HIDCOTE MANOR GARDEN

A-429

MORETON-IN-MARSH

TO STOW-ON-THE-WOLD

TO OXFORD & LONDON

A-46

A-439

A-45

M-6

A-444

TO YORK VIA M-1

TO CAMBRIDGE VIA A-14

COVENTRY

A-46

A-45

A-445

WARWICK

LEAMINGTON SPA

A-425

A-423

M-40

STRATFORD-UPON-AVON

A-422

B-4100

BANBURY

TO OXFORD & LONDON

N

MOTORWAY
OTHER ROAD
CASTLE

5 MILES
5 KM

DCH

London

of his castle. The greedy feel of the place is a little annoying, considering the already-steep admission. But—especially for kids—there just isn't a better medieval castle experience in England.

With a lush, green, grassy moat and fairy-tale fortifications, Warwick will entertain you from dungeon to lookout. Standing inside the castle gate, you can see the mound where the original Norman castle of 1068 stood. Under this "motte," the wooden stockade (or "bailey") defined the courtyard in the way the castle walls do today. The castle is a 14th- and 15th-century fortified shell, holding an 18th- and 19th-century royal residence, surrounded by another one of dandy "Capability" Brown's landscape jobs (like at Blenheim Palace).

Within the castle's mighty walls, there's something for every taste. The Great Hall and six lavish staterooms are the sumptuous highlights. You'll also find a Madame Tussauds–mastered re-creation of a royal weekend party—an 1898 game of statue-maker (look for a young Winston Churchill). You can ponder the weapons in the fine and educational armory, then see demonstrations outside of a trebuchet (like a catapult) and ballista (a type of giant slingshot). The "King Maker" exhibit (set in 1471, when the townsfolk are getting ready for battle) is highly promoted, but not quite as good as a

Disney ride. From the classic ramparts, the tower is a one-way, no-return, 250-step climb, offering a fun perch from which to fire your imaginary longbow. A recently restored mill and engine house come with an attendant who explains how the castle was electrified in 1894. Surrounding everything is a lush, peacock-patrolled, picnic-perfect park, complete with a Victorian rose garden. The castle grounds are often enlivened by a knight in shining armor on a horse that rotates with a merry band of musical jesters.

Cost and Hours: Steep £20 entry fee (£12 for kids under age 12, £13 for seniors), includes gardens and most castle attractions, add £6 to see the gory dungeon, discounted tickets available in advance on the castle's website and at the TI in Stratford. It's open daily April–Oct 10:00–18:00, Nov–March 10:00–17:00. Driving and parking tips are noted under "Warwick Connections—By

Car," later. For train travelers, it's a 15-minute, one-mile walk from the Warwick train station to the castle (recorded info tel. 0871-265-2000, www.warwick-castle.com).

Audioguide: Three audioguides provide descriptions of the State Apartments, the Royal Weekend Party exhibit, and A Knight's Tale (£3 apiece, or all three for £6, can be combined with online ticket purchase or rented upon arrival). The £5 guidebook

gives you nearly the same script in souvenir-booklet form. Either is worthwhile if you want to understand the various rooms. If you tour the castle without help, pick the brains of the earnest and talkative docents.

Events: During summer, special events (great for kids) are scheduled every half-hour throughout the day (jousting, longbow demo, sword fights, jester acts, and so on). Pick up the daily events flier (which also lists kiosks that sell snacks) and plan accordingly.

Eating in Warwick

The castle has three main lunch options. **The Coach House** has cafeteria fare and grungy seating (located just before the turnstiles). **The Undercroft** offers the best on-site cooked food, and has a sandwich buffet line (located inside, in basement of palace); you can sit under medieval vaults or escape with your food and picnic outside. The **riverside pavilion** sells sandwiches and fish-and-chips, and has fine outdoor seating (in park just before the bridge, behind castle).

Literally a hundred yards from the castle turnstiles—through a tiny gate in the wall—is the workaday commercial district of the town of **Warwick,** with several much more elegant and competitive eateries that serve fine lunches at non-Tussauds prices. It's worth the walk.

Warwick Connections

From Warwick by Train to: London (3/hour, 1.75 hours), **Stratford** (10/day, 30 minutes—buses are better, see below). Warwick's little train station is a 15-minute walk (or £3 taxi) from the castle. It has no official baggage check, but you can ask politely. The castle has a baggage-check facility. Train info: toll tel. 0845-748-4950, www.nationalrail.co.uk.

By Bus to: Stratford (hourly, 20 minutes, bus #X17, also slower #15/ #18), **Coventry** (10/day, 1 hour, bus #X17, www.stage coachbus.com).

By Car: The main Stratford–Coventry road cuts right through Warwick. Coming from Stratford (8 miles to the south), you'll hit the castle parking lots first (£4; if these are full, lurk until a few cars leave and they'll let you in). The four castle lots are expensive, and three of them are a 10- to 15-minute walk from the actual castle; "premium" £6 parking lot next to the entrance, off Castle Lane. Consider continuing into the town center (on the main road). At the TI (near the big square church spire), grab any streetside parking (free for 2 hours). The castle is a block behind the TI.

Coventry

Coventry, a ▲ sight, was bombed to smithereens in 1940 by the Nazi Luftwaffe. From that point on, the German phrase for "to

really blast the heck out of a place" was "to coventrate" it. But Coventry rose from its ashes, and its message to our world is one of forgiveness, reconciliation, and the importance of peace. Browse through Coventry, the closest thing to normal, everyday, urban England that most tourists will ever see. Get a map at the **TI,** located at the cathedral ruins (Mon–Fri 10:00–17:00, Sat 10:00–16:30, Sun 10:00–12:30 & 13:30–16:30, shorter hours off-season, tel. 02476/227-264, www .visitcoventryandwarwickshire.co.uk, tic@cvone.co.uk).

The symbol of Coventry is the bombed-out hulk of its old **cathedral,** with the huge new one adjoining it. The inspirational complex welcomes visitors. Climb the tower (£2.50, daily 10:30–16:00, 180 steps, tel. 02476/521-257, www.coventrycathedral .org.uk).

According to legend, Coventry's most famous hometown girl, Lady Godiva, rode bareback and bare-naked through the town in the 11th century to help lower taxes. You'll see her bronze statue a block from the cathedral (near Broadgate). Just beyond that is the **Coventry Transport Museum,** which features the first, fastest, and most famous cars and motorcycles that came from this "British Detroit" (free, daily 10:00–17:00, tel. 02476/234-270, www.transport-museum.com).

St. Mary's Guildhall has 14th-century tapestries, stained glass, and an ornate ceiling (free, Easter–Sept Sun–Thu 10:00–16:00, closed Fri–Sat, during events, and off-season, tel. 02476/833-325, www.coventry.gov.uk/stmarys).

Coventry Connections

From Coventry by Train to: Telford Central (near Ironbridge Gorge; 2/hour, 1.5 hours, change in Birmingham or Wolverhampton), **Warwick** (hourly, 30 minutes, change in Leamington Spa), **Stratford-upon-Avon** (at least hourly, 1.75 hrs, change in Leamington Spa or Birmingham). Train info: toll tel. 0845-748-4950, www.nationalrail.co.uk.

IRONBRIDGE GORGE

The Industrial Revolution was born in the Severn River Valley. In its glory days, this valley (blessed with abundant deposits of iron ore and coal, and a river for transport) gave the world its first iron wheels, steam-powered locomotive, and cast-iron bridge (begun in 1779). The museums in Ironbridge Gorge, which capture the flavor of the Victorian Age, take you back into the days when Britain was racing into the modern era, and pulling the rest of the West with her.

Near the end of the 20th century, the valley went through a second transformation: Photos taken just 30 years ago show an industrial wasteland. Today the Severn River Valley is lush and lined with walks and parkland. Even its bricks, while still smoke-stained, seem warmer and more inviting.

Planning Your Time

Without a car, Ironbridge Gorge isn't worth the headache. Drivers can slip it in between the Cotswolds/Stratford/Warwick and points north (such as the Lake District or North Wales). Speed demons zip in for a midday tour of the Blists Hill Victorian Town, look at the famous Iron Bridge and quaint Industrial Age town that sprawls around it, and speed out. For an overnight visit, arrive in the early evening to browse the town, see the bridge, and walk along the river. Spend the morning touring the Blists Hill Victorian Town, have lunch there, and head to your next destination.

With more time—say, a full month in Britain—I'd spend two nights and a leisurely day: 9:30–Iron Bridge and the town; 10:30–Museum of the Gorge; 11:30–Coalbrookdale Museum of

Ironbridge Gorge

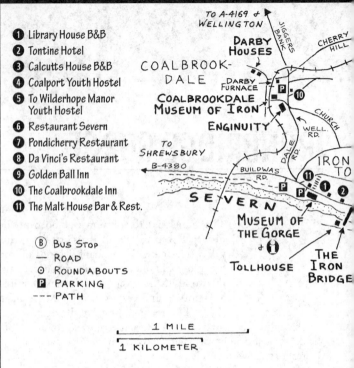

1 Library House B&B
2 Tontine Hotel
3 Calcutts House B&B
4 Coalport Youth Hostel
5 To Wilderhope Manor Youth Hostel
6 Restaurant Severn
7 Pondicherry Restaurant
8 Da Vinci's Restaurant
9 Golden Ball Inn
10 The Coalbrookdale Inn
11 The Malt House Bar & Rest.

B BUS STOP
— ROAD
O ROUNDABOUTS
P PARKING
--- PATH

DARBY HOUSES
COALBROOK-DALE
COALBROOKDALE MUSEUM OF IRON
ENGINUITY
DARBY FURNACE
TO A-4169 & WELLINGTON
JIGGERS BANK
CHERRY HILL
CHURCH
WELL RD.
DALE RD.
IRON TO
TO SHREWSBURY B-4380
BUILDWAS RD.
SEVERN
MUSEUM OF THE GORGE &
TOLLHOUSE
THE IRON BRIDGE

1 MILE
1 KILOMETER

Iron; 14:30–Blists Hill Victorian Town; then dinner at the recommended Golden Ball Inn.

Orientation to Ironbridge Gorge

(area code: 01952)
The town is just a few blocks gathered around the Iron Bridge, which spans the peaceful, tree-lined Severn River. While the smoke-belching bustle is long gone, knowing that this wooded, sleepy river valley was the "Silicon Valley" of the 19th century makes wandering its brick streets almost a pilgrimage. The actual museum sites are scattered over three miles. The modern cooling towers (for coal, not nuclear energy) that loom ominously over these red-brick remnants seem strangely appropriate.

Tourist Information
The TI is in the Museum of the Gorge, just west of the town center (Mon–Fri 9:00–17:00, Sat–Sun 10:00–17:00, tel. 01952/884-

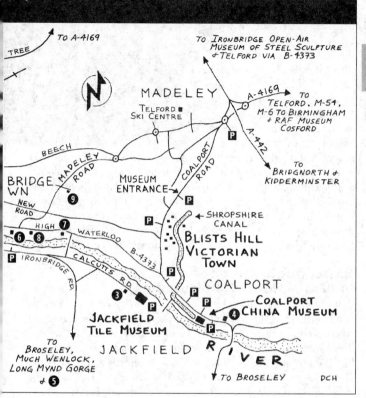

391, www.ironbridge.org.uk). The TI has lots of booklets for sale, including pamphlets describing nearby walks.

Getting Around Ironbridge Gorge

On weekends from Easter through October, **Gorge Connect** buses link the museum sites (£0.50/ride, £2.50 day ticket, free with Museum Passport—described below, 1–2/hour, 9:00–18:00 only, no buses Mon–Fri, several morning and afternoon runs go to the Telford rail station—schedule at www.visitironbridge.co.uk, tel. 01952/200-005).

Sights in Ironbridge Gorge

▲▲Iron Bridge

While England was at war with her American colonies, this first cast-iron bridge was built in 1779 to show off a wonderful new building material. Lacking experience with cast iron, the builders erred on the side of sturdiness and constructed it as if it were made out of wood. Notice that the original construction used traditional timber-jointing techniques rather than rivets. (Any rivets are from later repairs.) The valley's centerpiece is free, open all the time, and thought-provoking. Walk across the bridge to the tollhouse. Read the fee

schedule and notice the subtle slam against royalty. (England was not immune to the revolutionary sentiment brewing in the colonies at this time.) Pedestrians paid half a penny to cross; poor people crossed cheaper by coracle—a crude tub-like wood-and-canvas shuttle ferry. Cross back to the town and enjoy a pleasant walk downstream along the towpath. Where horses once dragged boats laden with Industrial Age cargo, locals now walk their dogs.

▲▲Ironbridge Gorge Industrial Revolution Museums

Ten museums located within a few miles of one another focus on the Iron Bridge and all that it represents. Not all the sights are worth your time. The Blists Hill Victorian Town is by far the best. The Museum of the Gorge attempts to give a historic overview, but the displays are humble—its most interesting feature is the 12-minute video. The Coalbrookdale Museum of Iron tells the story of iron—interesting to metalheads. Enginuity is just for kids. And the original Abraham Darby Furnace is a free shrine to 18th-century technology. The sights share the same opening hours and contact info (daily 10:00–17:00, tel. 01952/884-391, www.ironbridge .org.uk, tic@ironbridge.org.uk).

Museum Passport: This group of widely scattered sights has varied admission charges (usually £3–7; Blists Hill is £15). The £22 Museum Passport (families-£60) covers admission to all attractions. If you're visiting the area's top three sights—Blists Hill Victorian Town, the Museum of the Gorge, and the Coalbrookdale Museum of Iron—you'll save about £3 by using the £22 Passport.

Sightseeing Strategies: It helps to see the introductory movie at the Museum of the Gorge first, to help put everything else into context. To see the most significant sights by car, you'll park three times: once in town (either in the pay lot just over the bridge or in the lot at the Museum of the Gorge—the Iron Bridge and Gorge Museum are connected by an easy, flat walk); once at the Blists Hill parking lot; and once outside of the Coalbrookdale Museum of Iron (Enginuity is across the lot, and the Darby Houses are a three-minute uphill hike away). While you'll pay separately to park at the Museum of the Gorge, a single ticket is good for both "pay and display" lots at the Coalbrookdale Museum and Blists Hill.

If you're visiting on a weekend, you can leave your car in a town lot and take the Gorge Connect bus instead (runs Easter-Oct).

Museum of the Gorge

Orient yourself to the valley here in the Severn Warehouse (£4, daily 10:00–17:00, 500 yards upstream from the bridge, parking-£1.10). The 12-minute introductory movie (on a continuous loop) lays the groundwork for what you'll see in the other museums. Check out the exhibit and the model of the gorge in its heyday. Farther upstream from the museum parking lot is the fine riverside Dale End Park, with picnic areas and a playground.

Blists Hill Victorian Town

Save most of your time and energy for this wonderful town—an immersive, open-air folk museum. You'll wander through 50 acres

of Victorian industry, factories, and a re-created community from the 1890s. Pick up the Blists Hill guidebook for a good step-by-step rundown (£15, daily 10:00–17:00, closes at 16:00 in winter, tel. 01952/601-048).

The map you're given when entering is very important—it shows which stops in the big park are staffed with lively docents in Victorian dress. Pop in to say hello to the banker, the lady in the post office, the blacksmith, and the girl in the candy shop. Maybe the boys are singing in the pub. It's fine to take photos. Asking questions and chatting with the villagers is encouraged. What's a shilling? How was the pay? What about health care in the 1800s?

Stop by the pharmacy and check out the squirm-inducing setup of the dentist's chair—it'll make you appreciate the marvel of modern dental care. Down the street, kids like watching the candlemaker at work. Check the events in the barn across the path, where hands-on candle-making and other activities take place.

Just as it would've had in Victorian days, the village has a working pub, a greengrocer's shop, a fascinating squatter's cottage, and a snorty, slippery pigsty. Don't miss the explanation of the "winding engine" at the Blists Hill Mine (demos throughout the day). Walk along the canal to the "inclined plane."

Eating in Blists Hill: There are three places serving lunches: the New Inn Pub for beer and pub snacks, a traditional fish-and-chips joint, and the cafeteria near the children's old-time rides.

Coalbrookdale Museum of Iron and Abraham Darby's Furnace

The **museum,** while old-school, does a fine job of explaining the original iron-smelting process, and how iron (which makes up 95 percent of all industrial metal) changed our world. Compared to the fun and frolicking Blists Hill village, this museum is sleepy (£8.50, includes entry to the Darby Houses, listed later; £1 less in winter—when Darby Houses are closed for lack of light).

Across from the museum, standing like a shrine to the Industrial Revolution, is the **Abraham Darby Furnace.** The Coalbrookdale neighborhood is the birthplace of modern technology, where locals like to claim that mass production was invented. Darby's blast furnace sits inside a big glass pyramid (free), surrounded by evocative Industrial Age ruins. It was here that, in 1709, Darby first smelted iron, using coke as fuel. To me, "coke" is a drink, and "smelt" is the past tense of smell...but around here, these words recall the event that kicked off the modern Industrial Age.

All the ingredients of the recipe for big industry were here in abundance—iron ore, top-grade coal, and water for power and shipping. Wander around Abraham Darby's furnace. Before this furnace was built, iron ore was laboriously melted by charcoal. With huge waterwheel-powered bellows, Darby burned top-grade coal at super-hot temperatures (burning off the impurities to make "coke"). Local iron ore was dumped into the furnace and melted. Impurities floated to the top, while the pure iron sank to the bottom of a clay tub in the bottom of the furnace. Twice a day, the plugs were knocked off, allowing the "slag" to drain away on the top and the molten iron to drain out on the bottom. The low-grade slag was used locally on walls and paths. The high-grade iron trickled into molds formed in the sand below the furnace. It cooled into pig iron (named because the molds look like piglets suckling their mother). The pig-iron "planks" were broken off by sledgehammers and shipped away. The Severn River became one of Europe's busiest, shipping pig iron to distant foundries, where it was melted again and made into cast iron (for projects such as the Iron Bridge), or to forges, where it was worked like toffee into wrought iron.

Enginuity

Located across the parking lot from the Coalbrookdale Museum of Iron, Enginuity is a hands-on funfest for kids. Riffing on Ironbridge's engineering roots, this converted 1709 foundry is full of entertaining-to-kids water contraptions, pumps, magnets, and laser games. Build a dam, try your hand at earthquake-proof construction, navigate a water maze, operate a remote-controlled robot, or power a turbine with your own steam (£8).

Darby Houses

The Darby family, Quakers who were the area's richest residents by far, lived in these two homes located just above the Coalbrookdale Museum.

The 18th-century Darby mansion, **Rosehill House,** features a collection of fine china, furniture, and trinkets from various family members. It's decorated in the way the family home would have been in 1850. If the gilt-framed mirrors and fancy china seem a little ostentatious for the normally wealth-shunning Quakers, keep in mind that these folks were rich beyond reason, and—as docents will assure you—considering their vast wealth, this was relatively modest (included in £8.50 Coalbrookdale Museum of Iron ticket, otherwise £4.60, closed Nov–Easter).

Skip the adjacent **Dale House.** Dating from the 1780s, it's older than Rosehill, but almost completely devoid of interior furniture, and its exhibits are rarely open.

Coalport China Museum, Jackfield Tile Museum, and Broseley Pipeworks

Housed in their original factories, these showcase the region's porcelain, decorated tiles, and clay tobacco pipes. These industries were developed to pick up the slack when the iron industry shifted away from the Severn Valley in the 1850s. Each museum features finely decorated pieces, and the china and tile museums offer low-energy workshops (£5–8).

Ironbridge Open-Air Museum of Steel Sculpture

This park is a striking tribute to the region's industrial heritage. Stroll the 10-acre grounds and spot works by Roy Kitchin and other sculptors stashed in the forest and perched in rolling grasslands (£3, March–Nov Tue–Sun 10:00–17:00, closed Mon except bank holidays, closed Dec–Feb, 2 miles from Iron Bridge, Moss House, Cherry Tree Hill, Coalbrookdale, Telford, tel. 01952/433-152, www.go2.co.uk/steelsculpture).

Near Ironbridge Gorge

Skiing and Swimming—There's a small, brush-covered ski slope with two Poma lifts at Telford Snowboard and Ski Centre in Madeley, two miles from Ironbridge Gorge; you'll see signs for it as you drive into Ironbridge Gorge (£11/hour including gear, less for kids, open practice times Mon and Thu 10:00–20:00, Tue and

Fri 12:00–22:00, Wed 10:00–19:00, Sat 16:00–18:00, Sun 10:00–16:00, tel. 01952/382-688, www.telford.gov.uk/skicentre). A public swimming pool is up the road on Court Street (5-minute drive from town, Madeley Court Sports Centre, tel. 01952/382-770).

Royal Air Force (RAF) Museum Cosford—This Red Baron magnet displays more than 80 aircraft, from warplanes to rockets. Get the background on ejection seats and a primer on the principles of propulsion (free, daily 10:00–18:00, last entry at 17:00, Shifnal, Shropshire, on A41 near junction with M54, tel. 01902/376-200, www.rafmuseum.org.uk).

More Sights—If you're looking for reasons to linger in Ironbridge Gorge, these sights are all within a short drive: the medieval town of Shrewsbury, the abbey village of Much Wenlock, the scenic Long Mynd gorge at Church Stretton, the castle at Ludlow, and the steam railway at the river town of Bridgnorth. Shoppers like Chester (en route to points north).

Sleeping in Ironbridge Gorge

$$$ Library House is *Better Homes and Gardens* elegant. Located in the town center, a half-block downhill from the bridge, it's a classy, friendly gem that actually used to be a library. Each of its three rooms is a delight. The Chaucer Room, which includes a small garden, is the smallest and least expensive. Lizzie Steel offers a complimentary drink upon arrival (small Db-£75, larger Db–£90, £15 less for Sb, DVD library, Wi-Fi, free parking just up the road, 11 Severn Bank, Ironbridge Gorge, tel. 01952/432-299, www.libraryhouse.com, info@libraryhouse.com). Lizzie may be able to pick you up from the Telford train station if you request it in advance.

$$ Tontine Hotel is the town's big, 12-room, musty, Industrial Age hotel. Check out the historic photos in the bar (S-£25, Sb-£40, D-£40, Db-£56, en-suite rooms include breakfast—otherwise it's £5 extra, family rooms, 10 percent discount with this book if you ask while booking in advance, The Square, tel. 01952/432-127, fax 01952/432-094, www.tontine-hotel.com, tontinehotel@tiscali .co.uk).

Outside of Town

$$$ Calcutts House rents seven rooms in their 18th-century ironmaster's home and adjacent coach house. Rooms in the main house are elegant, while the coach-house rooms are bright, modern, and less expensive. Their inviting living room and garden are a plus. Ask the owners, Colin and Sarah Williams, how the rooms were named (Db-£52–85, price depends on room size, Wi-Fi, located on Calcutts Road, tel. 01952/882-631, www.calcuttshouse

Sleep Code

(£1 = about $1.60, country code: 44, area code: 01952)
S = Single, **D** = Double/Twin, **T** = Triple, **Q** = Quad, **b** = bathroom,
s = shower only. You can assume credit cards are accepted
and breakfast is included unless noted otherwise.

To help you sort easily through these listings, I've divided
the rooms into three categories based on the price for a
standard double room with bath during high season:

$$$ Higher Priced—Most rooms £65 or more.
$$ Moderately Priced—Most rooms between £45-65.
$ Lower Priced—Most rooms £45 or less.

Prices can change without notice; verify the hotel's
current rates online or by email. For other updates, see www
.ricksteves.com/update.

.co.uk, enquiries@calcuttshouse.co.uk). From Calcutts House, it's
a delightful 15-minute stroll down a former train track into town.

$ Coalport Youth Hostel, plush for a hostel, fills an old fac-
tory at the China Museum in Coalport (£15–20 bunks in mostly
4-bed dorms, bunk-bed Db-£32–48, £3 more for non-members,
includes sheets, kitchen, self-service laundry, tel. 01952/588-755,
ironbridge@yha.org.uk). Don't confuse this hostel with the area's
other hostel, Coalbrookdale, which is only available for groups.

$ Wilderhope Manor Youth Hostel, a beautifully remote
425-year-old manor house, is one of Europe's best hostels. On
Wednesday and Sunday afternoons, tourists actually pay to see
what hostelers get to sleep in (£19–23 bunks, under 18-£13.50, £3
more for non-members, single-sex dorms, family rooms available,
reservations recommended, reception closed 10:00–17:00, restaurant open 17:30–20:00, tel. 01694/771-363, wilderhope@yha.org
.uk). It's in Longville-in-the-Dale, six miles from Much Wenlock
down B4371 toward Church Stretton.

Eating in Ironbridge Gorge

Restaurant Severn is the local favorite for a place with style
that serves contemporary dishes. You'll choose from a £25 two-
course fixed-price meal or a £28 three-course offering (evenings
Wed–Sun, closed Mon–Tue, across from the Iron Bridge in the
town center, reservations smart—especially on weekends, 33 High
Street, tel. 01952/432-233).

Pondicherry, in a renovated former police station, serves
delicious Indian curries and a few British dishes to keep the

less adventurous happy. The mixed vegetarian sampler is popular even with meat-eaters. The basement holding cells are now little plush lounges—a great option if you'd like your pre-dinner drink "in prison" (£12–16 plates, Mon–Sat 17:00–23:00, Sun 17:00–21:30—starts to get hopping after 19:00, 57 Waterloo Street, tel. 01952/433-055).

Da Vinci's serves good, though pricey, Italian food and has a dressy ambience (£15–20 entrées, Tue–Sat 19:00–22:00, closed Sun–Mon, 26 High Street, tel. 01952/432-250).

Golden Ball Inn, a brewery back in the 18th century, is a popular pub known for its quality food and great atmosphere. Check out chef/owner Kevin Price's creative dishes listed on the big blackboard. You can dine with the friendly local crowd in the "bar," eat in back with the brewing gear in the more quiet—and formal—dining room, or munch on the lush garden patio. Kevin is serious about his beer, listing featured ales daily (£10–15 meals, daily 11:30–23:00, reservations smart on weekends, five-minute hike up Madeley Road from the town roundabout, 1 Newbridge Road, tel. 01952/432-179).

The Coalbrookdale Inn is filled with locals enjoying excellent ales and good food. This former "best pub in Britain" has a tradition of offering free samples from a lineup of featured beers. Ask which real ales are available (Mon–Thu 17:00–23:30, Fri–Sun 12:00–23:30, food served 12:00–14:00 & 18:00–21:00, no food Sun evening, reservations unnecessary for the bar but a good idea for the fancier restaurant, lively ladies' loo, across street from Coalbrookdale Museum of Iron, 1 mile from Ironbridge Gorge, 12 Wellington Road, tel. 01952/433-953, www.coalbrookdaleinn .co.uk).

The Malt House, located in an 18th-century beer house, is a very popular scene with the local twentysomething gang (£9–15 entrées, bar menu at their Jazz Bar, daily 12:00–21:30, Sun until 22:00, near Museum of the Gorge, 5-minute walk from center, The Wharfage, tel. 01952/433-712). For nighttime action, The Malt House is *the* vibrant spot in town, with live rock music and a fun crowd (generally Thu–Sat).

Ironbridge Gorge Connections

Ironbridge Gorge is five miles from Telford, which has the nearest train station. To get between Ironbridge Gorge and Telford, take bus #9, #39, #76, #77, or #99 (£5 "Day Saver" fare, 1–2/hour, 20–45 minutes, none on Sun) or a taxi (about £10). Although Telford's train and bus stations are an annoying 15-minute walk apart, you can connect them in five minutes on bus #44 (every 10 minutes, covered by "Day Saver") or #55 (every 15 minutes), or with a £3 cab ride. The Telford bus station is part of a large modern mall, an easy place to wait for the bus to Ironbridge Gorge. Buses are run by Arriva (www.arrivabus.co.uk), but you can also call Traveline for departure times and other information (toll tel. 0871-200-2233, www.traveline.org.uk).

The Gorge Connect bus service, which runs among Ironbridge Gorge sights on weekends, makes several morning and afternoon runs between Ironbridge Gorge and the Telford train station (doesn't run off-season, schedule at www.visitironbridge.co.uk). If you need a **taxi** while in Ironbridge Gorge, call Central Taxis at tel. 01952/501-050.

By Train from Telford to: Birmingham (2/hour, 1.25 hours, change in Wolverhampton), **Conwy** in North Wales (9/day, 2.25 hours, some change in Chester or Shrewsbury), **Blackpool** (hourly, 2.75 hours, 2 changes), **Keswick/Lake District** (every 1–2 hours, 5.5 hours; 3.5–4 hours to Penrith with 1–2 changes, then catch a bus to Keswick, hourly except Sun 6/day, 1.5 hours, www.stage coachbus.com), **Edinburgh** (every 1–2 hours, 4.5–5.5 hours, 1–2 changes). Train info: tel. 0845-748-4950, www.nationalrail.co.uk.

To Ironbridge Gorge by Car from the South: Driving in from the **Cotswolds** and **Stratford,** take M40 to Birmingham, then M6 (direction northwest) through Birmingham. The traffic northbound through Birmingham is miserable from 14:00 to 20:00, especially on Fridays. Take one of two M6 options: free with traffic through the city center; or M6 Toll, which, for £5, skirts you north of the center with nearly no traffic—a very good bet during rush hour. After Birmingham, follow signs to *Telford* via M54 (if on toll road, it'll be via A5). Leave M54 at the Telford/Ironbridge exit (Junction 4). Follow the brown *Ironbridge* signs through several roundabouts to Ironbridge Gorge. (Note: On maps, Ironbridge Gorge is often referred to as "Iron Bridge" or "Iron-Bridge.")

From Ironbridge Gorge by Car to North Wales: Heading from Ironbridge Gorge to North Wales is easy, with clear signs and good roads all the way. From Ironbridge Gorge, follow signs to M54. Get on M54 in the direction of Telford, and then Shrewsbury, as M54 becomes A5. You'll then follow signs to North Wales. In Wales, A483 takes you (direction Wrexham, then Chester) to A55, which leads to Conwy.

BLACKPOOL
AND LIVERPOOL

These two bustling cities—wedged between serene North Wales and the even-more-serene Lake District—provide an opportunity to sample the "real" England, both at work (Liverpool) and at play (Blackpool). Scream down roller coasters and eat "candy floss" until you're deliriously queasy in fun-loving Blackpool. In Liverpool, experience industrial England and relive the early mop-top days of some famous Liverpudlians...meet the Beatles.

Blackpool

Blackpool is Britain's tacky, laid-back underbelly. It's one of England's most-visited attractions, the private domain of its working class, a faded and sticky mix of Coney Island, Las Vegas, and Denny's. It can be fun or depressing, thought-provoking or mind-numbing. Some people love it...others hate it. But it is, without a doubt, an amazing spectacle.

Blackpool grew up with the Industrial Revolution. In the mid-1800s, entire mill towns would close down and take a two-week break here. They came to drink in the fresh air (much needed after a hard year in the mills) and—literally—the seawater. (Back then they figured it was healthy.) Supposedly, because Blackpool lies in a "rain shadow," it gets fewer rainy days than some other parts of England.

Blackpool's heyday is long past now, as more and more working people can afford the cheap charter flights to sunny Spain.

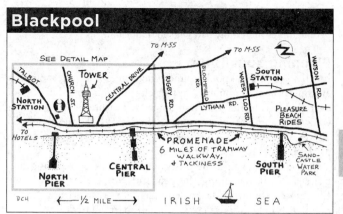

Blackpool

SEE DETAIL MAP
TO M-55
TO M-55
TALBOT
NORTH STATION
TOWER
CHURCH ST.
CENTRAL DRIVE
RIGBY RD.
BLOOMFIELD RD.
WATER-LOO RD.
LYTHAM RD.
SOUTH STATION
WATSON RD.
PLEASURE BEACH RIDES
TO HOTELS
PROMENADE
6 MILES OF TRAMWAY
WALKWAY,
& TACKINESS
NORTH PIER
CENTRAL PIER
SOUTH PIER
SAND-CASTLE WATER PARK
DCH
← ½ MILE →
IRISH SEA

BLACKPOOL

The resort has become popular for "stag" and "hen" (bachelor and bachelorette) parties—basically a cheap drunk weekend for the twentysomething crowd. Consequently, there are two Blackpools: the daytime Blackpool of kids riding roller coasters and grannies getting early-bird specials; and the drunken, debauched, late-night Blackpool of glass-dance-floor clubs and bars.

Blackpool is working to reinvent itself and draw more visitors. An overhaul of The Promenade has begun, as well as numerous renovations in the city center. No matter what, the town remains an accessible and affordable fun zone for the Flo and Andy Capps of northern England. People come year after year. They stay for a week, and they love it.

Be warned: Some of you will get to Blackpool and wonder, "Why did Rick send me *here*?" Most Americans don't even consider a stop in Blackpool. Many won't like it. It's an ears-pierced-while-you-wait, tipsy-toupee kind of place. Tacky, yes. Lowbrow, OK. More than a little run-down in parts, sure. If you're before or beyond kids, and not into kitsch and greasy spoons, skip it. But if you have kids, they'll enjoy Blackpool (hey, it's cheaper than Disneyland). And for those who are into nightlife, this town delivers. If you believe (as I do) that an itinerary should feature as many different facets of a culture as possible, consider a stop here. Blackpool is as English as the Queen—and considerably more fun.

Spend the day "muckin' about" the beach promenade of fortune-tellers, fish-and-chips joints, amusement piers, warped mirrors, and Englanders wearing hats with built-in ponytails. A million greedy doors try every trick to get you inside. Huge arcade halls advertise free toilets and broadcast bingo numbers into the streets; the wind machine under a wax Marilyn Monroe blows at a steady gale; and the smell of fries, tobacco, and sugar is everywhere. Milk comes in raspberry or banana in this land where people under incredibly bad wigs look normal.

Planning Your Time

Ideally, get to Blackpool around lunchtime for an afternoon and evening of making bubbles in this cultural mud puddle. A good overall plan is to ride the tram down to Pleasure Beach, and then walk back along the waterfront to the North Pier and Blackpool Tower, dipping into whatever fun zones appeal. To see a more pristine beach, just keep walking north.

The evening light here is great, with the sun setting over the sea. Walk out along the peaceful North Pier at twilight. Blackpool's Illuminations, when much of the waterfront is decorated with lights, draws crowds in fall, particularly on weekends (September through early November).

Blackpool is easy by car or train. Speed demons with a car can treat it as a midday break (it's just off M6 on M55) and continue north. If the weather's great and you love nature, the lakes are just a few hours north. A visit to Blackpool sharpens the wonders of Windermere.

Orientation to Blackpool

(area code: 01253)

Everything clusters along The Promenade, a tacky, glittering six-mile-long beachfront good-time strip mall punctuated by three fun-filled piers reaching out into the sea. The Pleasure Beach rides are near the South Pier. Jutting up near the North Pier is Blackpool's stubby Eiffel-type tower. The most interesting shops, eateries, and theaters are inland from the North Pier. For a break from glitz, walk north along The Promenade or sandy beach—a residential neighborhood stretches for miles. When you've had enough, just hop on the tram or a bus for a quick ride back.

Tourist Information

The TI sits about 50 yards inland from the North Pier (Mon–Sat 9:00–17:00, Easter–early Nov Sun 10:00–16:30, closed Sun off-season, 1 Clifton Street; tel. 01253/478-222—answered during the day, gives recorded entertainment info after hours; www.visitblackpool.com). There you'll find a city map, brochures on the amusement centers, and a helpful staff. The free *What's On* booklet lists local events; the TI can book shows for you for a £2 fee. If you're going to Sandcastle Waterpark, buy your tickets here to save a few pounds. The TI books rooms for no fee (but collects a 10 percent deposit, which hotels don't recoup; room-finding service closes at 16:30).

Arrival in Blackpool

The main (north) **train** station is three blocks from the town center (no maps given but one is posted). There's no luggage storage in town.

If arriving by **car,** the motorway funnels you down Yeadon Way into a giant parking zone. If you're just spending the day, head for one of the huge £6/day garages. If you're spending the night, drive to the waterfront and head north. My top accommodations are north on The Promenade (easy parking). Leaving Blackpool to go anywhere, follow signs to *M55*, which starts at Blackpool and zips you to M6 (for points north or south).

Helpful Hints

Markets: At the indoor **Abingdon Street Market,** vendors sell baked goods, fruit, bras, jewelry, eggs, and more (Mon–Sat 9:00–17:00, closed Sun). Eight miles north, the **Fleetwood Market** is huge, with two buildings full of produce, clothes, and crafts spilling out onto the street (May–Oct Mon–Tue and Thu–Sat 8:00–17:00, closed Wed and Sun; Nov–April Tue and Fri–Sat only; catch tram marked *Fleetwood*, 30 minutes, £2.70 one-way, www.fleetwoodmarket.co.uk).

Tipping: The pubs of Blackpool have a unique tradition of "and (name an amount) your own, luv." Say that here, and your barmaid will add that amount to your bill and drop it into her tip jar. (Say it anywhere else...and they won't know what you mean.)

Internet Access: The public library, in the big domed building on Queen Street, lets visitors stand and use its computers for 15 minutes (free, Mon and Fri 9:00–17:00, Tue and Thu 9:00–19:00, Wed and Sat 10:00–17:00, Sun 11:00–14:00, tel. 01253/478-111).

Post Office: The main P.O. is in the basement of the WH Smith store, at 12–16 Bank Hey Street (Mon–Sat 9:00–17:30, closed Sun).

Car Rental: In case you decide to tour the Lake District by car, you'll find plenty of rental agencies in Blackpool (closed Sat afternoon and Sun), including **Avis** (at the airport—just south of the South Pier, tel. 01253/408-003) and **Budget** (434 Waterloo Road—just north of the South Pier, tel. 01253/691-632).

Getting Around Blackpool

Trams trundle 13 miles up and down the waterfront, connecting all the sights. They come in all shapes and colors (some vintage, some modern, some dressed up like boats), but are all on the same system and take the same tickets. This electric tramway—the first in Europe—dates from 1885 (about £2 per ride depending on length of trip, pay conductor, trams come every 10–15 minutes or so year-round 6:00–23:15). Many **buses** also run along The Promenade—make sure you're not standing at a tram stop if you're waiting for a bus (similar prices, pay conductor, tel. 01253/473-001, www.blackpooltransport.com). For £6, you can purchase a day pass that covers both trams and buses; buy it on board, or at their office on Market Street.

City Sightseeing's one-hour, 16-stop **hop-on, hop-off bus** has a recorded commentary and leaves from the Blackpool Tower every 30 minutes (£7.50, June–early Nov daily from 9:00 until last departure at 19:00, mid-April–May Sat–Sun only, none off-season, tel. 01253/473-001, www.city-sightseeing.com).

Taxis are easy to snare in Blackpool, and three to five people travel cheaper by cab than by tram. Hotels can get you a taxi by phone within three minutes (no extra charge).

Sights in Blackpool

▲▲▲**People-Watching**—Blackpool's top sight is its people. You'll see England here as nowhere else. Grab someone's hand and a big baton of "rock" (candy), and stroll. Grown men walk around with huge teddy bears looking for places to play "bowlingo," a short-lane version of bowling. Ponder the thought of actually retiring here and spending your last years, day after day, wearing plaid pants and a bad toupee, surrounded by Blackpool. This place puts people in a talkative mood. Start up conversations. Ask a young couple on the street, "What's there to do here?" Find someone to explain the difference between tea and supper. Back at your hotel, join in the chat sessions in the lounge.

▲▲**The Piers**—Blackpool's famous piers were originally built for Victorian landlubbers who wanted to go to sea but were afraid of getting seasick. Each of the three amusement piers has its own personality and is a joy to wander. The sedate **North Pier** is most traditional and refreshingly uncluttered (open first Sat in March to first weekend in Nov, daily 10:00–23:00, £0.50 admission 10:00–17:30 includes discounts on an ice cream or drink and the carousel ride, free admission after 17:30). Dance down its empty planks at twilight to the early English rock playing on its speakers. Its **Carousel Bar** at the end is great for families—with a free kids' DJ nightly from 19:00 to 23:00 (parents drink good beer while the kids bunny-hop and boogie). The something-for-everyone **Central Pier** is lots of fun. Ride its great Ferris wheel for the best view in Blackpool (rich photography at twilight, get the operator to spin you as you bottom out). The family bar at the end of the pier is a hit with kids. The rollicking **South Pier** is all rides.

From the far end of any pier, look out at the horizon to see the natural-gas drilling platforms in the Irish Sea. In the distance, off the North Shore, a castaway gaggle of wind turbines capture energy.

▲**Blackpool Tower**—This mini–Eiffel Tower is a 100-year-old vertical fun center. You pay £17 to get in (£14 for kids, family tickets available); after that, the fun is free. Work your way up from the bottom through layer after layer of noisy entertainment: a circus (2–3 acts a day, runs Easter–first weekend in Nov), a 3-D cinema, an aquarium, and a wonderful old ballroom with barely live music and golden oldies dancing to golden oldies all day. Enjoy a break at the dance-floor-level pub or on a balcony perch. Kids love this place. With a little marijuana, adults would, too. Ride the elevator to the tip of the 500-foot-tall symbol of Blackpool for a chance to stroll across the "Walk of Fear" glass floor and enjoy a smashing view,

especially at sunset (Easter–June daily 10:00–17:00; July–early Nov daily 10:00–20:00; early Nov–Easter Wed 10:00–17:00, Sat–Sun 10:00–18:00; may be closed for events, top of tower closed when windy, tel. 01253/622-242, www.theblackpooltower.co.uk). If you want to leave and return, request a hand stamp.

▲**Pleasure Beach**—Rated ▲▲▲ for roller-coaster enthusiasts, these 42 acres across The Promenade from the beach attract nearly

six million visitors annually, and are littered with rides galore, an ice show, circus and illusion shows, and varied amusements. Many rides are tame enough for the under-10 set, but the top few offer some of the best thrills in Europe: the Pepsi Max Big One (with a peak of 235 feet and 85 mph, it's one of the world's fastest, highest, and steepest roller coasters), the Infusion (a twisty, loopy speed rush that you ride with feet dangling), and the IceBlast (which rockets you straight up before letting you bungee down). The Bling ride spins gondola riders in three different directions 100 feet above the ground at speeds of more than 60 mph. Also memorable is the Steeplechase—carousel horses stampeding down a roller coaster track (a dream come true for *National Velvet* and *Mary Poppins* fans). The Irn Bru Revolution speeds you over a steep drop and upside-down in a loop, then does it again backward. The Valhalla ride zips you on a Viking boat in watery darkness past scary

Nordic things like lutefisk. With two 80-foot drops and lots of hype, first you're scared, then you're soaked, and—finally—you're just glad you survived. The park also offers several old wooden-framed rides full of historic charm—but brittle travelers will want to consider their necks and backs. The tame-looking Wild Mouse, built in 1958, is the jerkiest, and has no doubt kept generations of Blackpool chiropractors in the money.

Admission to Pleasure Beach is £5, which includes a few attractions, then you can pay individually for rides with your £1 tickets (2–8 tickets per ride), or get unlimited rides with a £25–30 armband (price varies with season and day of week, cheaper if purchased in advance on their website). If you haven't pre-purchased your pass, pay the £5 entry fee and have a look around (check to see how long lines are for the top rides)—once you've paid admission to the park, you can upgrade to the armband by paying the difference (daily Easter–early Nov, also open some weekends in winter, opens at about 10:00 and closes as early as 17:00 or as late as 21:30, depending on season, weather, and demand—check website; toll tel. 0871-222-1234, www.pleasurebeachresort.com). Note: Pleasure Beach is about two miles (a 45-minute walk) south of the North Pier, so consider taking the tram or bus.

Sandcastle Waterpark—This popular indoor attraction, across the street from Pleasure Beach, has a big pool, long slides, a wave machine, and water, water, everywhere, at a constant temperature of 84 degrees. Featuring the longest tube waterslide in the world, this is a place where most kids could easily spend a day (£12 limited entry/£15 full admission, £10/£13 for kids, family passes, discount tickets online and at TI; roughly July–Aug daily 10:00–17:30; April–June and Sept–Oct Sat–Thu 10:00–17:00, Fri 13:30–20:00; Nov–March Sat–Sun only 10:00–16:30—confirm as hours may vary; last admission one hour before closing, tel. 01253/343-602, www.sandcastle-waterpark.co.uk).

▲**Illuminations**—Blackpool was the first town in England to "go electric" in 1879. Now, every fall, from early September through early November, Blackpool stretches its tourist season by illuminating its six miles of waterfront with countless lights, all blinking and twinkling (www.blackpool-illuminations.net). People here speak with wonder about these lights. The American in me kept saying, "I've seen bigger, and I've seen better," but I stuffed his mouth with cotton candy and just had some simple fun like everyone else on my specially decorated tram. Look for the animated tableaux up along the North Shore.

St. Annes-on-Sea—Had enough greasy food and flashing lights? The seaside village of St. Annes is an easy 20-minute bus ride away to the south, and offers a welcome break (buses #7 and #11 run from the Blackpool Tower every 10 minutes, covered by the all-day tram/bus pass). Get off at St. Annes Square, which is the first stop after the bus turns left following the long, dune-side straightaway. The town's promenade and the end of the simple Victorian pier (once you pass the noisy game arcade) feel like a breath of sanity. The broad sand beach is perfect for flying a kite, building a sand-castle, or watching happy dogs play in the surf. Consider stroll-ing the beach northward all the way to the southern edge of The Promenade (about three miles—you can see the Pleasure Beach roller coaster from here); if you max out on sand and sea before that, simply cross the dunes back to the seaside road and find the nearest bus stop.

Nightlife in Blackpool

▲**Showtime**—Blackpool always has a few razzle-dazzle music, dancing-girl, racy-humor, magic, and tumbling shows. Box offices around town can give you a rundown on what's available (£7–30 tickets). Your hotel has the latest. Blackpool is a staging ground for some London West End plays—giving you a chance to enjoy a show for a fraction of the London cost. You might try the Opera House for musicals (booking toll tel. 0844-856-1111, info tel. 01253/625-252) and the Grand Theatre for drama and ballet (£15–25, tel. 01253/290-190, www.blackpoolgrand.co.uk). Both are on Church Street, a couple of blocks behind the tower. For the latest in evening entertainment, see the window displays at the TI on The Promenade (www.blackpoollive.com).

▲▲**Funny Girls**—Blackpool's hot bar is in a dazzling venue a couple of blocks from the tower. Most nights from 20:00 to 23:30,

Funny Girls puts on a "glam bam thank you ma'am" burlesque-in-drag show that delights footballers and grannies alike. A troop of a dozen or so gorgeous guys go through an entire wardrobe, put-ting on skits and dances that range from the Charleston to Beyoncé to a very vampy *Sound of Music*. Between songs, the high-heeled MC entertains.

Get your drinks at the bar...unless the transvestites are danc-ing on it. The show, while racy, is not raunchy. The music is very loud. The crowd is young, old, straight, gay, very down-to-earth, and fun-loving. A weeknight is both a less-expensive and less-crushed experience, as Fridays and Saturdays are jammed. While the area up front can be a mosh pit, there are more sedate tables in back, where service comes with a vampish smile. If you want to experience the show without being immersed in a bar crowd, pay extra to sit.

There are two admissions: sitting and standing (Sun £4 to stand, £14 to sit; Tue–Thu £3.50 to stand, £11 to sit; Fri £6 to stand, £17.50 to sit; Sat £8 to stand, £19.50 to sit; no shows Mon). Getting dinner here before the show runs about £16 (dinner reservations required, must be 18 to enter, 5 Dickson Road, TI sells tickets; to reserve in advance, call 01253/624-901, or visit box office at 44 Queen Street—open 9:30–17:15, www.funnygirlsshowbar.co.uk).

Other Nightspots—The **Mitre Pub** serves beer in a truly rare, old-time Blackpool ambience. Drop in anytime to survey the fun photos of old Blackpool and for the great people scene (daily 11:00–23:00, 3 West Street, tel. 01253/623-718).

Blackpool's clubs and discos are cheap, with live bands and an interesting crowd (nightly 22:00–2:00 in the morning). With all the stag and hen parties, the late-night streets can be clotted with rude rowdies.

Sleeping in Blackpool

Blackpool's 140,000 people provide 120,000 beds in 3,500 mostly dumpy, cheap, nondescript hotels and B&Bs. Remember, this town's in the business of accommodating the people who can't afford to go to Spain. Most places have the same design—minimal character, maximum number of springy beds—and charge £20–25 per person. Empty beds abound except summer weekends and from September through early November (during Illuminations, when everyone bumps up prices). With the huge number of hotels in town, prices get really soft off-season. I've listed regular high-

---

Sleep Code

(£1 = about $1.60, country code: 44, area code: 01253)
S = Single, **D** = Double/Twin, **T** = Triple, **Q** = Quad, **b** = bathroom, **s** = shower only. You can assume credit cards are accepted unless otherwise noted.

To help you sort easily through these listings, I've divided the rooms into three categories based on the price for a standard double room with bath:

$$$ Higher Priced—Most rooms £90 or more.
$$ Moderately Priced—Most rooms between £45-90.
$ Lower Priced—Most rooms £45 or less.

Prices can change without notice; verify the hotel's current rates online or by email. For other updates, see www.ricksteves.co/update.

Central Blackpool

NOT TO SCALE
NORTH PIER TO CENTRAL PIER
IS ABOUT ½ MILE (800 METERS)

⊢+⊣ TROLLEY LINE

P PARKING

▢ PEDESTRIAN ZONE

BLACKPOOL NORTH TRAIN STN.

TO M-55

BUS STN.

DICKSON

TO M-55

TO SOUTH PIER

LIBRARY

OPERA HOUSE & WINTER GARDENS

CORONATION STREET

CORPORATION ST.

POST

MARKET ST.

WEST

CHURCH ST.

TOWER

P R O M E N A D E

TRAMWAY   BEACH   BEACH

NORTH PIER

CENTRAL PIER

I R I S H   S E A

DCH

❶ To Hotels North of the Tower

❷ To The Lonsdale & Valdene Hotels

❸ To Red Bank Road Eateries

❹ Clifton Street Eateries

❺ The Mitre Pub

❻ Marks & Spencer

❼ Funny Girls (Bar & Show)

❽ Funny Girls (Box Office)

BLACKPOOL

season prices. There's likely a launderette within a five-minute walk of your hotel; ask your host.

North of the Tower

These listings are on or near the waterfront in the quiet area they call "the posh end," a mile or two north of Blackpool Tower, with easy parking and easy access to the center by tram or bus. The first two listings have classy extras you wouldn't expect in Blackpool, and aren't far from the North Pier. The last two are B&Bs with welcoming owners and lots of stairs, a short tram ride or approximately 35-minute walk from the North Pier.

$$$ Barceló Imperial Hotel is where the Queen would stay in Blackpool. (They boast that every prime minister since they opened has visited their #10 Bar.) With dark-paneled Old World elegance, this splurge has all the comforts at its posh address (standard Db-£115–168 depending on size of room, season, and day of week—check website for deals but call front desk for best standard room available; children stay free, parking-£2.50/day, tram stop: Imperial Hotel, North Promenade, tel. 01253/623-971,

fax 01253/751-784, www.barcelo-hotels.co.uk, imperialblackpool
@barcelo-hotels.co.uk).

$$$ The **Hilton Hotel** is good if you need a splurge. Yes, I
know, staying at the Hilton in Blackpool is like wearing a tux to
eat falafel. But this is a grand 270-room place with lots of views,
a pool, sauna, gym, and comfortable rooms (Db-£110–170, "club
deal" Db with lots of extras-£25 more, ask if there are any "special
rates" being advertised, best deals online, call front desk to request
room with view for no extra charge, air-con, tram stop: Warley
Road, North Promenade, tel. 01253/623-434, fax 01253/627-864,
www.hilton.com).

$$ **Beechcliffe Private Hotel** has seven clean rooms run by
a friendly couple, Ken and Carol Selman. The rooms are tight and
simple, but this place has a homey touch, and the decor is being
nicely updated (Sb-£25, Db-£50, kids half-price, tram stop: Cabin;
turn left from tram stop, then right at Shaftesbury Avenue, and
walk a block away from beach; 16 Shaftesbury Avenue, North
Shore, tel. 01253/353-075, www.beechcliffe.co.uk, info@beech
cliffe.co.uk). Ken offers guests rides to or from the train station for
no charge.

$$ **Robin Hood Hotel** is a cheery place with a big, welcom-
ing living room and nine spacious rooms with big beds and sea
views. If you don't mind the stairs, the top room, #9, is great (Sb-
£25, Db-£50, discount for kids, under 6 free, facial and massage
treatments available, tram stop: St. Stephen's Avenue and walk a
block north, 1.5 miles north of tower across from a peaceful stretch
of beach, 100 Queens Promenade, North Shore, tel. 01253/351-599,
www.robinhoodhotel.co.uk, info@robinhoodhotel.co.uk, Paul and
Kathy).

Near the Train Station

Both of these hotels are located on quiet Cocker Street, which
provides an oasis of sanity and affordable comfort in a handy, if
rough, neighborhood just a few blocks from the train station and
the Blackpool Tower and North Pier. These hotels are family-run,
have strict security and noise standards, and cater to couples and
families rather than to revelers.

$$ **The Lonsdale Hotel** offers five rooms in an oasis of
peace behind a lush front porch garden. The plush lounge, with
Edwardian paintings and furnishings, takes you to another era.
Steve has managed the place for 25 years (Db-£60, Wi-Fi, free
parking, at the corner of Lord Street and Cocker Street at 25
Cocker Street, tel. 01253/621-628, www.blackpoolaccommodation
.net, lonsdalehotel@hotmail.co.uk).

$$ **The Valdene Hotel,** with a small garden facing the street,
rents 10 rooms above its generous and inviting lounge. Old-time

Blackpool photos on the walls create a peaceful and nostalgic atmosphere (Db-£50, 16 Cocker Street, tel. 01253/291-080, valdenehotel@aol.com, www.valdene-hotel.co.uk, Bob, Linda, and Simon Ablett).

Eating in Blackpool

Considering what's in demand here, I wouldn't hope for great food in Blackpool. Generally, food in the tower and along The Promenade is terrible.

Red Bank Road: Locals recommend riding the tram north to Bishpam, where Red Bank Road has several good eateries including Indian, Italian, and steakhouse choices. Try the Bishpam Kitchen (at #14-16) for good fish-and-chips.

Clifton Street: This street is lined with decent ethnic-food eateries, including Italian, Indian, and Chinese.

Supermarket: Marks & Spencer has a big supermarket in its basement (Mon–Wed and Fri 9:00–18:00, Thu 9:00–19:00, Sat 8:30–18:00, Sun 10:30–16:30, near recommended eateries, on Coronation Street and Church Street). Buy some food here and go picnic at the beach.

Blackpool Connections

If you're heading to (or from) Blackpool by train, you'll usually need to transfer at **Preston** (5/hour, 30 minutes). The following trains leave from Blackpool's main (north) station.

From Blackpool to: Liverpool (hourly, 1.5 hours), **Keswick/Lake District** (roughly hourly, allow at least 3.5 hours total for journey: transfer in Preston—30 minutes away, then 1 hour to Penrith, then catch a bus to Keswick, hourly except Sun 8/day, 40 minutes), **Conwy** in North Wales (roughly hourly, 3 hours, 3 transfers), **Edinburgh** (roughly hourly, 3.5 hours, transfer in Preston), **Glasgow** (1–2/hour, 3–3.5 hours, transfer in Preston), **York** (hourly, 3 hours, more with change in Manchester), **Moreton-in-Marsh** in the Cotswolds (hourly, 4.25–5 hours, 3 transfers), **Bath** (hourly, 4.5–4.75 hours, 2–3 transfers), **London**'s Euston Station (1–2/hour, 2.75–3.25 hours, 1–2 transfers), Telford near **Ironbridge Gorge** (hourly, 2.25 hours, 2 transfers), **Oban** (2/day, 7.25–7.75 hours, 3 transfers). Train info: toll tel. 0845-748-4950, www.nationalrail .co.uk.

Liverpool

Liverpool, a large, bustling city with a downtown full of shopping malls, is a fascinating stop for Beatles fans and those who would like to look urban England straight in the eye. The city, while long known as a depressed industrial center, has enjoyed a cultural renaissance. In 2008, Liverpool was one of the European Capitals of Culture; to prepare for the honor, the city rode a building-boom wave of new construction and architectural face-lifts. And today, it welcomes guests with a new confidence and energy.

Planning Your Time

For a quick visit (which basically ignores the core of this workaday city), every major sight is at or near the Albert Dock, and the Beatles bus tours also depart from there.

If you're a casual Beatles fan, make Liverpool an afternoon pit-stop: Spend most of your time at the Albert Dock, popping in to see The Beatles Story museum, having lunch at the Tate's lunchtime café (and appreciating the art upstairs), and visiting the Maritime Museum. Consider getting a ticket to ride the ferry across the Mersey, which leaves from the docks north of the Albert Dock.

Serious Beatles fan will need more time. There are three main Beatles-related activities: touring The Beatles Story, taking a Beatles bus tour, and visiting the boyhood homes of John and Paul. The first two are easy (and you'll see the homes from the outside on the tour). To actually visit the home interiors, you'll need to make arrangements in advance.

Orientation to Liverpool

(area code: 0151)

Tourist Information

Liverpool's main TI is on **Whitechapel Street,** a six-minute walk downhill from Lime Street Station. Ignore the pavilion with the information symbol on it—the real TI is a glossy silver storefront on this main shopping street (Mon–Sat 10:00–17:00, Sun 11:00–16:00, tel. 0151/233-2008, www.visitliverpool.com). There's another TI at the **Albert Dock** (daily 10:00–17:30, inland from

The Beatles Story, tel. 0151/707-0729). Get the free, small map at either place.

Arrival in Liverpool

By Train: Most trains use the **Lime Street train station.** Look for baggage-storage services on the station's main concourse (£7/item for 24 hours, open daily 7:00–21:00; most bus tours and private minivan/car tours are able to accommodate people with luggage). From this station to the Albert Dock, it's about a 20-minute walk, a short ride on bus #C4 (£1.60 one-way, £3.30 all-day ticket, 3/hour), or a £4 taxi trip. For public-transportation information, visit the Merseytravel center at the main bus center, between Lime Street Station and the TI (Mon–Sat 9:00–17:30, Sun 10:30–16:30, Queen Square, toll tel. 0871-200-2233, www.merseytravel.gov.uk).

Regional trains also arrive at the much smaller **Central Station,** which is essentially a subway stop, located just a few blocks south.

By Plane: From Liverpool John Lennon Airport, take bus #500 to the city center (£2.60, 2/hour).

By Car: Drivers approaching Liverpool follow signs to *City Center* and *Albert Dock,* where you'll find a huge parking lot at the dock. If coming from Wales, take the toll tunnel under the Mersey River (£1.40) and follow signs for *Albert Dock.*

Tours in Liverpool

Beatles Bus Tours

The "sights" covered by these tours are basically houses where the Fab Four grew up (exteriors only), places they performed, and spots made famous by the lyrics of their hits ("Penny Lane," "Strawberry Fields," the "Eleanor Rigby" grave-yard, and so on). While boring to anyone not into the Beatles, fans will enjoy the commentary and seeing the shelter on the roundabout, the fire station with the clean machine, and the barber who shaves another customer.

Magical Mystery Big Bus Tour—Beatles fans may want to invest a couple of hours taking this tour, which hits the lads' homes (from the outside), Penny Lane, and so on. With an enthusiastic, live commentary and Beatles tunes cued to famous landmarks, it leaves people happy (£15, 1.75 hours; Easter–Oct tours daily at 12:00, also at 14:30 on weekends and July–Aug; Oct–Easter Sat–Sun only at

Liverpool

LIVERPOOL

1 Sir Thomas Hotel
2 Premier Inns (2)
3 To Cocoon Pod Hotel & International Inn Hostel
4 National Trust Beatles Tour Pick-Up Point (Mornings Only)
5 Magical Mystery Tour Pick-Up Point
6 Yellow Duckmarine Tickets
7 Mathew Street & Site of Original Cavern Club

TO SOUTHPORT

LEEDS

NEW QUAY

CHAPEL TITHE

WATER

BRUNS.

STRAND

400 YARDS
400 METERS

ROYAL LIVER BLDG.

M

James Street

P

MERSEY FERRIES DOCK

MUSEUM OF LIVERPOOL

MARITIME & SLAVERY MUSEUMS

TATE GALLERY LIVERPOOL

i

L

6
2

B QUEEN SQUARE BUS HUB

M MERSEYRAIL SUBWAY STOP

P PARKING

THE BEATLES STORY

P

RIVER

MERSEY

DCH

LIVERPOOL

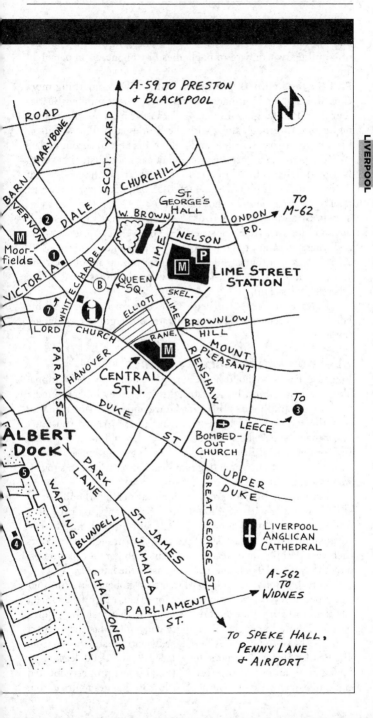

12:00; buses depart from the Albert Dock near The Beatles Story and TI, tel. 0151/233-2459, www.cavernclub.org). As these tours often fill up, you're wise to book ahead by phone, or in person at any TI.

Phil Hughes Mini-Bus Beatles Tours—For something more extensive, fun, and intimate, consider a four-hour minibus Beatles tour from Phil Hughes. It's longer because it includes information on historic Liverpool, along with the Beatles stuff. Phil organizes his tour to fit your schedule and will do his best to accommodate you (£17/person, £88/private group tour, can coordinate times with National Trust tour of Lennon and McCartney homes, 8-seat minibus, mobile 07961-511-223, tel. 0151/228-4565, www.tourliver pool.co.uk, tourliverpool@hotmail.com).

Jackie Spencer Private Tours—To tailor a visit to your schedule and interests, Jackie Spencer is at your service...just say when and where you want to go (up to five people in her minivan-£140, 2.5 hours, longer tours available, will pick you up at hotel or train station, mobile 0799-076-1478, www.beatleguides.com, jackie @beatleguides.com).

Beware of cheaper private-taxi tours promoted by some hotels—kickbacks, not quality, motivate concierges to recommend these tours.

▲Lennon and McCartney Homes

John and Paul's boyhood homes are now owned by the National Trust and have both been restored to how they looked during their 1950s childhoods. This isn't Graceland—you won't find an over-the-top rock-and-roll extravaganza here. And if you don't know the difference between John and Paul, you'll likely be bored. But for die-hard Beatles fans who want to get a glimpse into the time and place that created these musical masterminds, this tour is worth ▲▲▲.

Because the houses are in residential neighborhoods—and still share walls with neighbors—the National Trust runs only four tours per day in summer (Wed–Sun only), limited to 14 Beatlemaniacs each. Just 7,000 people pass through these doors each year. While some Beatles bus tours stop here for photo ops, only the National Trust tour gets you inside the homes.

Tour Options: From mid-March to October, tours run four times per day Wed–Sun (no tours Mon–Tue). Morning tours (at 10:00 and 10:50) follow a more scenic route that includes a quick pass by Penny Lane; these are more convenient, as they depart from the Jurys Inn at the Albert Dock (south of and visible from The Beatles Story). Afternoon tours (at 14:30 and 15:00) leave from Speke Hall, an out-of-the-way National Trust property located eight miles southeast of Liverpool. Allow 30 minutes to drive from the city center to Speke Hall—follow the brown *Speke Hall* signs through dozens of roundabouts, heading in the general direction of the airport. If you don't have a car, you'll need to hop a taxi.

Off-Season: From early to mid-March and in November, tours leave Wed–Sun at 10:00, 12:30, and 15:00, and all depart from the handy Jurys Inn at the Albert Dock. No tours run in winter (Dec–Feb).

Cost and Reservations: £17; because only 14 people are allowed on each tour, it's smart to make a reservation ahead of time, especially for the morning tours. You can reserve online (www.nationaltrust.org.uk/beatles), or by calling 0151/427-7231. If you haven't reserved ahead, you can try to book a same-day tour (for the morning tours, call 0151/707-0729). The afternoon tours generally don't fill up, but remember that it takes 30 minutes (by car or taxi) to reach the tour's starting point from central Liverpool.

Guides: Each home has a live-in caretaker who acts as your guide. These folks give an entertaining, insightful-to-fans 20- to 30-minute talk, and then leave you time (10–15 minutes) to wander through the house on your own. Ask lots of questions if their spiel peters out early—the docents are a wealth of information.

Mendips (John Lennon's Home)—Even though he sang about being a working-class hero, John grew up in the suburbs of

Liverpool, surrounded by doctors, lawyers, and—beyond the back fence—Strawberry Field (he added the "s" for the song).

This was the home of John's Aunt Mimi, who raised him in this house from the time he was five years old and once told him, "A guitar's all right, John, but you'll never earn a living by it." John moved out at age 23, but his first wife, Cynthia, bunked here for a while when John made his famous first trip to America. Yoko Ono bought the house in 2002, and gave it as a gift to the National Trust (generating controversy among the neighbors). The stewards, Colin and Sylvia, make this place come to life.

On the surface, it's just a 1930s house carefully restored to how it would have been in the past. But delve deeper. It's been lovingly cared for—restored to be the tidy, well-kept place Mimi would have recognized (down to her apron hanging in the kitchen). It's a lucky quirk of fate that the house's interior remained mostly unchanged after the Lennons left—the bachelor who owned it for the previous decades didn't upgrade much, so even the light switches are true to the time.

LIVERPOOL

If you're a John Lennon fan, it's fun to picture him as a young boy drawing and imagining at his dining room table. It also makes for an interesting comparison to Paul's humbler home, which is the second part of the tour.

20 Forthlin Road (Paul McCartney's Home)—In comparison to Aunt Mimi's house, the home where Paul grew up is simpler, much less "posh," and even a little ratty around the edges. Michael, Paul's brother, wanted it that way—their mother, Mary (famously mentioned in "Let It Be"), died when the boys were young, and it never had the tidiness of a woman's touch. It's been intentionally scuffed up around the edges to preserve the historical accuracy. Notice the differences—Paul has said that John's house was vastly different and more clearly middle class; at Mendips, there were books on the bookshelves.

More than a hundred Beatles songs were written in this house (including "I Saw Her Standing There") during days Paul and John spent skipping school. The photos from Michael, taken in this house, help make the scene of what's mostly a barren interior much more interesting.

Other Tours

City Bus Tour—The City Sightseeing bus is a hop-on, hop-off bus tour with a canned soundtrack, but considering the size of the city center, it's a quick way to get an overview that links all the major sights in 55 breezy minutes (£8, buy ticket from driver, valid for 24 hours, daily March–Oct 10:00–17:00, Jan–Feb 10:00–16:30, runs every 30 minutes, tel. 0151/203-3920, www.city-sightseeing .com).

Ferry Cruise—Mersey Ferries offers narrated cruises that depart from Mersey Dock, an easy five-minute walk from the Albert Dock. The 50-minute cruise makes two brief stops on the other side of the river; you can hop off and catch the next boat back (£6.50, year-round, Mon–Fri 10:00–15:00, Sat–Sun 10:00–18:00, leaves at top of hour, café, WCs onboard, tel. 0151/330-1444, www .merseyferries.co.uk).

Harbor and City Tour—The Yellow Duckmarine runs wacky tours of Liverpool's waterfront, city, and docks by land and by sea in its amphibious WWII-era tourist assault vehicles. Be prepared to quack (£12, or £10 midweek and off-peak, family deals, one hour, buy tickets at office on the Albert Dock near The Beatles Story, departs from the Albert Dock every 30 minutes daily 10:30–17:00, more frequently with demand, tel. 0151/708-7799, www .theyellowduckmarine.co.uk).

Sights in Liverpool

At the Albert Dock

All of the following sights are at the Albert Dock. Opened in 1852 by Prince Albert, and enclosing seven acres of water, the Albert Dock is surrounded by five-story brick warehouses. In its day, Liverpool was England's greatest seaport, but at the end of the 19th century, the port wasn't deep enough for the big new ships; trade declined after 1890, and by 1972 it was closed entirely. Like Liverpool itself, the docks have enjoyed a renaissance, and today, they contain the city's main attractions. A half-dozen trendy eateries are lined up here, out of the rain, and padded by lots of shopping mall–type dis-

LIVERPOOL

tractions. There's plenty of parking. And just strolling along the thriving harborside promenade, you'll find plenty of fun people-watching and local energy.

▲**The Beatles Story**—It's sad to think the Beatles are stuck in a museum (and their music turned into a Las Vegas show). Still,

this exhibit—while overpriced—is excellent, the story's a fascinating one, and even an avid fan will pick up some new information.

Listen to the included audioguide as you study the knickknacks. Cynthia Lennon, John's first wife, still marvels at the manic power of Beatlemania, while the narrator reminds listeners of all that made the group earth-shattering—and even a little edgy—at the time. For example, performing before the Queen Mother, John Lennon famously quips: "Will the people in the cheaper seats clap your hands? And the rest of you, if you'll just rattle your jewelry." The great audioguide captures the Beatles' charm and cheekiness in the way the stuffy wax mannequins can't.

The last few rooms trace the members' solo careers, and the last few steps are reserved for reverence about John's peace work, including a re-creation of the white room he used while writing "Imagine."

Cost and Hours: £13, includes audioguide, daily 9:00–19:00 in summer, 10:00–18:00 in winter, last entry two hours before closing, tel. 0151/709-1963, www.beatlesstory.com. The shop has an impressive pile of Beatles buyables.

▲Merseyside Maritime Museum and International Slavery Museum—These museums tell the story of Liverpool, once the second city of the British Empire. The port prospered in the 18th century as one corner of a commerce triangle with Africa and America. The British shippers profited greatly through exploitation: About 1.5 million enslaved African people passed through Liverpool's docks (if you have African ancestors who arrived in America as slaves, chances are high they came through here). From Liverpool, the British exported manufactured goods to Africa in exchange for enslaved Africans; the slaves were then shipped to the Americas, where they were traded for raw material (cotton, sugar, and tobacco); and the goods were then brought back to Britain. While the merchants on all three sides made money, the big profit came home to England. As Britain's economy boomed, so did Liverpool's. Not all the money made was above-board—a gallery in the basement discusses customs, duties, and the profitable business of smuggling.

Three galleries on the third floor make up the International Slavery Museum. They describe life in West Africa, enslavement and the Middle Passage to America, and the legacy of slavery. At the music desk, you can listen to more than 300 songs from many different genres that were influenced by African music.

After participation in the slave trade was outlawed in Britain in the early 1800s, Liverpool kept its port busy as a transfer point for emigrants. If your ancestors came from Scandinavia, Ukraine, or Ireland, they likely left Europe from this port. Between 1830 and 1930, nine million emigrants sailed from Liverpool to find their dreams in the New World. Awe-inspiring steamers such as the *Lusitania* called this port home. One exhibit shows footage and artifacts of three big Liverpool-related shipwrecks: the *Lusitania*, the *Empress of Ireland*, and the *Titanic*.

Cost and Hours: Free, daily 10:00–17:00, café, tel. 0151/478-4499, www.liverpoolmuseums.org.uk.

Tate Gallery Liverpool—This prestigious gallery of modern art is near the Maritime Museum. It won't entertain you as well as its London sister, the Tate Modern, but if you're into modern art, any Tate's great. Its two airy floors, dedicated to the rotating collection of statues and paintings from the 20th century, are free; the third floor is devoted to special exhibits (free but £3 suggested donation, £8 for special exhibits; Tue–Sun 10:00–17:50, closed Mon except in July–Aug; tel. 0151/702-7400, www.tate.org.uk/liverpool). The Tate has a nice, inexpensive café.

Museum of Liverpool—Opening in 2011, this museum promises to "capture Liverpool's vibrant character and demonstrate the city's unique contribution to the world." Displays will fill a big, splashy, white building on the harborfront next to the Albert Dock, and be divided into four main themes: Port City, Global City, People's City, and Creative City. On my last visit, the details of the new museum were uncertain...all anyone could tell me was that they were moving Ringo's house there, brick by brick (www.liverpool museums.org.uk/mol).

Sleeping in Liverpool

(£1 = about $1.60, country code: 44, area code: 0151)
Your best budget options in this thriving city are the boring, predictable, and central chain hotels. Many hotels, including the ones listed below, charge more on weekends, especially when Liverpool's soccer team plays a home game. Rates shoot up even higher two weekends a year: during the Grand National horse race (April 7–9 in 2011) and during Beatles Week at the end of August—avoid these times if you can.

$$ Sir Thomas Hotel is a centrally located hotel that was once a bank, and feels like it. The 39 recently renovated rooms are comfortable, and deluxe rooms are outfitted with stately, heavy decor (Db-£65 midweek, £85–99 on non-event weekends, includes breakfast, free Wi-Fi, 10-minute walk from station, 24 Sir Thomas Street at the corner of Victoria Street, tel. 0151/236-1366, fax 0151/ 227-1541, www.sirthomashotel.co.uk, reservations@sirthomas hotel.co.uk).

$$ Premier Inn, which has pleasant, American-style rooms and a friendly staff, is right on the Albert Dock (Db-£64–108, check website for specific rates, discounted parking in nearby lot-£7.50, next to The Beatles Story, toll tel. 0871-527-8622, www .premierinn.com). There's a second, downtown **$$ Premier Inn** as well. While it's a much less desirable location than the Albert Dock branch, it's just a 10-minute walk from the Lime Street train station (Vernon Street, just off Dale Street, tel. 0151/242-7650). Both locations can fill up quickly on weekends.

$$ Cocoon Pod Hotel, in the basement of the hostel (next listing), offers 32 no-nonsense, modern rooms with your choice of two twins or a king. As all the rooms are underground, there are no windows—but at least it's quiet (Sb or Db-£43 Sun–Thu, £53 Fri–Sat, 1- to 3-bedroom apartments from £65, free Wi-Fi, breakfast not included but café next door—with £1/30 minutes Internet access, laundry, same location and contact info as hostel below, www.cocoonliverpool.co.uk).

$ International Inn Hostel, run by the daughter of the Beatles' first manager, rents 100 budget beds in a former Victorian warehouse. Most nights, the hostel puts on fun, free food-themed events for guests—like a traditional Liverpudlian stew (Db-£36–45, bed in 2- to 10-bed room-£15–20, includes sheets and towels, all rooms have bathrooms, free toast and tea/coffee, free Wi-Fi, laundry room, games in lobby, TV lounge, video library, 24-hour reception, café, 4 South Hunter Street, tel. & fax 0151/709-8135, www.internationalinn.co.uk, info@internationalinn.co.uk). From the Lime Street Station, it's an easy 15-minute walk. Or take bus #80A or #86A (3–6/hour, direction: Liverpool Airport or Garston). If taking a taxi, tell them it's on South Hunter Street near Hardman Street.

Eating in Liverpool

Not much distinguishes restaurants in Liverpool. Your best bet is to survey your options at the **Albert Dock.** Here you'll find a slew of trendy restaurants that come alive with club energy at night, but are sedate and pleasant in the afternoon and early evening. For lunch, consider the café in the Tate Gallery (described earlier).

Liverpool Connections

By Train

From Liverpool by Train to: Blackpool (hourly, 1.5 hours), **Keswick/Lake District** (train to Penrith—roughly hourly with 1–2 changes, 1.75–2.25 hours; then bus to Keswick—hourly except Sun 8/day, 40 minutes), **York** (hourly, 2.25 hours), **Edinburgh** (hourly, 3.5–3.75 hours, 1–2 changes), **Glasgow** (1–2/hour, 3.5 hours, 1–2 changes), **London's** Euston Station (1–2/hour, 2.25–2.5 hours, some with change), **Crewe** (2/hour, 45 minutes), **Chester** (2/hour, 45 minutes). Train info: toll tel. 0845-748-4950, www .nationalrail.co.uk.

By Ferry

By Ferry to Dublin, Republic of Ireland: It's a seven- to eight-hour trip between Liverpool and Dublin by boat. Both ferry companies require you to check in 1.25–2 hours before the sailing time—call to confirm the details.

P&O Irish Sea Ferries runs a car ferry only—no foot passengers (prices vary widely, roughly £109–195 for car and 2 passengers, Tue–Sat at 9:30 and daily at 21:30, 8-hour trip, overnight ferry includes berth and meals, 20-minute drive north of the city center at Liverpool Freeport—Gladstone dock, toll tel. 0871-664-4777, www.poirishsea.com).

On foot or by car, you can use DFDS Seaways (formerly Norfolkline) from nearby Birkenhead. Ferries sail at 10:00 (Tue–Sat) and nightly at 22:00 (£25–30 for foot passengers on daytime ferry, £20 more for overnight ferry, sleeper cabins extra; prices vary widely, roughly £125–175 for car and 2 passengers on daytime ferry, £215–275 for overnight ferry includes cabin and meals; book online at least one day ahead to avoid additional £10 phone/in-person/day-of-sailing fee, 7-hour trip, Birkenhead Port, toll tel. 0871-230-0330, from the US dial 011-44-208-127-8303, www.norfolkline.com). Birkenhead's dock is a 15-minute walk from Hamilton Square Station on Merseyrail's Wirral Line. You can also take a ferry to Dublin via the Isle of Man (www.steam-packet.com).

By Ferry to Belfast, Northern Ireland: DFDS Seaways (formerly Norfolkline) sails most mornings (Tue–Sun) at 10:30, and every evening (Mon at 22:00, Tue–Sun at 22:30) year-round (8 hours, toll tel. 0871-230-0330, from the US dial 011-44-208-127-8303, www.norfolkline.com). You can also take a ferry to Belfast via the Isle of Man (www.steam-packet.com).

Route Tips for Drivers

From Liverpool to Blackpool: Leaving Liverpool, drive north along the waterfront, following signs to *M58* (Preston). Once on M58 (and not before), follow signs to *M6*, and then *M55* into Blackpool.

THE LAKE DISTRICT

In the pristine Lake District, William Wordsworth's poems still shiver in trees and ripple on ponds. This is a land where nature rules, and humanity keeps a wide-eyed but low profile. Relax, recharge, take a cruise or a hike, and maybe even write a poem. Renew your poetic license at Wordsworth's famous Dove Cottage.

The Lake District, about 30 miles long and 30 miles wide, is nature's lush, green playground. Explore it by foot, bike, bus, or car. While not impressive in sheer height (Scafell Pike, the tallest peak in England, is only 3,206 feet), there's a walking-stick charm about the way nature and the culture mix here. Locals are fond of declaring that their mountains are older than the Himalayas and were once as tall, but have been worn down by the ages. Walking along a windblown ridge or climbing over a rock fence to look into the eyes of a ragamuffin sheep, even tenderfeet get a chance to feel very outdoorsy. The tradition of staying close to the land remains true—albeit in an updated form—in the 21st century; you'll see restaurants serving organic foods as well as stickers advocating for environmental causes in the windows of homes.

Dress in layers, and expect rain mixed with brilliant "bright spells" (pubs offer atmospheric shelter at every turn). Drizzly days can be followed by delightful evenings.

Plan to spend the majority of your time in the unspoiled North Lake District. In this chapter, I focus on the town of Keswick, the lake called Derwentwater, and the vast, time-passed Newlands Valley. The North Lake District works great by car or by bus (with easy train access via Penrith), delights nature-lovers, and has good accommodations to boot.

The Lake District

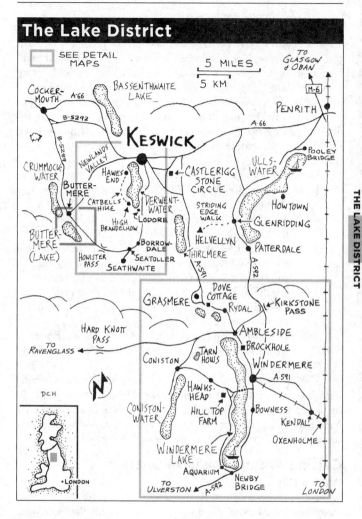

SEE DETAIL MAPS

5 MILES
5 KM

TO GLASGOW & OBAN

M-6

COCKER-MOUTH

A-66

BASSENTHWAITE LAKE

B-5292

PENRITH

A-66

KESWICK

POOLEY BRIDGE

CRUMMOCK WATER

NEWLANDS VALLEY

HAWES END

CASTLERIGG STONE CIRCLE

ULLS-WATER

BUTTER-MERE

CATBELLS HIKE

DERWENT-WATER

STRIDING EDGE WALK

HOWTOWN

GLENRIDDING

HIGH BRANDELHOW

LODORE

HELVELLYN

PATTERDALE

BUTTER-MERE (LAKE)

HONISTER PASS

BORROW-DALE

SEATOLLER

SEATHWAITE

THIRLMERE

A-591

A-592

DOVE COTTAGE

GRASMERE

RYDAL

KIRKSTONE PASS

HARD KNOTT PASS

AMBLESIDE

BROCKHOLE

TO RAVENGLASS

CONISTON

TARN HOWS

WINDERMERE

A-591

N

DCH

HAWKS-HEAD

CONISTON-WATER

HILL TOP FARM

BOWNESS

KENDAL

OXENHOLME

WINDERMERE LAKE

•LONDON

AQUARIUM

TO ULVERSTON

A-592

NEWBY BRIDGE

TO LONDON

THE LAKE DISTRICT

The South Lake District—famous primarily for its Words-worth and Beatrix Potter sights—is slightly closer to London, and gets the promotion, the tour crowds, and the tackiness that comes with them. I strongly recommend that you focus on the north. Ideally, enter the region from the north, via Penrith. Make your home base in or near Keswick, and side-trip from here into the South Lake District only if you're interested in the Wordsworth and Beatrix Potter sights.

Planning Your Time

On a three-week trip to Britain, I'd spend two days and two nights in this area. Penrith is the nearest train station, just 40 minutes by bus or car from Keswick. Those without a car will use Keswick as a springboard: Cruise the lake and take one of the many hikes in the Catbells area. Non-hikers can hop on a minibus tour. If great scenery is commonplace in your life, the Lake District can be more soothing (and rainy) than exciting. If you're rushed, you could make this area a one-night stand—or even a quick drive-through.

Two-Day Driving Plan: Here's the most exciting way for drivers coming from the south—who'd like to visit South Lake District sights en route to the North Lake District—to max out their time here:

Day 1: Get an early start, aiming to leave the motorway at Kendal by 10:30; drive along Windermere and through Ambleside.

11:30 Tour Dove Cottage and the Wordsworth Museum.

13:00 Backtrack to Ambleside, where a small road leads up and over the dramatic Kirkstone Pass (far more scenic northbound than southbound—get out and bite the wind) and down to Glenridding on Lake Ullswater.

15:00 Catch the Ullswater boat and ride to Howtown. Hike six miles (3–4 hours, roughly 15:30–19:00) from Howtown back to Glenridding.

19:00 Drive to your Keswick hotel or farmhouse B&B near Keswick, with a stop as the sun sets at Castlerigg Stone Circle.

Day 2: Spend the morning (3–4 hours) splicing the Catbells high-ridge hike into a circular boat trip around Derwentwater. In the afternoon, make the circular drive from Keswick through the Newlands Valley, Buttermere, Honister Pass, and Borrowdale. You could pitch-and-putt nine holes in Keswick before a late dinner.

Getting Around the Lake District
With a Car

Nothing is very far from Keswick and Derwentwater. Pick up a good map (any hotel can loan you one), get off the big roads, and leave the car, at least occasionally, for some walking. In summer, the Keswick–Ambleside–Windermere–Bowness corridor (A591) suffers from congestion.

Keswick Motor Company rents cars in Keswick (from £32/ day with insurance, Mon–Sat 8:30–17:15, closed Sun, ages 25–70 only, must have an International Driving Permit and passport, Lake Road, a block from Moot Hall in town center, tel. 017687/72064).

Parking is tight throughout the region. It's easiest to just park in the pay-and-display lots (gather small coins, as most machines don't make change). If you're parking free on the roadside, don't block the vital turnouts. Never park on double yellow lines.

Without a Car

Those based in Keswick without a car manage fine. Because of the region's efforts to "green up" travel and cut down on car traffic, the bus service is quite efficient for your hiking and sightseeing. (You could even make a case for leaving your car in town and using the bus for many sightseeing and hiking agendas.)

By Bus: Keswick has no real bus station; buses stop at a turnout in front of the Booths Supermarket. Local buses take you quickly and easily (if not always frequently) to all nearby points of interest. Check the schedule carefully to make sure you can catch the last bus home. The exhaustive *Cumbria & Lakes Rider* bus brochure (50 pages, free, at TI or on any bus) explains the schedules. On board, you can purchase one-day Explorer passes (£10), or get one-day passes for certain routes. A four-day pass is available at the Keswick TI/National Park Visitors Centre. For bus and rail info, visit www.traveline.org.uk.

Buses **#X4** and **#X5** connect Penrith train station to Keswick (hourly Mon–Sat, 8/day Sun, 40 minutes, £5.50).

Bus **#77/#77A,** the Honister Rambler, makes the gorgeous circle from Keswick around Derwentwater, over Honister Pass, through Buttermere, and down the Whinlatter Valley (4/day clockwise, 4/day "anticlockwise," daily Easter–Oct, weekends only in Nov, 1.5-hour loop, £6.50 Honister Dayrider all-day pass).

Bus **#78,** the Borrowdale Rambler, goes topless in the summer, affording a wonderful sightseeing experience in and of itself, heading from Keswick to Lodore Hotel, Grange, Rosthwaite, and Seatoller at the base of Honister Pass (hourly, 2/hour mid-July–Aug, 8/day on Sun, 25 minutes each way, £5.75 Borrowdale Dayrider all-day pass).

Bus **#108** runs between Penrith and Glenridding, stopping in Pooley Bridge (daily 4–6/day, no Sun service Sept–Easter, 45 minutes, £14 Ullswater Bus & Boat day pass covers this bus route as well as steamers on Ullswater).

Bus **#208** runs between Keswick and Glenridding (5/day mid-July–Aug, Sat–Sun only late May–mid-July, 45 minutes).

Bus **#505,** the Coniston Rambler, connects Windermere with Hawkshead (daily Easter–Oct, hourly, 35 minutes).

Bus **#517,** the Kirkstone Rambler, runs between Windermere and Glenridding (3/day mid-July–Aug, Sat–Sun only Easter–mid-July, 1 hour).

Buses **#555** and **#556** connect Keswick with the south (hourly, 1 hour to Windermere).

The Lake District at a Glance

North Lake District

In Keswick

▲▲**Theatre by the Lake** Top-notch theater a pleasant stroll from Keswick's main square. **Hours:** Shows at 20:00 in summer, usually 19:30 in spring and fall, 19:00 in winter; box office open from 9:30 until curtain time. See page 452.

▲**Derwentwater** Lake immediately south of Keswick, with good boat service and trails. See page 444.

▲**Pencil Museum** Peaen to graphite-filled wooden sticks. **Hours:** Daily 9:30–17:00. See page 444.

▲**Pitch-and-Putt Golf** Cheap, easygoing nine-hole course in Keswick's Hope Park. **Hours:** Daily from 9:30, last start at 19:45 or dusk, may close Nov–Easter. See page 445.

Bond Museum Vehicles and more from 007 films. **Hours:** Daily 10:00–17:00, closed roughly Jan–Easter. See page 445.

Near Keswick

▲▲▲ **Scenic Circle Drive South of Keswick** Hour-long drive through the best of the Lake District's scenery, with plenty of fun stops (including the fascinating Honister Slate Mine) and short side-trip options. See page 450.

▲▲**Castlerigg Stone Circle** Evocative and extremely old (even by British standards) ring of Neolithic stones. **Hours:** Always viewable. See page 445.

▲▲**Catbells High Ridge Hike** Two-hour hike along dramatic ridge southwest of Keswick. See page 446.

▲▲**Buttermere Hike** Four-mile, low-impact lakeside loop in a gorgeous setting. See page 448.

▲▲**More Hikes from Keswick** Scenic hikes with varying degrees of difficulty: Latrigg Peak, Latrigg Trail, and Walla Crag. See page 449.

▲▲**Ullswater Hike and Boat Ride** Long lake best enjoyed via steamer boat and seven-mile walk. **Hours:** Boats run June–Aug daily 9/day, April–May and Sept 6/day, fewer off-season. See page 460.

South Lake District

William Wordsworth Sights
▲▲**Dove Cottage and Wordsworth Museum** The poet's humble home, with a museum that tells the story of his remarkable life. **Hours:** Feb–Dec daily 9:30–17:30, closed Jan. See page 464.

Rydal Mount Wordsworth's later, more upscale home. **Hours:** March–Oct daily 9:30–17:00; Nov–Dec and Feb Wed–Sun 11:00–16:00, closed Mon–Tue; closed Jan. See page 466.

Beatrix Potter Sights
▲▲**Beatrix Potter Gallery** Collection of artwork by and background on the creator of Peter Rabbit. **Hours:** April–Oct Sat–Thu 10:30–16:30, mid-Feb–March Sat–Thu 11:00–15:30, closed Fri and Nov–mid-Feb. See page 467.

Hill Top Farm Potter's painstakingly preserved cottage. **Hours:** April–Oct Sat–Thu 10:30–16:30, mid-Feb–March Sat–Thu 11:00–15:30, closed Fri and Nov–mid-Feb, often a long wait to visit—call ahead. See page 467.

The World of Beatrix Potter Touristy exhibition about the author. **Hours:** Daily Easter–Sept 10:00–18:00, Oct–Easter 10:00–17:00. See page 468.

Other Sights
▲**Brockhole National Park Visitors Centre** Best place to gather info on Lake Windermere and the surrounding area, grandly situated in a lakeside mansion. **Hours:** Daily April–Oct 10:00–17:00, Nov–March 10:00–16:00. See page 469.

THE LAKE DISTRICT

Bus #599, the open-top Lakes Rider, runs along the main Windermere corridor, connecting the big tourist attractions in the south (3/hour daily Easter–Aug, 50 minutes each way, £6.50 Central Lakes Dayrider all-day pass, route: Grasmere and Dove Cottage–Rydal Mount–Ambleside–Brockhole–Windermere–Bowness Pier).

By Bike: Several shops in Keswick rent road bikes and mountain bikes. Bikes come with helmets, touring maps, and advice for good trips. Keswick works well as a springboard for several fine days out on a bike; consider a three-hour trip up Newlands Valley and the Latrigg loop up a former train track (now a biking path), and back via Castlerigg Stone Circle.

Good places to rent bikes in Keswick include **Whinlatter Bikes** (£12/half-day, £15/day, daily 10:00–17:00, 82 Main Street, tel. 017687/73940) and **Keswick Mountain Bikes** (£15–20/day depending on model, Mon–Sat 9:00–17:30, Sun 10:00–17:30; right off the town square, at the recommended Lakeland Pedlar Restaurant; tel. 017687/75202, www.keswickbikes.co.uk).

By Boat: A circular boat service glides you around Derwentwater, with several hiker-aiding stops along the way (for a cruise/hike option, see "Derwentwater Lakeside Walk," page 446).

By Foot: Hiking information is available everywhere. Don't hike without a good, detailed map (wide selection at Keswick TI and at the many outdoor gear stores, or borrow one from your B&B). Helpful fliers at TIs and B&Bs describe the most popular routes. For an up-to-date weather report, ask at TI or call 0844-846-2444. Wear suitable clothing and footwear (you can rent boots in town; B&Bs can often loan you a good coat if weather looks threatening). Plan for rain. Watch your footing. Injuries are common. And every year, several people die while hiking in the area (some from overexertion; others are blown off ridges).

By Tour: For organized bus tours that run the roads of the Lake District, see "Tours in Keswick."

Keswick and the North Lake District

As far as touristy Lake District towns go, Keswick (KEZ-ick, population 5,000) is far more enjoyable than Windermere, Bowness, or Ambleside. Many of the place

names around Keswick have Norse origins, inherited from the region's 10th-century settlers. An important mining center for slate, copper, and lead through the Middle Ages, Keswick became a resort in the 19th century. Its fine Victorian buildings recall those Romantic days when city slickers first learned about "communing with nature." Today, the compact town is lined with tearooms, pubs, gift shops, and hiking-gear shops. The lake called Derwentwater is a pleasant 10-minute walk from the town center.

Orientation to Keswick

(area code: 017687)

Keswick is an ideal home base, with plenty of good B&Bs, an easy bus connection to the nearest train station at Penrith, and a prime location near the best lake in the area, Derwentwater. In Keswick, everything is within a 10-minute walk of everything else: the pedestrian town square, the TI, recommended B&Bs, grocery stores, the wonderful municipal pitch-and-putt golf course, the main bus stop, a lakeside boat dock, the post office (with Internet access upstairs), and a central parking lot. Thursdays and Saturdays are market days in the town square, but the square is lively every day throughout the summer.

Keswick town is a delight for wandering. Its centerpiece, Moot Hall (meaning "meeting hall"), was a 16th-century copper warehouse upstairs with an arcade below (closed after World War II). "Keswick" means "cheese farm"—a legacy from the time when the town square was the spot to sell cheese. When the town square went pedestrians-only a few years back, locals were all abuzz about people tripping over the curbs. (The English, seemingly thrilled by ever-present danger, are endlessly warning visitors to "watch your head," "duck or grouse," "watch the step," and "mind the gap.")

THE LAKE DISTRICT

Keswick

THE LAKE DISTRICT

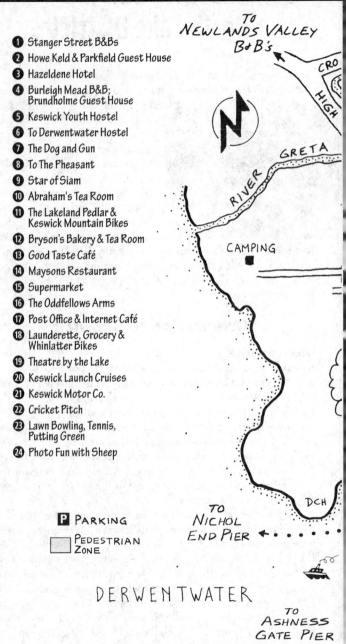

1. Stanger Street B&Bs
2. Howe Keld & Parkfield Guest House
3. Hazeldene Hotel
4. Burleigh Mead B&B; Brundholme Guest House
5. Keswick Youth Hostel
6. To Derwentwater Hostel
7. The Dog and Gun
8. To The Pheasant
9. Star of Siam
10. Abraham's Tea Room
11. The Lakeland Pedlar & Keswick Mountain Bikes
12. Bryson's Bakery & Tea Room
13. Good Taste Café
14. Maysons Restaurant
15. Supermarket
16. The Oddfellows Arms
17. Post Office & Internet Café
18. Launderette, Grocery & Whinlatter Bikes
19. Theatre by the Lake
20. Keswick Launch Cruises
21. Keswick Motor Co.
22. Cricket Pitch
23. Lawn Bowling, Tennis, Putting Green
24. Photo Fun with Sheep

P PARKING

PEDESTRIAN ZONE

TO NEWLANDS VALLEY B&B's

CRO
HIGH

RIVER GRETA

CAMPING

TO NICHOL END PIER

DCH

DERWENTWATER

TO ASHNESS GATE PIER

Keswick and the Lake District are popular with British holiday-makers who prefer to bring their dogs with them on vacation. The town square in Keswick can look like the Westminster Dog Show, and the recommended Dog and Gun pub, where "well-behaved dogs are welcomed," is always full of patient pups. If you are shy about connecting with people, pal up to a British pooch—you will often find they are happy to introduce you to their owners.

Tourist Information

The National Park Visitors Centre is in Moot Hall, right in the middle of the town square (daily Easter–Oct 9:30–17:30, Nov–Easter 9:30–16:30, tel. 017687/72645, www.lake-district.gov.uk and www.keswick.org). Staffers are pros at advising you about hiking routes. They'll also help you figure out public transportation to outlying sights, and book rooms (you'll pay a £4 booking fee; it's cheaper to call B&Bs direct).

The TI sells theater tickets, Keswick Launch tickets (at a £1 discount), fishing licenses, and brochures and maps that outline nearby hikes (£0.60–1.80, including a very simple and driver-friendly £1.70 *Lap Map* featuring sights, walks, and a mileage chart). The TI also has books and maps for hikers, cyclists, and drivers (more books are sold at shops all over town).

Check the "What's On Locally" boards (inside the TI's foyer) for information about walks, talks, and entertainment. The daily weather forecast is posted just outside the front door (weather tel. 0844-846-2444). For information about the TI's guided walks, see "Tours in Keswick," later.

Helpful Hints

Book in Advance: Keswick hosts a variety of festivals and conventions, especially during the summer, so it's smart to book ahead. Please honor your bookings—the B&B proprietors here lose out on much-needed business if you don't show up.

A sampling of events for 2011: The Keswick Jazz Festival mellows out the town in mid-May, followed immediately by the Mountain Festival, then a beer festival in early June (June 3–4 in 2011). The Keswick Religious Convention packs the town with 4,000 evangelical Christians the last three weeks in July.

Several Bank Holiday Mondays in spring and summer (May 2, May 30, and Aug 29 in 2011) draw vacationers from all over the island for three-day weekends.

If you have trouble finding a room (or a B&B that accepts small children), try www.keswick.org to search for available rooms.

Internet Access: U-Compute, located above the store that contains the post office, provides Internet access in a pleasant and airy perch (£2/30 minutes, £3/hour, unused time valid for 2 weeks, daily May–mid-Sept 8:30–21:00, mid-Sept–April 9:00–17:30, 16 terminals and Wi-Fi—same price, corner of Main and Bank streets, tel. 017687/75127). The **launderette** listed next also has Wi-Fi (£2/hour).

Laundry: It's around the corner from the bus station on Main Street, next to the Co-op grocery (self-service Mon–Fri 8:00–19:00, Sat–Sun 9:00–18:00, £6/load wash and dry, change machine and coin-op soap dispenser; full-service for a reasonable £1.20 service charge extra; tea and Wi-Fi for £2, tel. 017687/75448).

Midges: Tiny, biting insects might bug you from late May through September, particularly at dawn and dusk, but insect repellent fends them off.

Tours in Keswick

Guided Walks—Walks of varying levels of difficulty depart from the TI several times a week at 10:00. They're led by local guides, leave regardless of the weather, and sometimes incorporate a bus ride into the outing (£12, Easter–Oct, no tours during religious convention in July, wear suitable clothing and footwear, bring lunch and water, return by 17:00, tel. 017687/72645, www.keswick rambles.org.uk). TIs throughout the region also offer free walks led by "Voluntary Rangers" (generally from Keswick on Sun and Wed in summer, ask for the *Events Guide*).

Bus Tours—These are great for people with bucks who'd like to wring maximum experience out of their limited time and see the area without lots of hiking or messing with public transport. For a cheaper alternative, take public buses.

Mountain Goat Tours is the region's dominant tour company. Unfortunately, they run their minibus tours out of Windermere, with pick-ups in Ambleside and Grasmere, but not Keswick—adding about an extra hour of driving, round-trip, for those based in Keswick (£25/half-day, £35/day, year-round if there are sufficient sign-ups, minimum 4 to a maximum of 16 per hearty bus, book in advance by calling 015394/45161, www.mountain-goat .com).

Show Me Cumbria Private Tours runs personalized tours all around the area, and can pick you up in Keswick. They charge per tour, not per person (for 1–5 people), so their tours are a fine value for small groups (£35/first hour, £25/hour after that, tel. 01768/866-880, mobile 0780-902-6357, based in Penrith, www .showmecumbria.co.uk, andy@showmecumbria.co.uk).

Sights in Keswick

▲Derwentwater—One of Cumbria's most photographed and popular lakes, Derwentwater has four islands, good circular boat service, and plenty of trails. The pleas-

ant town of Keswick is a short stroll from the shore, near the lake's north end. The roadside views aren't much, and while you can walk around the lake (fine trail, floods in heavy rains, 9 miles, 4 hours), much of the walk is boring. You're better off mixing a hike and boat ride (see "Hikes and Drives in the North Lake District," later), or simply enjoy the circular boat tour of the lake (described next).

Boating on Derwentwater: Keswick Launch runs two **cruises** an hour, alternating clockwise and "anticlockwise" (departing on the half-hour, daily 10:00–16:30, July–Aug until 17:30, in winter 5/day weekends only, at end of Lake Road, tel. 017687/72263, www.keswick-launch.co.uk). Boats make seven stops on each one-hour round-trip. The boat trip costs £9 per circle (£1 less if you book through TI) with free stopovers, or about £2 per segment. Stand on the pier Gilligan-style, or the boat may not stop. Keswick Launch also rents **rowboats** for two (£8/30 minutes, £12/hour).

Keswick Launch's **evening cruise** is a delightful little trip that comes with a glass of wine and a mid-lake stop for a short commentary (£9.50, £21 family ticket, 1 hour, mid-July–Aug at 19:30 every evening—weather permitting and if enough people show up; 6 is the minimum). You're welcome to bring a picnic dinner and munch scenically as you cruise.

▲Pencil Museum—Graphite was first discovered centuries ago in Keswick. A hunk of the stuff proved great for marking sheep in the 15th century. In 1832, the first crude Keswick pencil factory opened, and the rest is history (which is what you'll learn about here). While you can't actually tour the 150-year-old factory where the famous Derwent pencils were made, you can enjoy the smell of thousands of pencils getting sharpened for the first time. The adjacent charming and kid-friendly museum is a good way to pass a rainy hour; you may even catch an artist's demonstration. Take a look at the "war pencils" made for WWII bomber crews (filled with tiny maps and compasses) and relax for 10 minutes watching *The Humble Pencil* video in the theater, followed by a sleepy animated-snowman short (£3.50, daily 9:30–17:00, last entry at 16:00, humble café on-site, 3-minute walk from the town center, signposted off Main Street, tel. 017687/73626, www.pencilmuseum.co.uk).

Bond Museum—Next door to the Pencil Museum, and dedicated to all things Bond...James Bond, this museum features an impressive collection of cars from each movie, from *Dr. No*'s dragon tank to *Quantum of Solace*'s Aston Martin DBS V12. For many, it's more exciting than pencils (£6, open "007 days a week" 10:00–17:00, closed roughly Jan–Easter, tel. 01768/775-007—what else?).

Fitz Park—An inviting, grassy park stretches alongside Keswick's tree-lined, duck-filled River Greta. There's plenty of room for kids to burn off energy. Consider an after-dinner stroll on the footpath. You may catch men in white (or frisky schoolboys in uniform) playing a game of cricket. There's the serious bowling green (where you're welcome to watch the experts play, and enjoy the cheapest cuppa—i.e., tea—in town), and the public one where tourists are welcome to give lawn bowling a go (£3). You can try tennis on a grass court (£7/hour for 2 people, includes rackets) or enjoy the putting green (£2). Find the rental pavilion across the road from the art gallery (open daily 9:30–19:45 or until dusk).

▲Golf—A lush nine-hole pitch-and-putt golf course near the gardens in Hope Park separates the town from the lake and offers a classy, cheap, and convenient chance to golf near the birthplace of the sport. This is a great, fun, and inexpensive experience—just right after a day of touring and before dinner (£3.70 for 9 holes, £2.20 for putting, £2.50 for 18 tame holes of "obstacle golf," daily from 9:30, last round starts at 19:45 or dusk, may close Nov–Easter, tel. 017687/73445).

Swimming—While the Leisure Centre doesn't have a serious adult pool, it does have an indoor pool kids love, with a huge water slide and a wave machine (pool-£4.75, kids-£3.75, family-£14, Mon–Tue 11:00–15:00, Wed 11:00–16:00, Thu 11:00–18:00, Fri 11:00–17:00, Sat–Sun 10:00–17:00, shorter hours off-season, longer during school break, no towels or suits for rent, lockers-£1 deposit, 10-minute walk from town center, follow Station Road past Fitz Park and veer left, tel. 017687/72760).

Near Keswick

▲▲Castlerigg Stone Circle—For some reason, 70 percent of England's stone circles are here in Cumbria. Castlerigg is one of the best and oldest in Britain, and an easy stop for drivers. The circle—90 feet across and 5,000 years old—has 38 stones mysteriously laid out on a line between the two tallest peaks on the horizon. They served as a celestial

calendar for ritual celebrations. Imagine the ambience here, as ancient people filled this clearing in spring to celebrate fertility, in late summer to commemorate the harvest, and in the winter to celebrate the winter solstice and the coming renewal of light. Festival dates were dictated by how the sun rose and set in relation to the stones. The more that modern academics study this circle, the more meaning they find in the placement of the stones. The two front stones face due north, toward a cut in the mountains. The rare-for-stone-circles "sanctuary" lines up with its center stone to mark where the sun rises on May Day. (Party!) For maximum "goose pimples" (as they say here), show up at sunset (free, open all the time, 3 miles east of Keswick—follow brown signs, 3 minutes off A66, easy parking).

Hikes and Drives in the North Lake District

From Keswick

Derwentwater Lakeside Walk—There's a trail all along Derwentwater, but much of it (especially the Keswick-to-Hawes End stretch) is not that interesting. The best hour-long section is the 1.5-mile path between the docks at High Brandelhow and Hawes End in Keswick, where you'll stroll a level trail through peaceful trees. This walk works best in conjunction with the lake boat (see "Boating on Derwentwater," earlier).

▲▲Catbells High Ridge Hike—For a great "king of the mountain" feeling, 360-degree views, and a close-up look at the weather

blowing over the ridge, hike above Derwentwater about two hours from Hawes End up along the ridge to Catbells (1,480 feet) and down to High Brandelhow. From there, you can catch the boat back to Keswick, or take the easy path along the shore of Derwentwater to your Hawes End starting point. (Extending the hike farther around the lake to Lodore takes you to a waterfall, rock climbers, a fine café, and another boat dock for a convenient return to Keswick—see "Car Hiking: A Scenic Circle Drive South of Keswick," later.)

Catbells is probably the most dramatic family walk in the area (but wear sturdy shoes, bring a raincoat, and watch your footing). From Keswick, the lake, or your farmhouse B&B, you can see silhouetted figures hiking along this ridge.

Derwentwater & Newlands Valley

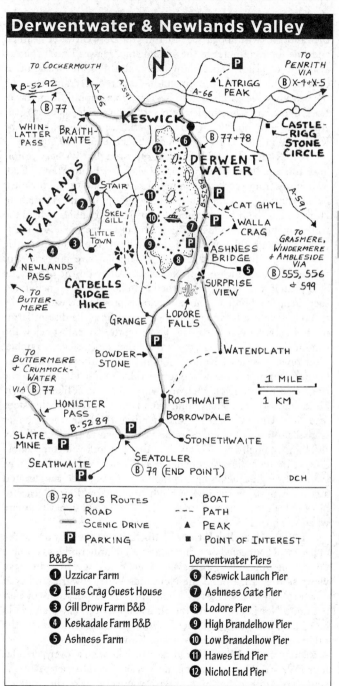

TO COCKERMOUTH

B-5292

(B) 77

WHIN-LATTER PASS

BRAITH-WAITE

NEWLANDS VALLEY

1 STAIR

2

SKEL-GILL

LITTLE TOWN

3

4

NEWLANDS PASS

TO BUTTER-MERE

CATBELLS RIDGE HIKE

A-66

A-591

KESWICK

(B) 77 + 78

DERWENT-WATER

12

6

11

10

9

8

7

B-5289

CAT GHYL

WALLA CRAG

ASHNESS BRIDGE

5

SURPRISE VIEW

GRANGE

LODORE FALLS

P BOWDER-STONE

WATENDLATH

TO BUTTERMERE & CRUMMOCK-WATER VIA (B) 77

HONISTER PASS

B-5289

SLATE MINE **P**

SEATHWAITE **P**

SEATOLLER
(B) 79 (END POINT)

ROSTHWAITE
BORROWDALE
STONETHWAITE

1 MILE
1 KM

TO PENRITH VIA (B) X-4 + X-5

P LATRIGG PEAK

CASTLE-RIGG STONE CIRCLE

A-591

TO GRASMERE, WINDERMERE & AMBLESIDE VIA (B) 555, 556 + 599

DCH

THE LAKE DISTRICT

(B) 78 BUS ROUTES
— ROAD
— SCENIC DRIVE
P PARKING

··· BOAT
--- PATH
▲ PEAK
■ POINT OF INTEREST

B&Bs
1 Uzzicar Farm
2 Ellas Crag Guest House
3 Gill Brow Farm B&B
4 Keskadale Farm B&B
5 Ashness Farm

Derwentwater Piers
6 Keswick Launch Pier
7 Ashness Gate Pier
8 Lodore Pier
9 High Brandelhow Pier
10 Low Brandelhow Pier
11 Hawes End Pier
12 Nichol End Pier

THE LAKE DISTRICT

Getting There: To reach the trailhead from Keswick, catch the "anticlockwise" boat (see "Boating on Derwentwater," earlier) and ride for 10 minutes to the second stop, Hawes End. (You can also ride to High Brandelhow and take this walk in the other direction, but I don't recommend it—two rocky scrambles along the way are easier, and safer, to navigate going uphill from Hawes End.) Note the schedule for your return boat ride, as boats generally run only hourly. Drivers can park free at Hawes End. The Keswick TI sells a *Catbells* brochure about the hike (£0.60).

The Route: The path is not signposted, but it's easy to follow, and you'll see plenty of other walkers. From Hawes End, walk away from the lake, through a kissing gate to the turn just before the car park. Then turn left and go up, up, up. After about 20 minutes, you'll hit the first of two short scrambles (where the trail vanishes into a cluster of steep rocks—the far-left route is easiest through this), which leads to a bluff. From the first little summit, and then along the ridge, you'll enjoy sweeping views of the lake on one side, and of Newlands Valley on the other. The bald peak in the distance is Catbells. Broken stones crunch under each step, wind buffets your ears, clouds prowl overhead, and the sheep baa comically. To anyone looking up from the distant farmhouse B&Bs, you are but a stick figure on the ridge. Just below the summit, the trail disintegrates into another short, steep, scramble. Your reward is just beyond: a magnificent hilltop perch. After Catbells summit, descend along the ridge to a saddle ahead. The ridge continues much higher, and while it may look like your only option, at its base a small, unmarked lane with comfortable steps leads left. Unless you're up for extending the hike (see "Longer Catbells Options," next), take this path down to the lake. To get to High Brandelhow Pier, take the first left fork you come across down through a forest to the lake. When you reach Abbot's Bay, go left through a swinging gate, following a lakeside trail around a gravelly bluff, to the idyllic High Brandelhow Pier, a peaceful place to wait for your boat back to Keswick. (You can pay your fare when you board.)

Longer Catbells Options: Catbells is just the first of a series of peaks all connected by a fine ridge trail. Hardier hikers continue up to nine miles along this same ridge, enjoying valley and lake views as they arc around the Newlands Valley toward (and even down to) Buttermere. After High Spy, you can descend an easy path into Newlands Valley. The ultimate, very full day-plan would be to take a bus to Buttermere, climb Robinson, and follow the ridge around to Catbells and back to Keswick.

▲▲**Buttermere Hike**—The ideal little lake with a lovely, circular four-mile stroll offers nonstop, no-sweat Lake District beauty. If you're not a hiker (but kind of wish you were), take this walk. If

you're very short on time, at least stop here and get your shoes dirty.

Buttermere is connected with Borrowdale and Derwentwater by a great road that runs over rugged Honister Pass. Buses #77/#77A make a 1.5-hour round-trip loop between Keswick and Buttermere that includes a trip over this pass. The two-pub hamlet of Buttermere has a pay-and-display parking lot, but many drivers park free along the side of the road. You're welcome to leave your car at the Fish Hotel if you eat in their pub. There's also a pay parking lot at the Honister Pass end of the lake (at Gatesgarth Farm, £3). The Syke Farm in Buttermere is popular for its homemade ice cream (tel. 01768/770-277).

▲▲**More Hikes from Keswick**—The area is riddled with wonderful hikes. B&Bs all have good advice, but consider these as well:

Latrigg Peak: For the easiest mountain-climbing sensation around, take the short drive to the Latrigg Peak parking lot just north of Keswick, and hike 15 minutes to the top of the 1,200-foot-high hill, where you'll be rewarded with a commanding view of the town and lake. At the traffic circle just outside of Keswick, take the A591 Carlisle exit, then an immediate right (direction: Ormathwaite/Underscar). Take the next right, a hard right, at the *Skiddaw* sign, where a long, steep, one-lane road leads to the Latrigg car park at the end of the lane.

Latrigg Trail: Right from downtown Keswick, you can walk the seven-mile Latrigg trail, which includes a stretch along an old train track and the Castlerigg Stone Circle described earlier (pick up £0.60 map/guide from TI).

Walla Crag: From your Keswick B&B, a fine two-hour walk to Walla Crag offers great fell (mountain) walking and a ridge-walk experience without the necessity of a bus or car. Start by

---

Buttermere Hike

TO CRUMMOCKWATER & COCKERMOUTH VIA Ⓑ 77

TO NEWLANDS VALLEY & KESWICK

B-5289

BUTTERMERE VILLAGE

BUTTER-MERE

GATESGARTH FARM

Ⓟ B-5289

TO HONISTER PASS & DERWENT-WATER VIA Ⓑ 77

SCENIC DRIVE
Ⓑ 77 BUS ROUTE
ROAD
Ⓟ PARKING
--- PATH

1 MILE
1 KM
DCH

THE LAKE DISTRICT

strolling along the lake to the Great Wood parking lot (or drive to this lot), and head up Cat Ghyl (where "fell runners"—trail-running enthusiasts—practice) to Walla Crag. You'll be treated to great panoramic views over Derwentwater and surrounding peaks. You can do a shorter version of this walk from the parking lot at Ashness Bridge.

▲▲▲Car Hiking: A Scenic Circle Drive South of Keswick—
This hour-long drive, which includes Newlands Valley, Buttermere, Honister Pass, and Borrowdale, gives you the best scenery you'll find in the North Lake District. (To do a similar route without a car from Keswick, take loop bus #77/#77A.) Distances are short, roads are narrow and have turn-outs, and views are rewarding. Get a good map and ask your B&B host for advice.

From Keswick, leave town on Crosthwaite Road, then, at the roundabout, head west on Cockermouth Road (A66). Don't take the first Newlands Valley exit, but do take the second one (through Braithwaite), and follow signs up the majestic **Newlands Valley.** If the place had a lake, it would be packed with tourists. But it doesn't—and it isn't.

The valley is dotted with 500-year-old family-owned farms. Shearing day is reason to rush home from school. Sons get school out of the way ASAP, and follow their dads into the family business. Neighbor girls marry those sons and move in. Grandparents retire to the cottage next door. With the price of wool depressed, most of the wives supplement the family income by running B&Bs (virtually every farm in the valley rents rooms). The road has one lane, with turnouts for passing. From the Newlands Pass summit, notice the glacial-shaped wilds, once forested, now not.

From the parking lot at Newlands Pass, at the top of Newlands Valley, there's an easy hike to a little waterfall. There's also an easy one-mile hike up to **Knottrigg,** which probably offers more TPCB (thrills per calorie burned) than any walk in the region. If you don't have time for even a short hike, at least get out of the car and get a feel for the setting.

After Newlands Pass, descend to **Buttermere** (scenic lake, tiny hamlet with a pub and ice-cream store—see "Buttermere Hike," earlier), turn left, and climb over rugged **Honister Pass**—strewn with glacial debris, remnants from the old slate mines, and curious, shaggy Swaledale sheep (looking more like goats with their curly horns). The valleys you'll see are textbook examples of those carved out by glaciers. Look high on the hillsides for "hanging valleys"—small glacial-shaped scoops cut off by the huge flow of the biggest glacier, which swept down the main valley.

The **Honister Slate Mine,** England's last still-functioning slate mine, stands at the summit of Honister Pass. The youth hos-

tel next to it was originally built to house miners in the 1920s. The mine closed in 1986, but was recently purchased and reopened by flamboyant entrepreneur Mark Weir, who now offers worthwhile tours. (As you await your tour, you'll see a video featuring views from Weir's helicopter ride to work.) You'll put on a hardhat, load onto a bus for a short climb, then hike into a shaft to learn about the region's slate industry. It's a long, stooped hike into the mountain, made interesting by the guide, and punctuated by the sound of your helmet scraping against low bits of the shaft. Standing deep in the mountain, surrounded by slate scrap and the beams of thirty headlamps fluttering around like fireflies, you'll learn of the hardships of miners' lives and how "green gold" is trendy once again, making the mine viable. Call ahead to confirm tour times and to book a spot (£10, 1.5-hour tour; departs daily at 10:30, 12:30, 14:00, and 15:30; Dec–Jan 12:30 tour only, tel. 017687/77230, www.honister.com). Even if you don't have time to take the tour, stop here for its slate-filled shop (café and nice WCs).

After stark and lonely Honister Pass, drop into sweet and homey **Borrowdale,** with a few lonely hamlets and fine hikes from Seathwaite. Circling back to Keswick past Borrowdale, B5289 takes you past a number of popular attractions: You can climb stairs to the top of the house-size **Bowder Stone** (signposted, a few minutes walk off the main road). Farther along, **Lodore Falls** is a short walk from the road (behind Lodore Hotel). **Shepherds Crag,** a cliff overlooking Lodore, was made famous by pioneer rock climbers. (Their descendants hang from little ridges on its face today.) This is serious climbing, with several fatalities a year.

For a great lunch, or tea and cakes, drop into the much-loved **High Lodore Farm Café,** where sheep farmer Martin is busy feeding hikers and day-trippers (Easter–Oct daily 9:00–17:00, closed Nov–Easter, short drive uphill from the main road and over a tiny bridge, tel. 017687/77221).

A hard right off B5289 (signposted *Ashness Bridge, Watendlath*) and a steep half-mile climb on a narrow lane takes you to the postcard-pretty **Ashness Packhorse Bridge** (a quintessential Lake District scene, parking lot just above on right). A half-mile farther up (parking lot on left, no sign), and you're startled by the "surprise

THE LAKE DISTRICT

view" of Derwentwater (great for a lakes photo op). Continuing from here, the road gets extremely narrow en route to the hamlet of **Watendlath,** which has a tiny lake and lazy farm animals.

Return to B5289, the Borrowdale Valley Road, and back to Keswick. If you have yet to see it, cap your drive with a short detour from Keswick to the Castlerigg Stone Circle (described earlier).

Nightlife in Keswick

▲▲Theatre by the Lake—Keswickians brag that they enjoy "London theater quality at Keswick prices." Their theater offers events year-round and a wonderful rotation of six plays through the summer (plays vary throughout the week, with music concerts on Sun). There are two stages: The main one seats 400, and the smaller "studio" theater seats 100 (and features edgier plays with rough language and nudity). Attending a play here is a fine opportunity to enjoy a classy night out (£10–23, box office open from 9:30 until curtain time, discounts for old and young, 20:00 shows in summer, usually at 19:30 in spring and fall, at 19:00 in winter, café, smart to book ahead, parking at the adjacent lot is free after 18:30, tel. 017687/74411; book by phone, at TI, or online: www.theatrebythelake.com).

▲▲Evening Activities—For a small and remote town, Keswick has lots going on in the evening. Remember, at this latitude it's light until 22:00 in midsummer. Along with the Theatre by the Lake (described above), you can **golf** (fine course, pitch-and-putt, goofy golf, or just enjoy the putting green, last start at 19:45) or **walk** among the grazing sheep in Hope Park as the sun gets ready to set (between the lake and the golf course, access from just above the beach, great photo ops on balmy evenings).

To socialize with locals, head to a pub for one of their special evenings: There's **quiz night** at The Dog and Gun (21:30 on most Thu; £1, proceeds go to Keswick's Mountain Rescue team, which rescues hikers and the occasional sheep). At a quiz night, tourists are more than welcome. Drop in, say you want to join a team, and you're in. If you like trivia, it's a great way to get to know people here.

Also in the town center, The Oddfellows Arms has free **live music** most nights (usually classic rock, from 21:30).

You can join Bob, the **Town Crier,** when he does his routine many summer Tuesday evenings (£2.50, 1.5 hours, usually starts at 19:30, weekly late May–early July, details at TI). Catch a **movie** at the Alhambra Cinema, a restored old-fashioned movie theater a few minutes' walk from the town center. An **evening lake cruise** is perfect for an extremely scenic and relaxing picnic dinner (£10, with narration, mid-July–Aug at 18:30 and 19:30, 55 minutes).

Sleeping in Keswick

The Lake District abounds with attractive B&Bs, guest houses, and hostels. It needs them all when summer hordes threaten the serenity of this Romantic mecca.

Reserve your room in advance in high season. From October through April, you should have no trouble finding a room. But to get a particular place (especially on Saturdays), call ahead. If you're using public transportation, you should sleep in Keswick. If you're driving, staying outside Keswick is your best chance for a remote farmhouse experience. Lakeland hostels offer £20 beds and come with an interesting crowd of all ages.

For Keswick, I've featured B&Bs and small hotels on two streets, each within three blocks of the bus station and town square. Stanger Street, a bit humbler but quiet and handy, has smaller homes and more moderately priced rooms. "The Heads" is a classier area lined with proud Victorian houses, close to the lake and theater, overlooking a golf course.

Many of my Keswick listings charge extra for a one-night stay. Most won't book one-night stays on weekends (but if you show up and they have a bed free, it's yours) and don't welcome children under 12 (unless extremely well-behaved). Owners are enthusiastic about offering plenty of advice to get you on the right walking trail. Most accommodations have inviting lounges with libraries of books on the region and loaner maps. Take advantage of these lounges to transform your humble B&B room into a suite.

This is still the countryside—expect huge breakfasts (often with a wide selection, including vegetarian options), no phones in

---

Sleep Code

(£1 = about $1.60, country code: 44, area code: 017687)
S = Single, **D** = Double/Twin, **T** = Triple, **Q** = Quad, **b** = bathroom, **s** = shower only. You can assume credit cards are accepted unless otherwise noted, and all B&B stays include breakfast.

To help you sort easily through these listings, I've divided the rooms into three categories based on the price for a double room with bath:

$$$ Higher Priced—Most rooms £75 or more.
 $$ Moderately Priced—Most rooms between £30-75.
  $ Lower Priced—Most rooms £30 or less.

Prices can change without notice; verify the hotel's current rates online or by email. For other updates, see www.ricksteves.com/update.

the rooms, and shower systems that might need to be switched on to get hot water. Parking is pretty easy (each place has a line on parking).

On Stanger Street

This street, quiet but just a block from Keswick's town center, is lined with B&Bs situated in Victorian slate townhouses. Each of these places is small, family-run, and only accepts cash. They are all good, offering comfortably sized rooms and a friendly welcome.

$$ Dunsford Guest House rents four rooms decorated with a Victorian feel, at a good price. Stained glass and wooden pews give the blue-and-cream breakfast room a country-chapel vibe (Db-£66, this price promised with this book in 2011, no children under age 16, free Wi-Fi, parking, 16 Stanger Street, tel. 017687/75059, www.dunsford.net, enquiries@dunsford.net, accommodating Richard and Linda).

$$ Heckberry House's two light, airy rooms are both on the first floor (Db-£64, 2-night minimum, no children, will pick up from bus station, 12 Stanger Street, tel. 017687/71277, www.heckberry.co.uk, enquiries@heckberry.co.uk, friendly Judith and David).

$$ Badgers Wood B&B, at the top of the street, has six modern, bright, un-frilly view rooms, each named after a different tree (Sb-£38, Db-£70, 2-night minimum, no children under age 12, special diets accommodated, Wi-Fi, 30 Stanger Street, tel. 017687/72621, www.badgers-wood.co.uk, enquiries@badgers-wood.co.uk, Andrew and Anne).

$$ Abacourt House, with a daisy-fresh breakfast room, has five pleasant doubles (Db-£68, no children, Wi-Fi, 26 Stanger Street, tel. 017687/72967, www.abacourt.co.uk, abacourt.keswick@btinternet.com, John and Heather).

On The Heads

These B&Bs are in an area known as The Heads. This area is classier, with bigger and grander Victorian architecture and great views overlooking the pitch-and-putt range and out into the hilly distance. The golf-course side of The Heads has free parking, if you can snare a spot (easy at night).

$$$ Howe Keld has the polished feel of a boutique hotel, but offers all the friendliness of a B&B. Its 14 contemporary-posh rooms are spacious and tastefully decked out in native woods and slate. It's warm, welcoming, and family-run, with one of the best breakfasts I've had anywhere in England (Sb-£45–50, standard Db-£80, superior Db-£95, cash preferred, 2 ground-floor rooms, family deals, free Wi-Fi, 017687/72417, www.howekeld.co.uk, david@howekeld.co.uk, run with care by David and Valerie Fisher).

THE LAKE DISTRICT

$$$ Parkfield Guest House, thoughtfully run and decorated by John and Susan Berry, is a big Victorian house. Its seven bright and pastel rooms have fine views (Sb-£55, Db-£78 with this book through 2011, Db suite-£98, 2-night minimum, no children under age 16, Wi-Fi, off-street parking available, tel. 017687/72328, www .parkfield-keswick.co.uk, susanberryparkfield@hotmail.com).

$$$ Burleigh Mead B&B is a slate mansion from 1892 with wild carpeting. Gill (pronounced "Jill," short for Gillian) rents seven lovely rooms for a great value, and offers a friendly welcome, as well as a lounge and peaceful front-yard sitting area that's perfect for enjoying the view (Db-£75, cash only, tel. 017687/75935, www.burleighmead.co.uk, info@burleighmead.co.uk).

$$$ Hazeldene Hotel, on the corner of The Heads, rents 10 spacious rooms, many with commanding views (Db-£70–90, Tb-£105, £5 extra for one-night stay, free Wi-Fi, tel. 017687/72106, www.hazeldene-hotel.co.uk, Helen).

$$ Brundholme Guest House has three bright and comfy rooms, all with grand views—especially from the front side—and a friendly and welcoming atmosphere (Db-£68 in 2011, cash only, tel. 017687/73305, www.brundholme.co.uk, barbara@brundholme .co.uk, the Thompsons).

Hostels in and near Keswick

The Lake District's inexpensive hostels, mostly located in great old buildings, are handy sources of information and social fun. These two hostels—both part of the Youth Hostels Association (www .yha.org.uk)—are former hotels, offering Internet access, laundry machines, and three cheap meals daily; at these, non-members pay about £3 extra a night, or buy a £16 membership.

$ Keswick Youth Hostel, with 85 beds in a converted old mill that overlooks the river, has a great riverside balcony and plenty of handy facilities, including a big lounge and library. Travelers of all ages feel at home here, but book ahead—beds here can be hard to come by from July through September (£22/bed, mostly 3- to 6-bed rooms, includes sheets and breakfast, café, bar, laundry, center of town just off Station Road before river, tel. 017687/72484, keswick@yha.org.uk).

$ Derwentwater Hostel, in a 200-year-old mansion on the shore of Derwentwater, is two miles south of Keswick and has 88 beds (£20 beds in 4- to 22-bed rooms, family rooms, 23:00 curfew, follow B5289 from Keswick, look for sign 100 yards after Ashness exit, tel. 017687/77246, derwentwater@yha.org.uk).

West of Keswick, in the Newlands Valley

If you have a car, drive 10 minutes past Keswick down the majestic Newlands Valley (described earlier, under "Car Hiking: Scenic

Circle Drive South of Keswick"). This valley is studded with 500-year-old farms that have been in the same family for centuries, and now rent rooms to supplement the family income. Each place offers easy parking, grand views, and perfect tranquility. The rooms are plainer and generally more dated than the B&Bs in town, and come with steep and gravelly roads, plenty of dogs, and an earthy charm. Traditionally, farmhouses lacked central heating, and while they are now heated, you can still request a hot-water bottle to warm up your bed.

Getting to the Newlands Valley: Leave Keswick via the roundabout at the end of Crosthwaite Road, and then head west on Cockermouth Road (A66). Take the second Newlands Valley exit through Braithwaite, and follow signs through Newlands Valley (drive toward Buttermere). All of my recommended B&Bs are on this road: Uzzicar Farm (under the shale field, which local kids love hiking up to glissade down), Ellas Crag Guest House, then Gill Brow Farm, and finally—the last house before the stark summit—Keskadale Farm (about four miles before Buttermere). The one-lane road has turnouts for passing. These are listed in geographical order, the first being a 10-minute drive from Keswick and the last being at the top of the valley (about a 15-minute drive from Keswick).

$$ Uzzicar Farm is a big, rustic place with a comfy B&B in a low-ceilinged, circa-1650 farmhouse—watch out for ducks. It's a particularly intimate and homey setting, where you'll feel like part of the family (S-£35, D or Db-£65, family deals, cash only, tel. 017687/78026, www.uzzicarfarm.co.uk, uzzicar@googlemail.com, Helen, David, and three daughters).

$$ Ellas Crag Guest House, with three rooms—each with a great view—is more of a comfortable stone house than a farm. This homey B&B offers a good mix of modern and traditional decor, including beautifully tiled bathrooms (Ss-£45, Sb-50, Ds-£60, Db-£64, these prices guaranteed with this book through 2011, cash only, 2-night minimum, local free-range meats and eggs for breakfast, sack lunches available, huge DVD library, laundry-£10, tel. 017687/78217, www.ellascrag.co.uk, info@ellascrag.co.uk, Jane and Ed Ma and their children).

$$ Gill Brow Farm is a rough-hewn, working farmhouse where Anne Wilson rents two simple but fine rooms (D or Db-£58, 10 percent discount with this book and 2-night stay in 2011, tel. 017687/78270, www.gillbrow-keswick.co.uk, wilson_gillbrow @hotmail.com).

$$ Keskadale Farm is another good farmhouse experience, with Ponderosa hospitality. One of the valley's oldest, the house—with two rooms to rent and a cozy lounge—is made from 500-year-old ship beams. This working farm is an authentic slice of

Lake District life and is your chance to get to know lots of curly-horned sheep and the dogs who herd them. Now that her boys are old enough to help Dad in the fields, Margaret Harryman runs the B&B (Sb-£40, Db-£60–70, £2 extra for one-night stays, cash only, closed Dec–Feb, tel. 017687/78544, www.keskadalefarm.co.uk, info@keskadalefarm.co.uk). They also rent a two-bedroom apartment (£400/week).

Southwest of Keswick, in Buttermere

$$$ Bridge Hotel, just beyond Newlands Valley at Buttermere, offers 21 beautiful rooms—most of them quite spacious—and a classic Old World countryside-hotel experience. On Fridays and Saturdays, a £31 dinner is required (standard Db-£130, fancier rooms for more, free Wi-Fi in lobby, tel. 017687/70252, fax 017687/70215, www.bridge-hotel.com, enquiries@bridge-hotel.com). There are no shops within 10 miles—only peace and quiet a stone's throw from one of the region's most beautiful lakes. The hotel has a dark-wood pub/restaurant on the ground floor.

$ Buttermere Hostel, a quarter-mile south of Buttermere village on Honister Pass Road, has good food, 70 beds, family rooms, and a peacefully rural setting (£20 beds in 4- to 6-bed rooms, £2 cheaper mid-week, includes breakfast, inexpensive lunches and dinners, laundry, office open 8:30–10:00 & 17:00–22:30, 23:00 curfew, toll tel. 0845-371-9508, buttermere@yha.org.uk).

South of Keswick, near Borrowdale

$$$ Ashness Farm sits alone, ruling its valley high above Derwentwater. If you want to be immersed in farm sounds and lakeland beauty, this is the place. On this 750-acre working farm, now owned by the National Trust, people have raised sheep and cattle for centuries. Today Anne and her son are "tenant farmers" keeping this farm operating, and renting five rooms to boot (Db-£75–86, less for 2 nights, cozy lounge, eggs and sausage literally fresh off the farm for breakfast, just above Ashness Bridge, tel. 017687/77361, www.ashnessfarm.co.uk, inquiries@ashnessfarm.co.uk).

$$ Seatoller Farm B&B is a rustic 17th-century house in a five-building hamlet where Christine Simpson rents three rooms. The old windows are small, but the abundant flower boxes keep things bright (Db-£70, less for 2 or more nights, tel. 017687/77232, www.seatollerfarm.co.uk, info@seatollerfarm.co.uk).

$ Borrowdale Hostel, in secluded Borrowdale Valley just south of Rosthwaite, is a well-run place surrounded by many ways to immerse yourself in nature. The hostel serves cheap dinners, offers sack lunches, and keeps the pantry well-stocked (86 beds, £18–22 beds in 2- to 8-bed dorms, D-£44, £3 more for non-members, family rooms, pay Internet access and Wi-Fi, laundry machines, 3 cheap meals daily, 23:00 curfew, toll tel. 0845-371-9624, borrowdale@yha.org.uk). To reach this hostel from Keswick by bus, take #78, the "Borrowdale Rambler" (hourly, 2/hour mid-July–Aug, 8/day on Sun; last bus from Keswick at 17:40 most of year, at 18:00 mid-July–Aug).

Eating in Keswick

Keswick has a huge variety of eateries catering to its many visitors, but I've found nothing particularly enticing at the top end; the places listed here are just good, basic values. Most stop serving by 21:00.

The Dog and Gun serves good pub food, but mind your head, and tread carefully: Low ceilings and wooden beams loom over-head, while paws poke out from under tables below, as Keswick's canines wait patiently for their masters to finish their beer (£6–10 meals, daily 12:00–21:00, goulash, no chips and proud of it, 2 Lake Road, tel. 017687/73463).

The Pheasant is a walk outside town, but locals trek here reg-ularly for the food. The menu offers Lake District pub standards (fish pie, Cumbrian sausage, guinea fowl), as well as more inventive choices. Check the walls for caricatures of pub regulars, sketched at these tables by a Keswick artist. While they have a small restau-rant section, I much prefer eating in the bar (£9–13 meals, daily 12:00–14:00 & 18:00–21:00, Crosthwaite Road, tel. 017687/72219). From the town square, walk past the Pencil Museum, hang a right onto Crosthwaite Road, and walk 10 minutes. For a more scenic route, cross the river into Fitz Park, go left along the riverside path until it ends at the gate to Crosthwaite Road, turn right, and walk five minutes.

Star of Siam serves wonderful and authentic Thai dishes in a tasteful dining room (£8–10 plates, daily 12:00–14:30 & 17:30–22:30, 89 Main Street, tel. 017687/71444).

Abraham's Tea Room, popular with townspeople, is a fine value for lunch. It's tucked away on the first floor of the giant George Fisher outdoor store (£4–6 soups and sandwiches, Mon–Fri 10:00–17:00, Sat 9:30–17:00, Sun 10:30–16:30, on the corner where Lake Road turns right).

The Lakeland Pedlar, a wholesome, pleasant café (with a bike shop upstairs), serves freshly baked vegan and vegetarian fare, including soups, organic bread, and daily specials. Their interior is cute. Outside tables face a big parking lot (£8 meals, daily 9:00–17:00, Thu–Sat until 21:00 in summer, Hendersons Yard, find the narrow walkway off Market Street between pink Johnson's sweet shop and The Golden Lion, tel. 017687/74492).

Bryson's Bakery and Tea Room has an enticing ground-floor bakery, with sandwiches and light lunches. The upstairs is a popular tearoom. Order lunch to go from the bakery, or for a few pence more, eat there, either sitting on stools or at a couple of sidewalk tables (£4–8 meals, Mon–Sat 8:30–17:30—tearoom opens at 9:30, Sun 9:30–17:00, 42 Main Street, tel. 017687/72257). Consider their £16 two-person Cumberland Cream Tea, which is like afternoon tea in London, but cheaper, and made with local products. Sandwiches, scones, and little cakes are served on a three-tiered platter with tea.

Good Taste has a small café space but a huge following, and is known for its fresh ingredients and its chef's expertise. Stop by for a light snack of homemade muffins and an espresso, or try a wild-boar burger (Mon–Sat 8:30–16:30, closed Sun, 19 Lake Road, tel. 017687/75973).

Maysons Restaurant, with Californian ambience, is fast and easy, with a buffet line of curry, Cajun, and vegetarian options. The food is cooked fresh on the premises, but it's nothing fancy: You point, and they dish up and microwave (£6–8 plates, cash only; April–Oct daily 11:30–20:45; Nov–March Mon–Thu 11:45–17:00, Fri–Sun 11:45–20:30; family-friendly, also take-out—great for evening cruise picnic, 33 Lake Road, tel. 017687/74104).

Picnic: The fine **Booths supermarket** is right where all the buses arrive (Mon–Sat 8:00–21:00, Sun 10:00–16:00, The Headlands). The recommended **Bryson's Bakery** does good sandwiches to go (described earlier). **The Keswickian,** on the town square, serves up old-fashioned fish-and-chips to go (daily 11:00–23:30, upstairs restaurant closes earlier). Just around the corner, **The Cornish Pasty** offers an enticing variety of fresh meat pies to go (£2–3 pies, daily 9:30–17:30 or until the pasties are all gone, across from The Dog and Gun on Borrowdale Road).

In the Newlands Valley

The farmhouse B&Bs of Newlands Valley don't serve dinner, so their guests have two good options: Go into Keswick, or take the lovely 10-minute drive to Buttermere for your evening meal at the **Fish Hotel Pub,** which has fine indoor and outdoor seating, but takes no reservations (£8–10 meals, daily 12:00–14:00 & 18:00–21:00, family-friendly, good fish and daily specials with fresh vegetables, tel. 017687/70253). The neighboring **Bridge Hotel Pub** is a bit cozier and serves "modern-day nibbles and good classic pub grub" (£10–12 meals, daily 12:00–21:30, tel. 017687/70252).

Keswick Connections

The nearest train station to Keswick is in Penrith (ticket window open Mon–Sat 5:30–21:00, Sun 11:30–21:00, no lockers). For train and bus info, check at a TI, visit www.traveline.org.uk, or call

0845-748-4950 (for train), or 0871-200-2233 (£0.10/minute). Most routes run less frequently on Sundays.

From Keswick by Bus: For connections, see page 435.

From Penrith by Bus to: Keswick (Mon–Sat roughly hourly 7:20–22:45, only 8/day on Sun, 40 minutes, £5.50, pay driver, Stagecoach buses #X4 and #X5), **Ullswater** and **Glenridding** (6/day, 45 minutes, bus #108). The Penrith bus stop is just outside the train station (bus schedules posted inside and outside station).

From Penrith by Train to: Blackpool (12/day, 1.75 hours, change in Preston), **Liverpool** (roughly hourly, 2 hours, change in Wigan or Preston), **Birmingham**'s New Street Station (roughly hourly, 2.5–3 hours, some with change in Preston), **Durham** (hourly, 2.5–3 hours, change in Carlisle and Newcastle), **York** (2/hour, 3.5–4 hours, 1–2 transfers), **London**'s Euston Station (9/day, 3–3.5 hours), **Edinburgh** (nearly hourly, 1.75 hours), **Glasgow** (10/day, 1.5–2 hours), **Oban** (2/day, morning train 5.75 hours, evening train 6.75 hours, both require changing stations in Glasgow, evening train requires additional change in Carlisle).

Route Tips for Drivers

Coming from (or Going to) the West: Only 1,300 feet above sea level, Hard Knott Pass is still a thriller, with a narrow, winding, steeply graded road. Just over the pass are the scant but evocative remains of the Hard Knott Roman fortress. The great views can come with miserable rainstorms, and it can be very slow and frustrating when the one-lane road with turnouts is clogged by traffic. Avoid it on summer weekends.

From Points South (such as Blackpool, Liverpool, or North Wales) to the Lake District: The direct, easy way to Keswick is to leave M6 at Penrith, and take the A66 highway for 16 miles to Keswick. For the scenic sightseeing drive through the south lakes to Keswick, exit M6 on A590/A591 through the towns of Kendal and Windermere to reach Brockhole National Park Visitors Centre. From Brockhole, the A road to Keswick is fastest, but the high road—the tiny road over Kirkstone Pass to Glenridding and lovely Ullswater—is much more dramatic.

Near Keswick: Ullswater

▲▲Ullswater Hike and Boat Ride

Long, narrow Ullswater, which some consider the loveliest lake in the area, offers eight miles of diverse and grand Lake District scenery. While you can drive it or cruise it, I'd ride the boat from the south tip halfway up (to Howtown—which is nothing more than a dock) and hike back. Or walk first, then enjoy an easy ride

back. Old-fashioned "steamer" boats (actually diesel-powered) leave **Glenridding** regularly for Howtown (£5.50 one-way, £9 round-trip, covered by £14 Ullswater Bus & Boat day pass, family rates, June–Aug daily 9/day 9:45–16:45, April–May and Sept 6/day 9:45–15:50, fewer off-season, 35 minutes one-way, drivers can use safe pay-and-display parking lot—£2/2 hours, £4/12 hours; take bus #108 from Penrith, bus #208 from Keswick, or bus #517 from Windermere; café at dock, brochure shows walking route, tel. 017684/82229, www.ullswater-steamers.co.uk).

From Howtown, spend three to four hours hiking and dawdling along the well-marked path by the lake south to Patterdale, and then along the road back to Glenridding. This is a serious seven-mile walk with good views, varied terrain, and a few bridges and farms along the way. For a shorter hike from Howtown Pier, consider a three-mile loop around Hallin Fell. A rainy-day plan is to ride the covered boat up and down the lake to Howtown and back, or to Pooley Bridge at the northern tip of the lake (£12 round-trip, 2–5/day, 2 hours). Boats don't run in really bad weather—call ahead if it looks iffy.

Helvellyn

Considered by many the best high-mountain hike in the Lake District, this breathtaking round-trip route from Glenridding includes the spectacular Striding Edge—about a half-mile along the ridge. Be careful; do this six-hour hike only in good weather, since the wind can be fierce. While it's not the shortest route, the Glenridding ascent is best. Get advice from the Keswick TI, which has a helpful *Helvellyn from Glenridding* leaflet on the hike (£0.60).

South Lake District

The South Lake District has a cheesiness similar to other popular English resort destinations. Here, piles of low-end vacationers suffer through terrible traffic, slurp ice cream, and get candy floss caught in their hair. The area around Windermere is worth a drive-through if you're a fan of Wordsworth or Beatrix Potter, but you'll still want to spend the majority of your Lake District time (and book your accommodations) up north.

Getting Around

By Car: Driving is your best option to see the small towns and sights clustered in the South Lake District; consider combining your drive with the bus trip mentioned below. If you're coming to or leaving the South Lake District from the west, you could take the Hard Knott Pass for a scenic introduction to the area.

By Bus: Buses are a fine and stress-less way to lace together this gauntlet of sights in the congested Lake Windermere neighborhood. The open-top Lakes Rider bus #599 stops at Bowness Pier (lake cruises), Windermere (train station), Brockhole (National Park Visitors Centre), Ambleside, Rydal Mount, and Grasmere (Dove Cottage). Consider leaving your car at Grasmere and enjoying the breezy and extremely scenic ride, hopping off and on as you like (3/hour daily Easter–Aug, 50 minutes each way, Central Lakes Dayrider all-day pass-£6.50—buy from driver). Buses #555 and #556 run between Windermere and Keswick.

Sights in the South Lake District

Wordsworth Sights

William Wordsworth was one of the first writers to reject fast-paced city life. During England's Industrial Age, hearts were muzzled and brains ruled. Science was in, machines were taming nature, and factory hours were taming humans. In reaction to these brainy ideals, a rare few—dubbed Romantics—began to embrace untamed nature and undomesticated emotions.

Back then, nobody climbed a mountain just because it was there—but Wordsworth did. He'd "wander lonely as a cloud" through the countryside, finding inspiration in "plain living and high thinking." He soon attracted a circle of like-minded creative friends.

The emotional highs the Romantics felt weren't all natural. Wordsworth and his poet friends Samuel Taylor Coleridge and Thomas de Quincey got stoned on opium and wrote poetry, combining their generation's standard painkiller drug with their

Wordsworth at Dove Cottage

William Wordsworth (1770–1850) was a Lake District home-boy. Born in Cockermouth (in a house now open to the public), he was schooled in Hawkshead. In adulthood, he married a local girl, settled down in Grasmere and Ambleside, and was buried in Grasmere's St. Oswald's churchyard.

But the 30-year-old man who moved into Dove Cottage in 1799 was not the carefree lad who'd roamed the district's lakes and fields. At Cambridge University, he'd been a C student, graduating with no job skills and no interest in a nine-to-five career. Instead, he and a buddy hiked through Europe, where Wordsworth had an epiphany of the "sublime" atop Switzerland's Alps. He lived a year in France, watching the Revolution rage. It stirred his soul. He fell in love with a Frenchwoman who bore his daughter Caroline. But lack of money forced him to return to England, and the outbreak of war with France kept them apart.

Pining away in London, William hung out in the pubs and coffeehouses with fellow radicals, where he met poet Samuel Taylor Coleridge. They inspired each other to write, edited each other's work, and jointly published a groundbreaking book of poetry.

In 1799, his head buzzing with words and ideas, William and his sister (and soul mate) Dorothy moved into the white-washed, slate-tiled former inn now known as Dove Cottage. He came into a small inheritance, and dedicated himself to poetry full time. In 1802, with the war over, William returned to France to finally meet his daughter. (He wrote of the rich experience: "It is a beauteous evening, calm and free.../Dear child! Dear Girl! that walkest with me here,/If thou appear untouched by solemn thought,/Thy nature is not therefore less divine.")

Having achieved closure, Wordsworth returned home to marry a former kindergarten classmate, Mary. She moved into Dove Cottage, along with an initially jealous Dorothy. Three of their five children were born here, and the cottage was also home to Mary's sister, the family dog Pepper (a gift from Sir Walter Scott; see Pepper's portrait), and frequent houseguests who bedded down in the pantry: Scott, Coleridge, and Thomas de Quincey, the Timothy Leary of opium.

After almost nine years here, Wordsworth's family and social status had outgrown the humble cottage. They moved first to a house in Grasmere before settling down in Rydal Hall. Wordsworth was changing. After the Dove years, he would write less, settle into a regular government job, quarrel with Coleridge, drift to the right politically, and endure criticism from old friends who branded him a sellout. Still, his poetry—most of it written at Dove—became increasingly famous, and he died honored as England's Poet Laureate.

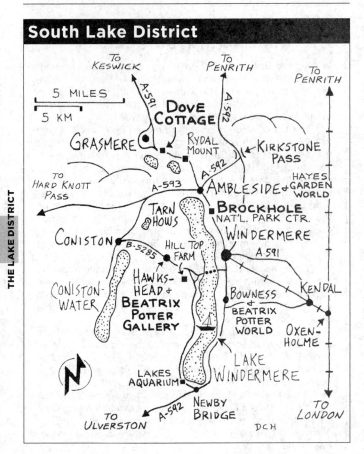

South Lake District

THE LAKE DISTRICT

tree-hugging passions. Today, opium is out of vogue, but the Romantic movement thrives as visitors continue to inundate the region.

▲▲**Dove Cottage and Wordsworth Museum**—For poets, this two-part visit is the top sight of the Lake District. Take a short tour of William Wordsworth's humble cottage and be inspired in its excellent museum, which displays original writings, sketches, personal items, and fine paintings.

The poet whose appreciation of nature and a back-to-basics lifestyle put this area on the map spent his most productive years (1799–1808) in this well-preserved stone cottage on the edge of Grasmere. After functioning as the Dove and Olive Bow pub for almost 200 years, it was bought by

Wordsworth's Poetry at Dove

At Dove Cottage, Wordsworth was immersed in the beauty of nature and the simple joy of his young, growing family. It was here that he reflected on both his idyllic childhood and his troubled twenties. The following are select lines from two well-known poems from this fertile time.

Ode: Intimations of Immortality

There was a time when meadow, grove, and stream,
The earth, and every common sight, to me did seem
Apparelled in celestial light, the glory and the freshness
    of a dream.
It is not now as it hath been of yore; turn wheresoe'er I
    may, by night or day,
The things which I have seen I now can see no more.
Now while the birds thus sing a joyous song...
To me alone there came a thought of grief...
Whither is fled the visionary gleam?
Where is it now, the glory and the dream?
Our birth is but a sleep and a forgetting:
The Soul...cometh from afar...
Trailing clouds of glory do we come
From God, who is our home.

I Wandered Lonely as a Cloud

I wandered lonely as a cloud
That floats on high o'er vales and hills,
When all at once I saw a crowd,
A host, of golden daffodils;
Beside the lake, beneath the trees,
Fluttering and dancing in the breeze...
For oft, when on my couch I lie
In vacant or in pensive mood,
They flash upon that inward eye
Which is the bliss of solitude;
And then my heart with pleasure fills,
And dances with the daffodils.

his family. This is where Wordsworth got married, had kids, and wrote much of his best poetry. Still owned by the Wordsworth family, the furniture was his, and the place comes with some amazing artifacts, including the poet's passport and suitcase (he packed light). Even during his lifetime, Wordsworth was famous, and Dove Cottage was turned into a museum in 1891—predating even the National Trust, which protects the house today.

Even if you're not a fan, Wordsworth's appreciation of nature, his Romanticism, and the ways his friends unleashed their creative talents with such abandon are appealing. The 30-minute cottage **tour** (departures on the hour and half-hour) and adjoining **museum**—with lots of actual manuscripts handwritten by Wordsworth and his illustrious friends—are both excellent. In dry weather, the garden where the poet was much inspired is worth a wander. (Visit this after leaving the cottage tour, and pick up the description at the back door. The garden is closed when wet.) Allow 1.5 hours for this visit.

Cost and Hours: £7.50, daily Feb–Dec 9:30–17:30, last entry at 17:00, last tour at 16:50, closed Jan, bus #555 or #556 from Keswick, tel. 015394/35544, www.wordsworth.org.uk. Parking costs £5 in the Dove Cottage lot facing the main road (A591), 50 yards from the site (coins only; grants you £4 rebate on Dove Cottage ticket).

Poetry Readings: On Tuesday evenings in summer, the Wordsworth Trust puts on poetry readings, where national poets read their own works. They're hoping to continue the poetry tradition of the Lake District. Readings are held at the St. Oswald's Church in Grasmere Village (every other Tue at 18:45, runs May–mid-Oct only, two 45-minute sessions followed by an optional dinner, £7 at the door or £6 pre-booked, £15 pre-booked dinner, tel. 015394/35544).

Rydal Mount—Located just down the road from Dove Cottage, this sight is well worthwhile for Wordsworth fans. The poet's final, higher-class home, with a lovely garden and view, lacks the humble charm of Dove Cottage, but still evokes the time and creative spirit of the literary giant who lived here for 37 years. His family repurchased it in 1969 (after a 100-year gap), and his great-great-great-  granddaughter still calls it home on occasion, as shown by recent family photos sprinkled throughout the house.

After a short intro by the attendant, you'll be given an explanatory flier and are welcome to roam. Wander through the garden William himself designed, which has changed little since then. Surrounded by his nature, you can imagine the poet enjoying them with you. "O happy gardens! Whose seclusion deep, so friendly to industrious hours; and to soft slumbers, that did gently steep our spirits carry with them dreams of flowers, and wild notes warbled among leafy bowers."

Cost and Hours: £6; March–Oct daily 9:30–17:00; Nov–Dec and Feb Wed–Sun 11:00–16:00, closed Mon–Tue; closed Jan, 1.5 miles north of Ambleside, well-signed, free and easy parking, bus #555 or #556 from Keswick, tel. 015394/33002, www.rydalmount .co.uk.

Beatrix Potter Sights

Of the many Beatrix Potter commercial ventures in the Lake District, there are two serious Beatrix Potter sights: her farm (Hill Top Farm); and her husband's former office, which is now the Beatrix Potter Gallery, filled with her sketches and paintings. The sights are two miles apart, in or near Hawkshead, a 20-minute drive south of Ambleside. If you're coming over from Windermere, catch the cute little 15-car ferry (runs constantly except when it's extremely windy, 10-minute trip, £4 car fare includes all passengers). Note that both of the major sights are closed on Friday.

On busy summer days, the wait to get into Hill Top Farm can last several hours (only eight people are allowed in every five minutes, and the timed-entry tickets must be bought in person). If you like cutesy tourist towns (Hawkshead), this can be a blessing. Otherwise, you'll wish you were in the woods somewhere with Wordsworth.

Hill Top Farm—A hit with Beatrix Potter fans (and skippable for others), this dark and intimate cottage, swallowed up in the inspirational and rough nature around it, provides an enjoyable if quick experience. The six-room farm was left just as it was when she died in 1943. At her request, the house is set as if she had just stepped out—flowers on the tables, fire on, low lights. While there's no printed information here, the room guides are eager to explain things.

Cost and Hours: £6.50, tickets often sell out by 14:00, April–Oct Sat–Thu 10:30–16:30, mid-Feb–March Sat–Thu 11:00–15:30, closed Fri and Nov–mid-Feb, last entry 30 minutes before closing, in Near Sawrey village, 2 miles south of Hawkshead, bus #505 or #525 from Hawkshead, Mountain Goat Tours' hourly shuttle bus from ferry dock, tel. 015394/36269, www.nationaltrust.org.uk /beatrixpotter. Drivers can park and buy tickets 150 yards down the road, and walk back to tour the place. Call the farm for the current wait times (if no one answers, leave a message for the administrator; someone will call you back).

▲▲**Beatrix Potter Gallery**—Located in the cute but extremely touristy town of Hawkshead, this gallery fills her husband's former law office with the wonderful and intimate drawings and watercolors that Potter did to illustrate her books. The best of the Potter sights, the gallery has plenty of explanation about her life and work. Even non-Potter fans find her art surprisingly interesting. Of about 700 works in the gallery's possession, a rotation of about 50 are shown at any one time. As you enter, pick up a page identifying each work of art—then you'll know (for example) that it's Mrs. Tittle Mouse meeting Bappity Bumble.

Cost and Hours: £4.50, tiny discount with Hill Top Farm, same hours as Hill Top Farm, bus #505 from Windermere, Main Street, drivers use the nearby pay-and-display lot and walk 200

Beatrix Potter
(1866–1943)

As a girl growing up in London, Beatrix Potter vacationed in the Lake District, where she became inspired to write her popular children's books. Unable to get a publisher, she self-published the first two editions of *The Tale of Peter Rabbit* in 1901 and 1902. When she finally landed a publisher, sales of her books were phenomenal. With the money she made, she bought Hill Top Farm, a 17th-century cottage, and fixed it up, living there from 1905 until she married in 1913. Potter was more than a children's book writer; she was a fine artist, an avid gardener, and a successful farmer. She married a lawyer and put her knack for business to use, amassing a 4,000-acre estate. An early conservationist, she used the garden-cradled cottage as a place to study nature. She willed it—along with the rest of her vast estate—to the National Trust, which she enthusiastically supported. The events of Potter's life were dramatized in the 2007 movie *Miss Potter*, starring Renée Zellweger as Beatrix.

yards to the town center, tel. 015394/36355, www.nationaltrust.org.uk/beatrixpotter.

Hawkshead—The town of Hawkshead is engulfed in Potter tourism, and the extreme quaintness of it all is off-putting. Just across from the pay-and-display parking lot is the interesting Hawkshead Grammar School Museum, founded in 1585, where William Wordsworth studied from 1779 to 1787. It shows off old school benches and desks whittled with penknife graffiti (£2 includes guided tour; April–Sept Mon–Sat 10:00–13:00 & 14:00–17:00, Sun 13:00–17:00; Oct Mon–Sat 10:00–13:00 & 14:00–15:30, Sun 13:00–15:30; closed Nov–March; bus #505 from Windermere, tel. 015394/36735, www.hawksheadgrammar.org.uk).

The World of Beatrix Potter—This tour, a hit with children, is a gimmicky exhibit with all the historical value of a Disney ride. The 45-minute experience features a 5-minute video trip into the world of Mrs. Tiggywinkle and company, a series of Lake District tableaux starring the same imaginary gang, and an all-about-Beatrix section, with an 8-minute video biography (£7, kids-£3.50, daily Easter–Sept 10:00–18:00, Oct–Easter 10:00–17:00, last entry 30 minutes before closing, in Bowness near Windermere town, tel. 015394/88444, www.hop-skip-jump.com).

More Sights at Lake Windermere

▲**Brockhole National Park Visitors Centre**—Set in a nicely groomed lakeside park, the center offers a free 30-minute video on life in the Lake District (played upon request), an information desk, organized walks (see the park's free *Visitor Guide*), exhibits, a bookshop (excellent selection of maps and guidebooks), a cafeteria, gardens, nature walks, and a large parking lot. Check the events board as you enter (free entry but steep £3 parking fee—coins only, or buy ticket at the Visitors Centre 100 yards away from parking lot; daily April–Oct 10:00–17:00, Nov–March 10:00–16:00, bus #555 from Keswick, buses #505 and #599 from Windermere, tel. 015394/46601, www.lake-district.gov.uk). It's in a stately old lakeside mansion between Ambleside and Windermere on A591. For a joyride around famous Windermere, catch the Brockhole "Green" cruise (£7, hourly April–Oct, more sailings mid-July–Aug, 45-minute circle, scant narration).

Lakes Aquarium—This aquarium gives a glimpse of the natural history of Cumbria. Exhibits describe the local wildlife living in lake and coastal environments, including otters, eels, pike, sharks, and the "much maligned brown rat." Experts give various talks throughout the day (£9, kids under 15-£6, family deals, daily 9:00–18:00, until 17:00 in winter, last entry one hour before closing, in Lakeside, by Newby Bridge, at south end of Lake Windermere, tel. 015395/30153, www.lakesaquarium.co.uk).

Hayes Garden World—This extensive gardening center, a popular weekend excursion for locals, offers garden supplies, a bookstore, a playground, and gorgeous grounds. Gardeners could wander this place all afternoon. Upstairs is a fine cafeteria-style restaurant (Mon–Sat 9:00–18:00, Sun 11:00–17:00, at south end of Ambleside on main drag, see *Garden Centre* signs, located at north end of Lake Windermere, tel. 015394/33434, www.hayesgarden world.co.uk).

THE LAKE DISTRICT

YORK

Historic York is loaded with world-class sights. Marvel at the York Minster, England's finest Gothic church. Ramble The Shambles, York's wonderfully preserved medieval quarter. Enjoy a walking tour led by an old Yorker. Hop a train at Europe's greatest railway museum, travel to the 1800s in the York Castle Museum, and head back a thousand years to Viking York at the Jorvik exhibit. And to get a taste of scenically desolate countryside, side-trip to the North York Moors.

York has a rich history. In A.D. 71, it was Eboracum, a Roman provincial capital—the northernmost city in the empire. Constantine was actually proclaimed emperor here in A.D. 306. In the fifth century, as Rome was toppling, a Roman emperor sent a letter telling England it was on its own, and York became Eoforwic, the capital of the Anglo-Saxon kingdom of Northumbria.

A church was built here in 627, and the town became an early Christian center of learning. The Vikings later took the town, and from the 9th through the 11th centuries, it was a Danish trading center called Jorvik. The invading and conquering Normans destroyed then rebuilt the city, fortifying it with a castle and the walls you see today.

Medieval York, with 9,000 inhabitants, grew rich on the wool trade and became England's second city. Henry VIII used the city's fine Minster as his Anglican Church's northern capital. (In today's Anglican Church, the Archbishop of York is second only to the Archbishop of Canterbury.)

In the Industrial Age, York was the railway hub of northern England. When it was built, York's train station was the world's largest. Today, York's leading industry is tourism.

Planning Your Time

York is the best sightseeing city in England after London. On even a 10-day trip through Great Britain, it deserves two nights and a day. For the best 36 hours, follow this plan: Catch the 18:45 free city walking tour on the evening of your arrival (evening tours offered mid-June through Aug). The next morning, be at the Castle Museum when it opens (at 9:30)—it's worth a good two hours. Then browse and sightsee the rest of town. Train buffs love the National Railway Museum, and the Yorkshire Museum displays artifacts from throughout the region's history. Tour the Minster at 16:00 before catching the 17:15 evensong service (16:00 on Sun, usually none on Mon). Finish your day with an early-evening stroll along the wall (wall gates close at 20:00), and perhaps through the abbey gardens. This schedule assumes you're here in the summer (when the evening orientation walk is going) and that there's an evensong on. Confirm your plans with the TI.

It's not worth going out of your way to visit the North York Moors (described at the end of this chapter), but it's handy to zip through that area if you're traveling between York and Durham.

Orientation to York

(area code: 01904)

York has about 190,000 people; about one in ten is a student. But despite the city's size, the sightseer's York is small. Virtually everything is within a few minutes' walk: sights, train station, TI, and B&Bs. The longest walk a visitor might take (from a B&B across the old town to the Castle Museum) is 30 minutes.

Bootham Bar, a gate in the medieval town wall, is the hub of your York visit. (In York, a "bar" is a gate and a "gate" is a street. Go ahead—blame the Vikings.) At Bootham Bar and on Exhibition Square, you'll find the starting points for most walking tours and bus tours, handy access to the medieval town wall, a public WC, and Bootham Street—which leads to the recommended B&Bs. To find your way around York, use the Minster's towers as a navigational landmark, or follow the strategically placed green signposts, which point out all places of interest to tourists.

Tourist Information

The **Museum Street** TI sells a £1 *York Map and Guide*. Ask for the free monthly *What's On* guide and the *York MiniGuide*, which includes a map and some discounts (April–Oct Mon–Sat 9:00–18:00, Sun 10:00–17:00; Nov–March Mon–Sat 9:00–17:00, Sun 10:00–16:00; 1 Museum Street, tel. 01904/550-099, www.visit york.org). The TI books rooms for a £4 fee. A screen lists "Today's Events in Town."

York and Yorkshire Pass: The TI sells an expensive pass that covers most York sights and a lot of other major sights in the region, and gives you discounts on the City Sightseeing hop-on, hop-off bus tours. You'd have to be a very busy sightseer to make this pass worth it—most will want to skip it (£28/1 day, £38/2 days, £44/3 days, £68/6 days, www.yorkshirepass.com).

Arrival in York

By Train: The train station is a 10-minute walk from town. Day-trippers can store baggage at the Europcar office on platform 1 (£5/24 hours, Mon–Sat 8:00–20:30, Sun 9:00–20:30). To walk downtown from the station, turn left down Station Road, and follow the crowd toward the Gothic towers of the Minster. After the bridge, a block before the Minster, you'll come upon the TI on your right. Recommended B&Bs are a 10-minute walk or a £5 taxi ride from the station—for specific walking directions to the B&Bs, see page 493.

By Car: As you near York (and your B&B), you'll hit the A1237 ring road. Follow this to the A19/Thirsk roundabout (next to river on northeast side of town). From the roundabout, follow signs for *York City*, traveling through Clifton into Bootham. All recommended B&Bs are four or five blocks before you hit the medieval city gate (see neighborhood map, page 494). If you're approaching York from the south, take M1 until it becomes A1M, exit at junction 45 onto A64, and follow it for 10 miles until you reach York's ring road (A1237), which allows you to avoid driving through the city center. If you have more time, A19 from Selby is a slower and more scenic route into York.

Helpful Hints

Festivals: Book a room well in advance during festival times, and on weekends any time of year. The **Viking Festival** features *lur* horn-blowing, warrior drills, and re-created battles in mid-February (www.jorvik-viking-centre.co.uk). The **Early Music Festival** (medieval minstrels, Renaissance dance, and so on) zings its strings in mid-July (July 8–16 in 2011, www.ncem.co.uk/yemf.shtml). York claims to be the "Ascot of the North," and the town fills up on horse-race weekends, especially during the **Ebor Races** in mid-August (once a month May–Oct, check schedules at www.yorkracecourse.co.uk). And the **York Festival of Food and Drink** takes a bite out of the last two weekends of September (www.yorkfoodfestival.com). For a complete list of festivals, see www.yorkfestivals.com.

Internet Access: Evil Eye Lounge has 10 terminals in a hip bar (Mon–Sat 10:00–23:00, Sun 11:00–23:00, upstairs at

42 Stonegate, tel. 01904/640-002). The **Basement Internet Café-Bar** overlooks the river (£3/hour, daily 11:00–18:00, 9 terminals, lower level of City Screens Cinema, at 13 Coney Street, tel. 01904/612-940). The **York Public Library**'s reference desk, on the first floor up, provides Internet access to visitors (£1/hour, Mon–Thu 9:00–19:45, Fri 9:00–18:00, Sat 9:00–17:00, Sun 11:00–16:00, Museum Street, tel. 01904/552-828).

Laundry: The nearest place is **Haxby Road Launderette,** a long 15-minute walk north of the town center (about £8/load self-service, about £1.50 more for drop-off service, Mon–Wed and Fri 9:00–17:45, Thu 10:00–18:00, Sat 9:00–17:15, Sun 9:00–16:15, start last loads 1.5 hours before closing, 124 Haxby Road, tel. 01904/623-379). Some B&Bs will do laundry for a small charge.

Bike Rental: With the exception of the pedestrian center, the town's not great for biking. But there are several fine countryside rides from York, and the riverside New Walk bike path is pleasant. **Bob Trotter Cycles,** just outside Monk Bar, rents bikes and has free cycling maps (£15/day, helmet and map free with this book in 2011, Mon–Sat 9:00–17:30, closed Sun, 13–15 Lord Mayor's Walk, tel. 01904/622-868, www.bobtrottercycles.com). **Europcar,** at platform 1 at the train station, also rents bikes (£10/day, includes helmet and lock, Mon–Sat 8:00–20:30, Sun 9:00–20:30, toll tel. 0844-846-4003, www.autohorn.co.uk).

Taxi: From the train station, taxis zip new arrivals to their B&Bs for £5. Queue up at the taxi stand, or call 01904/638-833; cabbies don't start the meter until you get in.

Car Rental: If you're nearing the end of your trip, consider dropping your car upon arrival in York. The money saved by turning it in early just about pays for the train ticket that whisks you effortlessly to London. In York, you'll find these agencies: **Avis** (Mon–Fri 8:00–18:00, Sat 8:00–13:00, closed Sun, 3 Layerthorpe, toll tel. 0844-544-6117); **Hertz** (Mon–Fri 8:00–17:00, Sat 9:00–13:00, closed Sun, at train station, tel. 01904/612-586); **Budget** (Mon–Fri 8:00–18:00, Sat 8:00–13:00, closed Sun, near the National Railway Museum at 75 Leeman Road, tel. 01904/644-919); and **Europcar** (Mon–Sat 8:00–20:30, Sun 9:00–20:30, train station platform 1, toll tel. 0844-846-4003).

Beware: Except for Europcar, most car-rental agencies close early on Saturday afternoons and all day Sunday—when dropping off is OK, but picking up is only possible by prior arrangement (and for a fee).

YORK

Tours in York

▲▲▲Walking Tours

Free Walks with Volunteer Guides—Charming locals give energetic, entertaining, and free two-hour walks through York (daily at 10:15 all year, plus 14:15 April–Oct, plus 18:45 June–Aug, depart from Exhibition Square in front of the art gallery). These tours often go long because the guides love to teach and tell stories. You're welcome to cut out early—but say so or they'll worry, thinking they lost you.

Yorkwalk Tours—These are more serious 1.5- to 2-hour walks with a history focus. They do four different walks: Essential York, Roman York, Secret York, and York's Snickelways (£5.50 each, Feb–Nov daily at 10:30 and 14:15, Dec–Jan weekends only, depart from Museum Gardens Gate, just show up, tel. 01904/622-303, www.yorkwalk.co.uk—check website, TI, or call for schedule). Tours go rain or shine, with as few as two participants.

Haunted Walks—Numerous ghost tours, all offered after dusk, are more fun than informative. "Haunted Walk" relies a bit more on storytelling and history than on masks and surprises (£4, Easter–Oct nightly at 20:00, weekends only Nov–Easter, 1.5 hours, just show up, depart from Exhibition Square in front of the art gallery, end in The Shambles, tel. 01904/621-003).

Local Guide—**Julian Cripps** offers good private walking tours (£25/hour, tel. 01904/709-755, mobile 077-6323-4156, travellers intime@googlemail.com), as well as guided day trips to the North York Moors, Whitby, and Goathland.

▲City Bus Tours

Two companies run hop-on, hop-off bus tours circling York. While you can hop on and off all day, these have no real transportation value because York is so compact. If taking a bus tour, I'd catch either one at Exhibition Square (near Bootham Bar) and ride it for an orientation all the way around. Consider getting off at the National Railway Museum, skipping the last five minutes.

City Sightseeing—This outfit's half-enclosed, bright-red, double-decker buses take tourists past secondary York sights that the city walking tours skip—the mundane perimeter of town. Buses that leave Exhibition Square at the top and bottom of each hour usually have live guides in summer—look for a sign in the front window (£9, £13.50 combo-ticket with boat cruise through YorkBoat—see below, pay driver cash, ticket good for 24 hours, can also buy tickets online or from TI with credit card, Easter–Sept buses run 9:15–17:00, every 10 minutes, less frequent off-season, tel. 01904/655-585, www.yorktourbuses.co.uk).

York Pullman Bus Tours—These classic old-time buses are slightly less expensive, with fewer stops, live guides, and two over-lapping routes (£7.50, buy ticket from driver, office, or TI; mid-June–Oct departs 6/hour from Exhibition Square daily 9:20–17:15, off-season 2–3/hour until about 16:00, 45 minutes, enclosed bus used when wet, tel. 01904/622-992, www.yorkpullmanbus.co.uk).

Boat Cruise

YorkBoat does a lazy, narrated 45-minute lap along the River Ouse (£7.50, £13.50 combo-ticket with City Sightseeing bus tours—see above, 4/day Feb–Nov 10:30–15:00; runs every 30–45 minutes April–Oct; 1.25-hour evening cruise at 21:15 for £9.50; leaves from Lendal Bridge and King's Staith landings, near Skeldergate Bridge, tel. 01904/628-324, www.yorkboat.co.uk).

Self-Guided Walk

Museum Gardens and Wall

Get a taste of Roman and medieval York on this easy stroll along a segment of York's wall.

YORK

• *Start just inside the Museum Gardens Gate (near the river, where Lendal Street hits Museum Street; gate closes at 20:00). About 20 yards to the right of the gate stands...*

Abbey Hospital: The 13th-century facade of the Abbey hospital is interesting mostly because of the ancient Roman tombs stacked just under its vault. These were buried outside the Roman city and discovered in the last century with the building of the train line.

• *Continue into the garden. About 50 yards ahead (on the right) is another remnant of ancient Rome, the...*

Multangular Tower: This 12-sided tower (A.D. 300) was likely a catapult station built to protect the town from enemy river traffic. The red ribbon of bricks was a Roman trademark—both structural and decorative. The lower stones are Roman, while the upper, bigger stones are medieval. After Rome fell, York suffered through two centuries of a dark age. Then the Vikings ruled from 780. They built with wood, so almost nothing from that period remains. The Normans came in 1066 and built in stone, gener-ally atop Roman structures (like this wall). The Roman wall that defined the ancient garrison town worked for the Norman town, too. From the 1600s on, no such fortified walls were needed in England's interior.

• *Continue about 100 yards (past the Neoclassical building holding the fine Yorkshire Museum on the right—worth a visit and described on page 489) to York's ruined...*

St. Mary's Abbey: This abbey dates to the age of William the

York

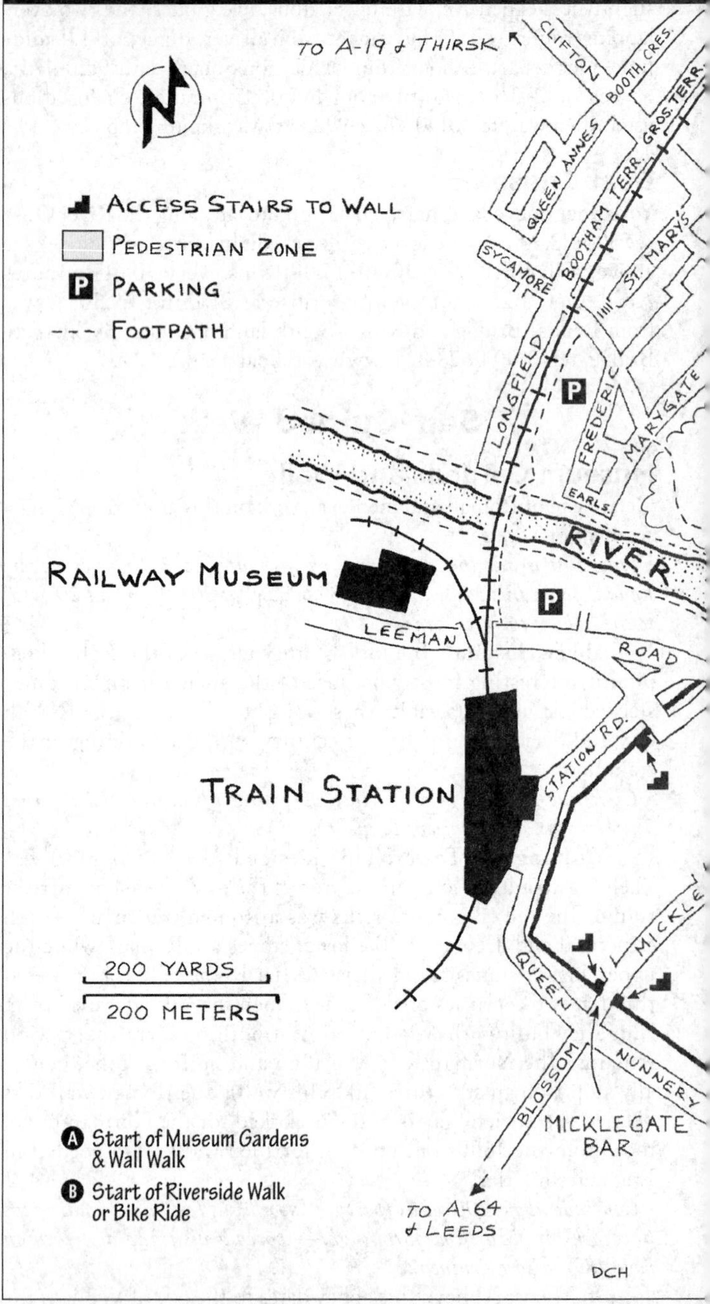

N

- ◢ ACCESS STAIRS TO WALL
- ▢ PEDESTRIAN ZONE
- 🅿 PARKING
- --- FOOTPATH

TO A-19 & THIRSK

CLIFTON
BOOTH. CRES.
GROS. TERR.
QUEEN ANNES
BOOTHAM TERR.
ST. MARYS
SYCAMORE
LONGFIELD
FREDERIC
MARYGATE
EARLS

🅿

RIVER

🅿

RAILWAY MUSEUM

LEEMAN

ROAD

STATION RD.

TRAIN STATION

MICKLE

200 YARDS
200 METERS

QUEEN

NUNNERY

BLOSSOM

MICKLEGATE
BAR

A Start of Museum Gardens
   & Wall Walk

B Start of Riverside Walk
   or Bike Ride

TO A-64
& LEEDS

DCH

YORK

Conqueror—whose harsh policies of massacres and destruction in this region (called the "Harrowing of the North") made him unpopular. His son Rufus, who tried to improve relations in the 12th century, established a great church here. The church became an abbey that thrived from the 13th century until the Dissolution of the Monasteries in the 16th century. The Dissolution, which came with the Protestant Reformation and break with Rome, was a power play by Henry VIII. He took over the land and riches of the monasteries. Upset with the pope, he wanted his subjects to pay him taxes rather than give the Church tithes. (For more information, see the sidebar on page 483.)

As you gaze at this ruin, imagine magnificent abbeys like this scattered throughout the realm. Henry VIII destroyed most of them, taking the lead from their roofs and leaving the stones to scavenging townsfolk. Scant as they are today, these ruins still evoke a time of immense monastic power. The one surviving wall was the west half of a very long, skinny nave. The tall arch marked the start of the transept. Stand on the plaque that reads *Crossing beneath central tower,* and look up at the air that now fills the space where a huge tower once stood.

YORK

• *Now, backtrack about 50 yards and turn left, walking between the museum and the Roman tower. Continuing between the abbot's palace and the town wall, you're walking along a "snickelway"—a small, characteristic York lane or footpath. The snickelway pops out on...*

Exhibition Square: With the Dissolution, the Abbot's Palace became the **King's Manor** (from the snickelway, make a U-turn to the left and through the gate). Today, it's part of the University of York. Because the northerners were slow to embrace the king's reforms, Henry VIII came here to enforce the Dissolution. He stayed 17 days in this mansion and brought along a thousand troops to make a statement of his determination. You can wander into the grounds and building. The Refectory Café serves cheap cakes, soup, and sandwiches to students, professors, and visitors like you (Mon–Fri 9:30–15:30, closed Sat–Sun).

Exhibition Square is the departure point for various walking and bus tours. You can see the towers of the **Minster** in the distance. (Travelers in the Middle Ages could see the Minster from miles away as they approached the city.) Across the street is a public WC, and **Bootham Bar**—one of the fourth-century Roman gates in York's wall—with access to the best part of the city walls (free, walls open 8:00–dusk).

• *Climb up and...*

Walk the Wall: Hike along the top of the wall behind the Minster to the first corner. York's 12th-century walls are three miles long. Norman kings built the walls to assert control over northern England. Notice the pivots in the crenellations (square notches at

York at a Glance

▲▲▲**York Minster** York's pride and joy, and one of England's finest churches, with stunning stained-glass windows, textbook Decorated Gothic design, and glorious evensong services. **Hours:** Open for worship daily from 7:00 and for sightseeing Mon–Sat from 9:00 (9:30 Nov–March), Sun from 12:00; flexible closing time (roughly May–Oct at 18:30, earlier off-season); shorter hours for tower and undercroft; evensong services Tue–Sat 17:15, Sun 16:00, occasionally on Mon, sometimes no services mid-July–Aug. See page 480.

▲▲▲**York Castle Museum** Excellent, far-ranging collection displaying everyday objects from Victorian times to the present. **Hours:** Daily 9:30–17:00. See page 486.

▲▲**National Railway Museum** Train buff's nirvana, tracing the history of all manner of rail-bound transport. **Hours:** Daily 10:00–18:00. See page 488.

▲▲**Yorkshire Museum** Sophisticated archaeology and natural history museum with York's best Viking exhibit, plus Roman, Saxon, Norman, and Gothic artifacts. **Hours:** Daily 10:00–17:00. See page 489.

▲**The Shambles** Atmospheric old butchers' quarter, with colorful, tipsy medieval buildings. **Hours:** Always open. See page 486.

▲**Jorvik** Cheesy, crowded, but not-quite-Disney-quality exhibit/ride exploring Viking lifestyles and artifacts. **Hours:** Daily April–Oct 10:00–17:00, Nov–March 10:00–16:00. See page 487.

▲**Fairfax House** Glimpse into an 18th-century Georgian family house, with enjoyably chatty docents. **Hours:** Mon–Thu and Sat 11:00–16:30, Sun 13:30–16:30, Fri by tour only at 11:00 and 14:00. See page 489.

the top of a medieval wall), which once held wooden hatches to provide cover for archers. At the corner with the benches—Robin Hood's Tower—you can lean out and see the moat outside. This was originally the Roman ditch that surrounded the fortified garrison town. Continue walking for a fine view of the Minster (better when the scaffolding comes down in 2014), with its truncated main tower and the pointy rooftop of its chapter house.

• *Continue on to the next gate,* **Monk Bar** *(skip the tacky museum in the tower house). Descend the wall at Monk Bar, and step past the portcullis* *to emerge outside the city's protective wall. Lean against the last bollard and gaze up at the tower, imagining 10 archers behind the arrow slits. Keep an eye on the 12th-century guards, with their stones raised and primed to protect the town. Return through the city wall and go left at the fork in the road to follow Goodramgate a couple of blocks into the old town center. Hiding off Goodramgate on the right is...*

Holy Trinity Church: This church holds rare box pews atop a floor that is sinking as bodies rot and coffins collapse (open Tue–Sun 10:00–16:00, closed Mon). The church is built in the late Perpendicular Gothic style, with lots of clear and precious stained glass from the 13th to 15th centuries. Enjoy the peaceful picnic-friendly gardens.

• *Goodramgate dead ends at...*

King's Square: This lively people-watching zone, with its inviting benches, is prime real estate for buskers and street performers. Just beyond (crossing the square diagonally) is the most characteristic and touristy street in old York: The Shambles (described on page 486). Our walk ends here, at the midpoint between York's main sights.

Sights in York

▲▲▲York Minster

The pride of York, this largest Gothic church north of the Alps (540 feet long, 200 feet tall) brilliantly shows that the High Middle Ages were far from dark. The word "minster" comes from the Old English for "monastery," but is now simply used to imply that it's an important church. As it's the seat of a bishop, York Minster is also a cathedral. While Henry VIII destroyed England's great abbeys, this was not part of a monastery and was therefore left standing. It seats 2,000 comfortably; on Christmas and Easter, at least 4,000 worshippers pack the place. Today, more than 250 employees and 500  volunteers work to preserve its heritage and welcome the 1.3 million visitors each year.

Cost and Hours: The cathedral opens for worship daily at 7:00. It's open for sightseeing Mon–Sat from 9:00 (9:30 Nov–March) and Sun from 12:00, when they begin charging £8 admission (includes free guided tour and entry to the undercroft, treasury, and crypt). Closing time flexes with activities (roughly May–Oct at 18:30, earlier off-season—check the day's closing time posted outside the church, or call for details, tel. 01904/557-

York Minster

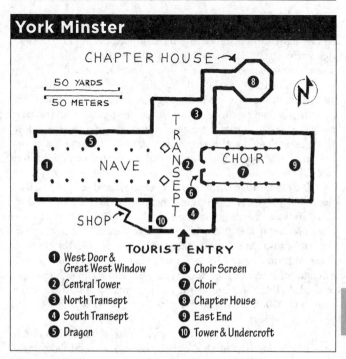

CHAPTER HOUSE

50 YARDS
50 METERS

T
R
A
N
S
E
P
T

NAVE

CHOIR

SHOP

TOURIST ENTRY

1. West Door & Great West Window
2. Central Tower
3. North Transept
4. South Transept
5. Dragon
6. Choir Screen
7. Choir
8. Chapter House
9. East End
10. Tower & Undercroft

217, www.yorkminster.org). The Minster may also close for special events (check calendar on their website). The tower (£5) and undercroft have shorter hours, typically opening a half-hour later and closing at 17:00 (as early as 16:45 for the tower).

Tours: After buying your ticket, go directly to the welcome desk, pick up the worthwhile *Welcome to the York Minster* flier, and ask when the next free guided tour departs (roughly 2/hour, Mon–Sat 10:30–15:00, one hour, they go even with just one or two people; you can join one in progress, or if none is scheduled, request a departure). The helpful Minster guides, some wearing blue badges, are happy to answer your questions. Stained-glass enthusiasts can take a special behind-the-scenes tour to learn about the restoration of the Minster's glass-terpiece, the Great East Window (£5, Wed and Fri at 14:00, one hour, 10-person maximum).

Evensong and Church Bells: To experience the cathedral in musical and spiritual action, attend an evensong (Tue–Sat at 17:15, Sun at 16:00, visiting choirs occasionally perform on Mon, 45 minutes). When the choir is off on school break (mid-July–Aug), visiting choirs usually fill in (confirm at church or TI). Arrive 10 minutes early and wait just outside the choir in the center of the church. You'll be ushered in and can sit in one of the big wooden stalls.

If you're a fan of church bells, you'll experience ding-dong ecstasy daily except Monday (Sun morning about 10:00, Tue practice 19:30–21:30, and Tue–Sat at 16:45 to announce evensong). These performances are especially impressive, as the church now holds a full carillon of 35 bells (it's the only English cathedral to have such a range). Stand in front of the church's west portal and imagine the gang pulling on a dozen ropes (halfway up the right tower—you can actually see the ropes through a little window) while one talented carillonneur plays 22 more bells with a baton-keyboard and foot pedals. On special occasions, you might even catch them playing a Beatles tune.

❍ **Self-Guided Tour:** Upon entering, head left, to the back (west end) of the church. Stand in front of the grand **west door** (used only on Sundays) on the *Deo Gratias 627–1927* plaque—a place of worship for 1,300 years, thanks to God. Flanking the door, the list of bishops goes unbroken back to the 600s. The statue of Peter with the key and Bible is a reminder that the church is dedicated to St. Peter, and the key to heaven is found through the word of God. While the Minster sits on the remains of a Romanesque church (c. 1100), today's church was begun in 1220 and took 250 years to complete.

Grab a chair and enjoy the nave. Looking down the church, your first impression might be the spaciousness and brightness of the nave (built 1280–1360). The nave—from the middle period of Gothic, called "Decorated Gothic"—is one of the widest Gothic naves in Europe. Rather than risk a stone roof, builders spanned the space with wood. Colorful shields on the arcades are the coats of arms of nobles who helped tall and formidable Edward I, known as "Longshanks," fight the Scots in the 13th century.

The coats of arms in the clerestory (upper-level) glass represent the nobles who helped his son, Edward II, in the same fight. There's more medieval glass in this building than in the rest of England combined. This precious glass survived World War II—hidden in stately homes throughout Yorkshire.

Walk to the very center of the church, under the **central tower.** Look up. Look down. Ask a Minster guide about how gifts and skill saved this tower—which weighs the equivalent of 40 jumbo jets—from collapse. (The first tower collapsed in 1407.) While the tower is 197 feet tall, it was intended to be much taller. Use the neck-saving mirror to marvel at it.

From here, you can survey many impressive features of the church:

In the **north transept,** the grisaille windows—dubbed the "Five Sisters"—are dedicated to British women who died in all wars. Made in 1260 (before colored glass was produced in England), these contain more than 100,000 pieces of glass.

England's Anglican Church

The Anglican Church (a.k.a. the Church of England) came into existence in 1534, when Henry VIII declared that he, and not Pope Clement VII, was the head of England's Catholics. The pope had refused to allow Henry to divorce his wife to marry his mistress Anne Boleyn (which Henry did anyway, resulting in the birth of Elizabeth I). Still, Henry regarded himself as a faithful Catholic—just not a *Roman* Catholic—and made relatively few changes in how and what Anglicans worshipped.

Henry's son, Edward VI, instituted many of the changes that Reformation Protestants were bringing about in continental Europe: an emphasis on preaching, people in the pews actually reading the Bible, clergy being allowed to marry, and a more "Protestant" liturgy in English from the revised Book of Common Prayer (1549). The next monarch, Edward's sister Mary I, returned England to the Roman Catholic Church (1553), earning the nickname of "Bloody Mary" for her brutal suppression of Protestant elements. When Elizabeth I succeeded Mary (1558), she soon broke from Rome again. Today, many regard the Anglican Church as a compromise between the Catholic and Protestant traditions.

Is the York Minster the leading Anglican church in England? Yes and no (but mostly no). After a long feud, the archbishops of Canterbury and York agreed that York's bishop would have the title "Primate of England" and Canterbury's would be the "Primate of All England," directing Anglicans on the national level.

The **south transept** features the tourists' entry, where stairs lead down to the undercroft. The new "bosses" (carved medallions decorating the point where the ribs meet on the ceiling) are a reminder that the roof of this wing of the church was destroyed by fire in 1984. Some believe the fire was God's angry response to a new bishop, David Jenkins, who questioned the literal truth of Jesus' miracles. Others blame an electricity box hit by lightning. Regardless, the entire country came to York's aid. *Blue Peter* (England's top kids' show) conducted a competition among their young viewers to design new bosses. Out of 30,000 entries, there were six winners (the blue ones—e.g., man on the moon, feed the children, save the whales).

Look back at the west end to marvel at the **Great West Window,** especially the stone tracery. While its nickname is the "Heart of Yorkshire," it represents the sacred heart of Christ, meant to remind people of his love for the world.

Find the **dragon** on the right of the nave (two-thirds of the way up). While no one is sure of its purpose, it pivots and has a hole through its neck—so it was likely a mechanism designed to raise a lid on a baptismal font.

The **choir screen** is an ornate wall of carvings separating the nave from the choir. It's lined with all the English kings from William I (the Conqueror) to Henry VI (during whose reign it was carved, 1461). Numbers indicate the years each reigned. To say "it's slathered in gold leaf" sounds impressive, but the gold is very thin...a nugget the size of a sugar cube is pounded into a sheet the size of a driveway.

Step into the **choir** (or "quire"), where a service is held daily. All the carving was redone after an 1829 fire, but its tradition of glorious evensong services (sung by choristers from the Minster School) goes all the way back to the eighth century.

In the **north transept,** the 18th-century astronomical clock is worth a look (a sign to its left helps you make sense of it). It's dedicated to the heroic Allied aircrews from bases here in northern England who died in World War II (as Britain kept the Nazis from invading in its "darkest hour"). The Book of Remembrance below the clock contains 18,000 names.

A corridor that functions as a small church museum leads to the Gothic, octagonal **Chapter House,** the traditional meet-

ing place of the governing body (or chapter) of the Minster. Above the doorway, the Virgin holds Baby Jesus while standing on the devilish serpent. Look for the panel of stained glass that is often on display here (it may also be in the undercroft). The panel is exquisitely detailed—its minute features would be invisible from the floor of the church and therefore would be "for God's eyes only."

The Chapter House, without an interior support, is remarkable (almost frightening) for its breadth. The fanciful carvings decorating the canopies above the stalls date from 1280 (80 percent are originals) and are some of the Minster's finest. Stroll slowly around the entire room and imagine that the tiny sculpted heads are a 14th-century parade—a fun glimpse of medieval society. Grates still send hot air up robes of attendees on cold winter mornings. A model of the wooden construction illustrates the impressive 1285 engineering.

The Chapter House was the site of an important moment

in England's parliamentary history. Fighting the Scots in 1295, Edward I (the "Longshanks" we met earlier) convened the "Model Parliament" here, rather than down south, in London. (The Model Parliament is the name for its early version, back before the legislature was split into the Houses of Commons and Lords.) The government met here through the 20-year reign of Edward II, before moving to London during Edward III's rule in the 14th century.

The church's **east end** is square, lacking a semicircular apse, typical of England's Perpendicular Gothic style (15th century). Monuments (almost no graves) were once strewn throughout the church, but in the Victorian Age, they were gathered into the east end, where you see them today.

The **Great East Window,** the size of a tennis court, is currently behind scaffolding. In the meantime, an interesting display explains the ongoing work. Also, a chart (on the right as you face the window) highlights the core Old Testament scenes in this masterpiece (hard to read from below, even when you can actually see the window). Because of the window's immense size, there's an extra layer of supportive stonework, parts of it wide enough to walk along. In fact, for special occasions, the choir sings from the walkway halfway up the window.

The tower and undercroft are two extra sights to consider, both accessed from the south transept. One gets you exercise and a view; the other is a basement full of history. You can scale the 275-step **tower** for the panoramic view (£5, last entry varies—can be as early as 16:45 in summer and 30 minutes before dusk in winter, no children under 8, not good for acrophobes, closes in bad weather). The **undercroft** consists of the crypt, treasury, and foundations (included in church admission, last entry at 17:00, no photos). The crypt is an actual bit of the Romanesque church, featuring 12th-century Romanesque art, excavated in modern times. The foundations give you a chance to climb down—archaeologically and physically—through the centuries to see the roots of the much smaller, but still huge, Norman (Romanesque) church from 1100 that stood on this spot and, below that, the Roman excavations. Today's Minster stands upon the remains of a Roman fort. Peek also at the modern concrete save-the-church foundations.

Outside the Minster entrance, you'll find the **Roman Column.** Erected in 1971, this column commemorates the 1,900th anniversary of the Roman founding of Eboracum (later renamed York). Across the street is a statue of Constantine, who was in York when his father died. The troops declared him the Roman emperor in A.D. 306 at this site, and six years later, he went to Rome to claim his throne. In A.D. 312, Constantine legalized Christianity, and in A.D. 314, York got its first bishop.

YORK

YORK

More Sights in York

▲**The Shambles**—This is the most colorful old street in the half-timbered, traffic-free core of town.

Walk to the midway point, at the intersection with Little Shambles. This 100-yard-long street, next to the old market, was once the "street of the butchers" (the name is derived from *shammell*—a butcher's cutting block). In the 16th century, it was busy with red meat. On the hooks under the eaves once hung rabbit, pheasant, beef, lamb, and pigs' heads. Fresh slabs were displayed on the fat sills. People lived above—as they did even in Roman times. All the garbage was flushed down the street to a mucky pond at the end—a favorite hangout for the town's cats and dogs. Tourist shops now fill the fine 16th-century, half-timbered Tudor buildings. Look above the modern crowds and storefronts to appreciate the classic old English architecture. The soil here wasn't great for building. Notice how things settled in the absence of a good soil engineer.

Little Shambles leads to the frumpy Newgate Market (popular for cheap produce and clothing), created in the 1960s with the demolition of a bunch of lanes as colorful as The Shambles. Return to The Shambles a little farther along, through a covered lane (one of York's "snickelways"). Study the 16th-century oak carpentry—mortise-and-tenon joints with wooden plugs rather than nails.

For a cheap lunch, consider the cute, tiny **St. Crux Parish Hall.** This medieval church is now used by a medley of charities that sell tea, homemade cakes, and light meals. They each book the church for a day, often a year in advance. Chat with the volunteers (Mon–Sat 10:00–16:00, closed Sun, on the left at bottom end of The Shambles, at intersection with Pavement).

▲▲▲**York Castle Museum**—Truly one of Europe's top museums, this is a Victorian home show, the closest thing to a time-tunnel experience Britain has to offer. Even a speedy museumgoer will want a couple of hours here.

Stroll down the museum's two re-created streets: Kirkgate, from the Victorian era, with roaming live guides in period dress; and a fun exhibit that depicts the spirit of the swinging 1960s—"a time when the cultural changes were massive but the cars and skirts were mini." The newest exhibit is the York Castle Prison, which re-creates the experiences of actual people who were thrown into the clink here. Actors are projected onto the walls of individual cells in eerie hologram-style scenes.

The "From Cradle to Grave" clothing exhibit and fine costume collection are also impressive. The one-way plan assures that you'll see everything: re-creations of rooms from the 17th to 20th centuries, the domestic side of World War II, a giant dollhouse from 1715, Victorian toys, and a century of swimsuit fashions.

The museum's £4 guidebook isn't necessary, but it makes a fine souvenir. The museum proudly offers no audioguides, as its roaming guides are enthusiastic about talking—engage them.

Cost and Hours: £8, ticket good for one year, £12 combo-ticket with Yorkshire Museum, kids under 16 free with paying adult, daily 9:30–17:00, cafeteria midway through museum, tel. 01904/687-687, www.yorkcastlemuseum.org.uk. It's at the bottom of the hop-on, hop-off bus route. The museum can call you a taxi (worthwhile if you're hurrying to the National Railway Museum).

Clifford's Tower—Perched high on a knoll across from the Castle Museum, this ruin is all that's left of York's 13th-century castle, the site of an 1190 massacre of local Jews (read about this at base of hill). If you climb inside, you can enjoy fine city views from the top of the ramparts (not worth the £3.50, daily April–Sept 10:00–18:00, Oct 10:00–17:00, Nov–March 10:00–16:00, last entry 15 minutes before closing, tel. 01904/646-940).

▲Jorvik—Take the "Pirates of the Caribbean," sail them northeast and back 1,000 years, and you get Jorvik—more a ride than a museum. Innovative 20 years ago, the commercial success of Jorvik (YOR-vik) inspired copycat ride/museums all over Great Britain. Some love this attraction, while others call it a gimmicky rip-off. If you're looking for a grown-up museum, skip Jorvik and head

YORK

instead to the Viking exhibit at the Yorkshire Museum. If you're thinking Disneyland with a splash of history, Jorvik's fun. To me, Jorvik is a commercial venture designed for kids, with nearly as much square footage devoted to its shop as to the museum. You'll ride a little Disney-type people-mover for 20 minutes through the re-created Viking street of Coppergate. It's the year 975, and you're in the village of Jorvik. Next, your little train takes you through the actual excavation site that inspired the reconstructed village. Everything is true to the dig—even the faces of the models are derived by computer from skulls dug up here. Finally, you'll browse through an impressive gallery of Viking shoes, combs, locks, and other intimate glimpses of that redheaded culture. More than 40,000 artifacts were dug out of the peat bog here in the 1970s. The exhibit on bone archaeology is fascinating.

Cost and Hours: £8.95, £13 combo-ticket with Dig—see below, daily April–Oct 10:00–17:00, Nov–March 10:00–16:00, these are last-entry times, tel. 01904/615-505, www.jorvik-viking-centre.co.uk.

Dig—This kid-oriented archaeological site gives young visitors an idea of what York looked like during Roman, medieval, Viking, and Victorian eras. Sift through "dirt" (actually shredded tires), reconstruct Roman wall plaster, and have a look at what archaeologists have dug up recently (£5.50, £13 combo-ticket with Jorvik, daily 10:00–17:00, last entry one hour before closing, St. Saviour's Church, Saviourgate, tel. 01904/615-505, www.digyork.com).

▲▲National Railway Museum—If you like model railways, this is train-car heaven. The thunderous museum shows 200 illustrious years of British railroad history. Fanning out from a grand roundhouse is an array of historic cars and engines, including Queen Victoria's lavish royal car and the very first "stagecoaches on rails," with a crude steam engine from 1830. A working steam engine is sliced open, showing cylinders, driving wheels, and smoke box in action. You'll trace the evolution of steam-powered transportation to the era of the aerodynamic Mallard, famous as the first train to travel at a startling two miles per minute (a marvel back in 1938). There's much more, including exhibits on dining cars, post cars, sleeping cars, train posters, and videos. At the Works section, you can see live train switchboards. And don't miss the English Channel Tunnel video (showing the first handshake at the breakthrough). Purple-shirted "explainers" are everywhere, eager to talk trains. This biggest and best railroad museum anywhere is interesting even to people who think "Pullman" means "don't push."

Cost and Hours: Free, £2.50 audioguide with 60 bits of railroad lore is worthwhile for train buffs, daily 10:00–18:00, tel. 08448/153-139, www.nrm.org.uk.

Getting There: It's about a 15-minute walk from the Minster (southwest of town, up the hill behind the train station). A cute little "road train" shuttles you more quickly between the Minster and the Railway Museum (£2 each way, runs daily Easter–Oct, leaves Railway Museum every 30 minutes 11:00–16:00 at the top and bottom of the hour; leaves the town—from Duncombe Place, 100 yards in front of the Minster—at :15 and :45 minutes after the hour).

▲▲**Yorkshire Museum**—Located in a lush, picnic-perfect park next to the stately ruins of St. Mary's Abbey, the Yorkshire Museum is the city's serious "archaeology of York" museum. While the hordes line up at Jorvik, this museum has no crowds and provides a better historical context (and includes a kid-friendly dinosaur exhibit to boot).

You can't dig a hole in York without hitting some remnant of the city's long past, and most of what's found ends up here. The museum has recently had a makeover, with freshly redone exhibits on life in York during prehistoric, Roman, and medieval times.

The Roman collection includes slice-of-life exhibits from Roman baths, a huge floor mosaic, and the skull of a man killed by a sword blow to the head. (The latter makes it graphically clear that the struggle between Romans and barbarians was a violent one.) These artifacts are particularly interesting when you consider that you're standing in one of the farthest reaches of that empire.

An eighth-century Anglo-Saxon helmet shows a bit of barbarian refinement; you'll notice that the Vikings wore some pretty decent shoes and actually combed their hair.

The Middleham Jewel, an exquisitely etched 15th-century pendant, is considered the finest piece of Gothic jewelry in Britain. The noble lady who wore this on a necklace believed that it helped her worship and protected her from illness. The back of the pendant, which rested near her heart, shows the Nativity. The front shows the Holy Trinity crowned by a sapphire (which people believed put their prayers at the top of God's to-do list).

Cost and Hours: £7, kids under 16 free with paying adult, ticket good for one year, £12 combo-ticket with York Castle Museum, daily 10:00–17:00, within Museum Gardens, tel. 01904/687-687, www.yorkshiremuseum.org.uk.

Nearby: Before leaving, enjoy the evocative ruins of St. Mary's Abbey in the park (described on page 475).

▲**Fairfax House**—This well-furnished townhouse is perfectly Georgian inside, with wonderfully pleasant docents in each room eager to talk with you. Built in 1740, the house is compact and bursting with stunning period furniture, all of it giving insights into aristocratic life in 18th-century England (£6, Mon–Thu and Sat 11:00–16:30, Sun 13:30–16:30, Fri by guided tour only at 11:00 and 14:00—the tours are worthwhile, closed Jan–mid-Feb, on Castlegate, near Jorvik, tel. 01904/655-543, www.fairfaxhouse .co.uk).

Traditional Tea—York is famous for its elegant teahouses. Drop into one at 16:00 for tea and cakes. Ladies love **Bettys Café Tea Rooms,** where you pay £8 for a Yorkshire Cream Tea (tea and scones with clotted Yorkshire cream and strawberry jam), or £17 for a full traditional English afternoon tea (tea, delicate sandwiches, scones, and sweets). Your table is so full of doily niceties that the food is served on a little three-tray tower. While you'll pay a little extra here (and the food's nothing special), the ambience and people-watching are hard to beat. If there's a line, it moves quickly (except at dinnertime). Wait for a seat by the windows on the ground level rather than in the much bigger basement (daily 9:00–21:00, "afternoon tea" served all day, piano music nightly 18:00–21:00, tel. 01904/659-142, St. Helen's Square, fine view of street scene from a window seat on the main floor). Near the WC downstairs is a mirror signed by WWII bomber pilots—read the story.

Riverside Walk or Bike Ride—The New Walk is a mile-long, tree-lined riverside lane created in the 1730s as a promenade for York's dandy class to stroll, see, and be seen—and is a fine place for today's visitors to walk or bike. This hour-long walk along a bike path is a great way to enjoy a dose of countryside away from York. It's clearly described in the TI's *New Walk* flier (£0.60). Start from the riverside under Skeldergate Bridge (near the York Castle Museum), and walk away from town for a mile until you hit the modern Millennium Bridge (check out its thin, modern, stainless-steel design). Cross the river and walk back home, passing through Rowntree Park (a great Edwardian park with lawn bowling for the public, plus family fun including a playground and adventure rides for kids). Energetic bikers can continue past the Millennium Bridge 18 miles to the market town of Selby.

Honorable Mentions

York has a number of other sights and activities (described in TI brochures) that, while interesting, pale in comparison to the biggies.

Merchant Adventurers' Hall—Claiming to be the finest surviving medieval guildhall in Britain (from 1357), it's basically a vast half-timbered building with marvelous exposed beams and 15 minutes' worth of interesting displays about life and commerce back in the days when York was England's second city (£5, includes audioguide; Easter–Sept Mon–Thu 9:00–17:00, Fri–Sat 9:00–15:30, Sun 12:00–16:00; Oct–Easter Mon–Sat 9:00–15:30, closed Sun; south of The Shambles off Piccadilly, tel. 01904/654-818, www.theyorkcompany.co.uk).

Barley Hall—Uncovered behind a derelict office block in the 1980s, this medieval house has been restored to replicate a 1483 dwelling (£5, combo-tickets with Jorvik or Dig, daily April–Oct 10:00–17:00, until 16:00 in winter, last entry one hour before closing, 2 Coffee Yard off Stonegate, tel. 01904/615-505, www.barley hall.org.uk).

Micklegate Bar Museum—This new museum, at one of the city's main gateways, gives a feel for how families lived here inside the city wall, and how enemies of the crown were punished in medieval, Tudor, and Stuart times (£3, 2 kids free with paying adult, daily Feb–Oct 10:00–15:00, closed Nov–Jan, tel. 01904/615-505, www.micklegatebar.com).

Richard III Museum—This goofy exhibit is like seeing a high school history project. It's interesting only for Richard III enthusiasts (£2.50, daily March–Oct 9:00–17:00, Nov–Feb 9:30–16:00, longer hours possible in summer, filling the top floors of Monk Bar, tel. 01904/634-191, www.richardiiimuseum.co.uk).

YORK

Shopping in York

With its medieval lanes lined with classy as well as tacky little shops, York is a hit with shoppers. I find the **antiques malls** interesting. Three places within a few blocks of each other are filled with stalls and cases owned by antiques dealers from the countryside. The malls sell the dealers' bygones on commission. Serious shoppers do better heading for the country, but York's shops are a fun browse: The **Antiques Centre York** (Mon–Sat 9:00–17:30, Sun 9:00–16:00, 41 Stonegate, tel. 01904/635-888, www.theantiques centreyork.co.uk), the **Red House Antiques Centre** (Mon–Fri 9:30–17:30, Sat 9:30–18:00, Sun 10:30–17:30, a block from Minster at Duncombe Place, tel. 01904/637-000, www.redhouseyork .co.uk), and **Cavendish Antiques and Jewellers** (Mon–Sat 9:30–17:30, Sun 10:00–17:00, 44 Stonegate, tel. 01904/621-666, www .cavendishjewellers.co.uk).

You'll find **thrift shops** run by various charity organizations from the beginning of Goodramgate by the wall to just past Deangate. Good deals abound on clothing, purses, accessories, children's toys, books, CDs, and maybe even a guitar. If you buy something, you're getting a bargain and at the same time helping the poor, elderly, or even a pet in need of a vet (Mon–Sat 9:30–17:00, Sun 11:00–16:00). On Goodramgate alone you'll find shops run by the British Heart Foundation, Save the Children, and Oxfam (selling donated items as well as free-trade products such as coffee, tea, culinary goods, stationery items, and jewelry and purses made in developing countries and purchased directly from the producers and artisans).

Nightlife in York

Theatre Royal—A full variety of dramas, comedies, and works by Shakespeare entertain the locals in either the main theater or the little 100-seat theater-in-the-round (£10–20, usually Tue–Sat at 19:30, tickets easy to get, on St. Leonard's Place near Bootham Bar and a 5- to 10-minute walk from recommended B&Bs, booking tel. 01904/623-568, www.yorktheatreroyal.co.uk). Those under 25 and students of any age get tickets for only £7.

Ghost Tours—You'll see flyers, signs, and promoters hawking a variety of not-so-spooky after-dark tours; of these, I'd go for the "Haunted Walks" (for details, see "Tours in York," earlier).

Pubs—Atmospheric, half-timbered pubs abound. One of my favorites for old-school York ambience is **The Blue Bell,** a tiny, traditional establishment with a time-warp Edwardian interior. This smallest pub in York serves no food. It has two distinct little rooms—each as cozy as can be—and the owners only recently allowed women to enter (near the east end of town at 53 Fossgate).

Movies—The centrally located City Screens Cinema is right on the river, playing both art-house and mainstream flicks (13 Coney Street, toll tel. 0871-704-2054).

Sleeping in York

I've listed peak-season, book-direct prices. Don't use the TI. Outside of July and August, some prices go soft. B&Bs will often charge £10 more for weekends and sometimes turn away one-night bookings, particularly for peak-season Saturdays. (York is worth two nights anyway.) Prices spike up for horse races and Bank Holidays (about 20 nights a season). Remember to book ahead during festival times (mid-Feb, early June, early July, mid-Aug, and late Sept—see "Helpful Hints" on page 472) and weekends year-round.

B&Bs and Small Hotels

These B&Bs are all small and family-run. They come with plenty of steep stairs (and no elevators) but no traffic noise. Rooms can be tight; if maneuverability is important to you, say so when booking. For a good selection, call well in advance. B&B owners will generally hold a room with a phone call and work hard to help their guests sightsee and eat smartly. Most have permits to lend for

---

Sleep Code

(£1 = about $1.60, country code: 44, area code: 01904)
S = Single, **D** = Double/Twin, **T** = Triple, **Q** = Quad, **b** = bathroom, **s** = shower only. You can assume credit cards are accepted unless otherwise noted.

To help you sort easily through these listings, I've divided the rooms into three categories based on the price for a standard double room with bath (during high season):

$$$ **Higher Priced**—Most rooms £90 or more.
$$ **Moderately Priced**—Most rooms between £65–90.
$ **Lower Priced**—Most rooms £65 or less.

Prices can change without notice; verify the hotel's current rates online or by email. For other updates, see www.ricksteves.com/update.

---

street parking.

The handiest B&B neighborhood is the quiet residential area just outside the old town wall's Bootham gate, along the road called Bootham. All of these are within a 10-minute walk of the Minster and TI, and a 10- to 15-minute walk or £5 taxi ride from the station. If driving, head for the cathedral and follow the medieval wall to the gate called Bootham Bar. The street called Bootham leads away from Bootham Bar.

Getting There: Here's the most direct way to walk to this B&B area from the train station: Exit the station to the left on Station Road. When the road swings right and goes through the old gate, turn left onto the busy street (Leeman Road). Just before that street goes under the rail bridge, turn right and follow the walkway along the tracks, then cross the bridge over the river. From the far end of the bridge, the Abbey Guest House is a few yards to your left, facing the river. To reach the B&Bs closer to the town wall, walk from the bridge along the river until just before the short ruined tower, then turn inland up onto Marygate. For other B&Bs, follow the path from the bridge, turning left immediately onto a path that skirts the big parking lot (parallel to the train tracks). At the end of the parking lot, you'll turn depending on your B&B: for the places on or near Bootham Terrace, turn left and go under the tracks; or, for B&Bs on St. Mary's Street, take the short stairway on your right.

On or near Bootham Terrace

$$ Abbeyfields Guest House has eight comfortable, bright rooms. This doily-free place, which lacks the usual B&B clutter,

York Accommodations

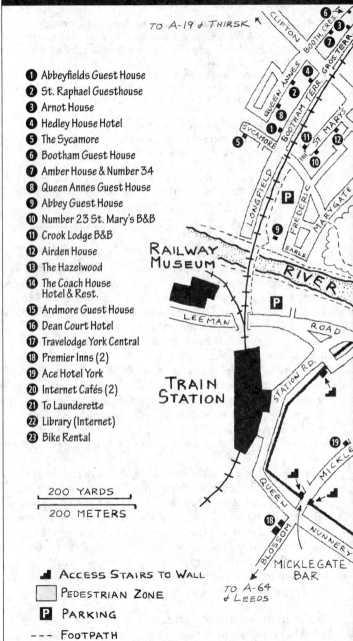

1. Abbeyfields Guest House
2. St. Raphael Guesthouse
3. Arnot House
4. Hedley House Hotel
5. The Sycamore
6. Bootham Guest House
7. Amber House & Number 34
8. Queen Annes Guest House
9. Abbey Guest House
10. Number 23 St. Mary's B&B
11. Crook Lodge B&B
12. Airden House
13. The Hazelwood
14. The Coach House Hotel & Rest.
15. Ardmore Guest House
16. Dean Court Hotel
17. Travelodge York Central
18. Premier Inns (2)
19. Ace Hotel York
20. Internet Cafés (2)
21. To Launderette
22. Library (Internet)
23. Bike Rental

TO A-19 & THIRSK

CLIFTON

BOOTH CRES.

QUEEN ANNES

BOOTHAM TERR.

GROS. TERR.

SYCAMORE

ST. MARY'S

MARYGATE

LONGFIELD

FREDERIC

EARLS

RAILWAY MUSEUM

RIVER

LEEMAN

ROAD

P

P

TRAIN STATION

STATION RD.

MICKLE

QUEEN

BLOSSOM

NUNNERY

MICKLEGATE BAR

TO A-64 & LEEDS

200 YARDS

200 METERS

ACCESS STAIRS TO WALL

PEDESTRIAN ZONE

P PARKING

--- FOOTPATH

YORK

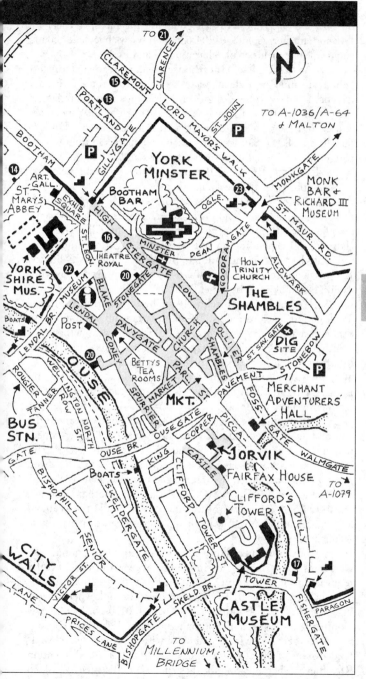

has been designed with care (Sun–Thu: Sb-£44, Db-£72; Fri–Sat: Sb-£49, Db-£82; doesn't price-gouge during races, free Wi-Fi, 19 Bootham Terrace, tel. 01904/636-471, www.abbeyfields.co.uk, enquire@abbeyfields.co.uk, charming Al and Les).

$$ At St. Raphael Guesthouse, young, creative, and energetic Dom and Zoe understand a traveler's needs. You'll be instant friends. Dom's graphic design training brings a dash of class to their seven comfy rooms, each themed after a different York street, and each lovingly accented with a fresh rose (Sb-£65; Db-£76 Sun–Thu, £88 Fri–Sat; less off-season, free drinks in their guests' fridge, family rooms, free Internet access and Wi-Fi, 44 Queen Annes Road, tel. 01904/645-028, www.straphaelguesthouse.co.uk, info@straphaelguesthouse.co.uk).

$$ Arnot House, run by a hardworking daughter-and-mother team, is homey and lushly decorated with Victorian memorabilia. The three well-furnished rooms even have little libraries (Db-£70–80 depending on size of room, 2-night minimum stay unless it's last-minute, no children, free Wi-Fi, huge DVD library, 17 Grosvenor Terrace, tel. 01904/641-966, www.arnothouseyork.co.uk, kim.robbins@virgin.net, Kim).

$$ Hedley House Hotel, well-run by a wonderful family, has 30 clean and spacious rooms. The outdoor hot tub is a fine way to end your day (Sb-£55–90, Db-£70–100, ask for a deal with stay of 3 or more nights, family rooms, good 3-course evening meals from £18, free Wi-Fi, free parking, 3 Bootham Terrace, tel. 01904/637-404, www.hedleyhouse.com, greg@hedleyhouse.com, Greg and Louise Harrand). They also have two luxury studio apartments—see their website for details.

$$ The Sycamore is a fine value, with six homey rooms at the end of a quiet street opposite a bowling green. A little cramped, it's friendly and well-run (Db-£60–75, Tb-£90–102, Qb-£110, lower price is for weekdays, these are special prices in 2011 if you mention this book when you reserve and pay cash, may be cheaper off-season, free Wi-Fi, 19 Sycamore Place off Bootham Terrace, tel. 01904/624-712, www.thesycamore.co.uk, mail@thesycamore.co.uk, accommodating Elizabeth and Spiros freely dispense sightseeing advice).

$ Bootham Guest House features gregarious Emma, who welcomes you to her eight simple but cheery and thoughtfully renovated rooms (S-£35; D-£56, £60 Fri–Sat; Db-£60, £70 Fri–Sat; these prices in 2011 if you mention this book when reserving, free Wi-Fi, 56 Bootham Crescent, tel. 01904/672-123, www.boothamguesthouse.com, boothamguesthouse1@hotmail.com).

$ Amber House is a small place with three breezy and well-tended rooms (Db-£64 Sun–Thu, £72 Fri–Sat; Tb-£90; mention Rick Steves when booking for these prices in 2011, free Wi-Fi, 36

Bootham Crescent, tel. 01904/620-275, www.amberhouse-york
.co.uk, amberhouseyork@hotmail.co.uk, John and Linda).

$ Number 34, run by hardworking Amy and Jason, has four
simple, light, and airy rooms at fair prices (May–Oct: Sb-£35–45,
Db-£60, Tb-£84; Nov–April: Sb-£35, Db-£56, Tb-£75; free
Wi-Fi, 34 Bootham Crescent, tel. 01904/645-818, www.number
34york.co.uk, enquiries@number34york.co.uk).

$ Queen Annes Guest House has nine basic rooms in
two adjacent houses at the best prices in the neighborhood. If
you're looking for plush beds and rich decor, look elsewhere. If
you'd simply like an affordable and clean place to sleep, this is it
(high season: S-£30, D-£48, Db-£55; off-season: S-£26, D-£44,
Db-£48; these prices with this book through 2011, family room,
ground-floor room, free Wi-Fi, lounge, 24 Queen Annes Road, tel.
01904/629-389, www.queen-annes-guesthouse.co.uk, info@queen
-annes-guesthouse.co.uk, Jason).

On the River

$$ Abbey Guest House is a peaceful refuge overlooking the River
Ouse, with five cheerful, beautifully updated rooms and a cute
little garden (Db-£78–86, four-poster Db with river view, less off-
season, ask for Rick Steves discount when booking, free Wi-Fi,
free parking, £7 laundry service, 13–14 Earlsborough Terrace, tel.
01904/627-782, www.abbeyghyork.co.uk, info@abbeyghyork.co.uk,
delightful couple Gill—pronounced "Jill"—and Alec Saville, and a
dog aptly named Loofah).

On St. Mary's Street

$$ Number 23 St. Mary's B&B is extravagantly decorated. Chris
and Julie Simpson have done everything just right and offer nine
spacious and tastefully comfy rooms, a classy lounge, and all the
doily touches (Sb-£48–55, Db-£80–95 depending on room size
and season, discount for longer stays, family room, DVD library
and DVD players, free Wi-Fi, 23 St. Mary's, tel. 01904/622-738,
www.23stmarys.co.uk, stmarys23@hotmail.com).

$$ Crook Lodge B&B, with seven tight but elegantly
charming rooms, serves breakfast in an old Victorian kitchen (Db-
£74–80, cheaper off-season, check for specials online, one ground-
floor room, free Internet access and Wi-Fi, parking, quiet, 26 St.
Mary's, tel. 01904/655-614, www.crooklodge.co.uk, crooklodge
@hotmail.com, Brian and Louise Aiken).

$$ Airden House rents nine nice rooms (Db-£70–78, this
price with 2-night minimum if you mention this book when reserv-
ing in 2011, cheaper off-season, lounge, free parking, 1 St. Mary's,
tel. 01904/638-915, www.airdenhouse.co.uk, info@airdenhouse
.co.uk).

Closer to the Town Wall

$$$ **The Hazelwood,** my most hotelesque listing, is plush and more formal than a B&B. This spacious house has 14 beautifully decorated rooms with modern furnishings and lots of thoughtful touches (Sb-£65, Db-£80–125 depending on room size and day of week, two ground-floor rooms, free Internet access and Wi-Fi, laundry service-£7, free parking, light breakfast option, garden patio; a fridge, ice, and travel library in the pleasant basement lounge; 24 Portland Street, tel. 01904/626-548, www.thehazelwoodyork.com, reservations @thehazelwoodyork.com, Ian and Carolyn). Ask about their bright top-floor two-bedroom apartment, great for families and those with strong legs (continental breakfast only).

$$$ **The Coach House Hotel** is a labyrinthine, well-located 17th-century coach house. Facing a bowling green and the abbey walls, it offers 14 huge ceiling-beamed rooms, some with views of the Minster (Sb-£55, Db-£85–100, family room for £150 sleeps up to 6, one ground-floor room, free Internet access and Wi-Fi, tea and cake at check-in, laundry service, free parking, 20–22 Marygate, tel. 01904/652-780, www.coachhousehotel-york.com, info@coachhousehotel-york.com, Julie). This is also a good place for a cozy pub dinner, with veggie options and homemade sweets (£9–13 dishes, nightly 17:00–21:00).

$$ **Ardmore Guest House** is a fine little four-room place enthusiastically run by Irishwoman Vera, who's given it a green theme. It's about 15 minutes' walk from the station, but only five minutes from Bootham Bar (Sb-£40, Db-£60–75, Tb-£75, discount off-season for 3 or more nights, cash only, 31 Claremont Terrace, tel. 01904/622-562, mobile 079-3928-3588, www.ardmore york.co.uk).

Hotels in the Center and Big-Budget Hotel Options

$$$ **Dean Court Hotel,** a Best Western facing the Minster, is a big, stately hotel with classy lounges and 37 comfortable rooms (Ss/ Sb-£105, small Db-£140, standard Db-£170, superior Db-£200, spacious deluxe Db-£220, cheaper midweek and off-season, elevator, free Wi-Fi, bistro, restaurant, Duncombe Place, tel. 01904/625-082, fax 01904/620-305, www.deancourt-york.co.uk).

$$ **Travelodge York Central** offers 93 identical, affordable, slightly worn rooms near the Castle Museum. If you book long in advance on their website, this can be amazingly cheap. River views make some rooms slightly less boring—after booking online, call the front desk to try to arrange a view (Db and Tb-£70 Sun–Thu, £65 Fri–Sat, often much lower with online deals, kids' bed free, continental breakfast-£4.50, pay Internet access and Wi-Fi, park-

ing-£6.50/day, 90 Piccadilly, central reservations toll tel. 08719-848-484, front desk tel. 01904/651-852, www.travelodge.co.uk).

$$ Premier Inn offers 200 rooms in two side-by-side hotels that I hate to recommend, but York has few budget options. They have little character (at one, you enter through a coffee shop), but they offer industrial-strength efficiency and a decent value (Db-£74 Sun–Thu, £85 Fri–Sat, check for specials online, up to 2 kids stay free, breakfast-£8 extra, pay Internet access and Wi-Fi, free parking, 5-minute walk to train station, 20 and 28–40 Blossom Street, toll tel. 0871-527-9194, www.premierinn.com, yorkcitycentre .pi@premierinn.com).

Hostel

$ Ace Hotel York is a boutique hostel in a large, classy, nicely renovated Georgian house that provides a much-needed option for backpackers. They rent 129 beds in 2- to 14-bed rooms, most with great views and all with private bathrooms and thoughtful touches such as reading lights for each bed. They also offer fancier, hotel-quality doubles (£20–30/bed depending on size of dorm, Db-£80, family room-£100, includes continental breakfast, air-con, pay Internet access, free Wi-Fi, laundry-£3, TV lounge, bar, lockers, no curfew, 5-minute walk from train station at 88–90 Mickelgate, tel. 01904/627-720, www.acehotelyork .co.uk, reception@ace-hotelyork.co.uk).

Eating in York

York is bursting with inviting eateries. There seems to be a pub serving grub on every corner. And in the last decade or so, the city has become a hot spot for the new British cuisine—every year seems to bring another bistro serving classy dishes made with fresh, local ingredients. I've listed five of my favorites here: Café No. 8, Café Concerto, The Blue Bicycle, J. Baker's, and Melton's Too. These places are each romantic, laid-back, and popular with natives (so reservations are wise for dinner). All have several creative vegetarian options on the menu. Main courses at these places cost about £15–20—not exorbitant by British standards, but not cheap, either.

Fortunately, picnic and light-meals-to-go options abound, and it's easy to find a churchyard, bench, or riverside perch upon which to munch cheaply. On a sunny day, perhaps the best picnic spot in town is under the evocative 12th-century ruins of St. Mary's Abbey in the Museum Gardens (near Bootham Bar).

Just Lunch

St. William's Tea Rooms, signed as the "York Minster Tea Rooms," are nestled just behind the Great East Window of the

York Restaurants

1 St. William's Tea Rooms
2 Grays Court Tea Rooms
3 Bettys Café Tea Rooms
4 York Hogroast (2)
5 Café Concerto
6 El Piano Restaurant
7 Evil Eye Lounge
8 Ask Restaurant
9 Siam House
10 Bengal Brasserie & Caesars
11 The Viceroy of India
12 Little Italy
13 Café No. 8
14 Mamma Mia
15 The Exhibition Hotel Pub & Sainsbury's Grocery
16 The Blue Bicycle
17 J. Baker's
18 Melton's Too
19 The Blue Bell
20 The Coach House

ACCESS STAIRS TO WALL

PEDESTRIAN ZONE

P PARKING

--- FOOTPATH

200 YARDS

200 METERS

York

Minster in a wonderful half-timbered 15th-century building (read the history on the menu). They serve quick and tasty lunches. Eat outside (with a scaffolded Minster view), inside (cafeteria under timbers), or in the peaceful cobbled courtyard (tea and pastries served daily 10:30–16:00, £7–8 lunches served daily 12:00–15:00, College Street, tel. 01904/634-830).

Grays Court is also tucked away behind the Minster, around the corner from St. William's Tea Rooms. For centuries, this was the residence of the Norman Treasurers of York Minster; today it's home to a pleasant tea room. Enjoy lunch or tea in the garden or in the Jacobean gallery—ask to see the medieval wall of the original Treasurer's House behind the oak paneling (daily 10:00–17:00, Chapter House Street, tel. 01904/612-613).

Bettys Café Tea Rooms, a favorite among local ladies, is popular for its traditional English afternoon tea (which works as a meal—£17 for tea, delicate sandwiches, scones, and sweets; for details, see page 490).

York Hogroast is a fixture, serving its delicious £3 hearty pork sandwiches with a choice of traditional fillings—try the apple (take-away only, Mon–Thu 11:00–16:00, Fri 11:00–16:00 & 20:00–24:00, Sat 11:00–24:00, Sun 11:00–17:00, 82–84 Goodramgate; second location with similar hours at 4 Stonegate). Grab a sandwich and munch in the yard at the nearby Holy Trinity Church (to your left as you exit, peaceful) or in King's Square (to your right as you exit, lively with buskers).

Near the Minster

Café Concerto, a casual bistro with a fun menu, wholesome food, and a charming musical theme, has an understandably loyal following (soup, sandwich, and salad meals-£9–10; fancier dinners-£12–17; daily 8:30–22:00, smart to reserve for dinner—try for a window seat, also offers take-away, facing the Minster, 21 High Petergate, tel. 01904/610-478).

El Piano Restaurant, a few blocks from the Minster on charming Grape Lane, is a popular veggie option that serves only vegan, gluten-free, and low-sodium dishes in tapas-style portions. The dishes have Indian/Asian/Middle Eastern flavors, and the inside ambience is bubble gum with blinking lights; they also have a pleasant patio out back. If you're eating family-style, three or four plates serve two. Save money at the take-away window (£3–4 to-go "bamboo boats," Mon–Sat 11:00–23:00, Sun 12:00–17:00, between Low Petergate and Swinegate at 15–17 Grape Lane, tel. 01904/610-676).

Evil Eye Lounge serves large portions of Southeast Asian cuisine to a hip crowd in a creaky, funky space (£7 entrées, Mon–Fri 10:00–21:00, Sat 12:00–19:00, 42 Stonegate, tel. 01904/640-002).

On Sundays, the Asian cuisine takes a break, and a full multi-course traditional Sunday roast is served instead (good deal at £7 for adults, £9 for "monsters," Sun 12:00–18:00).

Ask Restaurant is a cheap and cheery Italian chain, similar to those found in historic buildings all over England. But York's version lets you dine in the majestic marble-columned yellow hall of its Grand Assembly Rooms. The food may be Italian-chain dull—but the atmosphere is 18th-century deluxe (£8–9 pizza, pastas, and salads; daily, Blake Street, tel. 01904/637-254). Even if you're just walking past, peek inside to gape at the interior.

Along Goodramgate

Goodramgate is lined with a fun variety of competitive eateries dishing up everything from fish-and-chips and pub grub to tastes of Thailand, India, and Italy. Strolling this lane, you'll find plenty of good options. Working roughly from the center to the medieval gate, Monk Bar, my favorites are:

Siam House serves creative Thai food popular with locals (£7 lunches, £11–13 dinners, Sun–Fri 18:00–22:00, Wed–Fri also 12:00–14:00, Sat 12:00–15:00 & 17:00–23:00, 63a Goodramgate, tel. 01904/624-677).

Bengal Brasserie is a town favorite for Indian cuisine (Sun–Fri 18:00–24:00, Sat 12:00–24:00, 21 Goodramgate, tel. 01904/613-131). I also like the **Viceroy of India,** just outside Monk Bar and therefore outside the tourist zone (£6–11 plates, daily 18:00–24:00, out Monk Bar to 26 Monkgate, tel. 01904/622-370).

Two popular Italian places along Goodramgate offer pizzas and pastas for £8: **Little Italy** is a little more intimate and classy (Mon–Tue and Thu–Sat 10:30–22:00, Sun 11:30–21:00, closed Wed, at #12, tel. 01904/623-539), while **Caesars** is bright and boisterous (Mon–Fri 12:00–14:30 & 17:30–23:00, Sat–Sun 12:00–23:00, at #27, tel. 01904/670-914).

Near Bootham Bar and Recommended B&Bs

Café No. 8 is your best bistro choice on Gillygate, serving modern European and veggie options. Grab one of eight tables inside or enjoy a shaded little garden out back if the weather's good. No. 8 feels like Café Concerto (described earlier) but is more romantic, with jazz, modern art, candles, and hardworking Martin bringing it all together. Chef Chris Pragnell uses what's fresh in the market to shape his menu. The food is simple, elegant, and creative—with appetizers such as figs with Yorkshire bleu cheese (£6–10 lunches, £15–17 dinners, Mon–Fri 11:00–22:00, Sat–Sun 10:00–22:00, 8 Gillygate, tel. 01904/653-074).

Mamma Mia is the locals' choice for affordable Italian. The casual eating area features a tempting gelato bar, and in nice weather the back patio is *molto bella* (£8 pizza and pasta, daily 11:30–14:00 & 17:30–23:00, 20 Gillygate, tel. 01904/622-020).

The handsome **Exhibition Hotel pub** has a nice bar area inside, as well as a glassed-in conservatory and patio seating out back that's great for kids (pub grub served daily 12:00–21:00, just outside Bootham Bar at 19 Bootham Street, tel. 01904/624-248).

Supermarket: **Sainsbury's** grocery store is handy and open late (daily 7:00–23:00, 50 yards outside Bootham Bar, on Bootham).

At the East End of Town

This neighborhood is across town from my recommended B&Bs, but still central (and a short walk from the Castle Museum). All three of these places are worth the longer after-dinner stroll.

The Blue Bicycle is no longer a brothel (but if you explore downstairs, you can still imagine when the tiny privacy snugs needed their curtains). Today, it is passionate about fish. The energy of its happy eaters, its charming canalside setting, and its location just beyond the tourist zone make it worth the splurge. Of my recommended York restaurants, this wins the best ambience award. It's a velvety, hardwood scene, a little sultry but fresh...like its fish. Reservations are a must (£5–10 starters, £17–24 entrées, vegetarian and meat options, nightly 18:00–21:30, Thu–Sun also 12:00–14:30, 34 Fossgate, tel. 01904/673-990).

J. Baker's is popular for how it turns local produce into highbrow versions of classic dishes. At lunchtime, their "grazing menu" makes it affordable to sample several dishes (available à la carte, or £12 for three courses). At dinnertime, the two earth-tone dining rooms—one downstairs, one upstairs—tend to fill up fast, so reservations are smart (£25 two-course meals, £29 three-course meals, £33 seven-course "grazing" meal, Tue–Sat 12:00–14:30 & 18:00–22:00, closed Sun–Mon, near the end of The Shambles at 7 Fossgate, tel. 01904/622-688). Across the street is the recommended Blue Bell pub (see page 492).

Melton's Too is a fun and casual place to eat. This homey, spacious, youthful restaurant serves up elegantly simple meals and a nice a selection of tapas, all with a focus on local ingredients (£9-11 entrées, Mon–Sat 10:30–22:30, Sun 10:30–21:30, just past Fossgate at 25 Walmgate, tel. 01904/629-222).

York Connections

From York by Train to: Durham (3–4/hour, 45 minutes), **London**'s King's Cross Station (2/hour, 2 hours), **Bath** (2/hour, 4–4.5 hours, 1–2 changes), **Cambridge** (hourly, 2.5 hours, change in Peterborough), **Birmingham** (2/hour, 2–2.5 hours), **Keswick/Lake District** (train to Penrith: 1–2/hour, 3.5 hours, 1–2 transfers;

then bus, allow about 4.5 hours total), **Manchester Airport** (2/hour, 1.75 hours), **Edinburgh** (1–2/hour, 2.5–2.75 hours). Train info: toll tel. 0845-748-4950, www.nationalrail.co.uk.

Connections with London's Airports: Heathrow (allow 3 hours minimum; from airport take Heathrow Express train to London's Paddington Station, transfer by tube to King's Cross, train to York—2/hour, 2 hours; for details on cheaper but slower Tube or bus option from airports to London, see page 185), **Gatwick** (allow 3 hours minimum; from Gatwick South, catch First Capital Connect train to London's St. Pancras Station; from there, walk to neighboring King's Cross Station, and catch train to York—2/hour, 2 hours).

Near York: North York Moors

In the lonesome North York Moors, sheep seem to outnumber people. In this high, desolate-feeling plateau, with a spongy and inhospitable soil, bleating flocks jockey for position against scrubby heather for control of the terrain. You can almost imagine the mysterious Heathcliff (from *Wuthering Heights,* which was set here) plodding across this terrain. As you pass through this haunting landscape, crisscrossed by only a few roads, notice how the gloomy brown heather—which blooms briefly with purple flowers at summer's end—is actually burned back by wardens to clear the way for new growth. The vast, undulating expanses of nothingness are punctuated by greener, sparsely populated valleys called dales. Park your car and take a hike across the moors on any small road. You'll come upon a few tidy villages and maybe even old Roman roads.

Drivers can consider The Moors Centre; non-drivers can take the steam train from Pickering; and anyone might want to stop in Goathland.

The Moors Centre

This visitor facility near Danby provides the best orientation for exploring North York Moors National Park. (Unfortunately, it's at the northern end of the park—not as convenient if you're coming from York.) This grand old lodge offers exhibits, shows, nature walks, an information desk, plenty of books and maps, brass rubbing, a cheery cafeteria, and brochures on several good walks that start right outside the front door.

Cost and Hours: Free entry but £2.20 parking fee; April–Oct daily 10:00–17:00; March and Nov–Dec daily 11:00–16:00; Jan–Feb Sat–Sun 11:00–16:00, closed Mon–Fri; café, tel. 01439/772-737, www.northyorkmoors.org.uk.

Getting There: The Centre is three-fourths of a mile from

Danby in Esk Valley, in the northern part of the park (follow signs from Danby, which is a short drive from A171 running along the northern edge of the park).

▲North Yorkshire Moors Railway

This 18-mile, one-hour steam-engine ride between Pickering and Grosmont (GROW-mont) runs almost hourly through some of the best parts of the moors. Sometimes the train continues from Grosmont on to the seaside town of Whitby; otherwise, you might be able to transfer in Grosmont to another, non-steam train to reach Whitby (check schedules before you plan your trip). Once in Whitby, you can use the bus to connect along the coast (such as to Staithes) or to return to York. (For details on getting to Pickering, see the next section.)

Even with the small and dirty windows (try to wipe off the outside of yours before you roll), and with the track situated mostly in a scenic gully, it's a good ride. You can stop along the way for a walk on the moors (or at the appealing village of Goathland—described next) and catch the next train (£16 round-trip to Grosmont, or £21 round-trip to Whitby, includes hop-on, hop-off privileges; runs daily late March–Oct, and some Dec weekends, no trains Nov and Jan–late March, schedule flexes with the season but generally the first train departs Pickering at 9:00, last train departs Grosmont about 18:30; trip takes about one hour one-way to Grosmont, allow about 2.75 hours round-trip to come back on the same train; tel. 01751/472-508 or 24-hour timetable info at tel. 01751/472-508, www.nymr.co.uk). There's nowhere to leave luggage at any stop on the steam-train line—pack light if you decide to hike.

Pickering

This functional town is a major crossroads and a proud hub of sorts for this region's meager public transit (**TI** tel. 01751/473-791). The main reason to visit Pickering is to catch the **North Yorkshire Moors Railway** steam train into the moors (described above). Otherwise, you can browse its Monday market (produce, knick-knacks) and consider its rural-life museum (Hutton-le-Hole's is better)—but don't bother visiting Pickering unless you're passing through anyway.

With more time, consider stopping by Pickering's ruined 13th-century Norman **castle,** built on the site of a wooden castle from William the Conqueror's 11th-century heyday. Appreciate its textbook motte-and-bailey (stone fort on a grassy hilltop) design, and climb to the top to understand its strategic location (£3.70, April–Sept daily 10:00–17:00, closed Oct–March, on the ridge above town, tel. 01751/474-989, www.english-heritage.org.uk).

Getting There: Drivers find Pickering right on A169 north of York (en route to the coast). Or you can catch Coastliner bus #840 from York (every 1–2 hours Mon–Sat, fewer on Sun, 1.25 hours, www.yorkshiretravel.net); you can shave a few minutes off the trip by taking the train to Malton, then catching bus #840 from there.

Goathland

This tranquil village, huddled along a babbling brook, is worth considering for a sleepy stopover, either on the steam-train trip or for drivers (it's an easy detour from A169, which cuts through the moors). Movie buffs will enjoy Goathland's train station, which was used to film scenes at "Hogsmeade Station" for the early Harry Potter movies (for more on Harry Potter sights, see page 832). But Brits know and love Goathland as the setting for the beloved, long-running TV series *Heartbeat*, about a small Yorkshire town in the 1960s. You'll see TV sets intermingled with real buildings, and some shops are even labeled "Aidensfield," for the TV town's fictional name.

DURHAM AND NORTHEAST ENGLAND

Northeast England harbors some of the country's best historical sights. Go for a Roman ramble at Hadrian's Wall, a reminder that Britain was an important Roman colony 2,000 years ago. Make a pilgrimage to Holy Island, where Christianity gained its first toehold in Britain. Marvel at England's greatest Norman church, Durham's cathedral, and enjoy an evensong service. At the Beamish Museum, travel back in time to the year 1913.

Planning Your Time

For train travelers, Durham is the most convenient overnight stop in this region. If you like Roman ruins, visit Hadrian's Wall (doable with transfers, easiest Easter–Oct). The Beamish Museum is an easy day trip from Durham (25 minutes by car, one hour by bus). If you're traveling by train, note that it's problematic to visit Durham en route to another destination, since there's no baggage storage in Durham. Either stay overnight or do Durham as a day trip from York.

By car, you can easily visit Beamish Museum, Hadrian's Wall, Bamburgh Castle, and Holy Island. Spend a night in Durham and a night near Hadrian's Wall.

For the best quick visit, arrive in Durham by mid-afternoon in time to tour the cathedral and enjoy the evensong service (Tue–Sat at 17:15, Sun at 15:30). Sleep in Durham. Visit Beamish the next morning before continuing on to your next destination.

Durham

Without its cathedral, Durham would hardly be noticed. But this magnificently situated cathedral is hard to miss (even if you're zooming by on the train). Seemingly happy to go nowhere, Durham sits along its river, and below its castle and famous cathedral. It has a medieval, cobbled atmosphere and a scraggly peasant's indoor market just off the main square. Durham is the home to England's third-oldest university, with a student vibe jostling against its lingering working-class mining-town feel. You'll see tattooed and pierced people in search of job security and a good karaoke bar. Yet Durham has a youthful liveliness and a small-town warmth that shines—especially on sunny days, when most everyone is licking ice-cream cones.

Orientation to Durham

(area code: 0191)
As it has for a thousand years, tidy little Durham clusters everything safely under its castle, within the protective hairpin bend of the River Wear. The longest walk you'll make will be a 30-minute uphill hike from the train station to the cathedral (also doable by bus).

Tourist Information

The TI books rooms and regional event tickets, and provides train times (Mon–Sat 9:30–17:30, Sun 11:00–16:00, WC, café; 1 block north of Market Place, past St. Nicholas Church, in Gala Theatre building; tel. 0191/384-3720, www.durhamtourism.co.uk, tourist info@durhamcity.gov.uk).

Arrival in Durham

From the **train station,** follow the walkway along the road downhill to the second pedestrian turnoff (within sight of railway bridge), which leads almost immediately over a bridge above the busy road called Alexander Crescent. Then take North Road into town or to the first couple of B&Bs (take Alexander Crescent to the other B&Bs). Or just hop on the convenient Cathedral Bus at the train station (described later, under "Getting Around Durham").

    Drivers simply surrender to the wonderful 400-space Prince Bishops Shopping Centre parking lot (at the roundabout at the base of the old town). It's perfectly safe, with 24-hour access, and an elevator that deposits you right in the heart of Durham (£2/2 hours, £3.20/4 hours, £1.50 for overnight, a short block from Market Place, tel. 0191/383-9592, www.princebishops.co.uk).

Helpful Hints

Internet Access: The library, across huge Millennium Place from the TI, has about 40 terminals with free Internet access (Mon–Fri 9:30–19:00, Sat 9:00–17:00, Sun 10:30–16:30, must join for free—bring ID, tel. 0191/386-4003).

Laundry: Durham has none within walking distance; ask at the TI for details if you're willing to drive or take a taxi.

Tours: The TI offers 1.5-hour **city walking tours** on summer weekends (£4, schedule varies but usually May–Sept Sat–Sun at 14:00—confirm with TI). **David Butler,** the town historian, gives excellent private tours (reasonable prices, tel. 0191/386-1500, david@dhent.fsnet.co.uk) as well as a Durham Ghost Tour on Mondays in summer (£5, meet at TI at 19:30, July–Sept only).

Harry Potter Sights: Durham Cathedral was used in the films, as were other nearby locations. For details, see page 832.

Getting Around Durham

While all my recommended hotels, eateries, and sights are easily walkable in Durham, taxis are available to zip tired tourists to their B&Bs or back to the station (about £4, wait on west side of Framwellgate Bridge on Silver Street).

If you don't feel like walking Durham's hills, hop on the convenient **Cathedral Bus** (#40), which runs between the train station and the cathedral, with stops near the North Road bus station, Millburngate, Market Place, and some car parks (£0.50 all-day ticket, daily 3/hour, leaves train station Mon–Fri 7:55–17:30, Sat 9:10–17:30, Sun 9:50–16:50; last bus leaves cathedral Mon–Sat at 17:40, Sun at 17:00; toll tel. 0871-200-2222, www.durham.gov.uk).

Self-Guided Walk

Welcome to Durham

• *Begin at Framwellgate Bridge (which connects the train station with the center).*

Framwellgate Bridge was a wonder when it was built in the 12th century—much longer than the river is wide and higher than seemingly necessary. It was well-designed to connect stretches of solid high ground, and to avoid steep descents toward the marshy river. Note how elegantly today's Silver Street (which leads toward town) slopes into the Framwellgate Bridge. (Imagine that as late as the 1970s, this people-friendly lane was congested with traffic and buses.)

• *Follow Silver Street up the hill to the town's main square.*

Durham's **Market Place** retains the same plotting the prince bishop gave it when he moved villagers here in about 1100. Each

Durham

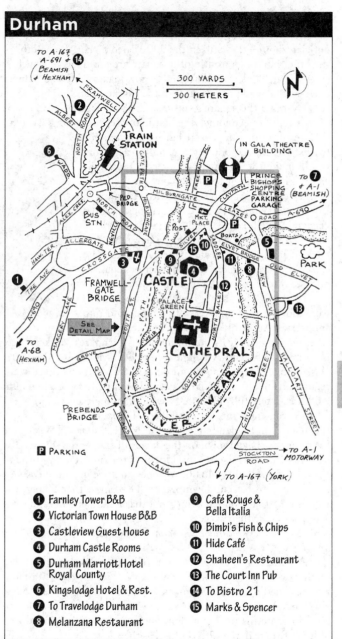

TO A-167
A-691 &
(BEAMISH
& HEXHAM) ❶❹

FRAMWELL

ALBERT
NORTH ROAD

❷

❻

TRAIN
STATION

300 YARDS
300 METERS

N

(IN GALA THEATRE
BUILDING)

PRINCE
BISHOP'S
SHOPPING
CENTRE
PARKING
GARAGE

TO ❼
& A-1
(BEAMISH)

GATE PETH

WADD

PED
BRIDGE

ALEX. CRES.

NORTH ROAD

HILBURNGATE

MILBURNGATE

FREEMAN'S PL.

CLAYPATH

LEAZES ROAD

A-690

BUS
STN.

NEVILLE

POST

MKT.
PLACE

SADLER

BOATS

SILVER

ELVET BRIDGE

OLD ELVET

❺

PARK

HAW. TER.

THE AVE.

❶

ALLERGATE

CROSSGATE

❸

⚓

❾

❿

⓫

❽

⓬

NEW ELVET

FRAMWELL-
GATE
BRIDGE

⓯

❹

CASTLE

TO
A-68
(HEXHAM)

MARGERY LANE

SOUTH ST.

PATH

WEIR

PALACE
GREEN

NORTH BAILEY

SEE
Detail Map

GROVE

QUARRY

CATHEDRAL

⓭

SOUTH BAILEY

CHURCH STREET

HALLGARTH STREET

PREBENDS
BRIDGE

HEADS

RIVER WEAR

P PARKING

STOCKTON
ROAD

TO A-1
MOTORWAY

TO A-167 (YORK)

LANE

❶ Farnley Tower B&B

❷ Victorian Town House B&B

❸ Castleview Guest House

❹ Durham Castle Rooms

❺ Durham Marriott Hotel
Royal County

❻ Kingslodge Hotel & Rest.

❼ To Travelodge Durham

❽ Melanzana Restaurant

❾ Café Rouge &
Bella Italia

❿ Bimbi's Fish & Chips

⓫ Hide Café

⓬ Shaheen's Restaurant

⓭ The Court Inn Pub

❹ To Bistro 21

⓯ Marks & Spencer

DURHAM

plot of land was the same width (about 8 yards). Find today's distinctly narrow buildings (Thomas Cook, Whittard, and the optician shop)—they still fit the 900-year-old plan. The widths of the other buildings fronting the square are multiples of that first shop width. Plots were long and skinny, maximizing the number of shops that could have a piece of the Market Place action.

Examine the square's **statues.** Coal has long been the basis of this region's economy. The statue of Neptune was part of an ill-fated attempt by a coal baron to bribe the townsfolk into embracing a canal project that would make the shipment of his coal more efficient. The statue of the fancy guy on the horse is Charles Stewart Vane, the Third Marquess of Londonderry. He was an Irish aristocrat, and a general in Wellington's army, who married a local coal heiress. A clever and aggressive businessman, he managed to create a vast business empire controlling every link in the coal business chain—mines, railroads, boats, harbors, and so on.

In the 1850s throughout England, towns were moving their markets off squares and into Industrial Age iron-and-glass market halls. Durham was no exception, and today its **indoor market** (which faces Market Place) is a funky 19th-century delight to explore (Mon–Sat 9:00–17:00, closed Sun). There are also outdoor markets in Market Square (Sat retail market 9:00–16:30, farmer's market third Thu of each month, 9:00–15:30, tel. 0191/384-6153, www.durhammarkets.co.uk).

Do you enjoy the sparse traffic in Durham's old town? It was the first city in England to institute a "congestion fee." Look where traffic enters the old town on the downhill side of the square. The bollards (short posts) are up, blocking traffic Monday through Saturday from 10:00 to 16:00. Anyone can drive in...but it costs £2 to get out. This has cut downtown traffic by more than 50 percent. Locals brag that London (which now has a similar congestion fee) was inspired by their success.

• *Head up to the cathedral along Saddler Street. On the left, you'll see a bridge.*

A 12th-century construction, **Elvet Bridge** led to a town market over the river. Like Framwellgate, it's very long (17 arches) and designed to avoid river muck and steep inclines. Even today, Elvet Bridge leads to an unusually wide road—once swollen to accommodate the market action. Shops lined the right-hand side of Elvet Bridge in the 12th century, as they do today. An alley separated the bridge from the buildings on the left. When the bridge was widened, it met the upper stories of the buildings on the left, which became "street level."

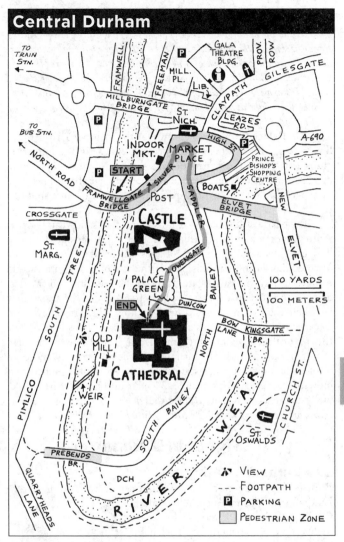

Central Durham

DURHAM

The Scots, living just 50 miles from here, were on the rampage in the 14th century. After their victory at Bannockburn in 1314, they pushed farther south and actually burned part of Durham. Wary of this new threat, Durham built these **city walls.** As people settled within the walls, the population density soared. Soon, open lanes were covered by residences and became tunnels (called "vennels"). A classic vennel leads to Saddlers Yard, a fine little 16th-century courtyard (immediately opposite Elvet Bridge). While the vennels are cute today, centuries ago they were

Dickensian nightmares—the filthiest of hovels.

• *Continue up Saddler Street. Between the two Georgian Window signs, go through the purple door to see a bit of the medieval wall incorporated into the brickwork of a newer building, and a turret from an earlier wall. Back on Saddler Street, you can see the ghost of the old wall. (It's exactly the width of the building now housing the Salvation Army.) Veer right at Owengate as you continue uphill, until you reach the Palace Green.*

The **Palace Green** was the site of the original 11th-century Saxon town, filling this green between the castle and an earlier church. Later, the town made way for 12th-century Durham's defenses, which now enclose the green. With the threat presented by the Vikings, it's no wonder people found comfort in a spot like this.

The **castle** still stands—as it has for a thousand years—on its motte (manmade mound). Like Oxford and Cambridge, Durham University is a collection of colleges scattered throughout the town, and even this castle is part of the school. Look into the old courtyard from the castle gate. It traces the very first and smallest bailey (protected area). As future bishops expanded the castle, they left their coats of arms as a way of "signing" the wing they built. Because the Norman kings appointed prince bishops here to rule this part of their realm, Durham was the seat of power for much of northern England. The bishops had their own army and even minted their own coins (castle entrance by 45-minute guided tour only, £5, call ahead for schedule, 24-hour info tel. 0191/334-3800, www.dur.ac.uk/university.college/tours).

• *This walk ends at Durham's stunning **cathedral**, described next.*

Sights in Durham

▲▲▲Durham's Cathedral

Built to house the much-venerated bones of St. Cuthbert from Lindisfarne, Durham's cathedral offers the best look at Norman architecture in England. ("Norman" is British for "Romanesque.") In addition to touring the cathedral and its attached sights, try to fit in an evensong service.

Cost and Hours: Entry to the cathedral itself is free, though a £4 donation is requested and you must pay to enter its several interior sights (described under "Other Cathedral Sights," later). The cathedral is open to visitors mid-July–Aug daily 9:30–20:00; Sept–mid-

---

Durham's Early Years

Durham's location, tucked inside a tight bend in the River Wear, was ideal for easy fortifications. But it wasn't settled until A.D. 995, with the arrival of St. Cuthbert's body (buried in Durham Cathedral). Shortly after that, a small church and fortification were built upon the site of today's castle and church to house the relic. The castle was a classic "motte-and-bailey" design (with the "motte," or mound, providing a lookout tower for the stockade encircling the protected area, or "bailey"). By 1100, the prince bishop's bailey was filled with villagers—and he wanted everyone out. This was *his* place! He provided a wider protective wall, and had the town resettle below, around today's Market Place. But this displaced the townsfolk's cows, so the prince bishop constructed a fine stone bridge (today's Framwellgate) to connect the new town to grazing land he established across the river. The bridge had a defensive gate, with a wall circling the peninsula and the river serving as a moat.

July Mon–Sat 9:30–18:00, Sun 12:30–17:30; opens daily at 7:15 for worship and prayer, tel. 0191/386-4266, www.durhamcathedral.co.uk. A bookshop, cafeteria, and WC are tucked away in the cloisters. No photos, videos, or mobile phones are allowed inside the cathedral.

Tours: The cathedral offers regular tours in summer. If one is already in session, you're welcome to join (£4; late July–late Sept Mon–Sat at 10:30, 11:00, and 14:30; tours also possible near Easter and during school vacations in May and Oct, call or check website to confirm schedule, tel. 0191/386-4266).

Evensong: For a thousand years, this cradle of English Christianity has been praising God. To really experience the cathedral, go for an evensong service. Arrive early and ask to be seated in the choir. It's a spiritual Oz, as the choristers (20 youngsters—now girls as well as boys—and 12 men) sing psalms—a red-and-white-robed pillow of praise, raised up by the powerful pipe organ. If you're lucky and the service goes well, the organist will run a spiritual musical victory lap as the congregation breaks up (Tue–Sat at 17:15, Sun at 15:30, 1 hour, sometimes sung on Mon; visiting choirs nearly always fill in when choir is off on school break mid-July–Aug; tel. 0191/386-4266).

Organ Recitals: On most Wednesday evenings in July and August you can catch a recital at the cathedral (£8, 19:30).

⊘ Self-Guided Tour: Begin your visit outside the cathedral. From the Palace Green, notice how this fortress of God stands boldly opposite the Norman keep of Durham's fortress of man.

DURHAM

Durham's Cathedral

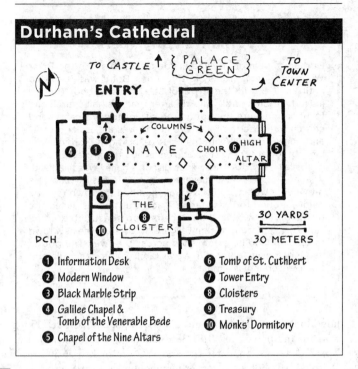

TO CASTLE | PALACE GREEN | TO TOWN CENTER

ENTRY

COLUMNS

NAVE   CHOIR   HIGH ALTAR

THE CLOISTER

DCH

❶ Information Desk
❷ Modern Window
❸ Black Marble Strip
❹ Galilee Chapel & Tomb of the Venerable Bede
❺ Chapel of the Nine Altars

❻ Tomb of St. Cuthbert
❼ Tower Entry
❽ Cloisters
❾ Treasury
❿ Monks' Dormitory

30 YARDS
30 METERS

The **exterior** of this awe-inspiring cathedral—if you look closely—has a serious skin problem. In the 1770s, as the stone was crumbling, they crudely peeled it back a few inches. The scrape marks give the cathedral a bad complexion to this day. For proof of this odd "restoration," study the masonry 10 yards to the right of the door. The L-shaped stones in the corner would normally never be found in a church like this—they only became L-shaped when the surface was cut back.

At the cathedral **door,** the big, bronze, lion-faced knocker (a replica of the 12th-century original—now in the treasury) was used by criminals seeking sanctuary (read the explanation).

Immediately inside, at the **information desk,** church attendants are standing by to happily answer questions. Ideally, follow a church tour. The £1 pamphlet, *A Short Guide to Durham Cathedral,* is informative but dull.

Notice the **modern window** with the novel depiction of the Last Supper (above and to the left of the entry door). It was given to the church by a local department store in 1984. The shapes of the apostles represent worlds and persons of every kind, from the shadowy Judas to the brightness of Jesus. This window is a good reminder that the cathedral remains a living part of the community.

Near the info desk, the **black marble strip** on the floor was as close to the altar as women were allowed in the days when this was a Benedictine church (until 1540). Sit down (ignoring the black line) and let the fine proportions of England's best Norman nave—and arguably Europe's best Romanesque nave—stir you. All the frilly woodwork and stonework were added in later centuries.

The architecture of the **nave** is particularly harmonious because it was built in a mere 40 years (1093–1133). The round arches and zigzag carved decorations are textbook Norman. The church was also proto-Gothic, built by well-traveled French masons and architects who knew the latest innovations from Europe. Its stone and ribbed roof, pointed arches, and flying buttresses were revolutionary in England. Notice the clean lines and simplicity. It's not as cluttered as other churches for several reasons: Out of respect for St. Cuthbert, for centuries no one else was buried here (so it's not filled with tombs). During Reformation times, sumptuous Catholic decor was cleaned out. And subsequent fires and wars destroyed what Protestants didn't.

Enter the **Galilee Chapel** (late Norman, from 1175) in the back of the nave. The paintings of St. Cuthbert and St. Oswald (seventh-century king of Northumbria) on the side walls of the side altar niche are rare examples of Romanesque (Norman) paintings. Facing this altar, look above to your right to see more faint paintings on the upper walls above the columns. Near the center of the chapel, the upraised tomb topped with a black slab contains the remains of the **Venerable Bede,** an eighth-century Christian scholar who wrote the first history of England. The Latin reads, "In this tomb are the bones of the Venerable Bede."

Back in the main church, stroll down the nave to the center, under the highest **bell tower** in Europe (218 feet). Gaze up. The ropes turn wheels upon which bells are mounted. If you're stirred by the cheery ringing of church bells, tune in to the cathedral on Sunday (9:15–10:00 & 14:30–15:30) or Thursday (19:30–21:00 practice, trained bell ringers welcome) when the resounding notes tumble merrily through the entire town.

Continuing east (all medieval churches faced east), you enter the **choir.** Monks worshipped many times a day, and the choir in the center of the church provided a cozy place to gather in this vast, dark, and chilly building. Mass has been said daily here in the heart of the cathedral for 900 years. The fancy wooden chairs are from the 17th century. Behind the altar is the delicately carved Neville Screen from 1380 (made of Normandy stone in London, shipped to Newcastle by sea, then brought here by wagon). Until the Reformation, the niches contained statues of 107 saints. Exit the choir from the far right side (south). Look for the stained-glass window (to your right) that commemorates the church's 1,000th anniversary in 1995. The colorful scenes depict England's history, from coal miners to cows to computers.

Step down behind the high altar into the east end of the church, which contains the 13th-century **Chapel of the Nine Altars.** Built later than the rest of the church, this is Gothic—taller, lighter, and relatively more extravagant than the Norman nave.

Climb a few steps to the **tomb of St. Cuthbert.** An inspirational leader of the early Christian Church in north England, St. Cuthbert lived in the Lindisfarne monastery on Holy Island (100 miles north of Durham). He died in 687. Eleven years later, his body was exhumed and found to be miraculously preserved. This stoked the popularity of his shrine, and pilgrims came in growing numbers. When Vikings raided Lindisfarne in 875, the monks fled with his body (and the famous illuminated *Lindisfarne Gospels,* now in the British Library in London). In 995, after 120 years of roaming, the monks settled in Durham on an easy-to-defend tight bend in the River Wear. This cathedral was built over Cuthbert's tomb.

Throughout the Middle Ages, a shrine stood here and was visited by countless pilgrims. In 1539, during the Reformation—whose proponents advocated focusing on God rather than saints—the shrine was destroyed. But pilgrims still come, especially on St. Cuthbert's feast day (March 20).

Other Cathedral Sights: The entry to the **tower** is in the south transept; the view from the tower will cost you 325 steps and £5 (Mon–Sat 10:00–16:00, closes at 15:00 in winter, closed Sun, last entry 20 minutes before closing; closed during events and in bad weather; must be at least 4'3" tall, no backless shoes). The following sights are within the **cloisters:** The **treasury,** filled with medieval bits and holy pieces (including Cuthbert's coffin, vestments, and cross), fleshes out this otherwise stark building. The actual relics from St. Cuthbert's tomb are at the far end (treasury well worth the £2.50 admission, Mon–Sat 10:00–16:30, Sun 14:00–16:30). The **Monks' Dormitory,** now a library with an original 14th-century timber roof filled with Anglo-Saxon stones, is worth its £1 admission (likely Mon–Sat 10:00–16:00, Sun 12:30–16:00). Skip the unexceptional **AV show** about St. Cuthbert in the unexceptional undercroft (£1, Mon–Sat 10:00–15:00, no showings Sun, off-season also no showings Fri, closed Nov–early Jan).

Near the treasury, you'll find the **WCs, bookshop** (in the old kitchen), and fine **Undercroft** cafeteria (daily 10:00–16:30, tel. 0191/386-3721).

Activities in Durham

Riverside Path—For a 20-minute woodsy escape, walk Durham's riverside path from busy Framwellgate Bridge to sleepy Prebends Bridge.

Boat Cruise and Rental—Hop on the *Prince Bishop* for a relaxing one-hour narrated cruise of the river that nearly surrounds Durham (£6, Easter–Oct, for schedule call 24-hour info line at 0191/386-9525, check at TI, or go down to dock at Brown's Boat House at Elvet Bridge, just east of old town, www.princebishoprc.co.uk). Sailings vary based on weather and tides. For some exercise with the same scenery, you can rent a rowboat at the same pier (£4/hour per person, £10 deposit, Easter–Sept daily 10:00–18:00, last boat rental one hour before dusk, tel. 0191/386-3779).

Sleeping in Durham

B&Bs

$$$ Farnley Tower, a luxurious B&B, has 13 large rooms with all the comforts. On a quiet street at the top of a hill, it's a 15-minute hike from the town center (Sb-£65, Db-£85, superior Db-£95, family room-£120, some rooms have cathedral views, paying with credit card costs 2 percent extra, free Wi-Fi, phones in rooms, easy free parking, inviting yard, The Avenue, tel. 0191/375-0011, fax 0191/383-9694, www.farnley-tower.co.uk, enquiries@farnley-tower.co.uk, Raj and Roopal Naik). The Naiks also run the adjacent, wildly inventive Gourmet Spot restaurant.

DURHAM

Sleep Code

(£1 = about $1.60, country code: 44, area code: 0191)
S = Single, **D** = Double/Twin, **T** = Triple, **Q** = Quad, **b** = bathroom, **s** = shower only. You can assume credit cards are accepted, and breakfast is included, unless otherwise noted.

To help you sort easily through these listings, I've divided the rooms into three categories based on the price for a standard double room with bath (during high season):

  $$$ Higher Priced—Most rooms £85 or more.
   $$ Moderately Priced—Most rooms between £50–85.
    $ Lower Priced—Most rooms £50 or less.

Prices can change without notice; verify the hotel's current rates online or by email. For other updates, see www.ricksteves.com/update.

$$ Victorian Town House B&B offers three spacious, tastefully updated rooms in an 1853 townhouse in a nice residential area just down the hill from the train station (Sb-£50–60, Db-£80–85, family room-£85–105, cash only, some view rooms, Wi-Fi, DVD library, 2 Victoria Terrace, 5-minute walk from train or bus station, tel. 05601/459-168, www.durhambedandbreakfast.com, stay @durhambedandbreakfast.com, friendly Jill and Andy).

$$ Castleview Guest House rents six airy, restful rooms in a well-located, 250-year-old guesthouse next door to a little church, close to Silver Street (Sb-£55–60, Db-£80–85, cash only, free Internet access and Wi-Fi, free street-parking permit, 4 Crossgate, tel. 0191/386-8852, www.castle-view.co.uk, castle_view@hotmail .com, Mike and Anne Williams).

$$ *Student Housing Open to Anyone:* Durham Castle, a student residence actually on the castle grounds facing the cathedral, rents rooms during the summer break (generally end of June–Sept only). Request a room in the stylish main building, or you may get one of the few bomb shelter–style modern dorm rooms (S-£28.50, Sb-£39, D-£51, Db-£70, fancier Db-£180, elegant breakfast hall, free parking down the hill at Prince Bishops Shopping Centre parking lot with voucher from reception, Palace Green, tel. 0191/334-4108 or 0191/334-4106, fax 0191/334-3801, www.dur.ac.uk /university.college, durham.castle@durham .ac.uk).

Hotels

$$$ Durham Marriott Hotel Royal County scatters its 150 posh, four-star rooms among several buildings sprawling across the river from the city center. The Leisure Club has a pool, sauna, Jacuzzi, and fitness equipment (Db-£150 is official rate—but check website for exact prices and deals, breakfast not included, elevator, 2 restaurants, bar, free parking, Old Elvet, tel. 0191/386-6821 or toll tel. 0870-400-7286, fax 0191/386-0704, www.marriott.co.uk).

$$ Kingslodge Hotel & Restaurant is a slightly worn but comfortable 21-room place with charming terraces, an attached restaurant, a pub, and a champagne-and-oyster bar. Located in a pleasantly woodsy setting, it's nevertheless convenient for train travelers (Sb-£60, Db-£75, family room-£95, breakfast-£7, free Wi-Fi, free parking, Waddington Street, Flass Vale, tel. 0191/370-9977, www.kingslodge.info, kingslodgehotel@yahoo.co.uk).

$$ Travelodge Durham's 57 simple rooms are in a converted 1844 train station, with the former waiting room now housing

DURHAM

the reception desk (Db-£55–65 but check website for deals, cold breakfast delivered to room—not worth price, Wi-Fi, half-mile northeast of cathedral, off A690 at Station Lane, Gilesgate, toll tel. 0871-984-6136, fax 0191/386-5461, www.travelodge.co.uk).

Eating in Durham

Durham is a university town with plenty of lively, inexpensive eateries. Stroll down North Road, across Framwellgate Bridge, through Market Place, and up Saddler Street, and consider these places.

Melanzana, just over Elvet Bridge on the other side of town, is an Italian restaurant with £8–9 pizzas and pastas and £11–17 dinners in an inviting setting (daily 9:00–21:00, Fri–Sat until 22:00, even cheaper during happy hour, 96 Elvet Bridge, tel. 0191/384-0096).

Café Rouge, a chain restaurant with French-bistro food and decor, is just east of Framwellgate Bridge (Mon–Sat 9:00–23:00, Sun 10:00–22:00, 21 Silver Street, tel. 0191/384-3429). **Bella Italia,** next door and down the stairs, overlooks the river. Although it's another chain, it's popular and has surprisingly good food (Tue–Sat 10:00–23:00, Sun–Mon 10:00–22:30, reservations recommended, 20 Silver Street, tel. 0191/386-1060). **Bimbi's,** on Market Place, is a standby for fish-and-chips (generally Mon–Wed 11:00–17:00, Thu–Sat 11:00–19:00, Sun 12:00–17:00).

Saddler Street, leading from Market Place up to the cathedral, is lined with eateries. The hip **Hide Café,** with youthful, jazz-filled ambience, serves the best modern continental cuisine in the old town (£6–10 lunches, £8–14 meals, Mon–Sat 12:00–15:00 & 18:00–21:30, Sun 12:00–15:00, reservations smart, 39 Saddler Street, tel. 0191/384-1999).

Shaheen's is the place for good Indian cuisine (£6–10 meals, Tue–Sat 17:00–22:00, closed Sun–Mon, 48 North Bailey Street, just past turnoff to cathedral, tel. 0191/386-0960).

The Court Inn, on the outskirts of town, is a local favorite for traditional pub grub (£7–12 meals, tapas, daily 11:00–22:20, 10-minute walk east of old town over Elvet Bridge, Court Lane, tel. 0191/384-7350).

Bistro 21, with modern French/Mediterranean fare and good seafood, works well for drivers looking for a nontouristy splurge (£15–22 entrées, £15–18 two- or three-course dinner specials, Mon–Sat 12:00–14:00 & 18:00–22:00, closed Sun, 1.5 miles northwest of town, Aykley Heads, tel. 0191/384-4354).

Supermarket: **Marks & Spencer** is in the old town, just off the main square (Mon–Sat 9:00–18:00, Sun 11:00–17:00, 4 Silver Street, across from post office). You can **picnic** in Market Square,

DURHAM

or on the benches and grass outside the cathedral entrance (but not on the Palace Green, unless the park police have gone home).

Durham Connections

From Durham by Train to: York (3–4/hour, 45 minutes), **Keswick/Lake District** (train to Penrith—hourly, 3 hours, change in Newcastle and Carlisle; then bus to Keswick—hourly Mon–Sat, Sun 8/day, 40 minutes), **London** (2/hour, 3 hours), **Hadrian's Wall** (take train to Newcastle—4/hour, 15 minutes, then a bus or a train/bus combination to near Hadrian's Wall), **Edinburgh** (2/hour, 2 hours, less frequent in winter). Train info: toll tel. 0845-748-4950, www.nationalrail.co.uk.

Near Durham: Beamish Museum

This huge 300-acre open-air museum, which re-creates the years 1825 and 1913 in northeast England, takes at least three hours to explore. Vintage trams and cool circa-1910 double-decker buses shuttle visitors to the four stations: Colliery Village, The Town, Pockerley Manor/Waggonway, and Home Farm. Tram routes are more plentiful than bus routes, but attendants on both are helpful and knowledgeable. Signs on the trams advertise a variety of 19th-century products, from "Borax, for washing everything" to "Murton's Reliable Travelling Trunks." This isn't a wax museum. If you touch the exhibits, they may smack you. Attendants at each stop happily explain everything. In fact, the place is only really interesting if you talk to the attendants. In 2008, the "Westoe netty"—a circa 1890 men's public WC—was acquired and rebuilt near the 1913 railway station. The loo became famous in 1972 as the subject in a painting by a local artist.

Cost and Hours: £16, £12 with bus receipt, £7.50 in winter, choose the Beamish Unlimited Pass at no extra charge for a 2-day visit; Easter–Oct open daily 10:00–17:00; in Nov–Easter only The Town, Colliery Village, and Tramway are open, Tue–Thu and Sat–Sun 10:00–16:00, closed Mon and Fri and mid-Nov–early Jan; check events schedule as you enter, last tickets sold at 15:00 year-round, tel. 0191/370-4000, www.beamish.org.uk, museum @beamish.org.uk.

Getting There: By **car,** the museum is five minutes off the A1/M1 motorway (one exit north of Durham at Chester-le-Street/Junction 63, well signposted, 12 miles and a 25-minute drive northwest of Durham).

Getting to Beamish from Durham by **bus** is a snap on peak-season weekends via the direct "Waggonway" bus #B1 (£3.70 day pass, 5/day, 30 minutes, runs April–Oct only, stops at Durham

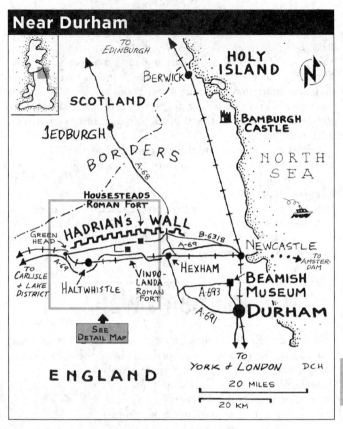

Near Durham

train and bus stations, tel. 0845/606-0260, www.simplygo.com).

Otherwise, catch **bus** #21 or #50/#50A from the Durham bus station (3–4/hour, 25 minutes, £3.70 day pass) and transfer at Chester-le-Street to bus #X8, #28, or #28A (2/hour Mon–Sat, hourly Sun, 15 minutes, leaves from central bus kiosk a half-block away; get handy bus schedule at Durham TI, toll tel. 0871-200-2233, www.traveline.org.uk). When you get off the bus at Beamish, the museum is a five-minute walk down the hill. Show your bus receipt for a 25 percent museum discount. To catch the bus leaving Beamish, the bus stop for bus #X8 is on the side of the street near the pub; the stop for #28 and #28A is on the opposite side of the street.

❸ **Self-Guided Tour:** Start with the **Colliery Village** (company town around a coal mine), with a school, a church, miners' homes, and a fascinating—if claustrophobic—20-minute tour into the Mahogany drift mine. Your guide will tell you about beams collapsing, gas exploding, and flooding; after that cheerful speech, you'll don a hard hat as you're led into the mine.

The Town is a bustling street featuring a 1913 candy shop (the chocolate room in back is worth a stop for chocolate fans), a dentist's office, a Masonic hall, a garage, a working pub (The Sun Inn, Mon–Sat 11:00–16:30, Sun 12:00–16:30), Barclays Bank, and a hardware store featuring a variety of "toilet sets" (not what you think). For lunch, try the Tea Rooms cafeteria (upstairs, daily 10:00–16:30). If the weather is good, picnic in the grassy pavilion next to the tram stop.

Pockerley Manor and the Waggonway has an 1820s manor house whose attendants have plenty to explain. Enjoy the lovely view from the gardens behind the manor, then enter through the kitchen, where bread is baked several times a week. Ask for a sample if you have a taste for tough rye. Adjacent is the re-created first-ever passenger train from 1825, which takes modern-day visitors for a spin on 1825 tracks—a hit with railway buffs. **Home Farm** is the least interesting section.

Hadrian's Wall

This is one of England's most thought-provoking sights. In about A.D. 122, during the reign of Emperor Hadrian, the Romans built this great stone wall. Its actual purpose is still debated. While Rome ruled Britain for 400 years, it never quite ruled its people. The wall may have been used for any number of reasons: to define the northern edge of the empire, to protect Roman Britain from invading Pict tribes from the north (or at least cut down on pesky border raids), to monitor the movement of people, or to simply give an otherwise bored army something to do. (Emperors understood that nothing's more dangerous than a bored army.) Stretching 73 miles coast to coast across the narrowest stretch of northern England, it  was built and defended by some 20,000 troops. Not just a wall, this was a military complex that included forts, ditches, settlements, and a road on the south side. At every mile of the wall, a castle guards a gate, and two turrets stand between each castle. The mile castles are numbered. (Eighty of them cover the 73 miles, because a Roman mile was slightly shorter than our mile.)

Today, several chunks of the wall, ruined forts, and museums thrill history buffs. About a dozen Roman sights cling along the wall's route; the best are Housesteads Roman Fort and Vindolanda.

Hadrian's Wall

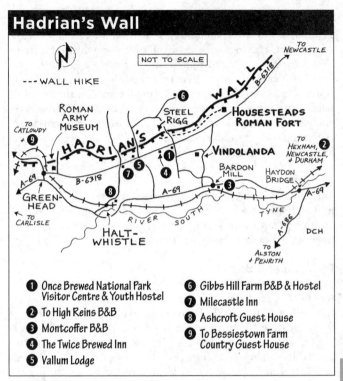

NOT TO SCALE

--- WALL HIKE

TO NEWCASTLE

B-6318

ROMAN ARMY MUSEUM

STEEL RIGG

HOUSESTEADS ROMAN FORT

TO CATLOWDY

HADRIAN'S WALL

VINDOLANDA

TO HEXHAM, NEWCASTLE, & DURHAM

A-69

B-6318

BARDON MILL

HAYDON BRIDGE

A-69

GREEN-HEAD

RIVER SOUTH TYNE

A-69

TO CARLISLE

HALT-WHISTLE

A-686

DCH

TO ALSTON & PENRITH

① Once Brewed National Park Visitor Centre & Youth Hostel
② To High Reins B&B
③ Montcoffer B&B
④ The Twice Brewed Inn
⑤ Vallum Lodge
⑥ Gibbs Hill Farm B&B & Hostel
⑦ Milecastle Inn
⑧ Ashcroft Guest House
⑨ To Bessiestown Farm Country Guest House

Housesteads shows you where the Romans lived; Vindolanda's museum shows you how they lived.

The Hadrian's Wall National Trail runs 84 miles, following the wall's route from coast to coast (for details, see www.national trail.co.uk/HadriansWall).

Tourist Information

Portions of the wall are in Northumberland National Park. The **Once Brewed National Park Visitor Centre** is located along the Hadrian's Wall bus #AD122 route and has information on the area, including walking guides to the wall (Easter–Oct daily 9:30–17:00, Nov–Easter 10:00–15:00 Sat–Sun only, parking-£3, Military Road, Bardon Mill, tel. 01434/344-396, www.north umberlandnationalpark.org.uk, tic.oncebrewed@nnpa.org.uk).

The helpful **TI** in Haltwhistle, right at the train station, has schedule information for Hadrian's Wall bus #AD122 (Easter–Oct Mon–Sat 9:30–13:00 & 14:00–17:00, Sun 13:00–17:00; Nov–Easter Mon–Sat 9:30–12:00 & 13:00–15:30, closed Sun; good selection of maps and guidebooks, tel. 01434/322-002, www.hadrians -wall.org).

Getting to Hadrian's Wall

Hadrian's Wall is anchored by Newcastle on the east and Carlisle on the west. Driving is the most convenient way to see Hadrian's Wall; if you're coming by train, consider renting a car for the day at either Newcastle or Carlisle; otherwise, you'll rely on a bus to connect the sights. If you're just passing through for the day using public transportation, it's impossible to stop and see all the sights—study the bus schedule carefully and prioritize. If you want to see everything—or even hike part of the wall—you'll need to stay at least one night along the bus route.

By Car

Take B6318; it parallels the wall and passes several viewpoints, minor sights, and "severe dips." (These road signs add a lot to a photo portrait.) Buy a good local map to help you explore this interesting area more easily and thoroughly.

By Train and Bus

To reach the Roman sights without a car, you'll take the made-for-tourists Hadrian's Wall **bus #AD122** (named for the year the wall was built; daily Easter–Oct only). Essential resources for navigating the wall by public transit include the *Hadrian's Wall Country Map,* the bus #AD122 schedule, and a local train timetable—all available at local visitor centers and train stations, or at www.hadrians-wall.org. If you arrive by train during the off-season (Nov-Easter), you'll need to take either a local bus or a taxi to visit the wall (explained later, under "Off-Season Options").

Bus Logistics: Bus #AD122 connects the Roman sights with the following train stations (west to east): **Carlisle, Haltwhistle, Hexham,** and **Newcastle** (£8 day pass, buy tickets on board or at any TI, tel. 01434/322-002, www.hadrians-wall.org). While the bus is handy for reaching the main sights (as well as several recommended accommodations), not every bus makes every stop; it's essential to get and study an up-to-date copy of the complete schedule. Two #AD122 buses a day have on-board guides (noted on the schedule).

Buses run most frequently between Haltwhistle and Hexham (6/day each way, plus 2 additional buses between the main sights). However, the bus runs less frequently from the end points: from Carlisle, five times a day; and from Newcastle, just once a day (at 9:00—if you miss this bus, take the train to Hexham and pick up the bus there).

From Newcastle by Train to: Hexham (Mon–Sat 2/hour, Sun hourly, 30 minutes), **Haltwhistle** (Mon–Sat hourly, Sun almost hourly, 1 hour); from either town, you can catch bus

#AD122. You can store your bags at the left-luggage office at the **Newcastle train station** (£5/bag per day, Mon–Sat 8:00–20:00, Sun 9:00–20:00, platform 12).

From Carlisle by Train to: Hexham (Mon–Sat hourly, Sun 11/day, 50 minutes), **Haltwhistle** (Mon–Sat hourly, Sun 11/day, 30 minutes)—bus #AD122 stops in both towns. In Carlisle, you can store your luggage across the street from the train station at **Bar Solo** (£2/bag per day, Mon–Wed 9:00–23:00, Thu–Sat 9:00–24:00, Sun 11:00–22:30, tel. 01228/631-600).

Taxi: If you're staying near the wall, your B&B host can arrange a taxi through Melvin's Taxi (tel. 01434/320-632, mobile 07903-760-230) or Turnbull Taxi (tel. 01434/320-105, mobile 07825-004-901; one-way about £11 from Haltwhistle to Housesteads Roman Fort, arrange for return pickup or have museum staff call a taxi).

Off-Season Options: Off-season (Nov–Easter), public transportation becomes trickier. For the train/bus option, take a train to Haltwhistle, then bus #681 to Housesteads Roman Fort 3/day. For local bus info, see www.traveline.info. To fill the gaps in the bus schedule, consider a taxi (described above).

Luggage: It's difficult to bring your luggage along with you. If you're side-tripping, store your luggage in Newcastle or Carlisle (see train information for each station, earlier). If you must travel with luggage, visit Housesteads Roman Fort, where you can ask to leave baggage at the entrance while exploring (Vindolanda may also agree to keep luggage, if asked nicely). Alternatively, if you want to walk the wall, **Hadrian's Haul** baggage-courier service will send your luggage ahead (£5/bag per pick-up, mobile 07967-564-823, www.hadrianshaul.com).

Sights at Hadrian's Wall

▲▲**Housesteads Roman Fort**—With its tiny museum, powerful scenery, and the best-preserved segment of the wall, this is your best single stop at Hadrian's Wall.

All Roman forts were the same rectangular shape and design, containing a commander's headquarters, barracks, and latrines (lower end); this fort even has a hospital. The fort was built right up to the wall, which is on the far side. From the parking lot and gift shop, it's a half-mile, mostly uphill walk to the entrance of the sprawling fort and minuscule museum.

At the car park are WCs, a snack bar, and a gift shop. Ask nicely if you want to leave your luggage at the gift shop (same hours as fort, tel. 01434/344-525).

Cost and Hours: £4.80 for sight and museum—pay up at fort, not at gift shop; daily April–Sept 10:00–18:00, Oct–March closes at 15:50 or dusk, parking-£3, tel. 01434/344-363, www.english -heritage.org.uk/housesteads).

▲▲Hiking the Wall—From Housesteads, hike west along the wall speaking Latin. For a good, craggy, three-mile walk along the wall, hike between Housesteads and Steel Rigg (free guides available at Once Brewed Visitor Centre). You'll pass a castle sitting in a nick in a crag (milecastle #39, called Castle Nick). There's a parking lot near Steel Rigg (take the little road up from the Twice Brewed Inn). East of Steel Rigg you'll see the "Robin Hood Tree," a large symmetrical tree (in a little roller-coaster gap) that was featured in the movie *Robin Hood: Prince of Thieves* (with Kevin Costner, 1991).

▲Vindolanda—This larger Roman fort (which actually predates the wall by 40 years) and museum are just south of the wall. Although Housesteads has better ruins and the wall, Vindolanda has the better museum, revealing intimate details of Roman life. It's an active dig—from Easter through September, you'll see the work in progress (usually daily, weather permitting).

Eight forts were built on this spot. The Romans, by carefully sealing the foundations from each successive fort, left modern-day archaeologists with seven yards of remarkably well-preserved arti-facts to excavate: keys, coins, brooches, scales, pottery, glass, tools, leather shoes, bits of cloth, and even a wig. Impressive examples of early Roman writing were discovered here in 1973. While the actual letters—written on thin pieces of wood—are in London's British Museum, see the interesting video here and read the trans-lations, including the first known example of a woman writing to a woman (an invitation to a birthday party). These varied let-ters, about parties held, money owed, and sympathy shared, bring Romans to life in a way that stones alone can't.

From the free parking lot, you'll pay at the entrance, then walk 500 yards of grassy parkland decorated by the foundation stones of the Roman fort and a full-size replica chunk of the wall. At the far side are the museum, gift shop, and cafeteria.

Cost and Hours: £5.90, £9 combo-ticket includes Roman Army Museum, daily April–Sept 10:00–18:00, mid-Feb–March and Oct 10:00–17:00, closed Nov–mid Feb, last entry 45 minutes before closing, free parking with entry, tel. 01434/344-277, www .vindolanda.com.

Roman Army Museum—This museum, a few miles farther west at Greenhead, is redundant if you've seen Vindolanda. Its film offers a good eagle-eye view of a portion of the wall (£4.50, or buy £9 combo-ticket that includes Vindolanda, same hours as Vindolanda, but closed Nov–early March, free parking with entry, tel. 016977/47485, www.vindolanda.com).

Sleeping and Eating near Hadrian's Wall

(£1 = about $1.60, country code: 44)

Near Hexham
(area code: 01434)
$$ High Reins offers four rooms in a stone house built by a shipping tycoon in the 1920s (Sb-£45, Db-£68, cash only, ground-floor bedrooms, lounge, 1 mile south of train station on the western outskirts of Hexham, Leazes Lane, tel. 01434/603-590, www.high reins.co.uk, pwalton@highreins.co.uk, Jan and Peter Walton).

In and near Bardon Mill
(area code: 01434)
The Twice Brewed Inn, Once Brewed Youth Hostel, Vallum Lodge, and Milecastle Inn are reachable with Hadrian's Wall bus (#AD122), which stops nearby several times a day.

$$ Montcoffer, a restored country home, is decorated with statues, old enameled advertising signs, and other artifacts collected by owner John McGrellis and his wife, Dehlia, whose textile art is displayed in the three guest rooms (Sb-£48, Db-£78, 2 ground-floor bedrooms, 200 yards from train station and 2 miles from Vindolanda, Bardon Mill, tel. 01434/344-138, mobile 07912-209-992, www.montcoffer.co.uk, john-dehlia@talk21.com).

$$ The Twice Brewed Inn, two miles west of Housesteads and a half-mile from the wall, rents 14 workable rooms and serves real ales and decent pub grub all day (pub open daily 11:00–23:00, food served daily 12:00–20:00, Fri–Sat until 20:30). It's a friendly pub that serves as the community gathering place (S-£33, D-£55, Db-£70–82, ask for a room away from the road, free Internet access for hotel guests, otherwise £1/30 minutes, Military Road, Bardon Mill, tel. 01434/344-534, www.twicebrewedinn.co.uk, info@twicebrewedinn.co.uk).

$ Once Brewed Youth Hostel is a comfortable place near the Twice Brewed Inn and right next door to the Once Brewed National Park Visitor Centre (£16–19/bed with sheets in 2- to 6-bed rooms, D-£30, £3 extra for non-members, breakfast-£4.65, packed lunch-£5, dinner-£9, reception open daily 8:00–10:00 & 16:00–22:00, closed Dec–Jan, laundry, Military Road, 2.5 miles north of Bardon Mill, tel. 01434/344-360, fax 01434/344-045, www.yha.org.uk, oncebrewed@yha.org.uk).

$$ Vallum Lodge is an almost-cushy, comfortable renovated base situated near the vallum (the ditch that forms part of the fortification a half-mile from the wall itself). The six cheery rooms are all on the ground floor, and it's near The Twice Brewed Inn—a handy dinner option, especially if you don't have a car (Sb-£65, Db-£80–85, closed late Oct–Easter, free Wi-Fi, lounge, Military Road, tel. 01434/344-248, www.vallum-lodge.co.uk, cheerful Ann).

$$ Gibbs Hill Farm B&B and Hostel is a friendly working sheep-and-cattle farm set on 700 acres in the stunning valley on the far side of the wall (works best for drivers). It offers four big, airy rooms in the main house, and three six-bed dorm rooms in a restored hay barn (hostel bed/bedding-£15, Sb-£45, Db-£70, laundry facilities, packed lunch-£5, bikes available for rent, 5-minute drive from Once Brewed National Park Visitor Centre, tel. 01434/344-030, www.gibbshillfarm.co.uk, val@gibbshillfarm .co.uk, warm Val). They also rent several cottages for two to six people by the week (£280–600).

Milecastle Inn cooks up all sorts of exotic game and offers the best dinner around, according to hungry national park rangers (daily 12:00–20:30, smart to reserve, North Road, tel. 01434/321-372).

In Haltwhistle
(area code: 01434)
$$ Ashcroft Guest House, a large Victorian and former vicarage in the middle of a cute village with several eating options and a launderette, is 400 yards from the Haltwhistle train station and 200 yards from a Hadrian's Wall bus #AD122 stop. The family-run B&B has nine rooms, huge terraced gardens, and views from the comfy lounge (Sb-£48, Db-£78, four-poster Db-£88, ask about family deals and two-bedroom suite, free Internet access and Wi-Fi, 1.5 miles from the wall, Lanty's Lonnen, tel. 01434/320-213, www.ashcroftguesthouse.co.uk, info@ashcroftguesthouse .co.uk, helpful Geoff and Christine James).

Near Carlisle
(area code: 01228)
$$$ Bessiestown Farm Country Guest House, located northwest of the Hadrian sights, is convenient for drivers connecting the Lake District and Scotland. It's a quiet and soothing stop in the middle of sheep pastures, with five bedrooms in the main house and two 2-bedroom apartments in the former stables (Sb-£57, Db-£90, Tb-£110, family room-£99–110, fancier suite-£130, discounts for 3-night stays, indoor pool; in Catlowdy, midway between Gretna Green and Hadrian's Wall, a 20-minute drive north of Carlisle; tel. 01228/577-219, fax 01228/577-019, www.bessiestown.co.uk, info@bessiestown.co.uk, gracious Margaret Sisson).

Holy Island and Bamburgh Castle

This area is worthwhile only for those with a car.

▲Holy Island

Twelve hundred years ago, this "Holy Island" was Christianity's

toehold on England. It was the home and original burial ground of St. Cuthbert (he's now in Durham). We know it today for the *Lindisfarne Gospels*, decorated by monks in the seventh century with some of the finest art from Europe's "Dark Ages" (now in the British Museum). It's a pleasant visit—a quiet town with a strik-

ing castle (not worth touring) and an evocative priory that was founded in 635.

Lindisfarne Priory: The museum in the priory is tiny but instructive. It's adjacent to the ruined abbey (£4.50; April–Sept daily 9:30–17:00; Oct daily 9:30–16:00; Nov–Jan Sat–Mon 10:00–14:00, closed Tue–Fri; Feb–March daily 10:00–16:00; tel. 01289/389-200, www.english-heritage.org.uk/lindisfarne). You can wander the abbey grounds and graveyard and pop in to the church without paying.

Holy Island is reached by a two-mile causeway that's cut off twice a day by high tides. Safe crossing times are posted at each end of the causeway (and on the priory's website), warning you when this holy place becomes Holy Island—and you become stranded.

For tourist and tide information, check with the **Berwick TI** (generally May–Sept Mon–Sat 10:00–17:00, Sun 11:00–15:00; Oct–April Mon–Sat 10:00–16:00, closed Sun; tel. 01289/330-733, www.visitnorthumberland.com, berwick.tic@northumberland .gov.uk). Park at the pay-and-display lot and walk five minutes into the town.

▲▲Bamburgh Castle

About 10 miles south of Holy Island, this grand castle dominates the Northumbrian countryside, and overlooks Britain's loveliest beach. The place was bought and passionately refurbished by Lord Armstrong, a big industrialist in the 1890s. Its interior, lined with well-described history, feels lived-in because it still is—with Armstrong family portraits and aristocratic-yet-homey knickknacks hanging everywhere. Take advantage of the talkative guides posted throughout the castle. The included **Armstrong Museum** features the inventions of the family that has owned the castle through modern times (£8, daily mid-Feb–Oct 11:00–17:00, winter Sat–Sun only 11:00–16:30, last entry one hour before closing, parking-£2, tel. 01668/214-515, www.bamburghcastle.com). Crisscrossed by walking paths, rolling dunes lead to a vast sandy beach and lots of families on holiday.

WALES

WALES

Wales, a country the size of Massachusetts, is located on a peninsula on the west coast of the Isle of Britain, facing the Irish Sea. Longer than it is wide (170 miles by 60 miles), it's shaped somewhat like a miniature Britain. The north is mountainous, rural, and sparsely populated. The south, with a less-rugged topography, is where two-thirds of the people live (including the capital, Cardiff, pop. 320,000). The country has 750 miles of scenic, windswept coastline and is capped by Mount Snowdon, which, at 3,560 feet, is taller than any mountain in England.

Despite centuries of English imperialism, the Welsh language (or Cymraeg, pronounced kum-RAH-ig) remains alive and well...better than its nearly dead Celtic cousin of Gaelic in Scotland. Though everyone in Wales speaks English, one in five can also speak the native tongue. In the northwest, well over half the population is fluent in Welsh, and uses it in everyday life. Listen in.

Most certainly *not* a dialect of English, the Celtic Welsh tongue sounds to foreign ears like the Middle Earth languages from *The Lord of the Rings*. One of Europe's oldest languages, Welsh has been written down since about A.D. 600, and was spoken 300 years before French or German. Today, the Welsh language and those who speak it are protected by law, the country is officially bilingual, and signs always display both languages (e.g., Cardiff/Caerdydd). In schools it's either the first or the required second language; in many areas, English isn't used in classes at all until middle school.

Though English has been the dominant language in Wales for many years (and most newspapers and media are in English), the Welsh people cherish their linguistic heritage as something that sets them apart. In fact, a line of the Welsh national anthem goes, "Oh, may the old language survive!"

Speaking Welsh

Welsh pronunciation is tricky. The common "ll" combination sounds roughly like "thl" (pronounced as if you were ready to make an "l" sound and then blew it out). As in Scotland, "ch" is a soft, guttural k, pronounced in the back of the throat. The Welsh "dd" sounds like the English "th," f = v, ff = f, w = the "u" in "push," y = i. Non-Welsh people often make the mistake of trying to say a long Welsh name too fast, and inevitably trip themselves up. A local tipped me off: Slow down and say each syllable separately, and it'll come out right. For example, Llangollen is thlang-GOT-hlen.

Although there's no need to learn any Welsh (because everyone also speaks English), make friends and impress the locals by learning a few polite phrases:

Hello	**Helo**	hee-LOH
Goodbye	**Hwyl**	hoo-il
Please	**Os gwelwch yn dda**	os GWELL-uck UN thah
Thank you	**Diolch**	dee-olkh
Wales	**Cymru**	KUM-ree
England	**Lloegr**	THLOY-ger

In a pub, toast the guy who just bought your drink with *Diolch* and *Yeach-hid dah* (YECH-id dah, "Good health to you").

Wales has some traditional foods worth looking for, particularly lamb dishes and leek soup *(cawl)*. In fact, the national symbol is the leek, ever since medieval warriors—who wore the vegetable on their helmets in battle—saved the land from Saxon invaders. Cheese on toast is known as "Welsh rarebit" (or "Welsh rabbit"; the name is a throwback to a time when the poor Welsh couldn't afford much meat in their diet). At breakfast you might get some "Welsh cakes," basically a small squashed scone. Cockles and seaweed bread were once common breakfast items—but don't expect your hotel to serve them.

Wales' three million people are mostly white and Christian (Presbyterian, Anglican, or Catholic). Like their UK counterparts, they enjoy football (soccer), but rugby is the unofficial Welsh sport, more popular in Wales than in any country outside of New Zealand. Other sports are cricket and snooker (similar to billiards).

The Welsh love their choirs. Every town has a choir (men's or mixed) that practices weekly. Visitors are usually welcome to observe, and very often they follow the choir down to the pub afterward for a good old-fashioned beer-lubricated sing-along. As this has become quite a tourist attraction, many choirs are asking for a small donation—which makes sense. Take in a weekly choir practice at one of the following towns in North Wales (note that some towns have more than one choir, and schedules are subject to change—confirm the schedule with a local TI or your B&B before making the trip, or go to www.welshassociationmalechoirs.com): **Ruthin** (mixed choir Thu 20:00 except Aug at Tabernacle Church, tel. 01824/703-757), **Llangollen** (two men's choirs: Fri 19:30 at Hand Hotel, 21:00 pub singsong afterward, hotel tel. 01978/861-482; the other choir meets Wed 20:00 at Memorial Hall on High Street, tel. 01691/600-242), **Denbigh** (men's choir Tue 19:30–21:30 at the Eirianfa Centre, tel. 01824/790-524, www.denbigh-choir .co.uk), **Llandudno** (men's choir rehearsals Mon 19:30–21:00 except Aug, near Conwy, tel. 01248/681-159), and **Caernarfon** (Tue 19:45 in the gallery at Victoria Dock, no practice in Aug, tel. 01286/672-633, www.cormeibioncaernarfon.org). Additionally, many of these groups regularly perform concerts—inquire for the latest schedule.

The Welsh flag features a red dragon on a field of green and white. The dragon has been a symbol of Wales since at least the ninth century (maybe even from Roman days). According to legend, King Arthur's men carried the dragon flag to battle.

Welsh history stretches back into the mists of prehistoric Britain. The original Celtic tribes were conquered by the Romans, who built forts and cities, and (later) introduced Christianity. As Rome fell, Saxon tribes like the Angles from Germany conquered "Angle-land" (England) but failed to penetrate Wales. Brave Welsh warriors, mountainous terrain, and the 177-mile man-made ditch-and-wall known as Offa's Dyke helped preserve the country's unique Celtic/Roman heritage. In 1216, Wales' medieval kingdoms unified under Llywelyn Fawr ("the Great").

This brief unification ended in 1282, however, when King Edward I of England invaded and conquered, forever ending Wales' sovereignty. To solidify his hold on the country, Edward built a string of castles (at Caernarfon, Conwy, and many other places—see sidebar on page 550). He then named his son and successor the "Prince of Wales," starting the tradition (which continues to today's Prince Charles) of England's heir to the throne

bearing that ceremonial title. Despite an unsuccessful rebellion in 1400, led by Owen Glendower (Owain Glyndwr), Wales has remained under English rule since 1282. In 1535, the annexation

WALES

was formalized under Henry VIII.

By the 19th century, Welsh coal and iron stoked the engines of Britain's Industrial Revolution, and its slate was exported to shingle roofs throughout Europe. The stereotype of the Welsh as poor, grimy-faced miners continued into the 20th century. They began the slow transition from mining, factories, and sheep-farming to the service-and-software economy of the global world.

In recent decades the Welsh have consciously tried to preserve their local traditions and language. In 1999, Wales was granted its own parliament, the National Assembly, with powers to distribute the national budget. Though still ruled by the UK government in London, Wales now has a measure of independence and self-rule.

Less urbanized and less wealthy than England, Wales consists of miles of green land where sheep graze (because the soil is too poor for crops).

Hikers, beware of midges. From late May through September, these tiny, biting insects like dawn, dusk, dampness, and you. Get insect repellent if they're a problem.

Because Wales is a cheap weekend destination spot, the country is becoming popular for English drinkers who pour over the border to drink the cheap beer, before stumbling home on Sunday. This can make some Welsh border towns surprisingly rowdy on Saturday nights.

I've focused my coverage of Wales on the north, which has the highest concentration of castles, natural beauty, and attractions. A few South Wales sights that are convenient to visit from Bath are covered in the Near Bath chapter.

Try to connect with Welsh culture in your itinerary. Clamber over a castle, eat a leek, count sheep in a field, catch a rugby match, or share a pint of bitter with a baritone. Open your ears to the sound of words as old as the legendary King Arthur. "May the old language survive!"

WALES

NORTH WALES

*Conwy • Caernarfon • Snowdonia National Park •
Blaenau Ffestiniog • Ruthin*

Wales' top historical, cultural, and natural wonders are found in the northern part of the country. From towering Mount Snowdon to lush forests to desolate moor country, North Wales is a poem written in landscape. For sightseeing thrills and diversity, North Wales is Britain's most interesting slice of the Celtic crescent. But be careful not to be waylaid by the many gimmicky sights and bogus "best of" lists. The region's economy is poor, and they're wringing every possible pound out of the tourist trade. Sort through your options carefully.

Planning Your Time

On a three-week Britain trip, give North Wales two nights and a day. It'll give you mighty castles, a giant slate mine, and some of Britain's most beautiful scenery. Many visitors are charmed and decide to stay an extra day.

Drivers staying in Conwy who have just one day can follow this plan:

  9:30 Leave after breakfast.

10:00 Visit Bodnant Garden.

12:00 Pop into Trefriw Woolen Mills.

13:00 Lunch in Llanberis and tour the Welsh Slate Museum, then drive to Caernarfon.

16:00 Catch the 16:00 Caernarfon Castle tour (castle open until 18:00 July-Aug).

18:00 Browse the town of Caernarfon.

19:00 Drive back to Conwy to follow my self-guided town walk (at 19:30) and have dinner (at 20:30).

For those relying on **public transportation,** Conwy is a good

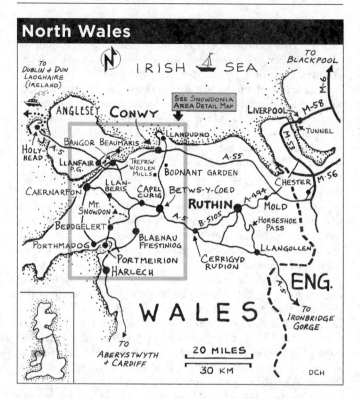

North Wales

home base for buses and trains. If you have one day, leave Conwy in the morning for a loop through the Snowdonia sights (possibly including Betws-y-Coed, Beddgelert, or Llanberis, depending on bus and train schedules—plan your route before heading out), then return to Conwy in the evening for the town walk and dinner. To see more in your limited time, consider hiring a local guide for a private driving tour (described on next page).

With a second day, slow down and consider the region's other sights: the train from Llanberis up Mount Snowdon, the slate-mine tour in Blaenau Ffestiniog, Beaumaris Castle and jail, and the town of Ruthin. With more time and a desire to hike, consider using the mountain village of Beddgelert as your base.

Getting Around North Wales

By Public Transportation: North Wales (except Ruthin) is surprisingly well-covered by a combination of buses and trains (though you'll want to get an early start to allow ample time to visit several destinations).

A main **train** line runs along the north coast from Chester to Holyhead via Llandudno Junction, Conwy, and Bangor, with hourly departures (toll tel. 0845-748-4950, www.nationalrail.co.uk or www.arrivatrainswales.co.uk). From Llandudno Junction, the Conwy Valley line goes scenically south to Betws-y-Coed and Blaenau Ffestiniog (5/day Mon–Sat, 3/day on Sun in summer, no Sun trains in winter, www.conwy.gov.uk/cvr). And the old-fashioned Welsh Highland Railway steam train goes from Caer-narfon to Beddgelert (2–4 trips/day, mid-March–Oct, 1.5 hours).

Public **buses** (run by various companies) pick up where the trains leave off. Get the *Public Transport Information* booklet at any local TI. Certain bus lines—dubbed "Sherpa" routes (the bus numbers begin with #S)—circle Snowdonia National Park with the needs of hikers in mind (www.snowdoniagreenkey.co.uk).

Schedules get sparse late in the afternoon and on Sundays; plan ahead and confirm times carefully at local TIs and bus and train stations. For any questions about public transportation, call the Wales Travel Line at toll tel. 0871-200-2233, or check www.traveline-cymru.info.

Your choices for money-saving public-transportation **passes** are confusing. The Red Rover Ticket—the simplest and probably the best bet for most travelers—covers all buses west of Llandudno, including Sherpa buses (£5/day, buy from driver). The £4 Snowdon Sherpa Day Ticket covers select buses that traverse the national park—but not connections between the park and Caernarfon or Conwy, so it's typically a worse deal than the Red Rover. The North Wales Rover Ticket covers trains and certain buses within a complex zone system (£7–22/day, depending on how many zones you need; buy on bus or train, www.taith.gov.uk).

By Private Tour: Mari Roberts, a Welsh guide, leads driving tours of the area tailored to your interests. Tours in her car are generally out of Conwy, but she will happily pick you up in Ruthin or Holyhead (£18/hour, 4-hour minimum, tel. 01824/702-713, marihr@talktalk.net).

Conwy

Along with the Conwy Castle, this garrison town was built in the 1280s to give Edward I a toehold in Wales. As there were no real cities in 13th-century Wales, this was an English town, planted with settlers for the king's political purposes. What's left today are the best medieval walls in Britain, surrounding a humble town, crowned by the bleak and barren hulk of a castle that was awe-some in its day (and still is). Conwy's charming High Street leads down to a fishy harbor that permitted Edward to restock his castle safely. Because the highway was tunneled under the town, a stroll-

ing ambience has returned to Conwy. Just beyond the castle, the mighty Telford Suspension Bridge was built in 1826 to better connect (and control) the route to Ireland. In that day, Dublin was the number-two city in all of Britain. These two major landmarks—the castle and 19th-century bridge—are both symbols of English imperialism.

Orientation to Conwy

(area code: 01492)

Conwy is an enjoyably small community of 4,000 people. The walled old town center is compact and manageable. Lancaster Square marks the center, where you'll find the bus "station" (a blue-and-white shelter), the unstaffed train station (the little white hut at the end of a sunken parking lot), and the start of the main drag, High Street—and my self-guided walk.

Tourist Information

The TI shares a building with the castle's ticket office and gift shop (daily April–Oct 9:00–17:00, Nov–March 9:30–16:00, tel. 01492/592-248, www.visitconwy.org.uk). Because Conwy's train and bus stations are unstaffed, ask at the TI about train or bus schedules for your departure. Don't confuse the TI with the tacky "Conwy Visitors Centre," a big gift shop near the station with a goofy little £1 video show.

Arrival in Conwy

Whether taking the bus or train, you need to tell the driver or conductor you want to stop at Conwy. Milk-run trains stop here only upon request; major trains don't stop here at all (instead, you'll get off at Llandudno Junction—see below). Consider getting train times and connections for your onward journey at a bigger station before you come here. In Conwy, train schedules are posted above the platforms. For train info in town, ask at the TI, call toll tel. 0871-200-2233, or see www.traveline-cymru.info.

For more frequent trains, use **Llandudno Junction,** visible a mile away beyond the bridges and a safer bet for more regular trains (catch the bus, take a £5 taxi, or walk a mile). Make sure to ask for trains that stop at Llandudno Junction, and not Llandudno proper, which is a seaside resort farther from Conwy.

Helpful Hints

Farmers' Market: It's held on the harborfront Wednesday mornings.

Medieval Festivals: The town is eager to emphasize its medieval history, with several events and festivals annually—ask at the TI or at your B&B to see what's going on during your visit.

Internet Access: Get online at the **library** at the bottom of High Street (free, Mon and Thu–Fri 10:00–17:30, Tue 10:00–19:00, Sat 10:00–13:00, closed Wed and Sun, tel. 01492/596-242). **Coffi Conway** has free Wi-Fi for paying customers (daily 10:00–17:00, 2 High Street, tel. 01492/596-436).

Car Rental: A dozen car-rental agencies in the city of Llandudno (a mile north of Llandudno Junction) offer cars for about £40 per day and can generally deliver to you in Conwy; the Conwy TI has a list. The closest is **Avis**, a 10-minute walk from Conwy (Conwy Road, Llandudno Junction, toll tel. 0844-544-6075).

Shoreline Walk: From the harborfront, there's a peaceful half-mile shoreline stroll along a promenade (from the Smallest House in Great Britain, walk through the wall gate and keep going).

Harbor Cruise: The **Queen Victoria tour boat** departs from the Conwy harborfront for a lazy, 30-minute cruise nearly hourly (£5, pay on boat, March–late Oct daily 11:00–17:00 depending on tides, closed off-season, mobile 07917-343-059).

Self-Guided Walk

Welcome to Conwy

This brief orientation walk introduces you to the essential Conwy in about an hour. As the town walls are open late, you can do this walk at any time—evening is a fine time.

• *Start at the top of High Street on the main square.*

❶ **Lancaster Square:** The square's centerpiece is a **column** honoring the town's founder, the Welsh prince Llywelyn the Great. Looking downhill, past the blue-and-white bus stop, find the cute pointed archway built into the medieval wall so the train could get through. Looking uphill, you can see Bangor Gate, built by the British engineer Thomas Telford in 1826 to accommodate traffic from his suspension bridge.

• *Walk uphill past Alfredo Restaurant to the end of the lane.*

❷ **Slate Memorials:** This wall of memorials recalls the 1937 coronation of King George VI (his wife, the Queen Consort Elizabeth, was the late "Queen Mum"). Notice the Welsh-language lesson here, given to the town by a citizen who never learned to read and wanted to inspire others to avoid his fate. It lists, in Welsh, the counties (shires, or *sir*), months (a few vaguely recognizable), days, numbers, and alphabet with its different letters. Much has changed since this memorial was posted. Today more people are speaking Welsh, and all children are taught Welsh in school until they are 12.

• *Turn left and walk uphill all the way to the wall, where steps lead to the town's tallest turret. Climb to the very top.*

❸ **Tallest Tower and Walls:** You're standing atop the most complete set of medieval town walls in Britain. In 1283, workers started to build them in conjunction with the castle. Four years later, they sent a message to London declaring, "Castle habitable, town defensible." Edward then sent in English settlers. Enjoy the view from the top. From here, guards could spot ships approaching by sea.

• *Walk two turrets downhill (toward the water) along the ramparts.*

The turrets were positioned about every 50 yards. They were connected by ramparts, and each one had a drawbridge that could be raised to bottle up any breach. Passing the second turret, you'll notice its wall is cracked. When they tunneled underneath this turret for the train, the construction accidentally undermined the foundation. Undermining was a common technique in medieval warfare. You can see its effectiveness here. (Unlike the town walls, Conwy Castle is built upon solid rock, so it can't be undermined.)

• *At the first opportunity (just after walking above Bangor Gate), take the steps back down to street level. Then leave the old town by passing through Bangor Gate, heading downhill, and crossing the street for the best wide view of the walls.*

❹ **The Walls (from Outside):** You are walking down Town Ditch Road, named for the dry moat that was the first line of defense from the highest tower down to the riverbank. As was the case with most walled towns, there was a clear swath of "dead ground" outside the walls, so no one could sneak up. Once England centralized and consolidated its rule, all the walls and castles in Britain were pretty useless. Most fell into disrepair—ravaged by time and by scavengers who used them as quarries. During the Napoleonic Wars, English aristocrats were unable to make their "Grand Tour" of the Continent, so they explored the far reaches of their own land. That's when ruined castles such as this were "discovered" and finally appreciated.

• *Stroll downhill to the bottom of Town Ditch Road. At the elderly-crossing sign (which can be considered a reminder to stand up straight), re-enter the old town, crossing through a hole cut in the wall by a modern mayor who wanted better access from his land, and walk down Berry Street. Originally called "Burial Street," it was a big ditch for mass burials during a 17th-century plague. After one block, turn right, climbing up Chapel Street to an austere stone structure.*

NORTH WALES

Conwy Self-Guided Walk

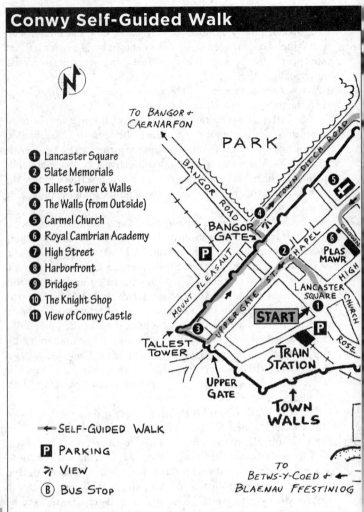

1. Lancaster Square
2. Slate Memorials
3. Tallest Tower & Walls
4. The Walls (from Outside)
5. Carmel Church
6. Royal Cambrian Academy
7. High Street
8. Harborfront
9. Bridges
10. The Knight Shop
11. View of Conwy Castle

TO BANGOR & CAERNARFON

PARK

BANGOR ROAD

TOWN DITCH ROAD

BANGOR GATE

MOUNT PLEASANT

UPPER GATE ST.

CHAPEL ST.

CROWN

PLAS MAWR

HIGH CHURCH

ROSE

LANCASTER SQUARE

START

TRAIN STATION

TALLEST TOWER

UPPER GATE

TOWN WALLS

TO BETWS-Y-COED & BLAENAU FFESTINIOG

← SELF-GUIDED WALK

P PARKING

⚲ VIEW

B BUS STOP

NORTH WALES

5 Carmel Church: This Presbyterian church is a fine example of stark "statement architecture"—stern, no frills, and typical of churches built in the early 20th century.

There are many different religious denominations in Welsh towns. (The Welsh often admit they can be contentious. They say, "Get two Welshmen together, and you'll have an argument. Get three together, and you'll have a fight.") In the 18th and 19th centuries, Welsh Christians who didn't want to worship in the official, English-style Anglican Church joined "nonconformist" congregations, such as Methodists, Congregationalists, Quakers,

or Presbyterians. You could say "nonconformist" is to "Anglican" as "Protestant" is to "Catholic." In Wales, the Anglican Church for many years was called "The Church of England"—which was not very attractive to Welsh nationalists. It's now called "The Church in Wales."

Religion can tell you a lot about politics in Wales. There are Welsh who think some of their countrymen kiss up to English rule by worshipping as Anglicans. And many are fond of saying, "The Anglican Church is the Conservative Party at prayer, and the nonconformist churches are the Labour Party at prayer."

• *Just beyond the church (on the left, at Seaview Terrace), in a modern building, is...*

❻ The Royal Cambrian Academy: This art academy, showing off two floors of contemporary Welsh painting, gives a fine glimpse into the region and its people through art (free, most paintings are for sale, Tue–Sat 11:00–17:00, Sun 13:00–16:30, closed Mon, on Crown Lane just above Plas Mawr, tel. 01492/593-413).

• *Continue on Crown Lane downhill past **Plas Mawr**. The first Welsh house built within the town walls, it dates from the time of Henry VIII (well worth touring, and described later, under "Sights in Conwy"). Turn left onto...*

❼ High Street: Wander downhill, enjoying this slice-of-Welsh-life scene—tearooms, bakery, butcher, newsstand, and old-timers. Across from the Castle Hotel is an old movie theater that is now the **Bingo Palace** (see "Nightlife in Conwy," later). All the colorful flags you see have no meaning—merchants are flying them simply to pump up the town's medieval feel. **Aberconwy House** marks the bottom of High Street. One of the oldest houses in

town, it's a museum (not worth touring). Conwy was once a garrison town filled with half-timbered buildings just like this one. At end of High Street, 20 yards to the right at 4 Castle Street, is the **Penny Farthing Sweet Shop**—filled with old-fashioned sweets.

• *Follow High Street through the gate and to the harbor.*

❽ Harborfront: The Harbor Gate, one of three original gates in the town walls, leads to the waterfront. The harbor dates from the 13th century, when it served Edward's castle and town. (The harborfront street is still called "King's Quay.") Conwy was once a busy slate port. Slate, barged downstream to here, was loaded onto big three-mast ships and transported to the Continent. Back when much of Europe was roofed with Welsh slate, Conwy was a boomtown. All the mud is new—the modern bridge caused this part of the river to silt up.

European Union money helped pay for the recently built promenade here, but EU regulations have helped mess up Conwy's economy too. New hygiene laws require that fish must be transported in refrigerated vehicles. They couldn't fit refrigerator trucks through the gate, so fishermen left Conwy's harbor and set up shop a few miles away.

Conwy's harbor is now a laid-back area that locals treat like a town square. On summer evenings, the action is on the quay. The scene is mellow, multi-generational, and perfectly Welsh. It's a small town, and everyone is here enjoying the local cuisine—"chips," ice cream, and beer—and savoring that great British pastime: torturing little crabs. (If you want to do more than photograph the action, the nearby lifeboat house sells gear. Mooch some bacon from others for bait, and join in. It's catch and release.)

The Liverpool Arms pub was built by a captain who ran a ferry service to Liverpool in the 19th century. Today it remains a salty and characteristic hangout—the only thriving pub in town. In 1900, Conwy had about 40 pubs. Back when this harbor was busy with quarrymen shipping their slate, mussel men carting their catch, and small farmers with their goods, Conwy's pubs were all thriving. Today, times are tough on the pubs, and this one depends on tourism.

• *Facing the harbor in front of The Liverpool Arms, turn left and walk along the promenade.*

It's easy to miss the **Smallest House in Great Britain.** It's red, 72 inches wide, 122 inches high, and worth £1 to pop in and listen to the short audioguide tour. No WC—but it did have a bedpan (April–Oct roughly Mon–Sat 10:00–17:30, Sun 11:00–16:30, closed Nov–March, tel. 01492/593-484).

• *Turn around and walk along the promenade toward the bridges and castle. On your right, you'll find a processing plant.*

Mussels, historically a big "crop" for Conwy, are processed "in the months with an 'R'" by the **Mussels Museum.** In the other months, it's open to visitors (free, Easter–Aug daily 10:30–16:30, tel. 01492/592-689). Also, check out the striking **sculpture** on the quay—a giant clump of mussels carved from dark-gray limestone. The benches are great for a picnic (two recommended fish-and-chips shops are back through the gate) or a visit with the noisy gulls.

The nearby **lifeboat house** welcomes visitors. Each coastal town has a house like this one, outfitted with a rescue boat suited to the area—in the shallow waters around Conwy, inflatable boats work best. You'll see *Lifeboats* stickers around town, marking homes of people who donate to the valuable cause of the Royal National Lifeboat Institution (RNLI)—Britain's all-volunteer and totally donation-funded answer to the Coast Guard.

• *Walk past the shrimp pots, up the stairs past EU signs and a giant red-and-white buoy, to the big street for a view of the castle and bridges. You can cross the road for a closer look at the...*

❾ **Bridges:** Three bridges cross the river, side by side. Behind the modern 1958 highway bridge is the historic 1826 Telford

Conwy

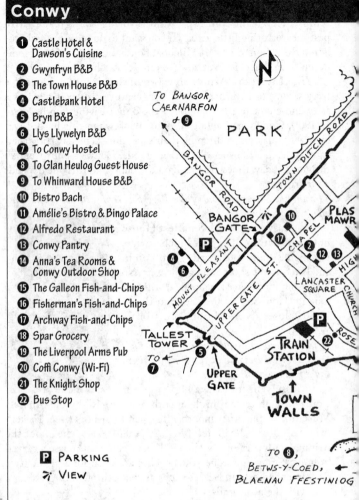

1. Castle Hotel & Dawson's Cuisine
2. Gwynfryn B&B
3. The Town House B&B
4. Castlebank Hotel
5. Bryn B&B
6. Llys Llywelyn B&B
7. To Conwy Hostel
8. To Glan Heulog Guest House
9. To Whinward House B&B
10. Bistro Bach
11. Amélie's Bistro & Bingo Palace
12. Alfredo Restaurant
13. Conwy Pantry
14. Anna's Tea Rooms & Conwy Outdoor Shop
15. The Galleon Fish-and-Chips
16. Fisherman's Fish-and-Chips
17. Archway Fish-and-Chips
18. Spar Grocery
19. The Liverpool Arms Pub
20. Coffi Conwy (Wi-Fi)
21. The Knight Shop
22. Bus Stop

P PARKING
⌐ VIEW

Suspension Bridge. This was an engineering marvel in its day, part of a big infrastructure project to connect Dublin with the rest of the realm. Just beyond that is Robert Stephenson's tube bridge for the train line (built in 1848). These days, 90 percent of traffic passes Conwy underground, unseen and unheard, in a modern tunnel.

• *On the town side of the big road, follow the sidewalk away from the water, under the ivy and an arch, to a tiny park around a well. Facing that square is...*

10 The Knight Shop: If you're in the market for a battleaxe or perhaps some chainmail, pop into The Knight Shop. Even if you're

not, it's a fun place to browse. The owner, Toby, is evangelical about mead, an ancient drink made from honey. (Most travelers just get the cheap stuff at tourist shops.) He offers free tastes so you can appreciate quality mead (Castle Square, tel. 01492/596-142).

• *Now, with a belly full of mead, set your bleary eyes on the...*

❶ **View of Conwy Castle:** Imagine this when newly built. Its eight mighty drum towers were brightly whitewashed, a power statement from the English king to the Welsh—who had no cities and little more than bows and arrows to fight with. The castle is built upon solid rock—making it impossible for invaders to tunnel

King Edward's Castles

In the 13th century, the Welsh, unified by two great princes named Llywelyn, created a united and independent Wales. The English king Edward I fought hard to end this Welsh sovereignty. In 1282, Llywelyn the Last was killed (and went to "where everyone speaks Welsh"). King Edward spent the next 20 years building or rebuilding 17 great castles to consolidate his English foothold in troublesome North Wales. The greatest of these  (such as Conwy Castle) were masterpieces of medieval engineering, with round towers (tough to undermine by tunneling), castle-within-a-castle defenses (giving defenders a place to retreat and wreak havoc on the advancing enemy...or just wait for reinforcements), and sea access (safe to restock from England).

These castles were English islands in the middle of angry Wales. Most were built with a fortified grid-plan town attached, and were filled with English settlers. (With this blatant abuse of Wales, you have to wonder, where was Greenpeace 700 years ago?) Edward I was arguably England's best monarch. By establishing and consolidating his realm (adding Wales to England), he made his kingdom big enough to compete with the other rising European powers.

Castle-lovers will want to tour each of Edward's five great-

underneath. The English paid dearly for its construction through heavy taxes. And today, with the Welsh flag proudly flying from its top, the English pay again just to visit. Notice the remains of the castle entry, which was within the town walls. There was once a steep set of stairs (designed so no horse could approach) up to the drawbridge. The castle (with its helpful guides) is by far the town's top sight (described next).

Sights in Conwy

▲▲Conwy Castle—Dramatically situated on a rock overlooking the sea with eight linebacker towers, this castle has an interesting story to tell. Finished in just four years, it had a water gate that allowed safe entry for English boats in a land of hostile Welsh subjects (£4.70, or £7 combo-ticket with Plas Mawr; March–Oct daily 9:30–17:00, July–Aug until 18:00; Nov–Feb Mon–Sat 10:00–16:00, Sun 11:00–16:00; last entry 30 minutes before closing, tel. 01492/592-358, www.cadw.wales.gov.uk). Guides wait inside to est castles (see map on page 539). With a car and two days, this makes one of Europe's best castle tours. I'd rate them in this order:

Conwy is attached to the cutest medieval town, and has the best public transport.

Caernarfon is the most entertaining and best presented (see page 562).

Harlech is the most dramatically situated, on a hilltop (£3.60, tel. 01766/780-552, TI open March–Oct, www.harlech.com).

Beaumaris, surrounded by a swan-filled moat, is the last, largest, and most romantic (see page 561).

Criccieth (KRICK-ith), built in 1230 by Llewelyn and later renovated by Edward, is also dramatic and remote (£3, tel. 01766/522-227).

All the above castles have the same opening hours: March–Oct daily 9:30–17:00, July-Aug until 18:00; Nov–Feb Mon–Sat 10:00–16:00, Sun 11:00–16:00; last entry 30 minutes before closing (with one exception: Criccieth is closed Mon–Thu in winter).

CADW, the Welsh version of the National Trust, sells a three-day Explorer Pass that covers many sights in Wales. If you're planning to visit at least three of the above castles, the pass will probably save you money (three-day pass: £11.50 for 1 person, £18.50 for 2 people, £26.50 for a family; seven-day pass for about £6 more per person; available at castle ticket desks). For photos and more information on the castles, as well as information on Welsh historic monuments in general, check www.cadw.wales.gov.uk.

take you on a one-hour, £1.50 tour. They bring the castle to life, putting the beams back in place, filling the fine arched windows, and stoking the big fireplaces. Tours usually depart about once per hour (no set schedule). If the guide booth is empty, look for the group and join it, or check the clock to see when the next tour departs.

▲**City Walls**—Most of the walls, with 22 towers and castle and harbor views, can be walked for free. Start at Upper Gate (the highest point) or Berry Street (the lowest), or do the small section at the castle entrance. (My favorite stretch is described on my "Self-Guided Walk," earlier.) In the evening, most of the walkways stay open.

▲**Plas Mawr**—A rare house from 1580, this was built during the reign of Elizabeth I. It was the first Welsh home to be built within

Conwy's walls. (The Tudor family had Welsh roots—and therefore relations between Wales and England warmed.) Billed as "the oldest house in Wales," Plas Mawr offers a delightful look at 16th-century domestic life, but you must be patient enough to spend an hour following the included audioguide. Historically accurate household items bring the rooms to life, as does the refreshing lack of velvet ropes—you're free to wander as you imagine life in this house. Docents, who are posted in some rooms, are happy to answer your questions.

Visitors stepping into the house in the 16th century were wowed by the heraldry over the fireplace. This symbol, now repainted in its original bright colors, proclaimed the family's rich lineage and princely stock. The kitchen came with all the circa-1600 conveniences: hay on the floor to add a little warmth and soak up spills; a hanging bread cage to keep food away from wandering critters; and a good supply of fresh meat in the pantry (take a whiff). Upstairs, the lady of the house's bedroom doubled as a sitting room—with a finely carved four-poster bed and a foot warmer by the chair. At night the bedroom's curtains were drawn to keep in warmth. In the great chamber next door, hearty evening feasting was followed by boisterous gaming, dancing, and music. And fixed above all of this extravagant entertainment was...more heraldry, pronouncing those important—if unproven—family connections and leaving a powerful impact on impressed guests. On the same floor is a well-done exhibit on health and hygiene in medieval Britain—you'll be grateful that you were born a few centuries later.

Cost and Hours: £5.10, or £7 combo-ticket with Conwy Castle, April–Sept Tue–Sun 9:30–17:00, closed Mon and Oct–March, tel. 01492/580-167, www.cadw.wales.gov.uk.

St. Mary's Parish Church—Sitting lonely in the town center, Conwy's church was the centerpiece of a Cistercian abbey that stood here a century before the town or castle. The Cistercians were French monks who built their abbeys in lonely places, "far from the haunts of man." Popular here because they were French and *not* English, the Cistercians taught locals farming and mussel-gathering techniques. Edward moved the monks 12 miles upstream but kept the church for his town. Notice the tombstone of a survivor of the 1805 Battle of Trafalgar who died in 1860 (two feet left of the north transept). On the other side of the church, a tomb containing seven brothers and sisters is marked "We Are Seven." It inspired William Wordsworth to write his poem of the same name. The slate tombstones look new even though many are hundreds of years old; slate weathers better than marble (cemetery always open, church may be staffed June–Aug Mon–Fri 10:00–12:00 & 14:00–16:00, tel. 01492/593-402).

NORTH WALES

Near Conwy

Llandudno—This genteel Victorian beach resort, a few miles away, is bigger and better known than Conwy. It was built after the advent of railroads, which made the Welsh seacoast easily accessible to the English industrial heartland. In the 1800s, the notion that bathing in seawater was good for your health was trendy, and the bracing sea air was just what the doctor ordered. These days, Llandudno remains popular with the English, but you won't see many other foreigners strolling its long pier and line of old-time hotels.

Hill Climb—For lovely views across the bay to Llandudno, take a pleasant walk (40 minutes one-way) along the footpath up Conwy Mount (follow Sychnant Pass Road past the Bryn B&B, look for fields on the right and a sign with a stick figure of a walker).

Nightlife in Conwy

No one goes to Conwy for wild nightlife. Nearby **Llandudno** has the fun you'd expect at a Coney-Island-type beach resort (see above). But there are some typically Welsh diversions here.

Music—The **Conwy Folk Music Club** plays at a Conwy pub Mondays at 20:00 (ask any local for this year's location). The **men's choir** puts on a casual practice/concert for visitors in nearby Llandudno (£5, May–Oct, Tue and Thu, 20:00, St. John's Church, between the two Marks & Spencer stores on Mostyn Street, toll tel. 0870-516-8767, www.malevoicechoir.net).

Bingo—Conwy's former cinema is now the **Bingo Palace,** where nearly every evening people who are very serious about their bingo gather. Visitors simply fill out a free membership card and buy in. Don't show up after 19:15, because you can't start late. As the woman announcer calls numbers with her mesmerizing tune ("eight and seven...eighty-seven; all the twos...twenty-two; only five...number five"), intense, dressed-up old ladies play blot-the-numbers. The tension breaks each time someone calls "Line!" (the British version of yelling "Bingo!"). It's keyed in with a national game, so you can really win big here. Note: As posted, "If you bring your own teabag, you'll still have to pay 40p" (£7–14 to play depending on the evening, Thu–Tue 18:00–22:00, closed Wed, across from Castle Hotel on High Street, tel. 01492/592-376).

Sleeping in Conwy

(area code: 01492)

Conwy's hotels are overpriced, but its B&Bs include some good-value gems. Nearly all have free parking (ask when booking), and most are happy to accommodate dietary needs in their breakfast

NORTH WALES

Sleep Code

(£1 = about $1.60, country code: 44)

S = Single, **D** = Double/Twin, **T** = Triple, **Q** = Quad, **b** = bathroom, **s** = shower only. You can assume credit cards are accepted and breakfast is included unless otherwise noted. Few of my accommodations in North Wales have elevators.

To help you sort easily through these listings, I've divided the rooms into three categories based on the price for a standard double room with bath:

$$$ Higher Priced—Most rooms £75 or more.
 $$ Moderately Priced—Most rooms between £45-75.
  $ Lower Priced—Most rooms £45 or less.

Prices can change without notice; verify the hotel's current rates online or by email. For other updates, see www.ricksteves.com/update.

offers (the local butcher, who supplies many of these B&Bs, even makes gluten-free sausages). There's no launderette in town.

Inside Conwy's Walled Old Town

$$$ Castle Hotel, along the main drag, rents 28 elegant rooms where Old World antique furnishings mingle with modern amenities. Peter and Bobbi Lavin, who co-own the hotel with chef Graham Tinsley, are eager to make your stay comfortable (Sb-£70–90, Db-£115–150, rates vary with season and room size, 10 percent discount if you show this book at check-in, free Wi-Fi, High Street, tel. 01492/582-800, fax 01492/582-300, www.castle wales.co.uk, mail@castlewales.co.uk). The hotel has a recommended restaurant and a bar.

$$ Gwynfryn B&B rents five bright, airy rooms, each with eclectic decor, a DVD player, and access to a DVD library. The location is dead-center in Conwy. It has a plush lounge, and out back there's a tiny patio for pleasant breakfasts in good weather (D-£60–65, Db-£65–80, price depends on season and room size, £5 extra for 1-night stays, no children under 12, free Internet access and Wi-Fi, fridge, 4 York Place, on the lane off Lancaster Square, tel. & fax 01492/576-733, www.gwynfrynbandb.co.uk, info @gwynfrynbandb.co.uk, energetic Monica and Colin).

$$ The Town House B&B is a colorful place renting five tidy, bright, updated rooms near the train and bus station at the top of the town (S-£45, D-£65, Db-£70, Tb-£100, discount with this book for 2 or more nights, cash only, no children under 12, free Wi-Fi, DVD library, 18 Rosehill Street, tel. 01492/596-454,

mobile 07974-650-609, www.thetownhousebb.co.uk, thetown
housebb@aol.com, friendly Alan and Elaine Naughton and shy
sheepdog Glenn).

Just Outside the Wall

The first three options are a two-minute walk from Conwy's old
town wall; the hostel is about 10 minutes beyond.

$$$ Castlebank Hotel is a small hotel with nine spacious
rooms, a small bar, and an inviting lounge with a wood-burning
fireplace that makes the Welsh winter cozy. Owners Jo and
Henrique have done a heroic job of rehabilitating a formerly
dumpy hotel into a dolled-up and comfortable home away from
home (S-£40, Sb-£55–80, Db-£80–85, depends on season, 10 per-
cent discount with this book for 2 or more nights—except on Bank
Holiday weekends, family rooms, free Internet access and Wi-Fi,
DVD library, easy parking, just outside town wall at Mount Plea-
sant, tel. 01492/593-888, www.castlebankhotel.co.uk, bookings
@castlebankhotel.co.uk).

$$ Bryn B&B offers four large, clutter-free rooms with castle
or mountain views in a big 19th-century house with the city wall
literally in the backyard. Owner Alison Archard runs the place
with style and energy, providing all the thoughtful touches—a
library of regional guides and maps; a glorious garden; fresh,
organic food for breakfast; and a very warm welcome (Sb-£50,
Db-£70, Tb-£90, £5 extra for 1-night stays, ground-floor room
available, free Wi-Fi, parking, on the right just outside upper gate
of wall on Sychnant Pass Road, tel. 01492/592-449, www.bryn
.org.uk, stay@bryn.org.uk).

$$ Llys Llywelyn B&B has five basic budget rooms. The
great prices—along with the humor and pleasant nature of Alan
Hughes, who's in his 70s and still a top-notch ski instructor—
make this a fine value (Sb-£35, top-floor D-£40, Db-£50, 10
percent discount with this book, cold breakfast included, cooked
breakfast for £2–5 extra, free Wi-Fi, cash only, easy parking,
Mount Pleasant, tel. 01492/593-257, no email but very easy phone
reservations).

$ Conwy Hostel, welcoming travelers of any age, has super
views from all 24 of its rooms (including eight twin-bed doubles),
and a spacious garden. Dorm rooms are equipped with either two
or four bunk beds and a full bathroom. The airy dining hall and
glorious rooftop deck make you feel like you're in the majestic
midst of Wales (beds in 4-bed rooms-£15–22 per person, Db-£40–
50, depends on season and age—under 18 is cheaper, non-members
pay £3 more, breakfast-£5, laundry, lockers, lunches and din-
ners, bar, elevator, parking, no lock-out times but office closed
10:00–14:00, Sychnant Pass Road, in Larkhill, tel. 01492/593-571,

fax 01492/593-580, www.yha.org.uk, conwy@yha.org.uk). It's a 10-minute uphill walk from the upper gate of Conwy's wall.

Beyond the Old Town

$$ Glan Heulog Guest House offers seven fresh, bright rooms, an inviting lounge, and a pleasant, enclosed sun porch. Practice speaking Welsh with your host, Stanley (Sb-£35–40, Db-£56–64, Tb-£75–80, family deals, price depends on room size, ask about healthy breakfast option, free Internet access and Wi-Fi, will pick up from train station, a 10-minute walk from town on Llanrwst Road on the way to Betws-y-Coed, tel. 01492/593-845, www .snowdoniabandb.co.uk, info@snowdoniabandb.co.uk, Stan and Viv Watson-Jones).

$$ Whinward House, a half-mile west of Conwy's town walls, works well for drivers. Because their three rooms lack any B&B formality—and because Chris and Janis quickly make you feel at home—staying here feels like sleeping in the spare room of old friends. Guests are encouraged to relax in the sunlit living room and the large garden. Hiking trails, two pubs, a marina, and a golf course are all within a short walk (Db-£70, free Internet access and Wi-Fi, laundry service available, Whinacres, tel. 01492/573-275, www.whinwardhouse.co.uk, whinwardhouse@aol .com). From the north gate in Conwy's town wall, head straight out along Bangor Road; after a minute's drive, turn right just before an overhead railroad bridge. Turn immediately right again onto Whinacres. Chris and Janis are happy to pick you up at the train station.

Eating in Conwy

All of these places are inside Conwy's walled old town. For dinner, consider strolling down High Street, comparing the cute teahouses and workaday eateries. Most pubs serve food, but none in town is currently worth recommending.

Bistro Bach, tucked away on Chapel Street, serves freshly prepared modern and traditional Welsh cuisine in a cozy wood-floor-and-candlelight setting. The menu (with tasty daily specials) is inventive, and the food is just possibly the best in town. Each meal starts with an amuse-bouche and finishes with a little Welsh cake and a shot of honey mead (£13–18 meals, Tue–Sat 18:30–21:00, closed Sun–Mon, reservations smart, tel. 01492/596-326).

Dawson's Cuisine, in the recommended Castle Hotel, serves up dishes from award-winning chef Graham Tinsley. It's a hit with locals and worth the splurge (£10–15 entrées, food served daily 12:00–21:30, reservations smart—especially weekends, High Street, tel. 01492/582-800). The hotel bar has the same menu with cozier and less formal ambience.

Amélie's, named for the French film, is a bistro with tasty modern dishes in a relaxed loft overlooking High Street (£4–8 lunches, £11–16 dinners; lunch Tue–Sat 11:00–14:15, closed Sun–Mon; dinner Thu–Sat 18:00–21:15, closed Sun–Wed; 10 High Street, tel. 01492/583-142).

Alfredo Restaurant, a thriving and family-friendly place right on Lancaster Square, serves good, reasonably priced Italian food (£7–9 pizzas, £8–10 pastas, £12–18 entrées, nightly from 18:00, last orders at 22:00, reservations recommended on weekends, York Place, tel. 01492/592-381, Christine).

Conwy Pantry dishes up cheap, hearty daily specials, salads, and homemade sweets in a cheery setting (£5–6 lunches, daily 9:00–17:00, until 16:30 in winter, 26 High Street, tel. 01492/596-445).

Anna's Tea Rooms, a frilly, doily, very feminine-feeling eatery located upstairs in the masculine-feeling Conwy Outdoor Shop, is popular with locals (£3–7 entrées and teas, daily 10:00–17:00, 9 Castle Street, tel. 01492/580-908).

Fish-and-Chips: At the bottom of High Street, on the intersecting Castle Street, are two chippies—**The Galleon** (daily, generally 11:30–15:00, mid-July–mid-Sept until 19:00, tel. 01492/593-391) and **Fisherman's** (daily generally 11:30–18:30, until 21:00 July–Aug, tel. 01492/593-792). **Archway Fish & Chips,** at the top of town just inside Bangor Gate, is open later (daily, restaurant until 18:30, take-out until 22:15, 12 Bangor Road, tel. 01492/592-458). Consider taking your fish-and-chips down to the harbor and sharing it with the noisy seagulls.

Picnic Fixings: The **Spar** grocery is conveniently located and well-stocked (daily 7:00–22:00, middle of High Street). Several other shops on High Street—including the bakery and the butcher nearby—sell meat pies and other microwaveables that can quickly flesh out a sparse picnic.

Conwy Connections

If you want to leave Conwy by train, be sure the schedule indicates the train can stop there, and then wave as it approaches; for more frequent trains, go to Llandudno Junction (see "Arrival in Conwy," earlier). For train info, call toll tel. 0871-200-2233, or see www.traveline-cymru.info. If hopping around by bus, simply buy the £5 Red Rover Ticket from the driver, and you're covered for the entire day on all Arriva buses. Remember, all of these connections are less frequent on Sundays.

From Conwy by Bus to: Llandudno Junction (4/hour, 5–20 minutes), **Caernarfon** (1–2/hour direct, more with change in

Bangor, 1.25 hours), **Betws-y-Coed** (at least hourly, 45 minutes), **Blaenau Ffestiniog** (hourly Mon–Sat, 4/day on Sun, 1.25 hours, transfer in Llandudno Junction to bus #X1, also stops in Betws-y-Coed; train is better—see below), **Beddgelert** (9/day Mon–Sat, 5/day on Sun, 1.75 hours total, transfer in Caernarfon), **Llangollen** (2/day, 2 hours, transfer in Llanrwst).

From Conwy by Train to: Llandudno Junction (nearly hourly, 3 minutes), **Chester** (nearly hourly, 50 minutes), **Holyhead** (nearly hourly, 1 hour), **London's Euston Station** (nearly hourly, 3.25 hours, transfer in Chester or Crewe).

From Llandudno Junction by Train to the Conwy Valley: Take the train to Llandudno Junction, where you'll board the scenic little Conwy Valley line, which runs up the pretty Conwy River Valley to **Betws-y-Coed** and **Blaenau Ffestiniog** (5/day Mon–Sat, 3/day on Sun, none on Sun in winter, 45 minutes to Betws-y-Coed, 1.25 hours to Blaenau Ffestiniog, www.conwyvalleyrailway .co.uk). If your train from Conwy to Llandudno Junction is late and you miss the Conwy Valley connection, tell a station employee at Llandudno Junction, who can arrange a taxi for you. Your taxi is free, as long as the missed connection is the Conwy train's fault *and* the next train doesn't leave for more than an hour (common on the infrequent Conwy Valley line).

From Llandudno Junction by Train to: Chester (2–3/hour, 1 hour), **Birmingham** (1–2/hour, 2.5–3 hours, 1–3 transfers), **London's Euston Station** (nearly hourly, 3–3.25 hours, some direct or change in Chester).

Between Conwy and Snowdonia

These two attractions are south of Conwy, on the route to Betws-y-Coed and Snowdonia National Park. Note that Bodnant Garden is on the east side of the Conwy River, on A470, and Trefriw is on the west side, along B5106. To see them both, you'll cross the river at Tal-y-Cafn.

▲Bodnant Garden

This sumptuous 80-acre display of floral color six miles south of Conwy is one of Britain's best gardens. Originally the private garden of the stately Bodnant Hall, this lush landscape was donated by the Bodnant family (who still live in the house) to the National Trust in 1949. The map you receive upon entering suggests a handy walking route. The highlight for

many is the famous "Laburnum Arch"—a 180-foot-long canopy made of bright-yellow laburnum, hanging like stalactites over the heads of garden-lovers who stroll beneath it (just inside the entry, blooms late May through early June). The garden is also famous for its magnolias, rhododendrons, camellias, and roses—and for the way that the buildings of the estate complement the carefully planned landscaping. The wild English-style plots seem to spar playfully with the more formal, Italian-style gardens. Consider your visit an extravagantly beautiful nature hike, and walk all the way to the old mill and waterfall.

Cost and Hours: £7.20, mid-Feb–mid-Nov daily 10:00–17:00, closed off-season, last entry 30 minutes before closing, café, WCs in parking lot and inside garden, best in spring, phone message tells what's blooming, tel. 01492/650-460, www.bodnant-garden.co.uk.

Getting There: To reach it by public transportation from Conwy, first head to Llandudno Junction and catch bus #25 (hourly Mon–Sat, 3/day on Sun) toward Eglwysbach, which will take you right to the garden in about 20 minutes.

Trefriw Woolen Mills

The mill in Trefriw (TREV-roo), five miles north of Betws-y-Coed, lets you peek into a working woolen mill. It's surprisingly interesting and rated ▲ if the machines are running (weekdays Easter–Oct). Various parts of the mill show off different processes and have different hours—but everything's free (tel. 01492/640-462, www.t-w-m.co.uk).

This mill buys wool from local farmers, and turns it into scarves, sweaters, bedspreads, caps, and more. You can peruse the finished products in the **shop** (daily June–Sept 9:30–17:30, Oct–May 10:00–17:00). The whole complex creates its own hydroelectric power; the **"turbine house"** in the cellar lets you take a peek at the enormous, fiercely spinning turbines, dating from the 1930s and 1940s, powered by streams that flow down the hillside above the mill. The **weaving looms,** with bobbin-loaded shuttles flying to and fro, allow you to watch a bedspread being created before your eyes (Mon–Fri). But the highlight is the **"working museum,"** which follows the 11 stages of wool transformation: blending, carding, spinning, doubling, hanking, spanking, warping, weaving, and so on. Follow a matted glob of fleece on its journey to becoming a fashionable cap or scarf. It's impressive that this Rube Goldberg–type process could have been so ingeniously designed and coordinated in an age before computers (mostly the 1950s and 1960s)—each machine seems to "know" how to do its rattling, clattering duty with amazing precision (some but not all machines are likely running at any one time; Easter–Oct Mon–Fri 10:00–13:00 & 14:00–17:00, closed Sat–Sun, closed Nov–Easter because they don't heat it in winter). In the summer, the **hand-spinning house** (next to the WC) has a charming spinster and a petting cupboard filled with all the various kinds of raw wool that can be spun into cloth (June–Sept only, Tue–Thu 10:00–17:00, closed Fri–Mon).

The grade school next door is rambunctious with Welsh-speaking kids—fun to listen to at recess.

The woolen mill at Penmachno (also near Betws-y-Coed) is smaller and much less interesting.

Getting There: Buses #19 and #19A go from Conwy and Llandudno Junction right to Trefriw (2/hour Mon–Sat, hourly on Sun, 30 minutes).

Between Conwy and Caernarfon: Beaumaris

The charming little town of Beaumaris is on the island of Anglesey, about a 40-minute drive from Conwy (and a short detour from the route to Caernarfon). The town itself originated, like other castle towns, as an English "green zone" in the 13th century surrounded by Welsh guerrillas. Today, it feels workaday Welsh, with a fine harborfront, lots of colorful shops and eateries, a fascinating Victorian prison (now a museum), and the remains of an idyllic castle. Around the castle are putt-putt-type amusements for the family and a swan-filled moat. Beaumaris has no tourist information center, but the island has a **TI** at the Holyhead Port Terminal (Mon–Sat 9:30–17:30, Sun 10:00–17:00, tel. 01407/762-622, www.visitanglesey.org).

Getting There: If driving, simply follow signs toward *Holyhead*, and immediately after crossing the big bridge onto the island, take the small coastal A545 highway for 10 minutes into Beaumaris.

Sights in Beaumaris

Beaumaris Gaol

The Beaumaris Gaol (jail), which was opened in 1829 as a result of new laws designed to give prisons more humane treatment, was in use until 1878. Under this "modern" ethic, inmates had their own cells, women prisoners were kept separate and attended by female guards, and prisoners worked to pay for their keep rather than suffer from jailers bilking their families for favors. This new standard of incarceration is the subject of this fascinating museum, where you'll see the prisoners' quarters, work yard, punishment cells, whipping rack, treadmill, and chapel (£3.75, guidebook-£0.60, Easter–Sept Sat–Thu 10:00–17:00, closed Fri, rarely open off-season—call for hours, tel. 01248/810-921).

▲Beaumaris Castle

Beaumaris, begun in 1295, was the last link in King Edward's "Iron Chain" of castles to enclose Gwynedd, the rebellious for-

mer kingdom of North Wales. There were no natural geological constraints here (like those that encumbered the castle designers at Caernarfon and Conwy), so its wall-within-a-wall design is almost perfectly concentric. The result is one of Britain's most beautiful castles. While Beaumaris shows medieval castle engineering at its best—four rings of defense, a moat, and a fortified dock—problems in Scotland changed the king's priorities. Construction stopped in 1330, and the castle was never finished. It looks ruined, but it was never ransacked or destroyed—it's simply unfinished. The site was overgrown until the last century, but today it's like a park; look for information boards explaining the architect's vision (£3.60; March–Oct daily 9:30–17:00, July–Aug until 18:00; Nov–Feb Mon–Sat 10:00–16:00, Sun 11:00–16:00; tel. 01248/810-361, www.cadw.wales.gov.uk).

Menai Suspension Bridge

The island of Anglesey is connected to the mainland by one of the engineering marvels of its day, the Menai Suspension Bridge. Designed by Thomas Telford and finished in 1826, at 580 feet it was the longest bridge of its day. It was built to be 100 feet above sea level at high tide—high enough to let Royal Navy ships sail beneath. With the Act of Union of 1800, London needed to be better connected to Dublin. And, as the economy of the island of Anglesey was mainly cattle farming (cows had to literally swim the Straits of Menai to get to market), there was a local need for this bridge. When it opened, the bridge cut the travel time from London to Holyhead from 36 to 27 hours. While it's next to a modern highway bridge today, the historic bridge still handles traffic.

Caernarfon

The small, lively little town of Caernarfon (kah-NAR-von) is famous for its striking castle—the place where the Prince of Wales is "invested" (given his title). Like Conwy, it has an Edward I garrison town marching out from the castle; it still follows the original, medieval grid plan laid within its well-preserved ramparts.

Caernarfon is mostly a 19th-century town. At that time, the most important thing in town wasn't the castle but the area—now a parking lot—that sprawls below the castle. This was once a booming slate port, shipping tidy bundles of slate from North Wales mining towns to roofs all over Europe.

The statue of local boy David Lloyd George looks over the town square. A member of Parliament from 1890 to 1945, he was the most important politician Wales ever sent to London, and ultimately became Britain's prime minister during the last years of World War I. Young Lloyd George began his career as a noisy nonconformist Liberal advocating Welsh rights. He ended up an eloquent spokesperson for the notion of Great Britain, convincing his slate-mining constituents that only as part of the Union would their industry boom.

Caernarfon bustles with shops, cafés, and people. Market-day activities fill its main square on Saturdays year-round; a smaller, sleepier market yawns on Monday from late May to September. The charming town is worth a wander.

Orientation to Caernarfon

(area code: 01286)

The small, walled old town of Caernarfon spreads out from its waterfront castle, its outer flanks fringed with modern sprawl (pop. 10,000). The main square, called Castle Square ("Y Maes" in Welsh), is fronted by the castle (with the TI across from its entry) and a post office. Public WCs are off the main square, on the road down to the riverfront and parking lot, where you'll find a bike-rental shop.

Tourist Information

The TI, facing the castle entrance, has a wonderful free town map/guide (with a good self-guided town walk) and train and bus

Conwy or Caernarfon?

Trying to decide between these two walled towns and their castles? Here are some comparisons:

The town of Conwy is more quaint, with a higgledy-piggledy medieval vibe and a modern workaday heart and soul—both of which feel diluted in busier, although more Welsh-feeling, Caernarfon. Conwy also has more accommodations and good eateries than Caernarfon. All of this makes it the better home base, which also means its castle is more convenient to see. Conwy's castle is a bit more ruined and less slickly presented than Caernarfon's—with fewer fancy exhibits—but some think that makes it more evocative. While Caernarfon's castle is the most famous in Wales, I find Conwy's castle more exciting.

schedules. They cheerfully dispense tips about all of the North Wales attractions, sell hiking books, and book rooms here and elsewhere for a £2 fee (April–Oct daily 9:30–16:30; Nov–March Mon–Sat 10:00–15:30, closed Sun; tel. 01286/672-232, www .caernarfon.com).

Arrival in Caernarfon

If you arrive by **bus,** walk straight ahead a few steps to Bridge Street, turn left, and walk two short blocks until you hit the main square and the castle. **Drivers** can park in the lot along the riverfront quay below the castle (£4/day July–Sept, cheaper rates rest of year) or follow signs as you enter town to a covered garage. The big lot under the Morrison Supermarket (near Victoria Dock) has free parking.

Helpful Hints

Internet Access: Get wired at the public **library** (£1/30 minutes for terminals, free Wi-Fi; Mon–Tue and Thu–Fri 9:30–19:00, Wed and Sat 9:30–13:00, closed Sun; just around the corner from Bridge Street—between the castle and the recommended Celtic Royal Hotel, tel. 01286/679-463, www.gwynedd.gov .uk/library).

Laundry: Pete's Launderette hides at the end of Skinner Street, a narrow lane branching off the main square (same-day full-service-£7/load, Mon–Thu 9:00–18:00, Fri–Sat 9:00–17:30, Sun 11:00–16:00, tel. 01286/678-395; Pete, Monica).

Bike Rental: Beics Menai Cycles rents good bikes on the riverfront, near the start of a handy bike path (£13/2 hours, £15/4 hours, £17/6 hours, £20/day, includes helmet and map of suggested routes, Mon–Sat 9:30–17:00, Sun 10:00–16:00,

Caernarfon

1 Celtic Royal Hotel
2 Caer Menai B&B
3 Victoria House B&B
4 Totters Hostel
5 Hole-in-the-Wall Street Eateries
6 High Street Eateries
7 J&C's Fish & Chips
8 Spar Supermarket
9 Iceland Supermarket
10 Morrisons Supermarket
11 The Anglesey Arms
12 Library (Internet)
13 Launderette
14 Bike Rental
15 Na-Nog Shop
16 Harbor Cruises
17 Bus Stop to/from Conwy

NORTH WALES

VICTORIA DOCK

THE GALLERY

BANK QUAY

NORTH.

THE PROMENADE

CHURCH

HIGH ST.

MARKET

CASTLE

PALACE

SHIREHALL

DITCH

CASTLE

MENAI STRAIT

CASTLE

RAMPARTS

P

16

ABER BRIDGE

SEIONT RIVER

P PARKING

100 YARDS

100 METERS

DCH

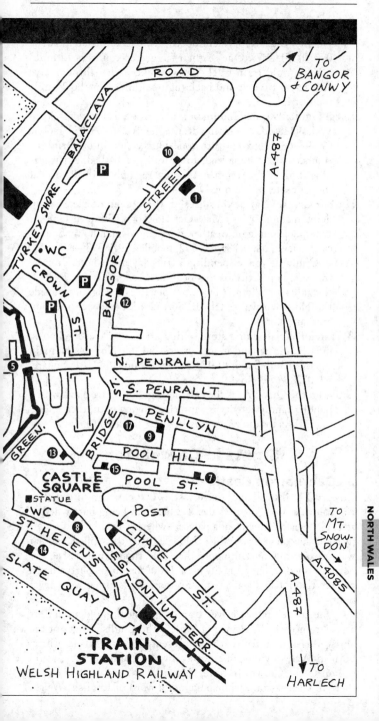

ROAD

TO
BANGOR
& CONWY

BALACLAVA

TURKEY SHORE

P

10

STREET

1

A-487

WC

CROWN ST.

P

BANGOR

P

12

N. PENRALLT

S. PENRALLT

5

BRIDGE ST.

PENLLYN

17

9

GREEN.

13

POOL HILL

15

POOL ST.

7

CASTLE
SQUARE

STATUE

WC

8

Post

CHAPEL ST.

TO
MT.
SNOW-
DON
A-4085

ST. HELEN'S

14

SEGONTIUM TERR.

SLATE QUAY

A-487

TRAIN
STATION
WELSH HIGHLAND RAILWAY

TO
HARLECH

NORTH WALES

closed Sun–Mon in winter, 1 Slate Quay—across the parking lot from the lot's payment booth, tel. 01286/676-804, mobile 07770-951-007). One of their suggested routes is 12 miles down an old train track—now a bike path—through five villages to Bryncir and back (figure 4 hours for the 24-mile round-trip).

Local Guide: Donna Goodman leads private day trips of North Wales (£180/day, book in advance, tel. 01286/677-059, mobile 07946-163-906, www.turnstone-tours.co.uk, info@turnstone -tours.co.uk). Donna leads town walks each Wednesday evening through the summer (£4, July-Aug only at 18:30, meet at the art center at Victoria Dock).

Harbor Cruise: Narrated cruises on the **Queen of the Sea** run daily in summer (£6, May–Oct 11:30 or 12:30 until 18:00 or 19:00, depending on weather, tides, and demand, 40 minutes, castle views, tel. 01286/672-772, mobile 07979-593-483).

Welsh Choir: If you're spending a Tuesday night here, drop by the weekly practice of the local men's choir (Tue at 19:45 in the gallery at Victoria Dock, no practice in Aug, just outside the old town walls, tel. 01286/672-633, www.cormeibion caernarfon.org).

A Taste of Welsh: For a store selling all things Welsh—books, movies, music, and more—check out **Na-Nog** on the main square (Mon–Sat 9:00–17:00, closed Sun, 16 Castle Square, tel. 01286/676-946).

Crabs on the Quay: As is the case in neighboring harbor towns, a popular family activity is capturing, toying with, then releasing little crabs (under the castle, along the harbor).

Sights in Caernarfon

▲▲Caernarfon Castle

Edward I built this impressive castle 700 years ago to establish English rule over North Wales. Rather than being purely defensive, it also had elements of a palace—where Edward and his family could stay on visits to Wales. Modeled after the striped, angular walls of ancient Constantinople, the castle, though impressive, was never finished and never really used. From the inner courtyard you can see the notched walls ready for more walls—that were never built.

The castle's fame derives from its physical grandeur and its association with the Prince of Wales. The English king got the angry Welsh to agree that if he presented them with "a prince, born in Wales, who spoke not a word of English," they would submit to the Crown. In time, Edward had a son born in Wales (here in Caernarfon), who spoke not a word of English, Welsh, or any other language—as an infant. In modern times, as another political maneuver, the Prince of Wales has been "invested" (given his title) here. This "tradition" actually dates only from the 20th century, and only two of 21 Princes of Wales have taken part.

Despite its disappointing history, it's fun to climb around. To bring the stones to life, catch the £2.50 guided tour (50-minute tours leave on the hour—and occasionally, with demand, on the half-hour—from the courtyard steps just beyond the ticket booth; if you're late, ask to join one in progress).

In the huge **Eagle Tower** (on the seaward side, to the far right as you enter), see the ground-floor "Prospect of Caernarfon" history exhibit (look for the model of the original castle); watch the 23-minute movie (*The Eagle and the Dragon,* a broad mix of Welsh legend and history enthusiastically enacted by an elfin narrator, shown upstairs on the hour and half-hour); and climb the tower for a great view. The nearby **Chamberlain's Tower** and **Queen's Tower** (ahead and to the right as you enter) house the mildly interesting "Museum of the Royal Welsh Fusiliers"—a military branch made up entirely of Welshmen. The museum shows off medals, firearms, uniforms, and information about various British battles and military strategies. The **northeast tower,** at the opposite end of the castle (to the left as you enter), has a "Princes of Wales" exhibit highlighting the investiture of Prince Charles in 1969.

Cost and Hours: £5.10; March–Oct daily 9:30–17:00, July–Aug until 18:00; Nov–Feb Mon–Sat 10:00–16:00, Sun 11:00–16:00; last entry 30 minutes before closing, tel. 01286/677-617, www.cadw .wales.gov.uk. Martin de Lewandowicz gives mind-bending tours of the castle (tel. 01286/674-369).

Near Caernarfon

Narrow-Gauge Steam Train—The Welsh Highland Railway steam train billows scenically through the countryside from Caernarfon to Beddgelert and beyond under the slopes of Mount Snowdon. The 1.5-hour ride to Beddgelert takes you along the original line that served a slate quarry; it makes a fine joyride. Those staying (or parking) in either town can ride the train one-way, look around, and catch bus #S4 back to save an hour (£15 one-way, £23 round-trip, 2–4 trips/day, mid-March–Oct, tel. 01766/516-000, www.festrail.co.uk).

Segontium Roman Fort—Dating from A.D. 77, this ruin is the westernmost Roman fort in Britain. It was manned for more than 300 years to keep the Welsh and the coast quiet. Little is left but foundations (free, Tue–Sun 12:30–16:30, closed Mon, small museum, 20-minute walk from town, tel. 01286/675-625, www .segontium.org.uk).

Horseback Riding—To ride a pony or horse, try **Snowdonia Riding Stables** (£17/hour, longer times available, 3 miles from Caernarfon, off the road to Beddgelert, bus #S4 from Caernarfon, tel. 01286/650-342, www.snowdonia2000.fsnet.co.uk, riding @snowdonia2000.fsnet.co.uk).

Sleeping in Caernarfon

(£1 = about $1.60, country code: 44, area code: 01286)
My listings favor traditional hotels and B&B, but if you're looking for a big hotel with cheap rooms, consider Caernarfon's branches of Premier Inn (www.premierinn.com) and Travelodge (www .travelodge.co.uk).

$$$ Celtic Royal Hotel rents 110 large, comfortable rooms and includes a restaurant, gym, pool, hot tub, and sauna; some top-floor rooms have castle views. Its grand, old-fashioned look comes with modern-day conveniences—but it's still overpriced (Db-£125, extra bed-£20, discounts for 2 or more nights, bar, restaurant; on Bangor Street; tel. 01286/674-477, fax 01286/674-139, www.celtic-royal.co.uk).

$$ Caer Menai B&B ("Fort of the Menai Strait") rents seven bright rooms one block from the harbor (Sb-£45, Db-£60, family room-£75–80, ask for seaview room, free Internet access and Wi-Fi, 15 Church Street, tel. 01286/672-612, www.caermenai .co.uk, info@caermenai.co.uk, Karen and Mark). Church Street is two blocks from the castle and the TI; with your back to the TI, turn right at the nearest corner and walk down Shirehall Street, which becomes Church Street after one block.

$$ Victoria House B&B, next door to the Caer Menai, rents five airy, fresh, large-for-Britain rooms with nice natural-stone bathrooms and in-room fridges stocked with free soft drinks. Generous breakfasts are served in a pleasant, woody room (Db-£65–70, £5 discount for 2 or more nights, free Internet access and Wi-Fi—even a loaner laptop for guests, 13 Church Street, tel. 01286/678-263, www.thevictoriahouse.co.uk, jan@thevictoriahouse.co.uk, friendly Jan Baker). For directions, see previous listing.

$ Totters Hostel is a creative little hostel well-run by Bob and Henriette (28 beds in 5 dorm rooms, £16/bed with sheets, includes continental breakfast, cash only, couples can have their own twin room when available-£38, beautiful and large top-floor Db-£45, open all day, lockers, welcoming cellar game room, inviting living room, DVD library, kitchen, a block from castle and sea at 2 High Street, tel. 01286/672-963, mobile 07979-830-470, www.totters .co.uk, totters.hostel@googlemail.com). They also own a three-bedroom house across the street (D-£36, Db-£45, entire house rents for £100/4 people, £125/6 people—perfect for families).

Eating in Caernarfon

The streets near Caernarfon's castle teem with inviting eateries. Rather than recommending a particular one, I'll point you in the direction of several good streets with reasonable options.

"**Hole-in-the-Wall Street**" (between Castle Square and TI) is lined with several charming cafés and bistros. Nearby **High Street** has plenty of cheap and cheery sandwich shops and tea-rooms. The pedestrianized but grubby **Pool Street** offers several budget options, including the popular **J&C's** fish-and-chips joint. And several places on the **main square** have outside tables from which you can watch the people scene while munching your toasted sandwich.

Picnic: For groceries, you'll find a small **Spar** supermarket on the main square, an **Iceland** supermarket near the bus stop, and a huge **Morrisons** supermarket a five-minute walk from the city center on Bangor Street (all of these are open long hours daily).

Pub Grub and Fun: The **Anglesey Arms** is a rough, old, characteristic pub serving basic lunches; it has picnic benches on the harborfront. The place is lively in the evening with darts, pool, and well-lubricated locals. There's live folk music Friday evenings from 21:30 (Harbour Front, tel. 01286/672-158).

Caernarfon Connections

Caernarfon is a handy hub for buses into Snowdonia National Park (such as to Llanberis, Beddgelert, and Betws-y-Coed). Bus info: toll tel. 0871-200-2233, www.gwynedd.gov.uk/bwsgwynedd. And the narrow-gauge steam train provides both sightseeing and transport from Caernarfon to **Beddgelert** (described earlier).

From Caernarfon by Bus to: Conwy (1–2/hour direct, more with change in Bangor, 1.25 hours), **Llanberis** (2/hour, 25 minutes, bus #88), **Beddgelert** (9/day Mon–Sat, 5/day on Sun, 30 minutes, bus #S4), **Betws-y-Coed** (hourly, 1–1.5 hours, 2 transfers), **Blaenau Ffestiniog** (at least hourly, 1.25 hours, change in Porthmadog).

Snowdonia National Park

This is Britain's second-largest national park, and its centerpiece—the tallest mountain in Wales or England—is Mount Snowdon (www.eryri-npa.co.uk). Each year, half a million people ascend one of seven different paths to the top of the 3,560-foot mountain. Hikes take from five to seven hours; if you're fit and the weather's good, it's an exciting day. Trail info abounds (local TIs sell the small £3 book *The Ascent*

of Snowdon, by E. G. Bowland, which describes the routes). As you explore, notice the slate roofs—the local specialty.

Betws-y-Coed

The resort center of Snowdonia National Park, Betws-y-Coed (BET-oos-uh-coyd) bursts with tour buses and souvenir shops.

This picturesque town is cuddled by wooded hills, made cozy by generous trees, and situated along a striking, waterfall-rippled stretch of the Conwy River. It verges on feeling overly manicured, with uniform checkerboard-stone houses yawning at each other from across a broad central green. There's little to do here except wander along the waterfalls (don't miss the old stone bridge—just up the river from the green—with the best waterfall views), have a snack or meal, or go for a walk in the woods.

Stop by Betws-y-Coed's good **National Park Centre/TI,** which books rooms for a £2 fee and sells the handy £2 *Forest Walks* map, outlining five different walks you can do from here. They show a free 13-minute video with aerial views of the park (daily April–Oct 9:30–17:30, Nov–March 9:30–12:30 & 13:30–16:30, tel. 01690/710-426, www.snowdonia-npa.gov.uk). In summer there's sometimes live entertainment in the TI's courtyard.

Arrival in Betws-y-Coed: Drivers can follow signs for *National Park* and *i* to find the main parking lot by the TI. **Trains** and **buses** arrive at the village green; with your back to the station, the TI is to the right of the green.

Snowdonia Area

- CASTLE
- IRISH SEA
- 5 MILES
- 5 KM
- LLANDUDNO
- CONWY
- LLANDUDNO JUNCTION
- TO HOLY-HEAD (FERRY TO IRELAND)
- MENAI SUSPENSION BRIDGE
- BEAUMARIS
- A-545
- A-55
- TO CHESTER & RUTHIN
- B-5106
- BODNANT GARDEN
- A-5
- LLANFAIR P.G.
- BANGOR
- TREFRIW WOOLEN MILLS
- A-470
- CAERNARFON
- LLANBERIS
- A-5
- CAPEL CURIG
- A-4085
- A-4086
- PEN-Y-PASS
- BETWS-Y-COED
- DINAS
- A-487
- PEN-Y-GWRYD HOTEL PUB
- A-470
- A-5
- TO LLAMGWN, RUTHIN & LLANGOLLEN
- MT. SNOWDON
- A-498
- BEDDGELERT
- LLECHWEDD SLATE MINE
- PORTH-MADOG
- A-498
- BLAENAU FFESTINIOG
- CRICCIETH
- FFESTINIOG
- PORTMEIRION
- A-496
- HARLECH
- TO ABERYSTWYTH

Nearby: If you drive west out of town on A5 (toward Beddgelert or Llanberis), after two miles you'll see the parking lot for scenic **Swallow Falls,** a pleasant five-minute walk from the road (£1.50 entry). A half-mile past the falls on the right, you'll see **The Ugly House,** built overnight to take advantage of a 15th-century law that let any quickie building avoid fees and taxes.

Betws-y-Coed Connections

Betws-y-Coed is connected to **Llandudno Junction** near Conwy (north, 45 minutes) and **Blaenau Ffestiniog** (south, 30 minutes) by the Conwy Valley train line (5/day Mon–Sat, 3/day Sun, no Sun trains in winter). Buses connect Betws-y-Coed with **Conwy** (at least hourly, 45 minutes), **Llanberis** (hourly, 45–70 minutes, transfer at Pen-y-Pass), **Beddgelert** (7/day, 1–2 hours, 1–2 changes), **Blaenau Ffestiniog** (8/day Mon–Sat, none on Sun, 20–35 minutes; usually bus #X1), **Caernarfon** (hourly, 1–1.5 hours, 2 transfers), and **Llangollen** (3/day Mon and Wed–Sat, 2/day Tue, none on Sun, 1 hour).

Beddgelert

This is the quintessential Snowdon village, rated ▲▲ and packing a scenic mountain punch without the tourist crowds (17 miles from Betws-y-Coed). Beddgelert (BETH-geh-lert) is a cluster of

stone houses lining a babbling brook in the shadow of Mount Snowdon and her sisters. Cute as a hobbit, Beddgelert will have you looking for The Shire around the next bend. Thanks to the fine variety of hikes from its doorstep and its decent bus service, Beddgelert makes a good stop for those wanting to experience the peace of Snowdonia.

There are no real "sights" here, but locals can recommend **walks.** You can follow the lane along the river (3 miles round-trip); walk down the river and around the hill (3 hours, 6 miles, 900-foot gain, via Cwm Bycham); hike along (or around) Llyn Gwynant Lake and four miles back to Beddgelert (ride the bus to the lake); or try the dramatic ridge walks on Moel Hebog (Hawk Hill).

The **Welsh Highland Railway** serves Beddgelert. This narrow-gauge joyride (12 miles and 1.5 hours to or from Caernarfon) is a popular excursion. Most people ride the train one-way and return by bus (described earlier—see "Sights in Caernarfon").

Orientation to Beddgelert

(area code: 01766)
Beddgelert clusters around its triple-arch stone bridge. The recommended B&Bs line up single-file along one side of the brook, while the hotels, most eateries, and the TI are on the other side.

The National Park Centre/TI is at the far end of town on the right, several blocks from the bridge. They can suggest tips for walks and hikes (April–Oct daily 9:30–17:30; Nov–March Fri–Sun 9:30–16:30—but closes for lunch, closed Mon–Thu; tel. 01766/890-615, www.snowdonia-npa.gov.uk or www.beddgelerttourism.com). There's Internet access inside the TI (£2/hour). For mountain-bike rental, try Beddgelert Bikes (2 miles from Beddgelert, tel. 01766/890-434, www.beddgelertbikes.co.uk).

Sleeping in Beddgelert

(£1 = about $1.60, country code: 44, area code: 01766)
The three recommended B&Bs all line up in a row at the bridge. They're quite different from each other—each seems to fill its own niche. The larger inn (listed first) is across the river.

$$$ Tanronnen Inn has seven hotelesque rooms above a pub that's been beautifully renovated from its interior medieval timbers to its exterior stone walls (Sb-£55, Db-£100, cheaper for longer stays, tel. 01766/890-347, fax 01766/890-606, www.tanronnen .co.uk, guestservice@tanronnen.co.uk).

$$$ Plas Tan y Graig Guest House is the best value in town: seven thoughtfully updated, calming, uncluttered rooms run with care and contemporary style by Tony and Sharon (Sb-£50, Db-£75–85 depending on season, 2-night minimum stay, fine lounge, free Wi-Fi, beautiful breakfast terrace overlooking the village, packed lunches offered, tel. 01766/890-310, www.plas -tanygraig.co.uk, plastanygraig@googlemail.com).

$$ Plas Gwyn Guest House rents six rooms in a cozy, cheery, 19th-century townhouse with a comfy lounge. Friendly Brian Wheatley is happy to dispense travel tips (S-£35, Db-£70, 10 percent discount with this book, cash only, Wi-Fi, tel. 01766/890-215, mobile 07815-549-708, www.plas-gwyn.com, bandb@beddgelert .fsbusiness.co.uk).

$$ Colwyn Guest House has five tight but slick and new-feeling rooms (S-£30–35, D-£55–65, Db-£60–70, 10 percent discount with this book, cash only, free Internet access, tel. 01766/890-276, www.beddgelertguesthouse.co.uk, colwynguest house@tiscali.co.uk, Colleen).

Near Beddgelert

Mountaineers note that this area was used by Sir Edmund Hillary and his men as they practiced for the first successful ascent of Mount Everest. They slept at **$$$ Pen-y-Gwryd Hotel Pub,** at the base of the road leading up to the Pen-y-Pass by Mount Snowdon, and today the bar is strewn with fascinating memorabilia from Hillary's 1953 climb. The 16 rooms, with dingy old furnishings and crampon ambience, are a poor value—aside from the impressive history (S-£40, Sb-£48, D-£80, Db-£96, old-time-elegant public rooms, some D rooms share museum-piece Victorian tubs and showers, natural pool and sauna for guests, £22 three-course dinners, £28 grand five-course dinners, tel. 01286/870-211, www.pyg.co.uk).

Eating in Beddgelert

Lyn's Café, just across the bridge from the B&Bs, serves nicely done home cookin' at good prices in a cozy one-room bistro (£3–8 lunches, £8–10 dinners, daily 9:00–20:00, Sat until 23:00, closes early off-season, so don't wait too late; tel. 01766/890-374).

The **Tanronnen Inn** serves up tasty food in an inviting pub setting, with several cozy, atmospheric rooms (£9–14 meals, cheaper snacks, tel. 01766/890-347).

And for Dessert: The **Glaslyn Homemade Ice Cream** shop (up the road from the Tanronnen Inn) offers good quality and selection.

Beddgelert Connections

Beddgelert is connected to **Caernarfon** by the scenic Welsh Highland Railway (2–4/day, 1.5 hours, no trains off-season) and handy bus #S4 (9/day Mon–Sat, 5/day Sun, 30 minutes). Bus connections to **Betws-y-Coed** are much less convenient (7/day, 1–2 hours, 1–2 changes). To reach **Conwy,** it's generally easiest to transfer in Caernarfon (9/day Mon–Sat, 5/day Sun, 1.75 hours total). Buses to **Blaenau Ffestiniog** involve one or two transfers (7/day Mon–Sat, 1–1.5 hours; 2/day Sun, 2.25–3.25 hours).

Llanberis

A town of 2,000 people with as many tourists on a sunny day, Llanberis (THLAN-beh-ris) is a popular base for Snowdon activi-

ties. Most people prefer to take the train from here to the summit, but Llanberis is also loaded with hikers, as it's the launchpad for the longest (five miles) but least strenuous hiking route to the Snowdon summit. (Routes from the nearby Pen-y-Pass, between here and Beddgelert, are steeper and even more scenic.)

NORTH WALES

Orientation to Llanberis

(area code: 01286)
Llanberis is a long, skinny, rugged, and functional town that feels like a frontier village. Drivers approaching Llanberis will find several parking lots, including one right by the Snowdon Mountain Railway, and a lakeside lot (marked with an *i*) across the road from the town center and TI.

Tourist Information

The TI, right on the colorful main street (High Street) in the center of the village, sells maps and offers tips for ascending Snowdon (Easter–Oct daily 9:30–16:30; Nov–Easter Fri–Mon 10:00–15:00, closed Tue–Thu; 41B High Street, tel. 01286/870-765, www.visit snowdonia.info).

Sights in Llanberis

▲▲**Snowdon Mountain Railway**—This is the easiest and most popular ascent of Mount Snowdon. You'll travel five miles from Llanberis to the summit on Britain's only rack-and-pinion railway (from 1896), climbing a total of 3,500 feet. On the way up, you'll hear a constant narration on legends, geology, and history. A mountaintop visitors center includes a café. On the way down, there's only engine noise (£25 round-trip, 2.5 hours, includes 30-minute stop at top, train departs from station along the main road at the south end of Llanberis town center, toll tel. 0844-493-8120, www.snowdonrailway.co.uk). Drivers should avoid the Royal Victoria Hotel's parking lot, which is pricey; instead, turn right after the station onto Victoria Terrace (£4/day) or park in one of several lakeside lots.

The first departure is often at 9:00. While the schedule flexes with weather and demand, they try to run several trips each day mid-March through October (up to 2/hour in peak season). On sunny summer days—especially in July and August—trains fill up fast. Designed for 54 Victorian gentry, these days the train is overrun with commoners. It's smart to reserve ahead (£3.50 reservation fee per party, ask about 20 percent discount with advance booking for 9:00 departure). Otherwise, show up early—the office opens at 8:30, and on very busy days, tickets can be sold out by mid-morning; even if you get one, you may have to wait until afternoon for your scheduled departure time. Occasionally, because of bad weather, the train doesn't run all the way to the summit. In that case, tickets are partially refunded or sold at a reduced rate.

Don't confuse this with the Llanberis Lake Railway, a different (and far less appealing) "Thomas the Tank Engine"-type steam train that fascinates kids and runs to the end of Padarn Lake and back.

▲▲**Welsh Slate Museum**—Across the lake from Llanberis yawns a giant slate quarry. To learn more, venture across to this free museum. The well-presented exhibit, displayed around the workshop that was used until 1969 to support the giant slate mine above, explains various aspects of this local industry. In addition to a giant water-wheel and the slate-splitting demo (lasts 30 minutes, starts

at :15 past each hour), the museum has a little row of modest quarrymen's houses from different eras, offering a thought-provoking glimpse into their hardy lifestyle. The big, 50-foot-high waterwheel turns a shaft that runs throughout the workshop, powering all the various belt-driven machinery. Historic photo galleries and a 12-minute video re-create what was—until the last generation—a thriving industry employing 3,000 workers. While not as in-depth (literally) as the Llechwedd Slate Mine in Blaenau Ffestiniog, this is as interesting and more convenient (free entry but £3 parking; Easter–Oct daily 10:00–17:00; Nov–Easter Sun–Fri 10:00–16:00, closed Sat; tel. 01286/870-630, www.museumwales.ac.uk/en /slate).

Electric Mountain—This attraction offers tours into a power plant burrowed into the mountain across the lake from town. After a 10-minute video, you'll load onto a bus and venture into Europe's biggest hydroelectric power station for a one-hour guided tour (£7.50, tours about hourly, open daily June–Aug 9:30–17:30, Sept–May 10:00–16:30, wear warm clothes and sturdy shoes, call in advance to reserve a spot, tel. 01286/870-636, www.electric mountain.co.uk).

Llanberis Connections

Llanberis is easiest to reach from **Caernarfon** (2/hour, 25 minutes, bus #88) or **Betws-y-Coed** (hourly, 45–70 minutes, transfer at Pen-y-Pass); from **Conwy,** transfer in one of these towns (Caernarfon is generally best). While it's a quick 30-minute drive from Llanberis to **Beddgelert,** the bus connection is more complicated, requiring a transfer at Pen-y-Pass, on the high road around Mount Snowdon (hourly, 50–75 minutes).

NORTH WALES

Blaenau Ffestiniog

Blaenau Ffestiniog (BLEH-nigh FES-tin-yog) is a quintessential Welsh slate-mining town, notable for its slate-mine tour and its old steam train. The town—a dark, poor place—seems to struggle on, oblivious to the tourists who nip in and out. Though it's tucked amidst a pastoral Welsh landscape, Blaenau Ffestiniog is surrounded by a gunmetal-gray wasteland of "tips," huge mountain-like piles of excess slate.

Take a walk. The shops are right out of the 1950s. Long rows of humble "two-up and two-down" houses (four rooms) feel a bit grim. The train station, bus stop, and parking lot all cluster along a one-block stretch in the heart of town. There's no TI.

Getting There: Blaenau Ffestiniog is conveniently connected to **Betws-y-Coed** and **Conwy** both by the Conwy Valley train line (5/day Mon–Sat, 3/day Sun, none on Sun in winter, 30 minutes to Betws-y-Coed, 1.25 hours to Conwy with transfer in Llandudno Junction) and by bus #X1 (8/day Mon–Sat, none on Sun, 20–35 minutes to Betws-y-Coed, 1 hour to Llandudno Junction near Conwy). To connect with **Beddgelert,** you must make one or two transfers (7/day Mon–Sat, 1–1.5 hours; 2/day Sun, 2.25–3.25 hours).

Sights in Blaenau Ffestiniog

▲▲Llechwedd Slate-Mine Tour

Slate mining played a blockbuster role in Welsh heritage, and this working slate mine on the northern edge of Blaenau Ffestiniog does a fine job of explaining the mining culture of Victorian Wales. The Welsh mined and split most of the slate roofs of Europe. For every ton of usable slate found, 10 tons were mined. You can wander around its basic exhibit, or join a guided tour. Dress warmly—I mean it. You'll freeze underground without a sweater. Lines are longer when rain drives in the hikers.

NORTH WALES

Hours: Daily March–Sept 10:00–18:00, Oct–Feb 10:00–17:00, cafeteria, tel. 01766/830-306, www.llechwedd-slate-caverns.co.uk.

Getting There: The slate mine is about a mile from the town center. Each arriving train on the Ffestiniog Railway from Porthmadog (described next) is met by bus #X1, which takes you to the mine (fewer buses on Sun). Unfortunately, buses don't meet the more useful Conwy Valley train line from Llandudno Junction and Betws-y-Coed, but you can walk 30 minutes to the mine, or take a taxi (about £5, reserve in advance, tel. 01766/831-781 or 01766/830-082).

Exhibit: The exhibit (£2) includes a tiny Victorian mining town (with a miners' pub and a view from "The Top of the Tip") and an engrossing slate-splitting demonstration. While this is generally timed to go with the finish of the tramway tour (explained next), anyone in the general exhibit is welcome to enjoy the demonstration. Don't miss this—check the posted schedule and plan your visit around it.

Tours: For a more in-depth visit, pay to join one or both of the two different tours (£10 for one tour, £16 for both tours, 2–6 tours per hour depending on demand, first tours at 10:15, last at 17:15, each about 40 minutes). The **"tramway"** tour is a level train ride with three stops, not much walking, and a live guide. It focuses on working life and traditional mining techniques. The **"deep mine"** tour descends deep into the mountain for an audiovisual dramatization of social life and a half-mile of walking with lots of stairs and some uneven footing. The tours overlap slightly, but the combo-ticket makes doing both worth considering.

Near Blaenau Ffestiniog

▲**Ffestiniog Railway**—This 13-mile narrow-gauge train line was built in 1836 for small horse-drawn wagons to transport the slate from the Ffestiniog mines to the port of Porthmadog. In the 1860s, horses gave way to steam trains. Today, hikers and tourists enjoy these tiny titans (tel. 01766/516-000, www.festrail.co.uk). After renovations are completed, possibly in 2011, this line will connect to the narrow-gauge Welsh Highland Railway from Caernarfon (see page 567). This is a novel steam-train experience, but the full-size Conwy Valley Line from Llandudno to Blaenau Ffestiniog is more scenic and works a little better for hikers (see page 558).

Portmeirion—Ten miles southwest of Blaenau Ffestiniog, this "Italian Village" was the life's work of a rich local architect who began building it in 1925. Set idyllically on the coast just beyond the poverty of the slate-mine towns, this flower-filled fantasy is extravagant. Surrounded by lush Welsh greenery and a windswept mudflat at low tide, the village is an artistic glob of palazzo arches, fountains, gardens, and promenades filled with cafés, tacky shops, a hotel, and local tourists who always wanted to go to Italy. Fans of the cultish British 1960s TV series *The Prisoner*, which was filmed here, will recognize the place (www.portmeirion.com).

Ruthin

Ruthin (RITH-in; "Rhuthun" in Welsh) is a low-key market town whose charm is in its ordinary Welshness. The town (pop. 5,000)

is situated atop a gentle hill surrounded by undulating meadows. Simple streets branch out from the central roundabout (at the former medieval marketplace, St. Peter's Square) like spokes on a wheel. It's so untouristy that it has no TI. The market square, jail, museum, bus station, and in-town accommodations are all within five blocks of one another. Ruthin is as Welsh as it can be, making it a distinctive stopover on your way to northern England and Scotland. The people are the sights, and admission is free if you start the conversation.

Ruthin has poor connections to just about everywhere. Skip it unless you have a car.

Sights in Ruthin

▲**Ruthin Gaol**—Get a glimpse into crime and punishment in 17th- to early-20th-century Wales in this 100-cell prison. Explore the "dark" and condemned cells, give the dreaded hand-crank a whirl, and learn about the men, women, and children who did time here before the prison closed in 1916. The included audioguide—partly narrated by a jovial "prisoner" named Will—is very good, informative, and engaging. You'll find out why prison kitchens came with a cat, why the bathtubs had a severe case of ring-around-the-tub, how they got prisoners to sit still for their mug shots (and why these photos often included the prisoners' hands), and why the prison was renovated into the "panopticon" style in the late 19th century (£3.50, family-£10; March–Oct daily 10:00–17:00; Nov–Feb Sat–Sun and school holidays only 10:00–17:00; last entry one hour before closing, Clwyd Street, tel. 01824/708-281, www.ruthingaol.co.uk).

Nantclwyd House—This Elizabethan-era "oldest timbered townhouse in Wales"—a white-and-brown half-timbered house

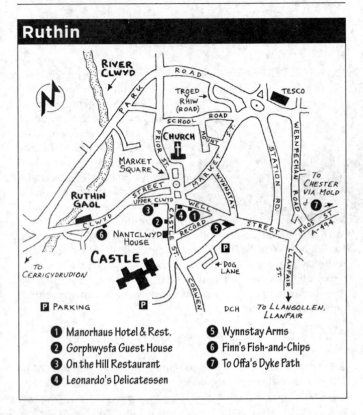

Ruthin

1. Manorhaus Hotel & Rest.
2. Gorphwysfa Guest House
3. On the Hill Restaurant
4. Leonardo's Delicatessen
5. Wynnstay Arms
6. Finn's Fish-and-Chips
7. To Offa's Dyke Path

between the castle and the market square—underwent an award-winning £600,000 renovation (funded partly by the EU) to convert it into a museum. Seven decorated rooms give visitors a peek into the history of the house, which was built in 1435 (£3.60, April–Sept Fri–Sun 10:00–17:00, last entry 45 minutes before closing, closed Mon–Thu and Oct–March, Castle Street, tel. 01824/709-822, www.nantclwydydre.co.uk).

Walks—For a scenic and interesting one-hour walk, try the Offa's Dyke Path to Moel Famau (the "Jubilee Tower," a 200-year-old war memorial on a peak overlooking stark moorlands). The trailhead is a 10-minute drive east of Ruthin on A494.

▲▲Welsh Choir—The mixed choir performs weekly at the Tabernacle Church (Thu 20:00 except Aug).

Sleeping in Ruthin

(£1 = about $1.60, country code: 44, area code: 01824)
For cheap sleeps, you'll have to stay at the youth hostels in Conwy or Caernarfon. Or, if you're driving, keep an eye out for rustic

hostel-like "bunkhouses" that dot the North Wales countryside. These not-so-cheap places each have their own individual charm.

$$$ Manorhaus rents the classiest rooms in Ruthin. Its eight rooms are impeccably appointed with artsy-contemporary decor, and the halls serve as gallery space for local artists. Guests enjoy use of the sauna, steam room, fitness room, library, and mini-cinema in the cellar. In fact, you could have a vacation and never leave the place (Sb-£70–95, "compact" Db-£95, standard Db-£115, superior Db-£135, pricier Db suite-£160, check website for discounts, free Wi-Fi, recommended restaurant, Well Street, tel. 01824/704-830, fax 01824/707-333, www.manorhaus.com, post @manorhaus.com). It's run by Chris (who played piano for years in London's West End theaters) and Gavin (an architect and former mayor of Ruthin)—together, it seems, they've brought Ruthin a splash of fun and style.

$$ Gorphwysfa Guest House ("Resting Place") is in a cozy 16th-century Tudor townhouse between the castle and the town square, next door to Ruthin's oldest house. The three rooms are huge, comfortable, and modern, while the public spaces are grand and Elizabethan—with wattle-and-daub construction, a library, a grand piano, and a breakfast room with a gigantic fireplace (Db-£60, Tb-£75, Qb-£85, less for 2-night stays, cash only, 8a Castle Street, tel. 01824/707-529, www.ruthinguesthouse.co.uk, marg @gorphwysfa.fsnet.co.uk, Margaret O'Riain).

Eating in Ruthin

On the Hill serves hearty £3–6 lunches and £10–15 dinners—mostly made with fresh, local ingredients—to an enthusiastic crowd. The Old World decor complements the good cuisine (Tue–Sat 12:00–14:00 & 18:30–21:00, closed Sun–Mon, 1 Upper Clwyd Street, tel. 01824/707-736).

Manorhaus is the town splurge in a recommended hotel (described above), with updated Welsh and British dinners served in a mod art-gallery space. Eating here—in the care of Chris and Gavin—is an evening in itself (£24 for two courses, £30 for three courses, food served daily 18:30–21:00, reservations recommended, Well Street, tel. 01824/704-830).

Leonardo's Delicatessen is *the* place to buy a top-notch gourmet picnic (made-to-order sandwiches, small salad bar, Mon–Sat 9:30–17:30, closed Sun, 4 Well Street, just off the main square).

Wynnstay Arms is a decent spot for pub grub (nightly, on Well Street, two blocks below the main square, tel. 01824/703-147).

Finn's is the local favorite for take-away fish-and-chips (£3, daily 11:00–22:00, near Ruthin Gaol at the bottom of Clwyd Street).

Near Ruthin: Llangollen

Worth a stop if you have a car, Llangollen (thlang-GOTH-lehn) is a red-brick riverside town that's equal parts blue collar and touristy. The town is famous for its **International Musical Eisteddfod,** a very popular and crowded festival of folk songs and dance (July 4–10 in 2011, tel. 01978/862-001, www.llangollen 2010.co.uk). The enthusiastic **TI** has the details on these events, the scenic steam-train trips, and other

attractions (daily 9:30–17:30, tel. 01978/860-828, www.llangollen .org.uk).

If you want to hear Welsh choral music, two **men's choirs** practice weekly: one on Friday nights (19:30 at the Hand Hotel on Bridge Street, 21:00 pub sing-along afterward, tel. 01978/861-482), and another on Wednesday nights (20:00 at Memorial Hall on High Street, tel. 01691/600-242).

Llangollen's most interesting attraction is the **Llangollen Canal,** a narrow, shallow waterway up the hill and across the bridge from the town center. You can stroll along the canal or take one of two different boat rides from Llangollen Wharf: a horse-drawn boat down to the Cistercian abbey (£6, Easter–Oct daily, 45 minutes, hourly from 11:00 in summer, less off-season, tel. 01978/860-702, www.horsedrawnboats.co.uk), or a longer, motor-ized canal-boat trip over the remarkable Pontcysyllte aqueduct (£11, Easter-Oct daily at 12:15 and 14:00, 2 hours).

If you take a walk or join the horse-drawn canal trip, you'll reach the lovely 13th-century Cistercian **Valle Crucis Abbey** (£2.70, April–Oct daily 10:00–17:00, last entry 30 minutes before closing, free access to grounds Nov–March, tel. 01978/860-326, www.llangollen.com/valle.html). An even older cross, **Eliseg's Pillar,** is nearby.

Sleeping in Llangollen: **$$ Glasgwm B&B** rents four spa-cious rooms in a Victorian townhouse (Sb-£35, Db-£55–65, Abbey Road, tel. 01978/861-975, www.glasgwm-llangollen.co.uk, glasgwm@llangollen.co.uk, John and Heather).

Llangollen Connections: From Llangollen, bus #X6 runs to **Betws-y-Coed** (3/day Mon and Wed–Sat, 2/day Tue, none on Sun, 1 hour). Llangollen is also connected by bus with train sta-tions at **Ruabon** (4/hour, 15 minutes) and **Wrexham** (4/hour, 35 minutes).

North Wales Connections

Two major transfer points out of (or into) North Wales are Crewe and Chester. Figure out your complete connection at www.national rail.co.uk.

From Crewe by Train to: London Euston Station (2/hour, 1.75 hours), **Bristol,** near Bath (2/hour, 2.5–3 hours), **Cardiff** (hourly, 2.75 hours), **Holyhead** (hourly, 2–2.5 hours), **Blackpool** (hourly, 1.5 hours), **Keswick** in the Lake District (nearly hourly, 1.75–2.75 hours to Penrith, some via Oxenholme or Manchester; then catch a bus to Keswick, hourly except 8/day Sun, 40 minutes, allow 3.5 hours total), **Glasgow** (nearly hourly, 3–4 hours, some via Lancaster or Preston).

From Chester by Train to: London Euston Station (2/hour, 2 hours), **Liverpool** (2/hour, 45 minutes), **Birmingham** (2/hour, 1.75 hours); points in North Wales including **Conwy** (nearly hourly, 50 minutes).

Ferry Connections Between North Wales and Ireland

Two companies make the crossing between Holyhead (in North Wales, beyond Caernarfon) and Ireland. Some boats go to Dublin, while others head for Dublin's southern suburb of Dun Laoghaire (pronounced "Dun Leary"). **Stena Line** sails from Holyhead to Dublin (2/day, 3.25 hours, plus 2 overnight) and also to Dun Laoghaire (1/day, 2 hours; one-way walk-on fare for either crossing-£25, cheaper if booked in advance, extra to use credit card but no fee for debit cards, reserve by phone or online—they book up long in advance on summer weekends, British toll tel. 0844-770-7070, or book online at www.stenaline.co.uk). **Irish Ferries** sails to Dublin (3/day—1 slow, 2 fast; plus 1 slow overnight sailing; slow boat 3.25 hours, fast boat 2 hours; one-way walk-on fare -£30 slow boat, £34 fast boat; extra to use credit card, reserve online for best fares; Britain toll tel. 08717-300-400, for Irish number dial 00-353-818-300-400 from Britain, www.irishferries.co.uk).

Sleeping near Holyhead Dock: The fine **$$ Monravon B&B** has seven rooms a 15-minute uphill walk from the dock (Sb-£35, Db-£50, family deals, £4 breakfast, free Wi-Fi, Porth-Y-Felin Road, tel. & fax 01407/762-944, www.monravon.co.uk, monravon @yahoo.co.uk). **$$ Celyn Villa B&B** is a lovely mid-19th-century house with views of the Dee estuary (Sb-£36–40, Db-£56–60, twin and family rooms available, 2-night minimum July–Aug, dinner available, Carmel Road, tel. 01352/710-853, www.celynvilla.co.uk, celynvilla@btinternet.com, Paulene and Les).

Route Tips for Drivers

From North Wales to Liverpool (40 miles): From Ruthin or A55, follow signs to the town of *Mold*, then *Queensferry*, then *Manchester M56*, then *Liverpool M53*, which tunnels under the Mersey River (£1.40).

From North Wales to Blackpool, Skipping Liverpool (100 miles): From A55, follow the blue signs to the motorway. The M56 road zips you to M6, where you'll turn north toward Preston and Lancaster (don't miss your turnoff). A few minutes after Preston, take the not-very-clearly signed next exit (#32, M55) into Blackpool, and drive as close as you can to the stubby Eiffel-type tower in the town center.

SCOTLAND

SCOTLAND

The country of Scotland makes up about a third of Britain's geographical area (30,400 square miles), but has less than a tenth of its population (just over five million). This sparsely populated chunk of land stretches to Norwegian latitudes. Its Shetland Islands, at about 60°N (similar to Anchorage, Alaska), are the northernmost point in Britain.

The southern part of Scotland, called the Lowlands, is relatively flat and urbanized. The northern area—the Highlands—

features a wild, severely undulating terrain, punctuated by lochs (lakes) and fringed by sea lochs (inlets) and islands. The Highland Boundary Fault that divides Scotland geologically also divides it culturally. Historically, there was a big difference between grizzled, kilt-wearing Highlanders in the northern wilderness, and the more refined Lowlanders in the southern flatlands and cities. The Highlanders spoke and acted like "true Scots," while the Lowlanders often seemed more "British" than Scottish. Although this division has faded over time, some Scots still cling to it today—city slickers down south think that Highlanders are crude and unrefined, and those who live at higher latitudes grumble about the soft, pampered urbanites in the Lowlands.

The Lowlands are dominated by a pair of rival cities: Edinburgh, the old royal capital, teems with Scottish history and is the country's best tourist attraction. Glasgow, once a gloomy industrial city, is becoming a hip, laid-back city of today, known for its modern architecture. The medieval university town and golf mecca of St. Andrews, the whisky village of Pitlochry, and the historic city of Stirling round out the Lowlands' top sights.

The Highlands provide your best look at traditional Scotland. The sights are subtle, but the warm culture and friendly people are engaging. There are a lot of miles, but they're scenic, the roads are

Scotland

••• FERRY ROUTES (NOT ALL SHOWN)

ATLANTIC OCEAN

ORKNEY
STROMNESS
KIRKWALL

50 MILES
30 KM

THURSO
JOHN O'GROATS

LEWIS

ULLAPOOL

NORTH UIST

MORAY FIRTH

KYLE OF LOCHALSH

CULLODEN

SOUTH UIST

PORTREE
SKYE

INVERNESS

HIGHLANDS
CALEDONIAN CANAL

LOCH NESS

ABERDEEN

RUM

BEN NEVIS

MALLAIG

COLL

FT. WILLIAM

PITLOCHRY

NORTH SEA

TIREE

MULL

GLENCOE

PERTH

DUNDEE

IONA

OBAN

LOCH LOMOND

ST. ANDREWS
EAST NEUK

JURA

STIRLING

FIRTH OF FORTH

ISLAY

BANNOCK-BURN

GLASGOW

EDINBURGH

CAMPBELTOWN

TROON

BERWICK-UPON-TWEED

ARRAN

AYR

LOWLANDS

ENGLAND

NORTHERN IRELAND

CAIRNRYAN
STRANRAER

CARLISLE

LARNE

HADRIAN'S WALL

NEW-CASTLE

BELFAST

DCH

TO DUBLIN

IRISH SEA

TO LAKE DISTRICT

TO YORK & LONDON

good, and the traffic is light. Generally, the Highlands are hungry
for the tourist dollar, and everything overtly Scottish is exploited to
the kilt. You'll need more than a quick visit to get away from that.
But if two days is all you have, you can get a feel for the area with
a quick drive to Oban, through Glencoe, then up the Caledonian
Canal to Inverness. With more time, the islands of Iona and Mull
(an easy day trip from Oban), the Isle of Skye, and countless brooding countryside castles will flesh out your Highlands experience.

The Highlands are more rocky and harsh than other parts
of the British Isles. It's no wonder that most of the scenes around
Hogwarts in the Harry Potter movies were filmed in this moody,
sometimes spooky landscape. Though Scotland's "hills" are

SCOTLAND

technically too short to be called "mountains," they do a convincing imitation. Scotland has 284 hills over 3,000 feet. A list of these was compiled in 1891 by Sir Hugh Munro, and to this day the Scots still call their high hills "Munros." According to the Scottish Mountaineering Club, more than 4,300 intrepid hikers can brag that they've climbed all of the Munros.

In this northern climate, cold and drizzly weather isn't uncommon—even in midsummer. The blazing sun can quickly be covered over by black clouds and howling wind. Scots warn visitors to prepare for "four seasons in one day." Because the Scots feel personally responsible for bad weather, they tend to be overly optimistic about forecasts. Take any Scottish promise of "sun by the afternoon" with a grain of salt—and bring your raincoat.

In the summer, the Highlands swarm with tourists...and midges. These tiny biting insects—like "no-see-ums" in some parts of North America—are bloodthirsty and determined. Depending on the weather, they can be an annoyance from late May through September. Hot sun or a stiff breeze blows the tiny buggers away, but they thrive in damp, shady areas. Locals suggest blowing or brushing them off, rather than swatting them—since killing them only seems to attract more (likely because of the smell of fresh blood). Scots say, "If you kill one midge, a million will come to his funeral." Even if you don't usually travel with bug spray, consider bringing or buying some for a summer visit—or your most vivid

memory of your Scottish vacation might be itchy arms and legs.

Keep an eye out for another Scottish animal: shaggy Highland cattle, with their hair falling in their eyes. Dubbed "hairy coos," these adorable beasts will melt your heart. With a heavy coat to keep them insulated, hairy coos graze on sparse vegetation that other animals ignore. And of course, there are a lot of sheep around.

The major theme of Scottish history is the drive for independence, especially from England. (Scotland's rabble-rousing national motto is *Nemo me impune lacessit*—"No one provokes me with impunity.") Like Wales, Scotland is a country of ragtag Celts sharing an island with wealthy and powerful Anglo-Saxons. Scotland's Celtic culture is a

SCOTLAND

result of its remoteness—the invading Romans were never able to conquer this rough-and-tumble people, and even built Hadrian's Wall to lock off this distant corner of their empire. The Anglo-Saxons, and their descendants the English, fared little better than the Romans did. Even King Edward I—who so successfully dominated Wales—was unable to hold on to Scotland for long, largely thanks to the relentlessly rebellious William Wallace (a.k.a. "Braveheart").

Failing to conquer Scotland by the blade, England eventually absorbed it politically. In 1603, England's Queen Elizabeth I died without an heir, so Scotland's King James VI took the throne, becoming King James I of England. It took another century or so of battles, both military and diplomatic, but the Act of Union in 1707 definitively (and controversially) unified the Kingdom of Great Britain. In 1745, Bonnie Prince Charlie attempted to reclaim the Scottish throne on behalf of the deposed Stuarts, but his army was slaughtered at the Battle of Culloden (described in the Inverness and the Northern Highlands chapter). This cemented English rule over Scotland, and is seen by many Scots as the last gasp of the traditional Highlands clan system.

Scotland has been joined—however unwillingly—to England ever since, and the Scots have often felt oppressed by their English countrymen (see "British, Scottish, and English" on page 609). During the Highland Clearances in the 18th and 19th centuries, landowners (mostly English) decided that vast tracks of land were more profitable as grazing land for sheep, than as farmland for people. Many Highlanders were forced to abandon their traditional homes and lifestyles and seek employment elsewhere. Large numbers ended up in North America, especially parts of eastern Canada, such as Prince Edward Island and Nova Scotia (literally, "New Scotland").

Today, Americans and Canadians of Scottish descent enjoy coming "home" to Scotland. If you're Scottish, your surname will tell you which clan your ancestors likely belonged to. The prefix "Mac" (or "Mc") means "son of"—so "MacDonald" means the same thing as "Donaldson." Tourist shops everywhere are happy

to help you track down your clan's tartan, or distinctive plaid pattern—many clans have several.

Is Scotland really a country? It's not a sovereign state, but it is a "nation" in that it has its own traditions, ethnic identity, languages (Gaelic and Scots, described below), and football league. To some extent, it even has its own

Scottish Words

Scotch may be the peaty drink the bartender serves you, but the nationality of the bartender is **Scots** or **Scottish.** Here are some other Scottish words that may come in handy during your time here:

aye	yes
auld	old
ben	mountain
blether	talk
bonnie	beautiful
brae	slope, hill
burn	creek or stream
cairn	pile of stones
close	an alley leading to a courtyard or square
craig	rock, cliff
firth	estuary
innis	island
inver	mouth of a river
ken	to know
kirk	church
kyle	strait
loch	lake
nae	no (as in "nae bother"—you're welcome)
neeps	turnips
ree	king, royal ("righ" in Gaelic)
tattie	potato
wee	small
wynd	tight, winding lane connecting major streets

A sharp intake of breath (like a little gasp), sometimes while saying "aye," means "yes."

government: Over the past several years, Scotland has enjoyed its greatest measure of political autonomy in centuries—a trend called "devolution." In 1998, the Scottish parliament opened its doors in Edinburgh for the first time in almost 300 years. Though the Scottish parliament's powers are limited (most major decisions are still made in London), the Scots are enjoying the refreshing breeze of increased independence. Today, some politicians are poised to ask the EU to recognize Scotland as a separate country.

Scotland even has its own currency. While Scots use the same coins as England, Scotland also prints its own bills (with Scottish rather than English people and landmarks). Just to confuse tourists, three different banks print Scottish pound notes, each with a different design. In the Lowlands (around Edinburgh and Glasgow), you'll receive both Scottish and English pounds from ATMs and in change. But in the Highlands, you'll almost never see English pounds. Though most merchants in England accept Scottish pound notes, a few might balk—especially at the rare one-pound note, which their cash registers don't have a slot for. (They are, however, legally required to accept your Scottish currency.)

The Scottish flag—a diagonal, X-shaped white cross on a blue field—represents the cross of Scotland's patron saint, the Apostle Andrew (who was crucified on an X-shaped cross). You may not realize it, but you see the Scottish flag every time you look at the Union Jack: England's flag (the red St. George's cross on a white field) superimposed on Scotland's (a blue field with a white diagonal cross). The diagonal red cross (St. Patrick's cross) over Scotland's white one represents Northern Ireland. (Wales gets no love on the Union Jack.)

Scots are known for their inimitable burr, but they are also proud of their old Celtic language, Scottish Gaelic (pronounced "gallic"; Ireland's closely related Celtic language is spelled the same but pronounced "gaylic"). Gaelic thrives only in the remotest corners of Scotland. In major towns and cities, virtually nobody speaks Gaelic every day, but the language is kept on life-support by a Scottish population keen to remember their heritage. New Gaelic schools are opening all the time, and Scotland recently passed a law to replace road signs with new ones listing both English and Gaelic spellings (e.g., Edinburgh/Dùn Èideann).

Scotland has another language of its own, called Scots (a.k.a. "Lowland Scots," to distinguish it from Gaelic). Aye, you're likely already a wee bit familiar with a few Scots words, ye lads and lassies. As you travel, you're sure to pick up a bit more (see sidebar) and enjoy the lovely musical lilt as well. Many linguists argue that Scots is technically an ancient dialect of English, rather than a distinct language. These linguists have clearly never heard a Scot read aloud the poetry of Robert Burns, who wrote in unfiltered (and often unintelligible) Scots. (Opening line of "To a Louse": *Ha! Whaur ye gaun, ye crowlin ferlie?*) Fortunately, you're unlikely to meet anyone quite that hard to understand; most Scots speak Scottish-accented standard English, peppered with their favorite Scots phrases. If you have a hard time understanding someone, ask them to translate—you may take home some new words as souvenirs.

Scottish cuisine is down-to-earth, often with an emphasis on local produce. Both seafood and "land food" (beef and chicken) are common. One Scottish mainstay—eaten more by tourists than by

Scots these days—is the famous haggis, a rich assortment of oats and sheep organs stuffed into a chunk of sheep intestine, liberally seasoned and boiled. Usually served with "neeps and tatties" (turnips and potatoes), it's tastier than it sounds and worth trying... once.

The "Scottish Breakfast" is similar to the English version, but they add a potato scone (like a flavorless, soggy potato pancake) and occasionally haggis (which is hard enough to get down at dinnertime).

Breakfast, lunch, or dinner, the Scots love their whisky—and touring one of the country's many distilleries is a sightseeing treat. The Scots are fiercely competitive with the Irish when it comes to this peaty spirit. Scottish "whisky" is distilled twice, whereas Irish "whiskey" adds a third distillation (and an extra *e*). Grain here is roasted over peat fires, giving it a smokier flavor than its Irish cousin. Also note that what we call "scotch"—short for "scotch whisky"—is just "whisky" here. I've listed several of the most convenient and interesting distilleries to visit, but if you're a whisky connoisseur, make a point of tracking down and touring your favorite.

Another unique Scottish flavor to sample is the soft drink called Irn-Bru (pronounced "Iron Brew"). This bright-orange beverage tastes not like orange soda, but like bubblegum with a slightly bitter aftertaste. (The diet version is even more bitter.) While Irn-Bru's appeal eludes non-Scots, it's hugely popular here, even outselling Coke. Be cautious sipping it—as the label understates, "If spilt, this product may stain."

Whether toasting with beer, whisky, or Irn-Bru, enjoy meeting the Scottish people. Many travelers fall in love with the irrepressible spirit and beautiful landscape of this faraway corner of Britain.

EDINBURGH

Edinburgh is the historical and cultural capital of Scotland. Once a medieval powerhouse sitting on a lava flow, it grew into Europe's first great grid-planned modern city. The colorful hometown of Robert Louis Stevenson, Sir Walter Scott, and Robert Burns, Edinburgh is Scotland's showpiece and one of Europe's most entertaining cities. Historic, monumental, fun, and well-organized, it's a tourist's delight—especially in August, when the Edinburgh Festival takes over the town.

Promenade down the Royal Mile through Old Town. Historic buildings pack the Royal Mile between the grand castle (on the top) and the Palace of Holyroodhouse (on the bottom). Medieval skyscrapers stand shoulder to shoulder, hiding peaceful courtyards connected to High Street by narrow lanes or even tunnels. This colorful jumble is the tourist's Edinburgh.

Edinburgh (ED'n-burah) was once the most crowded city in Europe—famed for its skyscrapers and filth. The rich and poor lived atop one another. In the Age of Enlightenment, a magnificent Georgian city (today's New Town) was laid out to the north, giving Edinburgh's upper class a respectable place to promenade. Georgian Edinburgh—like the city of Bath—shines with broad boulevards, straight streets, square squares, circular circuses, and elegant mansions decked out in colonnades, pediments, and sphinxes in the proud Neoclassical style of 200 years ago.

While the Georgian city celebrated the union of Scotland and England (with streets and squares named after English kings and emblems), "devolution" is the latest trend. For the past several centuries, Scotland was ruled from London, and Parliament had not met in Edinburgh since 1707. But in a 1998 election, the Scots

Greater Edinburgh

voted to gain more autonomy and bring their Parliament home. In 1999, Edinburgh resumed its position as home to the Scottish parliament (although London still calls the strategic shots). A strikingly modern Parliament building, which opened in 2004, is one more jewel in Edinburgh's crown. Today, you'll notice many references to the "nation" of Scotland.

Planning Your Time

While the major sights can be seen in a day, on a three-week tour of Britain, I'd give Edinburgh two days and three nights.

Day 1: Tour the castle (open from 9:30). Then consider catching one of the city bus tours for a one-hour loop (departing from a block below the castle at The Hub/Tolbooth Church; you could munch a sandwich from the top deck if you're into multitasking). Back at the castle, catch the 14:15 Mercat Tours walk (1.5 hours, leaves from Mercat Cross on the Royal Mile). Spend the remainder of your day enjoying the Royal Mile's shops and museums, or touring the Palace of Holyroodhouse (at the bottom of the Mile).

Day 2: Visit the Museum of Scotland. After lunch, stroll through the Princes Street Gardens and the National Gallery of Scotland. Then tour the good ship *Britannia*.

Evenings: Options include various "haunted Edinburgh" walks, literary pub crawls, or live music in pubs. Sadly, traditional folk shows are just about extinct, surviving only in excruciatingly schmaltzy variety shows put on for tour-bus groups. Perhaps the most authentic evening out is just settling down in a pub to sample the whisky and local beers while meeting the natives...and attempting to understand them through their thick Scottish accents.

Orientation to Edinburgh

(area code: 0131)

The center of Edinburgh, a drained lake bed, holds the Princes Street Gardens park and Waverley Bridge, where you'll find the TI, Princes Mall, the train station, the bus info office (starting point for most city bus tours), the National Gallery, and a covered dance-and-music pavilion. Weather blows in and out—bring your sweater and be prepared for rain. Locals say the bad weather is one of the disadvantages of living so close to England.

You might notice the city is pretty dug up. It's all in preparation for the city's new tram system, which is scheduled to begin running in 2012.

Tourist Information

The crowded TI is as central as can be atop the Princes Mall and train station (Mon–Sat 9:00–17:00, Sun 10:00–17:00, July–Aug daily until 19:00, tel. 0845-225-5121, www.edinburgh.org). The staff is knowledgeable and eager to help, but much of their information—including their assessment of museums and even which car-rental companies "exist"—is skewed by tourism payola. The TI at the airport is more helpful.

At either TI, pick up a free map or buy the excellent £4.50 *Collins Discovering Edinburgh* map (which comes with opinionated commentary and locates almost every major shop and sight). If you're interested in late-night music, ask for the free monthly entertainment *Gig Guide*. (The best monthly entertainment listing, *The List*, sells for a few pounds at newsstands.) The free *Essential Guide to Edinburgh,* while not truly essential, lists additional sights and services (when it's in stock). The TIs also sell the mediocre Edinburgh Pass, which provides unlimited travel on Lothian buses (includes the airport) and entry to dozens of B-list sights (£26.50/1 day, £39/2 days, £51.50/3 days, doesn't include Edinburgh Castle, www.edinburgh.org/pass).

Book your room direct, using my listings (the TIs charge you a £4 booking fee, and also take a 10 percent cut, which means that B&Bs end up charging more for rooms booked this way).

Browse the racks—tucked away in the hallway at the back of

the central TI—for brochures on the various Scottish folk shows, walking tours, regional bus tours, and other touristic temptations. Computers with Internet access are beyond the brochure racks (£1/30 minutes).

Arrival in Edinburgh

By Train: Arriving by train at Waverley Station puts you in the city center and below the TI. Taxis queue almost trackside; the ramp they come and go on leads to Waverley Bridge. If there's a long line for taxis, I hike up the ramp and hail one on the street. From the station, *Way Out-1-Princes Street* signs lead up to the TI and the city bus stop (for bus directions from here to my recommended B&Bs, see below). For picnic supplies, a **Marks & Spencer Simply Food** is near platform 2.

By Bus: Both Scottish Citylink and National Express buses use the bus station (with luggage lockers) in the New Town, two blocks north of the train station on St. Andrew Square.

By Plane: Edinburgh's slingshot of an airport is located 10 miles northwest of the center. Airport flight info: tel. 0870-040-0007, www.edinburghairport.com.

Taxis between the airport and the city center are pricey (£20–25, 20 minutes to downtown or to Dalkeith Road B&Bs). Fortunately, the airport is well-connected to central Edinburgh by the convenient, frequent, cheap Lothian **Airlink bus #100** (£3.50, £6 round-trip, 6/hour, 30 minutes, buses run all day and 2/hour through the night, tel. 0131/555-6363, www.flybybus.com). The bus drops you at the center of Waverley Bridge. From here, to reach my recommended B&Bs near Dalkeith Road, you can either take a taxi (about £7), or hop on a bus (during tram construction, you may have to walk over to North Bridge, on the other side of the train station, to catch the bus). Ride bus #14, #30, #33, or #48, and get off at the first or second stop after the bus makes a right turn onto Dalkeith Road (£1.20, have coins ready—drivers don't make change, buses leave frequently, confirm specific directions with your B&B).

If you're headed *to* the airport, you can take the same Airlink bus described above. To reach the Airlink bus stop from the Dalkeith Road B&Bs, ride the bus to the end of North Bridge and hop out just after the bus turns left at the grand Balmoral Hotel; exit the bus to your right and walk a short distance down Princes Street to the next bridge, Waverley, where you'll find the Airlink bus stop. (Rather than taking a £25 taxi all the way to the airport, you can save money by taking a £7 taxi to this stop, then hopping the bus to the airport.)

By Car: If you're arriving from the north, rather than drive through downtown Edinburgh to the recommended B&Bs, circle the city on the A720 City Bypass road. Approaching Edinburgh on M9, take M8 (direction: Glasgow) and quickly get onto A720 City Bypass (direction: Edinburgh South). After four miles, you'll hit a roundabout. Ignore signs directing you into *Edinburgh North* and stay on A720 for 10 more miles to the next and last roundabout, named *Sheriffhall*. Exit the roundabout on the first left (A7 Edinburgh). From here it's four miles to the B&B neighborhood. After a while, A7 becomes Dalkeith Road. If you see a huge building with a swimming pool (or a pool-shaped construction zone, if you're here before its renovation is complete), you've gone a couple of blocks too far (avoid this by referring to the map on page 640).

If you're driving in on A68 from the south, take the A7 Edinburgh exit off the roundabout and follow the directions above.

Helpful Hints

Sunday Activities: Many Royal Mile sights close on Sunday (except during August and the Edinburgh Festival), but other major sights are open. Sunday is a good day to catch a guided walking tour along the Royal Mile or a city bus tour (buses go faster in light traffic). Arthur's Seat is lively on weekends.

Festivals: August is a crowded, popular month to visit Edinburgh because of the multiple festivals hosted here, including the official Edinburgh Festival (Aug 12–Sept 4 in 2011). Book ahead if you'll be visiting during this month, and expect to pay significantly more for your accommodations. For all the details, see page 634.

Internet Access: Get online at the central TI (£1/30 minutes, see "Tourist Information," earlier); the recommended and atmospheric **Elephant House Café** (Mon–Fri 8:00–23:00, 4 stations, 24 George IV Bridge, off top of Royal Mile); or **E-Corner Internet Café and Call Shop,** a funky little place just off the Royal Mile, next to the Smart City Hostel (£1/30 minutes, Mon–Fri 9:00–21:30, Sat–Sun 10:00–21:30, in winter daily 10:00–21:00, packed with fast terminals and digital services, 54 Blackfriars Street, tel. 0131/558-7858).

Baggage Storage: At the train station, you'll find pricey, high-security luggage storage near platform 2 (£6/24 hours, daily 7:00–23:00). It's cheaper to use the lockers at the bus station on St. Andrew Square, just a five-minute walk from the train station (£3–5 depending on size—even smallest locker is plenty big, coins only, station open daily 6:00–24:00).

Laundry: Ace Cleaning Centre launderette is located near the recommended B&Bs (Mon–Fri 8:00–20:00, Sat 9:00–17:00, Sun 10:00–16:00, self-service or drop-off; along the bus route to the city center at 13 South Clerk Street, opposite Queens

Edinburgh at a Glance

▲▲▲**Edinburgh Castle** Iconic 11th-century hilltop fort and royal residence complete with crown jewels, Romanesque chapel, memorial, and fine military museum. **Hours:** Daily April–Oct 9:30–18:00, Nov–March 9:30–17:00. See page 605.

▲▲▲**Royal Mile** Historic road—good for walking—stretching from the castle down to the palace, lined with museums, pubs, and shops. **Hours:** Always open, but best during business hours, with walking tours daily. See page 612.

▲▲▲**National Museum of Scotland** Intriguing, well-displayed artifacts from prehistoric times to the 20th century. **Hours:** Daily 10:00–17:00. See page 625.

▲▲**Gladstone's Land** Sixteenth-century Royal Mile merchant's residence. **Hours:** Daily July–Aug 10:00–18:30, April–June and Sept–Oct 10:00–17:00, closed Nov–March. See page 615.

▲▲**St. Giles' Cathedral** Preaching grounds of Calvinist John Knox, with spectacular organ, Neo-Gothic chapel, and distinctive crown spire. **Hours:** May–Sept Mon–Fri 9:00–19:00, Sat 9:00–17:00, Sun 13:00–17:00; Oct–April Mon–Sat 9:00–17:00, Sun 13:00–17:00. See page 618.

▲▲**Scottish Parliament Building** New headquarters for the recently returned Parliament. **Hours:** Mon–Fri 10:00–17:30, until 16:30 Oct–March, Sat 11:00–17:30 year-round, closed Sun. See page 623.

▲▲**Georgian New Town** Elegant 1776 subdivision spiced with trendy shops, bars, and eateries. **Hours:** Always open. See page 628.

▲▲**Georgian House** Intimate peek at upper-crust life in the late 1700s. **Hours:** Daily July–Aug 10:00–18:30, April–June and Sept–Oct 10:00–17:00, March 11:00–16:00, Nov 11:00–15:00, closed Dec–Feb. See page 629.

▲▲**National Gallery of Scotland** Choice sampling of European masters and Scotland's finest. **Hours:** Daily 10:00–17:00, Thu until 19:00. See page 629.

▲▲*Britannia* The royal yacht with a history of distinguished passengers, a 15-minute trip out of town. **Hours:** Daily July–Sept

9:30–16:30, April–June and Oct 10:00–16:00, Nov–March 10:00–15:30 (these are last entry times). See page 632.

▲**Writers' Museum at Lady Stair's House** Tribute to Scottish literary triumvirate: Robert Burns, Sir Walter Scott, and Robert Louis Stevenson. **Hours:** Mon–Sat 10:00–17:00, closed Sun except during Festival 12:00–17:00. See page 616.

▲**Mary King's Close** Underground street and houses last occupied in the 17th century, viewable by guided tour. **Hours:** April–Oct daily 10:00–21:00; Nov–March Sun–Thu 10:00–17:00, Fri–Sat 10:00–21:00. See page 621.

▲**Museum of Childhood** Five stories of historic fun. **Hours:** Mon–Sat 10:00–17:00, Sun 12:00–17:00. See page 622.

▲**John Knox House** Reputed 16th-century digs of the great reformer. **Hours:** Mon–Sat 10:00–18:00, closed Sun except in July–Aug 12:00–18:00. See page 622.

▲**Cadenhead's Whisky Shop** Sample whisky straight from the distilleries. **Hours:** Mon–Sat 10:30–17:30, closed Sun except possibly in Aug 12:30–17:30. See page 622.

▲**People's Story** Proletarian life from the 18th to 20th centuries. **Hours:** Mon–Sat 10:00–17:00, closed Sun except during Festival 12:00–17:00. See page 623.

▲**Museum of Edinburgh** Historic mementos, from the original National Covenant inscribed on animal skin to early golf balls. **Hours:** Mon–Sat 10:00–17:00, closed Sun except during Festival 12:00–17:00. See page 623.

▲**Palace of Holyroodhouse** The Queen's splendid home away from home, with lavish rooms, 12th-century abbey, and gallery with rotating exhibits. **Hours:** Daily April–Oct 9:30–18:00, Nov–March 9:30–16:30, closed during royal visits. See page 624.

▲**Sir Walter Scott Monument** Climbable tribute to the famed novelist. **Hours:** April–Sept daily 10:00–19:00; Oct–March Mon–Sat 9:00–16:00, Sun 10:00–16:00. See page 631.

Hall; tel. 0131/667-0549). For a small extra fee, they collect and drop off laundry at the neighborhood B&Bs.

Bike Rental: The laid-back crew at **Cycle Scotland** offers bike tours and happily recommends good bike routes (£15/3 hours, £20/day, £25/24 hours, daily 10:00–18:00, just off Royal Mile at 29 Blackfriars Street, tel. 0131/556-5560, www.cycle scotland.co.uk).

Car Rental: All of these places have offices both in the town center and at the airport: **Avis** (5 West Park Place, tel. 0844-544-6059, airport tel. 0844-544-6004), **Europcar** (24 East London Street, tel. 0131/557-3456, airport tel. 0131/333-2588), **Hertz** (10 Picardy Place, tel. 0870-846-0013, airport tel. 0870-846-0009), and **Budget** (will meet you at train station and take you to their office at 1 Murrayburn Road, tel. 0131/455-7314, airport tel. 0844-544-4605). Some downtown offices are closed on Sunday, but the airport locations tend to be open daily—call ahead to confirm. If you're going to rent a car, pick it up on your way out of Edinburgh—you won't need it in town.

Blue Badge Local Guides: The following guides charge similar prices and offer half-day and full-day tours. **Ken Hanley** wears his kilt as if pants didn't exist, knows all the stories, and loves sharing his passion for Edinburgh and Scotland (£90/half-day, £120/day, extra charge if he uses his car—which fits up to 6, tel. 0131/666-1944, mobile 0771-034-2044, www.small-world-tours.co.uk, k.hanley@blueyonder.co.uk). Other good guides include **Jean Blair** (£130/day, £310/day with car, tel. 0150/682-5930, mobile 0798-957-0287, www.travelthrough scotland.com, jean@travelthroughscotland.com), **Sergio La Spina** (an Argentinean who adopted Edinburgh as his hometown more than 20 years ago, £130/day, tel. 0131/664-1731, mobile 0797-330-6579, sergiolaspina@aol.com), and **Anne Doig** (£120/day, mobile 0777-590-1792, annedoig2@hotmail.com).

Getting Around Edinburgh

Many of Edinburgh's sights are within walking distance of one another, but buses come in handy. Two companies handle the city routes: Lothian (which dominates) and First. Lothian sells a day pass valid only on their buses (£3, buy from driver). Buses run from about 6:00 to 23:00 (£1.20/ride, buy tickets on bus, Lothian Buses transit office at Old Town end of Waverley Bridge has schedules and route maps, tel. 0131/555-6363, www.lothianbuses.com). Tell the driver where you're going, have change handy (buses require exact change—you lose any extra you put in), take your ticket as you board, and ping the bell as you near your stop. Double-deckers come with fine views upstairs.

The 1,300 **taxis** cruising Edinburgh's streets are easy to flag down (a ride between downtown and the B&B neighborhood costs about £7). They can turn on a dime, so hail them in either direction.

Tours in Edinburgh

Royal Mile Walking Tours—**Edinburgh Tour Guides** offers your best basic historical walk (without all the ghosts and goblins). The staff of committed guides heads out as long as they have at least two people. Their Royal Mile tour is a gentle two-hour downhill stroll from the castle to the palace (£12; daily at 9:30, 14:00, and 19:00; meet outside Gladstone's Land, near the top of the Royal Mile—see map on page 614, call to confirm and reserve, tel. 0131/443-3200, mobile 0789/994-8585, www.edinburghtourguides.com).

Mercat Tours offers 1.5-hour guided walks of the Mile, which are more entertaining than intellectual (£9, daily at 14:15, leaves from Mercat Cross on the Royal Mile, tel. 0131/225-5445, www.mercattours.com). The guides, who enjoy making a short story long, ignore the big sights and take you behind the scenes with piles of barely historical gossip, bully-pulpit Scottish pride, and fun but forgettable trivia. These tours can move quickly, scaling the steep hills and steps of Edinburgh—wear good shoes. They also offer several ghost tours, as well as one focused on 18th-century underground vaults on the southern slope of the Royal Mile.

The **Voluntary Guides Association** offers free two-hour walks, but only during the Edinburgh Festival. You don't need a reservation, but it's a good idea to call the TI or drop by there to double-check details, such as departure point and time (daily at about 10:00 and 14:00, generally depart from Cannonball House at Castle Esplanade, www.edinburghfestivalguides.org).

The **Real Mary King's Close** runs Auld Town walking tours by a guide in the character of a 17th-century local (£7, £2 discount with recommended underground tour of Mary King's Close—see page 621, 1 hour; generally runs daily at 11:30, 13:00, and 15:00; leaves from Mary King's Close, across from St. Giles' Church; tel. 0845-070-6244, www.realmarykingsclose.com).

Evening **ghost walks** and **pub tours** are described later, under "Nightlife in Edinburgh" on page 635.

Edinburgh Bus Tours—Four different one-hour hop-on, hop-off bus tours circle the town center, stopping at the major sights. You can hop on and off at any stop all day with one ticket (pickups about every 10–15 minutes). All tours are narrated. Two of the tours have live guides: **Mac Tours' City Tour** (focuses on

Edinburgh

¼ MILE
400 METERS

VIEW

WATER OF LEITH

MORAY PLACE

QUEEN ST. GARDENS

QUEEN

NEW

GEORGIAN HOUSE →

HILL

ST. ANDREW'S

SEE DETAIL MAP

CHARLOTTE SQ.

GEORGE ST.

ST. ANDREW SQ.

ROSE

FREDERICK ST.

HANOVER ST.

❷

ST. DAVID ST.

CASTLE ST.

TOWN

SCOTT MON.

SHANDWICK PLACE

PRINCES STREET

LOTHIAN RD.

PRINCES ST. GARDENS

THE MOUND

❻

TO HAYMARKET STN., A-8, AIRPORT & GLASGOW

NATIONAL GALLERY

WAVERLEY BRIDGE

EDINBURGH → CASTLE

ESPLANADE ↗

ROYAL MILE

MORRISON

BREAD

GRASSMARKET

GEORGE IV BRIDGE

ST. GILES

COW-

FOUNTAINBRIDGE

OLD

TOWN

❶ Edinburgh City Centre Holiday Inn Express
❷ Travelodge Rose Street
❸ Travelodge Waterloo Place
❹ Edinburgh Central Youth Hostel
❺ Bus to Dalkeith Rd. B&Bs
❻ Half-Price Hut (Fringe Tickets)

LAURISTON PL.

NATIONAL MUSEUM OF SCOTLAND

Old Town, most comprehensive, live Mon–Fri with "vintage buses") and **Edinburgh Tour** (focuses on the wider city, more panoramic, always live). Avoid the **City Sightseeing Tours,** which have a recorded narration (better for non-English speakers). The tours all have virtually the same route, cost, and frequency, except the **Majestic Tour,** whose regular route is longer and includes a stop at the *Britannia* and the Royal Botanic Garden (£12/tour, £15 for all four tours, tick-

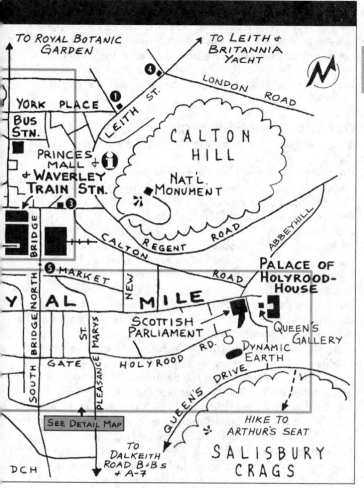

ets give small discounts on most sights along the route, valid 24 hours, buy on bus, tel. 0131/220-0770, www.edinburghtour.com). Buses run daily year-round; April–Oct in peak season, they leave Waverley Bridge every day between around 9:30 and 19:00 (hours shrink off-season). On sunny days they go topless (the buses), but come with increased traffic noise and exhaust fumes. All of these companies are actually run by Lothian Buses (which has to splinter its offerings this way because of local antimonopoly laws).

Busy sightseers might want to get the **Royal Edinburgh Ticket** (£40), which covers two days of unlimited travel on Lothian city buses—including all four tour buses, as well as admission to Edinburgh Castle (£14), the Palace of Holyroodhouse (£10.25), and the *Britannia* (£10.50). If you plan to visit all these sights and to use a tour bus both days, the ticket will save you a few pounds (and, in the summer, help you bypass any lines). You can buy these tickets online, from the TI, or from the staff at the tour-bus pick-up point on Waverley Bridge. If your main interest is seeing the Britannia, you'll save money by taking a regular bus instead (see page 632).

Day Trips from Edinburgh

Many companies run a variety of day trips to regional sights. Study the brochures at the TI's rack.

Highlands Tours—By far the most popular tour is the all-day Highlands trip. The standard Highlands tour gives those with limited time a chance to experience the wonders of Scotland's wild and legend-soaked Highlands in a single long day (about £35–45, roughly 8:30–20:30). You'll generally see the vast and brutal Rannoch Moor; Glencoe, still evocative with memories of the clan massacre; views of Britain's highest mountain, Ben Nevis; Fort Augustus on Loch Ness (some tours have a 1.5-hour stop here with an optional £9 boat ride); and a 45-minute tea or pub break in the fine town of Pitlochry. You learn about the Loch Ness monster, and a bit about Edinburgh to boot as you drive in and out. Various competing companies run these tours (each offering a slightly different combination of sights), including **Timberbush Highland Tours** (£37, 7- to 36-seat air-con buses, reliable, depart from entrance to Edinburgh Castle, tel. 0131/226-6066, www.timberbushtours.com); **Gray Line** (£39, tel. 0131/555-5558, www.graylinescotland.com); **Rabbie's Trail Burners** (£39-45, maximum 16 per tour, guaranteed departures, depart from their office at 207 High Street, tel. 0131/226-3133, www.rabbies.com); and **Heart of Scotland Tours** (£38, £3 Rick Steves discount on all their tours—mention when booking, departures daily at 8:00, leaves from opposite Travelodge on Waterloo Place near Waverley Station, tel. 01828/627-799, www.heartofscotlandtours.co.uk, run by Nick Roche). As Heart of Scotland is a small company, they may need to cancel if the requisite six people don't sign up. Be sure to leave a contact number so you can be notified. A final decision is made by 18:00 the night before.

Haggis Adventures runs cheap and youthful tours on 16- to 39-seat buses with a very Scottish driver/guide. Their day trips (£28–42) include a distillery visit and the northern Highlands, or Loch Lomond and the southern Highlands. Their overnight trips are designed for young backpackers, but they welcome travelers of any age who want a quick look at the countryside and are up for hosteling (2- to 10-day trips, office hours: Mon–Sat 9:00–18:00 in summer, until 17:00 in winter; Sun 9:00–12:00, often closed Sun

Edinburgh Castle

PRINCES ST. GARDENS

50 YARDS
50 METERS

CLIFFS

MIDDLE WARD

SHOP

ESPLANADE

CLIFFS

GARDENS

WALLS

CROWN SQUARE

START
ENTRY GATE

TO ROYAL MILE

WC

DITCH

DITCH

D.C.H

➡ ROUTE FROM ENTRY GATE TO CROWN SQUARE

MAIN BUILDINGS

OTHER BUILDINGS

VIEW

STAIRS

Tour
1. Crown Jewels
2. Royal Palace
3. Scottish National War Memorial
4. St. Margaret's Chapel
5. National War Museum Scotland

Other
6. Ticket Booth
7. Red Coat Café & Jacobite Room
8. Queen Anne Café
9. One O' Clock Gun
10. Dog Cemetery

in winter; 60 High Street, at Blackfriars Street, tel. 0131/557-9393, www.haggisadventures.com).

Sights in Edinburgh

▲▲▲Edinburgh Castle

The fortified birthplace of the city 1,300 years ago, this imposing symbol of Edinburgh sits proudly on a rock high above you.

While the castle has been both a fort and a royal residence since the 11th century, most of the buildings today are from its more recent use as a military garrison. This fascinating and multifaceted sight deserves several hours of your time.

Cost and Hours: £14, daily April–Oct 9:30–18:00, Nov–March 9:30–17:00, last entry 45 minutes before closing, National War Museum Scotland closes 15 minutes before rest of castle, tel. 0131/225-9846, www.edinburghcastle.gov.uk.

Avoiding Lines: The least crowded time is usually between 10:00 and 11:00. To avoid ticket lines (worst in August), book online and pick up your ticket at the machines just inside the entrance.

Tours: Twenty-minute guided introductory tours are free with admission (2–4/hour, depart from entry gate, see clock for next departure; fewer tours off-season). The excellent audioguide provides a good supplement to the live guided tour, offering four hours of quick-dial digital descriptions of the sights, including the National War Museum Scotland (£3.50, slightly cheaper if purchased with entry ticket, pay at the ticket booth and pick it up at the entry gate).

Services: The clean WC at the entry routinely wins "British Loo of the Year" awards. For lunch, you have two choices. **The Red Coat Café and Jacobite Room**—located within Edinburgh Castle—is a big, bright, efficient cafeteria with great views (£6 quick, healthy meals). Punctuate the two parts of your castle visit (the castle itself and the impressive National War Museum Scotland) with a smart break here. The **Queen Anne Café,** in a building at the top of the hill, right across from the crown jewels, serves sit-down meals in its small, tight space (last orders 30 minutes before castle complex closes).

Getting There: You can walk to the castle, catch a bus (which drops you off a short uphill walk away), or take a taxi (taxis let you off right at the bottom of the esplanade, in front of the gate).

● Self-Guided Tour: Start at the entry gate, where you can pick up your audioguide and enjoy the droll 20-minute introductory tour with a live guide. (It'd be a shame to miss this included and charmingly entertaining intro tour.)

The castle has five essential stops: the crown jewels, Royal Palace, Scottish National War Memorial, St. Margaret's Chapel (with a city view), and the excellent National War Museum Scotland. The first four are at the highest and most secure point—on or near the castle square, where your introductory guided tour ends (and the sights described below begin). The separate National War Museum Scotland is worth a serious look—allow at least a half-hour (50 yards below the cafeteria and big shop).

William Wallace
(c. 1270–1305)

In 1286, Scotland's king died without an heir, plunging the prosperous country into a generation of chaos. As Scottish nobles bickered over naming a successor, the English King Edward I—nicknamed "Longshanks" because of his height—invaded and assumed power (1296). He placed a figurehead on the throne, forced Scottish nobles to sign a pledge of allegiance to England (the "Ragman's Roll"), moved the British parliament north to York, and carried off the highly symbolic 336-pound Stone of Scone to London, where it would remain for the next seven centuries.

A year later, the Scots rose up against Edward, led by William Wallace (nicknamed "Braveheart"). A mix of history and legend portrays Wallace as the son of a poor-but-knightly family that refused to sign the Ragman's Roll. Exceptionally tall and strong, he learned Latin and French from two uncles, who were priests. In his teenage years, his father and older brother were killed by the English. Later, he killed an English sheriff to avenge the death of his wife, Marion. Wallace's rage inspired his fellow Scots to revolt.

In the summer of 1297, Wallace and his guerrillas scored a series of stunning victories over the English. On September 11, a large, well-equipped English army of 10,000 soldiers and 300 horsemen began crossing Stirling Bridge. Half of the army had made it across when Wallace's men attacked. In the chaos, the bridge collapsed, splitting the English ranks in two, and the ragtag Scots drove the confused English into the river. The Battle of Stirling Bridge was a rout, and Wallace was knighted and appointed Guardian of Scotland.

All through the winter, King Edward's men chased Wallace, continually frustrated by the Scots' hit-and-run tactics. Finally, at the Battle of Falkirk (1298), they drew Wallace's men out onto the open battlefield. The English with their horses and archers easily destroyed the spear-carrying Scots. Wallace resigned in disgrace and went on the lam, while his successors negotiated truces with the English, finally surrendering unconditionally in 1304. Wallace alone held out.

In 1305, the English tracked him down and took him to London, where he was convicted of treason and mocked with a crown of oak leaves as the "King of Scotland." On August 23, they stripped him naked and dragged him to the execution site. There he was strangled to near death, castrated, and dismembered. His head was stuck on a stick atop London Bridge, while his body parts were sent on tour around the realm to spook would-be rebels. But Wallace's martyrdom only served to inspire his countrymen, and the torch of independence was picked up by Robert the Bruce (see sidebar on page 610).

EDINBURGH

❶ **Crown Jewels:** There are two ways to get to the jewels. You can go in directly from the top palace courtyard, Crown Square, but there's often a line. To avoid the line, head to the left as you're facing the building and find the entrance near the WCs. This route takes you through the "Honors of Scotland" exhibition—an interesting, if Disney-esque, series of displays (which often moves at a very slow shuffle) telling the story of the crown jewels and how they survived the harrowing centuries.

Scotland's **crown jewels,** though not as impressive as England's, are older and treasured by the locals. Though Oliver Cromwell destroyed England's jewels, the Scots managed to hide theirs. Longtime symbols of Scottish nationalism, they were made in Edinburgh—in 1540 for a 1543 coronation—out of Scottish diamonds, gems, and gold...some say the personal gold of King Robert the Bruce. They were last used to crown Charles II in 1651. When the Act of Union was forced upon the Scots in 1707—dissolving Scotland's parliament into England's to create the United Kingdom—part of the deal was that the Scots could keep their jewels locked up in Edinburgh. The jewels remained hidden for more than 100 years. In 1818, Sir Walter Scott and a royal commission rediscovered them intact. In 1999, for the first time in nearly three centuries, the crown of Scotland was brought from the castle for the opening of the Scottish parliament (see photos on the wall where the "Honors of Scotland" exhibit meets the crown jewels room; a smiling Queen Elizabeth II presides over the historic occasion).

The **Stone of Scone** (a.k.a. the "Stone of Destiny") sits plain and strong next to the jewels. This big gray chunk of rock is the coronation stone of Scotland's ancient kings (ninth century). Swiped by the English, it sat under the coronation chair at Westminster Abbey from 1296 until 1996. Queen Elizabeth finally agreed to let the stone go home, on one condition: that it be returned to Westminster Abbey in London for all future coronations. With major fanfare, Scotland's treasured Stone of Scone returned to Edinburgh on Saint Andrew's Day, November 30, 1996. Talk to the guard for more details.

❷ **The Royal Palace:** Scottish royalty lived here only when safety or protocol required it (they preferred the Palace of Holyroodhouse at the bottom of the Royal Mile). The Royal Palace, facing the castle square under the flagpole, has two historic yet unimpressive rooms (through door marked "1566") and the Great Hall (separate entrance from opposite side of square; see below). Enter the **Mary, Queen of Scots room,** where in 1566 the queen gave birth to James VI of Scotland, who later became King James I of England. The Presence Chamber leads into **Laich Hall** (Lower Hall), the dining room of the royal family.

The **Great Hall** was the castle's ceremonial meeting place in

British, Scottish, and English

Scotland and England have been tied together for 300 years, since the Act of Union in 1707. For a century and a half afterward, Scottish nationalists rioted for independence in Edinburgh's streets and led rebellions in the Highlands. In this controversial union, history is clearly seen through two very different filters.

If you tour a British-oriented sight, such as the National War Museum Scotland, you'll find things told in a "happy union" way, which ignores the long history of Scottish resistance—from the ancient Picts through the time of Robert the Bruce. The official line: In 1706–1707, it was clear to England and some of Scotland (especially landowners from the Lowlands) that it was in their mutual interest to dissolve the Scottish government and fold it into Britain, to be ruled from London.

But talk to a cabbie or your B&B host, and you may get a different spin. In a clever move by England to deflate the military power of its little sister, Scottish Highlanders were often sent to fight and die for Britain in disproportionately higher numbers than their English counterparts. Poignant propaganda posters in the National War Museum Scotland show a happy lad with the message, "Hey, look! Willie's off to Singapore with the Queen's Own Highlanders."

Scottish independence is still a hot-button issue today. In 2007, the Scottish National Party (SNP) won a major election, and now has the largest majority in the fledgling Scottish parliament. Alex Salmond, SNP leader and the First Minister of Scotland, is widely expected to push for Scotland to be recognized as an independent nation within the EU. (English leaders are obviously not in favor of breaking up the "united kingdom," though there's a like-minded independence movement in Wales, as well.)

The deep-seated rift shows itself in sports, too. While the English may refer to a British team in international competition as "English," the Scots are careful to call it "British." If a Scottish athlete does well, the English call him "British." If he screws up...he's a clumsy Scot.

the 16th and 17th centuries. In later times, it was a barracks and a hospital. Although most of what you see is Victorian, two medieval elements survive: the fine hammer-beam roof and the big iron-barred peephole (above fireplace on right). This allowed the king to spy on his subjects while they partied.

❸ **The Scottish National War Memorial:** This commemorates the 149,000 Scottish soldiers lost in World War I, the 58,000 who died in World War II, and the nearly 800 (and counting) lost in British battles since. This is a somber spot (put away your

Robert the Bruce
(1274–1329)

William Wallace's story (see sidebar on page 607) paints the Scottish fight for independence in black-and-white terms—the oppressive English versus the plucky Scots. But Scotland had to overcome its own divisiveness, and no one was more divided than Robert the Bruce. As Earl of Carrick, he was born with blood ties to England and a long-standing family claim to the Scottish throne.

When England's King Edward I ("Longshanks") conquered Scotland in 1296, the Bruce family welcomed it, hoping Edward would defeat their rivals and put Bruce's father on the throne. They dutifully signed the "Ragman's Roll" of allegiance...and then Edward chose someone else as king.

Twentysomething Robert the Bruce (the "the" comes from his original family name of "de Bruce") then joined William Wallace's revolt against the English. Legend has it that it was he who knighted Wallace after the victory at Stirling Bridge. When Wallace fell from favor, Bruce became co-Guardian of Scotland (caretaker ruler in the absence of a king) and continued fighting the English. But when Edward's armies again got the upper hand in 1302, Robert—along with Scotland's other nobles—diplomatically surrendered and again pledged loyalty.

In 1306, Robert the Bruce murdered his chief rival and boldly claimed to be King of Scotland. Few nobles supported him. Edward crushed the revolt and kidnapped Bruce's wife, the Church excommunicated him, and Bruce went into hiding on a distant North Sea island. He was now the king of nothing. Legend says he gained inspiration by watching a spider patiently build its web.

The following year, Bruce returned to Scotland and weaved alliances with both nobles and the Church, slowly gaining acceptance as Scotland's king by a populace chafing under English rule. On June 24, 1314, he decisively defeated the English (now led by Edward's weak son, Edward II) at the Battle of Bannockburn. After a generation of turmoil (1286–1314), England was finally driven from Scotland, and the country was united under Robert I, King of Scotland.

As king, Robert the Bruce's priority was to stabilize the monarchy and establish clear lines of succession. His descendants would rule Scotland for the next 400 years, and even today, Bruce blood runs through the veins of Queen Elizabeth II, Prince Charles, and princes William and Harry.

camera, phone, etc.). Paid for by public donations, each bay is dedicated to a particular Scottish regiment. The main shrine, featuring a green Italian-marble memorial that contains the original WWI rolls of honor, sits—almost as if it were sacred—on an exposed chunk of the castle rock. Above you, the archangel Michael is busy slaying a dragon. The bronze frieze accurately shows the attire of various wings of Scotland's military. The stained glass starts with Cain and Abel on the left, and finishes with a celebration of peace on the right. To appreciate how important this place is, consider that Scottish soldiers died at twice the rate of other British soldiers in World War I.

❹ **St. Margaret's Chapel:** The oldest building in Edinburgh is dedicated to Queen Margaret, who died here in 1093 and was sainted in 1250. Built in 1130 in the Romanesque style of the Norman invaders, it's wonderfully simple, with classic Norman zigzags decorating the round arch that separates the tiny nave from the sacristy. It was used as a powder magazine for 400 years; very little survives. You'll see a facsimile of St. Margaret's 11th-century gospel book and small windows featuring St. Margaret, St. Columba (who brought Christianity to Scotland via Iona), and William Wallace (the brave-hearted defender of Scotland). The place is popular for weddings—and, as it seats only 20, it's particularly popular with brides' fathers.

Mons Meg, in front of the church, is a huge and once-upon-a-time frightening 15th-century siege cannon that fired 330-pound stones nearly two miles. It was a gift from the Belgians, who shared a common enemy with the Scots—England—and were eager to arm Scotland.

Belly up to the banister (outside the chapel, below the cannon) to enjoy the grand view. Beneath you are the guns—which fire the one o'clock salute—and a sweet little line of doggie tombstones, marking the soldiers' pet cemetery. Beyond stretches the Georgian New Town (read the informative plaque).

Crowds gather for the 13:00 gun blast, a tradition that gives ships in the bay something to set their navigational devices by. (The frugal Scots don't fire it at high noon, as that would cost 11 extra rounds a day.)

❺ **The National War Museum Scotland:** This museum is a pleasant surprise, thoughtfully covering four centuries of Scottish military history. Instead of the usual musty, dusty displays of endless armor, this museum has an interesting mix of short films, uniforms, weapons, medals, mementos, and eloquent excerpts from soldiers' letters. Just when you thought your castle visit was about over, you'll likely find yourself lingering at this stop, which rivals any military museum you'll see in Europe (closes 15 minutes before rest of castle complex).

Here you'll learn the story of how the fierce and courageous Scottish warrior changed from being a symbol of resistance against Britain to being a champion of that same empire. Along the way, these military men received many decorations for valor and did more than their share of dying in battle. But even when fighting for—rather than against—England, Scottish regiments still promoted their romantic, kilted-warrior image.

Queen Victoria fueled this ideal throughout the 19th century. (She was infatuated with the Scottish Highlands and the culture's untamed, rustic mystique.) Highland soldiers, especially officers, went to great personal expense to sport all their elaborate regalia, and the kilted men fought best to the tune of their beloved bagpipes. For centuries the stirring drone of bagpipes accompanied Highland soldiers into battle—inspiring them, raising their spirits, and announcing to the enemy that they were about to meet a fierce and mighty foe.

This museum shows the human side of war, and the cleverness of government-sponsored ad campaigns that kept the lads enlisting. Two centuries of recruiting posters make the same pitch that still works today: a hefty signing bonus, steady pay, and job security with the promise of a manly and adventurous life—all spiked with a mix of pride and patriotism.

Leaving the Castle: As you exit, turn around and look back at the gate. There stand King Robert the Bruce (on the left, 1274–1329) and Sir William Wallace (Braveheart—on the right, 1270–1305). Wallace—now well-known to Americans, thanks to Mel Gibson—fought long and hard against English domination before being executed in London. Bruce beat the English at Bannockburn in 1314. Bruce and Wallace still defend the spirit of Scotland. The Latin inscription above the gate between them reads, more or less, "What you do to us...we will do to you."

▲▲▲Royal Mile

The Royal Mile is one of Europe's most interesting historic walks. Consisting of a series of four different streets—Castlehill, Lawnmarket, High Street, and Canongate (each with its own set of street numbers)—the Royal Mile is actually 200 yards longer than a mile. And every inch is packed with shops, cafés, and lanes leading to tiny squares.

Start at the castle at the top and amble down to the palace. These sights are listed in walking order. Entertaining guided walks bring the legends and lore of the

Royal Mile alive (described earlier, under "Tours in Edinburgh").

As you walk, remember that originally there were two settlements here, divided by a wall: Edinburgh lined the ridge from the castle at the top. The lower end, Canongate, was outside the wall until 1856. By poking down the many side alleys, you'll find a few surviving rough edges of an Old Town well on its way to becoming a touristic mall. Be glad you're here now; in a few years it'll be all tartans and shortbread, with tourists slaloming through the postcard racks on bagpipe skateboards.

Royal Mile Terminology: A "close" is a tiny alley between two buildings (originally with a door that closed it at night). A close usually leads to a "court," or courtyard. A "land" is a tenement block of apartments. A "pend" is an arched gateway. A "wynd" is a narrow, winding lane. And "gate" is from an old Scandinavian word for street.

Castle Esplanade—At the top of the Royal Mile, the big parking lot leading up to the castle was created as a military parade ground in 1816. It's often cluttered with bleachers for the Military Tattoo—a spectacular massing of the bands, filling the square nightly for most of August. At the bottom, on the left (where the square hits the road), a plaque above the tiny witches' fountain memorializes 300 women who were accused of witchcraft and burned here. Scotland burned more witches per capita than any other country—17,000 between 1479 and 1722. The plaque shows two witches: one good and one bad.

Walking downhill, you'll pass a touristy "Weaving Mill and Exhibition" that was once the Old Town's reservoir (you'll see the wellheads it served all along this walk). At Ramsey Lane, the street just before the Camera Obscura, turn left and walk one block. At the corner, enjoy a commanding **Edinburgh view:** Nelson's column stands atop Calton Hill with a Greek temple folly from 1822 (they ran out of money to finish this memorial to the British victory over France in the Napoleonic era). The big clock tower marks the Balmoral Hotel—built as a terminal hotel above Waverley Station in 1903. The lacy Neo-Gothic Sir Walter Scott Memorial is to the left. Below, two Neoclassical buildings—the National Gallery and Royal Scottish Academy—stand on The Mound.

Now head back out to the Mile.

Camera Obscura—A big deal when it was built in 1853, this observatory topped with a mirror reflected images onto a disc before the wide eyes of people who had never seen a photograph or a captured image. Today, you can climb 100 steps for an entertaining 20-minute demonstration (3/hour). At the top, enjoy the best view anywhere of the Royal Mile. Then work your way down through five floors of illusions, holograms, and early photos. This is a big hit with kids, but sadly overpriced (£9.25, daily July–Aug

Edinburgh's Royal Mile

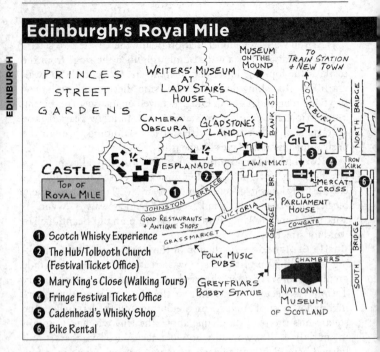

PRINCES STREET GARDENS

MUSEUM ON THE MOUND

TO TRAIN STATION & NEW TOWN

WRITERS' MUSEUM AT LADY STAIR'S HOUSE

CAMERA OBSCURA

GLADSTONE'S LAND

BANK ST.

COCKBURN ST.

NORTH BRIDGE

ST. GILES

CASTLE

TOP OF ROYAL MILE

ESPLANADE

LAWN MKT.

TRON KIRK

MERCAT CROSS

JOHNSTON TERRACE

VICTORIA

GEORGE IV BR.

OLD PARLIAMENT HOUSE

SOUTH BRIDGE

Good Restaurants + Antique Shops

GRASSMARKET

COWGATE

CHAMBERS

FOLK MUSIC PUBS

GREYFRIARS BOBBY STATUE

NATIONAL MUSEUM OF SCOTLAND

1 Scotch Whisky Experience
2 The Hub/Tolbooth Church (Festival Ticket Office)
3 Mary King's Close (Walking Tours)
4 Fringe Festival Ticket Office
5 Cadenhead's Whisky Shop
6 Bike Rental

9:30–19:30, April–June and Sept–Oct 9:30–18:00, Nov–March 10:00–17:00, last demonstration one hour before closing, tel. 0131/226-3709, www.camera-obscura.co.uk).

Scotch Whisky Experience (a.k.a. "Malt Disney")—This gimmicky ambush is designed only to distill £11.50 out of your pocket. You kick things off with a little whisky-barrel train-car ride that goes to great lengths to make whisky production seem thrilling (things get pretty psychedelic when you hit the yeast stage). A presentation on whisky in Scotland includes sampling a wee dram, and the chance to stand amid the world's largest Scotch whisky collection (almost 3,500 bottles). At the end, you'll find yourself in the bar, which is worth a quick look for its wall of unusually shaped whisky bottles. If you're visiting Oban, Pitlochry, or the Isle of Skye, you'll find cheaper, less hokey distillery tours there. People do seem to enjoy this place, but that might have something to do with the sample (daily 10:00–18:30, last tour at 17:00, tel. 0131/220-0441, www.scotchwhiskyexperience.co.uk). Serious connoisseurs of the Scottish firewater will want to pop into Cadenhead's Whisky Shop at the bottom of the Royal Mile (see page 622).

The Hub (Tolbooth Church)—This Neo-Gothic church (1844), with the tallest spire in the city, is now The Hub, Edinburgh's Festival Ticket and Information Centre (for ticket information,

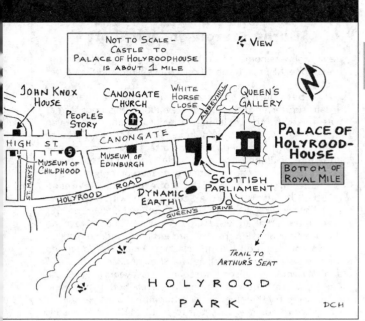

NOT TO SCALE –
CASTLE TO
PALACE OF HOLYROODHOUSE
IS ABOUT 1 MILE

VIEW

JOHN KNOX HOUSE

CANONGATE CHURCH

WHITE HORSE CLOSE

ABBEYHILL

QUEEN'S GALLERY

PEOPLE'S STORY

HIGH ST.

CANONGATE

PALACE OF HOLYROOD-HOUSE

BOTTOM OF ROYAL MILE

ST MARY'S

MUSEUM OF CHILDHOOD

MUSEUM OF EDINBURGH

HOLYROOD ROAD

DYNAMIC EARTH

SCOTTISH PARLIAMENT

QUEEN'S DRIVE

TRAIL TO ARTHUR'S SEAT

HOLYROOD PARK

DCH

see page 634). It also houses a handy café (£5–8 lunches).

▲▲**Gladstone's Land**—This is a typical 16th- to 17th-century merchant's house. "Land" means tenement, and these multistory buildings—in which merchants ran their shops on the ground floor and lived upstairs—were typical of the time. (For an interesting comparison of life in the Old Town versus the New Town, also visit the Georgian House—described later.) Gladstone's Land comes complete with an almost-lived-in, furnished interior and guides in each room who love to talk. Keep this place in mind as you stroll the rest of the Mile, imagining other houses as if they still looked like this

on the inside (£5.50, daily July–Aug 10:00–18:30, April–June and Sept–Oct 10:00–17:00, last entry 30 minutes before closing, closed Nov–March, no photos allowed, tel. 0844-493-2100, www.nts.org .uk/Property/25).

For a good Royal Mile photo, climb the curved stairway outside the museum to the left of the entrance (or to the right as you're leaving). Notice the snoozing pig outside the front door. Just

Scotland's Literary Greats: Burns, Stevenson, and Scott

Edinburgh was home to Scotland's three greatest literary figures: Robert Burns, Robert Louis Stevenson, and Sir Walter Scott.

Robert Burns (1759–1796) was Scotland's bard. An ardent supporter of the French Revolution, this poor farmer was tuned into the social inequities of the late 1700s. Even though Robby, as he's lovingly called even today, dared to speak up for the common man and attack social rank, he was a favorite of Edinburgh's high society, who'd gather in fine homes to hear the national poet recite his works.

One hundred years later, **Robert Louis Stevenson** (1850–1894) also stirred the Scottish soul with his pen. An avid traveler who always packed his notepad, Stevenson created settings that are vivid and filled with wonder. Traveling through Scotland, Europe, and around the world, he distilled his adventures into Romantic classics, including *Kidnapped* and *Treasure Island* (as well as *The Strange Case of Dr. Jekyll and Mr. Hyde*). Stevenson, who spent his last years in the South Pacific, wrote, "Youth is the time to travel—both in mind and in body—to try the manners of different nations." He said, "I travel not to go anywhere...but to simply go." Travel was his inspiration and his success.

Sir Walter Scott (1771–1832) wrote the *Waverley* novels, including *Ivanhoe* and *Rob Roy*. He's considered the father of the Romantic historical novel. Through his writing, he generated a worldwide interest in Scotland, and re-awakened his fellow countrymen's pride in their inheritance. An avid patriot, he wrote, "Every Scottish man has a pedigree. It is a national prerogative, as unalienable as his pride and his poverty." Scott is so revered in Edinburgh that his towering Neo-Gothic monument dominates the city center. With his favorite hound by his side, Sir Walter Scott overlooks the city that he inspired, and that inspired him.

The best way to learn about and experience these literary greats is to visit the Writers' Museum at Lady Stair's House (see below) and to take Edinburgh's Literary Pub Tour (see page 635).

like every house has a vacuum cleaner today, in the good old days a snorting rubbish collector was a standard feature of any well-equipped house.

▲**Writers' Museum at Lady Stair's House**—This aristocrat's house, built in 1622, is filled with well-described manuscripts and knickknacks of Scotland's three greatest literary figures: Robert Burns, Sir Walter Scott, and Robert Louis Stevenson. Edinburgh's high society would gather in homes like this in the 1780s to hear the great poet Robby Burns read his work. Burns' work is meant to be read aloud rather than to oneself. In the Burns room, you can hear his poetry—worth a few minutes for anyone, and essential for fans (free, Mon–Sat 10:00–17:00, closed Sun except during Festival 12:00–17:00, no photos, tel. 0131/529-4901).

Wander around the courtyard here. Edinburgh was a wonder in the 17th and 18th centuries. Tourists came here to see its skyscrapers, which towered 10 stories and higher. No city in Europe was as densely populated—or polluted—as "Auld Reekie."

Deacon Brodie's Tavern—Read the "Doctor Jekyll and Mister Hyde" story of this pub's notorious namesake on the wall facing

DEACON BRODIES

Bank Street. Then, to see his spooky split personality, check out both sides of the hanging signpost.

Deacon Brodie's Tavern lies at the intersection of the Royal Mile and George IV Bridge. At this point, you may want to consider several detours. If you head down the street to your right, you'll reach some recommended eateries (The Elephant House and The Outsider), as well as the excellent National Museum of Scotland, the famous Greyfriars Bobby statue, and

the photogenic Victoria Street, which leads to the fun pub-lined Grassmarket square (all described later in this chapter). To your left, down Bank Street, is the Museum on the Mound (free exhibit on banking history, described later). All are a five-minute walk from here.

Heart of Midlothian—Near the street in front of the cathedral, a heart-shaped outline in the brickwork marks the spot of a gallows and the entrance to a prison (now long gone). Traditionally, locals stand on the rim of the heart and spit into it. Hitting the middle brings good luck. Go ahead...do as the locals do.

Across the street is a seated green statue of hometown boy **David Hume** (1711–1776)—one of the most influential thinkers not only of the Scottish Enlightenment, but in all of Western philosophy. (Fun fact: Born David *Home*, he changed the spelling of his name after getting tired of hearing the English say it without the correct Scottish pronunciation.)

Look around to understand Royal Mile plumbing. About 65 feet uphill is a **wellhead** (the square stone with a pyramid cap). This was the neighborhood well, served by the reservoir up at the castle before buildings had plumbing. Imagine long lines of people in need of water standing here, until buildings were finally retrofitted with water pipes—the ones you see running outside of buildings.

EDINBURGH

▲▲St. Giles' Cathedral—This is Scotland's most important church. Its ornate spire—the Scottish crown steeple from 1495—is a proud part of Edinburgh's skyline. As the church functions as a kind of Westminster Abbey of Scotland, the interior is fascinating.

Cost and Hours: Free but donations encouraged, £2 to take photos; May–Sept Mon–Fri 9:00–19:00, Sat 9:00–17:00, Sun 13:00–17:00; Oct–April Mon–Sat 9:00–17:00, Sun 13:00–17:00; tel. 0131/225-9442, www.stgilescathedral.org.uk.

Concerts: St. Giles' busy concert schedule includes organ recitals and visiting choirs (frequent free events at 12:15, £8–10 concerts often Wed at 20:00 and Sun at 18:00, buy tickets at door or in gift shop, see schedule or ask for *Music at St. Giles'* pamphlet in gift shop).

◑ Self-Guided Tour: Today's facade is 19th-century Neo-Gothic, but most of what you'll see inside is from the 14th and

15th centuries. You'll also find cathedral guides trolling around, hoping you'll engage them in conversation. You'll be glad you did.

Just inside the entrance, turn around to see the modern stained-glass **Robert Burns window,** which celebrates Scotland's favorite poet. It was made in 1985 by the Icelandic artist Leifur Breiðfjörd. The green of the lower level symbolizes the natural world—God's creation. The middle zone with the circle shows the brotherhood of man—Burns was a great internationalist. The

top is a rosy red sunburst of creativity, reminding Scots of Burns' famous line, "My love is like a red, red rose"—part of a song near and dear to every Scottish heart.

To the right of the Burns window is a fine **Pre-Raphaelite window.** Like most in the church, it's a memorial to an important patron (in this case, John Marshall). From here stretches a great swath of war memorials.

As you walk along the north wall, find **John Knox's statue.** (There's no set location; they move him around like a six-foot-tall bronze chess piece.) Look into his eyes for 10 seconds from 10 inches away, and think of the Reformation struggles of the 16th century. Knox, the great Reformer and founder of austere Scottish Presbyterianism, first preached here in 1559. His insistence that every person should be able to read the word of God gave Scotland an educational system 300 years ahead of the rest of Europe (for more on Knox, see "The Scottish Reformation" on page 661).

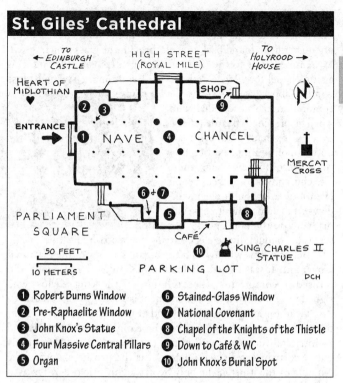

St. Giles' Cathedral

TO EDINBURGH CASTLE ←

HIGH STREET (ROYAL MILE)

TO HOLYROOD HOUSE →

HEART OF MIDLOTHIAN ♥

SHOP

❷ ❸

ENTRANCE ➡ ❶ NAVE ❹ CHANCEL

❾

N

MERCAT CROSS

❻ ✝ ❼

PARLIAMENT SQUARE

❺

❽

CAFÉ

KING CHARLES II STATUE

50 FEET

10 METERS

❿ PARKING LOT

DCH

❶ Robert Burns Window
❷ Pre-Raphaelite Window
❸ John Knox's Statue
❹ Four Massive Central Pillars
❺ Organ
❻ Stained-Glass Window
❼ National Covenant
❽ Chapel of the Knights of the Thistle
❾ Down to Café & WC
❿ John Knox's Burial Spot

Thanks partly to Knox, it was Scottish minds that led the way in math, science, medicine, and engineering. Voltaire called Scotland "the intellectual capital of Europe."

Knox preached Calvinism. Consider that the Dutch and the Scots both embraced this creed of hard work, frugality, and strict ethics. This helps explain why Scots are so different from the English (and why the Dutch and the Scots—both famous for their thriftiness and industriousness—are so much alike).

The oldest parts of the cathedral—the **four massive central pillars**—date from 1120. After the English burned the cathedral, in 1385, it was rebuilt bigger and better than ever, and in 1495 its famous crown spire was completed. During the Reformation—when Knox preached here (1559–1572)—the place was simplified and whitewashed. Before this, when the emphasis was on holy services provided by priests, there were lots of little niches. With the new focus on sermons rather than rituals, the grand pulpit took center stage. Knox even had the church's fancy medieval glass windows replaced with clear glass, but 19th-century Victorians took them out and installed the brilliantly colored ones you see today.

Cross over to the **organ** (1992, Austrian-built, one of Europe's finest) and take in its sheer might. For a peek into the realm of the organist, duck around back to look through the glass panel.

Immediately to the right of the organ (as you're facing it) is a tiny chapel for silence and prayer. The dramatic **stained-glass window** above (c. 1570) shows the commotion that surrounded Knox when he preached. Bearded, fiery-eyed Knox had a huge impact on this community. Notice how there were no pews back then. The church was so packed, people even looked through clear windows from across the street. With his hand on the holy book, Knox seems to conduct divine electricity to the Scottish faithful.

Between this window and the organ is a copy of the **National Covenant.** It was signed in blood in 1638 by Scottish heroes who refused to compromise their religion for the king's. Most who signed were martyred (their monument is nearby in Grassmarket).

Head toward the east (back) end of the church, and turn right to see the Neo-Gothic **Chapel of the Knights of the Thistle** and its intricate wood carving. Built in two years (1910–1911), entirely with Scottish materials and labor, it is the private chapel of the Knights of the Thistle, the only Scottish chivalric order. It's used about once a year to inaugurate new members. Scotland recognizes its leading citizens by bestowing upon them a membership. The Queen presides over the ritual from her fancy stall, marked by her Scottish coat of arms—a heraldic zoo of symbolism. Are there bagpipes in heaven? Find the tooting angel at a ceiling joint to the left of the altar.

Downstairs is an inviting, recommended café, along with handy public toilets.

Just outside, behind the church, is the **burial spot of John Knox**—with appropriate austerity, he's under the parking lot, at spot 23. The statue among the cars shows King Charles II riding to a toga party back in 1685.

• *Near parking spot 15, enter the...*

Old Parliament House—The building now holds the civil law courts, so you'll need to go through security first; stay to the left to allow lawyers to get waved through quickly. Step in to see the grand hall, with its fine 1639 hammer-beam ceiling and stained glass. This space housed the Scottish parliament until the Act of Union in 1707. Find the big stained-glass depiction of the initiation of the first Scottish High Court in 1532. Just under it, you'll find a history exhibition explaining the Scottish parliament. The building now holds the civil law courts and is busy with wigged and robed lawyers hard at work in the old library (peek through the door) or pacing the hall deep in discussion. Look for the "Box Corridor," a hallway filled with haphazard mailboxes for attorneys (the white dot indicates which lawyers have email). The friendly doorman is helpful (free, public welcome Mon–Fri 9:00–16:30, closed Sat–Sun, no photos, enter behind St. Giles' Cathedral; open-to-the-public trials are just across the street at the High Court—doorman has day's docket). The cleverly named Writz Café, in the basement, is literally their supreme court's restaurant (cheap, Mon–Fri 9:00–14:00, closed Sat–Sun).

▲**Mary King's Close**—For an unusual peek at Edinburgh's gritty, crowded past, join a costumed guide on a trip through a recently excavated underground street and buildings on the northern slope of the Royal Mile. Tours cover the standard goofy, crowd-pleasing ghost stories, but also provide authentic and interesting historical insight into a part of town entombed by later construction. It's best to book ahead—even though tours leave every 20 minutes, groups are small and the sight is popular (£11; April–Oct daily 10:00–21:00; Nov–March Sun–Thu 10:00–17:00, Fri–Sat 10:00–21:00; these are last tour times, no kids under 5, across from St. Giles' at 2 Warriston's Close, tel. 0845-070-6244, www.realmarykingsclose .com). The same company also runs Auld Town walking tours (see "Tours in Edinburgh," earlier).

Mercat Cross—This chunky pedestal, on the downhill side of St. Giles', holds a slender column topped with a white unicorn. Royal proclamations have been read at this market cross since the 14th century. In 1952 a town crier heralded the news that Britain had a new queen—three days (traditionally the time it took for a horse to speed here from London) after the actual event. Today, Mercat Cross is the meeting point of various walking tours—both historic and ghostly.

• *A few doors downhill is the...*

Police Information Center—This center provides a pleasant police presence (say that three times) and a little local law-and-order history to boot (free, daily May–Aug 10:00–21:30, April and Sept–Oct until 19:30, Nov–March until 18:00). Ask the officer on duty about the grave-robber William Burke's skin and creative poetic justice, Edinburgh-style. Seriously—drop in and discuss whatever law-and-order issue piques your curiosity.

Along this stretch of the Royal Mile, which is traffic-free most of the day (notice the bollards that raise and lower for permitted traffic), you'll see the Fringe Festival office (at #180), street musicians, and another wellhead (with horse "sippies," dating from 1675).

Cockburn Street—This street was cut through High Street's dense wall of medieval skyscrapers in the 1860s to give easy access to the Georgian New Town and the train station. Notice how the sliced buildings were thoughtfully capped with facades in a faux-16th-century Scottish baronial style. In the Middle Ages, only tiny lanes (like the Fleshmarket Lane just uphill from Cockburn Street) interrupted the long line of Royal Mile buildings.

• *Continue downhill 100 yards to the...*

▲**Museum of Childhood**—This five-story playground of historical toys and games is rich in nostalgia and history (free, Mon–Sat 10:00–17:00, Sun 12:00–17:00, last entry 30 minutes before closing). Just downhill is a fragrant fudge shop offering delicious free samples.

▲**John Knox House**—Intriguing for Reformation buffs, this

fine 16th-century house offers a well-explained look at the life of the great reformer. Although most contend he never actually lived here, preservationists called it "Knox's house" to save it from the wrecking ball in 1850. On the top floor, there's a fun cape, hat, and feather pen photo op (£4, Mon–Sat 10:00–18:00, closed Sun except in July–Aug 12:00–18:00, 43 High Street, tel. 0131/556-9579).

The World's End—For centuries, a wall halfway down the Royal Mile marked the end of Edinburgh and the beginning of Canongate, a community associated with Holyrood Abbey. Today, where the Mile hits St. Mary's and Jeffrey Streets, High Street becomes Canongate. Just below the John Knox House (at #43), notice the hanging sign showing the old gate. At the intersection, find the brass bricks that trace the gate (demolished in 1764). The cornerside Tass Pub is a great venue for live traditional music—pop in and see what's on tonight. Look down St. Mary's Street about 200 yards to see a surviving bit of that old wall.

• *Entering Canongate, you leave what was Edinburgh and head for...*

▲**Cadenhead's Whisky Shop**—The shop is not a tourist sight. Founded in 1842, this firm prides itself on bottling good malt whisky from casks straight from the best distilleries, without all the compromises that come with profitable mass production (coloring with sugar to fit the expected look, watering down to lessen the alcohol tax, and so on). Those drinking from Cadenhead-bottled whiskies will enjoy the pure product as the distilleries owners themselves do, not as the sorry public does.

If you want to learn about whisky—and perhaps pick up a bottle—chat up Mark and Alan, who love to talk. To buy whisky here, ask for a sample first. Sip once. Consider the flavor. Add a little water and sip again. Buy a small bottle of your favorite (£12 for about 7 ounces) and enjoy it in your hotel room night after night. Unlike wine, it has a long shelf life after it's opened. If you want to savor it post-trip, keep in mind that customs laws prohibit you from shipping whisky home, so you'll have to pack it in your checked luggage. Fortunately, the bottles are extremely durable—just ask Mark or Alan to demonstrate (Mon–Sat 10:30–17:30, closed Sun except possibly in Aug 12:30–17:30, 172 Canongate, tel. 0131/556-5864, www.wmcadenhead.com).

▲**People's Story**—This interesting exhibition traces the conditions of the working class through the 18th, 19th, and 20th centuries (free, Mon–Sat 10:00–17:00, last entry 15 minutes before closing, closed Sun except during Festival 12:00–17:00, tel. 0131/529-4057). Curiously, while this museum is dedicated to the proletariat, immediately around the back (embedded in the wall of the museum) is the tomb of Adam Smith—the author of *Wealth of Nations* and the father of modern free-market capitalism (1723–1790).

▲**Museum of Edinburgh**—Another old house full of old stuff, this one is worth a look for its early Edinburgh history and handy ground-floor WC. Don't miss the original copy of the National Covenant (written in 1638 on an animal skin), sketches of pre-Georgian Edinburgh (which show a lake, later filled in to become Princes Street Gardens when the New Town was built), and early golf balls. A favorite Scottish say-it-aloud joke: "Balls," said the queen. "If I had two, I'd be king." The king laughed—he had to (free, same hours as People's Story—listed above, tel. 0131/529-4143).

White Horse Close—Step into this 17th-century courtyard (bottom of Canongate, on the left, a block before the Palace of Holyroodhouse). It was from here that the Edinburgh stagecoach left for London. Eight days later, the horse-drawn carriage would pull into its destination: Scotland Yard.

• *Across the street is the…*

▲▲**Scottish Parliament Building**—Scotland's parliament originated in 1293 and was dissolved by England in 1707. In 1998

it was decided that "there shall be a Scottish parliament guided by justice, wisdom, integrity, and compassion," and in 1999 it was formally reopened by Queen Elizabeth. Except for matters of defense, foreign policy, and taxation, Scotland now enjoys home rule. The current government, run by the Scottish Nationalist Party (or at least until the elections in May 2011), is pushing for more independence.

In 2004 the Parliament moved into its striking new home. Although its cost ($800 million) and perceived extravagance made it controversial from the start, an in-person visit wins most people over. The eco-friendly building, by the Catalan architect Enric Miralles, mixes wild angles, lots of light, bold windows, oak, and local stone into a startling complex that would, as he envisioned, "arise from the sloping base of Arthur's Seat and arrive into the city as if almost surging out of the rock."

Since it celebrates Scottish democracy, the architecture is not a statement of authority. There are no statues of old heroes. There's not even a grand entry. You feel like you're entering an office park. The building is people-oriented. Signs are written in both English and Gaelic (the Scots' Celtic tongue). Anyone is welcome to attend the committee meetings (viewable by live video hookups throughout the nation's libraries).

For a peek at the building and a lesson in how the Scottish parliament works, drop in, pass through security, and find the visitors' desk. You're welcome into the public parts of the building, including the impressive "Debating Chambers." Worthwhile hour-long tours by proud locals are offered (free, call or check online for times and details). Or you can call or sign up online to witness the  Scottish parliament's hugely popular debates—best on Thursdays 12:00–12:30, when the First Minister is on the hot seat and has to field questions from members across all parties (other debate slots usually Wed 14:00–18:00, Thu 9:00–11:40 & 14:00–18:00, tel. 0131/348-5200).

Cost and Hours: Free, Mon–Fri 10:00–17:30, until 16:00 Oct–March, Tue–Thu 9:00–18:30 when Parliament in session, Sat 11:00–17:30 year-round, last entry 30 minutes before closing, closed Sun, www.scottish.parliament.uk. Generally Parliament is in recess for a week in February, from early July to early September, two weeks in October, and around Chrismas—dates are posted on their website.

▲**Palace of Holyroodhouse**—Since the 14th century, this palace has marked the end of the Royal Mile. An abbey—part of a 12th-century Augustinian monastery—originally stood in its place. It was named for a piece of the cross brought here as a relic by Queen (and later Saint) Margaret. Because Scotland's royalty preferred living at Holyroodhouse to the blustery castle on the rock, the palace evolved over time.

Consider touring the interior. The building, rich in history and decor, is filled with elegantly furnished rooms and a few darker, older rooms with glass cases of historic bits and Scottish pieces that locals find fascinating.

Bring the palace to life with the included one-hour **audio-guide.** You'll learn which of the kings featured in the 110 portraits lining the Great Gallery are real and which are fictional, what touches were added to the bedchambers to flatter King Charles II, and why the exiled Comte d'Artois took refuge in the palace. You'll also hear a goofy reenactment of the moment when conspirators—dispatched by Mary, Queen of Scots' jealous second husband—stormed into the queen's chambers and stabbed her male secretary. Royal diehards can pick up a palace guidebook for £4.50.

Cost and Hours: £10.25 includes a quality audioguide, £14.30 combo-ticket includes Queen's Gallery—listed below, tickets sold in Queen's Gallery, daily April–Oct 9:30–18:00, Nov–March 9:30–16:30, last entry one hour before closing, tel. 0131/556-5100, www.royalcollection.org.uk. It's still a working palace, so it's closed when the Queen or other VIPs are in residence.

Nearby: After exiting, you're free to stroll through the ruined abbey (destroyed by those dastardly English during the time of Mary, Queen of Scots, in the 16th century) and the queen's gardens (closed in winter). Hikers: Note that the wonderful trail up Arthur's Seat starts just across the street from the gardens (see page 631 for details).

Queen's Gallery—This small museum features rotating exhibits of artwork from the royal collection. For more than five centuries,

the royal family has amassed a wealth of art treasures. While the Queen keeps most in her many private palaces, she shares an impressive load of it here, with exhibits changing about every six months. Though the gallery occupies just a few rooms, it can be exquisite. The entry fee includes an excellent audioguide, written and read by the curator (£5.50, £14.30 combo-ticket includes Palace of Holyroodhouse, daily April–Oct 9:30–18:00, Nov–March until 16:30, café, last entry one hour before closing, on the palace grounds, to the right of the palace entrance, www.royalcollection.org.uk). Buses #35 and #36 stop outside, and can save you a walk to or from Princes Street/North Bridge.

Sights Just Off the Royal Mile

▲▲▲**National Museum of Scotland**—This huge museum has amassed more historic artifacts than every other place I've seen

in Scotland combined. It's all wonderfully displayed with fine descriptions offering a best-any-where hike through the history of Scotland. Start in the basement and work your way through the story: prehistoric, Roman, Viking, the "birth of Scotland," Edinburgh's witch-burning craze, clan massacres, all the way to life in the 20th century. Free audioguides offer a pleasant description of various rooms and exhibits, and even provide mood music for your wanderings.

The **Kingdom of the Scots** exhibit, on the first three floors, shows evidence of a vibrant young nation. While largely cut off from Europe by hostilities with England, Scotland connected with the Continent through trade, the Church, and their monarch, Mary, Queen of Scots. Throughout Scotland's long, underdog struggle with England, its people found inspiration from romantic (and almost legendary) Scottish leaders, including Mary. Educated and raised in France during the Renaissance, Mary brought refine-

ment to the Scottish throne. After she was imprisoned and then executed by the English, her countrymen rallied each other by invoking her memory. Pendants and coins with her portrait stoked the irrepressible Scottish spirit. Near the replica of Mary's tomb are tiny cameos, pieces of jewelry, and coins with her image.

The industry exhibit explains how (eventually) the Scots were tamed, and the union with England brought stability and investment to Scotland. Powered by the Scottish work ethic and the new opportunities that came from the Industrial Revolution, the country came into relative prosperity. Education and medicine thrived. Cast iron and foundries were huge, and this became one of the most industrialized places in Europe. With the dawn of the modern age came leisure time, the concept of "healthful sports," and golf—a Scottish invention. The first golf balls, which date from about 1820, were leather stuffed with feathers.

Cost and Hours: Free, daily 10:00–17:00; free 1-hour "Highlights" tours daily at 11:30 and 13:30, themed tours at 14:30—confirm tour schedule at info desk; 2 long blocks south of Royal Mile from St. Giles' Cathedral, Chambers Street, off George IV Bridge, tel. 0131/247-4422, www.nms.ac.uk.

Restaurant: On the museum's top floor, the upscale **Tower restaurant** serves surprisingly good food (£15 two-course lunch special, £16 afternoon tea 15:00–16:30, £15 early-dinner special 17:00–18:30, and fancy £18–25 meals, open daily 12:00–23:00—later than the museum itself, tel. 0131/225-3003).

Nearby: The **Royal Museum,** next door, fills a fine iron-and-glass Industrial Age building (built to house the museum in 1851) with all the natural sciences as it "presents the world to Scotland." It's great for school kids, but of no special interest to foreign visitors (closed until 2011).

Greyfriars Bobby—This famous statue of Edinburgh's favorite dog is across the street from the National Museum of Scotland. Every business nearby, it seems, is named for this terrier, who stood by his master's grave for 14 years and was immortalized in a 1960s Disney flick.

Grassmarket—Once Edinburgh's site for hangings (residents rented out their windows—above the rudely named "Last Drop" pub—for the view), today Grassmarket is being renovated into a people-friendly piazza. It was originally the city's garage, a depot for horses and cows (hence the name). It's rowdy here at night—a popular place for "hen" and "stag" parties. During the day, the literary pub tour departs from here. Budget shoppers might want to look at Armstrongs, a fun secondhand-clothing store. Victoria Street, built in the Victorian Age and lined with colorful little shops and eateries, was built to connect Grassmarket and High Street.

Hiding in the blur of traffic is a monument to the "Covenanters." These strict 17th-century Scottish Protestants were killed for refusing to accept the king's Episcopalian prayer book. To this day, Scots celebrate their emphatically democratic church government. Rather than big-shot bishops (as in the Anglican or Roman Catholic churches), they have a low-key "moderator" who's elected each year.

Museum on the Mound—Located in the basement of the grand Bank of Scotland building (easily spotted from a distance), this exhibit tells the story of the bank, which was founded in 1695 (making it only a year younger than the Bank of England). Featuring displays on cash production, safe technology, and bank robberies, this museum struggles mightily, with some success, to make banking interesting (the case holding £1 million is cool). It's worth popping in if you have some time or find the subject appealing. But no matter how well the information is presented, it's still about... yawn...banking (free, Tue–Fri 10:00–17:00, Sat–Sun 13:00–17:00, closed Mon, down Bank Street from the Royal Mile—follow the street around to the left and enter through the gate, tel. 0131/243-5464, www.museumonthemound.com).

Dynamic Earth—Located about a five-minute walk from the Palace of Holyroodhouse, this immense exhibit tells the story

of our planet, filling several underground floors under a white vast Gore-Tex tent. It's pitched, appropriately, at the base of the Salisbury Crags. The exhibit is designed for younger kids and does the same thing an American science exhibit would do—but with a charming Scottish accent. Standing

in a time tunnel, you watch the years rewind from Churchill to dinosaurs to the Big Bang. After viewing several short films on stars, tectonic plates, ice caps, and worldwide weather (in a new "4D" exhibit), you're free to wander past salty pools, a re-created rain forest, and various TV screens (£10.50; daily 10:00–17:30, Nov–March closed Mon–Tue; last ticket sold 2 hours before closing, on Holyrood Road, between the palace and mountain, tel. 0131/550-7800, www.dynamicearth.co.uk). Dynamic Earth is a stop on the hop-on, hop-off bus route.

Bonnie Wee Sights in the New Town

▲▲**Georgian New Town**—Cross Waverley Bridge and walk through the Georgian New Town. According to the 1776 plan, the New Town was three streets (Princes, George, and Queen) flanked by two squares (St. Andrew and Charlotte), woven together by alleys (Thistle and Rose). George Street—20 feet wider than the others (so a four-horse carriage could make a U-turn)—was the main drag. And, while Princes Street has gone down-market, George Street still maintains its old grace. The entire elegantly planned New Town—laid out when George III was king—celebrated the hard-to-sell notion that Scotland was an integral part of the United Kingdom. The streets and squares are named after the British royalty (Hanover was the royal family surname). Even Thistle and Rose Streets (the national flowers of Scotland and England, respectively) are emblems of the two happily paired nations. Mostly pedestrianized Rose Street is famous for its rowdy pubs; where it hits St. Andrew Square, the street is flanked by the venerable Jenners department store and a Sainsbury's supermarket. Sprinkled with popular restaurants and bars, the stately New Town is turning trendy.

Princes Street—Edinburgh's main drag will likely be torn up for tram construction during your visit. If it's patched up, it'll be busy with buses and taxis (and trams, if running). Jenners department store is an institution. Notice how statues of women support the building—just as real women support the business. The arrival of new fashions here was such a big deal that they'd announce it by flying flags on the Nelson Monument. Step inside. The central space—filled with a towering tree at Christmas—is classic Industrial Age architecture. The Queen's coat of arms high on the wall indicates she shops here.

St. Andrew Square—This green space bookends the Georgian New Town opposite Charlotte Square. In the early 19th century, there were no shops around here—just fine residences; this was a private garden for the fancy people living here. Now open to the public, the square is a popular lunch hangout for workers. The Melville Monument honors a powermonger Member of Parliament who, for four decades (around 1800), was nicknamed the "uncrowned king of Scotland."

St. Andrew's and St. George's Church—Designed as part of the New Town in the 1780s, the church is a product of the Scottish Enlightenment. It has an elliptical plan (the first in Britain) so that all can focus on the pulpit. A fine leaflet tells the story of the church, and a handy cafeteria downstairs serves cheap and cheery lunches (see page 651).

▲▲Georgian House—This refurbished Georgian house, set on Edinburgh's finest Georgian square, is a trip back to 1796. It recounts the era when a newly gentrified and well-educated Edinburgh was nicknamed the "Athens of the North." A volunteer guide in each of the five rooms shares stories and trivia—from the kitchen in the basement to the fully stocked medicine cabinet in the bedroom. Start your visit in the basement and view the interesting 16-minute video, which shows the life of one family who owned this property and touches on the architecture of the Georgian period. A walk down George Street after your visit here can be fun for the imagination.

Cost and Hours: £5.50, daily July–Aug 10:00–18:30, April–June and Sept–Oct 10:00–17:00, March 11:00–16:00, Nov 11:00–15:00, last entry 30 minutes before closing, closed Dec–Feb, 7 Charlotte Square, tel. 0131/226-3318, www.nts.org.uk/Property/56.

▲▲National Gallery of Scotland—The elegant Neoclassical building has a delightfully small but impressive collection of European masterpieces, from Raphael, Titian, and Peter Paul Rubens to Thomas Gainsborough, Claude Monet, and Vincent van Gogh. A highlight (along with guards in plaid trousers) is

Canova's exquisite *Three Graces*, and it offers the best look you'll get at Scottish paintings (in the basement). Check out one of Scotland's best-known paintings, *The Skating Minister*, by Sir Henry Raeburn. There's no audioguide, but each painting is well-described.

Cost and Hours: Free, daily 10:00–17:00, Thu until 19:00, no photos, tel. 0131/624-6200, recorded info 0131/624-6336, www.national galleries.org.

Related Sights: The skippable **Royal Scottish Academy,** next door, hosts temporary art exhibits and is connected to the National Gallery at the garden level (underneath the gallery) by the Weston Link building (same hours as the gallery, fine café and restaurant).

Two other museums are associated with the National Gallery, but are outside the downtown core: the Scottish National Portrait Gallery (closed until November 2011) and the Scottish National Gallery of Modern Art.

The Mound—The National Gallery sits upon what's known as "The Mound." When the lake was drained and the Georgian New Town was built, rubble from the excavations was piled into The Mound (c. 1770) to allay Old Town merchant concerns about being disconnected from the future heart of the city. The two fine Neoclassical buildings here (which house museums) date from the 1840s. From The Mound you can enjoy fine views of "Auld Reekie" (medieval Edinburgh), with its 14-story "skyscrapers."

Princes Street Gardens—The grassy park, a former lakebed, separates Edinburgh's New and Old Towns and offers a wonderful escape from the bustle of the city. Once the private domain of wealthy locals, it was opened to the public around 1870—not as a democratic gesture, but because it was thought that allowing the public into the park would increase sales for the Princes Street department stores. Join the office workers for a picnic lunch break, or see the oldest floral clock in the world. In summer you can also watch Scottish country dancing in the park (£3.50, May–July Mon and sometimes Tue 19:30–21:30, at Ross Bandstand, tel. 0131/228-8616, www.princesstreetgardensdancing.org.uk).

The big lake, Nor' Loch, was drained around 1800 as part of the Georgian expansion of Edinburgh. Before that, the lake was the town's sewer, water reservoir, and handy place for drowning witches. Much was written about the town's infamous stink (a.k.a. the "flowers of Edinburgh"). The town's nickname, "Auld Reekie," referred to both the smoke of its industry and the stench of its squalor.

Although the loch is now long gone, memories of the countless women drowned as witches remain. With their thumbs tied to their ankles, they'd be lashed to dunking stools. Those who survived the ordeal were considered "aided by the devil" and burned as witches. If they died, they were innocent and given a good Christian burial. Until 1720, Edinburgh was Europe's witch-burning mecca—any perceived "sign," including a small birthmark, could condemn you.

▲**Sir Walter Scott Monument**—Built in 1840, this elaborate Neo-Gothic monument honors the great author, one of Edinburgh's many illustrious sons. When Scott died in 1832, it was said that "Scotland never owed so much to one man." To all of Western literature, he's considered the father of the Romantic historical novel. The 200-foot monument shelters a marble statue of Scott and his favorite pet, Maida, a deerhound who was one of 30 canines this dog-lover owned during his lifetime. They're surrounded by busts of 16 great Scottish poets and 64 characters from his books. Climbing the tight, stony spiral staircase of 287 steps earns you a peek at a tiny museum midway, a fine city view at the top, and intimate encounters going up and down.

Cost and Hours: £3; April–Sept daily 10:00–19:00, Oct–March Mon–Sat 9:00–16:00, Sun 10:00–16:00; last entry one hour before closing, tel. 0131/529-4068.

Activities

▲▲**Arthur's Seat Hike**—A 45-minute hike up the 822-foot remains of an extinct volcano (surrounded by a fine park overlooking Edinburgh) starts from the Palace of Holyroodhouse. You can run up like they did in *Chariots of Fire*, or just stroll—at the summit you'll be rewarded with commanding views of the town and surroundings. On May Day, be on the summit at dawn and wash your face in the morning dew to commemorate the Celtic holiday of Beltaine, the celebration of spring. (Morning dew is supposedly very good for your complexion.)

From the parking lot below the Palace of Holyroodhouse, there are two trailheads. Take the wide path on the left (easier grade, through the abbey ruins and "Hunter's Bog"). After making the summit, you can return along the other path (to the right, with the steps), which skirts the base of the cliffs.

Those staying at my recommended B&Bs can enjoy a pre-breakfast or late-evening hike starting from the other side (in June, the sun comes up early, and it stays light until nearly midnight). From the Commonwealth Pool, take Holyrood Park Road, turn right on Queen's Drive, and continue to a small parking lot. From here it's a 20-minute hike.

If you have a car, you can drive up most of the way from behind (follow the one-way street from palace, park safely and for free by the little lake, and hike up).

Brush Skiing—If you like skiing, but not all that pesky snow, head a little south of town to Hillend, where the Midlothian Snowsports Centre has a hill with a chairlift, two slopes, a jump slope, and rentable skis, boots, and poles. It feels like snow-skiing on a slushy day, even though you're schussing over what seems like a million toothbrushes. Beware: Doctors are used to treating an ailment called "Hillend Thumb"—thumbs dislocated when people fall here and get tangled in the brush. Locals say that skiing here is "like falling on a carrot grater" (£9.50/first hour, then £4/hour, includes gear, beginners must take a lesson, generally Mon–Tue 18:30–21:00, Wed–Fri 13:00–21:00, Sat–Sun 10:00–19:00—but call to confirm before showing up, probably closes if it snows, Lothian bus #4 from Princes Street—garden side, tel. 0131/445-4433, www.midlothian.gov.uk).

More Hikes—You can hike along the river (called Water of Leith) through Edinburgh. Locals favor the stretch between Roseburn and Dean Village, but the 1.5-mile walk from Dean Village to the Royal Botanic Garden is also good. For more information on these and other hikes, ask at the TI for the free *Walks In and Around Edinburgh* one-page flier (if it's unavailable, consider their £2 guide to walks).

Prestonfield Golf Club—At the foot of Arthur's Seat, just a mile and a half from town, the Prestonfield Golf Club has golfers feeling like they're in a country estate (£32–38/person plus £10 for clubs, dress code enforced, 6 Priestfield Road North, tel. 0131/667-9665, www.prestonfieldgolf.com).

Shopping—The streets to browse are Princes Street (the elegant old Jenners department store is nearby on Rose Street, at St. Andrew Square), Victoria Street (antiques galore), Nicolson Street (south of the Royal Mile, line of interesting secondhand stores), and the Royal Mile (touristy but competitively priced). Shops are usually open from 10:00 to 18:00 (later on Thu).

Near Edinburgh

▲▲*Britannia*—This much-revered vessel, which transported Britain's royal family for more than 40 years and 900 voyages before being retired in 1997, is permanently moored at the Ocean Terminal Shopping Mall in Edinburgh's port of Leith. It's open to the public and worth the 15-minute bus or taxi ride from the center. Explore the museum, filled with engrossing royal-family-afloat history. Then, armed with your included audioguide, you're welcome aboard.

This was the last in a line of royal yachts that stretches back to 1660. With all its royal functions, the ship required a crew of more than 200. The captain's bridge feels like it's been preserved from the day it was launched in 1953. Queen Elizabeth II, who enjoyed the ship for 40 years, said, "This is the only place I can truly relax." The Sunny Lounge, just off the back Veranda Deck, was the queen's favorite, with teak from Burma (now Myanmar, in Southeast Asia) and the same phone system she was used to in Buckingham Palace.

The back deck was the favorite place for outdoor entertainment. Ronald Reagan, Boris Yeltsin, Bill Clinton, and Nelson Mandela all sipped champagne here with the Queen. When she wasn't entertaining, the Queen liked it quiet. The crew wore sneakers, communicated in hand signals, and (at least near the Queen's quarters) had to be finished with all their work by 8:00 in the morning.

The state dining room, decorated with gifts given by the ship's many noteworthy guests, enabled the Queen to entertain a good-size crowd. The silver pantry was just down the hall. The drawing room, while rather simple, was perfect for casual relaxing among royals. Princess Diana played the piano, which is bolted to the deck. Royal family photos evoke the fine times the Windsors enjoyed on the *Britannia*. Visitors can also see the crew's quarters and engine room.

Cost and Hours: £10.50, daily July–Sept 9:30–16:30, April–June and Oct 10:00–16:00, Nov–March 10:00–15:30, these are last entry times, tea room, tel. 0131/555-5566, www.royalyacht britannia.co.uk.

Getting There: From central Edinburgh, catch Lothian bus #1, #11, #22, #34, or #35 at Waverley Bridge to Ocean Terminal. If you're doing a city bus tour, consider the Majestic Tour, which includes transportation to the *Britannia* (see page 602).

Rosslyn Chapel—Founded in 1446 by the Knights Templar, this church became famous for its role in the final scenes of *The Da Vinci Code* (£7.50, Mon–Sat 9:30–18:00, until 17:00 Oct–March, Sun 12:00–16:45 year-round, last entry 30 minutes before closing, no photos, located in Roslin Village, www.rosslynchapel.org.uk). To get to the chapel by bus, ride Lothian bus #15 from the station at St. Andrew Square (1–2/hour). By car, take A701 to Penicuik/Peebles, and follow signs for *Roslin;* once you're in the village, you'll see signs for the chapel.

Royal Botanic Garden—Britain's second-oldest botanical garden (after Oxford) was established in 1670 for medicinal herbs, and this 70-acre refuge is now one of Europe's best (gardens free, greenhouse admission-£4, daily April–Sept 10:00–19:00, March and Oct 10:00–18:00, Nov–Feb 10:00–16:00, 1-hour tours April–Sept daily at 10:00 and 14:00 for £3, café, a mile north of the city center at Inverleith Row; take Lothian bus #8, #23, or #27; Majestic Tour stops here—see page 602, tel. 0131/552-7171, www.rbge.org.uk).

Experiences in Edinburgh

Edinburgh Festival

One of Europe's great cultural events, Edinburgh's annual festival turns the city into a carnival of the arts. There are enough music, dance, drama, and multicultural events to make even the most jaded traveler giddy with excitement. Every day is jammed with formal and spontaneous fun. A riot of festivals—official, fringe, book, and jazz and blues—rages simultaneously for about three weeks each August, with the Military Tattoo starting a week earlier (the best overall website is www.edinburghfestivals.co.uk). Many city sights run on extended hours, and those along the Royal Mile that are normally closed on Sunday are open in the afternoon. It's a glorious time to be in Edinburgh—if you have (and can afford) a room.

The official **Edinburgh International Festival** (Aug 12–Sept 4 in 2011) is the original, more formal, and most likely to get booked up. Major events sell out well in advance. The ticket office is at **The Hub,** located in the former Tolbooth Church, near the top of the Royal Mile (tickets-£8–64, booking from late March, office open Mon–Sat 10:00–17:00 or longer, in Aug 9:00–19:30 plus Sun 10:00–19:30, tel. 0131/473-2000, www.hubtickets.co.uk or www.eif.co.uk). Call and order your ticket through The Hub with your credit-card number. Pick up your ticket at the office on the day of the show or at the venue before showtime. Several publications—including the festival's official schedule, the *Edinburgh Festivals Guide Daily, The List,* the *Fringe Program,* and the *Daily Diary*—list and evaluate festival events.

The less-formal **Fringe Festival,** featuring "on the edge" comedy and theater, is huge—with 2,000 shows—and desperate for an audience (Aug 5–28 in 2011, ticket/info office just below St. Giles' Cathedral on the Royal Mile, 180 High Street, tel. 0131/226-0026, bookings tel. 0131/226-0000, can book online from mid-June on, www.edfringe.com). Tickets may be available at the door, and half-price tickets for some events are sold on the day of the show at the Half-Price Hut, located at the Mound, by the National Gallery (daily 10:00-21:00).

The **Military Tattoo** is a massing of bands, drums, and

bagpipes, with groups from all over the former British Empire. Displaying military finesse with a stirring lone-piper finale, this grand spectacle fills the Castle Esplanade nightly except Sunday, normally from a week before the festival starts until a week before it finishes (Aug 5–27 in 2011, Mon–Fri at 21:00, Sat at 19:30 and 22:30, £15–50, booking starts in Dec, Fri–Sat shows sell out first, all seats generally sold out many months ahead, some scattered same-day tickets may be available; office open Mon–Fri 10:00–16:30, closed Sat–Sun, during Tattoo open until show time and Sat 10:00–22:30, closed Sun; 32 Market Street, behind Waverley Station, tel. 0131/225-1188, www.edinburgh-tattoo.co.uk). The last day is broadcast as a big national television special.

The **Festival of Politics,** adding yet another dimension to Edinburgh's festival action, is held in August in the new Scottish Parliament building. It's a busy four days of discussions and lectures on environmentalism, globalization, terrorism, gender, and other issues (www.festivalofpolitics.org.uk).

Other summer festivals cover jazz and blues (early August, tel. 0131/467-5200, www.edinburghjazzfestival.co.uk), film (mid-June, tel. 0131/228-4051, www.edfilmfest.org.uk), and books (mid-late August, tel. 0131/718-5666, www.edbookfest.co.uk).

If you do manage to hit Edinburgh during a festival, book a room far in advance and extend your stay by a day or two. Once you know your dates, reserve tickets to any show you really want to see.

Nightlife in Edinburgh

▲▲**Literary Pub Tour**—This two-hour walk is interesting even if you think Sir Walter Scott was an Arctic explorer. You'll follow the witty dialogue of two actors as they debate whether the great literature of Scotland was high art or the creative re-creation of fun-loving louts fueled by a love of whisky. You'll wander from the Grassmarket, over the Old Town to the New Town, with stops in three pubs as your guides share their takes on Scotland's literary greats. The tour meets at The Beehive pub on Grassmarket (£10, book online and save £1, May–Sept nightly at 19:30, March–April and Oct Thu–Sun, Nov–Feb Fri only, call 0800-169-7410 to confirm, www.edinburghliterarypubtour.co.uk).

▲**Ghost Walks**—These walks are an entertaining and cheap night out (offered nightly, most around 19:00 and 21:00, easy socializing for solo travelers). The theatrical and creatively staged **Witchery Tours,** the most established outfit, offers two different walks: "Ghosts and Gore" (1.5 hours, May–early Sept only) and "Murder and Mystery" (1.25 hours, year-round). The former is better-suited for kids than the latter (either tour £7.50,

Sampling Whisky

While pub-hopping tourists generally think in terms of beer, many pubs are just as enthusiastic about serving whisky. If you are unfamiliar with whisky (what Americans call "Scotch"), it's a great conversation-starter. Many pubs (including Leslie's, described on next page) have lists of dozens of whiskies available. Lists include descriptions of their personalities (peaty, heavy iodine finish, and so on), which are much easier to discern than most wine flavors. A glass generally costs around £2.50. Let a local teach you how to drink it "neat," then add a little water. Learn how to swish it around and let your gums taste it, too. Keep experimenting until you discover "the nurse's knickers."

includes book of stories, leave from top of Royal Mile, outside the Witchery Restaurant, near Castle Esplanade, reservations required, tel. 0131/225-6745, www.witcherytours.com).

Auld Reekie Tours offers a scary array of walks daily and nightly (£8–12, 50–75 minutes, leaves from front steps of the Tron Kirk building on Cockburn Street, tel. 0131/557-4700, pick up brochure or visit www.auldreekietours.com). Auld Reekie is into the paranormal, witch covens, and pagan temples, taking groups into the "haunted vaults" under the old bridges "where it was so dark, so crowded, and so squalid that the people there knew each other not by how they looked, but by how they sounded, felt, and smelt." If you want more, there's plenty of it (complete with screaming Gothic "jumpers").

Scottish Folk Evenings—These £35–40 dinner shows, generally for tour groups intent on photographing old cultural clichés, are held in the huge halls of expensive hotels. (Prices are bloated to include 20 percent commissions.) Your "traditional" meal is followed by a full slate of swirling kilts, blaring bagpipes, and Scottish folk dancing with an "old-time music hall" emcee. If you like Lawrence Welk, you're in for a treat. But for most travelers, these are painfully cheesy variety shows. You can sometimes see the show without dinner for about two-thirds the price. The TI has fliers on all the latest venues.

Prestonfield House offers its kitschy Scottish folk evening—a plaid fantasy of smiling performers accompanied by electric keyboards—with or without dinner Sunday to Friday. For £40 you get the show with two drinks and a wad of haggis; £53 buys you the same, plus a four-course meal and wine (be there at 18:45, dinner at 19:00, show runs 20:00–22:00, May–Oct only). It's in the stables of "the handsomest house in Edinburgh," which is now home to the recommended Rhubarb Restaurant (Priestfield Road, a 10-minute walk from Dalkeith Road B&Bs, tel. 0131/225-7800, www.scottishshow.co.uk).

Theater—Even outside of festival time, Edinburgh is a fine place for lively and affordable theater. Pick up *The List* for a complete rundown of what's on (sold at newsstands for a few pounds).

▲**Live Music in Pubs**—Edinburgh used to be a good place for traditional folk music, but in the last few years, pub owners—out of economic necessity—are catering to college-age customers more interested in beer-drinking. Pubs that were regular venues for folk music have gone pop. Rather than list places likely to change their format in a few months, I'll simply recommend the monthly *Gig Guide* (free at TI, accommodations, and various pubs, www.gig guide.co.uk). This simple little sheet lists 8 or 10 places each night that have live music. Listings are divided by genre (pop, rock, world, and folk).

Pubs in the Old Town: The **Grassmarket** neighborhood (below the castle) bustles with live music and rowdy people spilling out of the pubs and into what was (once upon a time) a busy market square. It's fun to just wander through this area late at night and check out the scene at pubs such as Finnegans Wake, Biddy Mulligan, and White Hart Inn. Thanks to the music and crowds, you'll know where to go...and where not to. Have a beer and follow your ear.

Pubs on the Royal Mile: Several bars here feature live folk music every night. **Tass Pub** is a great and accessible little place with a love of folk and traditional music and free performances nearly every night from 21:00 (runs 18:00–21:00 on Sun, no music on Tue). Drop by during your sightseeing—as you walk the lower part of the Royal Mile—and ask what's on tonight (across from World's End, #1 High Street, tel. 0131/556-6338). **Whistlebinkies** is famous for live music (rock, pop, blues, South Bridge, tel. 0131/557-5114).

Pubs in the New Town: All the beer-drinkers seem to head for the pedestrianized Rose Street, famous for having the most pubs per square inch anywhere in Scotland—and plenty of live music.

Pubs near Dalkeith Road B&Bs: The first three listed below are classic pubs (without a lot of noisy machines and rowdy twentysomethings). Located near the Dalkeith Road B&B neighborhood, they cluster within 100 yards of each other around the intersection of Duncan Street and Causewayside.

Leslie's Pub, sitting between a working-class and an upper-class neighborhood, has two sides. Originally, the gang would go in on the right to gather around the great hardwood bar, glittering with a century of *Cheers* ambience. Meanwhile, the more delicate folks would slip in on the left, with its discreet doors, plush snugs (cozy private booths), and ornate ordering windows. Since 1896, this Victorian classic has been appreciated for both its "real ales" and its huge selection of fine whiskies (listed on a six-page menu). Dive into the whisky mosh pit on the right, and let them show you how whisky can become "a very good friend." (Leslie's is a block downhill from the next two pubs, at 49 Ratcliffe Terrace.)

The Old Bell Inn, with a nostalgic sports-bar vibe, serves only drinks after 19:00 (see "Scottish Grub and Pubs" on page 652).

Swanny's Pub is not quite as welcoming and plays music videos, but it's a quintessential hangout for the working-class boys of the neighborhood, with some fun characters to get to know.

A few blocks away, you'll find **Bierex,** a much younger and noisier scene. It's a favorite among young people for its cheap drinks (132 Causewayside, see "Scottish Grub and Pubs" on page 652).

Sleeping in Edinburgh

The advent of big, inexpensive hotels has made life more of a struggle for B&Bs, which are tending to go plush to compete. Still, book ahead, especially in August, when the annual festival fills Edinburgh. Conventions, rugby matches, school holidays, and weekends can make finding a room tough at almost any time of year. For the best prices, book direct rather than through the TI, which charges a higher room fee and levies a £4 booking fee. "Standard" rooms, with toilets and showers a tissue-toss away, are cheaper than "en suite" rooms (with a private bathroom). At B&Bs, you can usually save some money by paying cash; although most B&Bs take credit cards, many add the card service fee to your bill (about three percent of the price).

B&Bs off Dalkeith Road

South of town near the Royal Commonwealth Pool, these B&Bs—just off Dalkeith Road—are nearly all top-end, sporting three or four stars. While pricey, they come with uniformly friendly hosts and great cooked breakfasts, and are a good value for people with enough money. At these not-quite-interchangeable places, character is provided by the personality quirks of the hosts.

Most listings are on quiet streets and within a two-minute walk of a bus stop. Though you won't find phones in the rooms, most have Wi-Fi and several offer Internet access. Most can provide triples or even quads for families.

Sleep Code

(£1 = about $1.60, country code: 44, area code: 0131)
S = Single, **D** = Double/Twin, **T** = Triple, **Q** = Quad, **b** = bathroom,
s = shower only. You can assume credit cards are accepted
otherwise noted.

To help you sort easily through these listings, I've divided
the rooms into three categories based on the price for a
standard double room with bath (during high season):

$$$ Higher Priced—Most rooms £80 or more.
$$ Moderately Priced—Most rooms between £60-80.
$ Lower Priced—Most rooms £60 or less.

Prices can change without notice; verify the hotel's
current rates online or by email. For other updates, see www
.ricksteves.com/update.

The quality of all these B&Bs is more than adequate. Prices
listed are for most of peak season; if there's a range, prices slide up
with summer demand. *During the festival in August prices are higher;
B&Bs also do not accept bookings for one-night stays during this time.*
Conversely, in winter, when there's no demand, prices get really
soft (less than what's listed here). These prices are for cash; expect a
3–5 percent fee for using your credit card.

Near the B&Bs, you'll find plenty of great eateries (see "Eating
in Edinburgh," later) and several good, classic pubs (see "Nightlife
in Edinburgh," earlier). A few places have their own private parking spots; others offer access to easy, free street parking, though the
neighborhood may convert to metered parking (ask about it when
booking—better yet, don't rent a car for your time in Edinburgh).

If you bring in take-out food, your host would probably prefer
you eat it in the breakfast area rather than muck up your room—
ask. The nearest launderette is Ace Cleaning Centre (which picks
up and drops off; see page 597).

Getting There: This comfortable, safe neighborhood is a
10-minute bus ride from the Royal Mile. From the train station,
the nearest place to catch the bus (at least while tram construction
is underway), is around the corner on North Bridge (exit the station onto Princes Street, turn right, cross the street, and walk up
the bridge). If you're here after the Princes Street construction is
finished, use the bus stop in front of the H&M store (£1.20, use
exact change; catch Lothian bus #14, #30, #33, or #48, or First
bus #86). Tell the driver your destination is Dalkeith Road; about
10 minutes into the ride, after following South Clerk Street for
a while, the bus makes a left turn, then a right—depending on

Edinburgh's Dalkeith Road Neighborhood

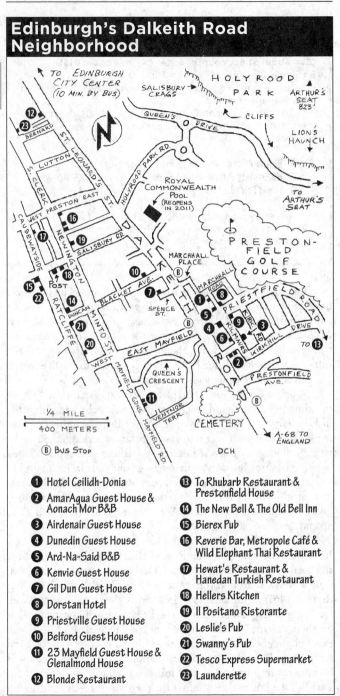

1. Hotel Ceilidh-Donia
2. AmarAgua Guest House & Aonach Mor B&B
3. Airdenair Guest House
4. Dunedin Guest House
5. Ard-Na-Said B&B
6. Kenvie Guest House
7. Gil Dun Guest House
8. Dorstan Hotel
9. Priestville Guest House
10. Belford Guest House
11. 23 Mayfield Guest House & Glenalmond House
12. Blonde Restaurant
13. To Rhubarb Restaurant & Prestonfield House
14. The New Bell & The Old Bell Inn
15. Bierex Pub
16. Reverie Bar, Metropole Café & Wild Elephant Thai Restaurant
17. Hewat's Restaurant & Hanedan Turkish Restaurant
18. Hellers Kitchen
19. Il Positano Ristorante
20. Leslie's Pub
21. Swanny's Pub
22. Tesco Express Supermarket
23. Launderette

where you're staying, you'll get off at the first or second stop after the turn. Ping the bell and hop out. These buses also stop at the corner of North Bridge and High Street on the Royal Mile. Buses run from 6:00 (9:00 on Sun) to 23:00. Taxi fare between the train station or Royal Mile and the B&Bs is about £7. Taxis are easy to hail on Dalkeith Road if it isn't raining.

$$$ Hotel Ceilidh-Donia rents 17 soothing, contemporary rooms with a pleasant back deck, a quiet bar, a free DVD lending library, and a guest-only restaurant (Sb-£50–60, Db-£70–100, more in Aug and for special events, less off-season, includes breakfast, restaurant open 18:00–20:00 Mon–Thu only, free Internet access and Wi-Fi for guests, 14–16 Marchhall Crescent, tel. 0131/667-2743, www.hotelceilidh-donia.co.uk, reservations @hotelceilidh-donia.co.uk, Max and Annette).

$$$ AmarAgua Guest House is an inviting Victorian home away from home, with five welcoming rooms and a Japanese garden. It's given a little extra sparkle by its energetic proprietors and former entertainers, Dawn-Ann and Tony Costa (Db-£74-98 in June–Sept, Db-£64–88 in April–May and Oct, less in winter, more for fancy four-poster rooms, 2-night minimum, free Internet access and Wi-Fi, 10 Kilmaurs Terrace, tel. 0131/667-6775, www .amaragua.co.uk, reservations@amaragua.co.uk).

$$ Airdenair Guest House, offering views and a friendly welcome, has five attractive rooms on the second floor with a lofty above-it-all feeling. Homemade scones are a staple here, and Jill's dad regularly makes batches of "tablet"—a Scottish delicacy that's sweet as can be (Sb-£40, Db-£70–80, Tb-£85–95, less off-season, free Wi-Fi, 29 Kilmaurs Road, tel. 0131/668-2336, www.airdenair .com, jill@airdenair.com, Jill and Doug McLennan).

$$ Dunedin Guest House (dun-EE-din) is a fine value: bright, plush, and elegantly Scottish, with seven nice, airy rooms and a spacious breakfast room (S with private b on hall-£45–55, Db-£75, family rooms for up to five, less off-season, free Wi-Fi, 8 Priestfield Road, tel. 0131/668-1949, www.dunedinguesthouse .co.uk, reservations@dunedinguesthouse.co.uk, David and Irene Wright).

$$ Ard-Na-Said B&B is an elegant 1875 Victorian house with a comfy lounge. It offers thoughtful touches and luxurious modern bathrooms in seven bright and spacious rooms—including one ground-floor room with a pleasant patio (Sb-£35–50, Db-£60–80, huge four-poster Db-£70–100, Tb-£90–120, prices depend on size of room as well as season, family room, free Internet access and Wi-Fi, DVD players, free parking, 5 Priestfield Road, tel. 0131/667-8754, www.ardnasaid.co.uk, jim@ardnasaid.co.uk, Jim and Olive Lyons).

$$ Aonach Mor B&B's plush rooms have views of either nearby Arthur's Seat or walled gardens (Db-£65–85, more in July–Aug, less Nov–March, online specials, free Wi-Fi, 14 Kilmaurs Terrace, tel. 0131/667-8694, www.aonachmor.com, info@aonachmor.com, Chris and Lee).

$$ Kenvie Guest House, expertly run by Dorothy Vidler, comes with six pleasant rooms (one small twin-£56, D-£58–64, Db-£66–74, these prices with cash and this book through 2011—must claim when you reserve, family deals, free Internet access and Wi-Fi, 16 Kilmaurs Road, tel. 0131/668-1964, www.kenvie.co.uk, dorothy@kenvie.co.uk).

$$ Gil Dun Guest House, with eight rooms on a quiet cul-de-sac just off Dalkeith Road, is comfortable, pleasant, and managed with care by Gerry McDonald and Bill (Sb-£35–40, Db-£70–80, or £120 in Aug, great bathrooms, family deals, free Wi-Fi, pleasant garden, 9 Spence Street, tel. 0131/667-1368, www.gildun.co.uk, gildun.edin@btinternet.com).

$$ Dorstan Hotel is a little bigger than my other listings in this area, but it's still friendly and relaxed. Several of its 14 thoughtfully decorated rooms are on the ground floor (S-£30–50, Sb-£35–55, Ds-£40–60, Db-£50–70, Tb-£60–100, family rooms and suites available, free Wi-Fi, lounge, parking lot, 7 Priestfield Road, tel. 0131/667-6721, www.dorstan-hotel.demon.co.uk, reservations@dorstan-hotel.demon.co.uk, Richard and Maki Stott).

$$ Priestville Guest House is homey, with a dramatic skylight above the stairs, a sunny breakfast room, and cozy charm—not fancy, but more than workable, and great for families. The six rooms have Wi-Fi, VCRs, and a free video library (D-£50–64, Db-£56–72, Tb-£100, Q-£120, discount for 2 or more nights, free Internet access and Wi-Fi, family rooms, 10 Priestfield Road, tel. 0131/667-2435, www.priestville.com, bookings@priestville.com, Trina and Colin Warwick and their "rescue dog" Torrie).

$ The Belford Guest House is a tidy, homey place offering three basic rooms with renovated bathrooms and a warm welcome. The two en-suite rooms are twins; the lone double has its own bathroom outside the room (Sb-£45, Db-£60, family room, cheaper for longer stays, cash only, free parking, 13 Blacket Avenue—no sign out front, tel. 0131/667-2422, www.belfordguesthouse.com, tom@belfordguesthouse.com, Tom Borthwick).

Guest Houses on Mayfield Gardens

These two very-well-run B&Bs are set back from a busy four-lane highway. They come with a little street noise, but are bigger buildings with more spacious rooms, finer public lounges, and nice comforts (such as iPod-compatible bedside radios).

$$ At **23 Mayfield Guest House,** Ross and Kathleen (and Grandma Mary) rent nine thoughtfully appointed rooms in an outstanding house. Every detail has been chosen with care, from the historically accurate paint colors to the "James Bond bathrooms." Being travelers themselves, they know the value of little extras, offering a wide breakfast selection and a comfy lounge with cold soft drinks at an "honesty bar" (Sb-£55-65, Db-£65–80, bigger Db-£70–100, 4-poster Db-£80–110, family room for up to 4, free Internet access and Wi-Fi, swap library, free parking, 23 Mayfield Gardens, tel. 0131/667-5806, www.23mayfield.co.uk, info@23mayfield.co.uk).

$$ Glenalmond House, run by Jimmy and Fiona Mackie, has 10 beautiful rooms with fancy modern bathrooms (Db-£70–80, bigger 4-poster Db up to £95, Tb-£75–105, Qb-£80–120, 5 percent Rick Steves discount if you book direct and pay cash, less off-season, discount for longer stays, free Internet access and Wi-Fi, free parking, 25 Mayfield Gardens, tel. 0131/668-2392, www.glenalmondhouse.com, enquiries@glenalmondhouse.com).

Big, Modern Hotels

The first listing's a splurge. The next four are cheaper than most of the city's other chain hotels, and offer more comfort than character. In each case I'd skip the institutional breakfast and eat out. To locate these hotels, see the maps on pages 602 and 644. You'll generally pay £10 a day to park near these hotels.

$$$ Macdonald Holyrood Hotel, my only fancy listing, is an opulent four-star splurge, with 156 rooms up the street from the new Parliament building. With its classy marble-and-wood decor, fitness center, and pool, it's hard to leave. On a gray winter day in Edinburgh, this could be worth it. Prices can vary wildly (Db-£110–170, breakfast extra, check for specials online, near bottom of Royal Mile, across from Dynamic Earth, 81 Holyrood Road, tel. 0131/550-4500, www.macdonaldhotels.co.uk).

$$$ Jurys Inn offers a more enjoyable feeling than the Ibis and Travelodge (listed next). A cookie-cutter place with 186 dependably comfortable and bright rooms, it is capably run and well-located a short walk from the station (Sb/Db/Tb-£99, less on weekdays, can be much cheaper off-season and for online bookings, 2 kids sleep free, breakfast-£10, some views, Wi-Fi, laundry service, pub/restaurant, on quiet street just off Royal Mile and just above the train station, 43 Jeffrey Street, tel. 0131/200-3300, www.jurysinns.com).

$$$ Ibis Hotel, at the middle of the Royal Mile, is well-run and perfectly located. It has 99 soulless but clean and comfy rooms drenched in prefab American "charm." Room rates vary widely—

Royal Mile Accommodations & Eateries

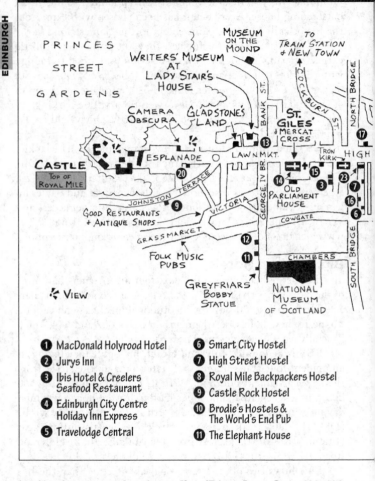

PRINCES STREET GARDENS

MUSEUM ON THE MOUND

TO TRAIN STATION & NEW TOWN

WRITERS' MUSEUM AT LADY STAIR'S HOUSE

CAMERA OBSCURA

GLADSTONE'S LAND

BANK ST.

COCKBURN ST.

NORTH BRIDGE

ST. GILES' & MERCAT CROSS

13

17

CASTLE

TOP OF ROYAL MILE

ESPLANADE

LAWN MKT.

TRON KIRK

HIGH

20

GEORGE IV BR.

14

OLD PARLIAMENT HOUSE

15

3

23

7

JOHNSTON TERRACE

VICTORIA

9

16

6

GOOD RESTAURANTS + ANTIQUE SHOPS

COWGATE

SOUTH BRIDGE

GRASSMARKET

12

CHAMBERS

FOLK MUSIC PUBS

11

GREYFRIARS BOBBY STATUE

NATIONAL MUSEUM OF SCOTLAND

VIEW

1 MacDonald Holyrood Hotel

2 Jurys Inn

3 Ibis Hotel & Creelers Seafood Restaurant

4 Edinburgh City Centre Holiday Inn Express

5 Travelodge Central

6 Smart City Hostel

7 High Street Hostel

8 Royal Mile Backpackers Hostel

9 Castle Rock Hostel

10 Brodie's Hostels & The World's End Pub

11 The Elephant House

book online to get their best offers (Db in June–Sept-£80–100, more during Festival, less off-season, breakfast-£7 extra, pay Internet access and Wi-Fi, 6 Hunter Square, tel. 0131/240-7000, fax 0131/240-7007, www.ibishotels.com, h2039@accor.com).

$$$ **Edinburgh City Centre Holiday Inn Express** rents 160 rooms with stark modern efficiency in a fine location, a five-minute walk from the train station. You can add up to two adults for £10 each, so two couples or a family can find a great deal here (Db-£95–135 depending on day, generally most expensive on Fri–Sat, much more during Festival, cheaper off-season, for best rates book online, includes breakfast, free Wi-Fi, just down Leith Street from the station at 16 Picardy Place, tel. 0131/558-2300, www.hiexpress

NOT TO SCALE —
CASTLE TO
PALACE OF HOLYROODHOUSE
IS ABOUT 1 MILE

JOHN KNOX HOUSE
CANONGATE CHURCH
WHITE HORSE CLOSE
QUEEN'S GALLERY
PEOPLE'S STORY
STREET
CANONGATE
PALACE OF HOLYROOD-HOUSE
BOTTOM OF ROYAL MILE
MUSEUM OF CHILDHOOD
MUSEUM OF EDINBURGH
ST. MARY'S
HOLYROOD RD.
DYNAMIC EARTH
SCOTTISH PARLIAMENT
QUEEN'S DRIVE
TRAIL TO ARTHUR'S SEAT
HOLYROOD PARK
DCH

⑫ The Outsider Restaurant
⑬ Deacon Brodie's Tavern
⑭ St. Giles' Cathedral Café
⑮ Always Sunday Food Co.
⑯ Piemaker Café
⑰ Dubh Prais Scottish Rest.
⑱ Wedgwood Restaurant
⑲ David Bann Restaurant
⑳ The Witchery by the Castle
㉑ Clarinda's Tea Room
㉒ Tass Pub
㉓ Whistlebinkies Pub

.co.uk). There's another location just off the Royal Mile (Db-£95–135, 300 Cowgate, tel. 0131/524-8400).

$$ Travelodge Central has 193 well-located, no-nonsense rooms, all decorated in dark blue. All rooms are the same and suitable for two adults with two kids, or three adults. While sleepable, it has a cheap feel with a quickly revolving staff (Sb/Db/Tb-£60–70, weekend Db-£70–85, Aug Db-£150, cheaper off-season and when booked online in advance, breakfast-£8 extra, 33 St. Mary's Street, a block off Royal Mile, tel. 0871-984-8484, www.travelodge.co.uk). They have two other locations in the New Town: at 37–43 Rose Street and at 3 Waterloo Place, on the east end of Princes Street.

Hostels

Edinburgh has two five-star hostels with dorm beds for about £20, slick modern efficiency, and careful management. They offer the best cheap beds in town. These places welcome families—travelers of any age feel comfortable here. Anyone on a tight budget wanting a twin room should think of these as simple hotels. The alternative is one of Edinburgh's scruffy bohemian hostels, each of which offers a youthful, mellow ambience and beds for around £15.

$ Edinburgh Central Youth Hostel rents 300 beds in rooms with one to eight beds (all with private bathrooms and lockers). Guests can eat cheap in the cafeteria or cook for the cost of groceries in the members' kitchen. Prices include sheets; towel rental costs extra (£16–28/person in 4- to 8-bed rooms, Sb-£34–49, Db-£51–95, Tb-£67–115, Qb-£89–145, depends on season, nonmembers pay £1 extra per night, single-sex dorms, £6 cooked breakfast, £4.25 continental breakfast, open 24/7, pay Internet access and Wi-Fi, laundry facilities, 10-minute walk to Waverley Station, Lothian bus #22 from station, 9 Haddington Place off Leith Walk, tel. 0131/524-2090. www.syha.org.uk).

$ Smart City Hostel is a godsend for backpackers and anyone looking for simple, efficient rooms in the old center for cheap. You'll pay £13–28 (depends on season) for a bed in an austere, industrial-strength 4- to 12-bed dorm—each with its own private bathroom. But it can get crazy with raucous weekend stag and hen parties. The Smart City Café in the basement has an inviting lounge with cheap meals. Half of the rooms function as a university dorm during the school year, becoming available just in time for the tourists (620 beds, Db-£50–125, bunky Qb-£70–150, includes linens and towels, £5 cooked breakfast, some female-only rooms, lockers, kitchen, lots of modern and efficient extras, free Wi-Fi, coin-op laundry, 50 Blackfriars Street, tel. 0131/524-1989, www.smartcityhostels.com, info@smartcityhostels.com).

Cheap and Scruffy Bohemian Hostels in the Center: These first three sister hostels—popular crash pads for young, hip backpackers—are beautifully located in the noisy center (£13.50–18 depending on time of year, twin D-£40–55, www.scotlandstop hostels.com): **High Street Hostel** (130 beds, 8 Blackfriars Street, just off High Street/Royal Mile, tel. 0131/557-3984); **Royal Mile Backpackers** (40 beds, dorms only—no private rooms, 105 High Street, tel. 0131/557-6120); and **Castle Rock Hostel** (200 beds, just below the castle and above the pubs, 15 Johnston Terrace, tel. 0131/225-9666). **Brodie's Hostels,** somewhere between spartan and dumpy in the middle of the Royal Mile, rents 130 cheap beds in 4- to 16-bed dorms (£10–13 beds, D-£39, Db-£45, includes linens, lockers, kitchen, Internet access-£1/20 minutes, laundry, 93 High Street, tel. 0131/556-2223, www.brodieshostels.co.uk).

Eating in Edinburgh

Reservations for restaurants are essential in August and on weekends, and a good idea anytime. All restaurants in Scotland are smoke-free.

Along the Royal Mile

Historic pubs and doily cafés with reasonable, unremarkable meals abound. Though the eateries along this most-crowded stretch of the city are invariably touristy, the scene is fun and competition makes a well-chosen place a good value. Here are some handy, affordable options for a good bite to eat (listed in downhill order; for locations, see map on pages 644–645). Sprinkled in this list are some places a block or two off the main drag offering better values—and correspondingly filled with more locals than tourists.

The first two restaurants are in a cluster of pleasant eateries happily removed from the Royal Mile melee. Consider stopping at one of these on your way to the National Museum of Scotland, which is a half-block away.

The Elephant House, two blocks out of the touristy zone with an unmarked front door, is a comfy neighborhood coffee shop where relaxed patrons browse newspapers in the stay-awhile back room, listen to soft rock, enjoy the castle and cemetery vistas, and sip coffee or munch a light meal. During the day you'll pick up food at the counter and grab your own seat; after 18:00, the café switches to table service. It's easy to imagine J. K. Rowling annoying waiters with her baby pram while spending long afternoons here writing the first Harry Potter book (£7 plates, "gourmet" pizza, great desserts, daily 8:00–23:00, 4 computers with cheap and fast Internet access, vegetarian options, 2 blocks south of Royal Mile near National Museum of Scotland at 21 George IV Bridge, tel. 0131/220-5355).

The Outsider, also without a hint of Royal Mile tourism, is a sleek spot serving creative and trendy cuisine (good fish and grilled meats and vegetables) in a minimalist, stylish, hardwood, candlelit castle-view setting. It's noisy with enthusiasm, and the service is crisp and youthful. As you'll be competing with yuppies, reserve for dinner (£6 lunch plates, £11–14 entrées, always a vegetarian course, good wines by the glass, daily 12:00–23:00, 30 yards up from Elephant House at 15 George IV Bridge, tel. 0131/226-3131).

Deacon Brodie's Tavern, at a dead-center location on the Royal Mile, is a sloppy pub on the ground floor with a sloppy restaurant upstairs serving basic £9 pub meals. While painfully touristy, it comes with a fun history (daily 10:00–22:00, hearty salads, kids' menu, kids welcome upstairs—but they're not allowed to enter after 20:00, tel. 0131/220-0317).

St. Giles' Cathedral Café, hiding under the landmark church, is *the* place for paupers to munch prayerfully. Stairs on the back side of the church lead into the basement, where you'll find simple, light lunches from 11:45 and coffee with cakes all day (Mon–Sat 9:00–17:00, Sun 11:00–16:30, open a little later during Festival, tel. 0131/225-5147).

Always Sunday Food Company is a tiny place with a wonderful formula. It's a flexible fantasy of Scottish and Mediterranean hot dishes, fresh salads, smoked salmon, sharp cheese, and homemade desserts. You're invited to mix and match at their user-friendly create-a-lunch buffet line. They use healthy ingredients and are sensitive to diet concerns. Sit inside or people-watch from Royal Mile tables outside (£6 lunches, Mon–Fri 8:00–18:00, Sat–Sun 9:00–18:00, 30 yards below St. Giles' Cathedral at 170 High Street, tel. 0131/622-0667).

Creelers Seafood Restaurant's Tim and Fran James have been fishing and feeding since 1995. This respected eatery creates a kind of rough, honest, unpretentious ambience with fresh seafood you'd expect from this salty part of Scotland (£18–20 entrées, £8–10 lunch and £17–20 early-dinner specials 17:30–18:45, open daily 12:00–14:30 & 17:30–22:00, open all day Sat, reservations smart, 30 yards off the Royal Mile at 3 Hunter Square, tel. 0131/220-4447).

Piemaker is a great place to grab a quick, cheap, and tasty meal, especially if you're in a hurry. Their meat pies and pastries—try the cherry—are "so fresh they'll pinch your bum and call you darlin'" (most everything under £3, Tue–Sat 9:00–24:00, Sun 11:00–18:00, Mon 9:00–19:00, about 100 yards off the Royal Mile at 38 South Bridge, tel. 0131/556-8566).

Dubh Prais Scottish Restaurant is a dressy nine-table place filling a cellar 10 steps and a world away from the High Street bustle. The owner-chef, James McWilliams, proudly serves Scottish "fayre" at its very best (including gourmet haggis). The daily specials are not printed, to guard against "zombie waiters." They like to get to know you a bit by explaining things (£16-19 entrées, £27 dinners, open Tue–Sat 17:00–22:30, closed Sun–Mon, reservations smart, opposite Radisson SAS Hotel at 123b High Street, tel. 0131/557-5732).

Wedgwood Restaurant is romantic, contemporary, chic, and as gourmet as possible with no pretense. Paul Wedgwood cooks while his partner Lisa serves with appetizing charm. The cuisine: creative, modern Scottish with an international twist and a whiff of Asia. The pigeon and haggis starter is scrumptious. Paul and

Lisa believe in making the meal the event of the evening—don't come here to eat and run. I like the ground level with the Royal Mile view, but the busy kitchen ambience in the basement is also fine (£10 two-course lunch, £7–9 starters, £17–24 entrées, fine wine by the glass, Mon–Sat 12:00–15:00 and 18:00–22:00, Sun 12:30–15:00, 267 Canongate on Royal Mile, tel. 0131/558-8737).

The World's End Pub, a colorful old place, dishes up hearty £8–10 meals from a creative menu in a fun, dark, and noisy space (daily 12:00–21:00, 4 High Street, tel. 0131/556-3628).

David Bann, just a three-minute walk off the Royal Mile, is a worthwhile stop for well-heeled vegetarians in need of a break from the morning fry. While vegetarian as can be, there's not a hint of hippie here. It's upscale (there's a cocktail bar), stylish (gorgeously presented dishes), serious about quality (David is busy in the kitchen), and organic—they serve polenta, tartlets, soups, and light meals (£6 starters, £11 entrées, decadent desserts, Mon–Fri 12:00–22:00, Sat–Sun 11:00–22:00, vegan options, 56–58 St. Mary's Street, tel. 0131/556-5888).

The Witchery by the Castle is set in a lushly decorated 16th-century building just below the castle on the Royal Mile, with wood paneling, antique candlesticks, tapestries, and opulent red leather upholstery. The emphasis is on fresh—and pricey—Scottish meats and seafood (£14 two-course, £30 three-course lunch specials 12:00–16:00, specials also good 17:30–18:30 & 22:30–23:30, £20–25 entrées, daily 12:00–16:00 & 17:30–23:30, reservations critical, tel. 0131/225-5613).

Clarinda's Tea Room, near the bottom of the Royal Mile, is charming and girlish—a fine and tasty place to relax after touring the Mile or the Palace of Holyroodhouse. Stop in for a £5 quiche, salad or soup lunch. It's also great for sandwiches and tea and cake anytime (Mon–Sat 8:30–16:45, Sun 9:30–16:45, 69 Canongate, tel. 0131/557-1888).

In the New Town

While most of your sightseeing will be along the Royal Mile, it's important that your Edinburgh experience stretches beyond this happy tourist gauntlet. Just a few minutes away, in the Georgian town, you'll find a bustling world of office workers, students, and pensioners doing their thing. And at midday, that includes eating. Simply hiking over to one of these places will give you a good helping of modern Edinburgh. All these places are within a few minutes' walk of the TI and main Waverley Bridge tour-bus depot.

Le Café St. Honoré, tucked away like a secret in the Georgian New Town, is a pricey but charming place with walls lined by tempting wine bottles. It serves French-Scottish cuisine in tight, Old World, cut-glass elegance to a dressy crowd (dinner specials

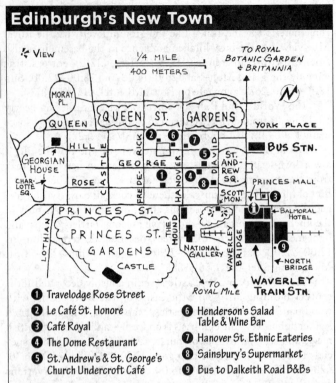

Edinburgh's New Town

➊ Travelodge Rose Street
➋ Le Café St. Honoré
➌ Café Royal
➍ The Dome Restaurant
➎ St. Andrew's & St. George's Church Undercroft Café
➏ Henderson's Salad Table & Wine Bar
➐ Hanover St. Ethnic Eateries
➑ Sainsbury's Supermarket
➒ Bus to Dalkeith Road B&Bs

Mon-Sat before 19:00, Sun all night; open Mon–Fri 12:00–14:00 & 17:15–22:00, Sat–Sun 18:00–22:00; reservations smart, down Thistle Street from Hanover Street, 34 Northwest Thistle Street Lane, tel. 0131/226-2211).

Café Royal is a movie producer's dream pub—the perfect *fin de siècle* setting for a coffee, beer, or light meal. (In fact, parts of *Chariots of Fire* were filmed here.) Drop in, if only to admire the 1880 tiles featuring famous inventors (daily 12:00–14:30 & 17:00–22:00, until 21:30 in winter, bar food available during the afternoon, 2 blocks from Princes Mall on 19 West Register Street, tel. 0131/556-1884). There are two eateries here: the noisy pub (£10–20 meals, Mon–Fri 11:00–21:45, Sat–Sun 12:30–22:00) and the dressier restaurant, specializing in oysters, fish, and game (£20 plates, daily 12:00–14:30 & 17:00–22:00, reserve for dinner—it's quite small and understandably popular).

The Dome Restaurant, in what was a fancy bank, serves decent meals around a classy bar and under the elegant 19th-century skylight dome. With soft jazz and chic, white-tablecloth ambience, it feels a world apart (£12–14 plates until 17:00, £12–20 dinners until 21:45, Sun–Wed 10:00–22:00, Thu–Sat 11:00–22:00, modern international cuisine, open for a drink anytime under the dome or in the adjacent Art Deco bar, 14 George Street, tel. 0131/624-8634, reserve for dinner). As you leave, look up to take in the facade of this former bank building—the pediment is filled with figures demonstrating various ways to make money, which they do with all the nobility of classical gods.

The **St. Andrew's and St. George's Church Undercroft Café,** in the basement of a fine old church, is the cheapest place in town for lunch—just £3.50 for sandwich and soup. Your tiny bill helps support the Church of Scotland (Mon–Fri 10:00–14:30, closed Sat–Sun, on George Street, just off St. Andrew Square, tel. 0131/225-3847).

Henderson's Salad Table and Wine Bar has fed a generation of New Town vegetarians hearty cuisine and salads. Even carnivores love this place for its delectable salads and desserts (two-course lunch for £9, Mon–Sat 8:00–22:00, Thu–Sat until 23:00, closed Sun except in July–Aug 10:00–17:00, strictly vegetarian, take-away available, pleasant live music nightly in wine bar—generally guitar or jazz; between Queen and George Streets at 94 Hanover Street, tel. 0131/225-2131). Henderson's two different seating areas use the same self-serve cafeteria line. For the same healthy food with more elegant seating and table service, eat at the attached **Henderson's Bistro** (daily 12:00–20:30, Thu–Sat until 21:30).

Fun Ethnic Eateries on Hanover Street: Hanover Street is lined with Thai, Greek, Turkish, Italian, and other restaurants. Stroll the block to eye your options.

Supermarket: The glorious **Sainsbury's** supermarket, with a tasty assortment of take-away food and specialty coffees, is just one block from the Sir Walter Scott Monument and the lovely picnic-perfect Princes Street Gardens (Mon–Sat 7:00–22:00, Sun 9:00–20:00, on corner of Rose Street on St. Andrew Square, across the street from Jenners, the classy department store).

The Dalkeith Road Area, near Your B&B

All of these places are within a 10-minute walk of my recommended B&Bs. Most are on or near the intersection of Newington Road and East Preston Street. Reserve on weekends and during the Festival. For locations, see the map on page 640. The nearest grocery store is **Tesco Express** (daily 6:00–23:00, 158 Causewayside). For a cozy drink after dinner, visit the recommended pubs in the area (see "Nightlife in Edinburgh," earlier).

Scottish/French Restaurants

Blonde Restaurant, with a modern Scottish and European menu, is less expensive, more crowded than the others, with no set-price dinners. It's a bit out of the way, but a hit with locals and tough to get into—make reservations (about £15–17 for two courses, Tue–Sun 12:00–14:30 & 18:00–22:00, open only for dinner on Mon, good vegetarian options, 75 St. Leonard's Street, tel. 0131/668-2917, Andy).

Rhubarb Restaurant is the hottest thing in Old World elegance. It's in "Edinburgh's most handsome house"—a riot of antiques, velvet, tassels, and fringes. The plush dark rhubarb color theme reminds visitors that this was the place where rhubarb was first grown in Britain. It's a 10-minute walk past the other recommended eateries behind Arthur's Seat, in a huge estate with big, shaggy Highland cattle enjoying their salads al fresco. At night, it's a candlelit wonder. While most spend a wad here (£20–34 plates), take advantage of the two-course lunch for £17, or at least consider the £30 three-course dinner (Sun–Thu 12:00–14:00 & 18:30–23:00, Fri–Sat 12:00–14:00 & 18:00–23:00, afternoon tea served 15:00-18:00, reserve in advance and dress up if you can, in Prestonfield House, Priestfield Road, tel. 0131/225-1333, www.prestonfield.com). For details on the Scottish folk evening offered here, see "Nightlife in Edinburgh," earlier.

The New Bell serves up filling modern Scottish fare, from steak and salmon to haggis, in a Victorian living-room setting above the lovable Old Bell Inn (see below). Along with wonderfully presented meals, you'll enjoy white tablecloths, Oriental carpets on hardwood floors, and a relaxing spaciousness under open beams (£14.50 two-course or £17.50 three-course special until 18:45, £15 plates, open Tue–Sun 17:30–21:30, Fri–Sun also 12:30–14:00, until 22:00 Fri–Sat, closed Mon, always a veggie option, 233 Causewayside, tel. 0131/668-2868).

Scottish Grub and Pubs

The Old Bell Inn, with an old-time sports-bar ambience—fishing, golf, horses—serves simpler £8 pub meals from the same fine kitchen as the fancier New Bell (which is just upstairs, described above). This is a classic snug pub, all dark woods and brass beer taps, littered with evocative knickknacks, and has live folk music Sundays at 20:00. It comes with sidewalk seating and a mixed-age crowd (open daily until 24:00; food served 12:00–14:30 & 17:00–19:00, until 19:30 Mon–Thu, 233 Causewayside, tel. 0131/668-1573).

Bierex, a youthful pub, is the neighborhood favorite for modern dishes (£7–9 plates), camaraderie, and cheap booze. It's a spacious, bright, mahogany-and-leather place popular for its long and varied happy hours (daily until late, food served Mon–Fri 11:00–21:00, Sat–Sun 10:00–21:00, Wi-Fi for customers, 132 Causewayside, tel. 0131/667-2335).

Reverie Bar is just your basic, fun pub with a focus on food rather than drinking and free live music most nights from 21:30 (every other Sun-jazz, Tue-traditional, Thu-blues; £7–9 main dishes, food served daily 12:00–21:00, 3 Newington Road, tel. 0131/667-8870).

Hewat's Restaurant is the neighborhood hit. Sample Scottish cuisine, or their popular steak dishes, in this elegantly whimsical dining space (£10 dinner deals Mon–Thu until 19:30; £14.50 for two courses, £17.50 for three courses until 18:45; open Wed–Sat 12:00–14:00 & 18:00–21:30, Fri–Sat until 22:00, Mon–Tue 18:00–21:30 only, closed Sun, 19–21b Causeway, tel. 0131/466-6660).

Hellers Kitchen is a casual blond-wood space specializing in dishes using local produce and fresh-baked breads and doughs. Check the big chalkboard to see what's on (£5–8 sandwiches, £8–10 pizzas, Mon–Fri 8:30–22:00, Sat 9:00–22:00, Sun 10:00–22:00, next to post office at 15 Salisbury Place, tel. 0130/667-4654).

Metropole Café is a fresh, healthy eatery with a Starbucks ambience, serving light bites for £4 and simple meals for £7 (daily 8:30–22:00, always a good vegetarian entrée, free Wi-Fi, 33 Newington Road, tel. 0131/668-4999).

Ethnic Options

Wild Elephant Thai Restaurant is a small, hardworking eatery that locals consider the best around for Thai (£11–14 entrées, £13 three-course meal available 17:00–19:00, also does take-away, open daily 12:00–14:30 & 17:00–23:00, 21 Newington Road, tel. 0131/662-8822).

Il Positano Ristorante has a spirited Italian ambience, as manager Giuseppe Votta injects a love of life and food into his little restaurant. The moment you step through the door, you know you're in for good, classic Italian cuisine (£7–9 pizzas and pastas, £11–15 plates, daily 12:00–14:00 & 17:00–23:00, 85–87 Newington Road, tel. 0131/662-9977).

Hanedan Turkish Restaurant is generating a huge buzz. This friendly, contemporary 10-table place serves great Turkish grills and vegetarian specials at a fine price (£9 two-course special anytime, £9 entrées, open Tue–Sun 12:00–15:00 & 17:30–24:00, closed Mon, 41 West Preston Street, tel. 0131/667-4242, chef Gürsel Bahar).

Edinburgh Connections

By Train or Bus

From Edinburgh by Train to: Glasgow (4/hour, 50 minutes), **St. Andrews** (train to Leuchars, 1–2/hour, 1–1.25 hours, then 10-minute bus into St. Andrews), **Stirling** (2/hour, 50 minutes),

Pitlochry (6/day direct, 2 hours, more with change in Stirling or Perth), **Inverness** (every 2 hours, 3.5–4 hours, some with change in Stirling or Perth), **Oban** (3/day, 4.25 hours, change in Glasgow), **York** (1–2/hour, 2.5 hours), **London** (1–2/hour, 4.5 hours), **Durham** (at least hourly, 1.75 hours), **Newcastle** (2/hour, 1.5 hours), **Keswick/Lake District** (8/day to Penrith—some via Carlisle, then catch bus to Keswick, fewer on Sun, 3 hours including bus transfer in Penrith), **Birmingham** (at least hourly, 4–5 hours, some with change in York), **Crewe** (every 2 hours, 3 hours), **Bristol** near Bath (hourly, 6–6.5 hours), **Blackpool** (roughly hourly, 3–3.5 hours, transfer in Preston). Train info: tel. 0845-748-4950, www .nationalrail.co.uk.

By Bus to: **Glasgow** (4/hour, 1.25 hours, £3–6.30), **Oban** (7/day Mon–Sat, 4–5 hours; 1 direct, rest with transfer in Glasgow, Perth, or Tyndrum), **Fort William** (7/day, 4–5 hours, 1 direct, rest with change in Glasgow or Tyndrum), **Portree** on the Isle of Skye (3/day, 7.5–8 hours, transfer in Inverness or Glasgow), **Inverness** (7/day, 3.5–4.5 hours). For bus info, call Scottish Citylink (tel. 0871-266-3333, www.citylink.co.uk) or National Express (tel. 0871-781-8181). You can get info and tickets at the bus desk inside the Princes Mall TI.

Route Tips for Drivers

To Hadrian's Wall: It's 100 miles south from Edinburgh to Hadrian's Wall; to Durham it's another 50 miles. From Edinburgh, Dalkeith Road leads south and eventually becomes A68 (handy Cameron Toll supermarket with cheap gas is on the left as you leave Edinburgh Town, 10 minutes south of Edinburgh; gas and parking behind store). The A68 road takes you to Hadrian's Wall in two hours. You'll pass Jedburgh and its abbey after one hour. (For one last shot of Scotland shopping, there's a coach tour's delight just before Jedburgh, with kilt-makers, woolens, and a sheepskin shop.) Across from Jedburgh's lovely abbey is a free parking lot, a good visitors center, and public toilets (£0.020 to pee). The England/ Scotland border is a fun, quick stop (great view, ice cream, and tea caravan). Just after the turn for Colwell, turn right onto A6079, and roller-coaster four miles down to Low Brunton. Then turn right onto B6318, and stay on it by turning left at Chollerford, following the Roman wall westward. (For information on Hadrian's Wall, see the Durham and Northeast England chapter.)

ST. ANDREWS

For many, St. Andrews is synonymous with golf. But there's more to this charming town than its famous links. Dramatically situated at the edge of a sandy bay, St. Andrews is the home of Scotland's most important university—think of it as the Scottish Cambridge. And centuries ago, the town was the religious capital of the country.

In its long history, St. Andrews has seen two boom periods. First, in the early Middle Ages, the relics of St. Andrew made the town cathedral one of the most important pilgrimage sites in Christendom. The faithful flocked here from all over Europe, leaving the town with a medieval all-roads-lead-to-the-cathedral street plan that survives today. But after the Scottish Reformation, the cathedral rotted away and the town became a forgotten backwater. A new wave of visitors arrived in the mid-19th century, when a visionary mayor named (appropriately enough) Provost Playfair began to promote the town's connection with the newly in-vogue game of golf. Most buildings in town date from this time (similar to Edinburgh's New Town).

Today St. Andrews remains a popular spot for both students and golf devotees (including professional golfers and celebrities such as Scotsman Sean Connery, often seen out on the links). With vast sandy beaches, golfing opportunities for pros and novices alike, playgrounds of ruins, a fun-loving student vibe, and a string of relaxing fishing villages nearby (the East Neuk), St. Andrews is an appealing place to take a vacation from your busy vacation.

Planning Your Time

St. Andrews, hugging the east coast of Scotland, is a bit off the main tourist track. But it's well-connected by train to Edinburgh (via bus from nearby Leuchars), making it a worthwhile day trip from the capital. Better yet, spend a night (or more, if you're a golfer) to enjoy this university town after dark.

If you're not here to golf, this is a good way to spend a day: Follow my self-guided walk, which connects the golf course, the university quad, the castle, and the cathedral. Dip into the Golf Museum, watch the golfers on the Old Course, and play a round at "the Himalayas" putting green. With more time, walk along the West Sands beach or take a spin by car or bus to the nearby East Neuk.

Orientation to St. Andrews

(area code: 01334)

St. Andrews (pop. 14,000), situated at the tip of a peninsula next to a broad bay, retains its old medieval street plan: Three main roads (North Street, Market Street, and South Street) converge at the cathedral, which overlooks the sea at the tip of town. The middle of these streets—Market Street—has the TI and many handy shops and eateries. North of North Street, the seafront street called The Scores connects the cathedral with the golf scene, which huddles along the West Sands beach at the base of the old town. It's an enjoyably compact town: You can stroll across town—from the cathedral to the historic golf course—in about 15 minutes.

Tourist Information

St. Andrews' helpful TI is on Market Street, about two blocks in front of the cathedral (July–Aug Mon–Sat 9:15–19:00, Sun 10:00–17:00; April–June and Sept–mid-Oct Mon–Sat 9:15–17:00, Sun 11:00–16:00; mid-Oct–March Mon–Sat 9:15–17:00, closed Sun; 70 Market Street, tel. 01334/472-021, www.visitfife.com or www.visitscotland.com). Pick up their stack of brochures on the town and region, and ask about other tours (such as ghost walks or witches walks). They also have Internet access (£1/20 minutes) and can find you a room for a £4 fee.

Arrival in St. Andrews

By Train and Bus: The nearest train station is in the village of Leuchars, five miles away. From there, a 10-minute bus ride takes you right into St. Andrews (£2.45, driver gives change for small bills; buses meet most trains, see schedule at bus shelter for next bus to St. Andrews; while waiting, read the historical info under the nearby flagpole). St. Andrews' bus station is near the base of

Market Street. To reach most B&Bs, turn left out of the station, right at the roundabout, and look for Murray Park on the left. To reach the TI, turn right out of the station, then take the next left and head up Market Street. Taxis from Leuchars into St. Andrews cost about £12.

By Car: For a short stay, drivers can simply head into the town center and park anywhere along the street. Easy-to-use meters dispense stickers (£0.85/hour, coins only, 2-hour limit, monitored Mon–Sat 9:00–17:00). For longer stays, you can park for free along certain streets near the center (such as along The Scores), or use one of the long-stay lots near the entrance to town.

Helpful Hints

Golf Events: Every five years, St. Andrews is swamped with about 100,000 visitors when it hosts the British Open (called simply "The Open" around here; the next one is in 2015). The town also fills up every year in early October for the Alfred Dunhill Links Championship. Unless you're a golf pilgrim, avoid the town at these times. If you are a golf pilgrim, expect room rates to skyrocket.

School Term: The University of St. Andrews has two terms: spring semester ("Candlemas"), from mid-February through May; and fall semester ("Martinmas"), from late September until mid-January. St. Andrews feels downright sleepy in summer, when most students leave and golfers take over the town.

Internet Access: You can get online for free at the **public library,** behind the church on South Street (Mon and Fri–Sat 9:30–17:00, Tue–Thu 9:30–19:00, closed Sun, tel. 01334/659-378). The TI also has two pay Internet terminals.

Walking Tour: June Riches offers good walking tours that bring St. Andrews' history to life. There's no set schedule, so call or email ahead to join a tour or arrange for one of your own (roughly £7/1.5 hours, prices vary by tour and group size, tel. 01334/850-638, june.riches@virgin.net).

Self-Guided Walk

Welcome to St. Andrews

This walk links all of St. Andrews' must-see sights and takes you down hidden medieval streets. Allow at least an hour, or more if you detour for the sights along the way.

• *Start at the base of the seaside street called The Scores, by the historical-information signpost near the green caddies' pavilion. (To get here from the bus station, turn left down City Road, then right onto North Street, then immediately left again onto Golf Place.)*

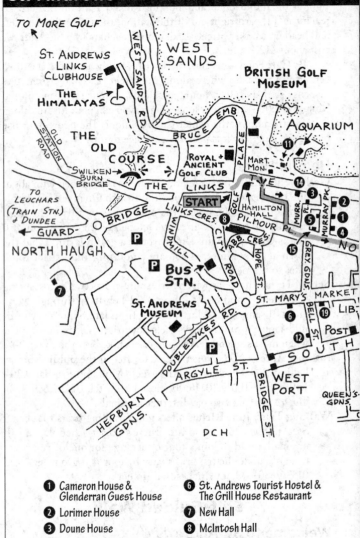

St. Andrews

TO MORE GOLF

ST. ANDREWS LINKS CLUBHOUSE

THE HIMALAYAS

WEST SANDS RD.

WEST SANDS

BRITISH GOLF MUSEUM

AQUARIUM

BRUCE EMB.

THE OLD COURSE

OLD STATION ROAD

SWILKEN BURN BRIDGE

ROYAL + ANCIENT GOLF CLUB

MART. MON.

THE LINKS

PLACE

AVE.

START

GOLF PL.

MURR. PL.

Murray Pk.

TO LEUCHARS (TRAIN STN.) & DUNDEE

GUARD-

BRIDGE

LINKS CRES.

HAMILTON HALL

PILMOUR PL.

NO.

NORTH HAUGH

WINDMILL

CITY ROAD

ABB. CRES.

HOPE ST.

GREY GDNS.

BUS STN.

ST. ANDREWS MUSEUM

DOUBLEDYKES RD.

ST. MARY'S

MARKET

BELL ST.

LIB.

POST

SOUTH

ARGYLE ST.

BRIDGE ST.

WEST PORT

QUEEN'S GDNS.

HEPBURN GDNS.

DCH

❶ Cameron House & Glenderran Guest House	❻ St. Andrews Tourist Hostel & The Grill House Restaurant
❷ Lorimer House	❼ New Hall
❸ Doune House	❽ McIntosh Hall
❹ Arran House	❾ The Doll's House Restaurant
❺ Hoppity House B&B	❿ The Glass House Restaurant

ST. ANDREWS

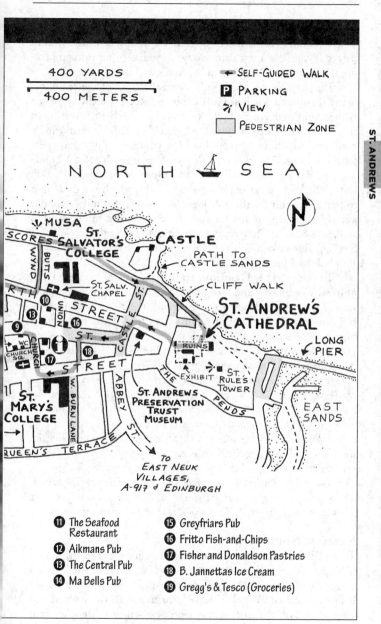

400 YARDS
400 METERS

← SELF-GUIDED WALK
P PARKING
↗ VIEW
PEDESTRIAN ZONE

NORTH ⛵ SEA

N

↓ MUSA
SCORES WYND
ST. SALVATOR'S COLLEGE
BUTTS WYND
CASTLE
PATH TO CASTLE SANDS
CLIFF WALK
ST. SALV. CHAPEL
⑩ UNION STREET
⑬ ⑯
⑨
WC CHURCH SQ.
ℹ
⑰ ⑱
ST. STREET
CASTLE ST.
ST. ANDREW'S CATHEDRAL
RUINS
EXHIBIT
ST. RULES TOWER
LONG PIER
EAST SANDS
NORTH
CHURCH
W. BURN LANE
ST. ANDREWS PRESERVATION TRUST MUSEUM
THE PENDS
ABBEY ST.
ST. MARY'S COLLEGE
QUEEN'S TERRACE
→ TO EAST NEUK VILLAGES, A-917 & EDINBURGH

⑪ The Seafood Restaurant
⑫ Aikmans Pub
⑬ The Central Pub
⑭ Ma Bells Pub
⑮ Greyfriars Pub
⑯ Fritto Fish-and-Chips
⑰ Fisher and Donaldson Pastries
⑱ B. Jannettas Ice Cream
⑲ Gregg's & Tesco (Groceries)

ST. ANDREWS

The Old Course

You're standing at the mecca of golf. The 18th hole of the world's first golf course is a few yards away, on your left (for info on playing the course, see "Golfing in St. Andrews," later).

The gray Neoclassical building to the right of the 18th hole is the **Royal and Ancient Golf Club** (or "R&A" for short), which is the world's governing body for golf (like the British version of the PGA). The R&A is closed to the public, and only men can be members (which might seem harmlessly quaint...if it weren't persisting into the 21st century). Women can enter the R&A building only during the Women's British Open on St. Andrew's Day (Nov 30). Anyone can enter the shop nearby, which is a great spot to buy a souvenir for the golf-lover back home. Even if you're not golfing, watch the action for a while. (Serious fans might want to walk around to the low-profile stone bridge across the creek called Swilken Burn, with golf's single most iconic view: back over the 18th hole and the R&A.)

To your right is **Hamilton Hall,** an old hotel long used as a university dormitory and now under renovation to become swanky timeshares. According to town legend, the tall red-sandstone building was built to upstage the R&A by an American upset over being declined membership to the exclusive club. Between Hamilton Hall and the beach is the low-profile **British Golf Museum** (described on page 670).

• *If the weather's decent and you've got the time, take a detour and stroll the* **West Sands,** *the two-mile-long, broad, sandy beach that stretches below the golf courses. It's a wonderful place for a relaxing and invigorating walk. Or jog the beach, humming the theme to* Chariots of Fire *(this is the beach they run along in the famous opening scene). To reach the sands, walk past the R&A and hang a left—just after you've crossed over the creek, you'll find the ramp leading down to the beach.*

To continue this walk, turn right and start walking up **The Scores.** *The street's name may sound golf-inspired, but comes instead from the Norse word for "cliff-top." When you see the obelisk, cross the street.*

Martyrs' Monument

This obelisk commemorates all those who died for their Protestant beliefs during the Scottish Reformation. Walk up to the benches to get a good look at the cliffs on your right. For a time, the sea below was called "Witches' Lake" because of all the women and men pushed off the cliff on suspicion of witchcraft. The Victorian bandstand gazebo recalls the town's genteel heyday as a seaside resort, when the train line ran all the way to town.

Cross back to the other side of the street. Find the covered **alleyway** near Alexander's Restaurant (you may see it next to the

The Scottish Reformation

It's easy to forget that during the 16th-century English Reformation—when King Henry VIII split with the Vatican and formed the Anglican Church (so he could get an officially recognized divorce)—Scotland was still its own independent nation. Like much of northern Europe, Scotland eventually chose a Protestant path, but it was more gradual and grassroots than Henry VIII's top-down, destroy-the-abbeys approach. While the English Reformation resulted in the Church of England (a.k.a. the Anglican Church, called "Episcopal" outside of England), with the monarch at its head, the Scottish Reformation created the Church of Scotland, which had groups of elected leaders (called "presbyteries" in church jargon).

One of the leaders of the Scottish Reformation was John Knox (1514–1572), who learned at the foot of the great Swiss Reformer John Calvin. Returning to Scotland, Knox hopped from pulpit to pulpit, and his feverish sermons incited riots of "born-again" iconoclasts who dismantled or destroyed Catholic churches and abbeys (including St. Andrew's Cathedral). Knox's newly minted Church of Scotland gradually spread from the Lowlands to the Highlands. The southern and eastern part of Scotland, around St. Andrews—just across the North Sea from the Protestant countries of northern Europe—embraced the Church of Scotland long before the more remote and Catholic-oriented part of the country to the north and west. Today about 40 percent of Scots claim affiliation with the Church of Scotland, compared with 20 percent who are Catholic (still mostly in the western Highlands).

blue Gillespie Terrace sign, if it's not obscured by shrubs). Step into the alley and take a quick look back at the magnificent view of the West Sands (in the spring, this archway frames a rainbow nearly every day). Then follow the alley as it winds through the back gardens of the city's stone houses. St. Andrews' street plan typifies that of a medieval pilgrimage town: All main roads lead to the cathedral; only tiny lanes, hidden alleys, and twisting "wynds" such as this one connect the main east-west streets, which converge at the cathedral.

• *The wynd pops you out onto North Street. Make like a pilgrim and head left toward the cathedral. As you walk, listen to the seagulls. Is it just me, or can you detect a Scottish brogue in their squawking?*

Once you've passed the small cinema on your left, you'll see the church tower with the red clock face. Walk past **Butt's Wynd** *(no joke). For some reason, this street sign often goes missing.*

You're standing outside St. Salvator's Chapel, part of...

St. Salvator's College

If you're a student, tread carefully over the cobbles here to avoid stepping on the initials *PH*. They mark the spot where St. Andrews alum and professor Patrick Hamilton—the Scottish Reformation's most famous martyr—was burned at the stake. According to student legend, as he suffered in the flames, Hamilton threatened that any students who stood on this spot would fail their exams. (And you thought you had hard-nosed teachers.)

St. Salvator's Chapel, dating from 1450, is the town's most beautiful medieval church. Try the door—if it's open, you'll be treated to a Gothic gem, with a wooden ceiling, 19th-century stained glass, and (supposedly) the pulpit of reformer John Knox.

• *If the chapel's not open, pass through the archway into the quad of St. Salvator's College—which isn't an institution itself, but rather a group of university buildings. (The archway may be closed off—if so, head to Butt's Wynd and enter at the gate there...which may also be closed. If so, have a peek at the quad through the gate.)*

This grassy square, known to students as **Sally's Quad,** is the heart of St. Andrews University. As most of the university's classrooms, offices, and libraries are spread out across the medieval town, this quad is the one focal point for student gatherings. It's where graduation is held every July, and where the free-for-all food fight of Raisin Monday takes place in November (see sidebar on pages 664–665). If you're feeling curious, push a few doors (some seemingly off-limits university buildings, many marked by blue doors, are actually open to the public).

On the outside wall of the chapel are cases holding notices and university information; if you're here in spring, you might see students nervously clustered here, looking to see if they've passed their exams. (Note the other door to the chapel, near the cases, which is worth trying if the one facing North Street is closed.)

Stroll the quad counterclockwise. On the east side, stop to check out the crazy faces on the heads above the second-floor windows. Find the **university's shield** over the door marked *School Six.* The diamonds are from the coat of arms of the bishop who issued the first university charter in 1411; the crescent moon is a shout-out to Pope Benedict XIII, who gave the OK in 1413 to found the university (his given name was Peter de Luna); the lion is from the Scottish coat of arms; and the cross is a stylized version of the Scottish flag (a.k.a. St. Andrew's Cross). On the next building to the left, facing the chapel, is St. Andrew himself (above door of building labeled *Upper & Lower College Halls*).

• *Exit the square at the west end, if the gate's open, and turn right into the wynd (if the gate's closed, backtrack out past Hamilton's initials and hang a right into Butt's Wynd). When the alley ends, you're back at The Scores. Cross the street and head to the right. The turreted stone build-*

ings along here are built in the Neo-Gothic Scots Baronial style, and most are academic departments. Head for the...

Museum of the University of St. Andrews (MUSA)

This free museum is worth a quick stop. The first room has some well-explained medieval paraphernalia, but the highlight is the earliest-known map of the town, made in 1580—back when the town walls led directly to countryside and the cathedral was intact. Notice that the street plan within the town walls has remained the same. The next room has some exhibits on student life; the rest is skippable. For another great view of the West Sands, when you leave the building walk out and around to the back to the small cliff-top patio (free; April–Sept Mon–Sat 10:00–17:00, Sun 12:00–16:00; Oct–March Thu–Sun 10:00–16:00, closed Mon–Wed; 7a The Scores, tel. 01334/461-660, www.st-andrews.ac.uk /musa).

• *Back on The Scores, walk left toward the castle. Along the way you'll pass stately St. Salvator's Hall (on your right, small sign on the wall), the most prestigious of the university residences and former dorm of Prince William. Just past St. Salvator's Hall are the remains of...*

▲St. Andrews' Castle

Overlooking the sea, the castle is basically just an evocative empty shell—another casualty of the Scottish Reformation. Built by a

bishop to entertain visiting diplomats in the late 12th century, the castle was home to the powerful bishops, archbishops, and cardinals of St. Andrews. In 1546, the cardinal burned a Protestant preacher at the stake in front of the castle. In retribution, Protestant Reformers took the castle and killed the cardinal. In 1547, the French came to attack the castle on behalf of their Catholic ally, Mary, Queen of Scots. During the ensuing siege, a young Protestant refugee named John Knox was captured and sent to France to row on a galley ship. Eventually he traveled to Switzerland and met the Swiss Protestant ringleader, John Calvin. Knox brought Calvin's ideas back home and became Scotland's greatest Reformer.

Today's castle is the ruined post-Reformation version. Your visit starts with a colorful, well-presented exhibit about the history of the castle. Afterward, head outside to explore the ruins. The most interesting parts are underground: the "bottle dungeon," where prisoners were sent never to return (peer down into it in

Student Life in St. Andrews

Although most people associate St. Andrews with golf, it's first and foremost a university town—the home of Scotland's most prestigious university. Founded in 1411, it's the third-oldest in the English-speaking world—only Oxford and Cambridge have been around longer.

The U. of St. A. has about 6,000 undergrads and 1,000 grad students. Though Scots attend for free, others (including students from England) must pay tuition. Some Scots resent the high concentration of upper-class English students (disparagingly dubbed "Yahs" for the snooty way they say "yes"), who treat St. Andrews as a "safety school" if rejected by Cambridge or Oxford. The school has even been called "England's northernmost university" because it has as many English students as Scottish ones. (Adding to the mix, about a quarter of the students come from overseas.) Its most famous recent graduate is Prince William (class of '05). Soon after he started here, the number of female applicants to study art history—his major—skyrocketed. (He later switched to geography.)

As with any venerable university, St. Andrews has its share of quirky customs—as if the university, like the town's street plan, insists on clinging to the Middle Ages. Most students own traditional red woolen academic "gowns" (woolen robes). Today these are only worn for special occasions (such as graduation), but in medieval times, students were required to wear them always—supposedly so they could be easily identified in brothels and pubs. (In a leap of faith, divinity students—apparently beyond temptation—wear black.) The way the robe is worn indicates the student's progress toward graduation: First-year students (called "bejants") wear them normally, on the shoulders; second-years

the Sea Tower); and, around under the main drawbridge, the tight "mine" and even tighter "counter-mine" tunnels (crawling is required to reach it all; go in as far as your claustrophobia allows). This shows how the besieging French army dug a mine to take the castle—but were followed at every turn by the Protestant counter-miners.

Just below the castle is a small beach called the Castle Sands, where university students take a traditional and chilly morning dip every May 1. Supposedly, doing this May Day swim is the only way to reverse the curse of having stepped on Patrick Hamilton's initials (explained earlier).

Cost and Hours: £5.20, £7.20 combo-ticket includes cathedral exhibit, daily April–Sept 9:30–17:30, Oct–March 9:30–16:30, last entry 30 minutes before closing, tel. 01334/477-196.

• *Leaving the castle, walk along the cliffside path, downhill toward the sea. Enter the gate to a graveyard. You're standing amid the ruins of...*

("semi-bejants") wear them slightly off the shoulders; third-years ("tertians") wear them off one shoulder (right shoulder for "scientists" and left shoulder for "artists"); and fourth-years ("magistrands") wear them off both shoulders.

There's no better time to see these robes than during the Pier Walk on Sunday afternoons during the university term. After church services (around noon), students clad in their gowns parade out to the end of the lonesome pier beyond the cathedral ruins. The tradition dates so far back that no one's sure how it started (either to commemorate a student who died rescuing victims of a shipwreck, or to bid farewell to a visiting dignitary). Today students participate mostly because it's fun to be a part of the visual spectacle of a long line of red robes flapping in the North Sea wind.

St. Andrews also clings to an antiquated family system, where underclassmen choose an "academic mother and father." In mid-November comes Raisin Monday, named for the raisins traditionally given as treats to one's "parents" (today students usually give wine to their "dad" and lingerie to their "mum"). After receiving their gifts, the upperclassmen dress up their "children" in outrageous costumes and parade them through town. The underclassmen are also obliged to carry around "receipts" for their gifts—often written on unlikely or unwieldy objects (e.g., plastic dinosaurs, microwave ovens, even refrigerators). Any upperclassmen they come across can demand a rendition of the school song (in Latin). The whole scene invariably turns into a free-for-all food fight in St. Salvator's quad (weapons include condiments, shaving cream, and, according to campus rumors, human entrails pilfered by med students).

▲▲St. Andrew's Cathedral

Between the Great Schism and the Reformation (roughly the 14th–16th centuries), St. Andrews was the ecclesiastical capital of Scotland—and this was its showpiece church. Today the site features the remains of the cathedral and cloister (with walls and spires pecked away by centuries of scavengers), a graveyard, and a small exhibit and climbable tower.

Cost and Hours: Cathedral ruins-free; exhibit and tower-£4.20, £7.20 combo-ticket includes castle; daily April–Sept 9:30–17:30, Oct–March 9:30–16:30, last entry 30 minutes before closing, tel. 01334/472-563.

Background: It was the relics of the Apostle Andrew that first put this town on the map and gave it its name. There are numerous legends associated with the relics. According to one of those (likely untrue), in the fourth century, St. Rule was directed in a dream to bring the relics northward from Constantinople. When the ship wrecked offshore from here, it was clear that this was a sacred place. Andrew's bones (an upper arm, a kneecap, some fingers, and a tooth) were kept on this site, and starting in 1160, the cathedral was built and pilgrims began to arrive. Since St. Andrew had a direct connection to Jesus, his relics were believed to possess special properties, making them worthy of pilgrimages on par with St. James' relics in Santiago de Compostela, Spain (of Camino de Santiago fame). St. Andrew became Scotland's patron saint; in fact, the white "X" on the blue Scottish flag evokes the diagonal cross on which St. Andrew was crucified (he chose this type of cross because he felt unworthy to die as Jesus had).

◐ **Self-Guided Tour:** You can stroll around the cathedral **ruins**—the best part of the complex—for free. First walk between

the two tall ends of the church, which used to be the apse (at the sea end) and the main entry (at the town end). Visually trace the gigantic footprint of the former church in the ground, including the bases of columns—like giant sawed-off tree trunks. Plaques identify where elements of the church once stood. Looking at the one wall that's still standing, you can see the architectural changes that were made over the 150 years the cathedral was built—from the rounded, Romanesque windows at the front to

the more highly decorated, pointed Gothic arches near the back. Mentally rebuild the church, and try to imagine it in its former majesty, when it played host to pilgrims from all over Europe. The church wasn't destroyed all at once, like all those ruined abbeys in England (demolished in a huff by Henry VIII when he broke with the pope). Instead, because the Scottish Reformation was more gradual, this church was slowly picked apart over time. First just the decorations were removed from inside the cathedral. Then the roof was pulled down to make use of its lead. Without a roof, the

cathedral fell further and further into disrepair, and was quarried by locals for its handy precut stones (which you'll still find in the walls of many old St. Andrews homes). The elements—a big storm in the 1270s and a fire in 1378—also contributed to the cathedral's demise.

The surrounding **graveyard,** dating from the post-Reformation Protestant era, is much more recent than the cathedral. In this golf-obsessed town, the game even infiltrates the cemeteries: Many notable golfers from St. Andrews are buried here (such as Young Tom—or "Tommy"—Morris, four-time British Open winner).

Go through the surviving wall into the former **cloister,** marked by a gigantic grassy square in the center. You can still see the cleats up on the wall, which once supported beams. Imagine the cloister back in its day, its passages filled with strolling monks.

At the end of the cloister is a small **exhibit** (entry fee required), with a relatively dull collection of old tombs and other carved-stone relics that have been unearthed on this site. Your ticket also includes entry to the surviving **tower of St. Rule's Church** (the rectangular tower beyond the cathedral ruins). If you feel like hiking up the 156 very claustrophobic steps for the view over St. Andrews' rooftops, it's worth the price. Up top, you can also look out to sea to find the pier where students traditionally walk out in their robes (see sidebar on page 664).

• *Leave the cathedral grounds through the gate on the town side of the cathedral. On your left, bending around the corner, is South Street, and the pointed stone arch of the gate called "the Pends"—which will supposedly collapse should the smartest man in Britain cross under it. Probably best not to test that legend—instead, head right to follow the road around to North Street. Just around the corner is the adorable...*

▲St. Andrews' Preservation Trust Museum and Garden

Filling a 17th-century fishing family's house that was protected from developers, this museum is a time capsule of an earlier, simpler era. The house itself seems built for Smurfs, but once housed 20 family members. The ground floor features replicas of a grocer's shop and a "chemist's" (pharmacy), using original fittings from actual stores. Upstairs are temporary exhibits, and out back is a tranquil garden (dedicated to the memory of a beloved professor) with "great-grandma's washhouse," featuring an exhibit about the history of soap and washing. Lovingly presented, this quaint, humble house provides a nice contrast to the big-money scene around the golf course at the other end of town (free but donation requested, late May–late Sept daily 14:00–17:00, closed off-season, 12 North Street, tel. 01334/477-629, www.standrewspreservation trust.org).

• *From the museum, hang a left around the corner (at the Castle Tavern) to South Castle Street. Just before you hit the top of Market Street, look for the tiny white house on your left, with the cute curved staircase. What's that on the roof?*

Turn right down Market Street (which leads directly to the town's center, but we'll take a curvier route). Notice how the streets and even the buildings are smaller at this end of town, as if the whole city is shrinking as the streets close in on the cathedral. Passing an antique bookstore on your right, turn left onto Baxter Wynd, a.k.a. Baker Lane. You'll pass a tiny garden on your right, before landing on South Street. To take an ice-cream detour, head left and walk 75 yards to the recommended **B. Jannettas.** *Otherwise, head right and immediately cross the street to take in the building marked by a university insignia.*

St. Mary's College

This is the home of the university's School of Divinity (theology). If the gate's open, find the peaceful quad, with its gnarled tree, purportedly planted by Mary, Queen of Scots. To get a feel of student life from centuries past, try poking your nose into one of the old classrooms.

• *Back on South Street, continue to your left. Some of the plainest buildings on this stretch of the street have the most interesting history—several of them were built to fund the Crusades. Our walk ends at charming Church Square, where you'll find the library (with Internet access; see "Helpful Hints," earlier) and recommended Fisher and Donaldson bakery (closed Sun). The TI, grocery store, and ATM are all nearby on North Street (a few yards down Church Street).*

If you want to do more sightseeing, there's one more museum just outside of the town center...

St. Andrews Museum

This small, modest museum, which traces St. Andrews' history from "A to Zed," is an enjoyable way to pass time on a rainy day. It's situated in an old mansion in Kinburn Park, a five-minute walk from the old town (free, daily April–Sept 10:00–17:00, Oct–March 10:30–16:00, café, Doubledykes Road, tel. 01334/659-380).

Golfing in St. Andrews

St. Andrews is the Cooperstown and Mount Olympus of golf, a mecca for the plaid-knickers-and-funny-hats crowd. Even if you're not a golfer, consider going with the flow and becoming one for your visit. While St. Andrews lays claim to founding the sport (the first record of golf being played here was in 1553), nobody knows exactly where and when golf was born. In the Middle Ages, St. Andrews traded with the Dutch, and some historians believe they picked up a golf-like Dutch game on ice, and translated it to the bonnie rolling hills of Scotland's east coast. Since the grassy beachfront strip just outside St. Andrews was too poor to support crops, it was used for playing the game—and, centuries later, it still is. Why do golf courses have 18 holes? Because that's how many fit at the Old Course in St. Andrews, golf's single most famous site.

The Old Course—The Old Course hosts the British Open every five years (next in 2015). At other times it's open to the public for golfing. Fortunately for women golfers, the men-only Royal and Ancient Golf Club doesn't actually own the course, which is public and managed by the St. Andrews Links Trust. Drop by their clubhouse, overlooking the beach near the Old Course (hours change frequently with the season—figure May–Aug daily 7:00–21:00, progressively shorter until 7:30–16:00 in Dec, www .standrews.org.uk).

Teeing Off at the Old Course: Playing at golf's pinnacle course is pricey (£130/person, less off-season), but accessible to the public—subject to lottery drawings for tee times and reserved spots by club members. You can play the Old Course only if you have a handicap of 24 (men) or 36 (women); bring along your certificate or card. If you don't know your handicap—or don't know what "handicap" means—then you're not good enough to play here (they want to keep the game moving, rather than wait for novices to spend 10 strokes on each hole). If you play, you'll do nine holes out, then nine more back in—however, all but four share the same greens.

Reserving a Tee Time: To ensure a specific tee time at the Old Course, it's smart to reserve a full year ahead. Call 01334/466-666 or email reservations@standrews.org.uk. Otherwise, some tee times are determined each day by a lottery. Call or visit in person by 14:00 the day before (or on Saturday, if you're looking to play on Monday) to put your name in (2 players minimum, 4 players max)—then keep your fingers crossed when they post the results online at 16:00 (or call to see if you made it). Note that no advance reservations are taken on Saturdays, and the courses are closed on Sundays—which is traditionally the day when townspeople can walk the course.

Other Courses: The trust manages six other courses (including two right next to the Old Course—the New Course and the Jubilee Course). These are cheaper, and it's much easier to get a tee time (£65 for New and Jubilee, £120 for Castle Course, £12–40 for others). It's usually possible to get a tee time for the same day or next day (if you want a guaranteed reservation, you'll need to make it at least 2 weeks in advance). The Castle Course has great views overlooking the town (but even more wind to blow your ball around).

▲The Himalayas—Named for its dramatically hilly terrain, "The Himalayas" is basically a very classy (but still relaxed) game of minigolf. Technically the "Ladies' Putting Green," this cute little patch of undulating grass presents the perfect opportunity for non-golfers (female or male) to say they've played the links at St. Andrews—for less than the cost of a Coke. It's remarkable how

the contour of the land can present even more challenging obstacles than the tunnels, gates, and distractions of a corny putt-putt course back home. Flat shoes are required (no high heels). You'll see it on the left as you walk toward the clubhouse from the R&A.

Cost and Hours: £2 for 18 holes. Except when it's open only to members, the putting green is open to the public June–July Mon–Sat 10:30–19:30; May and Aug Mon–Sat 10:30–19:00; April and Sept Mon–Sat 10:30–18:30. It's closed to the public (because members are using it) Mon–Tue and Fri 16:45–17:30, Wed 12:00–15:30, Thu 10:00–11:00, Sun before 12:00, and Oct–March. Tel. 01334/475-196.

British Golf Museum—This exhibit, which started as a small collection in the R&A across the street, is the best place in Britain to learn about the Scots' favorite sport. It's a bit tedious for those of us who reach for the remote when we see a golfer, but a must (and worth at least ▲▲) for golf-lovers.

The compact, one-way exhibit reverently presents a meticulous survey of the game's history—from the monarchs who loved and hated golf (including the king who outlawed it because it was distracting men from church and archery practice), right up to the "Golden Bear" and a certain Tiger. A constant two-and-a-quarter-hour loop film shows highlights of the British Open from 1923 to the present, and other video screens show scratchy black-and-white highlights from the days before corporate sponsorship. At the end, find items donated by the golfers of today, including Tiger Woods' shirt, hat, and glove.

Cost and Hours: £6, ticket good for 2 days and includes informative book about the history of golf; April–Oct Mon–Sat 9:30–17:00, Sun 10:00–17:00; Nov–March daily 10:00–16:00; last entry 45 minutes before closing; Bruce Embankment, in the blocky modern building squatting behind the R&A by the Old Course, tel. 01334/460-046, www.britishgolfmuseum.co.uk.

Sleeping in St. Andrews

Owing partly to the high-roller golf tourists flowing through the town, St. Andrews' accommodations are expensive. Note that during graduation week in June, hotels often require a four-night stay and book up quickly. Solo travelers are at a disadvantage, as many B&Bs don't have singles—and charge close to the double price for one person (I've listed "S" or "Sb" below for those that actually have single rooms). But the quality at my recommendations is

Sleep Code

(£1 = about $1.60, country code: 44, area code: 01334)
S = Single, **D** = Double/Twin, **T** = Triple, **Q** = Quad, **b** = bathroom,
s = shower only. Unless otherwise noted, you can assume
credit cards are accepted and breakfast is included.

To help you sort easily through these listings, I've divided
the rooms into two categories based on the price for a
standard double room with bath (during high season):

$$ Higher Priced—Most rooms £70 or more.
$ Lower Priced—Most rooms less than £70.

Prices can change without notice; verify the hotel's
current rates online or by email. For other updates, see www
.ricksteves.com/update.

high, and budget alternatives—including a hostel—are workable.
All of these, except the hostel and the dorms, are on the streets
called Murray Park and Murray Place, between North Street and
The Scores in the old town. If you need to find a room on the fly,
head for this same neighborhood, which has far more options than
just the ones I've listed below.

$$ Cameron House has five old-fashioned, paisley, masculine-feeling rooms (including two nice singles that share one bath-
room) around a beautiful stained-glass atrium (S-£40, Db-£80,
discount for longer stays, prices soft Nov–March, free Wi-Fi,
lounge, 11 Murray Park, tel. 01334/472-306, www.cameronhouse
-sta.co.uk, elizabeth@cameronhouse-sta.co.uk, Elizabeth and
Leonard Palompo).

$$ Lorimer Guest House has five comfortable, tastefully
decorated rooms, including one on the ground floor (Db-£94–104
July–Sept, Db-£88–94 spring and fall, cheaper in winter, higher
prices are for deluxe top-floor rooms, ask about discount for lon-
ger stays, free Internet access and Wi-Fi, 19 Murray Park, tel.
01334/476-599, www.lorimerhouse.com, info@lorimerhouse.com,
Mick and Chris Cordner).

$$ Doune Guest House is golfer-friendly, with six straightforward, comfy, plaid-heavy rooms. The helpful owners are happy
to arrange early breakfasts and airport transfers (S-£40–47,
Db-£80–94, price depends on season, cheaper off-season, cash only,
free Internet access and Wi-Fi, 5 Murray Place, tel. 01334/475-195,
www.dounehouse.com, info@dounehouse.com).

$$ Arran House has nine modern rooms, including a single
with a private bathroom across the hall (S-£50–55, Db-£80–90,
three ground-floor rooms, family rooms, free Wi-Fi, 5 Murray

Park, tel. 01334/474-724, mobile 07768-718-237, www.arranhouse standrews.co.uk, jmgmcgrory@btinternet.com, Anne and Jim McGrory).

$$ Glenderran Guest House offers five plush, golf-oriented rooms and a few nice breakfast extras (Sb-£40–50, Db-£80–90, free Internet access and Wi-Fi, same-day laundry-£8, 9 Murray Park, tel. 01334/477-951, www.glenderran.com, info@glenderran .com, Ray and Maggie).

$$ Hoppity House is a recently remodeled, bright, and contemporary place, with neutral tones and built-in furniture that makes good use of space. You may find a stuffed namesake bunny or two hiding out among its six rooms. Golfers appreciate the golf-bag lockers on the ground floor (Sb-£45–55, Db-£75–90, deluxe Db-£90–110, family room, lower prices off-season, fridges in rooms, free Wi-Fi, 4 Murray Park, tel. 01334/461-116, mobile 07701-099-100, www.hoppityhouse.co.uk, enquiries@hoppity house.co.uk, helpful Gordon and Heather).

Hostel: **$ St. Andrews Tourist Hostel** has 44 beds in colorful 4- to 8-bed rooms about a block from the base of Market Street. The high-ceilinged lounge is a comfy place for a break, and the friendly staff is happy to recommend their favorite pubs (£12–14/ bed, no breakfast, kitchen, free Wi-Fi, self-service laundry-£3.50, towels-£1, office open 7:00–23:00, office closed 15:00–18:00 outside of summer, no curfew, St. Mary's Place, tel. 01334/479-911, www.standrewshostel.com, info@standrewshostel.com).

University Accommodations

In the summer (mid-June–early Sept), two of the University of St. Andrews' student-housing buildings are tidied up and rented out to tourists (does not include breakfast; website for both: www .discoverstandrews.com; pay when reserving). **$$ New Hall** has double beds and private bathrooms; it's more comfortable, but also more expensive and less central (Sb-£56, Db-£83, tel. 01334/467-000, new.hall@st-andrews.ac.uk). **$ McIntosh Hall** is cheaper and more central, but it only has twin beds and shared bathrooms (Sb-£35, Db-£60, tel. 01334/467-035, mchall@st-andrews.ac.uk). Because true single rooms are rare in St. Andrews' B&Bs, these dorms are a good option for solo travelers.

Eating in St. Andrews

The first three listings—owned by the same group—are popular and serve up reliably good international cuisine. Comparing their early-dinner specials may help you choose (www.houserestaurants .com).

The Doll's House offers cuisine with a French flair, with two floors of indoor seating and a cozy, colorful, casual atmosphere; the sidewalk seating out front is across from Holy Trinity Church (£7–10 lunches, £9–16 dinners, £13 two-course early-bird special 17:00–18:30, open daily 12:00–15:00 & 17:00–22:00, a block from the TI at 3 Church Square, tel. 01334/477-422).

The Glass House serves pizza, pasta, and salads in a two-story glass building with an open-style layout (£6 lunches, £8-11 dinners, £12 two-course early-bird special 16:00–18:30, open daily 12:00-23:00, second-floor outdoor patio, near the castle on 80 North Street, tel. 01334/473-673).

The Grill House offers Mexican-style food in a vibrantly colored space (£5 lunches, £7-11 dinners, £11 two-course early-bird special 16:00–18:30, open daily 12:00–22:00, St. Mary's Place, tel. 01334/470-500).

The Seafood Restaurant is St. Andrews' favorite splurge. Situated in a modern glassy building overlooking the beach near the Old Course, it's like dining in an aquarium. The place serves locally caught seafood to a room full of tables that wrap around the busy open kitchen. Dinner reservations are recommended (£22 two-course lunch, £26 three-course lunch, £45 three-course dinner, daily 12:00–14:30 & 18:30–22:00, The Scores, tel. 01334/479-475).

On Market Street: In the area around the TI, you'll find a concentration of good restaurants—pubs, grill houses, coffee shops, Asian food, fish-and-chips (see later), and more...take your pick. A block down Market Street, you can stock up for a picnic at **Gregg's** and **Tesco**.

Pubs: There's no shortage in this college town. **Aikmans** features a cozy wood-table ambience and frequent live music (open-mic folk night once weekly, traditional Scottish music upstairs about twice per month, other live music generally Thu–Sat, £5–7 pub grub, open daily 11:00–24:00, 32 Bell Street, tel. 01334/477-425). **The Central** is a St. Andrews standby, with old lamps and lots of brass (£5 sandwiches, £7 burgers, Mon–Sat 11:30–24:00, Sun 12:30–24:00, food until 21:00, 77 Market Street, tel. 01334/478-296). **Ma Bells** is a sleek but friendly place that clings to its (pre-remodel) status as one of Prince William's favorites (£4–7 pub grub, pricier bistro meals, daily 11:00–24:00, a block from the Old Course and R&A at 40 The Scores, tel. 01334/472-622). **Greyfriars** is in a classy, modern hotel near the Murray Park B&Bs (£5 light meals, £7–10 entrées, daily 12:00–20:30, 129 North Street, tel. 01334/474-906).

Fish-and-Chips: **Fritto** is a local favorite for take-away fish-and-chips, centrally located on Market Street near the TI (£4 fish-and-chips, £3 burgers, Mon–Sat 11:00–23:00, Sun 12:00–23:00, at the corner of Union and Market, tel. 01334/476-425). Brave souls

ST. ANDREWS

will order a can of Irn-Bru with their fish (warning: it doesn't taste like orange soda—see page 592). For what's considered the country's best chippies, head for the famous place in the East Neuk (described at the end of this chapter).

Dessert: **Fisher and Donaldson** is beloved for its rich, affordable pastries and chocolates. Listen as the straw-hatted bakers chat with their regular customers, then try their Coffee Tower—like a giant cream puff filled with rich, lightly coffee-flavored cream (£1–2 pastries, Mon–Fri 6:00–17:15, Sat until 17:00, closed Sun, just around the corner from the TI at 13 Church Street, tel. 01334/472-201). **B. Jannettas,** which recently marked its 100th year, features a wide and creative range of 52 tasty ice-cream flavors (£1.30 per scoop, daily 9:00–21:00, 31 South Street, tel. 01334/473-285).

St. Andrews Connections

Remember, trains don't go into St. Andrews—instead, use the Leuchars station (5 miles from St. Andrews, connected by buses coordinated to meet most trains, 2–4/hour, see "Arrival in St. Andrews" on page 656). The TI has useful train schedules, which also list bus departure times from St. Andrews.

From Leuchars by Train to: Edinburgh (1–2/hour, 1–1.25 hours), **Glasgow** (2/hour, 2 hours, transfer in Edinburgh), **Inverness** (9/day, 3.25–4 hours, 1 direct, otherwise with 2 changes). Trains run less frequently on Sundays. Train info: toll tel. 0845-748-4950, www.nationalrail.co.uk.

Near St. Andrews: The East Neuk

On the lazy coastline meandering south from St. Andrews, the cute-as-a-pin East Neuk (pronounced "nook") is a collection of tidy fishing villages. While hardly earth-shattering, the East Neuk is a pleasant detour if you've got the time. The villages of Crail and Pittenweem have their fans, but Anstruther is worth most of your attention. The East  Neuk works best as a half-day side-trip (by either car or bus) from St. Andrews, though drivers can use it as a scenic detour between Edinburgh and St. Andrews.

Getting There: It's an easy **drive** from St. Andrews. For the scenic route, follow A917 south of town along the coast, past Crail, on the way to Anstruther and Pittenweem. For a shortcut directly to Anstruther, take B9131 across the peninsula (or return that way after driving the longer coastal route there). **Buses** connect St. Andrews to the East Neuk: Bus #95 goes hourly from St. Andrews to Crail and Anstruther (50 minutes to Anstruther, catch bus at St. Andrews bus station or from Church Street, around the corner from the TI). The hourly bus #X60 goes directly to Anstruther, then on to Edinburgh (20 minutes to Anstruther, 2.25 hours more to Edinburgh). Bus info: toll tel. 0871-200-2233, www.traveline scotland.com.

▲Anstruther

Stretched out along its harbor, colorful Anstruther (AN-stru-ther; pronounced ENT-ster by locals) is the centerpiece of the East Neuk. The main parking lot and bus stop are both right on the harbor. Anstruther's handy **TI,** which offers lots of useful information for the entire East Neuk area, is located inside the town's main sight, the Scottish Fisheries Museum (April–Sept Mon–Sat 10:00–17:00, Sun 11:00–16:00; Oct Mon–Sat 10:00–16:00, Sun 11:00–16:00; closed Nov–March; tel. 01333/311-073, www.visitfife .com). Stroll the harborfront to the end, detouring inland around the little cove (or crossing the causeway at low tide) to reach some colorful old houses, including one encrusted with seashells.

The **Scottish Fisheries Museum** is true to its slogan: "We are bigger than you think!" The endearingly hokey exhibit sprawls through several harborfront buildings, painstakingly tracing the history of Scottish seafaring from primitive dugout dinghies to modern vessels. You'll learn the story of Scotland's "Zulu" fishing boats and walk through vast rooms filled with boats. For a glimpse at humble fishing lifestyles, don't miss the Fisherman's Cottage, hiding upstairs from the courtyard (£6; April–Sept Mon–Sat 10:00–17:30, Sun 11:00–16:30; Oct–March Mon–Sat 10:00–16:00, Sun 12:00–16:00; last entry one hour before closing, tea room, Harbourhead, tel. 01333/310-628, www.scotfishmuseum.org).

Eating in Anstruther: Anstruther's claim to fame is its fish-and-chips, considered by many to be Scotland's best. Though there are several good "chippies" in town, the famous one is the **Anstruther Fish Bar,** facing the harbor just a block from the TI and Fisheries Museum. As you enter, choose whether you want to get takeout or dine in for a few pounds more. While more expensive than most chippies, the food here is good—so good the place has officially been named "UK's Fish and Chip Shop of the Year" multiple times (£5–7 takeout, £7–9 to dine in, dine-in prices include bread and a drink, daily 11:30–21:30, until 22:00 for takeaway, 42–44 Shore Street, tel. 01333/310-518).

GLASGOW

Glasgow (GLAS-goh), though bigger than Edinburgh, lives forever in the shadow of its more popular neighbor. Once a decrepit port city, Glasgow—astride the River Clyde—is both a workaday Scottish city and a cosmopolitan destination with an energetic dining and nightlife scene. The city is also a pilgrimage site of sorts for architecture buffs, thanks to a cityscape packed with Victorian architecture, early-20th-century touches, and modern flair (unfortunately, it also has some truly drab recent construction). Most beloved are the works by hometown boy Charles Rennie Mackintosh, the visionary turn-of-the-20th-century architect who left his mark all over Glasgow.

Edinburgh, a short train-trip away, may have the royal aura, but Glasgow has an unpretentious appeal. As my cab driver said, "The people of Glasgow have a better time at a funeral than the people of Edinburgh have at a wedding." In Glasgow, there's no upper-crust history, and no one puts on airs. Locals call sanded and polished concrete "Glasgow marble." You'll be hard-pressed to find a souvenir shop in Glasgow—and that's just how the natives like it. In this revitalized city, visitors are a novelty, and friendly locals do their best to introduce you to the fun-loving, laid-back Glaswegian (pronounced like "Norwegian") way of life.

Planning Your Time

For most visitors, a few hours are plenty to sample Glasgow. Focus on my self-guided walking tour in the city core, which includes Glasgow's two most interesting sights: Charles Rennie Mackintosh's Glasgow School of Art, and the time-warp Tenement House. With more time, add some of the outlying sights, such as

the cathedral area (to the east), Kelvingrove Gallery and the West End restaurant scene (to the west), and the Burrell Collection (a few miles out of town).

Day Trip from Edinburgh: For a full day, grab breakfast at your B&B in Edinburgh, then catch the 9:30 train to Glasgow (morning trains every 15 minutes; £10.70 same-day round-trip if leaving after 9:15 or on weekend); it arrives at Queen Street Train Station at 10:20. Call to reserve tickets to tour the Glasgow School of Art (aim for an early-afternoon time slot, so you can have lunch beforehand). Once in Glasgow, take my self-guided walk to hit all the major sights, making sure to reach the Tenement House by the last entry time (16:30). For dinner, consider heading out to the thriving West End restaurant scene, then hop the subway back to Queen Street Station (use the Buchanan Street stop) and catch the 21:00 train back to Edinburgh (evening trains every 30 minutes).

Orientation to Glasgow

(area code: 0141)

With a grid street plan, a downtown business zone, and more than its share of boxy office buildings, Glasgow feels more like a midsized American city than a big Scottish one—like Cleveland or Cincinnati with shorter skyscrapers, more sandstone, and more hills. While greater Glasgow is a sprawling city of 1.5 million people, the tourist's Glasgow has three main parts: the city center (including the Merchant City neighborhood), a cluster of minor sights near the cathedral (in the east), and the West End restaurant/nightlife/shopping zone. The easily walkable city center has a hilly northern area and two main drags, both lined with shops and crawling with shoppers: Sauchiehall Street (pronounced "Sockyhall," running west to east) and Buchanan Street (running north to south).

Tourist Information

The TI is opposite Queen Street Station in the southwest corner of George Square (at #11). They hand out an excellent free map, stock other Glasgow brochures, and can book you a room for a £4 fee. The TI sells tickets for the hop-on, hop-off bus tour; the Mackintosh Trail Ticket described below; and several Scotland sightseeing passes (Easter–May Mon–Sat 9:00–18:00, June and Sept until 19:00, July–Aug until 20:00, Oct–Easter until 17:00, Thu opens at 9:30 and Sun 10:00–18:00 year-round, tel. 0141/204-4400, www.seeglasgow.com or www.visitscotland.com). Buses to the West End depart from in front of the TI (see page 698), and the hop-on, hop-off bus tour leaves from across the square.

Mackintosh Trail Ticket: This ticket, sold by the TI and all Mackintosh sights, covers entry to all "Charles Rennie Mac" sights and public transportation to those outside the city limits (£16/day, www.crmsociety.com).

Arrival in Glasgow

By Train: Glasgow, a major Scottish transportation hub, has two main train stations, which are just a few blocks apart in the very heart of town: **Central Station** (with a grand, genteel interior) and **Queen Street Station** (more functional, with better connections to Edinburgh, and closer to the TI—take the exit marked *George Square* and continue straight across the square). Both stations have pay WCs (£0.30) and baggage storage (Central Station—at the head of track 1, £7/bag for 24 hours; Queen Street Station—near the head of track 7, £5–7/bag). Unless you're packing heavy, it's easier to walk the five minutes between the stations than to take the roundabout "RailLink" bus #398 between them (£0.75, or free if you have a ticket for a connecting train).

By Bus: Buchanan Street Bus Station is at Killermont Street, just two blocks up the hill behind Queen Street Train Station.

By Car: The M8 motorway, which slices through downtown Glasgow, is the easiest way in and out of the city. Ask your hotel for directions to and from M8, and connect with other highways from there.

By Air: For information on Glasgow's two airports, see "Glasgow Connections," at the end of this chapter.

Helpful Hints

Safety: The city center, which is packed with ambitious career types during the day, can feel deserted at night. Avoid the area near the River Clyde entirely (hookers and thugs), and confine yourself to the streets north of Argyle Street if you're in the downtown quarter. The Merchant City area (east of the train stations) and the West End bustle with crowded restaurants well into the evening and feel well-populated in the wee hours.

If you've picked up a football (soccer) jersey or scarf as a souvenir, don't wear it in Glasgow; local passions run very high, and most drunken brawls in town are between supporters of Glasgow's two rival soccer clubs: the Celtic in green and white, and the Rangers in blue and red. (For reasons no one can explain, the Celtic team name is pronounced "sell-tic"—the only place you'll find this pronunciation outside of Boston.)

Sightseeing: Glasgow's city-owned museums—including the sights near the cathedral but not the biggies like the Glasgow School of Art or Tenement House—are free (www.glasgow museums.com).

Sunday Travel: Bus and train schedules are dramatically reduced on Sundays—most routes have only half the departure times they have during the week (though Edinburgh is still easily accessible). If you plan to leave Glasgow for a remote destination on Sunday, check the schedules carefully when you arrive. All trains run less frequently in the off-season; if you want to get to the Highlands by bus on a Sunday in winter, forget it.

Internet Access: You'll see signs advertising Internet cafés around the city core (near Central Station and Buchanan Street). Try **Yeeha Internet Café** (Mon–Fri 9:30–19:00, Sat 10:00–18:00, Sun 11:00–18:00, 48 West George Street, go upstairs to first floor, tel. 0141/332-6543, www.yeeha-internet-cafe.co.uk).

Local Guide: Joan Dobbie, a native Glaswegian and registered Scottish Tourist Guide, will give you the insider's take on Glasgow's sights (£85/half-day, £125/day, tel. 01355/236-749, mobile 07773-555-151, joan.leo@lineone.net).

Getting Around Glasgow

By City Bus: Various companies run Glasgow's buses, but most city-center routes are operated by First (price depends on journey, £3.20 for any two single journeys, £3.75 for all-day ticket, buy ticket from driver, exact change required). Buses run every few minutes down Glasgow's main thoroughfares (such as Sauchiehall Street) to the downtown core (train stations). If you're waiting at a stop and a bus comes along, ask the driver if the bus is headed to Central Station; chances are the answer is yes. (For information on buses to the West End, see page 698.)

By Hop-on, Hop-off Bus Tour: This tour connects Glasgow's far-flung historic sights in a 1.25-hour loop (£11, ticket valid for 2 days; buy online, from driver, or at TI; daily 9:30–16:30, July–Aug 4/hour, spring and fall 3/hour, winter 2/hour until 16:00; stops in front of Central Station, George Square, and major hotels; tel. 0141/204-0444, www.citysightseeingglasgow.co.uk). If there's a particular sight you want to see, confirm that it's on the route.

By Taxi: Taxis are affordable, plentiful, and often come with nice, chatty cabbies—all speaking in the impenetrable local accent. Just smile and nod. Most taxi rides in the downtown area will cost about £5; from the West End, a one-way trip is about £6. Use taxis or public transport to connect Glasgow's more remote sights; splurge for a taxi (for safety) any time you're traveling late at night.

By Subway: The claustrophobic, orange-line subway runs in a loop around the edge of the city center. The "outer circle" runs clockwise, and the "inner circle" runs counterclockwise. (If you miss your stop, you can just wait it out—you'll come full circle in about 25 minutes. Or hop out and cross to the other side of the platform to go back the way you came.) Though the subway is essentially useless for connecting city-center sightseeing (Buchanan Street is the only downtown stop), it's handy for reaching sights farther out, including the Kelvingrove Gallery (Kelvinhall stop) and West End restaurant/nightlife neighborhood (Hillhead stop; £1.20 single trip, £3.50 Discovery Ticket lets you travel all day; subway runs Mon–Sat 6:30–23:30, Sun 10:00–18:00; www.spt .co.uk/subway).

Self-Guided Walk

Get to Know Glasgow

Glasgow isn't romantic, but it has an earthy charm, and architecture buffs love it. The trick to sightseeing here is to always look up—above the chain restaurants and mall stores, you'll see a wealth of imaginative facades, complete with ornate friezes and expressive sculptures. These buildings transport you to the heady days around the turn of the 20th century—when the rest of Great Britain was enthralled by Victorianism, but Glasgow set its own course, thanks largely to the artistic bravado of Charles Rennie Mackintosh and his friends (the "Glasgow Four"). This walking tour takes three to four hours, including one hour for Mackintosh's masterpiece, the Glasgow School of Art (in summer, consider calling ahead to reserve your tour there—see page 687).

• *Begin at Central Station. Exit the train station straight ahead from the tracks (to the north, onto Gordon Street), turn right, and cross busy Renfield/Union Street. Continue one block, then turn right down Mitchell Street, and look up on the left side of the street to see a multi-story brick water tower topped by a rounded cap. Turn left down a small alley (Mitchell Lane) just in front of the tower. Within about 25 yards, on the right, you'll see the entrance to...*

The Lighthouse

This facility, which houses the Scotland Center for Architecture and Design, has two parts: a water tower designed by Charles Rennie Mackintosh in the early 1900s, and a modern glass-and-metal museum built alongside it. The Lighthouse is filled mostly with design exhibitions, lonely floors of conference rooms, and funny icons directing desperate men and women to the bathrooms (free, open Mon and Wed–Sat 10:30–17:00, Tue 11:00–17:00, closed Sun, 11 Mitchell Lane, tel. 0141/276-5365,

www.glasgowarchitecture.co.uk). This sight is skippable for most, but it does offer a fine view over the city. You have two options for scaling the heights: Take the elevator to the sixth-floor windows, or even better, climb up yourself. Head to the third floor, which features information about Mackintosh, along with architectural plans and scale models (linger here only if you're planning to skip the Glasgow School of Art), then climb the 135 spiral steps inside the water tower. The top has a wraparound balcony with 360-degree views.

GLASGOW

• *Exit the Lighthouse to the right down the alley, then turn left onto the bustling pedestrian shopping drag called Buchanan Street—Glasgow's outdoor mall. One branch of the Mackintosh-designed Willow Tea Rooms is on your left at 97 Buchanan Street (two recreated Mackintosh interiors, tel. 0141/204-5242, other location described later in this walk). Across the street, find the second alley on the right, called Exchange Place. Before entering, look in the store windows of the former bank building to your left, at 98 Buchanan Street. A thousand antique sewing machines—count 'em—line three sides of the All Saints clothing store in a stunning geometric display worthy of this design-conscious city. Now walk down Exchange Place and pass through the arch, emerging onto the...*

Royal Exchange Square

This square—which marks the entrance to the shopping zone called Merchant City—is home to two interesting buildings. On your left as you enter the square is a stately Neoclassical bank-like building (today housing a Borders bookstore). This was once the **private mansion** of one of the tobacco lords, the super-rich businessmen who reigned here from the 1750s through the 1800s, stomping through the city with gold-tipped canes. During the port's heyday, these entrepreneurs helped make Glasgow Europe's sixth-biggest city.

In the middle of the square is the **Glasgow Gallery of Modern Art,** nicknamed GoMA. Walk around the GoMA building to the main entry (at the equestrian statue), and step back to take in the full Neoclassical facade. On the pediment (above the columns),

Glasgow Walk

① The Lighthouse
② Royal Exchange Square & Glasgow Gallery of Modern Art
③ George Square & Queen Victoria Statue
④ Nelson Mandela Place
⑤ Athenaeum
⑥ Art Nouveau Maidens
⑦ "Hatrack" Building
⑧ Wellington Street
⑨ Willow Tea Rooms (2)
⑩ Glasgow School of Art
⑪ Tenement House
⑫ Bus to Central Station

S SUBWAY STOP
B BUS STOP
P PARKING
◻ PEDESTRIAN ZONE

200 YARDS
200 METERS

TO EDINBURGH
TENEMENT HOUSE
WEST
M-8
GARN.
HILL
RENFREW
FINISH
SAUCHIEHA
CHARING CROSS STN.
BAT
WEST
TO KELVINGROVE MUSEUM
MOTORWAY
M-8
NEWTON ST.
ELMBANK ST.
HOLLAND
WES
VINC
BOTH
FOOT-BRIDGE
WATER-
A-814
ARGYLE
KINGSTON BRIDGE
BROOMIE
RIVER
TO AIRPORT & OBAN VIA A-82

notice the funky, mirrored mosaic—an example of how Glasgow refuses to take itself too seriously. The temporary exhibits inside GoMA are generally forgettable, but the museum does have an unusual charter: It displays only the work of living artists (free, Mon–Wed and Sat 10:00–17:00, Thu 10:00–20:00, Fri and Sun 11:00–17:00, tel. 0141/287-3050).

• *With the facade of GoMA behind you, turn left onto Queen Street. Within a block, you'll be at the southwest corner of...*

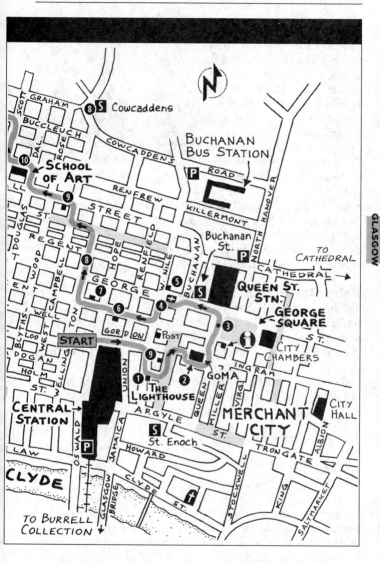

George Square

Here, in the heart of the city, you'll find the TI (just to your right as you come to the square), Queen Street Train Station, the Glasgow City Chambers (the big Neoclassical building to the east, not worth visiting), and—in front of that—a monument to Glaswegians killed fighting in the World Wars. The square is decorated with a *Who's Who* of statues depicting Glaswegians of note. Find James Watt (inventor of the steam engine), as well as Robert Burns and

Sir Walter Scott (Scotland's two most famous poets). Head north along the edge of the square to find a statue of an idealized, surprisingly skinny **Queen Victoria** riding a horse. But you won't see a statue of King George III, for whom the square is named. The stubborn Scots are still angry at George

for losing the colonies (i.e., us), and they never commissioned a statue of him.

• *Just past skinny Vic and Robert Peel, turn left onto West George Street and head for the tall church in the middle of the street (the Yeeha Internet Café—described earlier, under "Helpful Hints"—is on your right at #48). Cross Buchanan Street and go around the church on the left side, entering a little square called...*

Nelson Mandela Place

The area around this church features some interesting bits of architectural detail. First, as you stand along the left side of the church, look up and to the left (across from the church) to find the three circular friezes, on the first floor up, of the former **Stock Exchange** (built in 1875). These idealized heads, which were recently cleaned and restored, represent the industries that made Glasgow prosperous during its heyday: building, engineering, and mining.

• *Continue around to the back of the church and look to the right side of the street for the sandy-colored building at #8 (notice the low-profile label over the door). This is the...*

Athenaeum

Now a law office, this was founded in 1847 as a school and city library during Glasgow's golden age. (Charles Dickens gave the building's inaugural address.) Like Edinburgh, Glasgow was at the forefront of the 17th-century Scottish Enlightenment, a celebration of education and intellectualism. The Scots were known for their extremely practical brand of humanism; all members of society, including the merchant and working classes, were expected to be well-educated. (Tobacco lords, for example, often knew Latin and Greek.) Look above the door to find the symbolic statue of a reader sharing books with young children, an embodiment of this ideal.

• *Continue beyond the church and turn left onto West Nile Street; one block later, turn right onto St. Vincent Street. We'll enjoy more architectural Easter eggs as we continue along this street toward the Glasgow School of Art. After a block, on the left side of the street (at #115), look up to the second floor to see sculptures of...*

Art Nouveau Maidens

Their elongated, melancholy faces and downcast eyes seem to reflect Glasgow's difficult recent past, and decades of economic decline and urban decay. (They mirror similar faces in Art Nouveau paintings in the Glasgow School of Art, particularly in the artwork of Margaret MacDonald, Charles Rennie Mackintosh's wife and artistic partner.) As you walk along this street, keep your eyes above street level to take in classic Glaswegian sandstone architecture and the Mackintosh-influenced modern takes on it.

• *Another block down on the right (at #144) is the slender building locals have nicknamed the...*

"Hatrack" Building

At first glance it looks like most other sandstone buildings in the city. But look up at the very top to see the ornate rooftop and elaborate ironwork (Glasgow had roaring iron forges back in the day). The Hatrack is a prime example of the adventurous turn-of-the-century Glaswegian architecture: The building's internal framework bears all the weight, so the facade can use very little load-bearing stone. This "curtain wall" method allows for architectural creativity—here the huge bay windows let in plenty of light and contrast nicely with the recessed arches, making the building both unusual and still quintessentially Glaswegian. (The same method gave Antoni Gaudí the freedom to create his fantastical buildings in Barcelona.) Above the left doorway as you face the building, notice the stained-glass ship in turbulent seas, another fitting icon for a city that's seen more than its share of ups and downs.

• *At the end of the block, turn right up...*

Wellington Street

Climb this street to the crest of the hill, where the two- and three-story buildings have a pleasing, uniform look. These sandstone structures were the homes of Glasgow's upper-middle class, the factory managers who worked for the city's barons (such as the titan who owned the mansion back on Royal Exchange Square). In the strict Victorian class structure, the people who lived here were distinctly higher on the social scale than the people who lived in the tenements (which we'll see at the end of this tour).

• *Turn left onto Bath Street and then right onto West Campbell Street. It opens onto Sauchiehall, Glasgow's main commercial street. Turn left onto Sauchiehall. Half a block later, at #217 (on the left), you'll see a black-and-white Art Nouveau building with a sign reading...*

Willow Tea Rooms

Charles Rennie Mackintosh made his living from design commissions, including multiple tearooms for businesswoman Kate

Charles Rennie Mackintosh
(1868–1928)

During his lifetime, Charles Rennie Mackintosh brought an exuberant Art Nouveau influence to the architecture of his hometown. His designs challenged the city planners of this otherwise practical, working-class port city to create beauty in the buildings they commissioned. A radical thinker, he freely shared credit with his artist wife, Margaret MacDonald. (He once famously said, "I have the talent...Margaret has the genius.")

When Mackintosh was a young student at the Glasgow School of Art, the Industrial Age dominated life here. Factories belched black soot into the city as they burned coal and forged steel. Mackintosh and his circle of artist friends drew their solace and inspiration from nature (just as the Romantics had before them) and created some of the original Art Nouveau buildings, paintings, drawings, and furniture.

As a student traveling abroad in Italy, Mackintosh ignored the famous Renaissance paintings inside the museum walls, and set up his easel to paint the exteriors of churches and buildings instead. He rejected the architectural traditions of ancient Greece and Rome. In Venice and Ravenna, he fell under the spell of Byzantine design, and in Siena he saw a unified, medieval city design he would try to import—but with a Scottish flavor and Glaswegian palette—to his own hometown.

His first commission came in 1893, to design an extension to the Glasgow Herald building. More work soon followed, including the Glasgow School of Art and the Willow Tea Rooms 10 years later. Mackintosh envisioned a world without artistic borders, where an Islamic flourish could find its way onto a workaday building in a Scottish city. Inspired by the great buildings of the past and by his Art Nouveau peers, he in turn influenced others, such as painter Gustav Klimt and Bauhaus founder Walter Gropius. A century after Scotland's greatest architect set pencil to paper, his hometown is at last celebrating his unique vision.

Cranston. (You might also see fake "Mockintosh" tearooms sprinkled throughout the city—ignore them.) A well-known control freak, Mackintosh designed everything here—down to the furniture, lighting, and cutlery. He took his theme for the café from the name of the street it's on—*saugh* is Scots for willow, and

haugh for meadow.

In the design of these tearooms, there was a meeting of the (very modern) minds. Cranston wanted a place for women to be able to gather while unescorted, in a time when traveling solo could give a woman a less-than-desirable reputation. An ardent women's rights supporter, Cranston requested that the rooms be bathed in white, the suffragists' signature color.

Enter the Willow Tea Rooms and make your way past the tacky jewelry and trinket store that now inhabits the bottom floor. On the open mezzanine level you'll find 20 crowded tables run like a diner from a corner kitchen, serving bland meals to middle-class people—just as this place has since it opened in 1903 (£4–7 breakfasts, £4–5 sandwiches, £7 salads and entrées, £12.25 afternoon tea served all day). Don't leave without poking your head into the almost-hidden Room de Luxe. Head up the stairs (following signs for the toilet) to the first landing, and go left down the hall to see this peaceful tearoom space (only open for tea at certain times— call ahead). While some parts of the Room de Luxe are reproductions (such as the chairs and the doors, which were too fragile to survive), the rest is just as it was in Mackintosh's day (Mon–Sat 9:00–16:30, Sun 11:00–16:15, last orders 30 minutes before closing, 217 Sauchiehall Street, second location at 97 Buchanan Street, tel. 0141/332-0521, www.willowtearooms.co.uk).

• From here it's a five-minute, mostly uphill walk to the only must-see Mackintosh sight within the town center. Walk a block and a half west on Sauchiehall, and make a right onto Dalhousie Street; the big reddish-brown building on the left at the top of the hill is the Glasgow School of Art. Enter at the Dalhousie Street entrance.

If you have time to kill before your tour starts, consider eating lunch at one of my recommended restaurants: the student café **Where the Monkey Sleeps** *(closed Sat-Sun; go to the corner, cross Renfrew Street, and head left) or the* **CCA Terrace Bar and Courtyard Café** *(closed Sun-Mon; go around the corner, walk a block past the school, then turn left and go one block downhill). Or, if you have at least an hour before your tour, you can head to the Tenement Museum (listed at the end of this walk, closed mornings and Nov–Feb), a preserved home from the early 1900s—right when Mackintosh was doing his most important work.*

▲Glasgow School of Art

A pinnacle of artistic and architectural achievement, the Glasgow School of Art presented a unique opportunity for Charles Rennie Mackintosh to design a massive project entirely to his own liking, down to every last detail. These details—from a fireplace that looks like a kimono to windows that soar for multiple stories—are the beauty of the Glasgow School of Art.

Mackintosh loved the hands-on ideology of the Arts and Crafts movement, but he was also a practical Scot. Study the

outside of the building. Those protruding wrought-iron brackets that hover outside the multipaned windows were a new invention during the time of the Industrial Revolution; they reinforce the big, fragile glass windows, allowing natural light to pour in to the school. Mackintosh brought all the most recent technologies to this work and added them to his artistic palate—which also merged clean Modernist lines, Asian influences, and Art Nouveau flourishes.

Because the Glasgow School of Art is still a working school, the interior can only be visited by one-hour **guided tour,** though several exhibition galleries in the school are free and open to the public, even without a tour. Enter at the Dalhousie Street entrance, and buy your tour ticket at the shop.

Cost and Hours: £8.75 guided tour, April–Sept tours generally depart daily at the top of the hour 10:00–17:00, Oct–March tours daily at 11:00 and 15:00, no tours for one week in late May/early June during final exams; tip the starving students a pound or two if they give a good spiel. In the summer, tours are frequent, but they fill up quickly—it's smart to call or email the shop to confirm times and reserve a spot (shop open daily April–Sept 9:30–18:30, Oct–March 10:00–17:00). Tel. 0141/353-4526 (leave call-back number if leaving a message), www.gsa.ac.uk, shop@gsa.ac.uk. No cameras are allowed on the tour.

Background: When the building first opened, it was modern and minimalist. Other elements were added later, such as the lobby's tile mosaics depicting the artistic greats, including mustachioed Mackintosh (who hovers over the gift shop). As you tour the building, you'll see how Mackintosh—who'd been a humble art student himself not too long before he designed this building—strove to create a space that was both artistically innovative and completely functional for students. The plaster replicas of classical sculptures lining the halls were part of Mackintosh's vision to inspire students by the greats of the past. You'll likely see students and their canvases lining the halls. Do you smell oil paint?

Linking these useable spaces are clever artistic patterns and puzzles that Mackintosh embedded to spur creative thought. A resolute pagan in a very Protestant city, he romanticized the ideals of nature and included an abstract icon of a spiral-within-a-circle rose design on many of his works. In some cases, he designed a little alcove just big enough for a fresh, single-stem rose and placed it next to one of his stained-glass roses—so students could compare reality with the artistic form. (You'll even find these roses on the swinging doors in the bathroom.)

Mackintosh cleverly arranged the school so that every one of the cellar studios is bathed in intense natural light. And yet, as you climb to the top of the building—which should be the brightest, most light-filled area—the space becomes dark and gloomy, and the stairwell is encumbered by a cage-like structure. Then, reaching the top floor, the professors' offices are again full of sunrays—a literal and metaphorical "enlightenment" for the students after slogging through a dark spell.

During the tour, you'll be able to linger a few minutes in the major rooms, such as the remarkable forest-like library and the furniture gallery (including some original tables and chairs from the Willow Tea Rooms). Walking through the GSA, remember that all of this work was the Art Nouveau original, and that Frank Lloyd Wright, the Art Deco Chrysler Building, and everything that resembles it came well after "Charles Rennie Mack's" time.

• *To finish this walk, we'll do a wee bit of urban "hillwalking" (a popular Scottish pastime). Head north from the Glasgow School of Art on Scott Street (from the shop's exit, turn left, then left again on Renfrew Street; one block later, turn right onto Scott Street). Huff and puff your way over the crest of the hill, and make a left onto Buccleuch Street. After three blocks, the last house on the left is the...*

▲Tenement House

Packrats of the world, unite! A strange quirk of fate—the 10-year hospitalization of a woman who never redecorated—created this perfectly preserved middle-class residence. The Scottish National Trust bought this otherwise ordinary row home, located in a residential neighborhood, because of the peculiar tendencies of Miss Toward. For five decades, she kept her home essentially unchanged. The kitchen calendar is still set for 1935, and canisters of licorice powder (a laxative) still sit on the bathroom shelf. It's a time-warp experience, where Glaswegian old-timers enjoy coming to reminisce about how they grew up.

Buy your ticket on the main floor, and poke around the little museum. You'll learn that in Glasgow, a "tenement" isn't a slum—it's simply a stone apartment house. In fact, tenements like these were typical for every class except the richest. But with the city's economic decline, tenements went the way of the dodo bird as the city's population shrank.

Head upstairs to the apartment, which is staffed by caring volunteers. Ring the doorbell to be let in. Ask them why the bed is in the kitchen or why the rooms still smell like natural gas.

As you look through the rooms stuffed with lace and Victorian trinkets—such as the ceramic dogs on the living room's fireplace mantle—consider how different they are from Mackintosh's stark, minimalist designs from the same period.

Cost and Hours: £5.50, £3.50 guidebook, March–Oct 13:00–17:00, last entry 30 minutes before closing, closed Nov–Feb, 145 Buccleuch Street down off the top of Garnethill, toll tel. 0844-493-2197, www.nts.org.uk. No photos allowed.

• *Exit the Tenement House, cross the street, go left, and follow the sidewalk down the hill. Pass the pedestrian bridge on your left and curve around to arrive at the far end of Sauchiehall Street.*

To return to Central Station, turn left, walk to the second bus shelter, and take bus #44 (every 10 minutes, other buses also go to station—ask the driver if another bus pulls up while you're waiting). Taxis zip by on Sauchiehall; a ride to the station costs about £3.

To catch the bus from here straight out to the recommended restaurants in the West End (see page 697), cross Sauchiehall Street, turn left, and walk two blocks to Holland Street. Turn right and walk one short block to the bus stop near the corner of Holland and Bath streets, and wait for bus #16 (every 20 minutes, ask driver to let you off near the Hillhead subway stop).

More Sights in Glasgow

Away from the Center

▲**Kelvingrove Art Gallery and Museum**—This museum is like a Scottish Smithsonian—with everything from a pair of stuffed elephants to fine artwork by the great masters. The well-described collection is impressively displayed in an impressive 100-year-old Spanish Baroque-style building. It's divided into two sections. The "Life" section, in the West Court, features a menagerie of stuffed animals (including a giraffe, kanga-

roo, ostrich, and moose) with a WWII-era Spitfire fighter plane hovering overhead. Branching off are halls with exhibits ranging from Ancient Egypt to "Scotland's First Peoples" to weaponry ("Conflict and Consequence"), as well as several fine paintings (find Salvador Dalí's *Christ of St. John of the Cross*). The more serene "Expression" section, in the East Court, focuses on artwork, including Dutch, Flemish, French, and Italian paintings. It also has exhibits on "Scottish Identity in Art" and on Charles Rennie Mackintosh and the Glasgow School. The Kelvingrove claims to be one of the most-visited museums in Britain—presumably because of all the field-trip groups you'll see here. Watching all the excited Scottish kids—their imaginations ablaze—is as much fun as the collection itself (free, Mon–Thu and Sat 10:00–17:00, Fri and Sun 11:00–17:00, Argyle Street; subway to Kelvinhall stop—when you exit, turn left and walk 5 minutes; buses #9, #16, #23, #42, and #62 all stop nearby; tel. 0141/276-9599, www.glasgowmuseums.com).

▲**Burrell Collection**—This eclectic art collection of a wealthy local shipping magnate is one of Glasgow's top destinations, but

it's three miles outside the city center. If you'd like to visit, plan to make an afternoon of it, and leave time to walk around the surrounding park, where Highland cattle graze. The diverse contents of this museum include sculptures (from Roman to Rodin), stained glass, tapestries, furniture, Asian and Islamic works, and halls of paintings—starring Cézanne, Renoir, Degas, and a Rembrandt self-portrait (free, Mon–Thu and Sat 10:00–17:00, Fri and Sun 11:00–17:00, Pollok Country Park, 2060 Pollokshaws Road, tel. 0141/287-2550, www.glasgowmuseums.com). To get here from downtown, take bus #45, #47, #48, or #57 to Pollokshaws Road, or take a train to the Pollokshaws West train station; the entrance is a 10-minute walk from the bus stop and the train station. By car, follow M8 to exit at junction 22 onto M77 Ayr; exit junction 1 on M77 and follow signs.

East of Downtown: The Cathedral and Nearby

To reach these sights from the TI on George Square, head up North Hanover Street, turn right on Cathedral Street, and walk about 20 minutes (or hop a bus along the main drag—confirm with driver that the bus stops at the cathedral). All sights are free.

Glasgow Cathedral—This blackened, Gothic-to-the-extreme cathedral is a rare example of an intact pre-Reformation Scottish cathedral. Currently under renovation to remove dark soot and replace its mortar, the cathedral is open but covered with scaffolding until 2014. Inside, look up to see the wooden barrel-vaulted ceiling, and notice the beautifully decorated section over the choir ("quire"). Standing at the choir, turn around to look down the nave at the west wall, and notice how the right wall lists. (Don't worry; it's been standing for 800 years.) Peek into the lower church, and don't miss the Blacader Aisle (stairs down to the right as you face the choir), where you can look up to see the ceiling bosses—colorful carved demons, dragons, skulls, and more (April–Sept

Mon–Sat 9:30–17:30, Sun 13:00–17:00; Oct–March Mon–Sat 9:30–16:00, Sun 13:00–16:00, last entry 45 minutes before closing; near junction of Castle and Cathedral Streets, tel. 0141/552-6891, www.glasgowcathedral.org.uk).

Provand's Lordship—With low beams and medieval decor, this creaky home—supposedly the "oldest house in Glasgow"—displays the *Lifestyles of the Rich and Famous*...circa 1471. The interior shows off a few pieces of furniture from the 16th, 17th, and 18th centuries. Out back, explore the St. Nicholas Garden, which was once part of a hospital that dispensed herbal remedies. The plaques in each section show the part of the body each plant is used to treat (Tue–Thu and Sat 10:00–17:00, Fri and Sun 11:00–17:00, closed Mon, across the street from St. Mungo Museum at 3 Castle Street, tel. 0141/552-8819, www.glasgowmuseums.com).

St. Mungo Museum of Religious Life and Art—This museum, next to the cathedral, aims to promote religious understanding. Taking an ecumenical approach, it provides a handy summary of major and minor world religions, showing how each faith handles various rites of passage through the human life span: birth, puberty, marriage, death, and everything in between (same hours as Provand's Lordship, cheap ground-floor café, 2 Castle Street, tel. 0141/276-1625, www.glasgowmuseums.com).

Necropolis—Built to resemble Paris' Père Lachaise cemetery, Glasgow's huge burial hill next to the cathedral has a similarly wistful, ramshackle appeal, along with an occasional deer. Its gravestones seem poised to slide down the hill (open year-round, www.glasgownecropolis.org; if main black gates are closed, walk around to the side and see if you can get in and out through a side alleyway).

Nightlife in Glasgow

Glasgow is a young city, and its nightlife scene is renowned. Walking through the city center, you'll pass at least one club or bar on every block. For the latest, pick up a copy of *The List* (sold at newsstands).

In the West End: **Òran Mòr,** a converted 1862 church overlooking a busy intersection, is one of Glasgow's most popular hangouts. In addition to hosting an atmospheric bar, outdoor beer garden, and brasserie, the building's former nave (now decorated with funky murals) has a nightclub featuring everything from rock shows to traditional Scottish music nights (brasserie serves £10–20 entrées; pub with dressy conservatory or outdoor beer garden serves £7–10 pub grub; daily 9:00–very late, food served 12:00–15:00 & 17:00–22:00, top of Byres Road at 731–735 Great Western Road, tel. 0141/357-6226, www.oran-mor.co.uk).

In the City Center: **The Pot Still** is an award-winning malt whisky bar from 1835 that boasts a formidable selection of more than 300 choices. You'll see locals of all ages sitting in its leathery interior, watching football (soccer) and discussing their drinks. They have whisky aged in sherry casks, whisky preferred by wine drinkers, and whisky from every region of Scotland. Give the friendly bartenders a little background on your beverage tastes, and they'll narrow down a good choice for you from their long list (whisky runs £2-250 a glass, average price £4–5, no food served, Mon–Sat 11:00–24:00, Sun 12:30–24:00, 154 Hope Street, tel. 0141/333-0980).

Sleeping in Glasgow

On Renfrew Street

A batch of basic B&Bs lines Renfrew Street, a block away from the Glasgow School of Art. From here you can walk downhill into the downtown core in about 15 minutes (or take a £3–4 taxi). If approaching by car, you can't drive down one-way Renfrew Street from the city center. Instead, from busy Sauchiehall Street, go up Scott Street or Rose Street, turn left onto Buccleuch Street, and circle around to Renfrew Street.

$$ Rennie Mackintosh Art School Hotel has 24 nice-enough rooms and public spaces inspired by Glasgow's favorite architect (slippery rates change with demand, but generally Sb-£32–35; Db-£48–55 Sun–Thu, £55 Fri–Sat; includes breakfast, free Wi-Fi on ground floor, laundry services, 218–220 Renfrew Street, tel. 0141/333-9992, fax 0141/333-9995, www.rmghotels.com, rennie@rmghotels.com).

Sleep Code

(£1 = about $1.60, country code: 44, area code: 0141)
S = Single, **D** = Double/Twin, **T** = Triple, **Q** = Quad, **b** = bathroom, **s** = shower only. You can assume credit cards are accepted unless otherwise noted.

To help you sort easily through these listings, I've divided the rooms into two categories based on the price for a standard double room with bath (during high season):

  $$ Higher Priced—Most rooms £50 or more.
  $ Lower Priced—Most rooms less than £50.

Prices can change without notice; verify the hotel's current rates online or by email. For other updates, see www.ricksteves.com/update.

Central Glasgow Hotels & Restaurants

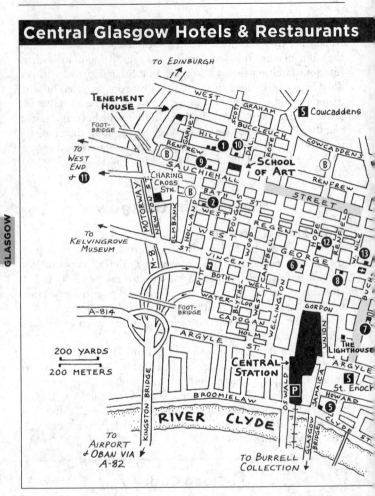

$ Victorian House Hotel is a crank-'em-out place with a friendly staff and 58 worn but workable rooms sprawling through several old townhouses (S-£32, Sb-£39, Db-£60, lots of stairs and no elevator, 212 Renfrew Street, tel. 0141/332-0129, www.the victorian.co.uk, info@thevictorian.co.uk).

Elsewhere in Central Glasgow

$$ Ibis Glasgow, part of the modern hotel chain, has 141 cookie-cutter rooms with blond wood and predictable comfort just three blocks downhill from the Renfrew Street B&Bs. It's a 10-minute, slightly uphill walk from downtown (Sb/Db-£55 on weeknights, £60 on weekends, £85 "event rate" during festivals and in Aug, breakfast-£7, air-con, pay Internet access and free Wi-Fi, eleva-

① Rennie Mackintosh Art School Hotel & Victorian House Hotel
② Ibis Glasgow
③ Premier Inn George Square
④ Babbity Bowster Rooms
⑤ Euro Hostel
⑥ Mussel Inn Restaurant
⑦ Rogano Restaurant
⑧ Wagamama Restaurant
⑨ CCA Terrace Bar & Courtyard Café
⑩ Where the Monkey Sleeps Cafeteria
⑪ To West End Eateries & Nightlife
⑫ The Pot Still Bar
⑬ Internet Café
⑭ Bus to West End

GLASGOW

BUCHANAN BUS STATION
Buchanan St.
QUEEN ST. STN.
GEORGE SQUARE
CITY CHAMBERS
GOMA
CITY HALL
HIGH ST. STN.
TRONGATE
Tolbooth Steeple
BARRAS MKT.
PROVAND'S LORDSHIP
GLASGOW CATHEDRAL
NECROPOLIS
ST. MUNGO'S MUSEUM
ROTTEN ROW
DUKE

S SUBWAY STOP
P PARKING
B BUS STOP
PEDESTRIAN ZONE

DCH

tor, restaurant, hiding behind a big Novotel at 220 West Regent Street, tel. 0141/225-6000, fax 0141/225-6010, www.ibishotel.com, h3139@accor.com).

$$ Premier Inn George Square is a family-friendly chain hotel in the Merchant City district, close to Queen Street Station (Db for up to 2 adults and 2 kids-£69, cheaper in winter—see page 30 for tips on getting the best deal, elevator, pay Wi-Fi, 187 George Street, tel. 08715-278-440, www.premierinn.com).

$$ Babbity Bowster, named for a traditional Scottish dance, is a pub and restaurant renting six basic rooms up top. It's located in the trendy Merchant City on the eastern fringe of downtown, near several clubs and restaurants (Sb-£45, Db-£60, lots of stairs and no elevator, 10-minute walk from Central Station, 16–18

Blackfriars Street, tel. 0141/552-5055, babbity@btinternet.com).
The ground-floor pub serves £5–9 pub grub (daily 12:00–22:00);
the first-floor restaurant, run by a French chef, offers £14–17
entrées (Thu–Sat only 18:30–21:30, closed Sun–Wed).

$ Euro Hostel is the best bet for hostel beds in the city cen-
ter. Part of a chain, this place is a lively hive of backpacker activity,
with 365 beds on nine floors, plus pay Internet access, free Wi-Fi
in the bar, a kitchen, and friendly staff (request a room on a higher
floor and in the back for maximum quiet; very slippery rates, but
figure Sb-£29–40, Db-£36–52, £13–16 bunk in 4- to 14-bed dorm
with bathroom, couples should request a double or you'll get a
bunk-bed, includes continental breakfast, elevator, laundry-£4/
load, 318 Clyde Street, tel. 0141/222-2828, www.euro-hostels
.co.uk, reservations@euro-hostels.co.uk). It's on the busy main
thoroughfare past Central Station, along the River Clyde, near
some seedy areas.

Eating in Glasgow

Many of Glasgow's fancier eateries serve "pre-theatre menus"—
affordable, fixed-price meals served before 19:00.

In the City Center

Mussel Inn offers light, good-value fish dinners and seafood plates
in an airy, informal environment. The restaurant is a cooperative, owned and run by shellfish farmers. Their £10 "kilo pot" of
Scottish mussels is popular with locals and big enough to share
(£7 small grilled platters, £11–17 meals, Mon–Fri 12:00–14:30 &
17:00–22:00, Sat 12:00–22:00, Sun 12:30–22:00, 157 Hope Street,
between St. Vincent and West George Streets, tel. 0141/572-1405).

Rogano is a time-warp Glasgow institution that retains much
of the same classy Art Deco interior it had when it opened in 1935.
You half-expect to see Bacall and Bogart at the next table. The restaurant has three parts. The bar in front has outdoor seating (£6
lunch sandwiches, £9–10 meals). The fancy dining room at the back
of the main floor smacks of the officers' mess on the *Queen Mary*,
which was built here on the Clyde during the same period (£20–24
meals with a focus on seafood). A more casual yet still dressy bistro in the cellar is filled with 1930s-Hollywood glamour (£11–14
meals, £15 afternoon tea; daily 12:00–22:30, fancy restaurant closed
14:30–18:00, 11 Exchange Place—just before giant archway from
Buchanan Street, reservations smart, tel. 0141/248-4055).

Wagamama is part of a reliably good UK chain that serves
delicious Asian noodle dishes at a reasonable price (£6–10 entrées,
Mon–Sat 12:00–23:00, Sun 12:30–22:00, 97–103 West George
Street, tel. 0141/229-1468).

And More: Dozens of restaurants line the main commercial areas of town: Sauchiehall Street, Buchanan Street, and the Merchant City area. Most are very similar, with trendy interiors, Euro disco-pop soundtracks, and dinner for about £15–20 per person.

Budget Options near the Glasgow School of Art

CCA Terrace Bar and Courtyard Café, located on the first floor of Glasgow's edgy contemporary art museum, has delicious designer food at art-student prices. An 18th-century facade, discovered when the site was excavated to build the museum, looms over the courtyard restaurant (£5–7 salads, sandwiches, and entrées; £9–13 early-bird specials 17:00–19:00; food served Tue–Thu 10:00–19:30, Fri–Sat 10:00–21:00; closed Sun–Mon, 350 Sauchiehall Street, tel. 0141/332-7959).

Where the Monkey Sleeps is a cheap student cafeteria across the street from the entrance to the Glasgow School of Art. This is a good spot for a subsidized lunch (open to the public, choice of two hot meals a day for £2–4, soups for £2, and sandwiches for £1–3). Nothing is ever more than £4. It's your chance to mingle with the city's next generation of artists and hear more of that lilting Glaswegian accent (Sept–June Mon–Fri 8:00–17:00, closed Sat–Sun, outside of the school year fewer foods to choose from, entrance is on the left as you face the multicolored windows, follow *refectory* signs, 166 Renfrew Street, tel. 0141/353-4728).

In the West End

The hip, lively residential neighborhood called the West End is worth exploring, particularly at dinnertime. A collection of fine and fun eateries lines Ashton Lane, a small street just off bustling Byres Road (the scene continues north along Cresswell Lane). Before choosing a place, make a point of strolling the whole scene to comparison-shop.

Local favorites (all open long hours daily) include the landmark **Ubiquitous Chip** (with various pubs and restaurants sprawling through a deceptively large building; £5–7 pub grub, £8–20 restaurant meals, tel. 0141/334-5007) and **The Loft** (£7–9 pizzas and pastas in the lobby of Grosvenor Cinema, a grand old movie theater; tel. 0141/339-0686). Up at Cresswell Lane, consider **Café Andaluz,** which offers £4–7 tapas and sangria behind lacy wooden screens, as the waitstaff clicks past on the cool tiles (2 Cresswell Lane, tel. 0141/339-1111). Back on Byres Road, **La Vallée Blanche** serves French cuisine with a Scottish twist, in a romantic dining area that resembles an upscale mountain lodge (£11–18 entrées, closed Mon, 360 Byres Road, tel. 0141/334-3333). Also note that the church-turned-pub **Òran Mòr**—described earlier, under "Nightlife in Glasgow"—is a five-minute walk away (at the intersection of Byres and Great Western Road).

Getting to the West End: It's easiest to take the subway to Hillhead, which is a two-minute walk from Ashton Lane (exit the station to the left, then take the first left to find the lane). From the city center, you can also take a £5–6 taxi or catch bus #20 or #66 (stops just in front of the TI and on Hope Street, near recommended Renfrew Street hotels, runs every 10 minutes; get out when you reach Byres Road).

Glasgow Connections

Traveline Scotland has a journey planner that's linked to all of Scotland's train and bus schedule info. Go online (www .travelinescotland.com); call them at toll tel. 0871-200-2233; or use the individual websites listed below. If you're connecting with Edinburgh, note that the train is faster but the bus is cheaper.

From Glasgow's Central Station by Train to: Keswick in the Lake District (about hourly, 1.5 hours to Penrith, then catch a bus to Keswick, roughly hourly, only 8/day on Sun, 40 minutes), **Stranraer** and ferry to Belfast (7/day, 2.5 hours, some direct, others with change in Ayr), **Troon** and ferry to Belfast (2/hour, 45 minutes), **Blackpool** (1–2/hour, 3–3.5 hours, transfer in Preston), **Liverpool** (1–2/hour, 3.5 hours, change in Wigan or Preston), **Durham** (1–2/hour, 2.75–3 hours, may require change in Edinburgh), **York** (2/hour, 3.5 hours, may require change in Edinburgh), **London** (1–2 hour, 4.5–5 hours direct). Train info: toll tel. 0845-748-4950, www.nationalrail.co.uk.

From Glasgow's Queen Street Station by Train to: Oban (3–5/day, just 1/day Sun in winter, 3.25 hours), **Inverness** (9/day, 3.25–3.5 hours, 3 direct, the rest change in Perth), **Edinburgh** (4/hour, 50 minutes), **Stirling** (3/hour, 30–45 minutes), **Pitlochry** (9/day, 1.5–1.75 hours, some with transfer in Perth).

From Glasgow by Bus to: Edinburgh (4/hour, 1.25 hour), **Oban** (6/day, 2.75 hours, some with transfer in Tyndrum), **Fort William** (buses #914, #915, and #916; 8/day, 3 hours), **Glencoe** (buses #914, #915, and #916; 8/day, 2.5 hours), **Inverness** (every 1–2 hours, 3.5–4.5 hours, some transfer in Perth), **Portree** on the Isle of Skye (buses #915 and #916, 3/day, 6.25 hours), **Pitlochry** (5/day, 2.25 hours, transfer in Perth). Bus info: toll tel. 0871-266-3333, www.citylink.co.uk.

Glasgow International Airport: Located eight miles west of the city, this airport has currency-exchange desks, a TI, Internet access, luggage storage, and ATMs (toll tel. 0844-481-5555, www .glasgowairport.com). Taxis connect downtown to the airport for about £20. Glasgow Flyer Bus #500 zips to central Glasgow (daily at least 4/hour 5:00–23:00, then hourly through the night, £4.50/one-way, £7/round-trip, 15–20 minutes to both train stations, 25 minutes to the bus station, catch at bus stop #1, www.glasgow flyer.com).

Prestwick Airport: A hub for Ryanair (as well as the US military, which refuels planes here), this airport is about 30 miles southwest of the city center (toll tel. 0871-223-0700, ext. 1006, www.gpia.co.uk). The best connection is by train, which runs between the airport and Central Station (Mon–Sat 2/hour, 45 minutes, half-price with Ryanair ticket). Stagecoach buses link the airport with Buchanan Street Station (£4–7, daily 1–2/hour plus a few nighttime buses, 45–60 minutes, check schedules at www .travelinescotland.com).

OBAN AND THE SOUTHERN HIGHLANDS

Oban • Mull • Iona • Glencoe • Fort William

The area north of Glasgow offers a fun and easy dip into the southern part of the Scottish Highlands. Oban is a fruit crate of Scottish traditions, with a handy pair of wind-bitten Hebrides islands (Mull and Iona) just a hop, skip, and jump away. Nearby, the evocative "Weeping Glen" of Glencoe aches with both history and natural beauty. Beyond that, Fort William anchors the southern end of the Caledonian Canal, offering a springboard to more Highlands scenery—this is where Britain's highest peak, Ben Nevis, keeps its head in the clouds, and where you'll find a valley made famous by a steam train carrying a young wizard named Harry.

Planning Your Time

Oban is a smart place to spend the night on a blitz tour of central Scotland; with more time to linger (and an interest in a day trip to the islands), spend two nights—Iona is worthwhile but adds a day to your trip. If you have a third night to spare, you can sleep in Iona and give yourself time to roam around Mull. Glencoe is worth considering as a very sleepy, rural overnight alternative to Oban, or if you have plenty of time and want a remote village experience on your way north.

Oban works well if you're coming from Glasgow, or even all the way from England's Lake District (for driving tips, see the end of this chapter). Assuming you're driving, here's an ambitious two-day plan for the Highlands (some of these sights are described in the next three chapters).

Day 1

Morning Drive up from the Lake District, or linger in Glasgow.

  11:30 Depart Glasgow.

  12:00 Rest stop on Loch Lomond, then joyride on.

  13:00 Lunch in Inveraray.

  16:00 Arrive in Oban, tour whisky distillery, and drop by the TI.

  20:00 Dine in Oban.

Day 2

  9:00 Leave Oban.

  10:00 Visit Glencoe museum and the valley's Visitors Centre.

  12:00 Drive to Fort William and follow the Caledonian Canal to Inverness, stopping at Fort Augustus to see the locks and along Loch Ness to search for monsters.

  16:00 Visit the Culloden Battlefield (closes earlier off-season) near Inverness.

  17:00 Drive south.

  20:00 Arrive in Edinburgh.

With More Time

While you'll see the Highlands on the above itinerary, you'll whiz past them in a misty blur. With more time, head north from Fort William to the Isle of Skye, spend a night or two there, head over to Inverness via Loch Ness, and consider a stop in Pitlochry.

Getting Around the Highlands

By Car: Drivers enjoy flexibility and plenty of tempting stopovers. Barring traffic, you'll make great time on good, mostly two-lane roads. Be careful, but don't be too timid about passing; otherwise, diesel fumes and large trucks might be your main memory of driving in Scotland. As you drive along Loch Ness, antsy locals may ride your bumper. For step-by-step instructions, read the "Route Tips for Drivers" at the end of this chapter.

    By Public Transportation: Glasgow is the gateway to this region (so you'll most likely have to transfer there if coming from Edinburgh). The **train** zips from Glasgow to Fort William, Oban, and Kyle of Lochalsh in the west; and up to Stirling, Pitlochry, and Inverness in the east. For more remote destinations (such as Glencoe), the bus is better.

    Most of the **buses** you'll need are operated by Scottish Citylink. Buy tickets at local TIs, pay the driver in cash when you board, or purchase tickets in advance online at www.citylink.co.uk. The nondescript town of Fort William serves as a hub for Highlands buses. Note that bus frequency is substantially reduced on Sundays and off-season—during these times, always carefully confirm schedules locally. Unless otherwise noted, I've listed bus information for summer weekdays.

These buses are particularly useful for connecting the sights in this book:

Buses **#976** and **#977** connect Glasgow with Oban (6/day, 2.75 hours, some with transfer in Tyndrum).

Bus **#913** runs one daily direct bus from Edinburgh to this region—stopping at Glasgow, Stirling, and Glencoe on the way to Fort William (allow 4 hours from Edinburgh to Fort William; 5 more/day with change in Glasgow on buses #900 and #914, 5 hours).

Bus **#978** connects Edinburgh with Oban, stopping in Stirling, but not Glencoe (1/day direct, 3.75 hours; 6 more/day with changes in Glasgow and/or Tyndrum, 4.75 hours).

Bus **#914** goes from Glasgow to Fort William, stopping at Glencoe (5/day, 3 hours).

Buses **#915** and **#916** follow the same route (Glasgow–Glencoe–Fort William), then continue all the way up to Portree on the Isle of Skye (3/day, 6.75 hours for the full run).

Bus **#918** goes from Oban to Fort William, stopping en route at Ballachulish near Glencoe (3/day in summer, 2/day off-season, never on Sun; 1 hour to Ballachulish, 1.5 hours total to Fort William).

Bus **#919** connects Fort William with Inverness (5/day, 2 hours).

By Plane: Seaplane service connects downtown Glasgow (on the River Clyde) and Oban Bay. While pricey—about £169 round-trip—the flight takes only about half an hour and provides a unique view of the Highlands you won't see any other way (on-demand morning or afternoon flights March–Nov, weather permitting, office hours daily 8:30–18:00, book far ahead in summer, tel. 0870-242-1457 or 01436/675-030, www.lochlomondseaplanes.com).

Oban

Oban (pronounced OH-bin) is called the "gateway to the isles." Equal parts functional and scenic, this busy little ferry-and-train terminal has no important sights, but makes up the difference in character. It's a low-key resort, with a winding promenade lined by gravel beaches, ice-cream stands, fish-and-chip take-away shops, and a surprising diversity of fine restaurants. When the rain clears, sun-starved Scots sit on benches along The Esplanade, leaning back to catch some rays. Wind, boats, gulls, layers of islands, and the promise of a wide-open Atlantic beyond give Oban a rugged charm.

Orientation to Oban

(area code: 01631)

Oban's business action, just a couple of streets deep, stretches along the harbor and its promenade. (The island just offshore is Kerrera,

with Mull looming behind it.) Everything in Oban is close together, and the town seems eager to please its many visitors. There's live music nightly in several bars and restaurants; wool and tweed are perpetually on sale (tourist shops stay open later than usual in summer—until 20:00—and many are even open on Sundays); and posters announce a variety of day tours to Scotland's wild and rabbit-strewn western islands.

OBAN

Tourist Information

Oban's impressive TI, located in a former church, sells bus and ferry tickets and has a fine bookshop. Stop by to get brochures and information on everything from bike rental to golf courses to horseback riding to rainy-day activities and more. They also offer coin-operated Internet access (£1/20 minutes) and can book you a room for a £4 fee (flexible hours, generally July–Aug daily 9:00–19:00; April–June Mon–Sat 9:00–17:30, Sun 10:00–17:00; Sept–Oct daily 10:00–17:00; Nov–March Mon–Sat 10:00–17:00, Sun 12:00–17:00; on Argyll Square, just off the harbor a block from the train station, tel. 01631/563-122, www.oban.org.uk). Wander through the TI's free exhibit (in the back) on the area, and pick up a few phones to hear hardy locals talk about their life on the wild western edge of Scotland. Check the "What's On" board for the latest on Oban's small-town evening scene (free live entertainment downstairs in the bar at the Great Western Hotel on the Esplanade—nightly at 20:30 generally year-round, Scottish Night generally every Thu, call for details, tel. 01631/563-101).

Helpful Hints

Internet Access: One option is at the **TI** (see above). **Fancy That** is a souvenir shop on the main drag with seven high-speed Internet terminals and Wi-Fi in the back room (£1/20 minutes, daily 9:30–17:00, until 22:00 July–Aug, 108 George Street, tel. 01631/562-996). To surf for free, get online at the

Oban

1. Strathaven Terrace Accommodations
2. To Glenburnie House, The Barriemore & Kilchrenan House
3. The Rowantree Hotel
4. Oban Backpackers
5. Oban Backpackers Annex
6. IYHF Hostel
7. Jeremy Inglis' Hostel
8. Ee'usk & Piazza Restaurants
9. To The Seafood Temple
10. Coast Restaurant
11. Cuan Mòr Gastro-Pub
12. Room 9 Restaurant
13. Ferry to Waypoint Bar & Grill
14. The Lorne Pub
15. Shellfish Shack
16. The Kitchen Garden Deli & Café
17. Tesco Supermarket
18. Skipinnish Ceilidh House
19. Great Western Hotel (Live Shows)
20. Fancy That Shop (Internet)
21. Bowman's Tours & West Coast Motors (Bag Storage)
22. Laundry
23. To Bike Rental
24. Whisky Distillery

OBAN

100 YARDS
100 METERS

‖‖‖ STAIRS
P PARKING

CORRAN

ST. COLUMBA'S

OBAN BAY

BOATS TO MULL & IONA

FERRY TERMINAL

SOUTH PIER

TO 9 & KERREA FERRY

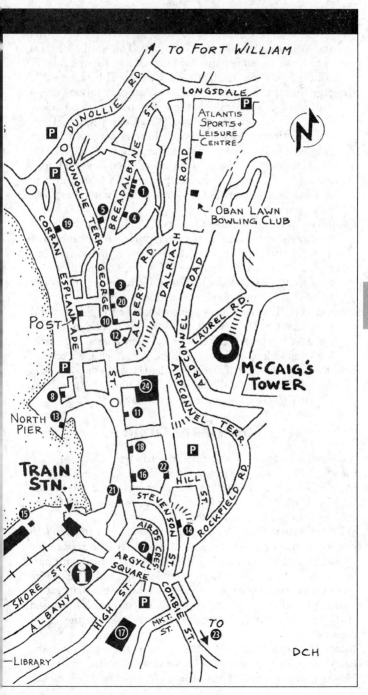

OBAN

library just above the ferry terminal; you can just show up, but it's smart to call ahead to book a 30-minute time slot (Mon and Wed 10:00–13:00 & 14:00–19:00, Thu until 18:00, Fri until 17:00, closed Sat afternoon and all day Tue and Sun, 77 Albany Street, tel. 01631/571-444, www.argyll-bute.gov.uk).

Baggage Storage: The train station has luggage lockers (£3–4 depending on bag size), but these have been known to close for security reasons. In this case, **West Coast Motors**, which sells bus tickets, has a pricey left-luggage service (£1/hour per piece, unsecured in main office, Mon–Fri 8:00–13:00 & 14:00–16:00, Sat 9:00–14:00, closed Sun, July–Aug open during lunch, can be sporadically closed Oct–May, next to Bowman's Tours at Queens Park Place, www.westcoast motors.co.uk).

Laundry: You'll find **Oban Quality Laundry** tucked a block behind the main drag, at the intersection of Stevenson and Tweedle Streets (£6–9 per load for same-day drop-off service, no self-service, Mon–Fri 9:00–17:00, Sat 9:00–13:00, closed Sun, tel. 01631/563-554). The **Oban Backpackers** and **IYHF** hostels have laundry service or facilities for guests.

Supermarket: **Tesco** is a five-minute walk from the TI (Mon–Fri 8:00–22:00, Sat 8:00–24:00, Sun 9:00–18:00, WC in front by registers, inexpensive cafeteria, look for entrance to large parking lot a block past TI on right-hand side, Lochside Street).

Bike Rental: Try **Flit Self Drive** (£10/half-day, £14/day, Mon–Fri 9:00–17:30, Sat 9:00–12:00, closed Sun, Glencruitten Road, tel. 01631/566-553, www.flitselfdrive.co.uk).

Tours near Oban

▲▲**Nearby Islands**—For the best day trip from Oban, tour the islands of Mull and Iona (offered daily Easter–Oct, described on page 715)—or consider staying overnight on remote and beautiful Iona. With more time or other interests, consider one of many other options you'll see advertised.

Wildlife Tours—Those more interested in nature than church history will enjoy trips to the wildly scenic Isle of Staffa with Fingal's Cave. The journey to Treshnish Island brims with puffins, seals, and other sea critters. Several groups, including Sealife Adventures and SeaFari, run whale-watching tours that feature rare minke whales, basking sharks, bottlenose dolphins, and porpoises. Departures and options abound—check at the TI for information.

Open-Top Bus Tours—If there's good weather and you don't have a car, take a spin out of Oban for views of nearby castles and islands, plus a stop at McCaig's Tower (£8, valid for 24 hours, late

May–late Sept daily at 11:00 and 14:00, no tours off-season, 2.5 hours, departs from rail station, tel. 01586/552-319, www.citysight seeingoban.com).

Sights in Oban

In Oban

▲**West Highland Malt Scotch Whisky Distillery Tours**—The 200-year-old Oban Whisky Distillery produces more than 16,000 liters a week. They offer serious and fragrant one-hour tours explaining the process from start to finish, with two smooth samples, a whisky glass (normally sells for £6), and a discount coupon for the shop. This is the handiest whisky tour you'll see, just a block off the harbor and better than anything in Edinburgh. The exhibition that precedes the tour gives a quick, whisky-centric history of Scotland (£7; July–Sept Mon–Fri 9:30–19:30, Sat-Sun 9:30–17:00; Easter–June and Oct Mon–Sat 9:30–17:00, closed Sun; March-Easter and Nov Mon–Fri 10:00–17:00, closed Sat–Sun; Dec and Feb Mon–Fri 12:30–16:00, closed Sat–Sun; closed Jan; last tour 1.25 hours before closing, tel. 01631/572-004). In high season, these very popular tours (which are limited to 15 people every 15 minutes) fill up quickly. Call or stop by the day before to reserve your time slot.

Skipinnish Ceilidh House—On most nights mid-June through mid-September, you can stroll into Skipinnish on the main drag for Highland music and storytelling. This venue, owned by professional musicians, invests in talented musicians and puts on a good show, with live bands, songs sung in Gaelic, and Highland dancing. For many, the best part is the chance to learn some *ceilidh* dancing. These group dances are a lot of fun—wallflowers and bad dancers are warmly welcomed, and the staff is happy to give you pointers (£8 music session, pricier for concerts with visiting big-name *ceilidh* bands, music 4–5 nights/week mid-June–mid-Sept at 20:00, Thu only in late May and late Sept, 2 hours, sidewalk ticket stall open daily 12:00–17:00, 34–38 George Street, tel. 01631/569-599, www.skipinnish.com).

McCaig's Tower—The unfinished "colosseum" on the hill overlooking town was an employ-the-workers-and-build-me-a-fine-memorial project undertaken by an early Oban tycoon in 1900. While the structure itself is nothing to see close-up, a 10-minute hike through a Victorian residential neighborhood leads you to a peaceful garden and a mediocre view.

Atlantis Leisure Centre—This industrial-type sports center is a good place to get some exercise on a rainy day or let the kids run wild for a few hours. There's an indoor swimming pool with a big water slide, a rock-climbing wall, tennis courts, and two playgrounds (Mon–Fri 7:00–21:00, Sat–Sun 8:30–18:00; open-swim pool hours vary by season—call or check online for exact times; pool entry: adults-£3.50, kids-£2.20, no rental towels or suits, lockers-£0.20, on the north end of Dalriach Road, tel. 01631/566-800, www.atlantisleisure.co.uk). The center's outdoor playground is free and open all the time; the indoor "soft play centre" for children under five costs £2 per kid.

Oban Lawn Bowling Club—The club has welcomed visitors since 1869. This elegant green is the scene of a wonderfully British spectacle of old men tiptoeing wishfully after their balls. It's fun to watch, and—if there's no match and the weather's dry—for £4 each, anyone can rent shoes and balls and actually play (informal hours, but generally daily 10:00–16:00 & 17:00 to "however long the weather lasts," just south of sports center on Dalriach Road, tel. 01631/570-808).

Near Oban

Kerrera—Just offshore from Oban, this stark but very green island offers a quick, easy opportunity to get that romantic island experience. Although Kerrera (KEH-reh-rah) dominates Oban's sea view, you'll have to head two miles south of town (follow the coast road past the ferry terminal) to catch the boat to the middle of the island (ferry-£5 round-trip, bikes free, 5-minute trip; Easter–Sept first ferry Mon–Sat at 8:45, then daily 2/hour 10:30–12:30 & 14:00–17:00, last ferry at 18:00; Oct–Easter 5–6/day, last ferry Mon–Fri at 17:50, Sat–Sun at 17:00—but changes with demand; at Gallanach's dock; tel. 01631/563-665, if no answer contact Oban TI for info; www.kerrera-ferry.co.uk). Bus #431 runs between the Oban train station and the Kerrera ferry twice a day in summer (late May–late Sept only, www.westcoastmotors.co.uk). The free shuttle service between Oban's North Pier and the Kerrera Marina is for customers of the Waypoint Bar & Grill (described on page 713), but you could always take a walk around the island after lunch.

Sleeping on Kerrera: To spend the night on the island, your only option is the **$ Kerrera Bunkhouse,** a converted 18th-century stable that has seven bunk beds in four compartments (£14 per person, £70 for the entire bunkhouse, includes bedding but not towels, cheaper for 2 nights or more, open year-round but book ahead in winter, kitchen, tel. 01631/570-223, ferry info at www.kerrerabunkhouse.co.uk, info@kerrerabunkhouse.co.uk, Susan). They also run a tea garden that serves meals (April–mid-Oct Wed–Sun 10:30–16:30, closed Mon-Tue and mid-Oct–March).

Isle of Seil—Enjoy a drive, a walk, some solitude, and the sea. Drive 12 miles south of Oban on A816 to B844 to the Isle of Seil (pronounced "seal"), connected to the mainland by a bridge (which, locals like to brag, "crosses the Atlantic"...well, maybe a small part of it).

Just over the bridge on the Isle of Seil is a pub called **Tigh-an-Truish** ("House of Trousers"). After a 1745 English law forbade the wearing of kilts on the mainland, Highlanders on the island used this pub to change from kilts to trousers before they made the crossing. The pub serves great meals and good seafood dishes to those either in kilts or pants (pub open daily April–Oct 11:00–23:00—food served 12:00–14:00 & 18:00–20:30, July–Aug all day until 21:00, Nov–March shorter hours and soup/sandwiches only, darts anytime, tel. 01852/300-242).

Five miles across the island, on a tiny second island and facing the open Atlantic, is **Easdale,** a historic, touristy, windy little slate-mining town—with a slate-town museum and incredibly tacky egomaniac's "Highland Arts" shop (shuttle ferry goes the 300 yards). An overpriced direct ferry runs from Easdale to Iona; but, at twice the cost of the Mull–Iona trip, the same time on the island, and very little time with a local guide, it's hardly worth it. For a better connection to Iona, see page 715.

Sleeping in Oban

(area code: 01631)

B&Bs

Oban's B&Bs offer a better value than its hotels. All of the places below are a very short walk from the town center. None of these B&Bs accepts credit cards.

On Strathaven Terrace

The following B&Bs line up on a quiet, flowery street that's nicely located two blocks off the harbor, three blocks from the center, and a 10-minute walk from the train station. By car, as you enter town, turn left after King's Knoll Hotel, and take your first right onto Breadalbane Street. ("Strathaven Terrace" is actually just the name for this row of houses on Breadalbane Street.) The alley behind the buildings has parking for all of these places.

$$ Sandvilla B&B rents six fine rooms—including one on the ground floor—with sleek contemporary decor (Db-£55, £65 in July–Aug, Tb-£83–90, free Wi-Fi, at #4, tel. 01631/562-803, www.holidayoban.co.uk, sandvilla@holidayoban.co.uk, Joyce and Scott).

$$ Gramarvin Guest House has five fresh and cheery rooms (Db-£55–60, £65 in Aug, Tb-£95, free Wi-Fi, at #5, tel. 01631/564-622, www.gramarvin.co.uk, mary@gramarvin.co.uk, Mary).

$$ Raniven Guest House has five simple, tastefully decorated rooms (Sb-£30–35, Db-£55–60, price depends on season,

Sleep Code

(£1 = about $1.60, country code: 44, area code: 01631)
S = Single, **D** = Double/Twin, **T** = Triple, **Q** = Quad, **b** = bathroom,
s = shower only. Unless otherwise noted, you can assume
credit cards are accepted at hotels and hostels—but not
B&Bs—and breakfast is included.

To help you sort easily through these listings, I've divided
the rooms into three categories based on the price for a
standard double room with bath (during high season):

$$$ Higher Priced—Most rooms £70 or more.
 $$ Moderately Priced—Most rooms between £30–70.
  $ Lower Priced—Most rooms £30 or less.

Prices can change without notice; verify the hotel's
current rates online or by email. For other updates, see www
.ricksteves.com/update.

OBAN

free Wi-Fi, at #1, tel. 01631/562-713, www.raniven.co.uk, info
@raniven.co.uk, Moyra and Stuart).

$$ Tanglin B&B, with five Grandma's house–homey rooms,
comes with lively, chatty hosts Liz and Jim Montgomery, who cre-
ate an easygoing atmosphere (S-£25, tiny D-£44, Db-£50, flexible
rates and family deals, free Wi-Fi, at #3, tel. 01631/563-247, mobile
0774/8305-891, jimtanglin@aol.com).

Guest Houses and Small Hotels

These options are a step up from the B&Bs—in terms of both ame-
nities and price. The first three, which are along The Esplanade
that stretches north of town above a cobble beach (with beautiful
bay views), are a 5- to 10-minute walk from the center. The last one
is on the main drag in town.

$$$ Glenburnie House, a stately Victorian home, has an
elegant breakfast room overlooking the bay. Its 12 spacious,
comfortable, classy rooms feel like plush living rooms. There's a
nice lounge and a tiny sunroom with a stuffed "hairy coo" head
(Sb-£50, Db-£84–100, price depends on size and view, closed
mid-Nov–Easter, free Wi-Fi, free parking, The Esplanade, tel. &
fax 01631/562-089, www.glenburnie.co.uk, graeme.strachan@bt
internet.com, Graeme).

$$$ The Barriemore is the last place on Oban's grand water-
front esplanade. Its woody, bright front-facing rooms—some with
bay views—are well-appointed, with furnishings that fit the house's
grand Victorian feel. Rooms in the modern addition in the back
have no views and simple furnishings, but are cheaper (Sb-£65–75,

Db-£92–102, Tb-£105–126, less off-season, price depends on view, free Wi-Fi, The Esplanade, tel. 01631/566-356, fax 01631/571-084, www.barriemore-hotel.co.uk, reception@barriemore-hotel.co.uk, friendly Nic and Sarah Jones, and Mara the complacent Great Dane).

$$$ Kilchrenan House, the turreted former retreat of a textile magnate, has 14 tastefully renovated, large rooms, most with bay views (Sb-£45, Db-£70–90, 2-night minimum, higher prices are for seaview rooms in June–Aug, lower prices are for back-facing rooms and Sept–May, stunning room #5 is worth the few extra pounds, welcome drink of whisky or sherry, different "breakfast special" every day, closed Dec–Jan, a few houses past the cathedral on The Esplanade, tel. 01631/562-663, www.kilchrenanhouse .co.uk, info@kilchrenanhouse.co.uk, Colin and Frances).

$$$ The Rowantree Hotel is a group-friendly place with 24 freshly renovated rooms reminiscent of a budget hotel in the US, and a central locale right on Oban's main drag (Sb-£50, Db-£90, prices may be soft for walk-ins and off-season, easy parking, George Street, tel. 01631/562-954, www.rowantreehoteloban.co.uk).

Hostels

Oban offers plenty of cheap dorm beds. Your choice: easygoing, institutional (but with fantastic views), or New Age.

$ Oban Backpackers is the most central, laid-back, and fun, with a wonderful, sprawling public living room and 48 beds. The giant mural of nearby islands in the lobby is useful for orientation, and the staff is generous with travel tips (£16/bed, 6–12 bunks per room, includes breakfast, pay Internet access, free Wi-Fi, £2.50 laundry service for guests only, 10-minute walk from station, on Breadalbane Street, tel. 01631/562-107, www.obanbackpackers .com, info@obanbackpackers.com, Peter). Their bunkhouse across the street has several basic but cheerful private rooms that share a kitchen (S-£19-22, D-£43, T-£57, same contact info as hostel).

$ The orderly **IYHF hostel,** on the scenic waterfront Esplanade, is in a grand building with 110 beds and smashing views of the harbor and islands from the lounges and all of the rooms. The smaller, private rooms—including several that can usually be rented as doubles—are in a separate newer building out back (£15–18/bed in 5- to 10-bed rooms, bunk-bed Db-£40–55, T-£55–65, Q-£70–85, price varies with demand, also has 8-bed apartment with kitchen, disabled access, £2 cheaper for members, breakfast-£4–6, pay Internet access and Wi-Fi, great facilities and public rooms with cushy sofas, one laundry machine, tel. 01631/562-025, www.syha.org.uk, oban@syha.org.uk).

$ Jeremy Inglis' Hostel has 37 beds located two blocks from the TI and train station. This loosely run place feels more like a

OBAN

commune than a youth hostel...and it's cheap (£15/bed, S-£22, D-£30, cash only, includes linens, kitchen, free Wi-Fi, breakfast comes with Jeremy's homemade jam, no curfew, second floor at 21 Airds Crescent, tel. 01631/565-065, jeremyinglis@mctavishs .freeserve.co.uk).

Eating in Oban

Oban calls itself the "seafood capital of Scotland," and there are plenty of good fish places in town.

Ee'usk (a phonetic rendering of *iasg*, Scottish Gaelic for "fish") is a popular, stylish, family-run place on the waterfront. It has tall tables, a casual-chic atmosphere, a bright and glassy interior, sweeping views on three sides, and fish dishes favored by both locals and tourists. Reservations are recommended every day in summer and on weekends off-season; if you have to wait for a table, find a seat on one of the comfy sofas in the loft bar (£5–9 lunches, £13–20 dinners, daily 12:00–15:00 & 18:00–21:00, North Pier, tel. 01631/565-666, MacLeod family).

Piazza, next door and also run by the MacLeods, has similar decor but serves Italian cuisine and offers a more family-friendly ambience (£7–10 pizzas and pastas, daily 12:00–15:00 & 17:30–21:00, smart to reserve ahead July–Aug, tel. 01631/563-628).

The Seafood Temple is worth the 15-minute walk from the town center (follow the road past the ferry terminal, or take a £3 taxi ride). This small eatery is situated in a beautifully restored former public toilet building from the Victorian era (no joke), with panoramic views across the bay to the Isle of Kerrera. Owner/chef John—who also runs the shellfish shack at the ferry dock (listed later)—prides himself on creating the best seafood dishes in town, listed on a limited, handwritten menu. Reservations are a must: To book a table, make a £10-per-person deposit at the shellfish shack (£12–21 meals, large portions, Thu–Sun seatings at 18:00 and 20:00, closed Mon–Wed, tel. 01631/566-000).

Coast proudly serves fresh local fish, meat, and veggies in a mod pine-and-candlelight atmosphere. As everything is prepared and presented with care by husband-and-wife team Richard and Nicola—who try to combine traditional Scottish elements in innovative new ways—come here only if you have time for a slow meal (£7–10 lunches, £13–18 dinners, £12 two-course and £15 three-course specials served for lunch and at 17:30–18:30, open daily 12:00–14:00 & 17:30–21:00, closed Sun for lunch, 104 George Street, tel. 01631/569-900).

Cuan Mòr is a popular gastropub that combines traditional Scottish with modern flair—both in its tasty cuisine and in its furnishings, made entirely of wood, stone, and metal scavenged from

OBAN

the beaches of Scotland's west coast (£6 lunches, £8–13 entrées, food served daily 12:00–22:00, brewery in the back, 60 George Street, tel. 01631/565-078).

Room 9 seats just 24 diners in one tiny light-wood room, and has a select menu of homemade nouvelle-cuisine dishes. It's owned and run with care by the chef (dinner only, £13–17 meals, Mon–Sat 17:30–21:30, closed Sun, reservations smart Fri–Sat, 9 Craigard Road, tel. 01631/564-200).

Waypoint Bar & Grill, just across the bay from Oban, is a laid-back patio at the Kerrera Marina with a no-nonsense menu of grilled seafood. It's not fancy, but the food is fresh and inexpensive, and on a nice day the open-air waterside setting is unbeatable (£8–10 plates, £15 seafood platter, May–Sept daily 12:00–14:00 & 17:00–21:00, closed Oct–April, tel. 08740/650-669). A free-for-customers eight-minute ferry to the marina leaves from Oban's North Pier—look for the sign near the recommended Piazza restaurant (departs hourly at :10 past each hour).

Pub Grub: **The Lorne** is a lively high-ceilinged pub known for its good grub and friendly service. After hours, it becomes the most happening nightspot in town...which isn't saying much (£7–9, food served Mon–Sat 12:00–15:00 & 17:30–21:00, Sun 12:30–15:30 & 17:30–21:00, outside seating, free Wi-Fi, tucked a couple of blocks off the main drag behind the stream at Stevenson Street, tel. 01631/570-020).

OBAN

Lunch

The green **shellfish shack** at the ferry dock is the best spot to pick up a seafood sandwich or a snack (often free salmon samples, inexpensive coffee, meal-size £3 salmon sandwiches, picnic tables nearby, open daily from 10:00 until the boat unloads from Mull around 17:45). This is a good place to pick up a sandwich for your island day—or get a light, early dinner (or "appetizer") when you return from the isles. For a full meal, check out the same folks' Seafood Temple restaurant, described earlier.

The Kitchen Garden is fine for soup, salad, or sandwiches. It's a deli and gourmet-foods store with a charming café upstairs (£3.50 sandwiches to go, £5–8 dishes upstairs, Mon–Sat 9:00–17:00, Sun 11:00–16:00, closed Sun Jan–mid-Feb, 14 George Street, tel. 01631/566-332).

Oban Connections

By Train from Oban: Trains link Oban to the nearest transportation hub in **Glasgow** (3–5/day, just 1/day Sun in winter, 3.25 hours); to get to **Edinburgh,** you'll have to transfer in Glasgow (3–5/day, 4.25 hours). To reach **Fort William** (a transit hub for the Highlands), you'll take the same Glasgow-bound train, but transfer in Crianlarich—the direct bus is easier (see below). Oban's small train station has limited hours (ticket window open Mon–Sat 7:15–18:00, Sun 10:45–18:00, same hours apply to lockers, train info tel. 08457-484-950, www.nationalrail.co.uk).

By Bus: Bus #918 passes through Ballachulish—a half-mile from **Glencoe**—on its way to **Fort William** (3/day in summer, 2/day off-season, never on Sun; 1 hour to Ballachulish, 1.5 hours total to Fort William). Take this bus to Fort William, then transfer to bus #919 to reach **Inverness** (3.75 hours total, with a 20-minute layover in Fort William) or **Portree** on the Isle of Skye (2/day, 4.5–5 hours total). A different bus (#976 or #977) connects Oban with **Glasgow** (6/day, 2.75 hours, some with transfer in Tyndrum), from where you can easily connect by bus or train to **Edinburgh** (figure 4.5 hours total). Buses arrive and depart in front of the Caledonian Hotel, across from the train station (toll tel. 08712/663-333, www.citylink.co.uk).

By Boat: Ferries fan out from Oban to the **southern Hebrides** (see information on the islands of Iona and Mull, later). Caledonian MacBrayne Ferry info: tel. 01631/566-688, free booking tel. 0800-066-5000, www.calmac.co.uk.

Between Glasgow and Oban

Drivers coming from the south can consider these stopovers, which are listed in order from Glasgow to Oban.

Loch Lomond

Leaving Glasgow on A82, you'll soon be driving along the scenic lake called Loch Lomond. The first picnic turnout has the best lake views, benches, a park, and a playground. Twenty-four miles long and speckled with islands, Loch Lomond is second in size only to Loch Ness. It's well-known mostly because of its easy proximity to Glasgow (about 15 miles away)—and also because its bonnie, bonnie banks inspired a beloved folk song: *Ye'll take the high road, and I'll take the low road, and I'll be in Scotland afore ye...* (You'll be humming that one all day. You're welcome.)

• *Halfway up the loch, at Tarbet, take the "tourist route" left onto A83, driving along Loch Long toward Inveraray.*

Rest-and-Be-Thankful Pass

A low-profile pull-out on A83 just west of A82 offers a pleasant opportunity to stretch your legs and get your first taste of that rugged Scottish countryside. The colorful name comes from the 1880s, when second- and third-class coach passengers got out and pushed the coach and first-class passengers up the hill.

Inveraray

Nearly everybody stops at this lovely, seemingly made-for-tourists castle town on Loch Fyne. Park near the pier and browse the wide selection of restaurants and tourist shops.

Inveraray's **TI** sells bus and ferry tickets, has Internet access, and offers a free mini-guide and an exhibit about the Argyll region (May–June Mon–Sat 9:00–17:00, Sun 12:00–17:00; July–Aug daily 9:00–8:00; April and Sept–Oct Mon–Sat 10:00–17:00, Sun 12:00–17:00; Nov–March daily 10:00–15:00; last entry to exhibit one hour before closing, Front Street, tel. 01499/302-063). Public WCs are at the end of the nearby pier (£0.20).

The town's main "sight" is the **Inveraray Jail,** an overpriced, corny, but mildly educational former jail converted into a museum. This "living 19th-century prison" includes a courtroom where mannequins argue the fate of the accused. You'll have the opportunity to be locked up for a photo op by a playful guard (£8.25, daily April–Oct 9:30–18:00, Nov–March 10:00–17:00, last entry one hour before closing, Church Square, tel. 01499/302-381, www .inveraryjail.co.uk).

You'll spot the dramatic **Inveraray Castle** on the right as you cross the bridge coming from Glasgow. This impressive-looking stronghold of one of the more notorious branches of the Campbell clan is striking from afar but dull inside; save your time for better Highlands castles elsewhere.

• *To continue on to Oban, leave Inveraray through a gate (at the Woolen Mill) to A819, and go through Glen Aray and along Loch Awe. A85 takes you into Oban.*

Islands near Oban: Mull and Iona

For the easiest one-day look at two of the dramatic and historic Hebrides (HEB-rid-eez) Islands, take the Iona/Mull tour from Oban. (For a more in-depth look, head north to Skye—see next chapter.)

Here's the game plan: You'll take a ferry from Oban to Mull (45 minutes), ride a Bowman's bus across Mull (1.25 hours), then board a quick ferry from Mull to Iona. The total round-trip travel time is 5.5 hours (all of it incredibly

Oban & the Southern Highlands

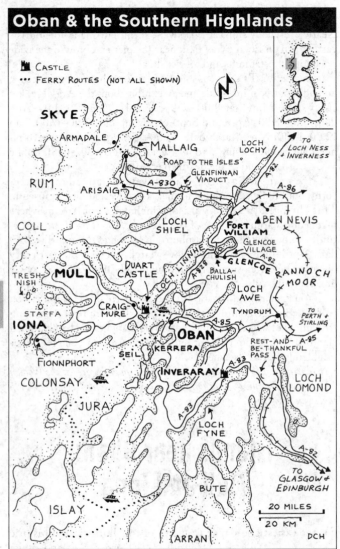

Castle

••• Ferry Routes (not all shown)

SKYE

ARMADALE

MALLAIG

"ROAD TO THE ISLES"

GLENFINNAN VIADUCT

A-830

LOCH LOCHY

TO LOCH NESS + INVERNESS

A-82

A-86

RUM

ARISAIG

COLL

LOCH SHIEL

FORT WILLIAM

BEN NEVIS

Glencoe Village

GLENCOE

A-82

TRESH-NISH

MULL

DUART CASTLE

LOCH LINNHE

A-828

BALLA-CHULISH

RANNOCH MOOR

STAFFA

CRAIG-MURE

LOCH AWE

TYNDRUM

TO PERTH + STIRLING

A-85

IONA

KERRERA

OBAN

A-85

REST-AND-BE-THANKFUL PASS

A-95

FIONNPHORT

SEIL

INVERARAY

A-83

COLONSAY

LOCH LOMOND

JURA

A-83

LOCH FYNE

A-82

BUTE

TO GLASGOW + EDINBURGH

ISLAY

20 MILES

20 KM

ARRAN

DCH

OBAN

scenic), plus about two hours of free time on Iona. Buy your set of six tickets—one for each leg—at the Bowman's office in Oban (£34, £2 discount with this book in 2011 for Iona/Mull tour, no tours Nov–Easter, book one day ahead in July–Sept if possible, bus tickets can sell out during busy summer weekends, office open daily 8:30–17:30, 1 Queens Park Place, a block from train station, tel. 01631/566-809 or 01631/563-221, www.bowmanstours.co.uk). For directions on how to buy individual tickets for various legs of this journey (for example, if you plan to sleep in Iona or spend a longer day there), see page 718.

You'll leave in the morning from the Oban pier on the huge Oban–Mull ferry run by Caledonian MacBrayne (boats depart Sun–Fri at 9:50, Sat at 9:30, board at least 20 minutes before departure; boats return daily around 17:45). As the schedule can change slightly from year to year, confirm your departure time carefully in Oban. The best inside seats on the ferry—with the biggest windows—are in the sofa lounge on the uppermost deck (Level 4) on the back end of the boat. (Follow signs for the toilets, and look for big staircase to the top floor; this floor also has its own small snack bar with £3 sandwiches and £4 box lunches.) On board, if it's a clear day, ask a local or a crew member to point out Ben Nevis, the tallest mountain in Great Britain. The ferry has a fine cafeteria and a bookshop (though guidebooks are cheaper in Oban). Five minutes before landing on Mull, you'll see the striking 13th-century Duart Castle on the left (www.duartcastle.com).

Upon arrival in Mull, find your tour company's bus for the entertaining and informative ride across the Isle of Mull. All drivers spend the entire ride chattering away about life on Mull. They are hardworking local boys who make historical trivia fascinating—or at least fun. Your destination is Mull's westernmost ferry terminal (Fionnphort), where you'll board a small, rocking ferry for the brief ride to Iona. Unless you stay overnight, you'll have only about two hours to roam freely around the island before taking the ferry–bus–ferry ride in reverse back to Oban.

OBAN

Mull

The Isle of Mull, the third-largest in Scotland, has 300 scenic miles of coastline and castles and a 3,169-foot-high mountain. Called Ben More ("Big Mountain" in Gaelic), it was once much

bigger. The last active volcano in northern Europe, it was 10,000 feet tall—making up the entire island of Mull—before it blew. It's calmer now, and, similarly, Mull has a notably laid-back population. My bus driver reported that there are no deaths from stress, and only a few from boredom.

With steep, fog-covered hillsides topped by cairns (piles of stones, sometimes indicating graves) and ancient stone circles, Mull has a gloomy, otherworldly charm. Bring plenty of rain protection and wear layers in case the sun peeks through the clouds. As my driver said, Mull is a place of cold, wet, windy winters and mild, wet, windy summers.

On the far side of Mull, the caravan of tour buses unloads at Fionnphort, a tiny ferry town. The ferry to the island of Iona takes about 200 walk-on passengers. Confirm the return time with your bus driver, then hustle to the dock to make the first trip over (otherwise, it's a 30-minute wait). There's a small ferry-passenger building/meager snack bar (and a pay WC); if it's closed, just buy your ticket from the ferry worker at the dock (cash or credit/debit cards accepted; leaving Iona, do the same as there's no ferry office). After the 10-minute ride, you wash ashore on sleepy Iona (free WC on this side), and the ferry mobs that crowded you on the boat seem to disappear up the main road and into Iona's back lanes.

The **About Mull Tours and Taxi** service can also get you around Mull (tel. 01681/700-507 or mobile 0788-777-4550, www.aboutmull.co.uk). They also do day tours of Mull (£35), focusing on local history and wildlife (half-day tours also available, shorter Mull tours can drop you off at Iona ferry dock at 15:00 for a quick Iona visit and pick you up at 18:00, minimum 2 people, smart to book ahead).

For directions on how to just buy ferry tickets to Mull and Iona (but not take the Bowman's bus tour), see "Staying Longer on Iona," later.

Iona

The tiny island of Iona, just 3 miles by 1.5 miles, is famous as the birthplace of Christianity in Scotland. You'll have about two hours

here on your own before you retrace your steps (your driver will tell you which return ferry to take back to Mull—don't miss this boat); you'll dock back in Oban about 17:45. And though the day is spectacular when it's sunny, it's worthwhile in any weather.

A pristine quality of light and a thoughtful peace pervade the stark, (nearly) car-free island and its tiny community. With buoyant clouds bouncing playfully off distant bluffs, sparkling-white crescents of sand, and lone tourists camped thoughtfully atop huge rocks just looking out to sea, Iona is a place perfect for meditation. Climb a peak—nothing's higher than 300 feet above the sea.

Staying Longer on Iona: For a chance to really experience peaceful, idyllic Iona, consider spending a night or two. Scots bring their kids and stay on this tiny island for a week. If you want to overnight in Iona, don't buy your tickets at Bowman's in Oban—they require a same-day return. Instead, buy each leg of the ferry–bus–ferry (and return) trip separately. Get your Oban–Mull ferry ticket in the Oban ferry office (one-way for walk-on passengers-£4.65, round-trip-£7.90, ticket good for 5 days). Once you arrive in Mull (Craignure), follow the crowds to the Bowman buses and buy a ticket directly from the driver (£10 round-trip). When you arrive at the ferry terminal (Fionnphort), walk into the small trailer ferry office to buy a ticket to Iona (£2.15 each way).

If you want to spend more time on Iona (about four hours) and return to Oban the same day, you have another option. Although taking the Bowman's tour bus guarantees a seat back the same day, you can also take an earlier Bowman's service bus (no tour narration, same price, buy each leg separately as described above) from the Mull ferry terminal to Fionnphort. Ask at the Bowman's office for details.

Orientation to Iona

The village, Baile Mòr, has shops, a restaurant/pub, enough beds, and no bank (get cash back with a purchase at the grocery store). The **Finlay Ross Shop** rents bikes (to the left as you depart the ferry, £4.50/4 hours, £8/day, £10 deposit per bike; open April–Oct Mon–Sat 9:30–17:00, Sun 11:30–16:00; shorter hours off-season, tel. 01681/700-357, www.finlayrossiona.co.uk). The only taxi on Iona is **Iona Taxi** (tel. 07810-325-990, www.ionataxi.co.uk). Up the road from the ferry dock is a little **Spar** grocery (Mon–Sat 9:00–17:15, Sun 12:00–16:00, shorter hours off-season and closed Sun, free island maps). Iona's official website (www.isle-of-iona.com) has good information about the island.

Sights on Iona

A single paved road leads from the ferry, passing through the village and up a small hill to the **nunnery ruins** (one of the best-preserved medieval nunneries in Britain) before heading to the **abbey,** with its graveyard. **St. Oran's Chapel** (next to the graveyard) is the oldest church building on the island. Inside you'll find several grave slabs carved in the distinctive Iona School style, developed by local stonecarvers in the 14th century. Look for the depictions of medieval warrior aristocrats. Many more of these carved graves have been moved to the abbey, where you can see them in its cloisters and old infirmary. It's free to see the nunnery ruins, graveyard, and chapel; the abbey itself has an admission fee, but it's worth the cost just to sit in the stillness of its lovely, peaceful interior courtyard (£4.70, not covered by bus tour ticket,

History of Iona

St. Columba, an Irish scholar, soldier, priest, and founder of monasteries, got into a small war over the possession of an illegally copied psalm book. Victorious but sickened by the bloodshed, Columba left Ireland, vowing never to return. According to legend, the first bit of land out of sight of his homeland was Iona. He stopped here in 563, and established an abbey.

Columba's monastic community flourished, and Iona became the center of Celtic Christianity. Missionaries from Iona spread the gospel throughout Scotland and northern England, while scholarly monks established Iona as a center of art and learning. The *Book of Kells*—perhaps the finest piece of art from "Dark Ages" Europe—was probably made on Iona in the eighth century. The island was so important that it was the legendary burial place for ancient Scottish and even Scandinavian kings (including Shakespeare's Macbeth).

Slowly, the importance of Iona ebbed. Vikings massacred 68 monks in 806. Fearing more raids, the monks evacuated most of Iona's treasures to Ireland (including the *Book of Kells*, which is now in Dublin). Much later, with the Reformation, the abbey was abandoned, and most of its finely carved crosses were destroyed. In the 17th century, locals used the abbey only as a handy quarry for other building projects.

Iona's population peaked at about 500 in the 1830s. In the 1840s, a potato famine hit, and in the 1850s, a third of the islanders emigrated to Canada or Australia. By 1900, the population was down to 210, and today it's only around 100.

But in our generation, a new religious community has given the abbey fresh life. The Iona Community is an ecumenical gathering of men and women who seek new ways of living the Gospel in today's world, with a focus on worship, peace and justice issues, and reconciliation.

includes 30-minute guided tour, £14 guidebook, daily April–Sept 9:30–17:00, Oct–March 9:30–16:00, tel. 01681/700-512, www.historic-scotland.gov.uk). While the present abbey, nunnery, and graveyard go back to the 13th century, much of what you'll see was rebuilt in the 20th century. (There may be scaffolding on the abbey tower during your visit, as the mortar is being replaced.)

Across from the abbey is the **Iona Community's information center** (free WCs), which runs the abbey with Historic Scotland and hosts modern-day pilgrims who come here to experience the birthplace of Scottish Christianity. Its gift shop is packed with books on the island's important role in Christian history.

If you have extra time, the **Heritage Center** is small but well done, with displays on local and natural history and a tiny tea room (£3, Mon–Sat 10:30–16:30, closed Sun; on the left past the nunnery ruins). You can also catch a **worship service** at the abbey (get times from Iona Community's information center, tel. 01681/700-404, www.iona.org.uk).

Sleeping and Eating on Iona

(£1 = about $1.60, country code: 44, area code: 01681)
In addition to the options listed below, there are many B&Bs, apartments, and a hostel on the island (see www.isle-of-iona.com /accommodation.htm).

$$$ Argyll Hotel, built in 1867, proudly overlooks the waterfront, with 16 rooms and pleasingly creaky hallways lined with bookshelves (Sb-£55-60, D-£70, Db-£96, larger Db-£130, cheaper off-season, extra bed for kids-£15, includes continental breakfast, closed Nov–March, free Wi-Fi, comfortable lounge and sunroom, tel. 01681/700-334, fax 01681/700-510, www.argyllhoteliona.co.uk, reception@argyllhoteliona.co.uk, Daniel and Claire). Its white-linen dining room is open to the public for lunch (12:30–13:30) and dinner (£12–16 entrées, 19:00–20:00).

$$$ St. Columba Hotel, situated in the middle of a peaceful garden with picnic tables, has 27 pleasant rooms and spacious lodge-like common spaces (Sb-£55–70, Db-£90–120, huge view Db-£150, front rooms have sea views but windows are small, includes continental breakfast, discounts for stays of 4 or more nights, extra bed for kids-£15, free Internet access, next door to abbey on road up from dock, open Easter–Oct only, tel. 01681/700-304, fax 01681/700-688, www.stcolumba-hotel.co.uk, info@stcolumba-hotel.co.uk). Their fine 14-table restaurant, open to the public, overlooks the water (£5–10 lunches, £10–13 dinners, daily 12:00–14:30 & 18:30–20:00). Even if you're not staying here, you can stop by to use the Internet (£0.50/15 minutes).

$$ Calva B&B, near the abbey, has three spacious rooms (Db-£55, second house on left past the abbey, look for sign in window and gnomes on porch, tel. 01681/700-340, friendly Janetta and Jack the bearded collie).

OBAN

Glencoe

This valley is the essence of the wild, powerful, and stark beauty of the Highlands. Along with its scenery, Glencoe offers a good dose of bloody clan history: In 1692, British Redcoats (led by a local Campbell commander) came to the valley, and were sheltered and fed for 12 days by the MacDonalds—whose leader had been late in swearing an oath to the British monarch. Then, the morning of February 13, the soldiers were ordered to rise up early and kill their sleeping hosts, violating the rules of Highland hospitality and earning the valley the name "The Weeping Glen." It's fitting that such an epic, dramatic incident should be set in this equally epic, dramatic valley, where the cliffsides seem to weep (with running streams) when it rains.

Orientation to Glencoe

(area code: 01855)

The valley of Glencoe is just off the main A828/A82 road between Oban and points north (such as Fort William and Inverness). (If you're coming from the north, the signage can be tricky—at the roundabout south of Fort William, follow signs to *Crianlarich* and *A82*.) The most appealing town here is the one-street Glencoe village, while the slightly larger and more modern town of Ballachulish (a half-mile away) has more services. Though not quite quaint, the very sleepy village of Glencoe is worth a stop for its folk museum and its status as the gateway to the valley. The town's hub of activity is its grocery store (ATM, daily 8:00–20:00).

Tourist Information

Your best source of information (especially for walks and hikes) is the **Glencoe Visitors Centre,** described later. The nearest **TI** is well-signed in Ballachulish (daily 9:00–17:00, opens at 10:00 on Sun in winter, bus timetables, free phone to call area B&Bs, café, shop, tel. 01855/811-866, www.glencoetourism.co.uk or www.discoverglencoe.com).

Sights in Glencoe

Glencoe Village

Glencoe village is just a line of houses sitting beneath the brooding mountains. Two tiny thatched-roof, early-18th-century croft houses are jammed with local history at the huggable **Glencoe and North Lorn Folk Museum.** It's filled with humble exhibits gleaned from the town's old closets and attics. When one house was being rethatched, its owner found a cache of 200-year-old swords and pistols hidden there from the British Redcoats after the disastrous battle of Culloden. Don't miss the museum's little door that leads out back, where you'll find more exhibits on the Glencoe Massacre, local slate, farm tools, and an infamous local murder that inspired Robert Louis Stevenson to write *Kidnapped* (£3, call ahead for hours—generally Easter–Oct Mon–Sat 10:00–17:30, closed Sun and off-season, tel. 01855/811-664).

In Glencoe Valley

▲▲**Driving Through Glencoe Valley**—If you have a car, spend an hour or so following A82 through the valley, past the Glencoe Visitors Centre (see next listing), into the desolate moor beyond, and back again. You'll enjoy grand views, flocks of "hairy coos" (shaggy Highland Cattle), and a chance to hear a bagpiper in the wind—roadside Highland buskers (most often seen on good-weather summer weekends). If you play the recorder (and no other tourists are there), ask to finger a tune while the piper does the hard work. At the end of the valley you hit the vast Rannoch

Moor—500 desolate square miles with barely enough decent land to graze a sheep.

Glencoe Visitors Centre—This modern facility, a mile up A82 past Glencoe village (off to the left) into the dramatic valley, is designed to resemble a *clachan*, or traditional Highlands settlement. The information desk inside the shop is your single best resource for advice (and maps or guidebooks) about local walks and hikes, some of which are described next. At the back of the complex you'll find a viewpoint with a handy 3-D model of the hills for orientation. There's also a pricey £5.50 exhibition about the surrounding landscape, local history, mountaineering, and conservation. It's worth the time to watch the more-interesting-than-it-sounds video on geology and the 14-minute film on the Glencoe Massacre, which thoughtfully traces the events leading up to the tragedy rather than simply recycling romanticized legends (April–Aug daily 9:30–17:30; Sept–Oct daily 10:00–17:00; Nov–mid-Dec and Feb-March Thu–Sun 10:00–16:00, closed Mon–Wed; closed mid-Dec–Jan; last entry 45 minutes before closing, café, tel. 01855/811-307, www.nts.org.uk).

Walks—For a steep one-mile hike, climb the Devil's Staircase (trailhead just off A82, 8 miles east of Glencoe). For a three-hour hike, ask at the Visitors Centre about the Lost Valley of the MacDonalds (trailhead just off A82, 3 miles east of Glencoe). For an easy walk above Glencoe, head to the mansion on the hill (over the bridge, turn left, fine loch views). This mansion was built in 1894 by Canadian Pacific Railway magnate Lord Strathcona for his wife, a Canadian with First Nations (Native American) ancestry. She was homesick for the Rockies, so he had the grounds landscaped to represent the lakes, trees, and mountains of her home country. It didn't work, and they eventually returned to Canada. The house originally had 365 windows, to allow a different view each day.

Glencoe's Burial Island and Island of Discussion—In the loch just outside Glencoe (near Ballachulish), notice the burial island—where the souls of those who "take the low road" are piped home. (Ask a local about "Ye'll take the high road, and I'll take the low road.") The next island was the Island of Discussion—where those in dispute went until they found agreement.

Sleeping in Glencoe

(£1 = about $1.60, country code: 44, area code: 01855)

Glencoe is an extremely low-key place to spend the night between Oban or Glasgow and the northern destinations. These places are accustomed to one-nighters just passing through, but some people stay here for several days to enjoy a variety of hikes. All of these B&Bs are along the main road through the middle of the village, and all are cash-only.

$$ Inchconnal B&B is a cute, renovated house with a bonnie wee potted garden out front, renting two bright rooms with views—one cottage-style, the other woodsy (Db-£48, £50 July–Aug, tel. 01855/811-958, warm Caroline Macdonald).

$$ Heatherlea B&B, at the end of the village, has three pleasant, modern rooms, homey public spaces, and a big board-game collection (Sb-£26–28, Db-£52–56, £52 in July–Aug, closed Nov–Easter, tel. 01855/811-799, heatherleaglencoe@gmail.com, friendly Ivan and Thea).

$$ Tulachgorm B&B has two comfortable rooms that share a bathroom in a modern house with fine mountain views (D-£42, tel. 01855/811-391, mellow Ann Blake and friendly West Highland terrier Jo).

$$$ Clachaig Inn, outside of town, works well for hikers who want a comfy mountain inn (Db-£88–92; see description below, under "Eating in Glencoe").

Eating in Glencoe

The choices in and near Glencoe are slim—this isn't the place for fine dining. But three options offer decent food a short walk or drive away. For evening fun, take a walk or ask your B&B host where to find music and dancing.

In Glencoe: The only choice in Glencoe village is **The Glencoe Hotel,** with lovely dining areas and a large outdoor deck (£8–10 entrées, food served daily 12:00–14:00 & 18:00–20:30, at junction of A82 and Glencoe village, tel. 01855/811-140).

Near Glencoe: **Clachaig Inn** is a Highlands pub in a stunning valley setting whose clientele is half locals and half tourists. This unpretentious and very popular social hub features billiards, jukeboxes, and pub grub (£5–13 entrées, open daily for lunch and dinner, tel. 01855/811-252, www.clachaig.com). Drive to the end of Glencoe village, cross the bridge, and follow the little single-track road for three miles, past campgrounds and hostels, until you reach the inn on the right.

In Ballachulish, near Glencoe: **Laroch Bar & Bistro,** in the next village over from Glencoe (toward Oban), is family-friendly (£6–9 pub grub, food served 12:00–14:30 & 17:30–21:00, tel. 01855/811-900). Drive into Ballachulish village, and you'll see it on the left.

Glencoe Connections

Unfortunately, buses don't actually drive down the main road through Glencoe village. Some buses (most notably those going between Glasgow and Fort William) stop near Glencoe village at a place called **"Glencoe Crossroads"**—a short walk into the village center. Other buses (such as those between Oban and Fort William) stop at the nearby town of **Ballachulish,** which is just a half-mile away (or a £3 taxi ride). Tell the bus driver where you're going ("Glencoe village") and ask to be let off as close to there as possible.

From **Glencoe Crossroads,** you can catch bus #914, #915, or #916 (8/day) to **Fort William** (30 minutes) or **Glasgow** (2.5 hours).

From **Ballachulish,** you can take bus #918 (3/day in summer, 2/day off-season, never on Sun) to **Fort William** (30 minutes) or **Oban** (1 hour). Bus info: Toll tel. 08712/663-333, www.citylink.co.uk.

To reach **Inverness** or **Portree** on the Isle of Skye, transfer in Fort William. To reach **Edinburgh,** transfer in Glasgow.

Near Glencoe: Fort William

Laying claim to the title of "outdoor capital of the UK," Fort William is well-positioned between Oban, Inverness, and the Isle of Skye. This crossroads town is a transportation hub and has a pleasant-enough, shop-studded, pedestrianized main drag, but few charms of its own. Most visitors just pass through...and should. But while you're here, consider buying lunch and stopping by the TI to get your questions answered.

Tourist Information: The TI is on the car-free main drag (June–Aug Mon–Sat 9:00–18:00, Sun 9:30–17:00; Easter–May and Sept–Oct Mon–Sat 9:00–17:00, Sun 10:00–16:00; shorter hours and closed Sun off-season; Internet access, free public WCs up the street next to parking lot, 15 High Street, tel. 01397/701-801).

Sights in and near Fort William

Fort William has no real sights, aside from a humble-but-well-presented **West Highland Museum,** with exhibits on local history, wildlife, dress, Jacobite memorabilia, and more (£4, guide-book-£2.50; June–Sept Mon–Sat 10:00–17:00, July–Aug also Sun 10:00–16:00; Oct–May Mon–Sat 10:00–16:00, closed Sun; on Cameron Square, tel. 01397/702-169, www.westhighlandmuseum .org.uk).

The appealing options described below lie just outside of town.

Ben Nevis

From Fort William, take a peek at Britain's highest peak, Ben Nevis (4,409 feet). Thousands walk to its summit each year. On a clear day, you can admire it from a distance. Scotland's only mountain cable cars—at the **Nevis Range Mountain Experience**—can take you to a not-very-lofty 2,150-foot perch on the slopes of Aonach Mor for a closer look (£10.50, daily July–Aug 9:30–18:00, Sept–June 10:00–17:00, 15-minute ride, shuts down in high winds and mid-Nov–mid-Dec—call ahead, signposted on A82 north of Fort William, tel. 01397/705-825, www.nevisrange.co.uk). They also have high-wire obstacle courses (£20, under age 17-£14, daily 10:00–16:00).

Toward the Isle of Skye: The Road to the Isles and the Jacobite Steam Train

The magical steam train that scenically transports Harry Potter to the wizarding school of Hogwarts runs along a real-life train line. The West Highland Railway Line chugs 42 miles from Fort William west to the ferry port at Mallaig. Along the way, it passes the iconic **Glenfinnan Viaduct,** with 416 yards of raised track over 21 supporting arches. This route is also graced with plenty of loch-and-mountain views and, near the end, passes along a beautiful stretch of coast with some fine sandy beaches. While many people take the Jacobite Steam Train to enjoy this stretch of Scotland, it can be more rewarding to drive the same route—especially if you're headed for the Isle of Skye.

By Train: The **Jacobite Steam Train** (they don't actually call it the "Hogwarts Express") offers a small taste of the Harry Potter experience...but many who take this trip for that reason alone are disappointed. (For more Harry Potter sights in Britain, see page 832.) Although one of the steam engines and some of the coaches were used in the films, don't expect a Harry Potter theme ride. However, you can expect beautiful scenery. Along the way, the train stops for 20 minutes at Glenfinnan station (just after the Glenfinnan Viaduct), and then gives you way too much time (1.75 hours) to poke around the dull port town of Mallaig before heading back to Fort William (one-way—£23.50 adults, £13.50 kids; round-trip—£31 adults, £17.50 kids; £2.50 booking fee, more for first class, tickets must be purchased in advance—see details next, 1/day Mon–Fri mid-May–late Oct, also Sat–Sun July–Aug, departs Fort William at 10:20 and returns at 16:00, about a 2-hour ride each way, WCs on board, tel. 08451/284-681 or 08451/284-685, www.westcoastrailways.co.uk).

Note: Trains leave Fort William from the main train station, but you must book ahead online or by phone—you cannot buy tickets for this train at the Fort William or Mallaig train-station ticket offices. There may be a limited amount of seats available each day on a first-come, first-served basis (cash only, buy from conductor), but in summer, trips are often sold out.

The 84-mile round-trip from Fort William takes the better part of a day to show you the same scenery twice. Modern "Sprinter" trains follow the same line—consider taking the steam train one-way to Mallaig, then speeding back on a regular train to avoid the long Mallaig layover and slow return (1.25 hours, 2-3/day, book at least two days ahead July–Aug, tel. 08457-550-033, www .scotrail.co.uk). Note that you can use this train to reach the Isle of Skye: Take the train to Mallaig, walk onto the ferry to Armadale (on Skye), then catch a bus in Armadale to your destination on Skye (toll tel. 08712/663-333, www.citylink.co.uk).

There are lockers for storing luggage at the Fort William train station (£4–5/24 hours, station open Mon–Sat 7:20–22:10, Sun 11:30–22:10).

By Car: While the train is time-consuming and expensive, driving the same **"Road to the Isles"** route (A830)—ideally on your way to Skye—can be a fun way to see the same famous scenery more affordably and efficiently. The key here is to be sure you leave enough time to make it to Mallaig before the Skye ferry departs—get timing advice from the Fort William TI. I'd allow at least 1 hour and 20 minutes to get from Fort William to the ferry landing in Mallaig (if you keep moving, with no stops en route)—and note that vehicles are required to arrive 30 minutes before the boat departs. As you leave Fort William on A830, a sign on the left tells you what time the next ferry will depart Mallaig. For more tips on the Mallaig–Armadale ferry, see "Getting to the Isle of Skye" on page 732.

Sleeping in Fort William

These two B&Bs are on Union Road, a five-minute walk up the hill above the main pedestrian street that runs through the heart of town. Each place has three rooms, one of which has a private bathroom on the hall.

$$ Glenmorven Guest House is a friendly, flower-bedecked, family-run place renting rooms with views of Loch Linnhe (Db-£60, free pick-up from train or bus station with advance notice, laundry service, Union Road, Fort William, tel. 01397/703-236, www.glenmorven.co.uk, glenmorven@yahoo.com, Anne and Colin Jamieson).

$$ Gowan Brae B&B ("Hill of the Big Daisy") has antique-filled rooms with loch or garden views in a hobbit-cute house (Db-£64 in high season, £50 off-season, Union Road, tel. 01397/704-399, www.gowanbrae.co.uk, gowan_brae@btinternet .com, Jim and Ann Clark).

Eating in Fort William

All three places listed below are on the main walking street, near the start of town; the first two serve only lunch.

Hot Roast Company sells beef, turkey, ham, or pork sandwiches, topped with some tasty extras (£3 take-away, a bit more for sit-down service, Mon–Sat 9:30–15:30, closed Sun, 127 High Street, tel. 01397/700-606).

Café 115 features good food and modern bistro decor (£4–8 meals, £8 fish-and-chips, daily 10:00–17:30, mid-July–Aug until 21:30, 115 High Street, tel. 01397/702-500).

The Grog & Gruel serves real ales, good pub grub, and Tex-Mex and Cajun dishes, with unusual meals such as vegetarian haggis with Drambuie sauce, boar burgers, and venison chili (£5–12 meals, food served daily 12:00–21:00, Sun in winter 17:00–21:00, free Wi-Fi, 66 High Street, tel. 01397/705-078). Their upstairs restaurant features the same menu (daily 17:00–21:00).

Fort William Connections

Fort William is a major transit hub for the Highlands, so you'll likely change buses here at some point during your trip.

From Fort William by Bus to: Glencoe (all Glasgow-bound buses—#914, #915, and #916; 8/day, 30 minutes), **Ballachulish** near Glencoe (Oban-bound bus #918, 3/day in summer, 2/day off-season, never on Sun, 30 minutes), **Oban** (bus #918, 3/day in summer, 2/day off-season, never on Sun, 1.5 hours), **Portree** on the Isle of Skye (buses #915 and #916, 4/day, 3 hours), **Inverness** (Citylink bus #919 or Stagecoach bus #19, 8/day, 2 hours), **Glasgow** (buses #914, #915, and #916; 8/day, 3 hours, some with change in Tyndrum), **Edinburgh** (bus #913, 3/day in evening, 4 hours, 1 direct, 2 with change in Tyndrum; more with transfer in Glasgow on buses #900 and #914/915, 5 hours). Bus info: toll tel. 08712/663-333, www.citylink.co.uk or www.stagecoachbus.com.

Route Tips for Drivers

From England's Lake District to Glasgow: From Keswick, take A66 for 18 miles to M6 and speed north nonstop (via Penrith and Carlisle), crossing Hadrian's Wall into Scotland. The road becomes M74 south of Glasgow. To slip through Glasgow quickly, leave M74 at Junction 4 onto M73, following signs to *M8/Glasgow*. Leave M73 at Junction 2, exiting onto M8. Stay on M8 west through Glasgow, exit on Junction 30, cross Erskine Bridge, and turn left on A82, following signs to *Crianlarich* and *Loch Lomond*. (For a scenic drive through Glasgow, take exit 17 off M8 and stay on A82 toward Dumbarton.)

From Oban to Glencoe and Fort William: From Oban, follow coastal A828 toward Fort William. After about 20 miles, you'll see the photogenic Castle Staulker marooned on a lonely island. At North Ballachulish, you'll reach a bridge spanning Loch Leven; rather than crossing the bridge, turn off and follow A82 into the Glencoe valley. After exploring the valley, make a U-turn and return through Glencoe. To continue on to Fort William, backtrack to the bridge at North Ballachulish and cross it, following A82 north. (For a scenic shortcut directly back to Glasgow or Edinburgh, head north only as far as Glencoe, and then cut to Glasgow or Edinburgh on A82 via Rannoch Moor and Tyndrum.)

From Fort William to Loch Ness and Inverness: Follow the Caledonian Canal north along A82, which goes through Fort Augustus (and its worthwhile Caledonian Canal Heritage Centre) and then follows the west side of Loch Ness on its way to Inverness. Along the way, A82 passes Urquhart Castle and two Loch Ness Monster exhibits in Drumnadrochit. These attractions are described in the Inverness and the Northern Highlands chapter.

From Fort William to the Isle of Skye: You have two options for this journey: Head west on A830 (the Road to the Isles), then catch the ferry from Mallaig to Armadale on the Isle of Skye (described on page 732); or head north on A82 to Invergarry, and turn left (west) on A87, which you'll follow (past Eilean Donan Castle) to Kyle of Lochalsh and the Skye Bridge to the island. Consider using one route one way, and the other on the return trip—for example, follow the "Road to the Isles" from Fort William to Mallaig, and take the ferry to Skye; later, leaving Skye, take A87 east from the Skye Bridge past Eilean Donan Castle to Loch Ness and Inverness.

ISLE OF SKYE

The rugged, remote-feeling Isle of Skye has a reputation for unpredictable weather ("Skye" means "cloudy" in Old Norse, and locals call it "The Misty Isle"). But it also offers some of Scotland's best scenery, and it rarely fails to charm its many visitors. Narrow, twisty roads wind around Skye in the shadows of craggy, black, bald mountains.

Skye seems to have more sheep than people; 200 years ago, many human residents were forced to move off the island to make room for more livestock during the Highland Clearances. The people who remain are some of the most ardently Gaelic Scots in Scotland. The island's Sleat Peninsula is home to a rustic but important Gaelic college. Half of all native island residents speak Gaelic (which they pronounce "gallic") as their first language. A generation ago, it was illegal to teach Gaelic in schools; today, Skye offers its residents the opportunity to enroll in Gaelic-only education, from primary school to college.

Set up camp in one of the island's home-base towns, Portree or Kyleakin. Then dive into Skye's attractions. Drive around the appealing Trotternish Peninsula, enjoying stark vistas of jagged rock formations with the mysterious Outer Hebrides looming on the horizon. Explore a gaggle of old-fashioned stone homes, learn about Skye's ancient farming lifestyles, and pay homage at the grave of a brave woman who rescued a bonnie prince. Climb the dramatic Cuillin Hills, and drive to a lighthouse at the end of the world. Visit a pair of castles—run-down but thought-provoking Dunvegan, and nearby but not on Skye, the photo-perfect Eilean Donan.

Planning Your Time

With a week in Scotland, Skye merits two nights, with a full day to hit its highlights (Trotternish Peninsula, Dunvegan Castle, Cuillin Hills, Talisker Distillery). Mountaineers enjoy extra time for hiking and hillwalking. Because it takes time to reach, Skye (the northernmost destination in this book) is skippable if you only have a few days in Scotland—instead, focus on Edinburgh and the more accessible Highlands sights near Oban.

Skye fits neatly into a Highlands itinerary between Oban/Glencoe and Loch Ness/Inverness. To avoid seeing the same scenery twice, it works well to drive the "Road to the Isles" from Fort William to Mallaig, then take the ferry to Skye; later, leave Skye via the Skye Bridge and follow A87 east toward Loch Ness and Inverness, stopping at Eilean Donan Castle en route.

Orientation to the Isle of Skye

The Isle of Skye is big (over 600 square miles), with lots of ins and outs—but you're never more than five miles from the sea. The island is punctuated by peninsulas and inlets (called "sea lochs"). Skye is covered with hills, but the most striking are the mountain-like Cuillin Hills in the south-central part of the island.

There are only about 11,000 people on the entire island; roughly a quarter live in the main village, Portree. Other population centers include Kyleakin (near the bridge connecting Skye with the mainland) and Broadford (a tidy string of houses on the road between Portree and the bridge, with the biggest and handiest grocery store on the island). A few of the villages—including Broadford and Dunvegan—have TIs, but the most useful one is in Portree.

Getting to the Isle of Skye

By Car: Your easiest bet is the slick, free **Skye Bridge** that crosses from Kyle of Lochalsh on the mainland to Kyleakin on Skye (for more on the bridge, see page 743).

The island can also be reached from the mainland via a pair of **car ferry** crossings. The major ferry line connects the mainland town of Mallaig (west of Fort William along the "Road to the Isles" and the Harry Potter steam-train line—see page 833) to Armadale on Skye (£20.30/car, £3.85/passenger, late March–late Oct 8/day each way, 4-6/day on Sun, late Oct–late March very limited Sat–Sun connections, check-in closes 30 minutes before sailing, can be cancelled in rough weather, 30-minute trip, operated by Caledonian MacBrayne, www.calmac.co.uk). A tiny six-car, proudly local "turntable" ferry crosses the short gap between the mainland Glenelg and Skye's Kylerhea (£12/car with up to 4

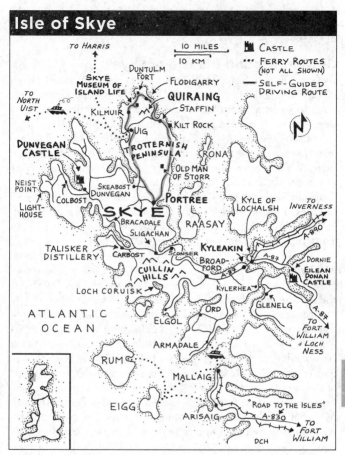

Isle of Skye

TO HARRIS

10 MILES
10 KM

🏰 CASTLE
••• FERRY ROUTES (NOT ALL SHOWN)
— SELF-GUIDED DRIVING ROUTE

DUNTULM FORT
SKYE MUSEUM OF ISLAND LIFE
FLODIGARRY
QUIRAING
STAFFIN
KILT ROCK

TO NORTH UIST

KILMUIR
UIG
TROTTERNISH PENINSULA

DUNVEGAN CASTLE

OLD MAN OF STORR
RONA

NEIST POINT
LIGHT-HOUSE
COLBOST
SKEABOST
DUNVEGAN

SKYE

PORTREE

KYLE OF LOCHALSH
TO INVERNESS

A-890

BRACADALE
SLIGACHAN
RAASAY

TALISKER DISTILLERY
CARBOST
SCONSER
KYLEAKIN
BROAD-FORD
A-87
DORNIE
EILEAN DONAN CASTLE

CUILLIN HILLS
A-87
KYLERHEA

LOCH CORUISK
ORD
GLENELG

ATLANTIC OCEAN
ELGOL
A-87
TO FORT WILLIAM & LOCH NESS

ARMADALE

RUM

MALLAIG

"ROAD TO THE ISLES"
A-830
TO FORT WILLIAM

EIGG
ARISAIG

DCH

ISLE OF SKYE

passengers, £15 round-trip, Easter–Oct daily every 20 minutes 10:00–18:00, June–Aug until 19:00, no need to book ahead, no boats off-season, Skye Ferry, www.skyeferry.co.uk).

By Public Transportation: Skye is connected to the outside world by a series of Scottish CityLink **buses** (www.citylink.co.uk), which use Portree as their Skye hub. From Portree, buses connect to **Inverness** (bus #917, 2–3/day, 3.25 hours, via Loch Ness), **Glasgow** (buses #915 and #916, 3/day, 6.25 hours, also stops at **Fort William** and **Glencoe**), and **Edinburgh** (3/day, 7.5–8 hours, transfer in Fort William or Glasgow).

There are also some more complicated connections possible for the determined: Take the train from Edinburgh, Glasgow, or Inverness to Fort William; transfer to the steam train to Mallaig; take the ferry across to Armadale; and catch a bus to Portree. Alternatively, you can take the train from Edinburgh or Glasgow to Inverness, take the train to Kyle of Lochalsh, then take the bus to Portree.

Getting Around the Isle of Skye

By Car: Once on Skye, you'll need a car to enjoy the island. (Even if you're doing the rest of your trip by public transportation, a car rental is worthwhile to bypass the frustrating public-transportation options; I've listed some car-rental options in Portree, page 746.) If you're driving, a good map is a must (look for a 1:130,000 map that covers the entire island with enough detail to point out side roads and attractions). You'll be surprised how long it takes to traverse this "small" island. Here are driving-time estimates for some likely trips: Kyleakin and Skye Bridge to Portree—45 minutes; Portree to Dunvegan—30 minutes; Portree to the tip of Trotternish Peninsula and back again—1.5–2 hours; Uig (on Trotternish Peninsula) to Dunvegan—45 minutes.

By Bus: Skye is frustrating by bus, especially on Sundays, when virtually no local buses run (except for a few long-distance buses to the ferry dock and mainland destinations). Portree is the hub for local bus traffic. Most Skye buses are operated by Stagecoach (www.stagecoachbus.com/highlands, timetable info from Traveline, toll tel. 0871-200-2233, www.traveline.org.uk). If you'll be using local buses a lot, consider a Skye Dayrider ticket (£6.50/1 day) or the Skye Megarider (£41/7 days, covers all of Skye plus trip to Eilean Donan, cheaper options available for just part of the island). You can buy either of these tickets from any driver. From Portree you can go around the **Trotternish Peninsula** (#57, Mon–Sat 4–5/day in each direction—clockwise and counterclockwise; none on Sun), to **Dunvegan** (#56, 5/day Mon–Fri, 3/day Sat, none on Sun, goes right to the castle, catch a bus that leaves no later than 12:35 to have enough time at the castle), and to **Kyleakin** (#50, 5/day Mon–Sat, 2/day Sun, transfer in Broadford).

By Tour: If you're without a car, consider taking a tour. Several operations on the island take visitors to hard-to-reach spots on a half-day or full-day tour. Some are more educational, while others are loose and informal. Look for brochures around the island, or ask locals for tips. The **Aros Centre** near Portree leads three-hour tours twice daily (£14, mid-April–mid-Oct Mon–Sat at 10:00 and 14:00, can pick you up in Portree, reserve ahead by calling 01478/613-649 or in person at the Portree TI, www.aros.co.uk). **Kathleen MacAskil** with Skye Tours gives private tours by car or minibus (about £100/4 hours, minimum 2 people, tel. 01470/582-306, kathleenmacaskil@aol.com).

The Trotternish Peninsula

This inviting peninsula north of Portree is packed with windswept castaway scenery, unique geological formations, and some offbeat sights. In good weather, a spin around Trotternish is the single best Skye activity (and you'll still have time to visit Dunvegan Castle or the Cuillin Hills later on).

Self-Guided Driving Tour

The following loop tour starts and ends in Portree, circling the peninsula counterclockwise. If you did it without stopping, you'd make it back to Portree within two hours—but it deserves the better part of a day.

Begin in the island's main town, Portree. (If you're heading up from Kyleakin, you'll enjoy some grand views of the Cuillin Hills on your way up—especially around the crossroads of Sligachan, described on page 740.) For sightseeing information on Portree—and the nearby Aros visitors center—see page 746. Note that from Portree to Uig, you'll be driving on a paved single-track road, with occasional "passing places" to allow cars to pull over.

• *Head north of Portree on A855, following signs for* Staffin. *About three miles out of town, you'll begin to enjoy some impressive views of the Trotternish Ridge. As you pass the small loch on your right, straight ahead is the distinctive feature called the...*

Old Man of Storr: This 160-foot-tall tapered slab of basalt stands proudly apart from the rest of the Storr. The unusual land-

scape of the Trotternish Peninsula is due to massive landslides (the largest that have ever occurred in Britain). This block slid down the cliff about 6,500 years ago and landed on its end, where it was slowly whittled by weather into a pinnacle. The lochs on your right have been linked together to spin the turbines at a nearby hydro-electric plant that once provided all of Skye's electricity.

• *After passing the Old Man, enjoy the scenery on your right, over-looking...*

Nearby Islands and the Mainland: Some of Skye's most appealing scenery isn't of the island itself, but of the surrounding terrain. In the distance, craggy mountains recede into the horizon. The long island in the foreground, a bit to the north, is called Rona. This military-owned island, and the channel behind it, were used to develop and test one of Margaret Thatcher's pet projects, the Sting Ray remote-control torpedo.

• *After about five miles, keep an eye out on the right for a large parking lot near a wee loch. Park and walk to the viewpoint to see...*

Kilt Rock: So named because of its resemblance to a Scotsman's tartan kilt, this 200-foot-tall sea cliff has a layer of

volcanic rock with vertical lava columns that resemble pleats, sitting atop a layer of horizontal sedimentary rock.

• *After continuing through the village of Staffin (whose name means "the pinnacle place"), you'll begin to see interesting rock formations high on the hill to your left. When you get to the crossroads, head left toward Quiraing (a rock formation). This crossroads is a handy pit stop—there's a public WC in the little white building behind the red phone box just up the main road.*

Now twist your way up the road to...

Quiraing: As you drive up, notice (on your left) a couple of modern cemeteries high in the hills, far above the village. It seems like a strange spot to bury the dead, in the middle of nowhere, but the earth here is less valuable for development, and (since it's not clay, like down by the water) it provides better drainage.

You'll enjoy fine views on the right of the jagged, dramatic northern end of the Trotternish Ridge, called the Quiraing—rated

▲▲. More landslides caused the dramatic scenery in this area, and each rock formation has a name, such as "The Needle" or "The Prison." As you approach the summit of this road, you'll reach a parking area on the left. This marks a popular trailhead for hiking out to get a closer look at the formations. If you've got the time, energy, and weather for a sturdy 30-minute uphill hike, here's your chance. You can either follow the trail along the base of the rock formations, or hike up to the top of the plateau and follow it to the end (both paths are faintly visible from the parking area). Once up top, your reward is a view of the secluded green plateau called "The Table," another landslide block, which isn't visible from the road.

• *You could continue on this road all the way to Uig, at the other end of the peninsula, but it's worth backtracking, then turning left onto the main road (A855), to see the...*

Tip of Trotternish: A few miles north, you'll pass a hotel called **Flodigarry,** with a cottage on the premises that was once home to Bonnie Prince Charlie's rescuer, Flora MacDonald (for her story, read "Monument to Flora MacDonald," later; cottage is now part of the hotel and not open to the public).

Soon after, at the top of the ridge at the tip of the peninsula, you'll see the remains of an old **fort**—not from the Middle Ages or the days of Bonnie Prince Charlie, but from World War II, when the Atlantic was monitored for U-boats from this position.

Then you'll pass (on the right) the crumbling remains of another fort, this one much older: **Duntulm Castle,** which was the first stronghold on Skye of the influential MacDonald clan. The castle was abandoned around 1730 for Armadale Castle on the southern end of Skye; according to a legend, the family left after a nursemaid accidentally dropped the infant heir out a window onto the rocks below. In the distance beyond, you can see the **Outer Hebrides**—the most rugged, remote, and Gaelic part of Scotland. (Skye, a bit closer to the mainland, belongs to the Inner Hebrides.)

• *A mile after the castle, you'll come to a place called Kilmuir. Watch for the turn-off on the left to the excellent...*

Skye Museum of Island Life: This fine little stand of seven thatched stone huts, organized into a family-run museum and

worth ▲▲, explains how a typical Skye family lived a century and a half ago (£2.50, Easter–Oct Mon–Sat 10:00–16:30, closed Sun and Nov–Easter, tel. 01470/552-206, www.skyemuseum.co.uk). Though there are ample posted explanations, the £1.25 guidebook is worthwhile.

The three huts closest to the sea are original (more than 200 years old). Most interesting is the one called The Old Croft House, which was the residence of the Graham family until 1957. Inside you'll find three rooms: kitchen (with peat-burning fire) on the right, parents' bedroom in the middle, and a bedroom for the 12 kids on the left. Nearby, The Old Barn displays farm implements, and the Ceilidh House contains some dense but very informative displays about crofting (the traditional tenant-farmer lifestyle on Skye—explained later), Gaelic, and other topics.

The four other huts were reconstructed here from elsewhere on the island, and now house exhibits about weaving and the village smithy (which was actually a gathering place for villagers). As you explore, admire the smart architecture of these humble but deceptively well-planned structures. Rocks hanging from the roof keep the thatch from blowing away, and the streamlined shape of the structure embedded in the ground encourages strong winds to deflect around the hut rather than hit it head-on.

• *After touring the museum, drive out to the very end of the small road that leads past the parking lot, to a lonesome cemetery. The tallest Celtic cross at the far end of the cemetery (you can enter the gate to reach it) is the...*

Monument to Flora MacDonald: This local heroine sup- posedly rescued beloved Scottish hero Bonnie Prince Charlie

at his darkest hour. After his loss at Culloden, and with a hefty price on his head, Charlie retreated to the Outer Hebrides. But the Hanover dynasty, which controlled the islands, was clos- ing in. Flora MacDonald rescued the prince, disguised him as her Irish maid, Betty Burke, and sailed him to safety on Skye. (Charlie pulled off the ruse thanks to his soft, feminine features—hence the nickname "Bonnie," which means "beautiful.") The flight inspired a popu- lar Scottish folk song: *Speed bonnie boat like a bird on the wing, / Onward, the sailors cry. / Carry the lad that's born to be king / Over the sea to Skye.* For more on Bonnie Prince Charlie, see page 769.

• *Return to the main road and proceed about six miles around the pen- insula. On the right, notice the big depression.*

The Missing Loch: This was once a large loch, but it was drained in the mid-20th century to create more grazing land for sheep. If you look closely, you may see a scattering of stones in the middle of the field. Once an island, this is the site of a former mon- astery...now left as high, dry, and forgotten as the loch. Beyond the missing loch is Prince Charlie's Point, where the bonnie prince supposedly came ashore on Skye with Flora MacDonald.

• *Soon after the loch, you'll drop down over the town of...*

Uig: Pronounced "OO-eeg," this village is the departure point for ferries to the Outer Hebrides (North Uist and Harris islands, 3/day). It's otherwise unremarkable, but does have a café with good £3 sandwiches (follow *Uig Pier* signs into town, blue building with white *café* sign, next to ferry terminal at entrance to town).

• *Continue past Uig, climbing the hill across the bay. Near the top is a large parking strip on the right. Pull over here and look back to Uig for a lesson about Skye's traditional farming system.*

Crofting: You'll hear a lot about crofts during your time on Skye. Traditionally, arable land on the island was divided into plots. If you look across to the hills above Uig, you can see strips

of demarcated land running up from the water—these are crofts. Crofts were generally owned by landlords (mostly English aristocrats or Scottish clan chiefs, and later the Scottish government) and rented to tenant farmers. The crofters lived and worked under very difficult conditions, and were lucky if they could produce enough potatoes, corn, and livestock to feed their families. Rights to farm the croft were passed down from father to son over generations, but always under the auspices of a wealthy landlord.

Finally, in 1976, new legislation kicked off a process of privatization called "decrofting." Suddenly crofters could have their land decrofted, then buy it for an affordable price (£130 per quarter-hectare, or about £8,000 for one of the crofts you see here). Many decroftees would quickly turn around and sell their old family home for a huge profit, but hang on to most of their land and build a new house at the other end. In the crofts you see here, notice that some have a house at the top of a strip of land, and another house at the bottom. Many crofts (like most of these) are no longer cultivated, but a new law might require crofters to farm their land... or lose it. In many cases, families who have other jobs still hang on to their traditional croft, which they use to grow produce for themselves or to supplement their income.

• *Our tour is finished. From here, you can continue along the main road south toward Portree (and possibly continue from there on to the Cuillin Hills). Or, take the shortcut road just after Kensaleyre (B8036), and head west on A850 to Dunvegan and its castle (both options described later in this chapter).*

More Sights on the Isle of Skye

▲▲Cuillin Hills

These dramatic, rocky "hills" (which look more like mountains to me) stretch along the southern coast of the island, dominating Skye's landscape. More craggy and alpine than anything else you'll see in Scotland, the Cuillin seem to rise directly from the deep. You'll see them from just about anywhere on the southern two-thirds of the island, but no roads actually take you through the heart of the Cuillin—that's reserved for hikers and climbers, who love this area. To get the best views with a car, consider these options:

ISLE OF SKYE

Near Sligachan: The road from the Skye Bridge to Portree is the easiest way to appreciate the Cuillin (you'll almost certainly drive along here at some point during your visit). These mountains are all that's left of a long-vanished volcano. As you approach, you'll clearly see that there are three separate ranges (from right to left): red, gray, and black. The steep and challenging Black Cuillin is the most popular for serious climbers; the granite Red Cuillin ridge is more rounded.

The crossroads of Sligachan, with an old triple-arched bridge and a landmark hotel (see page 748), is nestled at the foothills of the Cuillin, and is a popular launch pad for mountain fun. The 2,500-foot-tall cone-shaped hill looming over Sligachan, named Glamaig ("Greedy Lady"), is the site of an annual competition in July (www.carnethy.com): Speed hikers begin at the door of the Sligachan Hotel, race to the summit, run around a bagpiper, and scramble back down to the hotel. The record: 44 minutes (30 minutes up, 13 minutes down, 1 minute dancing a jig up top).

Elgol: For the best view of the Cuillin, locals swear by the drive from Broadford (on the Portree–Kyleakin road) to Elgol, at the tip of a small peninsula that faces the Black Cuillin head-on. While it's just 12 miles as the crow flies from Sligachan, give it a half-hour each way to drive into Elgol from Broadford. To get an even better Cuillin experience, take a boat excursion from Elgol into Loch Coruisk, a "sea loch" (fjord) surrounded by the Cuillin (April–Oct, various companies do the trip several times a day, fewer on Sun and off-season, generally 3 hours round-trip including 1.5 hours free time on the shore of the loch, figure £15–20 round-trip).

▲Dunvegan Castle

Perched on a rock overlooking a sea loch, this past-its-prime castle is a strange and intriguing artifact of Scotland's antiquated, nearly extinct clan system.  Dunvegan Castle is the residence of the MacLeod (pronounced "McCloud") clan—along with the MacDonalds, one of Skye's preeminent clans. Worth ▲▲▲ to people named MacLeod, and mildly interesting to anyone else, this is a good way to pass the time on a rainy day. The owners claim it is the oldest continuously inhabited castle in Scotland. They are restoring it, so the roof may be under a blue tarp during your visit.

Cost and Hours: £8, April–mid-Oct daily 10:00–17:30, last entry 30 minutes before closing, mid-Oct–March Mon–Fri open by appointment only, no photos, tel. 01470/521-206, www.dunvegan castle.com. Consider picking up the £2 guidebook by the late chief.

Getting There: It's near the small town of Dunvegan in the northwestern part of the island, well-signposted from A850. As you approach Dunvegan on A850, the two flat-topped plateaus you'll see are nicknamed the "MacLeod Tables."

You can also get to the castle by bus from Portree (#56, 5/day Mon–Fri, 3/day Sat, none on Sun; leave Portree no later than the 12:35 departure to have time to tour the castle).

Background: In Gaelic, *clann* means "children," and the clan system was the traditional Scottish way of passing along power—similar to England's dukes, barons, and counts. Each clan traces its roots to an ancestral castle, like Dunvegan. The MacLeods (or, as they prefer, "MacLeod of MacLeod") have fallen on hard times. Having run out of male heirs in 1935, Dame Flora MacLeod of MacLeod became the 28th clan chief. Her grandson, John MacLeod of MacLeod, became the 29th chief after her death in 1976. Their castle is rough around the edges, and to raise money to fix the leaky roof, John MacL of MacL actually pondered selling the Black Cuillin ridge of hills (which technically belong to him) to an American tycoon for £10 million a few years back. The deal fell through, and the chief passed away in early 2007. Now his son Hugh Magnus MacLeod of MacLeod, in his mid-thirties, has become clan chief of the MacLeods.

⊘ Self-Guided Tour: The interior feels a bit worn, but the MacLeods proudly display their family heritage—old photographs and portraits of former chiefs. You'll wander through halls, the dining room, the library, and look down into the dungeon's deep pit. Pick up the laminated flyer in each room to discover some of the history. In the **Drawing Room,** look for the tattered silk remains of the Fairy Flag, a mysterious swatch with about a dozen different legends attached to it (most say that it was a gift from a fairy, and somehow it's related to the Crusades). It's said that the clan chief can invoke the power of the flag three times, in the clan's darkest moments. It's worked twice before on the battlefield—which means there's just one use left.

The most interesting historical tidbits are in the **North Room,** which was built in 1360 as the original Great Hall. The family's coat of arms (in the middle of the carpet) has a confused-looking bull and the clan motto, "Hold Fast"—recalling an incident where a MacLeod saved a man from being gored by a bull when he grabbed its horns and forced it to stop. In the case nearby, find the Dunvegan Cup and the Horn of Rory Mor. Traditionally, this horn would be filled with nearly a half-gallon of claret (Bordeaux wine), which a potential heir had to drink without stopping (or falling) to prove himself fit for the role. (The late chief, John MacLeod of MacLeod, bragged that he did it in less than two minutes...but you have to wonder if Dame Flora chug-a-lugged.) Other artifacts in the North Room include bagpipes and several relics related to Bonnie Prince Charlie (including a lock of his hair and his vest). Look for a portrait of Flora MacDonald and some items that belonged to her.

At the end of the tour, you can wander out onto the **terrace** (overlooking a sea loch) and, in the cellar, watch a stuffy **video** about the clan. Between the castle and the parking lot are five acres of enjoyable **gardens** to stroll through while pondering the fading clan system. You can also take a boat ride on Loch Dunvegan to visit a seal colony on a nearby island (£5, 25-minute trip, mid-April–Sept only).

The flaunting of inherited wealth and influence in some English castles rubs me the wrong way. But here, seeing the rough edges of a Scottish clan chief's castle, I had the opposite feeling: sympathy and compassion for a proud way of life that's slipping into the sunset of history. You have to admire the way that they "hold fast" to this antiquated system (in the same way the Gaelic tongue is kept on life support). Paying admission here feels more like donating to charity than padding the pockets of a wealthy family. In fact, watered-down McClouds and McDonalds from America, eager to reconnect with their Scottish roots, help keep the Scottish clan system alive.

▲Neist Point and Lighthouse

To get a truly edge-of-the-world feeling, consider an adventure on the back lanes of the Duirinish Peninsula, west of Dunvegan. This trip is best for hardy drivers looking to explore the most remote corner of Skye and undertake a strenuous hike to a lighthouse. (The lighthouse itself is a letdown, so do this only if you believe a journey is its own reward.) Although it looks close on  the map, give this trip 30 minutes each way from Dunvegan, plus 30 minutes or more for the lighthouse hike.

Head west from Dunvegan, following signs for *Glendale*. You'll cross a moor, then twist around the Dunvegan sea loch, before heading overland and passing through rugged, desolate hamlets that seem like the setting for a BBC sitcom about backwater Britain. After passing through Glendale, carefully track *Neist Point* signs until you reach an end-of-the-road parking lot. The owner of this private property has signs on his padlocked gate stating that you enter at your own risk—which many walkers happily do. (It's laughably easy to walk around the unintimidating "wall.") From here you enjoy sheep and cliff views, but can't see the lighthouse itself unless you do the sturdy 30-minute hike (with a steep uphill return). After hiking around the cliff, the lighthouse springs into view, with the Outer Hebrides beyond.

It's efficient and fun to combine this trek with lunch or dinner at the recommended **Three Chimneys Restaurant,** on the road to Neist Point at Colbost (reservations essential; see page 749).

▲Talisker Distillery

Opened in 1830, Talisker is a Skye institution. If you've only tried mainland whisky, island whisky is worth a dram to appreciate the differences. Island whisky is known for having a strong smoky flavor, due to the amount of peat smoke used during the roasting of the barley. The Isle of Islay has the smokiest, and Talisker workers describe theirs as "medium smoky," which may be easier for non-connoisseurs to take. Talisker produces single-malt whisky only, so it's a favorite with whisky purists: On summer days, this tiny distillery down a tiny road in Carbost village swarms with visitors from all over the world (£5 for an hour-long tour and wee dram; Easter–Oct Mon–Sat 9:30–17:00, closed Sun except in July–Aug when it's open 11:00–17:00, last tour one hour before closing; Nov–Easter Mon–Fri 10:00–17:00, tours at 10:30, 12:00, 14:00 and 15:30, closed Sat–Sun, call ahead; no photos or cell phones, tel. 01478/614-308, www.taliskerwhisky.com).

Skye Bridge

Connecting Kyleakin on Skye with Kyle of Lochalsh on the mainland, the Skye Bridge severely damaged B&B business in the towns it connects. And environmentalists worry about the bridge disrupting the habitat for otters—keep an eye out for these furry native residents. But it's been a boon for Skye tourism—making a quick visit to the island possible without having to wait for a ferry.

The bridge, which was Europe's most expensive toll bridge when it opened in 1995, has stirred up a remarkable amount of controversy among island-dwellers. Here's the Skye natives' take on things: A generation ago, Lowlanders (city folk) began selling their urban homes and buying cheap property on Skye. Natives had grown to enjoy the slow-paced lifestyle that came with living life according to the whim of the ferry, but these new transplants found their commute into civilization too frustrating by boat. They demanded a new bridge be built. Finally a deal was struck to privately fund the bridge, but the toll wasn't established before construction began. So when the bridge opened—and the ferry line it replaced closed—locals were shocked to be charged upward of £5 per car each way to go to the mainland. A few years ago, the bridge was bought by the Scottish Executive, the fare was abolished, and the Skye natives were appeased...for now.

▲▲Near the Isle of Skye: Eilean Donan Castle

This postcard castle, watching over a sea loch from its island perch, is conveniently and scenically situated on the road between the Isle of Skye and Loch Ness.

Famous from such films as Sean Connery's *Highlander* (1986) and the James Bond movie *The World Is Not Enough* (1999), Eilean Donan (EYE-lan DOHN-an) might be Scotland's most photogenic countryside castle. Though it looks ancient, the castle is actually less than a century old. The original castle on this site (dating from 800 years ago) was destroyed in battle in 1719, then rebuilt between 1912 and 1932 by the MacRae family as their residence.

Even if you're not going inside, the castle warrants a five-minute photo stop. But the interior—with cozy rooms—is worth a peek if you have time. Walk across the bridge and into the castle complex, and make your way into the big, blocky keep. First you'll see the claustrophobic, vaulted Billeting Room (where soldiers had their barracks), then head upstairs to the inviting Banqueting Room. Docents posted in these rooms can tell you more. Another flight of stairs takes you to the circa-1930 bedrooms. Downstairs is the cute kitchen exhibit, with mannequins preparing a meal (read the recipes posted throughout). Finally, you'll head through a few more assorted exhibits to the exit.

Cost and Hours: £5.50, good £3.50 guidebook, early March–Oct daily 10:00–18:00, June opens at 9:30, July–Aug opens at 9:00, last entry one hour before closing; generally closed Nov–early March but may be open a few times a week—call; tel. 01599/555-202, www.eileandonancastle.com.

Getting There: It's not actually on the Isle of Skye, but it's quite close, in the mainland town of Dornie. Follow A87 about 15 minutes east of Skye Bridge, through Kyle of Lochalsh and toward Loch Ness and Inverness. The castle is on the right side of this road, just after a long bridge.

Portree

Skye's main attraction is its natural beauty, not its villages. But among them, the best home base is Portree (say poor-TREE fast, comes from Port Righ, literally, "Royal Port"). This village (with 3,000 people, too small to be considered a "town") is Skye's largest settlement and the hub of activity and transportation.

Orientation to Portree

(area code: 01478)

This functional village has a small harbor and, on the hill above it, a tidy main square (from which buses fan out across the island and to the mainland). Surrounding the central square are just a few streets. Homes, shops, and B&Bs line the roads to other settlements on the island.

Tourist Information

Portree's helpful TI is a block off the main square, along Bridge Road. They can help you sort through bus schedules, give you maps, and book you a room for a £4 fee (June–early Sept Mon–Sat 9:00–18:00, Aug until 20:00, Sun 10:00–16:00; early Sept–May Mon–Fri 9:00–17:00, Sat 10:00–16:00, closed Sun; just south of Bridge Street, tel. 01478/612-137 or toll tel. 0845-225-5121). Public WCs are across the street and down a block, across from the hostel.

Helpful Hints

Internet Access: The TI has two terminals in the back (£1/20 minutes), and the **Aros Centre** has four (£2/hour). You can get online at the **library** in Portree High School (free, picture ID required, Mon–Fri 9:15–17:00, Tue and Thu until 20:00, Sat 10:00–16:00, closed Sun, Viewfield Road, tel. 01478/614-823).

Laundry: The **Independent Hostel,** just off the main square, has a self-service launderette down below (about £4 self-service, £8 full-service, usually 11:00–21:00, last load starts at 20:00, tel. 01478/613-737).

Supermarket: A **Co-op** is on Bank Street (Mon–Sat 8:00–22:00, Sun 9:00–19:00).

ISLE OF SKYE

Bike Rental: Island Cycles rents bikes at the lower parking lot, along the water (£7.50/half-day, £14/24 hours, Mon–Sat 9:00–17:00, closed Sun, tel. 01478/613-121, www.isbuc.co.uk).

Car Rental: M2 Motors will pick you up at your B&B or the bus station (£35/day, half-day available, Dunvegan Road, tel. 01478/613-344, www.m2motors.co.uk). Other places to rent a car are the **MacRae Dealership,** a 10-minute walk from downtown Portree on the road toward Dunvegan (£38–42/day, Mon–Fri 8:30–17:30, Sat 9:00–12:30, closed Sun, call at least a week in advance in summer, tel. 01478/612-554). Farther along the same road are two more options: **Jansvans** (£43/day, Mon–Sat 8:00–17:30, closed Sun, tel. 01478/612-087, www.jans.co.uk) and **Portree Coachworks** (£38/day, Mon–Fri 8:30–17:30, weekends by appointment, tel. 01478/612-688, www.portreecoachworks.co.uk).

Parking: As you enter town, a free parking lot is off to the right; look for the sign.

Sights in Portree

Harbor—There's little to see in Portree itself, other than to wander along the colorful harbor, where boat captains offer £14 90-minute excursions out to the sea-eagle nests and around the bay (ask at TI).

Aros Centre—This visitors center and cinema, a mile outside of town on the road to Kyleakin and Skye Bridge, overlooks the sea loch. It offers a humble but earnest exhibit about the island's natural history and wildlife (when I visited it, there was a heron nest in the trees at the end of the parking lot). Enjoy the 20-minute movie with aerial photos of otherwise-hard-to-reach parts of Skye, and chat with the ranger. The exhibit also describes the local sea eagles. These raptors were hunted to extinction on Skye and have been reintroduced to the ecosystem from Scandinavia. A live webcam shows their nests nearby—or, if there are no active nests, a "greatest hits" video show of past fledglings (£4.50, daily 9:00–17:00, last entry 30 minutes before closing, café, gift shop, Internet access, a mile south of town center on Viewfield Road, tel. 01478/613-649, www.aros.co.uk).

Sleeping in Portree

(area code: 01478)

$$$ Almondbank Guest House, on the road into town from Kyleakin, works well for drivers and has great views of the loch from the public areas. It has four tidy, homey rooms (two with sea

Sleep Code

(£1 = about $1.60, country code: 44)
S = Single, **D** = Double/Twin, **T** = Triple, **Q** = Quad, **b** = bathroom, **s** = shower only. Unless otherwise noted, you can assume credit cards are accepted at hotels and hostels—but not B&Bs—and breakfast is included.

To help you sort easily through these listings, I've divided the rooms into three categories based on the price for a standard double room with bath (during high season):

$$$ Higher Priced—Most rooms £65 or more.
$$ Moderately Priced—Most rooms between £45–65.
$ Lower Priced—Most rooms £45 or less.

Prices can change without notice; verify the hotel's current rates online or by email. For other updates, see www .ricksteves.com/update.

views for no extra charge) run by friendly Effie Nicolson (Sb-£65, D-£64, Db-£72, free Wi-Fi, Viewfield Road, tel. 01478/612-696, fax 01478/613-114, j.n.almondbank@btconnect.com). She also rents a three-bedroom cottage next door that sleeps up to six (4-night minimum, www.fisherfield-self-catering.co.uk).

$$ Braeside B&B has three comfortable rooms at the top of town, up from the Bosville Hotel (Db-£55, cash only, closed Nov–Feb, steep stairs, Stormyhill, tel. 01478/612-613, www .braesideportree.co.uk, mail@braesideportree.co.uk, Judith and Philip Maughan).

$$ Bayview House has seven small, sterile, and basic rooms, well-located on the main road just below the square (Db-£50, no breakfast, tel. 01478/613-340, www.bayviewhouse.co.uk, info@bayviewhouse.co.uk, Murdo and Alison). If there's no answer, walk down the stairs to Bayfield Backpackers, described below.

$$ Marine House, run by sweet Skye native Fiona Stephenson, has two simple, homey rooms (one with a private bathroom down the hall) and great views of the harbor (Db-£60–65, cash only, 2 Beaumont Crescent, tel. 01478/611-557).

Hostel: **$ Bayfield Backpackers**—run by Murdo and Alison from the Bayview House, above—is a modern-feeling, institutional, cinderblock-and-metal hostel with 24 beds in four- to eight-bed rooms (£15 per bunk, pay Wi-Fi, kitchen, laundry, tel. 01478/612-231, www.skyehostel.co.uk, info@skyehostel.co.uk).

ISLE OF SKYE

Sleeping near Portree, in Sligachan

$$$ Sligachan Hotel—actually a compound of related sleeping and eating options—is a local institution and a haven for hikers. It's been in the Campbell family since 1913. The hotel's 21 renovated rooms are comfortable, if a bit simple for the price, while the nearby campground and bunkhouse offer a budget alternative. The setting—surrounded by the mighty Cuillin Hills—is remarkably scenic (Db-£118 May–Sept, £98 March–April and Oct, closed Nov–Feb, campground-£5 per person, bunkhouse-£16 per person, pay Internet access in pub, on A87 between Kyleakin and Portree in Sligachan, tel. 01478/650-204, www.sligachan.co.uk, reservations@sligachan.co.uk).

Eating in Portree

Note that Portree's few eateries tend to close early (21:00 or 22:00), and during busy times, lines begin to form soon after 19:00. Eating early works best here.

On the Waterfront: A pair of good eateries vie for your attention along Portree's little harbor. **Lower Deck** feels like a salty sailor's restaurant, decorated with the names of local ships (£5–9 lunches, £9–16 dinners, daily 12:30–14:30 & 18:00–21:30, closed Nov–March, tel. 01478/613-611).

Sea Breezes, with a more contemporary flair, serves tasty cuisine with an emphasis on seafood (£7–9 lunches, £13–18 dinners, £16 two-course early-bird specials 17:00–18:00, open daily 12:00–14:00 & 17:00–21:00, sometimes closed Sun, reserve ahead for dinner, tel. 01478/612-016).

Café Arriba tries hard to offer eclectic flavors in this small Scottish town. With an ambitious menu that includes local specialties, Mexican, Italian, and more, this youthful, colorful, easygoing eatery's hit-or-miss cuisine is worth trying. Drop in to see what's on the blackboard menu today (£4–7 lunches, £8–15 dinners, lots of vegetarian options, daily 7:00–17:00 & 18:00–21:00, Quay Brae, tel. 01478/611-830).

The Café, a few steps off the main square, is a busy, popular hometown diner serving good crank-'em-out food to an appreciative local crowd. The homemade ice-cream stand in the front is a nice way to finish your meal (£8–9 lunches and burgers, £10–15 dinners, also does take-away, daily 8:30–15:30 & 17:30–21:00, tel. 01478/612-553).

The Bosville Hotel has, according to locals, the best of Portree's many hotel restaurants. There are two parts: the inexpensive, casual **bistro** (£5 lunch sandwiches, £9–16 lunches and dinners, June–Aug daily 12:00–14:00 & 17:30–21:30, shorter hours off-season), and the well-regarded formal **Chandlery Restaurant**

(£36 two-course meal, £44 three-course meal, nightly 18:30–
20:30). While pricey, it's a suitable splurge (just up from the main
square, 9–11 Bosville Terrace, tel. 01478/612-846). Their 19 rooms,
also expensive, are worth considering (Db-£128, www.bosville
hotel.co.uk).

Eating Elsewhere on the Isle of Skye

In Sligachan

Sligachan Hotel (described earlier) has a restaurant and a micro-
brew pub serving up mountaineer-pleasing grub in an extremely
scenic setting nestled in the Cuillin Hills (traditional dinners in
restaurant—£25 for three courses, served nightly 18:30–21:00; pub
grub served until 21:00—£7–11; closed Nov–Feb, on A87 between
Kyleakin and Portree in Sligachan, tel. 01478/650-204).

In Colbost, near Dunvegan

Three Chimneys Restaurant is your big-splurge-on-a-small-
island meal. The high-quality Scottish cuisine, using local ingredients, earns rave reviews. Its 16 tables fill an old three-chimney
croft house, with a stone-and-timbers decor that artfully melds
old and new. It's cozy, classy, and candlelit, but not stuffy. Because
of its remote location—and the fact that it's almost always booked
up—reservations are absolutely essential, ideally several weeks
ahead, although it's worth calling in case of last-minute cancellations (lunch: £27.50 for two courses, £35 for three courses; dinner:
£55 for three courses, £80 for seven-course "showcase menu"; dinner served nightly 18:15–21:45, lunch mid-March–Oct Mon–Sat
12:15–13:45, no lunch Sun or Nov–mid-March, closed for 3 weeks
in Jan, tel. 01470/511-258, Eddie and Shirley Spear). They also
rent six swanky, pricey suites next door (Db-£285, less off-season,
www.threechimneys.co.uk).

Getting There: It's in the village of Colbost, about a 10- to
15-minute drive west of Dunvegan on the Duirinish Peninsula
(that's about 45 minutes each way from Portree). To get there, first
head for Dunvegan, then follow signs toward *Glendale*. This single-track road with "passing places" twists you through the countryside, over a moor, and past several dozen sheep before passing
through Colbost. You can combine this with a visit to the Neist
Point Lighthouse (described earlier), which is at the end of the
same road.

ISLE OF SKYE

Kyleakin

Kyleakin (kih-LAH-kin), the last town in Skye before the bridge, used to be a big tourist hub...until the bridge connecting it to the mainland made it much easier for people to get to Portree and other areas deeper in the island. Today this unassuming little village with a ruined castle (Castle Moil), a cluster of lonesome fishing boats, and a forgotten ferry slip still works well as a home base.

If you want to pick up information on the island before you drive all the way to Portree, stop by the tiny **TI** in Broadford, about 15 minutes up the road from Kyleakin (Mon–Fri 10:00–17:00, Sat 11:00–16:00, closed Sun and off-season, maps and hiking books, next to Co-op, WCs across street next to church, toll tel. 08452-255-121).

Helpful Hints

Internet Access: If you're desperate, **Saucy Mary's** store/bar has one laptop available for visitors to rent (Main Street, tel. 01599/534-845).

Laundry: There's none in town, but a launderette is in Broadford, next to the Co-op supermarket (daily 6:00–20:00, less in winter).

Supermarkets: A **Co-op** is across the bridge in Kyle of Lochalsh (Mon–Sat 8:00–22:00, Sun 9:00–18:00, Bridge Road, tel. 01599/530-190) or up the road in Broadford (Mon–Sat 8:00–22:00, Sun 9:00–18:00, Main Street, tel. 01471/820-420).

Car Rental: You can rent a car for the day from **Kyle Taxi** (about £45/day, Mon–Sat 9:00–17:00, closed Sun, will deliver in Kyleakin, tel. 01599/534-323, www.lochalsh.net/taxi).

Sleeping in Kyleakin

(£1 = about $1.60, country code: 44, area code: 01599)

$$$ MacKinnon Country House Hotel is my favorite countryside home base on Skye. It sits quietly in the middle of five acres of gardens just off the bustling Skye Bridge. Ian and the Tongs family have lovingly restored this old 1912 country home with Edwardian antiques and 18 clan-themed rooms, an inviting over-stuffed-sofa lounge, and a restaurant with garden views in nearly every direction (Sb-£50, Db-£100–135 depending on room size and amenities, 10 percent discount when you mention this book in 2011, about 20 percent cheaper Oct–Easter, room fridges, tel. 01599/534-180, www.mackinnonhotel.co.uk, info@mackinnon hotel.co.uk, a 10-minute walk from Kyleakin, at the turnoff for the bridge). Ian also serves a delicious dinner to guests and non-guests alike (see "Eating in Kyleakin," later). Moss, the border collie, will try to take you for a walk.

$$$ White Heather Hotel, run by friendly and helpful Gillian and Craig Glenwright, has nine small but nicely decorated rooms with woody pine bathrooms, across from the waterfront and the castle ruins (Sb-£50, Db-£70, family rooms, cheaper for stays longer than 2 nights, free Internet access and Wi-Fi, lounges, closed Nov–mid-March, The Harbour, tel. 01599/534-577, fax 01599/534-427, www.whiteheatherhotel.co.uk, info@whiteheather hotel.co.uk).

$$ Cliffe House B&B rents three rooms in a white house perched at the edge of the water. All of the rooms, and the breakfast room, enjoy wonderful views over the strait and the bridge (Db-£60, £70 in July–Aug, cash only, tel. 01599/534-019, www .cliffehousebedandbreakfast.co.uk, i.sikorski@btinternet.com, Ian and Mary Sikorski).

Hostel: **$ Dun-Caan Hostel,** named for a dormant volcano on a nearby island, is mellow and friendly. With woody ambience and 15 beds in three rooms, it's quieter and cozier than most hostels—enjoying a genuine camaraderie without an obnoxious party atmosphere (£16/bed, includes sheets, towels-£0.50, pleasant kitchen and lounge, free Wi-Fi, laundry service, The Pier Road, tel. 01599/534-087, www.skyerover.co.uk, info@skyerover.co.uk, Terry and Laila).

Eating in and near Kyleakin

Locals like the **Taste of India,** just past the roundabout outside Kyleakin on A87 toward Broadford (£6–10 entrées, also does takeaway, daily 12:00–14:00 & 17:00–23:00, tel. 01599/534-134). For a nice dinner, head up to the recommended **MacKinnon Country House Hotel** (listed earlier; £13–15 entrées, nightly 19:00–21:00, just outside Kyleakin at roundabout, tel. 01599/534-180). And there are a few pubs in little Kyleakin; ask your B&B host for advice.

In Kyle of Lochalsh: If you can get reservations, eat fresh Scottish cuisine at the **Waverly Restaurant,** a tiny six-table place with locally sourced food across the bridge from Kyleakin in Kyle of Lochalsh (£12–17 entrées, £11.50 two-course dinner special 17:30–19:00, open Fri–Wed 17:30–21:30, closed Thu, reservations essential, Main Street, across from Kyle Hotel and up the stairs, tel. 01599/534-337, Dutch chef/owner Ank).

In Broadford: Up the road in Broadford are more eateries,

ISLE OF SKYE

including the newly renovated **Broadford Hotel** overlooking the bay (£9–12 entrées, many Drambuie drinks, Torrin Road at junction with Elgol, tel. 01471/822-204). It was here that a secret elixir—supposedly once concocted for Bonnie Prince Charlie— caught on in the 19th century. Now known as Drambuie, the popular liqueur is made with Scottish whisky, honey, and spices.

ISLE OF SKYE

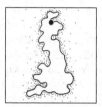

INVERNESS AND THE NORTHERN HIGHLANDS

Filled with more natural and historical mystique than people, the northern Highlands are where Scottish dreams are set. Legends of Bonnie Prince Charlie linger around crumbling castles as tunes played by pipers in kilts swirl around tourists. Explore the locks and lochs of the Caledonian Canal while the Loch Ness monster plays hide-and-seek. Hear the music of the Highlands in Inverness and the echo of muskets at Culloden, where the English drove Bonnie Prince Charlie into exile and conquered his Jacobite supporters.

I've focused my coverage on the handy hub of Inverness, with several day-trip options into the surrounding countryside. For Highlands sights to the south and west, see the Oban and the Southern Highlands chapter; for the Isle of Skye off Scotland's west coast, see the previous chapter.

Planning Your Time

Though it has little in the way of sights, Inverness does have a workaday charm and is a handy spot to spend a night or two en route to other Highland destinations. One night here gives you time to take a quick tour of nearby attractions. With two nights, you can find a full day's worth of sightseeing nearby.

Note that Loch Ness is on the way toward Oban or the Isle of Skye. If you're heading to one of those places, it makes sense to see Loch Ness en route, rather than as a side trip from Inverness.

For a speedy itinerary through the Highlands that includes Inverness and Loch Ness, see page 701.

Getting Around the Highlands

With a car, the day trips around Inverness are easy. Without a car, you can get to Inverness by train (better from Edinburgh or Pitlochry) or by bus (better from Skye, Oban, and Glencoe), then side-trip to Loch Ness, Culloden, and other nearby attractions by public bus or with a package tour.

Inverness

The only city in the north of Scotland, Inverness is pleasantly situated on the River Ness at the base of a castle (now a courthouse, not

a tourist attraction). Inverness' charm is its normalcy—it's a nice, midsize Scottish city that gives you a palatable taste of the "urban" Highlands, and is well-located for enjoying the surrounding countryside sights. Check out the bustling, pedestrian downtown or meander the picnic-friendly riverside paths—best at sunset, when the light hits the castle and couples hold hands while strolling along the water and over the many footbridges.

Orientation to Inverness

(area code: 01463)

Inverness, with about 70,000 people, is the fastest-growing city in Scotland. Marked by its castle, Inverness clusters along the River Ness. Where the main road crosses the river at Ness Bridge, you'll find the TI; within a few blocks (away from the river) are the train and bus stations and an appealing pedestrian shopping zone. The best B&Bs huddle atop a gentle hill behind the castle (a 15-minute mostly uphill walk, or a £5 taxi ride, from the city center).

Tourist Information

At the centrally located TI, you can pick up activity and day-trip brochures, the self-guided *Historic Trail* walking-tour leaflet, and the *What's On* events booklet for the latest theater, music, and film showings (both free). The office also books rooms for a £4 fee and tours for a £1 fee (July–mid-Sept Mon–Sat 9:00–18:30, Sun 9:30–18:30; mid-Sept–June Mon–Sat 9:00–17:00, Sun 10:00–16:00; Internet access, free WCs up behind TI, Castle Wynd, tel. 01463/234-353).

Tattoos and the Painted People

In Inverness, as in other Scottish cities such as Glasgow and Edinburgh, hip pubs are filled with tattooed kids. In parts of Scotland, however, tattoos aren't a recent phenomenon—this form of body art has been around longer than the buildings and sights. Some of the area's earliest known settlers of the Highlands were called the Picts, dubbed the "Painted People" by their enemies, the Romans. The Picts, who conquered the northeast corner of Scotland (including Inverness), were believed to have ruled from the first century A.D. to approximately the ninth century, when they united with the Scots and were lost to written history.

Picts were known for their elaborate full-body tattoos. The local plant they used for their ink, called *woad*, had built-in healing properties, helping to coagulate blood (a property particularly handy in battle). The tattoos gave rise to a truly remarkable fighting technique: going to war naked. The Picts saw their tattoos as a kind of psychological armor, a combination of symbols and magical signs that would protect them more than any metal could. Imagine a Scottish hillside teeming with screaming, head-to-toe dyed-blue warriors, most with complex tattooed designs—and all of them buck naked.

Helpful Hints

Festivals: In mid-June, the city fills up for the **RockNess Music Festival** (www.rockness.co.uk), and there's a **marathon** the first week of October (www.lochnessmarathon.com); book ahead for these times.

Internet Access: You can get online at the **TI** (£1/20 minutes), or for free at the Neoclassical **library** behind the bus station, though you'll be limited to a half-hour session (Mon and Fri 9:00–19:30, Tue and Thu 9:00–18:30, Wed 10:00–17:00, Sat 9:00–17:00, closed Sun, computers shut down 15 minutes before closing, tel. 01463/236-463). **Clanlan** is in the middle of town, between the train station and the river (£1.20/20 minutes, Mon–Fri 10:00–20:00, Sat 11:00–20:00, Sun 12:00–17:00, 22 Baron Taylor Street, tel. 01463/241-223). The launderette listed below also has Internet access (£1/30 minutes).

Baggage Storage: The train station has lockers (£3–5/24 hours, open Mon–Sat 6:30–19:45, Sun 10:45–18:15).

Laundry: New City Launderette is just across the Ness Bridge from the TI (self-service-£8, same-day full-service for £3.50 more, price calculated by weight, Internet access, Mon–Sat 8:00–18:00, until 20:00 Mon–Fri June–Oct, Sun 10:00–16:00, last load one hour before closing, 17 Young Street, tel. 01463/242-507).

INVERNESS

Inverness

1. Melness Guest House
2. Craigside Lodge B&B
3. Dionard Guest House
4. Ardconnel House & Crown Hotel Guest House
5. Ryeford Guest House
6. The Redcliffe Hotel & Rest.
7. Inverness Palace Hotel & Spa
8. To Premier Inn Inverness Centre
9. Inverness Student Hotel & Bazpackers Hostel
10. Café 1
11. Number 27 Restaurant
12. La Tortilla Asesina Rest.
13. Heathmount Hotel & Rest.
14. Hootananny Café/Bar
15. Rocpool Restaurant
16. The Mustard Seed Rest.
17. Rajah Indian Restaurant
18. Girvans Café & Délices de Bretagne Brasserie
19. Leakey's Bookshop & Café
20. Marks & Spencer (Groceries)
21. Co-op Supermarket
22. Library (Internet)
23. Clanlan (Internet)
24. Launderette (Internet)
25. Bus Stop for Culloden & Cawdor

P PARKING

TO A-862

TO A-82 FORT WILLIAM, LOCH NESS (WEST) & OBAN

400 YARDS
400 METERS

Supermarket: The **Co-operative** is handy for picnics (Mon–Sat 7:00–22:00, Sun 9:00–20:00, 59 Church Street).

Tours in Inverness

Walking Tour—Happy Tours offers guided historical walks in spring and summer (£10; April–Sept daily at 11:00, 13:00, and 15:00; one hour, leaves from the steps of the TI, in summer just show up, arrange in advance in winter, tel. 07828/154-683 or

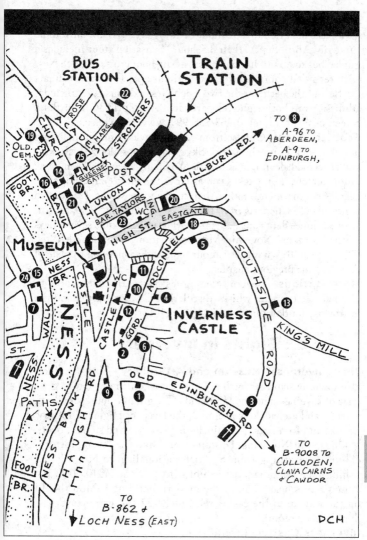

mobile 0782-815-4683, www.happy-tours.biz). They also do a one-hour "Crime and Punishment" tour nightly at 19:00 and 20:15.

Excursions from Inverness

While thin on sights of its own, Inverness is a great home base for day trips. The biggest attraction is Loch Ness, a 20-minute drive southwest. Tickets are available at the TI, and tours depart from somewhere nearby. It's smart to book ahead, especially in peak season.

Jacobite Tours—This outfit runs a variety of tours, from a one-hour basic boat ride to a 6.5-hour extravaganza (£11–37, most tours run daily April–Sept). Their 3.5-hour "Sensation" tour includes a guided bus tour with live narration, a half-hour cruise of Loch Ness with recorded commentary, and an hour apiece at the Urquhart Castle and the better of the two Loch Ness exhibits (£26, includes admissions to both sights, departs at 10:30 and 13:30 from Bank Street, near the TI, tel. 01463/233-999, www.jacobite.co.uk).

Scottish Tours—Choose from several daylong tours, including one that focuses on the Isle of Skye, with stops along Loch Ness and at scenic Eilean Donan Castle. You'll get a few hours on Skye; unfortunately, it only takes you as far as the Sleat Peninsula at the island's southern end, rather than to the more scenic Trotternish Peninsula (£38, departs from Inverness bus station at 9:30, returns at 19:30; June–Sept runs daily; mid-May and Oct runs several days a week; no tours Nov–mid-May, reservations recommended, tel. 0871-200-0601, www.scottishtours.co.uk). For more on the Isle of Skye, see the previous chapter.

More Options—Several companies host daily excursions to Culloden Battlefield, whisky distilleries, Cawdor Castle, and the nearby bay for dolphin-watching (ask at TI).

Sights in Inverness

"Imaginverness" Museum and Art Gallery—This free, likeable town museum is worth poking around on a rainy day to get a taste of Inverness and the Highlands. The ground-floor exhibits on geology and archaeology peel back the layers of Highland history: Bronze and Iron ages, Picts (including some carved stones), Scots, Vikings, and Normans. Upstairs you'll find the "social history" exhibit (everything from Scottish nationalism to hunting and fishing) and temporary art exhibits (free, Mon–Sat 10:00–17:00, closed Sun, cheap café, in the modern building behind the TI on the way up to the castle, tel. 01463/237-114, http://inverness .highland.museum).

Inverness Castle—Inverness' biggest nonsight has nice views from its front lawn, but the building itself isn't worth visiting. The statue outside depicts Flora MacDonald, who helped Bonnie Prince Charlie escape from the English (see page 770). The castle is used as a courthouse, and when trials are in session, loutish-looking men hang out here, waiting for their bewigged barristers to arrive.

Sleeping in Inverness

(area code: 01463)

B&Bs on and near Ardconnel Street and Old Edinburgh Road

These B&Bs are popular; book ahead for June through August (and during the marathon in early October—see "Festivals" under "Helpful Hints," earlier), and be aware that some require a two-night minimum during busy times. The rooms are all a 10-minute walk from the train station and town center. To get to the B&Bs, either catch a taxi (£5) or walk: From the train and bus stations, go left on Academy Street. At the first stoplight (the second if you're coming from the bus station), veer right onto Inglis Street in the pedestrian zone. Go up the Market Brae steps. At the top, turn right onto Ardconnel Street toward the B&Bs and hostels.

$$ Melness Guest House has two country-comfy rooms, a tartan-bedecked lounge, and an adorable West Highland Terrier named Rogie (Db-£70, 2-night minimum in summer, free Wi-Fi, 8 Old Edinburgh Road, tel. 01463/220-963, www.melnessie.co.uk, joy@melnessie.co.uk, welcoming Joy Joyce).

$$ Craigside Lodge B&B has five large, comfortable, cheery rooms remodeled with a tasteful modern flair. Guests share an inviting sunroom and a cozy lounge with a great city view (Sb-£35–40, Db-£65–70, prices depend on season, free Wi-Fi, just above Castle Street at 4 Gordon Terrace, tel. 01463/231-576,

---

Sleep Code

(£1 = about $1.60, country code: 44, area code: 01463)
S = Single, **D** = Double/Twin, **T** = Triple, **Q** = Quad, **b** = bathroom, **s** = shower only. Unless otherwise noted, you can assume credit cards are accepted at hotels and hostels—but not B&Bs—and breakfast is included.

   To help you sort easily through these listings, I've divided the rooms into three categories based on the price for a standard double room with bath (during high season):

$$$ Higher Priced—Most rooms £75 or more.
  $$ Moderately Priced—Most rooms between £30-75.
    $ Lower Priced—Most rooms £30 or less.

   Prices can change without notice; verify the hotel's current rates online or by email. For other updates, see www .ricksteves.com/update.

www.craigsideguesthouse.co.uk, enquiries@craigsideguesthouse
.co.uk, Ewan and Amy).

$$ Dionard Guest House, just up Old Edinburgh Road from
Ardconnel Street, has cheerful blue-toned common spaces and six
pleasant rooms, with two on the ground floor (Sb-£40, Db-£65–75
depending on size, 2-night minimum, no single-occupancy rate
during high season, free Wi-Fi, in-room fridges, laundry ser-
vice-£6-12, 39 Old Edinburgh Road, tel. 01463/233-557, www
.dionardguesthouse.co.uk, enquiries@dionardguesthouse.co.uk,
welcoming Val and John).

$$ Ardconnel House has six spacious and relaxing pastel rooms with lots of extra touches (Sb-£42, Db-£72, family
room-£95, family deals but no children under 10, slightly cheaper
off-season or for 2 or more nights, free Wi-Fi, nice lounge, 21
Ardconnel Street, tel. 01463/240-455, www.ardconnel-inverness
.co.uk, ardconnel@gmail.com, John and Elizabeth).

$$ Crown Hotel Guest House has six clean, bright rooms
and an enjoyable breakfast room (Sb-£35, Db-£60, family room-
£80–100, lounge, 19 Ardconnel Street, tel. 01463/231-135, www
.crownhotel-inverness.co.uk, reservations@crownhotel-inverness
.co.uk, friendly Catriona—pronounced "Katrina"—Barbour).

$$ Ryeford Guest House is a great value, with six flowery
rooms and plenty of teddy bears (Sb-£38, Db-£60, Tb-£90, fam-
ily deals, free Wi-Fi, vegetarian breakfast available, small twin
room #1 in back has fine garden view, above Market Brae steps,
go left on Ardconnel Terrace to #21, tel. 01463/242-871, www
.scotland-inverness.co.uk/ryeford, joananderson@uwclub.net, Joan
and George Anderson).

Hotels

The following hotels may have rooms when my recommended
B&Bs are full.

$$$ The Redcliffe Hotel, which is actually in the midst of
all the B&Bs described above, has 12 renovated, contemporary
rooms, some in a six-room townhouse annex across the street.
Though a lesser value than the B&Bs, it's fairly priced for a small
hotel (Sb-£50–60, Db-£80–100, Db suite-£100–130, depends on
season, some castle-view rooms, pay Wi-Fi, 1 Gordon Terrace,
tel. & fax 01463/232-767, www.redcliffe-hotel.co.uk, enquiry
@redcliffe-hotel.co.uk). They also have a good restaurant (listed
later, under "Eating in Inverness").

$$$ Inverness Palace Hotel & Spa, a Best Western, is a
fancy splurge with a pool, a gym, and 88 overpriced rooms. It's
located right on the River Ness, across from the castle (Db-£149,
but you can almost always get a much better rate—even half-
price—if you book a package deal on their website, £70 last-minute

rooms, prices especially soft on weekends, river/castle view rooms about £40 more than rest, breakfast extra, elevator, free Wi-Fi, free parking, 8 Ness Walk, tel. 01463/223-243, fax 01463/236-865, www.bw-invernesspalace.co.uk, palace@miltonhotels.com).

$$ Premier Inn Inverness Centre, a half-mile east of the train station along busy and dreary Millburn Road, offers 55 modern, identical rooms in a converted distillery. While it feels like a freeway rest-stop hotel (nondrivers should skip it), it's fairly affordable, especially for families. The appealing onsite restaurant, Slice, offers steaks, salads, and more (Db for up to 2 adults and 2 kids-about £75, check for specials online, cheaper in winter, continental breakfast-£5.25, full cooked breakfast-£7.75, elevator, Wi-Fi, B865/Millburn Road, just west of the A9 and A96 interchange, tel. 08701-977-141, fax 01463/717-826, www.premierinn.com).

Hostels on Culduthel Road

For inexpensive dorm beds near the center and the recommended Castle Street restaurants, consider these friendly side-by-side hostels, geared toward younger travelers. They're about a 12-minute walk from the train station.

$ Inverness Student Hotel has 57 beds in nine rooms and a cozy, inviting, laid-back lounge with a bay window overlooking the River Ness. The friendly staff welcome any traveler over 18. Dorms come in some interesting shapes, and each bunk has its own playful name (£14 beds in 6- to 10-bed rooms, price depends on season, breakfast-£2, free tea and coffee, cheap Internet access, free Wi-Fi, full-service laundry for £2.50, kitchen, 8 Culduthel Road, tel. 01463/236-556, www.scotlands-top-hostels.com, inverness @scotlands-top-hostels.com).

$ Bazpackers Hostel, a stone's throw from the castle, has a pleasant common room and 34 beds in basic 4- to 6-bed dorms (beds-£14–15, D-£38, cheaper Oct–May, linens provided, reception open 7:30–24:00, no curfew, Internet access, laundry service, 4 Culduthel Road, tel. 01463/717-663, www.bazpackershostel .co.uk).

Eating in Inverness

You'll find a lot of traditional Highland fare—game, fish, lamb, and beef. Reservations are smart at most of these places, especially on summer weekends.

Near the B&Bs, on or near Castle Street

The first three eateries line Castle Street, facing the back of the castle. The last two are right in the middle of the B&B neighborhood.

Café 1 serves up high-quality modern Scottish and international cuisine with a trendy, elegant bistro flair. This popular place fills up on weekends, so it's smart to call ahead (£9–19 entrées, lunch and early-bird dinner specials 17:30–18:45, Mon–Sat 12:00–14:00 & 17:30–21:30, closed Sun, 75 Castle Street, tel. 01463/226-200).

Number 27 is the Scottish version of T.G.I. Friday's. The straightforward, crowd-pleasing menu offers something for everyone—salads, burgers, seafood, and more (£9–14 entrées, Mon–Fri 12:00–14:45 & 17:00–21:00, Sat 12:00–21:30, Sun 12:30–14:45 & 17:00–21:00, generous portions, noisy bar up front not separated from restaurant in back, 27 Castle Street, tel. 01463/241-999).

La Tortilla Asesina has Spanish tapas, including spicy king prawns (the house specialty). It's an appealing and vivacious dining option (£3–5 cold and hot tapas, a few make a meal, cheap three-course specials; July–Sept daily 12:00–22:00; Oct–June Sun–Thu 12:00–21:00, Fri–Sat until 22:00; 99 Castle Street, tel. 01463/709-809).

The Redcliffe Hotel's restaurant is conveniently located (right on one of the B&B streets) and serves up good food in three areas: a bright and leafy sunroom, a pub, or an outdoor patio (£9–16 dinners, Mon–Sat 12:00–14:30 & 17:00–21:30, Sun 12:30–14:30 & 17:30–21:30, 1 Gordon Terrace, tel. 01463/232-767). Also nearby is the **Heathmount Hotel and Restaurant,** which serves good food in their quiet dining room (£5–9 lunch entrées, £9–17 dinner entrées, Mon–Fri 12:00–14:30 & 17:00–22:00, Sat–Sun 12:30–22:00, Kingsmills Road, tel. 01463/235-877).

In the Town Center

Hootananny is a cross-cultural experience, combining a lively pub atmosphere, nightly live music (Scottish traditional every night, plus rock, blues, and "bar music"), and Thai cuisine. It's got a great join-in-the-fun vibe at night (£6–7 Thai dishes, lunch deals, food served Mon–Sat 12:00–15:00 & 17:00–21:30, music begins every night at 21:30, closed Sun, good for take-away, 67 Church Street, tel. 01463/233-651, www.hootananny.co.uk). Upstairs is the Mad Hatter's nightclub (Thu-Sun only), complete with a "chill-out room."

Rocpool Restaurant is a hit with locals and good for a splurge. Owner/chef Steven Devlin serves creative modern European food in a sleek—and often crowded—chocolate/pistachio dining room (£12 lunch specials Mon–Sat, £14 pre-theater special before 18:45 Sun–Fri, £12–18 dinners, daily 12:00–14:30 & 17:45–22:00, reserve or be sorry, across the Ness Bridge from TI at 1 Ness Walk, tel. 01463/717-274).

The Mustard Seed serves Scottish food with a modern twist and a view of the river in an old church in a lively-at-lunch, mellow-at-dinner atmosphere. It's pricey but worth considering for a nice meal. Ask for a seat on the balcony if the weather is cooperating (£6 lunch specials, £12 early-bird specials before 19:00, £10–15 meals, daily 12:00–15:00 & 17:30–22:00, reservations essential on weekends, on the corner of Bank and Fraser Streets, 16 Fraser Street, tel. 01463/220-220).

Rajah Indian Restaurant provides a tasty break from meat and potatoes, with vegetarian options served in a classy red-velvet, white-linen atmosphere (£9–14 meals, 10 percent less for take-out, Mon–Sat 12:00–22:30, Sun 15:00–22:30, last dine-in order 30 minutes before closing, just off Church Street at 2 Post Office Avenue, tel. 01463/237-190).

Girvans serves sandwiches and tempting pastries in an easygoing atmosphere (£8–14 meals, Mon–Sat 9:00–21:00, Sun 10:00–21:00, 2 Stephens Brae, at the end of the pedestrian zone nearest the train station, tel. 01463/711-900).

Délices de Bretagne, next door to Girvans, is a tiny French brasserie serving £5 croque sandwiches, £3–6 crêpes, and its share of tasty pastries in a lighthearted, Art Nouveau space (Mon–Sat 9:00–17:00, closed Sun, 4A/6 Stephens Brae, tel. 01463/712-422).

Leakey's Bookshop and Café, located in a 1649 converted church, has the best lunch deal in town. Browse through stacks of old books and vintage maps, warm up by the wood-burning stove, and climb the spiral staircase to the loft for hearty home-made soups, sandwiches, and sweets (£3–4 light lunches, Mon–Sat 10:00–16:30, bookstore stays open until 17:30, closed Sun, in Greyfriar's Hall on Church Street, tel. 01463/239-947, Charles Leakey).

Picnic: The **Marks & Spencer** food hall is best (you can't miss it—on the main pedestrian mall, near the Market Brae steps at the corner of the big Eastgate Shopping Centre; Mon–Wed and Fri–Sat 9:00–18:00, Thu 9:00–20:00, Sun 11:00–17:00, tel. 01463/224-844).

Inverness Connections

From Inverness by Train to: Pitlochry (every 1.5-2 hours, 1.5 hours), **Stirling** (every 1.5–2 hours, 2.75–3 hours, some transfer in Perth), **Kyle of Lochalsh** near Isle of Skye (4/day, 2.5 hours), **Edinburgh** (every 2 hours, 3.5–4 hours, more with change in Perth), **Glasgow** (9/day, 3.5 hours, 3 direct, the rest change in Perth). ScotRail does a great sleeper service to **London** (generally £140–190 for first class/private compartment or £100–150 for standard class/shared compartment with breakfast, not available Sat night, www.firstscotrail.com). Consider dropping your car in

Inverness & the Northern Highlands

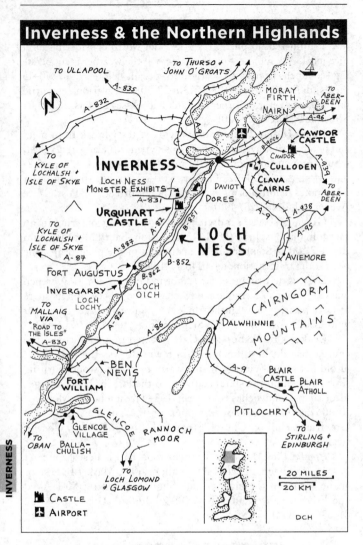

Inverness and riding to London by train. Train info: tel. 0845-748-4950.

By Bus: To reach most destinations in western Scotland, you'll first head for **Fort William** (5/day, 2 hours). For connections onward to **Oban** (figure 4 hours total) or **Glencoe** (3 hours total), see the "Fort William Connections" on page 729. To reach **Portree** on the Isle of Skye, you can either take the direct bus (3/day in summer, 2/day in winter, 3.25 hours direct), or transfer in Fort William. These buses are run by Scottish Citylink; for schedules, see www.citylink.co.uk. You can buy tickets in advance by calling

Citylink at tel. 0871-266-3333 or stopping by the Inverness bus station (Mon–Sat 7:00–18:45, Sun 9:00–17:30, £0.50 extra for credit cards, daily baggage storage-£4–5/bag, 2 blocks from train station on Margaret Street, tel. 01463/233-371). For bus travel to England, check www.nationalexpress.com.

Route Tips for Drivers

Inverness to Edinburgh (150 miles, 3 hours minimum): Leaving Inverness, follow signs to A9 (south, toward Perth). If you haven't seen the Culloden Battlefield yet (described later), it's an easy detour: Just as you leave Inverness, head four miles east off A9 on B9006. Back on A9, it's a wonderfully speedy, scenic highway (A9, M90, A90) all the way to Edinburgh. If you have time, consider stopping en route in Pitlochry (just off A9; see the Between Inverness and Edinburgh chapter).

  To Oban, Glencoe, or Isle of Skye: See the "Route Tips for Drivers" at the end of the Oban and the Southern Highlands chapter.

Near Inverness

Inverness puts you in the heart of the Highlands, within easy striking distance of a gaggle of famous and worthwhile sights: Squint across Loch Ness looking for Nessie—or, if you're a skeptic, just appreciate the majesty of Britain's largest body of water by volume. Commune with the Scottish soul at the historic Culloden Battlefield, where Scottish, English, and world history reached a turning point. Ponder three mysterious Neolithic cairns, reminding visitors that Scotland's history goes back even before Braveheart. And enjoy a homey country castle at Cawdor.

Loch Ness

I'll admit it: I had my zoom lens out and my eyes on the water. The local tourist industry thrives on the legend of the Loch Ness Monster. It's a thrilling thought, and there have been several seemingly reliable "sightings" (monks, police officers, and sonar images). But even if you ignore the monster stories, the loch is impressive: 23 miles long, less than a mile wide, the third-deepest in Europe (754 feet), and containing more water than in all the freshwater bodies of England and Wales combined.

  Getting There: The Loch Ness sights are a quick drive southwest of Inverness. Various buses go from Inverness to Urquhart

Castle in about a half-hour (8/day, various companies, ask at Inverness bus station or TI).

Sights on Loch Ness

Loch Ness Monster Exhibits—In July of 1933, a couple swore that they saw a giant sea monster shimmy across the road in front of their car by Loch Ness. Within days, ancient legends about giant monsters in the lake (dating as far back as the sixth century) were revived—and suddenly everyone was spotting "Nessie" poke its head above the waters of Loch Ness. In the last 75 years, further sightings and photographic "evidence" have bolstered the claim that there's something mysterious living in this unthinkably deep and murky lake. (Most sightings take place in the deepest part of the loch, near Urquhart Castle.) Most witnesses describe a waterbound dinosaur (resembling the real, but extinct, plesiosaur). Others cling to the slightly more plausible theory of a gigantic eel. And skeptics figure the sightings can be explained by a combination of reflections, boat wakes, and mass hysteria. The most famous photo of the beast (dubbed the "Surgeon's Photo") was later discredited—the "monster's" head was actually attached to a toy submarine. But that hasn't stopped various cryptozoologists from seeking photographic, sonar, and other proof.

And that suits the thriving local tourist industry just fine. The Nessie commercialization is so tacky that there are two different monster exhibits within 100 yards of each other, both in the town of Drumnadrochit. Each has a tour-bus parking lot and more square footage devoted to their kitschy shop than to the exhibit. The overpriced exhibitions are actually quite interesting—even though they're tourist traps, they'll appease that small part of you that knows the *real* reason you wanted to see Loch Ness.

The better option of the two—worth ▲—is the **Loch Ness Centre & Exhibition,** headed by a marine biologist who has spent more than 15 years researching lake ecology and scientific phenomena. With a 30-minute series of video bits and special effects, this exhibit explains the geological and historical environment that bred the monster story as well as the various searches that have been conducted. Refreshingly, it retains an air of healthy skepticism instead of breathless monster-chasing. It also has some artifacts related to the search, such as a hippo-foot ashtray used to fake monster footprints and the *Viperfish*—a harpoon-equipped

The Caledonian Canal

The Highlands are cut in two by the impressive Caledonian Canal, which connects lakes (lochs) that lie in the huge depression created by the Great Glen Fault (easily visible on any map as the diagonal slash across Scotland). The town of Fort William (described in a previous chapter) is located at the southwest end of the canal, and Inverness sits at its northeast end. The major sights—including the famous Loch Ness—cluster along the scenic 60-mile stretch between these two towns.

Three locks and a series of canals trace the fault. Oich, Loch, and Ness were connected in the early 1800s by the great British engineer Thomas Telford. Traveling between Fort William and Inverness, you'll follow Telford's work—20 miles of canals and locks between 40 miles of lakes, raising ships from sea level to 51 feet (Ness), 93 feet (Lochy), and to 106 feet (Oich).

While "Neptune's Staircase," a series of locks near Fort William, has been cleverly named to sound intriguing,  the best lock stop is midway, at Fort Augustus, where the canal hits the south end of Loch Ness. In Fort Augustus, the **Caledonian Canal Heritage Centre,** three locks above the main road, gives a good run-down on Telford's work (free, April-Oct daily 10:00-13:30 & 14:00-17:30, closed Nov-March, tel. 01320/366-493). Stroll past several shops and eateries to the top of the locks for a fine view.

submarine used in a 1969 Nessie search (£6.50, daily Easter–May 9:30–17:00, June–Oct 9:00–18:00, Nov–Easter 10:00–15:30, in the big stone mansion right on the main road to Inverness, tel. 01456/450-573, www.lochness.com).

The other exhibit, called the **Nessieland Castle Monster Centre** (up a side road closer to the town center, affiliated with a hotel), is less serious. It's basically a tacky high-school-quality photo report and a 30-minute *We Believe in the Loch Ness Monster* movie, which features credible-sounding locals explaining what they saw and a review of modern Nessie searches. (The most convincing reason for locals to believe: Look at the hordes of tourists around you.) It also has small exhibits on local history and on other "monsters" and hoaxes around the world (£5.50, daily May–Sept 9:00–18:00, Oct–April 9:00–17:00, tel. 01456/450-342, www.loch-ness-monster-nessieland.com).

▲**Urquhart Castle**—The ruins at Urquhart (UR-kurt), just up the loch from the Nessie exhibits, are gloriously situated with a view

of virtually the entire lake. Its visitors center has a tiny museum with interesting castle artifacts and a good eight-minute film, but the castle itself is a relatively empty shell. Its previous owners blew it up to keep the Jacobites from taking it. As you walk toward the ruins, take a close look at the trebuchet (a working replica of one of the most destructive weapons of English King Edward I), and ponder how this giant slingshot helped Edward grab almost every castle in the country away from the native Scots (£7, guidebook-£4, daily April–Sept 9:30–18:00, Oct 9:30–17:00, Nov–March 9:30–16:30, last entry 45 minutes before closing, café, tel. 01456/450-551, www.historic-scotland.gov.uk).

Culloden Battlefield

Jacobite troops under Bonnie Prince Charlie were defeated at Culloden (kuh-LAW-dehn) by supporters of the Hanover dynasty in 1746. This last major land battle fought on British soil spelled the end of Jacobite resistance and the beginning of the clan chiefs' fall from power. Wandering the desolate, solemn battlefield, you sense that something terrible occurred here. Locals still bring white roses and speak of "the '45" (as Bonnie Prince Charlie's entire campaign is called) as if it just happened. The battlefield at Culloden and its high-tech Visitors Centre together are worth ▲▲▲.

Orientation to Culloden

Cost and Hours: £10, plus £2 for parking. Daily April–Oct 9:00–18:00, Nov–March 10:00–16:00, closed in Jan.

Information and Services: £5 guidebook, café, tel. 01463/796-090, www.nts.org.uk/culloden.

Tours: Tours with live guides are included with your admission. Check for a schedule—there are generally 3–4/day, focusing on various aspects of the battle.

INVERNESS

Audioguide: It's free, with good information tied by GPS to important sites on the battlefield; pick it up at the end of the indoor exhibit.

Getting There: It's a 15-minute drive east of Inverness. Follow signs to *Aberdeen,* then *Culloden Moor,* and B9006 takes you right there (well-signed on the right-hand side). Public buses leave from Inverness' Queensgate street and drop you off in the parking lot (bus #1 or #1A, hourly, 30 minutes, confirm that bus is going all the way to the battlefield).

Length of This Tour: Allow 2 hours.

Background: The Battle of Culloden

The Battle of Culloden (April 16, 1746) marks the end of the power of the Scottish Highland clans and the start of years of repression of Scottish culture by the English. It was the culmination of a year's worth of battles, known collectively as "the '45." At the center of it all was the charismatic, enigmatic Bonnie Prince Charlie (1720–1788).

Charles Edward Stuart, from his first breath, was raised with a single purpose—to restore his family to the British throne. His grandfather was King James II, deposed in 1688 by Parliament for his tyranny and pro-Catholic bias. In 1745, young Charlie crossed the Channel from exile in France to retake the throne for the Stuarts. He landed on the west coast of Scotland and rallied support for the "Jacobite" cause (from the Latin for "James"). Though Charles was not Scottish-born, he was the rightful heir directly down the line from Mary, Queen of Scots—and so many Scots joined the Stuart family's rebellion out of resentment at being ruled by a foreign king (English royalty of German descent).

Bagpipes droned, and "Bonnie" (handsome) Charlie led an army of 2,000 tartan-wearing, Gaelic-speaking Highlanders across Scotland, seizing Edinburgh. They picked up other supporters of the Stuarts from the Lowlands and from England. Now 6,000 strong, they marched south toward London, and King George II made plans to flee the country. But anticipated support for the Jacobites failed to materialize in the numbers they were hoping for (both in England and from France). The Jacobites had so far been victorious in their battles against the Hanoverian government forces, but the odds now turned against them. Charles retreated to the Scottish Highlands, where many of his men knew the terrain and might gain an advantage when outnumbered. The English government troops followed closely on his heels.

Against the advice of his best military strategist, Charles' army faced the Hanoverian forces at Culloden Moor on flat, barren terrain that was unsuited to the Highlanders' guerrilla tactics. The Scots—many of them brandishing only broadswords and spears—were mowed down by English cannons and horsemen. In less than an hour, the government forces routed the Jacobite army, but that was just the start. They spent the next weeks methodically hunting down ringleaders and sympathizers (and many others in the Highlands who had nothing to do with the battle), ruthlessly killing, imprisoning, and banishing thousands.

Charles fled with a £30,000 price on his head. He escaped to the Isle of Skye, hidden by a woman named Flora MacDonald (her grave is on the Isle of Skye, and her statue is outside Inverness Castle). Flora dressed Charles in women's clothes and passed him off as her maid. Later, Flora was arrested and thrown in the Tower of London before being released and treated like a celebrity.

Charles escaped to France. He spent the rest of his life wandering Europe trying to drum up support to retake the throne. He drifted through short-lived romantic affairs and alcohol, and died in obscurity, without an heir, in Rome.

Though usually depicted as a battle of the Scottish versus the English, in truth Culloden was a civil war between two opposing dynasties: Stuart (Charlie) and Hanover (George). In fact, about one-fifth of the government's troops were Scottish, and several redcoat deserters fought along with the Jacobites. However, as the history has faded into lore, the battle has come to be remembered as a Scottish-versus-English standoff—or, in the parlance of the Scots, the Highlanders versus the Strangers.

The Battle of Culloden was the end of 60 years of Jacobite rebellions, the last major battle fought on British soil, and the final stand of the Highlanders. From then on, clan chiefs were deposed; kilts, tartans, and bagpipes became illegal paraphernalia; and farmers were cleared off their ancestral land, replaced by more-profitable sheep. Scottish culture would never recover from the events of the campaign called "the '45."

Self-Guided Tour

Culloden's Visitors Centre, opened in spring 2008, is a state-of-the-art £10 million facility. The ribbon was cut by two young local men, each descended from soldiers who fought in the battle (one from either side). On the way up to the door, look under your feet at the memorial stones for fallen soldiers and clans, mostly purchased by their American and Canadian descendants.

The initial part of the exhibit provides you with some background. As you pass the ticket desk, note the **family tree** of Bonnie Prince Charlie ("Prince Charles Edward") and George II, who were essentially distant cousins. Next you'll come across the first of the exhibit's shadowy-figure **touchscreens,** which connect you with historical figures who give you details from both the Hanoverian and Jacobite perspectives. A **map** here shows the other power struggles happening in and around Europe, putting this fight for political control of Britain in a wider context. This battle was no simple local skirmish, but rather a key part of a larger struggle between Britain and its neighbors, primarily France, for control over trade and colonial power. In the display case are **medals** from the early 1700s, made by both sides as propaganda.

Your path through this building is cleverly designed to echo the course of the Jacobite army. Your short march gets underway as Charlie sails from France to Scotland, then finagles the support of Highland clan chiefs. As he heads south with his army to take London, you, too, are walking south. Along the way, maps show the movement of troops, and wall panels cover the build-up to the attack, as seen from both sides. Note the clever division of information: To the left and in red is the story of the "government" (a.k.a. Hanoverians/Whigs/English, led by the Duke of Cumberland); to right, in blue, is the Jacobites' perspective (Prince Charlie and his Highlander/French supporters).

But you, like Charlie, don't make it to London—in the dark room at the end, you can hear Jacobite commanders arguing over whether to retreat back to Scotland. Pessimistic about their chances of receiving more French support, they decide to U-turn, and so do you. Heading back up north, you'll get some insight into some of the strategizing that went on behind the scenes.

By the time you reach the end of the hall, it's the night before the battle. Round another bend into a dark passage and listen to the voices of the anxious troops. While the English slept soundly in their tents (recovering from celebrating the Duke's 25th birthday), the scrappy and exhausted Jacobite Highlanders struggled through the night to reach the battlefield (abandoning their plan of a surprise attack at Nairn and instead retreating back toward Inverness).

At last the two sides meet. As you wait outside the theater for the next showing, study the chart depicting how the forces were arranged on the battlefield. Once inside the theater, you'll soon be surrounded by the views and sounds of a windswept moor. An impressive four-minute **360° movie** projects the reenacted battle with you right in the center of the action (the violence is realistic; young kids should probably sit this one out). If it hasn't hit you already, the movie drives home how truly outmatched the Jacobites were, and what a hopeless and tragic day it was for them.

Leave the movie, then enter the last room. Here you'll find **period weapons**, including ammunition and artifacts found on the battlefield, as well as **historical depictions** of the battle. You'll also find a section describing the detective work required to piece together the story from historical evidence. On the far end is a huge map, with narration explaining the combat you've just experienced while giving you a bird's-eye view of the field you're about to roam through. Collect your free battlefield **audioguide.** The doors in front of you lead outside.

From the back wall of the Visitors Centre, survey the battlefield. In the foreground is a cottage used as a makeshift hospital during the conflict (it's decorated as it would have been then). To the east (south of the River Nairn) is the site that Lord George Murray originally chose for the action. In the end, he failed to convince Prince Charlie of its superiority, and the battle was held here—with disastrous consequences. Although not far from Culloden, the River Nairn site was miles away tactically, and things might have turned out differently for the Jacobites had the battle taken place there instead.

Head left, down to the **battlefield.** Your GPS guide knows where you are, and the attendant will give you directions on where to start. As you walk along the path, stop each time you hear the "ping" sound (if you keep going, you'll confuse the satellite). The basic audioguide will stop you 10 times on the battlefield—at the Jacobite front line, the Hanoverian front line, and more—taking a minimum of 30 minutes to complete the walking tour. Each stop has additional information on everything from the Brown Bess musket to who was standing on what front line—how long this part of the tour takes depends on how much you want to hear. Notice how uneven and boggy the ground is in parts here, and imagine trying to run across this hummocky terrain with all your gear, toward your almost-certain death.

As you pass by the **mass graves,** marked by small headstones, realize that entire clans fought, died, and were buried together. (The fallen were identified by the clan badge on their caps.) The Mackintosh grave alone was 77 yards long.

When you've finished your walking tour, re-enter the hall where you left, return your audioguide (before 17:50), then catch the last part of the exhibit, which covers the aftermath of the battle. As you leave the building, hang a left to see the wall of **protruding bricks,** each representing a soldier who died. The handful of Hanoverian casualties are on the left (about 50); the rest of the long wall's raised bricks represent the multitude of dead Jacobites (about 1,500).

If you're having trouble grasping the significance of this battle, play a game of "What if?" If Bonnie Prince Charlie had persevered on this campaign and taken the throne, he likely wouldn't have plunged Britain into the Seven Years' War with France (his ally). And increased taxes on either side of that war led directly to the French and American revolutions. So if the Jacobites had won...the American colonies might still be part of the British Empire today.

Clava Cairns

Scotland is littered with reminders of prehistoric peoples—especially along the coast of the Moray Firth—but the Clava Cairns are

among the best-preserved, most interesting, and easiest to reach. You'll find them nestled in the spooky countryside just beyond Culloden Battlefield. These "Balnauran of Clava" are Neolithic burial chambers dating from 3,000 to 4,000 years ago. Although they simply look like giant piles of rocks in a sparsely forested clearing, they warrant a closer look to appreciate the prehistoric logic behind them. (The site is well-explained by informative plaques.) There are three structures: a central "ring cairn" with an open space in the center but no access to it, flanked by two "passage cairns," which were once covered. The entrance shaft in each passage cairn lines up with the setting sun at the winter solstice. Each cairn is surrounded by a stone circle, injecting this site with even more mystery.

Cost and Hours: Free, always open.

Getting There: Just after passing Culloden Battlefield on B9006 (coming from Inverness), signs on the right point to *Clava Cairns*. Follow this twisty road to the free parking lot by the stones. Skip it if you don't have a car.

Cawdor Castle

Homey and intimate, this castle is still the residence of the Dowager (read: widow) Countess of Cawdor, a local aristocratic

branch of the Campbell family. The castle's claim to fame is its connection to Shakespeare's *Macbeth*, in which the three witches correctly predict that the protagonist will be granted the title "Thane of Cawdor." The castle is not used as a setting in the play—which takes place in Inverness, 300 years before this castle was built—but Shakespeare's dozen or so references to "Cawdor" are enough for the marketing machine to kick in. Today, virtually nothing tangibly ties Cawdor to the Bard or to the real-life Macbeth. But even if you ignore the Shakespeare lore, the castle is worth a visit.

The chatty, friendly docents (including Jean at the front desk, who can say "welcome" and "mind your head" in 60 different languages) give the castle an air of intimacy—most are residents of the neighboring village of Cawdor, and act as though they're old friends with the Dowager Countess (many probably are). Entertaining posted explanations—written by the countess' late husband, the sixth Earl of Cawdor—bring the castle to life, and make you wish you'd known the old chap. While many of today's castles are still residences for the aristocracy, Cawdor feels even more lived-in than the norm—you can imagine the Dowager Countess stretching out in front of the fireplace with a good book. Notice her geraniums in every room.

Stops on the tour include a tapestry-laden bedroom and a "tartan passage" speckled with modern paintings. In another bedroom (just before the stairs back down) is a tiny pencil sketch by Salvador Dalí. Inside the base of the tower, near the end of the tour, is the castle's proud symbol: a holly tree dating from 1372. According to the beloved legend, a donkey leaned against this tree to mark the spot where the castle was to be built—which it was, around the tree. (The tree is no longer alive, but its withered trunk is still propped up in the same position. No word on the donkey.)

The **gardens,** included with the ticket, are also worth exploring, with some 18th-century linden trees, a hedge maze (not open to the public), and several surprising species (including sequoia and redwood). In May and June, the laburnum arbors drip with yellow blossoms.

The nearby remote-feeling **village of Cawdor**—with a few houses, a village shop, and a tavern—is also worth a look if you've got time to kill.

Cost and Hours: £8, good £3 guidebook explains the family and the rooms, May–early Oct daily 10:00–17:30, last entry at 17:00, gardens open until 18:00, closed early Oct–April, tel. 01667/404-401, www.cawdorcastle.com.

Getting There: It's on B9090, just off A96, about 10 miles east of Inverness (six miles beyond Culloden and the Clava Cairns). Without a car, you can either take a guided tour from Inverness (ask at the TI), or hop on public bus #1 or #1A—the same ones that go to Culloden—from central Inverness (hourly, 55 minutes, get on at Queensgate stop, check with driver that bus goes all the way to Cawdor, 15-minute walk from Cawdor Church bus stop to castle, last bus back to Inverness around 18:45).

BETWEEN INVERNESS AND EDINBURGH

Pitlochry and Stirling

To break up the trip between Inverness and Edinburgh (3 hours by car, 3.5 hours by train), consider stopping over at one of these two worthwhile destinations. The town of Pitlochry, right on the train route, mixes whisky and hillwalking with a dash of countryside charm. Farther south, the historic city of Stirling boasts an impressive castle, a monument to a Scottish hero (William "Braveheart" Wallace), and one of the country's most important battle sites (Bannockburn).

Planning Your Time

Visiting both Pitlochry and Stirling on a one-day drive from Inverness to Edinburgh is doable but busy (especially since part of Pitlochry's allure is slowing down to taste the whisky).

Pleasant Pitlochry is well-located, a quick detour off of the main A9 highway from Inverness to Edinburgh (via Perth) or an easy stop for train travelers. The town deserves an overnight for whisky-lovers, or for those who really want to relax in small-town Scotland. Though many find the town of Pitlochry appealing, it lacks the rugged Highlands scenery and easy access to other major sights found in Oban and Glencoe.

Stirling, off the busy A9/M9 motorway between Perth and Edinburgh, is well worth a sightseeing stop, especially for historians and romantics interested in Scottish history. (If skipping Stirling, notice that you can take M90 due south over the Firth of Forth to connect Perth and Edinburgh.) Stirling also works well as a stop-off between Edinburgh and points west (such as Glasgow or Oban)—just take the northern M9/A80 route instead of more direct M8.

Between Inverness & Edinburgh

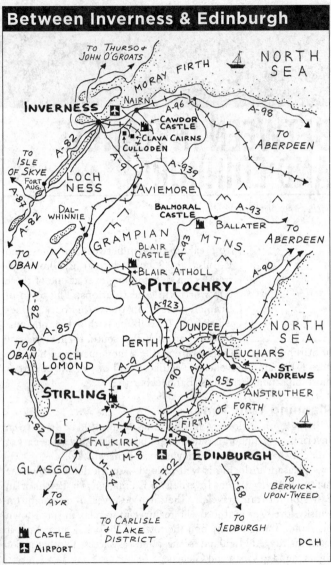

TO THURSO &
JOHN O'GROATS

MORAY FIRTH

NORTH
SEA

INVERNESS

NAIRN

A-96

A-98

CAWDOR
CASTLE

CLAVA CAIRNS

CULLODEN

TO
ABERDEEN

TO
ISLE
OF SKYE

A-82

A-9

A-939

FORT
AUG.

A-87

A-82

LOCH
NESS

DAL-
WHINNIE

AVIEMORE

BALMORAL
CASTLE

A-93

BALLATER

TO
ABERDEEN

TO
OBAN

GRAMPIAN

MTNS.

BLAIR
CASTLE

A-93

A-82

A-85

BLAIR ATHOLL

PITLOCHRY

A-923

A-90

TO
OBAN

PERTH

DUNDEE

NORTH
SEA

LOCH
LOMOND

A-9

A-92

M-90

LEUCHARS

ST.
ANDREWS

STIRLING

A-955

ANSTRUTHER

FIRTH
OF
FORTH

A-82

FALKIRK

M-8

GLASGOW

M-74

A-702

EDINBURGH

TO
AYR

TO CARLISLE
& LAKE
DISTRICT

A-68

TO
JEDBURGH

TO
BERWICK-
UPON-TWEED

🏰 CASTLE
✈ AIRPORT

DCH

Pitlochry

This likable tourist town, famous for its whisky and its hillwalking (both beloved by Scots), makes an enjoyable overnight stop

on the way between Inverness and Edinburgh. Just outside the craggy Highlands, Pitlochry is set amid pastoral rolling hills that offer plenty of forest hikes (brochures at TI). A salmon ladder climbs alongside the lazy river (free viewing area—best in May and June, 10-minute walk from town).

Orientation to Pitlochry

(area code: 01796)

Plucky little Pitlochry (pop. 2,500) lines up along its tidy, tourist-minded main road, where you'll find the train station, bus stops, the TI, and bike rental. The River Tummel runs parallel to the main road, a few steps away. Most distilleries are a short drive out of town, but you can walk to the two best; see my self-guided hillwalk, below. Navigate easily by following the black directional signs to Pitlochry's handful of sights.

Tourist Information

The helpful TI provides train schedules, books rooms for a £4 fee, and sells good maps for walks and scenic drives (July–mid-Sept Mon–Sat 9:00–19:00, Sun 9:30–17:30; mid-Sept–June Mon–Sat 9:30–17:30, Sun 10:00–16:00; exit from station and follow small road to the right with trains behind you, turn right on Atholl Road, and walk 5 minutes to TI on left, at #22; tel. 01796/472-215, pitlochry@visitscotland.com).

Helpful Hints

Bike Rental: Escape Route Bikes, located across the street and a block from the TI (away from town), rents a variety of bikes for adults and kids (£10/4 hours, £18/24 hours, price varies by type of bike and includes helmets and lock if you ask, Mon–Sat 9:00–17:30, Sun 10:00–17:00, shorter hours in winter, 3 Atholl Road, tel. 01796/473-859, www.escape-route.biz).

Self-Guided Hillwalk

Pitlochry Whisky Walk

If you've ever suspected you were a hobbit in a previous life, spend an afternoon hillwalking from downtown Pitlochry to a pair of top distilleries. The entire loop trip takes two to three hours, depending on how long you linger in the distilleries (at least 45 minutes to an hour of walking each way). It's a good way to see some green rolling hills, especially if you've only experienced urban Scotland. The walk is largely uphill on the way to the Edradour Distillery; wear good shoes, bring a rain jacket just in case, and be happy that you'll stroll easily downhill *after* you've had your whisky samples.

At the TI, pick up the *Pitlochry Walks* brochure (£1). You'll be taking the **Edradour Walk** (marked on directional signs with the yellow hiker icons; on the map it's a series of yellow dots). Leave the TI and head left along busy A924. The walk can be done by going either direction, but I'll describe it counterclockwise.

Within 10 minutes, you'll come to **Bell's Blair Athol Distillery.** If you're a whisky buff, stop in here (described under "Sights in Pitlochry"). Otherwise, hold out for the much more atmospheric Edradour. After passing a few B&Bs and suburban homes, you'll see a sign (marked *Edradour Walk*) on the left side of the road, leading you up and off the highway. You'll come to a clearing, and as the road gets steeper, you'll see signs directing you 50 yards off the main path to see the "Black Spout"—a wonderful waterfall well worth a few extra steps.

At the top of the hill, you'll arrive in another clearing, where a narrow path leads along a field. Low rolling hills surround you in all directions. It seems like there's not another person around for miles, with just thistles to keep you company. It's an easy 20 minutes to the distillery from here.

Stop into the **Edradour Distillery** (also described later). After the tour, leave the distillery, heading right, following the paved road (Old North Road). In about five minutes, there's a sign that seems to point right into the field. Take the small footpath that runs along the left side of the road. (If you see the driveway with stone lions on both sides, you've gone a few steps too far.) You'll walk parallel to the route you took getting to the distillery, and then you'll head back into the forest. Cross the footbridge and make a left (as the map indicates), staying on the wide road. You'll pass a B&B, and hear traffic noises as you emerge out of the forest. The trail leads back to the highway, with the TI a few blocks ahead on the right.

Sights in Pitlochry

Distillery Tours—The cute **Edradour Distillery** (ED-rah-dower), the smallest in Scotland, takes pride in making its whisky with a minimum of machinery. Small white-and-red buildings are nestled in an impossibly green Scottish hillside. Wander through the buildings and take the £5 guided tour (3/hour in summer, 2/hour in winter, 50 minutes). They offer a 10-minute A/V show and, of course, a free sample dram. Unlike the bigger distilleries, they allow you to take photos of the equipment. If you like the whisky, buy some here and support the local economy—this is one of the few independently owned distilleries left in Scotland (May–Oct Mon–Sat 10:00–17:00, Sun 12:00–17:00; June–Sept Mon–Sat opens at 9:30, Nov–April Mon–Sat 10:00–16:00, Sun 12:00–16:00, Jan–Feb closed Sun; last tour departs one hour before closing, tel. 01796/472-095, www.edradour.co.uk). Most come to the distillery by car (follow signs from the main road, 2.5 miles into the countryside), but you can also get there on a peaceful hiking trail that you'll have all to yourself (follow my "Pitlochry Whisky Walk," earlier).

The big, ivy-covered **Bell's Blair Athol Distillery** is more conveniently located (about a half-mile from the town center) and more corporate-feeling, offering £5 45-minute tours with a wee taste at the end (Easter–Oct tours depart 2/hour Mon–Sat 9:30–17:00, July-Aug until 17:30, June–Oct also Sun 12:00–17:00, last tour departs one hour before closing; Nov–Easter tours depart Mon–Fri at 11:00, 13:00, and 15:00, closed Sat–Sun; tel. 01796/482-003, www.discovering-distilleries.com/blairathol).

Pitlochry Power Station—The station, adjacent to the salmon ladder, offers a mildly entertaining exhibit about hydroelectric power in the region (free, April–Oct Mon–Fri 10:00–17:00, closed Sat–Sun, July–Aug also open weekends, closed Nov–March, tel. 01796/473-152). Although walkers can reach this easily by crossing the footbridge from the town center (about a 15-minute walk), drivers will head east out of town (toward Bell's Blair Athol Distillery), then turn right on Bridge Road, cross the river, and backtrack to the power station.

Theater—From May through October, the **Pitlochry Festival Theatre** presents a different play every night and concerts on some

PITLOCHRY AND STIRLING

Sundays (both £17–27 Sun–Thu, £18–28 Fri–Sat, purchase tickets online, at TI, or theater—same price, box office open daily 10:00–17:00, tel. 01796/484-626, www.pitlochryfestivaltheatre.com).

Garden—The **Explorers Garden,** adjacent to the theater, has a six-acre woodland garden with plants and wildflowers from around the world (£3, April–Oct daily 10:00–17:00, last entry at 16:15, tel. 01796/484-626, www.explorersgarden.com).

Near Pitlochry

Balmoral Castle—The Queen spends each August and September here on her 50,000-acre private estate, located within Cairngorms National Park. The grounds and the ballroom are open to visitors part of the year (except when the Queen's in residence), but they're overpriced (£8.70, audioguide requires £5 deposit, April–July 10:00–17:00, closed Aug–March, tel. 013397/42534, www.balmoral castle.com).

For a free peek at another royal landmark, stop at **Crathie Kirk,** the small but charming parish church where the royal family worships when they are at Balmoral, and where Queen Victoria's beloved servant John Brown is buried. The church is just across the highway from the Balmoral parking lot.

Getting There: Balmoral is on A93, midway between Ballater and Braemar, about 50 miles northeast of Pitlochry and about 75 miles southeast of Inverness.

Sleeping in Pitlochry

$$ Craigroyston House is a quaint, large Victorian country house with eight Laura Ashley–style bedrooms run by charming Gretta and Douglas Maxwell (Db-£70–90, less off-season, family

Sleep Code

(£1 = about $1.60, country code: 44, area code: 01796)
S = Single, **D** = Double/Twin, **T** = Triple, **Q** = Quad, **b** = bathroom, **s** = shower only.

To help you sort easily through these listings, I've divided the rooms into two categories based on the price for a standard double room with bath (during high season):

$$ Higher Priced—Most rooms £50 or more.
$ Lower Priced—Most rooms less than £50.

Prices can change without notice; verify the hotel's current rates online or by email. For other updates, see www .ricksteves.com/update.

room, cash only, above and behind the TI—small gate at back of parking lot—and next to the church at 2 Lower Oakfield, tel. & fax 01796/472-053, www.craigroyston.co.uk, reservations@craig royston.co.uk).

$ Pitlochry's fine **hostel** has 62 beds in 12 rooms, including some private and family rooms. It's on Knockard Road, well-signed from the town center, about a five-minute walk above the main drag and offering nice views (£18 bunks in 3- to 8-bed rooms, Db-£60; £2 more for non-members, breakfast-£4.25, packed lunch-£5, Internet access and Wi-Fi, self-service laundry, kitchen, office open 7:00–10:00 & 17:00–23:00, tel. 01796/472-308, www.syha.org.uk, pitlochry@syha.org.uk).

Eating in Pitlochry

Plenty of options line the main drag, including several bakeries selling picnic supplies. For a heartier meal, try **Victoria's** restaurant and coffee shop, located midway between the train station and the TI (£5–9 sandwiches, £9 pizzas, £8–12 lunch entrées, £11–20 dinners, daily 10:00–21:00, patio seating, at corner of memorial garden at 45 Atholl Road, tel. 01796/472-670) or **Fern Cottage**, just behind Victoria's (pre-theater £18–22 dinner specials 17:30–18:45, tel. 01796/473-840). **Port-na-Craig Inn** is a fancy option across from the theater (tel. 01796/472-777).

Pitlochry Connections

The train station is open daily 8:00–18:00 (maybe less in winter).

From Pitlochry by Train to: Inverness (every 1.5–2 hours, 1.5–1.75 hours), **Stirling** (every 1.5–2 hours, 1.25 hours, some transfer in Perth), **Edinburgh** (6/day direct, 2 hours), **Glasgow** (9/day, 1.5–1.75 hours, most transfer in Perth). Train info: tel. 08457-484-950, www.nationalrail.co.uk.

PITLOCHRY AND STIRLING

Stirling

Once the Scottish capital, the quaint city of Stirling (pop. 41,000) is a mini-Edinburgh with lots of character and a trio of attractions: a dramatic castle, dripping with history and boasting sweeping views; the William Wallace Monument, honoring the real-life Braveheart; and the Bannockburn Heritage Centre, marking the site of Robert the Bruce's victorious battle.

Orientation to Stirling

(area code: 01786)

Stirling's old town is situated along a long, narrow, steep hill, with the castle at its apex. The **TI** is near the base of the old town (daily 10:00–17:00, 41 Dumbarton Road, tel. 01786/475-019, stirling @visitscotland.com).

Getting Around Stirling

Stirling's three main sights (Stirling Castle, the Wallace Monument, and the Bannockburn Heritage Centre) are difficult to reach by foot from the center of town, but are easily accessible by frequent public bus (the bus station is a short walk from the train station) or by taxi (£4–5).

Sights in Stirling

▲Stirling Castle

"He who holds Stirling, holds Scotland." These fateful words have proven, more often than not, to be true. Stirling Castle's strategic position—perched on a volcanic crag overlooking a bridge over the River Forth, the primary passage between the Lowlands and the Highlands—has long been the key to Scotland. This castle of the Stuart kings is one of Scotland's most historic and popular. Offering spectacular views over a gentle countryside, and a mildly interesting but steadily improving exhibit inside, Stirling is worth a look.

Cost and Hours: £9, daily April–Sept 9:30–18:00, Oct–March 9:30–17:00, palace apartments reopen in spring 2011 after renovation, last entry 45 minutes before closing, tel. 01786/450-000, www.stirlingcastle.gov.uk.

Getting There: Similar to Edinburgh's castle, Stirling Castle sits at the very tip of a steep old town. If you enter Stirling by car, follow the *Stirling Castle* signs, twist up the mazelike roads to the esplanade, and park at the £2 lot just outside the castle gate. Without a car, it's a bit more complicated: From the train or bus station, you can either hike the 20-minute uphill route to the castle, or you can take a taxi (about £4 to castle).

Tours: Posted information is skimpy, so a tour or audioguide is important for bringing the site to life. You can take the included 45-minute guided tour (generally hourly April–June, 2/hour July–Sept, 4/day Oct–March, depart from the Castle Close just inside the entry, includes a tour of Argyll's Lodging, a 17th-century townhouse) or rent the very good £2 audioguide from the kiosk near the ticket window. Knowledgeable docents posted throughout can tell you more.

Background: Stirling marks the site of two epic medieval battles where famous Scotsmen defeated huge English armies despite impossible odds: In 1297, William Wallace (a.k.a. "Braveheart") fended off an invading English army at the Battle of Stirling Bridge. And in 1314, Robert the Bruce won the battle of nearby Bannockburn. Soon after, the castle became the primary residence of the Stuart monarchs, who turned it into a showpiece of Scotland (and a symbol of one-upmanship against England). But when the Crown moved to London, Stirling's prominence waned. The military, which took over the castle during the Jacobite Wars of the 18th century, bulked it up and converted it into a garrison—damaging much of its delicate beauty. Since 1966, the fortress has been undergoing an extensive and costly restoration to bring it back to its glory days and make it, once again, one of Britain's premier castles.

❍ Self-Guided Tour: From the parking lot at the esplanade, go through the gate to buy your ticket (ask about tour times, and consider renting the audioguide), then head up into the castle through another gate. If you have time to kill before your tour, dip into the grassy courtyard on the left to reach an introductory **castle exhibition** about the history of the town and its fortress. Historians at Stirling are proud of the work they've done to rebuild the castle—and they're not shy about saying so.

Then head up through the main gateway into the **Outer Close.** Tours depart from just to your right, near the Grand Battery, which boasts cannon-and-rampart views. Down the hill along this wall is the Great Kitchens exhibit (where mannequin cooks oversee medieval recipes); below that the North Gate leads to the Nether Bailey (dating from the castle's later days as a military base). Back in the Outer Close, at the top of the courtyard (to your left as you enter), is a narrow passageway lined with exhibits about Stirling's medieval craftspeople.

Hike up into the **Inner Close,** where you're surrounded by Scottish history. Each of the very different buildings in this complex was built by a different monarch. Facing downhill, you'll see the Great Hall straight ahead. This grand structure—Scotland's biggest medieval banqueting hall—was built by the great Renaissance king James IV. Step inside the grand, empty-feeling space to appreciate its fine flourishes. The Chapel Royal, where Mary, Queen of Scots was crowned in 1543, is to your left and also worth a visit. To your right is the Palace, which reopens in spring 2011 after the restoration of six ground-floor apartments, done up as they might have looked in the mid-16th century. Costumed performers play the role of palace attendants, happy to chat with you about palace life. Behind you is the King's Old Building, with a regimental (military) museum (closes 45 minutes before the castle).

▲William Wallace Monument

Commemorating the Scottish hero better known to Americans as "Braveheart," this sandstone tower—built during a wave of Scottish nationalism in the mid-19th century—marks the Abbey Craig hill on the outskirts of Stirling. This is where Wallace gathered forces for his largest-scale victory against England's King Edward I, in 1297. To learn more about William Wallace, see page 607.

From the base of the monument, you can see the Stirling Bridge—a stone version that replaced the original wooden one. Looking out from the same vantage point as Wallace, imagine how the famous battle played out, and consider why the location was so important in the battle (explained in more detail inside the monument).

After entering the monument, pick up the worthwhile £1 audioguide. You'll first encounter a passionate talking Wallace replica, explaining his defiant stand against Edward I. As you listen, ogle Wallace's five-and-a-half-foot-long broadsword (and try to imagine drawing it from a scabbard on your back at a dead run). Then take a spin through a hall of other Scottish heroes. Finally, climb the 246 narrow steps inside the tower for grand views. The stairways are extremely tight and require some maneuvering—claustrophobes be warned.

Cost and Hours: £7.50, £1 audioguide, daily July–Aug 10:00–18:00, April–June and Sept–Oct 10:00–17:00, Nov–March 10:30–16:00, last entry 45 minutes before closing, café and gift shop, tel. 01786/472-140, www.nationalwallacemonument.com.

Getting There: It's two miles northeast of Stirling on A8, signposted from the city center. You can catch a public bus from the Stirling bus station (a short walk south of the train station) to the the Monument's parking lot (10/hour on a number of different bus lines, 15 minutes). Taxis cost about £5. From the parking lot's Visitors Pavilion, you'll need to hike (a very steep 10 minutes) or take a shuttle bus up the hill to the monument itself.

PITLOCHRY AND STIRLING

▲Bannockburn Heritage Centre

Just to the south of Stirling proper is the Bannockburn Heritage Centre, commemorating what many Scots view as their nation's most significant military victory over the invading English: the Battle of Bannockburn, won by a Scottish army led by Robert the Bruce against England's King Edward II in 1314.

In simple terms, Robert—who was first and foremost a politician—found himself out of political options after years of failed diplomatic attempts to make peace with the strong-arming English. Wallace's execution left a vacuum in military leadership, and eventually Robert stepped in, waging a successful guerrilla campaign that came to a head as young Edward's army marched to Stirling. Although the Scots were greatly outnumbered, their strategy and use of terrain at Bannockburn allowed them to soundly beat the English and drive Edward out of Scotland for good. For more about Robert the Bruce, read the sidebar on page 610.

This victory is so legendary among the Scots that the country's unofficial national anthem, "Flower of Scotland"—written 600 years after the battle—focuses on this one event. (CDs with a version of this song performed by The Corries can be purchased at the Heritage Centre. Buy one and learn the song, and you might soon find yourself singing along at a pub.)

The Heritage Centre, though small, has excellent exhibits and a worthwhile film about the battle and events leading up to it. You can even try on a real chainmail shirt and helmet.

Cost and Hours: £5.50, March–Oct daily 10:00–17:00, April–Sept until 17:30, last entry 45 minutes before closing, closed Nov–Feb, tel. 0844/493-2139, www.nts.org.uk/Property/95.

Getting There: It's two miles south of Stirling on A872, off M80/M9. For non-drivers, it's an easy bus ride from the Stirling bus station (a short walk south from the train station; several bus lines run on this route, 6/hour, 9–15 minutes).

Stirling Connections

From Stirling by Train to: Edinburgh (2/hour, 50 minutes), **Glasgow** (3/hour, 30–45 minutes), **Pitlochry** (every 1.5–2 hours, 1.25 hours, most transfer in Perth), **Inverness** (every 1.5–2 hours, 2.75–3 hours, most transfer in Perth). Train info: tel. 08457-484-950, www.nationalrail.co.uk.

BRITISH HISTORY AND CULTURE

Britain was created by force and held together by force. It's really a nation of the 19th century, when this rich Victorian-era empire reached its financial peak. Its traditional industry, buildings, and the popularity of the notion of "Great" Britain are a product of its past wealth.

To best understand the many fascinating guides you'll encounter in your travels, have a basic handle on the sweeping story of this land. (Generally speaking, the nice and bad stories are not true... and the boring ones are.)

What's So Great About Britain?

Regardless of the revolution we had 230-some years ago, many American travelers feel that they "go home" to Britain. This most popular tourist destination has a strange influence and power over us. The more you know of Britain's roots, the better you'll get in touch with your own.

Geographically, the Isle of Britain is small (about the size of Uganda or Idaho)—600 miles long and 300 miles at its widest point. England occupies the southeastern part of Britain (with about 60 percent of its land—similar in size to Louisiana—and 80 percent of its population). England's highest mountain (Scafell Pike in the Lake District) is 3,206 feet, a foothill by our standards. The population is a fifth that of the United States. At its peak in the mid-1800s, Britain owned one-fifth of the world and accounted for more than half the planet's industrial output. Today, the Empire is down to the Isle of Britain itself and a few token, troublesome scraps, such as the Falklands, Gibraltar, and Northern Ireland.

Economically, Great Britain's industrial production is about 5 percent of the world's total. After emerging from a recession in 1992, Britain's economy enjoyed its longest period of expansion on record. But in 2008, the global economic slowdown, tight credit, and falling home prices pushed Britain back into a recession.

Culturally, Britain is still a world leader. Her heritage, culture, and people cannot be measured in traditional units of power. London is a major exporter of actors, movies, and theater; of rock and classical music; and of writers, painters, and sculptors.

Ethnically, the British Isles are a mix of the descendants of the early Celtic natives (in Scotland, Ireland, Wales, and Cornwall), descendants of the invading Anglo-Saxons who took southeast England in the Dark Ages, and descendants of the conquering Normans of the 11th century...not to mention more recent immigrants from around the world. Cynics call the United Kingdom an English Empire ruled by London, whose dominant Anglo-Saxon English (50 million) far outnumber their Celtic brothers and sisters (10 million).

Politically, Britain is ruled by the House of Commons, with some guidance from the mostly figurehead Queen and House of Lords. Just as the United States Congress is dominated by Democrats and Republicans, Britain's Parliament is dominated by two parties: left-leaning Labour and right-leaning Conservative ("Tories"). Recently the center-left Liberal Democrats ("Lib Dems") have made some inroads, but still remain a distant third.

Strangely, Britain's "constitution" is not one single document; the government's structures and policies are based on centuries of tradition, statues, and doctrine, and much of it is not actually in writing. While this might seem potentially troublesome—if not dangerous—the British body politic takes pride in its ethos of civility and mutual respect, which has long made this arrangement work.

The prime minister is the chief executive. He or she is not elected directly by voters; rather, he or she assumes power as the head of the party that wins a majority in Parliamentary elections. (If no party wins a clear majority—as none did in the 2010 election—it's a "hung parliament," and is usually resolved by at least two parties forming a coalition that adds up to a majority.) In the interest of protocol, the Queen symbolically "invites" the winner to form a "government" (administration). Instead of imposing term limits, the Brits allow their prime ministers to choose when to leave office. The ruling party also gets to choose when to hold elections, as long as it's within five years of the previous one—so prime ministers carefully schedule elections for times that (they hope) their party will win. (Breaking with tradition, the current coalition government has already announced an election for May 7, 2015.) When an election is announced, the Queen dissolves the parliament so the parties can focus on a short-and-sweet, one-month campaign.

In the 1980s, Conservatives were in charge under Prime Minister Margaret Thatcher and Prime Minister John Major. As proponents of traditional, Victorian values—community, family, hard work, thrift, and trickle-down economics—they took a Reaganesque approach to Britain's serious social and economic problems.

In 1997, a huge Labour victory brought Tony Blair to the prime ministership. Labour began shoring up a social-service system (health care, education, the minimum wage) undercut by years of Conservative rule. Blair started out as a respected and well-liked PM. But after he followed US President George W. Bush into war with Iraq, his popularity took a nosedive. In May of 2007, Blair announced that he would resign; a few weeks later, his Chancellor of the Exchequer and longtime colleague, Gordon Brown, was sworn in as Britain's new prime minister. Burdened with an economic crisis and lacking his predecessor's charisma, Brown never achieved a level of popularity anywhere near Blair's.

Elections in May of 2010 pitted Brown against a Conservative opponent, David Cameron, and a third-party Liberal Democrat challenger, Nick Clegg. Brown, Cameron, and Clegg participated in a series of three television debates—the first in UK history. Thanks to the economic crisis—and his own, characteristic stumbles (such as being caught on tape referring to a voter he'd just met as a "bigoted woman")—Brown failed to win a clear majority for his Labour Party. Clegg won acclaim for his performance in the debates, though ultimately his Lib Dems won barely more seats than in previous elections. Other smaller parties helped split the vote, and no party won the number of seats needed for a majority—resulting in the first "hung parliament" since 1974. After a few days of wrangling, the Conservatives and the Lib Dems formed a coalition government (the first since World War II), Gordon Brown stepped down, and David Cameron became the new prime minister.

Because of a huge—and growing—budget deficit, Cameron announced a program right after the election that would dramatically cut back spending and increase the VAT (Value-Added Tax—the national sales tax) from 17.5 to 20 percent. It remains to be seen whether these bold steps will return Britain to its previous prosperity, or douse the spark of economic recovery.

In the meantime, visitors to England might begin to notice the country's economic woes (locals grumbling about tax hikes or sudden closures of a tourist office or minor sight). However, Britain remains stronger, economically, than some of its fellow EU nations (such as Greece). And Brits are turning their attention to the summer of 2012, when the world's eyes will be on their capital city as London hosts the 30th Olympiad. As the city and country

Prime Minister David Cameron

David Cameron succeeded Gordon Brown as prime minister in May of 2010, and lives at #10 Downing Street with his wife, Samantha, and their young children. At 44, Cameron is the youngest PM in two centuries. He heads the Conservative Party (the "Tories"), but he has never quite fit the stodgy Conservative image. In his college days at Oxford, there were rumors of wild parties and illicit drugs. He's known as "Dave" to his friends, and he developed a habit of riding his bike to work. Cameron rose quickly through the political ranks: He worked to re-elect Conservative PM John Major (1992), assisted the finance minister at #11 Downing Street (1992–1994), and was himself elected to Parliament in 2001, becoming head of the Conservative Party in 2005. By 2008, he was on the cover of *Time* magazine, which hailed him as the future of conservatism.

In 2010, Cameron's Conservative Party came to power. The prime minister is not elected directly by popular vote (the way the American president is), but rules as leader of the party that garners the most votes in Parliamentary elections. The 2010 elections were hardly a sweeping Conservative mandate: Three parties split the vote, forcing Cameron's Conservatives to form a coalition with the (more left-leaning) Liberal Democrat Party. The Labour Party, which had held power in Britain for 13 years under Gordon Brown and Tony Blair, is the coalition's chief opposition.

Politically, Cameron is a moderate Conservative who is more pragmatic than ideological. Socially, he's "liberal," advocating for personal freedoms—gay rights, decriminalization of drugs, allowing hunting and smoking, and ensuring citizens' privacy against government intrusion. Fiscally, he rails against big-government waste. In his early days as PM, he delivered a sober speech about a time of austerity looming on Britain's horizon, when belts would need to be tightened to get the budget under control. His most right-of-center stance is his support for distancing Britain from the euro and the European Union.

Despite his personal appeal, Cameron can't quite shake the Conservatives' image as the party of the upper class. Cameron was born rich, married rich, and has worked within the corporate culture. His colleagues form an old boys' network from his days at Eton, England's most exclusive prep school. The Mayor of London, Boris Johnson, is not only an old Oxford frat buddy but also a distant cousin. As the Conservatives try to unite the country to solve Britain's severe economic and cultural problems, it remains to be seen whether David Cameron has brought a fresh enough approach to #10.

spiff up even more than usual for the Olympics, the Brits can look forward to an even brighter future.

Challenges Facing Today's Britain

Great as Britain is, the country has its share of challenges. You'll likely hear people talking about some of the following hot-button topics during your visit: the recession, the war in Afghanistan, terrorism, immigration, and binge-drinking.

From early 2008 to late 2009, the British economy shrank more than 6 percent—the largest decline since the Great Depression. While the country came out of its recession in early 2010, that summer it still suffered from a 7.8 percent unemployment rate. There's been talk of a "double-dip" downturn. In this era of uncertainty, British consumers don't seem to be spending much as they try to gauge the effects of Cameron's budget cuts.

While British forces ended combat operations in Iraq in April of 2009, its troops remain in Afghanistan, and every new casualty re-invigorates public debate about the merits and possible outcomes of this war.

Like the US, Britain has been coping with its own string of terrorist threats and attacks. On the morning of July 7, 2005, London's commuters were rocked by four different bombs that killed dozens across the city. In the summer of 2006, authorities foiled a plot to carry liquid bombs onto a plane (resulting in the liquid ban air travelers are still experiencing today). On June 29, 2007, two car bombs were discovered (and defused) near London's Piccadilly Circus, and the next day, a flaming car drove into the baggage-claim level at Glasgow Airport. Most Brits have accepted that they now live with the possibility of terrorism at home—and that life must go on.

Britain has taken aggressive measures to prevent future attacks, such as installing "CCTV" (closed-circuit) surveillance cameras everywhere, in both public and private places. (You'll frequently see signs warning you that you're being filmed.) These cameras have already proved helpful in piecing together the events leading up to an attack, but as Brits trade their privacy for security, many wonder if they've given up too much.

The terrorist threats have also highlighted issues relating to Britain's large immigrant population (nearly 4 million). Second-generation Muslims—born in Britain, but who strongly identify with other Muslims rather than their British neighbors—were responsible for the July 2005 bombs. Some Brits reacted to the event known as "7/7" as if all the country's Muslims were to blame. At the same time, a handful of radical Islamic clerics began to justify the bombers' violent actions. Unemployment and the economic downturn further stretch the already strained relations between communities within Britain.

The large Muslim population is just one thread in the tapestry of today's Britain. While nine out of ten Brits are white, the country has large minority groups, mainly from Britain's former overseas colonies: India, Pakistan, Bangladesh, Africa, the Caribbean, and many other places. But despite the tensions between some groups, for the most part Britain is well integrated, with minorities represented in most (if not all) walks of life.

Recently another wave of immigration has hit Britain. Throughout the British Isles, you'll see many Eastern Europeans (mostly Poles, Slovaks, and Lithuanians) working in restaurants, cafés, and B&Bs. These transplants—who started arriving after their home countries joined the EU in 2004—can make a lot more money working here than back home. British small-business owners have found these new arrivals to be polite, responsible, and affordable. While a few Brits complain that the new arrivals are taking jobs away from the natives, and others are frustrated that their English is often far from perfect, for the most part Britain has absorbed this new set of immigrants gracefully.

Over the last several years, Britain has seen an epidemic of binge-drinking among young people. A 2007 study revealed that one out of every three British men, and one out of every five British women, routinely drink to excess. It's become commonplace for young adults (typically from their mid-teens to mid-20s) to spend weekend nights drinking at pubs and carousing in the streets. (And they ratchet up the debauchery even more when celebrating a "stag night" or "hen night"—bachelor and bachelorette parties.) While sociologists and politicians scratch their heads about the causes and effects of this phenomenon, tourists are complaining about weekend noise and obnoxious (though generally harmless) young drunks on the streets.

Basic British History for the Traveler

When Julius Caesar landed on the misty and mysterious isle of Britain in 55 B.C., England entered the history books. The primitive Celtic tribes he conquered were themselves invaders (who had earlier conquered the even more mysterious people who built Stonehenge). The Romans built towns and roads, establishing their capital at Londinium. The Celtic natives in Scotland and Wales—consisting of Gaels, Picts, and Scots—were not easily subdued. The Romans built Hadrian's Wall near the Scottish border as protection against their troublesome northern neighbors. Even today, the Celtic language and influence are strongest in these far reaches of Britain.

As Rome fell, so fell Roman Britain, a victim of invaders and internal troubles. Barbarian tribes from Germany and Denmark,

Typical Castle Architecture

Castles were fortified residences for medieval nobles. Castles come in all shapes and sizes, but knowing a few general terms will help you understand them.

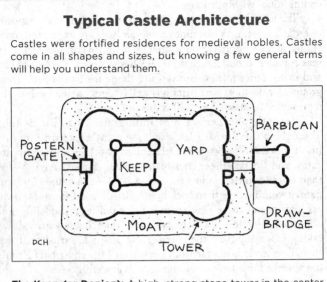

The Keep (or Donjon): A high, strong stone tower in the center of the castle complex that was the lord's home and refuge of last resort.

Great Hall: The largest room in the castle, serving as throne room, conference center, and dining hall.

The Yard (or Bailey or Ward): An open courtyard inside the castle walls.

Loopholes: Narrow slits in the walls (also called embrasures, arrow slits, or arrow loops) through which soldiers could

called Angles and Saxons, swept through the southern part of the island, establishing Angle-land. These were the days of the real King Arthur, possibly a Christianized Roman general who fought valiantly against invading barbarians, but in vain. In 793, England was hit with the first of two centuries of savage invasions by barbarians from Norway, called the Vikings or Norsemen. The island was plunged into 500 years of Dark Ages—wars, plagues, and poverty—lit only by the dim candle of a few learned Christian monks and missionaries trying to convert the barbarians. The sightseer sees little from this Anglo-Saxon period.

Modern England began with yet another invasion. William the Conqueror and his Norman troops crossed the English Channel from France in 1066. William crowned himself king in Westminster Abbey (where all subsequent coronations would take place) and began building the Tower of London. French-speaking Norman kings ruled the country for two centuries. Then followed two centuries of civil wars, with various noble families vying for shoot arrows at the enemy.

Towers: Tall structures serving as lookouts, chapels, living quarters, or the dungeon. Towers could be square or round, with either crenellated tops or conical roofs.

Turret: A small lookout tower projecting up from the top of the wall.

Moat: A ditch encircling the wall, often filled with water.

Wall Walk (or Allure): A pathway atop the wall where guards could patrol and where soldiers stood to fire at the enemy.

Parapet: Outer railing of the wall walk.

Crenellation: A gap-toothed pattern of stones atop the parapet.

Hoardings (or Gallery or Brattice): Wooden huts built onto the upper parts of the stone walls. They served as watch towers, living quarters, and fighting platforms.

Machicolation: A stone ledge jutting out from the wall, fitted with holes in the bottom. If the enemy was scaling the walls, soldiers could drop rocks or boiling oil down through the holes and onto the enemy below.

Barbican: A fortified gatehouse, sometimes a stand-alone building located outside the main walls.

Drawbridge: A bridge that could be raised or lowered, using counterweights or a chain-and-winch.

Portcullis: A heavy iron grille that could be lowered across the entrance.

Postern Gate: A small, unfortified side or rear entrance used during peacetime. In wartime, it could become a "sally-port" used to launch surprise attacks, or as an escape route.

---

the crown. In one of the most bitter feuds, the York and Lancaster families fought the Wars of the Roses, so-called because of the white and red flowers the combatants chose as their symbols. Rife with battles, intrigues, and kings, nobles, and ladies imprisoned and executed in the Tower, it's a wonder the country survived its rulers.

England was finally united by the "third-party" Tudor family. Henry VIII, a Tudor, was England's Renaissance king. He was handsome, athletic, highly sexed, a poet, a scholar, and a musician. He was also arrogant, cruel, gluttonous, and paranoid. He went through six wives in 40 years, divorcing, imprisoning, or beheading them when they no longer suited his needs.

Henry "divorced" England from the Catholic Church, establishing the Protestant Church of England (the Anglican Church) and setting in motion years of religious squabbles. He also "dissolved" the monasteries (circa 1540), left just the shells of many formerly glorious abbeys dotting the countryside, and

Royal Families: Past and Present

Royal Lineage

802-1066	Saxon and Danish kings
1066-1154	Norman invasion (William the Conqueror), Norman kings
1154-1399	Plantagenet (kings with French roots)
1399-1461	Lancaster
1462-1485	York
1485-1603	Tudor (Henry VIII, Elizabeth I)
1603-1649	Stuart (civil war and beheading of Charles I)
1649-1653	Commonwealth, no royal head of state
1653-1659	Protectorate, with Cromwell as Lord Protector
1660-1714	Stuart (Parliament replaces James II with Protestant heirs)
1714-1901	Hanover (four Georges, Victoria)
1901-1910	Saxe-Coburg (Edward VII)
1910-present	Windsor (George V, Edward VIII, George VI, Elizabeth II)

The Royal Family Today

It seems you can't pick up a British newspaper without some mention of the latest scandal or oddity involving the royal family. Here is the cast of characters:

Queen Elizabeth II wears the traditional crown of her great-great grandmother Victoria. Her husband is Prince Philip, who's not considered king.

pocketed their land and wealth for the crown.

Henry's daughter, Queen Elizabeth I, who reigned for 45 years, made England a great trading and naval power (defeating the Spanish Armada) and presided over the Elizabethan era of great writers (such as William Shakespeare) and scientists (such as Francis Bacon). But Elizabeth never married, so the English Parliament asked the Protestant ruler to the north, Scotland's King James (Elizabeth's cousin), if he'd like to inherit the English throne. The two nations have been tied together ever since.

The longstanding quarrel between England's divine-right kings and Parliament's nobles finally erupted into a civil war (1643). Parliament forces under the Protestant Puritan farmer Oliver Cromwell defeated—and beheaded—King Charles I. This civil war left its mark on much of what you'll see in Britain. Eventually, Parliament invited Charles' son to take the throne. This "restoration of the monarchy" was accompanied by a great colonial

Their son, Prince Charles (the Prince of Wales), is next in line to become king. In 1981, Charles married Lady Diana Spencer (Princess Di) who, after their bitter divorce, died in a car crash in 1997. Their two sons, William and Harry, are next in line to the throne after their father. In 2005, Charles married his longtime girlfriend, Camilla Parker Bowles, who is trying to gain respectability with the Queen and the public. But she's doesn't call herself a princess—she uses the title "Duchess of Cornwall."

Prince Charles' siblings are occasionally in the news: Princess Anne, Prince Andrew (who married and divorced Sarah "Fergie" Ferguson), and Prince Edward (who married Di look-alike Sophie Rhys-Jones).

But it's Prince Charles' sons who generate the tabloid buzz these days. Handsome Prince William (b. 1982), a graduate of Scotland's St. Andrews University and an officer in both the Royal Air Force and Royal Navy, serves as the royal family's public face at many charity events. There's endless speculation about his romantic interests, especially about his long-time, on-again-off-again girlfriend, Kate Middleton (a commoner he met at university). Whomever he marries may eventually become Britain's queen.

Redheaded Prince Harry (b. 1984) made a media splash as a bad boy when he wore a Nazi armband (as an ill-advised joke) to a costume party. Since then, he's proved his mettle as a career soldier, serving two months in Afghanistan (early 2008). In 2008, he and his regiment did charity work in Africa, and since then he's been training to become a pilot with the Army Air Corps. Harry's love life, like his brother's, is a popular topic for the tabloids.

For more on the monarchy, see www.royal.gov.uk.

---

expansion and the rebuilding of London (including Christopher Wren's St. Paul's Cathedral), which had been devastated by the Great Fire of 1666. Parliament gained ultimate authority over the throne when it deposed Catholic James II in 1688, guaranteeing a Protestant succession.

Britain grew as a naval superpower, colonizing and trading with all parts of the globe (although it lost its most important colony to ungrateful Americans in 1776). Admiral Horatio Nelson's victory over Napoleon's fleet at the Battle of Trafalgar secured her naval superiority ("Britannia rules the waves"), and 10 years later, the Duke of Wellington stomped Napoleon on land at Waterloo. Nelson and Wellington—both buried in London's St. Paul's Cathedral—are memorialized by many arches, columns, and squares throughout England.

Economically, Britain led the world into the Industrial Age with her mills, factories, coal mines, and trains. By the time of

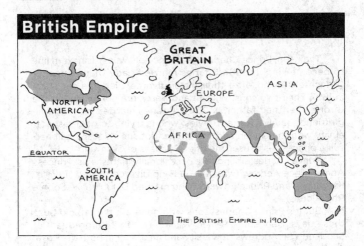

British Empire

GREAT BRITAIN

NORTH AMERICA

EUROPE

ASIA

AFRICA

EQUATOR

SOUTH AMERICA

THE BRITISH EMPIRE IN 1900

Queen Victoria's reign (1837–1901), Britain was at its zenith of power, with a colonial empire that covered one-fifth of the world.

The 20th century was not kind to Britain. After decades of rebellion, Ireland finally gained its independence—except for the more Protestant north. Two world wars devastated the population. The Nazi Blitz reduced much of London to rubble, although the freedom-loving world was inspired by Britain's determination to stand up to Hitler. After the war, the colonial empire dwindled to almost nothing, and Britain lost its superpower economic status.

One post-Empire hot spot—Northern Ireland, plagued by the "Troubles" between Catholics and Protestants—heated up, and then finally started cooling off. In the spring of 2007, the unthinkable happened when leaders of the ultra-nationalist party sat down with those of the ultra-unionist party. London returned control of Northern Ireland to the popularly elected Northern Ireland Assembly. Perhaps most important of all, after almost 40 years, the British Army withdrew from Northern Ireland that summer. Three years later, the British government formally apologized for the 1972 shooting of 26 civilians in Derry by British soldiers—a day of infamy known as "Bloody Sunday."

The tradition (if not the substance) of greatness continues, presided over by Queen Elizabeth II, her husband, Prince Philip, and their son Prince Charles. With economic problems, the marital turmoil of Charles and the late Princess Diana, and a relentless popular press, the royal family has had a tough time. But the queen has stayed above it all, and most British people still jump at an opportunity to see royalty. With the 1997 death of Princess Diana and the historic outpouring of grief, it was clear that the concept of royalty is still alive and well as Britain entered the third millennium.

HISTORY AND CULTURE

Queen Elizabeth, who turns 85 in 2011, marked her 58th year on the throne in 2010. While many wonder who will succeed her, the case is fairly straightforward: The queen sees her job as a lifelong position, and legally, Charles (who wants to be king) cannot be skipped over for his son William. Given the longevity in the family (the queen's mum, born in August of 1900, made it to 101 before she died in 2002), Charles is in for a long wait.

Architecture in Britain

From Stonehenge to Big Ben, travelers are storming castle walls, climbing spiral staircases, and snapping the pictures of 5,000 years of architecture. Let's sort it out.

The oldest ruins—mysterious and prehistoric—date from before Roman times back to 3000 B.C. The earliest sites, such as

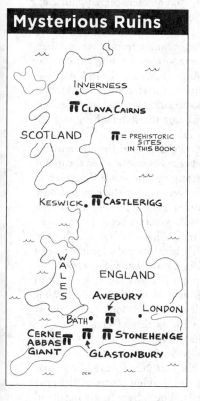

Mysterious Ruins

INVERNESS

π CLAVA CAIRNS

SCOTLAND   π = PREHISTORIC
                      SITES
                      IN THIS BOOK

KESWICK. π CASTLERIGG

WALES

ENGLAND

AVEBURY

BATH π   • LONDON

CERNE π π π STONEHENGE
ABBAS
GIANT   GLASTONBURY

DCH

Stonehenge and Avebury, were built during the Stone and Bronze ages. The remains from these periods are made of huge stones or mounds of earth, even man-made hills, and were created as celestial calendars and for worship or burial. Britain is crisscrossed with lines of these mysterious sights (ley lines). Iron Age people (600 B.C.–A.D. 50) left desolate stone forts. The Romans thrived in Britain from A.D. 50 to 400, building cities, walls, and roads. Evidence of Roman greatness can be seen in lavish villas with ornate mosaic floors, temples uncovered beneath great English churches, and Roman stones in medieval city walls. Roman roads sliced across the island in straight lines. Today, unusually straight rural roads are very likely laid directly on these ancient roads.

As Rome crumbled in the fifth century, so did Roman Britain. Little architecture survives from Dark Ages England, the Saxon period from 500 to 1000. Architecturally, the light was switched on with the Norman Conquest in 1066. As William earned his title "the Conqueror," his French architects built churches and castles in the European

Romanesque style.

English Romanesque is called Norman (1066–1200). Norman churches had round arches, thick walls, and small windows; Durham Cathedral and the Chapel of St. John in the Tower of London are prime examples. The Tower of London, with its square keep, small windows, and spiral stone stairways, is a typical Norman castle. You'll see plenty of Norman castles—all built to secure the conquest of these invaders from Normandy.

Gothic architecture (1200–1600) replaced the heavy Norman style with light, vertical buildings, pointed arches, soaring spires, and bigger windows. English Gothic is divided into three stages. Early English (1200–1300) features tall, simple spires; beautifully carved capitals; and elaborate chapter houses (such as the Wells Cathedral). Decorated Gothic (1300–1400) gets fancier, with more elaborate tracery, bigger windows, and ornately carved pinnacles, as you'll see at Westminster Abbey. Finally, the Perpendicular Gothic style (1400–1600, also called "rectilinear") returns to square towers and emphasizes straight, uninterrupted vertical lines from ceiling to floor, with vast windows and exuberant decoration, including fan-vaulted ceilings (King's College Chapel at Cambridge). Through this evolution, the structural ribs (arches meeting at the top of the ceilings) became more and more decorative and fanciful (the most fancy being the star vaulting and fan vaulting of the Perpendicular style).

As you tour the great medieval churches of Britain, remember that almost everything is symbolic. For instance, on the tombs of knights, if the figure has crossed legs, he was a Crusader. If his feet rest on a dog, he died at home; but if the legs rest on a lion, he died in battle. Local guides and books help us modern pilgrims understand at least a little of what we see.

Wales is particularly rich in English castles, which were needed to subdue the stubborn Welsh. Edward I built a ring of powerful castles in Wales, including Conwy and Caernarfon.

Gothic houses were a simple mix of woven strips of thin wood, rubble, and plaster called wattle and daub. The famous black-and-white Tudor (or "half-timbered") look came simply from filling in heavy oak frames with wattle and daub.

The Tudor period (1485–1560) was a time of relative peace (the Wars of the Roses were finally over), prosperity, and renaissance. Henry VIII broke with the Catholic Church and "dissolved" (destroyed) the monasteries, leaving scores of Britain's greatest churches as gutted shells. These hauntingly beautiful abbey ruins (Glastonbury, Tintern, Whitby, Rievaulx, Battle, St. Augustine's in Canterbury, St. Mary's in York, and lots more) surrounded by lush lawns are now pleasant city parks.

Although few churches were built during the Tudor period,

Typical Church Architecture

History comes to life when you visit a centuries-old church. Even if you wouldn't know your apse from a hole in the ground, learning a few simple terms will enrich your experience. Note that not every church has every feature, and that a "cathedral" isn't a type of church architecture, but rather a designation for a church that's a governing center for a local bishop.

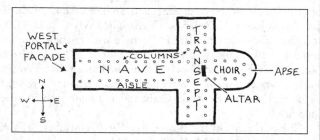

Aisles: The long, generally low-ceilinged arcades that flank the nave.

Altar: The raised area with a ceremonial table (often adorned with candles or a crucifix), where the priest prepares and serves the bread and wine for Communion.

Apse: The space beyond the altar, often bordered with small chapels.

Choir: A cozy area, often screened off, located within the church nave and near the high altar where services are sung in a more intimate setting.

Cloister: A square-shaped series of hallways surrounding an open-air courtyard, traditionally where monks and nuns got fresh air.

Facade: The outer wall of the church's main (west) entrance, viewable from outside and usually highly decorated.

Groin Vault: An arched ceiling formed where two equal barrel vaults meet at right angles. Less common usage: term for a medieval jock strap.

Narthex: The area (portico or foyer) between the main entry and the nave.

Nave: The long, central section of the church (running west to east, from the entrance to the altar) where the congregation stood through the service.

Transept: The north–south part of the church, which crosses (perpendicularly) the east–west nave. In a traditional Latin cross-shaped floor plan, the transept forms the "arms" of the cross.

West Portal: The main entry to the church (on the west end, opposite the main altar).

this was a time of house and mansion construction. Heating a home was becoming popular and affordable, and Tudor buildings featured small square windows and many chimneys. In towns, where land was scarce, many Tudor houses grew up and out, getting wider with each overhanging floor.

The Elizabethan and Jacobean periods (1560–1620) were followed by the English Renaissance style (1620–1720). English architects mixed Gothic and classical styles, then Baroque and classical styles. Although the ornate Baroque never really grabbed Britain, the classical style of the Italian architect Andrea Palladio did. Inigo Jones (1573–1652), Christopher Wren (1632–1723), and those they inspired plastered Britain with enough columns, domes, and symmetry to please a Caesar. The Great Fire of London (1666) cleared the way for an ambitious young Wren to put his mark on London forever with a grand rebuilding scheme, including the great St. Paul's Cathedral and more than 50 other churches.

The celebrants of the Boston Tea Party remember Britain's Georgian period (1720–1840) for its lousy German kings. Georgian architecture was rich and showed off by being very classical. Grand ornamental doorways, fine cast-ironwork on balconies and railings, Chippendale furniture, and white-on-blue Wedgwood ceramics graced rich homes everywhere. John Wood Jr. and Sr. led the way, giving the trendsetting city of Bath its crescents and circles of aristocratic Georgian row houses. "Georgian" is English for "Neoclassical."

The Industrial Revolution shaped the Victorian period (1840–1890) with glass, steel, and iron. Britain had a huge new erector set (so did France's Mr. Eiffel). This was also a Romantic period, reviving the "more Christian" Gothic style. London's Houses of Parliament are Neo-Gothic—just 140 years old but looking 700, except for the telltale modern precision and craftsmanship. Whereas Gothic was stone or concrete, Neo-Gothic was often red brick. These were Britain's glory days, and there was more building in this period than in all previous ages combined.

The architecture of modern times obeys the formula "form follows function"—it worries more about your needs than your eyes. Britain treasures its heritage and takes great pains to build tastefully in historic districts and to preserve its many "listed" buildings. With a booming tourist trade, these quaint reminders of its past—and ours—are becoming a valuable part of the British economy.

British TV

Although it has its share of lowbrow reality programming, much British television is still so good—and so British—that it deserves a mention as a sightseeing treat. After a hard day of castle climbing, watch the telly over tea in the living room of your village B&B.

There are currently five free channels that any television can receive. BBC-1 and BBC-2 are government-regulated and commercial-free. Broadcasting of these two channels (and of the five BBC radio stations) is funded by a mandatory £145.50-per-year-per-household television and radio license (hmmm, 65 cents per day to escape commercials and public-broadcasting pledge drives). Channels 3, 4, and 5 are privately owned, are a little more lowbrow, and have commercials—but those commercials are often clever and sophisticated, providing a fun look at British life. In addition, about 85 percent of households now receive digital cable or satellite television, which offer dozens of specialty channels, similar to those available in North America.

Like the US, Britain is joining the Digital Age, gradually converting its TV signals to digital-only, which requires a digitally equipped set or a converter. By 2013, the old analog signals will be switched off and only digital signals will be broadcast.

Whereas California "accents" fill our airwaves 24 hours a day, homogenizing the way our country speaks, Britain protects and promotes its regional accents by its choice of TV and radio announcers. See if you can tell where each is from (or ask a local for help).

Commercial-free British TV, while looser than it used to be, is still careful about what it airs and when. But after the 21:00 "watershed" hour, when children are expected to be in bed, some nudity and profanity are allowed, and may cause you to spill your tea.

American programs (such as *Mad Men, CSI, Oprah,* and trash-talk shows) are very popular. The visiting viewer should be sure to tune the TV to a few typical British shows, including a dose of British situation- and political-comedy fun, and the top-notch BBC evening news. British comedies have tickled the American funny bone for years, from sketch comedy *(Monty Python's Flying Circus)* to sitcoms (such as *Are You Being Served?, Fawlty Towers,* and *Absolutely Fabulous*). A more recent cross-the-pond mega-hit, *The Office,* has made its star Ricky Gervais the top name in British comedy today, and has spawned successful adaptations in the US, Germany, France, French Canada, Chile, and Israel. Quiz shows and reality shows are taken very seriously here (*Who Wants to Be a Millionaire?, American Idol,* and *Dancing with the Stars* are all based on British shows). Jonathan Ross is the David Letterman of Britain for sometimes edgy late-night talk—he left the BBC in 2010, but watch for his return on a private channel in 2011. For a tear-filled, slice-of-life taste of British soaps dealing in all the controversial issues, see the popular *Emmerdale, Coronation Street,* or *EastEnders.*

HISTORY AND CULTURE

APPENDIX

Contents

Tourist Information

Tourist Information Offices

The **Visit Britain** office in the US is a wealth of knowledge. Request free maps of London and Britain and any specific information you may want (such as regional information, a garden-tour map, urban cultural activities brochures, and so on). The phone line is mainly intended as a customer service number for their online shop and isn't staffed (but they do check their messages). For most questions, it's best to inquire by email (tel. 800-462-2748, www.visitbritain .com, travelinfo@visitbritain.org). Also try these official tourism board websites: www.visitengland.com, www.visitwales.com, and www.visitscotland.com.

In Britain, your best first stop in every town is generally the tourist information office—abbreviated **TI** in this book. (The **Britain and London Visitors Centre** in London is particularly good—see page 51.) A TI is a great place to get a city map, advice on public transportation (including bus and train schedules), walking-tour schedules, information on special events, and recommendations for nightlife. For all the help TIs offer, steer clear of their room-finding services (bloated prices, booking fee up to £4, no opinions, and they take a 10 percent cut from your B&B host). Many TIs have information on the entire country or at least the region, so try to pick up maps for destinations that you'll be visiting later in your trip. If you're arriving in town after the TI closes, call ahead or pick up a map in a neighboring town.

Communicating

Telephones

Smart travelers use the telephone to book or reconfirm rooms, get tourist information, reserve restaurants, confirm tour times, or phone home. Generally, the cheapest way to go is to buy an international phone card in Britain and make your calls from hotel-room phones or mobile phones, but not pay phones. The handiest—though pricier—way to make calls is by using a mobile phone (brought from home or purchased in Britain). This section covers dialing instructions, phone cards, and types of phones (for more in-depth information, see www.ricksteves.com/phoning).

How to Dial

Calling from the US to Britain, or vice versa, is simple—once you break the code. The European calling chart in this chapter will walk you through it.

Dialing Domestically Within Britain

Britain, like much of the US, uses an area-code dialing system. To make local calls, if you're calling within an area code, just dial the local number to be connected; if you're calling outside your area code, you have to dial both the area code (which starts with a 0) and the local number.

Area codes are listed in this book and by city on phone-booth walls, and are available from directory assistance (dial 118-500, £0.64/minute). It's most expensive to call within Britain between 8:00 and 13:00, and cheapest between 17:00 and 8:00. Still, a short call across the country is inexpensive; don't hesitate to call long distance.

Dialing Internationally to or from Britain

If you want to make an international call, follow these steps:

1. Dial the international access code (00 if you're calling from Britain, 011 from the US or Canada).

2. Dial the country code of the country you're calling (44 for Britain, or 1 for the US or Canada).

The British Accent

In the olden days, a British person's accent indicated his or her social standing. Eliza Doolittle had the right idea—elocution could make or break you. Wealthier families would send their kids to fancy private schools to learn proper pronunciation. But these days, in a sort of reverse snobbery that has gripped the nation, accents are back. Politicians, newscasters, and movie stars have been favoring deep accents over the Queen's English. While it's hard for American ears to pick out all of the variations, most Brits can determine where a person is from based on his or her accent...not just the region, but often the village, and even the part of town.

3. Dial the area code (without the initial zero) and the local number.

Calling from the US to Britain: To call a London hotel from the US, dial 011 (the US international access code), 44 (Britain's country code), 20 (London's area code without its initial 0), then 7730-8191 (the hotel's number).

Calling from any European Country to the US: To call my office in Edmonds, Washington, from anywhere in Europe, I dial 00 (Europe's international access code), 1 (the US country code), 425 (Edmonds' area code), and 771-8303.

Note: You might see a + in front of a European number. When dialing the number, replace the + with the international access code of the country you're calling from (00 from Europe, 011 from the US or Canada).

Public Phones and Hotel-Room Phones

To make a call from a public pay phone, you'll need a lot of coins (Britain doesn't use insertable phone cards, and calls are pricey). Even prepaid international phone cards are prohibitively expensive on public phones.

International Phone Cards: These cards are the cheapest way to make international calls from Britain (less than $0.10 a minute to the US; they also work for local calls). But there's a catch: British Telecom levies a hefty surcharge for using international calling cards from a pay phone (so instead of 100 minutes for a £5 card, you'll get less than 10 minutes—a miserable deal). But they're still a good deal if you use them when calling from a mobile phone or fixed line (e.g., a hotel-room phone; ask at the front desk if they charge any fees for toll-free calls). The cards are sold all over; look for them at newsstand kiosks and hole-in-the-wall long-distance shops. Ask the clerk which of the various brands has the best rates

European Calling Chart

Just smile and dial, using this key:
AC = Area Code, LN = Local Number.

European Country	Calling long distance within ...	Calling from the US or Canada to ...	Calling from a European country to ...
Austria	AC + LN	011 + 43 + AC (without the initial zero) + LN	00 + 43 + AC (without the initial zero) + LN
Belgium	LN	011 + 32 + LN (without initial zero)	00 + 32 + LN (without initial zero)
Bosnia-Herzegovina	AC + LN	011 + 387 + AC (without initial zero) + LN	00 + 387 + AC (without initial zero) + LN
Britain	AC + LN	011 + 44 + AC (without initial zero) + LN	00 + 44 + AC (without initial zero) + LN
Croatia	AC + LN	011 + 385 + AC (without initial zero) + LN	00 + 385 + AC (without initial zero) + LN
Czech Republic	LN	011 + 420 + LN	00 + 420 + LN
Denmark	LN	011 + 45 + LN	00 + 45 + LN
Estonia	LN	011 + 372 + LN	00 + 372 + LN
Finland	AC + LN	011 + 358 + AC (without initial zero) + LN	999 (or other 900 number) + 358 + AC (without initial zero) + LN
France	LN	011 + 33 + LN (without initial zero)	00 + 33 + LN (without initial zero)
Germany	AC + LN	011 + 49 + AC (without initial zero) + LN	00 + 49 + AC (without initial zero) + LN
Gibraltar	LN	011 + 350 + LN	00 + 350 + LN
Greece	LN	011 + 30 + LN	00 + 30 + LN
Hungary	06 + AC + LN	011 + 36 + AC + LN	00 + 36 + AC + LN
Ireland	AC + LN	011 + 353 + AC (without initial zero) + LN	00 + 353 + AC (without initial zero) + LN

APPENDIX

European Country	Calling long distance within ...	Calling from the US or Canada to ...	Calling from a European country to ...
Italy	LN	011 + 39 + LN	00 + 39 + LN
Montenegro	AC + LN	011 + 382 + AC (without initial zero) + LN	00 + 382 + AC (without initial zero) + LN
Morocco	LN	011 + 212 + LN (without initial zero)	00 + 212 + LN (without initial zero)
Netherlands	AC + LN	011 + 31 + AC (without initial zero) + LN	00 + 31 + AC (without initial zero) + LN
Norway	LN	011 + 47 + LN	00 + 47 + LN
Poland	LN	011 + 48 + LN (without initial zero)	00 + 48 + LN (without initial zero)
Portugal	LN	011 + 351 + LN	00 + 351 + LN
Slovakia	AC + LN	011 + 421 + AC (without initial zero) + LN	00 + 421 + AC (without initial zero) + LN
Slovenia	AC + LN	011 + 386 + AC (without initial zero) + LN	00 + 386 + AC (without initial zero) + LN
Spain	LN	011 + 34 + LN	00 + 34 + LN
Sweden	AC + LN	011 + 46 + AC (without initial zero) + LN	00 + 46 + AC (without initial zero) + LN
Switzerland	LN	011 + 41 + LN (without initial zero)	00 + 41 + LN (without initial zero)
Turkey	AC (if there's no initial zero, add one) + LN	011 + 90 + AC (without initial zero) + LN	00 + 90 + AC (without initial zero) + LN

- The instructions above apply whether you're calling a land line or mobile phone.
- The international access codes (the first numbers you dial when making an international call) are 011 if you're calling from the US or Canada, or 00 if you're calling from virtually anywhere in Europe (except Finland, where it's 999 or another 900 number, depending on the phone service you're using).
- To call the US or Canada from Europe, dial 00, then 1 (the country code for the US and Canada), then the area code and number. In short, 00 + 1 + AC + LN = Hi, Mom!

for calls to the US. Because cards are occasionally duds, avoid the more expensive denominations. These cards usually work only in the country where they're purchased (unless otherwise noted on the card).

Hotel-Room Phones: Phones are rare in B&Bs. If your room has a phone, it can be a cheap way to make local calls (ask for the rates at the front desk first), but is often a rip-off for long-distance calls, unless you use an international phone card. Incoming calls are free, making this an inexpensive way for friends and family to stay in touch (provided they have a good long-distance plan for calls to Europe—and a list of your hotels' phone numbers).

US Calling Cards: These cards, such as the ones offered by AT&T, Verizon, and Sprint, are the worst option. You'll nearly always save money by using a locally purchased phone card instead.

Mobile Phones

For most travelers in Britain, a mobile phone is the best option for making calls.

Using Your Mobile Phone: Your US mobile phone works in Britain if it's GSM-enabled, tri-band or quad-band, and on a calling plan that includes international calls. Phones from T-Mobile and AT&T, which use the same GSM technology that Europe does, are more likely to work overseas than Verizon or Sprint phones (if you're not sure, ask your service provider). Most US providers charge $1.29 per minute while roaming internationally to make or receive calls, and $0.20–0.50 to send or receive text messages.

You'll pay cheaper rates if your phone is electronically "unlocked" (ask your provider about this); then, in Britain, you can simply buy a tiny **SIM card,** which gives you a British phone number. SIM cards are available at mobile-phone stores and some newsstand kiosks. You might have to pay a nominal amount for these (around $5), but you'll often get one for free— they make their money selling you calling time, not the SIM card itself. When you buy a SIM card, you may need to show ID, such as your passport. Insert the SIM card in your phone (usually in a slot behind the battery), and it'll work like a British mobile phone. When buying a SIM card and calling credit, always ask about fees for domestic and international calls, roaming charges, and how to check your credit balance and buy more time. To call home, save money by using an international calling card (described earlier).

Many **smartphones,** such as the iPhone or BlackBerry, work in Europe—but beware of sky-high fees, especially for data downloading (checking email, browsing the Internet, watching streaming videos, and so on). Ask your provider in advance how to avoid unwittingly roaming your way to a huge bill. Some applications allow for cheap or free smartphone calls over a Wi-Fi connection (see "Calling over the Internet," later).

Using a European Mobile Phone: Mobile-phone shops all over Europe sell basic phones. (For example, Britain's Carphone Warehouse sells pay-as-you-go mobile phones for as little as £10 plus £10 for calling time.) You'll also need to get a SIM card and prepaid credit for making calls. If you remain in Britain, incoming calls are generally free, and outgoing domestic calls to a fixed line generally run about £0.15–0.20/minute—less than from a pay phone. (It's more expensive to call a mobile phone or a toll number.) You'll pay more if roaming in another country.

Calling over the Internet

Some things that seem too good to be true...actually are true. If you're traveling with a laptop, you can make calls using VoIP (Voice over Internet Protocol). With VoIP, two computers act as the phones, and the Internet-based calls are free (or you can pay a few cents to call from your computer to a telephone). If both computers have webcams, you can even see each other while you chat. The major providers are Skype (www.skype.com), followed by Google Talk (www.google.com/talk).

Useful Phone Numbers

Understand the various prefixes—numbers starting with 09 are telephone-sex–type expensive. Numbers that begin with 0800 are toll-free, but numbers with prefixes of 0844, 0845, 0870, and 0871 cost about £0.10 per minute from a fixed line (but can be much more expensive if calling from a mobile phone). If you have questions about a prefix, call 100 for free help.

Emergencies and Directory Assistance

Police and Ambulance: tel. 999
Operator Assistance: tel. 100 (free)
Directory Assistance: tel. 118-500 (£0.64/minute, plus £0.23/minute connection charge from fixed lines)
International Directory Assistance: tel. 118-505 (£1.99/minute, plus £0.69 connection charge)

Embassies and Consulates in London

US Consulate and Embassy: tel. 020/7499-9000, passport info tel. 020/7894-0563, passport services available Mon–Fri 8:30–11:30, Mon, Wed, Fri also 14:00–16:00 (24 Grosvenor Square, Tube: Bond Street, www.usembassy.org.uk)
Canadian High Commission: tel. 020/7258-6600, passport

services available Mon–Fri 9:30–13:30 (Trafalgar Square, Tube: Charing Cross, www.unitedkingdom.gc.ca)

Travel Advisories

US Department of State: US tel. 202/647-5225 (www.travel.state.gov)

Canadian Department of Foreign Affairs: Canadian tel. 800-267-6788 (www.dfait-maeci.gc.ca)

US Centers for Disease Control and Prevention: US tel. 800-CDC-INFO (800-232-4636, www.cdc.gov/travel)

Trains and Buses

Train Information for Trips Within Britain: toll tel. 0845-748-4950, overseas tel. 011-44-20-7278-5240 (www.nationalrail.co.uk)

Eurostar (Chunnel Info): toll tel. 0870-518-6186 (www.eurostar.com)

Trains to All Points in Europe: toll tel. 0870-584-8848 (www.raileurope.com)

National Express Buses: toll tel. 0871-781-8181 (www.nationalexpress.com)

Airports

For online information on the first three airports, check www.baa.co.uk.

Heathrow (flight info): toll tel. 0870-000-0123

Gatwick (general info): toll tel. 0870-000-2468 for all airlines, except British Airways—toll tel. 0870-551-1155 (flights) or 0870-850-9850 (booking)

Stansted (general info): toll tel. 0870-000-0303

Luton (general info): tel. 01582/405-100 (www.london-luton.com)

London City Airport (general info): tel. 020/7646-0088 (www.londoncityairport.com)

Airlines

Aer Lingus: toll tel. 0870-876-5000, US tel. 800-474-7424 (www.aerlingus.com)

Air Canada: toll tel. 0871-220-1111 (www.aircanada.com)

Alitalia: toll tel. 0871-424-1424 (www.alitalia.com)

American: toll tel. 0845-778-9789 (www.aa.com)

bmi: reservations toll tel. 0870-607-0555, flight info tel. 020/8745-7321 (www.flybmi.com)

British Airways: reservations toll tel. 0844-493-0787, flight info toll tel. 0844-493-0777 (www.ba.com)

Brussels Airlines: toll tel. 0905-609-5609, US tel. 516/740 5200, 40p/minute (www.brusselsairlines.com)

Continental Airlines: toll tel. 0845-607-6760 (www.continental.com)
easyJet: toll tel. 0871-244-2366, 10p/minute (www.easyjet.com)
KLM Royal Dutch/Northwest Airlines: toll tel. 0870-507-4074 (www.klm.com)
Lufthansa: toll tel. 0871-945-9747 (www.lufthansa.com)
Ryanair: toll tel. 0871-246-0000 (www.ryanair.com)
Scandinavian Airlines (SAS): toll tel. 0871-521-2772 (www.flysas.com)
United Airlines: toll tel. 0845-844-4777 (www.unitedairlines.co.uk)
US Airways: toll tel. 0845-600-3300 (www.usair.com)

Heathrow Airport Car-Rental Agencies
Avis: toll tel. 0844-544-6000 (www.avis.co.uk)
Budget: toll tel. 0844-544-4600 (www.budget.co.uk)
Enterprise: tel. 020/8897-2100 (www.enterprise.co.uk)
Europcar: tel. 020/8564-3500 (www.europcar.co.uk)
Hertz: toll tel. 0870-846-0006 (www.hertz.co.uk)

Internet Access
It's useful to get online periodically as you travel—to confirm trip plans, check train or bus schedules, get weather forecasts, catch up

on email, blog or post photos from your trip, or call folks back home (explained earlier, in "Calling over the Internet").

Some hotels and B&Bs offer a computer in the lobby with Internet access for guests. If you ask politely, smaller places may sometimes let you sit at their desk for a few minutes just to check your email. If your hotel doesn't have access, ask your hotelier to direct you to the nearest place to get online. Most of the towns where I've listed accommodations in this book also have Internet cafés. Many libraries offer free access, but they also tend to have limited opening hours, restrict your online time to 30 minutes, and may require reservations.

Traveling with a Laptop: With a laptop or netbook, it's easy to get online if your hotel has Wi-Fi (wireless Internet access) or a port in your room for plugging in a cable. Some hotels offer Wi-Fi for free; others charge by the minute or hour. A cellular modem—which lets your laptop access the Internet over a mobile phone network—provides more extensive coverage, but is much more expensive than Wi-Fi.

Mail

Get stamps at the neighborhood post office, newsstands within fancy hotels, and some mini-marts and card shops. You can arrange for mail delivery to your hotel (allow 10 days for a letter to arrive), but phoning and emailing are so easy that I've dispensed with mail stops altogether.

Transportation

By Car or Public Transportation?

Cars are best for three or more traveling together (especially families with small kids), those packing heavy, and those scouring the countryside. Trains and buses are best for solo travelers, blitz tourists, and city-to-city travelers. While a car gives you the ultimate in mobility and freedom, enables you to search for hotels more easily, and carries your bags for you, the train zips you effortlessly from city to city, usually dropping you in the center and near the tourist office.

Britain's 100-mph train system is one of Europe's best. Buses pick you up when the trains let you down. Travelers who don't want (or can't afford) to drive a rental car can enjoy an excellent tour using public transportation.

In Britain, my choice is to connect big cities by train and to explore rural areas (such as the Cotswolds, North Wales, the Lake District, and the Scottish Highlands) footloose and fancy-free by rental car. The mix works quite efficiently (e.g., London, Bath, York, Edinburgh, and Glasgow by train, with a rental car for the rest). You might consider a BritRail & Drive Pass, which gives you various combinations of rail days and car days to use within two months' time.

Trains

Regular tickets on Britain's great train system (15,000 departures from 2,400 stations daily) are the most expensive per mile in all of Europe. Those who save the biggest book in advance, leave after rush hour (after 9:30), or ride the bus. Now that Britain has privatized its railways, it can be tricky to track down all your options; a single bus or train route can be operated by several companies. However, one British website covers all train lines (www.nationalrail.co.uk), and another covers all bus and train routes in Britain (www.traveline.org.uk). Another good resource, which also has schedules for trains throughout Europe, is German Rail's timetable (http://bahn.hafas.de/bin/query.exe/en).

As with airline tickets, British train tickets can come at many different prices for the same journey. A clerk at any station can figure out the cheapest fare for your trip (or call the helpful National

Sample Train Journey

Here is a typical example of a personalized train schedule printed out at Britain's train stations. At the Llandudno
Junction station in North Wales, I told the clerk I wanted to
leave after 14:00 for Moreton-in-Marsh in the Cotswolds.

Stations	Arrive	Depart	Class
Llandudno Junction	—	15:27	Standard
Shrewsbury	17:15	17:22	Standard
Wolverhampton	17:58	18:18	Standard
Oxford	19:46	20:21	Standard
Moreton-in-Marsh	20:57	—	

Even though the trip involved three transfers, this schedule
allowed me to easily navigate the rails.

Train departures are listed on overhead boards at the station by their final destination (note that your destination could
be an intermediate stop on this route, and therefore not listed
on the overhead). It's helpful to ask at the info desk—or any
conductor—for the final destination of your next train so you'll
be able to figure out quickly which platform it's departing from.
For example, I knew that my Shrewsbury-to-Wolverhampton
train would eventually terminate at Birmingham (even though
I was disembarking at Wolverhampton). So, upon arrival at
Shrewsbury, I looked for *Birmingham* on the station's overhead train schedule to determine where to catch my train.

Often the conductor on your previous train can even tell
you which platform your next train will depart from, but it's
wise to confirm.

Britain's train system can experience delays, so don't
schedule your connections too tight if you need to be at your
destination at a specific time.

Rail folks at toll tel. 0845-748-4950, 24 hours daily). Savings can
be significant. For a London-to-Edinburgh round-trip (standard
class), if you book the day of departure for travel after 9:30, it's
around £108; the cheapest fare, booked a couple of months in
advance as two one-way tickets, can cost as little as £55.

While not required on British trains, reservations are free and
a good idea for long journeys or any train travel on Sunday. Make
them at any train station before 18:00 on the day before you travel.

Buying Train Tickets in Advance: The best fares go to those
who book their trips well in advance of their journey. (While only
a 7-day minimum advance booking is officially required for the
cheapest fares, these sell out fast—especially in summer—so a 6–8
week advance booking is often necessary.) Keep in mind that when

Public Transportation Routes in Britain

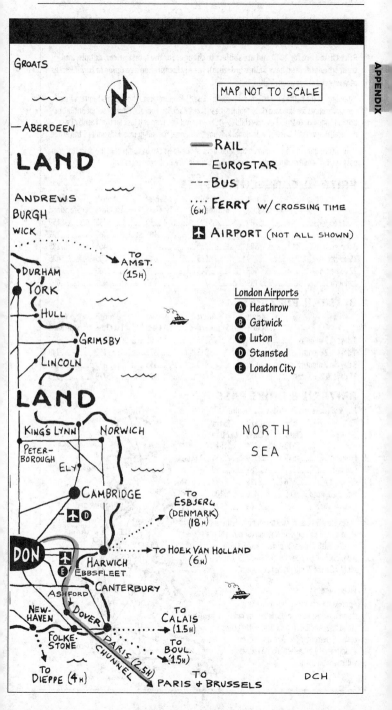

GROATS

MAP NOT TO SCALE

—ABERDEEN

LAND

ANDREWS
BURGH
WICK

—— RAIL
—— EUROSTAR
--- BUS
···· FERRY w/ CROSSING TIME
(6H)
✈ AIRPORT (NOT ALL SHOWN)

TO
AMST.
(15H)

•DURHAM
YORK
•HULL
●GRIMSBY
•LINCOLN

London Airports
Ⓐ Heathrow
Ⓑ Gatwick
Ⓒ Luton
Ⓓ Stansted
Ⓔ London City

LAND

KING'S LYNN   NORWICH
PETER-
BOROUGH   ELY
●CAMBRIDGE

NORTH
SEA

✈Ⓓ

TO
ESBJERG
(DENMARK)
(18H)

DON

✈
HARWICH
Ⓔ EBBSFLEET
CANTERBURY

→ TO HOEK VAN HOLLAND
(6H)

ASHFORD

NEW-
HAVEN   DOVER

TO
CALAIS
(1.5H)

FOLKE-
STONE

PARIS (2.5H)
CHUNNEL

TO
BOUL.
(1.5H)

TO
DIEPPE (4H)

TO
PARIS & BRUSSELS

DCH

Railpasses

Prices listed are for 2010 and are subject to change. For the latest prices, details, and train schedules (and easy online ordering), see my comprehensive *Guide to Eurail Passes* at www.ricksteves.com/rail.

"Standard" is the polite British term for "second" class. "Senior" refers to those age 60 and up. No senior discounts for standard class. "Youth" means under age 26. For each adult or senior BritRail or BritRail England pass you buy, one child (5–15) can travel free with you (ask for the "**Family Pass**," not available with all passes). Additional kids pay the normal half-adult rate. Kids under 5 travel free.

Note: Overnight journeys begun on the final night of your pass can be completed the day after your pass expires—only BritRail allows this trick. A bunk in a twin sleeper costs $75.

BRITRAIL CONSECUTIVE PASS

	Adult 1st Class	Adult Standard	Senior 1st Class	Youth 1st Class	Youth Standard
3 consec. days	$289	$199	$249	$235	$159
4 consec. days	365	249	305	289	199
8 consec. days	509	359	435	405	285
15 consec. days	759	535	649	609	425
22 consec. days	965	645	819	769	515
1 month	1139	759	965	909	605

BRITRAIL FLEXIPASS

	Adult 1st Class	Adult Standard	Senior 1st Class	Youth 1st Class	Youth Standard
3 days in 2 months	$359	$255	$305	$285	$205
4 days in 2 months	445	315	379	359	249
8 days in 2 months	649	459	555	519	365
15 days in 2 months	975	689	829	779	555

BRITRAIL & DRIVE PASS

Any 4 rail days and 2 car days in 2 months.

	1st Class	Standard Class	Extra Car Day
Mini	$513	$374	$44
Economy	519	380	50
Compact	527	389	59
Compact Auto	556	418	88
Intermed. Auto	569	430	100
Minivan Auto	644	505	175

Prices are per person, two traveling together. Third and fourth persons sharing car buy a regular BritRail pass. To order a Rail & Drive pass, call Rail Europe at 800-438-7245. *Not sold by Europe Through the Back Door.*

Map key:

Approximate point-to-point one-way standard-class fares in US dollars by rail (solid line) and bus (dashed line). First class costs 50 percent more. Add up fares for your itinerary to see whether a railpass will save you money.

BRITRAIL ENGLAND CONSECUTIVE PASS

	Adult 1st Class	Adult Standard	Senior 1st Class	Youth 1st Class	Youth Standard
3 consec. days	$229	$159	$195	$189	$129
4 consec. days	$285	$199	$245	$229	$159
8 consec. days	$409	$285	$349	$329	$229
15 consec. days	$615	$429	$525	$489	$345
22 consec. days	$775	$519	$665	$619	$415
1 month	$915	$609	$775	$729	$489

Covers travel only in England, not Scotland, Wales, or Ireland.

BRITRAIL ENGLAND FLEXIPASS

Type of Pass	Adult 1st Class	Adult Standard	Senior 1st Class	Youth 1st Class	Youth Standard
3 days in 2 months	$289	$205	$249	$235	$165
4 days in 2 months	$365	$255	$305	$289	$205
8 days in 2 months	$525	$369	$445	$419	$295
15 days in 2 months	$779	$549	$665	$625	$439

Covers travel only in England, not Scotland, Wales, or Ireland.

BRITRAIL LONDON PLUS PASS

	Adult 1st Class	Adult Standard
2 out of 8 days	$199	$139
4 out of 8 days	275	225
7 out of 15 days	355	269

Covers much of SE England (see London Plus Coverage Map at www.ricksteves.com/rail).Includes vouchers to cover two trips on the Heathrow, Stansted, or Gatwick Express, separate from your counted travel days, which can be used up to 6 months from the date you validate the pass in Britain (but not before pass is validated for the 8- or 15-day travel window). Many trains are standard class only. The 7 p.m. rule for night trains does not apply. Kids 5–15 half price; under 5 free.

BRITRAIL SCOTTISH FREEDOM PASS

4 out of 8 days	$235
8 out of 15 days	315

Valid in Scotland only, standard class only. Not valid on trains that depart before 9:15 a.m. Mon–Fri. Covers Caledonian MacBrayne and Strathclyde ferry service to popular islands. Discounts on some P&O ferries, some Citylink buses & more. Kids 5–15 half fare; under 5 free.

BRITRAIL CENTRAL SCOTLAND PASS

3 out of 7 days	$79

Passes are prevalidated at the time of purchase for a specific, 7-day travel window and cannot be refunded after that planned travel date! Covers frequent service between Edinburgh and Glasgow's Queen St Station (not Glasgow Central), some nearby side-trips (see Central Scotland Coverage Map at www.ricksteves.com/rail), and the Glasgow Underground (on your three travel days). Standard class only. No highlands or islands. Not valid on trains that depart before 9:15 a.m. Mon–Fri, Glasgow Airport Coach Links, excursion trains, nor private railways. The 7 p.m. rule for night trains does not apply. No child discount; under 5 free.

BRITRAIL PASS PLUS IRELAND

	First Class	Standard Class
5 days in 1 month	$665	$469
10 days in 1 month	1185	839

Covers the entire British Isles (England, Wales, Scotland, Northern Ireland, and the Republic of Ireland). No longer covers ferries. Kids 5-15 pay half fare; under 5 free. No Family Pass, Party Pass, Eurail Discount, nor Off-Peak Special. Consider the cost of separate BritRail and Ireland passes.

booking in advance, "return" (round-trip) fares are not always cheaper than buying two "single" (one-way) tickets. Also note that cheap advance tickets often come with the toughest refund restrictions, so be sure to nail down your travel plans before you reserve. To book ahead, you can go in person to any station, book online at www.nationalrail.co.uk, or call 0845-748-4950 (from the US, call 011-44-20-7278-5240, phone answered 24 hours) to find out the schedule and best fare for your journey; then you'll be referred to the appropriate number to call—depending on the particular rail company—to book your ticket. If you order online, be sure you know what you want; it's tough to reach a person who can change your online reservation. You'll pick up your ticket at the station (unless your order was lost—this service still has some glitches). If you want your ticket mailed to you in the US, you need to allow a couple of weeks and cover the shipping costs. (BritRail passholders, however, cannot use the Web to make reservations.)

A company called **Megabus** (through their subsidiary Megatrain) sells some discounted train tickets well in advance on a few specific routes, though their focus is mainly on selling bus tickets (toll tel. 0871-266-3333, www.megatrain.com).

Buying Train Tickets as You Travel: If you'd rather have the flexibility of booking tickets as you go, you can save a few pounds by buying a round-trip ticket, called a "return ticket" (a same-day round-trip, called a "day return," is particularly cheap); buying before 18:00 the day before you depart; traveling after the morning rush hour (this usually means after 9:30 Mon–Fri); and going standard class instead of first class. Preview your options at www.nationalrail.co.uk or www.thetrainline.com.

Senior, Youth, and Family Deals: To get a third off the price of most point-to-point rail tickets, seniors can buy a Senior Railcard (for ages 60 and above), and younger travelers can buy a 16–25 Railcard (for ages 16–25, or for full-time students 26 and above with a valid ISIC card). A Family Railcard allows adults to travel about 33 percent cheaper while their kids ages 5 to 15 receive a 60 percent discount for most trips (maximum of 4 adults and 4 kids). Each Railcard costs £26; see www.railcard.co.uk. Any of these cards are valid for a year on almost all trains except special runs, such as the Heathrow Express or the Eurostar to Paris or Brussels (fill out application at station, brochures on racks in info center, need to show passport; passport-type photo needed for 16–25 Railcard).

Railpasses: Consider getting a railpass. The BritRail pass comes in "consecutive day" and "flexi" versions, with price breaks for youths, seniors, off-season travelers, and groups of three of more. Most allow one child under 16 to travel free with a paying adult. If you're exploring Britain's backcountry with a BritRail pass, standard class is a good choice since many of the smaller train lines don't even offer first-class cars. BritRail passes cover England as well as Scotland and Wales.

More BritRail options include England-only passes, Scotland-only passes, Britain/Ireland passes, "London Plus" passes (good for travel in most of southeast England but not in London itself), and BritRail & Drive passes (which offer you some rail days and some car-rental days). These BritRail passes, as well as Eurailpasses, get you a discount on the Eurostar train that zips you to continental Europe under the English Channel. These passes are sold outside of Europe only. For specifics, see www.ricksteves.com/rail.

Buses

Although buses are about a third slower than trains, they're also a lot cheaper. Most buses are operated by **National Express** (toll tel. 0871-781-8181, www.nationalexpress.com). Note that Brits distinguish between "buses" (for in-city travel with lots of stops) and "coaches" (long-distance cross-country runs)—though for simplicity in this book, I call both "buses."

Round-trip bus tickets usually cost less than two one-way fares (e.g., London–York one-way costs about £26; round-trip cost about £40). And buses go many places that trains don't. Budget travelers can save a wad with a bus pass. National Express sells **Brit Xplorer bus passes** for unlimited travel on consecutive days (£79/7 days, £139/14 days, £219/28 days, sold over the counter, non-UK passport required, toll tel. 0871-781-8181, www.nationalexpress.com). Check their website to learn about online Funfare deals; senior/youth/family cards and fares; and discounts for advance booking.

If you want to take a bus from your last destination to the nearest airport, you'll find that National Express often offers **airport buses.** Bus stations are normally at or near train stations (in London, the main bus station is a block southwest of Victoria Station).

Megabus sells very cheap promotional fares on certain routes, often beating National Express in price. While this can save you some money, you have to book far ahead for the best rates, and journey times tend to be longer than those on National Express (toll tel. 0900-160-0900, www.megabus.com). They also sell discounted train tickets on selected routes.

A couple of companies offer **backpackers' bus circuits.** These easy hop-on, hop-off bus circuits take mostly youth hostelers around the country for super-cheap fares, with the assumption that they'll be sleeping in the hostels along the way. For instance, **Backpacker Tours** offers 1–19-day excursions through Britain (from about £65/1 day, £90/3 days, £266/5 days, toll tel. 0870-745-1046, www.backpackertours.co.uk, sales@backpackertours.co.uk).

Renting a Car

To rent a car in Britain, you must be at least 23 years old and have a valid license. Drivers under the age of 25 may incur a young-driver surcharge, and some companies do not rent to anyone 75 and over. If you're considered too young or old, look into leasing, which has less-stringent age restrictions (see "Leasing," later). To drive in Britain, an International Driving Permit is recommended, but not required ($15 through your local AAA, plus two passport-type photos, www.aaa.com); I've frequently rented cars in Britain without having or being asked to show this permit.

Research car rentals before you go. It's cheaper to arrange most car rentals from the US. Call several companies and look online to compare rates, or arrange a rental through your home-town travel agent. Most of the major US rental agencies—such as Enterprise, Alamo, National, Avis/Budget, Dollar, Hertz, and Thrifty—have offices in Britain (although some subcontract to Europcar). It can be cheaper to use a consolidator, such as Auto Europe (www.autoeurope.com) or Europe by Car (www.ebctravel.com), but by using a middleman, you risk trading customer service for lower prices; if you have a problem with the rental company, you can't count on the consolidator to intervene on your behalf.

For the best deal, rent by the week with unlimited mileage. If you want to save money on gas, ask for a diesel car. I normally rent the smallest, least-expensive model with a stick-shift. Almost all rentals are manual by default, so if you need an automatic, you must request one in advance; beware that these cars are usually larger models (not as maneuverable on narrow, winding roads). An automatic transmission adds about 50 percent to the car-rental cost over a manual transmission. But weigh this against the fact that in Britain, you'll be sitting on the right side of the car, and shifting with your left hand...while driving on the left side of the road. The floor pedals are in the same locations as in the US, and the gears are found in the same basic "H" pattern as at home (i.e., first gear, second, etc.).

Expect to pay about $900 per person (based on two people sharing) for a small economy car for three weeks with unlimited mileage, including gas, parking, and insurance. Consider leasing to save money on insurance and taxes.

Compare pick-up costs (downtown can be cheaper than the airport) and explore drop-off options. For a trip covering both Britain and Ireland, you're better off with two separate car rentals. If you pick up the car in a smaller city, such as Bath, you'll more likely survive your first day on the British roads. Returning a car at a big-city train station can be tricky; get precise details on the car drop-off location and hours. Note that rental offices usually close from midday Saturday until Monday.

If you drop the car off early or keep it longer, you'll be credited or charged at a fair, prorated price. But keep your receipts in case any questions arise about your billing.

When you pick up the car, check it thoroughly and make sure any damage is noted on your rental agreement. Find out how your car's lights, turn signals, wipers, and gas cap function. Ask what type of fuel your car takes before you fill up. When you return the car, make sure the agent verifies its condition with you.

Car Insurance Options

When you rent a car, you are liable for a very high deductible, sometimes equal to the entire value of the car. Limit your financial risk by choosing one of these three options: Buy Collision Damage Waiver (CDW) coverage from the car-rental company, get coverage through your credit card (free, if your card automatically includes zero-deductible coverage), or buy coverage through Travel Guard.

CDW includes a very high deductible (typically $1,000–1,500). Though each rental company has its own variation, basic CDW costs $15–25 a day (figure roughly 25 percent extra) and reduces your liability, but does not eliminate it. When you pick up the car, you'll be offered the chance to "buy down" the basic deductible to zero (for an additional $15–30/day; this is sometimes called "super CDW").

If you opt for **credit-card coverage,** there's a catch. You'll technically have to decline all coverage offered by the car-rental company, which means they can place a hold on your card (which can be up to the full value of the car). In case of damage, it can be time-consuming to resolve the charges with your credit-card company. Before you decide on this option, quiz your credit-card company about how it works.

Finally, you can buy CDW insurance from **Travel Guard** ($9/day plus a one-time $3 service fee covers you for up to $35,000, $250 deductible, tel. 800-826-4919, www.travelguard.com). It's valid everywhere in Europe except the Republic of Ireland, and some Italian car-rental companies refuse to honor it. Oddly, residents of Washington state and Texas aren't allowed to buy this coverage.

For more on car-rental insurance, see www.ricksteves.com/cdw.

Leasing

For trips of two and a half weeks or more, leasing (which automatically includes zero-deductible collision and theft insurance) is the best way to go. By technically buying and then selling back the car, you save lots of money on tax and insurance. Leasing provides you a brand-new car with unlimited mileage and a 24-hour emergency assistance program. You can lease for as little as 17 days to as long as six months. Car leases must be arranged from the US. One of many reliable companies offering affordable lease packages is Europe by Car (US tel. 800-223-1516, www.ebctravel.com).

Driving in Britain

Driving in Britain is basically wonderful—once you remember to stay on the left and after you've mastered the roundabouts. Every year, however, I get a few notes from traveling readers advising me that, for them, trying to drive in Britain was a nerve-racking and regrettable mistake. If you want to get a little slack on the roads, drop by a gas station or auto shop and buy a green *P* (probationary driver with license) sign to put in your car window (don't get the red *L* sign, which means you're a learner driver without a license and thus prohibited from driving on motorways).

Many Yankee drivers find the hardest part isn't driving on the left, but steering from the right. Your instinct is to put yourself on the left side of your lane, which means you

STOP **AND LEARN THESE ROAD SIGNS**

- (50) Speed Limit (mph)
- Yield
- No Passing
- End of No Passing Zone
- One Way
- Intersection
- Main Road
- Freeway
- Danger
- No Entry
- No Entry for cars
- All Vehicles Prohibited
- Parking
- No Parking
- Customs
- Peace

may spend your first day or two constantly drifting off the road to the left. It can help to remember that the driver always stays close to the center line.

Road Rules: Seat belts are mandatory for all, and kids under age 12 (or less than about 4.5 feet tall) must ride in an appropriate child-safety seat. It's illegal to use a mobile phone while driving—pull over if you need to chat or text. For more information about driving in Britain, read the Department for Transport's *Highway Code* (buy it in the UK or visit www.direct.gov.uk—click on "Motoring" and look for "The Highway Code" link).

Speed Limits: Speed limits are 30 mph in town, 70 mph on the motorways, and 50 or 60 mph elsewhere (though, as back home, many British drivers consider these limits advisory). The national sign for 60 mph is a white circle with a black slash. Motorways have electronic speed limit signs; posted speeds can change

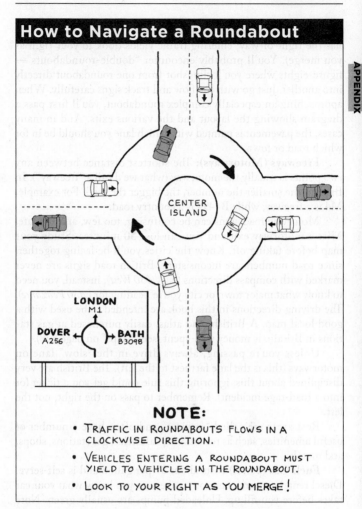

How to Navigate a Roundabout

LONDON
M1

DOVER
A256

BATH
B3098

NOTE:

- TRAFFIC IN ROUNDABOUTS FLOWS IN A CLOCKWISE DIRECTION.
- VEHICLES ENTERING A ROUNDABOUT MUST YIELD TO VEHICLES IN THE ROUNDABOUT.
- LOOK TO YOUR RIGHT AS YOU MERGE!

depending on traffic or the weather. Follow them accordingly.

Note that road-surveillance cameras strictly enforce speed

limits. Any driver (including foreigners renting cars) photographed speeding will get a nasty bill in the mail. (Cameras—you'll see the foreboding gray boxes—flash on your rear license plate in order not to invade the privacy of anyone sharing the front seat with someone he or she shouldn't be with.)

Roundabouts: Don't let a roundabout spook you. After all, you routinely merge into much faster traffic on American highways back home. Traffic in roundabouts has the right-of-way; entering traffic yields (look to your right as you merge). You'll probably encounter "double-roundabouts"—figure-eights where you'll slingshot from one roundabout directly into another. Just go with the flow and track signs carefully. When approaching an especially complex roundabout, you'll first pass a diagram showing the layout and the various exits. And in many cases, the pavement is painted with which lane you should be in for which road or town.

Freeways (Motorways): The shortest distance between any two points is usually the motorway (what we'd call a "freeway"). In Britain, the smaller the number, the bigger the road. For example, M4 is a freeway, while B4494 is a country road.

Motorway road signs can be confusing, too few, and too late. Miss a motorway exit and you can lose 30 minutes. Study your map before taking off. Know the cities you'll be lacing together, since road numbers are inconsistent. British road signs are never marked with compass directions (e.g., *A30 West*); instead, you need to know what major town or city you're heading for (*A30 Penzance*). The driving directions in this book are intended to be used with a good local map. A British road atlas, easily purchased at gas stations in Britain, is money well-spent (see "Maps" on page 828).

Unless you're passing, always drive in the "slow" lane on motorways (this is the lane farthest to the left). The British are very disciplined about this; ignoring this rule could get you a ticket (or into a road-rage incident). Remember to pass on the right, not the left.

Rest areas are called "services" and often have a number of useful amenities, such as restaurants, cafeterias, gas stations, shops, and motels.

Fuel: Gas (petrol) costs about $9 per gallon and is self-serve. Diesel rental cars are common; make sure you know what your car takes before you fill up. Unleaded pumps are usually green. Note that your US credit and debit cards are unlikely to work at self-service gas pumps, as well as toll bridges and automated parking garages. It might help if you know your PIN, but just in case, be sure to carry sufficient cash.

Driving in Cities: Whenever possible, avoid driving in cities. Be warned that London assesses a congestion charge (see page 56). Most cities have modern ring roads to skirt the congestion. Follow signs to the parking lots outside the city core—most are a 5- to 10-minute walk to the center—and avoid what can be an unpleasant grid of one-way streets (as in Bath) or roads that are only available to public transportation during the day (as in Oxford).

Britain by Car: Mileage and Time

m = miles
h = hours

Note: Your times may vary based on traffic, construction, and road conditions.

SCOTLAND

Portree
35m 1h
85m • 2h
Inverness
Kyle of Lochalsh
90m • 2.5h
85m • 3h
90m • 1.75h
Glencoe
90m • 2.75h
Pitlochry
35m • 1h →
60m • 1.5h
Oban
120m • 3h
St. Andrews
125m • 3.25h
70m • 1.5h
100m • 2.5h
50m • 1.5h
Glasgow
50m • 1h
Edinburgh
75m • 2h
Holy Island
90m • 2.25h
130m • 3h
125m • 2.75h
80m • 1.75h
135m • 2.5h
100m • 2.5h
Stranraer
145m • 3h
Hadrian's Wall (Housesteads Fort)
65m • 1.5h
50m • 1h
Durham
Keswick (N. Lake Dist.)
20m • .5h →
120m • 3h
85m • 2h
Windermere (S. Lake Dist.)
60m • 1.25h →
75m • 2h
Whitby
Blackpool
90m • 1.75h
120m • 2.5h
35m • 1h
York
55m 1.25h →
40m • .75h
60m • 1.25h
Liverpool
130m • 3.5h
160m • 3h
Holyhead
Conwy
25m • .5h →
30m • .25h
30m 1.25h
15m • .5h →
Caernarfon
Ruthin
75m • 2h
145m • 2.75h
220m • 4h
25m • .75h →
30m 1h
Snowdonia (Betws-y-Coed)
60m • 1.5h
Ironbridge Gorge
ENGLAND
170m • 4h
70m • 1.75h
Warwick
10m • .25h
110m
150m • 3.5h
Stratford
2h
Cambridge
10m • .5h
Cotswolds (Chipping Campden)
WALES
100m • 2h
65m 1.75h
115m • 2.5h
90m • 2h
1.25h
Cardiff
Bath
60m 1.5h
Avebury
London
55m 1.25h →
20m • .75h
30m • 1h
85m • 1.75h
Wells
30m 1h
75m • 1.5h
10m • .25h →
40m • 1h
100m • 2h
Glastonbury
50m • 1.25h
Salisbury (Stonehenge)
Dover

Driving in Rural Areas: Outside of the big cities and the motorways, British roads tend to be narrow. In towns, you may have to cross over the center line just to get past parked cars. Adjust your perceptions of personal space: It's not "my side of the road" or "your side of the road," it's just "the road"—and it's shared as a cooperative adventure. If the road's wide enough, both directions of traffic can pass parked cars simultaneously, but frequently you'll have to take turns—follow the locals' lead and drive defensively. Some narrow country lanes are barely wide enough for one car. Go slowly, and if you encounter an oncoming car, look for the nearest pullout (or "passing place")—the driver who's closest to one is expected to use it, even if they have to back up to reach it. If another car pulls over and blinks its headlights, that means, "Go ahead; I'll wait to let you pass." British drivers are quick to offer a friendly wave to thank you for letting them pass (and they appreciate it if you reciprocate). Pull over frequently—to let faster locals pass and to check the map.

Parking: Parking can be confusing. One yellow line marked on the pavement means no parking Monday through Saturday during work hours. Double yellow lines mean no parking at any time. Broken yellow lines mean short stops are OK, but you should always look for explicit signs or ask a passerby. White lines mean you're free to park.

In towns, rather than look for street parking, I generally just pull into the most central and handy "pay and display" parking lot I can find. To "pay and display," feed change into a machine, receive a timed ticket, and display it on the dashboard or stick it to the driver's-side window. Rates are reasonable by US standards, and locals love to share stickers that have time remaining. If you stand by the machine, someone on their way out with time left on their sticker will probably give it to you. Keep a bag of coins in the ashtray or glove box for these machines and for parking meters.

Traffic Alerts: If you want to stay up-to-date on traffic conditions, ask your rental-car company about turning on automatic traffic alerts that play on the car radio. Once these are enabled (look for the letters *TA* or *TP* on the radio readout), traffic reports for the area you are driving in will periodically interrupt programming.

The AA: An Automobile Association membership for Britain comes with most rentals (www.theaa.com). Understand its towing and emergency road-service benefits.

Stock Up: Set your car up for a fun road trip. Establish a cardboard-box munchies pantry. Buy a rack of liter boxes of juice for the trunk, and some Windex and a roll of paper towels (called a "kitchen roll" in Britain) for cleaner sightseeing.

Cheap Flights

London is the hub for many cheap, no-frills airlines, which affordably connect the city with other destinations in the British Isles and throughout Europe. While trains are still the best way to connect places that are close together, a flight can save both time and money on long journeys.

One of the best websites for comparing inexpensive flights is www.skyscanner.net. Other comparison search engines include www.wegolo.com and www.whichbudget.com. Buy tickets in advance. Although you can usually book right up until the flight departs, the cheap seats will often have sold out long before, leaving the most expensive seats for latecomers.

Be aware of the potential drawbacks of flying on the cheap: nonrefundable and nonchangeable tickets, minimal or nonexistent customer service, additional charges for everything (with Ryanair being the worst offender), treks to airports far outside town, and pricey baggage fees. Read the small print—especially baggage policies—before you book.

With **bmi,** you can fly inexpensively from London to destinations in the UK and beyond. Fares start at about £45 one-way to Edinburgh, Dublin, Brussels, or Amsterdam (toll tel. 0870-607-0555, US tel. 800-788-0555, www.flybmi.com).

Another low-cost airline, **easyJet** flies from Gatwick, Luton, and Stansted, as well as Liverpool. Prices are based on demand, so the least popular routes make for the cheapest fares, especially if you book early (toll tel. 0905-821-0905, calls £0.65/minute, www.easyjet.com).

Irish-owned **Ryanair** flies from London (mostly Stansted Airport, though also Gatwick and Luton), Liverpool, and Glasgow to often obscure airports near Dublin, Frankfurt, Stockholm, Oslo, Venice, Turin, and many others. Sample fares: London–Dublin—£50 round-trip (sometimes as low as £30), London–Frankfurt—£45 round-trip (Irish toll tel. 0818-303-030, British toll tel. 0871-246-0000, www.ryanair.com). However, be warned that Ryanair charges additional fees for nearly everything. The company requires a mandatory online-only check-in (£5 charge), from 15 days to four hours before your flight (no airport check-in). When checking in, you must also print out your boarding pass; if you show up without it, there's an additional £40 charge. You can carry on only a small day bag; you'll pay a fee for each checked bag (price depends on number of bags; up to three bags allowed per passenger).

Brussels Airlines (formerly Virgin Express) is a Brussels-based company with good rates and hubs in Bristol, Birmingham, Gatwick, Manchester, and Newcastle (book by phone and pick up ticket at airport an hour before your flight, US tel. 516/740-5200, British toll tel. 0905-609-5609—£0.40/minute, www.brussels airlines.com).

Resources

Resources from Rick Steves

Rick Steves' Great Britain 2011 is one of many books in my series on European travel, which includes country guidebooks (such as *Rick Steves' England*), city and regional guidebooks (including London), Snapshot guides (excerpted chapters from my country guides), Pocket guides (full-color little books on big cities), and my budget-travel skills handbook, *Rick Steves' Europe Through the Back Door*. My phrase books—for French, Italian, German, Spanish, and Portuguese—are practical and budget-oriented. My other books include *Europe 101* (a crash course on art and history) and *Travel as a Political Act* (a travelogue sprinkled with tips for bringing home a global perspective). For a list of my books, see the inside of the last page of this book.

Video: My public television series, *Rick Steves' Europe,* covers European destinations in 100 shows, with 10 episodes on Great Britain. To watch episodes, visit www.hulu.com/rick-steves -europe; for scripts and other details, see www.ricksteves.com/tv.

Audio: My weekly public radio show, *Travel with Rick Steves,* features interviews with travel experts from around the world. I've also produced free self-guided audio tours of the top sights and neighborhoods in London. All of this audio content is available for free at Rick Steves' Audio Europe, an extensive online library organized by destination. Choose whatever interests you, and download it for free to your iPod, smartphone, or computer at www.rick steves.com/audioeurope or iTunes.

Maps

The black-and-white maps in this book, drawn by Dave Hoerlein, are concise and simple. Dave, who is well-traveled in Britain, designed the maps to help you locate recommended places and get to local TIs, where you can pick up more in-depth maps of towns or regions (usually free). Better maps are sold at newsstands and

Begin Your Trip at www.ricksteves.com

At our travel website, you'll find a wealth of free information on European destinations, including fresh monthly news and helpful tips from thousands of fellow travelers. You'll also find my latest guidebook updates (www.ricksteves.com/update) and my travel blog.

Our **online Travel Store** offers travel bags and accessories specially designed by Rick Steves to help you travel smarter and lighter. These include Rick's popular carry-on bags (roll-aboard and rucksack versions), money belts, totes, toiletries kits, adapters, other accessories, and a wide selection of guidebooks, planning maps, and DVDs.

Choosing the right **railpass** for your trip—amidst hundreds of options—can drive you nutty. We'll help you choose the best pass for your needs, plus give you a bunch of free extras.

Rick Steves' Europe Through the Back Door travel company offers **tours** with more than three dozen itineraries and 400 departures reaching the best destinations in this book...and beyond. We offer a 14-day England tour, an 11-day Scotland tour, and a 7-day in-depth London city tour. You'll enjoy great guides, a fun bunch of travel partners (with small groups of around 28), and plenty of room to spread out in a big, comfy bus. You'll find European adventures to fit every vacation length. For all the details, and to get our Tour Catalog and a free Rick Steves Tour Experience DVD (filmed on location during an actual tour), visit www.ricksteves.com or call the Tour Department at 425/608-4217.

bookstores. Before you buy a map, look at it to be sure it has the level of detail you want.

If you'll be lingering in London, buy a city map at a London newsstand; the red *Benson's London Street Map* (£2.75) is excellent. Even the vending-machine maps sold in Tube stations are good. The *Rough Guide* map to London is well-designed (£5, sold at London bookstores). The *Rick Steves' Britain, Ireland & London City Map* has a good map of London ($6, www.ricksteves.com). Many Londoners, along with obsessive-compulsive tourists, rely on the highly detailed *London A–Z* map book (generally £5–7, called "A to Zed" by locals, available at newsstands).

If you're driving, get a road atlas (1 inch equals 3 miles) covering all of Britain. Ordnance Survey, AA, and Bartholomew editions are all available for about £7 at tourist information offices, gas stations, and bookstores. Drivers, hikers, and cyclists may want more in-depth maps for the Cotswolds, the Lake District, and Snowdonia (North Wales).

Other Guidebooks

If you're like most travelers, this book is all you need. But if you're heading beyond my recommended neighborhoods and destinations, $40 for extra maps and books is money well-spent. Especially for several people traveling by car, the extra weight and expense are negligible.

The following books are worthwhile, though not updated annually; check the publication date before you buy. The *Lonely Planet* and *Let's Go* guidebooks on London and on Britain are fine budget-travel guides. *Lonely Planet*'s guidebooks are more thorough and informative; *Let's Go* books are youth-oriented, with good coverage of nightlife, hostels, and cheap transportation deals. For cultural and sightseeing background, look into Michelin and Cadogan guides to London, England, and Britain. The readable Access guide for London is similarly well-researched. *Secret London* by Andrew Duncan leads the reader on unique walks through a less-touristy London. If you're a literature fan, consider picking up *The Edinburgh Literary Companion* (Lownie).

If you'll be focusing on London or traveling elsewhere in Britain, consider *Rick Steves' London 2011* or *Rick Steves' England 2011*.

Recommended Books and Movies

To learn more about Britain past and present, check out a few of these books and films.

Nonfiction

For a serious historical overview, wade into *A History of Britain*, a three-volume collection by Simon Schama. *Literary Trails* (Hardyment) reunites famous authors with the environments that inspired them. *A Traveller's History of England* (Daniell), *A Traveller's History of Scotland* (Fisher), and *A History of Wales* (Davies) provide good, succinct summaries of British history. Other possibilities include the humorous *Notes from a Small Island* (Bryson), *The Matter of Wales* (Morris), or any of the books by Susan Allen Toth on her British travels.

If you'll be spending time in the Cotswolds, try *Cider with Rosie,* Laurie Lee's boyhood memoir set just after World War I. If you'll be visiting Scotland, consider reading *Crowded with Genius* (Buchan) or *How the Scots Invented the Modern World* (Herman), which explains the influence the Scottish Enlightenment had on the rest of Europe. *The Guynd* is a memoir of a woman who married into a historic Highlands estate. And the obsessive world of British soccer is illuminated in Nick Hornby's memoir, *Fever Pitch.*

Fiction

For the classics of British fiction, read anything—and everything— by Charles Dickens, Jane Austen, and the Brontës. Mystery fans can't miss with any of the books by Agatha Christie. *Kidnapped,* by Robert Louis Stevenson, is a fantastic adventure story set in Scotland. Sharon Kay Penman brings 13th-century Wales to life in *Here Be Dragons.* And in the romantic, swashbuckling *Outlander* series (Gabaldon), the heroine time-travels between the Scotland of 1945 and 1743.

Pillars of the Earth (Follett) traces the building of a fictional 12th-century cathedral in southern England. For a big book on the era of King Richard III, try *The Sunne in Splendour,* one in a series by Sharon Kay Penman. *The Other Boleyn Girl* (Gregory) sets its intrigues in the court of Henry VIII, while *Restoration* (Tremain) returns readers to the time of King Charles II.

Set in the 19th-century Anglican church, *The Warden* (Trollope) dwells on moral dilemmas. *Brideshead Revisited* (Waugh) satirizes the British obsession with class, taking place between the World Wars. A rural village in the 1930s is the social battlefield for E. F. Benson's *Mapp and Lucia.*

Mystery novels have a long tradition in Britain. *A Morbid Taste for Bones* (Peters) features a Benedictine monk-detective in 12th-century Shropshire. Agatha Christie's Miss Marple was introduced in 1930 in *The Murder at the Vicarage.* And Ian Rankin's troubled Inspector Rebus first gets his man in *Knots and Crosses,* set in modern-day Edinburgh. For a modern mystery, try any of the books in the Inspector Lynley series by Elizabeth George. For a more contemporary read, check out *Bridget Jones's Diary* (Fielding), *Behind the Scenes at the Museum* (Atkinson), *White Teeth* (Smith),

Harry Potter Sights

Harry Potter's story is set in a magical Britain. Except for those in London, all of the places mentioned in the books are fictional—though you can still visit many real film locations. So quicker than you can say "Lumos," let's shine a light on where to get your Harry Potter fix if you're a die-hard fan.

Spoiler Warning: The following information will ruin surprises for the three of you who haven't yet read or seen any of the Harry Potter books or movies.

London

In the first film, Harry first realizes his wizard powers when talking with a boa constrictor, filmed at the **London Zoo's Reptile House** in Regent's Park (Tube: Great Portland Street).

London bustles along oblivious to the parallel universe of wizards, hidden in the magical Diagon Alley (filmed, like many of the other fictional settings, on a set at Leavesden Studios, north of London). The goblin-run Gringotts Wizarding Bank, though, was filmed in the real-life marble-floored Exhibition Hall of **Australia House** (Tube: Temple), home of the Australian Embassy.

Harry catches the train to Hogwarts at **King's Cross Station.**

Inside the glass-roofed train station, on a **pedestrian sky bridge** over the tracks, Hagrid gives Harry a train ticket. Harry heads to platform 9¾. You'll find a fun re-creation—complete with a *Platform 9¾* sign and a luggage cart that appears to be disappearing into the wall—on the way to platform 9. (Walk toward the pedestrian bridge and make a left at the arch.)

In film #3, Harry careens through London's lamp-lit streets on a purple three-decker bus that dumps him at the Leaky Cauldron pub. The exterior was shot on rough-looking Stoney Street at the southeast edge of **Borough Street Market,** by The Market Porter pub (Tube: London Bridge).

In film #5, the Order of the Phoenix takes to the night sky on broomsticks over London, passing over plenty of identifiable landmarks, including the **London Eye, Big Ben,** and **Buckingham Palace.**

In film #6, the **Millennium Bridge** is attacked and collapses into the Thames.

APPENDIX

Near Bath

The mysterious side of Hogwarts is often set in the elaborate, fan-vaulted corridors of the **Gloucester Cathedral** cloisters, 50 miles north of Bath. In film #1, when Harry and Ron set out to save Hermione, they look down a long, dark Gloucester hallway and spot a 20-foot troll at the far end.

Also in film #1, the scene showing Harry being chosen for Gryffindor's Quidditch team was shot in the halls of the 13th-century **Lacock Abbey,** 13 miles east of Bath. Harry attends Professor Snape's class in one of the Abbey's bare, peeling-plaster rooms—appropriate to Snape's temperament. (Mad Max tours include Lacock on its day-trip itinerary; for details, see page 238.)

Durham and Northeast England

In the first film, Harry walks with his white owl, Hedwig, through a snowy cloister courtyard located in **Durham's Cathedral** (see listing on page 514). The bird soars up and over the church's twin 13th-century towers.

Harry first learns to fly a broomstick on the green grass of Hogwarts school grounds, filmed inside the walls of **Alnwick Castle,** located 30 miles from Newcastle. In film #2, this is where the Weasleys' flying car crashes into the Whomping Willow.

Scotland

A lot of what you'll see in the exterior shots in the Harry Potter movies—especially scenes of the Hogwarts grounds—was filmed in craggy, cloudy, mysterious Scotland, much of it in the Fort William and Glencoe areas.

The **Hogwarts Express train** that carries Harry, Ron, and Hermione to school each year is filmed along an actual steam-train line that runs from Fort William to Mallaig (tourists can ride this Jacobite Steam Train—see page 726). The movies show the train chugging across the real-life **Glenfinnan Viaduct,** where, in film #4, the Dementors stall the train and torture Harry. A train bridge opposite Loch Shiel near Fort William was shown in film #2 and was used when the Dementor boarded the train in film #3. In film #3, Hogwarts Lake was filmed using Loch Shiel, Loch Eilt, and Loch Morar near Fort William, and Hagrid skips stones across the water at **Loch Eilt. Steal Falls,** a waterfall at the base of Ben Nevis, is the locale for Harry's battle with a dragon for the Triwizard Tournament in film #4.

Other scenes filmed in the Highlands include a desolate hillside with Hagrid's stone hut in **Glencoe,** which was the main location for outdoor filming in movie #3.

Saturday (McEwan), or anything by Nick Hornby (*High Fidelity*, *About a Boy*, etc.).

Films

Goodbye, Mr. Chips (1939) is set in a boys' boarding school during Victorian England. *Mrs. Miniver* (1942), a sentimental WWII picture, won the Academy Award for Best Picture, as did *How Green Was My Valley* (1941), set in a 19th-century Welsh mining village.

If Scotland is on your itinerary, consider viewing the Hitchcock mystery *The 39 Steps* (1935); *I Know Where I'm Going!* (1945), a charming love story filmed on the Island of Mull; the musical *Brigadoon* (1954); and/or the funny, fish-out-of-water flick *Local Hero* (1983). *The Wicker Man* (1973), a horror flick, shows a different side of a small Scottish town.

If you're in the mood for something completely different, try *Monty Python and the Holy Grail* (1975), a surreal take on the Arthurian legend. *Chariots of Fire* (1981) ran away with the Academy Award for Best Picture. *Hope and Glory* (1987) is a semi-autobiographical story of a boy growing up during WWII's Blitz.

A Room with a View (1985) and *The Remains of the Day* (1993) include scenes filmed in rural England. *Shadowlands* (1993) tells a fictionalized account of author C. S. Lewis' relationship with his future wife. Among the many versions of *Pride and Prejudice*, the 1995 BBC miniseries starring Colin Firth is the winner.

In 1995, Scottish history had a mini-renaissance, with *Braveheart*, winner of the Best Picture Oscar, and *Rob Roy*, which some historians consider the more accurate of the two films. The UK television series *Monarch of the Glen* (2000) features stunning Highland scenery and the eccentric family of a modern-day Laird.

For a taste of Tudor-era London, try *Shakespeare in Love* (1999), which is set in the original Globe Theatre. The all-star *Gosford Park* (2001) is part comedy, part murder mystery, and part critique of England's class stratification in the 1930s. In *The Queen* (2006), Helen Mirren expertly channels Elizabeth II during the days after Princess Diana's death. In *The Duchess* (2008), the 18th-century Duchess of Devonshire glides languidly through life in big skirts and even bigger wigs. *An Education* (2009), about a bright schoolgirl who falls for an older man, takes place in 1960s London.

Holidays and Festivals

This list includes many—but not all—big festivals in major cities, plus national holidays observed throughout Great Britain. Before planning a trip around a festival, make sure you verify its dates by checking the festival's website or contacting the Visit Britain

2011

JANUARY
S	M	T	W	T	F	S
						1
2	3	4	5	6	7	8
9	10	11	12	13	14	15
16	17	18	19	20	21	22
23/30	24/31	25	26	27	28	29

FEBRUARY
S	M	T	W	T	F	S
		1	2	3	4	5
6	7	8	9	10	11	12
13	14	15	16	17	18	19
20	21	22	23	24	25	26
27	28					

MARCH
S	M	T	W	T	F	S
		1	2	3	4	5
6	7	8	9	10	11	12
13	14	15	16	17	18	19
20	21	22	23	24	25	26
27	28	29	30	31		

APRIL
S	M	T	W	T	F	S
					1	2
3	4	5	6	7	8	9
10	11	12	13	14	15	16
17	18	19	20	21	22	23
24	25	26	27	28	29	30

MAY
S	M	T	W	T	F	S
1	2	3	4	5	6	7
8	9	10	11	12	13	14
15	16	17	18	19	20	21
22	23	24	25	26	27	28
29	30	31				

JUNE
S	M	T	W	T	F	S
			1	2	3	4
5	6	7	8	9	10	11
12	13	14	15	16	17	18
19	20	21	22	23	24	25
26	27	28	29	30		

JULY
S	M	T	W	T	F	S
					1	2
3	4	5	6	7	8	9
10	11	12	13	14	15	16
17	18	19	20	21	22	23
24/31	25	26	27	28	29	30

AUGUST
S	M	T	W	T	F	S
	1	2	3	4	5	6
7	8	9	10	11	12	13
14	15	16	17	18	19	20
21	22	23	24	25	26	27
28	29	30	31			

SEPTEMBER
S	M	T	W	T	F	S
				1	2	3
4	5	6	7	8	9	10
11	12	13	14	15	16	17
18	19	20	21	22	23	24
25	26	27	28	29	30	

OCTOBER
S	M	T	W	T	F	S
						1
2	3	4	5	6	7	8
9	10	11	12	13	14	15
16	17	18	19	20	21	22
23/30	24/31	25	26	27	28	29

NOVEMBER
S	M	T	W	T	F	S
		1	2	3	4	5
6	7	8	9	10	11	12
13	14	15	16	17	18	19
20	21	22	23	24	25	26
27	28	29	30			

DECEMBER
S	M	T	W	T	F	S
				1	2	3
4	5	6	7	8	9	10
11	12	13	14	15	16	17
18	19	20	21	22	23	24
25	26	27	28	29	30	31

office (tel. 800-462-2748, www.visitbritain.com). Many sights and banks close down on national holidays—keep this in mind when planning your itinerary.

Many British towns have holiday festivals in late November and early December, with markets, music, and entertainment in the Christmas spirit (for instance, Keswick's Victorian Fayre). Here are some major holidays in 2011:

Jan 1	New Year's Day
Jan 2	New Year's Holiday (Scotland)
Feb (one week)	London Fashion Week (www.london fashionweek.co.uk)
Mid-Feb	Jorvik Viking Festival, York (costumed warriors, battles; www.jorvik-viking -centre.co.uk)
Feb 26–March 6	Literature Festival, Bath (www.bathlit fest.org.uk)
April 22	Good Friday

April 24–25	Easter Sunday and Monday
May 2	Early May Bank Holiday
Mid-May	Jazz Festival, Keswick (www.keswick jazzfestival.co.uk)
Late May	Chelsea Flower Show, London (book tickets in advance for this popular event at www.rhs.org.uk/chelsea)
May 25–June 5	International Music Festival, Bath (www.bathmusicfest.org.uk)
Late May–early June	Fringe Festival, Bath (alternative music, dance, and theater; www.bathfringe.co.uk)
May 30	Spring Bank Holiday (last Monday in May)
June 3–4	Beer Festival, Keswick (music, shows; www.keswickbeerfestival.co.uk)
Early–mid-June	Trooping the Colour, London (military bands and pageantry, Queen's birthday parade; www.trooping-the-colour.co.uk)
June 14–18	Royal Ascot Horse Race, Ascot (near Windsor; www.ascot.co.uk)
Mid–late June	Golowan (Midsummer) Festival, Penzance (www.golowan.com)
Late June–early July	Wimbledon Tennis Championship, London (www.wimbledon.org)
June 24–27	Royal Highland Show (Scottish county fair, www.royalhighlandshow.org), Edinburgh
July 6–11	International Eisteddfod (folk songs, dances, www.international-eisteddfod.co.uk), Llangollen
July 8–16	Early Music Festival, York (www.ncem.co.uk)
Late July–early Aug	Cambridge Folk Festival (buy tickets early at www.cambridgefolkfestival.co.uk)
Aug 2	Summer Bank Holiday (Scotland only, not England or Wales)
Aug 6–28	Military Tattoo (massing of bands, www.edinburgh-tattoo.co.uk), Edinburgh
Aug 6–30	Fringe Festival (offbeat theater and comedy, www.edfringe.com), Edinburgh
Aug 13–Sept 35	Edinburgh International Festival (music, dance, shows, www.eif.co.uk)

Late Aug	Notting Hill Carnival, London (costumes, Caribbean music, www.thenottinghillcarnival.com)
Aug 29	Late Summer Bank Holiday (England and Wales only, not Scotland)
Sept–Nov	Illuminations, Blackpool (waterfront light festival, www.visitblackpool.com/illuminations)
Sept (one week)	London Fashion Week (www.london fashionweek.co.uk)
Mid-Sept	Jane Austen Festival, Bath (www.janeausten.co.uk)
Late Sept	York Festival of Food and Drink (www.yorkfoodfestival.com)
Nov 5	Bonfire Night, or Guy Fawkes Night, Britain (fireworks, bonfires, effigy-burning of 1605 traitor Guy Fawkes)
Nov 30	St. Andrew's Day, Scotland
Dec 24–26	Christmas holidays
Dec 31–Jan 2	Hogmanay (music, street theater, carnival, www.hogmanay.net), Scotland

Conversions and Climate

Numbers and Stumblers

- In Europe, dates appear as day/month/year, so Christmas is 25/12/11.
- What Americans call the second floor of a building is the first floor in Britain.
- On escalators and moving sidewalks, Brits keep the left "lane" open for passing. Keep to the right.
- When pointing, use your whole hand, palm down.
- When counting with fingers, start with your thumb. If you hold up your first finger to request one item, you'll probably get two.
- To avoid the British version of giving someone "the finger," don't hold up the first two fingers of your hand with your palm facing you. (It looks like a reversed victory sign.)
- And please...don't call your waist pack a "fanny pack."

Metric Conversions (approximate)

Britain uses the metric system for everything but driving measurements. Weight and volume are typically calculated in metric: A kilogram is 2.2 pounds, and a liter is about a quart. The weight of a person is measured by "stone" (one stone equals 14 pounds). Temperatures are generally given in both Celsius and Fahrenheit.

On the road, Britain uses miles and posts speed limits in miles per hour.

1 foot = 0.3 meter	1 square yard = 0.8 square meter
1 yard = 0.9 meter	1 square mile = 2.6 square kilometers
1 mile = 1.6 kilometers	1 ounce = 28 grams
1 centimeter = 0.4 inch	1 quart = 0.95 liter
1 meter = 39.4 inches	1 kilogram = 2.2 pounds
1 kilometer = 0.62 mile	32°F = 0°C

Weights and Measures

1 British pint = 1.2 US pints
1 imperial gallon = 1.2 US gallons or about 4.5 liters
1 stone = 14 pounds (a 168-pound person weighs 12 stone)

Clothing Sizes

When shopping for clothing, use these US-to-Britain comparisons as general guidelines (but note that no conversion is perfect).

- Women's dresses and blouses: Add 4
  (US women's size 10 = UK size 14)
- Men's suits and jackets: US and UK use the same sizing
- Men's shirts: US and UK use the same sizing
- Women's shoes: Subtract 2½
  (US size 8 = UK size 5½)
- Men's shoes: Subtract about ½
  (US size 9 = UK size 8½)

Climate

First line, average daily temperature; second line, average daily low; third line, average days without rain. For more detailed weather statistics for destinations in this book (as well as the rest of the world), check www.worldclimate.com.

	J	F	M	A	M	J	J	A	S	O	N	D
LONDON												
	43°	44°	50°	56°	62°	69°	71°	71°	65°	58°	50°	45°
	36°	36°	38°	42°	47°	53°	56°	56°	52°	46°	42°	38°
	16	15	20	18	19	19	19	20	17	18	15	16

	J	F	M	A	M	J	J	A	S	O	N	D

CARDIFF (SOUTH WALES)

45°	45°	50°	56°	61°	68°	69°	69°	64°	58°	51°	46°
35°	35°	38°	41°	46°	51°	54°	55°	51°	46°	41°	37°
13	14	18	17	18	17	17	16	14	15	13	13

YORK

43°	44°	49°	55°	61°	67°	70°	69°	64°	57°	49°	45°
33°	34°	36°	40°	44°	50°	54°	53°	50°	44°	39°	36°
14	13	18	17	18	16	16	17	16	16	13	14

EDINBURGH

42°	43°	46°	51°	56°	62°	65°	64°	60°	54°	48°	44°
34°	34°	36°	39°	43°	49°	52°	52°	49°	44°	39°	36°
14	13	16	16	17	15	14	15	14	14	13	13

Temperature Conversion: Fahrenheit and Celsius

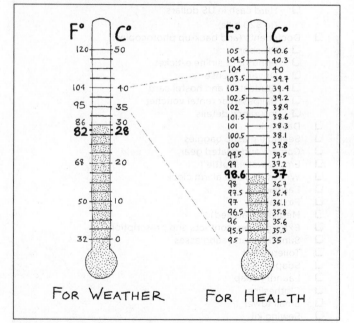

Britain uses both Celsius and Fahrenheit to take its temperature. For a rough conversion from Celsius to Fahrenheit, double the number and add 30. For weather, remember that 28°C is 82°F—perfect. For health, 37°C is just right.

Essential Packing Checklist

Whether you're traveling for five days or five weeks, here's what you'll need to bring. Remember to pack light to enjoy the sweet freedom of true mobility. Happy travels!

- ❑ 5 shirts
- ❑ 1 sweater or lightweight fleece jacket
- ❑ 2 pairs pants
- ❑ 1 pair shorts
- ❑ 1 swimsuit (women only—men can use shorts)
- ❑ 5 pairs underwear and socks
- ❑ 1 pair shoes
- ❑ 1 rain-proof jacket
- ❑ Tie or scarf
- ❑ Money belt
- ❑ Money—your mix of:
    - ❑ Debit card for ATM withdrawals
    - ❑ Credit card
    - ❑ Hard cash in US dollars (in $20 bills)
- ❑ Documents (and back-up photocopies):
    - ❑ Passport
    - ❑ Printout of airline e-ticket
    - ❑ Driver's license
    - ❑ Student ID and hostel card
    - ❑ Railpass/car rental voucher
    - ❑ Insurance details
- ❑ Daypack
- ❑ Sealable plastic baggies
- ❑ Camera and related gear
- ❑ Empty water bottle
- ❑ Wristwatch and alarm clock
- ❑ Earplugs
- ❑ First-aid kit
- ❑ Medicine (labeled)
- ❑ Extra glasses/contacts and prescriptions
- ❑ Sunscreen and sunglasses
- ❑ Toiletries kit
- ❑ Soap
- ❑ Laundry soap
- ❑ Clothesline
- ❑ Small towel
- ❑ Sewing kit
- ❑ Travel information
- ❑ Necessary map(s)
- ❑ Address list (email and mailing addresses)
- ❑ Postcards and photos from home
- ❑ Notepad and pen
- ❑ Journal

If you plan to carry on your luggage, note that all liquids must be in three-ounce or smaller containers and fit within a single quart-size baggie. For details, see www.tsa.gov/travelers.

Hotel Reservation

To: _____ _____
        hotel   *email or fax*

From: _____ _____
        name   *email or fax*

Today's date: _____ / _____ / _____
        day   *month*   *year*

Dear Hotel _____ ,
Please make this reservation for me:

Name: _____

Total # of people: _____   # of rooms: _____   # of nights: _____

Arriving: _____ / _____ / _____   My time of arrival (24-hr clock): _____
      day *month* *year*   (I will telephone if I will be late)

Departing: _____ / _____ / _____
      day *month* *year*

Room(s): Single___ Double ___ Twin ___ Triple ___ Quad ___

With: Toilet ___ Shower ___ Bath ___ Sink only___

Special needs: View___ Quiet___ Cheapest ___ Ground Floor___

Please email or fax confirmation of my reservation, along with the type of room reserved and the price. Please also inform me of your cancellation policy. After I hear from you, I will quickly send my credit-card information as a deposit to hold the room. Thank you.

_____
Name

_____
Address

_____
City   *State*   *Zip Code* *Country*

Before hoteliers can make your reservation, they want to know the information listed above. You can use this form as the basis for your email, or you can photocopy this page, fill in the information, and send it as a fax (also available online at www.ricksteves.com/reservation).

British-Yankee Vocabulary

For a longer list, plus a dry-witted primer on British culture, see *The Septic's Companion* (Chris Rae).

advert–advertisement

afters–dessert

anticlockwise–counterclockwise

Antipodean–An Australian or New Zealander

aubergine–eggplant

banger–sausage

bangers and mash–sausage and mashed potatoes

Bank Holiday–legal holiday

bap–small roll

bespoke–custom-made

billion–a thousand of our billions (a million million)

biro–ballpoint pen

biscuit–cookie

black pudding–sausage made from dried blood

bloody–damn

blow off–fart

bobby–policeman ("the Bill" is more common)

Bob's your uncle–there you go (with a shrug), naturally

boffin–nerd, geek

bollocks–testicles; also used as an exclamation of strong disbelief or disagreement

bolshy–argumentative

bomb–success or failure

bonnet–car hood

boot–car trunk

braces–suspenders

bridle way–path for walkers, bikers, and horse riders

brilliant–cool

brolly–umbrella

bubble and squeak–cabbage and potatoes fried together

bum–butt

candy floss–cotton candy

caravan–trailer

car-boot sale–temporary flea market, often for charity

car park–parking lot

cashpoint–ATM

casualty–emergency room

cat's eyes–road reflectors

ceilidh (KAY-lee)–informal evening of song and folk fun (Scottish and Irish)

cheap and cheerful–budget but adequate

cheap and nasty–cheap and bad quality

cheers–good-bye or thanks; also a toast

chemist–pharmacist

chicory–endive

chippie–fish-and-chips shop; carpenter

chips–French fries

chock-a-block–jam-packed

chuffed–pleased

cider–alcoholic apple cider

clearway–road where you can't stop

coach–long-distance bus

concession–discounted admission

concs (pronounced "conks")–short for "concession"

cos–romaine lettuce

cotton buds–Q-tips

courgette–zucchini

craic (pronounced "crack")–fun, good conversation (Irish/Scottish and spreading to England)

crisps–potato chips

cuppa–cup of tea

dear–expensive

dicey–iffy, risky

digestives–round graham cookies

dinner–lunch or dinner
diversion–detour
donkey's years–ages, long time
draughts–checkers
draw–marijuana
dual carriageway–divided highway (four lanes)
dummy–pacifier
elevenses–coffee-and-biscuits break before lunch
elvers–baby eels
face flannel–washcloth
fag–cigarette
fagged–exhausted
faggot–sausage
fancy–to like, to be attracted to (a person)
fanny–vagina
fell–hill or high plain (Lake District)
first floor–second floor
fizzy drink–pop or soda
flutter–a bet
football–soccer
force–waterfall (Lake District)
fortnight–two weeks (shortened from "fourteen nights")
fringe–hair bangs
Frogs–French people
fruit machine–slot machine
full Monty–whole shebang, everything
gallery–balcony
gammon–ham
gangway–aisle
gaol–jail (same pronunciation)
gateau (or gateaux)–cake
gear lever–stick shift
geezer–"dude"
give way–yield
glen–narrow valley (Scotland)
goods wagon–freight truck
green fingers–green thumbs
half eight–8:30 (not 7:30)
heath–open treeless land

hen night–bachelorette party
holiday–vacation
homely–homey or cozy
hoover–vacuum cleaner
ice lolly–Popsicle
interval–intermission
ironmonger–hardware store
ish–more or less
jacket potato–baked potato
jelly–Jell-O
Joe Bloggs–John Q. Public
jumble sale–rummage sale
jumper–sweater
just a tick–just a second
kipper–smoked herring
knackered–exhausted (Cockney: cream crackered)
knickers–ladies' panties
knocking shop–brothel
knock up–wake up or visit (old-fashioned)
ladybird–ladybug
lady fingers–flat, spongy cookie
lady's finger–okra
lager–light, fizzy beer
left luggage–baggage check
lemonade–lemon-lime pop like 7-Up, fizzy
lemon squash–lemonade, not fizzy
let–rent
licenced–restaurant authorized to sell alcohol
lift–elevator
listed–protected historic building
loo–toilet or bathroom
lorry–truck
mac–mackintosh raincoat
mangetout–snow peas
marrow–summer squash
mate–buddy (boy or girl)
mean–stingy
mental–wild, memorable

mews–former stables converted to two-story rowhouses (London)

mobile (MOH-bile)–cell phone

moggie–cat

motorway–freeway

naff–tacky or trashy

nappy–diaper

natter–talk on and on

neep–Scottish for turnip

newsagent–corner store

nought–zero

noughts & crosses–tic-tac-toe

off-licence–liquor store

on offer–for sale

panto, pantomime–fairy-tale play performed at Christmas (silly but fun)

pants–underwear, briefs

pasty (PASS-tee)–crusted savory (usually meat) pie from Cornwall

pavement–sidewalk

pear-shaped–messed up, gone wrong

petrol–gas

pillar box–mailbox

pissed (rude), **paralytic, bevvied, wellied, popped up, merry, trollied, ratted, rat-arsed, pissed as a newt**–drunk

pitch–playing field

plaster–Band-Aid

publican–pub owner

public school–private "prep" school (e.g., Eton)

pudding–dessert in general

pull, to be on the–on the prowl

punter–customer, especially in gambling

put a sock in it–shut up

queue–line

queue up–line up

quid–pound (£1)

randy–horny

rasher–slice of bacon

redundant, made–laid off

Remembrance Day–Veterans' Day

return ticket–round trip

revising; doing revisions–studying for exams

ring up–call (telephone)

roundabout–traffic circle

rubber–eraser

rubbish–bad

sausage roll–sausage wrapped in a flaky pastry

Scotch egg–hard-boiled egg wrapped in sausage meat

self-catering–accommodation with kitchen

Sellotape–Scotch tape

services–freeway rest area

serviette–napkin

setee–couch

shag–intercourse (cruder than in the US)

shandy–lager and 7-Up

silencer–car muffler

single ticket–one-way ticket

skip–Dumpster

sleeping policeman–speed bumps

smalls–underwear

snogging–kissing, making out

sod–mildly offensive insult

sod it, sod off–screw it, screw off

soda–soda water (not pop)

solicitor–lawyer

spanner–wrench

spend a penny–urinate

stag night–bachelor party

starkers–buck naked

starters–appetizers

state school–public school

sticking plaster–Band-Aid

sticky tape–Scotch tape

stone–14 pounds (weight)

stroppy–bad-tempered
subway–underground walkway
suet–fat from animal rendering (sometimes used in cooking)
sultanas–golden raisins
surgical spirit–rubbing alcohol
suspenders–garters
suss out–figure out
swede–rutabaga
ta–thank you
take the mickey/take the piss–tease
tatty–worn out or tacky
tattie scone–potato pancake
taxi rank–taxi stand
telly–TV
tenement–stone apartment house (not necessarily a slum)
tenner–£10 bill
theatre–live stage
tick–a check mark
tight as a fish's bum–cheapskate (watertight)
tights–panty hose
tin–can
tip–public dump
tipper lorry–dump truck
top hole–first rate
top up–refill (a drink, mobile-phone credit, petrol tank, etc.)
torch–flashlight
towel, press-on–panty liner
towpath–path along a river
trainers–sneakers
Tube–subway
twee–quaint, cutesy
twitcher–bird-watcher
Underground–subway
verge–grassy edge of road
verger–church official
way out–exit
wee (adj)–small (Scottish)
wee (verb)–urinate

Wellingtons, wellies–rubber boots
whacked–exhausted
whinge (rhymes with hinge)–whine
wind up–tease, irritate
witter on–gab and gab
yob–hooligan
zebra crossing–crosswalk
zed–the letter Z

INDEX

INDEX

INDEX

MAP INDEX

Free mobile app (and podcast)

With the **Rick Steves Audio Europe** app, your iPhone or smartphone becomes a powerful travel tool.

This exciting app organizes Rick's entire audio library by country—giving you a playlist of all his audio walking tours, radio interviews, and travel tips for wherever you're going in Europe.

Let the experts Rick interviews enrich your understanding. Let Rick's self-guided tours amplify your guidebook. With Rick in your ear, Europe gets even better.

Thanks Facebook fans for submitting photos while on location! From top: John Kuijper in Florence, Brenda Mamer with her mother in Rome, Angel Capobianco in London, and Alyssa Passey with her friend in Paris.

Find out more at ricksteves.com/audioeurope

▸ Plan Your Trip

Browse thousands of articles and a wealth of money-saving tips for planning your dream trip. You'll find up-to-date information on Europe's best destinations, packing smart, getting around, finding rooms, staying healthy, avoiding scams and more.

▸ Eurail Passes

Find out, step-by-step, if a railpass makes sense for your trip—and how to avoid buying more than you need. Get a bunch of free extras!

▸ Graffiti Wall & Travelers' Helpline

Learn, ask, share—our online community of savvy travelers is a great resource for first-time travelers to Europe, as well as seasoned pros.

Rick Steves' Europe Through the Back Door, Inc.

Rick Steves.

www.rickssteves.com

EUROPE GUIDES

Best of Europe
Eastern Europe
Europe Through the Back Door

COUNTRY GUIDES

Croatia & Slovenia
England
France
Germany
Great Britain
Ireland
Italy
Portugal
Scandinavia
Spain
Switzerland

CITY & REGIONAL GUIDES

Amsterdam, Bruges & Brussels
Budapest
Florence & Tuscany
Greece: Athens & the Peloponnese
Istanbul
London
Paris
Prague & the Czech Republic
Provence & the French Riviera
Rome
Venice
Vienna, Salzburg & Tirol

SNAPSHOT GUIDES

Barcelona
Berlin
Bruges & Brussels
Copenhagen & the Best of
  Denmark
Dublin
Dubrovnik
Hill Towns of Central Italy
Italy's Cinque Terre
Krakow, Warsaw & Gdansk
Lisbon
Madrid & Toledo
Munich, Bavaria & Salzburg
Naples & the Amalfi Coast
Northern Ireland
Norway
Scotland
Sevilla, Granada & Southern Spain
Stockholm

POCKET GUIDES

London
Paris
Rome

TRAVEL CULTURE

Europe 101
European Christmas
Postcards from Europe
Travel as a Political Act

Rick Steves guidebooks are published by Avalon Travel,
a member of the Perseus Books Group.

NOW AVAILABLE: eBOOKS, APPS, DVDS, & BLU-RAY

eBOOKS

Most guides available as eBooks
   from Amazon, Barnes & Noble,
   Borders, Apple iBook and Sony
   eReader, beginning January 2011

RICK STEVES' EUROPE DVDs

Austria & the Alps
Eastern Europe, Israel & Egypt
England & Wales
European Travel Skills & Specials
France
Germany, Benelux & More
Greece & Turkey
Iran
Ireland & Scotland
Italy's Cities
Italy's Countryside
Rick Steves' European Christmas
Scandinavia
Spain & Portugal

BLU-RAY

Celtic Charms
Eastern Europe Favorites
European Christmas
Italy Through the Back Door
Surprising Cities of Europe

PHRASE BOOKS & DICTIONARIES

French
French, Italian & German
German
Italian
Portuguese
Spanish

JOURNALS

Rick Steves' Pocket Travel Journal
Rick Steves' Travel Journal

APPS

Rick Steves' Ancient Rome Tour
Rick Steves' Historic Paris Walk
Rick Steves' Louvre Tour
Rick Steves' Orsay Museum Tour
Rick Steves' St. Peter's Basilica Tour
Rick Steves' Versailles

PLANNING MAPS

Britain, Ireland & London
Europe
France & Paris
Germany, Austria & Switzerland
Ireland
Italy
Spain & Portugal

Credits

Researchers

To help update this book, Rick relied on...

Cathy McDonald

Cathy, an editor and researcher for Rick Steves, considers Britain's natural history crucial to understanding the land and its people. She lives in Seattle, where she has written about the Pacific Northwest for more than 15 years as a freelancer for *The Seattle Times*.

Cameron Hewitt

Cameron writes and edits guidebooks for Rick Steves, specializing in Eastern Europe. For this book, he spent a week swinging through the urban jungle of London, studied up on England's great university towns, and overdosed on quaint in the Cotswolds. When he's not traveling, Cameron lives in Seattle with his wife, Shawna.

Lauren Mills

Lauren, a map editor and in-house search engine at Rick Steves, was an ardent Anglophile even before bringing home her British husband as a souvenir. They live in Seattle with their cat Annabel.

Contributor
Gene Openshaw

Gene is the co-author of seven Rick Steves books. For this book, he wrote material on Europe's art, history, and contemporary culture. When not traveling, Gene enjoys composing music, recovering from his 1973 trip to Europe with Rick, and living everyday life with his daughter.

Images

Location	Photographer
Title Page: Tower Bridge, London	Dominic Bonuccelli
England: Salisbury Cathedral	Cameron Hewitt
London: Houses of Parliament	Rick Steves
Greenwich, Windsor, and Cambridge: Windsor's Changing of the Guard	Lauren Mills
Bath: Pulteney Bridge	Lauren Mills
Near Bath: Avebury Stone Circle	David C. Hoerlein
The Cotswolds: Typical Cotswold Scene	Dominic Bonuccelli
Stratford-upon-Avon: Anne Hathaway's Cottage	Rick Steves
Ironbridge Gorge: The Iron Bridge	Lauren Mills
Blackpool and Liverpool: Blackpool	Rick Steves
The Lake District: Derwentwater	Rick Steves
York: York Minster	Rick Steves
Durham and Northeast England: Durham Cathedral	David C. Hoerlein
Wales: Snowdonia	Cameron Hewitt
North Wales: Snowdonia	David C. Hoerlein
Scotland: Neist Point	Cameron Hewitt
Edinburgh: Edinburgh Castle	Rick Steves
St. Andrews: The Old Course	Cameron Hewitt
Glasgow: Cityscape with the Lighthouse	David C. Hoerlein
Oban and the Southern Highlands: Oban	Jennifer Hauseman
Isle of Skye: Kyleakin Harbor	Cameron Hewitt
Inverness and the Northern Highlands: Inverness	Jennifer Hauseman
Between Inverness and Edinburgh: View from Stirling Castle	Cameron Hewitt

Acknowledgements

Thanks to Cameron Hewitt for his original work on several of the Scotland chapters (particularly St. Andrews and the Isle of Skye), to Jennifer Hauseman for the original version of the Glasgow chapter, and to friends listed in this book who put the "Great" in Great Britain.

Images

Rick Steves' Guidebook Series

Country Guides

Rick Steves' Best of Europe
Rick Steves' Croatia &
  Slovenia
Rick Steves' Eastern Europe
Rick Steves' England
Rick Steves' France
Rick Steves' Germany

Rick Steves' Great Britain
Rick Steves' Ireland
Rick Steves' Italy
Rick Steves' Portugal
Rick Steves' Scandinavia
Rick Steves' Spain
Rick Steves' Switzerland

City and Regional Guides

Rick Steves' Amsterdam,
  Bruges & Brussels
Rick Steves' Athens &
  the Peloponnese
Rick Steves' Budapest
Rick Steves' Florence &
  Tuscany
Rick Steves' Istanbul
Rick Steves' London

Rick Steves' Paris
Rick Steves' Prague &
  the Czech Republic
Rick Steves' Provence &
  the French Riviera
Rick Steves' Rome
Rick Steves' Venice
Rick Steves' Vienna,
  Salzburg & Tirol

Rick Steves' Phrase Books

French
French/Italian/German
German
Italian
Portuguese
Spanish

Snapshot Guides

Excerpted chapters from country guides, such as *Rick Steves' Snapshot Barcelona, Rick Steves' Snapshot Scotland,* and *Rick Steves' Snapshot Hill Towns of Central Italy.*

Pocket Guides (new in 2011)

Condensed, pocket-size, full-color guides to Europe's top cities: Paris, London, and Rome.

Other Books

Rick Steves' Europe 101: History and Art for the Traveler
Rick Steves' Europe Through the Back Door
Rick Steves' European Christmas
Rick Steves' Postcards from Europe
Rick Steves' Travel as a Political Act

Avalon Travel
a member of the Perseus Books Group
1700 Fourth Street
Berkeley, CA 94710

Text © 2011 by Rick Steves
Maps © 2011 by Europe Through the Back Door. All rights reserved.

Printed in the USA by Worzalla
First printing December 2010

ISBN 978-1-59880-667-0
ISSN 1090-6843

For the latest on Rick's lectures, guidebooks, tours, public radio show, and public television series, contact Europe Through the Back Door, Box 2009, Edmonds, WA 98020, 425/771-8303, fax 425/771-0833, www.ricksteves.com, rick@ricksteves.com.

Europe Through the Back Door Reviewing Editors: Cameron Hewitt, Risa Laib
ETBD Editors: Sarah McCormic, Gretchen Strauch, Tom Griffin, Cathy McDonald, Jennifer Madison Davis, Cathy Lu
Research Assistance: Cathy McDonald, Cameron Hewitt, Lauren Mills
Avalon Travel Senior Editor and Series Manager: Madhu Prasher
Avalon Travel Project Editor: Kelly Lydick
Copy Editor: Naomi Adler-Dancis
Proofreader: Jennifer Malnick
Indexer: Stephen Callahan
Production and Layout: McGuire Barber Design
Cover Design: Kimberly Glyder Design
Graphic Content Director: Laura VanDeventer
Maps and Graphics: David C. Hoerlein, Laura VanDeventer, Brice Ticen, Lauren Mills, Barb Geisler, Pat O'Connor, Mike Morgenfeld
Front Matter Color Photos: Cameron Hewitt, Sarah Murdoch, Rick Steves, Dominic Bonuccelli
Front Cover Photo: Snowdonia, North Wales © Cameron Hewitt
Additional Photography: Rick Steves, Cameron Hewitt, Gene Openshaw, Bruce VanDeventer, Lauren Mills, David C. Hoerlein, Jennifer Hauseman, Jennifer Schutte, Ken Hanley, Sarah Murdoch, Darbi Macy, Dominic Bonuccelli

Foldout Color Map ▶

The foldout map on the opposite page includes:
• A map of Great Britain on one side
• A city map of London on the other side